# ARISTOTELIS *Metaphysica*

# Contents

## Aristotelis Metaphysica

## Outline of Ancient Greek Grammar

# LIBER PRIMUS 1

(A)

[980α] [21] πάντες ἄνθρωποι τοῦ εἰδέναι ὀρέγονται φύσει. σημεῖον δ᾽ ἡ τῶν αἰσθήσεων ἀγάπησις· καὶ γὰρ χωρὶς τῆς χρείας ἀγαπῶνται δι᾽ αὐτάς, καὶ μάλιστα τῶν ἄλλων ἡ διὰ τῶν ὀμμάτων. οὐ γὰρ μόνον ἵνα πράττωμεν ἀλλὰ καὶ μηθὲν [25] μέλλοντες πράττειν τὸ ὁρᾶν αἱρούμεθα ἀντὶ πάντων ὡς εἰπεῖν τῶν ἄλλων. αἴτιον δ᾽ ὅτι μάλιστα ποιεῖ γνωρίζειν ἡμᾶς αὕτη τῶν αἰσθήσεων καὶ πολλὰς δηλοῖ διαφοράς.

Omnes homines natura scire desiderant. Signum autem, est sensuum dilectio; praeter enim et utilitatem propter se ipsos diliguntur, et maxime aliorum qui est per oculos. Non enim solum ut agamus sed et nihil agere debentes ipsum videre pre omnibus ut dicam aliis eligimus. Causa autem est quia hic maxime sensuum cognoscere nos facit et multas differentias demonstrat.

[980 a1] ALL men by nature desire to know. An indication of this is the delight we take in our senses; for even apart from their usefulness they are loved for themselves; and above all others the sense of sight. For not only with a view to action, but even when we are not going to do anything, we prefer seeing (one might say) to everything else. The reason is that this, most of all the senses, makes us know and brings to light many differences between things.

φύσει μὲν οὖν αἴσθησιν ἔχοντα γίγνεται τὰ ζῷα, ἐκ δὲ ταύτης τοῖς μὲν αὐτῶν οὐκ ἐγγίγνεται μνήμη, τοῖς δ᾽ ἐγγίγνεται. [980β] [21] καὶ διὰ τοῦτο ταῦτα φρονιμώτερα καὶ μαθητικώτερα τῶν μὴ δυναμένων μνημονεύειν ἐστί, φρόνιμα μὲν ἄνευ τοῦ μανθάνειν ὅσα μὴ δύναται τῶν ψόφων ἀκούειν (οἷον μέλιττα κἂν εἴ τι τοιοῦτον ἄλλο γένος ζῴων ἐστι), μανθάνει [25] δ᾽ ὅσα πρὸς τῇ μνήμῃ καὶ ταύτην ἔχει τὴν αἴσθησιν.

Animalia quidem igitur natura sensum habentia fiunt, ex sensu autem quibusdam quidem ipsorum memoria non infit, quibusdam vero fit. Et propter hoc alia quidem prudentia sunt, alia vero disciplinabiliora non potentibus memorari. Prudentia quidem sunt sine addiscere quecumque sonos audire non potentia sunt, ut apis et utique si aliquod aliud genus animalium huiusmodi est; addiscunt autem quaecumque cum memoria et hunc habent sensum.

By nature animals are born with the faculty of sensation, and from sensation memory is produced in some of them, though not in others. And therefore the former are more intelligent and apt at learning than those which cannot remember; those which are incapable of hearing sounds are intelligent though they cannot be taught, e.g. the bee, and any other race of animals that may be like it; and those which besides memory have this sense of hearing can be taught.

τὰ μὲν οὖν ἄλλα ταῖς φαντασίαις ζῇ καὶ ταῖς μνήμαις, ἐμπειρίας δὲ μετέχει μικρόν: τὸ δὲ τῶν ἀνθρώπων γένος καὶ τέχνῃ καὶ λογισμοῖς. γίγνεται δ᾽ ἐκ τῆς μνήμης ἐμπειρία τοῖς ἀνθρώποις: αἱ γὰρ πολλαὶ μνῆμαι τοῦ αὐτοῦ πράγματος μιᾶς ἐμπειρίας δύναμιν ἀποτελοῦσιν. [981a] [1] καὶ δοκεῖ σχεδὸν ἐπιστήμη καὶ τέχνῃ ὅμοιον εἶναι καὶ ἐμπειρία, ἀποβαίνει δ᾽ ἐπιστήμη καὶ τέχνῃ διὰ τῆς ἐμπειρίας τοῖς ἀνθρώποις: ἡ μὲν γὰρ ἐμπειρία τέχνην ἐποίησεν, ὡς φησὶ Πῶλος, ἡ [5] δ᾽ ἀπειρία τύχην. γίγνεται δὲ τέχνῃ ὅταν ἐκ πολλῶν τῆς ἐμπειρίας ἐννοημάτων μία καθόλου γένηται περὶ τῶν ὁμοίων ὑπόληψις. τὸ μὲν γὰρ ἔχειν ὑπόληψιν ὅτι Καλλίᾳ κάμνοντι τηνδὶ τὴν νόσον τοδὶ συνήνεγκε καὶ Σωκράτει καὶ καθ᾽ ἕκαστον οὕτω πολλοῖς, ἐμπειρίας ἐστίν: [10] τὸ δ᾽ ὅτι πᾶσι τοῖς τοιοῖσδε κατ᾽ εἶδος ἓν ἀφορισθεῖσι, κάμνουσι τηνδὶ τὴν νόσον, συνήνεγκεν, οἷον τοῖς φλεγματώδεσιν ἢ χολώδεσι [ἢ] πυρέττουσι καύσῳ, τέχνης.

Alia quidem igitur ymaginationibus et memoriis vivunt, experimenti autem parum participant; hominum autem genus arte et rationibus. Fit autem ex memoria hominibus experimentum; eiusdem namquae rei multe memorie unius experientie potentiam faciunt. Et fere videtur scientie et arti simile experimentum esse, hominibus autem scientia et ars per experientiam evenit; experientia quidem enim artem fecit, sicut ait Polus recte dicens, sed inexperientia casum. Fit autem ars cum ex multis experimentalibus conceptionibus una fit universalis de similibus acceptio. Acceptionem quidem enim habere quod callie et Socrati hac egritudine laborantibus hoc contulit et ita multis singularium, experimenti est; quod autem omnibus huiusmodi secundum autem unam speciem determinatis, hac egritudine laborantibus, contulit, ut flegmaticis aut colericis aut estu febricitantibus , artis est.

The animals other than man live by appearances and memories, and have but little of connected experience; but the human race lives also by art and reasonings. Now from memory experience is produced in men; for the several memories of the same thing produce finally the capacity for a single experience. [81a] And experience seems pretty much like science and art, but really science and art come to men through experience; for 'experience made art', as Polus says, 'but inexperience luck.' Now art arises when from many notions gained by experience one universal judgement about a class of objects is produced. For to have a judgement that when Callias was ill of this disease this did him good, and similarly in the case of Socrates and in many individual cases, is a matter of experience; but to judge that it has done good to all persons of a certain constitution, marked off in one class, when they were ill of this disease, e.g. to phlegmatic or bilious people when burning with fevers-this is a matter of art.

πρὸς μὲν οὖν τὸ πράττειν ἐμπειρία τέχνης οὐδὲν δοκεῖ διαφέρειν, ἀλλὰ καὶ μᾶλλον ἐπιτυγχάνουσιν οἱ ἔμπειροι τῶν ἄνευ τῆς ἐμπειρίας [15] λόγον ἐχόντων (αἴτιον δ᾽ ὅτι ἡ μὲν ἐμπειρία τῶν καθ᾽ ἕκαστόν ἐστι γνῶσις ἡ δὲ τέχνη τῶν καθόλου, αἱ δὲ πράξεις καὶ αἱ γενέσεις πᾶσαι περὶ τὸ καθ᾽ ἕκαστόν εἰσιν: οὐ γὰρ ἄνθρωπον ὑγιάζει ὁ ἰατρεύων ἀλλ᾽ ἢ κατὰ συμβεβηκός, ἀλλὰ Καλλίαν ἢ Σωκράτην ἢ τῶν ἄλλων τινὰ [20] τῶν οὕτω λεγομένων ᾧ συμβέβηκεν ἀνθρώπῳ εἶναι: ἐὰν οὖν ἄνευ τῆς ἐμπειρίας ἔχῃ τις τὸν λόγον, καὶ τὸ καθόλου μὲν γνωρίζῃ τὸ δ᾽ ἐν τούτῳ καθ᾽ ἕκαστον ἀγνοῇ, πολλάκις διαμαρτήσεται τῆς θεραπείας: θεραπευτὸν γὰρ τὸ καθ᾽ ἕκαστον):

Ad agere quidem igitur experientia nihil ab arte differre videtur, sed et expertos magis proficere videmus sine experientia rationem habentibus. Causa autem est quia experientia quidem singularium est cognitio, ars vero universalium, actus autem et omnes generationes circa singulare sunt. Non enim hominem medicans sanat nisi secundum accidens, sed Calliam aut Socratem aut aliquem sic dictorum cui esse hominem accidit. Si igitur sine experimento quis rationem habeat et universale quidem cognoscat, in hoc autem singulare ignoret, multotiens quidem curatione peccabit; singulare namque magis curabile est.

With a view to action experience seems in no respect inferior to art, and men of experience succeed even better than those who have theory without experience. (The reason is that experience is knowledge of individuals, art of universals, and actions and productions are all concerned with the individual; for the physician does not cure man, except in an incidental way, but Callias or Socrates or some other called by some such individual name, who happens to be a man. If, then, a man has the theory without the experience, and recognizes the universal but does not know the individual included in this, he will often fail to cure; for it is the individual that is to be cured.)

ἀλλ᾽ ὅμως τό γε εἰδέναι καὶ τὸ ἐπαΐειν τῇ [25] τέχνῃ τῆς ἐμπειρίας ὑπάρχειν οἰόμεθα μᾶλλον, καὶ σοφωτέρους τοὺς τεχνίτας τῶν ἐμπείρων ὑπολαμβάνομεν, ὡς κατὰ τὸ εἰδέναι μᾶλλον ἀκολουθοῦσαν τὴν σοφίαν πᾶσι: τοῦτο δ᾽ ὅτι οἱ μὲν τὴν αἰτίαν ἴσασιν οἱ δ᾽ οὔ. οἱ μὲν γὰρ ἔμπειροι τὸ ὅτι μὲν ἴσασι, διότι δ᾽ οὐκ ἴσασιν: οἱ δὲ τὸ διότι [30] καὶ τὴν αἰτίαν γνωρίζουσιν. διὸ καὶ τοὺς ἀρχιτέκτονας περὶ ἕκαστον τιμιωτέρους καὶ μᾶλλον εἰδέναι νομίζομεν τῶν χειροτεχνῶν καὶ σοφωτέρους, [981β] [1] ὅτι τὰς αἰτίας τῶν ποιουμένων ἴσασιν (τοὺς δ᾽, ὥσπερ καὶ τῶν ἀψύχων ἔνια ποιεῖ μέν, οὐκ εἰδότα δὲ ποιεῖ ἃ ποιεῖ, οἷον καίει τὸ πῦρ: τὰ μὲν οὖν ἄψυχα φύσει τινὶ ποιεῖν τούτων ἕκαστον τοὺς δὲ χειροτέχνας [5] δι᾽ ἔθος), ὡς οὐ κατὰ τὸ πρακτικοὺς εἶναι σοφωτέρους ὄντας ἀλλὰ κατὰ τὸ λόγον ἔχειν αὐτοὺς καὶ τὰς αἰτίας γνωρίζειν.

Sed tamen scire et intelligere magis arte quam experimento esse arbitramur, et artifices expertis sapientiores esse opinamur, tamquam magis secundum scire sapientia omnibus sequente. Hoc autem est quia hii quidem causam sciunt, illi vero non. Experti quidem enim ipsum quia sciunt, sed propter quid nesciunt; hii autem et propter quid et causam cognoscunt. Unde et architectores circa quodlibet honorabiliores et magis scire manu artificibus putamus et sapientio res, quia factorum causas sciunt; illos vero, sicut quedam inanimatorum faciunt quidem, non scientia autem faciunt quae faciunt, ut ignis exurit — inanimata igitur quidem natura quadam horum unumquodque facere, sed manu artifices propter consuetudinem. Tamquam non secundum practicos esse sapientiores sint, sed secundum quod rationem habent ipsi et causas cognoscunt.

But yet we think that knowledge and understanding belong to art rather than to experience, and we suppose artists to be wiser than men of experience (which implies that Wisdom depends in all cases rather on knowledge); and this because the former know the cause, but the latter do not. For men of experience know that the thing is so, but do not know why, while the others know the 'why' and the cause. Hence we think also that the masterworkers in each craft are more honourable and know in a truer sense and are wiser [81b] than the manual workers, because they know the causes of the things that are done (we think the manual workers are like certain lifeless things which act indeed, but act without knowing what they do, as fire burns, - but while the lifeless things perform each of their functions by a natural tendency, the labourers perform them through habit); thus we view them as being wiser not in virtue of being able to act, but of having the theory for themselves and knowing the causes.

ὅλως τε σημεῖον τοῦ εἰδότος καὶ μὴ εἰδότος τὸ δύνασθαι διδάσκειν ἐστίν, καὶ διὰ τοῦτο τὴν τέχνην τῆς ἐμπειρίας ἡγούμεθα μᾶλλον ἐπιστήμην εἶναι: δύνανται γάρ, οἱ δὲ οὐ δύνανται διδάσκειν. [10]

Et omnino scientis signum est posse docere, et ob hoc artem magis experimento scientiam esse existimamus; possunt enim hii, hii autem docere non possunt.

And in general it is a sign of the man who knows and of the man who does not know, that the former can teach, and therefore we think art more truly knowledge than experience is; for artists can teach, and men of mere experience cannot.

ἔτι δὲ τῶν αἰσθήσεων οὐδεμίαν ἡγούμεθα εἶναι σοφίαν: καίτοι κυριώταταί γ᾽ εἰσὶν αὗται τῶν καθ᾽ ἕκαστα γνώσεις: ἀλλ᾽ οὐ λέγουσι τὸ διὰ τί περὶ οὐδενός, οἷον διὰ τί θερμὸν τὸ πῦρ, ἀλλὰ μόνον ὅτι θερμόν.

Amplius autem sensuum neque unum sapientiam esse ponimus, cum et hiis singulorum cognitiones maxime proprie sint; sed propter quid de nullo dicunt, ut propter quid ignis calidus, sed quia calidus solum sit.

Again, we do not regard any of the senses as Wisdom; yet surely these give the most authoritative knowledge of particulars. But they do not tell us the 'why' of anything-e.g. why fire is hot; they only say that it is hot.

τὸ μὲν οὖν πρῶτον εἰκὸς τὸν ὁποιανοῦν εὑρόντα τέχνην παρὰ τὰς κοινὰς αἰσθήσεις θαυμάζεσθαι [15] ὑπὸ τῶν ἀνθρώπων μὴ μόνον διὰ τὸ χρήσιμον εἶναί τι τῶν εὑρεθέντων ἀλλ᾿ ὡς σοφὸν καὶ διαφέροντα τῶν ἄλλων· πλειόνων δ᾿ εὑρισκομένων τεχνῶν καὶ τῶν μὲν πρὸς τἀναγκαῖα τῶν δὲ πρὸς διαγωγὴν οὐσῶν, ἀεὶ σοφωτέρους τοὺς τοιούτους ἐκείνων ὑπολαμβάνεσθαι διὰ τὸ μὴ πρὸς [20] χρῆσιν εἶναι τὰς ἐπιστήμας αὐτῶν. ὅθεν ἤδη πάντων τῶν τοιούτων κατεσκευασμένων αἱ μὴ πρὸς ἡδονὴν μηδὲ πρὸς τἀναγκαῖα τῶν ἐπιστημῶν εὑρέθησαν, καὶ πρῶτον ἐν τούτοις τοῖς τόποις οὗ πρῶτον ἐσχόλασαν· διὸ περὶ Αἴγυπτον αἱ μαθηματικαὶ πρῶτον τέχναι συνέστησαν, ἐκεῖ γὰρ ἀφείθη σχολάζειν [25] τὸ τῶν ἱερέων ἔθνος.

Primum quidem igitur conveniens est quamlibet artem invenientem ultra communes sensus ab hominibus mirari, non 981b15 solum propter aliquam inventorum utilitatem, sed sicut sapientem et ab aliis differentem. Pluribus autem repertis artibus  et aliis quidem ad necessaria  aliis vero ad introductionem existentibus, semper tales sapientiores illis esse arbitrandum  est propter id quod illorum scientie ad usum non sunt. Unde iam omnibus talibus institutis, quae non ad voluptatem neque ad necessaria scientiarum reperte sunt, et primum  in hiis locis ubi vacabant. Unde circa Egyptum mathematice artes  primum constiterunt; ibi namque gens sacerdotum vacare dimissa est.

At first he who invented any art whatever that went beyond the common perceptions of man was naturally admired by men, not only because there was something useful in the inventions, but because he was thought wise and superior to the rest. But as more arts were invented, and some were directed to the necessities of life, others to recreation, the inventors of the latter were naturally always regarded as wiser than the inventors of the former, because their branches of knowledge did not aim at utility. Hence when all such inventions were already established, the sciences which do not aim at giving pleasure or at the necessities of life were discovered, and first in the places where men first began to have leisure. This is why the mathematical arts were founded in Egypt; for there the priestly caste was allowed to be at leisure.

εἴρηται μὲν οὖν ἐν τοῖς ἠθικοῖς τίς διαφορὰ τέχνης καὶ ἐπιστήμης καὶ τῶν ἄλλων τῶν ὁμογενῶν· οὗ δ᾿ ἕνεκα νῦν ποιούμεθα τὸν λόγον τοῦτ᾿ ἐστίν, ὅτι τὴν ὀνομαζομένην σοφίαν περὶ τὰ πρῶτα αἴτια καὶ τὰς ἀρχὰς ὑπολαμβάνουσι πάντες· ὥστε, καθάπερ εἴρηται πρότερον, [30] ὁ μὲν ἔμπειρος τῶν ὁποιανοῦν ἐχόντων αἴσθησιν εἶναι δοκεῖ σοφώτερος, ὁ δὲ τεχνίτης τῶν ἐμπείρων, χειροτέχνου δὲ ἀρχιτέκτων, αἱ δὲ θεωρητικαὶ τῶν ποιητικῶν μᾶλλον. [982α] [1] ὅτι μὲν οὖν ἡ σοφία περί τινας ἀρχὰς καὶ αἰτίας ἐστὶν ἐπιστήμη, δῆλον.

In Moralibus quidem igitur quae sit artis et scientie differentia et similium generum dictum est; cuius autem gratia nunc sermonem facimus hoc est, quia nominatam sapientiam circa primas causas et principia existimant omnes. Quare, sicut dictum est prius, expertus quidem quemcumque sensum habentibus sapientior esse videtur, artifex autem expertis, architecton autem manu artifice, speculative autem magis activis. Quod quidem igitur sapientia circa quasdam causas et principia sit scientia, manifestum est.

We have said in the Ethics what the difference is between art and science and the other kindred faculties; but the point of our present discussion is this, that all men suppose what is called Wisdom to deal with the first causes and the principles of things; so that, as has been said before, the man of experience is thought to be wiser than the possessors of any sense-perception whatever, the artist wiser than the men of experience, the masterworker than the mechanic, and the theoretical kinds of knowledge to be more of the nature of Wisdom than the productive. Clearly then Wisdom is knowledge about certain principles [82a] and causes.

### *Chapter* 2

ἐπεὶ δὲ ταύτην τὴν ἐπιστήμην ζητοῦμεν, τοῦτ᾽ ἂν εἴη [5] σκεπτέον, ἡ περὶ ποίας αἰτίας καὶ περὶ ποίας ἀρχὰς ἐπιστήμη σοφία ἐστίν. εἰ δὴ λάβοι τις τὰς ὑπολήψεις ἃς ἔχομεν περὶ τοῦ σοφοῦ, τάχ᾽ ἂν ἐκ τούτου φανερὸν γένοιτο μᾶλλον. ὑπολαμβάνομεν δὴ πρῶτον μὲν ἐπίστασθαι πάντα τὸν σοφὸν ὡς ἐνδέχεται, μὴ καθ᾽ ἕκαστον ἔχοντα ἐπιστήμην [10] αὐτῶν: εἶτα τὸν τὰ χαλεπὰ γνῶναι δυνάμενον καὶ μὴ ῥάδια ἀνθρώπῳ γιγνώσκειν, τοῦτον σοφόν (τὸ γὰρ αἰσθάνεσθαι πάντων κοινόν, διὸ ῥάδιον καὶ οὐδὲν σοφόν): ἔτι τὸν ἀκριβέστερον καὶ τὸν διδασκαλικώτερον τῶν αἰτιῶν σοφώτερον εἶναι περὶ πᾶσαν ἐπιστήμην: καὶ τῶν ἐπιστημῶν δὲ τὴν [15] αὑτῆς ἕνεκεν καὶ τοῦ εἰδέναι χάριν αἱρετὴν οὖσαν μᾶλλον εἶναι σοφίαν ἢ τὴν τῶν ἀποβαινόντων ἕνεκεν, καὶ τὴν ἀρχικωτέραν τῆς ὑπηρετούσης μᾶλλον σοφίαν: οὐ γὰρ δεῖν ἐπιτάττεσθαι τὸν σοφὸν ἀλλ᾽ ἐπιτάττειν, καὶ οὐ τοῦτον ἑτέρῳ πείθεσθαι, ἀλλὰ τούτῳ τὸν ἥττον σοφόν.

Quoniam autem scientiam hanc quaerimus, circa quales causas et circa qualia principia scientia sapientia sit, hoc utique erit considerandum. Si itaque accipiat aliquis existimationes quas de sapiente habemus, fortassis ex hiis manifestius fiet. Itaque primum existimamus sapientem omnia maxime scire ut contingit [accipimus], non singularem scientiam eorum habentem. Postea difficilia cognoscere potentem nec levia homini noscere, hunc dicimus sapientem; sentire enim omnium est commune, quare facile et non sophon. Adhuc certiorem et magis causas docentem sapientiorem circa omnem scientiam esse. Et scientiarum autem eam quae sui ipsius causa et sciendi gratia eligibilis est: magis est sapientia quam quae evenientium gratia. Et principaliorem subserviente magis esse sapientiam; non enim ordinari sed sapientem ordinare oportet, neque hunc ab altero, sed ab hoc minus sapientem suaderi.

Since we are seeking this knowledge, we must inquire of what kind are the causes and the principles, the knowledge of which is Wisdom. If one were to take the notions we have about the wise man, this might perhaps make the answer more evident. We suppose first, then, that the wise man knows all things, as far as possible, although he has not knowledge of each of them in detail; secondly, that he who can learn things that are difficult, and not easy for man to know, is wise (sense-perception is common to all, and therefore easy and no mark of Wisdom); again, that he who is more exact and more capable of teaching the causes is wiser, in every branch of knowledge; and that of the sciences, also, that which is desirable on its own account and for the sake of knowing it is more of the nature of Wisdom than that which is desirable on account of its results, and the superior science is more of the nature of Wisdom than the ancillary; for the wise man must not be ordered but must order, and he must not obey another, but the less wise must obey him.

τὰς μὲν οὖν [20] ὑπολήψεις τοιαύτας καὶ τοσαύτας ἔχομεν περὶ τῆς σοφίας καὶ τῶν σοφῶν· τούτων δὲ τὸ μὲν πάντα ἐπίστασθαι τῷ μάλιστα ἔχοντι τὴν καθόλου ἐπιστήμην ἀναγκαῖον ὑπάρχειν (οὗτος γὰρ οἶδέ πως πάντα τὰ ὑποκείμενα), σχεδὸν δὲ καὶ χαλεπώτατα ταῦτα γνωρίζειν τοῖς ἀνθρώποις, τὰ μάλιστα [25] καθόλου (πορρωτάτω γὰρ τῶν αἰσθήσεών ἐστιν), ἀκριβέσταται δὲ τῶν ἐπιστημῶν αἱ μάλιστα τῶν πρώτων εἰσίν (αἱ γὰρ ἐξ ἐλαττόνων ἀκριβέστεραι τῶν ἐκ προσθέσεως λεγομένων, οἷον ἀριθμητικὴ γεωμετρίας)·

Tales quidem igitur existimationes et tot de sapientia et sapientibus habemus. Istorum autem hoc quidem omnia scire universalem scientiam maxime habenti inesse necesse est; hic enim novit omnia aliqualiter subiecta. Fere autem et difficillima sunt ea hominibus ad cognoscendum quae maxime sunt universalia; nam a sensibus sunt remotissima. Scientiarum vero certissime sunt quae maxime primorum sunt; nam quae sunt ex paucioribus certiores sunt ex additione dictis, ut arismetica geometria.

Such and so many are the notions, then, which we have about Wisdom and the wise. Now of these characteristics that of knowing all things must belong to him who has in the highest degree universal knowledge; for he knows in a sense all the instances that fall under the universal. And these things, the most universal, are on the whole the hardest for men to know; for they are farthest from the senses. And the most exact of the sciences are those which deal most with first principles; for those which involve fewer principles are more exact than those which involve additional principles, e.g. arithmetic than geometry.

ἀλλὰ μὴν καὶ διδασκαλική γε ἡ τῶν αἰτιῶν θεωρητικὴ μᾶλλον (οὗτοι γὰρ διδάσκουσιν, οἱ τὰς [30] αἰτίας λέγοντες περὶ ἑκάστου), τὸ δ᾿ εἰδέναι καὶ τὸ ἐπίστασθαι αὐτῶν ἕνεκα μάλισθ᾿ ὑπάρχει τῇ τοῦ μάλιστα ἐπιστητοῦ ἐπιστήμῃ (ὁ γὰρ τὸ ἐπίστασθαι δι᾿ αὐτὸ αἱρούμενος τὴν μάλιστα ἐπιστήμην μάλιστα αἱρήσεται, [982β] [1] τοιαύτη δ᾿ ἐστὶν ἡ τοῦ μάλιστα ἐπιστητοῦ), μάλιστα δ᾿ ἐπιστητὰ τὰ πρῶτα καὶ τὰ αἴτια (διὰ γὰρ ταῦτα καὶ ἐκ τούτων τἆλλα γνωρίζεται ἀλλ᾿ οὐ ταῦτα διὰ τῶν ὑποκειμένων),

At vero et doctrinalis quae causarum est speculatrix magis; hii namque docent, qui causas de singulis dicunt. Et noscere et scire sui gratia maxime inest ei quae maxime scibilis scientie; nam qui scire propter se desiderat, ipsam maxime scientiam maxime desiderabit, talis autem est quae maxime scibilis. Maxime autem scibilia prima et cause; nam propter haec et ex hiis alia dinoscuntur, sed non haec per subiecta.

But the science which investigates causes is also instructive, in a higher degree, for the people who instruct us are those who tell the causes of each thing. And understanding and knowledge pursued for their own sake are found most in the knowledge of that which is most knowable (for he who chooses to know for the sake of knowing will choose most [82b] readily that which is most truly knowledge, and such is the knowledge of that which is most knowable); and the first principles and the causes are most knowable; for by reason of these, and from these, all other things come to be known, and not these by means of the things subordinate to them.

ἀρχικωτάτη δὲ τῶν ἐπιστημῶν, καὶ [5] μᾶλλον ἀρχικὴ τῆς ὑπηρετούσης, ἡ γνωρίζουσα τίνος ἕνεκέν ἐστι πρακτέον ἕκαστον· τοῦτο δ᾽ ἐστὶ τἀγαθὸν ἑκάστου, ὅλως δὲ τὸ ἄριστον ἐν τῇ φύσει πάσῃ.

Maxime vero principalis scientiarum, et magis principalis subserviente, quae cognoscit cuius causa sunt agenda singula; hoc autem est bonum uniuscuiusque, totaliter autem optimum in natura omni.

And the science which knows to what end each thing must be done is the most authoritative of the sciences, and more authoritative than any ancillary science; and this end is the good of that thing, and in general the supreme good in the whole of nature.

ἐξ ἁπάντων οὖν τῶν εἰρημένων ἐπὶ τὴν αὐτὴν ἐπιστήμην πίπτει τὸ ζητούμενον ὄνομα· δεῖ γὰρ ταύτην τῶν πρώτων ἀρχῶν καὶ αἰτιῶν εἶναι θεωρητικήν· [10] καὶ γὰρ τἀγαθὸν καὶ τὸ οὗ ἕνεκα ἓν τῶν αἰτίων ἐστίν.

Ex omnibus ergo quae dicta sunt in eandem cadit scientiam quesitum nomen; oportet enim hanc primorum principiorum et causarum esse speculativam; et enim bonum et quod cuius gratia una causarum est.

Judged by all the tests we have mentioned, then, the name in question falls to the same science; this must be a science that investigates the first principles and causes; for the good, i.e. the end, is one of the causes.

ὅτι δ᾽ οὐ ποιητική, δῆλον καὶ ἐκ τῶν πρώτων φιλοσοφησάντων· διὰ γὰρ τὸ θαυμάζειν οἱ ἄνθρωποι καὶ νῦν καὶ τὸ πρῶτον ἤρξαντο φιλοσοφεῖν, ἐξ ἀρχῆς μὲν τὰ πρόχειρα τῶν ἀτόπων θαυμάσαντες, εἶτα κατὰ μικρὸν οὕτω προϊόντες [15] καὶ

περὶ τῶν μειζόνων διαπορήσαντες, οἷον περί τε τῶν τῆς σελήνης παθημάτων καὶ τῶν περὶ τὸν ἥλιον καὶ ἄστρα καὶ περὶ τῆς τοῦ παντὸς γενέσεως.

Quia vero non activa, palam ex primis philosophantibus. Nam propter admirari homines et nunc et primum inceperunt philosophari, a principio quidem paratiora dubitabilium mirantes, deinde paulatim sic procedentes et de maioribus dubitantes, ut de lune passionibus et de hiis quae circa solem et astra et de universi generatione.

That it is not a science of production is clear even from the history of the earliest philosophers. For it is owing to their wonder that men both now begin and at first began to philosophize; they wondered originally at the obvious difficulties, then advanced little by little and stated difficulties about the greater matters, e.g. about the phenomena of the moon and those of the sun and of the stars, and about the genesis of the universe.

ὁ δ᾽ ἀπορῶν καὶ θαυμάζων οἴεται ἀγνοεῖν (διὸ καὶ ὁ φιλόμυθος φιλόσοφός πώς ἐστιν: ὁ γὰρ μῦθος σύγκειται ἐκ θαυμασίων): ὥστ᾽ εἴπερ διὰ [20] τὸ φεύγειν τὴν ἄγνοιαν ἐφιλοσόφησαν, φανερὸν ὅτι διὰ τὸ εἰδέναι τὸ ἐπίστασθαι ἐδίωκον καὶ οὐ χρήσεώς τινος ἕνεκεν.

Qui vero [Quoniam vero] dubitat et admiratur ignorare videtur. Quare et philomitos philosophus aliqualiter est; fabula namque ex miris constituitur. Quare si ad ignorantiam fugiendam philosophati sunt, palam quia propter scire studere persecuti sunt et non usus alicuius causa.

And a man who is puzzled and wonders thinks himself ignorant (whence even the lover of myth is in a sense a lover of Wisdom, for the myth is composed of wonders); therefore since they philosophized order to escape from ignorance, evidently they were pursuing science in order to know, and not for any utilitarian end.

μαρτυρεῖ δὲ αὐτὸ τὸ συμβεβηκός: σχεδὸν γὰρ πάντων ὑπαρχόντων τῶν ἀναγκαίων καὶ πρὸς ῥᾳστώνην καὶ διαγωγὴν ἡ τοιαύτη φρόνησις ἤρξατο ζητεῖσθαι. δῆλον οὖν ὡς δι᾽ [25] οὐδεμίαν αὐτὴν ζητοῦμεν χρείαν ἑτέραν, ἀλλ᾽ ὥσπερ ἄνθρωπος, φαμέν, ἐλεύθερος ὁ αὑτοῦ ἕνεκα καὶ μὴ ἄλλου ὤν, οὕτω καὶ αὐτὴν ὡς μόνην οὖσαν ἐλευθέραν τῶν ἐπιστημῶν: μόνη γὰρ αὕτη αὑτῆς ἕνεκέν ἐστιν.

Testatur autem ipsum quod accidit; nam fere cunctis existentibus quae sunt necessariorum et ad valitudinem et ad perductionem, talis prudentia inquiri cepit. Palam igitur quia propter nullam ipsam quaerimus aliam necessitatem, sed, ut dicimus, homo liber qui suimet et non alterius causa est, sic et haec sola liberaa est scientiarum; sola namque haec suimet causa est.

And this is confirmed by the facts; for it was when almost all the necessities of life and the things that make for comfort and recreation had been secured, that such knowledge began to be sought. Evidently then we do not seek it for the sake of any other advantage; but as the man is free, we say, who exists for his own sake and not for another's, so we pursue this as the only free science, for it alone exists for its own sake.

διὸ καὶ δικαίως ἂν οὐκ ἀνθρωπίνη νομίζοιτο αὐτῆς ἡ κτῆσις: πολλαχῇ γὰρ ἡ φύσις δούλη τῶν [30] ἀνθρώπων ἐστίν, κατὰ Σιμωνίδην "θεὸς ἂν μόνος τοῦτ᾽ ἔχοι γέρας", ἄνδρα δ᾽ οὐκ ἄξιον μὴ οὐ ζητεῖν τὴν καθ᾽ αὑτὸν ἐπιστήμην. εἰ δὴ λέγουσί τι οἱ ποιηταὶ καὶ πέφυκε φθονεῖν τὸ θεῖον, [983α] [1] ἐπὶ τούτου συμβῆναι μάλιστα εἰκὸς καὶ δυστυχεῖς [2] εἶναι πάντας τοὺς περιττούς. ἀλλ᾽ οὔτε τὸ θεῖον φθονερὸν ἐνδέχεται εἶναι, ἀλλὰ κατὰ τὴν παροιμίαν πολλὰ ψεύδονται ἀοιδοί, οὔτε τῆς τοιαύτης ἄλλην χρὴ νομίζειν τιμιωτέραν. [5] ἡ γὰρ θειοτάτη καὶ τιμιωτάτη: τοιαύτη δὲ διχῶς ἂν εἴη μόνη: ἥν τε γὰρ μάλιστ᾽ ἂν ὁ θεὸς ἔχοι, θεία τῶν ἐπιστημῶν ἐστί, κἂν εἴ τις τῶν θείων εἴη. μόνη δ᾽ αὕτη τούτων ἀμφοτέρων τετύχηκεν: ὅ τε γὰρ θεὸς δοκεῖ τῶν αἰτίων πᾶσιν εἶναι καὶ ἀρχή τις, καὶ τὴν τοιαύτην ἢ μόνος ἢ μάλιστ᾽ [10] ἂν ἔχοι ὁ θεός. ἀναγκαιότεραι μὲν οὖν πᾶσαι ταύτης, ἀμείνων δ᾽ οὐδεμία.

Propter quod et iuste non humana putetur eius possessio. Multipliciter enim hominum natura serva est, quare secundum Symonida "solus quidem Deus hunc habet honorem", virum vero non dignum non quaerere quae secundum se est scientiam. Si autem dicunt aliquid poete, quia divinum natum est inuidere, in hoc contingere maxime verisimile et infortunatos omnes superfluos esse. Sed nec divinum inuidum esse convenit, sed secundum proverbium multa mentiuntur poete, nec tali aliam honorabiliorem oportet existimare. Nam maxime divina et maxime honoranda. Talis autem dupliciter utique erit solum; quam enim maxime deus habet, divina scientiarum est, et utique si qua sit divinorum. Sola autem ista ambo haec sortita est; deus enim videtur causarum omnibus esse et principium quoddam, et talem aut solus aut maxime deus habet. Necessariores quidem igitur omnes ipsa, dignior vero nulla.

Hence also the possession of it might be justly regarded as beyond human power; for in many ways human nature is in bondage, so that according to Simonides 'God alone can have this privilege', and it is unfitting that man should not be content to seek the knowledge that is suited to him. If, then, there is something in what the poets say, and jealousy is natural to the divine power, it would probably [83a] occur in this case above all, and all who excelled in this knowledge would be unfortunate. But the divine power cannot be jealous (nay, according to the proverb, 'bards tell a lie'), nor should any other science be thought more honourable than one of this sort. For the most divine science is also most honourable; and this science alone must be, in two ways, most divine. For the science which it would be most meet for God to have is a divine science, and so is any science that deals with divine objects; and this science alone has both these qualities; for (1) God is thought to be among the causes of all

12

things and to be a first principle, and (2) such a science either God alone can have, or God above all others. All the sciences, indeed, are more necessary than this, but none is better.

δεῖ μέντοι πως καταστῆναι τὴν κτῆσιν αὐτῆς εἰς τοὐναντίον ἡμῖν τῶν ἐξ ἀρχῆς ζητήσεων. ἄρχονται μὲν γάρ, ὥσπερ εἴπομεν, ἀπὸ τοῦ θαυμάζειν πάντες εἰ οὕτως ἔχει, καθάπερ <περὶ τῶν θαυμάτων ταὐτόματα [τοῖς μήπω τεθεωρηκόσι [15] τὴν αἰτίαν] ἢ περὶ τὰς τοῦ ἡλίου τροπὰς ἢ τὴν τῆς διαμέτρου ἀσυμμετρίαν (θαυμαστὸν γὰρ εἶναι δοκεῖ πᾶσι <τοῖς μήπω τεθεωρηκόσι τὴν αἰτίαν εἴ τι τῷ ἐλαχίστῳ μὴ μετρεῖται): δεῖ δὲ εἰς τοὐναντίον καὶ τὸ ἄμεινον κατὰ τὴν παροιμίαν ἀποτελευτῆσαι, καθάπερ καὶ ἐν τούτοις ὅταν μάθωσιν: οὐθὲν γὰρ [20] ἂν οὕτως θαυμάσειεν ἀνὴρ γεωμετρικὸς ὡς εἰ γένοιτο ἡ διάμετρος μετρητή.

Oportet tamen aliqualiter constituere ordinem ipsius ad contrarium nobis earum quae a principio questionum. Incipiunt quidem enim, ut diximus, omnes ab admirari si ita habent, quemadmodum mirabilium automata, nondum speculantibus causam, aut circa solis conversiones aut diametri non commensurationem; mirum enim videtur esse omnibus si quid non minimorum non mensuratur. Oportet autem in contrarium et ad dignius iuxta proverbium consummare, quemadmodum et in hiis cum didicerint; nihil enim ita mirabitur vir geometricus quam si diameter commensurabilis fiat.

Yet the acquisition of it must in a sense end in something which is the opposite of our original inquiries. For all men begin, as we said, by wondering that things are as they are, as they do about self-moving marionettes, or about the solstices or the incommensurability of the diagonal of a square with the side; for it seems wonderful to all who have not yet seen the reason, that there is a thing which cannot be measured even by the smallest unit. But we must end in the contrary and, according to the proverb, the better state, as is the case in these instances too when men learn the cause; for there is nothing which would surprise a geometer so much as if the diagonal turned out to be commensurable.

τίς μὲν οὖν ἡ φύσις τῆς ἐπιστήμης τῆς ζητουμένης, εἴρηται, καὶ τίς ὁ σκοπὸς οὗ δεῖ τυγχάνειν τὴν ζήτησιν καὶ τὴν ὅλην μέθοδον.

Quae quidem igitur sit natura scientie quesite, dictum est, et quae sit intentio quam oportet adipisci questionem et totam methodum.

We have stated, then, what is the nature of the science we are searching for, and what is the mark which our search and our whole investigation must reach.

*Chapter* 3

ἐπεὶ δὲ φανερὸν ὅτι τῶν ἐξ ἀρχῆς αἰτίων δεῖ λαβεῖν [25] ἐπιστήμην (τότε γὰρ εἰδέναι φαμὲν ἕκαστον, ὅταν τὴν πρώτην αἰτίαν οἰώμεθα γνωρίζειν), τὰ δ᾽ αἴτια λέγεται τετραχῶς, ὧν μίαν μὲν αἰτίαν φαμὲν εἶναι τὴν οὐσίαν καὶ τὸ τί ἦν εἶναι (ἀνάγεται γὰρ τὸ διὰ τί εἰς τὸν λόγον ἔσχατον, αἴτιον δὲ καὶ ἀρχὴ τὸ διὰ τί πρῶτον), ἑτέραν δὲ τὴν ὕλην [30] καὶ τὸ ὑποκείμενον, τρίτην δὲ ὅθεν ἡ ἀρχὴ τῆς κινήσεως, τετάρτην δὲ τὴν ἀντικειμένην αἰτίαν ταύτῃ, τὸ οὗ ἕνεκα καὶ τἀγαθόν (τέλος γὰρ γενέσεως καὶ κινήσεως πάσης τοῦτ᾽ ἐστίν), τεθεώρηται μὲν οὖν ἱκανῶς περὶ αὐτῶν ἡμῖν ἐν τοῖς περὶ φύσεως,

Quoniam autem manifestum quod earum quae a principio causarum oportet sumere scientiam; tunc enim scire dicimus unumquodque, quando primam causam cognoscere putamus. Cause vero quadrupliciter dicuntur, quarum unam quidem causam dicimus esse substantiam et quod quid erat esse; reducitur enim ipsum quare primum ad rationem ultimam, causa autem et principium ipsum quare primum. Unam vero materiam et subiectum. Tertiam autem unde principium motus. Quartam vero causam ei oppositam: et quod est cuius causa et bonum; finis enim generationis et motus omnis hoc est. Sufficienter quidem igitur de hiis speculatum est in hiis quae de natura.

Evidently we have to acquire knowledge of the original causes (for we say we know each thing only when we think we recognize its first cause), and causes are spoken of in four senses. In one of these we mean the substance, i.e. the essence (for the 'why' is reducible finally to the definition, and the ultimate 'why' is a cause and principle); in another the matter or substratum, in a third the source of the change, and in a fourth the cause opposed to this, the purpose and the good (for this is the end of all generation and change). We have studied these causes sufficiently in [83b] our work on nature.

[983β] [1] ὅμως δὲ παραλάβωμεν καὶ τοὺς πρότερον ἡμῶν εἰς ἐπίσκεψιν τῶν ὄντων ἐλθόντας καὶ φιλοσοφήσαντας περὶ τῆς ἀληθείας. δῆλον γὰρ ὅτι κἀκεῖνοι λέγουσιν ἀρχάς τινας καὶ αἰτίας· ἐπελθοῦσιν οὖν ἔσται τι προὔργου τῇ μεθόδῳ τῇ νῦν· [5] ἢ γὰρ ἕτερόν τι γένος εὑρήσομεν αἰτίας ἢ ταῖς νῦν λεγομέναις μᾶλλον πιστεύσομεν.

Accipiamus tamen et nobis priores ad entium perscrutationem venientes et de veritate philosophantes. Palam enim quia et rilli dicunt principia quaedam et causas. Supervenientibus igitur erit aliquid pre opere methodo quae nunc ; aut enim aliud aliquod cause genus inveniemus aut modo dictis magis credemus.

But yet let us call to our aid those who have attacked the investigation of being [83b 4] and philosophized about reality before us. For obviously they too speak of certain principles and causes; to go over their views, then, will be of profit to the present inquiry, for we shall either find another kind of cause, or be more convinced of the correctness of those which we now maintain.

τῶν δὴ πρώτων φιλοσοφησάντων οἱ πλεῖστοι τὰς ἐν ὕλης εἴδει μόνας ᾠήθησαν ἀρχὰς εἶναι πάντων: ἐξ οὗ γὰρ ἔστιν ἅπαντα τὰ ὄντα καὶ ἐξ οὗ γίγνεται πρῶτου καὶ εἰς ὃ φθείρεται τελευταῖον, τῆς μὲν [10] οὐσίας ὑπομενούσης τοῖς δὲ πάθεσι μεταβαλλούσης, τοῦτο στοιχεῖον καὶ ταύτην ἀρχήν φασιν εἶναι τῶν ὄντων, καὶ διὰ τοῦτο οὔτε γίγνεσθαι οὐθὲν οἴονται οὔτε ἀπόλλυσθαι, ὡς τῆς τοιαύτης φύσεως ἀεὶ σωζομένης, ὥσπερ οὐδὲ τὸν Σωκράτην φαμὲν οὔτε γίγνεσθαι ἁπλῶς ὅταν γίγνηται καλὸς ἢ μουσικὸς [15] οὔτε ἀπόλλυσθαι ὅταν ἀποβάλλῃ ταύτας τὰς ἕξεις, διὰ τὸ ὑπομένειν τὸ ὑποκείμενον τὸν Σωκράτην αὐτόν, οὕτως οὐδὲ τῶν ἄλλων οὐδέν: ἀεὶ γὰρ εἶναί τινα φύσιν ἢ μίαν ἢ πλείους μιᾶς ἐξ ὧν γίγνεται τἆλλα σωζομένης ἐκείνης.

Primum igitur philosophantium plurimi solas eas quae in materie specie putaverunt omnium esse principia. Nam ex quo sunt omnia entia et ex quo fiunt primo et in quod corrumpuntur ultimo, substantia quidem manente in passionibus vero mutata, hoc elementum et id principium dicunt esse eorum quae sunt. Et propter hoc nec generari nihil putant nec corrumpi, quasi tali natura semper conservata; sicut nec dicimus Socratem neque generari simpliciter quando fit bonus aut musicus neque corrumpi quando deponit habitus istos, propterea quod subiectum maneat Socrates ipse, sic nec aliorum nihil. Oportet enim esse aliquam naturam aut unam aut plures una ex quibus fiunt alia, illa conservata.

Of the first philosophers, then, most thought the principles which were of the nature of matter were the only principles of all things. That of which all things that are consist, the first from which they come to be, the last into which they are resolved (the substance remaining, but changing in its modifications), this they say is the element and this the principle of things, and therefore they think nothing is either generated or destroyed, since this sort of entity is always conserved, as we say Socrates neither comes to be absolutely when he comes to be beautiful or musical, nor ceases to be when loses these characteristics, because the substratum, Socrates himself remains. just so they say nothing else comes to be or ceases to be; for there must be some entity-either one or more than one-from which all other things come to be, it being conserved.

τὸ μέντοι πλῆθος καὶ τὸ εἶδος τῆς τοιαύτης ἀρχῆς οὐ τὸ αὐτὸ [20] πάντες λέγουσιν, ἀλλὰ Θαλῆς μὲν ὁ τῆς τοιαύτης ἀρχηγὸς φιλοσοφίας ὕδωρ φησὶν εἶναι (διὸ καὶ τὴν γῆν ἐφ᾽ ὕδατος ἀπεφήνατο εἶναι),

Pluralitatem tamen et speciem talis principii non idem omnes dicunt. Sed thales quidem talis princeps philosophiae aquam ait esse, unde et terram esse super aquam asserebat;

Yet they do not all agree as to the number and the nature of these principles. Thales, the founder of this type of philosophy, says the principle is water (for which reason he declared that the earth rests on water),

λαβὼν ἴσως τὴν ὑπόληψιν ταύτην ἐκ τοῦ πάντων ὁρᾶν τὴν τροφὴν ὑγρὰν οὖσαν καὶ αὐτὸ τὸ θερμὸν ἐκ τούτου γιγνόμενον καὶ τούτῳ ζῶν (τὸ δ᾽ ἐξ οὗ γίγνεται, τοῦτ᾽ ἐστὶν [25] ἀρχὴ πάντων)—διά τε δὴ τοῦτο τὴν ὑπόληψιν λαβὼν ταύτην καὶ διὰ τὸ πάντων τὰ σπέρματα τὴν φύσιν ὑγρὰν ἔχειν, τὸ δ᾽ ὕδωρ ἀρχὴν τῆς φύσεως εἶναι τοῖς ὑγροῖς.

forsan [forsan enim] opinionem hanc accipiens quia cunctorum nuthmentum humidum videbat esse et ipsum calidum ex hoc factum et animal hoc vivere; ex quo vero fit , hoc est principium omnium. Propter hoc igitur eam est accipiens existimationem et quia cunctorum spermata naturam habent humidam, aqua vero nature principium est humidis.

getting the notion perhaps from seeing that the nutriment of all things is moist, and that heat itself is generated from the moist and kept alive by it (and that from which they come to be is a principle of all things). He got his notion from this fact, and from the fact that the seeds of all things have a moist nature, and that water is the origin of the nature of moist things.

εἰσὶ δέ τινες οἳ καὶ τοὺς παμπαλαίους καὶ πολὺ πρὸ τῆς νῦν γενέσεως καὶ πρώτους θεολογήσαντας οὕτως οἴονται περὶ τῆς φύσεως [30] ὑπολαβεῖν· Ὠκεανόν τε γὰρ καὶ Τηθὺν ἐποίησαν τῆς γενέσεως πατέρας, καὶ τὸν ὅρκον τῶν θεῶν ὕδωρ, τὴν καλουμένην ὑπ᾽ αὐτῶν Στύγα [τῶν ποιητῶν]· τιμιώτατον μὲν γὰρ τὸ πρεσβύτατον, ὅρκος δὲ τὸ τιμιώτατόν ἐστιν. [984α] εἰ μὲν οὖν ἀρχαία τις αὕτη καὶ παλαιὰ τετύχηκεν οὖσα περὶ τῆς φύσεως [1] ἡ δόξα, τάχ᾽ ἂν ἄδηλον εἴη, Θαλῆς μέντοι λέγεται οὕτως ἀποφήνασθαι περὶ τῆς πρώτης αἰτίας (Ἵππωνα γὰρ οὐκ ἄν τις ἀξιώσειε θεῖναι μετὰ τούτων διὰ τὴν εὐτέλειαν [5] αὐτοῦ τῆς διανοίας)·

Sunt autem aliqui qui antiquiores et multum ante eam quae nunc est generationem et primos theologizantes sic putant de natura existimandum. Occeanum enim et Thetim generationis parentes fecerunt, sacramentumque deorum aquam, Stigem ab ipsis poetis vocatam; honorabilius enim quod antiquius, sacramentum autem quod honorabilius. Si quidem igitur antiquior aliqua ista et senior fuit de natura opinio, forsan utique incertum erit; Thales quidem secundum hunc modum pronuntiasse dicitur de prima causa. Ypponem quidem enim non utique aliquis dignificabit posuisse cum hiis propter sui intellectus parvitatem.

Some think that even the ancients who lived long before the present generation, and first framed accounts of the gods, had a similar view of nature; for they made Ocean and Tethys the parents of creation, and described the oath of the gods as being by water, to which they give the name of Styx; for what is oldest is most honourable, and the most honourable thing is that by which one swears. [84a] It may perhaps be uncertain whether this opinion about nature is primitive and ancient, but Thales at any rate is said to have declared himself thus about the first cause. Hippo no one would think fit to include among these thinkers, because of the paltriness of his thought.

Ἀναξιμένης δὲ ἀέρα καὶ Διογένης πρότερον ὕδατος καὶ μάλιστ᾽ ἀρχὴν τιθέασι τῶν ἁπλῶν σωμάτων, Ἵππασος δὲ πῦρ ὁ Μεταποντῖνος καὶ Ἡράκλειτος ὁ Ἐφέσιος, Ἐμπεδοκλῆς δὲ τὰ τέτταρα, πρὸς τοῖς εἰρημένοις γῆν προστιθεὶς τέταρτον (ταῦτα γὰρ ἀεὶ διαμένειν καὶ οὐ [10] γίγνεσθαι ἀλλ᾽ ἢ πλήθει καὶ ὀλιγότητι, συγκρινόμενα καὶ διακρινόμενα εἰς ἕν τε καὶ ἐξ ἑνός):

Anaximenes autem et Diogenes aerem priorem aqua et maxime principium simplicium corporum ponunt. Ypassus autem Methapontinus et Eraclitus Ephesius ignem. Empedocles vero quatuor, cum dictis terram addens quartum; ea namque dixit semper manere et non fieri nisi pluralitate et paucitate, congregata et disgregata in unum et ex uno.

Anaximenes and Diogenes make air prior to water, and the most primary of the simple bodies, while Hippasus of Metapontium and Heraclitus of Ephesus say this of fire, and Empedocles says it of the four elements (adding a fourth-earth-to those which have been named); for these, he says, always remain and do not come to be, except that they come to be more or fewer, being aggregated into one and segregated out of one.

Ἀναξαγόρας δὲ ὁ Κλαζομένιος τῇ μὲν ἡλικίᾳ πρότερος ὢν τούτου τοῖς δ᾽ ἔργοις ὕστερος ἀπείρους εἶναί φησι τὰς ἀρχάς: σχεδὸν γὰρ ἅπαντα τὰ ὁμοιομερῆ καθάπερ ὕδωρ ἢ πῦρ οὕτω γίγνεσθαι καὶ [15] ἀπόλλυσθαί φησι, συγκρίσει καὶ διακρίσει μόνον, ἄλλως δ᾽ οὔτε γίγνεσθαι οὔτ᾽ ἀπόλλυσθαι ἀλλὰ διαμένειν ἀΐδια.

Anaxagoras vero Clazomenius isto quidem etate prior factis vero posterior infinita dixit esse principia; nam fere omnia partium consimilium ut ignem aut aquam ita generari et corrumpi ait, congregatione et disgregatione solum, aliter autem nec generari nec corrumpi sed permanere sempiterna.

Anaxagoras of Clazomenae, who, though older than Empedocles, was later in his philosophical activity, says the principles are infinite in number; for he says almost all the things that are made of parts like themselves, in the manner of water or fire, are generated and destroyed in this way, only by aggregation and segregation, and are not in any other sense generated or destroyed, but remain eternally.

ἐκ μὲν οὖν τούτων μόνην τις αἰτίαν νομίσειεν ἂν τὴν ἐν ὕλης εἴδει λεγομένην: προϊόντων δ᾽ οὕτως, αὐτὸ τὸ πρᾶγμα ὡδοποίησεν αὐτοῖς καὶ συνηνάγκασε ζητεῖν: εἰ γὰρ ὅτι μάλιστα [20] πᾶσα γένεσις καὶ φθορὰ ἔκ τινος ἑνὸς ἢ καὶ πλειόνων ἐστίν, διὰ τί τοῦτο συμβαίνει καὶ τί τὸ αἴτιον; οὐ γὰρ δὴ τό γε ὑποκείμενον αὐτὸ ποιεῖ μεταβάλλειν ἑαυτό: λέγω δ᾽ οἷον οὔτε τὸ ξύλον οὔτε ὁ χαλκὸς αἴτιος τοῦ μεταβάλλειν ἑκάτερον αὐτῶν, οὐδὲ ποιεῖ τὸ μὲν ξύλον κλίνην ὁ δὲ χαλκὸς ἀνδριάντα, [25] ἀλλ᾽ ἕτερόν τι τῆς μεταβολῆς αἴτιον. τὸ δὲ τοῦτο ζητεῖν ἐστι τὸ τὴν ἑτέραν ἀρχὴν ζητεῖν, ὡς ἂν ἡμεῖς φαίημεν, ὅθεν ἡ ἀρχὴ τῆς κινήσεως.

Ex hiis quidem igitur solam quis causam intelliget utique eam quae in materie specie dicitur. Procedentibus autem sic, res ipsa viam sibi fecit et quaerere coegit. Si enim quam maxime omnis corruptio et generatio ex aliquo uno aut pluribus est, quare hoc accidit et quae causa? Non enim utique facit ipsum subiectum transmutare se ipsum. Dico autem veluti neque lignum neque es utrumlibet ipsorum permutandi est causa; neque enim lignum facit lectum neque es statuam, sed aliud aliquid mutationis est causa. Hoc autem quaerere est aliud principium quaerere, ut si nos dicamus: unde principium motus.

From these facts one might think that the only cause is the so-called material cause; but as men thus advanced, the very facts opened the way for them and joined in forcing them to investigate the subject. However true it may be that all generation and destruction proceed from some one or (for that matter) from more elements, why does this happen and what is the cause? For at least the substratum itself does not make itself change; e.g. neither the wood nor the bronze causes the change of either of them, nor does the wood manufacture a bed and the bronze a statue, but something else is the cause of the change. And to seek this is to seek the second cause, as we should say,- that from which comes the beginning of the movement.

οἱ μὲν οὖν πάμπαν ἐξ ἀρχῆς ἁψάμενοι τῆς μεθόδου τῆς τοιαύτης καὶ ἓν φάσκοντες εἶναι τὸ ὑποκείμενον οὐθὲν ἐδυσχέραναν ἑαυτοῖς, ἀλλ᾽ ἔνιοί [30] γε τῶν ἓν λεγόντων, ὥσπερ ἡττηθέντες ὑπὸ ταύτης τῆς ζητήσεως, τὸ ἓν ἀκίνητόν φασιν εἶναι καὶ τὴν φύσιν ὅλην οὐ μόνον κατὰ γένεσιν καὶ φθοράν (τοῦτο μὲν γὰρ ἀρχαῖόν τε καὶ πάντες ὡμολόγησαν) ἀλλὰ καὶ κατὰ τὴν ἄλλην μεταβολὴν πᾶσαν: καὶ τοῦτο αὐτῶν ἴδιόν ἐστιν. [984β] [1] τῶν μὲν οὖν ἓν φασκόντων εἶναι τὸ πᾶν οὐθενὶ συνέβη τὴν τοιαύτην συνιδεῖν αἰτίαν πλὴν εἰ ἄρα Παρμενίδῃ, καὶ τούτῳ κατὰ τοσοῦτον ὅσον οὐ μόνον ἓν ἀλλὰ καὶ δύο πως τίθησιν αἰτίας εἶναι: [5] τοῖς δὲ δὴ πλείω ποιοῦσι μᾶλλον ἐνδέχεται λέγειν, οἷον τοῖς θερμὸν καὶ ψυχρὸν ἢ πῦρ καὶ γῆν: χρῶνται γὰρ ὡς κινητικὴν ἔχοντι τῷ πυρὶ τὴν φύσιν, ὕδατι δὲ καὶ γῇ καὶ τοῖς τοιούτοις τοὐναντίον.

Igitur omnino qui talem a principio viam tetigerunt et unum esse subiectum dixerunt nihil difficultatis sibimet fecerunt; verum quidam unum esse dicentium, quasi ab ea questione devicti, ipsum unum immobile dicunt esse et naturam totam non solum secundum generationem et corruptionem (hoc et enim antiquum est et quod omnes esse confessi sunt), verum et secundum aliam mutationem omnem; et hoc eorum est proprium. Unum ergo solum dicentium esse ipsum omne nulli talem intelligere causam convenit nisi forte Parmenidi, et huic in tantum quia non solum unum sed et duas aliqualiter ponit esse causas. Plura vero facientibus magis contingit dicere, ut ipsum calidum et frigidum aut ignem et terram; utuntur enim quasi motivam habente naturam igne, aqua vero et terra et huiusmodi econtrario.

Now those who at the very beginning set themselves to this kind of inquiry, and said the substratum was one, were not at all dissatisfied with themselves; but some at least of those who maintain it to be one-as though defeated by this search for the second cause-say the one and nature as a whole is unchangeable not only in respect of generation and destruction (for this is a primitive belief, and all agreed in it), but also of all [84a 34] other change; and this view is peculiar to them. [84b] Of those who said the universe was one, then none succeeded in discovering a cause of this sort, except perhaps Parmenides, and he only inasmuch as he supposes that there is not only one but also in some sense two causes. But for those who make more elements it is more possible to state the second cause, e.g. for those who make hot and cold, or fire and earth, the elements; for they treat fire as having a nature which fits it to move things, and water and earth and such things they treat in the contrary way.

μετὰ δὲ τούτους καὶ τὰς τοιαύτας ἀρχάς, ὡς οὐχ ἱκανῶν οὐσῶν γεννῆσαι τὴν τῶν ὄντων φύσιν, πάλιν [10] ὑπ᾽ αὐτῆς τῆς ἀληθείας, ὥσπερ εἴπομεν, ἀναγκαζόμενοι τὴν ἐχομένην ἐζήτησαν ἀρχήν. τοῦ γὰρ εὖ καὶ καλῶς τὰ μὲν ἔχειν τὰ δὲ γίγνεσθαι τῶν ὄντων ἴσως οὔτε πῦρ οὔτε γῆν οὔτ᾽ ἄλλο τῶν τοιούτων οὐθὲν οὔτ᾽ εἰκὸς αἴτιον εἶναι οὔτ᾽ ἐκείνους οἰηθῆναι· οὐδ᾽ αὖ τῷ αὐτομάτῳ καὶ τύχῃ τοσοῦτον ἐπιτρέψαι [15] πρᾶγμα καλῶς εἶχεν.

Post hos autem et talia principia, tamquam non sufficientibus existentium generare naturam, iterum ab ipsa veritate, velut aiebamus, coacti habitum quesierunt principium. Ipsius enim eu et bene haec quidem eorum quae sunt habere illa vero fieri forsan neque ignem neque terram neque aliud talium nihil nec verisimile causam esse, nec illos conveniens existimare; nec iterum ipsi automato et fortune tantam committere rem bene habere.

When these men and the principles of this kind had had their day, as the latter were found inadequate to generate the nature of things men were again forced by the truth itself, as we said, to inquire into the next kind of cause. For it is not likely either that fire or earth or any such element should be the reason why things manifest goodness and, beauty both in their being and in their coming to be, or that those thinkers should have supposed it was; nor again could it be right to entrust so great a matter to spontaneity and chance.

νοῦν δή τις εἰπὼν ἐνεῖναι, καθάπερ ἐν τοῖς ζῴοις, καὶ ἐν τῇ φύσει τὸν αἴτιον τοῦ κόσμου καὶ τῆς τάξεως πάσης οἷον νήφων ἐφάνη παρ᾽ εἰκῇ λέγοντας [18] τοὺς πρότερον. φανερῶς μὲν οὖν Ἀναξαγόραν ἴσμεν ἁψάμενον τούτων τῶν λόγων, αἰτίαν δ᾽ ἔχει πρότερον Ἑρμότιμος [20] ὁ Κλαζομένιος εἰπεῖν. οἱ μὲν οὖν οὕτως ὑπολαμβάνοντες ἅμα τοῦ καλῶς τὴν αἰτίαν ἀρχὴν εἶναι τῶν ὄντων ἔθεσαν, καὶ τὴν τοιαύτην ὅθεν ἡ κίνησις ὑπάρχει τοῖς οὖσιν.

Dicens et aliquis intellectum inesse, quemadmodum in animalibus et in natura, causam et mundi et ordinis totius ut excitans apparuit priores praeter convenientia dicentes. Palam quidem igitur Anaxagoram scimus hos sermones tetigisse, at tamen habet prius hermotimus clazomenius causam dicendi. Sic quidem igitur opinantes simul ipsius bene causam principium existentium esse posuerunt, et tale unde motus existentibus inest.

When one man said, then, that reason was present-as in animals, so throughout nature-as the cause of order and of all arrangement, he seemed like a sober man in contrast with the random talk of his predecessors. We know that Anaxagoras certainly adopted these views, but Hermotimus of Clazomenae is credited with expressing them earlier. Those who thought thus stated that there is a principle of things which is at the same time the cause of beauty, and that sort of cause from which things acquire movement.

## Chapter 4

ὑποπτεύσειε δ᾽ ἄν τις Ἡσίοδον πρῶτον ζητῆσαι τὸ τοιοῦτον, κἂν εἴ τις ἄλλος ἔρωτα ἢ ἐπιθυμίαν ἐν τοῖς οὖσιν ἔθηκεν [25] ὡς ἀρχήν, οἷον καὶ Παρμενίδης· καὶ γὰρ οὗτος κατασκευάζων τὴν τοῦ παντὸς γένεσιν

Suspicabitur autem utique aliquis Esiodum primum quesivisse huiusmodi, et utique si quis alius amorem aut desiderium in existentibus quasi principium posuisset, ut Parmenides; et enim hic temptans monstrare universi generationem, "primum quidem" ait

One might suspect that Hesiod was the first to look for such a thing-or some one else who put love or desire among existing things as a principle, as Parmenides, too, does; for he, in constructing the genesis of the universe, says:—

πρώτιστον μέν (φησιν) ἔρωτα θεῶν μητίσατο πάντων

Ἡσίοδος δὲ πάντων μὲν πρώτιστα χάος γένετ᾽, αὐτὰρ ἔπειτα γαῖ᾽ εὐρύστερνος... ἠδ᾽ ἔρος, ὃς πάντεσσι μεταπρέπει ἀθανάτοισιν,

"deorum amorem fore providentem omnibus". Esiodus vero "omnium primum chaos fuisse, deinde terram latam et amorem, qui omnia condecet immortalia",

Love first of all the Gods she planned. And Hesiod says:—

First of all things was chaos made, and then

Broad-breasted earth...

And love, 'mid all the gods pre-eminent,

ὡς δέον ἐν τοῖς [30] οὖσιν ὑπάρχειν τιν᾽ αἰτίαν ἥτις κινήσει καὶ συνάξει τὰ πράγματα. τούτους μὲν οὖν πῶς χρὴ διανεῖμαι περὶ τοῦ τίς πρῶτος, ἐξέστω κρίνειν ὕστερον· ἐπεὶ δὲ καὶ τἀναντία τοῖς ἀγαθοῖς ἐνόντα ἐφαίνετο ἐν τῇ φύσει, καὶ οὐ μόνον τάξις καὶ τὸ καλὸν ἀλλὰ καὶ ἀταξία καὶ τὸ αἰσχρόν, [985α] [1] καὶ πλείω τὰ κακὰ τῶν ἀγαθῶν καὶ τὰ φαῦλα τῶν καλῶν, οὕτως ἄλλος τις φιλίαν εἰσήνεγκε καὶ νεῖκος, ἑκάτερον ἑκατέρων αἴτιον τούτων. εἰ γάρ τις ἀκολουθοίη καὶ λαμβάνοι πρὸς τὴν διάνοιαν [5] καὶ μὴ πρὸς ἃ ψελλίζεται λέγων Ἐμπεδοκλῆς, εὑρήσει τὴν μὲν φιλίαν αἰτίαν οὖσαν τῶν ἀγαθῶν τὸ δὲ νεῖκος τῶν κακῶν· ὥστ᾽ εἴ τις φαίη τρόπον τινὰ καὶ λέγειν καὶ πρῶτον λέγειν τὸ κακὸν καὶ τὸ ἀγαθὸν ἀρχὰς Ἐμπεδοκλέα, τάχ᾽ ἂν λέγοι καλῶς, εἴπερ τὸ τῶν ἀγαθῶν ἁπάντων αἴτιον [10] αὐτὸ τἀγαθόν ἐστι [καὶ τῶν κακῶν τὸ κακόν].

quasi necessarium sit in existentibus esse causam quae res ipsas moveat et congreget. Hns quidem igitur quomodo oporteat distribuere de hoc quis primus, liceat iudicare posterius. Quoniam vero contraria bonis inesse videbantur in natura, et non solum ordinatio et bonum sed inordinatio et turpe, et plura mala melioribus et praua bonis, sic alius aliquis amorem induxit et litem, singula singulorum causam horum. si quis enim assequatur et accipiat ad intellectum et non ad quae balbutit dicens Empedocles, inveniet amorem quidem causam esse agathorum, litem vero malorum. Quare si quis dixerit quodam modo rdicere et primum dicere Empedoclem bonum et malum principia, forsan bene dicet, si bonorum omnium ei bonum est causa et malorum malum.

which implies that among existing things there must be from the first a cause which will move things and bring them together. How these thinkers should be arranged with regard to priority of discovery let us be allowed to decide later; but since the contraries of the various forms of good were also perceived to be present in nature-not only order and the beautiful, but also disorder and the ugly, and [85a] bad things in greater number than good, and ignoble things than beautiful-therefore another thinker introduced friendship and strife, each of the two the cause of one of these two sets of qualities. For if we were to follow out the view of Empedocles, and interpret it according to its meaning and not to its lisping expression, we should find that friendship is the cause of good things, and strife of bad. Therefore, if we said that

Empedocles in a sense both mentions, and is the first to mention, the bad and the good as principles, we should perhaps be right, since the cause of all goods is the good itself.

οὗτοι μὲν οὖν, ὥσπερ λέγομεν, καὶ μέχρι τούτου δυοῖν αἰτίαιν ὧν ἡμεῖς διωρίσαμεν ἐν τοῖς περὶ φύσεως ἡμμένοι φαίνονται, τῆς τε ὕλης καὶ τοῦ ὅθεν ἡ κίνησις, ἀμυδρῶς μέντοι καὶ οὐθὲν σαφῶς ἀλλ᾽ οἷον ἐν ταῖς μάχαις οἱ ἀγύμναστοι ποιοῦσιν· καὶ γὰρ ἐκεῖνοι περιφερόμενοι [15] τύπτουσι πολλάκις καλὰς πληγάς, ἀλλ᾽ οὔτε ἐκεῖνοι ἀπὸ ἐπιστήμης οὔτε οὗτοι ἐοίκασιν εἰδέναι ὅ τι λέγουσιν· σχεδὸν γὰρ οὐθὲν χρώμενοι φαίνονται τούτοις ἀλλ᾽ ἢ κατὰ μικρόν.

Isti quidem igitur, sicut diximus, et usque ad hoc duas causas tetigerunt quas in phisicis determinavimus, materiamque et id unde motus, obscure quidem et non manifeste sed qualiter in bellis ineruditi faciunt; et enim illi circumducti saepe bonas plagas faciunt, at nec illi ex scientia nec isti sunt assimilati scientibus dicere quod dicunt; hiis etenim fere usi videntur nihil nisi parum.

These thinkers, as we say, evidently grasped, and to this extent, two of the causes which we distinguished in our work on nature-the matter and the source of the movement-vaguely, however, and with no clearness, but as untrained men behave in fights; for they go round their opponents and often strike fine blows, but they do not fight on scientific principles, and so too these thinkers do not seem to know what they say; for it is evident that, as a rule, they make no use of their causes except to a small extent.

Ἀναξαγόρας τε γὰρ μηχανῇ χρῆται τῷ νῷ πρὸς τὴν κοσμοποιίαν, καὶ ὅταν ἀπορήσῃ διὰ τίν᾽ αἰτίαν [20] ἐξ ἀνάγκης ἐστί, τότε παρέλκει αὐτόν, ἐν δὲ τοῖς ἄλλοις πάντα μᾶλλον αἰτιᾶται τῶν γιγνομένων ἢ νοῦν,

Anaxagoras enim artificialiter ad mundi generationem utitur intellectu. Nam quando dubitat qua causa ex necessitate est, tunc attrahit ipsum, in aliis vero omnia magis causatur eorum quae fiunt quam intellectum.

For Anaxagoras uses reason as a deus ex machina for the making of the world, and when he is at a loss to tell from what cause something necessarily is, then he drags reason in, but in all other cases ascribes events to anything rather than to reason.

καὶ Ἐμπεδοκλῆς ἐπὶ πλέον μὲν τούτου χρῆται τοῖς αἰτίοις, οὐ μὴν οὔθ᾽ ἱκανῶς, οὔτ᾽ ἐν τούτοις εὑρίσκει τὸ ὁμολογούμενον. πολλαχοῦ γοῦν αὐτῷ ἡ μὲν φιλία διακρίνει τὸ δὲ νεῖκος συγκρίνει. [25] ὅταν μὲν γὰρ εἰς τὰ στοιχεῖα διίστηται τὸ πᾶν ὑπὸ τοῦ νείκους, τότε τὸ πῦρ εἰς ἓν συγκρίνεται καὶ τῶν ἄλλων στοιχείων ἕκαστον· ὅταν δὲ πάλιν ὑπὸ τῆς φιλίας συνίωσιν εἰς τὸ ἕν, ἀναγκαῖον ἐξ ἑκάστου τὰ μόρια διακρίνεσθαι πάλιν.

Et Empedocles plus quidem hoc utitur causis, sed tamen nec sufficienter, nec in hiis invenit quod confessum est. Multis igitur in locis apud ipsum amor disgregat, lis autem congregat. Nam cum in elementa quidem ipsum omne a lite distrahitur, tunc ignis in unum et aliorum elementorum singula concernuntur; cum autem iterum in unum ab amore conveniunt, necesse rursum ut ex singulis particule secernantur.

And Empedocles, though he uses the causes to a greater extent than this, neither does so sufficiently nor attains consistency in their use. At least, in many cases he makes love segregate things, and strife aggregate them. For whenever the universe is dissolved into its elements by strife, fire is aggregated into one, and so is each of the other elements; but whenever again under the influence of love they come together into one, the parts must again be segregated out of each element.

Ἐμπεδοκλῆς μὲν οὖν παρὰ τοὺς πρότερον πρῶτος [30] τὸ τὴν αἰτίαν διελεῖν εἰσήνεγκεν, οὐ μίαν ποιήσας τὴν τῆς κινήσεως ἀρχὴν ἀλλ᾽ ἑτέρας τε καὶ ἐναντίας, ἔτι δὲ τὰ ὡς ἐν ὕλης εἴδει λεγόμενα στοιχεῖα τέτταρα πρῶτος εἶπεν (οὐ μὴν χρῆταί γε τέτταρσιν ἀλλ᾽ ὡς δυσὶν οὖσι μόνοις, [985β] [1] πυρὶ μὲν καθ᾽ αὑτὸ τοῖς δ᾽ ἀντικειμένοις ὡς μιᾷ φύσει, γῇ τε καὶ ἀέρι καὶ ὕδατι: λάβοι δ᾽ ἄν τις αὐτὸ θεωρῶν ἐκ τῶν ἐπῶν):

Empedocles quidem igitur praeter priores primus hanc causam dividens induxit, non unum faciens motus principium sed diversa et contraria. Amplius autem quae in materie specie dicuntur elementa quatuor primus dixit; non tamen utitur quatuor sed ut duobus existentibus solis, igne quidem secundum se, oppositis vero quasi una natura: terra et aere et aqua. Sumet autem utique aliquis id speculans ex versibus.

Empedocles, then, in contrast with his precessors, was the first to introduce the dividing of this cause, not positing one source of movement, but different and contrary sources. Again, he was the first to speak of four material elements; yet he does not use four, but treats them as two only; [ 85b] he treats fire by itself, and its opposite-earth, air, and water-as one kind of thing. We may learn this by study of his verses.

οὗτος μὲν οὖν, ὥσπερ λέγομεν, οὕτω τε καὶ τοσαύτας εἴρηκε τὰς ἀρχάς:

Hic quidem igitur, sicut diximus, sic et tot dixit principia.

This philosopher then, as we say, has spoken of the principles in this way, and made them of this number.

Λεύκιππος δὲ καὶ ὁ ἑταῖρος [5] αὐτοῦ Δημόκριτος στοιχεῖα μὲν τὸ πλῆρες καὶ τὸ κενὸν εἶναί φασι, λέγοντες τὸ μὲν ὂν τὸ δὲ μὴ ὄν, τούτων δὲ τὸ μὲν πλῆρες καὶ στερεὸν τὸ ὄν, τὸ δὲ κενὸν τὸ μὴ ὄν (διὸ καὶ οὐθὲν μᾶλλον τὸ ὂν τοῦ μὴ ὄντος εἶναί φασιν, ὅτι οὐδὲ τοῦ κενοῦ τὸ σῶμα), αἴτια δὲ τῶν ὄντων ταῦτα ὡς [10] ὕλην.

Leucippus vero et collega eius Democritus elementa quidem plenum et inane dicunt esse, dicentes velut hoc quidem ens illud vero non ens, horum autem plenum quidem et solidum ens, inane vero non ens; propter quod et nihil magis ens non ente esse dicunt, quia nec inane corpore. Causas autem entium haec ut materiam.

Leucippus and his associate Democritus say that the full and the empty are the elements, calling the one being and the other non-being-the full and solid being being, the empty non-being (whence they say being no more is than non-being, because the solid no more is than the empty); and they make these the material causes of things.

καὶ καθάπερ οἱ ἓν ποιοῦντες τὴν ὑποκειμένην οὐσίαν τἆλλα τοῖς πάθεσιν αὐτῆς γεννῶσι, τὸ μανὸν καὶ τὸ πυκνὸν ἀρχὰς τιθέμενοι τῶν παθημάτων, τὸν αὐτὸν τρόπον καὶ οὗτοι τὰς διαφορὰς αἰτίας τῶν ἄλλων εἶναί φασιν. ταύτας μέντοι τρεῖς εἶναι λέγουσι, σχῆμά τε καὶ τάξιν καὶ [15] θέσιν: διαφέρειν γάρ φασι τὸ ὂν ῥυσμῷ καὶ διαθιγῇ καὶ τροπῇ μόνον: τούτων δὲ ὁ μὲν ῥυσμὸς σχῆμά ἐστιν ἡ δὲ διαθιγὴ τάξις ἡ δὲ τροπὴ θέσις: διαφέρει γὰρ τὸ μὲν Α τοῦ Ν σχήματι τὸ δὲ ΑΝ τοῦ ΝΑ τάξει τὸ δὲ Ζ τοῦ Η θέσει. περὶ δὲ κινήσεως, ὅθεν ἢ πῶς ὑπάρξει τοῖς οὖσι, καὶ [20] οὗτοι παραπλησίως τοῖς ἄλλοις ῥᾳθύμως ἀφεῖσαν.

Et quemadmodum qui unum faciunt subiectam substantiam alia passionibus eius generant, rarum et spissum principia passionum ponentes, eodem modo et hii differentias causas aliorum esse dicunt. Has vero tres dicunt esse: figuram et ordinem et positionem. Differre enim aiunt ens rismo et diathigi et tropi solum; horum autem rismos figura est et diathigi ordo et tropi positio. Differt enim a ab n figura, an autem a na ordine, z autem ab n positione. De motu vero, unde aut quomodo inest existentibus, et hii aliis consimiliter negligenter dimiserunt.

And as those who make the underlying substance one generate all other things by its modifications, supposing the rare and the dense to be the sources of the modifications, in the same way these philosophers say the differences in the elements are the causes of all other qualities. These differences, they say, are three-shape and order and position. For they say the real is differentiated only by 'rhythm and 'inter-contact' and 'turning'; and of these rhythm is shape, inter-contact is order, and turning is position; for A differs from N in shape, AN from NA in order, M from W in position. The question of movement-whence or how it is to belong to things – these thinkers, like the others, lazily neglected.

περὶ μὲν οὖν τῶν δύο αἰτιῶν, ὥσπερ λέγομεν, ἐπὶ τοσοῦτον ἔοικεν ἐζητῆσθαι παρὰ τῶν πρότερον.

De duabus quidem igitur causis, ut diximus, in tantum videtur quesitum esse prius.

Regarding the two causes, then, as we say, the inquiry seems to have been pushed thus far by the early philosophers.

*Chapter* 5

ἐν δὲ τούτοις καὶ πρὸ τούτων οἱ καλούμενοι Πυθαγόρειοι τῶν μαθημάτων ἁψάμενοι πρῶτοι ταῦτά τε προήγαγον, καὶ [25] ἐντραφέντες ἐν αὐτοῖς τὰς τούτων ἀρχὰς τῶν ὄντων ἀρχὰς ᾠήθησαν εἶναι πάντων. ἐπεὶ δὲ τούτων οἱ ἀριθμοὶ φύσει πρῶτοι, ἐν δὲ τούτοις ἐδόκουν θεωρεῖν ὁμοιώματα πολλὰ τοῖς οὖσι καὶ γιγνομένοις, μᾶλλον ἢ ἐν πυρὶ καὶ γῇ καὶ ὕδατι, ὅτι τὸ μὲν τοιονδὶ τῶν ἀριθμῶν πάθος δικαιοσύνη [30] τὸ δὲ τοιονδὶ ψυχή τε καὶ νοῦς ἕτερον δὲ καιρὸς καὶ τῶν ἄλλων ὡς εἰπεῖν ἕκαστον ὁμοίως,

In hiis autem et ante hos vocati Pytagorici mathematica tangentes primi ea produxerunt, et in eis nutriti horum principia omnium esse putaverunt. Horum autem quoniam numeri natura sunt primi, et in numeris videbantur multas speculari similitudines existentibus et factis, magis quam in igne et aqua et terra; quia talis quidem numerorum passio iustitia, talis autem anima et intellectus, alia vero tempus, et aliorum ut est dicere unumquodque similiter.

[85b 22] Contemporaneously with these philosophers and before them, the so-called Pythagoreans, who were the first to take up mathematics, not only advanced this study, but also having been brought up in it they thought its principles were the principles of all things. Since of these principles numbers are by nature the first, and in numbers they seemed to see many resemblances to the things that exist and come into being-more than in fire and earth and water (such and such a modification of numbers being justice, another being soul and reason, another being opportunity-and similarly almost all other things being numerically expressible).

ἔτι δὲ τῶν ἁρμονιῶν ἐν ἀριθμοῖς ὁρῶντες τὰ πάθη καὶ τοὺς λόγους, ἐπεὶ δὴ τὰ μὲν ἄλλα τοῖς ἀριθμοῖς ἐφαίνοντο τὴν φύσιν ἀφωμοιῶσθαι πᾶσαν, οἱ δ᾽ ἀριθμοὶ πάσης τῆς φύσεως πρῶτοι, [986α] [1] τὰ τῶν ἀριθμῶν στοιχεῖα τῶν ὄντων στοιχεῖα πάντων ὑπέλαβον εἶναι, καὶ τὸν ὅλον οὐρανὸν ἁρμονίαν εἶναι καὶ ἀριθμόν: καὶ ὅσα εἶχον ὁμολογούμενα ἔν τε τοῖς ἀριθμοῖς καὶ ταῖς ἁρμονίαις πρὸς [5] τὰ τοῦ οὐρανοῦ πάθη καὶ μέρη καὶ πρὸς τὴν ὅλην διακόσμησιν, ταῦτα συνάγοντες ἐφήρμοττον. κἂν εἴ τί που διέλειπε, προσεγλίχοντο τοῦ συνειρομένην πᾶσαν αὐτοῖς εἶναι τὴν πραγματείαν: λέγω δ᾽ οἷον, ἐπειδὴ τέλειον ἡ δεκὰς εἶναι δοκεῖ καὶ πᾶσαν περιειληφέναι τὴν τῶν ἀριθμῶν φύσιν, [10] καὶ τὰ φερόμενα κατὰ τὸν οὐρανὸν δέκα μὲν εἶναί φασιν, ὄντων δὲ ἐννέα μόνον τῶν φανερῶν διὰ τοῦτο δεκάτην τὴν ἀντίχθονα ποιοῦσιν. διώρισται δὲ περὶ τούτων ἐν ἑτέροις ἡμῖν ἀκριβέστερον.

Amplius autem et armoniarum in numeris speculantes passiones et rationes, quoniam et alia quidem numeris secundum naturam omnem videbantur assimilata esse, numeri autem omnis nature primi, elementa numerorum existentium elementa cunctorum esse existimaverunt, et totum celum armoniam esse et numerum. Et quaecumque habebant confessa monstrare et in numeris et in armoniis ad celi passiones et partes et ad totum ornatum, haec colligentes adaptabant. Et si quid alicubi deficiebat, adnectebant ut ipsis totum negotium esset connexum. Dico autem puta quoniam perfectus denarius esse videtur et omnem comprehendere numerorum naturam, et quae secundum celum feruntur decem quidem esse dicunt. Solum autem novem existentibus manifestis, ideo antixthonam decimam faciunt. De hiis autem certius est in aliis a nobis determinatum.

Since, again, they saw that the modifications and the ratios of the musical scales were expressible in numbers; – since, then, all other things seemed in their whole nature to be modelled on numbers, and numbers seemed to be the first things in the whole of [86a] nature, they supposed the elements of numbers to be the elements of all things, and the whole heaven to be a musical scale and a number. And all the properties of numbers and scales which they could show to agree with the attributes and parts and the whole arrangement of the heavens, they collected and fitted into their scheme; and if there was a gap anywhere, they readily made additions so as to make their whole theory coherent. E.g. as the number 10 is thought to be perfect and to comprise the whole nature of numbers, they say that the bodies which move through the heavens are ten, but as the visible bodies are only nine, to meet this they invent a tenth—the 'counter-earth'. We have discussed these matters more exactly elsewhere[3].

ἀλλ᾽ οὗ δὴ χάριν ἐπερχόμεθα, τοῦτό ἐστιν ὅπως λάβωμεν καὶ παρὰ τούτων τίνας εἶναι τιθέασι τὰς [15] ἀρχὰς καὶ πῶς εἰς τὰς εἰρημένας ἐμπίπτουσιν αἰτίας.

Sed cuius quidem gratia supervenimus, hoc est ut accipiamus et de hiis quae ponunt esse principia et quomodo in dictas cadunt causas.

But the object of our review is that we may learn from these philosophers also what they suppose to be the principles and how these fall under the causes we have named.

φαίνονται δὴ καὶ οὗτοι τὸν ἀριθμὸν νομίζοντες ἀρχὴν εἶναι καὶ ὡς ὕλην τοῖς οὖσι καὶ ὡς πάθη τε καὶ ἕξεις, τοῦ δὲ ἀριθμοῦ στοιχεῖα τό τε ἄρτιον καὶ τὸ περιττόν, τούτων δὲ τὸ μὲν πεπερασμένον τὸ δὲ ἄπειρον, τὸ δ᾽ ἓν ἐξ ἀμφοτέρων εἶναι τούτων [20] (καὶ γὰρ ἄρτιον εἶναι καὶ περιττόν), τὸν δ᾽ ἀριθμὸν ἐκ τοῦ ἑνός, ἀριθμοὺς δέ, καθάπερ εἴρηται, τὸν ὅλον οὐρανόν.

Videntur igitur [Videtur ergo] et hii numerum putare principium esse et quasi materiam existentibus et quasi passiones et habitus; numeri vero elementa par et impar, et horum hoc quidem finitum illud vero infinitum, unum autem ex hiis utrisque esse (et enim par esse et impar), numerum vero ex uno, numeros autem, sicut dictum est, totum celum.

Evidently, then, these thinkers also consider that number is the principle both as matter for things and as forming both their modifications and their permanent states, and hold that the elements of number are the even and the odd, and that of these the latter is limited, and the former unlimited; and that the One proceeds from both of these (for it is both even and odd), and number from the One; and that the whole heaven, as has been said, is numbers.

ἕτεροι δὲ τῶν αὐτῶν τούτων τὰς ἀρχὰς δέκα λέγουσιν εἶναι τὰς κατὰ συστοιχίαν λεγομένας, πέρας [καὶ] ἄπειρον, περιττὸν [καὶ] ἄρτιον, ἓν [καὶ] πλῆθος, δεξιὸν [καὶ] ἀριστερόν, ἄρρεν [25] [καὶ] θῆλυ, ἠρεμοῦν [καὶ] κινούμενον, εὐθὺ [καὶ] καμπύλον, φῶς [καὶ] σκότος, ἀγαθὸν [καὶ] κακόν, τετράγωνον [καὶ] ἑτερόμηκες·

Eorundem autem alii decem dicunt esse principia secundum coelementationem dicta: finitum infinitum, rimpar par, unum plurale, dextrum sinistrum, masculinum femininum, quiescens motum, rectum curuum, lucem tenebras, bonum malum, quadrangulare iongius altera parte.

Other members of this same school say there are ten principles, which they arrange in two columns of cognates-limit and unlimited, odd and even, one and plurality, right and left, male and female, resting and moving, straight and curved, light and darkness, good and bad, square and oblong.

ὅνπερ τρόπον ἔοικε καὶ Ἀλκμαίων ὁ Κροτωνιάτης ὑπολαβεῖν, καὶ ἤτοι οὗτος παρ᾽ ἐκείνων ἢ ἐκεῖνοι παρὰ τούτου παρέλαβον τὸν λόγον τοῦτον· καὶ γὰρ [ἐγένετο τὴν ἡλικίαν] Ἀλκμαίων [30] [ἐπὶ γέροντι Πυθαγόρᾳ,] ἀπεφήνατο [δὲ] παραπλησίως τούτοις· φησὶ γὰρ εἶναι δύο τὰ πολλὰ τῶν ἀνθρωπίνων, λέγων τὰς ἐναντιότητας οὐχ ὥσπερ οὗτοι διωρισμένας ἀλλὰ τὰς τυχούσας, οἷον λευκὸν μέλαν, γλυκὺ πικρόν, ἀγαθὸν κακόν, μέγα μικρόν. οὗτος μὲν οὖν ἀδιορίστως ἀπέρριψε περὶ τῶν λοιπῶν, [986β] [1] οἱ δὲ Πυθαγόρειοι καὶ πόσαι καὶ τίνες αἱ ἐναντιώσεις [2] ἀπεφήναντο.

Quemadmodum videtur Alemeon Crotoniatis suscipere, et aut hic ab illis aut illi ab hoc hunc sermonem acceperunt; et enim fuit etate alemeon sene existente Pytagora, hiis vero consimiliter enuntiavit. Nam ait esse duo multa humanorum, dicens contrarietates non sicut hii determinatas sed quascumque, ut album nigrum,

dulce amarum, bonum malum, magnum parvum. Hic quidem indeterminate proiecit de ceteris, Pytagorici vero et quot et quae contrarietates enuntiaverunt.

In this way Alcmaeon of Croton seems also to have conceived the matter, and either he got this view from them or they got it from him; for he expressed himself similarly to them. For he says most human affairs go in pairs, meaning not definite contrarieties such as the Pythagoreans speak of, but any chance contrarieties, e.g. white and black, sweet and bitter, good and bad, great and small. He threw out indefinite suggestions about the other [86b] contrarieties, but the Pythagoreans declared both how many and which their contrarieties are.

παρὰ μὲν οὖν τούτων ἀμφοῖν τοσοῦτον ἔστι λαβεῖν, ὅτι τἀναντία ἀρχαὶ τῶν ὄντων: τὸ δ᾽ ὅσαι παρὰ τῶν ἑτέρων, καὶ τίνες αὗταί εἰσιν. πῶς μέντοι πρὸς [5] τὰς εἰρημένας αἰτίας ἐνδέχεται συνάγειν, σαφῶς μὲν οὐ διήρθρωται παρ᾽ ἐκείνων, ἐοίκασι δ᾽ ὡς ἐν ὕλης εἴδει τὰ στοιχεῖα τάττειν: ἐκ τούτων γὰρ ὡς ἐνυπαρχόντων συνεστάναι καὶ πεπλάσθαι φασὶ τὴν οὐσίαν.

Ab hiis igitur ambobus tantum est accipere, quia contraria sunt existentium principia; quot vero ab aliis, et quae haec sint. Qualiter tamen ad dictas causas contingit adducere, plane quidem non est dearticulatum ab illis, videntur autem ut in materie specie elementa ordinare; ex hiis enim ut ex eis quae insunt constitui et plasmari dicunt substantiam.

From both these schools, then, we can learn this much, that the contraries are the principles of things; and how many these principles are and which they are, we can learn from one of the two schools. But how these principles can be brought together under the causes we have named has not been clearly and articulately stated by them; they seem, however, to range the elements under the head of matter; for out of these as immanent parts they say substance is composed and moulded.

τῶν μὲν οὖν παλαιῶν καὶ πλείω λεγόντων τὰ στοιχεῖα τῆς φύσεως ἐκ τούτων ἱκανόν [10] ἐστι θεωρῆσαι τὴν διάνοιαν: εἰσὶ δέ τινες οἳ περὶ τοῦ παντὸς ὡς μιᾶς οὔσης φύσεως ἀπεφήναντο, τρόπον δὲ οὐ τὸν αὐτὸν πάντες οὔτε τοῦ καλῶς οὔτε τοῦ κατὰ τὴν φύσιν. εἰς μὲν οὖν τὴν νῦν σκέψιν τῶν αἰτίων οὐδαμῶς συναρμόττει περὶ αὐτῶν ὁ λόγος (οὐ γὰρ ὥσπερ ἔνιοι τῶν φυσιολόγων ἓν ὑποθέμενοι [15] τὸ ὂν ὅμως γεννῶσιν ὡς ἐξ ὕλης τοῦ ἑνός, ἀλλ᾽ ἕτερον τρόπον οὗτοι λέγουσιν: ἐκεῖνοι μὲν γὰρ προστιθέασι κίνησιν, γεννῶντές γε τὸ πᾶν, οὗτοι δὲ ἀκίνητον εἶναί φασιν):

Antiquorum quidem igitur elementa nature plura dicentium ex hiis sufficiens est intellectum speculari. Sunt autem aliqui qui de omni quasi una existente natura enuntiaverunt, modo vero non eodem omnes neque ipsius bene neque ipsius secundum naturam. Ad presentem quidem igitur causarum perscrutationem nullatenus congruit de ipsis sermo;  non enim ut phisiologorum quidam qui unum posuerunt, ipsum ens tamen generant quasi ex materia ex uno, sed alio dicunt hii modo; illi namque  motum apponunt, ipsum omne generantes, hij vero immobile dicunt esse.

From these facts we may sufficiently perceive the meaning of the ancients who said the elements of nature were more than one; but there are some who spoke of the universe as if it were one entity, though they were not all alike either in the excellence of their statement or in its conformity to the facts of nature. The discussion of them is in no way appropriate to our present investigation of causes, for they do not, like some of the natural philosophers, assume being to be one and yet generate it out of the one as out of matter, but they speak in another way; those others add change, since they generate the universe, but these thinkers say the universe is unchangeable.

οὐ μὴν ἀλλὰ τοσοῦτόν γε οἰκεῖόν ἐστι τῇ νῦν σκέψει. Παρμενίδης μὲν γὰρ ἔοικε τοῦ κατὰ τὸν λόγον ἑνὸς ἅπτεσθαι, Μέλισσος [20] δὲ τοῦ κατὰ τὴν ὕλην (διὸ καὶ ὁ μὲν πεπερασμένον ὁ δ᾽ ἄπειρόν φησιν εἶναι αὐτό): Ξενοφάνης δὲ πρῶτος τούτων ἑνίσας (ὁ γὰρ Παρμενίδης τούτου λέγεται γενέσθαι μαθητής) οὐθὲν διεσαφήνισεν, οὐδὲ τῆς φύσεως τούτων οὐδετέρας ἔοικε θιγεῖν, ἀλλ᾽ εἰς τὸν ὅλον οὐρανὸν ἀποβλέψας τὸ ἓν εἶναί φησι τὸν [25] θεόν.

At tamen tantum conveniens est presenti speculationi. Parmenides quidem enim videtur unum secundum rationem tangere, mellissus vero ipsum secundum materiam; quare et hic quidem finitum, ille vero infinitum id ait esse. Xenophanes vero primus horum unum dixit. Parmenides enim qui huius dicitur  discipulus nihil explanavit, neque de natura horum neutra visus est tangere, sed ad totum celum respiciens ipsum unum dicit esse  deum.

Yet this much is germane to the present inquiry: Parmenides seems to fasten on that which is one in definition, Melissus on that which is one in matter, for which reason the former says that it is limited, the latter that it is unlimited; while Xenophanes, the first of these partisans of the One (for Parmenides is said to have been his pupil), gave no clear statement, nor does he seem to have grasped the nature of either of these causes, but with reference to the whole material universe he says the One is God.

οὗτοι μὲν οὖν, καθάπερ εἴπομεν, ἀφετέοι πρὸς τὴν νῦν ζήτησιν, οἱ μὲν δύο καὶ πάμπαν ὡς ὄντες μικρὸν ἀγροικότεροι, Ξενοφάνης καὶ Μέλισσος: Παρμενίδης δὲ μᾶλλον βλέπων ἔοικέ που λέγειν: παρὰ γὰρ τὸ ὂν τὸ μὴ ὂν οὐθὲν ἀξιῶν εἶναι, ἐξ ἀνάγκης ἓν οἴεται εἶναι, τὸ ὄν, καὶ [30] ἄλλο οὐθέν (περὶ οὗ σαφέστερον ἐν τοῖς περὶ φύσεως εἰρήκαμεν), ἀναγκαζόμενος δ᾽ ἀκολουθεῖν τοῖς φαινομένοις, καὶ τὸ ἓν μὲν κατὰ τὸν λόγον πλείω δὲ κατὰ τὴν αἴσθησιν ὑπολαμβάνων εἶναι, δύο τὰς αἰτίας καὶ δύο τὰς ἀρχὰς πάλιν τίθησι, θερμὸν καὶ ψυχρόν, οἷον πῦρ καὶ γῆν λέγων: [987α] [1] τούτων δὲ κατὰ μὲν τὸ ὂν τὸ θερμὸν τάττει θάτερον δὲ κατὰ τὸ μὴ ὄν.

Hii quidem igitur, sicut diximus, praetermittendi sunt ad presentem inquisitionem, duo quidem et penitus tamquam existentes parum agrestiores: xenophanes et mellissus. Parmenides autem magis videns visus est dicere. Nam praeter ens non ens nichij dignatus esse, ex necessitate ens opinatur unum esse et aliud nihil; de quo manifestius in phisicis diximus. Coactus vero apparentia sequi, et unum quidem secundum rationem pjura vero secundum sensum opinans esse, duas causas et duo principia rursus ponit, calidum et frigidum, ut ignem et terram dicens; horum autem quod quidem secundum ens calidum ordinat, alterum vero secundum non ens.

Now these thinkers, as we said, must be neglected for the purposes of the present inquiry-two of them entirely, as being a little too naive, viz. Xenophanes and Melissus; but Parmenides seems in places to speak with more insight. For, claiming that, besides the existent, nothing non-existent exists, he thinks that of necessity one thing exists, viz. the existent and nothing else (on this we have spoken more clearly in our work on nature), but being forced to follow the observed facts, and supposing the existence of that which is one in definition, but more than one according to our sensations, he now posits two causes and two principles, calling them hot and cold, i.e. fire and earth; and of these he ranges the hot with the existent, and the other with the [87a] non-existent.

ἐκ μὲν οὖν τῶν εἰρημένων καὶ παρὰ τῶν συνηδρευκότων ἤδη τῷ λόγῳ σοφῶν ταῦτα παρειλήφαμεν, παρὰ μὲν τῶν πρώτων σωματικήν τε τὴν ἀρχήν (ὕδωρ γὰρ καὶ [5] πῦρ καὶ τὰ τοιαῦτα σώματά ἐστιν), καὶ τῶν μὲν μίαν τῶν δὲ πλείους τὰς ἀρχὰς τὰς σωματικάς, ἀμφοτέρων μέντοι ταύτας ὡς ἐν ὕλης εἴδει τιθέντων, παρὰ δέ τινων ταύτην τε τὴν αἰτίαν τιθέντων καὶ πρὸς ταύτῃ τὴν ὅθεν ἡ κίνησις, καὶ ταύτην παρὰ τῶν μὲν μίαν παρὰ τῶν δὲ δύο.

Ex dictis quidem igitur <et de rationi consentientibus iam sapientibus haec accepimus. A primis quidem principium esse corporeum (aqua namque et ignis et similia corpora sunt), et ab hiis quidem unum ab illis vero plura principia corporea, utrisque tamen haec ut in materie specie ponentibus; a quibusdam vero hanc causam ponentibus et cum hac illam unde motus, et hanc ab hiis quidem unam ab illis vero duas.

From what has been said, then, and from the wise men who have now sat in council with us, we have got thus much-on the one hand from the earliest philosophers, who regard the first principle as corporeal (for water and fire and such things are bodies), and of whom some suppose that there is one corporeal principle, others that there are more than one, but both put these under the head of matter; and on the other hand from some who posit both this cause and besides this the source of movement, which we have got from some as single and from others as twofold.

μέχρι μὲν [10] οὖν τῶν Ἰταλικῶν καὶ χωρὶς ἐκείνων μοουχώτερον εἰρήκασιν οἱ ἄλλοι περὶ αὐτῶν, πλὴν ὥσπερ εἴπομεν δυοῖν τε αἰτίαιν τυγχάνουσι κεχρημένοι, καὶ τούτων τὴν ἑτέραν οἱ μὲν μίαν οἱ δὲ δύο ποιοῦσι, τὴν ὅθεν ἡ κίνησις:

Igitur usque ad Ytalicos et absque illis mediocrius dixerunt alii de ipsis; at tamen, ut diximus, duabus sunt causis usi, et harum alteram hii quidem unam illi vero duas faciunt: illam unde motus.

Down to the Italian school, then, and apart from it, philosophers have treated these subjects rather obscurely, except that, as we said, they have in fact used two kinds of cause, and one of these-the source of movement-some treat as one and others as two.

οἱ δὲ Πυθαγόρειοι δύο μὲν τὰς ἀρχὰς κατὰ τὸν αὐτὸν εἰρήκασι τρόπον, τοσοῦτον [15] δὲ προσεπέθεσαν ὃ καὶ ἴδιόν ἐστιν αὐτῶν, ὅτι τὸ πεπερασμένον καὶ τὸ ἄπειρον [καὶ τὸ ἓν] οὐχ ἑτέρας τινὰς ᾠήθησαν εἶναι φύσεις, οἷον πῦρ ἢ γῆν ἤ τι τοιοῦτον ἕτερον, ἀλλ᾽ αὐτὸ τὸ ἄπειρον καὶ αὐτὸ τὸ ἓν οὐσίαν εἶναι τούτων ὧν κατηγοροῦνται, διὸ καὶ ἀριθμὸν εἶναι τὴν οὐσίαν πάντων. περί τε [20] τούτων οὖν τοῦτον ἀπεφήναντο τὸν τρόπον, καὶ περὶ τοῦ τί ἐστιν ἤρξαντο μὲν λέγειν καὶ ὁρίζεσθαι, λίαν δ᾽ ἁπλῶς ἐπραγματεύθησαν. ὡρίζοντό τε γὰρ ἐπιπολαίως, καὶ ᾧ πρώτῳ ὑπάρξειεν ὁ λεχθεὶς ὅρος, τοῦτ᾽ εἶναι τὴν οὐσίαν τοῦ πράγματος ἐνόμιζον, ὥσπερ εἴ τις οἴοιτο ταὐτὸν εἶναι διπλάσιον καὶ τὴν [25] δυάδα διότι πρῶτον ὑπάρχει τοῖς δυσὶ τὸ διπλάσιον. ἀλλ᾽ οὐ ταὐτὸν ἴσως ἐστὶ τὸ εἶναι διπλασίῳ καὶ δυάδι· εἰ δὲ μή, πολλὰ τὸ ἓν ἔσται, ὃ κἀκείνοις συνέβαινεν. παρὰ μὲν οὖν τῶν πρότερον καὶ τῶν ἄλλων τοσαῦτα ἔστι λαβεῖν.

Pytagorici vero duo quidem principia dixerunt secundum eundem modum, tantum autem addiderunt quod et proprium eorum est: quia finitum et infinitum non alias aliquas putaverunt esse naturas, ut ignem aut terram aut aliud aliquid tale, sed infinitum ipsum et unum ipsum horum esse substantiam de quibus predicantur. Quapropter et numerum esse substantiam omnium. De hiis igitur secundum hunc enuntiaverunt modum, et de eo quod quid est dicere et diffinire ceperunt, valde autem simpliciter tractaverunt. Superficialiter enim diffinierunt, et cui primo inerat dictus terminus, hoc esse substantiam rei putaverunt, ut si quis existimet idem esse duplum et dualitatem eo quod primo inest duobus duplum. Sed fortasse duplo et dualitati non idem est esse; si autem non, multa ipsum unum erit, quod et illis accidit. De prioribus quidem igitur et aliis tot est accipere.

But the Pythagoreans have said in the same way that there are two principles, but added this much, which is peculiar to them, that they thought that finitude and infinity were not attributes of certain other things, e.g. of fire or earth or anything else of this kind, but that infinity itself and unity itself were the substance of the things of which they are predicated. This is why number was the substance of all things. On this subject, then, they expressed themselves thus; and regarding the question of essence they began to make statements and definitions, but treated the matter too simply. For they both defined superficially and thought that the first subject of which a given definition was predicable was the substance of the thing defined, as if one supposed that 'double' and '2' were the same, because 2 is the first thing of which 'double' is predicable. But surely to be double and to be 2 are not the same; if they are, one thing will be many-a consequence which they actually drew. From the earlier philosophers, then, and from their successors we can learn thus much.

## Chapter 6

μετὰ δὲ τὰς εἰρημένας φιλοσοφίας ἡ Πλάτωνος ἐπεγένετο [30] πραγματεία, τὰ μὲν πολλὰ τούτοις ἀκολουθοῦσα, τὰ δὲ καὶ ἴδια παρὰ τὴν τῶν Ἰταλικῶν ἔχουσα φιλοσοφίαν. ἐκ νέου τε γὰρ συνήθης γενόμενος πρῶτον Κρατύλῳ καὶ ταῖς Ἡρακλειτείοις δόξαις, ὡς ἁπάντων τῶν αἰσθητῶν ἀεὶ ῥεόντων καὶ ἐπιστήμης περὶ αὐτῶν οὐκ οὔσης, ταῦτα μὲν καὶ ὕστερον οὕτως ὑπέλαβεν: [987β] [1] Σωκράτους δὲ περὶ μὲν τὰ ἠθικὰ πραγματευομένου περὶ δὲ τῆς ὅλης φύσεως οὐθέν, ἐν μέντοι τούτοις τὸ καθόλου ζητοῦντος καὶ περὶ ὁρισμῶν ἐπιστήσαντος πρώτου τὴν διάνοιαν, ἐκεῖνον ἀποδεξάμενος διὰ τὸ τοιοῦτον [5] ὑπέλαβεν ὡς περὶ ἑτέρων τοῦτο γιγνόμενον καὶ οὐ τῶν αἰσθητῶν: ἀδύνατον γὰρ εἶναι τὸν κοινὸν ὅρον τῶν αἰσθητῶν τινός, ἀεί γε μεταβαλλόντων. οὗτος οὖν τὰ μὲν τοιαῦτα τῶν ὄντων ἰδέας προσηγόρευσε, τὰ δ' αἰσθητὰ παρὰ ταῦτα καὶ κατὰ ταῦτα λέγεσθαι πάντα: κατὰ μέθεξιν γὰρ εἶναι τὰ [10] πολλὰ ὁμώνυμα τοῖς εἴδεσιν. τὴν δὲ μέθεξιν τοὔνομα μόνον μετέβαλεν: οἱ μὲν γὰρ Πυθαγόρειοι μιμήσει τὰ ὄντα φασὶν εἶναι τῶν ἀριθμῶν, Πλάτων δὲ μεθέξει, τοὔνομα μεταβαλών. τὴν μέντοι γε μέθεξιν ἢ τὴν μίμησιν ἥτις ἂν εἴη τῶν εἰδῶν ἀφεῖσαν ἐν κοινῷ ζητεῖν.

Post dictas vero philosophias Platonis supervenit negotium, in multis quidem hos sequens, alia vero et propria praeter ytalicorum philosophiam habens. Nam ex nouo consentiens Cratilo et Eracliti opinionibus, quasi sensibilibus omnibus semper defluentibus et scientia de eis non existente, haec quidem et posterius ita suscepit. Socrate vero circa moralia negotiante et de tota natura nihil, in hiis tamen universale quaerente et de diffinitionibus primo intellectum firmante, illum suscipiens propter tale putavit quasi de aliis hoc factum et non de sensibilium aliquo; impossibile namque est communem rationem esse alicuius sensibilium, semper transmutantium. Sic itaque talia quidem entium ydeas et species appellavit, sensibilia vero propter haec et secundum haec dici omnia; nam secundum participationem esse multa univocorum speciebus. participationem vero secundum nomen transmutavit. Pytagorici quidem enim existentia dicunt esse numerorum imitatione, Plato vero participatione, nomen transmutans. Participationem tamen aut imitationem quae utique sit specierum dimiserunt in communi quaerere.

After the systems we have named came the philosophy of Plato, which in most respects followed these thinkers, but had peculiarities that distinguished it from the philosophy of the Italians. For, having in his youth first become familiar with Cratylus and with the Heraclitean doctrines (that all sensible things are ever in a state of flux and there is no knowledge about them), these views he held even in [87b] later years. Socrates, however, was busying himself about ethical matters and neglecting the world of nature as a whole but seeking the universal in these ethical matters, and fixed thought for the first time on definitions; Plato accepted his teaching, but held that the problem applied not to sensible things but to entities of another kind-for this reason, that the common definition could not be a definition of any sensible thing, as they were always changing. Things of this other sort, then, he called Ideas, and sensible things, he said, were all named after these, and in virtue of a relation to these; for the many existed by participation in the Ideas that have the same name as they. Only the name 'participation' was new; for the Pythagoreans say that things exist by 'imitation' of numbers, and Plato says they exist by participation, changing the name. But what the participation or the imitation of the Forms could be they left an open question.

ἔτι δὲ παρὰ τὰ αἰσθητὰ [15] καὶ τὰ εἴδη τὰ μαθηματικὰ τῶν πραγμάτων εἶναί φησι μεταξύ, διαφέροντα τῶν μὲν αἰσθητῶν τῷ ἀΐδια καὶ ἀκίνητα εἶναι, τῶν δ' εἰδῶν τῷ τὰ μὲν πόλλ' ἄττα ὅμοια εἶναι τὸ δὲ εἶδος αὐτὸ ἓν ἕκαστον μόνον.

Amplius autem praeter sensibilia et species mathematica rerum dicit esse intermedia, et differentia a sensibilibus quidem, quia sempiterna sunt et immobilia, a speciebus autem eo quod haec quidem multa quaedam similia sint, species autem ipsum unum unumquodque solum.

Further, besides sensible things and Forms he says there are the objects of mathematics, which occupy an intermediate position, differing from sensible things in being eternal and unchangeable, from Forms in that there are many alike, while the Form itself is in each case unique.

ἐπεὶ δ' αἴτια τὰ εἴδη τοῖς ἄλλοις, τἀκείνων στοιχεῖα πάντων ᾠήθη τῶν ὄντων εἶναι [20] στοιχεῖα. ὡς μὲν οὖν ὕλην τὸ μέγα καὶ τὸ μικρὸν εἶναι ἀρχάς, ὡς δ' οὐσίαν τὸ ἕν· ἐξ ἐκείνων γὰρ κατὰ μέθεξιν τοῦ ἑνὸς [τὰ εἴδη] εἶναι τοὺς ἀριθμούς.

Quoniam autem species cause sunt aliis, illarum elementa omnium putaverunt existentium elementa esse. Ut quidem igitur materiam magnum et parvum esse principia, ut autem substantiam unum; ex illis enim secundum participationem unius species esse numeros.

Since the Forms were the causes of all other things, he thought their elements were the elements of all things. As matter, the great and the small were principles; as essential reality, the One; for from the great and the small, by participation in the One, come the Numbers.

τὸ μέντοι γε ἓν οὐσίαν εἶναι, καὶ μὴ ἕτερόν γέ τι ὂν λέγεσθαι ἕν, παραπλησίως τοῖς Πυθαγορείοις ἔλεγε, καὶ τὸ τοὺς ἀριθμοὺς αἰτίους εἶναι τοῖς ἄλλοις [25] τῆς οὐσίας ὡσαύτως ἐκείνοις· τὸ δὲ ἀντὶ τοῦ ἀπείρου ὡς ἑνὸς δυάδα ποιῆσαι, τὸ δ᾽ ἄπειρον ἐκ μεγάλου καὶ μικροῦ, τοῦτ᾽ ἴδιον· καὶ ἔτι ὁ μὲν τοὺς ἀριθμοὺς παρὰ τὰ αἰσθητά, οἱ δ᾽ ἀριθμοὺς εἶναί φασιν αὐτὰ τὰ πράγματα, καὶ τὰ μαθηματικὰ μεταξὺ τούτων οὐ τιθέασιν.

Unum tamen esse substantiam, et non aliquid aliud ens dici unum, consimiliter Pytagoricis dixit, et numeros esse causas materie substantiae similiter ut illi; pro infinito autem ut uno dualitatem facere, et infinitum ex magno et parvo, hoc proprium. Amplius hic quidem numeros praeter sensibilia, illi vero numeros esse dicunt res ipsas, et mathematica intermedia horum non ponunt.

But he agreed with the Pythagoreans in saying that the One is substance and not a predicate of something else; and in saying that the Numbers are the causes of the reality of other things he agreed with them; but positing a dyad and constructing the infinite out of great and small, instead of treating the infinite as one, is peculiar to him; and so is his view that the Numbers exist apart from sensible things, while they say that the things themselves are Numbers, and do not place the objects of mathematics between Forms and sensible things.

τὸ μὲν οὖν τὸ ἓν καὶ τοὺς [30] ἀριθμοὺς παρὰ τὰ πράγματα ποιῆσαι, καὶ μὴ ὥσπερ οἱ Πυθαγόρειοι, καὶ ἡ τῶν εἰδῶν εἰσαγωγὴ διὰ τὴν ἐν τοῖς λόγοις ἐγένετο σκέψιν (οἱ γὰρ πρότεροι διαλεκτικῆς οὐ μετεῖχον), τὸ δὲ δυάδα ποιῆσαι τὴν ἑτέραν φύσιν διὰ τὸ τοὺς ἀριθμοὺς ἔξω τῶν πρώτων εὐφυῶς ἐξ αὐτῆς γεννᾶσθαι ὥσπερ ἔκ τινος ἐκμαγείου.

Unum quidem igitur et numeros praeter res facere, et non ut Pytagorici, et specierum introductio propter eam quae in rationibus perscrutationem evenit (priores enim dialetica non participaverunt); dualitatem autem facere alteram naturam, quia numeri extra primos naturaliter ex ea generantur velut ex aliquo ecmagio.

His divergence from the Pythagoreans in making the One and the Numbers separate from things, and his introduction of the Forms, were due to his inquiries in the region of definitions (for the earlier thinkers had no tincture of dialectic), and his making the other entity besides the One a dyad was due to the belief that the numbers, except those which were prime, could be neatly produced out of the dyad as out of some plastic material. [88a]

[988α] [1] καίτοι συμβαίνει γ᾽ ἐναντίως· οὐ γὰρ εὔλογον οὕτως. οἱ μὲν γὰρ ἐκ τῆς ὕλης πολλὰ ποιοῦσιν, τὸ δ᾽ εἶδος ἅπαξ γεννᾷ μόνον, φαίνεται δ᾽ ἐκ μιᾶς ὕλης μία τράπεζα, ὁ δὲ τὸ εἶδος ἐπιφέρων εἷς ὢν πολλὰς ποιεῖ. [5] ὁμοίως δ᾽ ἔχει καὶ τὸ ἄρρεν πρὸς τὸ θῆλυ· τὸ μὲν γὰρ ὑπὸ μιᾶς πληροῦται ὀχείας, τὸ δ᾽ ἄρρεν πολλὰ πληροῖ· καίτοι ταῦτα μιμήματα τῶν ἀρχῶν ἐκείνων ἐστίν.

Equidem econtrario [Attamen e contrario] contingit; non enim rationale ita. Nunc quidem enim ex materia multa faciunt, species vero semel generat solum; videtur autem ex una materia una mensa, speciem autem qui inducit unus existens multas facit. Similiter quoque se habet masculus ad feminam; haec enim ab uno impletur coitu, masculus vero multas implet; quamvis haec imitationes principiorum illorum sunt.

Yet what happens is the contrary; the theory is not a reasonable one. For they make many things out of the matter, and the form generates only once, but what we observe is that one table is made from one matter, while the man who applies the form, though he is one, makes many tables. And the relation of the male to the female is similar; for the latter is impregnated by one copulation, but the male impregnates many females; yet these are analogues of those first principles.

Πλάτων μὲν οὖν περὶ τῶν ζητουμένων οὕτω διώρισεν· φανερὸν δ᾽ ἐκ τῶν εἰρημένων ὅτι δυοῖν αἰτίαιν μόνον κέχρηται, τῇ τε [10] τοῦ τί ἐστι καὶ τῇ κατὰ τὴν ὕλην (τὰ γὰρ εἴδη τοῦ τί ἐστιν αἴτια τοῖς ἄλλοις, τοῖς δ᾽ εἴδεσι τὸ ἕν), καὶ τίς ἡ ὕλη ἡ ὑποκειμένη καθ᾽ ἧς τὰ εἴδη μὲν ἐπὶ τῶν αἰσθητῶν τὸ δ᾽ ἓν ἐν τοῖς εἴδεσι λέγεται, ὅτι αὕτη δυάς ἐστι, τὸ μέγα καὶ τὸ μικρόν, ἔτι δὲ τὴν τοῦ εὖ καὶ τοῦ κακῶς αἰτίαν τοῖς στοιχείοις [15] ἀπέδωκεν ἑκατέροις ἑκατέραν, ὥσπερ φαμὲν καὶ τῶν προτέρων ἐπιζητῆσαί τινας φιλοσόφων, οἷον Ἐμπεδοκλέα καὶ Ἀναξαγόραν.

Plato quidem igitur de quesitis ita diffinivit. Palam autem ex dictis quia duabus causis solum est usus, ipsa quae est eius quod quid est et ipsa materia; species enim eius quod quid est cause sunt aliis, speciebus vero unum. Et quae materia subiecta de qua species hae quidem in sensibilibus, hae autem in speciebus, unum vero in speciebus dicitur, quia haec dualitas est: magnum et parvum. Amplius bene et male causam dedit elementis singulis singulam, quod magis dicimus priorum investigare quosdam philosophorum, ut Empedoclem et Anaxagoram.

Plato, then, declared himself thus on the points in question; it is evident from what has been said that he has used only two causes, that of the essence and the material cause (for the Forms are the causes of the essence of all other things, and the One is the cause of the essence of the Forms); and it is evident what the underlying matter is, of which the Forms are predicated in the case of sensible things, and the One in the case of Forms, viz. that this is a dyad, the great and the small. Further, he has assigned the cause of good and that of evil to the elements, one to each of the two, as we say some of his predecessors sought to do, e.g. Empedocles and Anaxagoras.

*Chapter 7*

συντόμως μὲν οὖν καὶ κεφαλαιωδῶς ἐπεληλύθαμεν τίνες τε καὶ πῶς τυγχάνουσιν εἰρηκότες περί τε τῶν ἀρχῶν [20] καὶ τῆς ἀληθείας: ὅμως δὲ τοσοῦτόν γ᾽ ἔχομεν ἐξ αὐτῶν, ὅτι τῶν λεγόντων περὶ ἀρχῆς καὶ αἰτίας οὐθεὶς ἔξω τῶν ἐν τοῖς περὶ φύσεως ἡμῖν διωρισμένων εἴρηκεν, ἀλλὰ πάντες ἀμυδρῶς μὲν ἐκείνων δέ πως φαίνονται θιγγάνοντες.

Breviter igitur et capitaliter qui et quomodo de principiis et veritate dixerunt pertransivimus. At tamen ab eis tantum habemus, quia dicentium de principio et causa nullus praeter ea quae sunt in phisicis a nobis determinata dixit, sed omnes tenuiter quidem, videntur autem illa tangere aliqualiter.

Our review of those who have spoken about first principles and reality and of the way in which they have spoken, has been concise and summary; but yet we have learnt this much from them, that of those who speak about 'principle' and 'cause' no one has mentioned any principle except those which have been distinguished in our work on nature, but all evidently have some inkling of them, though only vaguely.

οἱ μὲν γὰρ ὡς ὕλην τὴν ἀρχὴν λέγουσιν, ἄν τε μίαν ἄν τε πλείους [25] ὑποθῶσι, καὶ ἐάν τε σῶμα ἐάν τε ἀσώματον τοῦτο τιθῶσιν (οἷον Πλάτων μὲν τὸ μέγα καὶ τὸ μικρὸν λέγων, οἱ δ᾽ Ἰταλικοὶ τὸ ἄπειρον, Ἐμπεδοκλῆς δὲ πῦρ καὶ γῆν καὶ ὕδωρ καὶ ἀέρα, Ἀναξαγόρας δὲ τὴν τῶν ὁμοιομερῶν ἀπειρίαν: οὗτοί τε δὴ πάντες τῆς τοιαύτης αἰτίας ἡμμένοι εἰσί, καὶ ἔτι ὅσοι [30] ἀέρα ἢ πῦρ ἢ ὕδωρ ἢ πυρὸς μὲν πυκνότερον ἀέρος δὲ λεπτότερον: καὶ γὰρ τοιοῦτόν τινες εἰρήκασιν εἶναι τὸ πρῶτον στοιχεῖον):

Hii quidem ut materiam principium dicunt, sive unam sive plures supponant, et sive corpus sive incorporea ponant; ut Plato quidem magnum et parvum dicens, Ytalici vero infinitum, et empedocjes ignem et terram et aquam et aerem, Anaxagoras autem similium partium infinitatem. Hii itaque omnes causam talem sunt tangentes, et amplius quicumque aerem aut ignem aut aquam aut igne spissius aere autem subtilius; et enim quidam tale primum elementum dixerunt.

For some speak of the first principle as matter, whether they suppose one or more first principles, and whether they suppose this to be a body or to be incorporeal; e.g. Plato spoke of the great and the small, the Italians of the infinite, Empedocles of fire, earth, water, and air, Anaxagoras of the infinity of things composed of similar parts. These, then, have all had a notion of this kind of cause, and so have all who speak of air or fire or water, or something denser than fire and rarer than air; for some have said the prime element is of this kind.

οὗτοι μὲν οὖν ταύτης τῆς αἰτίας ἥψαντο μόνον, ἕτεροι δέ τινες ὅθεν ἡ ἀρχὴ τῆς κινήσεως (οἷον ὅσοι φιλίαν καὶ νεῖκος ἢ νοῦν ἢ ἔρωτα ποιοῦσιν ἀρχήν):

Hii quidem igitur hanc causam solum tetigerunt; alii vero quidam unde principium motus, ut quicumque amicitiam et litem et intellectum aut amorem principium faciunt.

These thinkers grasped this cause only; but certain others have mentioned the source of movement, e.g. those who make friendship and strife, or reason, or love, a principle.

τὸ δὲ τί ἦν εἶναι [35] καὶ τὴν οὐσίαν σαφῶς μὲν οὐθεὶς ἀποδέδωκε, [988β] [1] μάλιστα δ᾽ οἱ τὰ εἴδη τιθέντες λέγουσιν (οὔτε γὰρ ὡς ὕλην τοῖς αἰσθητοῖς τὰ εἴδη καὶ τὸ ἓν τοῖς εἴδεσιν οὔθ᾽ ὡς ἐντεῦθεν τὴν ἀρχὴν τῆς κινήσεως γιγνομένην ὑπολαμβάνουσιν—ἀκινησίας γὰρ αἴτια μᾶλλον καὶ τοῦ ἐν ἠρεμίᾳ εἶναι φασιν— ἀλλὰ τὸ τί ἦν εἶναι [5] ἑκάστῳ τῶν ἄλλων τὰ εἴδη παρέχονται, τοῖς δ᾽ εἴδεσι τὸ ἕν):

Quod autem quid erat esse et substantiam plane nullus dedit. Maxime autem qui species ponunt dicunt; neque enim ut materiam sensibilibus species et quae in speciebus neque ut hinc principium motus proveniens existimant (immobilitatis enim causas magis et eius quod est in quiete esse dicunt), sed quod quid erat esse aliorum singulis species prestant, speciebus autem unum.

The essence, i.e. the substantial reality, no one has expressed distinctly. It is hinted at chiefly by those who believe [88b] in the Forms; for they do not suppose either that the Forms are the matter of sensible things, and the One the matter of the Forms, or that they are the source of movement (for they say these are causes rather of immobility and of being at rest), but they furnish the Forms as the essence of every other thing, and the One as the essence of the Forms.

τὸ δ᾽ οὗ ἕνεκα αἱ πράξεις καὶ αἱ μεταβολαὶ καὶ αἱ κινήσεις τρόπον μέν τινα λέγουσιν αἴτιον, οὕτω δὲ οὐ λέγουσιν οὐδ᾽ ὅνπερ πέφυκεν. οἱ μὲν γὰρ νοῦν λέγοντες ἢ φιλίαν ὡς ἀγαθὸν μὲν ταύτας τὰς αἰτίας τιθέασιν, οὐ μὴν ὡς [10] ἕνεκά γε τούτων ἢ ὂν ἢ γιγνόμενόν τι τῶν ὄντων ἀλλ᾽ ὡς ἀπὸ τούτων τὰς κινήσεις οὔσας λέγουσιν: ὡς δ᾽ αὕτως καὶ οἱ τὸ ἓν ἢ τὸ ὂν φάσκοντες εἶναι τὴν τοιαύτην φύσιν τῆς μὲν οὐσίας αἴτιόν φασιν εἶναι, οὐ μὴν τούτου γε ἕνεκα ἢ εἶναι ἢ γίγνεσθαι, ὥστε λέγειν τε καὶ μὴ λέγειν πως συμβαίνει αὐτοῖς [15] τἀγαθὸν αἴτιον: οὐ γὰρ ἁπλῶς ἀλλὰ κατὰ συμβεβηκὸς λέγουσιν.

Cuius vero causa actus et transmutationes et motus modo quodam dicunt causam, ita vero non dicunt neque quod vere natum est. Nam intellectum quidem dicentes aut amicitiam ut bonum quidem has ponunt causas; non tamen ut gratia horum aut existens aut factum aliquid entium, sed ut ab hiis horum esse motus dicunt. Similiter autem et unum aut ens dicentes esse talem naturam substantiae quidem causam dicunt esse, non tamen huius causa aut esse aut fieri. Quare dicere et non dicere aliqualiter accidit eis bonum causam; non enim simpliciter sed secundum accidens dicunt.

That for whose sake actions and changes and movements take place, they assert to be a cause in a way, but not in this way, i.e. not in the way in which it is its nature to be a cause. For those who speak of reason or friendship class these causes as goods; they do not speak, however, as if anything that exists either existed or came into being for the sake of these, but as if movements started from these. In the same way those who say the One or the existent is the good, say that it is the cause of substance, but not that substance either is or comes to be for the sake of this. Therefore it turns out that in a sense they both say and do not say the good is a cause; for they do not call it a cause qua good but only incidentally.

ὅτι μὲν οὖν ὀρθῶς διώρισται περὶ τῶν αἰτίων καὶ πόσα καὶ ποῖα, μαρτυρεῖν ἐοίκασιν ἡμῖν καὶ οὗτοι πάντες, οὐ δυνάμενοι θιγεῖν ἄλλης αἰτίας, πρὸς δὲ τούτοις ὅτι ζητητέαι αἱ ἀρχαὶ ἢ οὕτως ἅπασαι ἢ τινὰ τρόπον τοιοῦτον, δῆλον: [20] πῶς δὲ τούτων ἕκαστος εἴρηκε καὶ πῶς ἔχει περὶ τῶν ἀρχῶν, τὰς ἐνδεχομένας ἀπορίας μετὰ τοῦτο διέλθωμεν περὶ αὐτῶν.

Quod quidem igitur recte determinatum est de causis et quot et quae, testimonium prebere nobis videntur et hii omnes, aliam causam tangere non valentes. Ad haec autem quia quaerenda sunt principia aut sic omnia aut horum aliquo modo, palam. Quomodo etiam horum unusquisque dixit et quomodo habent de principiis, contingentes autem dubitationes post hoc pertranseamus de ipsis.

All these thinkers then, as they cannot pitch on another cause, seem to testify that we have determined rightly both how many and of what sort the causes are. Besides this it is plain that when the causes are being looked for, either all four must be sought thus or they must be sought in one of these four ways. Let us next discuss the possible difficulties with regard to the way in which each of these thinkers has spoken, and with regard to his situation relatively to the first principles.

## Chapter 8

ὅσοι μὲν οὖν ἕν τε τὸ πᾶν καὶ μίαν τινὰ φύσιν ὡς ὕλην τιθέασι, καὶ ταύτην σωματικὴν καὶ μέγεθος ἔχουσαν, δῆλον ὅτι πολλαχῶς ἁμαρτάνουσιν. τῶν γὰρ σωμάτων τὰ [25] στοιχεῖα τιθέασι μόνον, τῶν δ᾽ ἀσωμάτων οὔ, ὄντων καὶ ἀσωμάτων.

Quicumque quidem igitur unum ipsum omne et unam esse quandam naturam ut materiam ponunt, et eam corpoream et magnitudinem habentem, palam quia multiphciter delinquunt. Corporum enim elementa ponunt solum, incorporeorum vero non, existentibus et incorporeis.

Those, then, who say the universe is one and posit one kind of thing as matter, and as corporeal matter which has spatial magnitude, evidently go astray in many ways. For they posit the elements of bodies only, not of incorporeal things, though there are also incorporeal things.

καὶ περὶ γενέσεως καὶ φθορᾶς ἐπιχειροῦντες τὰς αἰτίας λέγειν, καὶ περὶ πάντων φυσιολογοῦντες, τὸ τῆς κινήσεως αἴτιον ἀναιροῦσιν. ἔτι δὲ τῷ τὴν οὐσίαν μηθενὸς αἰτίαν τιθέναι μηδὲ τὸ τί ἐστι, καὶ πρὸς τούτοις τῷ ῥᾳδίως τῶν [30] ἁπλῶν σωμάτων λέγειν ἀρχὴν ὁτιοῦν πλὴν γῆς, οὐκ ἐπισκεψάμενοι τὴν ἐξ ἀλλήλων γένεσιν πῶς ποιοῦνται, λέγω δὲ πῦρ καὶ ὕδωρ καὶ γῆν καὶ ἀέρα. τὰ μὲν γὰρ συγκρίσει τὰ δὲ διακρίσει ἐξ ἀλλήλων γίγνεται, τοῦτο δὲ πρὸς τὸ πρότερον εἶναι καὶ ὕστερον διαφέρει πλεῖστον.

De generatione quoque et corruptione causam dicere conantes, et de omnibus phisice tractantes, motus causam auferunt. Amplius autem substantiam nullius ponere causam nec quod quid est, et ad haec facile esse quodcumque simplicium corporum principium excepta terra, non considerantes eam quae ex invicem generationem aliqualiter faciunt; dico autem ignem et aquam et terram et aerem. Haec quidem enim congregatione illa vero disgregatione ex ad invicem fiunt; hoc autem ad prius esse et posterius plurimum differt.

And in trying to state the causes of generation and destruction, and in giving a physical account of all things, they do away with the cause of movement. Further, they err in not positing the substance, i.e. the essence, as the cause of anything, and besides this in lightly calling any of the simple bodies except earth the first principle, without inquiring how they are produced out of one anothers- I mean fire, water, earth, and air. For some things are produced out of each other by combination, others by separation, and this makes the greatest difference to their priority and posteriority.

τῇ μὲν γὰρ ἂν [35] δόξειε στοιχειωδέστατον εἶναι πάντων ἐξ οὗ γίγνονται συγκρίσει πρώτου, [989a] [1] τοιοῦτον δὲ τὸ μικρομερέστατον καὶ λεπτότατον ἂν εἴη τῶν σωμάτων (διόπερ ὅσοι πῦρ ἀρχὴν τιθέασι, μάλιστα ὁμολογουμένως ἂν τῷ λόγῳ τούτῳ λέγοιεν: τοιοῦτον δὲ καὶ τῶν ἄλλων ἕκαστος ὁμολογεῖ τὸ στοιχεῖον εἶναι τὸ τῶν σωμάτων:

Aliqualiter enim utique videbitur maxime elementale esse omnium ex quo primo fiunt congregatione, tale vero est quod minutissime partis et subtilissimum est corporum. Unde quicumque ponunt ignem principium, maxime confesse rationi huic dicunt. Tale vero et aliorum unusquisque confitetur elementum esse quod corporum.

For (1) in a way the property of being most elementary of all would seem to belong to the first thing [89a] from which they are produced by combination, and this property would belong to the most fine-grained and subtle of bodies. For this reason those who make fire the principle would be most in agreement with this argument. But each of the other thinkers agrees that the element of corporeal things is of this sort.

[5] οὐθεὶς γοῦν ἠξίωσε τῶν ἓν λεγόντων γῆν εἶναι στοιχεῖον, δηλονότι διὰ τὴν μεγαλομέρειαν, τῶν δὲ τριῶν ἕκαστον στοιχείων εἴληφέ τινα κριτήν, οἱ μὲν γὰρ πῦρ οἱ δ᾽ ὕδωρ οἱ δ᾽ ἀέρα τοῦτ᾽ εἶναί φασιν· καίτοι διὰ τί ποτ᾽ οὐ καὶ τὴν γῆν λέγουσιν, ὥσπερ οἱ πολλοὶ τῶν ἀνθρώπων; πάντα [10] γὰρ εἶναί φασι γῆν, φησὶ δὲ καὶ Ἡσίοδος τὴν γῆν πρώτην γενέσθαι τῶν σωμάτων· οὕτως ἀρχαίαν καὶ δημοτικὴν συμβέβηκεν εἶναι τὴν ὑπόληψιν)· κατὰ μὲν οὖν τοῦτον τὸν λόγον οὔτ᾽ εἴ τις τούτων τι λέγει πλὴν πυρός, οὔτ᾽ εἴ τις ἀέρος μὲν πυκνότερον τοῦτο τίθησιν ὕδατος δὲ [15] λεπτότερον, οὐκ ὀρθῶς ἂν λέγοι·

Nullus enim posteriorum et unum dicentium terram esse elementum voluit, palam quia propter magnitudinem partialitatis. Quodlibet autem trium elementorum iudicem quendam accepit; hii namque ignem illi vero aquam alii aerem hoc esse dicunt. Sed quare non et terram dicunt, quemadmodum hominum multi? Omnia namque terram esse dicunt. Dicit autem et Esiodus terram primam corporum factam esse; sic enim antiquam et popularem contingit esse existimationem. Secundum hanc igitur rationem nec si quis horum aliquid dicit praeter ignem, nec si quis aere quidem spissius hoc ponit aqua vero subtilius, non recte utique dicet.

At least none of those who named one element claimed that earth was the element, evidently because of the coarseness of its grain. (Of the other three elements each has found some judge on its side; for some maintain that fire, others that water, others that air is the element. Yet why, after all, do they not name earth also, as most men do? For people say all things are earth Hesiod says earth was produced first of corporeal things; so primitive and popular has the opinion been.) According to this argument, then, no one would be right who either says the first principle is any of the elements other than fire, or supposes it to be denser than air but rarer than water.

εἰ δ᾽ ἔστι τὸ τῇ γενέσει ὕστερον τῇ φύσει πρότερον, τὸ δὲ πεπεμμένον καὶ συγκεκριμένον ὕστερον τῇ γενέσει, τοὐναντίον ἂν εἴη τούτων, ὕδωρ μὲν ἀέρος πρότερον γῆ δὲ ὕδατος.

Si vero est quod generatione posterius natura prius, et quod est digestum et concretum posterius generatione, horum utique erit contrarium: aqua quidem aere prior et terra aqua.

But (2) if that which is later in generation is prior in nature, and that which is concocted and compounded is later in generation, the contrary of what we have been saying must be true,-water must be prior to air, and earth to water.

περὶ μὲν οὖν τῶν μίαν τιθεμένων αἰτίαν οἵαν εἴπομεν, ἔστω ταῦτ᾽ εἰρημένα· τὸ δ᾽ [20] αὐτὸ κἂν εἴ τις ταῦτα πλείω τίθησιν, οἷον Ἐμπεδοκλῆς τέτταρά φησιν εἶναι σώματα τὴν ὕλην. καὶ γὰρ τούτῳ τὰ μὲν ταὐτὰ τὰ δ᾽ ἴδια συμβαίνειν ἀνάγκη. γιγνόμενά τε γὰρ ἐξ ἀλλήλων ὁρῶμεν ὡς οὐκ ἀεὶ διαμένοντος πυρὸς καὶ γῆς τοῦ αὐτοῦ σώματος (εἴρηται δὲ ἐν τοῖς περὶ φύσεως περὶ αὐτῶν), [25] καὶ περὶ τῆς τῶν κινουμένων αἰτίας, πότερον ἓν ἢ δύο θετέον, οὔτ᾽ ὀρθῶς οὔτε εὐλόγως οἰητέον εἰρῆσθαι παντελῶς.

De ponentibus quidem igitur unam causam qualem diximus sint haec dicta. Idem autem [Idem quoque] et si quis haec plura ponit, velut Empedocles quatuor dicit esse corpora materiam. Et enim huic haec quidem eadem illa vero propria accidere necesse. Ex ad invicem enim generata cernimus quasi non semper igne et terra eodem corpore permanente (dictum est autem de eis in phisicis); et de moventium causa, utrum unum aut plura ponendum, nec recte nec irrationabiliter putandum est omnino dictum esse.

So much, then, for those who posit one cause such as we mentioned; but the same is true if one supposes more of these, as Empedocles says matter of things is four bodies. For he too is confronted by consequences some of which are the same as have been mentioned, while others are peculiar to him. For we see these bodies produced from one another, which implies that the same body does not always remain fire or earth (we have spoken about this in our works on nature); and regarding the cause of movement and the question whether we must posit one or two, he must be thought to have spoken neither correctly nor altogether plausibly.

ὅλως τε ἀλλοίωσιν ἀναιρεῖσθαι ἀνάγκη τοῖς οὕτω λέγουσιν· οὐ γὰρ ἐκ θερμοῦ ψυχρὸν οὐδὲ ἐκ ψυχροῦ θερμὸν ἔσται. τί γὰρ αὐτὰ ἂν πάσχοι τἀναντία, καὶ τίς εἴη ἂν μία φύσις ἡ γιγνομένη [30] πῦρ καὶ ὕδωρ, ὃ ἐκεῖνος οὔ φησιν.

Et ex toto alterationem auferri est necesse sic dicentibus; non enim ex calido frigidum nec ex frigido calidum erit. Quid enim haec patietur contraria, et quae est una natura quae fit ignis et aqua: quod ille non ait.

And in general, change of quality is necessarily done away with for those who speak thus, for on their view cold will not come from hot nor hot from cold. For if it did there would be something that accepted the contraries themselves, and there would be some one entity that became fire and water, which Empedocles denies.

Ἀναξαγόραν δ᾽ εἴ τις ὑπολάβοι δύο λέγειν στοιχεῖα, μάλιστ᾽ ἂν ὑπολάβοι κατὰ λόγον, ὃν ἐκεῖνος αὐτὸς μὲν οὐ διήρθρωσεν, ἠκολούθησε μέντ᾽ ἂν ἐξ ἀνάγκης τοῖς ἐπάγουσιν αὐτόν.

Anaxagoram vero si quis susceperit elementa duo dicere, suscipiat maxime secundum rationem, quam ille quidem non dearticulavit; secutus est enim ex necessitate dicentes eam.

As regards Anaxagoras, if one were to suppose that he said there were two elements, the supposition would accord thoroughly with an argument which Anaxagoras himself did not state articulately, but which he must have accepted if any one had led him on to it.

ἀτόπου γὰρ ὄντος καὶ ἄλλως τοῦ φάσκειν μεμῖχθαι τὴν ἀρχὴν πάντα, [989β] [1] καὶ διὰ τὸ συμβαίνειν ἄμικτα δεῖν προϋπάρχειν καὶ διὰ τὸ μὴ πεφυκέναι τῷ τυχόντι μίγνυσθαι τὸ τυχόν, πρὸς δὲ τούτοις ὅτι τὰ πάθη καὶ τὰ συμβεβηκότα χωρίζοιτ᾽ ἂν τῶν οὐσιῶν (τῶν γὰρ αὐτῶν μῖξίς ἐστι καὶ χωρισμός), ὅμως εἴ τις ἀκολουθήσειε [5] συνδιαρθρῶν ἃ βούλεται λέγειν, ἴσως ἂν φανείη καινοπρεπεστέρως λέγων. ὅτε γὰρ οὐθὲν ἦν ἀποκεκριμένον, δῆλον ὡς οὐθὲν ἦν ἀληθὲς εἰπεῖν κατὰ τῆς οὐσίας ἐκείνης, λέγω δ᾽ οἷον ὅτι οὔτε λευκὸν οὔτε μέλαν ἢ φαιὸν ἢ ἄλλο χρῶμα, ἀλλ᾽ ἄχρων ἦν ἐξ ἀνάγκης· εἶχε γὰρ ἄν τι τούτων [10] τῶν χρωμάτων· ὁμοίως δὲ καὶ ἄχυμον τῷ αὐτῷ λόγῳ τούτῳ, οὐδὲ ἄλλο τῶν ὁμοίων οὐθέν· οὔτε γὰρ ποιόν τι οἷόν τε αὐτὸ εἶναι οὔτε ποσὸν οὔτε τί. τῶν γὰρ ἐν μέρει τι λεγομένων εἰδῶν ὑπῆρχεν ἂν αὐτῷ, τοῦτο δὲ ἀδύνατον μεμιγμένων γε πάντων· ἤδη γὰρ ἂν ἀπεκέκριτο, φησὶ δ᾽ [15] εἶναι μεμιγμένα πάντα πλὴν τοῦ νοῦ, τοῦτον δὲ ἀμιγῆ μόνον καὶ καθαρόν. ἐκ δὴ τούτων συμβαίνει λέγειν αὐτῷ τὰς ἀρχὰς τό τε ἕν (τοῦτο γὰρ ἁπλοῦν καὶ ἀμιγές) καὶ θάτερον, οἷον τίθεμεν τὸ ἀόριστον πρὶν ὁρισθῆναι καὶ μετασχεῖν εἴδους τινός, ὥστε λέγει μὲν οὔτ᾽ ὀρθῶς οὔτε σαφῶς, βούλεται μέντοι [20] τι παραπλήσιον τοῖς τε ὕστερον λέγουσι καὶ τοῖς νῦν φαινομένοις μᾶλλον.

Nam absurdo existente et aliter dicere permixta esse a principio omnia, et quia oportet accidere quod impermixta preexistant et quia non aptum est cuilibet permisceri quodlibet. Ad haec autem quia passiones et accidentia separantur a substantiis; eorundem enim permixtio et separatio. Tamen si quis prosequitur dearticulans quae vult dicere, forsan apparebit mirabilius dicens. Quando namque nihil erat discretum, palam quia nihil erat verum dicere de substantia illa. Dico autem quia neque album neque nigrum aut fuscum aut alium colorem, sed non colorata erat ex necessitate; horum enim colorum aliquem haberet. Similiter autem et sine sapore eadem hac ratione, nec aliud similium nihil; nec enim quale aliquid id possibile esse nec quantum nec quid. Aliqua enim dictarum in parte specierum inesset utique ei, sed hoc impossibile permixtis omnibus; iam enim discreta essent, dicit autem permixta esse omnia praeter intellectum, hunc autem impermixtum solum et purum. Ex hiis itaque accidit ei dicere principia ipsum unum (hoc enim simplex et impermixtum) et alterum, quale ponimus indeterminatum antequam determinetur et quadam specie participet. Quare dicitur quidem nec recte nec plane, vult tamen aliquid simile posterius dicentibus et nunc apparentibus magis.

True, to say that in the beginning all things were mixed is absurd both on other grounds and because it follows that they must have existed before [89b] in an unmixed form, and because nature does not allow any chance thing to be mixed with any chance thing, and also because on this view modifications and accidents could be separated from substances (for the same things which are mixed can be separated); yet if one were to follow him up, piecing together what he means, he would perhaps be seen to be somewhat modern in his views. For when nothing was separated out, evidently nothing could be truly asserted of the substance that then existed. I mean, e.g. that it was neither white nor black, nor grey nor any other colour, but of necessity colourless; for if it had been coloured, it would have had one of these colours. And similarly, by this same argument, it was flavourless, nor had it any similar attribute; for it could not be either of any quality or of any size, nor could it be any definite kind of thing. For if it were, one of the particular forms would have belonged to it, and this is impossible, since all were mixed together; for the particular form would necessarily have been already separated out, but he all were mixed except reason, and this alone was unmixed and pure. From this it follows, then, that he must say the principles are the One (for this is simple and unmixed) and the Other, which is of such a nature as we suppose the indefinite to be before it is defined and partakes of some form. Therefore, while expressing himself neither rightly nor clearly, he means something like what the later thinkers say and what is now more clearly seen to be the case.

ἀλλὰ γὰρ οὗτοι μὲν τοῖς περὶ γένεσιν λόγοις καὶ φθορὰν καὶ κίνησιν οἰκεῖοι τυγχάνουσι μόνον (σχεδὸν γὰρ περὶ τῆς τοιαύτης οὐσίας καὶ τὰς ἀρχὰς καὶ τὰς αἰτίας ζητοῦσι μόνης):

Verum hii quidem  hiis qui circa generationem sermonibus et corruptionem et motum proprii sunt solum; fere namque circa talis substantiae principia et causas quaerunt solum.

But these thinkers are, after all, at home only in arguments about generation and destruction and movement; for it is practically only of this sort of substance that they seek the principles and the causes.

ὅσοι δὲ περὶ μὲν ἁπάντων τῶν ὄντων ποιοῦνται [25] τὴν θεωρίαν, τῶν δ᾽ ὄντων τὰ μὲν αἰσθητὰ τὰ δ᾽ οὐκ αἰσθητὰ τιθέασι, δῆλον ὡς περὶ ἀμφοτέρων τῶν γενῶν ποιοῦνται τὴν [27] ἐπίσκεψιν: διὸ μᾶλλον ἄν τις ἐνδιατρίψειε περὶ αὐτῶν, τί καλῶς ἢ μὴ καλῶς λέγουσιν εἰς τὴν τῶν νῦν ἡμῖν προκειμένων σκέψιν.

Quicumque vero de omnibus existentibus  faciunt theoriam, existentium autem haec quidem sensibilia illa vero insensibilia ponunt, palam quia de utrisque generibus perscrutationem faciunt. Propter quod magis utique immorabitur aliquis de eis, quid bene aut non bene dicunt ad presentem nobis propositorum perscrutationem.

But those who extend their vision to all things that exist, and of existing things suppose some to be perceptible and others not perceptible, evidently study both classes, which is all the more reason why one should devote some time to seeing what is good in their views and what bad from the standpoint of the inquiry we have now before us.

οἱ μὲν οὖν καλούμενοι Πυθαγόρειοι ταῖς μὲν [30] ἀρχαῖς καὶ τοῖς στοιχείοις ἐκτοπωτέροις χρῶνται τῶν φυσιολόγων (τὸ δ᾽ αἴτιον ὅτι παρέλαβον αὐτὰς οὐκ ἐξ αἰσθητῶν: τὰ γὰρ μαθηματικὰ τῶν ὄντων ἄνευ κινήσεώς ἐστιν ἔξω τῶν περὶ τὴν ἀστρολογίαν), διαλέγονται μέντοι καὶ πραγματεύονται περὶ φύσεως πάντα: γεννῶσί τε γὰρ τὸν οὐρανόν, [990α] [1] καὶ περὶ τὰ τούτου μέρη καὶ τὰ πάθη καὶ τὰ ἔργα διατηροῦσιν τὸ συμβαῖνον, καὶ τὰς ἀρχὰς καὶ τὰ αἴτια εἰς ταῦτα καταναλίσκουσιν, ὡς ὁμολογοῦντες τοῖς ἄλλοις φυσιολόγοις ὅτι τό γε ὂν τοῦτ᾽ ἐστὶν ὅσον αἰσθητόν ἐστι καὶ περιείληφεν ὁ [5] καλούμενος οὐρανός. τὰς δ᾽ αἰτίας καὶ τὰς ἀρχάς, ὥσπερ εἴπομεν, ἱκανὰς λέγουσιν ἐπαναβῆναι καὶ ἐπὶ τὰ ἀνωτέρω τῶν ὄντων, καὶ μᾶλλον ἢ τοῖς περὶ φύσεως λόγοις ἁρμοττούσας.

Pytagorici quidem igitur vocati principiis et elementis extranee a phisiologis sunt usi. Causa vero quia acceperunt ea ex non sensibilibus; nam mathematica existentium sine motu sunt, extra ea quae sunt circa astrologiam. Disputant tamen et tractant omnia de natura; generant enim celum, et quod circa huius partes et passiones et operationes accidit observant, et principia et causas in haec dispensant, quasi aliis phisiologis consentientes quia ens hoc est quodcumque sensibile est et comprehendit vocatum celum. Causas vero et principia, sicut diximus, dicunt sufficientia pertingere usque ad ea quae sunt entium superiora, et magis quam de natura rationibus convenientia.

The 'Pythagoreans' treat of principles and elements stranger than those of the physical philosophers (the reason is that they got the principles from non-sensible things, for the objects of mathematics, except those of astronomy, are of the class of things without movement); yet their discussions and investigations are all about nature; for they [90a] generate the heavens, and with regard to their parts and attributes and functions they observe the phenomena, and use up the principles and the causes in explaining these, which implies that they agree with the others, the physical philosophers, that the real is just all that [90a 4] which is perceptible and contained by the so-called 'heavens'. But the causes and the principles which they mention are, as we said, sufficient to act as steps even up to the higher realms of reality, and are more suited to these than to theories about nature.

ἐκ τίνος μέντοι τρόπου κίνησις ἔσται πέρατος καὶ ἀπείρου μόνων ὑποκειμένων καὶ περιττοῦ καὶ ἀρτίου, οὐθὲν [10] λέγουσιν, ἢ πῶς δυνατὸν ἄνευ κινήσεως καὶ μεταβολῆς γένεσιν εἶναι καὶ φθορὰν ἢ τὰ τῶν φερομένων ἔργα κατὰ τὸν οὐρανόν.

Ex quo tamen modo motus inerit fini et infinito solum suppositis et pari et impari, non dicunt, aut quomodo possibile sine motu et transmutatione generationem et corruptionem esse aut eorum quae feruntur opera circa celum.

They do not tell us at all, however, how there can be movement if limit and unlimited and odd and even are the only things assumed, or how without movement and change there can be generation and destruction, or the bodies that move through the heavens can do what they do.

ἔτι δὲ εἴτε δοίη τις αὐτοῖς ἐκ τούτων εἶναι μέγεθος εἴτε δειχθείη τοῦτο, ὅμως τίνα τρόπον ἔσται τὰ μὲν κοῦφα τὰ δὲ βάρος ἔχοντα τῶν σωμάτων; ἐξ ὧν γὰρ ὑποτίθενται [15] καὶ λέγουσιν, οὐθὲν μᾶλλον περὶ τῶν μαθηματικῶν λέγουσι σωμάτων ἢ τῶν αἰσθητῶν· διὸ περὶ πυρὸς ἢ γῆς ἢ τῶν ἄλλων τῶν τοιούτων σωμάτων οὐδ᾽ ὁτιοῦν εἰρήκασιν, ἅτε οὐθὲν περὶ τῶν αἰσθητῶν οἶμαι λέγοντες ἴδιον.

Amplius autem sive quis det eis ex hiis esse magnitudinem sive hoc ostendatur, tamen quomodo erunt haec corporum levia illa vero gravitatem habentia? Ex quibus enim supponunt et dicunt, nihil magis de mathematicis dicunt corporibus quam de sensibilibus; unde de igne aut terra aut aliis huiusmodi corporibus nihil dixerunt, sicut nihil de sensibilibus existimo dicentes proprium.

Further, if one either granted them that spatial magnitude consists of these elements, or this were proved, still how would some bodies be light and others have weight? To judge from what they assume and maintain they are speaking no more of mathematical bodies than of perceptible; hence they have said nothing whatever about fire or earth or the other bodies of this sort, I suppose because they have nothing to say which applies peculiarly to perceptible things.

ἔτι δὲ πῶς δεῖ λαβεῖν αἴτια μὲν εἶναι τὰ τοῦ ἀριθμοῦ πάθη καὶ τὸν ἀριθμὸν [20] τῶν κατὰ τὸν οὐρανὸν ὄντων καὶ γιγνομένων καὶ ἐξ ἀρχῆς καὶ νῦν, ἀριθμὸν δ᾽ ἄλλον μηθένα εἶναι παρὰ τὸν ἀριθμὸν τοῦτον ἐξ οὗ συνέστηκεν ὁ κόσμος; ὅταν γὰρ ἐν τῳδὶ μὲν τῷ μέρει δόξα καὶ καιρὸς αὐτοῖς ᾖ, μικρὸν δὲ ἄνωθεν ἢ κάτωθεν ἀδικία καὶ κρίσις ἢ μῖξις, ἀπόδειξιν δὲ λέγωσιν ὅτι [25] τούτων μὲν ἕκαστον ἀριθμός ἐστι, συμβαίνει δὲ κατὰ τὸν τόπον τοῦτον ἤδη πλῆθος εἶναι τῶν συνισταμένων μεγεθῶν διὰ τὸ τὰ πάθη ταῦτα ἀκολουθεῖν τοῖς τόποις ἑκάστοις, πότερον οὗτος ὁ αὐτός ἐστιν ἀριθμός, ὁ ἐν τῷ οὐρανῷ, ὃν δεῖ λαβεῖν ὅτι τούτων ἕκαστόν ἐστιν, ἢ παρὰ τοῦτον ἄλλος; ὁ μὲν γὰρ [30] Πλάτων ἕτερον εἶναί φησιν· καίτοι κἀκεῖνος ἀριθμοὺς οἴεται καὶ ταῦτα εἶναι καὶ τὰς τούτων αἰτίας, ἀλλὰ τοὺς μὲν νοητοὺς αἰτίους τούτους δὲ αἰσθητούς.

Amplius autem quomodo oportet accipere causas quidem esse numeri passiones et numerum circa celum existentium et factorum et ab initio et nunc, numerum vero alium nullum esse praeter numerum hunc ex quo constitit mundus? Nam cum in hac parte opinio et tempus sit eis, parum vero desuper aut subtus iniustitia et discretio aut permixtio, demonstrationem autem dicant quia horum unumquodque numerus est, accidit autem secundum hunc locum iam pluralitatem esse constitutarum magnitudinum, quia passiones hae sequuntur singula loca: utrum idem est hic numerus qui in celo est, quem oportet accipere quia horum unumquodque est, aut praeter hunc alius? Plato namque alium ait esse; existimat etiam quidem et ille numeros haec esse et horum causas, sed illos quidem intellectuales causas hos vero sensibiles.

Further, how are we to combine the beliefs that the attributes of number, and number itself, are causes of what exists and happens in the heavens both from the beginning and now, and that there is no other number than this number out of which the world is composed? When in one particular region they place opinion and opportunity, and, a little above or below, injustice and decision or mixture, and allege, as proof, that each of these is a number, and that there happens to be already in this place a plurality of the extended bodies composed of numbers, because these attributes of number attach to the various places, - this being so, is this number, which we must suppose each of these abstractions to be, the same number which is exhibited in the material universe, or is it another than this? Plato says it is different; yet even he thinks that both these bodies and their causes are numbers, but that the intelligible numbers are causes, while the others are sensible.

### Chapter 9

περὶ μὲν οὖν τῶν Πυθαγορείων ἀφείσθω τὰ νῦν (ἱκανὸν γὰρ αὐτῶν ἅψασθαι τοσοῦτον): [990β] [1] οἱ δὲ τὰς ἰδέας αἰτίας τιθέμενοι πρῶτον μὲν ζητοῦντες τωνδὶ τῶν ὄντων λαβεῖν τὰς αἰτίας ἕτερα τούτοις ἴσα τὸν ἀριθμὸν ἐκόμισαν, ὥσπερ εἴ τις ἀριθμῆσαι βουλόμενος ἐλαττόνων μὲν ὄντων οἴοιτο μὴ δυνήσεσθαι, πλείω δὲ ποιήσας ἀριθμοίη (σχεδὸν γὰρ ἴσα—ἢ οὐκ [5] ἐλάττω—ἐστὶ τὰ εἴδη τούτοις περὶ ὧν ζητοῦντες τὰς αἰτίας ἐκ τούτων ἐπ᾿ ἐκεῖνα προῆλθον: καθ᾿ ἕκαστον γὰρ ὁμώνυμόν τι ἔστι καὶ παρὰ τὰς οὐσίας, τῶν τε ἄλλων ἔστιν ἓν ἐπὶ πολλῶν, καὶ ἐπὶ τοῖσδε καὶ ἐπὶ τοῖς ἀϊδίοις):

De Pytagoricis ergo dimittatur ad presens; sufficit enim ipsa tangere tantum. Qui vero ydeas posuerunt primum quidem horum existentium accipere causas quaerentes alia hiis equalia numero attulerunt, ut si quis numerare volens paucioribus quidem existentibus putet non posse, plura vero faciens numeret. Nam fere equales, aut non pauciores, hiis sunt species de quibus quaerentes causas ab hiis ad illas provenerunt. Secundum unumquodque enim equivocum (omonimum) aliquid est, et circa substantias aliorum est in multis unum, et in hiis et in sempiternis.

Let us leave the Pythagoreans for the present; for it is enough to have touched on them as much as we have done. But as for those who posit the Ideas as causes, firstly, in seeking [90b] to grasp the causes of the things around us, they introduced others equal in number to these, as if a man who wanted to count things thought he would not be able to do it while they were few, but tried to count them when he had added to their number. For the Forms are practically equal to-or not fewer than-the things, in trying to explain which these thinkers proceeded from them to the Forms. For to each thing there answers an entity which has the same name and exists apart from the substances, and so also in the case of all other groups there is a one over many, whether the many are in this world or are eternal.

ἔτι δὲ καθ᾽ οὓς τρόπους δείκνυμεν ὅτι ἔστι τὰ εἴδη, κατ᾽ οὐθένα φαίνεται τούτων: [10] ἐξ ἐνίων μὲν γὰρ οὐκ ἀνάγκη γίγνεσθαι συλλογισμόν, ἐξ ἐνίων δὲ καὶ οὐχ ὧν οἰόμεθα τούτων εἴδη γίγνεται. κατά τε γὰρ τοὺς λόγους τοὺς ἐκ τῶν ἐπιστημῶν εἴδη ἔσται πάντων ὅσων ἐπιστῆμαί εἰσί, καὶ κατὰ τὸ ἓν ἐπὶ πολλῶν καὶ τῶν ἀποφάσεων, κατὰ δὲ τὸ νοεῖν τι φθαρέντος τῶν φθαρτῶν: φάντασμα [15] γάρ τι τούτων ἔστιν.

Amplius autem secundum quos modos ostendimus quia sunt species, secundum nullum videntur horum. Ex quibusdam   enim non est necesse fieri sillogismum, ex quibusdam vero  et non quorum putamus horum species fiunt; quia secundum rationes eas quae ex scientiis species omnium erunt quo rumcumque sunt scientie, et secundum unum in multis et negationibus, et secundum intelligere autem aliquid corrupti  corruptibilium; fantasma enim aliquid horum est.

Further, of the ways in which we prove that the Forms exist, none is convincing; for from some no inference necessarily follows, and from some arise Forms even of things of which we think there are no Forms. For according to the arguments from the existence of the sciences there will be Forms of all things of which there are sciences and according to the 'one over many' argument there will be Forms even of negations, and according to the argument that there is an object for thought even when the thing has perished, there will be Forms of perishable things; for we have an image of these.

ἔτι δὲ οἱ ἀκριβέστεροι τῶν λόγων οἱ μὲν τῶν πρός τι ποιοῦσιν ἰδέας, ὧν οὔ φαμεν εἶναι καθ᾽ αὑτὸ γένος, οἱ δὲ τὸν τρίτον ἄνθρωπον λέγουσιν.

Amplius autem rationum certissime aliae quidem eorum quae ad aliquid ydeas faciunu quorum non dicunt esse secundum se genus, aliae vero tertium hominem dicunt.

Further, of the more accurate arguments, some lead to Ideas of relations, of which we say there is no independent class, and others introduce the 'third man'.

ὅλως τε ἀναιροῦσιν οἱ περὶ τῶν εἰδῶν λόγοι ἃ μᾶλλον εἶναι βουλόμεθα [οἱ λέγοντες εἴδη] τοῦ τὰς ἰδέας εἶναι· συμβαίνει γὰρ μὴ [20] εἶναι τὴν δυάδα πρώτην ἀλλὰ τὸν ἀριθμόν, καὶ τὸ πρός τι τοῦ καθ᾽ αὑτό, καὶ πάνθ᾽ ὅσα τινὲς ἀκολουθήσαντες ταῖς περὶ τῶν ἰδεῶν δόξαις ἠναντιώθησαν ταῖς ἀρχαῖς.

Et omnino quae sunt de speciebus rationes auferunt quae magis esse volunt dicentes esse species quam ipsas ydeas esse. Accidit enim dualitatem non esse primam sed numerum, et ad aliquid ipso quod secundum se, et omnia quaecumque aliqui de speciebus opiniones sequentes opposuerunt principiis.

And in general the arguments for the Forms destroy the things for whose existence we are more zealous than for the existence of the Ideas; for it follows that not the dyad but number is first, i.e. that the relative is prior to the absolute,-besides all the other points on which certain people by following out the opinions held about the Ideas have come into conflict with the principles of the theory.

ἔτι κατὰ μὲν τὴν ὑπόληψιν καθ᾽ ἣν εἶναί φαμεν τὰς ἰδέας οὐ μόνον τῶν οὐσιῶν ἔσται εἴδη ἀλλὰ πολλῶν καὶ ἑτέρων (καὶ γὰρ τὸ [25] νόημα ἓν οὐ μόνον περὶ τὰς οὐσίας ἀλλὰ καὶ κατὰ τῶν ἄλλων ἐστί, καὶ ἐπιστῆμαι οὐ μόνον τῆς οὐσίας εἰσὶν ἀλλὰ καὶ ἑτέρων, καὶ ἄλλα δὲ μυρία συμβαίνει τοιαῦτα)· κατὰ δὲ τὸ ἀναγκαῖον καὶ τὰς δόξας τὰς περὶ αὐτῶν, εἰ ἔστι μεθεκτὰ τὰ εἴδη, τῶν οὐσιῶν ἀναγκαῖον ἰδέας εἶναι μόνον. οὐ [30] γὰρ κατὰ συμβεβηκὸς μετέχονται ἀλλὰ δεῖ ταύτῃ ἑκάστου μετέχειν ᾗ μὴ καθ᾽ ὑποκειμένου λέγεται (λέγω δ᾽ οἷον, εἴ τι αὐτοδιπλασίου μετέχει, τοῦτο καὶ ἀϊδίου μετέχει, ἀλλὰ κατὰ συμβεβηκός· συμβέβηκε γὰρ τῷ διπλασίῳ ἀϊδίῳ εἶναι),

Amplius autem secundum existimationem quidem secundum quam esse dicimus ydeas, esse non solum substantiarum species sed multorum et aliorum; et enim conceptus unus non solum circa substantias sed et de aliis est, et scientie non solum sunt ipsius substantiae sed et aliorum, accidunt autem et mille talia alia. Secundum vero necessitatem et opiniones de eis, si sunt participabiles species, substantiarum necesse ydeas esse solum. Non enim secundum accidens participantur, sed oportet hac uniuscuiusque participare in quantum non de subiecto dicitur. Dico autem ut si quid per se duplo participat, hoc et sempiterno participat, sed secundum accidens; accidit enim duplo sempiternum esse.

Further, according to the assumption on which our belief in the Ideas rests, there will be Forms not only of substances but also of many other things (for the concept is single not only in the case of substances but also in the other cases, and there are sciences not only of substance but also of other things, and a thousand other such difficulties confront them). But according to the necessities of the case and the opinions held about the Forms, if Forms can be shared in there must be Ideas of substances only. For they are not shared in incidentally, but a thing must share in its

Form as in something not predicated of a subject (by 'being shared in incidentally' I mean that e.g. if a thing shares in 'double itself', it shares also in 'eternal', but incidentally; for 'eternal' happens to be predicable of the 'double').

ὥστ' ἔσται οὐσία τὰ εἴδη· ταὐτὰ δὲ ἐνταῦθα οὐσίαν σημαίνει κἀκεῖ· [991α] [1] ἢ τί ἔσται τὸ εἶναί τι παρὰ ταῦτα, τὸ ἓν ἐπὶ πολλῶν; καὶ εἰ μὲν ταὐτὸ εἶδος τῶν ἰδεῶν καὶ τῶν μετεχόντων, ἔσται τι κοινόν (τί γὰρ μᾶλλον ἐπὶ τῶν φθαρτῶν δυάδων, καὶ τῶν πολλῶν μὲν ἀϊδίων δέ, τὸ [5] δυὰς ἓν καὶ ταὐτόν, ἢ ἐπί τ' αὐτῆς καὶ τῆς τινός;)· εἰ δὲ μὴ τὸ αὐτὸ εἶδος, ὁμώνυμα ἂν εἴη, καὶ ὅμοιον ὥσπερ ἂν εἴ τις καλοῖ ἄνθρωπον τόν τε Καλλίαν καὶ τὸ ξύλον, μηδεμίαν κοινωνίαν ἐπιβλέψας αὐτῶν.

Quare substantia erunt species; hae vero substantiam hic significant et ibi. Aut quid erit ipsum esse dicere aliquid praeter haec, unum in multis? Et si quidem eadem species ydearum et participantium, aliquid erit commune; quid enim magis in corruptibilibus dualitatibus, et dualitatibus multis quidem sed sempiternis, dualitas unum et idem, quam in hac et aliqua? Si vero non eadem species, equivocatio erit, et simile ut si quis vocat hominem Calliam et lignum, nullam eorum communitatem inspiciens.

Therefore the Forms will be substance; but the same terms indicate substance in this and in the ideal world [91a] (or what will be the meaning of saying that there is something apart from the particulars-the one over many?). And if the Ideas and the particulars that share in them have the same form, there will be something common to these; for why should '2' be one and the same in the perishable 2's or in those which are many but eternal, and not the same in the '2' itself' as in the particular 2? But if they have not the same form, they must have only the name in common, and it is as if one were to call both Callias and a wooden image a 'man', without observing any community between them.

πάντων δὲ μάλιστα διαπορήσειεν ἄν τις τί ποτε συμβάλλεται τὰ εἴδη τοῖς [10] ἀϊδίοις τῶν αἰσθητῶν ἢ τοῖς γιγνομένοις καὶ φθειρομένοις· οὔτε γὰρ κινήσεως οὔτε μεταβολῆς οὐδεμιᾶς ἐστιν αἴτια αὐτοῖς.

Omnium autem dubitabit aliquis maxime quid conferunt species sempiternis sensibilium aut hiis quae fiunt et corrumpuntur; nec enim motus nec transmutationis nullius sunt causa eis.

Above all one might discuss the question what on earth the Forms contribute to sensible things, either to those that are eternal or to those that come into being and cease to be. For they cause neither movement nor any change in them.

ἀλλὰ μὴν οὔτε πρὸς τὴν ἐπιστήμην οὐθὲν βοηθεῖ τὴν τῶν ἄλλων (οὐδὲ γὰρ οὐσία ἐκεῖνα τούτων· ἐν τούτοις γὰρ ἂν ἦν), οὔτε εἰς τὸ εἶναι, μὴ ἐνυπάρχοντά γε τοῖς μετέχουσιν: οὕτω μὲν [15] γὰρ ἂν ἴσως αἴτια δόξειεν εἶναι ὡς τὸ λευκὸν μεμιγμένον τῷ λευκῷ, ἀλλ᾽ οὗτος μὲν ὁ λόγος λίαν εὐκίνητος, ὃν Ἀναξαγόρας μὲν πρῶτος Εὔδοξος δ᾽ ὕστερον καὶ ἄλλοι τινὲς ἔλεγον (ῥάδιον γὰρ συναγαγεῖν πολλὰ καὶ ἀδύνατα πρὸς τὴν τοιαύτην δόξαν):

At vero nec ad scientiam nihil auxiliatur eis quae est aliorum (nec enim ille horum substantia; nam in hiis essent) nec ad esse, cum non insint participantibus; sic enim forsan causa videbitur esse album permixtum albo. Sed haec quidem ratio valde mobilis est, quam Anaxagoras prius et Eudoxus posterius et alii quidam dixerunt; facile namque colligere multa et impossibilia ad talem opinionem.

But again they help in no wise either towards the knowledge of the other things (for they are not even the substance of these, else they would have been in them), or towards their being, if they are not in the particulars which share in them; though if they were, they might be thought to be causes, as white causes whiteness in a white object by entering into its composition. But this argument, which first Anaxagoras and later Eudoxus and certain others used, is very easily upset; for it is not difficult to collect many insuperable objections to such a view.

ἀλλὰ μὴν οὐδ᾽ ἐκ τῶν εἰδῶν ἐστὶ τἄλλα [20] κατ᾽ οὐθένα τρόπον τῶν εἰωθότων λέγεσθαι. τὸ δὲ λέγειν παραδείγματα αὐτὰ εἶναι καὶ μετέχειν αὐτῶν τἄλλα κενολογεῖν ἐστὶ καὶ μεταφορὰς λέγειν ποιητικάς. τί γάρ ἐστι τὸ ἐργαζόμενον πρὸς τὰς ἰδέας ἀποβλέπον; ἐνδέχεταί τε καὶ εἶναι καὶ γίγνεσθαι ὅμοιον ὁτιοῦν καὶ μὴ εἰκαζόμενον [25] πρὸς ἐκεῖνο, ὥστε καὶ ὄντος Σωκράτους καὶ μὴ ὄντος γένοιτ᾽ ἂν οἷος Σωκράτης: ὁμοίως δὲ δῆλον ὅτι κἂν εἰ ἦν ὁ Σωκράτης ἀΐδιος. ἔσται τε πλείω παραδείγματα τοῦ αὐτοῦ, ὥστε καὶ εἴδη, οἷον τοῦ ἀνθρώπου τὸ ζῷον καὶ τὸ δίπουν, ἅμα δὲ καὶ τὸ αὐτοάνθρωπος. ἔτι οὐ μόνον τῶν αἰσθητῶν [30] παραδείγματα τὰ εἴδη ἀλλὰ καὶ αὐτῶν, οἷον τὸ γένος, ὡς γένος εἰδῶν: ὥστε τὸ αὐτὸ ἔσται παράδειγμα καὶ εἰκών.

At vero nec ex speciebus sunt alia secundum nullum modum dici consuetorum. Dicere vero exempla esse et eis alia participare vaniloquium est et metaphoras dicere poeticas. Quid enim est [Nam quid est] quod agitur ad ydeas respiciens? Contingit enim et esse et fieri simile quodcumque et non assimilatum ad illud; quare et existente Socrate et non existente fiet qualis Socrates. Similiter autem palam quia etiam si sit Socrates sempiternus. Erunt eiusdem exemplaria plura, quare et species, ut hominis animal et bipes, simul autem et autoanthropos. Amplius autem non solum sensibilium species exemplaria sed et ipsarum, ut genus specierum; quare idem erit exemplar et ymago.

But, further, all other things cannot come from the Forms in any of the usual senses of 'from'. And to say that they are patterns and the other things share in them is to use empty words and poetical metaphors. For what is it that works, looking to the

Ideas? And anything can either be, or become, like another without being copied from it, so that whether Socrates or not a man Socrates like might come to be; and evidently this might be so even if Socrates were eternal. And there will be several patterns of the same thing, and therefore several Forms; e.g. 'animal' and 'two-footed' and also 'man himself' will be Forms of man. Again, the Forms are patterns not only sensible things, but of Forms themselves also; i.e. the genus, as genus of various species, will be so; therefore the same thing will be pattern and copy.

[991β] [1] ἔτι δόξειεν ἂν ἀδύνατον εἶναι χωρὶς τὴν οὐσίαν καὶ οὗ ἡ οὐσία· ὥστε πῶς ἂν αἱ ἰδέαι οὐσίαι τῶν πραγμάτων οὖσαι χωρὶς εἶεν;

Amplius videbitur [Amplius opinabitur] utique impossibile esse separatim substantiam et cuius est substantia. Quare quomodo ydee substantiae rerum existentes separatim erunt?

[91b] Again, it would seem impossible that the substance and that of which it is the substance should exist apart; how, therefore, could the Ideas, being the substances of things, exist apart?

ἐν δὲ τῷ Φαίδωνι οὕτω λέγεται, ὡς καὶ τοῦ εἶναι καὶ τοῦ γίγνεσθαι αἴτια τὰ εἴδη ἐστίν· καίτοι τῶν εἰδῶν [5] ὄντων ὅμως οὐ γίγνεται τὰ μετέχοντα ἂν μὴ ᾖ τὸ κινῆσον, καὶ πολλὰ γίγνεται ἕτερα, οἷον οἰκία καὶ δακτύλιος, ὧν οὔ φαμεν εἴδη εἶναι· ὥστε δῆλον ὅτι ἐνδέχεται καὶ τἆλλα καὶ εἶναι καὶ γίγνεσθαι διὰ τοιαύτας αἰτίας οἵας καὶ τὰ ῥηθέντα νῦν.

In Fedone vero sic dicitur quasi ipsius esse et fieri cause sint species. Et etiam existentibus speciebus tamen non fiunt participantia, si non sit quod movit, et multa fiunt alia, ut domus et anulus, quorum non dicimus esse species. Quare palam quia contingit et alia et esse et fieri propter tales causas quales et nunc dicte.

In the Phaedo the case is stated in this way-that the Forms are causes both of being and of becoming; yet when the Forms exist, still the things that share in them do not come into being, unless there is something to originate movement; and many other things come into being (e.g. a house or a ring) of which we say there are no Forms. Clearly, therefore, even the other things can both be and come into being owing to such causes as produce the things just mentioned.

ἔτι εἴπερ εἰσὶν ἀριθμοὶ τὰ εἴδη, πῶς αἴτιοι ἔσονται; [10] πότερον ὅτι ἕτεροι ἀριθμοί εἰσι τὰ ὄντα, οἷον ὁδὶ μὲν <ὁ ἀριθμὸς ἄνθρωπος ὁδὶ δὲ Σωκράτης ὁδὶ δὲ Καλλίας; τί οὖν ἐκεῖνοι τούτοις αἴτιοί εἰσιν; οὐδὲ γὰρ εἰ οἱ μὲν ἀίδιοι οἱ δὲ μή, οὐδὲν διοίσει. εἰ δ᾽ ὅτι λόγοι ἀριθμῶν τἀνταῦθα, οἷον ἡ συμφωνία, δῆλον ὅτι ἐστιν ἕν γέ τι ὧν εἰσι λόγοι. εἰ δὴ [15] τι τοῦτο, ἡ ὕλη, φανερὸν ὅτι καὶ αὐτοὶ οἱ ἀριθμοὶ λόγοι τινὲς ἔσονται ἑτέρου πρὸς ἕτερον. λέγω δ᾽ οἷον, εἰ ἔστιν ὁ Καλλίας λόγος ἐν ἀριθμοῖς πυρὸς καὶ γῆς καὶ ὕδατος καὶ ἀέρος, καὶ ἄλλων τινῶν ὑποκειμένων ἔσται καὶ ἡ ἰδέα ἀριθμός: καὶ αὐτοάνθρωπος, εἴτ᾽ ἀριθμός τις ὢν εἴτε μή, ὅμως ἔσται λόγος [20] ἐν ἀριθμοῖς τινῶν καὶ οὐκ ἀριθμός, οὐδ᾽ ἔσται τις διὰ ταῦτα ἀριθμός.

Amplius si sunt numeri species, quomodo cause erunt? utrum quia alii numeri sunt ipsa existentia, ut hic quidem numerus homo ille vero Socrates et alius Callias? Quid igitur hiis sunt cause illi? Nec enim si hii quidem sempiterni illi vero non, non differunt. Si vero quia rationes numerorum et hic, ut symphonia, palam quia est unum quid quorum sunt rationes. Si itaque hoc materia, manifestum quia et ipsi numeri alique rationes erunt alius ad aliud. Dico autem ut si est Callias ratio in numeris ignis et terre et aque et aeris, et autoanthropos, sive numerus quis existens sive non, tamen erit ratio in numeris quorundam et non numerus, et non erit quis propter ea numerus.

Again, if the Forms are numbers, how can they be causes? Is it because existing things are other numbers, e.g. one number is man, another is Socrates, another Callias? Why then are the one set of numbers causes of the other set? It will not make any difference even if the former are eternal and the latter are not. But if it is because things in this sensible world (e.g. harmony) are ratios of numbers, evidently the things between which they are ratios are some one class of things. If, then, this—the matter— is some definite thing, evidently the numbers themselves too will be ratios of something to something else. E.g. if Callias is a numerical ratio between fire and earth and water and air, his Idea also will be a number of certain other underlying things; and man himself, whether it is a number in a sense or not, will still be a numerical ratio of certain things and not a number proper, nor will it be a of number merely because it is a numerical ratio.

ἔτι ἐκ πολλῶν ἀριθμῶν εἷς ἀριθμὸς γίγνεται, ἐξ εἰδῶν δὲ ἓν εἶδος πῶς; εἰ δὲ μὴ ἐξ αὐτῶν ἀλλ᾽ ἐκ τῶν ἐν τῷ ἀριθμῷ, οἷον ἐν τῇ μυριάδι, πῶς ἔχουσιν αἱ μονάδες; εἴτε γὰρ ὁμοειδεῖς, πολλὰ συμβήσεται ἄτοπα, εἴτε μὴ ὁμοειδεῖς, [25] μήτε αὐταὶ ἀλλήλαις μήτε αἱ ἄλλαι πᾶσαι πάσαις: τίνι γὰρ διοίσουσιν ἀπαθεῖς οὖσαι; οὔτε γὰρ εὔλογα ταῦτα οὔτε ὁμολογούμενα τῇ νοήσει.

Amplius ex multis numeris unus fit numerus, ex speciebus autem una species aliqualiter. Sed si nec ex ipsis sed ex unis , ut in millenario, quomodo se habent unitates? Sive enim eiusdem speciei, multa inconvenientia accidunt, sive non eiusdem speciei, nec eaedem sibi invicem nec aliae omnes omnibus; quo namque different impassibiles existentes? Nec enim rationabilia haec neque intelligentie confessa.

Again, from many numbers one number is produced, but how can one Form come from many Forms? And if the number comes not from the many numbers themselves but from the units in them, e.g. in 10,000, how is it with the units? If they are specifically alike, numerous absurdities will follow, and also if they are not alike (neither the units in one number being themselves like one another nor those in other numbers being all like to all); for in what will they differ, as they are without quality? This is not a plausible view, nor is it consistent with our thought on the matter.

ἔτι δ᾽ ἀναγκαῖον ἕτερον γένος ἀριθμοῦ κατασκευάζειν περὶ ὃ ἡ ἀριθμητική, καὶ πάντα τὰ μεταξὺ λεγόμενα ὑπό τινων, ἃ πῶς ἢ ἐκ τίνων [30] ἐστὶν ἀρχῶν; ἢ διὰ τί μεταξὺ τῶν δεῦρό τ᾽ ἔσται καὶ αὐτῶν; ἔτι αἱ μονάδες αἱ ἐν τῇ δυάδι ἑκατέρα ἔκ τινος προτέρας δυάδος: καίτοι ἀδύνατον. [992α] [1] ἔτι διὰ τί ἓν ὁ ἀριθμὸς συλλαμβανόμενος;

Amplius autem aliud aliquod genus numeri facere est necesse circa quod sit arismetica; et omnia intermedia dicta ab aliquibus simpliciter,  ex quibus sunt principiis? Aut quare intermedia eorum  quae hic et ipsorum erunt? Amplius unitates quae sunt in dualitate utraque est ex aliqua priore dualitate; quamvis impossibile. Amplius quare unum numerus est collectus?

Further, they must set up a second kind of number (with which arithmetic deals), and all the objects which are called 'intermediate' by some thinkers; and how do these exist or from what principles do they proceed? Or why must they be intermediate between the things in this sensible world and the things-themselves? Further, the units in must each come from a prior but this is impossible. [92a] Further, why is a number, when taken all together, one?

ἔτι δὲ πρὸς τοῖς εἰρημένοις, εἴπερ εἰσὶν αἱ μονάδες διάφοροι, ἐχρῆν οὕτω λέγειν ὥσπερ καὶ ὅσοι τὰ στοιχεῖα τέτταρα ἢ δύο λέγουσιν: καὶ γὰρ τούτων ἕκαστος οὐ [5] τὸ κοινὸν λέγει στοιχεῖον, οἷον τὸ σῶμα, ἀλλὰ πῦρ καὶ γῆν, εἴτ᾽ ἔστι τι κοινόν, τὸ σῶμα, εἴτε μή. νῦν δὲ λέγεται ὡς ὄντος τοῦ ἑνὸς ὥσπερ πυρὸς ἢ ὕδατος ὁμοιομεροῦς: εἰ δ᾽ οὕτως, οὐκ ἔσονται οὐσίαι οἱ ἀριθμοί, ἀλλὰ δῆλον ὅτι, εἴπερ ἐστί τι ἓν αὐτὸ καὶ τοῦτό ἐστιν ἀρχή, πλεοναχῶς λέγεται τὸ ἕν: ἄλλως [10] γὰρ ἀδύνατον.

Amplius cum dictis [Amplius autem], si sunt differentes unitates, oportebit ita dicere quemadmodum et quicumque elementa quatuor aut duo dicunt; et enim horum quilibet non commune dicit elementum,  ut corpus, sed ignem et terram, sive sit commune corpus ipsum sive non. Nunc autem dicitur quasi uno existente quemadmodum igne aut aqua similium partium; si vero sic, non erunt substantiae numeri. Sed palam quia, si omne est aliquid unum ipsum et hoc est principium, multipliciter dicitur ipsum unum; aliter enim impossibile.

Again, besides what has been said, if the units are diverse the Platonists should have spoken like those who say there are four, or two, elements; for each of these thinkers gives the name of element not to that which is common, e.g. to body, but to fire and earth, whether there is something common to them, viz. body, or not. But in fact the Platonists speak as if the One were homogeneous like fire or water; and if this is so, the numbers will not be substances. Evidently, if there is a One itself and this is a first principle, 'one' is being used in more than one sense; for otherwise the theory is impossible.

βουλόμενοι δὲ τὰς οὐσίας ἀνάγειν εἰς τὰς ἀρχὰς μήκη μὲν τίθεμεν ἐκ βραχέος καὶ μακροῦ, ἔκ τινος μικροῦ καὶ μεγάλου, καὶ ἐπίπεδον ἐκ πλατέος καὶ στενοῦ, σῶμα δ᾽ ἐκ βαθέος καὶ ταπεινοῦ. καίτοι πῶς ἕξει ἢ τὸ ἐπίπεδον γραμμὴν ἢ τὸ στερεὸν γραμμὴν καὶ ἐπίπεδον; ἄλλο [15] γὰρ γένος τὸ πλατὺ καὶ στενὸν καὶ βαθὺ καὶ ταπεινόν: ὥσπερ οὖν οὐδ᾽ ἀριθμὸς ὑπάρχει ἐν αὐτοῖς, ὅτι τὸ πολὺ καὶ ὀλίγον ἕτερον τούτων, δῆλον ὅτι οὐδ᾽ ἄλλο οὐθὲν τῶν ἄνω ὑπάρξει τοῖς κάτω. ἀλλὰ μὴν οὐδὲ γένος τὸ πλατὺ τοῦ βαθέος: ἦν γὰρ ἂν ἐπίπεδόν τι τὸ σῶμα. ἔτι αἱ στιγμαὶ ἐκ [20] τίνος ἐνυπάρξουσιν; τούτῳ μὲν οὖν τῷ γένει καὶ διεμάχετο Πλάτων ὡς ὄντι γεωμετρικῷ δόγματι, ἀλλ᾽ ἐκάλει ἀρχὴν γραμμῆς—τοῦτο δὲ πολλάκις ἐτίθει—τὰς ἀτόμους γραμμάς. καίτοι ἀνάγκη τούτων εἶναί τι πέρας: ὥστ᾽ ἐξ οὗ λόγου γραμμὴ ἔστι, καὶ στιγμὴ ἔστιν.

Volentes autem substantias ad principia reducere longitudines quidem ponimus ex producto et brevi ( ex aliquo paruo et magno) et planum ex lato et arto, corpus vero ex profundo et humili. Quamvis quomodo [attamen quomodo] habebit aut planum lineam aut solidum lineam et planum? Aliud enim genus et latum et artum et profundum et humile. Quemadmodum ergo nec numerus est in eis, quia multum et paucum ab hiis alterum , palam quia nec aliud nihil superiorum inerit inferioribus. At vero nec genus profundi latum; esset enim planum aliquod corpus. Amplius puncta ex quo inexistunt? Huic quidem igitur generi et Plato oppugnabat tamquam existente geometrico dogmati, sed lineae principium vocabat. Hic autem multotiens indivisibiles lineas posuit. Quamvis necesse terminum aliquem harum esse; quare ex qua ratione linea est, et punctum est.

When we wish to reduce substances to their principles, we state that lines come from the short and long (i.e. from a kind of small and great), and the plane from the broad and narrow, and body from the deep and shallow. Yet how then can either the plane contain a line, or the solid a line or a plane? For the broad and narrow is a different class from the deep and shallow. Therefore, just as number is not present in these, because the many and few are different from these, evidently no other of the higher classes will be present in the lower. But again the broad is not a genus which includes the deep, for then the solid would have been a species of plane. Further, from what principle will the presence of the points in the line be derived? Plato even used to object to this class of things as being a geometrical fiction. He gave the name of principle of the line-and this he often posited-to the indivisible lines. Yet these must have a limit; therefore the argument from which the existence of the line follows proves also the existence of the point.

ὅλως δὲ ζητούσης τῆς σοφίας περὶ [25] τῶν φανερῶν τὸ αἴτιον, τοῦτο μὲν εἰάκαμεν (οὐθὲν γὰρ λέγομεν περὶ τῆς αἰτίας ὅθεν ἡ ἀρχὴ τῆς μεταβολῆς), τὴν δ᾽ οὐσίαν οἰόμενοι λέγειν αὐτῶν ἑτέρας μὲν οὐσίας εἶναί φαμεν, ὅπως δ᾽ ἐκεῖναι τούτων οὐσίαι, διὰ κενῆς λέγομεν· τὸ γὰρ μετέχειν, ὥσπερ καὶ πρότερον εἴπομεν, οὐθέν ἐστιν.

Omnino autem sapientia de manifestis causam inquirente, hoc quidem praetermisimus; nihil enim de causa dicimus unde principium est transmutationis. Horum vero substantiam dicere putantes ipsorum alias quidem substantias esse dicimus, quomodo vero ille horum substantiae, uane dicimus; nam et participare, sicut prius diximus, nihil est.

In general, though philosophy seeks the cause of perceptible things, we have given this up (for we say nothing of the cause from which change takes its start), but while we fancy we are stating the substance of perceptible things, we assert the existence of a second class of substances, while our account of the way in which they are the substances of perceptible things is empty talk; for 'sharing', as we said before, means nothing.

οὐδὲ δὴ ὅπερ ταῖς [30] ἐπιστήμαις ὁρῶμεν ὂν αἴτιον, δι᾽ ὃ καὶ πᾶς νοῦς καὶ πᾶσα φύσις ποιεῖ, οὐδὲ ταύτης τῆς αἰτίας, ἥν φαμεν εἶναι μίαν τῶν ἀρχῶν, οὐθὲν ἅπτεται τὰ εἴδη, ἀλλὰ γέγονε τὰ μαθήματα τοῖς νῦν ἡ φιλοσοφία, φασκόντων ἄλλων χάριν αὐτὰ δεῖν πραγματεύεσθαι.

Nec quam in scientiis videmus, existens causa, propter quam et omnis intellectus et omnis natura facit, nec hanc causam quam esse dicimus unum principiorum, nihil tangunt species, sed facta est mathematica presentibus philosophia, dicentium aliorum gratia ea oportere tractari.

Nor have the Forms any connexion with what we see to be the cause in the case of the arts, that for whose sake both all mind and the whole of nature are operative,- with this cause which we assert to be one of the first principles; but mathematics has come to be identical with philosophy for modern thinkers, though they say that it should be studied for the sake of other things.

[992β] [1] ἔτι δὲ τὴν ὑποκειμένην οὐσίαν ὡς ὕλην μαθηματικωτέραν ἄν τις ὑπολάβοι, καὶ μᾶλλον κατηγορεῖσθαι καὶ διαφορὰν εἶναι τῆς οὐσίας καὶ τῆς ὕλης ἢ ὕλην, οἷον τὸ μέγα καὶ τὸ μικρόν, ὥσπερ καὶ οἱ φυσιολόγοι [5] φασὶ τὸ μανὸν καὶ τὸ πυκνόν, πρώτας τοῦ ὑποκειμένου φάσκοντες εἶναι διαφορὰς ταύτας· ταῦτα γὰρ ἐστιν ὑπεροχή τις καὶ ἔλλειψις. περί τε κινήσεως, εἰ μὲν ἔσται ταῦτα κίνησις, δῆλον ὅτι κινήσεται τὰ εἴδη· εἰ δὲ μή, πόθεν ἦλθεν; ὅλη γὰρ ἡ περὶ φύσεως ἀνῄρηται σκέψις.

Amplius autem substantiam subiectam ut materiam magis mathematicam aliquis suscipiet, et magis predicari et differentiam esse substantiae et materiei, ut magnum et parvum. Sicut phisiologi aiunt rarum et spissum, primas subiecti dicentes esse differentias has; haec namque sunt superhabundantia quaedam et defectio. Et de motu, si quidem haec erunt motus, palam quia moventur species; sin autem, unde venit? Tota namque de natura auferetur perscrutatio.

[92b] Further, one might suppose that the substance which according to them underlies as matter is too mathematical, and is a predicate and differentia of the substance, ie. of the matter, rather than matter itself; i.e. the great and the small are like the rare and the dense which the physical philosophers speak of, calling these the primary differentiae of the substratum; for these are a kind of excess and defect. And regarding movement, if the great and the small are to he movement, evidently the Forms will be moved; but if they are not to be movement, whence did movement come? The whole study of nature has been annihilated.

ὅ τε δοκεῖ ῥᾴδιον [10] εἶναι, τὸ δεῖξαι ὅτι ἓν ἅπαντα, οὐ γίγνεται· τῇ γὰρ ἐκθέσει οὐ γίγνεται πάντα ἓν ἀλλ᾽ αὐτό τι ἕν, ἂν διδῷ τις πάντα· καὶ οὐδὲ τοῦτο, εἰ μὴ γένος δώσει τὸ καθόλου εἶναι· τοῦτο δ᾽ ἐν ἐνίοις ἀδύνατον.

Et quod videtur esse facile: monstrare quod unum omnia non fiunt. Expositione enim non fiunt omnia unum sed id aliquid unum, si quis dat omnia, et nec hoc, si non genus dat universale esse; hoc autem in quibusdam impossibile.

And what is thought to be easy-to show that all things are one-is not done; for what is proved by the method of setting out instances is not that all things are one but that there is a One itself,-if we grant all the assumptions. And not even this follows, if we do not grant that the universal is a genus; and this in some cases it cannot be.

οὐθένα δ᾽ ἔχει λόγον οὐδὲ τὰ μετὰ τοὺς ἀριθμοὺς μήκη τε καὶ ἐπίπεδα καὶ στερεά, οὔτε ὅπως ἔστιν ἢ [15] ἔσται οὔτε τίνα ἔχει δύναμιν· ταῦτα γὰρ οὔτε εἴδη οἷόν τε εἶναι (οὐ γὰρ εἰσιν ἀριθμοί) οὔτε τὰ μεταξύ (μαθηματικὰ γὰρ ἐκεῖνα) οὔτε τὰ φθαρτά, ἀλλὰ πάλιν τέταρτον ἄλλο φαίνεται τοῦτό τι γένος.

Nullam autem [Nullam namque] rationem habent nec quae sunt post numeros longitudines, latitudines et solida, nec quomodo sunt aut futura sint, nec si aliquam habent virtutem; haec enim nec species possibile esse (non enim sunt numeri) nec intermedia (sunt enim illa mathematica) nec corruptibilia. Sed rursum quartum videtur aliud hoc genus.

Nor can it be explained either how the lines and planes and solids that come after the numbers exist or can exist, or what significance they have; for these can neither be Forms (for they are not numbers), nor the intermediates (for those are the objects of mathematics), nor the perishable things. This is evidently a distinct fourth class.

ὅλως τε τὸ τῶν ὄντων ζητεῖν στοιχεῖα μὴ διελόντας, πολλαχῶς λεγομένων, ἀδύνατον εὑρεῖν, ἄλλως [20] τε καὶ τοῦτον τὸν τρόπον ζητοῦντας ἐξ οἵων ἐστὶ στοιχείων. ἐκ τίνων γὰρ τὸ ποιεῖν ἢ πάσχειν ἢ τὸ εὐθύ, οὐκ ἔστι δήπου λαβεῖν, ἀλλ᾽ εἴπερ, τῶν οὐσιῶν μόνον ἐνδέχεται: ὥστε τὸ τῶν ὄντων ἀπάντων τὰ στοιχεῖα ἢ ζητεῖν ἢ οἴεσθαι ἔχειν οὐκ ἀληθές.

Et omnino existentium quaerere elementa non dividentem multipliciter dicta invenire impossibile est, et aliter secundum hunc modum quaerentes ex quibus sunt elementis. Ex quibus enim facere aut pati aut ipsum rectum non est accipere, sed siquidem, substantiarum solum esse contingit; quare existentium omnium elementa aut quaerere aut putare habere non est verum.

In general, if we search for the elements of existing things without distinguishing the many senses in which things are said to exist, we cannot find them, especially if the search for the elements of which things are made is conducted in this manner. For it is surely impossible to discover what 'acting' or 'being acted on', or 'the straight', is made of, but if elements can be discovered at all, it is only the elements of substances; therefore either to seek the elements of all existing things or to think one has them is incorrect.

πῶς δ᾽ ἄν τις καὶ μάθοι τὰ τῶν πάντων στοιχεῖα; [25] δῆλον γὰρ ὡς οὐθὲν οἷόν τε προϋπάρχειν γνωρίζοντα πρότερον. ὥσπερ γὰρ τῷ γεωμετρεῖν μανθάνοντι ἄλλα μὲν ἐνδέχεται προειδέναι, ὧν δὲ ἡ ἐπιστήμη καὶ περὶ ὧν μέλλει μανθάνειν οὐθὲν προγιγνώσκει, οὕτω δὴ καὶ ἐπὶ τῶν ἄλλων, ὥστ᾽ εἴ τις τῶν πάντων ἔστιν ἐπιστήμη, οἵαν δή τινές φασιν, [30] οὐθὲν ἂν προϋπάρχοι γνωρίζων οὗτος. καίτοι πᾶσα μάθησις διὰ προγιγνωσκομένων ἢ πάντων ἢ τινῶν ἐστί, καὶ ἡ δι᾽ ἀποδείξεως <καὶ ἡ δι᾽ ὁρισμῶν (δεῖ γὰρ ἐξ ὧν ὁ ὁρισμὸς προειδέναι καὶ εἶναι γνώριμα): ὁμοίως δὲ καὶ ἡ δι᾽ ἐπαγωγῆς. ἀλλὰ μὴν εἰ καὶ τυγχάνοι σύμφυτος οὖσα, [993α] [1] θαυμαστὸν πῶς λανθάνομεν ἔχοντες τὴν κρατίστην τῶν ἐπιστημῶν.

Quomodo autem aliquis discet omnium elementa? Palam enim quia non est possibile preexistere cognoscentem prius. Sicut enim geometrizare discentem alia quidem oportet prescire, quorum autem est scientia et de quibus debet discere non prenoscit, ita et in aliis. Quare si qua est omnium scientia, ut quidam aiunt, nihil utique preexistet hic cognoscens. quamvis sit omnis disciplina per precognita aut omnia aut quaedam, aut per demonstrationem aut per diffinitiones (oportet enim ex quibus est diffinitio prescire et esse nota); similiter autem et quae per inductionem. At vero et si existit connaturalis, mirum quomodo latemus habentes potissimam scientiarum.

And how could we learn the elements of all things? Evidently we cannot start by knowing anything before. For as he who is learning geometry, though he may know other things before, knows none of the things with which the science deals and about which he is to learn, so is it in all other cases. Therefore if there is a science of all things, such as some assert to exist, he who is learning this will know nothing before. Yet all learning is by means of premises which are (either all or some of them) known before,-whether the learning be [92b 32] by demonstration or by definitions; for the elements of the definition must be known before and be familiar; and learning by induction proceeds [93a] similarly. But again, if the science were actually innate, it were strange that we are unaware of our possession of the greatest of sciences.

ἔτι πῶς τις γνωριεῖ ἐκ τίνων ἐστί, καὶ πῶς ἔσται δῆλον; καὶ γὰρ τοῦτ᾽ ἔχει ἀπορίαν· ἀμφισβητήσειε γὰρ ἄν τις ὥσπερ καὶ περὶ ἐνίας [5] συλλαβάς· οἱ μὲν γὰρ τὸ ζα ἐκ τοῦ ς καὶ δ καὶ α φασὶν εἶναι, οἱ δέ τινες ἕτερον φθόγγον φασὶν εἶναι καὶ οὐθένα τῶν γνωρίμων.

Amplius autem quomodo aliquis cognoscit ex quibus est, et quomodo erit manifestum? Et enim hoc habet dubitationem. Ambiget enim aliquis quemadmodum et circa quasdam sillabas; hii namque SMA ex S et M et A dicunt esse, alii vero quendam alium sonum dicunt esse et cognitorum nullum.

Again, how is one to come to know what all things are made of, and how is this to be made evident? This also affords a difficulty; for there might be a conflict of opinion, as there is about certain syllables; some say za is made out of s and d and a, while others say it is a distinct sound and none of those that are familiar.

ἔτι δὲ ὧν ἐστιν αἴσθησις, ταῦτα πῶς ἄν τις μὴ ἔχων τὴν αἴσθησιν γνοίη; καίτοι ἔδει, εἴγε πάντων ταὐτὰ στοιχεῖά ἐστιν ἐξ ὧν, ὥσπερ αἱ σύνθετοι φωναί εἰσιν ἐκ τῶν [10] οἰκείων στοιχείων.

Amplius autem quorum est sensus, haec quomodo aliquis non habens sensum cognoscet? Quamvis oportebat, si omnium haec sunt elementa ex quibus, quemadmodum composite voces sunt ex propriis elementis

Further, how could we know the objects of sense without having the sense in question? Yet we ought to, if the elements of which all things consist, as complex sounds consist of the clements proper to sound, are the same.

*Chapter* 10

ὅτι μὲν οὖν τὰς εἰρημένας ἐν τοῖς φυσικοῖς αἰτίας ζητεῖν ἐοίκασι πάντες, καὶ τούτων ἐκτὸς οὐδεμίαν ἔχοιμεν ἂν εἰπεῖν, δῆλον καὶ ἐκ τῶν πρότερον εἰρημένων· ἀλλ᾽ ἀμυδρῶς ταύτας, καὶ τρόπον μέν τινα πᾶσαι πρότερον εἴρηνται τρόπον [15] δέ τινα οὐδαμῶς. ψελλιζομένη γὰρ ἔοικεν ἡ πρώτη φιλοσοφία περὶ πάντων, ἅτε νέα τε καὶ κατ᾽ ἀρχὰς οὖσα [καὶ τὸ πρῶτον], ἐπεὶ καὶ Ἐμπεδοκλῆς ὀστοῦν τῷ λόγῳ φησὶν εἶναι, τοῦτο δ᾽ ἐστὶ τὸ τί ἦν εἶναι καὶ ἡ οὐσία τοῦ πράγματος. ἀλλὰ μὴν ὁμοίως ἀναγκαῖον καὶ σάρκας καὶ τῶν ἄλλων [20] ἕκαστον εἶναι τὸν λόγον, ἢ μηδὲ ἕν· διὰ τοῦτο γὰρ καὶ σὰρξ καὶ ὀστοῦν ἔσται καὶ τῶν ἄλλων ἕκαστον καὶ οὐ διὰ τὴν ὕλην, ἣν ἐκεῖνος λέγει, πῦρ καὶ γῆν καὶ ὕδωρ καὶ ἀέρα. ἀλλὰ ταῦτα ἄλλου μὲν λέγοντος συνέφησεν ἂν ἐξ ἀνάγκης, σαφῶς δὲ οὐκ εἴρηκεν.

Quod quidem igitur [Quoniam ergo] dictas in phisicis causas quaerere visi sunt omnes, et extra has nullam habemus dicere, palam et ex prius dictis. Sed tenuiter hae, et modo quodam omnes prius dicte sunt modo vero quodam nullatenus. Balbutiens enim est visa prima philosophia de omnibus, velut noua existens circa principium et primo. Quoniam et Empedocles os dicit esse rationem. Hoc autem est quod quid erat esse et substantia rei. At vero similiter necessarium et carnis et aliorum singulorum esse rationem aut nihil; propter hoc enim et caro et os est et aliorum unumquodque, et non propter materiam quam ille dicit, ignem et terram et aerem et aquam. Sed haec alio quidem dicente simul dixit ex necessitate, manifeste vero non dixit.

It is evident, then, even from what we have said before, that all men seem to seek the causes named in the Physics, and that we cannot name any beyond these; but they seek these vaguely; and though in a sense they have all been described before, in a sense they have not been described at all. For the earliest philosophy is, on all subjects, like one who lisps, since it is young and in its beginnings. For even Empedocles says bone exists by virtue of the ratio in it. Now this is the essence and the substance of the thing. But it is similarly necessary that flesh and each of the other tissues should be the ratio of its elements, or that not one of them should; for it is on account of this that both flesh and bone and everything else will exist, and not on account of the matter, which he names,-fire and earth and water and air. But while he would necessarily have agreed if another had said this, he has not said it clearly.

περὶ μὲν οὖν τούτων δεδήλωται καὶ [25] πρότερον· ὅσα δὲ περὶ τῶν αὐτῶν τούτων ἀπορήσειεν ἄν τις, [26] ἐπανέλθωμεν πάλιν· τάχα γὰρ ἂν ἐξ αὐτῶν εὐπορήσαιμέν τι πρὸς τὰς ὕστερον ἀπορίας.

De talibus quidem igitur ostensum est et prius. Quaecumque vero de ipsis hiis dubitabit aliquis, resumamus iterum; nam forsan ex ipsis habundabimus aliquid ad posteriores dubitationes.

On these questions our views have been expressed before; but let us return to enumerate the difficulties that might be raised on these same points; for perhaps we may get from them some help towards our later difficulties.

2 (A1)

[993α] [30] ἡ περὶ τῆς ἀληθείας θεωρία τῇ μὲν χαλεπὴ τῇ δὲ ῥαδία.

De veritate theoria sic quidem difficilis est, sic vero facilis.

THE investigation of the truth is in one way hard, in another easy.

σημεῖον δὲ τὸ μήτ᾽ ἀξίως μηδένα δύνασθαι θιγεῖν αὐτῆς μήτε πάντας ἀποτυγχάνειν, [993β] [1] ἀλλ᾽ ἕκαστον λέγειν τι περὶ τῆς φύσεως,

Signum autem est neque digne nullum adipisci ipsam posse nec omnes exsortes esse, sed unumquemque aliquid de natura dicere,

An indication of this is found in the fact that no one is able to attain the truth adequately, while, on the other hand, we do not collectively fail, but every one says something true about the nature of things,

καὶ καθ᾽ ἕνα μὲν ἢ μηθὲν ἢ μικρὸν ἐπιβάλλειν αὐτῇ, ἐκ πάντων δὲ συναθροιζομένων γίγνεσθαί τι μέγεθος:

Et secundum unum quidem nihil aut parum ei immittere, ex omnibus autem coarticulatis fieri magnitudinem aliquam.

And while individually we contribute little or nothing to the truth, by the union of all a considerable amount is amassed.

ὥστ᾽ εἴπερ ἔοικεν ἔχειν καθάπερ τυγχάνομεν παροιμιαζόμενοι, [5] τίς ἂν θύρας ἁμάρτοι; ταύτῃ μὲν ἂν εἴη ῥαδία, τὸ δ᾽ ὅλον τι ἔχειν καὶ μέρος μὴ δύνασθαι δηλοῖ τὸ χαλεπὸν αὐτῆς.

Quare si videtur habere ut proverbialiter dicimus fcin foribus quis delinquet?', sic quidem utique erit facilis; habere autem totum et partem non posse difficultatem eius ostendit.

Therefore, since the truth seems to be like the proverbial door, which no one can fail to hit, in this respect it must be easy, but the fact that we can have a whole truth and not the particular part we aim at shows the difficulty of it.

ἴσως δὲ καὶ τῆς χαλεπότητος οὔσης κατὰ δύο τρόπους, οὐκ ἐν τοῖς πράγμασιν ἀλλ᾽ ἐν ἡμῖν τὸ αἴτιον αὐτῆς· ὥσπερ γὰρ τὰ τῶν νυκτερίδων ὄμματα πρὸς τὸ [10] φέγγος ἔχει τὸ μεθ᾽ ἡμέραν, οὕτω καὶ τῆς ἡμετέρας ψυχῆς ὁ νοῦς πρὸς τὰ τῇ φύσει φανερώτατα πάντων.

Forsan autem et difficultate secundum duos existente modos, non in rebus sed in nobis est eius causa. Sicut enim nicticoracum oculi ad lucem diei se habent, sic et anime nostre intellectus ad ea quae sunt omnium nature manifestissima.

Perhaps, too, as difficulties are of two kinds, the cause of the present difficulty is not in the facts but in us. For as the eyes of bats are to the blaze of day, so is the reason in our soul to the things which are by nature most evident of all.

οὐ μόνον δὲ χάριν ἔχειν δίκαιον τούτοις ὧν ἄν τις κοινώσαιτο ταῖς δόξαις, ἀλλὰ καὶ τοῖς ἐπιπολαιότερον ἀποφηναμένοις: καὶ γὰρ οὗτοι συνεβάλοντό τι: τὴν γὰρ ἕξιν προήσκησαν ἡμῶν: [15] εἰ μὲν γὰρ Τιμόθεος μὴ ἐγένετο, πολλὴν ἂν μελοποιίαν οὐκ εἴχομεν: εἰ δὲ μὴ Φρῦνις, Τιμόθεος οὐκ ἂν ἐγένετο. τὸν αὐτὸν δὲ τρόπον καὶ ἐπὶ τῶν περὶ τῆς ἀληθείας ἀποφηναμένων: παρὰ μὲν γὰρ ἐνίων παρειλήφαμέν τινας δόξας, οἱ δὲ τοῦ γενέσθαι τούτους αἴτιοι γεγόνασιν.

Non solum autem hiis dicere gratiam iustum est quorum aliquis opinionibus communicaverit, sed et hiis qui adhuc superficialiter enuntiaverunt; et enim hii conferunt aliquid, nam habitum nostrum preexercitati sunt. Nam si Thimotheus non fuisset, multam melodiam non haberemus; si autem non Phrinis, thimotheus non fuisset. Eodem vero modo et de enuntiantibus veritatem; a quibusdam enim opiniones quasdam accepimus, sed alii ut hii forent causa fuerunt.

It is just that we should be grateful, not only to those with whose views we may agree, but also to those who have expressed more superficial views; for these also contributed something, by developing before us the powers of thought. It is true that if there had been no Timotheus we should have been without much of our lyric poetry; but if there had been no Phrynis there would have been no Timotheus. The same holds good of those who have expressed views about the truth; for from some thinkers we have inherited certain opinions, while the others have been responsible for the appearance of the former.

ὀρθῶς δ᾽ ἔχει καὶ τὸ καλεῖσθαι [20] τὴν φιλοσοφίαν ἐπιστήμην τῆς ἀληθείας. θεωρητικῆς μὲν γὰρ τέλος ἀλήθεια πρακτικῆς δ᾽ ἔργον: καὶ γὰρ ἂν τὸ πῶς ἔχει σκοπῶσιν, οὐ τὸ ἀΐδιον ἀλλ᾽ ὃ πρός τι καὶ νῦν θεωροῦσιν οἱ πρακτικοί.

Vocari vero philosophiam veritatis scientiam recte habet. Nam theorice finis est veritas et practice opus; et enim si quomodo se habet intendant, non causam secundum se sed ad aliquid et nunc speculantur practici.

It is right also that philosophy should be called knowledge of the truth. For the end of theoretical knowledge is truth, while that of practical knowledge is action (for even if they consider how things are, practical men do not study the eternal, but what is relative and in the present).

οὐκ ἴσμεν δὲ τὸ ἀληθὲς ἄνευ τῆς αἰτίας: ἕκαστον δὲ μάλιστα αὐτὸ τῶν ἄλλων καθ᾽ ὃ καὶ [25] τοῖς ἄλλοις ὑπάρχει τὸ συνώνυμον (οἷον τὸ πῦρ θερμότατον: καὶ γὰρ τοῖς ἄλλοις τὸ αἴτιον τοῦτο τῆς θερμότητος): ὥστε καὶ ἀληθέστατον τὸ τοῖς ὑστέροις αἴτιον τοῦ ἀληθέσιν εἶναι. διὸ τὰς τῶν ἀεὶ ὄντων ἀρχὰς ἀναγκαῖον ἀεὶ εἶναι ἀληθεστάτας (οὐ γάρ ποτε ἀληθεῖς, οὐδ᾽ ἐκείναις αἴτιόν τί ἐστι τοῦ [30] εἶναι, ἀλλ᾽ ἐκεῖναι τοῖς ἄλλοις), ὥσθ᾽ ἕκαστον ὡς ἔχει τοῦ εἶναι, οὕτω καὶ τῆς ἀληθείας.

Nescimus autem verum sine causa. Unumquodque vero  rmaxime ipsum aliorum  secundum quod et aliis inest univocatio, puta ignis  calidissimus; et enim est causa aliis hic caloris.  quare et verissimum quod posterioribus est causa ut sint vera. Quapropter semper existentium principia semper esse verissima est necesse; non enim quandoque vera nec illis causa aliquid est ut sint, sed illa aliis. Quare unumquodque sicut se habet ut sit, ita et ad veritatem.

Now we do not know a truth without its cause; and a thing has a quality in a higher degree than other things if in virtue of it the similar quality belongs to the other things as well (e.g. fire is the hottest of things; for it is the cause of the heat of all other things); so that that causes derivative truths to be true is most true. Hence the principles of eternal things must be always most true (for they are not merely sometimes true, nor is there any cause of their being, but they themselves are the cause of the being of other things), so that as each thing is in respect of being, so is it in respect of truth.

*Chapter*  2

[994α] [1] ἀλλὰ μὴν ὅτι γ᾽ ἔστιν ἀρχή τις καὶ οὐκ ἄπειρα τὰ αἴτια τῶν ὄντων οὔτ᾽ εἰς εὐθυωρίαν οὔτε κατ᾽ εἶδος, δῆλον. οὔτε γὰρ ὡς ἐξ ὕλης τόδ᾽ ἐκ τοῦδε δυνατὸν ἰέναι εἰς ἄπειρον (οἷον σάρκα μὲν ἐκ γῆς, γῆν δ᾽ ἐξ ἀέρος, ἀέρα δ᾽ ἐκ πυρός, [5] καὶ τοῦτο μὴ ἵστασθαι), οὔτε ὅθεν ἡ ἀρχὴ τῆς κινήσεως (οἷον τὸν μὲν ἄνθρωπον ὑπὸ τοῦ ἀέρος κινηθῆναι, τοῦτον δ᾽ ὑπὸ τοῦ ἡλίου, τὸν δὲ ἥλιον ὑπὸ τοῦ νείκους, καὶ τούτου μηδὲν εἶναι πέρας): ὁμοίως δὲ οὐδὲ τὸ οὗ ἕνεκα εἰς ἄπειρον οἷόν τε ἰέναι, βάδισιν μὲν ὑγιείας ἕνεκα, ταύτην δ᾽ εὐδαιμονίας, τὴν δ᾽ εὐδαιμονίαν [10] ἄλλου, καὶ οὕτως ἀεὶ ἄλλο ἄλλου ἕνεκεν εἶναι: καὶ ἐπὶ τοῦ τί ἦν εἶναι δ᾽ ὡσαύτως.

At vero quod sit principium quoddam et non infinite cause existentium nec in directum  nec secundum speciem, palam. Nec enim ut ex materia hoc ex hoc in infinitum progredi est possibile, veluti carnem quidem ex terra, terram vero ex  aere, aerem autem ex igne, et hoc non stare. Nec unde principium motus, ut hominem ab aere moveri, et hunc a sole, solem vero a lite, et huius nullum esse finem. Similiter autem nec id cuius causa in infinitum ire est possibile; iter quidem sanitatis causa, ijjam vero felicitatis, et felicitatem alius, et ita semper aliud alius causam esse. Et in quid erat esse similiter.

[94a] But evidently there is a first principle, and the causes of things are neither an infinite series nor infinitely various in kind. For neither can one thing proceed from another, as from matter, ad infinitum (e.g. flesh from earth, earth from air, air from fire, and so on without stopping), nor can the sources of movement form an endless series (man for instance being acted on by air, air by the sun, the sun by Strife, and so on without limit). Similarly the final causes cannot go on ad infinitum,-walking being for the sake of health, this for the sake of happiness, happiness for the sake of something else, and so one thing always for the sake of another. And the case of the essence is similar.

τῶν γὰρ μέσων, ὧν ἐστί τι ἔσχατον καὶ πρότερον, ἀναγκαῖον εἶναι τὸ πρότερον αἴτιον τῶν μετ᾽ αὐτό. εἰ γὰρ εἰπεῖν ἡμᾶς δέοι τί τῶν τριῶν αἴτιον, τὸ πρῶτον ἐροῦμεν: οὐ γὰρ δὴ τό γ᾽ ἔσχατον, οὐδενὸς γὰρ τὸ [15] τελευταῖον: ἀλλὰ μὴν οὐδὲ τὸ μέσον, ἑνὸς γάρ (οὐθὲν δὲ διαφέρει ἓν ἢ πλείω εἶναι, οὐδ᾽ ἄπειρα ἢ πεπερασμένα). τῶν δ᾽ ἀπείρων τοῦτον τὸν τρόπον καὶ ὅλως τοῦ ἀπείρου πάντα τὰ μόρια μέσα ὁμοίως μέχρι τοῦ νῦν: ὥστ᾽ εἴπερ μηδέν ἐστι πρῶτον, ὅλως αἴτιον οὐδέν ἐστιν.

Mediorum enim, extra quae est aliquid ultimum et primum, necesse est esse quod prius est causam ipsorum post se. Nam si dicere nos oporteat quid trium causa, quod primum est dicemus; non enim quod est ultimum, nullius enim quod finale est; sed nec medium, nam unius. Nihil enim differt unum aut plura esse, nec infinita aut finita. Infinitorum vero secundum modum istum et omnino infiniti partes omnes medie sunt similiter usque modo; quare si ex toto nihil est aliquod primum, ex toto causa nulla est.

For in the case of intermediates, which have a last term and a term prior to them, the prior must be the cause of the later terms. For if we had to say which of the three is the cause, we should say the first; surely not the last, for the final term is the cause of none; nor even the intermediate, for it is the cause only of one. (It makes no difference whether there is one intermediate or more, nor whether they are infinite or finite in number.) But of series which are infinite in this way, and of the infinite in general, all the parts down to that now present are alike intermediates; so that if there is no first there is no cause at all.

ἀλλὰ μὴν οὐδ᾽ ἐπὶ τὸ κάτω [20] οἷόν τε εἰς ἄπειρον ἰέναι, τοῦ ἄνω ἔχοντος ἀρχήν, ὥστ᾽ ἐκ πυρὸς μὲν ὕδωρ, ἐκ δὲ τούτου γῆν, καὶ οὕτως ἀεὶ ἄλλο τι γίγνεσθαι γένος.

At vero neque in deorsum est possibile in infinitum ire, ipso sursum habente principium, ut ex igne quidem aquam, ex hoc vero terram, et ita semper aliquid aliud fieri genus.

Nor can there be an infinite process downwards, with a beginning in the upward direction, so that water should proceed from fire, earth from water, and so always some other kind should be produced.

διχῶς γὰρ γίγνεται τόδε ἐκ τοῦδε—μὴ ὡς τόδε λέγεται μετὰ τόδε, οἷον ἐξ Ἰσθμίων Ὀλύμπια, ἀλλ᾽ ἢ ὡς ἐκ παιδὸς ἀνὴρ μεταβάλλοντος ἢ ὡς ἐξ ὕδατος ἀήρ. [25] ὡς μὲν οὖν ἐκ παιδὸς ἄνδρα γίγνεσθαί φαμεν, ὡς ἐκ τοῦ γιγνομένου τὸ γεγονὸς ἢ ἐκ τοῦ ἐπιτελουμένου τὸ τετελεσμένον (ἀεὶ γάρ ἐστι μεταξύ, ὥσπερ τοῦ εἶναι καὶ μὴ εἶναι γένεσις, οὕτω καὶ τὸ γιγνόμενον τοῦ ὄντος καὶ μὴ ὄντος: ἔστι γὰρ ὁ μανθάνων γιγνόμενος ἐπιστήμων, καὶ τοῦτ᾽ ἐστὶν ὃ λέγεται, [30] ὅτι γίγνεται ἐκ μανθάνοντος ἐπιστήμων): τὸ δ᾽ ὡς ἐξ ἀέρος ὕδωρ, φθειρομένου θατέρου.

Dupliciter enim fit hoc ex hoc, non ut hoc dicitur post hoc, ut ex isthmiis olympia, sed ut aut ex puero mutato vir aut ex aqua aer. Ut quidem igitur ex puero fieri virum dicimus [Ergo sic ex puero], quomodo ex eo quod fit quod factum est aut ex eo quod perficitur perfectum. Semper enim est medium, ut esse et non esse generatio, ita et quod fit existentis et non existentis. Est autem addiscens qui fit sciens, et hoc est quod dicitur quia fit ex discente sciens. Hoc vero ut ex aere aquam: corrupto altero.

For one thing comes from another in two ways-not in the sense in which 'from' means 'after' (as we say 'from the Isthmian games come the Olympian' ), but either (i) as the man comes from the boy, by the boys changing, or (ii) as air comes from water. By 'as the man comes from the boy' we mean 'as that which has come to be from that which is coming to be' or 'as that which is finished from that which is being achieved' (for as becoming is between being and not being, so that which is becoming is always between that which is and that which is not; for the learner is a man of science in the making, and this is what is meant when we say that from a learner a man of science is being made); on the other hand, coming from another thing as water comes from air implies the destruction of the other thing.

διὸ ἐκεῖνα μὲν οὐκ ἀνακάμπτει εἰς ἄλληλα, [994β] [1] οὐδὲ γίγνεται ἐξ ἀνδρὸς παῖς (οὐ γὰρ γίγνεται ἐκ τῆς γενέσεως τὸ γιγνόμενον ἀλλ᾽ <ὃ ἔστι μετὰ τὴν γένεσιν: οὕτω γὰρ καὶ ἡμέρα ἐκ τοῦ πρωΐ, ὅτι μετὰ τοῦτο: διὸ οὐδὲ τὸ πρωΐ ἐξ ἡμέρας): θάτερα δὲ ἀνακάμπτει.

Propter quod illa quidem non reflectuntur ad invicem, nec fit ex viro puer; non enim fit ex generatione quod fit, sed est post generationem. Sic enim est dies ex aurora, quia post hanc; propter quod nec aurora ex die. Altera vero reflectuntur.

This is why changes of the former kind are not reversible, and the boy does not come from the man (for it is not that which comes to be something that comes to be as a result of [94b] coming to be, but that which exists after the coming to be; for it is thus that the day, too, comes from the morning-in the sense that it comes after the morning; which is the reason why the morning cannot come from the day); but changes of the other kind are reversible.

ἀμφοτέρως δὲ ἀδύνατον εἰς ἄπειρον ἰέναι: τῶν μὲν γὰρ ὄντων μεταξὺ [5] ἀνάγκη τέλος εἶναι, τὰ δ᾿ εἰς ἄλληλα ἀνακάμπτει: ἡ γὰρ θατέρου φθορὰ θατέρου ἐστὶ γένεσις.

Utroque autem modo impossibile [est] in infinitum ire. Existentium enim intermediorum necesse est finem esse. quaedam vero ad invicem reflectuntur; alterius enim corruptio alterius est generatio.

But in both cases it is impossible that the number of terms should be infinite. For terms of the former kind, being intermediates, must have an end, and terms of the latter kind change back into one another, for the destruction of either is the generation of the other.

ἅμα δὲ καὶ ἀδύνατον τὸ πρῶτον ἀΐδιον ὂν φθαρῆναι: ἐπεὶ γὰρ οὐκ ἄπειρος ἡ γένεσις ἐπὶ τὸ ἄνω, ἀνάγκη ἐξ οὗ φθαρέντος πρώτου τι ἐγένετο μὴ ἀΐδιον εἶναι.

Simul autem impossibile primum sempiternum corrumpi. Quoniam enim non est infinita generatio in sursum, necesse ex quo corrupto primo aliquid factum est non sempiternum esse.

At the same time it is impossible that the first cause, being eternal, should be destroyed; for since the process of becoming is not infinite in the upward direction, that which is the first thing by whose destruction something came to be must be non-eternal.

ἔτι δὲ τὸ οὗ ἕνεκα τέλος, τοιοῦτον δὲ ὃ μὴ ἄλλου [10] ἕνεκα ἀλλὰ τἆλλα ἐκείνου, ὥστ᾿ εἰ μὲν ἔσται τοιοῦτόν τι ἔσχατον, οὐκ ἔσται ἄπειρον, εἰ δὲ μηθὲν τοιοῦτον, οὐκ ἔσται τὸ οὗ ἕνεκα, ἀλλ᾿ οἱ τὸ ἄπειρον ποιοῦντες λανθάνουσιν ἐξαιροῦντες τὴν τοῦ ἀγαθοῦ φύσιν (καίτοι οὐθεὶς ἂν ἐγχειρήσειεν οὐδὲν πράττειν μὴ μέλλων ἐπὶ πέρας ἥξειν): οὐδ᾿ ἂν εἴη νοῦς ἐν [15] τοῖς οὖσιν: ἕνεκα γάρ τινος ἀεὶ πράττει ὅ γε νοῦν ἔχων, τοῦτο δέ ἐστι πέρας: τὸ γὰρ τέλος πέρας ἐστίν.

[i]Amplius autem quod est cuius causa[/i] finis est, tale vero quod non alius causa, sed alia illius. Quare si quidem fuerit tale ipsum ultimum, non erit infinitum; si vero nihil tale, non erit quod cuius causa. Sed qui infinitum faciunt, latent auferentes boni naturam (et nullus conabitur aliquid facere ad terminum non futurus venire). Neque utique erit intellectus in talibus; nam causa alicuius semper facit qui intellectum habet; hoc enim est terminus; finis enim terminus est.

Further, the final cause is an end, and that sort of end which is not for the sake of something else, but for whose sake everything else is; so that if there is to be a last term of this sort, the process will not be infinite; but if there is no such term, there will be no final cause, but those who maintain the infinite series eliminate the Good without knowing it (yet no one would try to do anything if he were not going to come to a limit); nor would there be reason in the world; the reasonable man, at least, always acts for a purpose, and this is a limit; for the end is a limit.

ἀλλὰ μὴν οὐδὲ τὸ τί ἦν εἶναι ἐνδέχεται ἀνάγεσθαι εἰς ἄλλον ὁρισμὸν πλεονάζοντα τῷ λόγῳ: ἀεί τε γὰρ ἔστιν ὁ ἔμπροσθεν μᾶλλον, ὁ δ᾽ ὕστερος οὐκ ἔστιν, οὗ δὲ τὸ πρῶτον μὴ ἔστιν, οὐδὲ [20] τὸ ἐχόμενον:

Sed nec quod quid erat esse convenit reduci ad aliam diffinitionem multiplicantem rationem. Semper enim quae ante est magis est, et quae posterior est non est; cuius autem primum non est, nec habitum est.

But the essence, also, cannot be reduced to another definition which is fuller in expression. For the original definition is always more of a definition, and not the later one; and in a series in which the first term has not the required character, the next has not it either.

ἔτι τὸ ἐπίστασθαι ἀναιροῦσιν οἱ οὕτως λέγοντες, οὐ γὰρ οἷόν τε εἰδέναι πρὶν εἰς τὰ ἄτομα ἐλθεῖν: καὶ τὸ γιγνώσκειν οὐκ ἔστιν, τὰ γὰρ οὕτως ἄπειρα πῶς ἐνδέχεται νοεῖν;

Amplius scire destruunt qui ita dicunt; non enim possibile scire priusquam ad individua perueniatur. Et cognoscere non est; nam quae sic sunt infinita, quomodo contingit intelligere?

Further, those who speak thus destroy science; for it is not possible to have this till one comes to the unanalysable terms. And knowledge becomes impossible; for how can one apprehend things that are infinite in this way?

οὐ γὰρ ὅμοιον ἐπὶ τῆς γραμμῆς, ἣ κατὰ τὰς διαιρέσεις μὲν οὐχ ἵσταται, νοῆσαι δ᾽ οὐκ ἔστι μὴ στήσαντα (διόπερ [25] οὐκ ἀριθμήσει τὰς τομὰς ὁ τὴν ἄπειρον διεξιών), ἀλλὰ καὶ τὴν ὅλην οὐ κινουμένῳ νοεῖν ἀνάγκη. καὶ ἀπείρῳ οὐδενί ἐστιν εἶναι: εἰ δὲ μή, οὐκ ἄπειρόν γ᾽ ἐστὶ τὸ ἀπείρῳ εἶναι.

Non enim simile in linea , quae secundum divisiones quidem non stat, intelligere vero non est non statuentem; propter quod non enumerabit sectiones qui per infinitam procedit. Sed materiam in eo quod movetur intelligere necesse; et infinito nihil est. Esse autem non. Non infinitumque est infinito esse.

For this is not like the case of the line, to whose divisibility there is no stop, but which we cannot think if we do not make a stop (for which reason one who is tracing the infinitely divisible line cannot be counting the possibilities of section), but the whole line also must be apprehended by something in us that does not move from part to part.-Again, nothing infinite can exist; and if it could, at least the notion of infinity is not infinite.

ἀλλὰ μὴν καὶ εἰ ἄπειρά γ᾽ ἦσαν πλήθει τὰ εἴδη τῶν αἰτίων, οὐκ ἂν ἦν οὐδ᾽ οὕτω τὸ γιγνώσκειν: τότε γὰρ εἰδέναι οἰόμεθα [30] ὅταν τὰ αἴτια γνωρίσωμεν: τὸ δ᾽ ἄπειρον κατὰ τὴν πρόσθεσιν οὐκ ἔστιν ἐν πεπερασμένῳ διεξελθεῖν.

Sed si infinitae essent pluralitate species causarum, non esset nec ita cognoscere; tunc enim scire putamus cum causas ipsas noverimus. Infinitum vero secundum adiectionem non est pertransire in finito.

But if the kinds of causes had been infinite in number, then also knowledge would have been impossible; for we think we know, only when we have ascertained the causes, that but that which is infinite by addition cannot be gone through in a finite time.

*Chapter* 3

αἱ δ᾽ ἀκροάσεις κατὰ τὰ ἔθη συμβαίνουσιν: ὡς γὰρ εἰώθαμεν οὕτως ἀξιοῦμεν λέγεσθαι, [995α] [1] καὶ τὰ παρὰ ταῦτα οὐχ ὅμοια φαίνεται ἀλλὰ διὰ τὴν ἀσυνήθειαν ἀγνωστότερα καὶ ξενικώτερα: τὸ γὰρ σύνηθες γνώριμον.

Contingunt autem auditiones secundum consuetudines entibus; nam ut consuevimus ita dignamur dici. Et quae praeter ea non similia videntur, sed propter inconsuetudinem minus nota et magis extranea; nam consuetum notius.

The effect which lectures produce on a hearer depends on his habits; for we demand the language we are [95a] accustomed to, and that which is different from this seems not in keeping but somewhat unintelligible and foreign because of its unwontedness. For it is the customary that is intelligible.

ἡλίκην δὲ ἰσχὺν ἔχει τὸ σύνηθες οἱ νόμοι δηλοῦσιν, ἐν οἷς τὰ μυθώδη καὶ [5] παιδαριώδη μεῖζον ἰσχύει τοῦ γινώσκειν περὶ αὐτῶν διὰ τὸ ἔθος.

Quantam vero vim habeat quod consuetum est leges ostendunt, in quibus fabularia et puerilia magis quidem valent cognitione de eis propter consuetudinem.

The force of habit is shown by the laws, in which the legendary and childish elements prevail over our knowledge about them, owing to habit.

οἱ μὲν οὖν ἐὰν μὴ μαθηματικῶς λέγῃ τις οὐκ ἀποδέχονται τῶν λεγόντων, οἱ δ᾽ ἂν μὴ παραδειγματικῶς, οἱ δὲ μάρτυρα ἀξιοῦσιν ἐπάγεσθαι ποιητήν. καὶ οἱ μὲν πάντα ἀκριβῶς, τοὺς δὲ λυπεῖ τὸ ἀκριβὲς ἢ διὰ τὸ μὴ δύνασθαι [10] συνείρειν ἢ διὰ τὴν μικρολογίαν: ἔχει γάρ τι τὸ ἀκριβὲς τοιοῦτον, ὥστε, καθάπερ ἐπὶ τῶν συμβολαίων, καὶ ἐπὶ τῶν λόγων ἀνελεύθερον εἶναί τισι δοκεῖ.

Alii ergo [vero], si non mathematicae quis dicit, non recipiunt dicentes. Alii, si non exemplariter. Et hii testem induci dignantur poetam. Et illi quidem omnia certe; hiis vero flebilis est certitudo aut propter impotentiam complectendi aut propter micrologiam. Habet enim aliquid quod certum est tale, ut quemadmodum in symbolis et rationibus non LIBERum esse quibusdam videtur.

Thus some people do not listen to a speaker unless he speaks mathematically, others unless he gives instances, while others expect him to cite a poet as witness. And some want to have everything done accurately, while others are annoyed by accuracy, either because they cannot follow the connexion of thought or because they regard it as pettifoggery. For accuracy has something of this character, so that as in trade so in argument some people think it mean.

διὸ δεῖ πεπαιδεῦσθαι πῶς ἕκαστα ἀποδεκτέον, ὡς ἄτοπον ἅμα ζητεῖν ἐπιστήμην καὶ τρόπον ἐπιστήμης: ἔστι δ᾽ οὐδὲ θάτερον ῥᾴδιον λαβεῖν.

Propter quod oportet erudiri quomodo singula sunt recipienda, et absurdum est simul quaerere scientiam et modum scientie; est autem neutrum facile accipere.

Hence one must be already trained to know how to take each sort of argument, since it is absurd to seek at the same time knowledge and the way of attaining knowledge; and it is not easy to get even one of the two.

τὴν [15] δ᾽ ἀκριβολογίαν τὴν μαθηματικὴν οὐκ ἐν ἅπασιν ἀπαιτητέον, [16] ἀλλ᾽ ἐν τοῖς μὴ ἔχουσιν ὕλην. διόπερ οὐ φυσικὸς ὁ τρόπος: ἅπασα γὰρ ἴσως ἡ φύσις ἔχει ὕλην. διὸ σκεπτέον πρῶτον τί ἐστιν ἡ φύσις: οὕτω γὰρ καὶ περὶ τίνων ἡ φυσικὴ δῆλον ἔσται [καὶ εἰ μιᾶς ἐπιστήμης ἢ πλειόνων τὰ αἴτια καὶ [20] τὰς ἀρχὰς θεωρῆσαί ἐστιν].

Acribologia vero mathematica non in omnibus est expetenda, sed in non habentibus materiam. Propter quod non naturalis est modus; omnis enim forsan natura materiam habet. Ideoque primum perscrutandum quid est natura. Ita namque et de quibus est phisica, manifestum erit; et si unius scientie aut plurium est causas et principia considerare.

The minute accuracy of mathematics is not to be demanded in all cases, but only in the case of things which have no matter. Hence method is not that of natural science; for presumably the whole of nature has matter. Hence we must inquire first what nature is: for thus we shall also see what natural science treats of (and whether it belongs to one science or to more to investigate the causes and the principles of things).

# METHAPHISICE ARISTOTILIS LIBER TERTIUS

## 3 (B)

[995α] [24] ἀνάγκη πρὸς τὴν ἐπιζητουμένην ἐπιστήμην ἐπελθεῖν ἡμᾶς [25] πρῶτον περὶ ὧν ἀπορῆσαι δεῖ πρῶτον: ταῦτα δ᾽ ἐστὶν ὅσα τε περὶ αὐτῶν ἄλλως ὑπειλήφασί τινες, κἂν εἴ τι χωρὶς τούτων τυγχάνει παρεωραμένον.

Necesse est ad quesitam scientiam nos aggredi primum de quibus dubitare primum oportet. Haec autem sunt quaecumque de ipsis aliter susceperunt quidam, et si quid extra haec est praetermissum.

WE must, with a view to the science which we are seeking, first recount the subjects that should be first discussed. These include both the other opinions that some have held on the first principles, and any point besides these that happens to have been overlooked.

ἔστι δὲ τοῖς εὐπορῆσαι βουλομένοις προὔργου τὸ διαπορῆσαι καλῶς: ἡ γὰρ ὕστερον εὐπορία λύσις τῶν πρότερον ἀπορουμένων ἐστί, λύειν δ᾽ οὐκ [30] ἔστιν ἀγνοοῦντας τὸν δεσμόν, ἀλλ᾽ ἡ τῆς διανοίας ἀπορία δηλοῖ τοῦτο περὶ τοῦ πράγματος: ἧ γὰρ ἀπορεῖ, ταύτῃ παραπλήσιον πέπονθε τοῖς δεδεμένοις: ἀδύνατον γὰρ ἀμφοτέρως προελθεῖν εἰς τὸ πρόσθεν. διὸ δεῖ τὰς δυσχερείας τεθεωρηκέναι πάσας πρότερον, τούτων τε χάριν καὶ διὰ τὸ τοὺς [35] ζητοῦντας ἄνευ τοῦ διαπορῆσαι πρῶτον ὁμοίους εἶναι τοῖς ποῖ δεῖ βαδίζειν ἀγνοοῦσι,

Inest autem investigare volentibus pre opere bene dubitare; posterior enim copia [investigatio] priorum est solutio dubitatorum, soluere vero non est ignorantis vinculum. Sed mentis dubitatio hoc de re demonstrat. In quantum enim dubitat, in tantum similiter ligatis est passa; impossibile enim utrisque procedere ad quod est ante. Propter quod oportet difficultates speculari omnes prius, horumque causa et quia quaerentes sine dubitatione primo similes sunt quo oportet ire ignorantibus;

For those who wish to get clear of difficulties it is advantageous to discuss the difficulties well; for the subsequent free play of thought implies the solution of the previous difficulties, and it is not possible to untie a knot of which one does not know. But the difficulty of our thinking points to a knot in the object; for in so far as our thought is in difficulties, it is in like case with those who are bound; for in either case it is impossible to go forward. Hence one should have surveyed all the difficulties beforehand, both for the purposes we have stated and because people who inquire without first stating the difficulties are like those who do not know where they have to go;

καὶ πρὸς τούτοις οὐδ᾽ εἴ ποτε τὸ ζητούμενον εὕρηκεν ἢ μὴ γιγνώσκειν: [995β] [1] τὸ γὰρ τέλος τούτῳ μὲν οὐ δῆλον τῷ δὲ προηπορηκότι δῆλον. ἔτι δὲ βέλτιον ἀνάγκη ἔχειν πρὸς τὸ κρῖναι τὸν ὥσπερ ἀντιδίκων καὶ τῶν ἀμφισβητούντων λόγων ἀκηκοότα πάντων.

et ad haec neque quando quesitum invenit aut non, cognoscit; finis enim huic est non manifestus, predubitanti vero manifestus. Amplius melius necesse est habere ad iudicandum eum qui audivit velut adversariorum et dubitantium omnes rationes.

besides, a man does not otherwise know even whether he has at any given time found what he is looking for [95b] or not; for the end is not clear to such a man, while to him who has first discussed the difficulties it is clear. Further, he who has heard all the contending arguments, as if they were the parties to a case, must be in a better position for judging.

ἔστι δ᾽ ἀπορία πρώτη [5] μὲν περὶ ὧν ἐν τοῖς πεφροιμιασμένοις διηπορήσαμεν, πότερον μιᾶς ἢ πολλῶν ἐπιστημῶν θεωρῆσαι τὰς αἰτίας: καὶ πότερον τὰς τῆς οὐσίας ἀρχὰς τὰς πρώτας ἐστὶ τῆς ἐπιστήμης ἰδεῖν μόνον ἢ καὶ περὶ τῶν ἀρχῶν ἐξ ὧν δεικνύουσι πάντες, οἷον πότερον ἐνδέχεται ταὐτὸ καὶ ἓν ἅμα φάναι καὶ ἀποφάναι [10] ἢ οὔ, καὶ περὶ τῶν ἄλλων τῶν τοιούτων: εἴ τ᾽ ἐστι περὶ τὴν οὐσίαν, πότερον μία περὶ πάσας ἢ πλείονές εἰσι, κἂν εἰ πλείονες πότερον ἅπασαι συγγενεῖς ἢ τὰς μὲν σοφίας τὰς δὲ ἄλλο τι λεκτέον αὐτῶν.

Est autem dubitatio prima quidem de quibus in prohemialiter dictis dubitavimus, utrum unius aut multarum est scientiarum causas speculari; et utrum substantiae principia prima est scientie huius scire solum aut etiam de principiis ex quibus ostendunt omnes, ut utrum contingit unum et idem simul dicere et negare aut non, et de aliis talibus. Et si est circa substantiam, utrum una circa omnes aut plures sunt, et si plures, utrum omnes cognate aut earum hae quidem sapientie ille vero aliquid aliud dicende sunt.

The first problem concerns the subject which we discussed in our prefatory remarks. It is this – (1) whether the investigation of the causes belongs to one or to more sciences, and (2) whether such a science should survey only the first principles of substance, or also the principles on which all men base their proofs, e.g. whether it is possible at the same time to assert and deny one and the same thing or not, and all other such questions; and (3) if the science in question deals with substance, whether one science deals with all substances, or more than one, and if more, whether all are akin, or some of them must be called forms of Wisdom and the others something else.

καὶ τοῦτο δ᾽ αὐτὸ τῶν ἀναγκαίων ἐστὶ ζητῆσαι, πότερον τὰς αἰσθητὰς οὐσίας εἶναι [15] μόνον φατέον ἢ καὶ παρὰ ταύτας ἄλλας, καὶ πότερον μοναχῶς ἢ πλείονα γένη τῶν οὐσιῶν, οἷον οἱ ποιοῦντες τά τε εἴδη καὶ τὰ μαθηματικὰ μεταξὺ τούτων τε καὶ τῶν αἰσθητῶν. περί τε τούτων οὖν,

Et hoc idem quoque necessarium est quaerere, utrum sensibiles substantiae esse solum dicende sunt aut  praeter has aliae, et utrum unice sunt aut plura genera substantiarum, ut facientes species et mathematica inter istas et sensibilia . De hiis igitur, ut dicimus, perscrutandum est.

And (4) this itself is also one of the things that must be discussed-whether sensible substances alone should be said to exist or others also besides them, and whether these others are of one kind or there are several classes of substances, as is supposed by those who believe both in Forms and in mathematical objects intermediate between these and sensible things. Into these questions, then, as we say, we must inquire,

καθάπερ φαμέν, ἐπισκεπτέον, καὶ πότερον περὶ τὰς οὐσίας ἡ θεωρία μόνον ἐστὶν ἢ καὶ περὶ [20] τὰ συμβεβηκότα καθ᾽ αὑτὰ ταῖς οὐσίαις, πρὸς δὲ τούτοις περὶ ταὐτοῦ καὶ ἑτέρου καὶ ὁμοίου καὶ ἀνομοίου καὶ ἐναντιότητος, καὶ περὶ προτέρου καὶ ὑστέρου καὶ τῶν ἄλλων ἁπάντων τῶν τοιούτων περὶ ὅσων οἱ διαλεκτικοὶ πειρῶνται σκοπεῖν ἐκ τῶν ἐνδόξων μόνων ποιούμενοι τὴν σκέψιν, τίνος [25] ἐστὶ θεωρῆσαι περὶ πάντων· ἔτι δὲ τούτοις αὐτοῖς ὅσα καθ᾽ αὑτὰ συμβέβηκεν, καὶ μὴ μόνον τί ἐστι τούτων ἕκαστον ἀλλὰ καὶ ἆρα ἓν ἑνὶ ἐναντίον·

Et utrum circa substantias solum est speculatio aut et circa quae accidunt secundum se substantiis. Adhuc autem de eodem et diverso, simili et dissimili et contrarietate et de priore et posteriore et aliis omnibus talibus de quibuscumque dialetici intendere temptant, ex probabilibus solum perscrutationem facientes, quorum theoria est de omnibus. Amplius autem hiis eisdem quaecumque  secundum se accidunt; et non solum quid est horum unumquodque, sed utrum uni est unum contrarium.

and also (5) whether our investigation is concerned only with substances or also with the essential attributes of substances. Further, with regard to the same and other and like and unlike and contrariety, and with regard to prior and posterior and all other such terms about which the dialecticians try to inquire, starting their investigation from probable premises only,-whose business is it to inquire [95b 25] into all these? Further, we must discuss the essential attributes of these themselves; and we must ask not only what each of these is, but also whether one thing always has one contrary.

καὶ πότερον αἱ ἀρχαὶ καὶ τὰ στοιχεῖα τὰ γένη ἐστὶν ἢ εἰς ἃ διαιρεῖται ἐνυπάρχοντα ἕκαστον· καὶ εἰ τὰ γένη, πότερον ὅσα ἐπὶ τοῖς ἀτόμοις λέγεται [30] τελευταῖα ἢ τὰ πρῶτα, οἷον πότερον ζῷον ἢ ἄνθρωπος ἀρχή τε καὶ μᾶλλον ἔστι παρὰ τὸ καθ᾽ ἕκαστον.

Et utrum principia et elementa genera sunt aut in quae dividitur existentium singulum. Et si genera, utrum quaecumque de individuis dicuntur finalia aut prima, ut utrum animal aut homo principiumque et magis est quam singulare.

Again (6), are the principles and elements of things the genera, or the parts present in each thing, into which it is divided; and (7) if they are the genera, are they the genera that are predicated proximately of the individuals, or the highest genera, e.g. is animal or man the first principle and the more independent of the individual instance?

μάλιστα δὲ ζητητέον καὶ πραγματευτέον πότερον ἔστι τι παρὰ τὴν ὕλην αἴτιον καθ᾽ αὑτὸ ἢ οὔ, καὶ τοῦτο χωριστὸν ἢ οὔ, καὶ πότερον ἓν ἢ πλείω τὸν ἀριθμόν, καὶ πότερον ἔστι τι παρὰ τὸ [35] σύνολον (λέγω δὲ τὸ σύνολον, ὅταν κατηγορηθῇ τι τῆς ὕλης) ἢ οὐθέν, ἢ τῶν μὲν τῶν δ᾽ οὔ, καὶ ποῖα τοιαῦτα τῶν ὄντων.

Maxime vero quaerendum est et tractandum utrum est aliquid praeter materiam causa secundum se aut non, et hoc separabile aut non, et utrum unum aut plura numero. Et utrum est aliquid praeter simul totum (dico autem synolon, quando predicatur aliquid de materia) aut nihil, aut horum quidem horum vero non, et qualia talia existentium.

And (8) we must inquire and discuss especially whether there is, besides the matter, any thing that is a cause in itself or not, and whether this can exist apart or not, and whether it is one or more in number, and whether there is something apart from the concrete thing (by the concrete thing I mean the matter with something already predicated of it), or there is nothing apart, or there is something in some cases though not in others, and what sort of cases these are.

[996α] [1] ἔτι αἱ ἀρχαὶ πότερον ἀριθμῷ ἢ εἴδει ὡρισμέναι, καὶ αἱ ἐν τοῖς λόγοις καὶ αἱ ἐν τῷ ὑποκειμένῳ· καὶ πότερον τῶν φθαρτῶν καὶ ἀφθάρτων αἱ αὐταὶ ἢ ἕτεραι, καὶ πότερον ἄφθαρτοι πᾶσαι ἢ τῶν φθαρτῶν φθαρταί; ἔτι δὲ τὸ πάντων [5] χαλεπώτατον καὶ πλείστην ἀπορίαν ἔχον, πότερον τὸ ἓν καὶ τὸ ὄν, καθάπερ οἱ

Πυθαγόρειοι καὶ Πλάτων ἔλεγεν, οὐχ ἕτερόν τί ἐστιν ἀλλ᾽ οὐσία τῶν ὄντων; ἢ οὔ, ἀλλ᾽ ἕτερόν τι τὸ ὑποκείμενον, ὥσπερ Ἐμπεδοκλῆς φησὶ φιλίαν ἄλλος δέ τις πῦρ ὁ δὲ ὕδωρ ἢ ἀέρα· καὶ πότερον αἱ ἀρχαὶ [10] καθόλου εἰσὶν ἢ ὡς τὰ καθ᾽ ἕκαστα τῶν πραγμάτων,

Amplius autem utrum principia numero aut specie determinata, et in rationibus et in subiecto, et utrum corruptibilium et incorruptibilium eadem aut diversa, et utrum incorruptibilia omnia aut corruptibilium corruptibilia. Amplius autem quod omnium difficillimum est et plurimam habet dubitationem: utrum unum aut ens, quemadmodum pytagorici et Plato dicebant, non alterum aliquid est sed entium substantia, aut non, sed alterum aliquid ipsum subiectum, ut Empedocles amorem dicit, alius vero ignem, alius aquam aut aerem.

[96a] Again (9) we ask whether the principles are limited in number or in kind, both those in the definitions and those in the substratum; and (10) whether the principles of perishable and of imperishable things are the same or different; and whether they are all imperishable or those of perishable things are perishable. Further (11) there is the question which is hardest of all and most perplexing, whether unity and being, as the Pythagoreans and Plato said, are not attributes of something else but the substance of existing things, or this is not the case, but the substratum is something else,-as Empedocles says, love; as some one else says, fire; while another says water or air. Again (12) we ask whether the principles are universal or like individual things,

καὶ δυνάμει ἢ ἐνεργείᾳ· ἔτι πότερον ἄλλως ἢ κατὰ κίνησιν· καὶ γὰρ ταῦτα ἀπορίαν ἂν παράσχοι πολλήν.

Et utrum principia sint universalia aut ut singularia rerum; et potestate aut actu. Amplius utrum aliter aut secundum motum; haec enim dubitationem prestant magnam.

and (13) whether they exist potentially or actually, and further, whether they are potential or actual in any other sense than in reference to movement; for these questions also would present much difficulty.

πρὸς δὲ τούτοις πότερον οἱ ἀριθμοὶ καὶ τὰ μήκη καὶ τὰ σχήματα καὶ αἱ στιγμαὶ οὐσίαι τινές εἰσιν ἢ οὔ, κἂν εἰ οὐσίαι πότερον [15] κεχωρισμέναι τῶν αἰσθητῶν ἢ ἐνυπάρχουσαι ἐν τούτοις; περὶ γὰρ τούτων ἁπάντων οὐ μόνον χαλεπὸν τὸ εὐπορῆσαι τῆς ἀληθείας ἀλλ᾽ οὐδὲ τὸ διαπορῆσαι τῷ λόγῳ ῥᾴδιον καλῶς.

Ad haec autem utrum numeri et longitudines et figure et puncta substantiae quaedam sunt aut non. Et si substantiae, utrum separata a sensibilibus aut in eis. De hiis enim omnibus non solum difficile veritatem ipsam inquirere sed nec dubitare ratione facile bene.

Further (14), are numbers and lines and figures and points a kind of substance or not, and if they are substances are they separate from sensible things or present in them? With regard to all these matters not only is it hard to get possession of the truth, but it is not easy even to think out the difficulties well.

## *Chapter* 2

πρῶτον μὲν οὖν περὶ ὧν πρῶτον εἴπομεν, πότερον μιᾶς ἢ πλειόνων ἐστὶν ἐπιστημῶν θεωρῆσαι πάντα τὰ γένη τῶν [20] αἰτίων. μιᾶς μὲν γὰρ ἐπιστήμης πῶς ἂν εἴη μὴ ἐναντίας οὔσας τὰς ἀρχὰς γνωρίζειν;

Primum ergo de quibus in primis diximus, utrum unius    aut plurium scientiarum sunt speculanda omnia genera causarum. Unius enim scientie quomodo erit non contraria existentia principia cognoscere?

(1) First then with regard to what we mentioned first, does it belong to one or to more sciences to investigate all the kinds of causes? How could it belong to one science to recognize the principles if these are not contrary?

ἔτι δὲ πολλοῖς τῶν ὄντων οὐχ ὑπάρχουσι πᾶσαι· τίνα γὰρ τρόπον οἷόν τε κινήσεως ἀρχὴν εἶναι τοῖς ἀκινήτοις ἢ τὴν τἀγαθοῦ φύσιν, εἴπερ ἅπαν ὃ ἂν ᾖ ἀγαθὸν καθ᾽ αὑτὸ καὶ διὰ τὴν αὑτοῦ φύσιν τέλος ἐστὶν [25] καὶ οὕτως αἴτιον ὅτι ἐκείνου ἕνεκα καὶ γίγνεται καὶ ἔστι τἆλλα, τὸ δὲ τέλος καὶ τὸ οὗ ἕνεκα πράξεώς τινός ἐστι τέλος, αἱ δὲ πράξεις πᾶσαι μετὰ κινήσεως· ὥστ᾽ ἐν τοῖς ἀκινήτοις οὐκ ἂν ἐνδέχοιτο ταύτην εἶναι τὴν ἀρχὴν οὐδ᾽ εἶναί τι αὐτοαγαθόν. διὸ καὶ ἐν τοῖς μαθήμασιν οὐθὲν δείκνυται διὰ [30] ταύτης τῆς αἰτίας, οὐδ᾽ ἔστιν ἀπόδειξις οὐδεμία διότι βέλτιον ἢ χεῖρον, ἀλλ᾽ οὐδὲ τὸ παράπαν μέμνηται οὐθεὶς οὐθενὸς τῶν τοιούτων, ὥστε διὰ ταῦτα τῶν σοφιστῶν τινὲς οἷον Ἀρίστιππος προεπηλάκιζεν αὐτάς· ἐν μὲν γὰρ ταῖς ἄλλαις τέχναις, καὶ ταῖς βαναύσοις, οἷον ἐν τεκτονικῇ καὶ σκυτικῇ, διότι [35] βέλτιον ἢ χεῖρον λέγεσθαι πάντα, τὰς δὲ μαθηματικὰς οὐθένα ποιεῖσθαι λόγον περὶ ἀγαθῶν καὶ κακῶν.

Amplius autem multis existentium non insunt omnibus omnia. Quo namque modo possibile est motus principium esse  in immobilibus aut boni naturam, siquidem omne quod est bonum secundum se et propter suam naturam finis est et ita  causa quod illius causa et fiunt et sunt cetera, finis autem et cuius causa actus cuiusdam est finis, sed actus omnes cum motu? Quare in immobilibus non continget hoc esse principium nec esse aliquid autoagathon. Unde et in mathematicis nihil per hanc ostenditur causam, nec est demonstratio nulla  eo quod melius aut deterius; sed nec omnino nullus talium alicuius reminiscitur. Quapropter et sophistarum quidam, ut aristippus, ipsas preneglexit. In aliis enim artibus et iliberalibus, ut tectonica et coriaria, eo quod melius vel deterius dici  omnia, mathematicas vero nullam de bonis et malis rationem facere.

Further, there are many things to which not all the principles pertain. For how can a principle of change or the nature of the good exist for unchangeable things, since everything that in itself and by its own nature is good is an end, and a cause in the sense that for its sake the other things both come to be and are, and since an end or purpose is the end of some action, and all actions imply change? So in the case of unchangeable things this principle could not exist, nor could there be a good itself. This is why in mathematics nothing is proved by means of this kind of cause, nor is there any demonstration of this kind – because it is better, or worse; indeed no one even mentions anything of the kind. And so for this reason some of the Sophists, e.g. Aristippus, used to ridicule mathematics; for in the arts (he maintained), even in the industrial arts, e.g. in carpentry and cobbling, the reason always given is because it is better, or worse, but the mathematical sciences take no account of goods and evils.

[996β] [1] - ἀλλὰ μὴν εἴ γε πλείους ἐπιστῆμαι τῶν αἰτίων εἰσὶ καὶ ἑτέρα ἑτέρας ἀρχῆς, τίνα τούτων φατέον εἶναι τὴν ζητουμένην, ἢ τίνα μάλιστα τοῦ πράγματος τοῦ ζητουμένου ἐπιστήμονα τῶν ἐχόντων [5] αὐτάς;

At vero si causarum scientie sunt plures et altera alterius principii, quae earum est dicenda quae quaeritur? Aut quis maxime rem quaesitam est sciens eas habentium?

[96b] But if there are several sciences of the causes, and a different science for each different principle, which of these sciences should be said to be that which we seek, or which of the people who possess them has the most scientific knowledge of the object in question?

ἐνδέχεται γὰρ τῷ αὐτῷ πάντας τοὺς τρόπους τοὺς τῶν αἰτίων ὑπάρχειν, οἷον οἰκίας ὅθεν μὲν ἡ κίνησις ἡ τέχνη καὶ ὁ οἰκοδόμος, οὗ δ᾽ ἕνεκα τὸ ἔργον, ὕλη δὲ γῆ καὶ λίθοι, τὸ δ᾽ εἶδος ὁ λόγος.

Contingit enim eidem omnes modos causarum inesse, ut domus unde quidem motus ars et edificator, cuius vero causa opus, et materia terra et lapides, species vero ratio.

The same thing may have all the kinds of causes, e.g. the moving cause of a house is the art or the builder, the final cause is the function it fulfils, the matter is earth and stones, and the form is the definition.

ἐκ μὲν οὖν τῶν πάλαι διωρισμένων τίνα χρὴ καλεῖν τῶν ἐπιστημῶν σοφίαν ἔχει λόγον ἑκάστην [10] προσαγορεύειν: ἡ μὲν γὰρ ἀρχικωτάτη καὶ ἡγεμονικωτάτη καὶ ἡ ὥσπερ δούλας οὐδ᾽ ἀντειπεῖν τὰς ἄλλας ἐπιστήμας δίκαιον, ἡ τοῦ τέλους καὶ τἀγαθοῦ τοιαύτη (τούτου γὰρ ἕνεκα τἄλλα),

Igitur ex dudum determinatis quam decet vocare scientiarum sapientiam habet rationem quamlibet appellari. In quantum enim senior quidem et principalior, cui veluti seruientes non contradicere scientias alias iustum est, quae finis et boni talis est; huius enim causa sunt cetera.

To judge from our previous discussion of the question which of the sciences should be called Wisdom, there is reason for applying the name to each of them. For inasmuch as it is most architectonic and authoritative and the other sciences, like slavewomen, may not even contradict it, the science of the end and of the good is of the nature of Wisdom (for the other things are for the sake of the end).

ἡ δὲ τῶν πρώτων αἰτίων καὶ τοῦ μάλιστα ἐπιστητοῦ διωρίσθη εἶναι, ἡ τῆς οὐσίας ἂν εἴη τοιαύτη· πολλαχῶς γὰρ [15] ἐπισταμένων τὸ αὐτὸ μᾶλλον μὲν εἰδέναι φαμὲν τὸν τῷ εἶναι γνωρίζοντα τί τὸ πρᾶγμα ἢ τῷ μὴ εἶναι, αὐτῶν δὲ τούτων ἕτερον ἑτέρου μᾶλλον, καὶ μάλιστα τὸν τί ἐστιν ἀλλ᾽ οὐ τὸν πόσον ἢ ποῖον ἢ τί ποιεῖν ἢ πάσχειν πέφυκεν. ἔτι δὲ καὶ ἐν τοῖς ἄλλοις τὸ εἰδέναι ἕκαστον καὶ ὧν ἀποδείξεις [20] εἰσί, τότ᾽ οἰόμεθα ὑπάρχειν ὅταν εἰδῶμεν τί ἐστιν (οἷον τί ἐστι τὸ τετραγωνίζειν, ὅτι μέσης εὕρεσις· ὁμοίως δὲ καὶ ἐπὶ τῶν ἄλλων),

In quantum vero primarum causarum et maxime scibilis 95 diffmita est esse, quae substantiae utique erit talis. Multis enim modis idem scientibus magis quidem scire dicimus eum qui novit in ipso esse quid res quam in non esse, et horum eorundem alium alio magis, sed maxime qui quid est et non quantum aut quale aut quid facere aut pati est apta nata. Amplius autem et in aliis scire singula et quorum demonstrationes sunt tunc putamus existere quando scimus quid est, ut tetragonizare quid est, quia medie inventio; similiter autem et in aliis.

But inasmuch as it was described as dealing with the first causes and that which is in the highest sense object of knowledge, the science of substance must be of the nature of Wisdom. For since men may know the same thing in many ways, we say that he who recognizes what a thing is by its being so and so knows more fully than he who recognizes it by its not being so and so, and in the former class itself one knows more fully than another, and he knows most fully who knows what a thing is, not he who knows its quantity or quality or what it can by nature do or have done to it. And further [96b 18]in all cases also we think that the knowledge of each even of the things of which demonstration is possible is present only when we know what the thing is, e.g. what squaring a rectangle is, viz. that it is the finding of a mean; and similarly in all other cases.

περὶ δὲ τὰς γενέσεις καὶ τὰς πράξεις καὶ περὶ πᾶσαν μεταβολὴν ὅταν εἰδῶμεν τὴν ἀρχὴν τῆς κινήσεως· τοῦτο δ᾽ ἕτερον καὶ ἀντικείμενον τῷ τέλει, ὥστ᾽ ἄλλης ἂν [25] δόξειεν ἐπιστήμης εἶναι τὸ θεωρῆσαι τῶν αἰτίων τούτων ἕκαστον.

Circa generationes vero et actus et circa omnem transmutationem, quando cognoscimus principium motus; hoc autem alterum et oppositum fini. Quapropter videbitur alius esse scientie causarum harum singulas speculari.

And we know about becomings and actions and about every change when we know the source of the movement; and this is other than and opposed to the end. Therefore it would seem to belong to different sciences to investigate these causes severally.

ἀλλὰ μὴν καὶ περὶ τῶν ἀποδεικτικῶν ἀρχῶν, πότερον μιᾶς ἐστιν ἐπιστήμης ἢ πλειόνων, ἀμφισβητήσιμόν ἐστιν (λέγω [28] δὲ ἀποδεικτικὰς τὰς κοινὰς δόξας ἐξ ὧν ἅπαντες δεικνύουσιν) οἷον ὅτι πᾶν ἀναγκαῖον ἢ φάναι ἢ ἀποφάναι, καὶ [30] ἀδύνατον ἅμα εἶναι καὶ μὴ εἶναι, καὶ ὅσαι ἄλλαι τοιαῦται προτάσεις, πότερον μία τούτων ἐπιστήμη καὶ τῆς οὐσίας ἢ ἑτέρα, κἂν εἰ μὴ μία, ποτέραν χρὴ προσαγορεύειν τὴν ζητουμένην νῦν.

At vero et de principiis demonstrationis, utrum unius est scientie aut plurium, dubitatio est. Dico autem demonstrativas comrnunes opiniones ex quibus omnes demonstrant. Ut quoniam omne necessarium aut dicere aut negare, et impossibile simul esse et non esse, et quaecumque aliae tales propositiones: utrum harum una scientia et substantiae aut alia, et si non una est, quam oportet appellare quae nunc est quaesita.

But (2), taking the starting-points of demonstration as well as the causes, it is a disputable question whether they are the object of one science or of more (by the starting-points of demonstration I mean the common beliefs, on which all men base their proofs); e.g. that everything must be either affirmed or denied, and that a thing cannot at the same time be and not be, and all other such premisses:-the question is whether the same science deals with them as with substance, or a different science, and if it is not one science, which of the two must be identified with that which we now seek.

μιᾶς μὲν οὖν οὐκ εὔλογον εἶναι: τί γὰρ μᾶλλον γεωμετρίας ἢ ὁποιασοῦν περὶ τούτων ἐστὶν ἴδιον τὸ ἐπαΐειν; [35] εἴπερ οὖν ὁμοίως μὲν ὁποιασοῦν ἐστίν, ἁπασῶν δὲ μὴ ἐνδέχεται, [997α] [1] ὥσπερ οὐδὲ τῶν ἄλλων οὕτως οὐδὲ τῆς γνωριζούσης τὰς οὐσίας ἴδιόν ἐστι τὸ γιγνώσκειν περὶ αὐτῶν.

Unius igitur esse non est rationabile; quid enim magis geometrie quam qualiscumque de hiis est proprium obaudire? Si igitur similiter quidem qualiscumque est, omnium vero non contingit, sicut nec aliarum ita nec ipsas substantias cognoscentis proprium est de ipsis cognoscere.

-It is not reasonable that these topics should be the object of one science; for why should it be peculiarly appropriate to geometry or to any other science to understand these matters? If then it belongs to every science [97a] alike, and cannot belong to all, it is not peculiar to the science which investigates substances, any more than to any other science, to know about these topics.

ἅμα δὲ καὶ τίνα τρόπον ἔσται αὐτῶν ἐπιστήμη; τί μὲν γὰρ ἔκαστον τούτων τυγχάνει ὂν καὶ νῦν γνωρίζομεν (χρῶνται γοῦν ὡς γιγνωσκομένοις [5] αὐτοῖς καὶ ἄλλαι τέχναι): εἰ δὲ ἀποδεικτικὴ περὶ αὐτῶν ἐστι, δεήσει τι γένος εἶναι ὑποκείμενον καὶ τὰ μὲν πάθη τὰ δ᾽ ἀξιώματ᾽ αὐτῶν (περὶ πάντων γὰρ ἀδύνατον ἀπόδειξιν εἶναι), ἀνάγκη γὰρ ἔκ τινων εἶναι καὶ περί τι καὶ τινῶν τὴν ἀπόδειξιν: ὥστε συμβαίνει πάντων εἶναι γένος ἕν [10] τι τῶν δεικνυμένων, πᾶσαι γὰρ αἱ ἀποδεικτικαὶ χρῶνται τοῖς ἀξιώμασιν.

Simul autem et quomodo erit ipsorum scientia? Quid quidem enim et unumquodque horum existit ens et nunc novimus; utuntur igitur eis ut notis artes aliae. Si autem de eis demonstratio est, oportebit aliquod genus esse subiectum et haec quidem passiones illa vero dignitates eorum. Nam de omnibus esse demonstrationem est impossibile. Necesse enim ex aliquibus esse et circa aliquid et aliquorum demonstrationem. Quare accidit omnium esse genus unum aliquid monstratorum1; omnes enim demonstrative dignitatibus utuntur.

-And, at the same time, in what way can there be a science of the first principles? For we are aware even now what each of them in fact is (at least even other sciences use them as familiar); but if there is a demonstrative science which deals with them, there will have to be an underlying kind, and some of them must be demonstrable attributes and others must be axioms (for it is impossible that there should be demonstration about all of them); for the demonstration must start from certain premises and be about a certain subject and prove certain attributes. Therefore it follows that all attributes that are proved must belong to a single class; for all demonstrative sciences use the axioms.

ἀλλὰ μὴν εἰ ἑτέρα ἡ τῆς οὐσίας καὶ ἡ περὶ τούτων, ποτέρα κυριωτέρα καὶ προτέρα πέφυκεν αὐτῶν; καθόλου γὰρ μάλιστα καὶ πάντων ἀρχαὶ τὰ ἀξιώματά ἐστιν, εἴ τ᾽ ἐστὶ μὴ τοῦ φιλοσόφου, τίνος ἔσται περὶ αὐτῶν ἄλλου τὸ [15] θεωρῆσαι τὸ ἀληθὲς καὶ ψεῦδος;

At vero si alia quae substantiae et quae de hiis, quae earum principalior et prior est earum? Universaliter enim maxime omnium principia sunt dignitates. Et si non est philosophi, cuius erit alius de eis speculari veritatem et falsitatem?

But if the science of substance and the science which deals with the axioms are different, which of them is by nature more authoritative and prior? The axioms are most universal and are principles of all things. And if it is not the business of the philosopher, to whom else will it belong to inquire what is true and what is untrue about them?

ὅλως τε τῶν οὐσιῶν πότερον μία πασῶν ἐστὶν ἢ πλείους ἐπιστῆμαι; εἰ μὲν οὖν μὴ μία, ποίας οὐσίας θετέον τὴν ἐπιστήμην ταύτην;

Totaliterque substantiarum utrum una omnium est aut plures scientie? Si quidem ergo non una, cuius substantiae ponenda est scientia ista?

(3) In general, do all substances fall under one science or under more than one? If the latter, to what sort of substance is the present science to be assigned?

τὸ δὲ μίαν πασῶν οὐκ εὔλογον· καὶ γὰρ ἂν ἀποδεικτικὴ μία περὶ πάντων εἴη τῶν συμβεβηκότων, εἴπερ πᾶσα ἀποδεικτικὴ περὶ [20] τι ὑποκείμενον θεωρεῖ τὰ καθ᾽ αὑτὰ συμβεβηκότα ἐκ τῶν κοινῶν δοξῶν. περὶ οὖν τὸ αὐτὸ γένος τὰ συμβεβηκότα καθ᾽ αὑτὰ τῆς αὐτῆς ἐστὶ θεωρῆσαι ἐκ τῶν αὐτῶν δοξῶν. περί τε γὰρ ὃ μιᾶς καὶ ἐξ ὧν μιᾶς, εἴτε τῆς αὐτῆς εἴτε ἄλλης, ὥστε καὶ τὰ συμβεβηκότα, εἴθ᾽ αὗται θεωροῦσιν εἴτ᾽ [25] ἐκ τούτων μία.

Unam vero omnium non est rationabile. Et enim demonstrativa una de omnibus erit utique accidentibus, siquidem omnis demonstrativa circa aliquod subiectum speculatur per se accidentia ex communibus opinionibus. Circa idem igitur genus accidentia per se eiusdem est speculari ex eisdem opinionibus. Nam circa ipsum quia unius et ex quibus unius, sive eiusdem sive alius; quare et accidentia deinde hae speculabuntur aut ex hiis una.

-On the other hand, it is not reasonable that one science should deal with all. For then there would be one demonstrative science dealing with all attributes. For ever demonstrative science investigates with regard to some subject its essential attributes, starting from the common beliefs. Therefore to investigate the essential attributes of one class of things, starting from one set of beliefs, is the business of one science. For the subject belongs to one science, and the premisses belong to one, whether to the same or to another; so that the attributes do so too, whether they are investigated by these sciences or by one compounded out of them.

ἔτι δὲ πότερον περὶ τὰς οὐσίας μόνον ἡ θεωρία ἐστὶν ἢ καὶ περὶ τὰ συμβεβηκότα ταύταις; λέγω δ᾽ οἷον, εἰ τὸ στερεὸν οὐσία τίς ἐστι καὶ γραμμαὶ καὶ ἐπίπεδα, πότερον τῆς αὐτῆς ταῦτα γνωρίζειν ἐστὶν ἐπιστήμης καὶ τὰ συμβεβηκότα περὶ ἕκαστον γένος περὶ ὧν αἱ μαθηματικαὶ [30] δεικνύουσιν, ἢ ἄλλης.

Amplius autem utrum circa substantias solum theoria est aut et circa ipsis accidentia? Dico autem ut si solidum quaedam substantia est et lineae et superficies, utrum eiusdem scientie est ea cognoscere et accidentia circa unumquodque genus de quibus mathematice ostendunt, aut alius.

(5) Further, does our investigation deal with substances alone or also with their attributes? I mean for instance, if the solid is a substance and so are lines and planes, is it the business of the same science to know these and to know the attributes of each of these classes (the attributes about which the mathematical sciences offer proofs), or of a different science?

εἰ μὲν γὰρ τῆς αὐτῆς, ἀποδεικτική τις ἂν εἴη καὶ ἡ τῆς οὐσίας, οὐ δοκεῖ δὲ τοῦ τί ἐστιν ἀπόδειξις εἶναι·

Nam si eiusdem, demonstrativa quaedam erit et quae est substantiae; non autem videtur eius quod quid est demonstratio esse.

If of the same, the science of substance also must be a demonstrative science, but it is thought that there is no demonstration of the essence of things.

εἰ δ᾽ ἑτέρας, τίς ἔσται ἡ θεωροῦσα περὶ τὴν οὐσίαν τὰ συμβεβηκότα; τοῦτο γὰρ ἀποδοῦναι παγχάλεπον.

Si vero diverse, quae erit speculans circa substantiam accidentia? Hoc enim reddere est valde difficile.

And if of another, what will be the science that investigates the attributes of substance? This is a very difficult question.

ἔτι δὲ πότερον τὰς αἰσθητὰς οὐσίας μόνας εἶναι [35] φατέον ἢ καὶ παρὰ ταύτας ἄλλας, καὶ πότερον μοναχῶς ἢ πλείω γένη τετύχηκεν ὄντα τῶν οὐσιῶν, [997β] [1] οἷον οἱ λέγοντες τά τε εἴδη καὶ τὰ μεταξύ, περὶ ἃ τὰς μαθηματικὰς εἶναί φασιν ἐπιστήμας;

Amplius autem utrum sensibiles substantiae sole esse sint dicende aut praeter eas aliae? Et utrum unice aut plura genera substantiarum sunt, ut dicentes species et intermedia, circa quae mathematicas dicunt esse scientias?

(4) Further, must we say that sensible substances alone exist, or that there are others besides these? And are substances of one kind or are there in fact several kinds of [97b] substances, as those say who assert the existence both of the Forms and of the intermediates, with which they say the mathematical sciences deal?

ὡς μὲν οὖν λέγομεν τὰ εἴδη αἰτιά τε καὶ οὐσίας εἶναι καθ᾽ ἑαυτὰς εἴρηται ἐν τοῖς πρώτοις λόγοις περὶ [5] αὐτῶν·

Quomodo ergo dicimus species causasque et substantias secundum se, dictum est in primis de ipsis sermonibus.

-The sense in which we say the Forms are both causes and self-dependent substances has been explained in our first remarks about them;

πολλαχῇ δὲ ἐχόντων δυσκολίαν, οὐθενὸς ἧττον ἄτοπον τὸ φάναι μὲν εἶναί τινας φύσεις παρὰ τὰς ἐν τῷ οὐρανῷ, ταύτας δὲ τὰς αὐτὰς φάναι τοῖς αἰσθητοῖς πλὴν ὅτι τὰ μὲν ἀΐδια τὰ δὲ φθαρτά. αὐτὸ γὰρ ἄνθρωπόν φασιν εἶναι καὶ ἵππον καὶ ὑγίειαν, ἄλλο δ᾽ οὐδέν, παραπλήσιον [10] ποιοῦντες τοῖς θεοὺς μὲν εἶναι φάσκουσιν ἀνθρωποειδεῖς δέ: οὔτε γὰρ ἐκεῖνοι οὐδὲν ἄλλο ἐποίουν ἢ ἀνθρώπους ἀϊδίους, οὔθ᾽ οὗτοι τὰ εἴδη ἀλλ᾽ ἢ αἰσθητὰ ἀΐδια.

Multis autem modis habentibus difficultatem, nullo minus absurdum dicere quidem aliquas esse naturas praeter eas quae sunt in celo, has autem easdem dicere sensibilibus nisi quia haec quidem sempiterna illa vero corruptibilia. Nam per se hominem dicunt esse et equum et sanitatem, aliud autem nihil, simile facientes deos esse dicentibus et humane speciei esse. Nihil enim aliud illi fecerunt quam homines sempiternos, nec hii species nisi sensibiles sempiternas.

while the theory presents difficulties in many ways, the most paradoxical thing of all is the statement that there are certain things besides those in the material universe, and that these are the same as sensible things except that they are eternal while the latter are perishable. For they say there is a man-himself and a horse-itself and health-itself, with no further qualification,-a procedure like that of the people who said there are gods, but in human form. For they were positing nothing but eternal men, nor are the Platonists making the Forms anything other than eternal sensible things.

ἔτι δὲ εἴ τις παρὰ τὰ εἴδη καὶ τὰ αἰσθητὰ τὰ μεταξὺ θήσεται, πολλὰς ἀπορίας ἕξει: δῆλον γὰρ ὡς ὁμοίως γραμμαί τε παρά τ᾽ αὐτὰς καὶ [15] τὰς αἰσθητὰς ἔσονται καὶ ἕκαστον τῶν ἄλλων γενῶν: ὥστ᾽ ἐπείπερ ἡ ἀστρολογία μία τούτων ἐστίν, ἔσται τις καὶ οὐρανὸς παρὰ τὸν αἰσθητὸν οὐρανὸν καὶ ἥλιός τε καὶ σελήνη καὶ τἆλλα ὁμοίως τὰ κατὰ τὸν οὐρανόν. καίτοι πῶς δεῖ πιστεῦσαι τούτοις; οὐδὲ γὰρ ἀκίνητον εὔλογον εἶναι, κινούμενον δὲ [20] καὶ παντελῶς ἀδύνατον: ὁμοίως δὲ καὶ περὶ ὧν ἡ ὀπτικὴ πραγματεύεται καὶ ἡ ἐν τοῖς μαθήμασιν ἁρμονική: καὶ γὰρ ταῦτα ἀδύνατον εἶναι παρὰ τὰ αἰσθητὰ διὰ τὰς αὐτὰς αἰτίας: εἰ γὰρ ἔστιν αἰσθητὰ μεταξὺ καὶ αἰσθήσεις, δῆλον ὅτι καὶ ζῷα ἔσονται μεταξὺ αὐτῶν τε καὶ τῶν φθαρτῶν.

Amplius autem si quis praeter species et sensibilia intermedia ponat, multas habebit dubitationes. Palam enim quia similiter lineae praeter ipsas et sensibiles erunt et unumquodque aliorum generum. Igitur quoniam astrologia harum una est, erit quoddam celum praeter sensibile celum et sol et luna et alia similiter celestia. Et quomodo hiis credere oportet? Neque enim immobile rationabile esse, mobile vero omnino impossibile. — Similiter autem et de quibus perspectiva tractat et in mathematicis armonica; et enim haec impossibile esse praeter sensibilia propter easdem causas. Nam si sunt sensibilia intermedia et sensus, palam quia et animalia erunt intermedia ipsorum et corruptibilium.

Further, if we are to posit besides the Forms and the sensibles the intermediates between them, we shall have many difficulties. For clearly on the same principle there will be lines besides the lines-themselves and the sensible lines, and so with each of the other classes of things; so that since astronomy is one of these mathematical sciences there will also be a heaven besides the sensible heaven, and a sun and a moon (and so with the other heavenly bodies) besides the sensible. Yet how are we to believe in these things? It is not reasonable even to suppose such a body immovable, but to suppose it moving is quite impossible.-And similarly with the things of which optics and mathematical harmonics treat; for these also cannot exist apart from the sensible things, for the same reasons. For if there are sensible things and sensations intermediate between Form and individual, evidently there will also be animals intermediate between animals-themselves and the perishable animals.

[25] ἀπορήσειε δ᾽ ἄν τις καὶ περὶ ποῖα τῶν ὄντων δεῖ ζητεῖν ταύτας τὰς ἐπιστήμας. εἰ γὰρ τούτῳ διοίσει τῆς γεωδαισίας ἡ γεωμετρία μόνον, ὅτι ἡ μὲν τούτων ἐστὶν ὧν αἰσθανόμεθα ἡ δ᾽ οὐκ αἰσθητῶν, δῆλον ὅτι καὶ παρ᾽ ἰατρικὴν ἔσται τις ἐπιστήμη καὶ παρ᾽ ἐκάστην τῶν ἄλλων μεταξὺ αὐτῆς τε ἰατρικῆς [30] καὶ τῆσδε τῆς ἰατρικῆς· καίτοι πῶς τοῦτο δυνατόν; καὶ γὰρ ἂν ὑγιείν᾽ ἄττα εἴη παρὰ τὰ αἰσθητὰ καὶ αὐτὸ τὸ ὑγιεινόν.

— Dubitabit autem aliquis et circa quae existentium quaerere oportet has scientias. Nam si in hoc differt geometria a geodesia solum, quia haec quidem horum est quae sentimus illa vero non sensibilium, palam quia et praeter medicinalem et alia erit scientia (et praeter unamquamque aliarum) inter ipsam medicinalem et hanc medicinalem. Sed quomodo hoc possibile? Et enim rsalubria quaedam utique erunt praeter sensibilia et autosanum.

-We might also raise the question, with reference to which kind of existing things we must look for these sciences of intermediates. If geometry is to differ from mensuration only in this, that the latter deals with things that we perceive, and the former with things that are not perceptible, evidently there will also be a science other than medicine, intermediate between medical-science-itself and this individual medical science, and so with each of the other sciences. Yet how is this possible? There would have to be also healthy things besides the perceptible healthy things and the healthy-itself.

ἅμα δὲ οὐδὲ τοῦτο ἀληθές, ὡς ἡ γεωδαισία τῶν αἰσθητῶν ἐστὶ μεγεθῶν καὶ φθαρτῶν· ἐφθείρετο γὰρ ἂν φθειρομένων.

Simul autem nec hoc verum quia geodesia sensibilium est magnitudinum et corruptibilium; corrupta enim utique esset corruptis.

And at the same time not even this is true, that mensuration deals with perceptible and perishable magnitudes; for then it would have perished when they perished.

ἀλλὰ μὴν οὐδὲ τῶν αἰσθητῶν ἂν εἴη μεγεθῶν [35] οὐδὲ περὶ τὸν οὐρανὸν ἡ ἀστρολογία τόνδε. [998α] [1] οὔτε γὰρ αἱ αἰσθηταὶ γραμμαὶ τοιαῦταί εἰσιν οἵας λέγει ὁ γεωμέτρης (οὐθὲν γὰρ εὐθὺ τῶν αἰσθητῶν οὕτως οὐδὲ στρογγύλον: ἅπτεται γὰρ τοῦ κανόνος οὐ κατὰ στιγμὴν ὁ κύκλος ἀλλ᾽ ὥσπερ Πρωταγόρας ἔλεγεν ἐλέγχων τοὺς γεωμέτρας), οὔθ᾽ αἱ κινήσεις καὶ [5] ἕλικες τοῦ οὐρανοῦ ὅμοιαι περὶ ὧν ἡ ἀστρολογία ποιεῖται τοὺς λόγους, οὔτε τὰ σημεῖα τοῖς ἄστροις τὴν αὐτὴν ἔχει φύσιν.

At vero nec sensibilium erit magnitudinum nec circa caelum hoc astrologia. Nec enim sensibiles lineae tales sunt quales dicit geometer. Nihil enim rectum sensibilium ita nec rotundum; tangit enim regulam non secundum punctum circulus, sed ut Protagoras ait geometras redarguens. Nec motus nec revolutiones celi similes de quibus astrologia facit sermones, nec astris puncta naturam habent eandem.

But on the other hand astronomy cannot be dealing with perceptible magnitudes nor with this heaven above us. For neither are perceptible lines such lines as the [98a]geometer speaks of (for no perceptible thing is straight or round in the way in which he defines straight and round ; for a hoop touches a straight edge not at a point, but as Protagoras used to say it did, in his refutation of the geometers), nor are the movements and spiral orbits in the heavens like those of which astronomy treats, nor have geometrical points the same nature as the actual stars.

εἰσὶ δέ τινες οἵ φασιν εἶναι μὲν τὰ μεταξὺ ταῦτα λεγόμενα τῶν τε εἰδῶν καὶ τῶν αἰσθητῶν, οὐ μὴν χωρίς γε τῶν αἰσθητῶν ἀλλ᾽ ἐν τούτοις: οἷς τὰ συμβαίνοντα ἀδύνατα πάντα [10] μὲν πλείονος λόγου διελθεῖν, ἱκανὸν δὲ καὶ τὰ τοιαῦτα θεωρῆσαι.

— Sunt autem aliqui qui dicunt esse quidem intermedia haec dicta infra species et sensibilia, non tamen sine sensibilibus sed in hiis. Quibus accidentia impossibilia omnia quidem pluris est orationis pertransire, sufficit autem et talia speculari.

-Now there are some who say that these so-called intermediates between the Forms and the perceptible things exist, not apart from the perceptible things, however, but in these; the impossible results of this view would take too long to enumerate, but it is enough to consider even such points as the following:

οὔτε γὰρ ἐπὶ τούτων εὔλογον ἔχειν οὕτω μόνον, ἀλλὰ δῆλον ὅτι καὶ τὰ εἴδη ἐνδέχοιτ᾽ ἂν ἐν τοῖς αἰσθητοῖς εἶναι (τοῦ γὰρ αὐτοῦ λόγου ἀμφότερα ταῦτά ἐστιν),

Non enim in talibus congruum est habere sic solum, sed palam quia et species convenit in sensibilibus esse; eiusdem enim rationis utraque haec sunt.

-It is not reasonable that this should be so only in the case of these intermediates, but clearly the Forms also might be in the perceptible things; for both statements are parts of the same theory.

ἔτι δὲ δύο στερεὰ ἐν τῷ αὐτῷ ἀναγκαῖον εἶναι τόπῳ,

Amplius autem duo solida in eodem necesse est esse loco,

Further, it follows from this theory that there are two solids in the same place,

καὶ μὴ εἶναι ἀκίνητα [15] ἐν κινουμένοις γε ὄντα τοῖς αἰσθητοῖς.

et non esse immobilia in motis existentia sensibilibus.

and that the intermediates are not immovable, since they are in the moving perceptible things.

ὅλως δὲ τίνος ἕνεκ᾽ ἄν τις θείη εἶναι μὲν αὐτά, εἶναι δ᾽ ἐν τοῖς αἰσθητοῖς; ταῦτὰ γὰρ συμβήσεται ἄτοπα τοῖς προειρημένοις: ἔσται γὰρ οὐρανός τις παρὰ τὸν οὐρανόν, πλήν γ᾽ οὐ χωρὶς ἀλλ᾽ ἐν τῷ αὐτῷ τόπῳ: ὅπερ ἐστὶν ἀδυνατώτερον. [20]

Totaliter autem cuius causa quis ponet utique esse quidem ipsa, esse autem in sensibilibus? Eadem enim contingent inconvenientia eis quae predicta sunt; erit enim celum aliquod preter celum, tamen non extra sed in eodem loco, quod magis est impossibile.

And in general to what purpose would one suppose them to exist indeed, but to exist in perceptible things? For the same paradoxical results will follow which we have already mentioned; there will be a heaven besides the heaven, only it will be not apart but in the same place; which is still more impossible.

*Chapter* 3

περί τε τούτων οὖν ἀπορία πολλὴ πῶς δεῖ θέμενον τυχεῖν τῆς ἀληθείας, καὶ περὶ τῶν ἀρχῶν πότερον δεῖ τὰ γένη στοιχεῖα καὶ ἀρχὰς ὑπολαμβάνειν ἢ μᾶλλον ἐξ ὧν ἐνυπαρχόντων ἐστὶν ἕκαστον πρώτων,

De hiis ergo dubitatio multa quomodo oportet positum habere veritatem. Et de principiis, utrum oportet genera elementa et principia suscipere aut magis ex quibus cum insint est unumquodque primis.

(6) Apart from the great difficulty of stating the case truly with regard to these matters, it is very hard to say, with regard to the first principles, whether it is the genera that should be taken as elements and principles, or rather the primary constituents of a thing;

οἷον φωνῆς στοιχεῖα καὶ ἀρχαὶ δοκοῦσιν εἶναι ταῦτ᾽ ἐξ ὧν σύγκεινται αἱ φωναὶ [25] πρώτων, ἀλλ᾽ οὐ τὸ κοινὸν ἡ φωνή· καὶ τῶν διαγραμμάτων ταῦτα στοιχεῖα λέγομεν ὧν αἱ ἀποδείξεις ἐνυπάρχουσιν ἐν ταῖς τῶν ἄλλων ἀποδείξεσιν ἢ πάντων ἢ τῶν πλείστων,

Ut vocis elementa et principia videntur esse ea ex quibus componuntur voces omnes primis, sed non commune vox; et diagramatum ea dicimus elementa quorum demonstrationes insunt in aliorum demonstrationibus aut omnium aut plurimorum.

e.g. it is the primary parts of which articulate sounds consist that are thought to be elements and principles of articulate sound, not the common genus-articulate sound; and we give the name of elements to those geometrical propositions, the proofs of which are implied in the proofs of the others, either of all or of most.

ἔτι δὲ τῶν σωμάτων καὶ οἱ πλείω λέγοντες εἶναι στοιχεῖα καὶ οἱ ἕν, ἐξ ὧν σύγκειται καὶ ἐξ ὧν συνέστηκεν ἀρχὰς λέγουσιν [30] εἶναι, οἷον Ἐμπεδοκλῆς πῦρ καὶ ὕδωρ καὶ τὰ μετὰ τούτων στοιχεῖά φησιν εἶναι ἐξ ὧν ἐστὶ τὰ ὄντα ἐνυπαρχόντων, ἀλλ᾽ οὐχ ὡς γένη λέγει ταῦτα τῶν ὄντων.

Amplius autem corporum qui dicunt esse plura elementa et qui unum, ex quibus componuntur et constant principia esse dicunt, ut Empedocles ignem et aquam et quae cum hiis elementa dicit esse ex quibus sunt entia inexistentibus, sed non ut genera dicit ea eorum quae sunt.

Further, both those who say there are several elements of corporeal things and those who say there is one, say the parts of which bodies are compounded and consist are principles; e.g. Empedocles says fire and water and the rest are the constituent elements of things, but does not describe these as genera of existing things.

πρὸς δὲ τούτοις καὶ τῶν ἄλλων εἴ τις ἐθέλει τὴν φύσιν ἀθρεῖν, [998β] [1] οἷον κλίνην ἐξ ὧν μορίων συνέστηκε καὶ πῶς συγκειμένων, τότε γνωρίζει τὴν φύσιν αὐτῆς. ἐκ μὲν οὖν τούτων τῶν λόγων οὐκ ἂν εἴησαν αἱ ἀρχαὶ τὰ γένη τῶν ὄντων·

ad haec autem et aliorum si quis vult naturam speculari, ut lectum ex quibus partibus est et quomodo compositis, tunc cognoscet eius naturam. Ex hiis quidem igitur rationibus non utique erunt principia genera existentium;

Besides this, if we want to examine the nature of anything else, we [98b]examine the parts of which, e.g. a bed consists and how they are put together, and then we know its nature. To judge from these arguments, then, the principles of things would not be the genera;

εἰ δ᾽ ἕκαστον μὲν [5] γνωρίζομεν διὰ τῶν ὁρισμῶν, ἀρχαὶ δὲ τὰ γένη τῶν ὁρισμῶν εἰσίν, ἀνάγκη καὶ τῶν ὁριστῶν ἀρχὰς εἶναι τὰ γένη.

in quantum autem cognoscimus unumquodque per diffinitiones, principia autem diffinitionum sunt ipsa genera, necesse et diffinitorum principia genera esse.

but if we know each thing by its definition, and the genera are the principles or starting-points of definitions, the genera must also be the principles of definable things.

κἂν [7] εἰ ἔστι τὴν τῶν ὄντων λαβεῖν ἐπιστήμην τὸ τῶν εἰδῶν λαβεῖν καθ᾽ ἃ λέγονται τὰ ὄντα, τῶν γε εἰδῶν ἀρχαὶ τὰ γένη εἰσίν.

Et si est eorum quae sunt accipere scientiam specierum scientiam accipere secundum quas dicuntur entia, specierum autem principia genera sunt.

And if to get the knowledge of the species according to which things are named is to get the knowledge of things, the genera are at least starting-points of the species.

φαίνονται δέ τινες καὶ τῶν λεγόντων στοιχεῖα τῶν ὄντων τὸ [10] ἓν ἢ τὸ ὂν ἢ τὸ μέγα καὶ μικρὸν ὡς γένεσιν αὐτοῖς χρῆσθαι.

Videntur autem quidam dicentium elementa existentium unum aut ens aut magnum aut parvum ut generibus eis uti.

And some also of those who say unity or being, or the great and the small, are elements of things, seem to treat them as genera.

ἀλλὰ μὴν οὐδὲ ἀμφοτέρως γε οἷόν τε λέγειν τὰς ἀρχάς. ὁ μὲν γὰρ λόγος τῆς οὐσίας εἷς· ἕτερος δ᾽ ἔσται ὁ διὰ τῶν γενῶν ὁρισμὸς καὶ ὁ λέγων ἐξ ὧν ἔστιν ἐνυπαρχόντων.

At vero neque utrobique possibile dicere principia . Ratio namque substantiae est una; diversa vero erit quae est per genera diffinitio et quae dicit ex quibus est inexistentibus.

But, again, it is not possible to describe the principles in both ways. For the formula of the essence is one; but definition by genera will be different from that which states the constituent parts of a thing.

πρὸς δὲ τούτοις εἰ καὶ ὅτι μάλιστα ἀρχαὶ τὰ γένη εἰσί, [15] πότερον δεῖ νομίζειν τὰ πρῶτα τῶν γενῶν ἀρχὰς ἢ τὰ ἔσχατα κατηγορούμενα ἐπὶ τῶν ἀτόμων; καὶ γὰρ τοῦτο ἔχει ἀμφισβήτησιν.

Ad haec autem si quam maxime principia genera sunt, quae oportet existimare: prima generum principia aut ultima predicata de individuis? Et enim hoc dubitationem habet.

(7) Besides this, even if the genera are in the highest degree principles, should one regard the first of the genera as principles, or those which are predicated directly of the individuals? This also admits of dispute.

εἰ μὲν γὰρ ἀεὶ τὰ καθόλου μᾶλλον ἀρχαί, φανερὸν ὅτι τὰ ἀνωτάτω τῶν γενῶν· ταῦτα γὰρ λέγεται κατὰ πάντων. τοσαῦται οὖν ἔσονται ἀρχαὶ τῶν ὄντων ὅσαπερ [20] τὰ πρῶτα γένη, ὥστ᾽ ἔσται τό τε ὂν καὶ τὸ ἓν ἀρχαὶ καὶ οὐσίαι· ταῦτα γὰρ κατὰ πάντων μάλιστα λέγεται τῶν ὄντων. οὐχ οἷόν τε δὲ τῶν ὄντων ἓν εἶναι γένος οὔτε τὸ ἓν οὔτε τὸ ὄν· ἀνάγκη μὲν γὰρ τὰς διαφορὰς ἑκάστου γένους καὶ εἶναι καὶ μίαν εἶναι ἑκάστην, ἀδύνατον δὲ κατηγορεῖσθαι ἢ τὰ εἴδη τοῦ [25] γένους ἐπὶ τῶν οἰκείων διαφορῶν ἢ τὸ γένος ἄνευ τῶν αὐτοῦ εἰδῶν, ὥστ᾽ εἴπερ τὸ ἓν γένος ἢ τὸ ὄν, οὐδεμία διαφορὰ οὔτε ὂν οὔτε ἓν ἔσται. ἀλλὰ μὴν εἰ μὴ γένη, οὐδ᾽ ἀρχαὶ ἔσονται, εἴπερ ἀρχαὶ τὰ γένη.

Nam si quia universalia sunt magis principia, palam quia suprema generum; haec namque dicuntur de omnibus. Tot igitur erunt entium principia quot genera prima, quare erunt ens et unum principia et substantiae; haec namque de omnibus maxime dicuntur existentibus. Non est autem possibile genus existentium unum esse neque unum neque ens. Nam necesse differentias cuiuslibet generis et esse et unam esse quamlibet, impossibile autem predicari aut species generis de propriis differentiis aut genus sine suis speciebus; quare si unum genus aut ens, nulla differentia nec unum nec ens erit. At vero si non genera, nec principia erunt, si principia genera.

For if the universals are always more of the nature of principles, evidently the uppermost of the genera are the principles; for these are predicated of all things. There will, then, be as many principles of things as there are primary genera, so that both being and unity will be principles and substances; for these are most of all predicated of all existing things. But it is not possible that either unity or being should be a single genus of things; for the differentiae of any genus must each of them both have being and be one, but it is not possible for the genus taken apart from its species (any more than for the species of the genus) to be predicated of its proper differentiae; so that if unity or being is a genus, no differentia will either have being or be one. But if unity and being are not genera, neither will they be principles, if the genera are the principles.

ἔτι καὶ τὰ μεταξὺ συλλαμβανόμενα μετὰ τῶν διαφορῶν ἔσται γένη μέχρι τῶν ἀτόμων [30] (νῦν δὲ τὰ μὲν δοκεῖ τὰ δ᾽ οὐ δοκεῖ): πρὸς δὲ τούτοις ἔτι μᾶλλον αἱ διαφοραὶ ἀρχαὶ ἢ τὰ γένη: εἰ δὲ καὶ αὗται ἀρχαί, ἄπειροι ὡς εἰπεῖν ἀρχαὶ γίγνονται, ἄλλως τε κἂν τις τὸ πρῶτον γένος ἀρχὴν τιθῇ.

— Amplius et intermedia coaccepta cum differentiis erunt genera usque ad individua; nunc autem haec quidem videntur illa vero non videntur. Ad haec autem adhuc magis differentie principia quam genera; si autem et hae principia, infinita ut si ita dicatur erunt principia, aliterque et si quis primum genus principium ponat.

Again, the intermediate kinds, in whose nature the differentiae are included, will on this theory be genera, down to the indivisible species; but as it is, some are thought to be genera and others are not thought to be so. Besides this, the differentiae are principles even more than the genera; and if these also are principles, there comes to be practically an infinite number of principles, especially if we suppose the [99a] highest genus to be a principle.

[999α] [1] ἀλλὰ μὴν καὶ εἰ μᾶλλόν γε ἀρχοειδὲς τὸ ἕν ἐστιν, ἓν δὲ τὸ ἀδιαίρετον, ἀδιαίρετον δὲ ἅπαν ἢ κατὰ τὸ ποσὸν ἢ κατ᾽ εἶδος, πρότερον δὲ τὸ κατ᾽ εἶδος, τὰ δὲ γένη διαιρετὰ εἰς εἴδη, μᾶλλον ἂν ἓν τὸ [5] ἔσχατον εἴη κατηγορούμενον: οὐ γάρ ἐστι γένος ἄνθρωπος τῶν τινῶν ἀνθρώπων.

At vero et si magis principii speciem habens est unum, unum autem indivisibile, indivisibile vero omne aut secundum quantitatem aut secundum speciem, prius autem quod secundum speciem, genera vero divisibilia in species: magis utique unum ultimum erit predicatum.

-But again, if unity is more of the nature of a principle, and the indivisible is one, and everything indivisible is so either in quantity or in species, and that which is so in species is the prior, and genera are divisible into species for man is not the genus of individual men), that which is predicated directly of the individuals will have more unity.

ἔτι ἐν οἷς τὸ πρότερον καὶ ὕστερόν ἐστιν, οὐχ οἷόν τε τὸ ἐπὶ τούτων εἶναί τι παρὰ ταῦτα (οἷον εἰ πρώτη τῶν ἀριθμῶν ἡ δυάς, οὐκ ἔσται τις ἀριθμὸς παρὰ τὰ εἴδη τῶν ἀριθμῶν: ὁμοίως δὲ οὐδὲ σχῆμα παρὰ τὰ εἴδη [10] τῶν σχημάτων: εἰ δὲ μὴ τούτων, σχολῇ τῶν γε ἄλλων ἔσται τὰ γένη παρὰ τὰ εἴδη: τούτων γὰρ δοκεῖ μάλιστα εἶναι γένη): ἐν δὲ τοῖς ἀτόμοις οὐκ ἔστι τὸ μὲν πρότερον τὸ δ᾽ ὕστερον.

Non enim est genus homo aliquorum hominum. — Amplius in quibus et prius et posterius est, non est possibile in hiis aliquid esse praeter haec; ut si prima numerorum est dualitas, non erit numerus aliquis praeter species numerorum, similiter autem nec figura aliqua praeter species figurarum. Si autem non horum, schola aliorum erunt genera praeter species; horum enim maxime genera esse videntur. In individuis vero non est hoc prius et illud posterius. —

-Further, in the case of things in which the distinction of prior and posterior is present, that which is predicable of these things cannot be something apart from them (e.g. if two is the first of numbers, there will not be a Number apart from the kinds of numbers; and similarly there will not be a Figure apart from the kinds of figures; and if the genera of these things do not exist apart from the species, the genera of other things will scarcely do so; for genera of these things are thought to exist if any do). But among the individuals one is not prior and another posterior.

ἔτι ὅπου τὸ μὲν βέλτιον τὸ δὲ χεῖρον, ἀεὶ τὸ βέλτιον πρότερον: ὥστ᾽ οὐδὲ τούτων ἂν εἴη γένος. ἐκ μὲν οὖν τούτων [15] μᾶλλον φαίνεται τὰ ἐπὶ τῶν ἀτόμων κατηγορούμενα ἀρχαὶ εἶναι τῶν γενῶν:

Amplius autem ubi hoc quidem melius illud vero vilius, semper quod est melius prius; quare neque horum erit utique genus. Ex hiis quidem igitur magis videntur quae de individuis sunt predicata esse principia generum.

Further, where one thing is better and another worse, the better is always prior; so that of these also no genus can exist. From these considerations, then, the species predicated of individuals seem to be principles rather than the genera.

πάλιν δὲ πῶς αὖ δεῖ ταύτας ἀρχὰς ὑπολαβεῖν οὐ ῥᾴδιον εἰπεῖν. τὴν μὲν γὰρ ἀρχὴν δεῖ καὶ τὴν αἰτίαν εἶναι παρὰ τὰ πράγματα ὧν ἀρχή, καὶ δύνασθαι εἶναι χωριζομένην αὐτῶν: τοιοῦτον δέ τι παρὰ τὸ καθ᾽ ἕκαστον [20] εἶναι διὰ τί ἄν τις ὑπολάβοι, πλὴν ὅτι καθόλου κατηγορεῖται καὶ κατὰ πάντων; ἀλλὰ μὴν εἰ διὰ τοῦτο, τὰ μᾶλλον καθόλου μᾶλλον θετέον ἀρχάς: ὥστε ἀρχαὶ τὰ πρῶτ᾽ ἂν εἴησαν γένη.

Iterum autem quomodo oportet haec existimare principia, non facile dicere. Principium enim et causam oportet esse praeter res quarum principium est, et possibile ab eis separatum esse; tale vero aliquid praeter singularia esse propter quid utique aliquis suscipiet, nisi quia universaliter et de omnibus predicatur? At vero si propter hoc, magis universalia magis ponenda sunt principia; quare principia prima erunt genera.

But again, it is not easy to say in what sense these are to be taken as principles. For the principle or cause must exist alongside of the things of which it is the principle, and must be capable of existing in separation from them; but for what reason should we suppose any such thing to exist alongside of the individual, except that it is predicated universally and of all? But if this is the reason, the things that are more universal must be supposed to be more of the nature of principles; so that the highest genera would be the principles.

## Chapter 4

ἔστι δ᾽ ἐχομένη τε τούτων ἀπορία καὶ πασῶν χαλεπωτάτη [25] καὶ ἀναγκαιοτάτη θεωρῆσαι, περὶ ἧς ὁ λόγος ἐφέστηκε νῦν.

Est autem habita hiis dubitatio et omnium difficillima et ad considerandum maxime necessaria, de qua ratio nunc extitit.

(8) There is a difficulty connected with these, the hardest of all and the most necessary to examine, and of this the discussion now awaits us.

εἴτε γὰρ μὴ ἔστι τι παρὰ τὰ καθ᾽ ἕκαστα, τὰ δὲ καθ᾽ ἕκαστα ἄπειρα, τῶν δ᾽ ἀπείρων πῶς ἐνδέχεται λαβεῖν ἐπιστήμην; ᾗ γὰρ ἕν τι καὶ ταὐτόν, καὶ ᾗ καθόλου τι ὑπάρχει, ταύτῃ πάντα γνωρίζομεν.

Nam si non est aliquid praeter singularia, singularia vero infinita, infinitorum quomodo contingit accipere scientiam? Nam in quantum unum aliquid et idem et in quantum universale aliquid est, in tantum omnia cognoscimus.

If, on the one hand, there is nothing apart from individual things, and the individuals are infinite in number, how then is it possible to get knowledge of the infinite individuals? For all things that we come to know, we come to know in so far as they have some unity and identity, and in so far as some attribute belongs to them universally.

ἀλλὰ μὴν εἰ τοῦτο [30] ἀναγκαῖόν ἐστι καὶ δεῖ τι εἶναι παρὰ τὰ καθ᾽ ἕκαστα, ἀναγκαῖον ἂν εἴη τὰ γένη εἶναι παρὰ τὰ καθ᾽ ἕκαστα, ἤτοι τὰ ἔσχατα ἢ τὰ πρῶτα: τοῦτο δ᾽ ὅτι ἀδύνατον ἄρτι διηπορήσαμεν.

At vero si hoc est necesse et oportet aliquid esse praeter singularia, necesse utique erit genera esse praeter singularia, aut ujtima aut prima; hoc autem quia impossibile nunc dubitavimus.

But if this is necessary, and there must be something apart from the individuals, it will be necessary that the genera exist apart from the individuals, either the lowest or the highest genera; but we found by discussion just now that this is impossible.

ἔτι εἰ ὅτι μάλιστα ἔστι τι παρὰ τὸ σύνολον ὅταν κατηγορηθῇ τι τῆς ὕλης, πότερον, εἰ ἔστι, παρὰ πάντα δεῖ εἶναί τι, ἢ παρὰ μὲν ἔνια εἶναι παρὰ δ᾽ ἔνια μὴ εἶναι, ἢ παρ᾽ οὐδέν;

Amplius autem si quam maxime est aliquid praeter simul totum quando predicatur aliquid de materia, utrum, si est aliquid, praeter omnia oportet aliquid esse, aut praeter quaedam esse et praeter quaedam non esse, aut praeter nihil?

Further, if we admit in the fullest sense that something exists apart from the concrete thing, whenever something is predicated of the matter, must there, if there is something apart, be something apart from each set of individuals, [99b] or from some and not from others, or from none?

[999β] [1] εἰ μὲν οὖν μηδέν ἐστι παρὰ τὰ καθ' ἕκαστα, οὐθὲν ἂν εἴη νοητὸν ἀλλὰ πάντα αἰσθητὰ καὶ ἐπιστήμη οὐδενός, εἰ μή τις εἶναι λέγει τὴν αἴσθησιν ἐπιστήμην.

Si quidem igitur nihil est praeter singularia, nil utique erit intellectuale sed omnia sensibilia et scientia nullius, nisi quis dicat esse sensum scientiam.

(A) If there is nothing apart from individuals, there will be no object of thought, but all things will be objects of sense, and there will not be knowledge of anything, unless we say that sensation is knowledge.

ἔτι δ' οὐδ' ἀΐδιον οὐθὲν οὐδ' ἀκίνητον (τὰ γὰρ αἰσθητὰ [5] πάντα φθείρεται καὶ ἐν κινήσει ἐστίν):

— Amplius autem nec sempiternum est aliquid nec immobile; nam sensibilia omnia corrumpuntur et in motu sunt.

Further, nothing will be eternal or unmovable; for all perceptible things perish and are in movement.

μὴν εἴ γε ἀΐδιον μηθέν ἐστιν, οὐδὲ γένεσιν εἶναι δυνατόν. ἀνάγκη γὰρ εἶναί τι τὸ γιγνόμενον καὶ ἐξ οὗ γίγνεται καὶ τούτων τὸ ἔσχατον ἀγένητον, εἴπερ ἵσταταί τε καὶ ἐκ μὴ ὄντος γενέσθαι ἀδύνατον:

At vero si sempiternum nihil est, nec generationem esse possibile est; necesse est enim aliquid esse quod fit et ex quo fit et horum ultimum ingenitum, si stat et ex non ente generari impossibile.

But if there is nothing eternal, neither can there be a process of coming to be; for there must be something that comes to be, i.e. from which something comes to be, and the ultimate term in this series cannot have come to be, since the series has a limit and since nothing can come to be out of that which is not.

ἔτι δὲ γενέσεως οὔσης καὶ κινήσεως ἀνάγκη καὶ πέρας εἶναι (οὔτε [10] γὰρ ἄπειρός ἐστιν οὐδεμία κίνησις ἀλλὰ πάσης ἔστι τέλος, γίγνεσθαί τε οὐχ οἷόν τε τὸ ἀδύνατον γενέσθαι:

Amplius autem, cum sit generatio et motus, finem esse est necesse; motus enim nullus est infinitus sed omnis est finis, generarique non possibile quod impossibile est factum esse; quod autem est generatum est esse necesse quando primum factum est.

Further, if generation and movement exist there must also be a limit; for no movement is infinite, but every movement has an end, and that which is incapable of completing its coming to be cannot be in process of coming to be; and that which has completed its coming to be must he as soon as it has come to be.

τὸ δὲ γεγονὸς ἀνάγκη εἶναι ὅτε πρῶτον γέγονεν): ἔτι δ᾽ εἴπερ ἡ ὕλη ἔστι διὰ τὸ ἀγένητος εἶναι, πολὺ ἔτι μᾶλλον εὔλογον εἶναι τὴν οὐσίαν, ὅ ποτε ἐκείνη γίγνεται: εἰ γὰρ μήτε τοῦτο ἔσται [15] μήτε ἐκείνη, οὐθὲν ἔσται τὸ παράπαν, εἰ δὲ τοῦτο ἀδύνατον, ἀνάγκη τι εἶναι παρὰ τὸ σύνολον, τὴν μορφὴν καὶ τὸ εἶδος.

Amplius autem si materia est quia est ingenita, multo rationabilius est esse substantiam, quando illa fit esse; nam si nec haec erit nec illa, nihil erit omnino. Sed si hoc est impossibile, necesse est aliquid esse praeter sinolon: formam et speciem.

Further, since the matter exists, because it is ungenerated, it is a fortiori reasonable that the substance or essence, that which the matter is at any time coming to be, should exist; for if neither essence nor matter is to be, nothing will be at all, and since this is impossible there must be something besides the concrete thing, viz. the shape or form.

εἰ δ᾽ αὖ τις τοῦτο θήσει, ἀπορία ἐπὶ τίνων τε θήσει τοῦτο καὶ ἐπὶ τίνων οὔ. ὅτι μὲν γὰρ ἐπὶ πάντων οὐχ οἷόν τε, φανερόν: οὐ γὰρ ἂν θείημεν εἶναί τινα οἰκίαν παρὰ τὰς τινὰς [20] οἰκίας.

Sed si hoc iterum quis ponit, dubitatio in quibus hoc ponet et in quibus non. Nam quod in omnibus non sit possibile, manifestum; non enim utique ponemus domum aliquam praeter domos aliquas.

But again (B) if we are to suppose this, it is hard to say in which cases we are to suppose it and in which not. For evidently it is not possible to suppose it in all cases; we could not suppose that there is a house besides the particular houses.

πρὸς δὲ τούτοις πότερον ἡ οὐσία μία πάντων ἔσται, οἷον τῶν ἀνθρώπων; ἀλλ᾽ ἄτοπον: ἓν γὰρ πάντα ὧν ἡ οὐσία μία. ἀλλὰ πολλὰ καὶ διάφορα;

Ad haec autem utrum substantia una erit omnium, ut hominum? Sed inconveniens est; non enim unum omnia quorum substantia una. Sed multa et differentia?

-Besides this, will the substance of all the individuals, e.g. of all men, be one? This is paradoxical, for all the things whose substance is one are one. But are the substances many and different?

ἀλλὰ καὶ τοῦτο ἄλογον.

Sed et hoc extra rationem.

This also is unreasonable.

ἅμα δὲ καὶ πῶς γίγνεται ἡ ὕλη τούτων ἕκαστον καὶ ἔστι τὸ σύνολον ἄμφω ταῦτα;

Simul autem et quomodo fit materia horum singulum et est sinolon ambo haec?

-At the same time, how does the matter become each of the individuals, and how is the concrete thing these two elements?

ἔτι δὲ περὶ τῶν ἀρχῶν [25] καὶ τόδε ἀπορήσειεν ἄν τις. εἰ μὲν γὰρ εἴδει εἰσὶν ἕν, οὐθὲν ἔσται ἀριθμῷ ἕν, οὐδ᾽ αὐτὸ τὸ ἕν καὶ τὸ ὄν: καὶ τὸ ἐπίστασθαι πῶς ἔσται, εἰ μή τι ἔσται ἕν ἐπὶ πάντων;

Amplius autem et de principiis et hoc dubitabit aliquis.Nam  si specie sunt unum, nihil erit numero unum, nec  iterum unum ipsum et ens. Et scire quomodo erit, si non aliquid erit unum in omnibus?

(9) Again, one might ask the following question also about the first principles. If they are one in kind only, nothing will be numerically one, not even unity-itself and being-itself; and how will knowing exist, if there is not to be something common to a whole set of individuals?

ἀλλὰ μὴν εἰ ἀριθμῷ ἕν καὶ μία ἑκάστη τῶν ἀρχῶν, καὶ μὴ ὥσπερ ἐπὶ τῶν αἰσθητῶν ἄλλαι ἄλλων (οἷον τῆσδε τῆς συλλαβῆς [30] τῷ εἴδει τῆς αὐτῆς οὔσης καὶ αἱ ἀρχαὶ εἴδει αἱ αὐταί: καὶ γὰρ αὗται ὑπάρχουσιν ἀριθμῷ ἕτεραι), εἰ δὲ μὴ οὕτως ἀλλ᾽ αἱ τῶν ὄντων ἀρχαὶ ἀριθμῷ ἕν εἰσιν, οὐκ ἔσται παρὰ τὰ στοιχεῖα οὐθὲν ἕτερον: τὸ γὰρ ἀριθμῷ ἕν ἢ τὸ καθ᾽ ἕκαστον λέγειν διαφέρει οὐθέν: οὕτω γὰρ λέγομεν τὸ καθ᾽ ἕκαστον, τὸ ἀριθμῷ ἕν, καθόλου δὲ τὸ ἐπὶ τούτων. [1000α] [1] ὥσπερ οὖν εἰ τὰ τῆς φωνῆς ἀριθμῷ ἦν στοιχεῖα ὡρισμένα, ἀναγκαῖον ἦν ἂν τοσαῦτα εἶναι τὰ πάντα γράμματα ὅσαπερ τὰ στοιχεῖα, μὴ ὄντων γε δύο τῶν αὐτῶν μηδὲ πλειόνων.

At vero si numero unum et unum quodlibet principiorum, et non quemadmodum in sensibilibus alia aliorum (ut in hac sillaba specie eadem existente et principia specie eadem; et enim  haec sunt numero diversa), si autem non ita sed quae sunt existentium numero unum sunt, non erit praeter elementa nihil aliud. Nam numero unum aut singulare dicere nihil differt. Sic enim dicimus singulare: numero unum; universale vero quod in hiis est. Sicut igitur si quae vocis unum numero essent elementa determinata, tot omnes litteras esse necesse esset quot elementa, non existentibus quidem duobus eisdem nec pluribus.

But if there is a common element which is numerically one, and each of the principles is one, and the principles are not as in the case of perceptible things different for different things (e.g. since this particular syllable is the same in kind whenever it occurs, the elements it are also the same in kind; only in kind, for these also, like the syllable, are numerically different in different contexts),-if it is not like this but the principles of things are numerically one, there will be nothing else besides the elements (for there is no difference of meaning between numerically one and individual ; for this is just what we mean by the individual-the numerically one, and by the universal we [00a] mean that which is predicable of the individuals). Therefore it will be just as if the elements of articulate sound were limited in number; all the language in the world would be confined to the ABC, since there could not be two or more letters of the same kind.

οὐθενὸς δ᾽ ἐλάττων ἀπορία παραλέλειπται καὶ τοῖς νῦν καὶ τοῖς πρότερον, πότερον αἱ αὐταὶ τῶν φθαρτῶν καὶ τῶν ἀφθάρτων ἀρχαί εἰσιν ἢ ἕτεραι.

Non minor autem dubitatio modernis et prioribus relinquitur, utrum eadem corruptibilium et incorruptibilium sunt principia aut diversa.

(10) One difficulty which is as great as any has been neglected both by modern philosophers and by their predecessors-whether the principles of perishable and those of imperishable things are the same or different.

εἰ μὲν γὰρ αἱ αὐταί, πῶς τὰ μὲν φθαρτὰ τὰ δὲ ἄφθαρτα, καὶ διὰ τίν᾽ αἰτίαν;

Nam si eadem sunt, quomodo haec quidem incorruptibilia illa vero corruptibilia, et propter quam causam?

If they are the same, how are some things perishable and others imperishable, and for what reason?

οἱ μὲν οὖν περὶ Ἡσίοδον καὶ πάντες ὅσοι θεολόγοι [10] μόνον ἐφρόντισαν τοῦ πιθανοῦ τοῦ πρὸς αὑτούς, ἡμῶν δ᾽ ὠλιγώρησαν (θεοὺς γὰρ ποιοῦντες τὰς ἀρχὰς καὶ ἐκ θεῶν γεγονέναι, τὰ μὴ γευσάμενα τοῦ νέκταρος καὶ τῆς ἀμβροσίας θνητὰ γενέσθαι φασίν,

Qui quidem igitur circa Esyodum et omnes quicumque theologi solum ad ipsos persuasionem curaverunt, nos autem neglexerunt. Deos enim facientes principia et ex deis esse facta, quae non gustaverunt nectar et manna mortalia facta esse dicunt.

The school of Hesiod and all the theologians thought only of what was plausible to themselves, and had no regard to us. For, asserting the first principles to be gods and born of gods, they say that the beings which did not taste of nectar and ambrosia became mortal;

δῆλον ὡς ταῦτα τὰ ὀνόματα γνώριμα λέγοντες αὐτοῖς· καίτοι περὶ αὐτῆς τῆς προσφορᾶς [15] τῶν αἰτίων τούτων ὑπὲρ ἡμᾶς εἰρήκασιν· εἰ μὲν γὰρ χάριν ἡδονῆς αὐτῶν θιγγάνουσιν, οὐθὲν αἴτια τοῦ εἶναι τὸ νέκταρ καὶ ἡ ἀμβροσία, εἰ δὲ τοῦ εἶναι, πῶς ἂν εἶεν ἀΐδιοι δεόμενοι τροφῆς):

Palam quod haec nomina sibi nota dicentes; equidem de allatione harum causarum super nos dixerunt. Nam si gratia voluptatis ipsa tangunt, non est causa existendi nectar et manna. Si vero existendi, quomodo erunt sempiterni cibo egentes?

and clearly they are using words which are familiar to themselves, yet what they have said about the very application of these causes is above our comprehension. For if the gods taste of nectar and ambrosia for their pleasure, these are in no wise the causes of their existence; and if they taste them to maintain their existence, how can gods who need food be eternal?

ἀλλὰ περὶ μὲν τῶν μυθικῶς σοφιζομένων οὐκ ἄξιον μετὰ σπουδῆς σκοπεῖν·

Sed de fabulose sophizantibus non est dignum cum studio intendere;

-But into the subtleties of the mythologists it is not worth our while to inquire seriously;

παρὰ δὲ τῶν δι᾽ [20] ἀποδείξεως λεγόντων δεῖ πυνθάνεσθαι διερωτῶντας τί δή [21] ποτ᾽ ἐκ τῶν αὐτῶν ὄντα τὰ μὲν ἀΐδια τὴν φύσιν ἐστὶ τὰ δὲ φθείρεται τῶν ὄντων. ἐπεὶ δὲ οὔτε αἰτίαν λέγουσιν οὔτε εὔλογον οὕτως ἔχειν, δῆλον ὡς οὐχ αἱ αὐταὶ ἀρχαὶ οὐδὲ αἰτίαι αὐτῶν ἂν εἶεν.

a dicentibus vero per demonstrationem oportet sciscitari interrogantes quare ex eisdem existentia haec quidem sempiterna secundum naturam sunt, illa vero corrumpuntur existentium. Quoniam autem nec causam dicunt nec rationabile est sic habere, palam quod nec eadem principia nec cause ipsorum erunt.

those, however, who use the language of proof we must cross-examine and ask why, after all, things which consist of the same elements are, some of them, eternal in nature, while others perish. Since these philosophers mention no cause, and it is unreasonable that things should be as they say, evidently the principles or causes of things cannot be the same.

καὶ γὰϱ ὅνπεϱ οἰηθείη λέγειν [25] ἄν τις μάλιστα ὁμολογουμένως αὐτῷ, Ἐμπεδοκλῆς, καὶ οὗτος ταὐτὸν πέπονθεν: τίθησι μὲν γὰϱ ἀϱχήν τινα αἰτίαν τῆς φθοϱᾶς τὸ νεῖκος,

Et enim quem existimabit utique aliquis dicere maxime ipsi confesse, Empedocles , et hic idem passus est. Ponit enim principium quoddam causam corruptionis odium,

Even the man whom one might suppose to speak most [00a 25]consistently-Empedocles, even he has made the same mistake; for he maintains that strife is a principle that causes destruction,

δόξειε δ᾽ ἂν οὐθὲν ἧττον καὶ τοῦτο γεννᾶν ἔξω τοῦ ἑνός: ἅπαντα γὰϱ ἐκ τούτου τἆλλά ἐστι πλὴν ὁ θεός. λέγει γοῦν ἐξ ὧν πάνθ᾽ ὅσα τ᾽ ἦν ὅσα τ᾽ [30] ἔσθ᾽ ὅσα τ᾽ ἔσται ὀπίσσω, δένδϱεά τ᾽ ἐβλάστησε καὶ ἀνέϱες ἠδὲ γυναῖκες, θῆϱές τ᾽ οἰωνοί τε καὶ ὑδατοθϱέμμονες ἰχθῦς, καί τε θεοὶ δολιχαίωνες.

videbitur nihil minus et hoc generare extra unum; nam omnia ex hoc alia sunt praeter deum. Dicit ergo: "ex quibus omnia et quaecumque erant et quaecumque erunt, et arbores pullulaverunt et viri et femine, bestieque et vultures et aqua nutriti pisces, et dei longevi".

but even strife would seem no less to produce everything, except the One; for all things excepting God proceed from strife. At least he says:

From which all that was and is and will be hereafter

Trees, and men and women, took their growth,

And beasts and birds and water-nourished fish,

And long-aged gods.

καὶ χωϱὶς δὲ τούτων δῆλον: [1000β] [1] εἰ γὰϱ μὴ ἦν ἐν τοῖς πϱάγμασιν, ἓν ἂν ἦν ἅπαντα, ὡς φησίν: ὅταν γὰϱ συνέλθῃ, "τότε δ᾽ ἔσχατον ἵστατο νεῖκος."

Et praeter haec palam quia si non esset in rebus, essent unum omnia, ut ait; nam quando convenerunt, tunc " ultimum stabat odium".

The implication is evident even apart from these words; [00b] for if strife had not been present in things, all things would have been one, according to him; for when they have come together, "then strife stood outermost".

διὸ καὶ συμβαίνει αὐτῷ τὸν εὐδαιμονέστατον θεὸν ἧττον φϱόνιμον εἶναι τῶν ἄλλων: οὐ γὰϱ γνωϱίζει [5] ἅπαντα: τὸ γὰϱ νεῖκος οὐκ ἔχει, ἡ δὲ γνῶσις τοῦ

ὁμοίου τῷ ὁμοίῳ. γαίῃ μὲν γάρ, (φησί,) γαῖαν ὀπώπαμεν, ὕδατι δ᾽ ὕδωρ, αἰθέρι δ᾽ αἰθέρα δῖον, ἀτὰρ πυρὶ πῦρ ἀΐδηλον, στοργὴν δὲ στοργῇ, νεῖκος δέ τε νείκεϊ λυγρῷ.

Propter quod et accidit ipsi felicissimum deum minus prudentem esse aliis; non enim cognoscit elementa omnia; nam odium non habet, notitia vero similis simili. "Terram namque", ait, "per terram cognovimus, et per aquam aquam, et per affectum affectum, et adhuc odium per odium difficile".

Hence it also follows on his theory that God most blessed is less wise than all others; for he does not know all the elements; for he has in him no strife, and knowledge is of the like by the like. "For by earth", he says,

we see earth, by water water,

By ether godlike ether, by fire wasting fire,

Love by love, and strife by gloomy strife.

ἀλλ᾽ ὅθεν δὴ ὁ λόγος, τοῦτό γε φανερόν, ὅτι [10] συμβαίνει αὐτῷ τὸ νεῖκος μηθὲν μᾶλλον φθορᾶς ἢ τοῦ εἶναι αἴτιον:

Sed unde ratio, hoc etiam palam quia accidit ei odium non magis corruptionis quam existendi causam.

But-and this is the point we started from this at least is evident, that on his theory it follows that strife is as much the cause of existence as of destruction.

ὁμοίως δ᾽ οὐδ᾽ ἡ φιλότης τοῦ εἶναι, συνάγουσα γὰρ εἰς τὸ ἓν φθείρει τὰ ἄλλα.

similiter autem nec amor existendi; colligens enim in unum corrumpit alia.

And similarly love is not specially the cause of existence; for in collecting things into the One it destroys all other things.

καὶ ἅμα δὲ αὐτῆς τῆς μεταβολῆς αἴτιον οὐθὲν λέγει ἀλλ᾽ ἢ ὅτι οὕτως πέφυκεν:

Simul quoque ipsius transmutationis causam nullam dicit, nisi quia sic aptum natum fuit:

And at the same time Empedocles mentions no cause of the change itself, except that things are so by nature.

ἀλλ᾽ ὅτε δὴ μέγα νεῖκος ἐνὶ μελέεσσιν ἐθρέφθη, εἰς τιμάς [15] τ᾽ ἀνόρουσε τελειομένοιο χρόνοιο ὅς σφιν ἀμοιβαῖος πλατέος παρ᾽ ἐλήλαται ὅρκου:

"alias itaque magnum odium in membris nutritum est, et ad honorem intendebat perfecto tempore, qui mutabilis dissolvit sacramentum".

But when strife at last waxed great in the limbs of the Sphere,

And sprang to assert its rights as the time was fulfilled

Which is fixed for them in turn by a mighty oath.

ὡς ἀναγκαῖον μὲν ὂν μεταβάλλειν: αἰτίαν δὲ τῆς ἀνάγκης οὐδεμίαν δηλοῖ. ἀλλ᾽ ὅμως τοσοῦτόν γε μόνος λέγει ὁμολογουμένως: οὐ γὰρ τὰ μὲν φθαρτὰ τὰ δὲ ἄφθαρτα ποιεῖ τῶν ὄντων ἀλλὰ πάντα [20] φθαρτὰ πλὴν τῶν στοιχείων. ἡ δὲ νῦν λεγομένη ἀπορία ἐστὶ διὰ τί τὰ μὲν τὰ δ᾽ οὔ, εἴπερ ἐκ τῶν αὐτῶν ἐστίν.

Quasi necessarium ens transmutari; causam vero necessitatis nullam ostendit. At tamen tantum solum dicit confesse; non enim existentium haec quidem corruptibilia illa vero incorruptibilia facit, sed omnia corruptibilia praeter elementa. Dicta vero nunc dubitatio est cur haec quidem illa vero non, si ex eisdem sunt.

This implies that change was necessary; but he shows no cause of the necessity. But yet so far at least he alone speaks consistently; for he does not make some things perishable and others imperishable, but makes all perishable except the elements. The difficulty we are speaking of now is, why some things are perishable and others are not, if they consist of the same principles.

ὅτι μὲν οὖν οὐκ ἂν εἴησαν αἱ αὐταὶ ἀρχαί, τοσαῦτα εἰρήσθω: εἰ μὲν γὰρ φθαρταί, δῆλον ὡς [25] ἀναγκαῖον καὶ ταύτας ἔκ τινων εἶναι (πάντα γὰρ φθείρεται εἰς ταῦτ᾽ ἐξ ὧν ἔστιν), ὥστε συμβαίνει τῶν ἀρχῶν ἑτέρας ἀρχὰς εἶναι προτέρας, τοῦτο δ᾽ ἀδύνατον, καὶ εἰ ἵσταται καὶ εἰ βαδίζει εἰς ἄπειρον: ἔτι δὲ πῶς ἔσται τὰ φθαρτά, εἰ αἱ ἀρχαὶ ἀναιρεθήσονται; εἰ δὲ ἄφθαρτοι, διὰ [30] τί ἐκ μὲν τούτων ἀφθάρτων οὐσῶν φθαρτὰ ἔσται, ἐκ δὲ τῶν ἑτέρων ἄφθαρτα; τοῦτο γὰρ οὐκ εὔλογον, ἀλλ᾽ ἢ ἀδύνατον ἢ πολλοῦ λόγου δεῖται.

Quod quidem igitur non utique erunt eadem principia, tot dicta sint. Si vero diversa principia, una quidem dubitatio utrum incorruptibilia et haec erunt aut corruptibilia. Nam si corruptibilia, manifestum quia necessarium et ea ex aliquibus esse; omnia enim corrumpuntur in ea ex quibus sunt. Quare contingit principiorum alia principia esse priora. Hoc autem impossibile, sive stet sive in infmitum vadat. — Amplius autem quomodo erunt ipsa corruptibilia, si destruentur principia? Si vero incorruptibilia, cur ex hiis quidem incorruptibilibus existentibus corruptibilia erunt, ex diversis vero incorruptibilia? Hoc enim non rationabile est, sed aut impossibile aut multa ratione eget.

Let this suffice as proof of the fact that the principles cannot be the same. But if there are different principles, one difficulty is whether these also will be imperishable or perishable. For if they are perishable, evidently these also must consist of certain elements (for all things that perish, perish by being resolved into the elements of which they consist); so that it follows that prior to the principles there are other principles. But this is impossible, whether the process has a limit or proceeds to infinity. Further, how will perishable things exist, if their principles are to be annulled? But if the principles are imperishable, why will things composed of some imperishable principles be perishable, while those composed of the others are imperishable? This is not probable, but is either impossible or needs much proof.

ἔτι δὲ οὐδ᾽ ἐγκεχείρηκεν οὐδεὶς ἑτέρας, ἀλλὰ τὰς αὐτὰς ἁπάντων λέγουσιν ἀρχάς. [1001a] [1] ἀλλὰ τὸ πρῶτον ἀπορηθὲν ἀποτρώγουσιν ὥσπερ τοῦτο μικρόν τι λαμβάνοντες.

Amplius autem nec conatus est aliquis diversa dicere, sed eadem omnium dicunt principia. Verum primum dubitatum corrodunt tamquam hoc parvum aliquid accipientes.

Further, no one has even tried to maintain different principles; they maintain the same principles for all things. [01a] But they swallow the difficulty we stated first as if they took it to be something trifling.

πάντων δὲ καὶ θεωρῆσαι χαλεπώτατον καὶ πρὸς τὸ [5] γνῶναι τἀληθὲς ἀναγκαιότατον πότερόν ποτε τὸ ὂν καὶ τὸ ἓν οὐσίαι τῶν ὄντων εἰσί, καὶ ἑκάτερον αὐτῶν οὐχ ἕτερόν τι ὂν τὸ μὲν ἓν τὸ δὲ ὂν ἐστιν, ἢ δεῖ ζητεῖν τί ποτ᾽ ἐστὶ τὸ ὂν καὶ τὸ ἓν ὡς ὑποκειμένης ἄλλης φύσεως. οἱ μὲν γὰρ ἐκείνως οἱ δ᾽ οὕτως οἴονται τὴν φύσιν ἔχειν.

Omnium autem ad considerandum difficillimum et ad cognoscendum veritatem maxime necessarium est, utrum unum et ens substantiae existentium sunt, et utrumque ipsorum non alterum aliquid ens, hoc quidem unum hoc autem ens est, aut oportet quaerere quid est ipsum ens et unum quasi subiecta alia natura.

(11) The inquiry that is both the hardest of all and the most necessary for knowledge of the truth is whether being and unity are the substances of things, and whether each of them, without being anything else, is being or unity respectively, or we must inquire what being and unity are, with the implication that they have some other underlying nature.

Πλάτων [10] μὲν γὰρ καὶ οἱ Πυθαγόρειοι οὐχ ἕτερόν τι τὸ ὂν οὐδὲ τὸ ἓν ἀλλὰ τοῦτο αὐτῶν τὴν φύσιν εἶναι, ὡς οὔσης τῆς οὐσίας αὐτοῦ τοῦ ἑνὶ εἶναι καὶ ὄντι: οἱ δὲ περὶ φύσεως, οἷον Ἐμπεδοκλῆς ὡς εἰς γνωριμώτερον ἀνάγων λέγει ὅ τι τὸ ἓν ἐστιν: δόξειε γὰρ ἂν λέγειν τοῦτο τὴν φιλίαν εἶναι (αἰτία [15] γοῦν ἐστιν αὕτη τοῦ ἓν εἶναι πᾶσιν), ἕτεροι δὲ πῦρ, οἱ δ᾽ ἀέρα φασὶν εἶναι τὸ ἓν τοῦτο καὶ τὸ ὄν, ἐξ οὗ τὰ ὄντα εἶναί τε καὶ γεγονέναι. ὡς δ᾽ αὔτως καὶ οἱ πλείω τὰ στοιχεῖα τιθέμενοι· ἀνάγκη γὰρ καὶ τούτοις τοσαῦτα λέγειν τὸ ἓν καὶ τὸ ὂν ὅσας περ ἀρχὰς εἶναί φασιν.

Hii namque illo modo illi hoc modo putant naturam se habere. Plato namque et pytagorici non aliud aliquid ens nec unum sed hoc ipsorum naturam esse, quasi existente substantia  ipsum unum esse et ens aliquid. Alii vero de natura, ut Empedocles ut ad notius reducens dicit quia unum ens est; videbitur enim utique dicere hoc amorem esse; causa  namque est hic unum omnibus esse. Alii vero ignem, alii aerem dicunt esse unum hoc et ens, ex quo entia esse et facta esse. Similiter et qui plura ponunt elementa; necesse namque et hiis tot dicere ens et unum quot principia dicunt esse.

For some people think they are of the former, others think they are of the latter character. Plato and the Pythagoreans thought being and unity were nothing else, but this was their nature, their essence being just unity and being. But the natural philosophers take a different line; e.g. Empedocles-as though reducing to something more intelligible-says what unity is; for he would seem to say it is love: at least, this is for all things the cause of their being one. Others say this unity and being, of which things consist and have been made, is fire, and others say it is air. A similar view is expressed by those who make the elements more than one; for these also must say that unity and being are precisely all the things which they say are principles.

συμβαίνει [20] δέ, εἰ μέν τις μὴ θήσεται εἶναί τινα οὐσίαν τὸ ἓν καὶ τὸ ὄν, μηδὲ τῶν ἄλλων εἶναι τῶν καθόλου μηθέν (ταῦτα γὰρ ἐστι καθόλου μάλιστα πάντων, εἰ δὲ μὴ ἔστι τι ἓν αὐτὸ μηδ᾽ αὐτὸ ὄν, σχολῇ τῶν γε ἄλλων τι ἂν εἴη παρὰ τὰ λεγόμενα καθ᾽ ἕκαστα), ἔτι δὲ μὴ ὄντος τοῦ ἑνὸς οὐσίας, [25] δῆλον ὅτι οὐδ᾽ ἂν ἀριθμὸς εἴη ὡς κεχωρισμένη τις φύσις τῶν ὄντων (ὁ μὲν γὰρ ἀριθμὸς μονάδες, ἡ δὲ μονὰς ὅπερ ἕν τί ἐστιν):

Accidit autem, si quidem quis non ponit esse quandam substantiam unum et ens, nec aliorum esse universalium nullum; haec namque universalia sunt maxime omnium. Si vero non est aliquid unum ipsum neque ipsum ens, neque aliorum aliquid erit praeter ea quae dicta sunt singularia. Amplius autem non  existente unius substantia, palam quia nec numerus erit quasi natura aliqua ab existentibus separata; numerus enim unitates, unitas vero quod vere unum aliquid est.

(A) If we do not suppose unity and being to be substances, it follows that none of the other universals is a substance; for these are most universal of all, and if there is no unity itself or being-itself, there will scarcely be in any other case anything apart from what are called the individuals. Further, if unity is not a substance, evidently number also will not exist as an entity separate from the individual things; for number is units, and the unit is precisely a certain kind of one.

εἰ δ᾽ ἔστι τι αὐτὸ ἓν καὶ ὄν, ἀναγκαῖον οὐσίαν αὐτῶν εἶναι τὸ ἓν καὶ τὸ ὄν· οὐ γὰρ ἕτερόν τι καθόλου κατηγορεῖται ἀλλὰ ταῦτα αὐτά.

Si autem aliquid est ipsum unum et ens, necesse est substantiam ipsorum esse ens et unum; non enim aliquid aliud universaliter predicatur sed haec ipsa.

But (B) if there is a unity-itself and a being itself, unity and being must be their substance; for it is not something else that is predicated universally of the things that are and are one, but just unity and being.

ἀλλὰ μὴν εἴ γ᾽ ἔσται [30] τι αὐτὸ ὂν καὶ αὐτὸ ἕν, πολλὴ ἀπορία πῶς ἔσται τι παρὰ ταῦτα ἕτερον, λέγω δὲ πῶς ἔσται πλείω ἑνὸς τὰ ὄντα. τὸ γὰρ ἕτερον τοῦ ὄντος οὐκ ἔστιν, ὥστε κατὰ τὸν Παρμενίδου συμβαίνειν ἀνάγκη λόγον ἓν ἅπαντα εἶναι τὰ ὄντα καὶ τοῦτο εἶναι τὸ ὄν.

At vero si erit aliquid ens ipsum et ipsum unum, multa erit dubitatio quomodo erit diversum aliquid praeter haec. Dico autem quomodo erunt uno plura entia. Quod enim diversum est ab ente non est; quare secundum Parmenidis rationem accidere est necesse unum omnia esse entia et hoc esse ens.

But if there is to be a being-itself and a unity-itself, there is much difficulty in seeing how there will be anything else besides these,-I mean, how things will be more than one in number. For what is different from being does not exist, so that it necessarily follows, according to the argument of Parmenides, that all things that are are one and this is being.

[1001β] [1] ἀμφοτέρως δὲ δύσκολον· ἄν τε γὰρ μὴ ᾖ τὸ ἓν οὐσία ἄν τε ᾖ τὸ αὐτὸ ἕν, ἀδύνατον τὸν ἀριθμὸν οὐσίαν εἶναι. ἐὰν μὲν οὖν μὴ ᾖ, εἴρηται πρότερον δι᾽ ὅ· ἐὰν δὲ ᾖ, ἡ αὐτὴ ἀπορία καὶ περὶ τοῦ ὄντος. ἐκ τίνος γὰρ [5] παρὰ τὸ ἓν ἔσται αὐτὸ ἄλλο ἕν; ἀνάγκη γὰρ μὴ ἓν εἶναι· ἅπαντα δὲ τὰ ὄντα ἢ ἓν ἢ πολλὰ ὧν ἓν ἕκαστον.

Utrobiquae vero difficile; sive namque non sit unum substantia sive sit ipsum unum, substantiam esse numerum est impossibile. Si quidem igitur non sit, dictum est prius propter quod; si autem fuerit, eadem est dubitatio et de ente. Ex aliquo namque et praeter ens erit ipsum aliud unum. Nihil enim esse est necesse; omnia autem entia aut unum aut multa quorum unum unumquodque.

[01b] There are objections to both views. For whether unity is not a substance or there is a unity-itself, number cannot be a substance. We have already said why this result follows if unity is not a substance; and if it is, the same difficulty arises as arose

with regard to being. For whence is there to be another one besides unity-itself? It must be not-one; but all things are either one or many, and of the many each is one.

ἔτι εἰ ἀδιαίρετον αὐτὸ τὸ ἕν, κατὰ μὲν τὸ Ζήνωνος ἀξίωμα οὐθὲν ἂν εἴη (ὃ γὰρ μήτε προστιθέμενον μήτε ἀφαιρούμενον ποιεῖ μεῖζον μηδὲ ἔλαττον, οὔ φησιν εἶναι τοῦτο τῶν ὄντων, [10] ὡς δηλονότι ὄντος μεγέθους τοῦ ὄντος: καὶ εἰ μέγεθος, σωματικόν: τοῦτο γὰρ πάντῃ ὄν: τὰ δὲ ἄλλα πὼς μὲν προστιθέμενα ποιήσει μεῖζον, πὼς δ᾽ οὐθέν, οἷον ἐπίπεδον καὶ γραμμή, στιγμὴ δὲ καὶ μονὰς οὐδαμῶς):

Amplius si indivisibile est ipsum unum, secundum Zenonis dignitatem nihil utique erit. Quod enim nec additum nec ablatum facit maius nec minus, non ait esse hoc existentium, tamquam palam quod existente magnitudine ipso ente. Et si magnitudo, corporalis; hoc enim omnino ens, alia vero aliqualiter quidem addita facient maius, aliqualiter autem nihil, ut superficies et linea, punctum vero et unitas nullatenus.

Further, if unity-itself is indivisible, according to Zeno's postulate it will be nothing. For that which neither when added makes a thing greater nor when subtracted makes it less, he asserts to have no being, evidently assuming that whatever has being is a spatial magnitude. And if it is a magnitude, it is corporeal; for the corporeal has being in every dimension, while the other objects of mathematics, e.g. a plane or a line, added in one way will increase what they are added to, but in another way will not do so, and a point or a unit does so in no way.

ἀλλ᾽ ἐπειδὴ οὗτος θεωρεῖ φορτικῶς, καὶ ἐνδέχεται εἶναι ἀδιαίρετόν τι [15] ὥστε [καὶ οὕτως] καὶ πρὸς ἐκεῖνόν τιν᾽ ἀπολογίαν ἔχειν (μεῖζον μὲν γὰρ οὐ ποιήσει πλεῖον δὲ προστιθέμενον τὸ τοιοῦτον):

Sed quoniam hic speculatur onerose et non contingit esse indivisibile, ut et sic ad illum aliqua habeatur responsio: maius enim non faciet sed plus additum tale.

But, since his theory is of a low order, and an indivisible thing can exist in such a way as to have a defence even against him (for the indivisible when added will make the number, though not the size, greater),

ἀλλὰ πῶς δὴ ἐξ ἑνὸς τοιούτου ἢ πλειόνων τοιούτων ἔσται μέγεθος;

Sed quomodo ex uno tali aut pluribus erit magnitudo? Simile namque est et lineam ex punctis esse dicere.

-yet how can a magnitude proceed from one such indivisible or from many? It is like saying that the line is made out of points.

ὅμοιον γὰρ καὶ τὴν γραμμὴν ἐκ στιγμῶν εἶναι φάσκειν. ἀλλὰ μὴν καὶ εἴ τις οὕτως ὑπολαμβάνει ὥστε [20] γενέσθαι, καθάπερ λέγουσί τινες, ἐκ τοῦ ἑνὸς αὐτοῦ καὶ ἄλλου μὴ ἑνός τινος τὸν ἀριθμόν, οὐθὲν ἧττον ζητητέον διὰ τί καὶ πῶς ὁτὲ μὲν ἀριθμὸς ὁτὲ δὲ μέγεθος ἔσται τὸ γενόμενον, εἴπερ τὸ μὴ ἓν ἡ ἀνισότης καὶ ἡ αὐτὴ φύσις ἦν. οὔτε γὰρ ὅπως ἐξ ἑνὸς καὶ ταύτης οὔτε ὅπως ἐξ ἀριθμοῦ [25] τινὸς καὶ ταύτης γένοιτ᾽ ἂν τὰ μεγέθη, δῆλον.

At vero et si quis ita putat ut factus sit, ut quidam dicunt, ex uno ipso et alio non uno aliquo numerus, nihil minus est quaerendum quare et quomodo quandoque quidem numerus quandoque autem magnitudo erit quod factum est, si non unum inequalitas et eadem natura erat. Nec enim quomodo ex uno et hac nec quomodo ex numero aliquo et hac fient utique magnitudines, palam.

But even if one supposes the case to be such that, as some say, number proceeds from unity-itself and something else which is not one, none the less we must inquire why and how the product will be sometimes a number and sometimes a magnitude, if the not-one was inequality and was the same principle in either case. For it is not evident how magnitudes could proceed either from the one and this principle, or from some number and this principle.

## *Chapter* 5

τούτων δ᾽ ἐχομένη ἀπορία πότερον οἱ ἀριθμοὶ καὶ τὰ σώματα καὶ τὰ ἐπίπεδα καὶ αἱ στιγμαὶ οὐσίαι τινές εἰσιν ἢ οὔ.

Hiis autem habita dubitatio utrum numeri et corpora et superficies et puncta substantiae alique sunt aut non.

(14) A question connected with these is whether numbers and bodies and planes and points are substances of a kind, or not.

εἰ μὲν γὰρ μή εἰσιν, διαφεύγει τί τὸ ὂν καὶ τίνες αἱ οὐσίαι τῶν ὄντων· τὰ μὲν γὰρ πάθη καὶ αἱ κινήσεις [30] καὶ τὰ πρός τι καὶ αἱ διαθέσεις καὶ οἱ λόγοι οὐθενὸς δοκοῦσιν οὐσίαν σημαίνειν (λέγονται γὰρ πάντα καθ᾽ ὑποκειμένου τινός, καὶ οὐθὲν τόδε τι)· ἃ δὲ μάλιστ᾽ ἂν δόξειε σημαίνειν οὐσίαν, ὕδωρ καὶ γῆ καὶ πῦρ καὶ ἀήρ, ἐξ ὧν τὰ σύνθετα σώματα συνέστηκε, [1002α] [1] τούτων θερμότητες μὲν καὶ ψυχρότητες καὶ τὰ τοιαῦτα πάθη, οὐκ οὐσίαι, τὸ δὲ σῶμα τὸ ταῦτα πεπονθὸς μόνον ὑπομένει ὡς ὄν τι καὶ οὐσία τις οὖσα.

Nam si non sunt, diffugit aliquid ipsum ens et quaedam entium substantiae. Passiones enim et motus et ad aliquid et dispositiones et orationes nullius videntur substantiam significare; dicuntur enim omnia de subiecto aliquo, et nihil hoc aliquid. Quae vero maxime substantiam significare videntur, aqua et ignis et terra looiai ex quibus composita corpora constant, horum calores quidem et frigiditates et similes

passiones non sunt substantiae. Corpus vero haec patiens solum remanet ut ens aliquod et substantia aliqua existens.

If they are not, it baffles us to say what being is and what the substances of things are. For modifications and movements and relations and dispositions and ratios do not seem to indicate the substance of anything; for all are predicated of a subject, and none is a this . And as to the things which might seem most of all to indicate substance, water and earth and fire and air, of which composite bodies [02a] consist, heat and cold and the like are modifications of these, not substances, and the body which is thus modified alone persists as something real and as a substance.

ἀλλὰ μὴν τό γε σῶμα ἧττον οὐσία τῆς ἐπιφανείας, [5] καὶ αὕτη τῆς γραμμῆς, καὶ αὕτη τῆς μονάδος καὶ τῆς στιγμῆς: τούτοις γὰρ ὥρισται τὸ σῶμα, καὶ τὰ μὲν ἄνευ σώματος ἐνδέχεσθαι δοκεῖ εἶναι τὸ δὲ σῶμα ἄνευ τούτων ἀδύνατον.

At vero corpus est minus substantia superficie,  et haec linea, et haec unitate et puncto. Hiis enim diffmitur corpus, et haec quidem sine corpore contingere videntur esse corpus vero sine hiis  impossibile.

But, on the other hand, the body is surely less of a substance than the surface, and the surface than the line, and the line than the unit and the point. For the body is bounded by these; and they are thought to be capable of existing without body, but body incapable of existing without these.

διόπερ οἱ μὲν πολλοὶ καὶ οἱ πρότερον τὴν οὐσίαν καὶ τὸ ὂν ᾤοντο τὸ σῶμα εἶναι τὰ δὲ ἄλλα [10] τούτου πάθη, ὥστε καὶ τὰς ἀρχὰς τὰς τῶν σωμάτων τῶν ὄντων εἶναι ἀρχάς: οἱ δ᾽ ὕστεροι καὶ σοφώτεροι τούτων εἶναι δόξαντες ἀριθμούς. καθάπερ οὖν εἴπομεν, εἰ μὴ ἔστιν οὐσία ταῦτα, ὅλως οὐδέν ἐστιν οὐσία οὐδὲ ὂν οὐθέν: οὐ γὰρ δὴ τά γε συμβεβηκότα τούτοις ἄξιον ὄντα καλεῖν.

Propter quod multi quidem et  priores substantiam et ens putabant corpus esse alia vero huius passiones, quare et principia corporum entium esse  principia; posteriores vero et sapientiores hiis esse opinabantur numeros. Quemadmodum ergo dicebamus, si non sunt substantia haec, omnino nulla substantia est nec ens nullum; non enim horum accidentia dignum est vocare entia.

This is why, while most of the philosophers and the earlier among them thought that substance and being were identical with body, and that all other things were modifications of this, so that the first principles of the bodies were the first principles of being, the more recent and those who were held to be wiser thought numbers were the first principles. As we said, then, if these are not substance, there is no substance and no being at all; for the accidents of these it cannot be right to call beings.

[15] —ἀλλὰ μὴν εἰ τοῦτο μὲν ὁμολογεῖται, ὅτι μᾶλλον οὐσία τὰ μήκη τῶν σωμάτων καὶ αἱ στιγμαί, ταῦτα δὲ μὴ ὁρῶμεν ποίων ἂν εἶεν σωμάτων (ἐν γὰρ τοῖς αἰσθητοῖς ἀδύνατον εἶναι), οὐκ ἂν εἴη οὐσία οὐδεμία.

At vero si hoc quidem confessum est, quia magis sunt substantia longitudines corporibus et puncta, haec autem non videmus qualium utique erunt corporum (nam in sensibilibus impossibile esse), non utique erit substantia nulla.

But if this is admitted, that lines and points are substance more than bodies, but we do not see to what sort of bodies these could belong (for they cannot be in perceptible bodies), there can be no substance.

ἔτι δὲ φαίνεται ταῦτα πάντα διαιρέσεις ὄντα τοῦ σώματος, τὸ μὲν εἰς πλάτος [20] τὸ δ᾽ εἰς βάθος τὸ δ᾽ εἰς μῆκος.

Amplius haec omnia videntur divisiones esse corporis, hoc quidem ad latitudinem, hoc vero ad profunditatem, aliud ad longitudinem.

-Further, these are all evidently divisions of body,-one in breadth, another in depth, another in length.

πρὸς δὲ τούτοις ὁμοίως ἔνεστιν ἐν τῷ στερεῷ ὁποιονοῦν σχῆμα: ὥστ᾽ εἰ μηδ᾽ ἐν τῷ λίθῳ Ἑρμῆς, οὐδὲ τὸ ἥμισυ τοῦ κύβου ἐν τῷ κύβῳ οὕτως ὡς ἀφωρισμένον: οὐκ ἄρα οὐδ᾽ ἐπιφάνεια (εἰ γὰρ ὁποιαοῦν, κἂν αὕτη ἂν ἦν ἡ ἀφορίζουσα τὸ ἥμισυ), ὁ δ᾽ [25] αὐτὸς λόγος καὶ ἐπὶ γραμμῆς καὶ στιγμῆς καὶ μονάδος, ὥστ᾽ εἰ μάλιστα μὲν οὐσία τὸ σῶμα, τούτου δὲ μᾶλλον ταῦτα, μὴ ἔστι δὲ ταῦτα μηδὲ οὐσίαι τινές, διαφεύγει τί τὸ ὂν καὶ τίς ἡ οὐσία τῶν ὄντων.

Ad haec autem similiter inest in solido quaecumque figura. Quare si nec in lapide Mercurius, nec medietas cubi in cubo sic ut segregata; non igitur nec superficies. Nam si quaecumque, et utique haec erat determinans medietatem. eadem autem ratio est et in linea et in puncto et in unitate. quare si maxime quidem substantia est corpus, hoc autem magis haec, nec sunt autem haec nec substantiae alique, diffugit quid ipsum ens et quae substantia entium. Nam cum dictis et circa generationem et corruptionem accidunt irrationabilia.

Besides this, no sort of shape is present in the solid more than any other; so that if the Hermes is not in the stone, neither is the half of the cube in the cube as something determinate; therefore the surface is not in it either; for if any sort of surface were in it, the surface which marks off the half of the cube would be in it too. And the same account applies to the line and to the point and the unit. Therefore, if on the one hand body is in the highest degree substance, and on the other hand these things are so more than body, but these are not even instances of substance, it baffles us to say what being is and what the substance of things is.

πρὸς γὰρ τοῖς εἰρημένοις καὶ τὰ περὶ τὴν γένεσιν καὶ τὴν φθορὰν συμβαίνει ἄλογα. [30] δοκεῖ μὲν γὰρ ἡ οὐσία, ἐὰν μὴ οὖσα πρότερον νῦν ᾖ ἢ πρότερον οὖσα ὕστερον μὴ ᾖ, μετὰ τοῦ γίγνεσθαι καὶ φθείρεσθαι ταῦτα πάσχειν: τὰς δὲ στιγμὰς καὶ τὰς γραμμὰς καὶ τὰς ἐπιφανείας οὐκ ἐνδέχεται οὔτε γίγνεσθαι οὔτε φθείρεσθαι, ὁτὲ μὲν οὔσας ὁτὲ δὲ οὐκ οὔσας. ὅταν γὰρ ἅπτηται ἢ διαιρῆται τὰ σώματα, [1002β] [1] ἅμα ὁτὲ μὲν μία ἁπτομένων ὁτὲ δὲ δύο διαιρουμένων γίγνονται: ὥστ᾽ οὔτε συγκειμένων ἔστιν ἀλλ᾽ ἔφθαρται, διῃρημένων τε εἰσὶν αἱ πρότερον οὐκ οὖσαι (οὐ γὰρ δὴ ἥ γ᾽ ἀδιαίρετος στιγμὴ διῃρέθη εἰς δύο), εἴ τε γίγνονται καὶ [5] φθείρονται, ἐκ τίνος γίγνονται;

Videtur enim substantia non ens prius nunc esse aut prius existens posterius non, cum fieri et corrumpi haec pati; puncta vero et lineas et superficies non contingit neque fieri neque corrumpi, quandoque quidem existentes quandoque vero non existentes. Nam quando copulantur aut dividuntur corpora simul, quandoque quidem una copulatorum quandoque due divisorum fiunt; quare non compositorum est sed corruptum est, divisorumque sunt prius non existentes (non enim indivisibile punctum divisum est in duo). Et si generantur et corrumpuntur, ex aliquo generantur.

-For besides what has been said, the questions of generation and instruction confront us with further paradoxes. For if substance, not having existed before, now exists, or having existed before, afterwards does not exist, this change is thought to be accompanied by a process of becoming or perishing; but points and lines and surfaces cannot be in process either of becoming or of perishing, when they at one time exist and at another do not. For when bodies come into contact or [02b] are divided, their boundaries simultaneously become one in the one case when they touch, and two in the other-when they are divided; so that when they have been put together one boundary does not exist but has perished, and when they have been divided the boundaries exist which before did not exist (for it cannot be said that the point, which is indivisible, was divided into two). And if the boundaries come into being and cease to be, from what do they come into being?

παραπλησίως δ᾽ ἔχει καὶ περὶ τὸ νῦν τὸ ἐν τῷ χρόνῳ: οὐδὲ γὰρ τοῦτο ἐνδέχεται γίγνεσθαι καὶ φθείρεσθαι, ἀλλ᾽ ὅμως ἕτερον ἀεὶ δοκεῖ εἶναι, οὐκ οὐσία τις οὖσα. ὁμοίως δὲ δῆλον ὅτι ἔχει καὶ περὶ τὰς στιγμὰς καὶ τὰς γραμμὰς καὶ τὰ ἐπίπεδα: ὁ γὰρ [10] αὐτὸς λόγος: ἅπαντα γὰρ ὁμοίως ἢ πέρατα ἢ διαιρέσεις εἰσίν.

Similiter autem se habet circa nunc in tempore; non enim hoc contingit fieri et corrumpi, at tamen aliud videtur semper esse, non substantia aliqua existens. Similiter autem palam quia se habet et circa puncta et lineas et superficies; eadem enim ratio, nam omnia similiter aut termini aut divisiones sunt.

A similar account may also be given of the now in time; for this also cannot be in process of coming into being or of ceasing to be, but yet seems to be always different, which shows that it is not a substance. And evidently the same is true of points and lines and planes; for the same argument applies, since they are all alike either limits or divisions.

### Chapter 6

ὅλως δ᾽ ἀπορήσειεν ἄν τις διὰ τί καὶ δεῖ ζητεῖν ἄλλ᾽ ἄττα παρά τε τὰ αἰσθητὰ καὶ τὰ μεταξύ, οἷον ἃ τίθεμεν εἴδη.

Omnino vero dubitabit aliquis quare et oportet quaerere alia quaedam praeter sensibilia et intermedia, ut quas ponimus species.

In general one might raise the question why after all, besides perceptible things and the intermediates, we have to look for another class of things, i.e. the Forms which we posit.

εἰ γὰρ διὰ τοῦτο, ὅτι τὰ μὲν μαθηματικὰ [15] τῶν δεῦρο ἄλλῳ μέν τινι διαφέρει, τῷ δὲ πόλλ᾽ ἄττα ὁμοειδῆ εἶναι οὐθὲν διαφέρει, ὥστ᾽ οὐκ ἔσονται αὐτῶν αἱ ἀρχαὶ ἀριθμῷ ἀφωρισμέναι (ὥσπερ οὐδὲ τῶν ἐνταῦθα γραμμάτων ἀριθμῷ μὲν πάντων οὐκ εἰσὶν αἱ ἀρχαὶ ὡρισμέναι, εἴδει δέ, ἐὰν μὴ λαμβάνῃ τις τησδὶ τῆς συλλαβῆς [20] ἢ τησδὶ τῆς φωνῆς· τούτων δ᾽ ἔσονται καὶ ἀριθμῷ ὡρισμέναι— ὁμοίως δὲ καὶ ἐπὶ τῶν μεταξύ· ἄπειρα γὰρ κἀκεῖ τὰ ὁμοειδῆ), ὥστ᾽ εἰ μὴ ἔστι παρὰ τὰ αἰσθητὰ καὶ τὰ μαθηματικὰ ἕτερ᾽ ἄττα οἷα λέγουσι τὰ εἴδη τινές, οὐκ ἔσται μία ἀριθμῷ ἀλλ᾽ εἴδει οὐσία, οὐδ᾽ αἱ ἀρχαὶ τῶν [25] ὄντων ἀριθμῷ ἔσονται ποσαί τινες ἀλλὰ εἴδει· εἰ οὖν τοῦτο ἀναγκαῖον, καὶ τὰ εἴδη ἀναγκαῖον διὰ τοῦτο εἶναι τιθέναι. καὶ γὰρ εἰ μὴ καλῶς διαρθροῦσιν οἱ λέγοντες, ἀλλ᾽ ἔστι γε τοῦθ᾽ ὃ βούλονται, καὶ ἀνάγκη ταῦτα λέγειν αὐτοῖς, ὅτι τῶν εἰδῶν οὐσία τις ἕκαστόν ἐστι καὶ οὐθὲν κατὰ συμβεβηκός.

Nam si ideo, quia mathematica a presentibus in alio quodam differunt, in esse vero plura similis speciei nihil differunt. Quare non erunt ipsorum principia numero determinata, quemadmodum nec presentium litterarum numero quidem omnium non sunt principia determinata sed specie, si non lateat quis huius sillabe aut huius vocis, harum enim erunt et numero determinata. Similiter autem et in intermediis; infinita namque et illic quae eiusdem speciei. Quare si non sunt praeter sensibilia et mathematica alia quaedam qualia dicunt species ipsas quidam, non erit una numero et specie substantia, nec principia entium numero erunt quanta aliqua sed specie. Ergo si hoc est necessarium, et species necessarium est propter hoc esse. Et enim si non bene dearticulant dicentes, sed hoc est quod volunt, et necesse haec ipsos dicere, quia specierum substantia quaedam unumquodque est et nihil secundum accidens.

If it is for this reason, because the objects of mathematics, while they differ from the things in this world in some other respect, differ not at all in that there are many of the same kind, so that their first principles cannot be limited in number (just as the elements of all the language in this sensible world are not limited in number, but in kind, unless one takes the elements of this individual syllable or of this individual articulate sound-whose elements will be limited even in number; so is it also in the case of the intermediates; for there also the members of the same kind are infinite in number), so that if there are not-besides perceptible and mathematical objects-others such as some maintain the Forms to be, there will be no substance which is one in number, but only in kind, nor will the first principles of things be determinate in number, but only in kind:-if then this must be so, the Forms also must therefore be held to exist. Even if those who support this view do not express it articulately, still this is what they mean, and they must be maintaining the Forms just because each of the Forms is a substance and none is by accident.

ἀλλὰ μὴν εἴ γε θήσομεν τά τε εἴδη εἶναι καὶ ἐν ἀριθμῷ τὰς ἀρχὰς ἀλλὰ μὴ εἴδει, εἰρήκαμεν ἃ συμβαίνειν ἀναγκαῖον ἀδύνατα.

At vero si ponimus species esse et  numero principia et non specie, diximus quae contingere necesse est impossibilia.

But if we are to suppose both that the Forms exist and that the principles are one in number, not in kind, we have mentioned the impossible results that necessarily follow.

σύνεγγυς δὲ τούτων ἐστὶ τὸ διαπορῆσαι πότερον δυνάμει ἔστι τὰ στοιχεῖα ἢ τιν᾽ ἕτερον τρόπον.

Hiis autem affine est quaerere utrum potestate sunt elementa aut aliquo ajio modo.

(13) Closely connected with this is the question whether the elements exist potentially or in some other manner.

εἰ μὲν γὰρ ἄλλως πως, πρότερόν τι ἔσται τῶν ἀρχῶν ἄλλο (πρότερον [1003α] [1] γὰρ ἡ δύναμις ἐκείνης τῆς αἰτίας, τὸ δὲ δυνατὸν οὐκ ἀναγκαῖον ἐκείνως πᾶν ἔχειν):

Nam si aliter aliqualiter, prius aliquid  erit principiis aliud; prior enim  potestas causa illa, possibile autem non est necessarium illo modo omne se habere.

If in some other way, there will be something else prior to the first [03a] principles; for the potency is prior to the actual cause, and it is not necessary for everything potential to be actual.

εἰ δ᾽ ἔστι δυνάμει τὰ στοιχεῖα, ἐνδέχεται μηθὲν εἶναι τῶν ὄντων: δυνατὸν γὰρ εἶναι καὶ τὸ μήπω ὄν: γίγνεται μὲν γὰρ τὸ [5] μὴ ὄν, οὐθὲν δὲ γίγνεται τῶν εἶναι ἀδυνάτων.

Si vero potestate sunt elementa, nihil entium esse contingit. Nam possibile est esse et quod nondum ens; fit enim non ens, nihil autem fit impossibilium esse.

-But if the elements exist potentially, it is possible that everything that is should not be. For even that which is not yet is capable of being; for that which is not comes to be, but nothing that is incapable of being comes to be.

ταύτας τε οὖν τὰς ἀπορίας ἀναγκαῖον ἀπορῆσαι περὶ τῶν ἀρχῶν, καὶ πότερον καθόλου εἰσὶν ἢ ὡς λέγομεν τὰ καθ᾽ ἕκαστα.

Has igitur dubitationes necessarium est dubitare de principiis, et utrum universalia sint aut ut dicimus singularia.

(12) We must not only raise these questions about the first principles, but also ask whether they are universal or what we call individuals.

εἰ μὲν γὰρ καθόλου, οὐκ ἔσονται οὐσίαι (οὐθὲν γὰρ τῶν κοινῶν τόδε τι σημαίνει ἀλλὰ τοιόνδε, ἡ δ᾽ οὐσία τόδε τι:

Nam si universalia, non erunt substantiae; nihil enim communium hoc aliquid significat sed tale , substantia vero hoc aliquid est.

If they are universal, they will not be substances; for everything that is common indicates not a this but a such , but substance is a this .

δ᾽ [10] ἔσται τόδε τι καὶ ἓν θέσθαι τὸ κοινῇ κατηγορούμενον, πολλὰ ἔσται ζῷα ὁ Σωκράτης, αὐτός τε καὶ ὁ ἄνθρωπος καὶ τὸ ζῷον, εἴπερ σημαίνει ἕκαστον τόδε τι καὶ ἕν): εἰ μὲν οὖν καθόλου αἱ ἀρχαί, ταῦτα συμβαίνει:

Sed si est hoc aliquid et ponitur quod communiter predicatur, multa erit animalia Socrates, ipseque homo et animal, si significat singulum hoc aliquid et unum.

And if we are to be allowed to lay it down that a common predicate is a this and a single thing, Socrates will be several animals-himself and man and animal , if each of these indicates a this and a single thing.

εἰ δὲ μὴ καθόλου ἀλλ᾽ ὡς τὰ καθ᾽ ἕκαστα, οὐκ ἔσονται ἐπιστηταί (καθόλου [15] γὰρ ἡ ἐπιστήμη πάντων), ὥστ᾽ ἔσονται ἀρχαὶ ἕτεραι πρότεραι τῶν ἀρχῶν αἱ καθόλου κατηγορούμεναι, ἄνπερ μέλλῃ ἔσεσθαι αὐτῶν ἐπιστήμη.

Si igitur universalia sunt principia, haec contingunt. Si autem non universalia sed quasi singularia, non erunt scibilia; universales enim sunt omnium scientie. Quare erunt principia diversa priora principiis universaliter predicata, si futura est esse eorum scientia.

If, then, the principles are universals, these universal. Therefore if there is to be results follow; if they are not universals but of knowledge of the principles there must be the nature of individuals, they will not be other principles prior to them, namely those knowable; for the knowledge of anything is that are universally predicated of them.

# METHAPHISICE ARISTOTILIS LIBER QUARTUS

4 (G)

[1003α] [21] ἔστιν ἐπιστήμη τις ἣ θεωρεῖ τὸ ὂν ᾗ ὂν καὶ τὰ τούτῳ ὑπάρχοντα καθ᾿ αὑτό.

Est scientia quaedam quae speculatur ens in quantum est ens et quae huic insunt secundum se.

THERE is a science which investigates being as being and the attributes which belong to this in virtue of its own nature.

αὕτη δ᾿ ἐστὶν οὐδεμιᾷ τῶν ἐν μέρει λεγομένων ἡ αὐτή: οὐδεμία γὰρ τῶν ἄλλων ἐπισκοπεῖ καθόλου περὶ τοῦ ὄντος ᾗ ὄν, ἀλλὰ μέρος αὐτοῦ τι ἀποτεμόμεναι [25] περὶ τούτου θεωροῦσι τὸ συμβεβηκός, οἷον αἱ μαθηματικαὶ τῶν ἐπιστημῶν.

Haec autem nulli in parte dictarum eadem; aliarum enim nulla intendit universaliter de ente in quantum est ens. Verum partem eius abscindentes aliquam circa hanc speculantur accidens, velut scientiarum mathematice.

Now this is not the same as any of the so-called special sciences; for none of these others treats universally of being as being. They cut off a part of being and investigate the attribute of this part; this is what the mathematical sciences for instance do.

ἐπεὶ δὲ τὰς ἀρχὰς καὶ τὰς ἀκροτάτας αἰτίας ζητοῦμεν, δῆλον ὡς φύσεώς τινος αὐτὰς ἀναγκαῖον εἶναι καθ᾿ αὑτήν. εἰ οὖν καὶ οἱ τὰ στοιχεῖα τῶν ὄντων ζητοῦντες ταύτας τὰς ἀρχὰς ἐζήτουν, ἀνάγκη καὶ τὰ [30] στοιχεῖα τοῦ ὄντος εἶναι μὴ κατὰ συμβεβηκὸς ἀλλ᾿ ᾗ ὄν: διὸ καὶ ἡμῖν τοῦ ὄντος ᾗ ὂν τὰς πρώτας αἰτίας ληπτέον.

Quoniam autem principia et extremas quaerimus causas, palam quia naturae cuiusdam ipsas secundum se esse est necesse. Si ergo et entium elementa quaerentes haec quesierunt principia, necesse et entis elementa esse non secundum accidens sed in quantum entia. Unde et nobis entis in quantum est ens prime cause sunt accipiende.

Now since we are seeking the first principles and the highest causes, clearly there must be some thing to which these belong in virtue of its own nature. If then those who sought the elements of existing things were seeking these same principles, it is necessary that the elements must be elements of being not by accident but just because it is being. Therefore it is of being as being that we also must grasp the first causes.

*Chapter* 2

τὸ δὲ ὂν λέγεται μὲν πολλαχῶς, ἀλλὰ πρὸς ἓν καὶ μίαν τινὰ φύσιν καὶ οὐχ ὁμωνύμως ἀλλ᾽ ὥσπερ καὶ τὸ [35] ὑγιεινὸν ἅπαν πρὸς ὑγίειαν, τὸ μὲν τῷ φυλάττειν τὸ δὲ τῷ ποιεῖν τὸ δὲ τῷ σημεῖον εἶναι τῆς ὑγιείας τὸ δ᾽ ὅτι δεκτικὸν αὐτῆς, [1003β] [1] καὶ τὸ ἰατρικὸν πρὸς ἰατρικήν (τὸ μὲν γὰρ τῷ ἔχειν ἰατρικὴν λέγεται ἰατρικὸν τὸ δὲ τῷ εὐφυὲς εἶναι πρὸς αὐτὴν τὸ δὲ τῷ ἔργον εἶναι τῆς ἰατρικῆς), ὁμοιοτρόπως δὲ καὶ ἄλλα ληψόμεθα λεγόμενα τούτοις, [5] οὕτω δὲ καὶ τὸ ὂν λέγεται πολλαχῶς μὲν ἀλλ᾽ ἅπαν πρὸς μίαν ἀρχήν: τὰ μὲν γὰρ ὅτι οὐσίαι, ὄντα λέγεται, τὰ δ᾽ ὅτι πάθη οὐσίας, τὰ δ᾽ ὅτι ὁδὸς εἰς οὐσίαν ἢ φθοραὶ ἢ στερήσεις ἢ ποιότητες ἢ ποιητικὰ ἢ γεννητικὰ οὐσίας ἢ τῶν πρὸς τὴν οὐσίαν λεγομένων, ἢ τούτων τινὸς [10] ἀποφάσεις ἢ οὐσίας: διὸ καὶ τὸ μὴ ὂν εἶναι μὴ ὂν φαμεν.

Ens autem multis quidem dicitur modis, sed ad unum et ad unam aliquam naturam et non equivoce. Sed quemadmodum salubre omne ad sanitatem, hoc quidem in conservatione, aliud vero in actione, aliud quia est signum sanitatis, hoc autem quia illius est susceptibile. Et medicinale ad medicativam, hoc enim in habendo medicativam dicitur medicinale, illud vero in existendo bene natum ad ipsam, et aliud per esse opus medicative. Similiter autem et alia sumemus hiis dicta. ita vero et ens multipliciter dicitur quidem, sed omne ad unum principium. Haec enim quia substantiae, entia dicuntur, illa vero quia passiones substantiae, alia quia via ad substantiam, aut corruptiones aut privationes aut qualitates, aut effectiva aut generativa substantiae, aut ad substantiam dictorum, aut horum cuiusdam negationes aut substantiae. Quapropter et non ens esse non ens dicimus.

There are many senses in which a thing may be said to be, but all that is is related to one central point, one definite kind of thing, and is not said to be by a mere ambiguity. Everything which is healthy is related to health, one thing in the sense that it preserves health, another in the sense that it produces it, another in the sense that it is a symptom of health, another because it is [03b] capable of it. And that which is medical is relative to the medical art, one thing being called medical because it possesses it, another because it is naturally adapted to it, another because it is a function of the medical art. And we shall find other words used similarly to these. So, too, there are many senses in which a thing is said to be, but all refer to one starting-point; some things are said to be because they are substances, others because they are affections of substance, others because they are a process towards substance, or destructions or privations or qualities of substance, or productive or generative of substance, or of things which are relative to substance, or negations of one of these thing of substance itself. It is for this reason that we say even of non-being that it is nonbeing.

καθάπερ οὖν καὶ τῶν ὑγιεινῶν ἁπάντων μία ἐπιστήμη ἔστιν, ὁμοίως τοῦτο καὶ ἐπὶ τῶν ἄλλων. οὐ γὰρ μόνον τῶν καθ᾽ ἓν λεγομένων ἐπιστήμης ἐστὶ θεωρῆσαι μιᾶς ἀλλὰ καὶ τῶν πρὸς μίαν λεγομένων φύσιν· καὶ γὰρ ταῦτα τρόπον τινὰ [15] λέγονται καθ᾽ ἕν. δῆλον οὖν ὅτι καὶ τὰ ὄντα μιᾶς θεωρῆσαι ᾗ ὄντα.

Quemadmodum ergo et salubrium omnium una est scientia, ita hoc et in aliis. Non enim solum eorum quae secundum unum dictorum est unius scientie speculari, sed et dictorum ad unam naturam; et enim haec modo  quodam secundum unum dicuntur.

As, then, there is one science which deals with all healthy things, the same applies in the other cases also. For not only in the case of things which have one common notion does the investigation belong to one science, but also in the case of things which are related to one common nature; for even these in a sense have one common notion.

πανταχοῦ δὲ κυρίως τοῦ πρώτου ἡ ἐπιστήμη, καὶ ἐξ οὗ τὰ ἄλλα ἤρτηται, καὶ δι᾽ ὃ λέγονται. εἰ οὖν τοῦτ᾽ ἐστὶν ἡ οὐσία, τῶν οὐσιῶν ἂν δέοι τὰς ἀρχὰς καὶ τὰς αἰτίας ἔχειν τὸν φιλόσοφον.

Palam ergo quia et entia unius est speculari in quantum entia. Ubique vero proprie primi est scientia, et ex quo alia pendent et propter quod dicuntur. Ergo si hoc est substantia, substantiarum oportet principia et causas habere philosophum .

It is clear then that it is the work of one science also to study the things that are, qua being. But everywhere science deals chiefly with that which is primary, and on which the other things depend, and in virtue of which they get their names. If, then, this is substance, it will be of substances that the philosopher must grasp the principles and the causes.

ἅπαντος δὲ γένους καὶ αἴσθησις μία ἑνὸς [20] καὶ ἐπιστήμη, οἷον γραμματικὴ μία οὖσα πάσας θεωρεῖ τὰς φωνάς· διὸ καὶ τοῦ ὄντος ᾗ ὂν ὅσα εἴδη θεωρῆσαι μιᾶς ἐστὶν ἐπιστήμης τῷ γένει, τά τε εἴδη τῶν εἰδῶν.

Omnis autem generis et sensus unus unius et scientia; ut gramatica una ens omnes speculatur voces. Quapropter et entis in quantum ens quascumque species speculari unius est scientie genere, species autem specierum.

Now for each one class of things, as there is one perception, so there is one science, as for instance grammar, being one science, investigates all articulate sounds. Hence to investigate all the species of being qua being is the work of a science which is generically one, and to investigate the several species is the work of the specific parts of the science.

εἰ δὴ τὸ ὂν καὶ τὸ ἓν ταὐτὸν καὶ μία φύσις τῷ ἀκολουθεῖν ἀλλήλοις ὥσπερ ἀρχὴ καὶ αἴτιον, ἀλλ᾽ οὐχ ὡς ἑνὶ λόγῳ δηλούμενα [25] (διαφέρει δὲ οὐθὲν οὐδ᾽ ἂν ὁμοίως ὑπολάβωμεν, ἀλλὰ καὶ πρὸ ἔργου μᾶλλον):

Si igitur ens et unum idem et una natura eo quod se ad invicem consequuntur sicut principium et causa, sed non ut una ratione ostensa (nil autem differt nec si similiter suscipiamus, sed et pre opere magis).

If, now, being and unity are the same and are one thing in the sense that they are implied in one another as principle and cause are, not in the sense that they are explained by the same definition (though it makes no difference even if we suppose them to be like that-in fact this would even strengthen our case);

ταὐτὸ γὰρ εἷς ἄνθρωπος καὶ ἄνθρωπος, [27] καὶ ὢν ἄνθρωπος καὶ ἄνθρωπος, καὶ οὐχ ἕτερόν τι δηλοῖ κατὰ τὴν λέξιν ἐπαναδιπλούμενον τὸ εἷς ἄνθρωπος καὶ εἷς ὢν ἄνθρωπος (δῆλον δ᾽ ὅτι οὐ χωρίζεται οὔτ᾽ ἐπὶ γενέσεως οὔτ᾽ [30] ἐπὶ φθορᾶς), ὁμοίως δὲ καὶ ἐπὶ τοῦ ἑνός, ὥστε φανερὸν ὅτι ἡ πρόσθεσις ἐν τούτοις ταὐτὸ δηλοῖ, καὶ οὐδὲν ἕτερον τὸ ἓν παρὰ τὸ ὄν,

Idem enim unus homo et homo, et ens homo et homo, et non diversum aliquid ostendit secundum dictionem repetitam 'est homo et homo et unus homo'; palam autem quia non separatur nec in generatione nec in corruptione. Similiter autem et in uno, quare palam quia additio in hiis idem ostendit, et nihil aliud unum praeter ens.

for one man and man are the same thing, and so are existent man and man, and the doubling of the words in one man and one existent man does not express anything different (it is clear that the two things are not separated either in coming to be or in ceasing to be); and similarly one existent man adds nothing to existent man, and that it is obvious that the addition in these cases means the same thing, and unity is nothing apart from being;

ἔτι δ᾽ ἡ ἑκάστου οὐσία ἕν ἐστιν οὐ κατὰ συμβεβηκός, ὁμοίως δὲ καὶ ὅπερ ὄν τι:

Amplius autem cuiusque substantia unum est non secundum accidens, similiter autem et quod quidem ens aliquid.

and if, further, the substance of each thing is one in no merely accidental way, and similarly is from its very nature something that is:

ὥσθ᾽ ὅσα περ τοῦ ἑνὸς εἴδη, τοσαῦτα καὶ τοῦ ὄντος· περὶ ὧν τὸ τί ἐστι τῆς [35] αὐτῆς ἐπιστήμης τῷ γένει θεωρῆσαι, λέγω δ᾽ οἷον περὶ ταὐτοῦ καὶ ὁμοίου καὶ τῶν ἄλλων τῶν τοιούτων. σχεδὸν δὲ πάντα ἀνάγεται τἀναντία εἰς τὴν ἀρχὴν ταύτην· [1004α] [1] τεθεωρήσθω δ᾽ ἡμῖν ταῦτα ἐν τῇ ἐκλογῇ τῶν ἐναντίων.

Quare quotcumque unius sunt species, tot et entis. De quibus quod quid est eiusdem scientie genere speculari. Dico autem ut de eodem et simili et aliis talibus. Fere autem omnia reducuntur contraria in principium hoc; speculata sunt autem a nobis haec in ecloga contrariorum.

All this being so, there must be exactly as many species of being as of unity. And to investigate the essence of these is the work of a science which is generically one-I mean, for instance, the discussion of the same and the similar and the other concepts of this sort; and nearly all contraries may be referred [04a] to this origin; let us take them as having been investigated in the Selection of Contraries.

καὶ τοσαῦτα μέρη φιλοσοφίας ἔστιν ὅσαι περ αἱ οὐσίαι· ὥστε ἀναγκαῖον εἶναί τινα πρώτην καὶ ἐχομένην αὐτῶν. ὑπάρχει [5] γὰρ εὐθὺς γένη ἔχον τὸ ὂν [καὶ τὸ ἕν]· διὸ καὶ αἱ ἐπιστῆμαι ἀκολουθήσουσι τούτοις. ἔστι γὰρ ὁ φιλόσοφος ὥσπερ ὁ μαθηματικὸς λεγόμενος· καὶ γὰρ αὕτη ἔχει μέρη, καὶ πρώτη τις καὶ δευτέρα ἔστιν ἐπιστήμη καὶ ἄλλαι ἐφεξῆς ἐν τοῖς μαθήμασιν.

Et tot partes sunt philosophiae quot substantiae, quare necessarium esse aliquam primam et habitam ipsis. Existunt enim statim genera habentia ens et unum; quapropter et scientie haec sequuntur. Est enim philosophus ut mathematicus dictus; et enim haec partes habet, et prima quaedam et secunda est scientia et aliae consequenter in mathematibus.

And there are as many parts of philosophy as there are kinds of substance, so that there must necessarily be among them a first philosophy and one which follows this. For being falls immediately into genera; for which reason the sciences too will correspond to these genera. For the philosopher is like the mathematician, as that word is used; for mathematics also has parts, and there is a first and a second science and other successive ones within the sphere of mathematics.

ἐπεὶ δὲ μιᾶς τἀντικείμενα [10] θεωρῆσαι, τῷ δὲ ἑνὶ ἀντίκειται πλῆθος— ἀπόφασιν δὲ καὶ στέρησιν μιᾶς ἐστι θεωρῆσαι διὰ τὸ ἀμφοτέρως θεωρεῖσθαι τὸ ἓν οὗ ἡ ἀπόφασις ἢ ἡ στέρησις (ἢ <γὰρ ἁπλῶς λέγομεν ὅτι οὐχ ὑπάρχει ἐκεῖνο, ἤ τινι γένει· ἔνθα μὲν οὖν τῷ ἑνὶ ἡ διαφορὰ πρόσεστι παρὰ τὸ ἐν τῇ ἀποφάσει, ἀπουσία γὰρ [15] ἡ ἀπόφασις ἐκείνου ἐστίν, ἐν δὲ τῇ στερήσει καὶ ὑποκειμένη τις φύσις γίγνεται καθ᾽ ἧς λέγεται ἡ στέρησις)

Quoniam autem unius est opposita speculari, uni autem opponitur pluralitas, negationem autem et privationem unius est speculari propter utroque modo speculari unum cuius negatio aut privatio, aut simpliciter dicta quia non inest illi aut alicui generi; hic quidem igitur uni differentia adest praeter quod in negatione, illius enim absentia negatio est, in privatione vero et subiecta quaedam fit natura de qua dicitur privatio.

Now since it is the work of one science to investigate opposites, and plurality is opposed to unity-and it belongs to one science to investigate the negation and the privation because in both cases we are really investigating the one thing of which the negation or the privation is a negation or privation (for we either say simply that that thing is not present, or that it is not present in some particular class; in the latter case difference is present over and above what is implied in negation; for negation means just the absence of the thing in question, while in privation there is also employed an underlying nature of which the privation is asserted):

[τῷ δ᾽ ἑνὶ πλῆθος ἀντίκειται]—ὥστε καὶ τἀντικείμενα τοῖς εἰρημένοις, τό τε ἕτερον καὶ ἀνόμοιον καὶ ἄνισον καὶ ὅσα ἄλλα λέγεται ἢ κατὰ ταῦτα ἢ κατὰ πλῆθος καὶ τὸ ἕν, [20] τῆς εἰρημένης γνωρίζειν ἐπιστήμης· ὧν ἐστι καὶ ἡ ἐναντιότης· διαφορὰ γάρ τις ἡ ἐναντιότης, ἡ δὲ διαφορὰ ἑτερότης.

Uni autem pluralitas opponitur, quare et opposita dictis, diversumque et dissimile et inequale et quaecumque alia dicuntur aut secundum eadem aut secundum pluralitatem et unum, est dicte cognoscere scientie. Quorum unum quidem aliquid et contrarietas est; differentia enim quaedam contrarietas est, differentia autem diversitas.

-in view of all these facts, the contraries of the concepts we named above, the other and the dissimilar and the unequal, and everything else which is derived either from these or from plurality and unity, must fall within the province of the science above named. And contrariety is one of these concepts; for contrariety is a kind of difference, and difference is a kind of otherness.

ὥστ᾽ ἐπειδὴ πολλαχῶς τὸ ἐν λέγεται, καὶ ταῦτα πολλαχῶς μὲν λεχθήσεται, ὅμως δὲ μιᾶς ἅπαντά ἐστι γνωρίζειν· οὐ γὰρ εἰ πολλαχῶς, ἑτέρας, ἀλλ᾽ εἰ μήτε καθ᾽ ἐν μήτε [25] πρὸς ἐν οἱ λόγοι ἀναφέρονται. ἐπεὶ δὲ πάντα πρὸς τὸ πρῶτον ἀναφέρεται, οἷον ὅσα ἐν λέγεται πρὸς τὸ πρῶτον ἕν, ὡσαύτως φατέον καὶ περὶ ταὐτοῦ καὶ ἑτέρου καὶ τῶν ἐναντίων ἔχειν· ὥστε διελόμενον ποσαχῶς λέγεται ἕκαστον, οὕτως ἀποδοτέον πρὸς τὸ πρῶτον ἐν ἑκάστῃ κατηγορίᾳ πῶς πρὸς ἐκεῖνο

115

[30] λέγεται· τὰ μὲν γὰρ τῷ ἔχειν ἐκεῖνο τὰ δὲ τῷ ποιεῖν τὰ δὲ κατ᾽ ἄλλους λεχθήσεται τοιούτους τρόπους.

Quare quoniam unum multipliciter dicitur, et haec multipliciter quidem dicentur, at tamen unius omnia cognoscere est; non enim si multipliciter, alterius, sed si nec secundum unum nec ad unum rationes referuntur, alterius tunc. Quoniam vero omnia ad primum referuntur, ut quaecumque unum dicuntur ad primum unum, similiter dicendum est et de eodem et de diverso et contrariis se habere. Ergo divisum quotiens dicitur singulum, sic reddendum est ad primum in singulis predicamentis quomodo ad illud dicitur; haec enim in habendo illud, illa vero in faciendo, alia vero secundum alios dicentur tales modos.

Therefore, since there are many senses in which a thing is said to be one, these terms also will have many senses, but yet it belongs to one science to know them all; for a term belongs to different sciences not if it has different senses, but if it has not one meaning and its definitions cannot be referred to one central meaning. And since all things are referred to that which is primary, as for instance all things which are called one are referred to the primary one, we must say that this holds good also of the same and the other and of contraries in general; so that after distinguishing the various senses of each, we must then explain by reference to what is primary in the case of each of the predicates in question, saying how they are related to it; for some will be called what they are called because they possess it, others because they produce it, and others in other such ways.

φανερὸν οὖν [ὅπερ ἐν ταῖς ἀπορίαις ἐλέχθη] ὅτι μιᾶς περὶ τούτων καὶ τῆς οὐσίας ἐστὶ λόγον ἔχειν (τοῦτο δ᾽ ἦν ἓν τῶν ἐν τοῖς ἀπορήμασιν),

Palam ergo, quod in dubitationibus dictum est, quia unius est de hiis et de substantia sermonem habere; hoc autem erat unum eorum quae in dubitationibus.

It is evident, then, that it belongs to one science to be able to give an account of these concepts as well as of substance (this was one of the questions in our book of problems),

καὶ ἔστι τοῦ φιλοσόφου περὶ πάντων δύνασθαι θεωρεῖν. [1004β] [1] εἰ γὰρ μὴ τοῦ φιλοσόφου, τίς ἔσται ὁ ἐπισκεψόμενος εἰ ταὐτὸ Σωκράτης καὶ Σωκράτης καθήμενος, ἢ εἰ ἓν ἑνὶ ἐναντίον, ἢ τί ἐστι τὸ ἐναντίον ἢ ποσαχῶς λέγεται; ὁμοίως δὲ καὶ περὶ τῶν ἄλλων τῶν τοιούτων. [5] ἐπεὶ οὖν τοῦ ἑνὸς ᾗ ἓν καὶ τοῦ ὄντος ᾗ ὂν ταῦτα καθ᾽ αὑτά ἐστι πάθη, ἀλλ᾽ οὐχ ᾗ ἀριθμοὶ ἢ γραμμαὶ ἢ πῦρ, δῆλον ὡς ἐκείνης τῆς ἐπιστήμης καὶ τί ἐστι γνωρίσαι καὶ τὰ συμβεβηκότ᾽ αὐτοῖς. καὶ οὐ ταύτῃ ἁμαρτάνουσιν οἱ περὶ αὐτῶν σκοπούμενοι ὡς οὐ φιλοσοφοῦντες, ἀλλ᾽ ὅτι πρότερον ἡ οὐσία, [10] περὶ ἧς οὐθὲν ἐπαΐουσιν, ἐπεὶ ὥσπερ ἔστι καὶ ἀριθμοῦ ᾗ ἀριθμὸς ἴδια πάθη, οἷον περιττότης ἀρτιότης, συμμετρία ἰσότης, ὑπεροχὴ ἔλλειψις, καὶ ταῦτα καὶ καθ᾽ αὑτοὺς καὶ πρὸς ἀλλήλους ὑπάρχει τοῖς ἀριθμοῖς (ὁμοίως δὲ καὶ στερεῷ καὶ ἀκινήτῳ καὶ κινουμένῳ ἀβαρεῖ τε καὶ βάρος [15] ἔχοντι ἔστιν ἕτερα ἴδια), οὕτω καὶ τῷ ὄντι ᾗ ὄν ἐστι τινὰ ἴδια, καὶ ταῦτ᾽ ἐστὶ περὶ ὧν τοῦ φιλοσόφου ἐπισκέψασθαι τὸ ἀληθές.

Et philosophi est de omnibus posse speculari. Nam si non philosophi, quis erit qui investigabit si idem Socrates et Socrates sedens, aut si unum uni contrarium, aut quid est contrarium aut quotiens dicitur? Similiter autem et de aliis talibus. quoniam ergo unius in quantum est unum et entis in quantum est ens eaedem secundum se passiones sunt, sed non in quantum numeri aut lineae aut ignis, palam quia illius scientie et quid sunt cognoscere et accidentia ipsis. Et non sic peccant qui de ipsis intendebant quasi non philosophantes, sed quia primum est substantia de qua nihil audiunt. Quoniam sicut sunt et numeri et in quantum numerus proprie passiones , ut imparitas paritas, commensuratio equalitas, excedentia defectio, et haec secundum se et ad invicem insunt numeris (similiter autem et solido et immobili et mobili et levi et gravi sunt alia propria), sic et enti in quantum est ens sunt quaedam propria, et ea sunt de quibus est philosophi perscrutari veritatem.

and that it is the function of the philosopher to be able to [04b] investigate all things. For if it is not the function of the philosopher, who is it who will inquire whether Socrates and Socrates seated are the same thing, or whether one thing has one contrary, or what contrariety is, or how many meanings it has? And similarly with all other such questions. Since, then, these are essential modifications of unity qua unity and of being qua being, not qua numbers or lines or fire, it is clear that it belongs to this science to investigate both the essence of these concepts and their properties. And those who study these properties err not by leaving the sphere of philosophy, but by forgetting that substance, of which they have no correct idea, is prior to these other things. For number qua number has peculiar attributes, such as oddness and evenness, commensurability and equality, excess and defect, and these belong to numbers either in themselves or in relation to one another. And similarly the solid and the motionless and that which is in motion and the weightless and that which has weight have other peculiar properties. So too there are certain properties peculiar to being as such, and it is about these that the philosopher has to investigate the truth.

σημεῖον δέ: οἱ γὰρ διαλεκτικοὶ καὶ σοφισταὶ τὸ αὐτὸ μὲν ὑποδύονται σχῆμα τῷ φιλοσόφῳ: ἡ γὰρ σοφιστικὴ φαινομένη μόνον σοφία ἐστί, καὶ οἱ διαλεκτικοὶ [20] διαλέγονται περὶ ἁπάντων, κοινὸν δὲ πᾶσι τὸ ὄν ἐστιν, διαλέγονται δὲ περὶ τούτων δῆλον ὅτι διὰ τὸ τῆς φιλοσοφίας ταῦτα εἶναι οἰκεῖα. περὶ μὲν γὰρ τὸ αὐτὸ γένος στρέφεται ἡ σοφιστικὴ καὶ ἡ διαλεκτικὴ τῇ φιλοσοφίᾳ,

Signum autem: dialetici namque et sophiste eandem subinduunt figuram philosopho, quia sophistica apparens solum est sophia, et dialetici de omnibus disputant; omnibus autem commune ens est. Disputant autem et de hiis, videlicet quia

philosophiae sunt ipsa propria. Nam circa idem genus versatur et sophistica et dialetica cum philosophia,

-An indication of this may be mentioned: dialecticians and sophists assume the same guise as the philosopher, for sophistic is Wisdom which exists only in semblance, and dialecticians embrace all things in their dialectic, and being is common to all things; but evidently their dialectic embraces these subjects because these are proper to philosophy.-For sophistic and dialectic turn on the same class of things as philosophy,

ἀλλὰ διαφέρει τῆς μὲν τῷ τρόπῳ τῆς δυνάμεως, τῆς δὲ τοῦ βίου [25] τῇ προαιρέσει· ἔστι δὲ ἡ διαλεκτικὴ πειραστικὴ περὶ ὧν ἡ φιλοσοφία γνωριστική, ἡ δὲ σοφιστικὴ φαινομένη, οὖσα δ᾽ οὔ.

sed differt ab hac quidem modo potestatis, ab illa vero vite proheresi. Est autem dialetica temptativa de quibus philosophia est sciens. Et sophistica visa quidem, ens vero non.

but this differs from dialectic in the nature of the faculty required and from sophistic in respect of the purpose of the philosophic life. Dialectic is merely critical where philosophy claims to know, and sophistic is what appears to be philosophy but is not.

ἔτι τῶν ἐναντίων ἡ ἑτέρα συστοιχία στέρησις, καὶ πάντα ἀνάγεται εἰς τὸ ὂν καὶ τὸ μὴ ὄν, καὶ εἰς ἓν καὶ πλῆθος, οἷον στάσις τοῦ ἑνὸς κίνησις δὲ τοῦ πλήθους·

Amplius contrariorum altera coelementatio privatio, et omnia referuntur ad ens et non ens et ad unum et pluralitatem, ut status unius et motus pluralitatis.

Again, in the list of contraries one of the two columns is privative, and all contraries are reducible to being and non-being, and to unity and plurality, as for instance rest belongs to unity and movement to plurality.

δ᾽ ὄντα καὶ τὴν [30] οὐσίαν ὁμολογοῦσιν ἐξ ἐναντίων σχεδὸν ἅπαντες συγκεῖσθαι· πάντες γοῦν τὰς ἀρχὰς ἐναντίας λέγουσιν· οἱ μὲν γὰρ περιττὸν καὶ ἄρτιον, οἱ δὲ θερμὸν καὶ ψυχρόν, οἱ δὲ πέρας καὶ ἄπειρον, οἱ δὲ φιλίαν καὶ νεῖκος.

Entia vero et substantiam confitentur ex contrariis fere omnes componi. Omnes enim principia contraria dicunt; hii namque par et impar, illi vero calidum et frigidum, alii finem et infinitum, alii amorem et odium.

And nearly all thinkers agree that being and substance are composed of contraries; at least all name contraries as their first principles-some name odd and even, some hot and cold, some limit and the unlimited, some love and strife.

πάντα δὲ καὶ τἆλλα ἀναγόμενα φαίνεται εἰς τὸ ἓν καὶ πλῆθος (εἰλήφθω γὰρ ἡ ἀναγωγὴ ἡμῖν), [1005a] [1] αἱ δ᾽ ἀρχαὶ καὶ παντελῶς αἱ παρὰ τῶν ἄλλων ὡς εἰς γένη ταῦτα πίπτουσιν.

Omnia vero et alia reducta videntur ad unum et pluralitatem. Sumatur enim ipsa reductio nobis. Principia vero et omnino quae ab aliis ut in genera haec cadunt.

And all the others as well are evidently reducible to unity and [05a] plurality (this reduction we must take for granted), and the principles stated by other thinkers fall entirely under these as their genera.

φανερὸν οὖν καὶ ἐκ τούτων ὅτι μιᾶς ἐπιστήμης τὸ ὂν ᾗ ὂν θεωρῆσαι. πάντα γὰρ ἢ ἐναντία ἢ ἐξ ἐναντίων, ἀρχαὶ δὲ τῶν ἐναντίων τὸ ἓν [5] καὶ πλῆθος. ταῦτα δὲ μιᾶς ἐπιστήμης, εἴτε καθ᾽ ἓν λέγεται εἴτε μή, ὥσπερ ἴσως ἔχει καὶ τἀληθές. ἀλλ᾽ ὅμως εἰ καὶ πολλαχῶς λέγεται τὸ ἕν, πρὸς τὸ πρῶτον τἆλλα λεχθήσεται καὶ τὰ ἐναντία ὁμοίως, [καὶ διὰ τοῦτο] καὶ εἰ μὴ ἔστι τὸ ὂν ἢ τὸ ἓν καθόλου καὶ ταὐτὸ ἐπὶ πάντων ἢ [10] χωριστόν, ὥσπερ ἴσως οὐκ ἔστιν ἀλλὰ τὰ μὲν πρὸς ἓν τὰ δὲ τῷ ἐφεξῆς.

Palam igitur et ex hiis quia unius est scientie ens in quantum ens speculari. Omnia namque aut contraria aut ex contrariis, principia vero contrariorum unum et pluralitas. Haec autem unius scientie, sive secundum unum dicuntur sive non, ut forsan habet veritas. At tamen et si multipliciter dicitur unum, ad primum alia dicuntur, et contraria similiter; et propter hoc et si non est ens aut unum universaliter et idem in omnibus aut separabile, ut forsan non est, sed haec quidem ad unum illa vero in eo quod consequenter.

It is obvious then from these considerations too that it belongs to one science to examine being qua being. For all things are either contraries or composed of contraries, and unity and plurality are the starting-points of all contraries. And these belong to one science, whether they have or have not one single meaning. Probably the truth is that they have not; yet even if one has several meanings, the other meanings will be related to the primary meaning (and similarly in the case of the contraries), even if being or unity is not a universal and the same in every instance or is not separable from the particular instances (as in fact it probably is not; the unity is in some cases that of common reference, in some cases that of serial succession).

διὰ τοῦτο οὐ τοῦ γεωμέτρου θεωρῆσαι τί τὸ ἐναντίον ἢ τέλειον ἢ ἓν ἢ ὂν ἢ ταὐτὸν ἢ ἕτερον, ἀλλ᾽ ἢ ἐξ ὑποθέσεως.

Et ideo non est geometre speculari quid contrarium aut perfectum aut unum aut ens aut idem aut diversum, nisi ex suppositione.

And for this reason it does not belong to the geometer to inquire what is contrariety or completeness or unity or being or the same or the other, but only to presuppose these concepts and reason from this starting-point.

ὅτι μὲν οὖν μιᾶς ἐπιστήμης τὸ ὂν ᾗ ὂν θεωρῆσαι καὶ τὰ ὑπάρχοντα αὐτῷ ᾗ ὄν, δῆλον, καὶ ὅτι [15] οὐ μόνον τῶν οὐσιῶν ἀλλὰ καὶ τῶν ὑπαρχόντων ἡ αὐτὴ θεωρητική, τῶν τε εἰρημένων καὶ περὶ προτέρου καὶ ὑστέρου, καὶ γένους καὶ εἴδους, καὶ ὅλου καὶ μέρους καὶ τῶν ἄλλων τῶν τοιούτων.

Quod quidem igitur unius est scientie ens in quantum est ens speculari et quae insunt ei in quantum est ens, manifestum, et quia non solum substantiarum sed et existentium eadem est theorica, et de dictis et de priore et posteriore, et genere et specie, et toto et parte et aliis talibus.

Obviously then it is the work of one science to examine being qua being, and the attributes which belong to it qua being, and the same science will examine not only substances but also their attributes, both those above named and the concepts prior and posterior, genus and species , whole and part, and the others of this sort.

## Chapter 3

λεκτέον δὲ πότερον μιᾶς ἢ ἑτέρας ἐπιστήμης περί τε [20] τῶν ἐν τοῖς μαθήμασι καλουμένων ἀξιωμάτων καὶ περὶ τῆς οὐσίας.

Dicendum autem utrum unius aut diverse scientie de vocatis in mathematibus dignitatibus et de substantia.

We must state whether it belongs to one or to different sciences to inquire into the truths which are in mathematics called axioms, and into substance.

φανερὸν δὴ ὅτι μιᾶς τε καὶ τῆς τοῦ φιλοσόφου καὶ ἡ περὶ τούτων ἐστὶ σκέψις:

Palam autem quia unius est et eius quae est philosophi quae de hiis perscrutatio.

Evidently, the inquiry into these also belongs to one science, and that the science of the philosopher;

ἅπασι γὰρ ὑπάρχει τοῖς οὖσιν ἀλλ᾽ οὐ γένει τινὶ χωρὶς ἰδίᾳ τῶν ἄλλων. καὶ χρῶνται μὲν πάντες, ὅτι τοῦ ὄντος ἐστὶν ᾗ ὄν, ἕκαστον δὲ τὸ γένος [25] ὄν: ἐπὶ τοσοῦτον δὲ χρῶνται ἐφ᾽ ὅσον αὐτοῖς ἱκανόν, τοῦτο δ᾽ ἐστὶν ὅσον ἐπέχει τὸ γένος περὶ οὗ φέρουσι τὰς ἀποδείξεις: ὥστ᾽ ἐπεὶ δῆλον ὅτι ᾗ ὄντα ὑπάρχει πᾶσι (τοῦτο γὰρ αὐτοῖς τὸ κοινόν), τοῦ περὶ τὸ ὂν ᾗ ὂν γνωρίζοντος καὶ περὶ τούτων ἐστὶν ἡ θεωρία.

Omnibus enim insunt existentibus, sed non generi alicui seorsum separatim ab aliis. Et utuntur omnes, quia entis sunt in quantum est ens; unumquodque autem genus   ens. In tantum vero utuntur in quantum eis sufficiens est; hoc autem est quantum continet genus de quo demonstrationes ferunt. Quare quoniam manifestum quod in quantum sunt entia insunt omnibus (hoc enim eis est commune), de ente  in quantum est ens cognoscentis et de hiis est speculatio.

for these truths hold good for everything that is, and not for some special genus apart from others. And all men use them, because they are true of being qua being and each genus has being. But men use them just so far as to satisfy their purposes; that is, as far as the genus to which their demonstrations refer extends. Therefore since these truths clearly hold good for all things qua being (for this is what is common to them), to him who studies being qua being belongs the inquiry into these as well.

διόπερ οὐθεὶς τῶν κατὰ μέρος ἐπισκοπούντων [30] ἐγχειρεῖ λέγειν τι περὶ αὐτῶν, εἰ ἀληθῆ ἢ μή, οὔτε γεωμέτρης οὔτ᾽ ἀριθμητικός,

Unde  nullus particulariter intendentium nititur dicere de eis aliquid, si vera aut non, nec geometra nec arismeticus.

And for this reason no one who is conducting a special inquiry tries to say anything about their truth or falsity,-neither the geometer nor the arithmetician.

ἀλλὰ τῶν φυσικῶν ἔνιοι, εἰκότως τοῦτο δρῶντες· μόνοι γὰρ ᾤοντο περί τε τῆς ὅλης φύσεως σκοπεῖν καὶ περὶ τοῦ ὄντος. ἐπεὶ δ᾽ ἔστιν ἔτι τοῦ φυσικοῦ τις ἀνωτέρω (ἓν γάρ τι γένος τοῦ ὄντος ἡ φύσις), [35] τοῦ καθόλου καὶ τοῦ περὶ τὴν πρώτην οὐσίαν θεωρητικοῦ καὶ ἡ περὶ τούτων ἂν εἴη σκέψις· [1005β] [1] ἔστι δὲ σοφία τις καὶ ἡ φυσική, ἀλλ᾽ οὐ πρώτη.

Sed phisicorum quidam, merito hoc facientes; soli namque putantur de tota natura intendere et de ente. Sed quoniam est adhuc phisico aliquis superior (unum enim aliquod genus est entis natura),   universalis et circa primam substantiam theorizantis et de hiis utique erit perscrutatio. Est autem sophia quaedam phisica, sed non prima.

Some natural philosophers indeed have done so, and their procedure was intelligible enough; for they thought that they alone were inquiring about the whole of nature and about being. But since there is one kind of thinker who is above even the natural philosopher (for nature is only one particular genus of being), the discussion of these truths also will belong to him whose inquiry is universal and deals with [05b] primary substance. Physics also is a kind of Wisdom, but it is not the first kind.

ὅσα δ' ἐγχειροῦσι τῶν λεγόντων τινὲς περὶ τῆς ἀληθείας ὃν τρόπον δεῖ ἀποδέχεσθαι, δι' ἀπαιδευσίαν [4] τῶν ἀναλυτικῶν τοῦτο δρῶσιν· δεῖ γὰρ περὶ τούτων [5] ἥκειν προεπισταμένους ἀλλὰ μὴ ἀκούοντας ζητεῖν.

Quaecumque vero conantur  dicentium quidam de veritate quo oportet modo recipere, propter ignorantiam analeticorum  hoc faciunt. Oportet enim de hiis prescientes venire sed non audientes quaerere.

-And the attempts of some of those who discuss the terms on which truth should be accepted, are due to a want of training in logic; for they should know these things already when they come to a special study, and not be inquiring into them while they are listening to lectures on it.

ὅτι μὲν οὖν τοῦ φιλοσόφου, καὶ τοῦ περὶ πάσης τῆς οὐσίας θεωροῦντος ᾗ πέφυκεν, καὶ περὶ τῶν συλλογιστικῶν ἀρχῶν ἐστιν ἐπισκέψασθαι, δῆλον·

Quod quidem igitur philosophi, et de omni substantia speculantis in quantum congruit, et de omnibus sillogisticis principiis est perscrutari, palam.

Evidently then it belongs to the philosopher, i.e. to him who is studying the nature of all substance, to inquire also into the principles of syllogism.

προσήκει δὲ τὸν μάλιστα γνωρίζοντα περὶ ἕκαστον γένος ἔχειν λέγειν τὰς βεβαιοτάτας ἀρχὰς [10] τοῦ πράγματος, ὥστε καὶ τὸν περὶ τῶν ὄντων ᾗ ὄντα τὰς πάντων βεβαιοτάτας. ἔστι δ' οὗτος ὁ φιλόσοφος.

Congruit autem maxime cognoscentem circa unumquodque genus habere dicere firmissima rei  principia, quare et de entibus in quantum sunt entia omnium firmissima. Est autem hic philosophus ipse.

But he who knows best about each genus must be able to state the most certain principles of his subject, so that he whose subject is existing things qua existing must be able to state the most certain principles of all things. This is the philosopher,

βεβαιοτάτη δ' ἀρχὴ πασῶν περὶ ἣν διαψευσθῆναι ἀδύνατον· γνωριμωτάτην τε γὰρ ἀναγκαῖον εἶναι τὴν τοιαύτην (περὶ γὰρ ἃ μὴ γνωρίζουσιν ἀπατῶνται πάντες) καὶ ἀνυπόθετον. [15] ἣν γὰρ ἀναγκαῖον ἔχειν τὸν ὁτιοῦν ξυνιέντα τῶν ὄντων, τοῦτο οὐχ ὑπόθεσις· ὃ δὲ γνωρίζειν ἀναγκαῖον τῷ ὁτιοῦν γνωρίζοντι, καὶ ἥκειν ἔχοντα ἀναγκαῖον. ὅτι μὲν οὖν βεβαιοτάτη ἡ τοιαύτη πασῶν ἀρχή, δῆλον·

Firmissimum autem omnium principium est circa quod mentiri impossibile est; notissimum enim esse tale est necesse (nam circa ea quae ignorant decipiuntur omnes), et non condicionale. Quod enim  necessarium habere quodcumque entium intelligentem, hoc non condicio; quod autem cognoscere est necessarium quodcumque

cognoscentem, et venire habentem est necesse. Quod quidem igitur tale principium omnium est firmissimum, palam.

and the most certain principle of all is that regarding which it is impossible to be mistaken; for such a principle must be both the best known (for all men may be mistaken about things which they do not know), and non-hypothetical. For a principle which every one must have who understands anything that is, is not a hypothesis; and that which every one must know who knows anything, he must already have when he comes to a special study. Evidently then such a principle is the most certain of all;

τίς δ᾽ ἔστιν αὕτη, μετὰ ταῦτα λέγωμεν. τὸ γὰρ αὐτὸ ἅμα ὑπάρχειν τε καὶ μὴ [20] ὑπάρχειν ἀδύνατον τῷ αὐτῷ καὶ κατὰ τὸ αὐτό (καὶ ὅσα ἄλλα προσδιορισαίμεθ᾽ ἄν, ἔστω προσδιωρισμένα πρὸς τὰς λογικὰς δυσχερείας): αὕτη δὴ πασῶν ἐστὶ βεβαιοτάτη τῶν ἀρχῶν: ἔχει γὰρ τὸν εἰρημένον διορισμόν. ἀδύνατον γὰρ ὁντινοῦν ταὐτὸν ὑπολαμβάνειν εἶναι καὶ μὴ εἶναι, καθάπερ [25] τινὲς οἴονται λέγειν Ἡράκλειτον. οὐκ ἔστι γὰρ ἀναγκαῖον, ἅ τις λέγει, ταῦτα καὶ ὑπολαμβάνειν: εἰ δὲ μὴ ἐνδέχεται ἅμα ὑπάρχειν τῷ αὐτῷ τἀναντία (προσδιωρίσθω δ᾽ ἡμῖν καὶ ταύτῃ τῇ προτάσει τὰ εἰωθότα), ἐναντία δ᾽ ἐστὶ δόξα δόξῃ ἡ τῆς ἀντιφάσεως, φανερὸν ὅτι ἀδύνατον ἅμα [30] ὑπολαμβάνειν τὸν αὐτὸν εἶναι καὶ μὴ εἶναι τὸ αὐτό: ἅμα γὰρ ἂν ἔχοι τὰς ἐναντίας δόξας ὁ διεψευσμένος περὶ τούτου. διὸ πάντες οἱ ἀποδεικνύντες εἰς ταύτην ἀνάγουσιν ἐσχάτην δόξαν: φύσει γὰρ ἀρχὴ καὶ τῶν ἄλλων ἀξιωμάτων αὕτη πάντων. [35]

Quid vero sit illud, post haec dicamus. Idem enim simul inesse et non inesse eidem et secundum idem est impossibile; et quaecumquae alia determinaremus utique, sint determinata ad logicas difficultates. Hoc autem omnium firmissimum est principiorum; habet enim dictam determinationem. Impossibile namque quemcumque idem existimare esse et non esse, quemadmodum quidam putant dicere Eraclitum. Non enim est necesse, quae aliquis dicit, haec et existimare. Si vero non contingit simul inesse eidem contraria (addeterminata sint autem nobis et huic propositioni consueta), contraria vero est opinio opinioni quae contradictionis, palam quod impossibile simul existimare eundem esse et non esse idem; simul enim habebit contrarias opiniones qui de hoc est mentitus. Quapropter omnes demonstrantes in hanc reducunt ultimam opinionem; natura namque principium et aliarum dignitatum hoc omnium.

which principle this is, let us proceed to say. It is, that the same attribute cannot at the same time belong and not belong to the same subject and in the same respect; we must presuppose, to guard against dialectical objections, any further qualifications which might be added. This, then, is the most certain of all principles, since it answers to the definition given above. For it is impossible for any one to believe the same thing to be and not to be, as some think Heraclitus says. For what a man says, he does not necessarily believe; and if it is impossible that contrary attributes should belong at the same time to the same subject (the usual qualifications must be presupposed in this premiss too), and if an opinion which contradicts another is contrary to it, obviously it is impossible for the same man at the same time to believe the same thing to be and not to be; for if a man were mistaken on this point he would have contrary opinions at the same time. It is for this reason that all who are carrying out a demonstration reduce it to this as an ultimate belief; for this is naturally the starting-point even for all the other axioms.

### Chapter 4

εἰσὶ δέ τινες οἵ, καθάπερ εἴπομεν, αὐτοί τε ἐνδέχεσθαί φασι τὸ αὐτὸ εἶναι καὶ μὴ εἶναι, [1006α] [1] καὶ ὑπολαμβάνειν οὕτως. χρῶνται δὲ τῷ λόγῳ τούτῳ πολλοὶ καὶ τῶν περὶ φύσεως. ἡμεῖς δὲ νῦν εἰλήφαμεν ὡς ἀδυνάτου ὄντος ἅμα εἶναι καὶ μὴ εἶναι, καὶ διὰ τούτου ἐδείξαμεν ὅτι βεβαιοτάτη [5] αὕτη τῶν ἀρχῶν πασῶν.

Sunt autem quidam qui, ut diximus, dicebant contingere idem esse et non esse et existimare ita. Utuntur autem ratione hac multi eorum qui de natura. Nos autem nunc accepimus quasi impossibili existente simul esse et non esse; et per hoc ostendimus quod firmissimum hoc principiorum omnium est.

There are some who, as we said, both themselves assert that it is possible for the same thing to be and not to be, [06a] and say that people can judge this to be the case. And among others many writers about nature use this language. But we have now posited that it is impossible for anything at the same time to be and not to be, and by this means have shown that this is the most indisputable of all principles.

ἀξιοῦσι δὴ καὶ τοῦτο ἀποδεικνύναι τινὲς δι᾽ ἀπαιδευσίαν: ἔστι γὰρ ἀπαιδευσία τὸ μὴ γιγνώσκειν τίνων δεῖ ζητεῖν ἀπόδειξιν καὶ τίνων οὐ δεῖ: ὅλως μὲν γὰρ ἁπάντων ἀδύνατον ἀπόδειξιν εἶναι (εἰς ἄπειρον γὰρ ἂν βαδίζοι, ὥστε μηδ᾽ οὕτως εἶναι ἀπόδειξιν), [10] εἰ δέ τινων μὴ δεῖ ζητεῖν ἀπόδειξιν, τίνα ἀξιοῦσιν εἶναι μᾶλλον τοιαύτην ἀρχὴν οὐκ ἂν ἔχοιεν εἰπεῖν.

Volunt autem et hoc demonstrare quidam propter ineruditionem; est enim ineruditio non cognoscere quorum oportet quaerere demonstrationem et quorum non oportet. Totaliter quidem enim omnium esse demonstrationem est impossibile; nam in infinitum procederet, ut nec ita foret demonstratio. Si vero quorundam non oportet demonstrationem quaerere, quod volunt magis esse tale principium non habent dicere.

Some indeed demand that even this shall be demonstrated, but this they do through want of education, for not to know of what things one should demand demonstration, and of what one should not, argues want of education. For it is impossible that there should be demonstration of absolutely everything (there would be an infinite regress, so that there would still be no demonstration); but if there are things of which one should not demand demonstration, these persons could not say what principle they maintain to be more self-evident than the present one.

ἔστι δ᾽ ἀποδεῖξαι ἐλεγκτικῶς καὶ περὶ τούτου ὅτι ἀδύνατον, ἂν μόνον τι λέγῃ ὁ ἀμφισβητῶν· ἂν δὲ μηθέν, γελοῖον τὸ ζητεῖν λόγον πρὸς τὸν μηθενὸς ἔχοντα λόγον, ᾗ μὴ ἔχει· ὅμοιος [15] γὰρ φυτῷ ὁ τοιοῦτος ᾗ τοιοῦτος ἤδη. τὸ δ᾽ ἐλεγκτικῶς ἀποδεῖξαι λέγω διαφέρειν καὶ τὸ ἀποδεῖξαι, ὅτι ἀποδεικνύων μὲν ἂν δόξειεν αἰτεῖσθαι τὸ ἐν ἀρχῇ, ἄλλου δὲ τοῦ τοιούτου αἰτίου ὄντος ἔλεγχος ἂν εἴη καὶ οὐκ ἀπόδειξις.

p; quaerere rationem ad nullius habentem rationem, in quantum  non habet rationem. Similis enim plante talis in quantum talis iam est. Elenchice autem dico demonstrare differre et demonstrare, quia demonstrans quidem utique videbitur petere quod  in principio, sed nec tali existente causa elenchus utique erit et non demonstratio.

We can, however, demonstrate negatively even that this view is impossible, if our opponent will only say something; and if he says nothing, it is absurd to seek to give an account of our views to one who cannot give an account of anything, in so far as he cannot do so. For such a man, as such, is from the start no better than a vegetable. Now negative demonstration I distinguish from demonstration proper, because in a demonstration one might be thought to be begging the question, but if another person is responsible for the assumption we shall have negative proof, not demonstration.

ἀρχὴ δὲ πρὸς ἅπαντα τὰ τοιαῦτα οὐ τὸ ἀξιοῦν ἢ εἶναί τι λέγειν [20] ἢ μὴ εἶναι (τοῦτο μὲν γὰρ τάχ᾽ ἄν τις ὑπολάβοι τὸ ἐξ ἀρχῆς αἰτεῖν), ἀλλὰ σημαίνειν γέ τι καὶ αὑτῷ καὶ ἄλλῳ· τοῦτο γὰρ ἀνάγκη, εἴπερ λέγοι τι. εἰ γὰρ μή, οὐκ ἂν εἴη τῷ τοιούτῳ λόγος, οὔτ᾽ αὐτῷ πρὸς αὑτὸν οὔτε πρὸς ἄλλον. ἂν δέ τις τοῦτο διδῷ, ἔσται ἀπόδειξις· ἤδη γάρ τι [25] ἔσται ὡρισμένον. ἀλλ᾽ αἴτιος οὐχ ὁ ἀποδεικνὺς ἀλλ᾽ ὁ ὑπομένων· ἀναιρῶν γὰρ λόγον ὑπομένει λόγον. ἔτι δὲ ὁ τοῦτο συγχωρήσας συγκεχώρηκέ τι ἀληθὲς εἶναι χωρὶς ἀποδείξεως [ὥστε οὐκ ἂν πᾶν οὕτως καὶ οὐχ οὕτως ἔχοι].

Principium vero ad omnia talia non velle aut esse aliquid  dicere aut non esse (hoc enim forsan utique quis opinabitur quod a principio petere), sed significare quidem aliquid et ipsi et alii; hoc enim necesse est, si dicat aliquid. Si enim non, cum tali non utique erit sermo; nec ipsi ad se ipsum nec ad alium. Si quis autem hoc dederit, erit demonstratio; iam  enim aliquid erit diffinitum. Sed causa non demonstrans sed sustinens; interimens enim rationem sustinet rationem.

The starting-point for all such arguments is not the demand that our opponent shall say that something either is or is not (for this one might perhaps take to be a begging of the question), but that he shall say something which is significant both for himself and for another; for this is necessary, if he really is to say anything. For, if he means nothing, such a man will not be capable of reasoning, either with himself or with another. But if any one grants this, demonstration will be possible; for we shall already have something definite. The person responsible for the proof, however, is not he who demonstrates but he who listens; for while disowning reason he listens to reason. [1]

And again he who admits this has admitted that something is true apart from demonstration (so that not everything will be so and not so).

πρῶτον μὲν οὖν δῆλον ὡς τοῦτό γ᾽ αὐτὸ ἀληθές, ὅτι σημαίνει τὸ [30] ὄνομα τὸ εἶναι ἢ μὴ εἶναι τοδί, ὥστ᾽ οὐκ ἂν πᾶν οὕτως καὶ οὐχ οὕτως ἔχοι:

Primum quidem igitur manifestum quod hoc idem verum ,  quod significat nomen 'esse' aut 'non esse' hoc , quare non  utique omne sic et non sic se habebit.

First then this at least is obviously true, that the word be or not be has a definite meaning, so that not everything will be so and not so.

ἔτι εἰ τὸ ἄνθρωπος σημαίνει ἕν, ἔστω τοῦτο τὸ ζῷον δίπουν.

Amplius si homo significat unum, sit hoc animal bipes.

Again, if man has one meaning, let this be two-footed animal;

λέγω δὲ τὸ ἓν σημαίνειν τοῦτο: εἰ τοῦτ᾽ ἔστιν ἄνθρωπος, ἂν ᾖ τι ἄνθρωπος, τοῦτ᾽ ἔσται τὸ ἀνθρώπῳ εἶναι (διαφέρει δ᾽ οὐθὲν οὐδ᾽ εἰ πλείω τις φαίη σημαίνειν μόνον δὲ ὡρισμένα, [1006β] [1] τεθείη γὰρ ἂν ἐφ᾽ ἑκάστῳ λόγῳ ἕτερον ὄνομα: λέγω δ᾽ οἷον, εἰ μὴ φαίη τὸ ἄνθρωπος ἓν σημαίνειν, πολλὰ δέ, ὧν ἑνὸς μὲν εἷς λόγος τὸ ζῷον δίπουν, εἶεν δὲ καὶ ἕτεροι πλείους, ὡρισμένοι δὲ τὸν ἀριθμόν: [5] τεθείη γὰρ ἂν ἴδιον ὄνομα καθ᾽ ἕκαστον τὸν λόγον: εἰ δὲ μή [τεθείη], ἀλλ᾽ ἄπειρα σημαίνειν φαίη, φανερὸν ὅτι οὐκ ἂν εἴη λόγος: τὸ γὰρ μὴ ἓν σημαίνειν οὐθὲν σημαίνειν ἐστίν, μὴ σημαινόντων δὲ τῶν ὀνομάτων ἀνῄρηται τὸ διαλέγεσθαι πρὸς ἀλλήλους, κατὰ δὲ τὴν ἀλήθειαν καὶ πρὸς αὐτόν: [10] οὐθὲν γὰρ ἐνδέχεται νοεῖν μὴ νοοῦντα ἕν, εἰ δ᾽ ἐνδέχεται, τεθείη ἂν ὄνομα τούτῳ τῷ πράγματι ἕν).

Dico autem  unum significare hoc: si hoc est homo, si sit aliquid homo, hoc est homini esse. Nil autem differt nec si plura quis dicat significare, solum autem diffinita; ponetur enim utique in singulis  rationibus alterum nomen. Dico autem ut si non dicat hominem unum significare sed multa, quorum unius quidem una  ratio animal bipes; sunt autem et aliae plures, sed diffinite numero; ponetur enim utique proprium nomen secundum unamquamque rationem. Si autem non ponatur, sed infinita significare dicat, palam quia non utique erit ratio; nam non unum significare nihil significare est. Non significantibus autem nominibus aufertur ad invicem disputare, secundum veritatem autem et ad se ipsum. Nihil enim contingit intelligere nihil intelligentem unum; si autem contingit, ponatur huic rei nomen unum.

by having one meaning I understand this:-if man means X , then if A is a man X will be what being a man means for him. (It makes no difference even if one were to say a word has several meanings, if only they are limited in number; [06b] for to each definition there might be assigned a different word. For instance, we might say that man has not one meaning but several, one of which would have one definition, viz. two-footed animal, while there might be also several other definitions if only they were limited in number; for a peculiar name might be assigned to each of the definitions. If, however, they were not limited but one were to say that the word has an infinite number of meanings, obviously reasoning would be impossible; for not to have one meaning is to have no meaning, and if words have no meaning our reasoning with one another, and indeed with ourselves, has been annihilated; for it is impossible to think of anything if we do not think of one thing; but if this is possible, one name might be assigned to this thing.)

ἔστω δή, ὥσπερ ἐλέχθη κατ᾽ ἀρχάς, σημαῖνόν τι τὸ ὄνομα καὶ σημαῖνον ἕν:

Sit itaque, sicut a principio dictum est, significans aliquid nomen et significans unum.

Let it be assumed then, as was said at the beginning, that the name has a meaning and has one meaning;

οὐ δὴ ἐνδέχεται τὸ ἀνθρώπῳ εἶναι σημαίνειν ὅπερ ἀνθρώπῳ μὴ εἶναι, εἰ τὸ ἄνθρωπος σημαίνει μὴ μόνον καθ᾽ ἑνὸς [15] ἀλλὰ καὶ ἕν (οὐ γὰρ τοῦτο ἀξιοῦμεν τὸ ἓν σημαίνειν, τὸ καθ᾽ ἑνός, ἐπεὶ οὕτω γε κἂν τὸ μουσικὸν καὶ τὸ λευκὸν καὶ τὸ ἄνθρωπος ἓν ἐσήμαινεν, ὥστε ἓν ἅπαντα ἔσται: συνώνυμα γάρ).

Non itaque contingit homini esse significare quod quidem non esse homini, si homo significat non solum de uno sed et unum. Non enim hoc dignificamus unum significare quod de uno, quoniam sic utique musicum et album et homo unum significarent, quare unum omnia erunt; synonima namque.

it is impossible, then, that being a man should mean precisely not being a man, if man not only signifies something about one subject but also has one significance (for we do not identify having one significance with signifying something about one subject, since on that assumption even musical and white and man would have had one significance, so that all things would have been one; for they would all have had the same significance).

καὶ οὐκ ἔσται εἶναι καὶ μὴ εἶναι τὸ αὐτὸ ἀλλ᾽ ἢ καθ᾽ ὁμωνυμίαν, ὥσπερ ἂν εἰ ὃν ἡμεῖς ἄνθρωπον [20] καλοῦμεν, ἄλλοι μὴ ἄνθρωπον καλοῖεν: τὸ δ᾽ ἀπορούμενον οὐ τοῦτό ἐστιν, εἰ ἐνδέχεται τὸ αὐτὸ ἅμα εἶναι καὶ μὴ εἶναι ἄνθρωπον τὸ ὄνομα, ἀλλὰ τὸ πρᾶγμα.

Et non erit esse et non esse idem nisi secundum equivocationem, ut si quem nos hominem vocamus, alii non hominem vocent. Dubitatum vero non hoc est, si contingit simul idem esse et non esse hominem scilicet nomen, sed rem.

And it will not be possible to be and not to be the same thing, except in virtue of an ambiguity, just as if one whom we call man , others were to call not-man; but the point in question is not this, whether the same thing can at the same time be and not be a man in name, but whether it can in fact.

δὲ μὴ σημαίνει ἕτερον τὸ ἄνθρωπος καὶ τὸ μὴ ἄνθρωπος, δῆλον ὅτι καὶ τὸ μὴ εἶναι ἀνθρώπῳ τοῦ εἶναι ἀνθρώπῳ, ὥστ᾽ ἔσται τὸ ἀνθρώπῳ [25] ι εἶναι μὴ ἀνθρώπῳ εἶναι: ἓν γὰρ ἔσται. τοῦτο γὰρ σημαίνει τὸ εἶναι ἕν, τὸ ὡς λώπιον καὶ ἱμάτιον, εἰ ὁ λόγος εἷς: εἰ δὲ ἔσται ἕν, ἓν σημανεῖ τὸ ἀνθρώπῳ εἶναι καὶ μὴ ἀνθρώπῳ. ἀλλ᾽ ἐδέδεικτο ὅτι ἕτερον σημαίνει.

Si autem non significet alterum homo et non homo, palam quia non esse homini ab esse homini, quare erit homini esse non homini esse; unum enim erunt. Hoc enim significat esse unum, ut uestimentum et indumentum, si ratio una. Si vero erunt unum, unum significat homini esse et non homini. Sed ostensum est quod alterum significat.

Now if man and not-man mean nothing different, obviously not being a man will mean nothing different from being a man; so that being a man will be not being a man; for they will be one. For being one means this-being related as raiment and dress are, if their definition is one. And if being a man and being a not-man are to be one, they must mean one thing. But it was shown earlier that they mean different things.

ἀνάγκη τοίνυν, εἴ τί ἐστιν ἀληθὲς εἰπεῖν ὅτι ἄνθρωπος, ζῷον εἶναι δίπουν [30] (τοῦτο γὰρ ἦν ὃ ἐσήμαινε τὸ ἄνθρωπος): εἰ δ᾽ ἀνάγκη τοῦτο, οὐκ ἐνδέχεται μὴ εἶναι <τότε τὸ αὐτὸ ζῷον δίπουν (τοῦτο γὰρ σημαίνει τὸ ἀνάγκη εἶναι, τὸ ἀδύνατον εἶναι μὴ εἶναι [ἄνθρωπον]): οὐκ ἄρα ἐνδέχεται ἅμα ἀληθὲς εἶναι εἰπεῖν τὸ αὐτὸ ἄνθρωπον εἶναι καὶ μὴ εἶναι ἄνθρωπον.

Necesse itaque, si quid est verum dicere quia homo, animal esse bipes; hoc enim erat quod significabat homo. Sed si hoc necesse, non contingit non esse hoc ipsum animal bipes; hoc enim significat necesse esse: impossibile non esse hominem. non igitur contingit simul verum esse dicere idem hominem esse et non esse hominem.

Therefore, if it is true to say of anything that it is a man, it must be a two-footed animal (for this was what man meant); and if this is necessary, it is impossible that the same thing should not at that time be a two-footed animal; for this is what being necessary means –that it is impossible for the thing not to be. It is, then, impossible that it should be at the same time true to say the same thing is a man and is not a man.

ὁ δ᾽ αὐτὸς λόγος καὶ ἐπὶ τοῦ μὴ εἶναι ἄνθρωπον·

Eadem autem ratio et in non esse hominem;

The same account holds good with regard to not being a man, [07a]

[1007α] [1] τὸ γὰρ ἀνθρώπῳ εἶναι καὶ τὸ μὴ ἀνθρώπῳ εἶναι ἕτερον σημαίνει, εἴπερ καὶ τὸ λευκὸν εἶναι καὶ τὸ ἄνθρωπον εἶναι ἕτερον· πολὺ γὰρ ἀντίκειται ἐκεῖνο μᾶλλον, ὥστε σημαίνειν ἕτερον. εἰ δὲ καὶ [5] τὸ λευκὸν φήσει τὸ αὐτὸ καὶ ἓν σημαίνειν, πάλιν τὸ αὐτὸ ἐροῦμεν ὅπερ καὶ πρότερον ἐλέχθη, ὅτι ἓν πάντα ἔσται καὶ οὐ μόνον τὰ ἀντικείμενα. εἰ δὲ μὴ ἐνδέχεται τοῦτο, συμβαίνει τὸ λεχθέν,

nam homini esse et non homini esse alterum significat, siquidem album esse et hominem esse alterum; multum enim opponitur illud magis, quare significat diversum. Si autem  et album dixerit idem significare et unum, item idem dicemus quod et prius dictum est, quia unum omnia sunt et non solum opposita. Si autem hoc non contingit, contingit  quod dictum est,

for being a man and being a not-man mean different things, since even being white and being a man are different; for the former terms are much more different so that they must a fortiori mean different things. And if any one says that white means one and the same thing as man , again we shall say the same as what was said before, that it would follow that all things are one, and not only opposites. But if this is impossible, then what we have maintained will follow,

ἂν ἀποκρίνηται τὸ ἐρωτώμενον. ἐὰν δὲ προστιθῇ ἐρωτῶντος ἁπλῶς καὶ τὰς ἀποφάσεις, οὐκ ἀποκρίνεται [10] τὸ ἐρωτώμενον. οὐθὲν γὰρ κωλύει εἶναι τὸ αὐτὸ καὶ ἄνθρωπον καὶ λευκὸν καὶ ἄλλα μυρία τὸ πλῆθος· ἀλλ᾽ ὅμως ἐρομένου εἰ ἀληθὲς εἰπεῖν ἄνθρωπον τοῦτο εἶναι ἢ οὔ, ἀποκριτέον τὸ ἓν σημαῖνον καὶ οὐ προσθετέον ὅτι καὶ λευκὸν καὶ μέγα. καὶ γὰρ ἀδύνατον ἄπειρά γ᾽ ὄντα τὰ [15] συμβεβηκότα διελθεῖν· ἢ οὖν ἅπαντα διελθέτω ἢ μηθέν. ὁμοίως τοίνυν εἰ καὶ μυριάκις ἐστὶ τὸ αὐτὸ ἄνθρωπος καὶ [17] οὐκ ἄνθρωπος, οὐ προσαποκριτέον τῷ ἐρομένῳ εἰ ἔστιν ἄνθρωπος, ὅτι ἐστὶν ἅμα καὶ οὐκ ἄνθρωπος, εἰ μὴ καὶ τἆλλα ὅσα συμβέβηκε προσαποκριτέον, ὅσα ἐστὶν ἢ μὴ ἔστιν· ἐὰν [20] δὲ τοῦτο ποιῇ, οὐ διαλέγεται.

si respondeatur interrogatum. Si autem apponatur interrogante simpliciter et negationes, non respondetur interrogatum. Nihil enim prohibet esse idem et hominem et album et alia mille secundum pluralitatem. At tamen interrogante si verum est dicere hominem hoc esse aut non, respondendum est unum significans et non addendum quia et album et magnum. Et enim impossibile infinita entia accidentia permeare; aut igitur omnia permeentur aut nullum. Similiter ergo et si milies est idem homo et non homo, non est correspondendum interroganti si est homo, quia est simul et non homo, si non et alia quaecumque acciderunt sunt correspondenda, quaecumque sunt aut non sunt. Si autem hoc fecerit, non disputat.

if our opponent will only answer our question. And if, when one asks the question simply, he adds the contradictories, he is not answering the question. For there is nothing to prevent the same thing from being both a man and white and countless other things: but still, if one asks whether it is or is not true to say that this is a man, our opponent must give an answer which means one thing, and not add that it is also white and large. For, besides other reasons, it is impossible to enumerate its accidental attributes, which are infinite in number; let him, then, enumerate either all or none. Similarly, therefore, even if the same thing is a thousand times a man and a not-man, he must not, in answering the question whether this is a man, add that it is also at the same time a not-man, unless he is bound to add also all the other accidents, all that the subject is or is not; and if he does this, he is not observing the rules of argument.

ὅλως δ᾽ ἀναιροῦσιν οἱ τοῦτο λέγοντες οὐσίαν καὶ τὸ τί ἦν εἶναι. πάντα γὰρ ἀνάγκη συμβεβηκέναι φάσκειν αὐτοῖς, καὶ τὸ ὅπερ ἀνθρώπῳ εἶναι ἢ ζῴῳ εἶναι μὴ εἶναι. εἰ γὰρ ἔσται τι ὅπερ ἀνθρώπῳ εἶναι, τοῦτο οὐκ ἔσται μὴ ἀνθρώπῳ εἶναι ἢ μὴ εἶναι ἀνθρώπῳ [25] (καίτοι αὗται ἀποφάσεις τούτου): ἓν γὰρ ἦν ὃ ἐσήμαινε, καὶ ἦν τοῦτό τινος οὐσία. τὸ δ᾽ οὐσίαν σημαίνειν ἐστὶν ὅτι οὐκ ἄλλο τι τὸ εἶναι αὐτῷ. εἰ δ᾽ ἔσται αὐτῷ τὸ ὅπερ ἀνθρώπῳ εἶναι ἢ ὅπερ μὴ ἀνθρώπῳ εἶναι ἢ ὅπερ μὴ εἶναι ἀνθρώπῳ, ἄλλο ἔσται, ὥστ᾽ ἀναγκαῖον αὐτοῖς [30] λέγειν ὅτι οὐθενὸς ἔσται τοιοῦτος λόγος, ἀλλὰ πάντα κατὰ συμβεβηκός: τούτῳ γὰρ διώρισται οὐσία καὶ τὸ συμβεβηκός: τὸ γὰρ λευκὸν τῷ ἀνθρώπῳ συμβέβηκεν ὅτι ἔστι μὲν λευκὸς ἀλλ᾽ οὐχ ὅπερ λευκόν.

Omnino vero destruunt qui hoc dicunt substantiam et quod quid erat esse. Omnia namque dicere accidere eis est necesse, et quod vere homini esse aut animali esse non esse. Nam si erit <quid quod vere homini esse, hoc non erit non homini esse aut non esse homini (quamvis hae negationes huius); unum enim erat quod significabat, et erat hoc alicuius substantia. Significare vero substantiam est quia non aliud aliquid esse ipsi. Si autem erit ipsi quod vere homini esse quod vere non homini esse aut quod vere non esse homini, aliud erit. Quare dicere eos est necesse quia nullius erit talis ratio, sed omnia secundum accidens. Hoc enim determinata est substantia et accidens; album enim accidit homini, quia est albus sed non quod vere album.

And in general those who say this do away with substance and essence. For they must say that all attributes are accidents, and that there is no such thing as being essentially a man or an animal. For if there is to be any such thing as being essentially a man this will not be being a not-man or not being a man (yet these are negations of it); for there was one thing which it meant, and this was the substance of something. And denoting the substance of a thing means that the essence of the thing is nothing else. But if its being essentially a man is to be the same as either being essentially a not-man or essentially not being a man, then its essence will be something else. Therefore our opponents must say that there cannot be such a definition of anything, but that all attributes are accidental; for this is the distinction between substance and accident – white is accidental to man, because though he is white, whiteness is not his essence.

εἰ δὲ πάντα κατὰ συμβεβηκὸς λέγεται, οὐθὲν ἔσται πρῶτον τὸ καθ᾽ οὗ, εἰ ἀεὶ [35] τὸ συμβεβηκὸς καθ᾽ ὑποκειμένου τινὸς σημαίνει τὴν κατηγορίαν. [1007β] [1] ἀνάγκη ἄρα εἰς ἄπειρον ἰέναι. ἀλλ᾽ ἀδύνατον: οὐδὲ γὰρ πλείω συμπλέκεται δυοῖν: τὸ γὰρ συμβεβηκὸς οὐ συμβεβηκότι συμβεβηκός, εἰ μὴ ὅτι ἄμφω συμβέβηκε ταὐτῷ, λέγω δ᾽ οἷον τὸ λευκὸν μουσικὸν καὶ τοῦτο λευκὸν [5] ὅτι ἄμφω τῷ ἀνθρώπῳ συμβέβηκεν. ἀλλ᾽ οὐχ ὁ Σωκράτης μουσικὸς οὕτως, ὅτι ἄμφω συμβέβηκεν ἑτέρῳ τινί. ἐπεὶ τοίνυν τὰ μὲν οὕτως τὰ δ᾽ ἐκείνως λέγεται συμβεβηκότα, ὅσα οὕτως λέγεται ὡς τὸ λευκὸν τῷ Σωκράτει, οὐκ ἐνδέχεται ἄπειρα εἶναι ἐπὶ τὸ ἄνω, οἷον τῷ Σωκράτει τῷ λευκῷ [10] ἕτερόν τι συμβεβηκός: οὐ γὰρ γίγνεταί τι ἓν ἐξ ἁπάντων. οὐδὲ δὴ τῷ λευκῷ ἕτερόν τι ἔσται συμβεβηκός, οἷον τὸ μουσικόν: οὐθέν τε γὰρ μᾶλλον τοῦτο ἐκείνῳ ἢ ἐκεῖνο τούτῳ συμβέβηκεν, καὶ ἅμα διώρισται ὅτι τὰ μὲν οὕτω συμβέβηκε τὰ δ᾽ ὡς τὸ μουσικὸν Σωκράτει: ὅσα δ᾽ οὕτως, οὐ [15] συμβεβηκότι συμβέβηκε συμβεβηκός, ἀλλ᾽ ὅσα ἐκείνως, ὥστ᾽ οὐ πάντα κατὰ συμβεβηκὸς λεχθήσεται. ἔσται ἄρα τι καὶ ὡς οὐσίαν σημαῖνον. εἰ δὲ τοῦτο, δέδεικται ὅτι ἀδύνατον ἅμα κατηγορεῖσθαι τὰς ἀντιφάσεις.

Si vero omnia secundum accidens dicuntur, nullum erit primum universale; si autem semper accidens de subiecto aliquo significat predicationem, in infinitum igitur ire necesse est. Sed impossibile; neque enim plura duobus complectitur. Accidens enim non accidenti accidens, nisi quia ambo eidem accidunt. Dico autem ut album musicum et hoc album, quia ambo homini accidunt. Sed non Socrates musicus ita, quia ambo accidunt alicui alterl quoniam igitur haec quidem ita illa vero illo modo dicuntur accidentia, quaecumque sic dicuntur ut album Socrati, non contingit infinita esse in superius, ut Socrati albo alterum aliquid accidens; non enim fit aliquid unum ex omnibus. Nec itaque albo aliquod aliud erit accidens, ut musicum. Nihil enim magis hoc illi quam illud huic accidit. Et simul determinatum est quia haec quidem ita accidunt haec autem ut musicum Socrati; quaecumque vero sic, non accidenti accidit accidens, sed quaecumque illo modo, quare non omnia secundum accidens dicuntur. Erit igitur aliquid et ut substantiam significans. Si autem hoc, ostensum est quia impossibile simul predicari contradictiones.

But if all statements are accidental, there will be nothing primary about which they are made, if the accidental always implies predication [07b] about a subject. The predication, then, must go on ad infinitum. But this is impossible; for not even more than two terms can be combined in accidental predication. For (1) an accident is not an accident of an accident, unless it be because both are accidents of the same subject. I mean, for instance, that the white is musical and the latter is white, only because both are accidental to man. But (2) Socrates is musical, not in this sense, that both terms are accidental to something else. Since then some predicates are accidental in this and some in that sense, (a) those which are accidental in the latter sense, in which white is accidental to Socrates, cannot form an infinite series in the upward direction; e.g. Socrates the white has not yet another accident; for no unity can be got out of such a sum. Nor again (b) will white have another term accidental to it, e.g. musical . For this is no more accidental to that than that is to this; and at the same time we have drawn the distinction, that while some predicates are accidental in this sense, others are so in the sense in which musical is accidental to Socrates; and the accident is an accident of an accident not in cases of the latter kind, but only in cases of the other kind, so that not all terms will be accidental. There must, then, even so be something which denotes substance. And if this is so, it has been shown that contradictories cannot be predicated at the same time.

ἔτι εἰ ἀληθεῖς αἱ ἀντιφάσεις ἅμα κατὰ τοῦ αὐτοῦ πᾶσαι, δῆλον ὡς [20] ἅπαντα ἔσται ἕν. ἔσται γὰρ τὸ αὐτὸ καὶ τριήρης καὶ τοῖχος καὶ ἄνθρωπος, εἰ κατὰ παντός τι ἢ καταφῆσαι ἢ ἀποφῆσαι ἐνδέχεται,

Amplius si contradictiones simul de eodem vere sunt omnes, palam quod omnia erunt unum. Erit enim idem trieris et murus et homo, si de omni aliquid aut affirmare aut negare contingit;

Again, if all contradictory statements are true of the same subject at the same time, evidently all things will be one. For the same thing will be a trireme, a wall, and a man, if of everything it is possible either to affirm or to deny anything

καθάπερ ἀνάγκη τοῖς τὸν Πρωταγόρου λέγουσι λόγον. εἰ γὰρ τῷ δοκεῖ μὴ εἶναι τριήρης ὁ ἄνθρωπος, δῆλον ὡς οὐκ ἔστι τριήρης: ὥστε καὶ ἔστιν, εἴπερ [25] ἡ ἀντίφασις ἀληθής. καὶ γίγνεται δὴ τὸ τοῦ Ἀναξαγόρου, ὁμοῦ πάντα χρήματα: ὥστε μηθὲν ἀληθῶς ὑπάρχειν. τὸ ἀόριστον οὖν ἐοίκασι λέγειν, καὶ οἰόμενοι τὸ ὂν λέγειν περὶ τοῦ μὴ ὄντος λέγουσιν: τὸ γὰρ δυνάμει ὂν καὶ μὴ ἐντελεχείᾳ τὸ ἀόριστόν ἐστιν.

quemadmodum est necesse dicentibus rationem Protagore. Nam alicui si videtur non esse trieris homo, palam quia non est trieris; quare et est, si contradictio vera. Et fit itaque quod Anaxagore: simul res omnes esse; ut nihil vere unum sit.

Indefinitum igitur videntur dicere, et putantes ens dicere de non ente dicunt; nam potestate ens et non endelichia indefinitum est.

(and this premiss must be accepted by those who share the views of Protagoras). For if any one thinks that the man is not a trireme, evidently he is not a trireme; so that he also is a trireme, if, as they say, contradictory statements are both true. And we thus get the doctrine of Anaxagoras, that all things are mixed together; so that nothing really exists. They seem, then, to be speaking of the indeterminate, and, while fancying themselves to be speaking of being, they are speaking about non-being; for it is that which exists potentially and not in complete reality that is indeterminate.

ἀλλὰ μὴν λεκτέον γ᾿ αὐτοῖς κατὰ [30] παντὸς <παντὸς τὴν κατάφασιν ἢ τὴν ἀπόφασιν· ἄτοπον γὰρ εἰ ἑκάστῳ ἡ μὲν αὐτοῦ ἀπόφασις ὑπάρξει, ἡ δ᾿ ἑτέρου ὃ μὴ ὑπάρχει αὐτῷ οὐχ ὑπάρξει· λέγω δ᾿ οἷον εἰ ἀληθὲς εἰπεῖν τὸν ἄνθρωπον ὅτι οὐκ ἄνθρωπος, δῆλον ὅτι καὶ ἢ τριήρης ἢ οὐ τριήρης. εἰ μὲν οὖν ἡ κατάφασις, ἀνάγκη καὶ τὴν ἀπόφασιν· [35] εἰ δὲ μὴ ὑπάρχει ἡ κατάφασις, ἥ γε ἀπόφασις ὑπάρξει μᾶλλον ἢ ἡ αὐτοῦ. [1008α] [1] εἰ οὖν κἀκείνη ὑπάρχει, ὑπάρξει καὶ ἡ τῆς τριήρους· εἰ δ᾿ αὕτη, καὶ ἡ κατάφασις. ταῦτά τε οὖν συμβαίνει τοῖς λέγουσι τὸν λόγον τοῦτον,

At vero dicenda est ipsis de omni affirmatio aut negatio. Inconveniens enim si unicuique sua quidem negatio inest, quae vero alterius quod non inest ei non inerit. Dico autem ut si verum est dicere hominem quia non homo, palam quod et non trieris. Ergo si affirmatio, necesse et negationem; si autem non existat affirmatio, negatio inerit magis quam quae sua. Ergo si et illa inest, inerit et quae ipsius trieris; si autem haec, et affirmatio. Haec ergo contingunt hanc dicentibus rationem.

But they must predicate of every subject the affirmation or the negation of every attribute. For it is absurd if of each subject its own negation is to be predicable, while the negation of something else which cannot be predicated of it is not to be predicable of it; for instance, if it is true to say of a man that he is not a man, evidently it is also true to say that he is either a trireme or not a trireme. If, then, the affirmative can be predicated, the negative must be predicable too; and if the affirmative is not predicable, the negative, at least, will be [08a] more predicable than the negative of the subject itself. If, then, even the latter negative is predicable, the negative of trireme will be also predicable; and, if this is predicable, the affirmative will be so too. Those, then, who maintain this view are driven to this conclusion,

καὶ ὅτι οὐκ ἀνάγκη ἢ φάναι ἢ ἀποφάναι. εἰ γὰρ ἀληθὲς ὅτι ἄνθρωπος καὶ [5] οὐκ ἄνθρωπος, δῆλον ὅτι καὶ οὔτ᾿ ἄνθρωπος οὔτ᾿ οὐκ ἄνθρωπος ἔσται· τοῖν γὰρ δυοῖν δύο ἀποφάσεις, εἰ δὲ μία ἐξ ἀμφοῖν ἐκείνη, καὶ αὕτη μία ἂν εἴη ἀντικειμένη.

Et quia non necesse aut dicere aut negare. Nam si verum quia homo et non homo, palam quia nec homo nec non homo erit. Nam duorum due negationes; si autem una ex utrisque, illi et haec una utique erit opposita.

and to the further conclusion that it is not necessary either to assert or to deny. For if it is true that a thing is a man and a not-man, evidently also it will be neither a man nor a not-man. For to the two assertions there answer two negations, and if the former is treated as a single proposition compounded out of two, the latter also is a single proposition opposite to the former.

ἔτι ἤτοι περὶ ἅπαντα οὕτως ἔχει, καὶ ἔστι καὶ λευκὸν καὶ οὐ λευκὸν καὶ ὂν καὶ οὐκ ὄν, καὶ περὶ τὰς ἄλλας φάσεις καὶ [10] ἀποφάσεις ὁμοιοτρόπως, ἢ οὒ ἀλλὰ περὶ μέν τινας, περί τινας δ᾽ οὒ. καὶ εἰ μὲν μὴ περὶ πάσας, αὗται ἂν εἶεν ὁμολογούμεναι· εἰ δὲ περὶ πάσας, πάλιν ἤτοι καθ᾽ ὅσων τὸ φῆσαι καὶ ἀποφῆσαι καὶ καθ᾽ ὅσων ἀποφῆσαι καὶ φῆσαι, ἢ κατὰ μὲν ὧν φῆσαι καὶ ἀποφῆσαι, καθ᾽ ὅσων δὲ ἀποφῆσαι [15] οὐ πάντων φῆσαι. καὶ εἰ μὲν οὕτως, εἴη ἄν τι παγίως οὐκ ὄν, καὶ αὕτη βεβαία δόξα, καὶ εἰ τὸ μὴ εἶναι βέβαιόν τι καὶ γνώριμον, γνωριμωτέρα ἂν εἴη ἡ φάσις ἡ ἀντικειμένη:

Amplius aut circa omnia ita se habet, et est album et non album et ens et non ens, et circa alias dictiones et negationes looxa10 modo simili, aut non, sed circa quasdam quidem et circa quasdam non. Et si quidem non circa omnes, hae utique erunt confesse; si vero circa omnes, iterum aut de quibuscumque dicere et negare et de quibuscumque negare et dicere, aut de quibus quidem dicere et negare, sed de quibuscumque negare non de omnibus dicere. Et si sic, erit aliquid firmiter non ens, et haec erit firma opinio; et si ipsum non esse firmum aliquid sit et notum, notior utique erit dictio quam opposita negatio.

Again, either the theory is true in all cases, and a thing is both white and not-white, and existent and non-existent, and all other assertions and negations are similarly compatible or the theory is true of some statements and not of others. And if not of all, the exceptions will be contradictories of which admittedly only one is true; but if of all, again either the negation will be true wherever the assertion is, and the assertion true wherever the negation is, or the negation will be true where the assertion is, but the assertion not always true where the negation is. And (a) in the latter case there will be something which fixedly is not, and this will be an indisputable belief; and if non-being is something indisputable and knowable, the opposite assertion will be more knowable.

εἰ δὲ ὁμοίως καὶ ὅσα ἀποφῆσαι φάναι, ἀνάγκη ἤτοι ἀληθὲς διαιροῦντα λέγειν, οἷον ὅτι [20] λευκὸν καὶ πάλιν ὅτι οὐ λευκόν, ἢ οὒ. καὶ εἰ μὲν μὴ ἀληθὲς διαιϱοῦντα λέγειν, οὐ λέγει τε ταῦτα καὶ οὐκ ἔστιν οὐθέν (τὰ δὲ μὴ ὄντα πῶς ἂν φθέγξαιτο ἢ βαδίσειεν;), καὶ πάντα δ᾽ ἂν εἴη ἕν, ὥσπερ καὶ πρότερον εἴϱηται, καὶ ταὐτὸν ἔσται καὶ ἄνθϱωπος καὶ θεὸς καὶ τϱιήϱης [25] καὶ αἱ ἀντιφάσεις αὐτῶν (εἰ γὰϱ ὁμοίως καθ᾽ ἑκάστου, οὐδὲν διοίσει ἕτεϱον ἑτέϱου: εἰ γὰϱ διοίσει, τοῦτ᾽ ἔσται ἀληθὲς καὶ ἴδιον): ὁμοίως δὲ καὶ εἰ διαιϱοῦντα ἐνδέχεται ἀληθεύειν, συμβαίνει τὸ λεχθέν,

Si vero similiter et quaecumque negare dicere, necesse aut verum dividentem dicere, ut quod album et iterum quod non album, aut non. Et si quidem non verum dividentem dicere, non dicet haec et non est nihil; non entia autem quomodo utique pronuntiabunt aut ibunt? Et omnia utique erunt unum, ut et prius dictum est, et idem erit et homo et deus et trieris et ipsorum contradictiones. Si autem similiter de unoquoque, nihil differret aliud ab alio; nam si differret, hoc erit verum et proprium. Similiter autem et si dividentem contingit verum esse, accidit quod dictum est.

But (b) if it is equally possible also to assert all that it is possible to deny, one must either be saying what is true when one separates the predicates (and says, for instance, that a thing is white, and again that it is not-white), or not. And if (i) it is not true to apply the predicates separately, our opponent is not saying what he professes to say, and also nothing at all exists; but how could non-existent things speak or walk, as he does? Also all things would on this view be one, as has been already said, and man and God and trireme and their contradictories will be the same. For if contradictories can be predicated alike of each subject, one thing will in no wise differ from another; for if it differ, this difference will be something true and peculiar to it. And (ii) if one may with truth apply the predicates separately, the above-mentioned result follows none the less,

πϱὸς δὲ τούτῳ ὅτι πάντες ἂν ἀληθεύοιεν καὶ πάντες ἂν ψεύδοιντο, καὶ αὐτὸς αὑτὸν ὁμολογεῖ [30] ψεύδεσθαι. ἅμα δὲ φανεϱὸν ὅτι πεϱὶ οὐθενός ἐστι πϱὸς τοῦτον ἡ σκέψις: οὐθὲν γὰϱ λέγει. οὔτε γὰϱ οὕτως οὔτ᾽ οὐχ οὕτως λέγει, ἀλλ᾽ οὕτως τε καὶ οὐχ οὕτως: καὶ πάλιν γε ταῦτα ἀπόφησιν ἄμφω, ὅτι οὔθ᾽ οὕτως οὔτε οὐχ οὕτως: εἰ γὰϱ μή, ἤδη ἄν τι εἴη ὡϱισμένον.

Ad hoc autem quia omnes verum dicent et omnes mentientur, et ipse se ipsum falsum dicere confitetur. Simul autem palam quia de nullo est ad hunc perscrutatio; nihil enim dicit. Nec enim ita nec non ita dicit, sed ita et non ita; et iterum haec negat ambo, quia nec ita nec non ita; nam si non, iam utique erit aliquid determinatum.

and, further, it follows that all would then be right and all would be in error, and our opponent himself confesses himself to be in error. And at the same time our discussion with him is evidently about nothing at all; for he says nothing. For he says neither yes nor no, but yes and no; and again he denies both of these and says neither yes nor no; for otherwise there would already be something definite.

ἔτι εἰ ὅταν ἡ φάσις [35] ἀληθὴς ᾖ, ἡ ἀπόφασις ψευδής, κἂν αὕτη ἀληθὴς ᾖ, ἡ κατάφασις ψευδής, οὐκ ἂν εἴη τὸ αὐτὸ ἅμα φάναι καὶ ἀποφάναι ἀληθῶς. [1008β] [1] ἀλλ᾽ ἴσως φαῖεν ἂν τοῦτ᾽ εἶναι τὸ ἐξ ἀρχῆς κείμενον.

Amplius si quando affirmatio vera est, negatio est falsa, et si haec vera, affirmatio falsa, non erit utique simul idem dicere  et negare vere. Sed forsan dicet utique hoc esse quod a principio positum.

Again if when the assertion is true, the negation is false, and when this is true, the affirmation is false, it will not be possible to assert and deny the same thing truly at the same [08b] time. But perhaps they might say this was the very question at issue.

ἔτι ἄρα ὁ μὲν ἢ ἔχειν πως ὑπολαμβάνων ἢ μὴ ἔχειν διέψευσται, ὁ δὲ ἄμφω ἀληθεύει; εἰ γὰρ ἀληθεύει, τί ἂν εἴη τὸ λεγόμενον ὅτι τοιαύτη τῶν ὄντων ἡ [5] φύσις; εἰ δὲ μὴ ἀληθεύει, ἀλλὰ μᾶλλον ἀληθεύει ἢ ὁ ἐκείνως ὑπολαμβάνων, ἤδη πως ἔχοι ἂν τὰ ὄντα, καὶ τοῦτ᾽ ἀληθὲς ἂν εἴη, καὶ οὐχ ἅμα καὶ οὐκ ἀληθές. εἰ δὲ ὁμοίως ἅπαντες καὶ ψεύδονται καὶ ἀληθῆ λέγουσιν, οὔτε φθέγξασθαι οὔτ᾽ εἰπεῖν τῷ τοιούτῳ ἔσται· ἅμα γὰρ ταῦτά τε καὶ [10] οὐ ταῦτα λέγει. εἰ δὲ μηθὲν ὑπολαμβάνει ἀλλ᾽ ὁμοίως οἴεται καὶ οὐκ οἴεται, τί ἂν διαφερόντως ἔχοι τῶν γε φυτῶν;

Amplius igitur qui quidem aut habere aliqualiter existimans aut non habere mentitus est, qui autem ambo verum dicit? Nam si verum dicit, quid utique erit  quod dicitur  quia talis est entium natura? Si vero non verum dicit, sed magis verum dicit qui illo modo existimat, iam aliqualiter se habebunt entia, et hoc verum utique erit, et non simul et non verum. Si autem similiter  omnes mentiuntur et vera dicunt, nec pronuntiandum nec dicendum est tali; similiter enim haec  et non haec dicit. Si autem nihil suscipit sed similiter existimat et non existimat, quid utique differenter habebit a natis?

Again, is he in error who judges either that the thing is so or that it is not so, and is he right who judges both? If he is right, what can they mean by saying that the nature of existing things is of this kind? And if he is not right, but more right than he who judges in the other way, being will already be of a definite nature, and this will be true, and not at the same time also not true. But if all are alike both wrong and right, one who is in this condition will not be able either to speak or to say anything intelligible; for he says at the same time both yes and no. And if he makes no judgement but thinks and does not think , indifferently, what difference will there be between him and a vegetable?

ὅθεν καὶ μάλιστα φανερόν ἐστιν ὅτι οὐδεὶς οὕτω διάκειται οὔτε τῶν ἄλλων οὔτε τῶν λεγόντων τὸν λόγον τοῦτον. διὰ τί γὰρ βαδίζει Μέγαράδε ἀλλ᾽ οὐχ ἡσυχάζει, οἰόμενος [15] βαδίζειν δεῖν; οὐδ᾽ εὐθέως ἕωθεν πορεύεται εἰς φρέαρ ἢ εἰς φάραγγα, ἐὰν τύχῃ, ἀλλὰ φαίνεται εὐλαβούμενος, ὡς οὐχ ὁμοίως οἰόμενος μὴ ἀγαθὸν εἶναι τὸ ἐμπεσεῖν καὶ ἀγαθόν; δῆλον ἄρα ὅτι τὸ μὲν βέλτιον ὑπολαμβάνει τὸ δ᾽ οὐ βέλτιον. εἰ δὲ τοῦτο, καὶ τὸ μὲν ἄνθρωπον τὸ δ᾽ οὐκ ἄνθρωπον [20] καὶ τὸ μὲν γλυκὺ τὸ δ᾽ οὐ γλυκὺ ἀνάγκη ὑπολαμβάνειν. οὐ γὰρ ἐξ ἴσου ἅπαντα ζητεῖ καὶ ὑπολαμβάνει, ὅταν οἰηθεὶς βέλτιον εἶναι τὸ πιεῖν ὕδωρ καὶ ἰδεῖν ἄνθρωπον εἶτα ζητῇ αὐτά· καίτοι ἔδει γε, εἰ ταὐτὸν ἦν ὁμοίως καὶ ἄνθρωπος καὶ οὐκ ἄνθρωπος. ἀλλ᾽ ὅπερ ἐλέχθη, οὐθεὶς ὃς οὐ [25] φαίνεται τὰ μὲν εὐλαβούμενος τὰ δ᾽ οὔ· ὥστε, ὡς ἔοικε, πάντες ὑπολαμβάνουσιν ἔχειν ἁπλῶς, εἰ μὴ περὶ ἅπαντα, ἀλλὰ περὶ τὸ ἄμεινον καὶ χεῖρον.

Unde et maxime manifestum est quia nullus ita disponitur nec aliorum nec dicentium hanc rationem. Quare namque uadit  domum et non quiescit putans ire? Nequepstatim diluculo uadit  in puteum aut torrentem, si contingat, sed videtur timens, tamquam non similiter putans non bonum esse incidere et bonum? Palam ergo quia hoc quidem melius existimat hoc autem non melius. Si autem hoc, et hoc quidem hominem  illud autem non hominem, et hoc quidem dulce illud autem non dulce putare est necesse. Non enim ex equo omnia quaerit et existimat, quando putans melius esse aquam bibere et hominem videre deinde ea quaerit; quamvis oportebat, si idem erat similiter homo et non homo. Sed quod dictum est: nullus qui non videtur haec quidem timens illa vero non. Quare, sicut  videtur, omnes existimant habere simpliciter, si non circa omnia, sed circa melius et deterius.

-Thus, then, it is in the highest degree evident that neither any one of those who maintain this view nor any one else is really in this position. For why does a man walk to Megara and not stay at home, when he thinks he ought to be walking there? Why does he not walk early some morning into a well or over a precipice, if one happens to be in his way? Why do we observe him guarding against this, evidently because he does not think that falling in is alike good and not good? Evidently, then, he judges one thing to be better and another worse. And if this is so, he must also judge one thing to be a man and another to be not-a-man, one thing to be sweet and another to be not-sweet. For he does not aim at and judge all things alike, when, thinking it desirable to drink water or to see a man, he proceeds to aim at these things; yet he ought, if the same thing were alike a man and not-a-man. But, as was said, there is no one who does not obviously avoid some things and not others. Therefore, as it seems, all men make unqualified judgements, if not about all things, still about what is better and worse.

εἰ δὲ μὴ ἐπιστάμενοι [28] ἀλλὰ δοξάζοντες, πολὺ μᾶλλον ἐπιμελητέον ἂν εἴη τῆς ἀληθείας, ὥσπερ καὶ νοσώδει ὄντι ἢ ὑγιεινῷ τῆς ὑγιείας· [30] καὶ γὰρ ὁ δοξάζων πρὸς τὸν ἐπιστάμενον οὐχ ὑγιεινῶς διάκειται πρὸς τὴν ἀλήθειαν.

Si autem non scientes sed opinantes, multo magis curandum utique erit de veritate, quemadmodum infirmo existenti  quam sano de sanitate; et  enim opinans ad scientem non salubriter disponitur ad veritatem.

And if this is not knowledge but opinion, they should be all the more anxious about the truth, as a sick man should be more anxious about his health than one who is healthy; for he who has opinions is, in comparison with the man who knows, not in a healthy state as far as the truth is concerned.

ἔτι εἰ ὅτι μάλιστα πάντα οὕτως ἔχει καὶ οὐχ οὕτως, ἀλλὰ τό γε μᾶλλον καὶ ἧττον ἔνεστιν ἐν τῇ φύσει τῶν ὄντων: οὐ γὰρ ἂν ὁμοίως φήσαιμεν εἶναι τὰ δύο ἄρτια καὶ τὰ τρία, οὐδ᾽ ὁμοίως διέψευσται ὁ τὰ [35] τέτταρα πέντε οἰόμενος καὶ ὁ χίλια. εἰ οὖν μὴ ὁμοίως, δῆλον ὅτι ἅτερος ἧττον, ὥστε μᾶλλον ἀληθεύει. εἰ οὖν τὸ μᾶλλον ἐγγύτερον, [1009α] [1] εἴη γε ἄν τι ἀληθὲς οὗ ἐγγύτερον τὸ μᾶλλον ἀληθές. κἂν εἰ μὴ ἔστιν, ἀλλ᾽ ἤδη γέ τι ἔστι βεβαιότερον καὶ ἀληθινώτερον, καὶ τοῦ λόγου ἀπηλλαγμένοι ἂν εἴημεν τοῦ ἀκράτου καὶ κωλύοντός τι τῇ διανοίᾳ [5] ὁρίσαι.

Amplius si quam maxime omnia sic se habent et non sic, sed magis et minus unum est in natura entium; non enim utique similiter dicemus esse duo paria et tria, nec similiter mentitus est qui quatuor pente opinatus est et qui mille. Si igitur non similiter, palam quia alter minus, quare magis verum dicit. Si ergo quod magis affinius, erit utique aliquid verum cuius affinius quod magis verum. Et utique si non est, sed iam aliquid est firmius et verius, et a ratione remoti utique erimus incondita et prohibente aliquid mente determinare.

Again, however much all things may be so and not so , still there is a more and a less in the nature of things; for we should not say that two and three are equally even, nor is he who thinks four things are five equally wrong with him who thinks they are a thousand. If then they are not equally wrong, obviously one is less wrong and therefore more right. If then that which has more of any quality is [09a] nearer the norm, there must be some truth to which the more true is nearer. And even if there is not, still there is already something better founded and liker the truth, and we shall have got rid of the unqualified doctrine which would prevent us from determining anything in our thought.

## Chapter 5

ἔστι δ᾽ ἀπὸ τῆς αὐτῆς δόξης καὶ ὁ Πρωταγόρου λόγος, καὶ ἀνάγκη ὁμοίως αὐτοὺς ἄμφω ἢ εἶναι ἢ μὴ εἶναι: εἴτε γὰρ τὰ δοκοῦντα πάντα ἐστὶν ἀληθῆ καὶ τὰ φαινόμενα, ἀνάγκη εἶναι πάντα ἅμα ἀληθῆ καὶ ψευδῆ (πολλοὶ γὰρ [10] τἀναντία ὑπολαμβάνουσιν ἀλλήλοις, καὶ τοὺς μὴ ταὐτὰ δοξάζοντας ἑαυτοῖς διεψεῦσθαι νομίζουσιν: ὥστ᾽ ἀνάγκη τὸ αὐτὸ εἶναί τε καὶ μὴ εἶναι), καὶ εἰ τοῦτ᾽ ἔστιν, ἀνάγκη τὰ δοκοῦντα εἶναι πάντ᾽ ἀληθῆ (τὰ ἀντικείμενα γὰρ δοξάζουσιν ἀλλήλοις οἱ διεψευσμένοι καὶ ἀληθεύοντες: εἰ οὖν ἔχει τὰ [15] ὄντα οὕτως, ἀληθεύσουσι πάντες).

Est autem et ab eadem opinione Protagore ratio, et necesse similiter ipsas ambas aut esse aut non esse. Nam si quae videntur omnia sunt vera et apparentia, necesse omnia simul vera et falsa esse. Multi namque contraria invicem 1009a10 existimant, et non eadem opinantes sibi ipsis mentiri putant; quare necesse idem esse et non esse. Et si hoc est, necesse putata esse omnia vera. Opposita namque invicem opinantur mentientes et verum dicentes; ergo entia si sic se habent, verum dicunt omnes.

From the same opinion proceeds the doctrine of Protagoras, and both doctrines must be alike true or alike untrue. For on the one hand, if all opinions and appearances are true, all statements must be at the same time true and false. For many men hold beliefs in which they conflict with one another, and think those mistaken who have not the same opinions as themselves; so that the same thing must both be and not be. And on the other hand, if this is so, all opinions must be true; for those who are mistaken and those who are right are opposed to one another in their opinions; if, then, reality is such as the view in question supposes, all will be right in their beliefs.

ὅτι μὲν οὖν ἀπὸ τῆς αὐτῆς εἰσὶ διανοίας ἀμφότεροι οἱ λόγοι, δῆλον:

Quod quidem igitur ab eodem sunt intellectu utreque rationes, palam.

Evidently, then, both doctrines proceed from the same way of thinking.

ἔστι δ᾽ οὐχ ὁ αὐτὸς τρόπος πρὸς ἅπαντας τῆς ἐντεύξεως: οἱ μὲν γὰρ πειθοῦς δέονται οἱ δὲ βίας. ὅσοι μὲν γὰρ ἐκ τοῦ ἀπορῆσαι ὑπέλαβον οὕτως, τούτων εὐΐατος ἡ ἄγνοια (οὐ γὰρ πρὸς τὸν [20] λόγον ἀλλὰ πρὸς τὴν διάνοιαν ἡ ἀπάντησις αὐτῶν): ὅσοι δὲ λόγου χάριν λέγουσι, τούτων δ᾽ ἔλεγχος ἴασις τοῦ ἐν τῇ φωνῇ λόγου καὶ τοῦ ἐν τοῖς ὀνόμασιν.

Est autem non idem modus <intercessionis ad omnes; hii namque persuasione egent illi vi. Quicumque enim ex dubitasse existimaverunt ita, horum bene curabilis ignorantia; non enim ad orationem sed ad mentem obviatio ipsorum. Quicumque vero orationis causa dicunt, horum arguitio curatio et eius quae in voce orationis et eius quae in nominibus.

But the same method of discussion must not be used with all opponents; for some need persuasion, and others compulsion. Those who have been driven to this position by difficulties in their thinking can easily be cured of their ignorance; for it is not their expressed argument but their thought that one has to meet. But those who argue for the sake of argument can be cured only by refuting the argument as expressed in speech and in words.

ἐλήλυθε δὲ τοῖς διαποροῦσιν αὕτη ἡ δόξα ἐκ τῶν αἰσθητῶν, ἡ μὲν τοῦ ἅμα τὰς ἀντιφάσεις καὶ τἀναντία ὑπάρχειν ὁρῶσιν ἐκ ταὐτοῦ [25] γιγνόμενα τἀναντία: εἰ οὖν μὴ ἐνδέχεται γίγνεσθαι τὸ μὴ ὄν, προϋπῆρχεν ὁμοίως τὸ πρᾶγμα ἄμφω ὄν,

ὥσπερ καὶ Ἀναξαγόρας μεμῖχθαι πᾶν ἐν παντί φησι καὶ Δημόκριτος· καὶ γὰρ οὗτος τὸ κενὸν καὶ τὸ πλῆρες ὁμοίως καθ' ὁτιοῦν ὑπάρχειν μέρος, καίτοι τὸ μὲν ὂν τούτων εἶναι τὸ δὲ [30] μὴ ὄν.

Venit autem dubitantibus haec opinio ex sensibilibus, quae quidem eius quod simul contradictiones et contraria existere videntibus ex eodem facta contraria. Ergo si non contingit fieri non ens, preextitit similiter res ambo ens, ut et Anaxagoras misceri omne in omni ait et Democritus; et enim hic inane et plenum similiter secundum quamcumque existere partem, quamvis hoc quidem horum esse ens illud vero non ens.

Those who really feel the difficulties have been led to this opinion by observation of the sensible world. (1) They think that contradictories or contraries are true at the same time, because they see contraries coming into existence out of the same thing. If, then, that which is not cannot come to be, the thing must have existed before as both contraries alike, as Anaxagoras says all is mixed in all, and Democritus too; for he says the void and the full exist alike in every part, and yet one of these is being, and the other non-being.

πρὸς μὲν οὖν τοὺς ἐκ τούτων ὑπολαμβάνοντας ἐροῦμεν ὅτι τρόπον μέν τινα ὀρθῶς λέγουσι τρόπον δέ τινα ἀγνοοῦσιν· τὸ γὰρ ὂν λέγεται διχῶς, ὥστ' ἔστιν ὂν τρόπον ἐνδέχεται γίγνεσθαί τι ἐκ τοῦ μὴ ὄντος, ἔστι δ' ὂν οὔ, καὶ ἅμα τὸ αὐτὸ εἶναι καὶ ὂν καὶ μὴ ὄν, ἀλλ' οὐ κατὰ ταὐτό [ὄν]· δυνάμει [35] μὲν γὰρ ἐνδέχεται ἅμα ταὐτὸ εἶναι τὰ ἐναντία, ἐντελεχείᾳ δ' οὔ.

Ad eos quidem igitur qui ex hiis existimant dicemus quia modo quodam recte dicunt et modo quodam ignorant. Ens enim dupliciter dicitur; est ergo quomodo contingit fieri aliquid ex non ente, est autem quomodo non, et simul idem esse ens et non ens, sed non secundum idem ens. Potestate namque contingit simul idem esse contraria, actu vero non.

To those, then, whose belief rests on these grounds, we shall say that in a sense they speak rightly and in a sense they err. For 'that which is' has two meanings, so that in some sense a thing can come to be out of that which is not, while in some sense it cannot, and the same thing can at the same time be in being and not in being – but not in the same respect. For the same thing can be potentially at the same time two contraries, but it cannot actually.

ἔτι δ' ἀξιώσομεν αὐτοὺς ὑπολαμβάνειν καὶ ἄλλην τινὰ οὐσίαν εἶναι τῶν ὄντων ᾗ οὔτε κίνησις ὑπάρχει οὔτε φθορὰ οὔτε γένεσις τὸ παράπαν.

Amplius autem dignificemus ipsos existimare et aliam substantiam esse entium cui nec motus existit nec corruptio nec generatio omnino.

And again we shall ask them to believe that among existing things there is also another kind of substance to which neither movement nor destruction nor generation at all belongs.

[1009β] [1] —ὅμοιως δὲ καὶ ἡ περὶ τὰ φαινόμενα ἀλήθεια ἐνίοις ἐκ τῶν αἰσθητῶν ἐλήλυθεν. τὸ μὲν γὰρ ἀληθὲς οὐ πλήθει κρίνεσθαι οἴονται προσήκειν οὐδὲ ὀλιγότητι, τὸ δ᾽ αὐτὸ τοῖς μὲν γλυκὺ γευομένοις δοκεῖν εἶναι τοῖς δὲ πικρόν, ὥστ᾽ εἰ πάντες ἔκαμνον [5] ἢ πάντες παρεφρόνουν, δύο δ᾽ ἢ τρεῖς ὑγίαινον ἢ νοῦν εἶχον, δοκεῖν ἂν τούτους κάμνειν καὶ παραφρονεῖν τοὺς δ᾽ ἄλλους οὔ:

Similiter autem et quae  circa apparentia veritas quibusdam ex sensibilibus venit. Verum enim non pluralitate iudicari  putant oportere nec paucitate, idem vero hiis quidem dulce gustantibus esse videtur illis vero amarum, quare si omnes laboraverint aut omnes desipuerint, duo autem vel tres sani sint  aut intellectum habeant, hos quidem videri laborare et desipere alios vero non.

[09b] And (2) similarly some have inferred from observation of the sensible world the truth of appearances. For they think that the truth should not be determined by the large or small number of those who hold a belief, and that the same thing is thought sweet by some when they taste it, and bitter by others, so that if all were ill or all were mad, and only two or three were well or sane, these would be thought ill and mad, and not the others.

ἔτι δὲ καὶ πολλοῖς τῶν ἄλλων ζῴων τἀναντία [περὶ τῶν αὐτῶν] φαίνεσθαι καὶ ἡμῖν, καὶ αὐτῷ δὲ ἑκάστῳ πρὸς αὑτὸν οὐ ταὐτὰ κατὰ τὴν αἴσθησιν ἀεὶ δοκεῖν. ποῖα οὖν τούτων ἀληθῆ [10] ἢ ψευδῆ, ἄδηλον: οὐθὲν γὰρ μᾶλλον τάδε ἢ τάδε ἀληθῆ, ἀλλ᾽ ὁμοίως. διὸ Δημόκριτός γέ φησιν ἤτοι οὐθὲν εἶναι ἀληθὲς ἢ ἡμῖν γ᾽ ἄδηλον.

Amplius autem multis aliorum animalium contraria videri et nobis, et ipsi autem unicuique ad se ipsum non eadem secundum sensum semper videri. Quae igitur horum vera  aut falsa, non manifestum ; nihil enim magis haec quam  illa vera, sed similiter. Propter quod Democritus ait aut nihil esse verum aut nobis non manifestum.

And again, they say that many of the other animals receive impressions contrary to ours; and that even to the senses of each individual, things do not always seem the same. Which, then, of these impressions are true and which are false is not obvious; for the one set is no more true than the other, but both are alike. And this is why Democritus, at any rate, says that either there is no truth or to us at least it is not evident.

ὅλως δὲ διὰ τὸ ὑπολαμβάνειν φρόνησιν μὲν τὴν αἴσθησιν, ταύτην δ᾽ εἶναι ἀλλοίωσιν, τὸ φαινόμενον κατὰ τὴν αἴσθησιν ἐξ ἀνάγκης ἀληθὲς εἶναί [15] φασιν:

141

Omnino vero propter existimare prudentiam quidem sensum, hunc autem esse alterationem, quod videtur secundum sensum ex necessitate verum esse dicunt.

And in general it is because these thinkers suppose knowledge to be sensation, and this to be a physical alteration, that they say that what appears to our senses must be true;

ἐκ τούτων γὰρ καὶ Ἐμπεδοκλῆς καὶ Δημόκριτος καὶ τῶν ἄλλων ὡς ἔπος εἰπεῖν ἕκαστος τοιαύταις δόξαις γεγένηνται ἔνοχοι. καὶ γὰρ Ἐμπεδοκλῆς μεταβάλλοντας τὴν ἕξιν μεταβάλλειν φησὶ τὴν φρόνησιν· πρὸς παρεὸν γὰρ μῆτις ἐναύξεται ἀνθρώποισιν.

καὶ ἐν ἑτέροις δὲ λέγει [20] ὅτι ὅσσον <δ᾿ ἀλλοῖοι μετέφυν, τόσον ἄρ σφισιν αἰεὶ καὶ τὸ φρονεῖν ἀλλοῖα παρίστατο. καὶ Παρμενίδης δὲ ἀποφαίνεται τὸν αὐτὸν τρόπον· ὡς γὰρ ἑκάστοτ᾿ ἔχει κρᾶσιν μελέων πολυκάμπτων, τὼς νόος ἀνθρώποισι παρίσταται· τὸ γὰρ αὐτό ἐστιν ὅπερ φρονέει, μελέων φύσις ἀνθρώποισιν [25] καὶ πᾶσιν καὶ παντί· τὸ γὰρ πλέον ἐστὶ νόημα.

Ex hiis enim Empedocles et Democritus et aliorum ut consequens dicere unusquisque talibus opinionibus facti sunt rei. Et enim Empedocles permutantes habitum permutare dicit prudentiam: "Ad presens enim consilium augetur hominibus". Et in aliis dicit quia "quantum alteri transformati sunt, tantum ipsis et semper sapere altera affuit". Parmenides vero enuntiat eodem modo: "ut enim quandocumque habuerint membrorum complexionem multe flexionis, intellectus hominibus adest; idem enim est quod quidem sapit, membrorum natura hominibus et omnibus et omni; quod enim plus est intelligentia".

for it is for these reasons that both Empedocles and Democritus and, one may almost say, all the others have fallen victims to opinions of this sort. For Empedocles says that when men change their condition they change their knowledge;

For wisdom increases in men according to what is before them.

And elsewhere he says that:

So far as their nature changed, so far to them always

Came changed thoughts into mind.

And Parmenides also expresses himself in the same way:For as at each time the much-bent limbs are composed,

So is the mind of men; for in each and all men'Tis one thing thinks-the substance of their limbs:

For that of which there is more is thought.

Ἀναξαγόρου δὲ καὶ ἀπόφθεγμα μνημονεύεται πρὸς τῶν ἑταίρων τινάς, ὅτι τοιαῦτ᾽ αὐτοῖς ἔσται τὰ ὄντα οἷα ἂν ὑπολάβωσιν. φασὶ δὲ καὶ τὸν Ὅμηρον ταύτην ἔχοντα φαίνεσθαι τὴν δόξαν, ὅτι ἐποίησε τὸν Ἕκτορα, ὡς ἐξέστη ὑπὸ [30] τῆς πληγῆς, κεῖσθαι ἀλλοφρονέοντα, ὡς φρονοῦντας μὲν καὶ τοὺς παραφρονοῦντας ἀλλ᾽ οὐ ταὐτά.

Anaxagore quoque pronuntium recordatur ad quosdam sociorum, quia talia ipsis erunt entia qualia utique existimaverunt. Dicunt autem et Homerum videri hanc habentem opinionem, quia fecit hectorem, tamquam in extasi fuerit a plaga, iacere aliud sapientem; tamquam sapientes quidem et desipientes, sed non eadem. Palam ergo quod, si utreque prudentie, et entia simul sic et non sic se habent.

A saying of Anaxagoras to some of his friends is also related,– that things would be for them such as they supposed them to be. And they say that Homer also evidently had this opinion, because he made Hector, when he was unconscious from the blow, lie 'thinking other thoughts',– which implies that even those who are bereft of thought have thoughts, though not the same thoughts. Evidently, then, if both are forms of knowledge, the real things also are at the same time both so and not so.

δῆλον οὖν ὅτι, εἰ ἀμφότεραι φρονήσεις, καὶ τὰ ὄντα ἅμα οὕτω τε καὶ οὐχ οὕτως ἔχει. ἢ καὶ χαλεπώτατον τὸ συμβαῖνόν ἐστιν· εἰ γὰρ οἱ μάλιστα τὸ ἐνδεχόμενον ἀληθὲς ἑωρακότες—οὗτοι [35] δ᾽ εἰσὶν οἱ μάλιστα ζητοῦντες αὐτὸ καὶ φιλοῦντες—οὗτοι τοιαύτας ἔχουσι τὰς δόξας καὶ ταῦτα ἀποφαίνονται περὶ τῆς ἀληθείας, πῶς οὐκ ἄξιον ἀθυμῆσαι τοὺς φιλοσοφεῖν ἐγχειροῦντας; τὸ γὰρ τὰ πετόμενα διώκειν τὸ ζητεῖν ἂν εἴη τὴν ἀλήθειαν.

Qua et gravissimum accidens est. Nam si qui maxime contingens verum viderunt (hii autem sunt maxime quaerentes ipsum et amantes), hii tales habent opiniones et talia enuntiant de veritate, quomodo non est dignum respuere philosophari conantes? Nam volantia persequi erit utique veritatem inquirere.

And it is in this direction that the consequences are most difficult. For if those who have seen most of such truth as is possible for us (and these are those who seek and love it most)-if these have such opinions and express these views about the truth, is it not natural that beginners in philosophy should lose heart? For to seek the truth would be to follow flying game.

[1010α] [1] —αἴτιον δὲ τῆς δόξης τούτοις ὅτι περὶ τῶν ὄντων μὲν τὴν ἀλήθειαν ἐσκόπουν, τὰ δ᾽ ὄντα ὑπέλαβον εἶναι τὰ αἰσθητὰ μόνον· ἐν δὲ τούτοις πολλὴ ἡ τοῦ ἀορίστου φύσις ἐνυπάρχει καὶ ἡ τοῦ ὄντος οὕτως ὥσπερ εἴπομεν· [5] διὸ εἰκότως μὲν λέγουσιν, οὐκ ἀληθῆ δὲ λέγουσιν (οὕτω γὰρ ἁρμόττει μᾶλλον εἰπεῖν ἢ ὥσπερ Ἐπίχαρμος εἰς Ξενοφάνην).

Hiis autem opinionis causa quia de entibus quidem veritatem intendebant, entia autem putaverunt esse sensibilia solum; in hiis vero multa quae indeterminati natura existit et quae entis sic ut diximus. Propter quod decenter quidem dicunt, non vera autem dicunt (sic enim congruit magis dicere quam sicut Epicharmus ad Xenophanem).

[10a] But the reason why these thinkers held this opinion is that while they were inquiring into the truth of that which is, they thought, that which is was identical with the sensible world; in this, however, there is largely present the nature of the indeterminate-of that which exists in the peculiar sense which we have explained; and therefore, while they speak plausibly, they do not say what is true (for it is fitting to put the matter so rather than as Epicharmus put it against Xenophanes).

ἔτι δὲ πᾶσαν ὁρῶντες ταύτην κινουμένην τὴν φύσιν, κατὰ δὲ τοῦ μεταβάλλοντος οὐθὲν ἀληθευόμενον, περί γε τὸ πάντη πάντως μεταβάλλον οὐκ ἐνδέχεσθαι ἀληθεύειν. [10] ἐκ γὰρ ταύτης τῆς ὑπολήψεως ἐξήνθησεν ἡ ἀκροτάτη δόξα τῶν εἰρημένων, ἡ τῶν φασκόντων ἡρακλειτίζειν καὶ οἵαν Κρατύλος εἶχεν, ὃς τὸ τελευταῖον οὐθὲν ᾤετο δεῖν λέγειν ἀλλὰ τὸν δάκτυλον ἐκίνει μόνον, καὶ Ἡρακλείτῳ ἐπετίμα εἰπόντι ὅτι δὶς τῷ αὐτῷ ποταμῷ οὐκ ἔστιν ἐμβῆναι· αὐτὸς [15] γὰρ ᾤετο οὐδ᾽ ἅπαξ.

Amplius autem omnem videntes hanc motam naturam, de permutante autem nihil verum dicimus, circa vero omnino semper permutans non contingere verum dicere. Nam ex hac existimatione pullulavit dictorum summa opinio quae est dicentium eraclizare et qualem cratylus habuit, qui tandem nihil opinatus est oportere dicere sed digitum movebat solum, et Eraclitum increpuit dicentem bis in eodem flumine non est intrare; ipse enim existimavit nec semel.

And again, because they saw that all this world of nature is in movement and that about that which changes no true statement can be made, they said that of course, regarding that which everywhere in every respect is changing, nothing could truly be affirmed. It was this belief that blossomed into the most extreme of the views above mentioned, that of the professed Heracliteans, such as was held by Cratylus, who finally did not think it right to say anything but only moved his finger, and criticized Heraclitus for saying that it is impossible to step twice into the same river; for he thought one could not do it even once.

ἡμεῖς δὲ καὶ πρὸς τοῦτον τὸν λόγον ἐροῦμεν ὅτι τὸ μὲν μεταβάλλον ὅτε μεταβάλλει ἔχει τινὰ αὐτοῖς λόγον μὴ οἴεσθαι εἶναι,

Nos autem et ad hanc rationem dicemus quia permutans quando permutat habet quandam ipsis veram rationem non existimari esse,

But we shall say in answer to this argument also that while there is some justification for their thinking that the changing, when it is changing, does not exist,

καίτοι ἔστι γε ἀμφισβητήσιμον: τό τε γὰρ ἀποβάλλον ἔχει τι τοῦ ἀποβαλλομένου, καὶ τοῦ γιγνομένου ἤδη ἀνάγκη τι εἶναι, ὅλως [20] τε εἰ φθείρεται, ὑπάρξει τι ὄν, καὶ εἰ γίγνεται, ἐξ οὗ γίγνεται καὶ ὑφ᾽ οὗ γεννᾶται ἀναγκαῖον εἶναι, καὶ τοῦτο μὴ ἰέναι εἰς ἄπειρον.

equidem est dubitabilissimum; abiciens enim habet aliquid eius quod abicitur, et eius quod fit iam necesse aliquid esse. Omninoque si corrumpitur, existet aliquid ens; et si fit, ex quo fit et a quo generatur necesse esse, et hoc non esse in infinitum.

yet it is after all disputable; for that which is losing a quality has something of that which is being lost, and of that which is coming to be, something must already be. And in general if a thing is perishing, will be present something that exists; and if a thing is coming to be, there must be something from which it comes to be and something by which it is generated, and this process cannot go on ad infinitum.

ἀλλὰ ταῦτα παρέντες ἐκεῖνα λέγωμεν, ὅτι οὐ ταὐτό ἐστι τὸ μεταβάλλειν κατὰ τὸ ποσὸν καὶ κατὰ τὸ ποιόν: κατὰ μὲν οὖν τὸ ποσὸν ἔστω μὴ μένον, [25] ἀλλὰ κατὰ τὸ εἶδος ἅπαντα γιγνώσκομεν.

Sed haec praetermittentes illa dicamus, quia non idem est permutare secundum quantitatem et secundum qualitatem; secundum quantitatem quidem igitur sit non manens, sed secundum speciem omnia cognoscimus.

-But, leaving these arguments, let us insist on this, that it is not the same thing to change in quantity and in quality. Grant that in quantity a thing is not constant; still it is in respect of its form that we know each thing.

ἔτι δ᾽ ἄξιον ἐπιτιμῆσαι τοῖς οὕτως ὑπολαμβάνουσιν, ὅτι καὶ αὐτῶν τῶν αἰσθητῶν ἐπὶ τῶν ἐλαττόνων τὸν ἀριθμὸν ἰδόντες οὕτως ἔχοντα περὶ ὅλου τοῦ οὐρανοῦ ὁμοίως ἀπεφήναντο: ὁ γὰρ περὶ ἡμᾶς τοῦ αἰσθητοῦ τόπος ἐν φθορᾷ καὶ γενέσει διατελεῖ [30] μόνος ὤν, ἀλλ᾽ οὗτος οὐθὲν ὡς εἰπεῖν μόριον τοῦ παντός ἐστιν, ὥστε δικαιότερον ἂν δι᾽ ἐκεῖνα τούτων ἀπεψηφίσαντο ἢ διὰ ταῦτα ἐκείνων κατεψηφίσαντο.

amplius autem dignum  increpare sic existimantes, quod sensibilium in minoribus numerum scientes  sic habentem de toto celo similiter enuntiaverunt. Nam circa nos sensibilis locus in generatione et corruptione perseuerat solus ens; sed  iste ut dicatur nulla pars est omnis, quare iustius utique propter illa haec reueriti fuissent quam propter haec de illis erraverunt.

-And again, it would be fair to criticize those who hold this view for asserting about the whole material universe what they saw only in a minority even of sensible things. For only that region of the sensible world which immediately surrounds us is always in process of destruction and generation; but this is-so to speak-not even a fraction of the whole, so that it would have been juster to acquit this part of the world because of the other part, than to condemn the other because of this.

ἔτι δὲ δῆλον ὅτι καὶ πρὸς τούτους ταὐτὰ τοῖς πάλαι λεχθεῖσιν ἐροῦμεν: ὅτι [34] γὰρ ἔστιν ἀκίνητός τις φύσις δεικτέον αὐτοῖς καὶ πειστέον [35] αὐτούς.

Amplius autem palam quia et ad hos eadem olim dictis dicemus; quod enim est immobilis natura quaedam ostendendum ipsis et credendum est eis.

And again, obviously we shall make to them also the same reply that we made long ago; we must show them and persuade them that there is something whose nature is changeless.

καίτοι γε συμβαίνει τοῖς ἅμα φάσκουσιν εἶναι καὶ μὴ εἶναι ἠρεμεῖν μᾶλλον φάναι πάντα ἢ κινεῖσθαι: οὐ γὰρ ἔστιν εἰς ὅ τι μεταβαλεῖ: ἅπαντα γὰρ ὑπάρχει πᾶσιν.

Equidem contingit simul dicentibus esse et non esse quiescere magis dicere omnia quam moveri; non enim est in quod aliquid permutetur, nam omnia insunt omnibus.

Indeed, those who say that things at the same time are and are not, should in consequence say that all things are at rest rather than that they are in movement; for there is nothing into which they can change, since all attributes belong already to all subjects.

[1010β] [1] —περὶ δὲ τῆς ἀληθείας, ὡς οὐ πᾶν τὸ φαινόμενον ἀληθές, πρῶτον μὲν ὅτι οὐδ᾽ <εἰ ἡ αἴσθησις <μὴ ψευδὴς τοῦ γε ἰδίου ἐστίν, ἀλλ᾽ ἡ φαντασία οὐ ταὐτὸν τῇ αἰσθήσει.

De veritate vero, quod non omne apparens verum; primum quidem quia neque sensus falsus proprii est, sed phantasia non idem sensui.

[10b] Regarding the nature of truth, we must maintain that not everything which appears is true; firstly, because even if sensation-at least of the object peculiar to the sense in question-is not false, still appearance is not the same as sensation.

εἶτ᾽ ἄξιον θαυμάσαι εἰ τοῦτ᾽ ἀποροῦσι, πότερον τηλικαῦτά ἐστι [5] τὰ μεγέθη καὶ τὰ χρώματα τοιαῦτα οἷα τοῖς ἄπωθεν φαίνεται ἢ οἷα τοῖς ἐγγύθεν, καὶ πότερον οἷα τοῖς ὑγιαίνουσιν ἢ οἷα τοῖς κάμνουσιν, καὶ βαρύτερα πότερον ἃ τοῖς ἀσθενοῦσιν ἢ ἃ τοῖς ἰσχύουσιν, καὶ ἀληθῆ πότερον ἃ τοῖς καθεύδουσιν ἢ ἃ τοῖς ἐγρηγορόσιν. ὅτι μὲν γὰρ οὐκ οἴονταί [10] γε, φανερόν· οὐθεὶς γοῦν, ἐὰν ὑπολάβῃ νύκτωρ Ἀθήνησιν εἶναι ὢν ἐν Λιβύῃ, πορεύεται εἰς τὸ ᾠδεῖον.

Deinde dignum mirari si hoc dubitant, utrum tante sunt magnitudines et colores tales quales a remotis videntur aut quales de prope, et utrum qualia sanis aut qualia laborantibus, et graviora utrum qualia debilibus aut qualia robustis, et vera utrum qualia dormientibus aut qualia vigilantibus. Quod quidem enim non putant, palam; nullus ergo, si putaverit de nocte Athenis esse ens in Libia, uadit ad Odium.

Again, it is fair to express surprise at our opponents raising the question whether magnitudes are as great, and colours are of such a nature, as they appear to people at a distance, or as they appear to those close at hand, and whether they are such as they appear to the healthy or to the sick, and whether those things are heavy which appear so to the weak or those which appear so to the strong, and those things true which appear to the slee ing or to the waking. For obviously they do not think these to be open questions; no one, at least, if when he is in Libya he has fancied one night that he is in Athens, starts for the concert hall.

ἔτι δὲ περὶ τοῦ μέλλοντος, ὥσπερ καὶ Πλάτων λέγει, οὐ δήπου ὁμοίως κυρία ἡ τοῦ ἰατροῦ δόξα καὶ ἡ τοῦ ἀγνοοῦντος, οἷον περὶ τοῦ μέλλοντος ἔσεσθαι ὑγιοῦς ἢ μὴ μέλλοντος.

Amplius autem de futuro, ut et Plato dicit, nequaquam similiter propria medici opinio et ignorantis, velut de futuro fore sanos aut non futuro.

And again with regard to the future, as Plato says, surely the opinion of the physician and that of the ignorant man are not equally weighty, for instance, on the question whether a man will get well or not.

ἔτι δὲ ἐπ᾿ αὐτῶν [15] τῶν αἰσθήσεων οὐχ ὁμοίως κυρία ἡ τοῦ ἀλλοτρίου καὶ ἰδίου ἢ τοῦ πλησίον καὶ τοῦ αὑτῆς, ἀλλὰ περὶ μὲν χρώματος ὄψις, οὐ γεῦσις, περὶ δὲ χυμοῦ γεῦσις, οὐκ ὄψις·

Amplius autem et in sensibus non similiter propria alieni et proprii aut propinqui et eius quod ipsius, sed de coloribus quidem visus, non gustus, de saporibus vero gustus, non visus;

-And again, among sensations themselves the sensation of a foreign object and that of the appropriate object, or that of a kindred object and that of the object of the sense in question, are not equally authoritative, but in the case of colour sight, not taste, has the authority, and in the case of flavour taste, not sight;

ὧν ἑκάστη ἐν τῷ αὐτῷ χρόνῳ περὶ τὸ αὐτὸ οὐδέποτε φησιν ἅμα οὕτω καὶ οὐχ οὕτως ἔχειν. ἀλλ᾽ οὐδὲ ἐν ἑτέρῳ [20] χρόνῳ περί γε τὸ πάθος ἠμφισβήτησεν, ἀλλὰ περὶ τὸ ᾧ συμβέβηκε τὸ πάθος. λέγω δ᾽ οἷον ὁ μὲν αὐτὸς οἶνος δόξειεν ἂν ἢ μεταβαλὼν ἢ τοῦ σώματος μεταβαλόντος ὁτὲ μὲν εἶναι γλυκὺς ὁτὲ δὲ οὐ γλυκύς· ἀλλ᾽ οὐ τό γε γλυκύ, οἷόν ἐστιν ὅταν ᾖ, οὐδεπώποτε μετέβαλεν, ἀλλ᾽ ἀεὶ ἀληθεύει [25] περὶ αὐτοῦ, καὶ ἔστιν ἐξ ἀνάγκης τὸ ἐσόμενον γλυκὺ τοιοῦτον.

quorum unusquisque in eodem tempore circa idem numquam dicit simul ita et non ita habere. Sed nec in altero tempore circa passionem dubitavit, sed circa id cui accidit passio. Dico autem puta idem quidem vinum videbitur utique, aut mutatum aut corpore mutato, quandoque quidem esse dulce quandoque autem non dulce. Sed non quod dulce, quale est quando fuerit, numquam mutavit, sed semper de ipso verum dicit, et est ex necessitate futurum dulce tale.

each of which senses never says at the same time of the same object that it simultaneously is so and not so. But not even at different times does one sense disagree about the quality, but only about that to which the quality belongs. I mean, for instance, that the same wine might seem, if either it or one's body changed, at one time sweet and at another time not sweet; but at least the sweet, such as it is when it exists, has never yet changed, but one is always right about it, and that which is to be sweet is of necessity of such and such a nature.

καίτοι τοῦτο ἀναιροῦσιν οὗτοι οἱ λόγοι ἅπαντες, ὥσπερ καὶ οὐσίαν μὴ εἶναι μηθενός, οὕτω μηδ᾽ ἐξ ἀνάγκης μηθέν· τὸ γὰρ ἀναγκαῖον οὐκ ἐνδέχεται ἄλλως καὶ ἄλλως ἔχειν, ὥστ᾽ εἴ τι ἔστιν ἐξ ἀνάγκης, οὐχ ἕξει οὕτω τε καὶ [30] οὐχ οὕτως.

Quamvis hoc hae rationes omnes destruant, quemadmodum et substantiam non esse nullius, ita nec ex necessitate nihil; necessarium enim non contingit aliter et aliter se habere, quare si quid est ex necessitate, non habebit ita et non ita.

Yet all these views destroy this necessity, leaving nothing to be of necessity, as they leave no essence of anything; for the necessary cannot be in this way and also in that, so that if anything is of necessity, it will not be both so and not so.

ὅλως τ᾽ εἴπερ ἔστι τὸ αἰσθητὸν μόνον, οὐθὲν ἂν εἴη μὴ ὄντων τῶν ἐμψύχων· αἴσθησις γὰρ οὐκ ἂν εἴη. τὸ μὲν οὖν μήτε τὰ αἰσθητὰ εἶναι μήτε τὰ αἰσθήματα ἴσως ἀληθές (τοῦ γὰρ αἰσθανομένου πάθος τοῦτό ἐστι), τὸ δὲ τὰ ὑποκείμενα μὴ εἶναι, ἃ ποιεῖ τὴν αἴσθησιν, καὶ ἄνευ αἰσθήσεως, [35] ἀδύνατον. οὐ γὰρ δὴ ἥ γ᾽ αἴσθησις αὐτὴ ἑαυτῆς ἐστίν, ἀλλ᾽ ἔστι τι καὶ ἕτερον παρὰ τὴν αἴσθησιν, ὃ ἀνάγκη πρότερον εἶναι τῆς αἰσθήσεως· [1011α] [1] τὸ γὰρ κινοῦν τοῦ κινουμένου φύσει πρότερόν ἐστι, κἂν εἰ λέγεται πρὸς ἄλληλα ταῦτα, οὐθὲν ἧττον.

Totaliterque si est sensibile solum, nihil utique erit solum non existentibus animatis; sensus enim non erit. Neque quidem igitur sensibilia esse neque sensiones forsan verum ; sentientis enim passio hoc est. Subiecta vero non esse quae sensum faciunt et sine sensu, impossibile. Non enim sensus suimet est, sed est aliquid alterum praeter sensum, quod ionai prius esse sensu est necesse; movens enim moto prius est natura, et utique si ad invicem dicuntur haec ipsa, nihil minus.

And, in general, if only the sensible exists, there would be nothing if animate things were not; for there would be no faculty of sense. Now the view that neither the sensible qualities nor the sensations would exist is doubtless true (for they are affections of the perceiver), but that the substrata which cause the sensation should not exist even apart from sensation is impossible. For sensation is surely not the sensation of itself, but there is something beyond the sensation, which must be prior to the sensation; for that [11a] which moves is prior in nature to that which is moved, and if they are correlative terms, this is no less the case.

## Chapter 6

εἰσὶ δέ τινες οἳ ἀποροῦσι καὶ τῶν ταῦτα πεπεισμένων καὶ τῶν τοὺς λόγους τούτους μόνον λεγόντων: ζητοῦσι γὰρ [5] τίς ὁ κρινῶν τὸν ὑγιαίνοντα καὶ ὅλως τὸν περὶ ἕκαστα κρινοῦντα ὀρθῶς. τὰ δὲ τοιαῦτα ἀπορήματα ὅμοιά ἐστι τῷ ἀπορεῖν πότερον καθεύδομεν νῦν ἢ ἐγρηγόραμεν, δύνανται δ᾽ αἱ ἀπορίαι αἱ τοιαῦται πᾶσαι τὸ αὐτό: πάντων γὰρ λόγον ἀξιοῦσιν εἶναι οὗτοι: ἀρχὴν γὰρ ζητοῦσι, καὶ ταύτην [10] δι᾽ ἀποδείξεως λαμβάνειν, ἐπεὶ ὅτι γε πεπεισμένοι οὐκ εἰσί, φανεροὶ εἰσιν ἐν ταῖς πράξεσιν. ἀλλ᾽ ὅπερ εἴπομεν, τοῦτο αὐτῶν τὸ πάθος ἐστίν: λόγον γὰρ ζητοῦσιν ὧν οὐκ ἔστι λόγος: ἀποδείξεως γὰρ ἀρχὴ οὐκ ἀπόδειξίς ἐστιν. οὗτοι μὲν οὖν ῥᾳδίως ἂν τοῦτο πεισθεῖεν (ἔστι γὰρ οὐ χαλεπὸν λαβεῖν):

Sunt autem quidam qui dubitant haec persuasorum et has rationes solum dicentium; quaerunt enim quis est qui iudicat sanum et omnino circa singula recte iudicantem. Tales vero dubitationes similes sunt dubitationi utrum dormimus nunc aut vigilamus. Possunt autem omnes dubitationes tales idem. Omnium enim rationem hii dignificant esse; principium enim quaerunt, et hoc per demonstrationem accipere, quoniamque quod non persuasi sunt, manifesti sunt in actibus. Sed quod quidem diximus, hoc ipsorum passio est: rationem enim quaerunt quorum non est ratio; demonstrationis enim principium non est demonstratio. Hii quidem igitur facile utique hoc credent; est enim non difficile sumere.

There are, both among those who have these convictions and among those who merely profess these views, some who raise a difficulty by asking, who is to be the judge of the healthy man, and in general who is likely to judge rightly on each class of questions. But such inquiries are like puzzling over the question whether we are now asleep or awake. And all such questions have the same meaning. These people demand that a reason shall be given for everything; for they seek a starting-point, and they seek to get this by demonstration, while it is obvious from their actions that they have no conviction. But their mistake is what we have stated it to be; they seek a reason for things for which no reason can be given; for the starting-point of demonstration is not demonstration. These, then, might be easily persuaded of this truth, for it is not difficult to grasp;

[15] οἱ δ᾽ ἐν τῷ λόγῳ τὴν βίαν μόνον ζητοῦντες ἀδύνατον ζητοῦσιν: ἐναντία γὰρ εἰπεῖν ἀξιοῦσιν, εὐθὺς ἐναντία λέγοντες.

In sermone autem  vim solum quaerentes impossibile quaerunt; contraria namque dicere dignificant, statim contraria dicentes.

but those who seek merely compulsion in argument seek what is impossible; for they demand to be allowed to contradict themselves – a claim which contradicts itself from the very first.

εἰ δὲ μὴ ἔστι πάντα πρός τι, ἀλλ᾽ ἔνιά ἐστι καὶ αὐτὰ καθ᾽ αὑτά, οὐκ ἂν εἴη πᾶν τὸ φαινόμενον ἀληθές: τὸ γὰρ φαινόμενον τινί ἐστι φαινόμενον: ὥστε ὁ λέγων ἅπαντα τὰ [20] φαινόμενα εἶναι ἀληθῆ ἅπαντα ποιεῖ τὰ ὄντα πρός τι. διὸ καὶ φυλακτέον τοῖς τὴν βίαν ἐν τῷ λόγῳ ζητοῦσιν, ἅμα δὲ καὶ ὑπέχειν λόγον ἀξιοῦσιν, ὅτι οὐ τὸ φαινόμενον ἔστιν ἀλλὰ τὸ φαινόμενον ᾧ φαίνεται καὶ ὅτε φαίνεται καὶ ᾗ καὶ ὥς. ἂν δ᾽ ὑπέχωσι μὲν λόγον, μὴ οὕτω δ᾽ [25] ὑπέχωσι, συμβήσεται αὐτοῖς τἀναντία ταχὺ λέγειν. ἐνδέχεται γὰρ τὸ αὐτὸ κατὰ μὲν τὴν ὄψιν μέλι φαίνεσθαι τῇ δὲ γεύσει μή, καὶ τῶν ὀφθαλμῶν δυοῖν ὄντοιν μὴ ταὐτὰ ἑκατέρᾳ τῇ ὄψει, ἂν ὦσιν ἀνόμοιαι: ἐπεὶ πρός γε τοὺς διὰ τὰς πάλαι εἰρημένας αἰτίας τὸ φαινόμενον φάσκοντας [30] ἀληθὲς εἶναι, καὶ διὰ τοῦτο πάνθ᾽ ὁμοίως εἶναι ψευδῆ καὶ ἀληθῆ: οὔτε γὰρ ἅπασι ταὐτὰ φαίνεσθαι οὔτε ταὐτῷ ἀεὶ ταὐτά, ἀλλὰ πολλάκις τἀναντία κατὰ τὸν αὐτὸν χρόνον (ἡ μὲν γὰρ ἁφὴ δύο λέγει ἐν τῇ ἐπαλλάξει τῶν δακτύλων ἡ δ᾽ ὄψις ἕν): ἀλλ᾽ οὔ τι τῇ αὐτῇ γε καὶ [35] κατὰ τὸ αὐτὸ αἰσθήσει καὶ ὡσαύτως καὶ ἐν τῷ αὐτῷ χρόνῳ, ὥστε τοῦτ᾽ ἂν εἴη ἀληθές. [1011β] [1] ἀλλ᾽ ἴσως διὰ τοῦτ᾽ ἀνάγκη λέγειν τοῖς μὴ δι᾽ ἀπορίαν ἀλλὰ λόγου χάριν λέγουσιν, ὅτι οὐκ ἔστιν ἀληθὲς τοῦτο ἀλλὰ τούτῳ ἀληθές.

Si autem non omnia sunt ad aliquid, sed quaedam sunt et ipsa secundum se, non utique erit omne quod apparet ; nam quod apparet alicui apparet. Quare qui dicit omnia quae apparent esse vera, omnia quae sunt facit ad aliquid. Propter quod et observandum vim in sermone quaerentibus, simul autem et sustinere sermonem dignificantibus; quod non quod apparet est, sed quod apparet cui apparet et quando apparet et in quantum et ut. Si autem sustineant quidem sermonem, non sic autem sustineant, accidet ipsis contraria cito  dicere. Contingit enim eidem secundum visum quidem mel apparere, gustu vero non, et oculis duobus existentibus non eadem utrique visui, si sint dissimiles. Quoniam ad  dicentes   propter olim dictas causas quod apparet verum esse, et propter hoc omnia similiter esse falsa et vera; neque enim omnibus eadem apparere contingit neque ipsi semper eadem, sed multotiens contraria

secundum idem tempus (tactus enim duo dicit in digitorum variatione, visus autem unum): — Sed non quid  eidem et secundum idem sensui et similiter et in eodem tempore; quare hoc utique erit verum. Sed forsan propter hoc  necesse dicere hiis qui non propter dubitationem sed orationis causa dicentibus: quod hoc non est verum sed huic verum.

-But if not all things are relative, but some are self-existent, not everything that appears will be true; for that which appears is apparent to some one; so that he who says all things that appear are true, makes all things relative. And, therefore, those who ask for an irresistible argument, and at the same time demand to be called to account for their views, must guard themselves by saying that the truth is not that what appears exists, but that what appears exists for him to whom it appears, and when, and to the sense to which, and under the conditions under which it appears. And if they give an account of their view, but do not give it in this way, they will soon find themselves contradicting themselves. For it is possible that the same thing may appear to be honey to the sight, but not to the taste, and that, since we have two eyes, things may not appear the same to each, if their sight is unlike. For to those who for the reasons named some time ago say that what appears is true, and therefore that all things are alike false and true, for things do not appear either the same to all men or always the same to the same man, but often have contrary appearances at the same time (for touch says there are two objects when we cross our fingers, while sight says there is one) – to these we shall say yes, but not to the same sense and in the same part of it and under the same conditions and at the same time, so that what appears will be with these [11b] qualifications true. But perhaps for this reason those who argue thus not because they feel a difficulty but for the sake of argument, should say that this is not true, but true for this man.

καὶ ὥσπερ δὴ πρότερον εἴρηται, ἀνάγκη πρός τι ποιεῖν [5] ἅπαντα καὶ πρὸς δόξαν καὶ αἴσθησιν, ὥστ᾽ οὔτε γέγονεν οὔτ᾽ ἔσται οὐθὲν μηθενὸς προδοξάσαντος. εἰ δὲ γέγονεν ἢ ἔσται, δῆλον ὅτι οὐκ ἂν εἴη ἅπαντα πρὸς δόξαν.

Et sicut prius dictum est, necesse ad aliquid facere omnia et ad opinionem et sensum; quare nec factum est nec erit nihil nullo preopinante. Si vero factum est aut erit, palam quia non erunt omnia ad opinionem.

And as has been said before, they must make everything relative-relative to opinion and perception, so that nothing either has come to be or will be without some one's first thinking so. But if things have come to be or will be, evidently not all things will be relative to opinion.

ἔτι εἰ ἕν, πρὸς ἓν ἢ πρὸς ὡρισμένον· καὶ εἰ τὸ αὐτὸ καὶ ἥμισυ καὶ ἴσον, ἀλλ᾽ οὐ πρὸς τὸ διπλάσιόν γε τὸ ἴσον. πρὸς δὴ τὸ δοξάζον [10] εἰ ταὐτὸ ἄνθρωπος καὶ τὸ

δοξαζόμενον, οὐκ ἔσται ἄνθρωπος τὸ δοξάζον ἀλλὰ τὸ δοξαζόμενον. εἰ δ᾽ ἕκαστον ἔσται πρὸς τὸ δοξάζον, πρὸς ἄπειρα ἔσται τῷ εἴδει τὸ δοξάζον.

Amplius si unum, ad unum aut ad determinatum; et si idem et dimidium et equale, sed ionbio non ad duplum equale. Ad opinans itaque si idem est homo et opinatum, non est homo opinans sed opinatum. Si vero unumquodque fuerit ad opinans, infinita erit specie opinans.

-Again, if a thing is one, it is in relation to one thing or to a definite number of things; and if the same thing is both half and equal, it is not to the double that the equal is correlative. If, then, in relation to that which thinks, man and that which is thought are the same, man will not be that which thinks, but only that which is thought. And if each thing is to be relative to that which thinks, that which thinks will be relative to an infinity of specifically different things.

ὅτι μὲν οὖν βεβαιοτάτη δόξα πασῶν τὸ μὴ εἶναι ἀληθεῖς ἅμα τὰς ἀντικειμένας φάσεις, καὶ τί συμβαίνει τοῖς οὕτω [15] λέγουσι, καὶ διὰ τί οὕτω λέγουσι, τοσαῦτα εἰρήσθω·

Quod quidem igitur firmissima opinio omnium non esse simul veras oppositas dictiones, et quid accidit ita dicentibus, et quare ita dicunt, tot sint dicta.

Let this, then, suffice to show (1) that the most indisputable of all beliefs is that contradictory statements are not at the same time true, and (2) what consequences follow from the assertion that they are, and (3) why people do assert this.

ἐπεὶ δ᾽ ἀδύνατον τὴν ἀντίφασιν ἅμα ἀληθεύεσθαι κατὰ τοῦ αὐτοῦ, φανερὸν ὅτι οὐδὲ τἀναντία ἅμα ὑπάρχειν ἐνδέχεται τῷ αὐτῷ· τῶν μὲν γὰρ ἐναντίων θάτερον στέρησίς ἐστιν οὐχ ἧττον, οὐσίας δὲ στέρησις· ἡ δὲ στέρησις ἀπόφασίς ἐστιν ἀπό [20] τινος ὡρισμένου γένους· εἰ οὖν ἀδύνατον ἅμα καταφάναι καὶ ἀποφάναι ἀληθῶς, ἀδύνατον καὶ τἀναντία ὑπάρχειν ἅμα, ἀλλ᾽ ἢ πῇ ἄμφω ἢ θάτερον μὲν πῇ θάτερον δὲ ἁπλῶς.

Quoniam autem impossibile est contradictionem esse simul veram de eodem, palam quia nec contraria simul inesse eidem contingit. Contrariorum enim alterum est privatio non minus; substantiae autem privatio negatio est ab aliquo determinato genere. Si igitur impossibile est simul affirmare et negare vere, impossibile et contraria simul inesse, sed aut quo ambo, vel alterum quo, alterum vero simpliciter.

Now since it is impossible that contradictories should be at the same time true of the same thing, obviously contraries also cannot belong at the same time to the same thing. For of contraries, one is a privation no less than it is a contrary-and a privation of the essential nature; and privation is the denial of a predicate to a determinate genus. If, then, it is impossible to affirm and deny truly at the same time, it is also impossible that contraries should belong to a subject at the same time, unless both belong to it in particular relations, or one in a particular relation and one without qualification.

*Chapter 7*

ἀλλὰ μὴν οὐδὲ μεταξὺ ἀντιφάσεως ἐνδέχεται εἶναι οὐθέν, ἀλλ᾽ ἀνάγκη ἢ φάναι ἢ ἀποφάναι ἓν καθ᾽ ἑνὸς ὁτιοῦν. [25] δῆλον δὲ πρῶτον μὲν ὁρισαμένοις τί τὸ ἀληθὲς καὶ ψεῦδος. τὸ μὲν γὰρ λέγειν τὸ ὂν μὴ εἶναι ἢ τὸ μὴ ὂν εἶναι ψεῦδος, τὸ δὲ τὸ ὂν εἶναι καὶ τὸ μὴ ὂν μὴ εἶναι ἀληθές, ὥστε καὶ ὁ λέγων εἶναι ἢ μὴ ἀληθεύσει ἢ ψεύσεται: ἀλλ᾽ οὔτε τὸ ὂν λέγεται μὴ εἶναι ἢ εἶναι οὔτε τὸ μὴ ὄν.

At vero nec medium contradictionis nihil esse contingit, sed necessarium aut dicere aut negare unum de uno quodcumque. Palam autem primum quidem diffmientibus quid verum et falsum. Dicere namque ens non esse aut hoc esse falsum , ens autem esse et non ens non esse verum ; quare et dicens esse aut non verum dicet aut mentietur; sed neque ens dicit non esse aut esse neque non ens,

But on the other hand there cannot be an intermediate between contradictories, but of one subject we must either affirm or deny any one predicate. This is clear, in the first place, if we define what the true and the false are. To say of what is that it is not, or of what is not that it is, is false, while to say of what is that it is, and of what is not that it is not, is true; so that he who says of anything that it is, or that it is not, will say either what is true or what is false; but neither what is nor what is not is said to be or not to be.

ἔτι [30] ἤτοι μεταξὺ ἔσται τῆς ἀντιφάσεως ὥσπερ τὸ φαιὸν μέλανος καὶ λευκοῦ, ἢ ὡς τὸ μηδέτερον ἀνθρώπου καὶ ἵππου. εἰ μὲν οὖν οὕτως, οὐκ ἂν μεταβάλλοι (ἐκ μὴ ἀγαθοῦ γὰρ εἰς ἀγαθὸν μεταβάλλει ἢ ἐκ τούτου εἰς μὴ ἀγαθόν), νῦν δ᾽ ἀεὶ φαίνεται (οὐ γὰρ ἔστι μεταβολὴ ἀλλ᾽ ἢ εἰς τὰ ἀντικείμενα [35] καὶ μεταξύ): εἰ δ᾽ ἔστι μεταξύ, καὶ οὕτως εἴη ἄν τις εἰς λευκὸν οὐκ ἐκ μὴ λευκοῦ γένεσις, νῦν δ᾽ οὐχ ὁρᾶται.

Amplius aut medium erit contradictionis quemadmodum pallidum albi et nigri, aut quemadmodum neutrum hominis et equi. Si quidem igitur sic, non permutabitur (nam ex non bono in bonum permutatur aut ex hoc in non bonum); nunc autem semper videtur. Non est enim permutatio nisi in contraria et media. Si autem est medium, et sic utique erit aliqua in album 1012a1 non ex non albo generatio; nunc autem non videtur.

Again, the intermediate between the contradictories will be so either in the way in which grey is between black and white, or as that which is neither man nor horse is between man and horse. (a) If it were of the latter kind, it could not change into the extremes (for change is from not-good to good, or from good to not-good), but as a matter of fact when there is an intermediate it is always observed to change into the extremes. For there is no change except to opposites and to their intermediates. (b) But if it is really intermediate, in this way too there would have to be a change to white, which was not from not-white; but as it [12a] is, this is never seen.

[1012α] [1] ἔτι πᾶν τὸ διανοητὸν καὶ νοητὸν ἡ διάνοια ἢ κατάφησιν ἢ ἀπόφησιν—τοῦτο δ᾽ ἐξ ὁρισμοῦ δῆλον—ὅταν ἀληθεύῃ ἢ ψεύδηται· ὅταν μὲν ὡδὶ συνθῇ φᾶσα ἢ ἀποφᾶσα, ἀληθεύει, [5] ὅταν δὲ ὡδί, ψεύδεται.

Amplius omne intellectuale et intelligibile mens aut affirmat aut negat. Hoc autem ex diffinitione palam, cum verum dicit aut mentitur. Quando quidem sic componit dicens aut negans, verum dicit, quando autem sic, mentitur.

Again, every object of understanding or reason the understanding either affirms or denies – this is obvious from the definition – whenever it says what is true or false. When it connects in one way by assertion or negation, it says what is true, and when it does so in another way, what is false.

ἔτι παρὰ πάσας δεῖ εἶναι τὰς ἀντιφάσεις, εἰ μὴ λόγου ἕνεκα λέγεται· ὥστε καὶ οὔτε ἀληθεύσει [7] τις οὔτ᾽ οὐκ ἀληθεύσει, καὶ παρὰ τὸ ὂν καὶ τὸ μὴ ὂν ἔσται, ὥστε καὶ παρὰ γένεσιν καὶ φθορὰν μεταβολή τις ἔσται.

Amplius praeter omnes oportet esse contradictiones, nisi orationis causa dicatur. Quare et nec verum dicet aliquis nec non verum dicet, et praeter ens et non ens erit, quare et praeter generationem et corruptionem transmutatio quaedam erit.

-Again, there must be an intermediate between all contradictories, if one is not arguing merely for the sake of argument; so that it will be possible for a man to say what is neither true nor untrue, and there will be a middle between that which is and that which is not, so that there will also be a kind of change intermediate between generation and destruction.

ἔτι ἐν ὅσοις γένεσιν ἡ ἀπόφασις τὸ ἐναντίον ἐπιφέρει, [10] καὶ ἐν τούτοις ἔσται, οἷον ἐν ἀριθμοῖς οὔτε περιττὸς οὔτε οὐ περιττὸς ἀριθμός· ἀλλ᾽ ἀδύνατον· ἐκ τοῦ ὁρισμοῦ δὲ δῆλον.

Amplius in quibuscumque generibus negatio contrarium infert, et in hiis erit, ut in numeris neque impar neque non impar numerus. Sed impossibile; ex diffinitione vero palam.

Again, in all classes in which the negation of an attribute involves the assertion of its contrary, even in these there will be an intermediate; for instance, in the sphere of numbers there will be number which is neither odd nor not-odd. But this is impossible, as is obvious from the definition.

ἔτι εἰς ἄπειρον βαδιεῖται, καὶ οὐ μόνον ἡμιόλια τὰ ὄντα ἔσται ἀλλὰ πλείω. πάλιν γὰρ ἔσται ἀποφῆσαι τοῦτο πρὸς τὴν φάσιν καὶ τὴν ἀπόφασιν, καὶ τοῦτ᾽ ἔσται τι· ἡ [15] γὰρ οὐσία ἐστί τις αὐτοῦ ἄλλη.

Amplius in infinitum vadet; et non solum emyolia quae sunt erunt sed plura. Iterum enim est hoc negare ad dictionem et negationem, et hoc erit aliquid; nam substantia est quaedam ipsius alia.

Again, the process will go on ad infinitum, and the number of realities will be not only half as great again, but even greater. For again it will be possible to deny this intermediate with reference both to its assertion and to its negation, and this new term will be some definite thing; for its essence is something different.

ἔτι ὅταν ἐρομένου εἰ λευκόν ἐστιν εἴπῃ ὅτι οὔ, οὐθὲν ἄλλο ἀποπέφηκεν ἢ τὸ εἶναι· ἀπόφασις δὲ τὸ μὴ εἶναι.

Amplius quando interrogante si est album dicit quia non , nihil aliud negavit quam ipsum esse; negatio vero est quod non esse.

Again, when a man, on being asked whether a thing is white, says no, he has denied nothing except that it is; and its not being is a negation.

ἐλήλυθε δ᾽ ἐνίοις αὕτη ἡ δόξα ὥσπερ καὶ ἄλλαι τῶν παραδόξων· ὅταν γὰρ λύειν μὴ δύνωνται λόγους ἐριστικούς, ἐνδόντες τῷ λόγῳ σύμφασιν ἀληθὲς [20] εἶναι τὸ συλλογισθέν. οἱ μὲν οὖν διὰ τοιαύτην αἰτίαν λέγουσιν, οἱ δὲ διὰ τὸ πάντων ζητεῖν λόγον.

Venit autem quibusdam haec opinio sicut et aliae inopinabilium; quando enim soluere non possunt orationes contentiosas, annuentes orationi confirmant verum esse quod est sillogizatum. Hii quidem igitur propter talem causam dicunt, illi vero propter omnium rationem inquirere.

Some people have acquired this opinion as other paradoxical opinions have been acquired; when men cannot refute eristical arguments, they give in to the argument and agree that the conclusion is true. This, then, is why some express this view; others do so because they demand a reason for everything.

ἀρχὴ δὲ πρὸς ἅπαντας τούτους ἐξ ὁρισμοῦ. ὁρισμὸς δὲ γίγνεται ἐκ τοῦ σημαίνειν τι ἀναγκαῖον εἶναι αὐτούς· ὁ γὰρ λόγος οὗ τὸ ὄνομα σημεῖον ὁρισμὸς ἔσται.

Principium autem ad hos omnes ex diffinitione. Diffinitio vero fit ex ipsos significare aliquid necessarium esse; ratio namque cuius nomen est signum diffinitio fit.

And the starting-point in dealing with all such people is definition. Now the definition rests on the necessity of their meaning something; for the form of words of which the word is a sign will be its definition.

ἔοικε δ᾽ ὁ μὲν Ἡρακλείτου [25] λόγος, λέγων πάντα εἶναι καὶ μὴ εἶναι, ἅπαντα ἀληθῆ ποιεῖν, ὁ δ᾽ Ἀναξαγόρου, εἶναί τι μεταξὺ τῆς ἀντιφάσεως, πάντα ψευδῆ· ὅταν γὰρ μιχθῇ, οὔτε ἀγαθὸν οὔτε οὐκ ἀγαθὸν τὸ μῖγμα, ὥστ᾽ οὐδὲν εἰπεῖν ἀληθές.

Videtur autem Eracliti quidem oratio, dicens omnia esse et non esse, omnia vera facere; quae vero est Anaxagore, esse aliquid medium contradictionis, quare omnia falsa. Nam quando miscentur, nec bonum nec non bonum est mixtum, quare nihil dicere verum.

-While the doctrine of Heraclitus, that all things are and are not, seems to make everything true, that of Anaxagoras, that there is an intermediate between the terms of a contradiction, seems to make everything false; for when things are mixed, the mixture is neither good nor not-good, so that one cannot say anything that is true.

## Chapter 8

διωρισμένων δὲ τούτων φανερὸν ὅτι καὶ τὰ μοναχῶς [30] λεγόμενα καὶ κατὰ πάντων ἀδύνατον ὑπάρχειν ὥσπερ τινὲς λέγουσιν, οἱ μὲν οὐθὲν φάσκοντες ἀληθὲς εἶναι (οὐθὲν γὰρ κωλύειν φασὶν οὕτως ἅπαντα εἶναι ὥσπερ τὸ τὴν διάμετρον σύμμετρον εἶναι), οἱ δὲ πάντ᾽ ἀληθῆ. σχεδὸν γὰρ οὗτοι οἱ λόγοι οἱ αὐτοὶ τῷ Ἡρακλείτου· ὁ γὰρ λέγων [35] ὅτι πάντ᾽ ἀληθῆ καὶ πάντα ψευδῆ, καὶ χωρὶς λέγει τῶν λόγων ἑκάτερον τούτων, [1012β] [1] ὥστ᾽ εἴπερ ἀδύνατα ἐκεῖνα, καὶ ταῦτα ἀδύνατον εἶναι.

Determinatis autem hiis palam quod uno modo dicta et de omnibus impossibile est esse sicut quidam dicunt. Hii quidem nihil dicentes verum esse; nihil enim prohibere dicunt sic omnia esse sicut dyametrum commensurabilem esse. Illi vero omnia vera. Fere namque ipsis rationes eaedem Eraclito; nam qui dicit quia omnia sunt vera et omnia falsa, et seorsum rdicit rationem utramque horum1, quare si sunt impossibilia illa, et haec impossibile esse.

In view of these distinctions it is obvious that the one-sided theories which some people express about all things cannot be valid-on the one hand the theory that nothing is true (for, say they, there is nothing to prevent every statement from being like the statement 'the diagonal of a square is commensurate with the side'), on the other hand the theory that everything is true. These views are practically the same as that of Heraclitus; for he who says that all things are true and all are false also makes each of [12b] these statements separately, so that since they are impossible, the double statement must be impossible too.

ἔτι δὲ φανερῶς ἀντιφάσεις εἰσὶν ἃς οὐχ οἷόν τε ἅμα ἀληθεῖς εἶναι—οὐδὲ δὴ ψευδεῖς πάσας· καίτοι δόξειέ γ᾽ ἂν μᾶλλον ἐνδέχεσθαι ἐκ τῶν εἰρημένων.

Amplius autem evidenter contradictiones sunt quas non est possibile simul esse veras, nec itaque falsas omnes; et quidem utique putabitur magis contingere ex dictis.

Again, there are obviously contradictories which cannot be at the same time true-nor on the other hand can all statements be false; yet this would seem more possible in the light of what has been said.

ἀλλὰ πρὸς πάντας τοὺς τοιούτους λόγους αἰτεῖσθαι δεῖ, καθάπερ ἐλέχθη καὶ ἐν τοῖς ἐπάνω λόγοις, οὐχὶ εἶναί τι ἢ μὴ εἶναι ἀλλὰ σημαίνειν τι, ὥστε ἐξ ὁρισμοῦ διαλεκτέον λαβόντας τί σημαίνει τὸ ψεῦδος ἢ τὸ ἀληθές. εἰ δὲ μηθὲν ἄλλο τὸ ἀληθὲς φάναι ἢ <ὃ ἀποφάναι; ψεῦδός ἐστιν, ἀδύνατον [10] πάντα ψευδῆ εἶναι· ἀνάγκη γὰρ τῆς ἀντιφάσεως θάτερον εἶναι μόριον ἀληθές.

Sed ad omnes tales orationes oportet quaerere, quemadmodum in superioribus sermonibus dictum est, non esse aliquid aut non esse sed significare aliquid, quare ex diffinitione disputandum accipientes quid significat verum aut falsum. Si autem nihil aliud quam verum dicere aut negare falsum est, impossibile omnia falsa esse; est enim necesse contradictionis partem alteram esse veram.

-But against all such views we must postulate, as we said above, not that something is or is not, but that something has a meaning, so that we must argue from a definition, viz. by assuming what falsity or truth means. If that which it is true to affirm is nothing other than that which it is false to deny, it is impossible that all statements should be false; for one side of the contradiction must be true.

ἔτι εἰ πᾶν ἢ φάναι ἢ ἀποφάναι ἀναγκαῖον, ἀδύνατον ἀμφότερα ψευδῆ εἶναι· θάτερον γὰρ μόριον τῆς ἀντιφάσεως ψεῦδός ἐστιν.

Amplius si omne aut dicere aut negare est necesse, utraque falsa esse impossibile est; altera namque pars contradictionis est falsa.

Again, if it is necessary with regard to everything either to assert or to deny it, it is impossible that both should be false; for it is one side of the contradiction that is false.

συμβαίνει δὴ καὶ τὸ θρυλούμενον πᾶσι τοῖς τοιούτοις λόγοις, αὐτοὺς [15] ἑαυτοὺς ἀναιρεῖν. ὁ μὲν γὰρ πάντα ἀληθῆ λέγων καὶ τὸν ἐναντίον αὑτοῦ λόγον ἀληθῆ ποιεῖ, ὥστε τὸν ἑαυτοῦ οὐκ ἀληθῆ (ὁ γὰρ ἐναντίος οὔ φησιν αὐτὸν ἀληθῆ), ὁ δὲ πάντα ψευδῆ καὶ αὐτὸς αὑτόν. ἐὰν δ᾽ ἐξαιρῶνται ὁ μὲν τὸν ἐναντίον ὡς οὐκ ἀληθὴς μόνος ἐστίν, ὁ δὲ τὸν αὑτοῦ ὡς οὐ ψευδής, [20] οὐδὲν ἧττον ἀπείρους συμβαίνει αὐτοῖς αἰτεῖσθαι λόγους ἀληθεῖς καὶ ψευδεῖς· ὁ γὰρ λέγων τὸν ἀληθῆ λόγον ἀληθῆ ἀληθής, τοῦτο δ᾽ εἰς ἄπειρον βαδιεῖται.

Accidit itaque et quod famatum est de omnibus talibus orationibus: ipsas se ipsas destruere. Nam qui omnia vera dicit orationis sue contrariam veram facit, quare suam non veram; contraria enim non dicit ipsam esse veram. Qui vero omnia falsa, et ipse se ipsum. Si autem excipiant, hic quidem contrariam quod non vera sola est, ille vero suam propriam quod non falsa, nihil minus infinitas accidit ipsis petere orationes veras et falsas. Nam qui dicit veram orationem veram verus est, hoc autem in infinitum vadet.

Therefore all such views are also exposed to the often expressed objection, that they destroy themselves. For he who says that everything is true makes even the statement contrary to his own true, and therefore his own not true (for the contrary statement denies that it is true), while he who says everything is false makes himself also false.-And if the former person excepts the contrary statement, saying it alone is not true, while the latter excepts his own as being not false, none the less they are driven to postulate the truth or falsity of an infinite number of statements; for that which says the true statement is true is true, and this process will go on to infinity.

φανερὸν δ᾽ ὅτι οὐδ᾽ οἱ πάντα ἠρεμεῖν λέγοντες ἀληθῆ λέγουσιν οὐδ᾽ οἱ πάντα κινεῖσθαι.

Palam autem quia nec qui omnia quiescere dicunt vera dicunt nec qui omnia moveri.

Evidently, again, those who say all things are at rest are not right, nor are those who say all things are in movement.

εἰ μὲν γὰρ ἠρεμεῖ πάντα, ἀεὶ ταὐτὰ ἀληθῆ καὶ [25] ψευδῆ ἔσται, φαίνεται δὲ τοῦτο μεταβάλλον (ὁ γὰρ λέγων ποτὲ αὐτὸς οὐκ ἦν καὶ πάλιν οὐκ ἔσται):

Nam si quiescunt omnia, semper haec vera et falsa erunt, videtur autem hoc transmutatum; nam qui dicit aliquando ipse non erat et iterum non erit.

For if all things are at rest, the same statements will always be true and the same always false,-but this obviously changes; for he who makes a statement, himself at one time was not and again will not be.

εἰ δὲ πάντα κινεῖται, οὐθὲν ἔσται ἀληθές· πάντα ἄρα ψευδῆ· ἀλλὰ δέδεικται ὅτι ἀδύνατον.

Si vero omnia moventur, nihil erit verum; ergo omnia falsa. Sed ostensum est quia impossibile est.

And if all things are in motion, nothing will be true; everything therefore will be false. But it has been shown that this is impossible.

ἔτι ἀνάγκη τὸ ὂν μεταβάλλειν: ἔκ τινος γὰρ εἴς τι ἡ μεταβολή.

Amplius ens permutari est necesse; nam ex aliquo in aliquid est permutatio.

Again, it must be that which is that changes; for change is from something to something.

ἀλλὰ μὴν οὐδὲ πάντα ἠρεμεῖ [30] ἢ κινεῖται ποτέ, ἀεὶ δ᾽ οὐθέν: ἔστι γάρ τι ὃ ἀεὶ κινεῖ τὰ κινούμενα, καὶ τὸ πρῶτον κινοῦν ἀκίνητον αὐτό.

At vero nec omnia quiescunt aut moventur aliquando, semper autem nihil; est enim aliquid quod semper movet quae moventur, et primum movens immobile ipsum.

But again it is not the case that all things are at rest or in motion sometimes, and nothing for ever; for there is something which always moves the things that are in motion, and the first mover is itself unmoved.

# METHAPHISICE ARISTOTILIS LIBER QUINTUS

## 5 (D)

[1012β] [34] ἀρχὴ λέγεται ἡ μὲν ὅθεν ἄν τις τοῦ πράγματος [35] κινηθείη πρῶτον, οἷον τοῦ μήκους καὶ ὁδοῦ ἐντεῦθεν μὲν αὕτη ἀρχή, ἐξ ἐναντίας δὲ ἑτέρα: [1013α] [1] ἡ δὲ ὅθεν ἂν κάλλιστα ἕκαστον γένοιτο, οἷον καὶ μαθήσεως οὐκ ἀπὸ τοῦ πρώτου καὶ τῆς τοῦ πράγματος ἀρχῆς ἐνίοτε ἀρκτέον ἀλλ᾽ ὅθεν ῥᾷστ᾽ ἂν μάθοι: ἡ δὲ ὅθεν πρῶτον γίγνεται ἐνυπάρχοντος, οἷον ὡς πλοίου [5] τρόπις καὶ οἰκίας θεμέλιος, καὶ τῶν ζῴων οἱ μὲν καρδίαν οἱ δὲ ἐγκέφαλον οἱ δ᾽ ὅ τι ἂν τύχωσι τοιοῦτον ὑπολαμβάνουσιν: ἡ δὲ ὅθεν γίγνεται πρῶτον μὴ ἐνυπάρχοντος καὶ ὅθεν πρῶτον ἡ κίνησις πέφυκεν ἄρχεσθαι καὶ ἡ μεταβολή, οἷον τὸ τέκνον ἐκ τοῦ πατρὸς καὶ τῆς μητρὸς καὶ ἡ μάχη [10] ἐκ τῆς λοιδορίας: ἡ δὲ οὗ κατὰ προαίρεσιν κινεῖται τὰ κινούμενα καὶ μεταβάλλει τὰ μεταβάλλοντα, ὥσπερ αἵ τε κατὰ πόλεις ἀρχαὶ καὶ αἱ δυναστεῖαι καὶ αἱ βασιλεῖαι καὶ τυραννίδες ἀρχαὶ λέγονται καὶ αἱ τέχναι, καὶ τούτων αἱ ἀρχιτεκτονικαὶ μάλιστα. ἔτι ὅθεν γνωστὸν τὸ πρᾶγμα [15] πρῶτον, καὶ αὕτη ἀρχὴ λέγεται τοῦ πράγματος, οἷον τῶν ἀποδείξεων αἱ ὑποθέσεις. ἰσαχῶς δὲ καὶ τὰ αἴτια λέγεται: πάντα γὰρ τὰ αἴτια ἀρχαί.

Principium dicitur aliud quidem unde utique aliquid rei movebitur primum, ut longitudinis et vie hinc quidem rhoc principium1, ex opposito autem alterum. Aliud unde utique optime fiet unumquodque, ut doctrine non a primo et rei principio aliquando inchoandum est sed unde facillime utique addiscet. Aliud unde primum generatur inexistente, ut navis sedile et domus fundamentum, et animalium alii cor alii cerebrum alii quodcumque sortiantur tale putant. Aliud unde fit primum non inexistente et unde primum motus natus initiari et permutatio, ut puer ex patre et matre et bellum ex conuicio. Aliud cuius secundum voluntatem moventur quae moventur et mutantur quae mutantur, ut secundum civitates principatus et potestates et imperia et tyrannides; principia dicuntur et artes, et harum architectonice maxime. Amplius unde cognoscibilis res primum, et hoc principium dicitur re, ut demonstrationum suppositiones. Totiens autem et causae dicuntur; omnes enim causae principia.

BEGINNING means (1) that part of a thing from which one would start first, e.g a line or a road has a beginning [13a] in either of the contrary directions. (2) That from which each thing would best be originated, e.g. even in learning we must sometimes begin not from the first point and the beginning of the subject, but from the point from which we should learn most easily. (3) That from which, as an immanent part, a thing first comes to be, e,g, as the keel of a ship and the foundation of a house, while in animals some suppose the heart, others the brain, others some other part, to be of this nature. (4) That from which, not as an immanent part, a thing first comes to be, and from which the movement or the change naturally first begins, as a child comes from its father and its mother, and a fight from abusive language. (5) That at whose will that which is moved is moved and that which changes changes, e.g. the magistracies in cities, and oligarchies and monarchies and tyrannies, are called arhchai, and so are the arts, and of these especially the architectonic arts. (6) That from which a thing can first be known, – this also is called the beginning of the thing, e.g. the hypotheses are the beginnings of demonstrations. (Causes are spoken of in an equal number of senses; for all causes are beginnings.)

πασῶν μὲν οὖν κοινὸν τῶν ἀρχῶν τὸ πρῶτον εἶναι ὅθεν ἢ ἔστιν ἢ γίγνεται ἢ γιγνώσκεται· τούτων δὲ αἱ μὲν ἐνυπάρχουσαί εἰσιν αἱ δὲ [20] ἐκτός. διὸ ἥ τε φύσις ἀρχὴ καὶ τὸ στοιχεῖον καὶ ἡ διάνοια καὶ ἡ προαίρεσις καὶ οὐσία καὶ τὸ οὗ ἕνεκα· πολλῶν γὰρ καὶ τοῦ γνῶναι καὶ τῆς κινήσεως ἀρχὴ τἀγαθὸν καὶ τὸ καλόν.

Omnium igitur principiorum commune est primum esse unde aut est aut fit aut cognoscitur. Horum autem haec quidem inexistentia sunt illa vero extra. Quapropter et natura principium et elementum et mens et voluntas et substantia et quod cuius causa; multorum enim et cognitionis et motus principium est bonum et malum.

It is common, then, to all beginnings to be the first point from which a thing either is or comes to be or is known; but of these some are immanent in the thing and

160

others are outside. Hence the nature of a thing is a beginning, and so is the element of a thing, and thought and will, and essence, and the final cause – for the good and the beautiful are the beginning both of the knowledge and of the movement of many things.

### Chapter 2 Cause

αἴτιον λέγεται ἕνα μὲν τρόπον ἐξ οὗ γίγνεταί τι ἐνυπάρχοντος, [25] οἷον ὁ χαλκὸς τοῦ ἀνδριάντος καὶ ὁ ἄργυρος τῆς φιάλης καὶ τὰ τούτων γένη: ἄλλον δὲ τὸ εἶδος καὶ τὸ παράδειγμα, τοῦτο δ᾽ ἐστὶν ὁ λόγος τοῦ τί ἦν εἶναι καὶ τὰ τούτου γένη (οἷον τοῦ διὰ πασῶν τὸ δύο πρὸς ἕν καὶ ὅλως ὁ ἀριθμός) καὶ τὰ μέρη τὰ ἐν τῷ λόγῳ. ἔτι ὅθεν ἡ [30] ἀρχὴ τῆς μεταβολῆς ἡ πρώτη ἢ τῆς ἠρεμήσεως, οἷον ὁ βουλεύσας αἴτιος, καὶ ὁ πατὴρ τοῦ τέκνου καὶ ὅλως τὸ ποιοῦν τοῦ ποιουμένου καὶ τὸ μεταβλητικὸν τοῦ μεταβάλλοντος. ἔτι ὡς τὸ τέλος: τοῦτο δ᾽ ἐστὶ τὸ οὗ ἕνεκα, οἷον τοῦ περιπατεῖν ἡ ὑγίεια. διὰ τί γὰρ περιπατεῖ; φαμέν. ἵνα ὑγιαίνῃ. καὶ [35] εἰπόντες οὕτως οἰόμεθα ἀποδεδωκέναι τὸ αἴτιον. καὶ ὅσα δὴ κινήσαντος ἄλλου μεταξὺ γίγνεται τοῦ τέλους, [1013β] [1] οἷον τῆς ὑγιείας ἡ ἰσχνασία ἢ ἡ κάθαρσις ἢ τὰ φάρμακα ἢ τὰ ὄργανα: πάντα γὰρ ταῦτα τοῦ τέλους ἕνεκά ἐστι, διαφέρει δὲ ἀλλήλων ὡς ὄντα τὰ μὲν ὄργανα τὰ δ᾽ ἔργα. τὰ μὲν οὖν αἴτια σχεδὸν τοσαυταχῶς λέγεται,

Causa vero dicitur uno quidem modo ex quo fit aliquid inexistente, ut es statue et argentum fiale et horum genera. alio vero species et exemplar; hoc autem est ratio ipsius quid erat esse et huius genera (ut eius quod diapason duo ad unum et totaliter numerus) et partes quae in ratione. Amplius unde principium permutationis primum aut quietis, ut consiliator causa, et pater pueri et omnino efficiens facti et permutans permutati. Amplius ut finis; hoc autem est quod cuius causa, ut ambulandi sanitas. Nam propter quid ambulat? Dicimus: ut sanetur; et dicentes ita putamus reddidisse causam. Et quaecumque movente alio intermedia fiunt finis, ut sanitatis attenuatio aut purgatio aut pharmaca aut organa; haec namque omnia finis gratia sunt, differunt autem ab invicem tamquam entia haec quidem ut organa illa vero ut opera.

Cause means (1) that from which, as immanent material, a thing comes into being, e.g. the bronze is the cause of the statue and the silver of the saucer, and so are the classes which include these. (2) The form or pattern, i.e. the definition of the essence, and the classes which include this (e.g. the ratio 2:1 and number in general are causes of the octave), and the parts included in the definition. (3) That from which the change or the resting from change first begins; e.g. the adviser is a cause of the action, and the father a cause of the child, and in general the maker a cause of the thing made and the change-producing of the changing. (4) The end, i.e. that for the sake of which a thing is; e.g. health is the cause of walking. For "Why does one walk?" we say; "that one may be healthy"; and in speaking thus we think we have given the cause. The same is true of all the means that intervene before the end, when something else has put the process in motion, as e.g. [13b] thinning or purging or drugs or instruments intervene before health is reached; for all these are for the sake of the end, though they differ from one another in that some are instruments and others are actions.

συμβαίνει δὲ πολλαχῶς [5] λεγομένων τῶν αἰτίων καὶ πολλὰ τοῦ αὐτοῦ αἴτια εἶναι οὐ κατὰ συμβεβηκός (οἷον τοῦ ἀνδριάντος καὶ ἡ ἀνδριαντοποιητικὴ καὶ ὁ χαλκὸς οὐ καθ᾽ ἕτερόν τι ἀλλ᾽ ἢ ἀνδριάς: ἀλλ᾽ οὐ τὸν αὐτὸν τρόπον ἀλλὰ τὸ μὲν ὡς ὕλη τὸ δ᾽ ὡς ὅθεν ἡ κίνησις),

Ergo causae fere totiens dicuntur. Accidit autem multotiens dictis causis et multas eiusdem esse causas non secundum accidens, ut statue statue factiva et es non secundum aliquid aliud sed in quantum statua; sed non eodem modo, sed hoc quidem ut materia illud vero ut unde motus.

These, then, are practically all the senses in which causes are spoken of, and as they are spoken of in several senses it follows both that there are several causes of the same thing, and in no accidental sense (e.g. both the art of sculpture and the bronze are causes of the statue not in respect of anything else but qua statue; not, however, in the same way, but the one as matter and the other as source of the movement),

καὶ ἀλλήλων αἴτια (οἷον τὸ πονεῖν [10] τῆς εὐεξίας καὶ αὕτη τοῦ πονεῖν: ἀλλ᾽ οὐ τὸν αὐτὸν τρόπον ἀλλὰ τὸ μὲν ὡς τέλος τὸ δ᾽ ὡς ἀρχὴ κινήσεως).

Et ad invicem causae sunt, ut laborare causa est euexie et haec laborandi; sed non eodem modo, verum hoc quidem ut finis illud vero ut principium motus.

and that things can be causes of one another (e.g. exercise of good condition, and the latter of exercise; not, however, in the same way, but the one as end and the other as source of movement).

ἔτι δὲ ταὐτὸ τῶν ἐναντίων ἐστίν: ὃ γὰρ παρὸν αἴτιον τουδί, τοῦτ᾽ ἀπὸν αἰτιώμεθα ἐνίοτε τοῦ ἐναντίου, οἷον τὴν ἀπουσίαν τοῦ κυβερνήτου τῆς ἀνατροπῆς, οὗ ἦν ἡ παρουσία αἰτία τῆς [15] σωτηρίας: ἄμφω δέ, καὶ ἡ παρουσία καὶ ἡ στέρησις, αἴτια ὡς κινοῦντα.

Amplius autem idem quandoque contrariorum est causa; quod enim presens huius est causa, hoc absens causamur quandoque de contrario, ut absentiam gubernatoris deperditionis, cuius erat presentia causa salutis; utraque vero, et presentia et privatio, causae sunt ut moventes.

Again, the same thing is the cause of contraries; for that which when present causes a particular thing, we sometimes charge, when absent, with the contrary, e.g. we impute the shipwreck to the absence of the steersman, whose presence was the cause of safety; and both the presence and the privation are causes as sources of movement.

ἄπαντα δὲ τὰ νῦν εἰρημένα αἴτια εἰς τέτταρας τρόπους πίπτει τοὺς φανερωτάτους. τὰ μὲν γὰρ στοιχεῖα τῶν συλλαβῶν καὶ ἡ ὕλη τῶν σκευαστῶν καὶ τὸ πῦρ καὶ ἡ γῆ καὶ τὰ τοιαῦτα πάντα τῶν σωμάτων καὶ τὰ [20] μέρη τοῦ ὅλου καὶ αἱ ὑποθέσεις τοῦ συμπεράσματος ὡς τὸ [21] ἐξ οὗ αἰτιά ἐστιν· τούτων δὲ τὰ μὲν ὡς τὸ ὑποκείμενον, οἷον τὰ μέρη, τὰ δὲ ὡς τὸ τί ἦν εἶναι, τό τε ὅλον καὶ ἡ σύνθεσις καὶ τὸ εἶδος. τὸ δὲ σπέρμα καὶ ὁ ἰατρὸς καὶ ὁ βουλεύσας καὶ ὅλως τὸ ποιοῦν, πάντα ὅθεν ἡ ἀρχὴ τῆς μεταβολῆς [25] ἢ στάσεως. τὰ δ᾽ ὡς τὸ τέλος καὶ τἀγαθὸν τῶν ἄλλων· τὸ γὰρ οὗ ἕνεκα βέλτιστον καὶ τέλος τῶν ἄλλων ἐθέλει εἶναι· διαφερέτω δὲ μηδὲν αὐτὸ εἰπεῖν ἀγαθὸν ἢ φαινόμενον ἀγαθόν.

Omnes vero causae dictae in quatuor modos cadunt manifestissimos. Nam elementa sillabarum et materia factorum et ignis et terra et talia omnia corporum et partes totius et suppositiones conclusionis ut ex quo causae sunt. Horum autem haec quidem quasi subiectum, ut partes; illa vero ut quod quid erat esse: et totum et compositio et species. Sperma vero et medicus et consiliator et omnino efficiens, omnia unde principium permutationis aut status. Alia vero ut finis et bonum aliorum; nam quod cuius causa optimum et finis aliorum vult esse; nil autem differat dicere sive bonum sive apparens bonum.

All the causes now mentioned fall under four senses which are the most obvious. For the letters are the cause of syllables, and the material is the cause of manufactured things, and fire and earth and all such things are the causes of bodies, and the parts are causes of the whole, and the hypotheses are causes of the conclusion, in the sense that they are that out of which these respectively are made; but of these some are cause as the substratum (e.g. the parts), others as the essence (the whole, the synthesis, and the form). The semen, the physician, the adviser, and in general the agent, are all sources of change or of rest. The remainder are causes as the end and the good of the other things; for that for the sake of which other things are tends to be the best and the end of the other things; let us take it as making no difference whether we call it good or apparent good.

τὰ μὲν οὖν αἴτια ταῦτα καὶ τοσαῦτά ἐστι τῷ εἴδει, τρόποι δὲ τῶν αἰτίων ἀριθμῷ μέν [30] εἰσι πολλοί, κεφαλαιούμενοι δὲ καὶ οὗτοι ἐλάττους. λέγονται γὰρ αἴτια πολλαχῶς, καὶ αὐτῶν τῶν ὁμοειδῶν προτέρως καὶ ὑστέρως ἄλλο ἄλλου, οἷον ὑγιείας ὁ ἰατρὸς καὶ ὁ τεχνίτης, καὶ τοῦ διὰ πασῶν τὸ διπλάσιον καὶ ἀριθμός, καὶ ἀεὶ τὰ περιέχοντα ὁτιοῦν τῶν καθ᾽ ἕκαστα.

Causae quidem igitur hae et tot sunt specie. Modi vero causarum numero quidem multi sunt, capitulati vero et hii pauciores. Dicuntur enim causae multipliciter, et ipsarum eiusdem speciei prius et posterius alia quam alia, ut sanitatis medicus et artifex, et eius quod dyapason duplum et numerus, et semper continentia quodcumque singularium.

These, then, are the causes, and this is the number of their kinds, but the varieties of causes are many in number, though when summarized these also are comparatively few. Causes are spoken of in many senses, and even of those which are of the same kind some are causes in a prior and others in a posterior sense, e.g. both the physician and the professional man are causes of health, and both the ratio 2:1 and number are causes of the octave, and the classes that include any particular cause are always causes of the particular effect.

ἔτι δ᾽ ὡς τὸ συμβεβηκὸς [35] καὶ τὰ τούτων γένη, οἷον ἀνδριάντος ἄλλως Πολύκλειτος καὶ ἄλλως ἀνδριαντοποιός, ὅτι συμβέβηκε τῷ ἀνδριαντοποιῷ Πολυκλείτῳ εἶναι: [1014α] [1] καὶ τὰ περιέχοντα δὲ τὸ συμβεβηκός, οἷον ἄνθρωπος αἴτιος ἀνδριάντος, ἢ καὶ ὅλως ζῷον, ὅτι ὁ Πολύκλειτος ἄνθρωπος ὁ δὲ ἄνθρωπος ζῷον. ἔστι δὲ καὶ τῶν συμβεβηκότων ἄλλα ἄλλων πορρώτερον καὶ [5] ἐγγύτερον, οἷον εἰ ὁ λευκὸς καὶ ὁ μουσικὸς αἴτιος λέγοιτο τοῦ ἀνδριάντος, ἀλλὰ μὴ μόνον Πολύκλειτος ἢ ἄνθρωπος. παρὰ πάντα δὲ καὶ τὰ οἰκείως λεγόμενα καὶ τὰ κατὰ συμβεβηκός, τὰ μὲν ὡς δυνάμενα λέγεται τὰ δ᾽ ὡς ἐνεργοῦντα, οἷον τοῦ οἰκοδομεῖσθαι οἰκοδόμος ἢ οἰκοδομῶν οἰκοδόμος. [10] ὁμοίως δὲ λεχθήσεται καὶ ἐφ᾽ ὧν αἴτια τὰ αἴτια τοῖς εἰρημένοις, οἷον τοῦδε τοῦ ἀνδριάντος ἢ ἀνδριάντος ἢ ὅλως εἰκόνος, καὶ χαλκοῦ τοῦδε ἢ χαλκοῦ ἢ ὅλως ὕλης: καὶ ἐπὶ τῶν συμβεβηκότων ὡσαύτως. ἔτι δὲ συμπλεκόμενα καὶ ταῦτα κἀκεῖνα λεχθήσεται, οἷον οὐ Πολύκλειτος οὐδὲ ἀνδριαντοποιὸς [15] ἀλλὰ Πολύκλειτος ἀνδριαντοποιός.

Amplius autem ut accidens et horum genera, veluti statue aliter Policlitus et aliter statue factor, quia accidit statue factori Policlitum esse. Et continentia autem accidens, ut homo causa statue aut et totaliter animal, quia Policlitus homo et homo animal. Sunt autem et accidentium alia aliis remotius et propinquius, ut si albus et musicus causa dicuntur statue, et non solum Policlitus aut homo. Praeter omnia autem et proprie dicta et secundum accidens, haec quidem ut potentia dicuntur illa vero ut agentia, ut ipsius edificari edificator aut edificans edificator. Similiter autem dicuntur et in quibus causae causae dictis, ut huius statue aut statue aut omnino ymaginis, aut eris huius aut eris aut omnino materie; et in accidentibus similiter. Amplius autem complexa et haec et illa dicuntur, ut nec Policlitus nec statue factor, sed Policlitus statue factor.

Again, there are accidental causes and the classes which include these; e.g. while in one sense the sculptor causes the statue, in another sense Polyclitus causes it, because the sculptor happens to be [14a] Polyclitus; and the classes that include the accidental cause are also causes, e.g. man – or in general animal – is the cause of the statue, because Polyclitus is a man, and man is an animal. Of accidental causes also some are more remote or nearer than others, as, for instance, if the white and the musical were called causes of the statue, and not only Polyclitus or man . But besides all these varieties of causes, whether proper or accidental, some are called causes as being able to act, others as acting; e.g. the cause of the house's being built is a builder, or a builder who is building. The same variety of language will be found with regard to the effects of causes; e.g. a thing may be called the cause of this statue or of a statue or in general of an image, and of this bronze or of bronze or of matter in general; and similarly in the case of accidental effects. Again, both accidental and proper causes may be spoken of in combination; e.g. we may say not Polyclitus nor the sculptor but Polyclitus the sculptor .

ἀλλ᾽ ὅμως ἅπαντά γε ταῦτ᾽ ἐστὶ τὸ μὲν πλῆθος ἕξ, λεγόμενα δὲ διχῶς· ἢ γὰρ ὡς τὸ καθ᾽ ἕκαστον ἢ ὡς τὸ γένος, ἢ ὡς τὸ συμβεβηκὸς ἢ ὡς τὸ γένος τοῦ συμβεβηκότος, ἢ ὡς συμπλεκόμενα ταῦτα ἢ ὡς ἁπλῶς λεγόμενα, πάντα δὲ ἢ ὡς [20] ἐνεργοῦντα ἢ κατὰ δύναμιν. διαφέρει δὲ τοσοῦτον, ὅτι τὰ μὲν ἐνεργοῦντα καὶ τὰ καθ᾽ ἕκαστον ἅμα ἔστι καὶ οὐκ ἔστι καὶ ὧν αἴτια, οἷον ὅδε ὁ ἰατρεύων τῷδε τῷ ὑγιαζομένῳ καὶ ὅδε ὁ οἰκοδόμος τῷδε τῷ οἰκοδομουμένῳ, τὰ δὲ κατὰ δύναμιν οὐκ ἀεί· φθείρεται γὰρ οὐχ ἅμα ἡ οἰκία καὶ ὁ [25] οἰκοδόμος.

At tamen omnia haec sunt pluralitate sex, dupliciter autem  dicta. Aut enim ut singulare aut ut genus, et ipsius secundum se aut secundum accidens aut ut genus accidentis, aut ut complexa haec aut ut simpliciter dicta. Amplius ut agentia aut secundum potentiam. Differunt autem in tantum, quod agentia quidem et singularia simul sunt et non sunt, et ipsa et quorum causae, ut hic medens cum hoc conualescente et hic edificator cum hoc edificio. Quod autem secundum potestatem non semper; corrumpuntur enim non simul domus et edificator.

Yet all these are but six in number, while each is spoken of in two ways; for (A) they are causes either as the individual, or as the genus, or as the accidental, or as the genus that includes the accidental, and these either as combined, or as taken simply; and (B) all may be taken as acting or as having a capacity. But they differ inasmuch as the acting causes, i.e. the individuals, exist, or do not exist, simultaneously with the things of which they are causes, e.g. this particular man who is healing, with this particular man who is recovering health, and this particular builder with this particular thing that is being built; but the potential causes are not always in this case; for the house does not perish at the same time as the builder.

*Chapter* 3 Element

στοιχεῖον λέγεται ἐξ οὗ σύγκειται πρώτου ἐνυπάρχοντος ἀδιαιρέτου τῷ εἴδει εἰς ἕτερον εἶδος, οἷον φωνῆς στοιχεῖα ἐξ ὧν σύγκειται ἡ φωνὴ καὶ εἰς ἃ διαιρεῖται ἔσχατα, ἐκεῖνα δὲ μηκέτ᾽ εἰς ἄλλας φωνὰς ἑτέρας τῷ [30] εἴδει αὐτῶν, ἀλλὰ κἂν διαιρῆται, τὰ μόρια ὁμοειδῆ, οἷον ὕδατος τὸ μόριον ὕδωρ, ἀλλ᾽ οὐ τῆς συλλαβῆς. ὁμοίως δὲ καὶ τὰ τῶν σωμάτων στοιχεῖα λέγουσιν οἱ λέγοντες εἰς ἃ διαιρεῖται τὰ σώματα ἔσχατα, ἐκεῖνα δὲ μηκέτ᾽ εἰς ἄλλα εἴδει διαφέροντα: καὶ εἴτε ἓν εἴτε πλείω τὰ τοιαῦτα, [35] ταῦτα στοιχεῖα λέγουσιν. παραπλησίως δὲ καὶ τὰ τῶν διαγραμμάτων στοιχεῖα λέγεται, καὶ ὅλως τὰ τῶν ἀποδείξεων: αἱ γὰρ πρῶται ἀποδείξεις καὶ ἐν πλείοσιν ἀποδείξεσιν ἐνυπάρχουσαι, [1014β] [1] αὗται στοιχεῖα τῶν ἀποδείξεων λέγονται: εἰσὶ δὲ τοιοῦτοι συλλογισμοὶ οἱ πρῶτοι ἐκ τῶν τριῶν δι᾽ ἑνὸς μέσου.

Elementum dicitur ex quo componitur primo inexistente indivisibili specie in aliam speciem, ut vocis elementa ex quibus vox componitur et in quae dividitur ultima, illa vero non adhuc in alias voces ab ipsis specie diversas. Sed et si dividantur, particule eiusdem speciei, ut aque particula aqua; sed non sillabe. Similiter autem et corporum elementa dicunt dicentes in quae dividuntur corpora ultima, illa autem non adhuc in alia specie differentia corpora; et sive unum sive plura talia, haec elementa dicunt. Propinque autem et quae dyagrammatum dicuntur elementa, et omnino quae demonstrationum; nam prime demonstrationes et in pluribus demonstrationibus existentes, hae elementa demonstrationum dicuntur; sunt autem tales sillogismi primi rex tribus per unum medium.

Element means (1) the primary component immanent in a thing, and indivisible in kind into other kinds; e.g. the elements of speech are the parts of which speech consists and into which it is ultimately divided, while they are no longer divided into other forms of speech different in kind from them. If they are divided, their parts are of the same kind, as a part of water is water (while a part of the syllable is not a syllable). Similarly those who speak of the elements of bodies mean the things into which bodies are ultimately divided, while they are no longer divided into other things differing in kind; and whether the things of this sort are one or more, they call these elements. The so-called elements of geometrical proofs, and in general the elements of demonstrations, have a similar character; for the primary demonstrations, each of which is implied in [14b] many demonstrations, are called elements of demonstrations; and the primary syllogisms, which have three terms and proceed by means of one middle, are of this nature.

καὶ μεταφέροντες δὲ στοιχεῖον καλοῦσιν ἐντεῦθεν ὃ ἂν ἓν ὂν καὶ μικρὸν ἐπὶ πολλὰ ᾖ χρήσιμον, [5] διὸ καὶ τὸ μικρὸν καὶ ἁπλοῦν καὶ ἀδιαίρετον στοιχεῖον λέγεται. ὅθεν ἐλήλυθε τὰ μάλιστα καθόλου στοιχεῖα εἶναι, ὅτι ἕκαστον αὐτῶν ἓν ὂν καὶ ἁπλοῦν ἐν πολλοῖς ὑπάρχει ἢ πᾶσιν ἢ ὅτι πλείστοις, καὶ τὸ ἓν καὶ τὴν στιγμὴν ἀρχάς τισι δοκεῖν εἶναι. ἐπεὶ οὖν τὰ καλούμενα γένη [10] καθόλου καὶ ἀδιαίρετα (οὐ γὰρ ἔστι λόγος αὐτῶν), στοιχεῖα τὰ γένη λέγουσί τινες, καὶ μᾶλλον ἢ τὴν διαφορὰν ὅτι καθόλου μᾶλλον τὸ γένος: ᾧ μὲν γὰρ ἡ διαφορὰ ὑπάρχει, καὶ τὸ γένος ἀκολουθεῖ, ᾧ δὲ τὸ γένος, οὐ παντὶ ἡ διαφορά. ἁπάντων δὲ κοινὸν τὸ εἶναι στοιχεῖον ἑκάστου τὸ [15] πρῶτον ἐνυπάρχον ἑκάστῳ.

Et transferentes autem elementum vocant hinc: quodcumquae unum ens et parvum ad multa fuerit utile; quapropter et parvum et simplex et indivisibile dicitur elementum. Unde venit maxime universalia elementa esse, quia unumquodque eorum unum ens et simplex in multis inest aut omnibus aut quam plurimis, et unum et punctum principia quibusdam videri  esse. Quoniam ergo vocata genera universalia et indivisibilia (una enim est ipsorum ratio), elementa genera dicunt aliqui, no et magis quam differentiam, quoniam universale magis genus; nam cui differentia inest, et genus sequitur, sed cui genus, non omne differentia. Omnium autem commune  esse elementum cuiuslibet quod primo inest cuique.

(2) People also transfer the word element from this meaning and apply it to that which, being one and small, is useful for many purposes; for which reason what is small and simple and indivisible is called an element. Hence come the facts that the most universal things are elements (because each of them being one and simple is present in a plurality of things, either in all or in as many as possible), and that unity and the point are thought by some to be first principles. Now, since the so-called genera are universal and indivisible (for there is no definition of them), some say the genera are elements, and more so than the differentia, because the genus is more universal; for where the differentia is present, the genus accompanies it, but where the genus is present, the differentia is not always so. It is common to all the meanings that the element of each thing is the first component immanent in each.

### *Chapter*  4 Nature

φύσις λέγεται ἕνα μὲν τρόπον ἡ τῶν φυομένων γένεσις, οἷον εἴ τις ἐπεκτείνας λέγοι τὸ υ, ἕνα δὲ ἐξ οὗ φύεται πρώτου τὸ φυόμενον ἐνυπάρχοντος: ἔτι ὅθεν ἡ κίνησις ἡ πρώτη ἐν ἑκάστῳ τῶν φύσει ὄντων ἐν αὐτῷ ᾗ αὐτὸ [20] ὑπάρχει: φύεσθαι δὲ λέγεται ὅσα αὔξησιν ἔχει δι᾽ ἑτέρου τῷ ἅπτεσθαι καὶ συμπεφυκέναι ἢ προσπεφυκέναι ὥσπερ τὰ ἔμβρυα: διαφέρει δὲ σύμφυσις ἁφῆς, ἔνθα μὲν γὰρ οὐδὲν παρὰ τὴν ἁφὴν ἕτερον ἀνάγκη εἶναι, ἐν δὲ τοῖς συμπεφυκόσιν ἔστι τι ἐν τὸ αὐτὸ ἐν ἀμφοῖν ὃ ποιεῖ ἀντὶ τοῦ [25] ἅπτεσθαι συμπεφυκέναι καὶ εἶναι ἓν κατὰ τὸ συνεχὲς καὶ ποσόν, ἀλλὰ μὴ κατὰ τὸ ποιόν. ἔτι δὲ φύσις λέγεται ἐξ οὗ πρώτου ἢ ἔστιν ἢ γίγνεταί τι τῶν φύσει ὄντων, ἀρρυθμίστου ὄντος καὶ ἀμεταβλήτου ἐκ τῆς δυνάμεως τῆς αὑτοῦ, οἷον ἀνδριάντος καὶ τῶν σκευῶν τῶν χαλκῶν ὁ χαλκὸς ἡ [30] φύσις λέγεται, τῶν δὲ ξυλίνων ξύλον: ὁμοίως δὲ καὶ ἐπὶ τῶν ἄλλων: ἐκ τούτων γὰρ ἔστιν ἕκαστον διασωζομένης τῆς πρώτης ὕλης: τοῦτον γὰρ τὸν τρόπον καὶ τῶν φύσει ὄντων τὰ στοιχεῖά φασιν εἶναι φύσιν, οἱ μὲν πῦρ οἱ δὲ γῆν οἱ δ᾽ ἀέρα οἱ δ᾽ ὕδωρ οἱ δ᾽ ἄλλο τι τοιοῦτον λέγοντες, οἱ δ᾽ [35] ἔνια τούτων οἱ δὲ πάντα ταῦτα. ἔτι δ᾽ ἄλλον τρόπον λέγεται ἡ φύσις ἡ τῶν φύσει ὄντων οὐσία, οἷον οἱ λέγοντες τὴν φύσιν εἶναι τὴν πρώτην σύνθεσιν, [1015a] [1] ἢ ὥσπερ Ἐμπεδοκλῆς λέγει ὅτι φύσις ; οὐδενὸς ἔστιν ἐόντων, ἀλλὰ μόνον μῖξίς τε διάλλαξίς τε μιγέντων ἔστι, φύσις δ᾽ ἐπὶ τοῖς ὀνομάζεται ἀνθρώποισιν.

διὸ καὶ ὅσα φύσει ἔστιν ἢ γίγνεται, ἤδη ὑπάρχοντος ἐξ οὗ πέφυκε γίγνεσθαι ἢ εἶναι, οὔπω φαμὲν [5] τὴν φύσιν ἔχειν ἐὰν μὴ ἔχῃ τὸ εἶδος καὶ τὴν μορφήν. φύσει μὲν οὖν τὸ ἐξ ἀμφοτέρων τούτων ἐστίν, οἷον τὰ ζῷα καὶ τὰ μόρια αὐτῶν:

Natura vero dicitur uno quidem modo nascentium generatio, ut si quis extendens dicat le Y. Vno vero ex quo generatur primum quod nascitur inexistente. Amplius unde motus primus in quolibet natura entium in ipso in quantum ipsum existit. Nasci vero dicuntur quaecumque augmentum habent per alterum in tangendo et connasci aut adnasci, ut embria. differt autem connascentia a tactu; hic enim nihil praeter tactum alterum necesse esse, in simul natis autem est aliquid unum idem in ambobus quod facit pro tangi simul nasci et unum esse secundum continuum et quantum, sed non secundum quale. Amplius autem natura dicitur ex quo primo aut est aut fit aliquid entium natura, inordinato existente et immutabili a sua propria potestate, ut statue et uasorum ereorum es natura dicitur, et ligneorum lignum, similiter autem et in aliis; ex hiis enim est unumquodque saluata prima materia. Hoc enim modo et existentium natura elementa dicunt esse naturam, alii ignem, alii terram, alii aquam, alii aerem, alii aliud aliquid tale dicentes, alii quaedam horum alii vero hec omnia. amplius autem alio modo dicitur natura existentium natura substantia, ut dicentes naturam primam compositionem esse, ut Empedocles dicit quod " natura nullius est inexistentium, sed solum mixtio et permutatio permixtorum est, natura vero in hominibus nominatur". Quapropter et quaecumque natura sunt aut fiunt, iam existente ex quo nata sunt fieri aut esse, non dicimus naturam habere, si non habent speciem et formam. natura quidem igitur quod ex hiis utrisque est, ut animalia et eorum partes.

Nature means (1) the genesis of growing things – the meaning which would be suggested if one were to pronounce the u in phusis long. (2) That immanent part of a growing thing, from which its growth first proceeds. (3) The source from which the primary movement in each natural object is present in it in virtue of its own essence. Those things are said to grow which derive increase from something else by contact and either by organic unity, or by organic adhesion as in the case of embryos. Organic unity differs from contact; for in the latter case there need not be anything besides the contact, but in organic unities there is something identical in both parts, which makes them grow together instead of merely touching, and be one in respect of continuity and quantity, though not of quality.(4) Nature means the primary material of which any natural object consists or out of which it is made, which is relatively unshaped and cannot be changed from its own potency, as e.g. bronze is said to be the nature of a statue and of bronze utensils, and wood the nature of wooden things; and so in all other cases; for when a product is made out of these materials, the first matter is preserved throughout. For it is in this way that people call the elements of natural objects also their nature, some naming fire, others earth, others air, others water, others something else of the sort, and some naming more than one of these, and others all of them. (5) Nature means the essence of natural objects, as with those who say the nature is the primary mode of composition, or as Empedocles says: [15a] "Nothing that is has a nature, But only mixing and parting of the mixed, And nature is but a name given them by men". Hence as regards the things that are or come to be by nature, though that from which they naturally come to be or are is already present, we say they have not their nature yet, unless they have their form or shape. That which comprises both of these exists by nature, e.g. the animals and their parts;

φύσις δὲ ἥ τε πρώτη ὕλη (καὶ αὕτη διχῶς, ἢ ἡ πρὸς αὐτὸ πρώτη ἢ ἡ ὅλως πρώτη, οἷον τῶν χαλκῶν ἔργων πρὸς αὐτὰ μὲν πρῶτος ὁ χαλκός, ὅλως δ᾽ [10] ἴσως ὕδωρ, εἰ πάντα τὰ τηκτὰ ὕδωρ) καὶ τὸ εἶδος καὶ ἡ οὐσία: τοῦτο δ᾽ ἐστὶ τὸ τέλος τῆς γενέσεως. μεταφορᾷ δ᾽ ἤδη καὶ ὅλως πᾶσα οὐσία φύσις λέγεται διὰ ταύτην, ὅτι καὶ ἡ φύσις οὐσία τίς ἐστιν.

Natura autem materia prima; et haec dupliciter, aut quae ad ipsum prima aut omnino prima, ut operum ereorum ad ipsa quidem primum es, totaliter vero forsan aqua, si omnia liquabilia aqua. Et species et substantia; hoc autem est finis generationis. Methaphora vero iam et omnino omnis substantia natura dicitur propter hanc, quia et natura substantia quaedam est.

and not only is the first matter nature (and this in two senses, either the first, counting from the thing, or the first in general; e.g. in the case of works in bronze, bronze is first with reference to them, but in general perhaps water is first, if all things that can be melted are water), but also the form or essence, which is the end of the process of becoming. (6) By an extension of meaning from this sense of nature every essence in general has come to be called a nature , because the nature of a thing is one kind of essence.

ἐκ δὴ τῶν εἰρημένων ἡ πρώτη φύσις καὶ κυρίως λεγομένη ἐστὶν ἡ οὐσία ἡ τῶν ἐχόντων [15] ἀρχὴν κινήσεως ἐν αὑτοῖς ᾗ αὑτά: ἡ γὰρ ὕλη τῷ ταύτης δεκτικὴ εἶναι λέγεται φύσις, καὶ αἱ γενέσεις καὶ τὸ φύεσθαι τῷ ἀπὸ ταύτης εἶναι κινήσεις. καὶ ἡ ἀρχὴ τῆς κινήσεως τῶν φύσει ὄντων αὕτη ἐστίν, ἐνυπάρχουσά πως ἢ δυνάμει ἢ ἐντελεχείᾳ. [20]

Ex dictis igitur prima natura et proprie dicta est substantia quae principium motus habentium in se in quantum ipsa; materia namque, quia huius est susceptiva, esse dicitur natura, et generationes et nasci, quia sunt ab hac motus. Et principium motus natura existentium haec est, inexistens aut potestate aut actu.

From what has been said, then, it is plain that nature in the primary and strict sense is the essence of things which have in themselves, as such, a source of movement; for the matter is called the nature because it is qualified to receive this, and processes of becoming and growing are called nature because they are movements proceeding from this. And nature in this sense is the source of the movement of natural objects, being present in them somehow, either potentially or in complete reality.

*Chapter* 5 Necessary

ἀναγκαῖον λέγεται οὗ ἄνευ οὐκ ἐνδέχεται ζῆν ὡς συναιτίου (οἷον τὸ ἀναπνεῖν καὶ ἡ τροφὴ τῷ ζῴῳ ἀναγκαῖον, ἀδύνατον γὰρ ἄνευ τούτων εἶναι),

Necessarium dicitur sine quo non contingit vivere quasi concausali, ut respirare et cibus animali necessarium; nam sine hiis esse est impossibile.

We call necessary (1) (a) that without which, as a condition, a thing cannot live; e.g. breathing and food are necessary for an animal; for it is incapable of existing without these;

καὶ ὧν ἄνευ τὸ ἀγαθὸν μὴ ἐνδέχεται ἢ εἶναι ἢ γενέσθαι, ἢ τὸ κακὸν ἀποβαλεῖν ἢ στερηθῆναι (οἷον τὸ πιεῖν τὸ φάρμακον ἀναγκαῖον [25] ἵνα μὴ κάμνῃ, καὶ τὸ πλεῦσαι εἰς Αἴγιναν ἵνα ἀπολάβῃ τὰ χρήματα).

Et sine quibus bonum non contingit aut esse aut fieri, aut aliquod malum expellere aut privari, veluti bibere farmacum necessarium ut non laboret, et ad eginam navigare ut pecuniam recipiat.

(b) the conditions without which good cannot be or come to be, or without which we cannot get rid or be freed of evil; e.g. drinking the medicine is necessary in order that we may be cured of disease, and a man _ s sailing to Aegina is necessary in order that he may get his money.

ἔτι τὸ βίαιον καὶ ἡ βία: τοῦτο δ᾽ ἐστὶ τὸ παρὰ τὴν ὁρμὴν καὶ τὴν προαίρεσιν ἐμποδίζον καὶ κωλυτικόν, τὸ γὰρ βίαιον ἀναγκαῖον λέγεται, διὸ καὶ λυπηρόν (ὥσπερ καὶ Εὔηνός φησι πᾶν γὰρ ἀναγκαῖον πρᾶγμ᾽ ἀνιαρὸν [30] ἔφυ),

καὶ ἡ βία ἀνάγκη τις (ὥσπερ καὶ Σοφοκλῆς λέγει [31] ἀλλ᾽ ἡ βία με ταῦτ᾽ ἀναγκάζει ποιεῖν),

1. 954;αὶ δοκεῖ ἡ ἀνάγκη ἀμετάπειστόν τι εἶναι, ὀρθῶς: ἐναντίον γὰρ τῇ κατὰ τὴν προαίρεσιν κινήσει καὶ κατὰ τὸν λογισμόν.

Amplius vim faciens et vis; hoc autem est quod praeter impetum et preuoluntatem impediens et prohibens. Violentum enim necessarium dicitur, quapropter et triste, sicut et euenus ait: " omnis enim res necessaria tristis est ". Et vis necessitas quaedam, ut sophocles dicit: "sed vis me haec facere cogit". Et videtur necessitas non increpabile aliquid esse, recte; contrarium enim motui secundum prevoluntatem et secundum cogitationem.

(2) The compulsory and compulsion, i.e. that which impedes and tends to hinder, contrary to impulse and purpose. For the compulsory is called necessary (whence the necessary is painful, as Evenus says: 'For every necessary thing is ever irksome'), and compulsion is a form of necessity, as Sophocles says: "But force necessitates me to this act" . And necessity is held to be something that cannot be persuaded – and rightly, for it is contrary to the movement which accords with purpose and with reasoning.

ἔτι τὸ μὴ ἐνδεχόμενον ἄλλως ἔχειν ἀναγκαῖόν φαμεν οὕτως [35] ἔχειν: καὶ κατὰ τοῦτο τὸ ἀναγκαῖον καὶ τἆλλα λέγεταί πως ἅπαντα ἀναγκαῖα:

Amplius quod non contingit aliter se habere necessarium dicimus sic se habere.

(3) We say that that which cannot be otherwise is necessarily as it is.

τό τε γὰρ βίαιον ἀναγκαῖον λέγεται ἢ ποιεῖν ἢ πάσχειν τότε, [1015β] [1] ὅταν μὴ ἐνδέχηται κατὰ τὴν ὁρμὴν διὰ τὸ βιαζόμενον, ὡς ταύτην ἀνάγκην οὖσαν δι᾽ ἣν μὴ ἐνδέχεται ἄλλως, καὶ ἐπὶ τῶν συναιτίων τοῦ ζῆν καὶ τοῦ ἀγαθοῦ ὡσαύτως: ὅταν γὰρ μὴ ἐνδέχηται ἔνθα [5] μὲν τὸ ἀγαθὸν ἔνθα δὲ τὸ ζῆν καὶ τὸ εἶναι ἄνευ τινῶν, ταῦτα ἀναγκαῖα καὶ ἡ αἰτία ἀνάγκη τίς ἐστιν αὕτη.

Et secundum hoc necessarium et alia dicuntur aliqualiter oinnia necessaria; violentum enim necessarium dicitur aut facere aut pati tunc, quando non contingit secundum impetum propter cogens, ut hanc necessitatem existentem propter quam non contingit aliter. Et in concausalibus vivendi et boni similiter; nam cum non contingit hic quidem bonum illic vero vivere et esse sine aliquibus, haec necessaria; causa necessitas quaedam est haec.

And from this sense of necessary all the others are somehow derived; for a thing is said to do or suffer what [15b] is necessary in the sense of compulsory, only when it cannot act according to its impulse because of the compelling forces – which implies that necessity is that because of which a thing cannot be otherwise; and similarly as regards the conditions of life and of good; for when in the one case good, in the other life and being, are not possible without certain conditions, these are necessary, and this kind of cause is a sort of necessity.

ἔτι ἡ ἀπόδειξις τῶν ἀναγκαίων, ὅτι οὐκ ἐνδέχεται ἄλλως ἔχειν, εἰ ἀποδέδεικται ἁπλῶς: τούτου δ᾽ αἴτια τὰ πρῶτα, εἰ ἀδύνατον ἄλλως ἔχειν ἐξ ὧν ὁ συλλογισμός.

Amplius demonstratio necessariorum est, quia non contingit aliter se habere, si demonstratum est simpliciter; huius autem causa est quae prima sunt, si impossibile est aliter se habere ex quibus est sillogismus.

Again, demonstration is a necessary thing because the conclusion cannot be otherwise, if there has been demonstration in the unqualified sense; and the causes of this necessity are the first premisses, i.e. the fact that the propositions from which the syllogism proceeds cannot be otherwise.

τῶν μὲν [10] δὴ ἕτερον αἴτιον τοῦ ἀναγκαῖα εἶναι, τῶν δὲ οὐδέν, ἀλλὰ διὰ ταῦτα ἕτερά ἐστιν ἐξ ἀνάγκης. ὥστε τὸ πρῶτον καὶ κυρίως ἀναγκαῖον τὸ ἁπλοῦν ἐστίν· τοῦτο γὰρ οὐκ ἐνδέχεται πλεοναχῶς ἔχειν, ὥστ᾽ οὐδὲ ἄλλως καὶ ἄλλως· ἤδη γὰρ πλεοναχῶς ἂν ἔχοι. εἰ ἄρα ἔστιν ἄττα ἀΐδια καὶ ἀκίνητα, [15] οὐδὲν ἐκείνοις ἐστὶ βίαιον οὐδὲ παρὰ φύσιν.

horum quidem itaque altera causa essendi necessaria , horum autem nulla, sed propter haec alia sunt ex necessitate. quare primum et proprie necessarium quod simplex est; hoc enim non contingit pluribus modis habere, quare nec aliter et aliter; iam enim pluribus modis utique haberet. Ergo si  qua sunt sempiterna et immobilia, nihil illis est violentum nec praeter naturam.

Now some things owe their necessity to something other than themselves; others do not, but are themselves the source of necessity in other things. Therefore the necessary in the primary and strict sense is the simple; for this does not admit of more states than one, so that it cannot even be in one state and also in another; for if it did it would already be in more than one. If, then, there are any things that are eternal and unmovable, nothing compulsory or against their nature attaches to them.

*Chapter* 6 One

ἓν λέγεται τὸ μὲν κατὰ συμβεβηκὸς τὸ δὲ καθ᾽ αὑτό, κατὰ συμβεβηκὸς μὲν οἷον Κορίσκος καὶ τὸ μουσικόν, καὶ Κορίσκος μουσικός (ταὐτὸ γὰρ εἰπεῖν Κορίσκος καὶ τὸ μουσικόν, καὶ Κορίσκος μουσικός), καὶ τὸ μουσικὸν καὶ τὸ [20] δίκαιον, καὶ μουσικὸς <Κορίσκος καὶ δίκαιος Κορίσκος· πάντα γὰρ ταῦτα ἓν λέγεται κατὰ συμβεβηκός, τὸ μὲν δίκαιον καὶ τὸ μουσικὸν ὅτι μιᾷ οὐσίᾳ συμβέβηκεν, τὸ δὲ μουσικὸν καὶ Κορίσκος ὅτι θάτερον θατέρῳ συμβέβηκεν· ὁμοίως δὲ τρόπον τινὰ καὶ ὁ μουσικὸς Κορίσκος τῷ Κορίσκῳ ἓν ὅτι θάτερον [25] τῶν μορίων θατέρῳ συμβέβηκε τῶν ἐν τῷ λόγῳ, οἷον τὸ μουσικὸν τῷ Κορίσκῳ· καὶ ὁ μουσικὸς Κορίσκος δικαίῳ Κορίσκῳ ὅτι ἑκατέρου μέρος τῷ αὐτῷ ἑνὶ συμβέβηκεν ἕν. ὡσαύτως δὲ κἂν ἐπὶ γένους κἂν ἐπὶ τῶν καθόλου τινὸς ὀνομάτων λέγηται τὸ συμβεβηκός, οἷον ὅτι ἄνθρωπος τὸ αὐτὸ [30] καὶ μουσικὸς ἄνθρωπος· ἢ γὰρ ὅτι τῷ ἀνθρώπῳ μιᾷ οὔσῃ οὐσίᾳ συμβέβηκε τὸ μουσικόν, ἢ ὅτι ἄμφω τῶν καθ᾽ ἕκαστόν τινι συμβέβηκεν, οἷον Κορίσκῳ. πλὴν οὐ τὸν αὐτὸν τρόπον ἄμφω ὑπάρχει, ἀλλὰ τὸ μὲν ἴσως ὡς γένος καὶ ἐν τῇ οὐσίᾳ τὸ δὲ ὡς ἕξις ἢ πάθος τῆς οὐσίας. ὅσα μὲν [35] οὖν κατὰ συμβεβηκὸς λέγεται ἕν, τοῦτον τὸν τρόπον λέγεται·

Unum dicitur aliud secundum accidens aliud secundum se. Secundum accidens quidem ut Coriscus et musicum, et Coriscus musicus (idem enim est dicere Coriscus et musicum et Coriscus musicus), et musicum et iustum, et musicus iustus Coriscus. Omnia enim haec unum dicuntur secundum accidens, iustum quidem et musicum, quia uni substantiae acciderunt, musicum vero et Coriscus, quia alterum alteri accidit. Similiter autem et modo quodam musicus Coriscus cum Corisco unum, quia altera partium alteri accidit earum quae sunt in oratione, ut musicum Corisco. Et musicus Coriscus iusto Corisco, quia utriusque pars eidem uni accidit, unum. Nihil enim differt quam Corisco musicum accidere. Similiter autem sive in genere sive in universalis alicuius nominibus dicatur accidens, ut quia homo idem et musicus homo; aut enim quia homini uni existenti substantiae accidit musicum, aut quia ambo singularium alicui accidunt, ut Corisco. Tamen non eodem modo ambo insunt, sed hoc quidem forsan ut genus et in substantia, illud vero ut habitus aut passio substantiae.

One means (1) that which is one by accident, (2) that which is one by its own nature. (1) Instances of the accidentally one are Coriscus and what is musical , and musical Coriscus (for it is the same thing to say Coriscus and what is musical , and musical Coriscus ), and what is musical and what is just , and musical Coriscus and just Coriscus . For all of these are called one by virtue of an accident, what is just and what is musical because they are accidents of one substance, what is musical and Coriscus because the one is an accident of the other; and similarly in a sense musical Coriscus is one with Coriscus because one of the parts of the phrase is an accident of the other, i.e. musical is an accident of Coriscus; and musical Coriscus is one with just Coriscus because one part of each is an accident of one and the same subject. The case is similar if the accident is predicated of a genus or of any universal name, e.g. if one says that man is the same as musical man ; for this is either because musical is an accident of man, which is one substance, or because both are accidents of some individual, e.g. Coriscus. Both, however, do not belong to him in the same way, but one presumably as genus and included in his substance, the other as a state or affection of the substance.

τῶν δὲ καθ᾽ ἑαυτὰ ἓν λεγομένων τὰ μὲν λέγεται τῷ συνεχῆ εἶναι, οἷον φάκελος δεσμῷ καὶ ξύλα κόλλῃ: [1016α] [1] καὶ γραμμή, κἂν κεκαμμένη ᾖ, συνεχὴς δέ, μία λέγεται, ὥσπερ καὶ τῶν μερῶν ἕκαστον, οἷον σκέλος καὶ βραχίων. αὐτῶν δὲ τούτων μᾶλλον ἓν τὰ φύσει συνεχῆ ἢ τέχνῃ. [5] συνεχὲς δὲ λέγεται οὗ κίνησις μία καθ᾽ αὑτὸ καὶ μὴ οἷόν τε ἄλλως: μία δ᾽ οὗ ἀδιαίρετος, ἀδιαίρετος δὲ κατὰ χρόνον.

Ergo quaecumque secundum accidens dicuntur unum, hoc modo dicuntur. Secundum se vero unum dictorum alia dicuntur eo quod continua sint, ut honus vinculo et ligna cum visco; et linea, et si flexa sit, continua autem, una dicitur, sicut et partium singule, tibia et brachium. Ipsorum autem horum magis unum natura continua quam arte. Continuum vero dicitur cuius motus unus secundum se et non possibile aliter; unus autem cuius indivisibilis, indivisibilis autem secundum tempus.

The things, then, that are called one in virtue of an accident, are called so in this way. (2) Of things that are called one in virtue of their own nature some (a) are so called because [16a] they are continuous, e.g. a bundle is made one by a band, and pieces of wood are made one by glue; and a line, even if it is bent, is called one if it is continuous, as each part of the body is, e.g. the leg or the arm. Of these themselves, the continuous by nature are more one than the continuous by art. A thing is called continuous which has by its own nature one movement and cannot have any other; and the movement is one when it is indivisible, and it is indivisible in respect of time.

καθ᾽ αὐτὰ δὲ συνεχῆ ὅσα μὴ ἀφῇ ἕν· εἰ γὰρ θείης ἁπτόμενα ἀλλήλων ξύλα, οὐ φήσεις ταῦτα εἶναι ἓν οὔτε ξύλον οὔτε σῶμα οὔτ᾽ ἄλλο συνεχὲς οὐδέν. τά τε δὴ ὅλως συνεχῆ [10] ἓν λέγεται κἂν ἔχῃ κάμψιν, καὶ ἔτι μᾶλλον τὰ μὴ ἔχοντα κάμψιν, οἷον κνήμη ἢ μηρὸς σκέλους, ὅτι ἐνδέχεται μὴ μίαν εἶναι τὴν κίνησιν τοῦ σκέλους. καὶ ἡ εὐθεῖα τῆς κεκαμμένης μᾶλλον ἕν· τὴν δὲ κεκαμμένην καὶ ἔχουσαν γωνίαν καὶ μίαν καὶ οὐ μίαν λέγομεν, ὅτι ἐνδέχεται καὶ μὴ ἅμα τὴν [15] κίνησιν αὐτῆς εἶναι καὶ ἅμα· τῆς δ᾽ εὐθείας ἀεὶ ἅμα, καὶ οὐδὲν μόριον ἔχον μέγεθος τὸ μὲν ἠρεμεῖ τὸ δὲ κινεῖται, ὥσπερ τῆς κεκαμμένης.

Secundum se autem continua quaecumque non tactu sunt unum; nam si ponis se tangentia ligna, non dices haec unum esse nec lignum nec corpus nec aliud continuum nullum. Quae itaque omnino sunt continua unum dicuntur quamvis reflexionem habeant, et adhuc magis quae non habent reflexionem, ut tibia aut crus quam skelos, quia contingit non unum esse motum skeli. Et recta quam flexa magis unum. Reflexam vero et angulum habentem unam et non unam dicimus, quia contingit et non simul esse motum eius et simul recte vero semper simul, et nulla pars habens magnitudinem haec quidem quiescit illa vero movetur, quemadmodum reflexe.

Those things are continuous by their own nature which are one not merely by contact; for if you put pieces of wood touching one another, you will not say these are one piece of wood or one body or one continuum of any other sort. Things, then, that are continuous in any way called one, even if they admit of being bent, and still more those which cannot be bent; e.g. the shin or the thigh is more one than the leg, because the movement of the leg need not be one. And the straight line is more one than the bent; but that which is bent and has an angle we call both one and not one, because its movement may be either simultaneous or not simultaneous; but that of the straight line is always simultaneous, and no part of it which has magnitude rests while another moves, as in the bent line.

ἔτι ἄλλον τρόπον ἓν λέγεται τῷ τὸ ὑποκείμενον τῷ εἴδει εἶναι ἀδιάφορον· ἀδιάφορον δ᾽ ὧν ἀδιαίρετον τὸ εἶδος κατὰ τὴν αἴσθησιν· τὸ δ᾽ ὑποκείμενον [20] ἢ τὸ πρῶτον ἢ τὸ τελευταῖον πρὸς τὸ τέλος· καὶ γὰρ οἶνος εἷς λέγεται καὶ ὕδωρ ἕν, ᾗ ἀδιαίρετον κατὰ τὸ εἶδος, καὶ οἱ χυμοὶ πάντες λέγονται ἕν (οἷον ἔλαιον οἶνος) καὶ τὰ τηκτά, ὅτι πάντων τὸ ἔσχατον ὑποκείμενον τὸ αὐτό· ὕδωρ γὰρ ἢ ἀὴρ πάντα ταῦτα.

Amplius alio modo dicitur  eo quod subiectum sit specie  indifferens; indifferens vero quorum indivisibilis  species secundum sensum. Subiectum autem aut primum aut ultimum ad finem. Vinum enim unum dicitur et aqua una in quantum indivisibile secundum speciem, et iiquores omnes unum dicuntur (ut oleum, vinum) et fluida, quia omnium ultimum subiectum  idem; nam aqua aut aer omnia haec sunt.

(b)(i) Things are called one in another sense because their substratum does not differ in kind; it does not differ in the case of things whose kind is indivisible to sense. The substratum meant is either the nearest to, or the farthest from, the final state. For, one the one hand, wine is said to be one and water is said to be one, qua indivisible in kind; and, on the other hand, all juices, e.g. oil and wine, are said to be one, and so are all things that can be melted, because the ultimate substratum of all is the same; for all of these are water or air.

λέγεται δ᾽ ἓν καὶ ὧν τὸ γένος ἓν [25] διαφέρον ταῖς ἀντικειμέναις διαφοραῖς—καὶ ταῦτα λέγεται πάντα ἓν ὅτι τὸ γένος ἓν τὸ ὑποκείμενον ταῖς διαφοραῖς (οἷον ἵππος ἄνθρωπος κύων ἕν τι ὅτι πάντα ζῷα), καὶ τρόπον δὴ παραπλήσιον ὥσπερ ἡ ὕλη μία. ταῦτα δὲ ὁτὲ μὲν οὕτως ἓν λέγεται, ὁτὲ δὲ τὸ ἄνω γένος ταὐτὸν λέγεται [30] —ἂν ᾖ τελευταῖα τοῦ γένους εἴδη—τὸ ἀνωτέρω τούτων, οἷον τὸ ἰσοσκελὲς καὶ τὸ ἰσόπλευρον ταὐτὸ καὶ ἓν σχῆμα ὅτι ἄμφω τρίγωνα· τρίγωνα δ᾽ οὐ ταὐτά.

Dicuntur  autem unum et quorum genus unum differens oppositis differentiis. Et haec dicuntur omnia unum quia genus unum quod subicitur differentiis, ut equus, homo, canis unum quid, quia omnia animalia. Et modo itaque simili sicut materia una. Haec autem quandoque quidem ita unum dicuntur, quandoque vero  genere superiore quod idem dicitur, si sint ultime species generis superiores hiis; ut isoskeles et isopleurus rsunt una et eadem1 figura, quia ambo triangulus; sed trianguli non iidem.

(ii) Those things also are called one whose genus is one though distinguished by opposite differentiae – these too are all called one because the genus which underlies the differentiae is one (e.g. horse, man, and dog form a unity, because all are animals), and indeed in a way similar to that in which the matter is one. These are sometimes called one in this way, but sometimes it is the higher genus that is said to be the same (if they are infimae species of their genus) – the genus above the proximate genera; e.g.

the isosceles and the equilateral are one and the same figure because both are triangles; but they are not the same triangles.

ἔτι δὲ ἓν λέγεται ὅσων ὁ λόγος ὁ τὸ τί ἦν εἶναι λέγων ἀδιαίρετος πρὸς ἄλλον τὸν δηλοῦντα [τί ἦν εἶναι] τὸ πρᾶγμα (αὐτὸς γὰρ καθ᾽ αὑτὸν [35] πᾶς λόγος διαιρετός). οὕτω γὰρ καὶ τὸ ηὐξημένον καὶ φθῖνον ἕν ἐστιν, ὅτι ὁ λόγος εἷς, ὥσπερ ἐπὶ τῶν ἐπιπέδων ὁ τοῦ εἴδους.

Amplius autem unum dicuntur quorumcumque ratio quae quod quid erat esse dicit indivisibilis est ad aliam significantem quid erat esse rem (ipsa enim secundum se omnis ratio divisibilis). Sic enim augmentatum et minutum unum sunt, quia ratio una, sicut in superficiebus quae speciei una.

(c) Two things are called one, when the definition which states the essence of one is indivisible from another definition which shows us the other (though in itself every definition is divisible). Thus even that which has increased or is diminishing is one, because its definition is one, as, in [16b] the case of plane figures, is the definition of their form.

[1016β] [1] ὅλως δὲ ὧν ἡ νόησις ἀδιαίρετος ἡ νοοῦσα τὸ τί ἦν εἶναι, καὶ μὴ δύναται χωρίσαι μήτε χρόνῳ μήτε τόπῳ μήτε λόγῳ, μάλιστα ταῦτα ἕν, καὶ τούτων ὅσα οὐσίαι:

Omnino vero quorum intelligentia indivisibilis intelligens quid erat esse, et non potest separari neque tempore neque loco neque ratione, maxime haec unum, et horum quaecumque substantia.

In general those things the thought of whose essence is indivisible, and cannot separate them either in time or in place or in definition, are most of all one, and of these especially those which are substances.

καθόλου γὰρ ὅσα μὴ ἔχει διαίρεσιν, ᾗ μὴ ἔχει, ταύτῃ ἓν λέγεται, [5] οἷον εἰ ᾗ ἄνθρωπος μὴ ἔχει διαίρεσιν, εἷς ἄνθρωπος, εἰ δ᾽ ᾗ ζῷον, ἓν ζῷον, εἰ δὲ ᾗ μέγεθος, ἓν μέγεθος. τὰ μὲν οὖν πλεῖστα ἓν λέγεται τῷ ἕτερόν τι ἢ ποιεῖν ἢ ἔχειν ἢ πάσχειν ἢ πρός τι εἶναι ἕν, τὰ δὲ πρώτως λεγόμενα ἓν ὧν ἡ οὐσία μία, μία δὲ ἢ συνεχείᾳ ἢ εἴδει ἢ λόγῳ: καὶ γὰρ [10] ἀριθμοῦμεν ὡς πλείω ἢ τὰ μὴ συνεχῆ ἢ ὧν μὴ ἓν τὸ εἶδος ἢ ὧν ὁ λόγος μὴ εἷς.

Universaliter enim quaecumque non habent divisionem, in quantum non habent, sic unum dicuntur; ut si in quantum homo non habet divisionem, unus homo, si vero in quantum animal, unum animal, et si in quantum magnitudo, una magnitudo. Plurima quidem igitur unum dicuntur per alterum aliquid facere aut pati aut habere aut ad aliquid esse unum, quae autem primo dicuntur unum quorum substantia una, una vero aut continuatione aut specie aut ratione; et enim numeramus ut plura  aut quae non continua aut quorum non una species aut quorum ratio non una.

For in general those things that do not admit of division are called one in so far as they do not admit of it; e.g. if two things are indistinguishable qua man, they are one kind of man; if qua animal, one kind of animal; if qua magnitude, one kind of magnitude. Now most things are called one because they either do or have or suffer or are related to something else that is one, but the things that are primarily called one are those whose substance is one, – and one either in continuity or in form or in definition; for we count as more than one either things that are not continuous, or those whose form is not one, or those whose definition is not one.

ἔτι δ᾽ ἔστι μὲν ὡς ὁτιοῦν ἕν φαμεν εἶναι ἂν ᾖ ποσὸν καὶ συνεχές, ἔστι δ᾽ ὡς οὔ, ἂν μή τι ὅλον ᾖ, τοῦτο δὲ ἂν μὴ τὸ εἶδος ἔχῃ ἕν: οἷον οὐκ ἂν φαῖμεν ὁμοίως ἓν ἰδόντες ὁπωσοῦν τὰ μέρη συγκείμενα τοῦ ὑποδήματος, [15] ἐὰν μὴ διὰ τὴν συνέχειαν, ἀλλ᾽ ἐὰν οὕτως ὥστε ὑπόδημα εἶναι καὶ εἶδός τι ἔχειν ἤδη ἕν: διὸ καὶ ἡ τοῦ κύκλου μάλιστα μία τῶν γραμμῶν, ὅτι ὅλη καὶ τέλειός ἐστιν.

Amplius autem est quidem ut quodcumque unum continuitate dicimus esse, si sit quantum et continuum, est autem ut non, si non aliquod totum sit, hoc autem si non speciem habeat unam; ut non utique dicemus rsimiliter unum videntes1 qualitercumque partes compositas calciamenti, nisi propter continuitatem, sed si sic ut calciamentum sit et 1016b 15 speciem habeat aliquam iam unam. Quapropter et quae circuli maxime una linearum, quia tota et perfecta est.

While in a sense we call anything one if it is a quantity and continuous, in a sense we do not unless it is a whole, i.e. unless it has unity of form; e.g. if we saw the parts of a shoe put together anyhow we should not call them one all the same (unless because of their continuity); we do this only if they are put together so as to be a shoe and to have already a certain single form. This is why the circle is of all lines most truly one, because it is whole and complete.

τὸ δὲ ἑνὶ εἶναι ἀρχῇ τινί ἐστιν ἀριθμοῦ εἶναι: τὸ γὰρ πρῶτον μέτρον ἀρχή, ᾧ γὰρ πρώτῳ γνωρίζομεν, τοῦτο πρῶτον μέτρον [20] ἑκάστου γένους: ἀρχὴ οὖν τοῦ γνωστοῦ περὶ ἕκαστον τὸ ἕν. οὐ ταὐτὸ δὲ ἐν πᾶσι τοῖς γένεσι τὸ ἕν. ἔνθα μὲν γὰρ δίεσις ἔνθα δὲ τὸ φωνῆεν ἢ ἄφωνον: βάρους δὲ ἕτερον καὶ κινήσεως ἄλλο. πανταχοῦ δὲ τὸ ἓν ἢ τῷ ποσῷ ἢ τῷ εἴδει ἀδιαίρετον. τὸ μὲν οὖν κατὰ τὸ ποσὸν ἀδιαίρετον, [25] τὸ μὲν πάντῃ καὶ ἄθετον λέγεται μονάς, τὸ δὲ πάντῃ καὶ θέσιν ἔχον στιγμή, τὸ δὲ μοναχῇ γραμμή, τὸ δὲ διχῇ ἐπίπεδον, τὸ δὲ πάντῃ καὶ τριχῇ διαιρετὸν κατὰ τὸ ποσὸν σῶμα: καὶ ἀντιστρέψαντι δὴ τὸ μὲν διχῇ διαιρετὸν ἐπίπεδον, τὸ δὲ μοναχῇ γραμμή, τὸ δὲ μηδαμῇ διαιρετὸν κατὰ [30] τὸ ποσὸν στιγμὴ καὶ μονάς, ἡ μὲν ἄθετος μονὰς ἡ δὲ θετὸς στιγμή.

Uni vero esse principium alicui est numero esse; prima namque mensura principium; nam quo primo cognoscimus, hoc est prima mensura cuiusque generis; principium ergo cognoscibilis circa quodlibet unum. Non idem autem in omnibus generibus unum. Hic quidem enim est diesis, illic autem vocalis aut consonans; gravitatis autem alterum et motus aliud. Vbique vero unum aut quantitate aut specie indivisibile. secundum quantum quidem igitur et in quantum quantum indivisibile: quod quidem omnino et sine positione dicitur unitas, quod autem omnino et positionem habens punctum; quod autem secundum unum linea, quod vero secundum duo superficies, omnino vero et tripliciter divisibile secundum quantitatem corpus. Facta autem conversione: dualiter quidem divisibile superficies, unice autem linea, nullatenus divisibile secundum quantitatem punctum et unitas; hoc quidem non habens positionem unitas, illud vero habens positionem punctum.

(3) The essence of what is one is to be some kind of beginning of number; for the first measure is the beginning, since that by which we first know each class is the first measure of the class; the one, then, is the beginning of the knowable regarding each class. But the one is not the same in all classes. For here it is a quarter-tone, and there it is the vowel or the consonant; and there is another unit of weight and another of movement. But everywhere the one is indivisible either in quantity or in kind. Now that which is indivisible in quantity is called a unit if it is not divisible in any dimension and is without position, a point if it is not divisible in any dimension and has position, a line if it is divisible in one dimension, a plane if in two, a body if divisible in quantity in all i.e. in three dimensions. And, reversing the order, that which is divisible in two dimensions is a plane, that which is divisible in one a line, that which is in no way divisible in quantity is a point or a unit, – that which has not position a unit, that which has position a point.

ἔτι δὲ τὰ μὲν κατ᾽ ἀριθμόν ἐστιν ἕν, τὰ δὲ κατ᾽ εἶδος, τὰ δὲ κατὰ γένος, τὰ δὲ κατ᾽ ἀναλογίαν, ἀριθμῷ μὲν ὧν ἡ ὕλη μία, εἴδει δ᾽ ὧν ὁ λόγος εἷς, γένει δ᾽ ὧν τὸ αὐτὸ σχῆμα τῆς κατηγορίας, κατ᾽ ἀναλογίαν δὲ ὅσα ἔχει ὡς [35] ἄλλο πρὸς ἄλλο. ἀεὶ δὲ τὰ ὕστερα τοῖς ἔμπροσθεν ἀκολουθεῖ, οἷον ὅσα ἀριθμῷ καὶ εἴδει ἕν, ὅσα δ᾽ εἴδει οὐ πάντα ἀριθμῷ: [1017α] [1] ἀλλὰ γένει πάντα ἕν ὅσαπερ καὶ εἴδει, ὅσα δὲ γένει οὐ πάντα [2] εἴδει ἀλλ᾽ ἀναλογίᾳ: ὅσα δὲ ἀνολογίᾳ οὐ πάντα γένει.

Amplius autem alia secundum numerum sunt unum, alia secundum speciem, alia secundum genus, alia secundum analogiam; numero quidem quorum materia una, specie quorum ratio una, genere quorum eadem figura predicationis, secundum proportionem quaecumque se habent ut aliud ad aliud. Semper itaque posteriora precedentia sequuntur, ut quaecumque numero specie unum, sed quaecumque specie non omnia numero; sed genere omnia unum quaecumque et specie, quaecumque vero genere non omnia specie sed proportione; et quaecumque unum proportione non omnia genere.

Again, some things are one in number, others in species, others in genus, others by analogy; in number those whose matter is one, in species those whose definition is one, in genus those to which the same figure of predication applies, by analogy those which are related as a third thing is to a fourth. The latter kinds of unity are always found when the former are; e.g. things that are one in number are also one in species, while things that are one in species are not [17a] all one in number; but things that are one in species are all one in genus, while things that are so in genus are not all one in species but are all one by analogy; while things that are one by analogy are not all one in genus.

φανερὸν δὲ καὶ ὅτι τὰ πολλὰ ἀντικειμένως λεχθήσεται τῷ ἑνί· τὰ μὲν γὰρ τῷ μὴ συνεχῆ εἶναι, τὰ δὲ τῷ διαιρετὴν [5] ἔχειν τὴν ὕλην κατὰ τὸ εἶδος, ἢ τὴν πρώτην ἢ τὴν τελευταίαν, τὰ δὲ τῷ τοὺς λόγους πλείους τοὺς τί ἦν εἶναι λέγοντας.

Palam autem et quod multa opposite dicentur uni; nam alia non existendo continua, alia in habendo materiam divisibilem secundum speciem, aut primam aut ultimam, alia in habendo rationes plures quid erat esse dicentes.

Evidently many will have meanings opposite to those of one ; some things are many because they are not continuous, others because their matter – either the proximate matter or the ultimate – is divisible in kind, others because the definitions which state their essence are more than one.

### *Chapter* 7 Being

τὸ ὂν λέγεται τὸ μὲν κατὰ συμβεβηκὸς τὸ δὲ καθ᾽ αὑτό,

Ens dicitur hoc quidem secundum accidens illud vero secundum se.

Things are said to be (1) in an accidental sense, (2) by their own nature.

κατὰ συμβεβηκὸς μέν, οἷον τὸν δίκαιον μουσικὸν εἶναί φαμεν καὶ τὸν ἄνθρωπον μουσικὸν καὶ τὸν μουσικὸν [10] ἄνθρωπον, παραπλησίως λέγοντες ὥσπερεὶ τὸν μουσικὸν οἰκοδομεῖν ὅτι συμβέβηκε τῷ οἰκοδόμῳ μουσικῷ εἶναι ἢ τῷ μουσικῷ οἰκοδόμῳ (τὸ γὰρ τόδε εἶναι τόδε σημαίνει τὸ συμβεβηκέναι τῷδε τόδε), οὕτω δὲ καὶ ἐπὶ τῶν εἰρημένων· τὸν γὰρ ἄνθρωπον ὅταν μουσικὸν λέγωμεν καὶ τὸν μουσικὸν ἄνθρωπον, [15] ἢ τὸν λευκὸν μουσικὸν ἢ τοῦτον λευκόν, τὸ μὲν ὅτι ἄμφω τῷ αὐτῷ συμβεβήκασι, τὸ δ᾽ ὅτι τῷ ὄντι συμβέβηκε, τὸ δὲ μουσικὸν ἄνθρωπον ὅτι τούτῳ τὸ μουσικὸν συμβέβηκεν (οὕτω δὲ λέγεται καὶ τὸ μὴ λευκὸν εἶναι, ὅτι ᾧ συμβέβηκεν, ἐκεῖνο ἔστιν)· τὰ μὲν οὖν κατὰ συμβεβηκὸς [20] εἶναι λεγόμενα οὕτω λέγεται ἢ διότι τῷ αὐτῷ ὄντι ἄμφω ὑπάρχει, ἢ ὅτι ὄντι ἐκείνῳ ὑπάρχει, ἢ ὅτι αὐτὸ ἔστιν ᾧ ὑπάρχει οὗ αὐτὸ κατηγορεῖται·

Secundum accidens quidem, ut iustum musicum esse dicimus et hominem musicum et musicum hominem, similiter dicentes ut musicum edificare, quia accidit edificatori musicum esse aut musico edificatorem; hoc enim esse hoc significat accidere hoc huic. Sic autem et in dictis; hominem quando musicum dicimus et musicum hominem, aut album musicum aut hunc album: hoc quidem quia ambo eidem acciderunt, illud vero quia enti accidit, hoc autem musicum hominem quia huic musicum accidit (sic autem dicitur et album esse, quia cui accidit, ille est). Quae quidem igitur secundum accidens esse dicuntur sic dicuntur aut eo quod eidem enti ambo insunt, aut quia enti illud inest, aut quia ipsum est cui inest de quo ipsum predicatur.

(1) In an accidental sense, e.g. we say "the righteous doer is musical", and "the man is musical", and "the musician is a man", just as we say "the musician builds", because the builder happens to be musical or the musician to be a builder; for here "one thing is another" means "one is an accident of another". So in the cases we have mentioned; for when we say "the man is musical" and "the musician is a man", or "he who is pale is musical" or "the musician is pale", the last two mean that both attributes are accidents of the same thing; the first that the attribute is an accident of that which is, while "the musical is a man" means that musical is an accident of a man. (In this sense, too, the not-pale is said to be, because that of which it is an accident is.) Thus when one thing is said in an accidental sense to be another, this is either because both belong to the same thing, and this is, or because that to which the attribute belongs is, or because the subject which has as an attribute that of which it is itself predicated, itself is.

καθ᾽ αὑτὰ δὲ εἶναι λέγεται ὅσαπερ σημαίνει τὰ σχήματα τῆς κατηγορίας· ὁσαχῶς γὰρ λέγεται, τοσαυταχῶς τὸ εἶναι σημαίνει. ἐπεὶ οὖν τῶν [25] κατηγορουμένων τὰ μὲν τί ἐστι σημαίνει, τὰ δὲ ποιόν, τὰ δὲ ποσόν, τὰ δὲ πρός τι, τὰ δὲ ποιεῖν ἢ πάσχειν, τὰ δὲ πού, τὰ δὲ ποτέ, ἑκάστῳ τούτων τὸ εἶναι ταὐτὸ σημαίνει· οὐθὲν γὰρ διαφέρει τὸ ἄνθρωπος ὑγιαίνων ἐστὶν ἢ τὸ ἄνθρωπος ὑγιαίνει, οὐδὲ τὸ ἄνθρωπος βαδίζων ἐστὶν ἢ τέμνων τοῦ ἄνθρωπος [30] βαδίζει ἢ τέμνει, ὁμοίως δὲ καὶ ἐπὶ τῶν ἄλλων.

Secundum se vero esse dicuntur quaecumque significant figuras predicationis; quotiens enim dicitur, totiens esse significat. Quoniam ergo predicatorum alia quid est significant, alia quale, alia quantum, alia ad aliquid, alia facere, alia pati, alia ubi, alia quando, horum unicuique esse idem significant. Nil enim refert 'homo conualescens esf aut 'homo convalescit', vel 'homo vadens est aut secans' aut 'hominem vadere aut secare'; similiter autem et in aliis.

(2) The kinds of essential being are precisely those that are indicated by the figures of predication; for the senses of being are just as many as these figures. Since, then, some predicates indicate what the subject is, others its quality, others quantity,

others relation, others activity or passivity, others its where , others its when, being has a meaning answering to each of these. For there is no difference between the man is recovering and the man recovers , nor between the man is walking or cutting and the man walks or cuts ; and similarly in all other cases.

ἔτι τὸ εἶναι σημαίνει καὶ τὸ ἔστιν ὅτι ἀληθές, τὸ δὲ μὴ εἶναι ὅτι οὐκ ἀληθὲς ἀλλὰ ψεῦδος, ὁμοίως ἐπὶ καταφάσεως καὶ ἀποφάσεως, οἷον ὅτι ἔστι Σωκράτης μουσικός, ὅτι ἀληθές τοῦτο, ἢ ὅτι ἔστι Σωκράτης οὐ λευκός, ὅτι ἀληθές· τὸ δ᾽ οὐκ [35] ἔστιν ἡ διάμετρος σύμμετρος, ὅτι ψεῦδος.

Amplius esse et est significant quia verum,  non esse autem quia non verum sed falsum, similiter in affirmatione et negatione; ut quod 'est Socrates musicus' quia hoc verum, aut quod 'est Socrates non albus', quod  verum; hoc autem 'non est dyameter incommensurabilis', quod falsum.

(3) Again, being and is mean that a statement is true, not being that it is not true but falses – and this alike in the case of affirmation and of negation; e.g. Socrates is musical means that this is true, or Socrates is not-pale means that this is true; but the diagonal of the square is not commensurate with the side means that it is false to say it is.

[1017β] [1] ἔτι τὸ εἶναι σημαίνει καὶ τὸ ὂν τὸ μὲν δυνάμει ῥητὸν τὸ δ᾽ ἐντελεχείᾳ τῶν εἰρημένων τούτων· ὁρῶν τε γὰρ εἶναί φαμεν καὶ τὸ δυνάμει ὁρῶν καὶ τὸ ἐντελεχείᾳ, καὶ [τὸ] ἐπίστασθαι ὡσαύτως καὶ τὸ δυνάμενον χρῆσθαι τῇ ἐπιστήμῃ καὶ τὸ [5] χρώμενον, καὶ ἠρεμοῦν καὶ ᾧ ἤδη ὑπάρχει ἠρεμία καὶ τὸ δυνάμενον ἠρεμεῖν. ὁμοίως δὲ καὶ ἐπὶ τῶν οὐσιῶν· καὶ γὰρ Ἑρμῆν ἐν τῷ λίθῳ φαμὲν εἶναι, καὶ τὸ ἥμισυ τῆς γραμμῆς, καὶ σῖτον τὸν μήπω ἁδρόν. πότε δὲ δυνατὸν καὶ πότε οὔπω, ἐν ἄλλοις διοριστέον. [10]

Amplius esse significat et ens: ens hoc quidem potestate  dicibile illud vero actu. Horum dictorum terminorum enim esse dicimus: et quod potestate est dicibile terminorum et quod est actu; et scire similiter: et potens uti scientia et utens;  et quiescens: et cui iam inest quies et potens quiescere. Similiter autem et in substantiis; et enim Mercurium in lapide dicimus esse, et medietatem lineae, et frumentum nondum perfectum. Quando vero potens et quando nondum, in aliis determinandum.

(4) Again, being and that which is mean that some [17b] of the things we have mentioned are potentially, others in complete reality. For we say both of that which sees potentially and of that which sees actually, that it is seeing , and both of that which can actualize its knowledge and of that which is actualizing it, that it knows, and both of that to which rest is already present and of that which can rest, that it rests. And similarly in the case of substances; we say the Hermes is in the stone, and the half

of the line is in the line, and we say of that which is not yet ripe that it is corn. When a thing is potential and when it is not yet potential must be explained elsewhere.

*Chapter*  8 Substance

οὐσία λέγεται τά τε ἁπλᾶ σώματα, οἷον γῆ καὶ πῦρ καὶ ὕδωρ καὶ ὅσα τοιαῦτα, καὶ ὅλως σώματα καὶ τὰ ἐκ τούτων συνεστῶτα ζῷά τε καὶ δαιμόνια καὶ τὰ μόρια τούτων: ἅπαντα δὲ ταῦτα λέγεται οὐσία ὅτι οὐ καθ᾽ ὑποκειμένου λέγεται ἀλλὰ κατὰ τούτων τὰ ἄλλα.

Substantia dicitur et simplicia corpora, ut terra et ignis et aqua et quaecumque talia, et universaliter corpora et ex hiis consistentia, animalia et demonia et partes horum; haec autem omnia dicuntur substantia, quia non de subiecto dicuntur sed de hiis alia.

We call substance (1) the simple bodies, i.e. earth and fire and water and everything of the sort, and in general bodies and the things composed of them, both animals and divine beings, and the parts of these. All these are called substance because they are not predicated of a subject but everything else is predicated of them.

ἄλλον δὲ [15] τρόπον ὃ ἂν ᾖ αἴτιον τοῦ εἶναι, ἐνυπάρχον ἐν τοῖς τοιούτοις ὅσα μὴ λέγεται καθ᾽ ὑποκειμένου, οἷον ἡ ψυχὴ τῷ ζῴῳ.

Alio vero modo quodcumque fuerit causa essendi, inexistens in talibus quaecumque non dicuntur de subiecto, ut anima animali.

(2) That which, being present in such things as are not predicated of a subject, is the cause of their being, as the soul is of the being of an animal.

ἔτι ὅσα μόρια ἐνυπάρχοντά ἐστιν ἐν τοῖς τοιούτοις ὁρίζοντά τε καὶ τόδε τι σημαίνοντα, ὧν ἀναιρουμένων ἀναιρεῖται τὸ ὅλον, οἷον ἐπιπέδου σῶμα, ὥς φασί τινες, καὶ ἐπίπεδον [20] γραμμῆς: καὶ ὅλως ὁ ἀριθμὸς δοκεῖ εἶναί τισι τοιοῦτος (ἀναιρουμένου τε γὰρ οὐδὲν εἶναι, καὶ ὁρίζειν πάντα):

Amplius quaecumque particule existentes sunt in talibus et terminantes et hoc aliquid significantes, quibus destructis destruitur totum, ut superficie corpus, ut dicunt quidam, et superficies linea; et totaliter numerus videtur esse quibusdam talis; nam destructo nihil esse, et terminare omnia.

(3) The parts which are present in such things, limiting them and marking them as individuals, and by whose destruction the whole is destroyed, as the body is by the

destruction of the plane, as some say, and the plane by the destruction of the line; and in general number is thought by some to be of this nature; for if it is destroyed, they say, nothing exists, and it limits all things.

ἔτι τὸ τί ἦν εἶναι, οὗ ὁ λόγος ὁρισμός, καὶ τοῦτο οὐσία λέγεται ἑκάστου.

Amplius quod quid erat esse, cuius ratio est diffinitio, et hoc substantia dicitur uniuscuiusque.

(4) The essence, the formula of which is a definition, is also called the substance of each thing.

συμβαίνει δὴ κατὰ δύο τρόπους τὴν οὐσίαν λέγεσθαι, τό θ᾽ ὑποκείμενον ἔσχατον, ὃ μηκέτι κατ᾽ ἄλλου λέγεται, καὶ ὃ [25] ἂν τόδε τι ὂν καὶ χωριστὸν ᾖ: τοιοῦτον δὲ ἑκάστου ἡ μορφὴ καὶ τὸ εἶδος.

Accidit itaque secundum duos modos substantiam dici: subiectum ultimum quod non adhuc de alio dicitur, et quodcumque hoc aliquid ens et separabile fuerit; tale vero uniuscuiusque forma et species.

It follows, then, that substance has two senses, (A) ultimate substratum, which is no longer predicated of anything else, and (B) that which, being a this , is also separable and of this nature is the shape or form of each thing.

*Chapter* 9 The same

ταὐτὰ λέγεται τὰ μὲν κατὰ συμβεβηκός, οἷον τὸ λευκὸν καὶ τὸ μουσικὸν τὸ αὐτὸ ὅτι τῷ αὐτῷ συμβέβηκε, καὶ ἄνθρωπος καὶ μουσικὸν ὅτι θάτερον θατέρῳ συμβέβηκεν, [30] τὸ δὲ μουσικὸν ἄνθρωπος ὅτι τῷ ἀνθρώπῳ συμβέβηκεν: ἑκατέρῳ δὲ τοῦτο καὶ τούτῳ ἑκάτερον ἐκείνων, καὶ γὰρ τῷ ἀνθρώπῳ τῷ μουσικῷ καὶ ὁ ἄνθρωπος καὶ τὸ μουσικὸν ταὐτὸ λέγεται, καὶ τούτοις ἐκεῖνο (διὸ καὶ πάντα ταῦτα καθόλου οὐ λέγεται: οὐ γὰρ ἀληθὲς εἰπεῖν ὅτι πᾶς ἄνθρωπος ταὐτὸ [35] καὶ τὸ μουσικόν: τὰ γὰρ καθόλου καθ᾽ αὑτὰ ὑπάρχει, τὰ δὲ συμβεβηκότα οὐ καθ᾽ αὑτά: [1018α] [1] ἀλλ᾽ ἐπὶ τῶν καθ᾽ ἕκαστα ἁπλῶς λέγεται: ταὐτὸ γὰρ δοκεῖ Σωκράτης καὶ Σωκράτης εἶναι μουσικός: τὸ δὲ Σωκράτης οὐκ ἐπὶ πολλῶν, διὸ οὐ πᾶς Σωκράτης λέγεται ὥσπερ πᾶς ἄνθρωπος): καὶ τὰ μὲν οὕτως [5] λέγεται ταὐτά,

Eadem vero dicuntur haec quidem secundum accidens, ut album et musicum idem quia eidem accidunt, et homo et musicum quia alterum alteri accidit, musicum autem homo quia musicum homini accidit; utrique autem hoc et horum utrumque illi, et enim homini musico et homo et musicum idem dicitur, et hiis illud. Quapropter et omnia haec universaliter non dicuntur; non enim est verum dicere quia omnis homo idem  et musicum (nam universalia secundum se existunt, accidentia autem non secundum se); sed in singularibus simpliciter dicuntur. Idem enim videtur Socrates et Socrates esse musicus; nam Socrates non in multis, propter quod non 'omnis Socrates' dicitur quemadmodum 'omnis homo'

The same means (1) that which is the same in an accidental sense, e.g. the pale and the musical are the same because they are accidents of the same thing, and a man and musical because the one is an accident of the other; and the musical is a man because it is an accident of the man. (The complex entity is the same as either of the simple ones and each of these is the same as it; for both the man and the musical are said to be the same as the musical man , and this the same as they.) This is why all of these statements are made not universally; for it is not true to say that every man is the same as the musical (for universal attributes belong to things in virtue of [18a] their own nature, but accidents do not belong to them in virtue of their own nature); but of the individuals the statements are made without qualification. For Socrates and musical Socrates are thought to be the same; but Socrates is not predicable of more than one subject, and therefore we do not say every Socrates as we say every man .

τὰ δὲ καθ᾽ αὑτὰ ὁσαχῶσπερ καὶ τὸ ἕν: καὶ γὰρ ὧν ἡ ὕλη μία ἢ εἴδει ἢ ἀριθμῷ ταὐτὰ λέγεται καὶ ὧν ἡ οὐσία μία, ὥστε φανερὸν ὅτι ἡ ταυτότης ἑνότης τίς ἐστιν ἢ πλειόνων τοῦ εἶναι ἢ ὅταν χρῆται ὡς πλείοσιν, οἷον ὅταν λέγῃ αὐτὸ αὑτῷ ταὐτόν: ὡς δυσὶ γὰρ χρῆται αὐτῷ.

et haec quidem sic dicuntur  eadem. Alia vero secundum se quaecumque quemadmodum et unum; et enim quorum materia una aut specie aut numero eadem dicuntur, et quorum substantia una. Quare palam quia ydemptitas unitas quaedam est aut plurium essendi  aut quando utitur ut pluribus, veluti quando dixerit ipsum ipsi idem; nam ut duobus utitur eodem.

Some things are said to be the same in this sense, others (2) are the same by their own nature, in as many senses as that which is one by its own nature is so; for both the things whose matter is one either in kind or in number, and those whose essence is one, are said to be the same. Clearly, therefore, sameness is a unity of the being either of more than one thing or of one thing when it is treated as more than one, ie. when we say a thing is the same as itself; for we treat it as two.

ἕτερα [10] δὲ λέγεται ὧν ἢ τὰ εἴδη πλείω ἢ ἡ ὕλη ἢ ὁ λόγος τῆς οὐσίας: καὶ ὅλως ἀντικειμένως τῷ ταὐτῷ λέγεται τὸ ἕτερον.

Diversa vero dicuntur quorum aut species sunt plures aut materia aut ratio substantiae; et omnino opposite eidem dicitur diversum.

Things are called other if either their kinds or their matters or the definitions of their essence are more than one; and in general other has meanings opposite to those of the same .

διάφορα δὲ λέγεται ὅς᾽ ἕτερά ἐστι τὸ αὐτό τι ὄντα, μὴ μόνον ἀριθμῷ ἀλλ᾽ ἢ εἴδει ἢ γένει ἢ ἀναλογίᾳ· ἔτι ὧν ἕτερον τὸ γένος, καὶ τὰ ἐναντία, καὶ ὅσα ἔχει ἐν τῇ οὐσίᾳ [15] τὴν ἑτερότητα.

Differentia vero dicuntur quaecumque diversa sunt idem aliquid entia, et non solum numero sed aut specie aut genere aut proportione. Amplius quorum diversum genus, et contraria, et quaecumque habent in substantia diversitatem.

Different is applied (1) to those things which though other are the same in some respect, only not in number but either in species or in genus or by analogy; (2) to those whose genus is other, and to contraries, and to an things that have their otherness in their essence.

ὅμοια λέγεται τά τε πάντῃ ταὐτὸ πεπονθότα, καὶ τὰ πλείω ταὐτὰ πεπονθότα ἢ ἕτερα, καὶ ὧν ἡ ποιότης μία·

Similia dicuntur quae idem passa, et plura idem passa aut diversa, et quorum qualitas una;

Those things are called like which have the same attributes in every respect, and those which have more attributes the same than different, and those whose quality is one;

καὶ καθ᾽ ὅσα ἀλλοιοῦσθαι ἐνδέχεται τῶν ἐναντίων, τούτων τὸ πλείω ἔχον ἢ κυριώτερα ὅμοιον τούτῳ. ἀντικειμένως δὲ τοῖς ὁμοίοις τὰ ἀνόμοια. [20]

et secundum quaecumque alterari contingit contrariorum, horum quod plura habet aut magis propria huic est simile. Opposite vero similibus dissimilia.

and that which shares with another thing the greater number or the more important of the attributes (each of them one of two contraries) in respect of which things are capable of altering, is like that other thing. The senses of unlike are opposite to those of like .

*Chapter* 10 Opposite

ἀντικείμενα λέγεται ἀντίφασις καὶ τἀναντία καὶ τὰ πρός τι καὶ στέρησις καὶ
ἕξις καὶ ἐξ ὧν καὶ εἰς ἃ ἔσχατα αἱ γενέσεις καὶ φθοραί:

Opposita dicuntur contradictio et contraria et ad aliquid et privatio et habitus et
ex quibus et ad quae ultima, ut generationes et corruptiones;

The term opposite is applied to contradictories, and to contraries, and to relative
terms, and to privation and possession, and to the extremes from which and into
which generation and dissolution take place;

καὶ ὅσα μὴ ἐνδέχεται ἅμα παρεῖναι τῷ ἀμφοῖν δεκτικῷ, ταῦτα ἀντικεῖσθαι
λέγεται ἢ αὐτὰ ἢ ἐξ ὧν ἐστίν. φαιὸν γὰρ καὶ λευκὸν ἅμα τῷ [25] αὐτῷ οὐχ ὑπάρχει:
διὸ ἐξ ὧν ἐστὶν ἀντίκειται.

et quaecumque non contingunt simul adesse amborum susceptibili, haec opponi
dicuntur aut ipsa aut ex quibus sunt. Nam pallidum et album simul eidem  non insunt;
propter quod ex quibus sunt opponuntur hiis.

and the attributes that cannot be present at the same time in that which is
receptive of both, are said to be opposed, – either themselves of their constituents.
Grey and white colour do not belong at the same time to the same thing; hence their
constituents are opposed.

ἐναντία λέγεται τά τε μὴ δυνατὰ ἅμα τῷ αὐτῷ παρεῖναι τῶν διαφερόντων
κατὰ γένος, καὶ τὰ πλεῖστον διαφέροντα τῶν ἐν τῷ αὐτῷ γένει, καὶ τὰ πλεῖστον
διαφέροντα τῶν ἐν ταὐτῷ δεκτικῷ, καὶ τὰ πλεῖστον διαφέροντα τῶν ὑπὸ τὴν αὐτὴν
[30] δύναμιν, καὶ ὧν ἡ διαφορὰ μεγίστη ἢ ἁπλῶς ἢ κατὰ γένος ἢ κατ᾽ εἶδος.

Contraria dicuntur quae non possunt simul adesse eidem differentium
secundum genus, et quae plurimum differunt eorum quae sunt in eodem genere, et
quae plurimum differunt eo quod in eodem susceptibili, et quae plurimum differunt
eorum quae sunt sub eadem potestate, et quorum differentia maxima aut simpliciter
aut secundum genus aut secundum speciem.

The term contrary is applied (1) to those attributes differing in genus which
cannot belong at the same time to the same subject, (2) to the most different of the
things in the same genus, (3) to the most different of the attributes in the same
recipient subject, (4) to the most different of the things that fall under the same faculty,
(5) to the things whose difference is greatest either absolutely or in genus or in species.

τὰ δ᾽ ἄλλα ἐναντία λέγεται τὰ μὲν τῷ τὰ τοιαῦτα ἔχειν, τὰ δὲ τῷ δεκτικὰ εἶναι τῶν τοιούτων, τὰ δὲ τῷ ποιητικὰ ἢ παθητικὰ εἶναι τῶν τοιούτων, ἢ ποιοῦντα ἢ πάσχοντα, ἢ ἀποβολαὶ ἢ λήψεις, ἢ ἕξεις ἢ στερήσεις [35] εἶναι τῶν τοιούτων.

Alia vero contraria dicuntur haec quidem in talia habere, alia in talium susceptiva esse, alia in activa aut passiva esse talium, aut agentia aut patientia, aut abiectiones aut acceptiones, aut habitus aut privationes esse talium.

The other things that are called contrary are so called, some because they possess contraries of the above kind, some because they are receptive of such, some because they are productive of or susceptible to such, or are producing or suffering them, or are losses or acquisitions, or possessions or privations, of such.

ἐπεὶ δὲ τὸ ἓν καὶ τὸ ὂν πολλαχῶς λέγεται, ἀκολουθεῖν ἀνάγκη καὶ τἆλλα ὅσα κατὰ ταῦτα λέγεται, ὥστε καὶ τὸ ταὐτὸν καὶ τὸ ἕτερον καὶ τὸ ἐναντίον, ὥστ᾽ εἶναι ἕτερον καθ᾽ ἑκάστην κατηγορίαν.

Quoniam autem ens et unum multipliciter dicitur, sequi est necesse et alia quaecumque secundum haec dicuntur, quare et idem et diversum et contrarium, ut sit diversum secundum unamquamquae cathegoriam.

Since one and being have many senses, the other terms which are derived from these, and therefore same , other , and contrary , must correspond, so that they must be different for each category.

τερα δὲ τῷ εἴδει λέγεται ὅσα τε ταὐτοῦ γένους ὄντα μὴ ὑπάλληλά ἐστι, [1018β] [1] καὶ ὅσα ἐν τῷ αὐτῷ γένει ὄντα διαφορὰν ἔχει, καὶ ὅσα ἐν τῇ οὐσίᾳ ἐναντίωσιν ἔχει· καὶ τὰ ἐναντία ἕτερα τῷ εἴδει ἀλλήλων ἢ πάντα ἢ τὰ λεγόμενα πρώτως, καὶ ὅσων ἐν τῷ [5] τελευταίῳ τοῦ γένους εἴδει οἱ λόγοι ἕτεροι (οἷον ἄνθρωπος καὶ ἵππος ἄτομα τῷ γένει οἱ δὲ λόγοι ἕτεροι αὐτῶν), καὶ ὅσα ἐν τῇ αὐτῇ οὐσίᾳ ὄντα ἔχει διαφοράν. ταὐτὰ δὲ τῷ εἴδει τὰ ἀντικειμένως λεγόμενα τούτοις.

Diversa vero specie dicuntur quaecumque eiusdem generis existentia non sub invicem sunt, et quaecumque in eodem genere existentia differentiam habent, et quaecumque in substantia contrarietatem habent; et contraria diversa sunt specie ab invicem aut omnia aut dicta primum, et quorumcumque in finali generis specie rationes diverse (ut homo et equus individua genere et rationes eorum diverse), et quaecumque in eadem substantia entia differentiam habent. Eadem vero specie opposite hiis dicta.

The term other in species is applied to things which being of the same genus are not subordinate the one to the [18b] other, or which being in the same genus have a difference, or which have a contrariety in their substance; and contraries are other than one another in species (either all contraries or those which are so called in the primary sense), and so are those things whose definitions differ in the infima species of the genus (e.g. man and horse are indivisible in genus, but their definitions are different), and those which being in the same substance have a difference. The same in species has the various meanings opposite to these.

*Chapter* 11 Prior, posterior

πρότερα καὶ ὕστερα λέγεται ἔνια μέν, ὡς ὄντος τινὸς [10] πρώτου καὶ ἀρχῆς ἐν ἑκάστῳ γένει, τῷ ἐγγύτερον <εἶναι ἀρχῆς τινὸς ὡρισμένης ἢ ἁπλῶς καὶ τῇ φύσει ἢ πρός τι ἢ ποὺ ἢ ὑπό τινων,

Priora et posteriora dicuntur quaedam quidem, tamquam existente aliquo primo et principio in unoquoque genere, quod propinquius principio cuidam determinato aut simpliciter et natura aut ad aliquid aut ubi aut ab aliquibus;

The words prior and posterior are applied (1) to some things (on the assumption that there is a first, i.e. a beginning, in each class) because they are nearer some beginning determined either absolutely and by nature, or by reference to something or in some place or by certain people;

οἷον τὰ μὲν κατὰ τόπον τῷ εἶναι ἐγγύτερον ἢ φύσει τινὸς τόπου ὡρισμένου (οἷον τοῦ μέσου ἢ τοῦ ἐσχάτου) ἢ πρὸς τὸ τυχόν, τὸ δὲ πορρώτερον ὕστερον:

ut haec quidem secundum locum in existendo propinquius aut natura alicui loco determinato (ut medio aut ultimo) aut sicut evenit; quod vero remotius posterius.

e.g. things are prior in place because they are nearer either to some place determined by nature (e.g. the middle or the last place), or to some chance object; and that which is farther is posterior.

τὰ δὲ κατὰ [15] χρόνον (τὰ μὲν γὰρ τῷ πορρώτερον τοῦ νῦν, οἷον ἐπὶ τῶν γενομένων, πρότερον γὰρ τὰ Τρωϊκὰ τῶν Μηδικῶν ὅτι πορρώτερον ἀπέχει τοῦ νῦν: τὰ δὲ τῷ ἐγγύτερον τοῦ νῦν, οἷον ἐπὶ τῶν μελλόντων, πρότερον γὰρ Νέμεα Πυθίων ὅτι ἐγγύτερον τοῦ νῦν τῷ νῦν ὡς ἀρχῇ καὶ πρώτῳ χρησαμένων):

Alia secundum tempus; haec quidem enim eo quod remotiora a nunc, ut in factis (priora namque troica medis, quia remotiora a nunc), haec autem eo quod propinquius nunc, ut in futuris (prius enim Nemia Pythion, quia propinquius nunc, ipso nunc ut principio et primo usis).

Other things are prior in time; some by being farther from the present, i.e. in the case of past events (for the Trojan war is prior to the Persian, because it is farther from the present), others by being nearer the present, i.e. in the case of future events (for the Nemean games are prior to the Pythian, if we treat the present as beginning and first point, because they are nearer the present).

τὰ [20] δὲ κατὰ κίνησιν (τὸ γὰρ ἐγγύτερον τοῦ πρώτου κινήσαντος πρότερον, οἷον παῖς ἀνδρός· ἀρχὴ δὲ καὶ αὕτη τις ἁπλῶς)· τὰ δὲ κατὰ δύναμιν (τὸ γὰρ ὑπερέχον τῇ δυνάμει πρότερον, καὶ τὸ δυνατώτερον· τοιοῦτον δ᾽ ἐστὶν οὗ κατὰ τὴν προαίρεσιν ἀνάγκη ἀκολουθεῖν θάτερον καὶ τὸ ὕστερον, ὥστε μὴ κινοῦντός [25] τε ἐκείνου μὴ κινεῖσθαι καὶ κινοῦντος κινεῖσθαι· ἡ δὲ προαίρεσις ἀρχή)·

Alia secundum motum; propinquius enim primo moventi est prius, ut puer viro; principium autem et hoc quoddam simpliciter . Alia secundum potestatem; excedens enim potestate prius , et quod potentius; tale vero est cuius secundum preuoluntatem sequi est necesse alterum et posterius, ut non movente illo non moveatur et movente moveatur; et est prevoluntas principium.

Other things are prior in movement; for that which is nearer the first mover is prior (e.g. the boy is prior to the man); and the prime mover also is a beginning absolutely. Others are prior in power; for that which exceeds in power, i.e. the more powerful, is prior; and such is that according to whose will the other – i.e. the posterior – must follow, so that if the prior does not set it in motion the other does not move, and if it sets it in motion it does move; and here will is a beginning.

τὰ δὲ κατὰ τάξιν (ταῦτα δ᾽ ἐστὶν ὅσα πρός τι ἓν ὡρισμένον διέστηκε κατά τινα λόγον, οἷον παραστάτης τριτοστάτου πρότερον καὶ παρανήτη νήτης· ἔνθα μὲν γὰρ ὁ κορυφαῖος ἔνθα δὲ ἡ μέση ἀρχή)· ταῦτα μὲν οὖν πρότερα [30] τοῦτον λέγεται τὸν τρόπον,

Alia secundum ordinem; haec autem sunt quaecumque ad aliquid unum determinatum distant secundum rationem, ut parastata tritostata prius et paraniti nitis; hic quidem enim qui summus hic autem quae media principium. Haec quidem igitur priora dicuntur hoc modo.

Others are prior in arrangement; these are the things that are placed at intervals in reference to some one definite thing according to some rule, e.g. in the chorus the second man is prior to the third, and in the lyre the second lowest string is prior to the lowest; for in the one case the leader and in the other the middle string is the beginning.

ἄλλον δὲ τρόπον τὸ τῇ γνώσει πρότερον ὡς καὶ ἁπλῶς πρότερον. τούτων δὲ ἄλλως τὰ κατὰ τὸν λόγον καὶ τὰ κατὰ τὴν αἴσθησιν. κατὰ μὲν γὰρ τὸν λόγον τὰ καθόλου πρότερα κατὰ δὲ τὴν αἴσθησιν τὰ καθ᾽ ἕκαστα·

Alio vero modo quod cognitione est prius ut et simpliciter prius. Horum autem aliter et quae secundum rationem et quae secundum sensum. Nam secundum rationem universalia priora, secundum autem sensum singularia.

These, then, are called prior in this sense, but (2) in another sense that which is prior for knowledge is treated as also absolutely prior; of these, the things that are prior in definition do not coincide with those that are prior in relation to perception. For in definition universals are prior, in relation to perception individuals.

καὶ κατὰ τὸν λόγον δὲ τὸ συμβεβηκὸς τοῦ ὅλου [35] πρότερον, οἷον τὸ μουσικὸν τοῦ μουσικοῦ ἀνθρώπου· οὐ γὰρ ἔσται ὁ λόγος ὅλος ἄνευ τοῦ μέρους· καίτοι οὐκ ἐνδέχεται μουσικὸν εἶναι μὴ ὄντος μουσικοῦ τινός.

Et secundum rationem accidens toto prius, ut musicum musico homine; non enim erit ratio tota sine parte; equidem non contingit musicum esse non existente aliquo musico.

And in definition also the accident is prior to the whole, e.g. musical to musical man , for the definition cannot exist as a whole without the part; yet musicalness cannot exist unless there is some one who is musical.

ἔτι πρότερα λέγεται τὰ τῶν προτέρων πάθη, οἷον εὐθύτης λειότητος· τὸ μὲν γὰρ γραμμῆς καθ᾽ αὑτὴν πάθος τὸ δὲ ἐπιφανείας. [1019α] [1] τὰ μὲν δὴ οὕτω λέγεται πρότερα καὶ ὕστερα,

Amplius priora dicuntur priorum passiones, ut rectitudo levitate; hoc enim lineae secundum se passio est illud vero superficiei.

(3) The attributes of prior things are called prior, e.g. straightness is prior to smoothness; for one is an attribute of a line as such, and the other of a surface.

τὰ δὲ κατὰ φύσιν καὶ οὐσίαν, ὅσα ἐνδέχεται εἶναι ἄνευ ἄλλων, ἐκεῖνα δὲ ἄνευ ἐκείνων μή· ᾗ διαιρέσει ἐχρήσατο Πλάτων. (ἐπεὶ δὲ τὸ εἶναι [5] πολλαχῶς, πρῶτον μὲν τὸ ὑποκείμενον πρότερον, διὸ ἡ οὐσία πρότερον, ἔπειτα ἄλλως τὰ κατὰ δύναμιν καὶ κατ᾽ ἐντελέχειαν· τὰ μὲν γὰρ κατὰ δύναμιν πρότερά ἐστι τὰ δὲ κατὰ ἐντελέχειαν, οἷον κατὰ δύναμιν μὲν ἡ ἡμίσεια τῆς ὅλης καὶ τὸ μόριον τοῦ ὅλου καὶ ἡ ὕλη τῆς οὐσίας, κατ᾽ [10] ἐντελέχειαν δ᾽ ὕστερον· διαλυθέντος γὰρ κατ᾽ ἐντελέχειαν ἔσται.)

Haec quidem itaque sic dicuntur priora et posteriora.Alia vero secundum naturam et substantiam, quaecumque contingit esse sine aliis et illa non sine illis; qua divisione usus est Plato. Quoniam autem esse multipliciter, primum quidem subiectum prius, propter quod et substantia prius, deinde aliter quae secundum potentiam et secundum actum; nam alia secundum potestatem priora sunt alia secundum actum, ut secundum potestatem quidem dimidietas toto et pars toto et materia substantia, secundum actum vero posterius; nam dissoluti secundum actum erunt.

[19a] Some things then are called prior and posterior in this sense, others (4) in respect of nature and substance, i.e. those which can be without other things, while the others cannot be without them, – a distinction which Plato used. (If we consider the various senses of being , firstly the subject is prior, so that substance is prior; secondly, according as potency or complete reality is taken into account, different things are prior, for some things are prior in respect of potency, others in respect of complete reality, e.g. in potency the half line is prior to the whole line, and the part to the whole, and the matter to the concrete substance, but in complete reality these are posterior; for it is only when the whole has been dissolved that they will exist in complete reality.)

τρόπον δή τινα πάντα τὰ πρότερον καὶ ὕστερον λεγόμενα κατὰ ταῦτα λέγεται: τὰ μὲν γὰρ κατὰ γένεσιν ἐνδέχεται ἄνευ τῶν ἑτέρων εἶναι, οἷον τὸ ὅλον τῶν μορίων, τὰ δὲ κατὰ φθοράν, οἷον τὸ μόριον τοῦ ὅλου. ὁμοίως δὲ καὶ τἆλλα. [15]

Modo itaque quodam omnia prius et posterius dicta secundum haec dicuntur; haec quidem enim secundum generationem sine aliis esse contingit, ut totum partibus, haec autem secundum corruptionem, ut pars toto. Similiter autem et alia.

In a sense, therefore, all things that are called prior and posterior are so called with reference to this fourth sense; for some things can exist without others in respect of generation, e.g. the whole without the parts, and others in respect of dissolution, e.g. the part without the whole. And the same is true in all other cases.

*Chapter* 12 Potency

δύναμις λέγεται ἡ μὲν ἀρχὴ κινήσεως ἢ μεταβολῆς ἡ ἐν ἑτέρῳ ἢ ᾗ ἕτερον, οἷον ἡ οἰκοδομικὴ δύναμίς ἐστιν ἢ οὐχ ὑπάρχει ἐν τῷ οἰκοδομουμένῳ, ἀλλ᾽ ἡ ἰατρικὴ δύναμις οὖσα ὑπάρχοι ἂν ἐν τῷ ἰατρευομένῳ, ἀλλ᾽ οὐχ ᾗ ἰατρευόμενος.

Potestas dicitur haec quidem principium motus aut mutationis aut in altero aut in quantum alterum; ut edificativa potestas est quae non existit in edificato, sed ars medicinalis potestas ens existet utique in sanato, sed non in quantum sanatum est.

Potency means (1) a source of movement or change, which is in another thing than the thing moved or in the same thing qua other; e.g. the art of building is a potency which is not in the thing built, while the art of healing, which is a potency, may be in the man healed, but not in him qua healed.

ἡ μὲν οὖν ὅλως ἀρχὴ μεταβολῆς ἢ κινήσεως λέγεται δύναμις [20] ἐν ἑτέρῳ ἢ ᾗ ἕτερον, ἡ δ᾿ ὑφ᾿ ἑτέρου ἢ ᾗ ἕτερον (καθ᾿ ἢν γὰρ τὸ πάσχον πάσχει τι, ὁτὲ μὲν ἐὰν ὁτιοῦν, δυνατὸν αὐτό φαμεν εἶναι παθεῖν, ὁτὲ δ᾿ οὐ κατὰ πᾶν πάθος ἀλλ᾿ ἂν ἐπὶ τὸ βέλτιον):

Ergo totaliter principium mutationis aut motus dicitur potestas in altero aut in quantum alterum. Haec autem ab altero aut in quantum alterum; secundum quam enim patiens patitur aliquid, quandoque quidem si quodcumque pati sit possibile dicimus esse autopathein, quandoque autem non secundum omnem passionem sed si ad melius.

Potency then means the source, in general, of change or movement in another thing or in the same thing qua other, and also (2) the source of a thing's being moved by another thing or by itself qua other. For in virtue of that principle, in virtue of which a patient suffers anything, we call it capable of suffering; and this we do sometimes if it suffers anything at all, sometimes not in respect of everything it suffers, but only if it suffers a change for the better.

ἔτι ἡ τοῦ καλῶς τοῦτ᾿ ἐπιτελεῖν ἢ κατὰ προαίρεσιν: ἐνίοτε γὰρ τοὺς μόνον ἂν πορευθέντας ἢ εἰπόντας, μὴ [25] καλῶς δὲ ἢ μὴ ὡς προείλοντο, οὐ φαμεν δύνασθαι λέγειν ἢ βαδίζειν: ὁμοίως δὲ καὶ ἐπὶ τοῦ πάσχειν.

Adhuc aut ut bene hoc efficiatur aut secundum voluntatem; quandoque enim solum utique ambulantes aut loquentes, non bene autem aut non ut vellent, non dicimus posse loqui aut ambulare. Similiter autem et in pati.

(3) The capacity of performing this well or according to intention; for sometimes we say of those who merely can walk or speak but not well or not as they intend, that they cannot speak or walk. So too (4) in the case of passivity.

ἔτι ὅσαι ἕξεις καθ᾿ ἃς ἀπαθῆ ὅλως ἢ ἀμετάβλητα ἢ μὴ ῥᾳδίως ἐπὶ τὸ χεῖρον εὐμετακίνητα, δυνάμεις λέγονται: κλᾶται μὲν γὰρ καὶ συντρίβεται καὶ κάμπτεται καὶ ὅλως φθείρεται οὐ τῷ [30] δύνασθαι ἀλλὰ τῷ μὴ δύνασθαι καὶ ἐλλείπειν τινός: ἀπαθῆ δὲ τῶν τοιούτων ἃ μόλις καὶ ἠρέμα πάσχει διὰ δύναμιν καὶ τῷ δύνασθαι καὶ τῷ ἔχειν πώς.

Amplius quicumque habitus secundum quos impassibilia omnino aut immutabilia aut non facile in peius mobilia, potestates dicuntur; franguntur enim et conteruntur, curuantur et omnino corrumpuntur non per posse sed per non posse et deficere in aliquo, impassibilia vero talium aut vix et modicum patiuntur propter potentiam et posse et aliqualiter habere.

(5) The states in virtue of which things are absolutely impassive or unchangeable, or not easily changed for the worse, are called potencies; for things are broken and crushed and bent and in general destroyed not by having a potency but by not having one and by lacking something, and things are impassive with respect to such processes if they are scarcely and slightly affected by them, because of a potency and because they can do something and are in some positive state.

λεγομένης δὲ τῆς δυνάμεως τοσαυταχῶς, καὶ τὸ δυνατὸν ἕνα μὲν τρόπον λεχθήσεται τὸ ἔχον κινήσεως ἀρχὴν ἢ μεταβολῆς (καὶ γὰρ [35] τὸ στατικὸν δυνατόν τι) ἐν ἑτέρῳ ἢ ᾗ ἕτερον, ἕνα δ᾽ ἐὰν ἔχῃ τι αὐτοῦ ἄλλο δύναμιν τοιαύτην,

Dicta vero potestate totiens, et potens uno quidem modo dicetur quod habet motus principium aut mutationis (et enim sistitivum potens aliquid in altero aut in quantum alterum); uno vero si quid ab ipso aliud potestatem habet talem.

Potency having this variety of meanings, so too the potent or capable in one sense will mean that which can begin a movement (or a change in general, for even that which can bring things to rest is a potent thing) in another thing or in itself qua other; and in one sense [19b] that over which something else has such a potency;

[1019β] [1] ἕνα δ᾽ ἐὰν ἔχῃ μεταβάλλειν ἐφ᾽ ὁτιοῦν δύναμιν, εἴτ᾽ ἐπὶ τὸ χεῖρον εἴτ᾽ ἐπὶ τὸ βέλτιον (καὶ γὰρ τὸ φθειρόμενον δοκεῖ δυνατὸν εἶναι φθείρεσθαι, ἢ οὐκ ἂν φθαρῆναι εἰ ἦν ἀδύνατον· νῦν δὲ ἔχει τινὰ [5] διάθεσιν καὶ αἰτίαν καὶ ἀρχὴν τοῦ τοιούτου πάθους· ὁτὲ μὲν δὴ τῷ ἔχειν τι δοκεῖ, ὁτὲ δὲ τῷ ἐστερῆσθαι τοιοῦτον εἶναι·

Uno autem si habet permutari in quodlibet potestatem, sive in peius sive in melius. Et enim corruptibile videtur esse possibile corrumpi, aut non utique corrumpi si erat impossibile; nunc autem dispositionem quandam habet et causam et principium talis passionis. Aliquando quidem itaque per habere aliquid videtur, aliquando per privari tale esse;

and in one sense that which has a potency of changing into something, whether for the worse or for the better (for even that which perishes is thought to be capable of perishing, for it would not have perished if it had not been capable of it; but, as a matter of fact, it has a certain disposition and cause and principle which fits it to suffer this; sometimes it is thought to be of this sort because it has something, sometimes because it is deprived of something;

εἰ δ᾽ ἡ στέρησίς ἐστιν ἕξις πως, πάντα τῷ ἔχειν ἂν εἴη τι, [εἰ δὲ μὴ] ὥστε τῷ τε ἔχειν ἕξιν τινὰ καὶ ἀρχήν ἐστι δυνατὸν [ὁμωνύμως] καὶ τῷ ἔχειν τὴν τούτου στέρησιν, εἰ ἐνδέχεται [10] ἔχειν στέρησιν· <εἰ δὲ μή, ὁμωνύμως):

si autem privatio est habitus aliquo modo, omnia in habendo utique erunt aliquid. Equivoce vero dicimus ens, quare in habendo habitum quendam et principium est possibile et habendo huius privationem, si contingit habere privationem.

but if privation is in a sense having or habit , everything will be capable by having something, so that things are capable both by having a positive habit and principle, and by having the privation of this, if it is possible to have a privation;

ἕνα δὲ τῷ μὴ ἔχειν αὐτοῦ δύναμιν ἢ ἀρχὴν ἄλλο ἢ ᾗ ἄλλο φθαρτικήν. ἕνα δὲ τῷ μὴ ἔχειν αὐτοῦ δύναμιν ἢ ἀρχὴν ἄλλο ἢ ᾗ ἄλλο φθαρτικήν. ἕνα δὲ τῷ μὴ ἔχειν αὐτοῦ δύναμιν ἢ ἀρχὴν ἄλλο ἢ ᾗ ἄλλο φθαρτικήν.

Uno in non habendo ipsius potestatem aut principium in alio in quantum est aliud corruptivum.

and if privation is not in a sense habit , capable is used in two distinct senses); and a thing is capable in another sense because neither any other thing, nor itself qua other, has a potency or principle which can destroy it.

ἔτι δὲ ταῦτα πάντα ἢ τῷ μόνον ἂν συμβῆναι γενέσθαι ἢ μὴ γενέσθαι, ἢ τῷ καλῶς. καὶ γὰρ ἐν τοῖς ἀψύχοις ἔνεστιν ἡ τοιαύτη δύναμις, οἷον ἐν τοῖς ὀργάνοις: τὴν μὲν γὰρ δύνασθαί φασι [15] φθέγγεσθαι λύραν, τὴν δ᾽ οὐδέν, ἂν ᾖ μὴ εὔφωνος.

Amplius autem haec omnia aut in solum accidere fieri aut non fieri, aut in bene. Nam in inanimatis inest talis potestas, ut in organis; aliam enim dicunt posse sonare liram, aliam non, si est non bene sonans.

Again, all of these are capable either merely because the thing might chance to happen or not to happen, or because it might do so well. This sort of potency is found even in lifeless things, e.g. in instruments; for we say one lyre can speak, and another cannot speak at all, if it has not a good tone.

ἀδυναμία δὲ ἐστι στέρησις δυνάμεως καὶ τῆς τοιαύτης ἀρχῆς οἵα εἴρηται, ἢ ὅλως ἢ τῷ πεφυκότι ἔχειν, ἢ καὶ ὅτε πέφυκεν ἤδη ἔχειν: οὐ γὰρ ὁμοίως ἂν φαῖεν ἀδύνατον εἶναι γεννᾶν παῖδα καὶ ἄνδρα καὶ εὐνοῦχον.

Impotentia autem est privatio potentiae et talis principii sublatio quaedam qualis dicta est, aut omnino aut apto nato habere aut quando aptum natum est iam habere; non enim similiter dicunt impossibile generare puerum et virum eunuchum.

Incapacity is privation of capacity – i.e. of such a principle as has been described either in general or in the case of something that would naturally have the capacity, or even at the time when it would naturally already have it; for the senses in which we should call a boy and a man and a eunuch incapable of begetting are distinct.

ἔτι δὲ καθ᾽ ἑκατέραν [20] δύναμιν ἔστιν ἀδυναμία ἀντικειμένη, τῇ τε μόνον κινητικῇ καὶ τῇ καλῶς κινητικῇ.

Amplius autem secundum alteram potentiam est impotentia opposita, ei quae solum motive et ei quae bene motive.

Again, to either kind of capacity there is an opposite incapacity – both to that which only can produce movement and to that which can produce it well.

καὶ ἀδύνατα δὴ τὰ μὲν κατὰ τὴν ἀδυναμίαν ταύτην λέγεται, τὰ δὲ ἄλλον τρόπον, οἷον δυνατόν τε καὶ ἀδύνατον, ἀδύνατον μὲν οὗ τὸ ἐναντίον ἐξ ἀνάγκης ἀληθές (οἷον τὸ τὴν διάμετρον σύμμετρον εἶναι [25] ἀδύνατον ὅτι ψεῦδος τὸ τοιοῦτον οὗ τὸ ἐναντίον οὐ μόνον ἀληθὲς ἀλλὰ καὶ ἀνάγκη [ἀσύμμετρον εἶναι]: τὸ ἄρα σύμμετρον οὐ μόνον ψεῦδος ἀλλὰ καὶ ἐξ ἀνάγκης ψεῦδος):

Et impossibilia vero haec quidem secundum impotentiam hanc dicuntur, alia alio modo, puta possibile et impossibile. Impossibile quidem cuius contrarium ex necessitate verum, ut dyametrum commensurabilem esse est impossibile, quia falsum quod tale cuius contrarium non solum verum sed et necesse non commensurabile esse; ergo commensurabile non solum falsum sed ex necessitate falsum.

Some things, then, are called adunata in virtue of this kind of incapacity, while others are so in another sense; i.e. both dunaton and adunaton are used as follows. The impossible is that of which the contrary is of necessity true, e.g. that the diagonal of a square is commensurate with the side is impossible, because such a statement is a falsity of which the contrary is not only true but also necessary; that it is commensurate, then, is not only false but also of necessity false.

τὸ δ᾽ ἐναντίον τούτῳ, τὸ δυνατόν, ὅταν μὴ ἀναγκαῖον ᾖ τὸ ἐναντίον ψεῦδος εἶναι, οἷον τὸ καθῆσθαι ἄνθρωπον δυνατόν: οὐ [30] γὰρ ἐξ ἀνάγκης τὸ μὴ καθῆσθαι ψεῦδος. τὸ μὲν οὖν δυνατὸν ἕνα μὲν τρόπον, ὥσπερ εἴρηται, τὸ μὴ ἐξ ἀνάγκης ψεῦδος σημαίνει, ἕνα δὲ τὸ ἀληθές [εἶναι], ἕνα δὲ τὸ ἐνδεχόμενον ἀληθὲς εἶναι.

Contrarium vero huic, possibile, quando non necesse fuerit contrarium falsum esse, ut sedere hominem possibile; non enim ex necessitate non sedere falsum. ergo possibile quidem uno modo, sicut dictum est, quod non ex necessitate falsum significat, alio vero verum esse, alio contingens verum iam.

The contrary of this, the possible, is found when it is not necessary that the contrary is false, e.g. that a man should be seated is possible; for that he is not seated is not of necessity false. The possible, then, in one sense, as has been said, means that which is not of necessity false; in one, that which is true; in one, that which may be true.

κατὰ μεταφορὰν δὲ ἡ ἐν γεωμετρίᾳ λέγεται δύναμις. ταῦτα μὲν οὖν τὰ δυνατὰ οὐ κατὰ δύναμιν:

Secundum methaphoram autem quae in geometria dicitur potentia. Haec quidem igitur possibilia non secundum potentiam.

A potency or power in geometry is so called by a change of meaning. – These senses of capable or possible involve no reference to potency.

[35] τὰ δὲ λεγόμενα κατὰ δύναμιν πάντα λέγεται πρὸς τὴν πρώτην [μίαν]: [1020α] [1] αὕτη δ᾽ ἐστὶν ἀρχὴ μεταβολῆς ἐν ἄλλῳ ἢ ᾗ ἄλλο. τὰ γὰρ ἄλλα λέγεται δυνατὰ τῷ τὰ μὲν ἔχειν αὐτῶν ἄλλο τι τοιαύτην δύναμιν τὰ δὲ μὴ ἔχειν τὰ δὲ ὡδὶ ἔχειν. ὁμοίως δὲ καὶ τὰ ἀδύνατα. ὥστε ὁ κύριος ὅρος [5] τῆς πρώτης δυνάμεως ἂν εἴη ἀρχὴ μεταβλητικὴ ἐν ἄλλῳ ἢ ᾗ ἄλλο.

Quae vero secundum potentiam omnia dicuntur ad primam unam; haec autem est principium mutationis in alio in quantum aliud. Alia namque dicuntur possibilia, haec quidem eorum in habendo aliud aliquid talem potentiam, illa vero in non habendo, alia in sic habendo. Similiter autem et impossibilia. Quare propria diffinitio prime potentie utique erit: principium permutativum in alio in quantum aliud.

But the senses which involve a reference to potency all refer to the primary [20a] kind of potency; and this is a source of change in another thing or in the same thing qua other. For other things are called capable , some because something else has such a potency over them, some because it has not, some because it has it in a particular way. The same is true of the things that are incapable. Therefore the proper definition of the primary kind of potency will be a source of change in another thing or in the same thing qua other .

*Chapter* 13 Quantum

ποσὸν λέγεται τὸ διαιρετὸν εἰς ἐνυπάρχοντα ὧν ἑκάτερον ἢ ἕκαστον ἕν τι καὶ τόδε τι πέφυκεν εἶναι. πλῆθος μὲν οὖν ποσόν τι ἐὰν ἀριθμητὸν ᾖ, μέγεθος δὲ ἂν μετρητὸν [10] ᾖ.

Quantum dicitur quod est divisibile in ea quae insunt, quorum utrumque aut singulum unum aliquid et hoc aliquid natum est esse. Multitudo ergo quantum aliquid si numerabilis fuerit, magnitudo autem si mensurabilis fuerit.

Quantum means that which is divisible into two or more constituent parts of which each is by nature a one and a this . A quantum is a plurality if it is numerable, a magnitude if it is a measurable.

λέγεται δὲ πλῆθος μὲν τὸ διαιρετὸν δυνάμει εἰς μὴ συνεχῆ, μέγεθος δὲ τὸ εἰς συνεχῆ: μεγέθους δὲ τὸ μὲν ἐφ᾽ ἓν συνεχὲς μῆκος τὸ δ᾽ ἐπὶ δύο πλάτος τὸ δ᾽ ἐπὶ τρία βάθος. τούτων δὲ πλῆθος μὲν τὸ πεπερασμένον ἀριθμὸς μῆκος δὲ γραμμὴ πλάτος δὲ ἐπιφάνεια βάθος δὲ σῶμα.

Dicitur autem multitudo quidem divisibile potestate in non continua, magnitudo autem quod in continua; magnitudinis vero quae quidem ad unum continua longitudo, quae autem ad duo latitudo, quae autem ad tria profunditas. Horum autem pluralitas quidem finita numerus, sed longitudo linea et latitudo superficies et profundum corpus.

Plurality means that which is divisible potentially into non-continuous parts, magnitude that which is divisible into continuous parts; of magnitude, that which is continuous in one dimension is length; in two breadth, in three depth. Of these, limited plurality is number, limited length is a line, breadth a surface, depth a solid.

ἔτι τὰ [15] μὲν λέγεται καθ᾽ αὑτὰ ποσά, τὰ δὲ κατὰ συμβεβηκός, οἷον ἡ μὲν γραμμὴ ποσόν τι καθ᾽ ἑαυτό, τὸ δὲ μουσικὸν κατὰ συμβεβηκός.

Amplius alia dicuntur secundum se quanta quaedam, alia secundum accidens, ut linea quantum aliquid secundum se, musicum vero secundum accidens.

Again, some things are called quanta in virtue of their own nature, others incidentally; e.g. the line is a quantum by its own nature, the musical is one incidentally.

τῶν δὲ καθ᾽ αὑτὰ τὰ μὲν κατ᾽ οὐσίαν ἐστίν, οἷον ἡ γραμμὴ ποσόν τι (ἐν γὰρ τῷ λόγῳ τῷ [19] τί ἐστι λέγοντι τὸ ποσόν τι ὑπάρχει), τὰ δὲ πάθη καὶ ἕξεις [20] τῆς τοιαύτης ἐστὶν οὐσίας, οἷον τὸ πολὺ καὶ τὸ ὀλίγον, καὶ μακρὸν καὶ βραχύ, καὶ πλατὺ καὶ στενόν, καὶ βαθὺ καὶ ταπεινόν, καὶ βαρὺ καὶ κοῦφον, καὶ τὰ ἄλλα τὰ τοιαῦτα. ἔστι δὲ καὶ τὸ μέγα καὶ τὸ μικρὸν καὶ μεῖζον καὶ ἔλαττον, καὶ καθ᾽ αὑτὰ καὶ πρὸς ἄλληλα λεγόμενα, τοῦ [25] ποσοῦ πάθη καθ᾽ αὑτά: μεταφέρονται μέντοι καὶ ἐπ᾽ ἄλλα ταῦτα τὰ ὀνόματα.

Eorum vero quae secundum se sunt alia secundum substantiam sunt, ut linea quantum quid (nam in ratione quid est dicente quantum quid existit), alia passiones et habitus talis sunt substantiae, ut multum et paucum, et productum et breve, et latum et strictum, et profundum et humile, et grave et leve, et alia talia. Sunt autem et magnum et parvum et maius et minus, et secundum se et ad invicem dicta, quanti passiones secundum se; transferuntur etiam et ad alia haec nomina.

Of the things that are quanta by their own nature some are so as substances, e.g. the line is a quantum (for a certain kind of quantum is present in the definition which states what it is), and others are modifications and states of this kind of substance, e.g. much and little, long and short, broad and narrow, deep and shallow, heavy and light, and all other such attributes. And also great and small, and greater and smaller, both in themselves and when taken relatively to each other, are by their own nature attributes of what is quantitative; but these names are transferred to other things also.

τῶν δὲ κατὰ συμβεβηκὸς λεγομένων ποσῶν τὰ μὲν οὕτως λέγεται ὥσπερ ἐλέχθη ὅτι τὸ μουσικὸν ποσὸν καὶ τὸ λευκὸν τῷ εἶναι ποσόν τι ᾧ ὑπάρχουσι, τὰ δὲ ὡς κίνησις καὶ χρόνος· καὶ γὰρ ταῦτα πός᾿ ἄττα λέγεται [30] καὶ συνεχῆ τῷ ἐκεῖνα διαιρετὰ εἶναι ὧν ἐστι ταῦτα πάθη. λέγω δὲ οὐ τὸ κινούμενον ἀλλ᾿ ὃ ἐκινήθη· τῷ γὰρ ποσὸν εἶναι ἐκεῖνο καὶ ἡ κίνησις ποσή, ὁ δὲ χρόνος τῷ ταύτην.

Secundum accidens vero dictorum quantorum hoc quidem sic dicitur sicut dictum est quia musicum quantum  et album per esse quantum quid cui insunt, haec autem ut motus et tempus; et enim haec quanta quaedam dicuntur et continua eo quod illa divisibilia sint quorum sunt  haec passiones. Dico autem non quod movetur sed quod motum est; nam per esse quantum illud et motus est quantus, tempus vero per ipsum.

Of things that are quanta incidentally, some are so called in the sense in which it was said that the musical and the white were quanta, viz. because that to which musicalness and whiteness belong is a quantum, and some are quanta in the way in which movement and time are so; for these also are called quanta of a sort and continuous because the things of which these are attributes are divisible. I mean not that which is moved, but the space through which it is moved; for because that is a quantum movement also is a quantum, and because this is a quantum time is one.

## *Chapter*  14 Quality

[τὸ] ποιὸν λέγεται ἕνα μὲν τρόπον ἡ διαφορὰ τῆς οὐσίας, οἷον ποιόν τι ἄνθρωπος ζῷον ὅτι δίπουν, ἵππος δὲ τετράπουν, [35] καὶ κύκλος ποιόν τι σχῆμα ὅτι ἀγώνιον, ὡς τῆς διαφορᾶς τῆς κατὰ τὴν οὐσίαν ποιότητος οὔσης· [1020β] [1] —ἕνα μὲν δὴ τρόπον τοῦτον λέγεται ἡ ποιότης διαφορὰ οὐσίας,

Quale dicitur  uno quidem modo differentia substantiae, ut quale quid homo animal quia bipes, equus vero quadrupes, et circulus qualis quaedam figura quia agonion, quasi  differentia secundum substantiam qualitate existente. Uno quidem itaque modo hoc dicitur qualitas differentia substantiae.

Quality means (1) the differentia of the essence, e.g. man is an animal of a certain quality because he is two-footed, and the horse is so because it is four-footed; and a circle is a figure of particular quality because it is without [20b] angles, – which shows that the essential differentia is a quality. This, then, is one meaning of quality – the differentia of the essence,

ἕνα δὲ ὡς τὰ ἀκίνητα καὶ τὰ μαθηματικά, ὥσπερ οἱ ἀριθμοὶ ποιοί τινες, οἷον οἱ σύνθετοι καὶ μὴ μόνον ἐφ᾽ ἓν ὄντες ἀλλ᾽ ὧν μίμημα [5] τὸ ἐπίπεδον καὶ τὸ στερεόν (οὗτοι δ᾽ εἰσὶν οἱ ποσάκις ποσοὶ ἢ ποσάκις ποσάκις ποσοί), καὶ ὅλως ὃ παρὰ τὸ ποσὸν ὑπάρχει ἐν τῇ οὐσίᾳ· οὐσία γὰρ ἑκάστου ὃ ἅπαξ, οἷον τῶν ἓξ οὐχ ὃ δὶς ἢ τρὶς εἰσιν ἀλλ᾽ ὃ ἅπαξ· ἓξ γὰρ ἅπαξ ἕξ.

Alio vero ut immobilia et mathematica, sicut numeri quales quidam, quemadmodum compositi et non solum ad unum entes sed quorum imitatio superficies et solidum (hii vero sunt quotiens quanti aut quotiens quotiens quanti), et totaliter quod praeter quantitatem existit in substantia; nam substantia cuiuslibet quod semel, ut ipsorum sex non qui bis aut ter sunt sed qui semel; sex enim semel sex.

but (2) there is another sense in which it applies to the unmovable objects of mathematics, the sense in which the numbers have a certain quality, e.g. the composite numbers which are not in one dimension only, but of which the plane and the solid are copies (these are those which have two or three factors); and in general that which exists in the essence of numbers besides quantity is quality; for the essence of each is what it is once, e.g. that of is not what it is twice or thrice, but what it is once; for 6 is once 6.

ἔτι ὅσα πάθη τῶν κινουμένων οὐσιῶν, οἷον θερμότης καὶ ψυχρότης, [10] καὶ λευκότης καὶ μελανία, καὶ βαρύτης καὶ κουφότης, καὶ ὅσα τοιαῦτα, καθ᾽ ἃ λέγονται καὶ ἀλλοιοῦσθαι τὰ σώματα μεταβαλλόντων.

Amplius quaecumque passiones earum quae moventur substantiarum, ut calor et frigiditas, et albedo et nigredo, et gravitas et levitas, et quaecumque talia, secundum quae dicuntur mutari corpora permutantium.

(3) All the modifications of substances that move (e.g. heat and cold, whiteness and blackness, heaviness and lightness, and the others of the sort) in virtue of which, when they change, bodies are said to alter.

ἔτι κατ᾽ ἀρετὴν καὶ κακίαν καὶ ὅλως τὸ κακὸν καὶ ἀγαθόν.

Amplius secundum virtutem et vitium et omnino bonum et malum.

(4) Quality in respect of virtue and vice, and in general, of evil and good.

σχεδὸν δὴ κατὰ δύο τρόπους λέγοιτ᾽ ἂν τὸ ποιόν, καὶ τούτων ἕνα τὸν κυριώτατον· πρώτη μὲν γὰρ [15] ποιότης ἡ τῆς οὐσίας διαφορά (ταύτης δέ τι καὶ ἡ ἐν τοῖς ἀριθμοῖς ποιότης μέρος· διαφορὰ γάρ τις οὐσιῶν, ἀλλ᾽ ἢ οὐ κινουμένων ἢ οὐχ ᾗ κινούμενα), τὰ δὲ πάθη τῶν κινουμένων ᾗ κινούμενα, καὶ αἱ τῶν κινήσεων διαφοραί. ἀρετὴ δὲ καὶ κακία τῶν παθημάτων μέρος τι· διαφορὰς γὰρ δηλοῦσι τῆς [20] κινήσεως καὶ τῆς ἐνεργείας, καθ᾽ ἃς ποιοῦσιν ἢ πάσχουσι καλῶς ἢ φαύλως τὰ ἐν κινήσει ὄντα· τὸ μὲν γὰρ ὡδὶ δυνάμενον κινεῖσθαι ἢ ἐνεργεῖν ἀγαθὸν τὸ δ᾽ ὡδὶ καὶ ἐναντίως μοχθηρόν. μάλιστα δὲ τὸ ἀγαθὸν καὶ τὸ κακὸν σημαίνει τὸ ποιὸν ἐπὶ τῶν ἐμψύχων, καὶ τούτων μάλιστα ἐπὶ τοῖς ἔχουσι [25] προαίρεσιν.

Fere itaque secundum duos modos dicetur quale, et horum uno principalissimo. Prima quidem qualitas substantiae differentia, huius autem quaedam et quae in numeris qualitas pars; nam differentia quaedam substantiarum, sed aut non motorum aut non in quantum sunt mota. Haec autem passiones motorum in quantum mota, et motuum differentie. Virtus autem et vitium passionum pars quaedam; differentias enim ostendunt motus et actus, secundum quos faciunt aut patiuntur bene aut prave quae sunt in motu; possibile namque sic moveri aut agere bonum, quod autem sic et contrarie prauum. Maxime vero bonum et malum significant quale in animatis, et horum maxime in habentibus proheresim.

Quality, then, seems to have practically two meanings, and one of these is the more proper. The primary quality is the differentia of the essence, and of this the quality in numbers is a part; for it is a differentia of essences, but either not of things that move or not of them qua moving. Secondly, there are the modifications of things that move, qua moving, and the differentiae of movements. Virtue and vice fall among these modifications; for they indicate differentiae of the movement or activity, according to which the things in motion act or are acted on well or badly; for that which can be moved or act in one way is good, and that which can do so in another the contrary way is vicious. Good and evil indicate quality especially in living things, and among these especially in those which have purpose.


*Chapter* 15 Relative

πρός τι λέγεται τὰ μὲν ὡς διπλάσιον πρὸς ἥμισυ καὶ τριπλάσιον πρὸς τριτημόριον, καὶ ὅλως πολλαπλάσιον πρὸς πολλοστημόριον καὶ ὑπερέχον πρὸς ὑπερεχόμενον· τὰ δ᾽ ὡς τὸ θερμαντικὸν πρὸς τὸ θερμαντὸν καὶ τὸ τμητικὸν πρὸς τὸ [30] τμητόν, καὶ ὅλως τὸ ποιητικὸν πρὸς τὸ παθητικόν· τὰ δ᾽ ὡς τὸ μετρητὸν πρὸς τὸ μέτρον καὶ ἐπιστητὸν πρὸς ἐπιστήμην καὶ αἰσθητὸν πρὸς αἴσθησιν.

Ad aliquid dicuntur alia ut duplum ad dimidium et triplum ad tertiam partem, et totaliter multiplicatum ad multiplicati partem et continens ad contentum. Alia ut calefactivum ad calefactibile et sectivum ad secabile, et omne activum ad passivum. Alia ut mensurabile ad mensuram et scibile ad scientiam et sensibile ad sensum.

Things are relative (1) as double to half, and treble to a third, and in general that which contains something else many times to that which is contained many times in something else, and that which exceeds to that which is exceeded; (2) as that which can heat to that which can be heated, and that which can cut to that which can be cut, and in general the active to the passive; (3) as the measurable to the measure, and the knowable to knowledge, and the perceptible to perception.

λέγεται δὲ τὰ μὲν πρῶτα κατ᾽ ἀριθμὸν ἢ ἁπλῶς ἢ ὡρισμένως, πρὸς αὑτοὺς ἢ πρὸς ἕν (οἷον τὸ μὲν διπλάσιον πρὸς ἓν ἀριθμὸς ὡρισμένος, τὸ δὲ πολλαπλάσιον [35] κατ᾽ ἀριθμὸν πρὸς ἕν, οὐχ ὡρισμένον δέ, οἷον τόνδε ἢ τόνδε: [1021α] [1] τὸ δὲ ἡμιόλιον πρὸς τὸ ὑφημιόλιον κατ᾽ ἀριθμὸν πρὸς ἀριθμὸν ὡρισμένον: τὸ δ᾽ ἐπιμόριον πρὸς τὸ ὑπεπιμόριον κατὰ ἀόριστον, ὥσπερ τὸ πολλαπλάσιον πρὸς τὸ ἕν: τὸ δ᾽ ὑπερέχον πρὸς τὸ ὑπερεχόμενον ὅλως ἀόριστον κατ᾽ ἀριθμόν: [5] ὁ γὰρ ἀριθμὸς σύμμετρος, κατὰ μὴ συμμέτρου δὲ ἀριθμὸς οὐ λέγεται, τὸ δὲ ὑπερέχον πρὸς τὸ ὑπερεχόμενον τοσοῦτόν τέ ἐστι καὶ ἔτι, τοῦτο δ᾽ ἀόριστον: ὁπότερον γὰρ ἔτυχέν ἐστιν, ἢ ἴσον ἢ οὐκ ἴσον): ταῦτά τε οὖν τὰ πρός τι πάντα κατ᾽ ἀριθμὸν λέγεται καὶ ἀριθμοῦ πάθη,

Dicuntur autem prima quidem secundum numerum aut simpliciter aut determinate, ad ipsos aut ad unum. Ut duplum quidem ad unum numerus determinatus; multiplex vero secundum numerum ad unum, non determinatum autem, ut hunc aut hunc; emiolium autem ad subemiolium secundum numerum ad numerum determinatum; superparticulare autem ad subsuperparticulare secundum indeterminatos, ut multiplex ad unum . Continens autem ad contentum omnino indeterminatum secundum numerum; numerus enim commensurabilis, secundum non commensurabilem autem numerum dicuntur; continens enim ad contentum tantumque est et amplius, hoc autem indeterminatum; quodcumque enim evenit est, aut equale aut non equale. Haec igitur ad aliquid omnia secundum numerum dicuntur et numeri passiones.

(1) Relative terms of the first kind are numerically related either indefinitely or definitely, to numbers themselves or to 1. E.g. the double is in a definite numerical relation to 1, and that which is many times as great is in a numerical, but not a definite, relation to 1, i.e. not in this [21a] or in that numerical relation to it; the relation of that which is half as big again as something else to that something is a definite numerical relation to a number; that which is n+1/n times something else is in an indefinite relation to that something, as that which is many times as great is in an indefinite relation to 1; the relation of that which exceeds to that which is exceeded is numerically quite indefinite; for number is always commensurate, and number is not predicated of that which is not commensurate, but that which exceeds is, in relation to

that which is exceeded, so much and something more; and this something is indefinite; for it can, indifferently, be either equal or not equal to that which is exceeded. – All these relations, then, are numerically expressed and are determinations of number,

καὶ ἔτι τὸ ἴσον καὶ [10] ὅμοιον καὶ ταὐτὸ κατ᾽ ἄλλον τρόπον (κατὰ γὰρ τὸ ἓν λέγεται πάντα, ταὐτὰ μὲν γὰρ ὧν μία ἡ οὐσία, ὅμοια δ᾽ ὧν ἡ ποιότης μία, ἴσα δὲ ὧν τὸ ποσὸν ἕν· τὸ δ᾽ ἓν τοῦ ἀριθμοῦ ἀρχὴ καὶ μέτρον, ὥστε ταῦτα πάντα πρός τι λέγεται κατ᾽ ἀριθμὸν μέν, οὐ τὸν αὐτὸν δὲ τρόπον):

Et amplius equale et simile et idem secundum alium modum; secundum enim unum dicuntur omnia. Eadem namque quorum una est substantia, similia vero quorum qualitas est una, equalia vero quorum quantitas est una; unum autem numeri principium et metrum, quare haec omnia ad aliquid dicuntur secundum numerum quidem, non eodem autem modo.

and so in another way are the equal and the like and the same. For all refer to unity. Those things are the same whose substance is one; those are like whose quality is one; those are equal whose quantity is one; and 1 is the beginning and measure of number, so that all these relations imply number, though not in the same way.

τὰ δὲ [15] ποιητικὰ καὶ παθητικὰ κατὰ δύναμιν ποιητικὴν καὶ παθητικὴν καὶ ἐνεργείας τὰς τῶν δυνάμεων, οἷον τὸ θερμαντικὸν πρὸς τὸ θερμαντὸν ὅτι δύναται, καὶ πάλιν τὸ θερμαῖνον πρὸς τὸ θερμαινόμενον καὶ τὸ τέμνον πρὸς τὸ τεμνόμενον ὡς ἐνεργοῦντα. τῶν δὲ κατ᾽ ἀριθμὸν οὐκ εἰσὶν ἐνέργειαι ἀλλ᾽ [20] ἢ ὃν τρόπον ἐν ἑτέροις εἴρηται· αἱ δὲ κατὰ κίνησιν ἐνέργειαι οὐχ ὑπάρχουσιν. τῶν δὲ κατὰ δύναμιν καὶ κατὰ χρόνους ἤδη λέγονται πρός τι οἷον τὸ πεποιηκὸς πρὸς τὸ πεποιημένον καὶ τὸ ποιῆσον πρὸς τὸ ποιησόμενον. οὕτω γὰρ καὶ πατὴρ υἱοῦ λέγεται πατήρ· τὸ μὲν γὰρ πεποιηκὸς τὸ δὲ πεπονθός [25] τί ἐστιν. ἔτι ἔνια κατὰ στέρησιν δυνάμεως, ὥσπερ τὸ ἀδύνατον καὶ ὅσα οὕτω λέγεται, οἷον τὸ ἀόρατον.

Activa vero et passiva secundum potentiam activam et passivam sunt et actiones potentiarum; ut calefactivum ad calefactibile quia potest, et iterum calefaciens ad id quod calefit et secans ad id quod secatur tamquam agentia. Eorum vero quae sunt secundum numerum non sunt actiones sed aut quomodo in aliis dictum est; quae autem secundum motum actiones non existunt. Eorum autem quae secundum potentiam et secundum tempora iam dicuntur ad aliquid, ut quod fecit ad factum et facturum ad faciendum. Sic enim pater filii dicitur pater; hoc quidem enim fecit, illud autem passum quid est. Amplius quaedam secundum privationem potentie, ut impossibile et quaecumque sic dicuntur, ut invisibile.

(2) Things that are active or passive imply an active or a passive potency and the actualizations of the potencies; e.g. that which is capable of heating is related to that which is capable of being heated, because it can heat it, and, again, that which

heats is related to that which is heated and that which cuts to that which is cut, in the sense that they actually do these things. But numerical relations are not actualized except in the sense which has been elsewhere stated; actualizations in the sense of movement they have not. Of relations which imply potency some further imply particular periods of time, e.g. that which has made is relative to that which has been made, and that which will make to that which will be made. For it is in this way that a father is called the father of his son; for the one has acted and the other has been acted on in a certain way. Further, some relative terms imply privation of potency, i.e. incapable and terms of this sort, e.g. invisible .

τὰ μὲν οὖν κατ' ἀριθμὸν καὶ δύναμιν λεγόμενα πρός τι πάντα ἐστὶ πρός τι τῷ ὅπερ ἐστὶν ἄλλου λέγεσθαι αὐτὸ ὅ ἐστιν, ἀλλὰ μὴ τῷ ἄλλο πρὸς ἐκεῖνο· τὸ δὲ μετρητὸν καὶ τὸ ἐπιστητὸν καὶ τὸ [30] διανοητὸν τῷ ἄλλο πρὸς αὐτὸ λέγεσθαι πρός τι λέγονται. τό τε γὰρ διανοητὸν σημαίνει ὅτι ἔστιν αὐτοῦ διάνοια, οὐκ ἔστι δ' ἡ διάνοια πρὸς τοῦτο οὗ ἐστὶ διάνοια (δὶς γὰρ ταὐτὸν εἰρημένον ἂν εἴη), ὁμοίως δὲ καὶ τινός ἐστιν ἡ ὄψις ὄψις, οὐχ οὗ ἐστὶν ὄψις (καίτοι γ' ἀληθὲς τοῦτο εἰπεῖν) ἀλλὰ πρὸς χρῶμα ἢ πρὸς ἄλλο τι τοιοῦτον. ἐκείνως δὲ δὶς τὸ αὐτὸ λεχθήσεται, ὅτι ἐστὶν οὗ ἐστὶν ἡ ὄψις. [1021β] [1] τὰ μὲν οὖν καθ' ἑαυτὰ λεγόμενα πρός τι τὰ μὲν οὕτω λέγεται,

Secundum numerum quidem igitur et potentiam dicta ad aliquid omnia sunt ad aliquid eo quod quod quidem est alterius dicitur ipsum quod est, sed non eo quod aliud ad illud; mensurabile vero et scibile et intellectuale eo quod aliud ad ipsum dicitur ad aliquid dicuntur. Nam intellectuale significat quia ipsius est intellectus, non est autem intellectus ad hoc cuius est intellectus; bis enim idem dictum utique erit. Similiter autem et alicuius visus est visus, non cuius est visus ( quamvis verum hoc dicere) sed ad colorem aut ad aliud aliquid tale. Illo vero modo bis idem dicetur: quia est visus cuius est visus.

Relative terms which imply number or potency, therefore, are all relative because their very essence includes in its nature a reference to something else, not because something else involves a reference to it; but (3) that which is measurable or knowable or thinkable is called relative because something else involves a reference to it. For that which is thinkable implies that the thought of it is possible, but the thought is not relative to that of which it is the thought ; for we should then have said the same thing twice. Similarly sight is the sight of something, not of that of which it is the sight (though of course it is true [21b] to say this); in fact it is relative to colour or to something else of the sort. But according to the other way of speaking the same thing would be said twice, – the sight is of that of which it is.

τὰ δὲ ἂν τὰ [5] γένη αὐτῶν ἦ τοιαῦτα, οἷον ἡ ἰατρικὴ τῶν πρός τι ὅτι τὸ γένος αὐτῆς ἡ ἐπιστήμη δοκεῖ εἶναι πρός τι· ἔτι καθ' ὅσα τὰ ἔχοντα λέγεται πρός τι, οἷον ἰσότης ὅτι τὸ ἴσον καὶ ὁμοιότης ὅτι τὸ ὅμοιον·

Secundum se quidem igitur dicta ad aliquid haec quidem sic dicuntur, illa vero si ipsorum genera sint talia, ut medicina eorum quae ad aliquid quia ipsius genus scientia videtur esse eorum quae ad aliquid. Amplius secundum quaecumque habentia dicuntur ad aliquid, ut equalitas quia equale et similitudo quia simile.

Things that are by their own nature called relative are called so sometimes in these senses, sometimes if the classes that include them are of this sort; e.g. medicine is a relative term because its genus, science, is thought to be a relative term. Further, there are the properties in virtue of which the things that have them are called relative, e.g. equality is relative because the equal is, and likeness because the like is.

τὰ δὲ κατὰ συμβεβηκός, οἷον ἄνθρωπος πρός τι ὅτι συμβέβηκεν αὐτῷ διπλασίῳ εἶναι, [10] τοῦτο δ᾿ ἐστὶ τῶν πρός τι· ἢ τὸ λευκόν, εἰ τῷ αὐτῷ συμβέβηκε διπλασίῳ καὶ λευκῷ εἶναι.

Alia vero secundum accidens, ut homo ad aliquid quia ei accidit duplum esse, hoc autem est eorum quae ad aliquid; aut album, si accidit eidem album et duplum esse.

Other things are relative by accident; e.g. a man is relative because he happens to be double of something and double is a relative term; or the white is relative, if the same thing happens to be double and white.

### *Chapter* 16 Complete

τέλειον λέγεται ἓν μὲν οὗ μὴ ἔστιν ἔξω τι λαβεῖν μηδὲ ἓν μόριον (οἷον χρόνος τέλειος ἑκάστου οὗτος οὗ μὴ ἔστιν ἔξω λαβεῖν χρόνον τινὰ ὃς τούτου μέρος ἐστὶ τοῦ χρόνου), καὶ τὸ [15] κατ᾿ ἀρετὴν καὶ τὸ εὖ μὴ ἔχον ὑπερβολὴν πρὸς τὸ γένος, οἷον τέλειος ἰατρὸς καὶ τέλειος αὐλητὴς ὅταν κατὰ τὸ εἶδος τῆς οἰκείας ἀρετῆς μηθὲν ἐλλείπωσιν (οὕτω δὲ μεταφέροντες καὶ ἐπὶ τῶν κακῶν λέγομεν συκοφάντην τέλειον καὶ κλέπτην τέλειον, ἐπειδὴ καὶ ἀγαθοὺς λέγομεν αὐτούς, οἷον κλέπτην [20] ἀγαθὸν καὶ συκοφάντην ἀγαθόν· καὶ ἡ ἀρετὴ τελείωσίς τις· ἕκαστον γὰρ τότε τέλειον καὶ οὐσία πᾶσα τότε τελεία, ὅταν κατὰ τὸ εἶδος τῆς οἰκείας ἀρετῆς μηδὲν ἐλλείπῃ μόριον τοῦ κατὰ φύσιν μεγέθους):

Perfectum vero dicitur unum quidem cuius non est extra aliquid accipere nullam particulam, ut tempus perfectum uniuscuiusque hoc extra quod non est accipere tempus aliquod quod sit huius temporis pars. Et quod secundum virtutem et quod eius quod bene non habens excedentiam ad genus, ut perfectus medicus et perfectus fistulator quando secundum speciem proprie virtutis in nullo deficiunt. Sic autem transferentes et ad mala dicimus calumpniatorem perfectum et latronem perfectum, quoniam et bonos dicimus ipsos, ut latronem bonum et calumpniatorem bonum. et virtus perfectio quaedam; unumquodque enim tunc perfectum et

substantia omnis tunc perfecta, quando secundum speciem proprie virtutis   nulla defecerit pars  eius quae secundum naturam magnitudinis.

What is called complete is (1) that outside which it is not possible to find any, even one, of its parts; e.g. the complete time of each thing is that outside which it is not possible to find any time which is a part proper to it. (2) That which in respect of excellence and goodness cannot be excelled in its kind; e.g. we have a complete doctor or a complete flute-player, when they lack nothing in respect of the form of their proper excellence. And thus, transferring the word to bad things, we speak of a complete scandal-monger and a complete thief; indeed we even call them good, i.e. a good thief and a good scandal-monger. And excellence is a completion; for each thing is complete and every substance is complete, when in respect of the form of its proper excellence it lacks no part of its natural magnitude.

ἔτι οἷς ὑπάρχει τὸ τέλος, σπουδαῖον <ὂν, ταῦτα λέγεται τέλεια: κατὰ γὰρ τὸ ἔχειν τὸ [25] τέλος τέλεια, ὥστ᾽ ἐπεὶ τὸ τέλος τῶν ἐσχάτων τί ἐστι, καὶ ἐπὶ τὰ φαῦλα μεταφέροντες λέγομεν τελείως ἀπολωλέναι καὶ τελείως ἐφθάρθαι, ὅταν μηδὲν ἐλλείπῃ τῆς φθορᾶς καὶ τοῦ κακοῦ ἀλλ᾽ ἐπὶ τῷ ἐσχάτῳ ᾖ: διὸ καὶ ἡ τελευτὴ κατὰ μεταφορὰν λέγεται τέλος, ὅτι ἄμφω ἔσχατα: τέλος δὲ [30] καὶ τὸ οὗ ἕνεκα ἔσχατον.

Amplius quibus inest finis studiosus, haec dicuntur perfecta;  secundum habere enim finem perfecta. Quare quoniam finis ultimorum aliquid est, et ad praua transferentes dicimus perfecte perditum esse et perfecte corruptum esse, quando nil deest corruptionis et mali sed in ultimo est. Quapropter et mors secundum methaphoram dicitur finis, quia ambo ultima.  Finis autem et cuius causa ultimum.

(3) The things which have attained their end, this being good, are called complete; for things are complete in virtue of having attained their end. Therefore, since the end is something ultimate, we transfer the word to bad things and say a thing has been completely spoilt, and completely destroyed, when it in no wise falls short of destruction and badness, but is at its last point. This is why death, too, is by a figure of speech called the end, because both are last things. But the ultimate purpose is also an end.

τὰ μὲν οὖν καθ᾽ αὑτὰ λεγόμενα τέλεια τοσαυταχῶς λέγεται, τὰ μὲν τῷ κατὰ τὸ εὖ μηδὲν ἐλλείπειν μηδ᾽ ἔχειν ὑπερβολὴν μηδὲ ἔξω τι λαβεῖν, τὰ δ᾽ [33] ὅλως κατὰ τὸ μὴ ἔχειν ὑπερβολὴν ἐν ἑκάστῳ γένει μηδ᾽ εἶναί τι ἔξω:

Secundum se dicta quidem igitur perfecta totiens dicuntur, alia quidem quia secundum bene in nullo deficiunt nec yperbolem habent nec extra aliquid accipitur, alia omnino secundum quod non habent yperbolem in unoquoque genere nec aliquid est extra.

Things, then, that are called complete in virtue of their own nature are so called in all these senses, some because in respect of goodness they lack nothing and cannot be excelled and no part proper to them can be found outside them, others in general because they cannot be exceeded in their several classes and no part proper to them is out[22a]side them;

[1022α] [1] τὰ δὲ ἄλλα ἤδη κατὰ ταῦτα τῷ ἢ ποιεῖν τι τοιοῦτον ἢ ἔχειν ἢ ἁρμόττειν τούτῳ ἢ ἁμῶς γέ πως λέγεσθαι πρὸς τὰ πρώτως λεγόμενα τέλεια.

Alia vero iam secundum ipsa aut in faciendo aliquid tale aut habendo aut congruendo tali aut in aliter qualiter dici ad primo dicta perfecta.

the others presuppose these first two kinds, and are called complete because they either make or have something of the sort or are adapted to it or in some way or other involve a reference to the things that are called complete in the primary sense.

*Chapter* 17 Limit

πέρας λέγεται τό τε ἔσχατον ἑκάστου καὶ οὗ ἔξω μηδὲν [5] ἔστι λαβεῖν πρώτου καὶ οὗ ἔσω πάντα πρώτου,

Terminus dicitur quod est cuiuslibet ultimum et cuius extra nihil est accipere primi et cuius infra omnia primi.

Limit means (1) the last point of each thing, i.e. the first point beyond which it is not possible to find any part, and the first point within which every part is;

καὶ ὃ ἂν ᾖ εἶδος μεγέθους ἢ ἔχοντος μέγεθος, καὶ τὸ τέλος ἑκάστου (τοιοῦτον δ᾽ ἐφ᾽ ὃ ἡ κίνησις καὶ ἡ πρᾶξις, καὶ οὐκ ἀφ᾽ οὗ—ὁτὲ δὲ ἄμφω, καὶ ἀφ᾽ οὗ καὶ ἐφ᾽ ὃ καὶ τὸ οὗ ἕνεκα), καὶ ἡ οὐσία ἡ ἑκάστου καὶ τὸ τί ἦν εἶναι ἑκάστῳ: τῆς γνώσεως γὰρ τοῦτο [10] πέρας: εἰ δὲ τῆς γνώσεως, καὶ τοῦ πράγματος.

Et quodcumque fuerit species magnitudinis aut habentis magnitudinem. Et finis cuiusque, tale vero ad quod motus et actus et non a quo; et quandoque ambo, et a quo et in quod. Et cuius causa. Et substantia cuiuslibet et quod quid erat esse cuique; cognitionis enim hoc terminus; si autem cognitionis, et rei.

(2) the form, whatever it may be, of a spatial magnitude or of a thing that has magnitude; (3) the end of each thing (and of this nature is that towards which the movement and the action are, not that from which they are – though sometimes it is both, that from which and that to which the movement is, i.e. the final cause); (4) the substance of each thing, and the essence of each; for this is the limit of knowledge; and if of knowledge, of the object also.

ὥστε φανερὸν ὅτι ὁσαχῶς τε ἡ ἀρχὴ λέγεται, τοσαυταχῶς καὶ τὸ πέρας, καὶ ἔτι πλεοναχῶς· ἡ μὲν γὰρ ἀρχὴ πέρας τι, τὸ δὲ πέρας οὐ πᾶν ἀρχή.

Quare palam quia quotiens principium dicitur totiens terminus, et adhuc amplius; principium enim terminus quidam est, sed terminus non omnis principium.

Evidently, therefore, limit has as many senses as beginning , and yet more; for the beginning is a limit, but not every limit is a beginning.

*Chapter* 18 That in virtue of which

τὸ καθ᾽ ὃ λέγεται πολλαχῶς, ἕνα μὲν τρόπον τὸ εἶδος [15] καὶ ἡ οὐσία ἑκάστου πράγματος, οἷον καθ᾽ ὃ ἀγαθός, αὐτὸ ἀγαθόν, ἕνα δὲ ἐν ᾧ πρώτῳ πέφυκε γίγνεσθαι, οἷον τὸ χρῶμα ἐν τῇ ἐπιφανείᾳ. τὸ μὲν οὖν πρώτως λεγόμενον καθ᾽ ὃ τὸ εἶδός ἐστι, δευτέρως δὲ ὡς ἡ ὕλη ἑκάστου καὶ τὸ ὑποκείμενον ἑκάστῳ πρῶτον. ὅλως δὲ τὸ καθ᾽ ὃ ἰσαχῶς καὶ [20] τὸ αἴτιον ὑπάρξει· κατὰ τί γὰρ ἐλήλυθεν ἢ οὗ ἕνεκα ἐλήλυθε λέγεται, καὶ κατὰ τί παραλελόγισται ἢ συλλελόγισται, ἢ τί τὸ αἴτιον τοῦ συλλογισμοῦ ἢ παραλογισμοῦ. ἔτι δὲ τὸ καθ᾽ ὃ τὸ κατὰ θέσιν λέγεται, καθ᾽ ὃ ἕστηκεν ἢ καθ᾽ ὃ βαδίζει· πάντα γὰρ ταῦτα τόπον σημαίνει καὶ θέσιν.

Secundum quod dicitur multipliciter, uno quidem modo species et substantia cuiusque rei, ut secundum quod bonus per se bonum, alio vero in quo primo aptum natum est fieri, ut color in superficie. Primo quidem igitur dictum secundum quod species est, secundo autem ut materia cuiusque et subiectum unicuique primum. Omnino vero ipsum secundum quod totiens et causa existet; nam secundum quid venit aut cuius causa venit dicitur, et secundum quid paralogizatum est aut sillogizatum est aut quia causa sillogismi aut paralogismi. Amplius secundum quod quod secundum positionem dicitur, secundum quod stetit aut secundum quod uadit; haec namque omnia positionem significant et locum.

*Chapter* 18. That in virtue of which has several meanings: (1) the form or substance of each thing, e.g. that in virtue of which a man is good is the good itself, (2) the proximate subject in which it is the nature of an attribute to be found, e.g. colour in a surface. That in virtue of which , then, in the primary sense is the form, and in a secondary sense the matter of each thing and the proximate substratum of each. In general that in virtue of which will found in the same number of senses as cause ; for we say indifferently (3) in virtue of what has he come? or for what end has he come? ; and (4) in virtue of what has he inferred wrongly, or inferred? or "what is the cause of the inference, or of the wrong inference?" Further (5) Kath _ d is used in reference to position, e.g. at which he stands or along which he walks; for all such phrases indicate place and position.

ὥστε καὶ [25] τὸ καθ᾽ αὑτὸ πολλαχῶς ἀνάγκη λέγεσθαι. ἓν μὲν γὰρ καθ᾽ αὑτὸ τὸ τί ἦν εἶναι ἑκάστῳ, οἷον ὁ Καλλίας καθ᾽ αὑτὸν Καλλίας καὶ τὸ τί ἦν εἶναι

Καλλίᾳ· ἓν δὲ ὅσα ἐν τῷ τί ἐστιν ὑπάρχει, οἷον ζῷον ὁ Καλλίας καθ᾽ αὑτόν· ἐν γὰρ τῷ λόγῳ ἐνυπάρχει τὸ ζῷον· ζῷον γάρ τι ὁ Καλλίας. ἔτι [30] δὲ εἰ ἐν αὑτῷ δέδεκται πρώτῳ ἢ τῶν αὑτοῦ τινί, οἷον ἡ ἐπιφάνεια λευκὴ καθ᾽ ἑαυτήν, καὶ ζῇ ὁ ἄνθρωπος καθ᾽ αὑτόν· ἡ γὰρ ψυχὴ μέρος τι τοῦ ἀνθρώπου, ἐν ᾗ πρώτῃ τὸ ζῆν. ἔτι οὗ μὴ ἔστιν ἄλλο αἴτιον· τοῦ γὰρ ἀνθρώπου πολλὰ αἴτια, τὸ ζῷον, τὸ δίπουν, ἀλλ᾽ ὅμως καθ᾽ αὑτὸν ἄνθρωπος ὁ ἄνθρωπός [35] ἐστιν. ἔτι ὅσα μόνῳ ὑπάρχει καὶ ᾗ μόνον δι᾽ αὐτὸ κεχωρισμένον καθ᾽ αὑτό. [1022β] [1]

Quare et secundum se multipliciter dici est necesse. Uno quidem enim secundum se quod quid erat esse unicuique, ut Callias et quod quid erat esse Calliam. Alio vero quaecumque in eo quod quid est existunt, ut animal Callias secundum se; nam in ratione inest animal; animal enim quoddam Callias. amplius autem si in ipso ostensum est primo aut in ipsius aliquo, ut superficies alba secundum se, et vivens secundum se homo; anima namque pars quaedam est hominis, in qua prima est ipsum vivere. Amplius cuius non est aliqua alia causa; hominis enim multe sunt causae, animal, bipes, at tamen secundum se homo homo est. Amplius quaecumque soli insunt, et in quantum solum quia separatum secundum se.

Therefore "in virtue of itself" must likewise have several meanings. The following belong to a thing in virtue of itself: (1) the essence of each thing, e.g. Callias is in virtue of himself Callias and what it was to be Callias; (2) whatever is present in the what , e.g. Callias is in virtue of himself an animal. For animal is present in his definition; Callias is a particular animal. (3) Whatever attribute a thing receives in itself directly or in one of its parts; e.g. a surface is white in virtue of itself, and a man is alive in virtue of himself; for the soul, in which life directly resides, is a part of the man. (4) That which has no cause other than itself; man has more than one cause animal, two-footed but yet man is man in virtue of himself. (5) Whatever attributes belong to a thing alone, and in so far as they belong to it merely by virtue of itself considered apart by itself.

*Chapter*   19 Disposition

διάθεσις λέγεται τοῦ ἔχοντος μέρη τάξις ἢ κατὰ τόπον ἢ κατὰ δύναμιν ἢ κατ᾽ εἶδος· θέσιν γὰρ δεῖ τινὰ εἶναι, ὥσπερ καὶ τοὔνομα δηλοῖ ἡ διάθεσις.

Dispositio dicitur habentis partes ordo aut secundum locum aut secundum potentiam aut secundum speciem; positionem enim oportet quandam esse, sicut et ipsum hoc nomen ostendit dispositio.

*Chapter*  19. [22b] Disposition means the arrangement of that which has parts, in respect either of place or of potency or of kind; for there must be a certain position, as even the word disposition shows.

*Chapter*  20 Having

ξις δὲ λέγεται ἕνα μὲν τρόπον οἷον ἐνέργειά τις τοῦ [5] ἔχοντος καὶ ἐχομένου, ὥσπερ πρᾶξίς τις ἢ κίνησις (ὅταν γὰρ τὸ μὲν ποιῇ τὸ δὲ ποιῆται, ἔστι ποίησις μεταξύ· οὕτω καὶ τοῦ ἔχοντος ἐσθῆτα καὶ τῆς ἐχομένης ἐσθῆτος ἔστι μεταξὺ ἕξις)· ταύτην μὲν οὖν φανερὸν ὅτι οὐκ ἐνδέχεται ἔχειν ἕξιν (εἰς ἄπειρον γὰρ βαδιεῖται, εἰ τοῦ ἐχομένου ἔσται ἔχειν τὴν [10] ἕξιν), ἄλλον δὲ τρόπον ἕξις λέγεται διάθεσις καθ᾿ ἣν ἢ εὖ ἢ κακῶς διάκειται τὸ διακείμενον, καὶ ἢ καθ᾿ αὑτὸ ἢ πρὸς ἄλλο, οἷον ἡ ὑγίεια ἕξις τις· διάθεσις γάρ ἐστι τοιαύτη. ἔτι ἕξις λέγεται ἂν ᾖ μόριον διαθέσεως τοιαύτης· διὸ καὶ ἡ τῶν μερῶν ἀρετὴ ἕξις τίς ἐστιν. [15]

Habitus vero dicitur uno quidem modo tamquam actio quaedam habentis et habiti, ut actus quidam aut motus. Nam quando hoc quidem facit illud vero fit, est factio intermedia; sic et habentis uestem et habite uestis est intermedius habitus. Hanc quidem igitur manifestum quod non contingit habere habitum; in infinitum enim uadet, si habiti fuerit  habere habitum. Alio vero modo habitus dispositio dicitur secundum quam bene aut male disponitur dispositum, et aut secundum se aut ad aliud, ut sanitas habitus quidam; dispositio namque talis. Amplius habitus dicitur, si est pars dispositionis talis; quapropter et partium virtus habitus quidam est.

*Chapter*  20. Having means (1) a kind of activity of the haver and of what he has – something like an action or movement. For when one thing makes and one is made, between them there is a making; so too between him who has a garment and the garment which he has there is a having. This sort of having, then, evidently we cannot have; for the process will go on to infinity, if it is to be possible to have the having of what we have. (2) Having or habit means a disposition according to which that which is disposed is either well or ill disposed, and either in itself or with reference to something else; e.g. health is a habit; for it is such a disposition. (3) We speak of a habit if there is a portion of such a disposition; and so even the excellence of the parts is a habit of the whole thing.

*Chapter*  21 Affection

πάθος λέγεται ἕνα μὲν τρόπον ποιότης καθ᾽ ἣν ἀλλοιοῦσθαι ἐνδέχεται, οἷον τὸ λευκὸν καὶ τὸ μέλαν, καὶ γλυκὺ καὶ πικρόν, καὶ βαρύτης καὶ κουφότης, καὶ ὅσα ἄλλα τοιαῦτα· ἕνα δὲ αἱ τούτων ἐνέργειαι καὶ ἀλλοιώσεις ἤδη. ἔτι τούτων μᾶλλον αἱ βλαβεραὶ ἀλλοιώσεις καὶ κινήσεις, [20] καὶ μάλιστα αἱ λυπηραὶ βλάβαι. ἔτι τὰ μεγέθη τῶν συμφορῶν καὶ λυπηρῶν πάθη λέγεται.

Passio dicitur uno quidem modo qualitas secundum quam alterari contingit, ut album et nigrum, et dulce et amarum, et gravitas et levitas, et quaecumque alia talia. Alio vero horum actiones et alterationes iam. Amplius horum magis nocive alterationes et motus, et maxime tristes nocive. amplius magnitudines calamitatum et tristium passiones dicuntur.

*Chapter* 21. Affection means (1) a quality in respect of which a thing can be altered, e.g. white and black, sweet and bitter, heaviness and lightness, and all others of the kind. (2) The actualization of these – the already accomplished alterations.(3) Especially, injurious alterations and movements, and, above all painful injuries.(4) Misfortunes and painful experiences when on a large scale are called affections.

*Chapter* 22 Privation

στέρησις λέγεται ἕνα μὲν τρόπον ἂν μὴ ἔχῃ τι τῶν πεφυκότων ἔχεσθαι, κἂν μὴ αὐτὸ ᾖ πεφυκὸς ἔχειν, οἷον φυτὸν ὀμμάτων ἐστερῆσθαι λέγεται· ἕνα δὲ ἂν πεφυκὸς [25] ἔχειν, ἢ αὐτὸ ἢ τὸ γένος, μὴ ἔχῃ, οἷον ἄλλως ἄνθρωπος ὁ τυφλὸς ὄψεως ἐστέρηται καὶ ἀσπάλαξ, τὸ μὲν κατὰ τὸ γένος τὸ δὲ καθ᾽ αὐτό. ἔτι ἂν πεφυκὸς καὶ ὅτε πέφυκεν ἔχειν μὴ ἔχῃ· ἡ γὰρ τυφλότης στέρησίς τις, τυφλὸς δ᾽ οὐ κατὰ πᾶσαν ἡλικίαν, ἀλλ᾽ ἐν ᾗ πέφυκεν ἔχειν, ἂν μὴ ἔχῃ. [30] ὁμοίως δὲ καὶ ἐν ᾧ ἂν ᾖ <πεφυκὸς καὶ καθ᾽ ὃ καὶ πρὸς ὃ καὶ ὥς, ἂν μὴ ἔχῃ [πεφυκός]. ἔτι ἡ βιαία ἑκάστου ἀφαίρεσις στέρησις λέγεται.

Privatio dicitur uno quidem modo, si non habet aliquid natorum haberi, et si non ipsum sit aptum natum habere, ut oculis privari dicitur planta. Alio vero si aptum natum habere, aut ipsum aut genus, non habet, ut aliter homo cecus visu privari dicitur et talpa; hoc quidem secundum genus illud vero secundum se. Amplius si aptum natum et quando aptum natum est habere, non habet; caecitas enim privatio quaedam est, sed cecus non est secundum omnem etatem, sed in qua aptum natum est habere, si non habet. Similiter autem et in quocumque fuerit et secundum quod et ad quod et ut, si non habet aptum natum. Amplius cuiusque per vim ablatio privatio dicitur.

*Chapter* 22. We speak of privation (1) if something has not one of the attributes which a thing might naturally have, even if this thing itself would not naturally have it; e.g. a plant is said to be deprived of eyes.(2) If, though either the thing itself or its genus would naturally have an attribute, it has it not; e.g. a blind man and a mole are in different senses deprived of sight; the latter in contrast with its genus, the former in contrast with his own normal nature.(3) If, though it would naturally have the attribute, and when it would naturally have it, it has it not; for blindness is a privation, but one is not blind at any and every age, but only if one has not sight at the age at which one would naturally have it. Similarly a thing is called blind if it has not sight in the medium in which, and in respect of the organ in respect of which, and with reference to the object with reference to which, and in the circumstances in which, it would naturally have it.(4) The violent taking away of anything is called privation.

καὶ ὁσαχῶς δὲ αἱ ἀπὸ τοῦ <α ἀποφάσεις λέγονται, τοσαυταχῶς καὶ αἱ στερήσεις λέγονται· ἄνισον μὲν γὰρ τῷ μὴ ἔχειν ἰσότητα πεφυκὸς λέγεται, ἀόρατον δὲ [35] καὶ τῷ ὅλως μὴ ἔχειν χρῶμα καὶ τῷ φαύλως, καὶ ἄπουν καὶ τῷ μὴ ἔχειν ὅλως πόδας καὶ τῷ φαύλους. ἔτι καὶ τῷ μικρὸν ἔχειν, οἷον τὸ ἀπύρηνον· [1023α] [1] τοῦτο δ᾽ ἐστὶ τὸ φαύλως πως ἔχειν. ἔτι τῷ μὴ ῥᾳδίως ἢ τῷ μὴ καλῶς, οἷον τὸ ἄτμητον οὐ μόνον τῷ μὴ τέμνεσθαι ἀλλὰ καὶ τῷ μὴ ῥᾳδίως ἢ μὴ καλῶς. ἔτι τῷ πάντη μὴ ἔχειν· τυφλὸς γὰρ οὐ λέγεται ὁ [5] ἑτερόφθαλμος ἀλλ᾽ ὁ ἐν ἀμφοῖν μὴ ἔχων ὄψιν· διὸ οὐ πᾶς ἀγαθὸς ἢ κακός, ἢ δίκαιος ἢ ἄδικος, ἀλλὰ καὶ τὸ μεταξύ.

Et quotiens autem ab eo quod a negationes dicuntur, totiens et privationes dicuntur; nam inequale non habere equalitatem aptum natum dicitur, inuisibile vero et eo quod omnino non habeat colorem et eo quod turpiter, et sine pede et eo quod non habeat omnino pedes et eo quod turpes. Amplius et eo quod parum habeat, ut non igneum; hoc autem est in prave aliquo modo habere. Amplius quod non facile aut non bene, ut insecabile non solum quia non secatur sed quia non facile aut quia non bene. Amplius omnino non habere; cecus enim non dicitur monoculus sed qui in ambobus non habet visum. Propter quod non omnis bonus aut malus, aut iustus aut iniustus, sed et medium.

Indeed there are just as many kinds of privations as there are of words with negative prefixes; for a thing is called unequal because it has not equality though it would naturally have it, and invisible either because it has no colour at all or because it has a poor colour, and apodous either because it has no feet at all or because it has imperfect feet. Again, a privative term may be used because the thing has [23a] little of the attribute (and this means having it in a sense imperfectly), e.g. kernel-less; or because it has it not easily or not well (e.g. we call a thing uncuttable not only if it cannot be cut but also if it cannot be cut easily or well); or because it has not the attribute at all; for it is not the one-eyed man but he who is sightless in both eyes that is called blind. This is why not every man is good or bad , just or unjust , but there is also an intermediate state.

*Chapter*   23 To have

τὸ ἔχειν λέγεται πολλαχῶς, ἕνα μὲν τρόπον τὸ ἄγειν κατὰ τὴν αὑτοῦ φύσιν ἢ κατὰ τὴν αὑτοῦ ὁρμήν, διὸ [10] λέγεται πυρετός τε ἔχειν τὸν ἄνθρωπον καὶ οἱ τύραννοι τὰς πόλεις καὶ τὴν ἐσθῆτα οἱ ἀμπεχόμενοι· ἕνα δ᾽ ἐν ᾧ ἄν τι ὑπάρχῃ ὡς δεκτικῷ, οἷον ὁ χαλκὸς ἔχει τὸ εἶδος τοῦ ἀνδριάντος καὶ τὴν νόσον τὸ σῶμα· ἕνα δὲ ὡς τὸ περιέχον τὰ περιεχόμενα· ἐν ᾧ γάρ ἐστι περιέχοντι, ἔχεσθαι ὑπὸ [15] τούτου λέγεται, οἷον τὸ ἀγγεῖον ἔχειν τὸ ὑγρόν φαμεν καὶ τὴν πόλιν ἀνθρώπους καὶ τὴν ναῦν ναύτας, οὕτω δὲ καὶ τὸ ὅλον ἔχειν τὰ μέρη. ἔτι τὸ κωλῦον κατὰ τὴν αὑτοῦ ὁρμήν τι κινεῖσθαι ἢ πράττειν ἔχειν λέγεται τοῦτο αὐτό, οἷον καὶ οἱ κίονες τὰ ἐπικείμενα βάρη, καὶ ὡς οἱ ποιηταὶ [20] τὸν Ἄτλαντα ποιοῦσι τὸν οὐρανὸν ἔχειν ὡς συμπεσόντ᾽ ἂν ἐπὶ τὴν γῆν, ὥσπερ καὶ τῶν φυσιολόγων τινές φασιν· τοῦτον δὲ τὸν τρόπον καὶ τὸ συνέχον λέγεται ἃ συνέχει ἔχειν, ὡς διαχωρισθέντα ἂν κατὰ τὴν αὑτοῦ ὁρμὴν ἕκαστον. καὶ τὸ ἔν τινι δὲ εἶναι ὁμοτρόπως λέγεται καὶ ἑπομένως τῷ [25] ἔχειν.

Habere multipliciter dicitur; uno quidem  ducere secundum suam naturam aut secundum suum impetum, propter  quod febris dicitur habere hominem et tyranni civitates et vestimentum induti. Alio in quo utique aliquid extiterit ut susceptibili, ut es habet speciem statue et infirmitatem corpus. Alio ut continens contentum; nam in quo est contentum ,  haberi ab hoc dicitur, ut lagenam habere humidum dicimus et civitatem homines et navem nautas; sic autem et totum habet partes. Amplius prohibens secundum suum impetum aliquid moveri aut operari habere dicitur hoc ipsum, ut  columpne ponderosa superposita, ut poete Athlantem faciunt celum habere tamquam casurum super terram, quemadmodum phisiologorum quidam dicunt. Hoc autem modo continens dicitur quae continet habere, quasi separata utique secundum suum impetum singula. Et in aliquo autem esse simili modo dicitur  et consequenter ipsi habere.

*Chapter*   23. To have or hold means many things:(1) to treat a thing according to one's own nature or according to one's own impulse; so that fever is said to have a man, and tyrants to have their cities, and people to have the clothes they wear.(2) That in which a thing is present as in something receptive of it is said to have the thing; e.g.

the bronze has the form of the statue, and the body has the disease.(3) As that which contains holds the things contained; for a thing is said to be held by that in which it is as in a container; e.g. we say that the vessel holds the liquid and the city holds men and the ship sailors; and so too that the whole holds the parts. (4) That which hinders a thing from moving or acting according to its own impulse is said to hold it, as pillars hold the incumbent weights, and as the poets make Atlas hold the heavens, implying that otherwise they would collapse on the earth, as some of the natural philosophers also say. In this way also that which holds things together is said to hold the things it holds together, since they would otherwise separate, each according to its own impulse. Being in something has similar and corresponding meanings to holding or having .

*Chapter*  24 To come from

τὸ ἔκ τινος εἶναι λέγεται ἕνα μὲν τρόπον ἐξ οὗ ἐστιν ὡς ὕλης, καὶ τοῦτο διχῶς, ἢ κατὰ τὸ πρῶτον γένος ἢ κατὰ τὸ ὕστατον εἶδος, οἷον ἔστι μὲν ὡς ἅπαντα τὰ τηκτὰ ἐξ ὕδατος, ἔστι δ᾽ ὡς ἐκ χαλκοῦ ὁ ἀνδριάς· ἕνα δ᾽ ὡς ἐκ τῆς [30] πρώτης κινησάσης ἀρχῆς (οἷον ἐκ τίνος ἡ μάχη; ἐκ λοιδορίας, ὅτι αὕτη ἀρχὴ τῆς μάχης)· ἕνα δ᾽ ἐκ τοῦ συνθέτου ἐκ τῆς ὕλης καὶ τῆς μορφῆς, ὥσπερ ἐκ τοῦ ὅλου τὰ μέρη καὶ ἐκ τῆς Ἰλιάδος τὸ ἔπος καὶ ἐκ τῆς οἰκίας οἱ λίθοι· τέλος μὲν γάρ ἐστιν ἡ μορφή, τέλειον δὲ τὸ ἔχον τέλος. [35] τὰ δὲ ὡς ἐκ τοῦ μέρους τὸ εἶδος, οἷον ἄνθρωπος ἐκ τοῦ δίποδος καὶ ἡ συλλαβὴ ἐκ τοῦ στοιχείου· ἄλλως γὰρ τοῦτο καὶ ὁ ἀνδριὰς ἐκ χαλκοῦ· [1023β] [1] ἐκ τῆς αἰσθητῆς γὰρ ὕλης ἡ συνθετὴ οὐσία, ἀλλὰ καὶ τὸ εἶδος ἐκ τῆς τοῦ εἴδους ὕλης. τὰ μὲν οὖν οὕτω λέγεται, τὰ δ᾽ ἐὰν κατὰ μέρος τι τούτων τις ὑπάρχῃ τῶν τρόπων, οἷον ἐκ πατρὸς καὶ μητρὸς τὸ τέκνον [5] καὶ ἐκ γῆς τὰ φυτά, ὅτι ἔκ τινος μέρους αὐτῶν. ἕνα δὲ μεθ᾽ ὃ τῷ χρόνῳ, οἷον ἐξ ἡμέρας νὺξ καὶ ἐξ εὐδίας χειμών, ὅτι τοῦτο μετὰ τοῦτο· τούτων δὲ τὰ μὲν τῷ ἔχειν μεταβολὴν εἰς ἄλληλα οὕτω λέγεται, ὥσπερ καὶ τὰ νῦν εἰρημένα, τὰ δὲ τῷ κατὰ τὸν χρόνον ἐφεξῆς μόνον, οἷον ἐξ ἰσημερίας [10] ἐγένετο ὁ πλοῦς ὅτι μετ᾽ ἰσημερίαν ἐγένετο, καὶ ἐκ Διονυσίων Θαργήλια ὅτι μετὰ τὰ Διονύσια.

Ex aliquo esse dicitur uno quidem modo ex quo est ut materia; et hoc dupliciter, aut secundum primum genus aut secundum ultimam speciem, puta sunt quidem ut omnia liquabilia ex aqua, est autem veluti ex ere statua. Alio vero ex  primo movente principio; ut ex quo pugna? Ex conuicio, hoc enim est principium pugne. Alio ex composito ex materia et forma, ut ex toto partes et ex Yliade versus et ex domo lapides; finis enim est forma, perfectum vero habens finem. Haec autem ut ex parte species, ut homo ex bipede et sillaba ex elemento;  aliter enim hoc et statua ex ere; nam ex sensibili materia est composita substantia, sed et species ex speciei materia. Haec quidem igitur sic dicuntur. Alia vero si secundum partem aliquam horum aliquis extiterit modorum, ut ex patre et matre puer et ex terra plante, quia ex aliqua parte ipsorum. Alio vero post quod tempore, ut ex die nox, ex serenitate hyemps, quia hoc post hoc. Horum autem haec quidem quia habent transmutationem ad invicem ita dicuntur, ut et quae nunc sunt dicta, haec autem eo quod secundum tempus consequenter solum, ut ex equinoctio fiebat navigatio quia post equinoctium fiebat, et ex Dyonisiis targelia quia post Dyonisia.

*Chapter* 24. To come from something means (1) to come from something as from matter, and this in two senses, either in respect of the highest genus or in respect of the lowest species; e.g. in a sense all things that can be melted come from water, but in a sense the statue comes from bronze.(2) As from the first moving principle; e.g. what did the fight come from? From abusive language, because this was the origin of the fight.(3) From the compound of matter and shape, as the parts come from the whole, and the verse from the Iliad, and the stones from the house; (in every such case the whole is a compound of matter and shape,) for the shape is the end, and only that which attains an end is complete.(4) As the form from its part, e.g. man from two-footed and syllable from letter ; for this is a different sense from that in which the statue comes [23b] from bronze; for the composite substance comes from the sensible matter, but the form also comes from the matter of the form.Some things, then, are said to come from something else in these senses; but (5) others are so described if one of these senses is applicable to a part of that other thing; e.g. the child comes from its father and mother, and plants come from the earth, because they come from a part of those things.(6) It means coming after a thing in time, e.g. night comes from day and storm from fine weather, because the one comes after the other. Of these things some are so described because they admit of change into one another, as in the cases now mentioned; some merely because they are successive in time, e.g. the voyage took place from the equinox, because it took place after the equinox, and the festival of the Thargelia comes from the Dionysia, because after the Dionysia.

*Chapter* 25 Part

μέρος λέγεται ἕνα μὲν τρόπον εἰς ὃ διαιρεθείη ἂν τὸ ποσὸν ὁπωσοῦν (ἀεὶ γὰρ τὸ ἀφαιρούμενον τοῦ ποσοῦ ᾗ ποσὸν μέρος λέγεται ἐκείνου, οἷον τῶν τριῶν τὰ δύο μέρος λέγεταί [15] πως), ἄλλον δὲ τρόπον τὰ καταμετροῦντα τῶν τοιούτων μόνον: διὸ τὰ δύο τῶν τριῶν ἔστι μὲν ὡς λέγεται μέρος, ἔστι δ' ὡς οὔ. ἔτι εἰς ἃ τὸ εἶδος διαιρεθείη ἂν ἄνευ τοῦ ποσοῦ, καὶ ταῦτα μόρια λέγεται τούτου: διὸ τὰ εἴδη τοῦ γένους φασὶν εἶναι μόρια. ἔτι εἰς ἃ διαιρεῖται ἢ ἐξ ὧν σύγκειται [20] τὸ ὅλον, ἢ τὸ εἶδος ἢ τὸ ἔχον τὸ εἶδος, οἷον τῆς σφαίρας τῆς χαλκῆς ἢ τοῦ κύβου τοῦ χαλκοῦ καὶ ὁ χαλκὸς μέρος (τοῦτο δ᾽ ἐστὶν ἡ ὕλη ἐν ᾗ τὸ εἶδος) καὶ ἡ γωνία μέρος. ἔτι τὰ ἐν τῷ λόγῳ τῷ δηλοῦντι ἕκαστον, καὶ ταῦτα μόρια τοῦ ὅλου: διὸ τὸ γένος τοῦ εἴδους καὶ μέρος λέγεται, ἄλλως δὲ τὸ [25] εἶδος τοῦ γένους μέρος.

Pars dicitur uno quidem modo in quam dividetur utique quantum quantacumque; semper enim ablatum a quanto in quantum quantum pars illius dicitur, ut trium duo pars dicuntur aliqualiter. Alio vero modo quae talia mensurant solum; propter quod duo trium sunt quidem ut dicitur pars, sunt autem ut non. Amplius in quae dividetur utique species sine quantitate, et haec partes huius dicuntur; quare species generis dicunt esse partes. Amplius in quae dividitur aliquid aut ex quibus componitur totum, aut species aut habens speciem, ut spere eree aut cubi erei et es pars (hoc autem est materia in qua species) et angulus pars. Amplius quae sunt in ratione unumquodque ostendente, et haec partes totius; propter quod genus speciei et pars dicitur, aliter autem species generis pars.

*Chapter* 25. Part means (1) (a) that into which a quantum can in any way be divided; for that which is taken from a quantum qua quantum is always called a part of it, e.g. two is called in a sense a part of three. It means (b), of the parts in the first sense, only those which measure the whole; this is why two, though in one sense it is, in another is not, called a part of three.(2) The elements into which a kind might be divided apart from the quantity are also called parts of it; for which reason we say the species are parts of the genus.(3) The elements into which a whole is divided, or of which it consists – the whole meaning either the form or that which has the form; e.g. of the bronze sphere or of the bronze cube both the bronze – i.e. the matter in which the form is – and the characteristic angle are parts.(4) The elements in the definition which explains a thing are also parts of the whole; this is why the genus is called a part of the species, though in another sense the species is part of the genus.

*Chapter* 26 Whole

ὅλον λέγεται οὗ τε μηθὲν ἄπεστι μέρος ἐξ ὧν λέγεται ὅλον φύσει, καὶ τὸ περιέχον τὰ περιεχόμενα ὥστε ἕν τι εἶναι ἐκεῖνα:

Totum dicitur et cuius nulla pars abest ex quibus dicitur totum natura, et continens contenta ut unum aliquid sunt illa;

*Chapter* 26. A whole means (1) that from which is absent none of the parts of which it is said to be naturally a whole, and (2) that which so contains the things it contains that they form a unity;

τοῦτο δὲ διχῶς: ἢ γὰρ ὡς ἕκαστον ἓν ἢ ὡς ἐκ τούτων τὸ ἕν.

hoc autem dupliciter; aut enim ut unumquodque unum aut ut ex hiis unum.

and this in two senses – either as being each severally one single thing, or as making up the unity between them.

τὸ μὲν γὰρ καθόλου, καὶ τὸ ὅλως λεγόμενον [30] ὡς ὅλον τι ὄν, οὕτως ἐστὶ καθόλου ὡς πολλὰ περιέχον τῷ κατηγορεῖσθαι καθ᾽ ἑκάστου καὶ ἓν ἅπαντα εἶναι ὡς ἕκαστον, οἷον ἄνθρωπον ἵππον θεόν, διότι ἅπαντα ζῷα:

Universale quidem enim, et quod totaliter dicitur ut totum aliquid ens, sic est universale quasi multa continens in predicari de unoquoque et unum omnia esse ut unumquodque, puta hominem, equum, deum, quia omnia animalia.

For (a) that which is true of a whole class and is said to hold good as a whole (which implies that it is a kind whole) is true of a whole in the sense that it contains many things by being predicated of each, and by all of them, e.g. man, horse, god, being severally one single thing, because all are living things.

τὸ δὲ συνεχὲς καὶ πεπερασμένον, ὅταν ἕν τι ἐκ πλειόνων ᾖ, ἐνυπαρχόντων μάλιστα μὲν δυνάμει, εἰ δὲ μή, ἐνεργείᾳ.

Continuum vero et finitum, quando unum aliquid ex pluribus est quae insunt maxime quidem potentia, si autem non et energia.

But (b) the continuous and limited is a whole, when it is a unity consisting of several parts, especially if they are present only potentially, but, failing this, even if they are present actually.

τούτων [35] δ᾽ αὐτῶν μᾶλλον τὰ φύσει ἢ τέχνῃ τοιαῦτα, ὥσπερ καὶ ἐπὶ τοῦ ἑνὸς ἐλέγομεν, ὡς οὔσης τῆς ὁλότητος ἑνότητός τινος.

Horum vero eorundem magis quae sunt natura quam arte talia, quemadmodum et in uno dicimus, tamquam existente totalitate unione aliqua.

Of these things themselves, those which are so by nature are wholes in a higher degree than those which are so by art, as we said in the case of unity also, wholeness being in fact a sort of oneness.

[1024a] [1] ἔτι τοῦ ποσοῦ ἔχοντος δὲ ἀρχὴν καὶ μέσον καὶ ἔσχατον, ὅσων μὲν μὴ ποιεῖ ἡ θέσις διαφοράν, πᾶν λέγεται, ὅσων δὲ ποιεῖ, ὅλον. ὅσα δὲ ἄμφω ἐνδέχεται, καὶ ὅλα καὶ πάντα· ἔστι δὲ ταῦτα ὅσων ἡ μὲν φύσις ἡ αὐτὴ μένει τῇ μεταθέσει, ἡ [5] δὲ μορφὴ οὔ, οἷον κηρὸς καὶ ἱμάτιον· καὶ γὰρ ὅλον καὶ πᾶν λέγεται· ἔχει γὰρ ἄμφω. ὕδωρ δὲ καὶ ὅσα ὑγρὰ καὶ ἀριθμὸς πᾶν μὲν λέγεται, ὅλος δ᾽ ἀριθμὸς καὶ ὅλον ὕδωρ οὐ λέγεται, ἂν μὴ μεταφορᾷ. πάντα δὲ λέγεται ἐφ᾽ οἷς τὸ πᾶν ὡς ἐφ᾽ ἑνί, ἐπὶ τούτοις τὸ πάντα ὡς ἐπὶ διῃρημένοις· [10] πᾶς οὗτος ὁ ἀριθμός, πᾶσαι αὗται αἱ μονάδες.

Amplius quanto habente principium et medium et ultimum, quorum quidem non facit positio differentiam, omne dicitur, quorum vero facit, totum. Et quaecumque ambo, dicuntur et totum et omne. Sunt autem haec quorumcumque natura quidem eadem manet transpositione, forma vero non, ut cera et uestis; et enim totum et omne dicuntur, habent enim ambo. Aqua vero et quaecumque sunt humida et numerus omne quidem dicuntur, totus vero numerus et tota aqua non dicitur nisi methaphora, omnia vero dicuntur in quibus 'omne' ut in uno, in hiis 'omnia' ut in divisis: omnis hic numerus, omnes hae unitates.

[24a] Again (3) of quanta that have a beginning and a middle and an end, those to which the position does not make a difference are called totals, and those to which it does, wholes. Those which admit of both descriptions are both wholes and totals. These are the things whose nature remains the same after transposition, but whose form does not, e.g. wax or a coat; they are called both wholes and totals; for they have both characteristics. Water and all liquids and number are called totals, but the whole number or the whole water one does not speak of, except by an extension of meaning. To things, to which qua one the term total is applied, the term all is applied when they are treated as separate; this total number, all these units.

*Chapter* 27 Mutilated

κολοβὸν δὲ λέγεται τῶν ποσῶν οὐ τὸ τυχόν, ἀλλὰ μεριστόν τε δεῖ αὐτὸ εἶναι καὶ ὅλον. τά τε γὰρ δύο οὐ κολοβὰ θατέρου ἀφαιρουμένου ἑνός (οὐ γὰρ ἴσον τὸ κολόβωμα καὶ τὸ λοιπὸν οὐδέποτ᾽ ἐστίν) οὐδ᾽ ὅλως ἀριθμὸς οὐδείς· καὶ [15] γὰρ τὴν οὐσίαν δεῖ μένειν· εἰ κύλιξ κολοβός, ἔτι εἶναι κύλικα· ὁ δὲ ἀριθμὸς οὐκέτι ὁ αὐτός. πρὸς δὲ τούτοις κἂν ἀνομοιομερῆ ᾖ, οὐδὲ ταῦτα πάντα (ὁ γὰρ ἀριθμὸς ἔστιν ὡς καὶ ἀνόμοια ἔχει μέρη, οἷον δυάδα τριάδα), ἀλλ᾽ ὅλως ὧν μὴ ποιεῖ ἡ θέσις διαφορὰν οὐδὲν κολοβόν, οἷον ὕδωρ ἢ πῦρ, [20] ἀλλὰ δεῖ τοιαῦτα εἶναι ἃ κατὰ τὴν

οὐσίαν θέσιν ἔχει. ἔτι συνεχῆ: ἡ γὰρ ἁρμονία ἐξ ἀνομοίων μὲν καὶ θέσιν ἔχει,
κολοβὸς δὲ οὐ γίγνεται.

Colobon vero dicitur quantorum non quodcumque, sed partibile oportet illud esse et totum. Nam duo non sunt coloba altero ablato uno (non enim equale coloboma et reliquum numquam est) nec totaliter numerus nullus; et enim substantiam oportet manere; si calix colobos, adhuc oportet esse calicem, numerus autem non adhuc idem. Ad haec autem et si partium dissimilium sint, nec haec omnia (numerus enim est ut dissimiles habet partes, ut dualitatem et trinitatem), sed totaliter quorum non facit positio differentiam nullum est colobon, ut aqua aut ignis; sed oportet talia esse quae in substantia positionem habeant. Amplius continua; nam armonia est ex eis quae sunt dissimilium partium et positionem habent, coloba autem non fit.

*Chapter* 27. It is not any chance quantitative thing that can be said to be mutilated ; it must be a whole as well as divisible. For not only is two not mutilated if one of the two ones is taken away (for the part removed by mutilation is never equal to the remainder), but in general no number is thus mutilated; for it is also necessary that the essence remain; if a cup is mutilated, it must still be a cup; but the number is no longer the same. Further, even if things consist of unlike parts, not even these things can all be said to be mutilated, for in a sense a number has unlike parts (e.g. two and three) as well as like; but in general of the things to which their position makes no difference, e.g. water or fire, none can be mutilated; to be mutilated, things must be such as in virtue of their essence have a certain position. Again, they must be continuous; for a musical scale consists of unlike parts and has position, but cannot become mutilated.

πρὸς δὲ τούτοις οὐδ᾽ ὅσα ὅλα, οὐδὲ ταῦτα ὁτουοῦν μορίου στερήσει κολοβά. οὐ γὰρ δεῖ οὔτε τὰ κύρια τῆς οὐσίας οὔτε τὰ ὁπουοῦν ὄντα: οἷον ἂν τρυπηθῇ ἡ [25] κύλιξ, οὐ κολοβός, ἀλλ᾽ ἂν τὸ οὖς ἢ ἀκρωτήριόν τι, καὶ ὁ ἄνθρωπος οὐκ ἐὰν σάρκα ἢ τὸν σπλῆνα, ἀλλ᾽ ἐὰν ἀκρωτήριόν τι, καὶ τοῦτο οὐ πᾶν ἀλλ᾽ ὃ μὴ ἔχει γένεσιν ἀφαιρεθὲν ὅλον. διὰ τοῦτο οἱ φαλακροὶ οὐ κολοβοί.

Ad haec autem nec quaelibet tota, nec haec cuiuscumque particule privatione coloba. Non enim oportet neque quae principalia substantiae nec ubicumque entia; ut si perforetur calix, non colobos, sed si auris aut extremitas aliqua, et homo non si carnem aut splenem, sed si extremitatem, et hoc non omne sed quae non habet generationem ablata tota. Quapropter calui non sunt colobi.

Besides, not even the things that are wholes are mutilated by the privation of any part. For the parts removed must be neither those which determine the essence nor any chance parts, irrespective of their position; e.g. a cup is not mutilated if it is bored through, but only if the handle or a projecting part is removed, and a man is mutilated not if the flesh or the spleen is removed, but if an extremity is, and that not every extremity but one which when completely removed cannot grow again. Therefore baldness is not a mutilation.

*Chapter*   28 Genus

γένος λέγεται τὸ μὲν ἐὰν ᾖ ἡ γένεσις συνεχὴς τῶν τὸ [30] εἶδος ἐχόντων τὸ αὐτό, οἷον λέγεται ἕως ἂν ἀνθρώπων γένος ᾖ, ὅτι ἕως ἂν ᾖ ἡ γένεσις συνεχὴς αὐτῶν: τὸ δὲ ἀφ᾽ οὗ ἂν ὦσι πρώτου κινήσαντος εἰς τὸ εἶναι: οὕτω γὰρ λέγονται Ἕλληνες τὸ γένος οἱ δὲ Ἴωνες, τῷ οἱ μὲν ἀπὸ Ἕλληνος οἱ δὲ ἀπὸ Ἴωνος εἶναι πρώτου γεννήσαντος: καὶ μᾶλλον οἱ ἀπὸ [35] τοῦ γεννήσαντος ἢ τῆς ὕλης (λέγονται γὰρ καὶ ἀπὸ τοῦ θήλεος τὸ γένος, οἷον οἱ ἀπὸ Πύρρας). [1024β] [1] ἔτι δὲ ὡς τὸ ἐπίπεδον τῶν σχημάτων γένος τῶν ἐπιπέδων καὶ τὸ στερεὸν τῶν στερεῶν: ἕκαστον γὰρ τῶν σχημάτων τὸ μὲν ἐπίπεδον τοιονδὶ τὸ δὲ στερεόν ἐστι τοιονδί: τοῦτο δ᾽ ἐστὶ τὸ ὑποκείμενον ταῖς διαφοραῖς. ἔτι ὡς ἐν τοῖς λόγοις τὸ πρῶτον ἐνυπάρχον, ὃ [5] λέγεται ἐν τῷ τί ἐστι, τοῦτο γένος, οὗ διαφοραὶ λέγονται αἱ ποιότητες. τὸ μὲν οὖν γένος τοσαυταχῶς λέγεται, τὸ μὲν κατὰ γένεσιν συνεχῆ τοῦ αὐτοῦ εἴδους, τὸ δὲ κατὰ τὸ πρῶτον κινῆσαν ὁμοειδές, τὸ δ᾽ ὡς ὕλη: οὗ γὰρ ἡ διαφορὰ καὶ ἡ ποιότης ἐστί, τοῦτ᾽ ἔστι τὸ ὑποκείμενον, ὃ λέγομεν ὕλην.

Genus dicitur hoc quidem si sit generatio continua speciem eandem habentium, ut dicitur 'donec utique hominum genus sit, quia donec est generatio continua ipsorum. Illud vero a quo sunt primo movente ad esse; sic enim dicuntur ellines genere et iones, quia hii ab elline et illi a ione primo generante. Et magis qui a generante quam qui a materia; dicuntur enim et a femina genere, ut a pirra, amplius autem ut superficies figurarum genus superficialium et solidum solidarum; figurarum enim unaqueque haec quidem superficies talis haec autem solidum tale; hoc autem est quod subicitur differentiis. Amplius ut in rationibus quod primum inest, quod dicitur in eo quod quid est, hoc genus, cuius differentie dicuntur qualitates. Genus igitur totiens dicitur: aliud quidem secundum generationem continuam eiusdem speciei, aliud quidem secundum primum movens eiusdem speciei, aliud ut materia; cuius enim differentia et qualitas est, hoc est subiectum, quod dicimus materiam.

*Chapter*   28. The term race or genus is used (1) if generation of things which have the same form is continuous, e.g. while the race of men lasts means "while the generation of them goes on continuously".(2) It is used with reference to that which first brought things into existence; for it is thus that some are called Hellenes by race and others Ionians, because the former proceed from Hellen and the latter from Ion as their first begetter. And the word is used in reference to the begetter more than to the matter, though people also get a race-name from the female, e.g. the descendants of Pyrrha .(3) There is genus in the sense in which [24b] plane is the genus of plane figures and solid of solids; for each of the figures is in the one case a plane of such and such a kind, and in the other a solid of such and such a kind; and this is what underlies the differentiae. Again (4) in definitions the first constituent element, which is included in the what , is the genus, whose differentiae the qualities are said to be Genus then is used in all these ways, (1) in reference to continuous generation of the same kind, (2) in reference to the first mover which is of the same kind as the things it moves, (3) as matter; for that to which the differentia or quality belongs is the substratum, which we call matter.

ἕτερα [10] δὲ τῷ γένει λέγεται ὧν ἕτερον τὸ πρῶτον ὑποκείμενον καὶ μὴ ἀναλύεται θάτερον εἰς θάτερον μηδ᾽ ἄμφω εἰς ταὐτόν, οἷον τὸ εἶδος καὶ ἡ ὕλη ἕτερον τῷ γένει, καὶ ὅσα καθ᾽ ἕτερον σχῆμα κατηγορίας τοῦ ὄντος λέγεται (τὰ μὲν γὰρ τί ἐστι σημαίνει τῶν ὄντων τὰ δὲ ποιόν τι τὰ δ᾽ ὡς διῄρηται [15] πρότερον)· οὐδὲ γὰρ ταῦτα ἀναλύεται οὔτ᾽ εἰς ἄλληλα οὔτ᾽ εἰς ἕν τι.

Diversa vero  genere dicuntur quorum diversum primum  subiectum et non resolvitur alterum in alterum nec ambo in idem, ut species et materia diversum genere, et quaecumque secundum diversam figuram cathegorie entis dicuntur (alia namque quid est significant entium, alia quale quid, alia ut  divisum est prius); nec enim haec resoluuntur neque in invicem neque in unum aliquod.

Those things are said to be other in genus whose proximate substratum is different, and which are not analysed the one into the other nor both into the same thing (e.g. form and matter are different in genus); and things which belong to different categories of being (for some of the things that are said to be signify essence, others a quality, others the other categories we have before distinguished); these also are not analysed either into one another or into some one thing.

*Chapter*   29 False

τὸ ψεῦδος λέγεται ἄλλον μὲν τρόπον ὡς πρᾶγμα ψεῦδος, καὶ τούτου τὸ μὲν τῷ μὴ συγκεῖσθαι ἢ ἀδύνατον εἶναι συντεθῆναι (ὥσπερ λέγεται τὸ τὴν διάμετρον εἶναι [20] σύμμετρον ἢ τὸ σὲ καθῆσθαι· τούτων γὰρ ψεῦδος τὸ μὲν ἀεὶ τὸ δὲ ποτέ· οὕτω γὰρ οὐκ ὄντα ταῦτα), τὰ δὲ ὅσα ἔστι μὲν ὄντα, πέφυκε μέντοι φαίνεσθαι ἢ μὴ οἷά ἐστιν ἢ ἃ μὴ ἔστιν (οἷον ἡ σκιαγραφία καὶ τὰ ἐνύπνια· ταῦτα γὰρ ἔστι μέν τι, ἀλλ᾽ οὐχ ὧν ἐμποιεῖ τὴν φαντασίαν): πράγματα [25] μὲν οὖν ψευδῆ οὕτω λέγεται, ἢ τῷ μὴ εἶναι αὐτὰ ἢ τῷ τὴν ἀπ᾽ αὐτῶν φαντασίαν μὴ ὄντος εἶναι:

Falsum dicitur uno modo ut res falsa, et huius hoc quidem per non componi aut per impossibile esse componi, sicut dicitur dyametrum esse commensurabilem aut te sedere; horum enim falsum hoc quidem semper illud vero quandoque; sic enim non entia haec. Alia vero quae sunt quidem entia, et apta nata sunt videri aut non qualia sunt aut quae non sunt, ut scyagraphia et sompnia; haec namque sunt aliquid quidem, sed non quorum faciunt phantasiam. Res ergo false sic dicuntur, aut quia non sunt ipse aut quia ab eis phantasia non entis est.

*Chapter* 29. The false means (1) that which is false as a thing, and that (a) because it is not put together or cannot be put together, e.g. that the diagonal of a square is commensurate with the side or that you are sitting ; for one of these is false always, and the other sometimes; it is in these two senses that they are non-existent. (b) There are things which exist, but whose nature it is to appear either not to be such as they are or to be things that do not exist, e.g. a sketch or a dream; for these are something, but are not the things the appearance of which they produce in us. We call things false in this way, then, – either because they themselves do not exist, or because the appearance which results from them is that of something that does not exist.

λόγος δὲ ψευδὴς ὁ τῶν μὴ ὄντων, ᾗ ψευδής, διὸ πᾶς λόγος ψευδὴς ἑτέρου ἢ οὗ ἐστιν ἀληθής, οἷον ὁ τοῦ κύκλου ψευδὴς τριγώνου. ἑκάστου δὲ λόγος ἔστι μὲν ὡς εἷς, ὁ τοῦ τί ἦν εἶναι, ἔστι δ᾽ ὡς [30] πολλοί, ἐπεὶ ταὐτό πως αὐτὸ καὶ αὐτὸ πεπονθός, οἷον Σωκράτης καὶ Σωκράτης μουσικός (ὁ δὲ ψευδὴς λόγος οὐθενός ἐστιν ἁπλῶς λόγος): διὸ Ἀντισθένης ᾤετο εὐήθως μηθὲν ἀξιῶν λέγεσθαι πλὴν τῷ οἰκείῳ λόγῳ, ἓν ἐφ᾽ ἑνός: ἐξ ὧν συνέβαινε μὴ εἶναι ἀντιλέγειν, σχεδὸν δὲ μηδὲ ψεύδεσθαι. ἔστι [35] δ᾽ ἕκαστον λέγειν οὐ μόνον τῷ αὑτοῦ λόγῳ ἀλλὰ καὶ τῷ ἑτέρου, ψευδῶς μὲν καὶ παντελῶς, ἔστι δ᾽ ὡς καὶ ἀληθῶς, ὥσπερ τὰ ὀκτὼ διπλάσια τῷ τῆς δυάδος λόγῳ. [1025α] [1] τὰ μὲν οὖν οὕτω λέγεται ψευδῆ,

Ratio vero falsa quae est non entium, in quantum falsa; unde omnis ratio falsa alterius quam cuius est vera, ut quae circuli falsa trigoni. Cuiuslibet autem ratio est quidem ut una, quae eius quod quid erat esse, est autem ut multe, quoniam idem aliqualiter ipsum et ipsum passum, ut Socrates et Socrates musicus. Falsa autem ratio nullius est simpliciter ratio. Quapropter antistenes opinatus est fatue nihil dici dignatus nisi propria ratione, unum in uno; ex quibus accidit non esse contradicere, fere autem neque mentiri. Est autem unumquodque dicere non solum sua ratione sed et ea quae alterius, falso quidem et omnino, est autem ut et vere, sicut octo dupla dualitatis ratione.

(2) A false account is the account of non-existent objects, in so far as it is false. Hence every account is false when applied to something other than that of which it is

true; e.g. the account of a circle is false when applied to a triangle. In a sense there is one account of each thing, i.e. the account of its essence, but in a sense there are many, since the thing itself and the thing itself with an attribute are in a sense the same, e.g. Socrates and musical Socrates (a false account is not the account of anything, except in a qualified sense). Hence Antisthenes was too simple-minded when he claimed that nothing could be described except by the account proper to it, – one predicate to one subject; from which the conclusion used to be drawn that there could be no contradiction, and almost that there could be no error. But it is possible to describe each thing not only by the account of itself, but also by that of something else. This may be done altogether falsely indeed, but there is also a way in which it may be done truly; e.g. eight may be described as a double number by the use of the definition of two.

ἄνθρωπος δὲ ψευδὴς ὁ εὐχερὴς καὶ προαιρετικὸς τῶν τοιούτων λόγων, μὴ δι᾽ ἕτερόν τι ἀλλὰ δι᾽ αὐτό, καὶ ὁ ἄλλοις ἐμποιητικὸς τῶν τοιούτων λόγων, [5] ὥσπερ καὶ τὰ πράγματά φαμεν ψευδῆ εἶναι ὅσα ἐμποιεῖ φαντασίαν ψευδῆ.

Haec quidem igitur ita dicuntur falsa. Homo autem falsus qui promptus et electivus talium rationum, non propter aliud aliquid sed propter id ipsum, et qui aliis talium factor rationum, sicut res dicimus esse falsas  quaecumque falsam faciunt phantasiam.

[25a] These things, then, are called false in these senses, but (3) a false man is one who is ready at and fond of such accounts, not for any other reason but for their own sake, and one who is good at impressing such accounts on other people, just as we say things are which produce a false appearance.

διὸ ὁ ἐν τῷ Ἱππίᾳ λόγος παρακρούεται ὡς ὁ αὐτὸς ψευδὴς καὶ ἀληθής. τὸν δυνάμενον γὰρ ψεύσασθαι λαμβάνει ψευδῆ (οὗτος δ᾽ ὁ εἰδὼς καὶ ὁ φρόνιμος):

Quare et in Ippia oratio refutatur ut eadem vera et falsa. Potentem enim mentiri accipit falsum, hic autem sciens et prudens.

This is why the proof in the Hippias that the same man is false and true is misleading.

ἔτι τὸν ἑκόντα φαῦλον βελτίω. τοῦτο δὲ ψεῦδος [10] λαμβάνει διὰ τῆς ἐπαγωγῆς—ὁ γὰρ ἑκὼν χωλαίνων τοῦ ἄκοντος κρείττων—τὸ χωλαίνειν τὸ μιμεῖσθαι λέγων, ἐπεὶ εἴ γε χωλὸς ἑκών, χείρων ἴσως, ὥσπερ ἐπὶ τοῦ ἤθους, καὶ οὗτος.

Amplius volentem prava meliorem. Hoc autem falsum accipit per inductionem; nam  voluntarius claudicans non voluntario  melior, claudicare imitari dicens; quoniam si claudus voluntarius, deterior forsan, sicut in more et hoc.

For it assumes that he is false who can deceive (i.e. the man who knows and is wise); and further that he who is willingly bad is better. This is a false result of induction – for a man who limps willingly is better than one who does so unwillingly – by limping Plato means mimicking a limp , for if the man were lame willingly, he would presumably be worse in this case as in the corresponding case of moral character.

*Chapter*   30 Accident

συμβεβηκὸς λέγεται ὃ ὑπάρχει μέν τινι καὶ ἀληθὲς [15] εἰπεῖν, οὐ μέντοι οὔτ᾽ ἐξ ἀνάγκης οὔτε <ὡς ἐπὶ τὸ πολύ, οἷον εἴ τις ὀρύττων φυτῷ βόθρον εὗρε θησαυρόν. τοῦτο τοίνυν συμβεβηκὸς τῷ ὀρύττοντι τὸν βόθρον, τὸ εὑρεῖν θησαυρόν: οὔτε γὰρ ἐξ ἀνάγκης τοῦτο ἐκ τούτου ἢ μετὰ τοῦτο, οὔθ᾽ ὡς ἐπὶ τὸ πολὺ ἄν τις φυτεύῃ θησαυρὸν εὑρίσκει. καὶ μουσικός γ᾽ [20] ἄν τις εἴη λευκός: ἀλλ᾽ ἐπεὶ οὔτε ἐξ ἀνάγκης οὔθ᾽ ὡς ἐπὶ τὸ πολὺ τοῦτο γίγνεται, συμβεβηκὸς αὐτὸ λέγομεν. ὥστ᾽ ἐπεὶ ἔστιν ὑπάρχον τι καὶ τινί, καὶ ἔνια τούτων καὶ πού καὶ ποτέ, ὅ τι ἂν ὑπάρχῃ μέν, ἀλλὰ μὴ διότι τοδὶ ἦν ἢ νῦν ἢ ἐνταῦθα, συμβεβηκὸς ἔσται. οὐδὲ δὴ αἴτιον ὡρισμένον οὐδὲν [25] τοῦ συμβεβηκότος ἀλλὰ τὸ τυχόν: τοῦτο δ᾽ ἀόριστον. συνέβη τῷ εἰς Αἴγιναν ἐλθεῖν, εἰ μὴ διὰ τοῦτο ἀφίκετο ὅπως ἐκεῖ ἔλθῃ, ἀλλ᾽ ὑπὸ χειμῶνος ἐξωσθεὶς ἢ ὑπὸ λῃστῶν ληφθείς. γέγονε μὲν δὴ ἢ ἔστι τὸ συμβεβηκός, ἀλλ᾽ οὐχ ᾗ αὐτὸ ἀλλ᾽ ᾗ ἕτερον: ὁ γὰρ χειμὼν αἴτιος τοῦ μὴ ὅπου ἔπλει ἐλθεῖν, [30] τοῦτο δ᾽ ἦν Αἴγινα. λέγεται δὲ καὶ ἄλλως συμβεβηκός, οἷον ὅσα ὑπάρχει ἑκάστῳ καθ᾽ αὑτὸ μὴ ἐν τῇ οὐσίᾳ ὄντα, οἷον τῷ τριγώνῳ τὸ δύο ὀρθὰς ἔχειν. καὶ ταῦτα μὲν ἐνδέχεται ἀΐδια εἶναι, ἐκείνων δὲ οὐδέν. λόγος δὲ τούτου ἐν ἑτέροις.

Accidens dicitur quod inest alicui et verum est dicere, non tamen neque ex necessitate nec secundum magis, puta iam aliquis fodiens plante fossam thesaurum invenit. Hoc igitur accidens fodienti fossam, invenire thesaurum; nec enim ex necessitate hoc ex hoc aut post hoc, nec ut secundum magis si quis plantat inveniet thesaurum. Et musicus utique quis  erit albus; sed quoniam nec ex necessitate nec ut secundum magis hoc fit, accidens ipsum dicimus. Quare quoniam est existens aliquid et alicui, et horum quaedam et alicubi et quandoque, quodcumque extiterit quidem, sed non quia hoc  aut nunc aut hic, accidens erit. Nec est aliqua causa determinata accidentis sed contingens; hoc autem  indeterminatum.   Accidit enim alicui eginam venire,  si non propter hoc advenit ut illuc veniat, sed ab hyeme expulsus aut a latronibus captus. Evenit quidem et est accidens, at non in quantum ipsum sed in quantum alterum; hyemps enim est causa veniendi non  quo navigabat, hoc autem erat egina. Dicitur et aliter accidens, ut quaecumque existunt unicuique secundum se non in substantia entia, velut  triangulo duos rectos habere. Et haec quidem contingit sempiterna esse, illorum vero nullum. Huius autem ratio  in aliis.

*Chapter*   30. Accident means (1) that which attaches to something and can be truly asserted, but neither of necessity nor usually, e.g. if some one in digging a hole for a plant has found treasure. This – the finding of treasure – is for the man who dug the hole an accident; for neither does the one come of necessity from the other or after the other, nor, if a man plants, does he usually find treasure. And a musical man might be pale; but since this does not happen of necessity nor usually, we call it an accident. Therefore since there are attributes and they attach to subjects, and some of them attach to these only in a particular place and at a particular time, whatever attaches to a subject, but not because it was this subject, or the time this time, or the place this place, will be an accident. Therefore, too, there is no definite cause for an accident, but a chance cause, i.e. an indefinite one. Going to Aegina was an accident for a man, if he went not in order to get there, but because he was carried out of his way by a storm or captured by pirates. The accident has happened or exists, – not in virtue of the subject's nature, however, but of something else; for the storm was the cause of his coming to a place for which he was not sailing, and this was Aegina. Accident has also (2) another meaning, i.e. all that attaches to each thing in virtue of itself but is not in its essence, as having its angles equal to two right angles attaches to the triangle. And accidents of this sort may be eternal, but no accident of the other sort is. This is explained elsewhere.

# METHAPHISICE ARISTOTILIS LIBER SEXTUS

6 (E)

[1025β] [3] αἱ ἀρχαὶ καὶ τὰ αἴτια ζητεῖται τῶν ὄντων, δῆλον δὲ ὅτι ἦ ὄντα. ἔστι γάρ τι αἴτιον ὑγιείας καὶ εὐεξίας, καὶ τῶν [5] μαθηματικῶν εἰσὶν ἀρχαὶ καὶ στοιχεῖα καὶ αἴτια, καὶ ὅλως δὲ πᾶσα ἐπιστήμη διανοητικὴ ἢ μετέχουσά τι διανοίας περὶ αἰτίας καὶ ἀρχάς ἐστιν ἢ ἀκριβεστέρας ἢ ἁπλουστέρας.

Principia et causae quaeruntur entium, palam autem quod in quantum entia. Est enim aliqua causa sanitatis et convalescentiae, sunt etiam mathematicorum principia et elementa et  causae, et totaliter omnis scientia intellectualis participans aliquid intellectus circa causas et principia est aut certiora aut simpliciora.

WE are seeking the principles and the causes of the things that are, and obviously of them qua being. For, while there is a cause of health and of good condition, and the objects of mathematics have first principles and elements and causes, and in general every science which is ratiocinative or at all involves reasoning deals with causes and principles, more or less precise,

ἀλλὰ πᾶσαι αὗται περὶ ὄν τι καὶ γένος τι περιγραψάμεναι περὶ τούτου πραγματεύονται, ἀλλ᾽ οὐχὶ περὶ ὄντος ἁπλῶς οὐδὲ ᾗ [10] ὄν, οὐδὲ τοῦ τί ἐστιν οὐθένα λόγον ποιοῦνται, ἀλλ᾽ ἐκ τούτου, αἱ μὲν αἰσθήσει ποιήσασαι αὐτὸ δῆλον αἱ δ᾽ ὑπόθεσιν λαβοῦσαι τὸ τί ἐστιν, οὕτω τὰ καθ᾽ αὑτὰ ὑπάρχοντα τῷ γένει περὶ ὅ εἰσιν ἀποδεικνύουσιν ἢ ἀναγκαιότερον ἢ μαλακώτερον· διόπερ φανερὸν ὅτι οὐκ ἔστιν ἀπόδειξις οὐσίας οὐδὲ τοῦ τί ἐστιν [15] ἐκ τῆς τοιαύτης ἐπαγωγῆς, ἀλλά τις ἄλλος τρόπος τῆς δηλώσεως. ὁμοίως δὲ οὐδ᾽ εἰ ἔστιν ἢ μὴ ἔστι τὸ γένος περὶ ὅ πραγματεύονται οὐδὲν λέγουσι, διὰ τὸ τῆς αὐτῆς εἶναι διανοίας τό τε τί ἐστι δῆλον ποιεῖν καὶ εἰ ἔστιν.

Sed omnes iste circa unum quid et genus aliquod circumscripte de hoc tractant, sed non de ente simpliciter nec in quantum est ens, nec de ipso quod quid est nullam rationem faciunt; sed ex hoc, aliae quidem sensu facientes ipsum manifestum aliae autem suppositionem accipientes quod quid est, sic que secundum se insunt generi circa quod sunt demonstrant aut magis necessarie aut infirmius. Quapropter palam quia non est demonstratio substantiae nec eius quod quid est ex tali inductione, sed quidam alius modus ostensionis. Similiter autem nec si est aut non est genus circa quod versantur nihil dicunt, propter eiusdem rationis esse ipsum  quod quid est manifestum facere et si est hoc.

all these sciences mark off some particular being – some genus, and inquire into this, but not into being simply nor qua being, nor do they offer any discussion of the essence of the things of which they treat; but starting from the essence – some making it plain to the senses, others assuming it as a hypothesis – they then demonstrate, more or less cogently, the essential attributes of the genus with which they deal. It is obvious, therefore, that such an induction yields no demonstration of substance or of the essence, but some other way of exhibiting it. And similarly the sciences omit the question whether the genus with which they deal exists or does not exist, because it belongs to the same kind of thinking to show what it is and that it is.

ἐπεὶ δὲ καὶ ἡ φυσικὴ ἐπιστήμη τυγχάνει οὖσα περὶ γένος τι τοῦ ὄντος (περὶ [20] γὰρ τὴν τοιαύτην ἐστὶν οὐσίαν ἐν ᾗ ἡ ἀρχὴ τῆς κινήσεως καὶ στάσεως ἐν αὐτῇ), δῆλον ὅτι οὔτε πρακτική ἐστιν οὔτε ποιητική (τῶν μὲν γὰρ ποιητῶν ἐν τῷ ποιοῦντι ἡ ἀρχή, ἢ νοῦς ἢ τέχνη ἢ δύναμίς τις, τῶν δὲ πρακτῶν ἐν τῷ πράττοντι, ἡ προαίρεσις· τὸ αὐτὸ γὰρ τὸ πρακτὸν καὶ προαιρετόν), [25] ὥστε εἰ πᾶσα διάνοια ἢ πρακτικὴ ἢ ποιητικὴ ἢ θεωρητική, ἡ φυσικὴ θεωρητική τις ἂν εἴη, ἀλλὰ θεωρητικὴ περὶ τοιοῦτον ὂν ὅ ἐστι δυνατὸν κινεῖσθαι, καὶ περὶ οὐσίαν τὴν κατὰ τὸν λόγον ὡς ἐπὶ τὸ πολὺ ὡς οὐ χωριστὴν μόνον.

Quoniam vero phisica scientia est circa genus quoddam entis (nam circa talem est substantiam in qua est principium motus et status in ea), palam quia neque activa est neque factiva. Factivarum enim in faciente principium, aut intellectus aut ars aut potentia quaedam, activarum vero quae in agente proheresis; idem enim agibile et eligibile. Quare si omnis scientia aut activa aut factiva aut theorica, phisica theorica quaedam est; sed theorica circa tale ens quod est possibile moveri, et circa substantiam quae secundum rationem ut secundum magis non separabilem solum.

And since natural science, like other sciences, is in fact about one class of being, i.e. to that sort of substance which has the principle of its movement and rest present in itself, evidently it is neither practical nor productive. For in the case of things made the principle is in the maker – it is either reason or art or some faculty, while in the case of things done it is in the doer – viz. will, for that which is done and that which is willed are the same. Therefore, if all thought is either practical or productive or theoretical, physics must be a theoretical science, but it will theorize about such being as admits of being moved, and about substance-as-defined for the most part only as not separable from matter.

δεῖ δὲ τὸ τί ἦν εἶναι καὶ τὸν λόγον πῶς ἐστὶ μὴ λανθάνειν, ὡς ἄνευ γε [30] τούτου τὸ ζητεῖν μηδέν ἐστι ποιεῖν. ἔστι δὲ τῶν ὁριζομένων καὶ τῶν τί ἐστι τὰ μὲν ὡς τὸ σιμὸν τὰ δ᾽ ὡς τὸ κοῖλον. διαφέρει δὲ ταῦτα ὅτι τὸ μὲν σιμὸν συνειλημμένον ἐστὶ μετὰ τῆς ὕλης (ἔστι γὰρ τὸ σιμὸν κοίλη ῥίς), ἡ δὲ κοιλότης ἄνευ ὕλης αἰσθητῆς. [1026α] [1] εἰ δὴ πάντα τὰ φυσικὰ ὁμοίως τῷ σιμῷ λέγονται, οἷον ῥὶς ὀφθαλμὸς πρόσωπον σάρξ ὀστοῦν, ὅλως ζῷον, φύλλον ῥίζα φλοιός, ὅλως φυτόν (οὐθενὸς γὰρ ἄνευ κινήσεως ὁ λόγος αὐτῶν, ἀλλ᾽ ἀεὶ ἔχει ὕλην), δῆλον πῶς δεῖ ἐν τοῖς φυσικοῖς τὸ τί ἐστι ζητεῖν καὶ ὁρίζεσθαι, [5] καὶ διότι καὶ περὶ ψυχῆς ἐνίας θεωρῆσαι τοῦ φυσικοῦ, ὅση μὴ ἄνευ τῆς ὕλης ἐστίν. ὅτι μὲν οὖν ἡ φυσικὴ θεωρητική ἐστι, φανερὸν ἐκ τούτων:

Oportet autem quid erat esse et rationem quomodo est non latere, tamquam sine hoc quaerere nihil 30 facere sit. Diffinientium autem et ipsorum quid est haec quidem ita sunt ut simum illa vero ut concauum. Differunt autem haec quia simum quidem conceptum est cum materia (est enim simum nasus concavus), concavitas vero sine materia sensibili. Si igitur omnia phisica similiter simo dicuntur, ut nasus, oculus, facies, caro, os, totaliter animal, folium, radix, cortex, totaliter planta (nullius enim ipsorum sine motu ratio, sed semper habet materiam), palam quomodo oportet in phisicis ipsum quid est quaerere et diffinire. Ideoque et de anima quadam est speculari phisici, quaecumque non sine materia est. Ergo quia est phisica theorica, manifestum ex hiis.

Now, we must not fail to notice the mode of being of the essence and of its definition, for, without this, inquiry is but idle. Of things defined, i.e. of whats , some are like snub , and some like concave . And these differ because snub is bound up with matter (for what is snub is a concave nose), while concavity is independent of perceptible matter. If then all natural things are a analogous [26a] to the snub in their nature; e.g. nose, eye, face, flesh, bone, and, in general, animal; leaf, root, bark, and, in general, plant (for none of these can be defined without reference to movement – they always have matter), it is clear how we must seek and define the what in the case of natural objects, and also that it belongs to the student of nature to study even soul in a certain sense, i.e. so much of it as is not independent of matter. That physics, then, is a theoretical science, is plain from these considerations.

ἀλλ᾽ ἔστι καὶ ἡ μαθηματικὴ θεωρητική: ἀλλ᾽ εἰ ἀκινήτων καὶ χωριστῶν ἐστί, νῦν ἄδηλον, ὅτι μέντοι ἔνια μαθήματα ᾗ ἀκίνητα καὶ ᾗ χωριστὰ [10] θεωρεῖ, δῆλον.

Sed est et mathematica theorica . Sed si immobilium et separabilium est, nunc adhuc non manifestum; quia tamen quaedam mathematica in quantum immobilia et in quantum separabilia speculatur, palam.

Mathematics also, however, is theoretical; but whether its objects are immovable and separable from matter, is not at present clear; still, it is clear that some mathematical theorems consider them qua immovable and qua separable from matter.

εἰ δέ τί ἐστιν ἀΐδιον καὶ ἀκίνητον καὶ χωριστόν, φανερὸν ὅτι θεωρητικῆς τὸ γνῶναι, οὐ μέντοι φυσικῆς γε (περὶ κινητῶν γάρ τινων ἡ φυσικὴ) οὐδὲ μαθηματικῆς, ἀλλὰ προτέρας ἀμφοῖν. ἡ μὲν γὰρ φυσικὴ περὶ χωριστὰ μὲν ἀλλ᾽ οὐκ ἀκίνητα, τῆς δὲ μαθηματικῆς ἔνια [15] περὶ ἀκίνητα μὲν οὐ χωριστὰ δὲ ἴσως ἀλλ᾽ ὡς ἐν ὕλῃ: ἡ δὲ πρώτη καὶ περὶ χωριστὰ καὶ ἀκίνητα. ἀνάγκη δὲ πάντα μὲν τὰ αἴτια ἀΐδια εἶναι, μάλιστα δὲ ταῦτα: ταῦτα γὰρ αἴτια τοῖς φανεροῖς τῶν θείων.

Si vero est immobile aliquid et sempiternum et separabile, palam quia est theorice id nosse, non tamen phisice (nam de mobilibus quibusdam est phisica) nec mathematice, sed prioris ambarum. Phisica namque circa inseparabilia quidem sed non immobilia, mathematice autem quaedam circa immobilia quidem sed inseparabilia forsan, verum quasi in materia; prima vero circa separabilia et immobilia. Necesse vero omnes quidem causas sempiternas, et maxime has; hae namque causae manifestis sensibilium .

But if there is something which is eternal and immovable and separable, clearly the knowledge of it belongs to a theoretical science, – not, however, to physics (for physics deals with certain movable things) nor to mathematics, but to a science prior to both. For physics deals with things which exist separately but are not immovable, and some parts of mathematics deal with things which are immovable but presumably do not exist separately, but as embodied in matter; while the first science deals with things which both exist separately and are immovable. Now all causes must be eternal, but especially these; for they are the causes that operate on so much of the divine as appears to us.

ὥστε τρεῖς ἂν εἶεν φιλοσοφίαι θεωρητικαί, μαθηματική, φυσική, θεολογική

Quare tres erunt philosophiae theorice: mathematica, phisica, theologia.

There must, then, be three theoretical philosophies, mathematics, physics, and what we may call theology,

(οὐ γὰρ [20] ἄδηλον ὅτι εἴ που τὸ θεῖον ὑπάρχει, ἐν τῇ τοιαύτῃ φύσει ὑπάρχει),

Non enim immanifestum quia si alicubi divinum existit, in tali natura existit;

since it is obvious that if the divine is present anywhere, it is present in things of this sort.

καὶ τὴν τιμιωτάτην δεῖ περὶ τὸ τιμιώτατον γένος εἶναι. αἱ μὲν οὖν θεωρητικαὶ τῶν ἄλλων ἐπιστημῶν αἱρετώταται, αὕτη δὲ τῶν θεωρητικῶν.

et honorabilissimam scientiam oportet circa honorabilissimum genus esse. Ergo theorice aliis scientiis desiderabiliores sunt, haec autem theoricis.

And the highest science must deal with the highest genus. Thus, while the theoretical sciences are more to be desired than the other sciences, this is more to be desired than the other theoretical sciences.

ἀπορήσειε γὰρ ἄν τις πότερόν ποθ᾽ ἡ πρώτη φιλοσοφία καθόλου ἐστὶν ἢ περί τι γένος [25] καὶ φύσιν τινὰ μίαν (οὐ γὰρ ὁ αὐτὸς τρόπος οὐδ᾽ ἐν ταῖς μαθηματικαῖς, ἀλλ᾽ ἡ μὲν γεωμετρία καὶ ἀστρολογία περί τινα φύσιν εἰσίν, ἡ δὲ καθόλου πασῶν κοινή):

Dubitabit enim [/autem] utique aliquis utrum prima philosophia sit universalis aut circa aliquod genus et naturam unam; non enim idem modus nec in mathematicis, quia geometria et astrologia circa aliquam naturam sunt, illa vero universaliter omnium est communis.

For one might raise the question whether first philosophy is universal, or deals with one genus, i.e. some one kind of being; for not even the mathematical sciences are all alike in this respect, – geometry and astronomy deal with a certain particular kind of thing, while universal mathematics applies alike to all.

εἰ μὲν οὖν μὴ ἔστι τις ἑτέρα οὐσία παρὰ τὰς φύσει συνεστηκυίας, ἡ φυσικὴ ἂν εἴη πρώτη ἐπιστήμη: εἰ δ᾽ ἔστι τις οὐσία ἀκίνητος, [30] αὕτη προτέρα καὶ

φιλοσοφία πρώτη, καὶ καθόλου οὕτως ὅτι πρώτη: καὶ περὶ τοῦ ὄντος ᾗ ὂν ταύτης ἂν εἴη θεωρῆσαι, καὶ τί ἐστι καὶ τὰ ὑπάρχοντα ᾗ ὄν.

Si quidem igitur non est aliqua altera substantia praeter natura consistentes, phisica utique erit prima scientia. Sed si est aliqua substantia immobilis, haec prior et philosophia prima, et universalis sic quia prima; et de ente in quantum ens huius utique erit speculari, et quae est et quae insunt in quantum ens.

We answer that if there is no substance other than those which are formed by nature, natural science will be the first science; but if there is an immovable substance, the science of this must be prior and must be first philosophy, and universal in this way, because it is first. And it will belong to this to consider being qua being – both what it is and the attributes which belong to it qua being.

*Chapter* 2

ἀλλ᾽ ἐπεὶ τὸ ὂν τὸ ἁπλῶς λεγόμενον λέγεται πολλαχῶς, ὧν ἓν μὲν ἦν τὸ κατὰ συμβεβηκός, ἕτερον δὲ τὸ [35] ὡς ἀληθές, καὶ τὸ μὴ ὂν ὡς τὸ ψεῦδος, παρὰ ταῦτα δ᾽ ἐστὶ τὰ σχήματα τῆς κατηγορίας (οἷον τὸ μὲν τί, τὸ δὲ ποιόν, τὸ δὲ ποσόν, τὸ δὲ πού, τὸ δὲ ποτέ, καὶ εἴ τι ἄλλο σημαίνει τὸν τρόπον τοῦτον), [1026β] [1] ἔτι παρὰ ταῦτα πάντα τὸ δυνάμει καὶ ἐνεργείᾳ:

Sed quoniam ens simpliciter dictum dicitur multipliciter, quorum unum quidem erat quod secundum accidens, et aliud quod ut verum et non ens ut falsum, praeter haec autem sunt figure cathegorie (ut quid, quale, quantum, ubi, quando, et si quid aliud significat hoc modo), amplius praeter haec omnia quod potestate et actu:

But since the unqualified term being has several meanings, of which one was seen to be the accidental, and another the true ( non-being being the false), while besides these there are the figures of predication (e.g. the what , quality, quantity, place, time, and any similar meanings which being [26b] may have), and again besides all these there is that which is potentially or actually:

ἐπεὶ δὴ πολλαχῶς λέγεται τὸ ὄν, πρῶτον περὶ τοῦ κατὰ συμβεβηκὸς λεκτέον, ὅτι οὐδεμία ἐστὶ περὶ αὐτὸ θεωρία. σημεῖον δέ: οὐδεμιᾷ γὰρ ἐπιστήμῃ ἐπιμελὲς [5] περὶ αὐτοῦ οὔτε πρακτικῇ οὔτε ποιητικῇ οὔτε θεωρητικῇ. οὔτε γὰρ ὁ ποιῶν οἰκίαν ποιεῖ ὅσα συμβαίνει ἅμα τῇ οἰκίᾳ γιγνομένῃ (ἄπειρα γάρ ἐστιν: τοῖς μὲν γὰρ ἡδεῖαν τοῖς δὲ βλαβερὰν τοῖς δ᾽ ὠφέλιμον οὐθὲν εἶναι κωλύει τὴν

ποιηθεῖσαν, καὶ ἑτέραν ὡς εἰπεῖν πάντων τῶν ὄντων· ὧν οὐθενός [10] ἐστιν ἡ οἰκοδομικὴ ποιητική), τὸν αὐτὸν δὲ τρόπον οὐδ᾽ ὁ γεωμέτρης θεωρεῖ τὰ οὕτω συμβεβηκότα τοῖς σχήμασιν, οὐδ᾽ εἰ ἕτερόν ἐστι τρίγωνον καὶ τρίγωνον δύο ὀρθὰς ἔχον.

quoniam itaque multipliciter dicitur ens, primum de eo quod secundum accidens est dicendum, quia nulla est circa id speculatio. Signum autem: nulla enim scientia studiosa est de eo, neque activa neque factiva nec theorica. non enim faciens domum facit quaecumque accidunt simul domui facte; infinita enim sunt: hiis quidem enim voluptuosam illis autem nocivam aliis autem utilem nihil esse prohibet factam, et alteram ut est dicere ab omnibus entibus; quorum nullius est edificativa factiva. Eodem vero modo nec geometer speculatur sic accidentia figuris, nec si alterum est trigonum et trigonum duos rectos habens.

since being has many meanings, we must say regarding the accidental, that there can be no scientific treatment of it. This is confirmed by the fact that no science practical, productive, or theoretical troubles itself about it. For on the one hand he who produces a house does not produce all the attributes that come into being along with the house; for these are innumerable; the house that has been made may quite well be pleasant for some people, hurtful for some, and useful to others, and different – to put it shortly from all things that are; and the science of building does not aim at producing any of these attributes. And in the same way the geometer does not consider the attributes which attach thus to figures, nor whether triangle is different from triangle whose angles are equal to two right angles.

καὶ τοῦτ᾽ εὐλόγως συμπίπτει· ὥσπερ γὰρ ὄνομά τι μόνον τὸ συμβεβηκός ἐστιν.

Et hoc rationabiliter concidit; quemadmodum enim nomine solum accidens est.

And this happens naturally enough; for the accidental is practically a mere name.

διὸ Πλάτων τρόπον τινὰ οὐ κακῶς τὴν σοφιστικὴν [15] περὶ τὸ μὴ ὂν ἔταξεν. εἰσὶ γὰρ οἱ τῶν σοφιστῶν λόγοι περὶ τὸ συμβεβηκὸς ὡς εἰπεῖν μάλιστα πάντων, πότερον ἕτερον ἢ ταὐτὸν μουσικὸν καὶ γραμματικόν, καὶ μουσικὸς Κορίσκος καὶ Κορίσκος, καὶ εἰ πᾶν ὃ ἂν ᾖ, μὴ ἀεὶ δέ, γέγονεν, ὥστ᾽ εἰ μουσικὸς ὢν γραμματικὸς γέγονε, καὶ γραμματικὸς [20] ὢν μουσικός, καὶ ὅσοι δὴ ἄλλοι τοιοῦτοι τῶν λόγων εἰσίν· φαίνεται γὰρ τὸ συμβεβηκὸς ἐγγύς τι τοῦ μὴ ὄντος.

Unde Plato modo quodam non male sophisticam circa non ens ordinavit. Sunt enim sophistarum rationes circa accidens ut est dicere maxime omnium: utrum diversum an idem musicum et gramaticum, et musicus Coriscus et Coriscus, et si omne quod est et non semper, factum est, quare si musicus ens gramaticus est factus,

et gramaticus ens  musicus, et quaecumque aliae rationum tales sunt; videtur enim accidens propinquum quid non enti.

And so Plato was in a sense not wrong in ranking sophistic as dealing with that which is not. For the arguments of the sophists deal, we may say, above all with the accidental; e.g. the question whether musical and lettered are different or the same, and whether musical Coriscus and Coriscus are the same, and whether "everything which is, but is not eternal, has come to be", with the paradoxical conclusion that if one who was musical has come to be lettered, he must also have been lettered and have come to be musical, and all the other arguments of this sort; the accidental is obviously akin to non-being.

δῆλον δὲ καὶ ἐκ τῶν τοιούτων λόγων: τῶν μὲν γὰρ ἄλλον τρόπον ὄντων ἔστι γένεσις καὶ φθορά, τῶν δὲ κατὰ συμβεβηκὸς οὐκ ἔστιν.

Palam autem et ex huiusmodi rationibus: nam alio modo entium generatio est et corruptio, eorum vero quae sunt secundum accidens non est.

And this is clear also from arguments such as the following: things which are in another sense come into being and pass out of being by a process, but things which are accidentally do not.

ἀλλ᾽ ὅμως λεκτέον ἔτι περὶ τοῦ συμβεβηκότος [25] ἐφ᾽ ὅσον ἐνδέχεται, τίς ἡ φύσις αὐτοῦ καὶ διὰ τίν᾽ αἰτίαν ἔστιν: ἅμα γὰρ δῆλον ἴσως ἔσται καὶ διὰ τί ἐπιστήμη οὐκ ἔστιν αὐτοῦ.

At tamen dicendum est  amplius de accidente in quantum contingit, quae eius natura et propter quam causam est; simul enim forsan palam erit et quare eius non est scientia.

But still we must, as far as we can, say further, regarding the accidental, what its nature is and from what cause it proceeds; for it will perhaps at the same time become clear why there is no science of it.

ἐπεὶ οὖν ἐστιν ἐν τοῖς οὖσι τὰ μὲν ἀεὶ ὡσαύτως ἔχοντα καὶ ἐξ ἀνάγκης, οὐ τῆς κατὰ τὸ βίαιον λεγομένης ἀλλ᾽ ἣν λέγομεν τῷ μὴ ἐνδέχεσθαι ἄλλως, τὰ δ᾽ [30] ἐξ ἀνάγκης μὲν οὐκ ἔστιν οὐδ᾽ ἀεί, ὡς δ᾽ ἐπὶ τὸ πολύ, αὕτη ἀρχὴ καὶ αὕτη αἰτία ἐστὶ τοῦ εἶναι τὸ συμβεβηκός:

Quoniam igitur sunt in entibus haec quidem semper similiter se habentia et ex necessitate,  non secundum vim dicta sed  quam dicimus in non contingere aliter, illa vero ex necessitate quidem non sunt nec semper, sed quasi secundum magis, hoc principium et haec causa est eius quod est accidens esse;

Since, among things which are, some are always in the same state and are of necessity (not necessity in the sense of compulsion but that which we assert of things because they cannot be otherwise), and some are not of necessity nor always, but for the most part, this is the principle and this the cause of the existence of the accidental;

ὃ γὰρ [32] ἂν ᾖ μήτ᾽ ἀεὶ μήθ᾽ ὡς ἐπὶ τὸ πολύ, τοῦτό φαμεν συμβεβηκὸς εἶναι. οἷον ἐπὶ κυνὶ ἂν χειμὼν γένηται καὶ ψῦχος, τοῦτο συμβῆναί φαμεν, ἀλλ᾽ οὐκ ἂν πνῖγος καὶ ἀλέα, ὅτι [35] τὸ μὲν ἀεὶ ἢ ὡς ἐπὶ τὸ πολύ τὸ δ᾽ οὔ. καὶ τὸν ἄνθρωπον λευκὸν εἶναι συμβέβηκεν (οὔτε γὰρ ἀεὶ οὔθ᾽ ὡς ἐπὶ τὸ πολύ), ζῷον δ᾽ οὐ κατὰ συμβεβηκός. καὶ τὸ ὑγιάζειν δὲ τὸν οἰκοδόμον συμβεβηκός, [1027α] [1] ὅτι οὐ πέφυκε τοῦτο ποιεῖν οἰκοδόμος ἀλλὰ ἰατρός, ἀλλὰ συνέβη ἰατρὸν εἶναι τὸν οἰκοδόμον. καὶ ὀψοποιὸς ἡδονῆς στοχαζόμενος ποιήσειεν ἄν τι ὑγιεινόν, ἀλλ᾽ οὐ κατὰ τὴν ὀψοποιητικήν: διὸ συνέβη, φαμέν, καὶ [5] ἔστιν ὡς ποιεῖ, ἁπλῶς δ᾽ οὔ. τῶν μὲν γὰρ ἄλλων [ἐνίοτε] δυνάμεις εἰσὶν αἱ ποιητικαί, τῶν δ᾽ οὐδεμία τέχνη οὐδὲ δύναμις ὡρισμένη: τῶν γὰρ κατὰ συμβεβηκὸς ὄντων ἢ γιγνομένων καὶ τὸ αἴτιόν ἐστι κατὰ συμβεβηκός.

quod enim nec semper nec quasi secundum magis est, hoc dicimus accidens esse. Ut sub cane si fuerit hyemps et frigus, hoc accidere dicimus, sed non si estuatio et calor, quia hoc quidem semper aut secundum magis illud vero non. Et hominem album esse accidit (nec enim semper nec secundum magis), animal vero non secundum accidens. Et edificatorem sanitatem facere accidens, quia non est natus hoc facere edificator sed medicus, sed accidit medicum esse edificatorem. Et coquus voluptatem coniectans faciet utique alicui salubre, sed non secundum pulmentariam; quapropter accidens dicimus, et est ut facit, simpliciter autem non. Aliorum enim aliae quandoque potentie factive sunt, horum vero nulla ars nec potentia determinata; nam secundum accidens entium aut factorum causa est secundum accidens.

for that which is neither always nor for the most part, we call accidental. For instance, if in the dog-days there is wintry and cold weather, we say this is an accident, but not if there is sultry heat, because the latter is always or for the most part so, but not the former. And it is an accident that a man is pale (for this is neither always nor for the most part so), but it is not by accident that he is an animal. And [27a] that the builder produces health is an accident, because it is the nature not of the builder but of the doctor to do this, – but the builder happened to be a doctor. Again, a confectioner, aiming at giving pleasure, may make something wholesome, but not in virtue of the confectioner's art; and therefore we say it was an accident , and while there is a sense in which he makes it, in the unqualified sense he does not. For to other things answer faculties productive of them, but to accidental results there corresponds no determinate art nor faculty; for of things which are or come to be by accident, the cause also is accidental.

ὥστ᾽ ἐπεὶ οὐ πάντα ἐστὶν ἐξ ἀνάγκης καὶ ἀεὶ ἢ ὄντα ἢ γιγνόμενα, ἀλλὰ τὰ [10] πλεῖστα ὡς ἐπὶ τὸ πολύ, ἀνάγκη εἶναι τὸ κατὰ συμβεβηκὸς ὄν· οἷον οὔτ᾽ ἀεὶ οὔθ᾽ ὡς ἐπὶ τὸ πολὺ ὁ λευκὸς μουσικός ἐστιν, ἐπεὶ δὲ γίγνεταί ποτε, κατὰ συμβεβηκὸς ἔσται (εἰ δὲ μή, πάντ᾽ ἔσται ἐξ ἀνάγκης)· ὥστε ἡ ὕλη ἔσται αἰτία ἡ ἐνδεχομένη παρὰ τὸ ὡς ἐπὶ τὸ πολὺ ἄλλως τοῦ συμβεβηκότος. [15] ἀρχὴν δὲ τηνδὶ ληπτέον, πότερον οὐδέν ἐστιν οὔτ᾽ αἰεὶ οὔθ᾽ ὡς ἐπὶ τὸ πολύ. ἢ τοῦτο ἀδύνατον; ἔστιν ἄρα τι παρὰ ταῦτα τὸ ὁπότερ᾽ ἔτυχε καὶ κατὰ συμβεβηκός. ἀλλὰ πότερον τὸ ὡς ἐπὶ τὸ πολύ, τὸ δ᾽ ἀεὶ οὐθενὶ ὑπάρχει, ἢ ἔστιν ἄττα ἀΐδια; περὶ μὲν οὖν τούτων ὕστερον σκεπτέον,

Quare quoniam quidem non omnia sunt ex necessitate et semper aut entia aut quae fiunt, sed plurima secundum magis, necesse esse quod secundum accidens est ens; ut nec semper nec secundum magis albus musicus est, quoniam vero fit aliquando, secundum accidens erit (si autem non, omnia erunt ex necessitate). Quare materia erit causa contingens praeter quod ut in pluribus aliter accidentis. Principium autem hoc oportet sumere, utrum nihil est nec semper nec secundum magis, aut hoc impossibile. Est igitur aliquid praeter haec quod utcumque contingit et secundum accidens. Sed utrum hoc quod ut in pluribus et quod semper nulli insunt, aut sunt quaedam sempiterna? De hiis quidem igitur posterius perscrutandum est.

Therefore, since not all things either are or come to be of necessity and always, but, the majority of things are for the most part, the accidental must exist; for instance a pale man is not always nor for the most part musical, but since this sometimes happens, it must be accidental (if not, everything will be of necessity). The matter, therefore, which is capable of being otherwise than as it usually is, must be the cause of the accidental. And we must take as our starting-point the question whether there is nothing that is neither always nor for the most part. Surely this is impossible. There is, then, besides these something which is fortuitous and accidental. But while the usual exists, can nothing be said to be always, or are there eternal things? This must be considered later,

ὅτι δ᾽ [20] ἐπιστήμη οὐκ ἔστι τοῦ συμβεβηκότος φανερόν· ἐπιστήμη μὲν γὰρ πᾶσα ἢ τοῦ ἀεὶ ἢ τοῦ ὡς ἐπὶ τὸ πολύ—πῶς γὰρ ἢ μαθήσεται ἢ διδάξει ἄλλον; δεῖ γὰρ ὡρίσθαι ἢ τῷ ἀεὶ ἢ τῷ ὡς ἐπὶ τὸ πολύ, οἷον ὅτι ὠφέλιμον τὸ μελίκρατον τῷ πυρέττοντι ὡς ἐπὶ τὸ πολύ—τὸ δὲ παρὰ τοῦτο οὐχ ἕξει λέγειν, [25] πότε οὔ, οἷον νουμηνίᾳ· ἢ γὰρ ἀεὶ ἢ ὡς ἐπὶ τὸ πολὺ καὶ τὸ τῇ νουμηνίᾳ· τὸ δὲ συμβεβηκός ἐστι παρὰ ταῦτα. τί μὲν οὖν ἐστι τὸ συμβεβηκὸς καὶ διὰ τίν᾽ αἰτίαν καὶ ὅτι ἐπιστήμη οὐκ ἔστιν αὐτοῦ, εἴρηται.

Quod autem scientia non est accidentis, palam; scientia namque omnis aut est eius quod est semper aut eius quod secundum magis — Etenim quomodo docebitur aut docebit alium? Oportet enim diffiniri aut per semper aut per magis, ut quia utile mellicratum febricitanti ut secundum magis. Quod autem praeter hoc non habebit

233

dicere quando , puta noua luna; aut enim semper aut ut  in pluribus et quod noua luna; accidens autem est praeter haec. Quid quidem igitur est accidens et propter quam causam et quia scientia non est eius, dictum est.

but that there is no science of the accidental is obvious; for all science is either of that which is always or of that which is for the most part. (For how else is one to learn or to teach another? The thing must be determined as occurring either always or for the most part, e.g. that honey-water is useful for a patient in a fever is true for the most part.) But that which is contrary to the usual law science will be unable to state, i.e. when the thing does not happen, e.g. on the day of new moon ; for even that which happens on the day of new moon happens then either always or for the most part; but the accidental is contrary to such laws. We have stated, then, what the accidental is, and from what cause it arises, and that there is no science which deals with it.

*Chapter*  3

ὅτι δ᾽ εἰσὶν ἀρχαὶ καὶ αἴτια γενητὰ καὶ φθαρτὰ [30] ἄνευ τοῦ γίγνεσθαι καὶ φθείρεσθαι, φανερόν. εἰ γὰρ μὴ τοῦτ᾽, ἐξ ἀνάγκης πάντ᾽ ἔσται, εἰ τοῦ γιγνομένου καὶ φθειρομένου μὴ κατὰ συμβεβηκὸς αἴτιόν τι ἀνάγκη εἶναι. πότερον γὰρ ἔσται τοδὶ ἢ οὔ; ἐάν γε τοδὶ γένηται: εἰ δὲ μή, οὔ. τοῦτο δὲ ἐὰν ἄλλο. καὶ οὕτω δῆλον ὅτι ἀεὶ χρόνου ἀφαιρουμένου ἀπὸ πεπερασμένου χρόνου ἥξει ἐπὶ τὸ νῦν, [1027β] [1] ὥστε ὁδὶ ἀποθανεῖται [νόσῳ ἢ] βίᾳ, ἐάν γε ἐξέλθῃ: τοῦτο δὲ ἐὰν διψήσῃ: τοῦτο δὲ ἐὰν ἄλλο: καὶ οὕτως ἥξει εἰς ὃ νῦν ὑπάρχει, ἢ εἰς τῶν γεγονότων τι. οἷον ἐὰν διψήσῃ: τοῦτο δὲ εἰ ἐσθίει δριμέα: [5] τοῦτο δ᾽ ἤτοι ὑπάρχει ἢ οὔ: ὥστ᾽ ἐξ ἀνάγκης ἀποθανεῖται ἢ οὐκ ἀποθανεῖται. ὁμοίως δὲ κἂν ὑπερπηδήσῃ τις εἰς τὰ γενόμενα, ὁ αὐτὸς λόγος: ἤδη γὰρ ὑπάρχει τοῦτο ἔν τινι, λέγω δὲ τὸ γεγονός: ἐξ ἀνάγκης ἄρα πάντα ἔσται τὰ ἐσόμενα, οἷον τὸ ἀποθανεῖν τὸν ζῶντα: ἤδη γάρ τι γέγονεν, [10] οἷον τὰ ἐναντία ἐν τῷ αὐτῷ. ἀλλ᾽ εἰ νόσῳ ἢ βίᾳ, οὔπω, ἀλλ᾽ ἐὰν τοδὶ γένηται. δῆλον ἄρα ὅτι μέχρι τινὸς βαδίζει ἀρχῆς, αὕτη δ᾽ οὐκέτι εἰς ἄλλο.

Quod autem sint principia et causae generabilia et  corruptibilia sine generari et corrumpi, palam. Si enim non hoc, ex necessitate omnia erunt, si eius quod fit et corrumpitur non secundum accidens causam aliquam necesse est esse. Vtrum enim erit hoc aut non? Si hoc fiat; si autem non, non. Hoc autem si aliud. Et ita manifestum quia semper tempore ablato a finito tempore veniet usque ad nunc. Quare hic moritur infirmitate aut vi, si exit; hoc autem si sitit; sed hoc si aliud; et ita veniet ad quod nunc est, aut in factorum  aliquid; ut si sitit; hoc autem si comedit mordicantia; sed hoc aut est aut non; quare ex necessitate morietur aut non morietur. Similiter autem et si supersiliat aliquis ad facta, eadem ratio; iam enim est hoc in aliquo, dico autem factum. Ex necessitate ergo omnia erunt quae futura, ut moriturum fore viventem; iam enim aliquid factum est, ut contraria in eodem corpore. Sed si infirmitate aut vi, nondum, nisi hoc factum fuerit.

That there are principles and causes which are generable and destructible without ever being in course of being generated or destroyed, is obvious. For otherwise all things will be of necessity, since that which is being generated or destroyed must have a cause which is not accidentally its cause. Will A exist or not? It will if B happens; and if not, not. And B will exist if C happens. And thus if time is constantly subtracted from a limited extent of time, one will obviously come to the present. [27b] This man, then, will die by violence, if he goes out; and he will do this if he gets thirsty; and he will get thirsty if something else happens; and thus we shall come to that which is now present, or to some past event. For instance, he will go out if he gets thirsty; and he will get thirsty if he is eating pungent food; and this is either the case or not; so that he will of necessity die, or of necessity not die. And similarly if one jumps over to past events, the same account will hold good; for this – I mean the past condition – is already present in something. Everything, therefore, that will be, will be of necessity; e.g. it is necessary that he who lives shall one day die; for already some condition has come into existence, e.g. the presence of contraries in the same body. But whether he is to die by disease or by violence is not yet determined, but depends on the happening of something else.

ἔσται οὖν ἡ τοῦ ὁπότερ᾽ ἔτυχεν αὕτη, καὶ αἴτιον τῆς γενέσεως αὐτῆς ἄλλο οὐθέν.

Palam ergo quia usque ad aliquod vadit principium, hoc autem non adhuc ad aliud. Erit ergo quod eius quod utcumque evenit ipsum, et causa generationis ipsius nulla.

Clearly then the process goes back to a certain starting-point, but this no longer points to something further. This then will be the starting-point for the fortuitous, and will have nothing else as cause of its coming to be.

ἀλλ᾽ εἰς ἀρχὴν ποίαν καὶ αἴτιον ποῖον ἡ ἀναγωγὴ ἡ [15] τοιαύτη, πότερον ὡς εἰς ὕλην ἢ ὡς εἰς τὸ οὗ ἕνεκα ἢ ὡς εἰς τὸ κινῆσαν, μάλιστα σκεπτέον.

Sed ad principium quale et causam qualem reductio talis, utrum ut ad materiam aut ut ad id quod cuius gratia aut ut ad movens, maxime perscrutandum.

But to what sort of starting-point and what sort of cause we thus refer the fortuitous – whether to matter or to the purpose or to the motive power, must be carefully considered.

περὶ μὲν οὖν τοῦ κατὰ συμβεβηκὸς ὄντος ἀφείσθω (διώρισται γὰρ ἱκανῶς):

Ergo de ente secundum accidens praetermittatur; determinatum enim est sufficienter.

*Chapter* 4 Let us dismiss accidental being; for we have sufficiently determined its nature.

τὸ δὲ ὡς ἀληθὲς ὄν, καὶ μὴ ὂν ὡς ψεῦδος, ἐπειδὴ παρὰ σύνθεσίν ἐστι καὶ διαίρεσιν, τὸ δὲ σύνολον [20] περὶ μερισμὸν ἀντιφάσεως (τὸ μὲν γὰρ ἀληθὲς τὴν κατάφασιν ἐπὶ τῷ συγκειμένῳ ἔχει τὴν δ᾽ ἀπόφασιν ἐπὶ τῷ διῃρημένῳ, τὸ δὲ ψεῦδος τούτου τοῦ μερισμοῦ τὴν ἀντίφασιν:

Quod autem ut verum ens et non ens ut falsum, quoniam secundum compositionem est et divisionem, totaliter vero circa partitionem contradictionis; verum quidem enim affirmationem in composito habet negationem vero in disiuncto, sed falsum huius partitionis contradictionem.

But since that which is in the sense of being true, or is not in the sense of being false, depends on combination and separation, and truth and falsity together depend on the allocation of a pair of contradictory judgements (for the true judgement affirms where the subject and predicate really are combined, and denies where they are separated, while the false judgement has the opposite of this allocation;

πῶς δὲ τὸ ἅμα ἢ τὸ χωρὶς νοεῖν συμβαίνει, ἄλλος λόγος, λέγω δὲ τὸ ἅμα καὶ τὸ χωρὶς ὥστε μὴ τὸ ἐφεξῆς [25] ἀλλ᾽ ἕν τι γίγνεσθαι):

Quomodo autem quod simul aut quod separatim intelligere accidit, alius sermo; dico autem quod simul et quod separatim ut non eo quod consequenter sed in unum aliquid fieri.

it is another question, how it happens that we think things together or apart; by together and apart I mean thinking them so that there is no succession in the thoughts but they become a unity);

οὐ γάρ ἐστι τὸ ψεῦδος καὶ τὸ ἀληθὲς ἐν τοῖς πράγμασιν, οἷον τὸ μὲν ἀγαθὸν ἀληθὲς τὸ δὲ κακὸν εὐθὺς ψεῦδος, ἀλλ᾽ ἐν διανοίᾳ, περὶ δὲ τὰ ἁπλᾶ καὶ τὰ τί ἐστιν οὐδ᾽ ἐν διανοίᾳ: ὅσα μὲν οὖν δεῖ θεωρῆσαι περὶ τὸ οὕτως ὂν καὶ μὴ ὄν, ὕστερον ἐπισκεπτέον:

Non enim est falsum et verum in rebus, ut quod quidem bonum verum quod autem malum falsum, sed in mente; circa vero simplicia et quid est nec in mente est. Ergo quaecumque oportet speculari circa sic ens et non ens, posterius perscrutandum est.

for falsity and truth are not in things – it is not as if the good were true, and the bad were in itself false – but in thought; while with regard to simple concepts and whats falsity and truth do not exist even in thought – this being so, we must consider later what has to be discussed with regard to that which is or is not in this sense.

ἐπεὶ δὲ ἡ συμπλοκὴ [30] ἐστιν καὶ ἡ διαίρεσις ἐν διανοίᾳ ἀλλ᾽ οὐκ ἐν τοῖς πράγμασι, τὸ δ᾽ οὕτως ὂν ἕτερον ὂν τῶν κυρίως (ἢ γὰρ τὸ τί ἐστιν ἢ ὅτι ποιὸν ἢ ὅτι ποσὸν ἤ τι ἄλλο συνάπτει ἢ ἀφαιρεῖ ἡ διάνοια), τὸ μὲν ὡς συμβεβηκὸς καὶ τὸ ὡς ἀληθὲς ὂν ἀφετέον—τὸ γὰρ αἴτιον τοῦ μὲν ἀόριστον τοῦ δὲ τῆς διανοίας τι πάθος, [1028α] [1] καὶ ἀμφότερα περὶ τὸ λοιπὸν γένος τοῦ ὄντος, καὶ οὐκ ἔξω δηλοῦσιν οὖσάν τινα φύσιν τοῦ ὄντος—διὸ ταῦτα μὲν ἀφείσθω, σκεπτέον δὲ τοῦ ὄντος αὐτοῦ τὰ αἴτια καὶ τὰς ἀρχὰς ᾗ ὄν. [φανερὸν δ᾽ ἐν οἷς διωρισάμεθα περὶ [5] τοῦ ποσαχῶς λέγεται ἕκαστον, ὅτι πολλαχῶς λέγεται τὸ ὄν.]

Quoniam autem complexio est et divisio in mente et non in rebus, quod autem ita ens alterum ens a propriis (aut enim quod quid est aut quia quale aut quia quantum aut si quid aliud copulat aut dividit mens), quod quidem ut accidens et quod ut verum ens praetermittendum. Causa enim huius quidem indefinita illius vero mentis aliqua passio, et utraque circa reliquum genus entis, et non extra ostendunt entem aliquam naturam entis. Quapropter ea quidem praetermittantur, perscrutande vero sunt entis ipsius causae et principia in quantum ens . Palam autem in quibus determinavimus de quotiens unumquodque dicitur, quia multipliciter dicitur ens. Significat enim hoc quidem quid est.

But since the combination and the separation are in thought and not in the things, and that which is in this sense is a different sort of being from the things that are in the full sense (for the thought attaches or removes either the subject's what or its having a certain quality or quantity or something else), that which is accidentally and that which is in the sense of being true must be dismissed. For the cause of the former is indeterminate, and that of the latter is some affection of the thought [28a], and both are related to the remaining genus of being, and do not indicate the existence of any separate class of being. Therefore let these be dismissed, and let us consider the causes and the principles of being itself, qua being. (It was clear in our discussion of the various meanings of terms, that being has several meanings.)

# METAPHISICE ARISTOTILIS LIBER SEPTIMUS

Aristotle's Metaphysics book seven

[1028α] [10] τὸ ὂν λέγεται πολλαχῶς, καθάπερ διειλόμεθα πρότερον ἐν τοῖς περὶ τοῦ ποσαχῶς: σημαίνει γὰρ τὸ μὲν τί ἐστι καὶ τόδε τι, τὸ δὲ ποιὸν ἢ ποσὸν ἢ τῶν ἄλλων ἕκαστον τῶν οὕτω κατηγορουμένων. τοσαυταχῶς δὲ λεγομένου τοῦ ὄντος φανερὸν ὅτι τούτων πρῶτον ὂν τὸ τί ἐστιν, ὅπερ σημαίνει [15] τὴν οὐσίαν

ENS dicitur multipliciter, sicut prius divisimus in hiis quae de quotiens. Significat enim hoc quidem quid est et hoc aliquid, illud vero quod quale aut quantum aut aliorum unumquodque sic predicatorum. Totiens autem dicto palam quia horum primum ens quod quid est, quod significat substantiam.

THERE are several senses in which a thing may be said to 'be', as we pointed out previously in our book on the various senses of words;' for in one sense the 'being' meant is 'what a thing is' or a 'this', and in another sense it means a quality or quantity or one of the other things that are predicated as these are. While 'being' has all these senses, obviously that which 'is' primarily is the 'what', which indicates the substance of the thing.

(ὅταν μὲν γὰρ εἴπωμεν ποιόν τι τόδε, ἢ ἀγαθὸν λέγομεν ἢ κακόν, ἀλλ᾽ οὐ τρίπηχυ ἢ ἄνθρωπον: ὅταν δὲ τί ἐστιν, οὐ λευκὸν οὐδὲ θερμὸν οὐδὲ τρίπηχυ, ἀλλὰ ἄνθρωπον ἢ θεόν), τὰ δ᾽ ἄλλα λέγεται ὄντα τῷ τοῦ οὕτως ὄντος τὰ μὲν ποσότητες εἶναι, τὰ δὲ ποιότητες, τὰ δὲ πάθη, τὰ δὲ [20] ἄλλο τι.

Nam quando dicimus quale quid hoc, aut bonum dicimus aut malum, sed non tricubitum aut hominem; quando vero quid est, nec album nec calidum nec tricubitum, sed hominem aut deum. Alia vero dicuntur entia eo quod taliter entis haec quidem qualitates esse, illa vero quantitates, alia passiones, alia aliud quid tale.

For when we say of what quality a thing is, we say that it is good or bad, not that it is three cubits long or that it is a man; but when we say what it is, we do not say 'white' or 'hot' or 'three cubits long', but 'a man' or 'a 'god'. And all other things are said to be because they are, some of them, quantities of that which is in this primary sense, others qualities of it, others affections of it, and others some other determination of it.

διὸ κἂν ἀπορήσειέ τις πότερον τὸ βαδίζειν καὶ τὸ ὑγιαίνειν καὶ τὸ καθῆσθαι ἕκαστον αὐτῶν ὂν σημαίνει, ὁμοίως δὲ καὶ ἐπὶ τῶν ἄλλων ὁτουοῦν τῶν τοιούτων: οὐδὲν γὰρ αὐτῶν ἐστιν οὔτε καθ᾽ αὐτὸ πεφυκὸς οὔτε χωρίζεσθαι δυνατὸν τῆς οὐσίας, ἀλλὰ μᾶλλον, εἴπερ, τὸ βαδίζον [25] τῶν ὄντων καὶ τὸ καθήμενον καὶ τὸ ὑγιαῖνον. ταῦτα δὲ μᾶλλον φαίνεται ὄντα, διότι ἔστι τι τὸ ὑποκείμενον αὐτοῖς ὡρισμένον (τοῦτο δ᾽ ἐστὶν ἡ οὐσία καὶ τὸ καθ᾽ ἕκαστον), ὅπερ ἐμφαίνεται ἐν τῇ κατηγορίᾳ τῇ τοιαύτῃ· τὸ ἀγαθὸν γὰρ ἢ τὸ καθήμενον οὐκ ἄνευ τούτου λέγεται.

Unde et utique dubitabit aliquis utrum vadere et sanare et sedere unumquodque ipsorum sit ens aut non ens; similiter autem et in aliis talibus. Nihil enim ipsorum est secundum se aptum natum nec separari possibile a substantia, sed magis siquidem vadens entium est aliquid et sedens et sanans. Hec autem magis apparent entia, quia est aliquid subiectum ipsis determinatum, hoc autem est substantia et unumquodque quod autem in cathegorica tali apparet; bonum enim aut sedens non sine hoc dicitur.

And so one might even raise the question whether the words 'to walk', 'to be healthy', 'to sit' imply that each of these things is existent, and similarly in any other case of this sort; for none of them is either self-subsistent or capable of being separated from substance, but rather, if anything, it is that which walks or sits or is healthy that is an existent thing. Now these are seen to be more real because there is something definite which underlies them (i.e. the substance or individual), which is implied in such a predicate; for we never use the word 'good' or 'sitting' without implying this.

δῆλον οὖν ὅτι διὰ [30] ταύτην κἀκείνων ἕκαστον ἔστιν, ὥστε τὸ πρώτως ὂν καὶ οὐ τὶ ὂν ἀλλ᾽ ὂν ἁπλῶς ἡ οὐσία ἂν εἴη.

Palam ergo quia propter eam et illorum singula sunt. Quare primo ens et non aliquid ens sed ens simpliciter substantia utique erit.

Clearly then it is in virtue of this category that each of the others also is. Therefore that which is primarily, i.e. not in a qualified sense but without qualification, must be substance.

πολλαχῶς μὲν οὖν λέγεται τὸ πρῶτον· ὅμως δὲ πάντως ἡ οὐσία πρῶτον, καὶ λόγῳ καὶ γνώσει καὶ χρόνῳ. τῶν μὲν γὰρ ἄλλων κατηγορημάτων οὐθὲν χωριστόν, αὕτη δὲ μόνη· καὶ τῷ λόγῳ δὲ τοῦτο [35] πρῶτον (ἀνάγκη γὰρ ἐν τῷ ἑκάστου λόγῳ τὸν τῆς οὐσίας ἐνυπάρχειν)· καὶ εἰδέναι δὲ τότ᾽ οἰόμεθα ἕκαστον μάλιστα, ὅταν τί ἐστιν ὁ ἄνθρωπος γνῶμεν ἢ τὸ πῦρ, [1028β] [1] μᾶλλον ἢ τὸ ποιὸν ἢ τὸ ποσὸν ἢ τὸ πού, ἐπεὶ καὶ αὐτῶν τούτων τότε ἕκαστον ἴσμεν, ὅταν τί ἐστι τὸ ποσὸν ἢ τὸ ποιὸν γνῶμεν.

Multipliciter quidem igitur dicitur quod primum. Sed substantia omnium primum, ratione et notitia et tempore. Aliorum enim cathegoreumatum nullum est separabile, hec autem sola. Et ratione autem hoc primum. Necesse enim in uniuscuiusque ratione substantiae rationem inesse. Et scire autem tunc singula maxime putamus, quando quid est homo cognoscimus aut ignis, magis quam quale aut quantum aut ubi; quoniam tunc horum eorundem singula scimus, quando quid est ipsum quale aut quantum scimus.

Now there are several senses in which a thing is said to be first; yet substance is first in every sense – (1) in definition, (2) in order of knowledge, (3) in time. For (3) of the other categories none can exist independently, but only substance. And (1) in definition also this is first; for in the definition of each term the definition of its substance must be present. And (2) we think we know each thing most fully, when we know what it is, e.g. what man is or what fire is, rather than when we know its quality, its quantity, or its place; since we know each of these predicates also, only when we know what the quantity or the quality is.

καὶ δὴ καὶ τὸ πάλαι τε καὶ νῦν καὶ ἀεὶ ζητούμενον καὶ ἀεὶ ἀπορούμενον, τί τὸ ὄν, τοῦτό ἐστι τίς ἡ οὐσία (τοῦτο γὰρ οἱ μὲν ἓν εἶναί [5] φασιν οἱ δὲ πλείω ἢ ἕν, καὶ οἱ μὲν πεπερασμένα οἱ δὲ ἄπειρα), διὸ καὶ ἡμῖν καὶ μάλιστα καὶ πρῶτον καὶ μόνον ὡς εἰπεῖν περὶ τοῦ οὕτως ὄντος θεωρητέον τί ἐστιν.

Et quod olim et nunc et semper quaesitum est et semper dubitatum, quid ens, hoc est que substantia. Hoc enim hii quidem unum esse dicunt illi vero plura quam unum, et hii quidem finita illi vero infinita. Quapropter nobis maxime et primum et solum ut est dicere de sic ente speculandum est quid est.

And indeed the question which was raised of old and is raised now and always, and is always the subject of doubt, viz. what being is, is just the question, what is substance? For it is this that some assert to be one, others more than one, and that some assert to be limited in number, others unlimited. And so we also must consider chiefly and primarily and almost exclusively what that is which is in this sense.

*Chapter*  2

δοκεῖ δ' ἡ οὐσία ὑπάρχειν φανερώτατα μὲν τοῖς σώμασιν (διὸ τά τε ζῷα καὶ τὰ φυτὰ καὶ τὰ μόρια αὐτῶν [10] οὐσίας εἶναί φαμεν, καὶ τὰ φυσικὰ σώματα, οἷον πῦρ καὶ ὕδωρ καὶ γῆν καὶ τῶν τοιούτων ἕκαστον, καὶ ὅσα ἢ μόρια τούτων ἢ ἐκ τούτων ἐστίν, ἢ μορίων ἢ πάντων, οἷον ὅ τε οὐρανὸς καὶ τὰ μόρια αὐτοῦ, ἄστρα καὶ σελήνη καὶ ἥλιος): πότερον δὲ αὗται μόναι οὐσίαι εἰσὶν ἢ καὶ ἄλλαι, ἢ τούτων τινὲς [15] ἢ καὶ ἄλλαι, ἢ τούτων μὲν οὐθὲν ἕτεραι δέ τινες, σκεπτέον.

Videtur autem substantia existere manifestissime quidem corporibus. Unde animalia et plante et eorum partes  substantias esse dicimus, et naturalia corpora, ut ignem et aquam et terram et talium singular, et quaecumque aut partes eorum aut ex hiis sunt, aut partibus aut omnibus, ut caelum et partes eius, astra et luna et sol. Utrum vero hee sole substantiae sunt aut et aliae, aut horum quidem nullum alterae quaedem, perscrutandum.

Substance is thought to belong most obviously to bodies; and so we say that not only animals and plants and their parts are substances, but also natural bodies such as fire and water and earth and everything of the sort, and all things that are either parts of these or composed of these (either of parts or of the whole bodies), e.g. the physical universe and its parts, stars and moon and sun. But whether these alone are substances, or there are also others, or only some of these, or others as well, or none of these but only some other things, are substances, must be considered.

δοκεῖ δέ τισι τὰ τοῦ σώματος πέρατα, οἷον ἐπιφάνεια καὶ γραμμὴ καὶ στιγμὴ καὶ μονάς, εἶναι οὐσίαι, καὶ μᾶλλον ἢ τὸ σῶμα καὶ τὸ στερεόν. ἔτι παρὰ τὰ αἰσθητὰ οἱ μὲν οὐκ οἴονται εἶναι οὐδὲν τοιοῦτον, οἱ δὲ πλείω καὶ μᾶλλον ὄντα ἀΐδια, ὥσπερ Πλάτων [20] τά τε εἴδη καὶ τὰ μαθηματικὰ δύο οὐσίας, τρίτην δὲ τὴν τῶν αἰσθητῶν σωμάτων οὐσίαν, Σπεύσιππος δὲ καὶ πλείους οὐσίας ἀπὸ τοῦ ἑνὸς ἀρξάμενος, καὶ ἀρχὰς ἑκάστης οὐσίας, ἄλλην μὲν ἀριθμῶν ἄλλην δὲ μεγεθῶν, ἔπειτα ψυχῆς· καὶ τοῦτον δὴ τὸν τρόπον ἐπεκτείνει τὰς οὐσίας. ἔνιοι δὲ [25] τὰ μὲν εἴδη καὶ τοὺς ἀριθμοὺς τὴν αὐτὴν ἔχειν φασὶ φύσιν, τὰ δὲ ἄλλα ἐχόμενα, γραμμὰς καὶ ἐπίπεδα, μέχρι πρὸς τὴν τοῦ οὐρανοῦ οὐσίαν καὶ τὰ αἰσθητά.

Videntur autem quibusdam corporis termini, ut superficies et linea et punctus et unitas, esse substantiae, et magis quam corpus et solidum. Amplius praeter sensibilia hii quidem non opiniantur esse aliquid talium vero plura et magis entia sempiterna, ut Plato species ipsas et mathematica duas  substantias, tertiam vero sensibilium corporum substantiam. Sed Speucippus plures substantias ab uno inchoans et principia cuiusque  substantiae, aliud quidem numerorum, aliud autem magnitudinum, deinde animae; et hoc modo protendit substantias.  Quidam vero species et numeros eandem habere dicunt naturam, alia vero habita, lineas et superficies, usque ad primam caeli substantiam et sensibilia.

Some think the limits of body, i.e. surface, line, point, and unit, are substances, and more so than body or the solid. Further, some do not think there is anything substantial besides sensible things, but others think there are eternal substances which are more in number and more real; e.g. Plato posited two kinds of substance – the Forms and objects of mathematics – as well as a third kind, viz. the substance of sensible bodies. And Speusippus made still more kinds of substance, beginning with the One, and assuming principles for each kind of substance, one for numbers, another for spatial magnitudes, and then another for the soul; and by going on in this way he multiplies the kinds of substance. And some say Forms and numbers have the same nature, and the other things come after them – lines and planes – until we come to the substance of the material universe and to sensible bodies.

περὶ δὴ τούτων τί λέγεται καλῶς ἢ μὴ καλῶς, καὶ τίνες εἰσὶν οὐσίαι, καὶ πότερον εἰσί τινες παρὰ τὰς αἰσθητὰς ἢ οὐκ εἰσί, καὶ αὗται πῶς [30] εἰσί, καὶ πότερον ἔστι τις χωριστὴ οὐσία, καὶ διὰ τί καὶ πῶς, ἢ οὐδεμία, παρὰ τὰς αἰσθητάς, σκεπτέον, ὑποτυπωσαμένοις τὴν οὐσίαν πρῶτον τί ἐστιν.

De hiis igitur quid dicitur bene aut non bene, et quae sunt substantiae, et utrum sunt aliquae praeter sensibiles aut non sunt, et iste quomodo sunt, et utrum est aliqua separabilis substantia, et quare et quomodo, aut nulla praeter sensibiles, perscrutandum, cum descripsimus primo substantiam quid est.

Regarding these matters, then, we must inquire which of the common statements are right and which are not right, and what substances there are, and whether there are or are not any besides sensible substances, and how sensible substances exist, and whether there is a substance capable of separate existence (and if so why and how) or no such substance, apart from sensible substances; and we must first sketch the nature of substance.

*Chapter* 3

λέγεται δ᾽ ἡ οὐσία, εἰ μὴ πλεοναχῶς, ἀλλ᾽ ἐν τέτταρσί γε μάλιστα: καὶ γὰρ τὸ τί ἦν εἶναι καὶ τὸ καθόλου [35] καὶ τὸ γένος οὐσία δοκεῖ εἶναι ἑκάστου, καὶ τέταρτον τούτων τὸ ὑποκείμενον. τὸ δ᾽ ὑποκείμενόν ἐστι καθ᾽ οὗ τὰ ἄλλα λέγεται, ἐκεῖνο δὲ αὐτὸ μηκέτι κατ᾽ ἄλλου: διὸ πρῶτον περὶ τούτου διοριστέον: [1029α] [1] μάλιστα γὰρ δοκεῖ εἶναι οὐσία τὸ ὑποκείμενον πρῶτον.

Dicitur autem substantia, si non multiplicius, de quatuor maxime. Et enim quid erat esse et universale et genus videtur substantia esse cuiusque, et quartum horum subiectum. Subiectum vero est de quo alia dicuntur, et illud ipsum non adhuc de alio. Propter quod primum de hoc determinandum est; maxime namque videtur esse substantia subiectum primum.

The word 'substance' is applied, if not in more senses, still at least to four main objects; for both the essence and the universal and the genus, are thought to be the substance of each thing, and fourthly the substratum. Now the substratum is that of

which everything else is predicated, while it is itself not predicated of anything else. And so we must first determine the nature of this; for that which underlies [29a]a thing primarily is thought to be in the truest sense its substance.

τοιοῦτον δὲ τρόπον μέν τινα ἡ ὕλη λέγεται, ἄλλον δὲ τρόπον ἡ μορφή, τρίτον δὲ τὸ ἐκ τούτων (λέγω δὲ τὴν μὲν ὕλην οἷον τὸν χαλκόν, τὴν δὲ μορφὴν τὸ σχῆμα τῆς [5] ἰδέας, τὸ δ᾽ ἐκ τούτων τὸν ἀνδριάντα τὸ σύνολον),

Tale vero modo quodam materia dicitur, et alio modo forma, tertio vero quod ex hiis. Dico autem materiam quidem es, formam autem figuram speciei, quod autem ex hiis statuam totam.

And in one sense matter is said to be of the nature of substratum, in another, shape, and in a third, the compound of these. (By the matter I mean, for instance, the bronze, by the shape the pattern of its form, and by the compound of these the statue, the concrete whole.)

ὥστε εἰ τὸ εἶδος τῆς ὕλης πρότερον καὶ μᾶλλον ὄν, καὶ τοῦ ἐξ ἀμφοῖν πρότερον ἔσται διὰ τὸν αὐτὸν λόγον.

Quare si species materia est prior et magis ens, et ipso quod ex utrisque prior erit propter eandem rationem.

Therefore if the form is prior to the matter and more real, it will be prior also to the compound of both, for the same reason.

νῦν μὲν οὖν τύπῳ εἴρηται τί ποτ᾽ ἐστὶν ἡ οὐσία, ὅτι τὸ μὴ καθ᾽ ὑποκειμένου ἀλλὰ καθ᾽ οὗ τὰ ἄλλα: δεῖ δὲ μὴ μόνον οὕτως: οὐ γὰρ ἱκανόν: [10] αὐτὸ γὰρ τοῦτο ἄδηλον, καὶ ἔτι ἡ ὕλη οὐσία γίγνεται. εἰ γὰρ μὴ αὕτη οὐσία, τίς ἐστιν ἄλλη διαφεύγει: περιαιρουμένων γὰρ τῶν ἄλλων οὐ φαίνεται οὐδὲν ὑπομένον: τὰ μὲν γὰρ ἄλλα τῶν σωμάτων πάθη καὶ ποιήματα καὶ δυνάμεις, τὸ δὲ μῆκος καὶ πλάτος καὶ βάθος ποσότητές τινες ἀλλ᾽ [15] οὐκ οὐσίαι (τὸ γὰρ ποσὸν οὐκ οὐσία), ἀλλὰ μᾶλλον ᾧ ὑπάρχει ταῦτα πρώτῳ, ἐκεῖνό ἐστιν οὐσία. ἀλλὰ μὴν ἀφαιρουμένου μήκους καὶ πλάτους καὶ βάθους οὐδὲν ὁρῶμεν ὑπολειπόμενον, πλὴν εἴ τί ἐστι τὸ ὁριζόμενον ὑπὸ τούτων, ὥστε τὴν ὕλην ἀνάγκη φαίνεσθαι μόνην οὐσίαν οὕτω σκοπουμένοις.

Nunc quidem igitur typo dictum est quid est substantia, quia quod non de subiecto sed de quo alia. Oportet autem non solum ita; non enim sufficiens. Ipsum enim hoc immanifestum, et adhuc materia substantia fit. Si enim non ipsa substantia, quae est alia diffugit. Aliis enim sublatis nil apparet remanens. Nam alia quidem corporum sunt passiones et factiones et potentiae, longitudo vero et latitudo et profunditas quantitates quaedam sunt sed non substantiae (quantitas enim non substantia); sed magis cui insunt haec ipsa primum, illo modo est substantia. At vero

ablata longitudine et latitudine et profundo nihil videmus remanens, nisi si quid est determinatum ab hiis; quare materiam necesse videri solam substantiam sic intendentibus.

We have now outlined the nature of substance, showing that it is that which is not predicated of a stratum, but of which all else is predicated. But we must not merely state the matter thus; for this is not enough. The statement itself is obscure, and further, on this view, matter becomes substance. For if this is not substance, it baffles us to say what else is. When all else is stripped off evidently nothing but matter remains. For while the rest are affections, products, and potencies of bodies, length, breadth, and depth are quantities and not substances (for a quantity is not a substance), but the substance is rather that to which these belong primarily. But when length and breadth and depth are taken away we see nothing left unless there is something that is bounded by these; so that to those who consider the question thus matter alone must seem to be substance.

[20] λέγω δ᾽ ὕλην ἣ καθ᾽ αὑτὴν μήτε τὶ μήτε ποσὸν μήτε ἄλλο μηδὲν λέγεται οἷς ὥρισται τὸ ὄν. ἔστι γάρ τι καθ᾽ οὗ κατηγορεῖται τούτων ἕκαστον, ᾧ τὸ εἶναι ἕτερον καὶ τῶν κατηγοριῶν ἑκάστῃ (τὰ μὲν γὰρ ἄλλα τῆς οὐσίας κατηγορεῖται, αὕτη δὲ τῆς ὕλης), ὥστε τὸ ἔσχατον καθ᾽ αὑτὸ οὔτε τὶ οὔτε ποσὸν [25] οὔτε ἄλλο οὐδέν ἐστιν: οὐδὲ δὴ αἱ ἀποφάσεις, καὶ γὰρ αὗται ὑπάρξουσι κατὰ συμβεβηκός. ἐκ μὲν οὖν τούτων θεωροῦσι συμβαίνει οὐσίαν εἶναι τὴν ὕλην: ἀδύνατον δέ:

Dico autem materiam quae secundum se neque quid neque quantitas neque aliud aliquid dicitur quibus ens est determinatum. Est enim quoddam de quo praedicatur horum quodlibet, cui est esse alterum et cathegoriarum unicuique; alia namque de substantia praedicantur, haec vero de materia. Quare quod est ultimum secundum se neque quid neque quantitas neque aliud est; neque itaque negationes, et enim hee erunt secundum accidens. Ex hiis ergo speculantibus accidit substantiam esse materiam.

By matter I mean that which in itself is neither a particular thing nor of a certain quantity nor assigned to any other of the categories by which being is determined. For there is something of which each of these is predicated, whose being is different from that of each of the predicates (for the predicates other than substance are predicated of substance, while substance is predicated of matter). Therefore the ultimate substratum is of itself neither a particular thing nor of a particular quantity nor otherwise positively characterized; nor yet is it the negations of these, for negations also will belong to it only by accident. If we adopt this point of view, then, it follows that matter is substance.

καὶ γὰρ τὸ χωριστὸν καὶ τὸ τόδε τι ὑπάρχειν δοκεῖ μάλιστα τῇ οὐσίᾳ, διὸ τὸ εἶδος καὶ τὸ ἐξ ἀμφοῖν οὐσία δόξειεν ἂν εἶναι μᾶλλον [30] τῆς ὕλης.

Sed impossibile; et enim separabile et hoc aliquid inesse videtur maxime substantiae. Quapropter species et quod ex ambobus substantia videbitur esse magis quam materia.

But this is impossible; for both separability and 'thisness' are thought to belong chiefly to substance. And so form and the compound of form and matter would be thought to be substance, rather than matter.

τὴν μὲν τοίνυν ἐξ ἀμφοῖν οὐσίαν, λέγω δὲ τὴν ἔκ τε τῆς ὕλης καὶ τῆς μορφῆς, ἀφετέον, ὑστέρα γὰρ καὶ δήλη· φανερὰ δέ πως καὶ ἡ ὕλη· περὶ δὲ τῆς τρίτης σκεπτέον, αὕτη γὰρ ἀπορωτάτη.

At tamen eam quae nunc ex ambobus substantiam, dico autem eam quae ex materia et forma, dimittendum; posterior enim est et aperta. Manifesta autem aliqualiter et materia. De tertia autem perscrutandum est, haec namque maxime dubitabilis.

The substance compounded of both, i.e. of matter and shape, may be dismissed; for it is posterior and its nature is obvious. And matter also is in a sense manifest. But we must inquire into the third kind of substance; for this is the most perplexing.

ὁμολογοῦνται δ᾽ οὐσίαι εἶναι τῶν αἰσθητῶν τινές, ὥστε ἐν ταύταις ζητητέον πρῶτον.

Confitentur autem substantiae esse sensibilium quaedam, quare in hiis quaerendum prius.

Some of the sensible substances are generally admitted to be substances, so that we must look first among these.

*Chapter* 4

πρὸ ἔργου γὰρ τὸ μεταβαίνειν εἰς τὸ γνωριμώτερον. ἡ γὰρ μάθησις οὕτω γίγνεται πᾶσι διὰ τῶν ἧττον γνωρίμων φύσει [5] εἰς τὰ γνώριμα μᾶλλον· καὶ τοῦτο ἔργον ἐστίν, ὥσπερ ἐν ταῖς πράξεσι τὸ ποιῆσαι ἐκ τῶν ἑκάστῳ ἀγαθῶν τὰ ὅλως ἀγαθὰ ἑκάστῳ ἀγαθά, οὕτως ἐκ τῶν αὐτῷ γνωριμωτέρων τὰ τῇ φύσει γνώριμα αὐτῷ γνώριμα. τὰ δ᾽ ἑκάστοις γνώριμα καὶ πρῶτα πολλάκις ἠρέμα ἐστὶ γνώριμα, καὶ μικρὸν ἢ [10] οὐθὲν ἔχει τοῦ ὄντος· ἀλλ᾽ ὅμως ἐκ τῶν φαύλως μὲν γνωστῶν αὐτῷ δὲ γνωστῶν τὰ ὅλως γνωστὰ γνῶναι πειρατέον, μεταβαίνοντας, ὥσπερ εἴρηται, διὰ τούτων αὐτῶν. [1] ἐπεὶ δ᾽ ἐν ἀρχῇ διειλόμεθα πόσοις ὁρίζομεν τὴν οὐσίαν, καὶ τούτων ἕν τι ἐδόκει εἶναι τὸ τί ἦν εἶναι, θεωρητέον περὶ [13] αὐτοῦ.

Quoniam autem in principio divisimus quot determinamus substantiam, et horum unum quidem videtur esse quod quid erat esse, speculandam est de ipso. Praeopere enim ad transeundum ad quod notius est. Disciplina enim ita fit omnibus per minus nota naturae ad nota magis. Et hoc opus est: quemadmodum in actibus facere ex unicuique bonis totaliter bona unicuique bona, sic ex ipsi notioribus quae naturae quidem nota ipsi nota. Quae autem singulis nota et prima multotiens debiliter nota, et parum aut nihil entis habent. At tamen ex male quidem noscibilibus ipsi autem noscibilibus quae omnino noscibilia noscere temptandum, procedentis, sicut dictum est, per haec ipsa.

Since at the start we distinguished the various marks by which we determine substance, and one of these was thought to be the essence, we must investigate this. For it is an advantage to advance to that which is more knowable. For learning proceeds for all in this way – through that which is less knowable by nature to that which is more knowable; and just as in conduct our task is to start from what is good for each and make what is without qualification good good for each, so it is our task to start from what is more knowable to oneself and make what is knowable by nature knowable to oneself. Now what is knowable and primary for particular sets of people is often knowable to a very small extent, and has little or nothing of reality. But yet one must start from that which is barely knowable but knowable to oneself, and try to know what is knowable without qualification, passing, as has been said, by way of those very things which one does know.

καὶ πρῶτον εἴπωμεν ἔνια περὶ αὐτοῦ λογικῶς, ὅτι ἐστὶ τὸ τί ἦν εἶναι ἑκάστου ὃ λέγεται καθ᾽ αὑτό. οὐ γάρ ἐστι τὸ σοὶ [15] εἶναι τὸ μουσικῷ εἶναι· οὐ γὰρ κατὰ σαυτὸν εἶ μουσικός. ὃ ἄρα κατὰ σαυτόν.

Et primo dicemus quaedam de eo logicae, quid est quod quid erat esse unumquodque quod dicitur secundum se. Non enim est tibi esse musicum esse; non enim secundum te ipsum es musicus. Quod ergo secundum te ipsum.

And first let us make some linguistic remarks about it. The essence of each thing is what it is said to be propter se. For being you is not being musical, since you are not by your very nature musical. What, then, you are by your very nature is your essence.

οὐδὲ δὴ τοῦτο πᾶν· οὐ γὰρ τὸ οὕτως καθ᾽ αὑτὸ ὡς ἐπιφανείᾳ λευκόν, ὅτι οὐκ ἔστι τὸ ἐπιφανείᾳ εἶναι τὸ λευκῷ εἶναι. ἀλλὰ μὴν οὐδὲ τὸ ἐξ ἀμφοῖν, τὸ ἐπιφανείᾳ λευκή, ὅτι πρόσεστιν αὐτό. ἐν ᾧ ἄρα μὴ ἐνέσται λόγῳ [20] αὐτό, λέγοντι αὐτό, οὗτος ὁ λόγος τοῦ τί ἦν εἶναι ἑκάστῳ, ὥστ᾽ εἰ τὸ ἐπιφανείᾳ λευκῇ εἶναί ἐστι τὸ ἐπιφανείᾳ εἶναι λεία, τὸ λευκῷ καὶ λείῳ εἶναι τὸ αὐτὸ καὶ ἕν.

Neque etiam hoc omne; non enim quod ita secundum se ut superficiei album, quia non est superficiei esse album esse. At vero neque quod ex utrisque: superficiei albe esse. Quare? Quia adest haec. In qua igitur non inerit ratione ipsum dicente ipsu, haec ratio eius quod quid erat esse singulis. Quare si superficiei albe esse est superficiei esse, semper albo et levi esse idem et unum.

Nor yet is the whole of this the essence of a thing; not that which is propter se as white is to a surface, because being a surface is not identical with being white. But again the combination of both – 'being a white surface' – is not the essence of surface, because 'surface' itself is added. The formula, therefore, in which the term itself is not present but its meaning is expressed, this is the formula of the essence of each thing. Therefore if to be a white surface is to be a smooth surface, to be white and to be smooth are one and the same.

ἐπεὶ δ᾽ ἔστι καὶ κατὰ τὰς ἄλλας κατηγορίας σύνθετα (ἔστι γάρ τι ὑποκείμενον ἑκάστῳ, οἷον τῷ ποιῷ καὶ τῷ ποσῷ καὶ τῷ [25] ποτὲ καὶ τῷ ποὺ καὶ τῇ κινήσει), σκεπτέον ἆρ᾽ ἔστι λόγος τοῦ τί ἦν εἶναι ἑκάστῳ αὐτῶν, καὶ ὑπάρχει καὶ τούτοις τὸ τί ἦν εἶναι, οἷον λευκῷ ἀνθρώπῳ [τί ἦν λευκῷ ἀνθρώπῳ]. ἔστω δὴ ὄνομα αὐτῷ ἱμάτιον. τί ἐστι τὸ ἱματίῳ εἶναι;

Quoniam vero sunt et secundum alias cathegorias composita (est enim aliquid subiectum cuique, ut qualitati et quantitati et quando et ubi et motui), perscrutandum ergo si est ratio ipsius quid erat cuiusque ipsorum esse, et inest hiis ipsum quid erat esse, ut albo homini quid erat albo homini. Sit itaque nomen ipsi 'vestis'. Quid est vesti esse?

But since there are also compounds answering to the other categories (for there is a substratum for each category, e.g. for quality, quantity, time, place, and motion), we must inquire whether there is a formula of the essence of each of them, i.e. whether to these compounds also there belongs an essence, e.g. 'white man'. Let the compound be denoted by 'cloak'. What is the essence of cloak?

ἀλλὰ μὴν οὐδὲ τῶν καθ᾽ αὑτὸ λεγομένων οὐδὲ τοῦτο. ἢ τὸ οὐ καθ᾽ αὑτὸ [30] λέγεται διχῶς, καὶ τούτου ἐστὶ τὸ μὲν ἐκ προσθέσεως τὸ δὲ οὔ. τὸ μὲν γὰρ τῷ αὐτὸ ἄλλῳ προσκεῖσθαι λέγεται ὃ ὁρίζεται, οἷον εἰ τὸ λευκῷ εἶναι ὁριζόμενος λέγοι λευκοῦ ἀνθρώπου λόγον· τὸ δὲ τῷ ἄλλο αὐτῷ, οἷον εἰ σημαίνοι τὸ ἱμάτιον λευκὸν ἄνθρωπον, ὁ δὲ ὁρίζοιτο ἱμάτιον ὡς λευκόν. τὸ δὴ λευκὸς ἄνθρωπος ἔστι μὲν λευκόν, [1030α] [1] οὐ μέντοι <τὸ τί ἦν εἶναι λευκῷ εἶναι. ἀλλὰ τὸ ἱματίῳ εἶναι ἆρά ἐστι τί ἦν εἶναί τι [ἢ] ὅλως; ἢ οὔ; ὅπερ γάρ τί ἐστι τὸ τί ἦν εἶναι· ὅταν δ᾽ ἄλλο κατ᾽ ἄλλου λέγηται, οὐκ ἔστιν ὅπερ τόδε τι, οἷον ὁ [5] λευκὸς ἄνθρωπος οὐκ ἔστιν ὅπερ τόδε τι, εἴπερ τὸ τόδε ταῖς οὐσίαις ὑπάρχει μόνον· ὥστε τὸ τί ἦν εἶναί ἐστιν ὅσων ὁ λόγος ἐστὶν ὁρισμός. ὁρισμὸς δ᾽ ἐστὶν οὐκ ἂν ὄνομα λόγῳ ταὐτὸ σημαίνῃ (πάντες γὰρ ἂν εἶεν οἱ λόγοι ὅροι· ἔσται γὰρ ὄνομα ὁτῳοῦν λόγῳ, ὥστε καὶ ἡ Ἰλιὰς ὁρισμὸς ἔσται), [10] ἀλλ᾽ ἐὰν πρώτου τινὸς ᾖ· τοιαῦτα δ᾽ ἐστὶν ὅσα λέγεται μὴ τῷ ἄλλο κατ᾽ ἄλλου λέγεσθαι. οὐκ ἔσται ἄρα οὐδενὶ τῶν μὴ γένους εἰδῶν ὑπάρχον τὸ τί ἦν εἶναι, ἀλλὰ τούτοις μόνον (ταῦτα γὰρ δοκεῖ οὐ κατὰ μετοχὴν λέγεσθαι καὶ πάθος οὐδ᾽ ὡς συμβεβηκός)· ἀλλὰ λόγος μὲν ἔσται ἑκάστου [15] καὶ τῶν ἄλλων τί σημαίνει, ἐὰν ᾖ ὄνομα, ὅτι τόδε τῷδε ὑπάρχει, ἢ ἀντὶ λόγου ἁπλοῦ ἀκριβέστερος· ὁρισμὸς δ᾽ οὐκ ἔσται οὐδὲ τὸ τί ἦν εἶναι.

At vero neque secundum se dictorum nec hoc. Aut ipsum 'non secundum se' dicitur dupliciter, et huius est aliquid hoc quidem ex additione illud vero non. Hoc quidem enim eo quod ipsum alii addi dicitur quod diffinitur, ut si albo esse diffiniens dicat albi hominis rationem; hoc autem eo quod aliud ipsi, ut si significat vestis album hominem, diffiniat vestem ut album. Albus itaque homo est quidem album, non tamen quid erat esse albo esse, sed vesti esse.Ergo est quid erat esse aliquid, aut totaliter aut non. Quod quidem enim quid erat esse est id quod aliquid erat esse. Quando vero aliud de alio dicitur, non est quod quidem hoc aliquid, ut albus homo non est quod vere hoc aliquid, siquidem le hoc substantiis inest solum. Quare quid erat esse est quorumcumque ratio est diffinitio. Diffinitio vero est non si nomen rationi idem significet (omnes enim essent rationes termini; erit enim nomen quod cuilibet rationi idem, quare et Ylias diffinitio erit), sed si primi alicuius fuerit; talia vero sunt quaecumque dicuntur non eo quod aliud de alio dicatur. Non erit igitur nulli non generis specierum existens quid erat esse, sed hiis solum; haec namque videntur non secundum participationem dici et passionum nec ut accidens. Sed ratio quidem erit cuiuslibet et aliorum quid significat, si est nomen, quia hoc huic inest, aut pro sermone simplici certior; diffinitio vero non erit nec quod quid erat esse.

But, it may be said, this also is not a propter se expression. We reply that there are just two ways in which a predicate may fail to be true of a subject propter se, and one of these results from the addition, and the other from the omission, of a determinant. One kind of predicate is not propter se because the term that is being defined is combined with another determinant, e.g. if in defining the essence of white one were to state the formula of white man; the other because in the subject another determinant is combined with that which is expressed in the formula, e.g. if 'cloak' meant 'white man', and one were to define cloak as white; white man is white indeed [30a], but its essence is not to be white.But is being-a-cloak an essence at all? Probably not. For the essence is precisely what something is; but when an attribute is asserted of a subject other than itself, the complex is not precisely what some 'this' is, e.g. white man is not precisely what some 'this' is, since thisness belongs only to substances. Therefore there is an essence only of those things whose formula is a definition. But we have a definition not where we have a word and a formula identical in meaning (for in that case all formulae or sets of words would be definitions; for there will be some name for any set of words whatever, so that even the Iliad will be a definition), but where there is a formula of something primary; and primary things are those which do not imply the predication of one element in them of another element. Nothing, then, which is not a species of a genus will have an essence – only species will have it, for these are thought to imply not merely that the subject participates in the attribute and has it as an affection, or has it by accident; but for ever thing else as well, if it has a name, there be a formula of its meaning – viz. that this attribute belongs to this subject; or instead of a simple formula we shall be able to give a more accurate one; but there will be no definition nor essence.

ἢ καὶ ὁ ὁρισμὸς ὥσπερ καὶ τὸ τί ἐστι πλεοναχῶς λέγεται; καὶ γὰρ τὸ τί ἐστιν ἕνα μὲν τρόπον σημαίνει τὴν οὐσίαν καὶ τὸ τόδε τι, ἄλλον δὲ ἕκαστον [20] τῶν κατηγορουμένων, ποσὸν ποιὸν καὶ ὅσα ἄλλα τοιαῦτα. ὥσπερ γὰρ καὶ τὸ ἔστιν ὑπάρχει πᾶσιν, ἀλλ᾽ οὐχ ὁμοίως ἀλλὰ τῷ μὲν πρώτως τοῖς δ᾽ ἑπομένως, οὕτω καὶ τὸ τί ἐστιν ἁπλῶς μὲν τῇ οὐσίᾳ πῶς δὲ τοῖς ἄλλοις: καὶ γὰρ τὸ ποιὸν ἐροίμεθ᾽ ἂν τί ἐστιν, ὥστε καὶ τὸ ποιὸν τῶν τί ἐστιν, ἀλλ᾽ [25] οὐχ ἁπλῶς, ἀλλ᾽ ὥσπερ ἐπὶ τοῦ μὴ ὄντος λογικῶς φασί τινες εἶναι τὸ μὴ ὄν, οὐχ ἁπλῶς ἀλλὰ μὴ ὄν, οὕτω καὶ τὸ ποιόν.

Aut et diffinitio sicut et quod quid est multipliciter dicitur? Et enim quod quid est uno quidem modo significat substantiam et hoc aliquid, alio vero quodcumque praedicamentorum, quantitatem, qualitatem et alia quaecumque talia. Sicut enim et le existit omnibus, sed non similiter sed huic quidem primum illis vero consequenter, ita et quod quid est simpliciter quidem substantiae aliquo vero modo aliis. Et enim qualitatem dicemus utique quid est, quare et qualitas eorum quae quid est quidem, sed non simpliciter, sed sicut de non ente logice dicunt quidam esse non ens, non simpliciter sed non ens, sic et qualitatem.

Or has 'definition', like 'what a thing is', several meanings? 'What a thing is' in one sense means substance and the 'this', in another one or other of the predicates, quantity, quality, and the like. For as 'is' belongs to all things, not however in the same sense, but to one sort of thing primarily and to others in a secondary way, so too 'what a thing is' belongs in the simple sense to substance, but in a limited sense to the other categories. For even of a quality we might ask what it is, so that quality also is a 'what a thing is', – not in the simple sense, however, but just as, in the case of that which is not, some say, emphasizing the linguistic form, that that is which is not is – not is simply, but is non-existent; so too with quality.

δεῖ μὲν οὖν σκοπεῖν καὶ τὸ πῶς δεῖ λέγειν περὶ ἕκαστον, οὐ μὴν μᾶλλόν γε ἢ τὸ πῶς ἔχει: διὸ καὶ νῦν ἐπεὶ τὸ λεγόμενον φανερόν, καὶ τὸ τί ἦν εἶναι ὁμοίως ὑπάρξει πρώτως [30] μὲν καὶ ἁπλῶς τῇ οὐσίᾳ, εἶτα καὶ τοῖς ἄλλοις, ὥσπερ καὶ τὸ τί ἐστιν, οὐχ ἁπλῶς τί ἦν εἶναι ἀλλὰ ποιῷ ἢ ποσῷ τί ἦν εἶναι. δεῖ γὰρ ἢ ὁμωνύμως ταῦτα φάναι εἶναι ὄντα, ἢ προστιθέντας καὶ ἀφαιροῦντας, ὥσπερ καὶ τὸ μὴ ἐπιστητὸν ἐπιστητόν, ἐπεὶ τό γε ὀρθόν ἐστι μήτε ὁμωνύμως φάναι [35] μήτε ὡσαύτως ἀλλ᾽ ὥσπερ τὸ ἰατρικὸν τῷ πρὸς τὸ αὐτὸ μὲν καὶ ἕν, οὐ τὸ αὐτὸ δὲ καὶ ἕν, οὐ μέντοι οὐδὲ ὁμωνύμως: [1030β] [1] οὐδὲ γὰρ ἰατρικὸν σῶμα καὶ ἔργον καὶ σκεῦος λέγεται οὔτε ὁμωνύμως οὔτε καθ᾽ ἓν ἀλλὰ πρὸς ἕν. ἀλλὰ ταῦτα μὲν ὁποτέρως τις ἐθέλει λέγειν διαφέρει οὐδέν:

Oportet quidem igitur intendere et quomodo oportet dicere circa unumquodque, non tamen quam quomodo habet. Quapropter et nunc, quoniam quod dicitur  manifestum, et quod quid erat esse similiter inerit primum quidem et simpliciter substantiae, deinde aliis, quemadmodum quid est, non simpliciter quid erat esse sed qualitati aut quantitati quid erat esse. Oportet enim equivoce haec dicere esse entia, aut addentes et auferentes, quemadmodum et quod non scibile scibile. Quoniam hoc quidem rectum est: neque  equivoce dicere neque eodem modo, sed quemadmodum  medicinale eo quod ad idem quidem et unum, non idem autem et unum, non tamen neque equivoce. Nihil enim medicativum corpus et opus et vas dicitur nec equivoce nec secundum unum, sed ad unum. Haec quidem igitur quocumque modo quis velit  dicere differet nihil.

We must no doubt inquire how we should express ourselves on each point, but certainly not more than how the facts actually stand. And so now also, since it is evident what language we use, essence will belong, just as 'what a thing is' does, primarily and in the simple sense to substance, and in a secondary way to the other categories also, – not essence in the simple sense, but the essence of a quality or of a quantity. For it must be either by an equivocation that we say these are, or by adding to and taking from the meaning of 'are' (in the way in which that which is not known may be said to be known), – the truth being that we use the word neither ambiguously nor in the same sense, but just as we apply the word 'medical' by virtue of a reference to one and the same thing, not meaning one [30b] and the same thing, nor yet speaking ambiguously; for a patient and an operation and an instrument are called medical neither by an ambiguity nor with a single meaning, but with reference to a common end. But it does not matter at all in which of the two ways one likes to describe the facts;

ἐκεῖνο δὲ φανερὸν [5] ὅτι ὁ πρώτως καὶ ἁπλῶς ὁρισμὸς καὶ τὸ τί ἦν εἶναι τῶν οὐσιῶν ἐστίν. οὐ μὴν ἀλλὰ καὶ τῶν ἄλλων ὁμοίως ἐστί, πλὴν οὐ πρώτως. οὐ γὰρ ἀνάγκη, ἂν τοῦτο τιθῶμεν, τούτου ὁρισμὸν εἶναι ὃ ἂν λόγῳ τὸ αὐτὸ σημαίνῃ, ἀλλὰ τινὶ λόγῳ: τοῦτο δὲ ἐὰν ἑνὸς ᾖ, μὴ τῷ συνεχεῖ ὥσπερ ἡ Ἰλιὰς ἢ ὅσα συνδέσμω [10] ι, ἀλλ᾽ ἐὰν ὁσαχῶς λέγεται τὸ ἕν: τὸ δ᾽ ἓν λέγεται ὥσπερ τὸ ὄν: τὸ δὲ ὂν τὸ μὲν τόδε τι τὸ δὲ ποσὸν τὸ δὲ ποιόν τι σημαίνει. διὸ καὶ λευκοῦ ἀνθρώπου ἔσται λόγος καὶ ὁρισμός, ἄλλον δὲ τρόπον καὶ τοῦ λευκοῦ καὶ οὐσίας.

Illud autem palam quia quae primo et simpliciter diffinitio et quod quid erat esse substantiarum est. Et non solum et aliorum similiter est, verumtamen non primo. Non enim est necesse, si hoc ponimus, huius diffinitionem esse quod utique rationi idem significat, sed cuidam rationi. Hoc autem si unius fuerit, non eo quod continuum sicut Ylias aut quaecumque colligatione, sed si quotiens dicitur unum. Unum vero dicitur sicut ens. Ens autem hoc quidem hoc aliquid, aliud vero quantitatem, aliud qualitatem significat. Quapropter erit albi hominis ratio et diffinitio, alio vero modo et albi et substantiae.

this is evident, that definition and essence in the primary and simple sense belong to substances. Still they belong to other things as well, only not in the primary sense. For if we suppose this it does not follow that there is a definition of every word which means the same as any formula; it must mean the same as a particular kind of formula; and this condition is satisfied if it is a formula of something which is one, not by continuity like the Iliad or the things that are one by being bound together, but in one of the main senses of 'one', which answer to the senses of 'is'; now 'that which is' in one sense denotes a 'this', in another a quantity, in another a quality. And so there can be a formula or definition even of white man, but not in the sense in which there is a definition either of white or of a substance.

*Chapter* 5

ἔχει δ᾽ ἀπορίαν, ἐάν τις μὴ φῇ ὁρισμὸν εἶναι τὸν ἐκ [15] προσθέσεως λόγον, τίνος ἔσται ὁρισμὸς τῶν οὐχ ἁπλῶν ἀλλὰ συνδεδυασμένων: ἐκ προσθέσεως γὰρ ἀνάγκη δηλοῦν. λέγω δὲ οἷον ἔστι ῥὶς καὶ κοιλότης, καὶ σιμότης τὸ ἐκ τῶν δυοῖν λεγόμενον τῷ τόδε ἐν τῷδε, καὶ οὐ κατὰ συμβεβηκός γε οὔθ᾽ ἡ κοιλότης οὔθ᾽ ἡ σιμότης πάθος τῆς ῥινός, ἀλλὰ καθ᾽ [20] αὐτήν: οὐδ᾽ ὡς τὸ λευκὸν Καλλίᾳ, ἢ ἀνθρώπῳ, ὅτι Καλλίας λευκὸς ᾧ συμβέβηκεν ἀνθρώπῳ εἶναι, ἀλλ᾽ ὡς τὸ ἄρρεν τῷ ζῴῳ καὶ τὸ ἴσον τῷ ποσῷ καὶ πάντα ὅσα λέγεται καθ᾽ αὐτὰ ὑπάρχειν. ταῦτα δ᾽ ἐστὶν ἐν ὅσοις ὑπάρχει ἢ ὁ λόγος ἢ τοὔνομα οὗ ἐστὶ τοῦτο τὸ πάθος, καὶ μὴ ἐνδέχεται δηλῶσαι [25] χωρίς, ὥσπερ τὸ λευκὸν ἄνευ τοῦ ἀνθρώπου ἐνδέχεται ἀλλ᾽ οὐ τὸ θῆλυ ἄνευ τοῦ ζῴου: ὥστε τούτων τὸ τί ἦν εἶναι καὶ ὁρισμὸς ἢ οὐκ ἔστιν οὐδενὸς ἤ, εἰ ἔστιν, ἄλλως, καθάπερ εἰρήκαμεν.

Habet autem dubitationem, si quis non dicit diffinitionem esse ex additione rationem, cuius erit diffinitio ipsorum non simplicium sed copulatorum; ex additione enim necesse palam facere. Dico autem ut est nasus et concavitas, et simitas ex duobus dictum eo quod hoc in hoc, hoc in hoc; et non secundum accidens nec concavitas neque simitas passio nasi, sed secundum se; nec ut album Calliae aut homini, quia Callias albus cui accidit hominem esse, sed ut masculinum animali et quantitate aequale et omnia quaecumque secundum se dicuntur existere. Haec autem sunt in quibusque existit aut ratio aut nomen cuius haec passio, et non contingit ostendere separatim, sicut album sine homine contingit sed non feminum sine animali. Quare horum quod quid erat esse et diffinitio aut non est alicuius aut, si est, aliter est, quemadmodum diximus.

It is a difficult question, if one denies that a formula with an added determinant is a definition, whether any of the terms that are not simple but coupled will be definable. For we must explain them by adding a determinant. E.g. there is the nose, and concavity, and snubness, which is compounded out of the two by the presence of the one in the other, and it is not by accident that the nose has the attribute either of concavity or of snubness, but in virtue of its nature; nor do they attach to it as whiteness does to Callias, or to man (because Callias, who happens to be a man, is white), but as 'male' attaches to animal and 'equal' to quantity, and as all so-called 'attributes propter se' attach to their subjects. And such attributes are those in which is involved either the formula or the name of the subject of the particular attribute, and which cannot be explained without this; e.g. white can be explained apart from man, but not female apart from animal. Therefore there is either no essence and definition of any of these things, or if there is, it is in another sense, as we have said.

ἔστι δὲ ἀπορία καὶ ἑτέρα περὶ αὐτῶν. εἰ μὲν γὰρ τὸ αὐτό ἐστι σιμὴ ῥὶς καὶ κοίλη ῥίς, τὸ αὐτὸ ἔσται τὸ σιμὸν καὶ τὸ [30] κοῖλον· εἰ δὲ μή, διὰ τὸ ἀδύνατον εἶναι εἰπεῖν τὸ σιμὸν ἄνευ τοῦ πράγματος οὗ ἐστι πάθος καθ᾽ αὑτό (ἔστι γὰρ τὸ σιμὸν κοιλότης ἐν ῥινί), τὸ ῥῖνα σιμὴν εἰπεῖν ἢ οὐκ ἔστιν ἢ δὶς τὸ αὐτὸ ἔσται εἰρημένον, ῥὶς ῥὶς κοίλη (ἡ γὰρ ῥὶς ἡ σιμὴ ῥὶς ῥὶς κοίλη ἔσται), διὸ ἄτοπον τὸ ὑπάρχειν τοῖς τοιούτοις τὸ τί [35] ἦν εἶναι· εἰ δὲ μή, εἰς ἄπειρον εἴσιν· ῥινὶ γὰρ ῥινὶ σιμῇ ἔτι ἄλλο ἐνέσται.

Est autem et alia dubitatio de eis. Si enim [/autem] idem simus nasus et concavus nasus, idem erit simum et concavum. Si vero non, quia impossibile est dicere simum sine re cuius est passio secundum se (et est simum concavitas in naso), nasum simum dicere aut non est aut bis idem erit dictum, nasus nasus concavus; nasis enim simus: nasus nasus concavus erit. Propter quod inconveniens est inesse talibus quod quid erat esse. Si autem non, in infinitum sunt; naso namque nasi, si non, adhuc aliud inerit.

But there is also a second difficulty about them. For if snub nose and concave nose are the same thing, snub and concave will be the thing; but if snub and concave are not the same (because it is impossible to speak of snubness apart from the thing of which it is an attribute propter se, for snubness is concavity-in-a-nose), either it is impossible to say 'snub nose' or the same thing will have been said twice, concave-nose nose; for snub nose will be concave-nose nose. And so it is absurd that such things should have an essence; if they have, there will be an infinite regress; for in snub-nose nose yet another 'nose' will be involved.

[1031α] [1] δῆλον τοίνυν ὅτι μόνης τῆς οὐσίας ἐστὶν ὁ ὁρισμός. εἰ γὰρ καὶ τῶν ἄλλων κατηγοριῶν, ἀνάγκη ἐκ προσθέσεως εἶναι, οἷον τοῦ ποιοῦ καὶ περιττοῦ· οὐ γὰρ ἄνευ ἀριθμοῦ, οὐδὲ τὸ θῆλυ ἄνευ ζῴου (τὸ δὲ ἐκ προσθέσεως λέγω ἐν οἷς [5] συμβαίνει δὶς τὸ αὐτὸ λέγειν ὥσπερ ἐν τούτοις). εἰ δὲ τοῦτο ἀληθές, οὐδὲ συνδυαζομένων ἔσται, οἷον ἀριθμοῦ περιττοῦ·

Palam itaque quia solius substantiae est diffinitio. Nam et si aliarum cathegoriarum, necesse est ex additione esse, ut qualitatis et imparis; non enim sine numero, nec quae est feminini sine animali. Ex additione vero dico in quibus accidit idem bis dicere, sicut in hiis. Si vero hoc verum, non copulatorum erit, ut numeri imparis;

Clearly, then, only substance is definable [31a]. For if the other categories also are definable, it must be by addition of a determinant, e.g. the qualitative is defined thus, and so is the odd, for it cannot be defined apart from number; nor can female be defined apart from animal. (When I say 'by addition' I mean the expressions in which it turns out that we are saying the same thing twice, as in these instances.) And if this is true, coupled terms also, like 'odd number', will not be definable

ἀλλὰ λανθάνει ὅτι οὐκ ἀκριβῶς λέγονται οἱ λόγοι. εἰ δ᾽ εἰσὶ καὶ τούτων ὅροι, ἤτοι ἄλλον τρόπον εἰσὶν ἢ καθάπερ ἐλέχθη πολλαχῶς λεκτέον εἶναι τὸν ὁρισμὸν καὶ τὸ τί ἦν [10] εἶναι, ὥστε ὡδὶ μὲν οὐδενὸς ἔσται ὁρισμὸς οὐδὲ τὸ τί ἦν εἶναι οὐδενὶ ὑπάρξει πλὴν ταῖς οὐσίαις, ὡδὶ δ᾽ ἔσται. ὅτι μὲν οὖν ἐστιν ὁ ὁρισμὸς ὁ τοῦ τί ἦν εἶναι λόγος, καὶ τὸ τί ἦν εἶναι ἢ μόνων τῶν οὐσιῶν ἐστιν ἢ μάλιστα καὶ πρώτως καὶ ἁπλῶς, δῆλον. [15]

sed latet, quia non certe dicuntur rationes. Si vero sunt et horum termini, aut alio modo sunt aut, quemadmodum dictum est, multipliciter oportet dicere esse diffinitionem et quid erat esse. Quare sic quidem nullius erit diffinitio nec quid erat esse alicui inerit nisi substantiis, sic autem erit. Quod quidem igitur est diffinitio quae ipsius quid erat esse ratio, et quid erat esse aut solum substantiarum est aut maximeet primum et simpliciter, palam.

but this escapes our notice because our formulae are not accurate.). But if these also are definable, either it is in some other way or, as we definition and essence must be said to have more than one sense. Therefore in one sense nothing will have a definition and nothing will have an essence, except substances, but in another sense other things will have them. Clearly, then, definition is the formula of the essence, and essence belongs to substances either alone or chiefly and primarily and in the unqualified sense.

*Chapter* 6

πότερον δὲ ταὐτόν ἐστιν ἢ ἕτερον τὸ τί ἦν εἶναι καὶ ἕκαστον, σκεπτέον. ἔστι γάρ τι πρὸ ἔργου πρὸς τὴν περὶ τῆς οὐσίας σκέψιν·

Utrum autem idem est aut alterum quod quid erat esse et unumquodque, perscrutandum est Est enim aliquid pre opere ad de substantia perscrutationem.

We must inquire whether each thing and its essence are the same or different. This is of some use for the inquiry concerning substance;

ἕκαστόν τε γὰρ οὐκ ἄλλο δοκεῖ εἶναι τῆς ἑαυτοῦ οὐσίας, καὶ τὸ τί ἦν εἶναι λέγεται εἶναι ἡ ἑκάστου οὐσία.

Singulum enim non aliud videtur esse a suimet substantia, et quod quid erat esse dicitur singuli substantia.

for each thing is thought to be not different from its substance, and the essence is said to be the substance of each thing.

ἐπὶ μὲν δὴ τῶν λεγομένων κατὰ συμβεβηκὸς δόξειεν ἂν [20] ἕτερον εἶναι, οἷον λευκὸς ἄνθρωπος ἕτερον καὶ τὸ λευκῷ ἀνθρώπῳ εἶναι (εἰ γὰρ τὸ αὐτό, καὶ τὸ ἀνθρώπῳ εἶναι καὶ τὸ λευκῷ ἀνθρώπῳ τὸ αὐτό· τὸ αὐτὸ γὰρ ἄνθρωπος καὶ λευκὸς ἄνθρωπος, ὡς φασίν, ὥστε καὶ τὸ λευκῷ ἀνθρώπῳ καὶ τὸ ἀνθρώπῳ· ἢ οὐκ ἀνάγκη ὅσα κατὰ συμβεβηκὸς εἶναι [25] ταὐτά, οὐ γὰρ ὡσαύτως τὰ ἄκρα γίγνεται ταὐτά· ἀλλ᾽ ἴσως γε ἐκεῖνο δόξειεν ἂν συμβαίνειν, τὰ ἄκρα γίγνεσθαι ταὐτὰ τὰ κατὰ συμβεβηκός, οἷον τὸ λευκῷ εἶναι καὶ τὸ μουσικῷ·

In dictis quidem itaque secundum accidens videbitur utique diversum esse, ut albus homo alterum et albo homini esse. Si enim idem, homini esse et albo homini idem; idem enim homo et albus homo, ut dicunt; quare et albo homini et homini. Aut non necesse est quaecumque secundum accidens esse eadem; non enim similiter extremitates fiunt eedem. Sed forsan illud videtur accidere: extremitates fieri easdem secundum accidens, ut albo esse et musico; videtur autem non.

Now in the case of accidental unities the two would be generally thought to be different, e.g. white man would be thought to be different from the essence of white man. For if they are the same, the essence of man and that of white man are also the same; for a man and a white man are the same thing, as people say, so that the essence of white man and that of man would be also the same. But perhaps it does not follow that the essence of accidental unities should be the same as that of the simple terms. For the extreme terms are not in the same way identical with the middle term. But perhaps this might be thought to follow, that the extreme terms, the accidents, should turn out to be the same, e.g. the essence of white and that of musical; but this is not actually thought to be the case.

δοκεῖ δὲ οὔ): ἐπὶ δὲ τῶν καθ᾽ αὑτὰ λεγομένων ἆρ᾽ ἀνάγκη ταὐτὸ εἶναι, οἷον εἴ τινες εἰσὶν οὐσίαι ὧν ἕτεραι [30] μὴ εἰσὶν οὐσίαι μηδὲ φύσεις ἕτεραι πρότεραι, οἵας φασὶ τὰς ἰδέας εἶναί τινες; εἰ γὰρ ἔσται ἕτερον αὐτὸ τὸ ἀγαθὸν καὶ τὸ ἀγαθῷ εἶναι, καὶ ζῷον καὶ τὸ ζῴῳ, καὶ τὸ ὄντι καὶ τὸ ὄν, [1031β] [1] ἔσονται ἄλλαι τε οὐσίαι καὶ φύσεις καὶ ἰδέαι παρὰ τὰς λεγομένας, καὶ πρότεραι οὐσίαι ἐκεῖναι, εἰ τὸ τί ἦν εἶναι οὐσία ἐστίν.

In dictis vero secundum se semper necesse idem esse, ut si quae sunt substantiae a quibus alterae non sunt substantiae nec alterae naturae priores, quales dicunt ydeas esse quidam. Si enim erit alterum ipsum bonum et quod bono esse, animal et quod animali et ens quod enti, erunt aliae substantiae et naturae et ydee praeter dictas, et priores substantiae illae, si quod quid erat esse substantiae est.

But in the case of so-called self-subsistent things, is a thing necessarily the same as its essence? E.g. if there are some substances which have no other substances nor entities prior to them – substances such as some assert the Ideas to be? – If the essence of good is to be different from good-itself, and the essence of animal from animal-itself, and the essence of being from being-itself [31b], there will, firstly, be other substances and entities and Ideas besides those which are asserted, and, secondly, these others will be prior substances, if essence is substance.

καὶ εἰ μὲν ἀπολελυμέναι ἀλλήλων, τῶν μὲν οὐκ ἔσται ἐπιστήμη τὰ δ᾽ οὐκ ἔσται ὄντα (λέγω δὲ τὸ ἀπολελύσθαι [5] εἰ μήτε τῷ ἀγαθῷ αὐτῷ ὑπάρχει τὸ εἶναι ἀγαθῷ μήτε τούτῳ τὸ εἶναι ἀγαθόν): ἐπιστήμη τε γὰρ ἑκάστου ἔστιν ὅταν τὸ τί ἦν ἐκείνῳ εἶναι γνῶμεν, καὶ ἐπὶ ἀγαθοῦ καὶ τῶν ἄλλων ὁμοίως ἔχει, ὥστε εἰ μηδὲ τὸ ἀγαθῷ εἶναι ἀγαθόν, οὐδὲ τὸ ὄντι ὂν οὐδὲ τὸ ἑνὶ ἕν: ὁμοίως δὲ πάντα ἔστιν ἢ οὐθὲν τὰ [10] τί ἦν εἶναι, ὥστ᾽ εἰ μηδὲ τὸ ὄντι ὄν, οὐδὲ τῶν ἄλλων οὐδέν. ἔτι ᾧ μὴ ὑπάρχει ἀγαθῷ εἶναι, οὐκ ἀγαθόν.

Et si quidem absolute ab invicem, harum quidem non erit scientia, haec autem non erunt entia. (Dico autem absolvi, si nec bono ipsi existit esse bono nec huic esse bonum). Scientia enim cuiuslibet haec: quod quid erat illi esse. Et in bono et in aliis similiter se habet; quare si nec bono esse bonum, nec quod enti ens nec quod uni unum. Similiter autem omnia sunt aut nullum quae quid erat esse; quare si neque quod enti ens, nec aliorum nullum. Amplius cui non inest bono esse, non bonum.

And if the posterior substances and the prior are severed from each other, (a) there will be no knowledge of the former, and (b) the latter will have no being. (By 'severed' I mean, if the good-itself has not the essence of good, and the latter has not

255

the property of being good.) For (a) there is knowledge of each thing only when we know its essence. And (b) the case is the same for other things as for the good; so that if the essence of good is not good, neither is the essence of reality real, nor the essence of unity one. And all essences alike exist or none of them does; so that if the essence of reality is not real, neither is any of the others. Again, that to which the essence of good does not belong is not good.

ἀνάγκη ἄρα ἓν εἶναι τὸ ἀγαθὸν καὶ ἀγαθῷ εἶναι καὶ καλὸν καὶ καλῷ εἶναι, <καὶ ὅσα μὴ κατ᾽ ἄλλο λέγεται, ἀλλὰ καθ᾽ αὑτὰ καὶ πρῶτα: καὶ γὰρ τοῦτο ἱκανὸν ἂν ὑπάρχῃ, κἂν μὴ ᾖ εἴδη, [15] μᾶλλον δ᾽ ἴσως κἂν ᾖ εἴδη (ἅμα δὲ δῆλον καὶ ὅτι εἴπερ εἰσὶν αἱ ἰδέαι οἵας τινές φασιν, οὐκ ἔσται τὸ ὑποκείμενον οὐσία: ταύτας γὰρ οὐσίας μὲν ἀναγκαῖον εἶναι, μὴ καθ᾽ ὑποκειμένου δέ: ἔσονται γὰρ κατὰ μέθεξιν). ἔκ τε δὴ τούτων τῶν λόγων ἓν καὶ ταὐτὸ οὐ κατὰ συμβεβηκὸς αὐτὸ ἕκαστον [20] καὶ τὸ τί ἦν εἶναι, καὶ ὅτι γε τὸ ἐπίστασθαι ἕκαστον τοῦτό ἐστι, τὸ τί ἦν εἶναι ἐπίστασθαι, ὥστε καὶ κατὰ τὴν ἔκθεσιν ἀνάγκη ἕν τι εἶναι ἄμφω

Necesse igitur unum esse benignum et benigno esse et bonum et bono esse, quaecumque non secundum aliud dicuntur, sed prima et secundum se. Et enim hoc sufficiens si extiterit, quamquam non sint species; magis autem forsan et si sint species. Simulque palam quia si sunt ydee quales quidam dicunt, non erit subiectum substantia. Has enim substantias esse est necesse, non de subiecto autem; erunt enim secundum participationem. Ex hiis itaque rationibus unum et idem non secundum accidens ipsum unumquodque et quod quid erat esse, et quod scire unumquodque horum est quod quid erat esse scire; quare secundum expositionem necesse unum aliquid esse ambo.

The good, then, must be one with the essence of good, and the beautiful with the essence of beauty, and so with all things which do not depend on something else but are self-subsistent and primary. For it is enough if they are this, even if they are not Forms; or rather, perhaps, even if they are Forms. (At the same time it is clear that if there are Ideas such as some people say there are, it will not be substratum that is substance; for these must be substances, but not predicable of a substratum; for if they were they would exist only by being participated in.) Each thing itself, then, and its essence are one and the same in no merely accidental way, as is evident both from the preceding arguments and because to know each thing, at least, is just to know its essence, so that even by the exhibition of instances it becomes clear that both must be one.

(τὸ δὲ κατὰ συμβεβηκὸς λεγόμενον, οἷον τὸ μουσικὸν ἢ λευκόν, διὰ τὸ διττὸν σημαίνειν [24] οὐκ ἀληθὲς εἰπεῖν ὡς ταὐτὸ τὸ τί ἦν εἶναι καὶ αὐτό: καὶ [25] γὰρ ᾧ συμβέβηκε λευκὸν καὶ τὸ συμβεβηκός, ὥστ᾽ ἔστι μὲν ὡς ταὐτόν, ἔστι δὲ ὡς οὐ ταὐτὸ τὸ τί ἦν εἶναι καὶ αὐτό: τῷ μὲν γὰρ ἀνθρώπῳ καὶ τῷ λευκῷ ἀνθρώπῳ οὐ ταὐτό, τῷ πάθει δὲ ταὐτό).

Secundum accidens vero dictum, ut musicum aut album, propter duplex signficare non est verum dicere quia idem quod quid erat esse et ipsum. Et enim cui accidit album  et accidens, quare est quidem ut idem, est autem ut non idem  quod quid erat esse et ipsum; nam homini et albo homini non idem, passioni autem idem.

(But of an accidental term, e.g.'the musical' or 'the white', since it has two meanings, it is not true to say that it itself is identical with its essence; for both that to which the accidental quality belongs, and the accidental quality, are white, so that in a sense the accident and its essence are the same, and in a sense they are not; for the essence of white is not the same as the man or the white man, but it is the same as the attribute white.)

ἄτοπον δ᾽ ἂν φανείη κἂν εἴ τις ἑκάστῳ ὄνομα θεῖτο τῶν τί ἦν εἶναι: ἔσται γὰρ καὶ παρ᾽ ἐκεῖνο [30] ἄλλο, οἷον τῷ τί ἦν εἶναι ἵππῳ τί ἦν εἶναι [ἵππῳ] ἕτερον. καίτοι τί κωλύει καὶ νῦν εἶναι ἔνια εὐθὺς τί ἦν εἶναι, εἴπερ οὐσία τὸ τί ἦν εἶναι; ἀλλὰ μὴν οὐ μόνον ἕν, ἀλλὰ καὶ ὁ λόγος ὁ αὐτὸς αὐτῶν, ὡς δῆλον καὶ ἐκ τῶν εἰρημένων: [1032α] [1] οὐ γὰρ κατὰ συμβεβηκὸς ἓν τὸ ἑνὶ εἶναι καὶ ἕν.

Absurdum vero apparebit et si quis unicuique nomen  imposuerit ipsorum quid erat esse. Erit enim et praeter illud aliud ei quod quid erat esse equo: ipsi quod quid erat esse equo alterum. Et quid prohibet et nunc esse quaedam statim quid erat esse, siquidem substantia est quod quid erat esse? At vero  non solum unum, sed et ratio eadem ipsorum, sicut palam est ex dictis; non enim secundum accidens unum quod uni esse et unum.

The absurdity of the separation would appear also if one were to assign a name to each of the essences; for there would be yet another essence besides the original one, e.g. to the essence of horse there will belong a second essence. Yet why should not some things be their essences from the start, since essence is substance? But indeed not only are a thing and its essence one, but the formula of them is also [32a] the same, as is clear even from what has been said; for it is not by accident that the essence of one, and the one, are one.

ἔτι εἰ ἄλλο ἔσται, εἰς ἄπειρον εἶσιν: τὸ μὲν γὰρ ἔσται τί ἦν εἶναι τοῦ ἑνὸς τὸ δὲ τὸ ἕν, ὥστε καὶ ἐπ᾽ ἐκείνων ὁ αὐτὸς ἔσται λόγος. ὅτι [5] μὲν οὖν ἐπὶ τῶν πρώτων καὶ καθ᾽ αὑτὰ λεγομένων τὸ ἑκάστῳ εἶναι καὶ ἕκαστον τὸ αὐτὸ καὶ ἕν ἐστι, δῆλον:

Amplius si aliud erit, in infinitum sunt; hoc quidem erit quid erat esse le uni esse illud vero unum,  quare et in illis erit eadem ration. Quod quidem igitur in primis et secundum se dictis unicuique esse et unumquodque idem et unum, palam.

Further, if they are to be different, the process will go on to infinity; for we shall have (1) the essence of one, and (2) the one, so that to terms of the former kind the same argument will be applicable. Clearly, then, each primary and self-subsistent thing is one and the same as its essence.

οἱ δὲ σοφιστικοὶ ἔλεγχοι πρὸς τὴν θέσιν ταύτην φανερὸν ὅτι τῇ αὐτῇ λύονται λύσει καὶ εἰ ταὐτὸ Σωκράτης καὶ Σωκράτει εἶναι· οὐδὲν γὰρ διαφέρει οὔτε ἐξ ὧν ἐρωτήσειεν ἄν τις οὔτε ἐξ ὧν [10] λύων ἐπιτύχοι. πῶς μὲν οὖν τὸ τί ἦν εἶναι ταὐτὸν καὶ πῶς οὐ ταὐτὸν ἑκάστῳ, εἴρηται.

Sophisti autem elenchi ad positionem hanc palam quod eadem solvuntur solutione, et si idem Socrates et Socrati esse; nihil enim differt  nec ex quibus interrogabit utique aliquis nec ex quibus solvens fuerit. Quomodo quidem igitur quod quid erat esse idem et quomodo non idem unicuique, dictum est.

The sophistical objections to this position, and the question whether Socrates and to be Socrates are the same thing, are obviously answered by the same solution; for there is no difference either in the standpoint from which the question would be asked, or in that from which one could answer it successfully. We have explained, then, in what sense each thing is the same as its essence and in what sense it is not.

*Chapter* 7

τῶν δὲ γιγνομένων τὰ μὲν φύσει γίγνεται τὰ δὲ τέχνῃ τὰ δὲ ἀπὸ ταὐτομάτου,

Eorum autem quae fiunt haec quidem natura fiunt haec autem arte alia autem casu.

Of things that come to be, some come to be by nature, some by art, some spontaneously.

πάντα δὲ τὰ γιγνόμενα ὑπό τέ τινος γίγνεται καὶ ἔκ τινος καὶ τί· τὸ δὲ τὶ λέγω καθ᾽ [15] ἑκάστην κατηγορίαν· ἢ γὰρ τόδε ἢ ποσὸν ἢ ποιὸν ἢ πού.

Omnia vero quae fiunt ab aliquo fiunt et ex aliquo et aliquid. Hoc autem aliquid dico  secundum quamlibet cathegoriam; aut enim hoc aut quantum aut quale aut quando.

Now everything that comes to be comes to be by the agency of something and from something and comes to be something. And the something which I say it comes to be may be found in any category; it may come to be either a 'this' or of some size or of some quality or somewhere.

αἱ δὲ γενέσεις αἱ μὲν φυσικαὶ αὗταί εἰσιν ὧν ἡ γένεσις ἐκ φύσεώς ἐστιν,

Et generationes autem naturales quidem hee sunt quarum generatio ex natura est.

Now natural comings to be are the comings to be of those things which come to be by nature;

τὸ δ᾽ ἐξ οὗ γίγνεται, ἣν λέγομεν ὕλην, τὸ δὲ ὑφ᾽ οὗ τῶν φύσει τι ὄντων, τὸ δὲ τὶ ἄνθρωπος ἢ φυτὸν ἢ ἄλλο τι τῶν τοιούτων, ἃ δὴ μάλιστα λέγομεν οὐσίας εἶναι

Hoc autem ex quo fit, quam dicimus materiam; hoc autem a quo eorum quae natura aliquid sunt; hoc autem aliquid homo aut planta aut aliud quid talium, quae maxime dicimus substantias esse.

and that out of which they come to be is what we call matter; and that by which they come to be is something which exists naturally; and the something which they come to be is a man or a plant or one of the things of this kind, which we say are substances if anything is –

[20] —ἅπαντα δὲ τὰ γιγνόμενα ἢ φύσει ἢ τέχνῃ ἔχει ὕλην· δυνατὸν γὰρ καὶ εἶναι καὶ μὴ εἶναι ἕκαστον αὐτῶν, τοῦτο δ᾽ ἐστὶν ἡ ἐν ἑκάστῳ ὕλη—

Omnia vero quae fiunt aut natura aut arte habent materiam; possibile enim et esse et non esse eorum quodlibet, hoc autem est quae in unoquoque materia.

all things produced either by nature or by art have matter; for each of them is capable both of being and of not being, and this capacity is the matter in each –

καθόλου δὲ καὶ ἐξ οὗ φύσις καὶ καθ᾽ ὃ φύσις (τὸ γὰρ γιγνόμενον ἔχει φύσιν, οἷον φυτὸν ἢ ζῷον) καὶ ὑφ᾽ οὗ ἡ κατὰ τὸ εἶδος λεγομένη φύσις ἡ ὁμοειδής [25] (αὕτη δὲ ἐν ἄλλῳ)· ἄνθρωπος γὰρ ἄνθρωπον γεννᾷ· οὕτω μὲν οὖν γίγνεται τὰ γιγνόμενα διὰ τὴν φύσιν,

Universaliter vero et ex quo natura et secundum quod natura (factum enim habet naturam, ut planta aut animal) et a quo quae secundum speciem dicta natura quae eiusdem speciei (haec autem in alio); homo namque hominem generat. Sic quidem igitur fiunt quae fiunt propter naturam.

and, in general, both that from which they are produced is nature, and the type according to which they are produced is nature (for that which is produced, e.g. a plant or an animal, has a nature), and so is that by which they are produced—the so-called 'formal' nature, which is specifically the same (though this is in another individual); for man begets man. Thus, then, are natural products produced;

αἱ δ᾽ ἄλλαι γενέσεις λέγονται ποιήσεις. πᾶσαι δὲ εἰσὶν αἱ ποιήσεις ἢ ἀπὸ τέχνης ἢ ἀπὸ δυνάμεως ἢ ἀπὸ διανοίας. τούτων δέ τινες γίγνονται καὶ ἀπὸ ταὐτομάτου καὶ ἀπὸ τύχης παραπλησίως [30] ὥσπερ ἐν τοῖς ἀπὸ φύσεως γιγνομένοις· ἔνια γὰρ κἀκεῖ ταὐτὰ καὶ ἐκ σπέρματος γίγνεται καὶ ἄνευ σπέρματος. περὶ μὲν οὖν τούτων ὕστερον ἐπισκεπτέον,

Generationes vero aliae dicuntur factiones. Omnes autem factiones sunt aut ab arte aut a potestate aut a mente. Harum autem quaedam fiunt et a casu et a fortuna, similiter ut in factis a natura; quaedam enim et illic eadem et ex spermate fiunt et sine spermate. De hiis quidem igitur posterius perscrutandam.

All other productions are called 'makings'. And all makings proceed either from art or from a faculty or from thought. Some of them happen also spontaneously or by luck just as natural products sometimes do; for there also the same things sometimes are produced without seed as well as from seed. Concerning these cases, then, we must inquire later,

[1032β] [1] ἀπὸ τέχνης δὲ γίγνεται ὅσων τὸ εἶδος ἐν τῇ ψυχῇ (εἶδος δὲ λέγω τὸ τί ἦν εἶναι ἑκάστου καὶ τὴν πρώτην οὐσίαν)· καὶ γὰρ τῶν ἐναντίων τρόπον τινὰ τὸ αὐτὸ εἶδος· τῆς γὰρ στερήσεως οὐσία ἡ οὐσία ἡ ἀντικειμένη, οἷον ὑγίεια νόσου, ἐκείνης γὰρ ἀπουσία [5] ἡ νόσος, ἡ δὲ ὑγίεια ὁ ἐν τῇ ψυχῇ λόγος καὶ ἡ ἐπιστήμη.

Ab arte vero fiunt quorumcumque species est in anima. Speciem autem dico quid erat esse cuiusque et primam substantiam. Et enim contrariorum modo quodam eadem species. Privationis enim substantia quae substantiae opposita, ut sanitas infirmitatis; illius enim absentia ostenditur infirmitas, sanitas autem quae in anima ratio et in scientia.

but from art proceed the things of which the form is in the soul of the artist. (By form I mean the essence of each [32b] thing and its primary substance.) For even contraries have in a sense the same form; for the substance of a privation is the opposite substance, e.g. health is the substance of disease (for disease is the absence of health); and health is the formula in the soul or the knowledge of it.

γίγνεται δὲ τὸ ὑγιὲς νοήσαντος οὕτως· ἐπειδὴ τοδὶ ὑγίεια, ἀνάγκη εἰ ὑγιὲς ἔσται τοδὶ ὑπάρξαι, οἷον ὁμαλότητα, εἰ δὲ τοῦτο, θερμότητα· καὶ οὕτως ἀεὶ νοεῖ, ἕως ἂν ἀγάγῃ εἰς τοῦτο ὃ αὐτὸς δύναται ἔσχατον ποιεῖν. εἶτα ἤδη [10] ἡ ἀπὸ τούτου κίνησις ποίησις καλεῖται, ἡ ἐπὶ τὸ ὑγιαίνειν. ὥστε συμβαίνει τρόπον τινὰ τὴν ὑγίειαν ἐξ ὑγιείας γίγνεσθαι καὶ τὴν οἰκίαν ἐξ οἰκίας, τῆς ἄνευ ὕλης τὴν ἔχουσαν ὕλην· ἡ γὰρ ἰατρικὴ ἐστι καὶ ἡ οἰκοδομικὴ τὸ εἶδος τῆς ὑγιείας καὶ τῆς οἰκίας, λέγω δὲ οὐσίαν ἄνευ ὕλης τὸ τί ἦν εἶναι.

Fit itaque sanitas intelligente ita: quoniam hoc sanitas, necesse si sanitas erit, hoc existere, puta regularitatem, sed si hoc, calorem; et ita semper intelligit, donec utique adducat in hod quod ipse valet ultimum facere. Deinde iam ab hoc motus factio vocatur ad sanandum. Quare accidit modo quodam ex sanitate sanitatem fieri et domum ex domo, sine materia materiam habentem; medicinalis enim ese et aedificatoria species sanitatis et domus, dico autem substantiam sine materia quod quid erat esse.

The healthy subject is produced as the result of the following train of thought: – since this is health, if the subject is to be healthy this must first be present, e.g. a uniform state of body, and if this is to be present, there must be heat; and the physician goes on thinking thus until he reduces the matter to a final something which he himself can produce. Then the process from this point onward, i.e. the process towards health, is called a 'making'. Therefore it follows that in a sense health comes from health and house from house, that with matter from that without matter; for the medical art and the building art are the form of health and of the house, and when I speak of substance without matter I mean the essence.

[15] τῶν δὴ γενέσεων καὶ κινήσεων ἡ μὲν νόησις καλεῖται ἡ δὲ ποίησις, ἡ μὲν ἀπὸ τῆς ἀρχῆς καὶ τοῦ εἴδους νόησις ἡ δ᾽ ἀπὸ τοῦ τελευταίου τῆς νοήσεως ποίησις. ὁμοίως δὲ καὶ τῶν ἄλλων τῶν μεταξὺ ἕκαστον γίγνεται. λέγω δ᾽ οἷον εἰ ὑγιανεῖ, δέοι ἂν ὁμαλυνθῆναι. τί οὖν ἐστὶ τὸ ὁμαλυνθῆναι; τοδί, [20] τοῦτο δ᾽ ἔσται εἰ θερμανθήσεται. τοῦτο δὲ τί ἐστι; τοδί. ὑπάρχει δὲ τοδὶ δυνάμει· τοῦτο δὲ ἤδη ἐπ᾽ αὐτῷ. τὸ δὴ ποιοῦν καὶ ὅθεν ἄρχεται ἡ κίνησις τοῦ ὑγιαίνειν, ἂν μὲν ἀπὸ τέχνης, τὸ εἶδός ἐστι τὸ ἐν τῇ ψυχῇ,

Generationum vero et motuum haec quidem intelligentia vocatur illa vero factio. Quae quidem a principio et a specie intelligentia, quae vero ab ultimo intelligentiae factio. Similiter autem et in aliis intermediis unumquodque fit. Dico autem ut si convalescit, oportet adaequari. Quid igitur est adaequari? Hoc. Hoc autem erit, si calefactum fuerit. Hoc vero quid est? Hoc. Existit autem hoc potestate; hoc autem iam in ipso. Faciens itaque et unde inchoat motus sanandi, si quidem ab arte, species est quae in anima;

Of the productions or processes one part is called thinking and the other making, – that which proceeds from the starting-point and the form is thinking, and that which proceeds from the final step of the thinking is making. And each of the other, intermediate, things is produced in the same way. I mean, for instance, if the subject is to be healthy his bodily state must be made uniform. What then does being made uniform imply? This or that. And this depends on his being made warm. What does this imply? Something else. And this something is present potentially; and what is present potentially is already in the physician's power.The active principle then and the starting point for the process of becoming healthy is, if it happens by art, the form in the soul,

ἐὰν δ' ἀπὸ ταὐτομάτου, ἀπὸ τούτου ὅ ποτε τοῦ ποιεῖν ἄρχει τῷ ποιοῦντι ἀπὸ [25] τέχνης, ὥσπερ καὶ ἐν τῷ ἰατρεύειν ἴσως ἀπὸ τοῦ θερμαίνειν ἡ ἀρχή (τοῦτο δὲ ποιεῖ τῇ τρίψει): ἡ θερμότης τοίνυν ἡ ἐν τῷ σώματι ἢ μέρος τῆς ὑγιείας ἢ ἔπεταί τι αὐτῇ τοιοῦτον ὅ ἐστι μέρος τῆς ὑγιείας, ἢ διὰ πλειόνων: τοῦτο δ' ἔσχατόν ἐστι, τὸ ποιοῦν τὸ μέρος τῆς ὑγιείας, καὶ τῆς οἰκίας [30] (οἷον οἱ λίθοι) καὶ τῶν ἄλλων:

si vero a casu, ab hoc quod quidem faciendi est principium facienti ab arte, ut quod in mederi forsam a calefactione principium; hoc autem facit fricatione. Calor itaque in corpore aut pars est sanitatis aut sequitur eum aliquid tale quod est pars sanitatis, aut per plura; hoc autem ultimum faciens, et quod est ita, pars est sanitatis et domus (ut lapides) et aliorum.

and if spontaneously, it is that, whatever it is, which starts the making, for the man who makes by art, as in healing the starting-point is perhaps the production of warmth (and this the physician produces by rubbing). Warmth in the body, then, is either a part of health or is followed (either directly or through several intermediate steps) by something similar which is a part of health; and this, viz. that which produces the part of health, is the limiting-point—and so too with a house (the stones are the limiting-point here) and in all other cases.

ὥστε, καθάπερ λέγεται, ἀδύνατον γενέσθαι εἰ μηδὲν προϋπάρχοι. ὅτι μὲν οὖν τι μέρος ἐξ ἀνάγκης ὑπάρξει φανερόν: ἡ γὰρ ὕλη μέρος (ἐνυπάρχει γὰρ καὶ γίγνεται αὕτη). [1033a] [1] ἀλλ' ἄρα καὶ τῶν ἐν τῷ λόγῳ; ἀμφοτέρως δὴ λέγομεν τοὺς χαλκοῦς κύκλους τί εἰσι, καὶ τὴν ὕλην λέγοντες ὅτι χαλκός, καὶ τὸ εἶδος ὅτι σχῆμα τοιόνδε, καὶ τοῦτό ἐστι τὸ γένος εἰς ὃ πρῶτον τίθεται. ὁ δὴ [5] χαλκοῦς κύκλος ἔχει ἐν τῷ λόγῳ τὴν ὕλην.

Quare, sicut dicitur, impossibile factum esse, si nihil praeextiterit. Quod quidem igitur pars ex necessitate existet, palam; materia namque pars, inest enim et fit haec. Sed igitur et eorum quae in ratione. Utroque autem modo dicimus multos circulos quid sunt: et materiam dicentes quia es, et speciem quia talis, et hoc est genus in quod primum ponitur. Aereus itaque circulus habet in ratione materiam.

Therefore, as the saying goes, it is impossible that anything should be produced if there were nothing existing before. Obviously then some part of the result will pre-exist of necessity; for the matter is a part; for this is present in the process and it is this that becomes [33a] something. But is the matter an element even in the formula? We certainly describe in both ways what brazen circles are; we describe both the matter by saying it is brass, and the form by saying that it is such and such a figure; and figure is the proximate genus in which it is placed. The brazen circle, then, has its matter in its formula.

ἐξ οὗ δὲ ὡς ὕλης γίγνεται ἔνια λέγεται, ὅταν γένηται, οὐκ ἐκεῖνο ἀλλ᾽ ἐκείνινον, οἷον ὁ ἀνδριὰς οὐ λίθος ἀλλὰ λίθινος, ὁ δὲ ἄνθρωπος ὁ ὑγιαίνων οὐ λέγεται ἐκεῖνο ἐξ οὗ· αἴτιον δὲ ὅτι γίγνεται ἐκ τῆς στερήσεως καὶ τοῦ ὑποκειμένου, ὃ λέγομεν τὴν [10] ὕλην (οἷον καὶ ὁ ἄνθρωπος καὶ ὁ κάμνων γίγνεται ὑγιής), μᾶλλον μέντοι λέγεται γίγνεσθαι ἐκ τῆς στερήσεως, οἷον ἐκ κάμνοντος ὑγιὴς ἢ ἐξ ἀνθρώπου, διὸ κάμνων μὲν ὁ ὑγιὴς οὐ λέγεται, ἄνθρωπος δέ, καὶ ὁ ἄνθρωπος ὑγιής· ὧν δ᾽ ἡ στέρησις ἄδηλος καὶ ἀνώνυμος, οἷον ἐν χαλκῷ σχήματος ὁποιουοῦν ἢ [15] ἐν πλίνθοις καὶ ξύλοις οἰκίας, ἐκ τούτων δοκεῖ γίγνεσθαι ὡς ἐκεῖ ἐκ κάμνοντος· διὸ ὥσπερ οὐδ᾽ ἐκεῖ ἐξ οὗ τοῦτο, ἐκεῖνο οὐ λέγεται, οὐδ᾽ ἐνταῦθα ὁ ἀνδριὰς ξύλον, ἀλλὰ παράγεται ξύλινος, [οὐ ξύλον,] καὶ χαλκοῦς ἀλλ᾽ οὐ χαλκός, καὶ λίθινος ἀλλ᾽ οὐ λίθος, καὶ ἡ οἰκία πλινθίνη ἀλλ᾽ οὐ πλίνθοι, ἐπεὶ οὐδὲ [20] ὡς ἐκ ξύλου γίγνεται ἀνδριὰς ἢ ἐκ πλίνθων οἰκία, ἐάν τις ἐπιβλέπῃ σφόδρα, οὐκ ἂν ἁπλῶς εἴπειεν, διὰ τὸ δεῖν μεταβάλλοντος γίγνεσθαι ἐξ οὗ, ἀλλ᾽ οὐχ ὑπομένοντος. διὰ μὲν οὖν τοῦτο οὕτως λέγεται.

Ex quo vero ut materia fit quaedam dicuntur, quando fiunt, non illud sed illius modi; ut statua non lapis sed lapidea, homo autem convalescens non dicitur illud ex quo. Causa vero quia fit ex privatione et subiecto, quod dicimus materiam, ut et homo et laborens fit sanus. Magis tamen dicimus fieri ex privatione, ut ex laborante sanus quam ex homine; propter quod laborens quidem qui sanus non dicitur, sed homo, et homo sanus. Quorum vero privatio non manifesta et innominabilis, ut in aere figurae cuiuslibet aut in lateribus et lignis domus, ex hiis videtur fieri ut illic ex laborante. Propter quod sicut nec ibi ex quo hoc, illud non dicitur, nec hic statua lignum, sed producitur lignea, non lignum, et enea, non es, et lapidea sed non lapis, et domus latericia sed non lateres. Quoniam neque quod ex ligno fit statua aut ex lateribus domus, si quis valde inspexerit, non utique simpliciter dicet, quia oportet permutato fieri ex quo, sed non permanente. Propter hoc quidem igitur ita dicitur.

As for that out of which as matter they are produced, some things are said, when they have been produced, to be not that but 'thaten'; e.g. the statue is not gold but golden. And a healthy man is not said to be that from which he has come. The reason is that though a thing comes both from its privation and from its substratum, which we call its matter (e.g. what becomes healthy is both a man and an invalid), it is said to come rather from its privation (e.g. it is from an invalid rather than from a man that a healthy subject is produced). And so the healthy subject is not said to he an invalid, but to be a man, and the man is said to be healthy. But as for the things whose privation is obscure and nameless, e.g. in brass the privation of a particular shape or in bricks and timber the privation of arrangement as a house, the thing is thought to be produced from these materials, as in the former case the healthy man is produced from an invalid. And so, as there also a thing is not said to be that from which it comes, here the statue is not said to be wood but is said by a verbal change to be wooden, not brass but brazen, not gold but golden, and the house is said to be not bricks but bricken (though we should not say without qualification, if we looked at the matter carefully, even that a statue is produced from wood or a house from bricks, because coming to be implies change in that from which a thing comes to be, and not permanence). It is for this reason, then, that we use this way of speaking.

*Chapter*  8

ἐπεὶ δὲ ὑπό τινός τε γίγνεται τὸ γιγνόμενον (τοῦτο δὲ [25] λέγω ὅθεν ἡ ἀρχὴ τῆς γενέσεώς ἐστι) καὶ ἔκ τινος (ἔστω δὲ μὴ ἡ στέρησις τοῦτο ἀλλ᾽ ἡ ὕλη· ἤδη γὰρ διώρισται ὃν τρόπον τοῦτο λέγομεν) καὶ τὶ γίγνεται (τοῦτο δ᾽ ἐστὶν ἢ σφαῖρα ἢ κύκλος ἢ ὅ τι ἔτυχε τῶν ἄλλων), ὥσπερ οὐδὲ τὸ ὑποκείμενον ποιεῖ, τὸν χαλκόν, οὕτως οὐδὲ τὴν σφαῖραν, εἰ μὴ [30] κατὰ συμβεβηκὸς ὅτι ἡ χαλκῆ σφαῖρα σφαῖρά ἐστιν ἐκείνην δὲ ποιεῖ. τὸ γὰρ τόδε τι ποιεῖν ἐκ τοῦ ὅλως ὑποκειμένου τόδε τι ποιεῖν ἐστίν (λέγω δ᾽ ὅτι τὸν χαλκὸν στρογγύλον ποιεῖν ἐστιν οὐ τὸ στρογγύλον ἢ τὴν σφαῖραν ποιεῖν ἀλλ᾽ ἕτερόν τι, οἷον τὸ εἶδος τοῦτο ἐν ἄλλῳ· εἰ γὰρ ποιεῖ, ἔκ τινος ἂν ποιοίη ἄλλου, τοῦτο γὰρ ὑπέκειτο· [1033β] [1] οἷον ποιεῖ χαλκῆν σφαῖραν, τοῦτο δὲ οὕτως ὅτι ἐκ τουδί, ὅ ἐστι χαλκός, τοδὶ ποιεῖ, ὅ ἐστι σφαῖρα)· εἰ οὖν καὶ τοῦτο ποιεῖ αὐτό, δῆλον ὅτι ὡσαύτως ποιήσει, καὶ βαδιοῦνται αἱ γενέσεις εἰς ἄπειρον. [5] φανερὸν ἄρα ὅτι οὐδὲ τὸ εἶδος, ἢ ὁτιδήποτε χρὴ καλεῖν τὴν ἐν τῷ αἰσθητῷ μορφήν, οὐ γίγνεται, οὐδ᾽ ἔστιν αὐτοῦ γένεσις, [7] οὐδὲ τὸ τί ἦν εἶναι (τοῦτο γάρ ἐστιν ὃ ἐν ἄλλῳ γίγνεται ἢ ὑπὸ τέχνης ἢ ὑπὸ φύσεως ἢ δυνάμεως).

Quoniam vero ab aliquo fit quod fit (hoc autem dico  unde principium generationis est) et ex aliquo (sit autem non privatio hod sed materia; iam enim diffinitum est quomodo hoc dicimus) et quod fit (hoc autem est spera aut circulus aut quodcumque evenit aliorum), quemadmodum nec subiectum facit es, sic nec speram, nisi secundum accidens quia aenea  spera est et illam facit. Nam hoc aliquid facere ex totaliter subiecto hoc facere est. Dico autem quia es rotundum facere est non quod rotundum aut speram facere sed alterum aliquid ut speciem hanc in alio. Nam si facit, ex aliquo facit alio,  hoc enim subiciebatur; ut facere eneam speram, hoc autem ita quia ex hoc quod est es, hoc facit quod spera. Si igitur et hoc facit ipsum, palam quia similiter faciet, et ibunt generationes in infinitum. Palam ergo quod nec species, aut quodcumque oportet vocare in sensibili formam, non fit, nec est eius generatio, neque quod quid erat esse huic; hoc enim est quod in alio fit aut ab arte aut a natura aut a potestate.

Since anything which is produced is produced by something (and this I call the starting-point of the production), and from something (and let this be taken to be not the privation but the matter; for the meaning we attach to this has already been explained), and since something is produced (and this is either a sphere or a circle or whatever else it may chance to be), just as we do not make the substratum (the brass), so we do not make the sphere, except incidentally, because the brazen sphere is a sphere and we make the forme. For to make a 'this' is to make a 'this' out of the substratum in the full sense of the word. (I mean that to make the brass round is not to make the round or the sphere, but something else, i.e. to produce this form in something different from itself. For if we make the form, we must make it out of something else; for this was assumed. [33b] E.g. we make a brazen sphere; and that in the sense that out of this, which is brass, we make this other, which is a sphere.) If, then, we also make the substratum itself, clearly we shall make it in the same way, and the processes of making will regress to infinity. Obviously then the form also, or whatever we ought to call the shape present in the sensible thing, is not produced, nor is there any production of it, nor is the essence produced; for this is that which is made to be in something else either by art or by nature or by some faculty.

τὸ δὲ χαλκῆν σφαῖραν εἶναι ποιεῖ: ποιεῖ γὰρ ἐκ χαλκοῦ καὶ σφαίρας: [10] εἰς τοδὶ γὰρ τὸ εἶδος ποιεῖ, καὶ ἔστι τοῦτο σφαῖρα χαλκῆ. τοῦ δὲ σφαῖρα εἶναι ὅλως εἰ ἔσται γένεσις, ἔκ τινος τὶ ἔσται. δεήσει γὰρ διαιρετὸν εἶναι ἀεὶ τὸ γιγνόμενον, καὶ εἶναι τὸ μὲν τόδε τὸ δὲ τόδε, λέγω δ᾽ ὅτι τὸ μὲν ὕλην τὸ δὲ εἶδος. εἰ δή ἐστι σφαῖρα τὸ ἐκ τοῦ μέσου σχῆμα ἴσον, τούτου τὸ μὲν [15] ἐν ᾧ ἔσται ὃ ποιεῖ, τὸ δ᾽ ἐν ἐκείνῳ, τὸ δὲ ἅπαν τὸ γεγονός, οἷον ἡ χαλκῆ σφαῖρα. φανερὸν δὴ ἐκ τῶν εἰρημένων ὅτι τὸ μὲν ὡς εἶδος ἢ οὐσία λεγόμενον οὐ γίγνεται, ἡ δὲ σύνολος ἡ κατὰ ταύτην λεγομένη γίγνεται, καὶ ὅτι ἐν παντὶ τῷ γεννωμένῳ ὕλη ἔνεστι, καὶ ἔστι τὸ μὲν τόδε τὸ δὲ τόδε.

Aeream vero speram esse facit. Facit enim ex aere et spera; nam in hoc hanc speciem facit, et est hoc spera aenea; hoc autem sperae esse. Eius vero quod est sperae esse omnino si est generatio, ex aliquo aliquid erit. Oportebit enum divisibile esse semper quod fit, et esse hoc quidem hoc et hoc hoc; dico autem quod hoc quidem materiam illud vero speciem. Si igitur est spera ex medio figura aequalis, huius hoc quidem est in quo erit quod facit, hoc autem in illo, hoc autem omne quod factum est, ut aenea spera. Palam igitur ex dictis quia quod quidem ut species aut ut substantia dicitur non fit, synodus autem secundum hanc dicta fit, et quod in omni generato materia inest, et est hoc quidem hoc et hoc hoc.

But that there is a brazen sphere, this we make. For we make it out of brass and the sphere; we bring the form into this particular matter, and the result is a brazen sphere. But if the essence of sphere in general is to be produced, something must be produced out of something. For the product will always have to be divisible, and one part must be this and another that; I mean the one must be matter and the other form.

If, then, a sphere is 'the figure whose circumference is at all points equidistant from the centre', part of this will be the medium in which the thing made will be, and part will be in that medium, and the whole will be the thing produced, which corresponds to the brazen sphere. It is obvious, then, from what has been said, that that which is spoken of as form or substance is not produced, but the concrete thing which gets its name from this is produced, and that in everything which is generated matter is present, and one part of the thing is matter and the other form.

πότερον [20] οὖν ἔστι τις σφαῖρα παρὰ τάσδε ἢ οἰκία παρὰ τὰς πλίνθους; ἢ οὐδ᾽ ἄν ποτε ἐγίγνετο, εἰ οὕτως ἦν, τόδε τι, ἀλλὰ τὸ τοιόνδε σημαίνει, τόδε δὲ καὶ ὡρισμένον οὐκ ἔστιν, ἀλλὰ ποιεῖ καὶ γεννᾷ ἐκ τοῦδε τοιόνδε, καὶ ὅταν γεννηθῇ, ἔστι τόδε τοιόνδε; τὸ δὲ ἅπαν τόδε, Καλλίας ἢ Σωκράτης, ἐστὶν ὥσπερ [25] ἡ σφαῖρα ἡ χαλκῆ ἡδί, ὁ δ᾽ ἄνθρωπος καὶ τὸ ζῷον ὥσπερ σφαῖρα χαλκῆ ὅλως. φανερὸν ἄρα ὅτι ἡ τῶν εἰδῶν αἰτία, ὡς εἰώθασί τινες λέγειν τὰ εἴδη, εἰ ἔστιν ἄττα παρὰ τὰ καθ᾽ ἕκαστα, πρός γε τὰς γενέσεις καὶ τὰς οὐσίας οὐθὲν χρησίμη· οὐδ᾽ ἂν εἶεν διά γε ταῦτα οὐσίαι καθ᾽ αὑτάς.

Utrum igitur est quaedam spera praeter has aut domus praeter lateres? Aut numquam facta est, si sic erat, hoc aliquid, sed quia tale significat, hoc autem et determinatum non est, sed facit et generat ex hoc tale, et quando generatum est, est hoc tale. Hoc autem omne hoc Callias aut Socrates est, quemadmodum spera aenea haec, homo vero et animal quemadmodum spera aenea totaliter. Manifestum ergo quia specierum causa, sicut consueti sunt quidam dicere species, si sunt quaedam praeter singularia, ad generationes et substantias nihil utiles; neque utique erunt propter haec substantiae secundum se.

Is there, then, a sphere apart from the individual spheres or a house apart from the bricks? Rather we may say that no 'this' would ever have been coming to be, if this had been so, but that the 'form' means the 'such', and is not a 'this' – a definite thing; but the artist makes, or the father begets, a 'such' out of a 'this'; and when it has been begotten, it is a 'this such'. And the whole 'this', Callias or Socrates, is analogous to 'this brazen sphere', but man and animal to 'brazen sphere' in general. Obviously, then, the cause which consists of the Forms (taken in the sense in which some maintain the existence of the Forms, i.e. if they are something apart from the individuals) is useless, at least with regard to comings-to-be and to substances; and the Forms need not, for this reason at least, be self-subsistent substances.

ἐπὶ μὲν δή [30] τινων καὶ φανερὸν ὅτι τὸ γεννῶν τοιοῦτον μὲν οἷον τὸ γεννώμενον, οὐ μέντοι τὸ αὐτό γε, οὐδὲ ἓν τῷ ἀριθμῷ ἀλλὰ τῷ εἴδει, οἷον ἐν τοῖς φυσικοῖς—ἄνθρωπος γὰρ ἄνθρωπον γεννᾷ—ἂν μή τι παρὰ φύσιν γένηται, οἷον ἵππος ἡμίονον (καὶ ταῦτα δὲ ὁμοίως· ὁ γὰρ ἂν κοινὸν εἴη ἐφ᾽ ἵππου καὶ ὄνου οὐκ ὠνόμασται, τὸ ἐγγύτατα γένος, εἴη δ᾽ ἂν ἄμφω ἴσως, οἷον ἡμίονος): [1034α] [1] ὥστε φανερὸν ὅτι οὐθὲν δεῖ ὡς παράδειγμα εἶδος κατασκευάζειν (μάλιστα γὰρ ἂν ἐν τούτοις ἐπεζητοῦντο: οὐσίαι γὰρ αἱ μάλιστα αὗται) ἀλλὰ ἱκανὸν τὸ γεννῶν ποιῆσαι [5] καὶ τοῦ εἴδους αἴτιον εἶναι ἐν τῇ ὕλῃ. τὸ δ᾽ ἅπαν ἤδη, τὸ τοιόνδε εἶδος ἐν ταῖσδε ταῖς σαρξὶ καὶ ὀστοῖς, Καλλίας καὶ Σωκράτης: καὶ ἕτερον μὲν διὰ τὴν ὕλην (ἑτέρα γάρ), ταὐτὸ δὲ τῷ εἴδει (ἄτομον γὰρ τὸ εἶδος).

In quibusdam vero palam quia generans tale quidem est quale generatum, nec tamen idem nec unum numero, sed unum specie, ut in phisicis (homo namque hominem generat) nisi quid praeter naturam fiat, ut equus mulum. Et haec quoque similiter; quod enim commune est super equum et asinum non est nominatum, proximum genus, sunt autem ambo forsan, velut mulus. Quare palam quia non oportet quasi exemplum speciem probare (maxime enim in hiis exquirerentur, nam substantiae maxime hee), sed sufficiens est generans facere et speciei causam esse in materia. Omnis vero iam talis species in hiis carnibus et ossibus, Callias et Socrates; et diversa quidem propter materiam (diversa namque), idem vero specie; nam individua species.

In some cases indeed it is even obvious that the begetter is of the same kind as the begotten (not, however, the same nor one in number, but in form), i.e. in the case of natural products (for man begets man), unless something happens contrary to nature, e.g. the production of a mule by a horse. (And even these cases are similar; for that which would be found to be common to horse and ass, the genus next above them, [34a] has not received a name, but it would doubtless be both in fact something like a mule.) Obviously, therefore, it is quite unnecessary to set up a Form as a pattern (for we should have looked for Forms in these cases if in any; for these are substances if anything is so); the begetter is adequate to the making of the product and to the causing of the form in the matter. And when we have the whole, such and such a form in this flesh and in these bones, this is Callias or Socrates; and they are different in virtue of their matter (for that is different), but the same in form; for their form is indivisible.

*Chapter* 9

ἀπορήσειε δ᾽ ἄν τις διὰ τί τὰ μὲν γίγνεται καὶ τέχνῃ [10] καὶ ἀπὸ ταὐτομάτου, οἷον ὑγίεια, τὰ δ᾽ οὔ, οἷον οἰκία.

Dubitabit autem aliquis quare alia fiunt arte et a casu, ut sanitas, alia non, ut domus.

The question might be raised, why some things are produced spontaneously as well as by art, e.g. health, while others are not, e.g. a house.

αἴτιον δὲ ὅτι τῶν μὲν ἡ ὕλη ἡ ἄρχουσα τῆς γενέσεως ἐν τῷ ποιεῖν καὶ γίγνεσθαί τι τῶν ἀπὸ τέχνης, ἐν ᾗ ὑπάρχει τι μέρος τοῦ πράγματος, ἡ μὲν τοιαύτη ἐστὶν οἵα κινεῖσθαι ὑφ᾽ αὑτῆς ἡ δ᾽ οὔ, καὶ ταύτης ἡ μὲν ὡδὶ οἵα τε ἡ δὲ ἀδύνατος: πολλὰ [15] γὰρ δυνατὰ μὲν ὑφ᾽ αὑτῶν κινεῖσθαι ἀλλ᾽ οὐχ ὡδί, οἷον ὀρχήσασθαι. ὅσων οὖν τοιαύτη ἡ ὕλη, οἷον οἱ λίθοι, ἀδύνατον ὡδὶ κινηθῆναι εἰ μὴ ὑπ᾽ ἄλλου, ὡδὶ μέντοι ναί—καὶ τὸ πῦρ. διὰ τοῦτο τὰ μὲν οὐκ ἔσται ἄνευ τοῦ ἔχοντος τὴν τέχνην τὰ δὲ ἔσται: ὑπὸ γὰρ τούτων κινηθήσεται τῶν οὐκ ἐχόντων [20] τὴν τέχνην, κινεῖσθαι δὲ δυναμένων αὐτῶν ὑπ᾽ ἄλλων οὐκ ἐχόντων τὴν τέχνην ἢ ἐκ μέρους.

Causa vero est quia horum quidem est materia incipiens generationis in facere et fieri aliquid eorum quae ab arte, in qua existit aliqua pars rei, haec quidem talis est qualis moveri ab ea illa vero non, et huius quidem sic potens haec autem impotens. Multa namque possunt quidem ab ipsis moveri sed non sic, puta saltare. Quorum igitur talis est materia, ut lapides, impossibile sic moveri nisi ab alio; sic tamen utique et ignis. Propter hoc haec quidem non erunt sine habente artem, haec autem erunt; ab hiis enim movebuntur non habentibus quasi artem, moveri vero potentibus eis aut ab aliis non habentibus artem aut ex parte

The reason is that in some cases the matter which governs the production in the making and producing of any work of art, and in which a part of the product is present, – some matter is such as to be set in motion by itself and some is not of this nature, and of the former kind some can move itself in the particular way required, while other matter is incapable of this; for many things can be set in motion by themselves but not in some particular way, e.g. that of dancing. The things, then, whose matter is of this sort, e.g. stones, cannot be moved in the particular way required, except by something else, but in another way they can move themselves – and so it is with fire. Therefore some things will not exist apart from some one who has the art of making them, while others will; for motion will be started by these things which have not the art but can themselves be moved by other things which have not the art or with a motion starting from a part of the product.

δῆλον δ᾽ ἐκ τῶν εἰρημένων καὶ ὅτι τρόπον τινὰ πάντα γίγνεται ἐξ ὁμωνύμου, ὥσπερ τὰ φύσει, ἢ ἐκ μέρους ὁμωνύμου (οἷον ἡ οἰκία ἐξ οἰκίας, ἢ ὑπὸ νοῦ: ἡ γὰρ τέχνη τὸ εἶδος) [ἢ ἐκ μέρους] ἢ [25] ἔχοντός τι μέρος, ἐὰν μὴ κατὰ συμβεβηκὸς γίγνηται:

Palam vero ex dictis quia modo quodam omnia fiunt ex univoco, quemadmodum naturalia, aut ex parte univoco, ut domus ex domo aut ab intellectu (ars enim species), aut ex parte aut habente aliquam partem, nisi secundum accidens fiat.

And it is clear also from what has been said that in a sense every product of art is produced from a thing which shares its name (as natural products are produced), or from a part of itself which shares its name (e.g. the house is produced from a house, qua produced by reason; for the art of building is the form of the house), or from something which contains a art of it, – if we exclude things produced by accident;

γὰρ αἴτιον τοῦ ποιεῖν πρῶτον καθ᾽ αὑτὸ μέρος. θερμότης γὰρ ἡ ἐν τῇ κινήσει θερμότητα ἐν τῷ σώματι ἐποίησεν: αὕτη δὲ ἐστιν ἢ ὑγίεια ἢ μέρος, ἢ ἀκολουθεῖ αὐτῇ μέρος τι τῆς ὑγιείας ἢ αὐτὴ ἡ ὑγίεια: διὸ καὶ λέγεται ποιεῖν, ὅτι ἐκεῖνο [30] ποιεῖ [τὴν ὑγίειαν] ᾧ ἀκολουθεῖ καὶ συμβέβηκε [θερμότης]. ὥστε, ὥσπερ ἐν τοῖς συλλογισμοῖς, πάντων ἀρχὴ ἡ οὐσία: ἐκ γὰρ τοῦ τί ἐστιν οἱ συλλογισμοί εἰσιν, ἐνταῦθα δὲ αἱ γενέσεις.

Causa namque faciendi prima secundum se pars. Calor enim in motu calorem in corpore fecit; is vero est aut sanitas aut pars, aut sequitur eum pars aliqua sanitatis aut sanitas ipsa. Propter quod et dicitur facere, quia illud facit sanitatem, cui consequitur et accidit calor. Quare, quemadmodum in syllogismis, omnium principium est substantia; nam ex quid est syllogismi sunt, et hic generationes.

for the cause of the thing's producing the product directly per se is a part of the product. The heat in the movement caused heat in the body, and this is either health, or a part of health, or is followed by a part of health or by health itself. And so it is said to cause health, because it causes that to which health attaches as a consequence.Therefore, as in syllogisms, substance is the starting-point of everything. It is from 'what a thing is' that syllogisms start; and from it also we now find processes of production to start.

ὁμοίως δὲ καὶ τὰ φύσει συνιστάμενα τούτοις ἔχει. τὸ μὲν γὰρ σπέρμα ποιεῖ ὥσπερ τὰ ἀπὸ τέχνης (ἔχει γὰρ δυνάμει τὸ εἶδος, [1034β] [1] καὶ ἀφ᾽ οὗ τὸ σπέρμα, ἐστί πως ὁμώνυμον—οὐ γὰρ πάντα οὕτω δεῖ ζητεῖν ὡς ἐξ ἀνθρώπου ἄνθρωπος: καὶ γὰρ γυνὴ ἐξ ἀνδρός—ἐὰν μὴ πήρωμα ᾖ: διὸ ἡμίονος οὐκ ἐξ ἡμιόνου): ὅσα δὲ ἀπὸ ταὐτομάτου ὥσπερ ἐκεῖ γίγνεται, [5] ὅσων ἡ ὕλη δύναται καὶ ὑφ᾽ αὑτῆς κινεῖσθαι ταύτην τὴν κίνησιν ἣν τὸ σπέρμα κινεῖ: ὅσων δὲ μή, ταῦτα ἀδύνατα γίγνεσθαι ἄλλως πως ἢ ἐξ αὐτῶν.

Similiter itaque hiis et quae sunt natura constituta se habent. Nam sperma facit sicut quae ab arte. Habet enim potestate speciem, et a quo sperma est aliqualiter univocum – non enim omnia sic oportet quaerare ut ex homine homo; et enim femina ex viro, unde mulus non ex mulo – sed si non orbatio fuerit. Quaecumque autem a casu, sicut ibi fit, quorumcumque materia potest a se ipsa moveri hoc motu quo sperma movet; quorumcumque vero non, ea impossibilia sunt fieri aliter quam ex ipsis.

Things which are formed by nature are in the same case as these products of art. For the seed is productive in the same way as the things that work by art; for it has the form potentially, and that from which the seed comes [34b] has in a sense the same name as the offspring only in a sense, for we must not expect parent and offspring always to have exactly the same name, as in the production of 'human being' from 'human' for a 'woman' also can be produced by a 'man' – unless the offspring be an imperfect form; which is the reason why the parent of a mule is not a mule. The natural things which (like the artificial objects previously considered) can be produced spontaneously are those whose matter can be moved even by itself in the way in which the seed usually moves it; those things which have not such matter cannot be produced except from the parent animals themselves.

οὐ μόνον δὲ περὶ τῆς οὐσίας ὁ λόγος δηλοῖ τὸ μὴ γίγνεσθαι τὸ εἶδος, ἀλλὰ περὶ πάντων ὁμοίως τῶν πρώτων κοινὸς ὁ λόγος, οἷον ποσοῦ [10] ποιοῦ καὶ τῶν ἄλλων κατηγοριῶν. γίγνεται γὰρ ὥσπερ ἡ χαλκῆ σφαῖρα ἀλλ᾽ οὐ σφαῖρα οὐδὲ χαλκός, καὶ ἐπὶ χαλκοῦ, εἰ γίγνεται (ἀεὶ γὰρ δεῖ προϋπάρχειν τὴν ὕλην καὶ τὸ εἶδος), οὕτως καὶ ἐπὶ τοῦ τί ἐστι καὶ ἐπὶ τοῦ ποιοῦ καὶ ποσοῦ καὶ τῶν ἄλλων ὁμοίως κατηγοριῶν: οὐ γὰρ γίγνεται [15] τὸ ποιὸν ἀλλὰ τὸ ποιὸν ξύλον, οὐδὲ τὸ ποσὸν ἀλλὰ τὸ ποσὸν ξύλον ἢ ζῷον.

Non solum autem de substantia ratio ostendit non fieri speciem, sed de omnibus similiter primis communis ratio, ut quantitate, qualitate et aliis cathegoriis. Fit enim velut aenea spera, sed non spera nec es, et in aere si fit (semper enim oportet praeexistere materiam et speciem): et in quid et in qualitate et quantitate et in aliis similiter cathegoriis. Non enim fit quale sed quale lignum, nec quantum sed quantum lignum aut animal.

But not only regarding substance does our argument prove that its form does not come to be, but the argument applies to all the primary classes alike, i.e. quantity, quality, and the other categories. For as the brazen sphere comes to be, but not the sphere nor the brass, and so too in the case of brass itself, if it comes to be, it is its concrete unity that comes to be (for the matter and the form must always exist before), so is it both in the case of substance and in that of quality and quantity and the other categories likewise; for the quality does not come to be, but the wood of that quality, and the quantity does not come to be, but the wood or the animal of that size.

ἀλλ᾽ ἴδιον τῆς οὐσίας ἐκ τούτων λαβεῖν ἔστιν ὅτι ἀναγκαῖον προϋπάρχειν ἑτέραν οὐσίαν ἐντελεχείᾳ οὖσαν ἣ ποιεῖ, οἷον ζῷον εἰ γίγνεται ζῷον: ποιὸν δ᾽ ἢ ποσὸν οὐκ ἀνάγκη ἀλλ᾽ ἢ δυνάμει μόνον. [20]

Sed proprium substantiae ex hiis accipere est quia necesse praeexistere semper alteram substantiam actu existentem quae facit, ut animal, si fit animal; quale vero aut quantum non necessarium nisi potestate solum.

But we may learn from these instances a peculiarity of substance, that there must exist beforehand in complete reality another substance which produces it, e.g. an animal if an animal is produced; but it is not necessary that a quality or quantity should pre-exist otherwise than potentially.

*Chapter* 10

ἐπεὶ δὲ ὁ ὁρισμὸς λόγος ἐστί, πᾶς δὲ λόγος μέρη ἔχει, ὡς δὲ ὁ λόγος πρὸς τὸ πρᾶγμα, καὶ τὸ μέρος τοῦ λόγου πρὸς τὸ μέρος τοῦ πράγματος ὁμοίως ἔχει, ἀπορεῖται ἤδη πότερον δεῖ τὸν τῶν μερῶν λόγον ἐνυπάρχειν ἐν τῷ τοῦ ὅλου λόγῳ ἢ οὔ. ἐπ᾽ ἐνίων μὲν γὰρ φαίνονται ἐνόντες ἐνίων δ᾽ οὔ. τοῦ μὲν [25] γὰρ κύκλου ὁ λόγος οὐκ ἔχει τὸν τῶν τμημάτων, ὁ δὲ τῆς συλλαβῆς ἔχει τὸν τῶν στοιχείων: καίτοι διαιρεῖται καὶ ὁ κύκλος εἰς τὰ τμήματα ὥσπερ καὶ ἡ συλλαβὴ εἰς τὰ στοιχεῖα. ἔτι δὲ εἰ πρότερα τὰ μέρη τοῦ ὅλου, τῆς δὲ ὀρθῆς ἡ ὀξεῖα μέρος καὶ ὁ δάκτυλος τοῦ ζώου, πρότερον ἂν εἴη ἡ ὀξεῖα [30] τῆς ὀρθῆς καὶ ὁ δάκτυλος τοῦ ἀνθρώπου. δοκεῖ δ᾽ ἐκεῖνα εἶναι πρότερα: τῷ λόγῳ γὰρ λέγονται ἐξ ἐκείνων, καὶ τῷ εἶναι δὲ ἄνευ ἀλλήλων πρότερα.

Quoniam vero diffinitio ratio est et omnis ratio partes habet, ut autem ratio ad rem et pars rationis ad partem rei similiter se habet, dubitatur iam an oportet partium rationem esse in totius ratione an non In quibusdam enim videntur esse, in quibusdam non. Nam circuli ratio non habet eam quae incisionum, quae autem syllabe habet quae elementorum. Et tamen dividitur circulus in incisiones ut syllaba in elementa. Amplius autem si priores sunt partes toto, et recti acutus est pars et digitus hominis, prior erit acutus recto et digitus homine. Videntur autem illa esse priora; secundum rationem namque dicuntur ex illis, et in esse sine invicem priora.

Since a definition is a formula, and every formula has parts, and as the formula is to the thing, so is the part of the formula to the part of the thing, the question is already being asked whether the formula of the parts must be present in the formula of the whole or not. For in some cases the formulae of the parts are seen to be present, and in some not. The formula of the circle does not include that of the segments, but that of the syllable includes that of the letters; yet the circle is divided into segments as the syllable is into letters. – And further if the parts are prior to the whole, and the acute angle is a part of the right angle and the finger a part of the animal, the acute angle will be prior to the right angle and finger to the man. But the latter are thought to be prior; for in formula the parts are explained by reference to them, and in respect also of the power of existing apart from each other the wholes are prior to the parts.

ἢ πολλαχῶς λέγεται τὸ μέρος, ὧν εἷς μὲν τρόπος τὸ μετροῦν κατὰ τὸ ποσόν—ἀλλὰ τοῦτο μὲν ἀφείσθω: ἐξ ὧν δὲ ἡ οὐσία ὡς μερῶν, τοῦτο σκεπτέον. [1035α] [1] εἰ οὖν ἐστὶ τὸ μὲν ὕλη τὸ δὲ εἶδος τὸ δ᾽ ἐκ τούτων, καὶ οὐσία ἥ τε ὕλη καὶ τὸ εἶδος καὶ τὸ ἐκ τούτων, ἔστι μὲν ὡς καὶ ἡ ὕλη μέρος τινὸς λέγεται, ἔστι δ᾽ ὡς οὔ, ἀλλ᾽ ἐξ ὧν ὁ τοῦ εἴδους λόγος. οἷον τῆς μὲν κοιλότητος οὐκ ἔστι μέρος [5] ἡ σάρξ (αὕτη γὰρ ἡ ὕλη ἐφ᾽ ἧς γίγνεται), τῆς δὲ σιμότητος μέρος: καὶ τοῦ μὲν συνόλου ἀνδριάντος μέρος ὁ χαλκὸς τοῦ δ᾽ ὡς εἴδους λεγομένου ἀνδριάντος οὔ (λεκτέον γὰρ τὸ εἶδος καὶ ἡ εἶδος ἔχει ἕκαστον, τὸ δ᾽ ὑλικὸν οὐδέποτε καθ᾽ αὑτὸ λεκτέον): διὸ ὁ μὲν τοῦ κύκλου λόγος οὐκ ἔχει [10] τὸν τῶν τμημάτων, ὁ δὲ τῆς συλλαβῆς ἔχει τὸν τῶν στοιχείων: τὰ μὲν γὰρ στοιχεῖα τοῦ λόγου μέρη τοῦ εἴδους καὶ οὐχ ὕλη, τὰ δὲ τμήματα οὕτως μέρη ὡς ὕλη ἐφ᾽ ἧς ἐπιγίγνεται: ἐγγυτέρω μέντοι τοῦ εἴδους ἢ ὁ χαλκὸς ὅταν ἐν χαλκῷ ἡ στρογγυλότης ἐγγένηται. ἔστι δ᾽ ὡς οὐδὲ τὰ στοιχεῖα πάντα [15] τῆς συλλαβῆς ἐν τῷ λόγῳ ἐνέσται, οἷον ταδὶ τὰ κήρινα ἢ τὰ ἐν τῷ ἀέρι: ἤδη γὰρ καὶ ταῦτα μέρος τῆς συλλαβῆς ὡς ὕλη αἰσθητή. καὶ γὰρ ἡ γραμμὴ οὐκ εἰ διαιρουμένη [18] εἰς τὰ ἡμίση φθείρεται, ἢ ὁ ἄνθρωπος εἰς τὰ ὀστᾶ καὶ νεῦρα καὶ σάρκας, διὰ τοῦτο καὶ εἰσὶν ἐκ τούτων οὕτως [20] ὡς ὄντων τῆς οὐσίας μερῶν, ἀλλ᾽ ὡς ἐξ ὕλης, καὶ τοῦ μὲν συνόλου μέρη, τοῦ εἴδους δὲ καὶ οὗ ὁ λόγος οὐκέτι: διόπερ οὐδ᾽ ἐν τοῖς λόγοις. τῷ μὲν οὖν ἐνέσται ὁ τῶν τοιούτων μερῶν λόγος, τῷ δ᾽ οὐ δεῖ ἐνεῖναι, ἂν μὴ ᾖ τοῦ συνειλημμένου: διὰ γὰρ τοῦτο ἔνια μὲν ἐκ τούτων ὡς ἀρχῶν ἐστὶν εἰς ἃ [25] φθείρονται, ἔνια δὲ οὐκ ἔστιν. ὅσα μὲν οὖν συνειλημμένα τὸ εἶδος καὶ ἡ ὕλη ἐστίν, οἷον τὸ σιμὸν ἢ ὁ χαλκοῦς κύκλος, ταῦτα μὲν φθείρεται εἰς ταῦτα καὶ μέρος αὐτῶν ἡ ὕλη: ὅσα δὲ μὴ συνείληπται τῇ ὕλῃ ἀλλὰ ἄνευ ὕλης, ὧν οἱ λόγοι τοῦ εἴδους μόνον, ταῦτα δ᾽ οὐ φθείρεται, ἢ ὅλως ἢ [30] οὗτοι οὕτω γε: ὥστ᾽ ἐκείνων μὲν ἀρχαὶ καὶ μέρη ταῦτα τοῦ δὲ εἴδους οὔτε μέρη οὔτε ἀρχαί. καὶ διὰ τοῦτο φθείρεται ὁ πήλινος ἀνδριὰς εἰς πηλὸν καὶ ἡ σφαῖρα εἰς χαλκὸν καὶ ὁ Καλλίας εἰς σάρκα καὶ ὀστᾶ, ἔτι δὲ ὁ κύκλος εἰς τὰ τμήματα: ἔστι γάρ τις ὃς συνείληπται τῇ ὕλῃ: [1035β] [1] ὁμωνύμως γὰρ λέγεται κύκλος ὅ τε ἁπλῶς λεγόμενος καὶ ὁ καθ᾽ ἕκαστα διὰ τὸ μὴ εἶναι ἴδιον ὄνομα τοῖς καθ᾽ ἕκαστον.

Aut multipliciter dicitur pars, quorum unus quidem modus est quod mensurat secundum quantitatem. Sed hoc quidem praetermittatur; ex quibus vero substantia est ut partibus, perscrutandum est. Si igitur est hoc quidem materia illud vero species, aliud ex hiis, et substantia est materia et species et quod ex hiis: est quidem ut materia pars alicuius dicitur, est autem ut non, sed ex quibus speciei ratio. Ut concavitatis non est pars caro (haec namque materia in qua fit), simitatis vero pars aliqua est. Et totius quidem statuae pars est es, eius autem quod ut species dicitur statuae non. Dicendum enim speciem et in quantum speciem habet unumquodque, sed materiale numquam secundum se est dicendum. Quapropter circuli ratio non habet eam quae est incisionum, sed quae syllabe eam quae est elementorum. Nam elementa rationis partes sunt speciei et non materia, incisiones vero huius sic partes ut materia in quibus fiunt; propinquius tamen speciei quam es, quando in aere fit rotunditas. Est autem ut neque elementa omnia syllabe in ratione insunt, ut haec cerea aut quae sunt in aere;

iam enum et haec pars syllabae quasi materia sensibilis. Et enim linea non, si divisa in dimidia corrumpitur, aut homo in ossa et nervos et carnes, propter hoc et sunt ex hiis sic ut entibus substantiae  partibus, sed ut ex materia, et eius quidem quod simul totum partes, speciei vero et cuius ratio non adhuc; quapropter nec  in rationibus. Horum quidem igitur inerit talium partium ratio, horum vero non oportet inesse, si non fuerit simul sumpti. Nam propter hoc quaedam quidem ex hiis ut principiis  sunt in quae corrumpuntur, quaedam vero non sunt. Quaecumque quidem igitur simul sumpta species et materia sunt, ut simum aut aeneus circulus, haec quidem corrumpuntur in haec et pars ipsorum materia; quaecumque vero non concipiuntur cum materia sed sine materia, ut rationes speciei solum, haec  non corrumpuntur, aut omnino aut non taliter. Quare illorum quidem principia haec. Et ideo corrumpitur lutea statua in lutum et spera in aes et Callias in carnem et ossa. Amplius autem circulus in incisiones; est enim aliquis qui concipitur  cum materia. Aequivoce namque dicitur circulus: qui simpliciter dicitur et singuli, quia non est proprium nomen singulorum.

Perhaps we should rather say that 'part' is used in several senses. One of these is 'that which measures another thing in respect of quantity'. But let this sense be set aside; let us inquire about the parts of which substance [35a] consists. If then matter is one thing, form another, the compound of these a third, and both the matter and the form and the compound are substance even the matter is in a sense called part of a thing, while in a sense it is not, but only the elements of which the formula of the form consists. E.g. of concavity flesh (for this is the matter in which it is produced) is not a part, but of snubness it is a part; and the bronze is a part of the concrete statue, but not of the statue when this is spoken of in the sense of the form. (For the form, or the thing as having form, should be said to be the thing, but the material element by itself must never be said to be so.) And so the formula of the circle does not include that of the segments, but the formula of the syllable includes that of the letters; for the letters are parts of the formula of the form, and not matter, but the segments are parts in the sense of matter on which the form supervenes; yet they are nearer the form than the bronze is when roundness is produced in bronze. But in a sense not even every kind of letter will be present in the formula of the syllable, e.g. particular waxen letters or the letters as movements in the air; for in these also we have already something that is part of the syllable only in the sense that it is its perceptible matter. For even if the line when divided passes away into its halves, or the man into bones and muscles and flesh, it does not follow that they are composed of these as parts of their essence, but rather as matter; and these are parts of the concrete thing, but not also of the form, i.e. of that to which the formula refers; wherefore also they are not present in the formulae. In one kind of formula, then, the formula of such parts will be present, but in another it must not be present, where the formula does not refer to the concrete object. For it is for this reason that some things have as their constituent principles parts into which they pass away, while some have not. Those things which are the form and the matter taken together, e.g. the snub, or the bronze circle, pass away into these materials, and the matter is a part of them; but those things which do not involve matter but are without matter, and whose formulae are formulae of the form only, do not pass away, – either not at all or at any rate not in this way. Therefore these materials are principles and parts of the concrete things, while of the form they are neither parts nor principles. And therefore the clay statue is resolved into clay and the ball into bronze and Callias into flesh and bones, and again the circle into its segments; for there is a sense of 'circle' in which involves matter. [35b] For 'circle' is used ambiguously, meaning both the circle, unqualified, and the individual circle, because there is no name peculiar to the individuals.

εἴρηται μὲν οὖν καὶ νῦν τὸ ἀληθές, ὅμως δ᾽ ἔτι σαφέστερον εἴπωμεν ἐπαναλαβόντες. ὅσα μὲν γὰρ τοῦ λόγου [5] μέρη καὶ εἰς ἃ διαιρεῖται ὁ λόγος, ταῦτα πρότερα ἢ πάντα ἢ ἔνια· ὁ δὲ τῆς ὀρθῆς λόγος οὐ διαιρεῖται εἰς ὀξείας λόγον, ἀλλ᾽ <ὁ τῆς ὀξείας εἰς ὀρθήν· χρῆται γὰρ ὁ ὁριζόμενος τὴν ὀξεῖαν τῇ ὀρθῇ· "ἐλάττων" γὰρ "ὀρθῆς"ἡ ὀξεῖα. ὁμοίως δὲ καὶ ὁ κύκλος καὶ τὸ ἡμικύκλιον ἔχουσιν· τὸ [10] γὰρ ἡμικύκλιον τῷ κύκλῳ ὁρίζεται καὶ ὁ δάκτυλος τῷ ὅλῳ· "τὸ"γὰρ "τοιόνδε μέρος ἀνθρώπου"δάκτυλος. ὥσθ᾽ ὅσα μὲν μέρη ὡς ὕλη καὶ εἰς ἃ διαιρεῖται ὡς ὕλην, ὕστερα· ὅσα δὲ ὡς τοῦ λόγου καὶ τῆς οὐσίας τῆς κατὰ τὸν λόγον, πρότερα ἢ πάντα ἢ ἔνια.

Dictum est quidem igitur et nunc ipsum verum, et tamen amplius manifestius dicamus repetentes. Nam quaecumque sunt rationis partes et in quas dividitur ratio, hee sunt priores aut omnes aut quaedam. Recti vero ratio non dividitur in acuti rationem, sed quae est acuti in quae est recti; utitur enim diffiniens acutum recto: minor enim recto acutus. Similiter autem et circulus et semicirculus se habent; semicirculus enim diffinitur circulo et digitus toto: talis enim hominis pars digitus. Quare quaecumque sunt partes ut materia et in quae dividitur ut in materiam, sunt posteriora; quaecumque vero ut rationis et substantiae secundum rationem, priora aut omnia aut quaedam.

The truth has indeed now been stated, but still let us state it yet more clearly, taking up the question again. The parts of the formula, into which the formula is divided, are prior to it, either all or some of them. The formula of the right angle, however, does not include the formula of the acute, but the formula of the acute includes that of the right angle; for he who defines the acute uses the right angle; for the acute is 'less than a right angle'. The circle and the semicircle also are in a like relation; for the semicircle is defined by the circle; and so is the finger by the whole body, for a finger is 'such and such a part of a man'. Therefore the parts which are of the nature of matter, and into which as its matter a thing is divided, are posterior; but those which are of the nature of parts of the formula, and of the substance according to its formula, are prior, either all or some of them.

ἐπεὶ δὲ ἡ τῶν ζῴων ψυχή [15] (τοῦτο γὰρ οὐσία τοῦ ἐμψύχου) ἡ κατὰ τὸν λόγον οὐσία καὶ τὸ εἶδος καὶ τὸ τί ἦν εἶναι τῷ τοιῷδε σώματι (ἕκαστον γοῦν τὸ μέρος ἐὰν ὁρίζηται καλῶς, οὐκ ἄνευ τοῦ ἔργου ὁριεῖται, ὃ οὐχ ὑπάρξει ἄνευ αἰσθήσεως), ὥστε τὰ ταύτης μέρη πρότερα ἢ πάντα ἢ ἔνια τοῦ συνόλου ζῴου, καὶ καθ᾽ ἕκαστον [20] δὴ ὁμοίως, τὸ δὲ σῶμα καὶ τὰ τούτου μόρια ὕστερα ταύτης τῆς οὐσίας, καὶ διαιρεῖται εἰς ταῦτα ὡς εἰς ὕλην οὐχ ἡ οὐσία ἀλλὰ τὸ σύνολον, τοῦ μὲν οὖν συνόλου πρότερα ταῦτ᾽ ἐστιν ὥς, ἔστι δ᾽ ὡς οὔ (οὐδὲ γὰρ εἶναι δύναται χωριζόμενα: οὐ γὰρ ὁ πάντως ἔχων δάκτυλος ζῴου, ἀλλ᾽ [25] ὁμώνυμος ὁ τεθνεώς): ἔνια δὲ ἅμα, ὅσα κύρια καὶ ἐν ᾧ πρώτῳ ὁ λόγος καὶ ἡ οὐσία, οἷον εἰ τοῦτο καρδία ἢ ἐγκέφαλος: διαφέρει γὰρ οὐθὲν πότερον τοιοῦτον. ὁ δ᾽ ἄνθρωπος καὶ ὁ ἵππος καὶ τὰ οὕτως ἐπὶ τῶν καθ᾽ ἕκαστα, καθόλου δέ, οὐκ ἔστιν οὐσία ἀλλὰ σύνολόν τι ἐκ τουδὶ τοῦ λόγου καὶ τησδὶ [30] τῆς ὕλης ὡς καθόλου: καθ᾽ ἕκαστον δ᾽ ἐκ τῆς ἐσχάτης ὕλης ὁ Σωκράτης ἤδη ἐστίν, καὶ ἐπὶ τῶν ἄλλων ὁμοίως.

Quoniam vero animalium anima (hoc enim substantia est animati) quae secundum rationem substantia et species et quod quid erat esse tali corpori (uniuscuiusque enim pars si diffiniatur bene, non sine opere diffinietur, quod non existet sine sensu), quare huius partes priores aut omnes aut quaedam simul toto animali; et secundum unumquodque itaque similiter. Corpus vero et huius partes posteriora sunt hac substantia est dividitur in haec ut in materiam non substantia sed simul totum. Eo quidem igitur quod simul totum priora haec, est ut, est autem ut non. Neque enim possunt esse separata; non enim qui quocumque modo se habens digitus animalis, sed equivocus qui mortuus. Quaedam vero simul: quaecumque principalia et in quo primo ratio et substantia, puta si hoc cor aut cerebrum; nihil enim differt, utrum tale. Homo vero et equus et quae ita in singularibus, universaliter autem, non sunt substantia sed simul totum quoddam ex hac ratione et hac materia ut universaliter. Singulare vero ex ultima materia Socrates iam est, et in aliis similiter.

And since the soul of animals (for this is the substance of a living being) is their substance according to the formula, i.e. the form and the essence of a body of a certain kind (at least we shall define each part, if we define it well, not without reference to its function, and this cannot belong to it without perception), so that the parts of soul are prior, either all or some of them, to the concrete 'animal', and so too with each individual animal; and the body and parts are posterior to this, the essential substance, and it is not the substance but the concrete thing that is divided into these parts as its matter: – this being so, to the concrete thing these are in a sense prior, but in a sense they are not. For they cannot even exist if severed from the whole; for it is not a finger in any and every state that is the finger of a living thing, but a dead finger is a finger only in name. Some parts are neither prior nor posterior to the whole, i.e. those which are dominant and in which the formula, i.e. the essential substance, is immediately present, e.g. perhaps the heart or the brain; for it does not matter in the least which of the two has this quality. But man and horse and terms which are thus applied to individuals, but universally, are not substance but something composed of this particular formula and this particular matter treated as universal; and as regards the individual, Socrates already includes in him ultimate individual matter; and similarly in all other cases.

μέρος μὲν οὖν ἐστὶ καὶ τοῦ εἴδους (εἶδος δὲ λέγω τὸ τί ἦν εἶναι) καὶ τοῦ συνόλου τοῦ ἐκ τοῦ εἴδους καὶ τῆς ὕλης <καὶ τῆς ὕλης αὐτῆς.

Pars quidem igitur est et speciei (speciem autem dico quod quid erat esse) et simul totius, eius quod ex specie et materia ipsa.

'A part' may be a part either of the form (i.e. of the essence), or of the compound of the form and the matter, or of the matter itself.

ἀλλὰ τοῦ λόγου μέρη τὰ τοῦ εἴδους μόνον ἐστίν, ὁ δὲ λόγος ἐστὶ τοῦ καθόλου: [1036α] [1] τὸ γὰρ κύκλῳ εἶναι καὶ κύκλος καὶ ψυχῇ εἶναι καὶ ψυχὴ ταὐτό. τοῦ δὲ συνόλου ἤδη, οἷον κύκλου τουδὶ καὶ τῶν καθ᾽ ἕκαστά τινος ἢ αἰσθητοῦ ἢ νοητοῦ—λέγω δὲ νοητοὺς μὲν οἷον τοὺς μαθηματικούς, αἰσθητοὺς δὲ οἷον τοὺς χαλκοῦς [5] καὶ τοὺς ξυλίνους—τούτων δὲ οὐκ ἔστιν ὁρισμός, ἀλλὰ μετὰ νοήσεως ἢ αἰσθήσεως γνωρίζονται, ἀπελθόντες δὲ ἐκ τῆς ἐντελεχείας οὐ δῆλον πότερον εἰσὶν ἢ οὐκ εἰσίν: ἀλλ᾽ ἀεὶ λέγονται καὶ γνωρίζονται τῷ καθόλου λόγῳ. ἡ δ᾽ ὕλη ἄγνωστος καθ᾽ αὑτήν. ὕλη δὲ ἡ μὲν αἰσθητή ἐστιν ἡ δὲ [10] νοητή, αἰσθητὴ μὲν οἷον χαλκὸς καὶ ξύλον καὶ ὅση κινητὴ ὕλη, νοητὴ δὲ ἡ ἐν τοῖς αἰσθητοῖς ὑπάρχουσα μὴ ᾗ αἰσθητά, οἷον τὰ μαθηματικά. πῶς μὲν οὖν ἔχει περὶ ὅλου καὶ μέρους καὶ περὶ τοῦ προτέρου καὶ ὑστέρου, εἴρηται:

Sed rationis partes quae speciei solum sunt, ratio vero est ipsius universalis; circulo enim esse et circulus et animae esse et anima idem. Simul totius autem, puta circuli huius et singularium alicuius aut sensibilis aut intellectualis – intellectuales vero dico ut mathematicos, et sensibiles ut aereos et ligneos –, horum autem non est diffinitio, sed cum intelligentia aut sensu cognoscuntur. Abeuntes vero ex actu non palam utrum quidem sunt aut non sunt; sed semper dicuntur et cognoscuntur universalis ratione. Materia quidem ignota secundum se. Materia vero alia sensibilis alia intellectualis; sensibilis quidem ut es et lignum et quaelibet mobilis materia, intellectualis vero quae in sensibilibus existit non in quantum sensibilia, ut mathematica. Quomodo igitur habet de toto et parte et priore et posteriore, dictum est.

But only the parts of the form are parts of the formula, and the formula is of the universal; for [36a] 'being a circle' is the same as the circle, and 'being a soul' the same as the soul. But when we come to the concrete thing, e.g. this circle, i.e. one of the individual circles, whether perceptible or intelligible (I mean by intelligible circles the mathematical, and by perceptible circles those of bronze and of wood), – of these there is no definition, but they are known by the aid of intuitive thinking or of perception;

and when they pass out of this complete realization it is not clear whether they exist or not; but they are always stated and recognized by means of the universal formula. But matter is unknowable in itself. And some matter is perceptible and some intelligible, perceptible matter being for instance bronze and wood and all matter that is changeable, and intelligible matter being that which is present in perceptible things not qua perceptible, i.e. the objects of mathematics. We have stated, then, how matters stand with regard to whole and part, and their priority and posteriority.

πρὸς δὲ τὴν ἐρώτησιν ἀνάγκη ἀπαντᾶν, ὅταν τις ἔρηται πότερον ἡ ὀρθὴ [15] καὶ ὁ κύκλος καὶ τὸ ζῷον πρότερον ἢ εἰς ἃ διαιροῦνται καὶ ἐξ ὧν εἰσί, τὰ μέρη, ὅτι οὐχ ἁπλῶς. εἰ μὲν γάρ ἐστι καὶ ἡ ψυχὴ ζῷον ἢ ἔμψυχον, ἢ ἕκαστον ἢ ἑκάστου, καὶ κύκλος τὸ κύκλῳ εἶναι, καὶ ὀρθὴ τὸ ὀρθῇ εἶναι καὶ ἡ οὐσία ἡ τῆς ὀρθῆς, τὶ μὲν καὶ τινὸς φατέον ὕστερον, οἷον [20] τῶν ἐν τῷ λόγῳ καὶ τινὸς ὀρθῆς (καὶ γὰρ ἡ μετὰ τῆς ὕλης, ἡ χαλκῆ ὀρθή, καὶ ἡ ἐν ταῖς γραμμαῖς ταῖς καθ᾽ ἕκαστα), ἡ δ᾽ ἄνευ ὕλης τῶν μὲν ἐν τῷ λόγῳ ὑστέρα τῶν δ᾽ ἐν τῷ καθ᾽ ἕκαστα μορίων προτέρα, ἁπλῶς δ᾽ οὐ φατέον: εἰ δ᾽ ἕτερα καὶ μὴ ἔστιν ἡ ψυχὴ ζῷον, καὶ οὕτω τὰ μὲν [25] φατέον τὰ δ᾽ οὐ φατέον, ὥσπερ εἴρηται.

Interrogationi vero obviare est necesse, quando quis interrogat utrum rectus et circulus et animal priora aut in quas interrogat utrum rectus et circulus et animal priora aut in quas dividuntur et ex quibus sunt partes, quia non simpliciter. Si quidem enim est et anima aut animatum, aut unumquodque quae uniuscuiusque, et circulus quod circulo esse, et rectus quod recto esse et substantia recti: quid quidem et quo dicendum est posterius, puta hiis quae in ratione et quo recto (et enim hic quidem cum materia qui aeuneus rectus, et qui in lineis singularibus); hic autem sine materia hiis quidem quae in ratione posterior, eis vero quae in singularibus partibus prior, simpliciter autem non dicendum. Si vero altera et non est anima animal, et sic haec quidem dicendum haec autem non dicendum, sicut dictum est.

But when any one asks whether the right angle and the circle and the animal are prior, or the things into which they are divided and of which they consist, i.e. the parts, we must meet the inquiry by saying that the question cannot be answered simply. For if even bare soul is the animal or the living thing, or the soul of each individual is the individual itself, and 'being a circle' is the circle, and 'being a right angle' and the essence of the right angle is the right angle, then the whole in one sense must be called posterior to the art in one sense, i.e. to the parts included in the formula and to the parts of the individual right angle (for both the material right angle which is made of bronze, and that which is formed by individual lines, are posterior to their parts); while the immaterial right angle is posterior to the parts included in the formula, but prior to those included in the particular instance, and the question must not be answered simply. If, however, the soul is something different and is not identical with the animal, even so some parts must, as we have maintained, be called prior and others must not.

ἀπορεῖται δὲ εἰκότως καὶ ποῖα τοῦ εἴδους μέρη καὶ ποῖα οὔ, ἀλλὰ τοῦ συνειλημμένου. καίτοι τούτου μὴ δήλου ὄντος οὐκ ἔστιν ὁρίσασθαι ἕκαστον: τοῦ γὰρ καθόλου καὶ τοῦ εἴδους ὁ ὁρισμός: ποῖα οὖν ἐστι τῶν μερῶν ὡς ὕλη καὶ ποῖα [30] οὔ, ἐὰν μὴ ᾖ φανερά, οὐδὲ ὁ λόγος ἔσται φανερὸς ὁ τοῦ πράγματος.

Dubitatur autem merito quae speciei sunt partes et quae non, sed simul sumpti. Hoc enim non manifesto existente non est diffinire unumquodque; universalis enim et speciei est diffinitio. Quae igitur sunt partium ut materia et quae non, si non fuerint manifeste, nec ratio erit manifesta quae rei.

Another question is naturally raised, viz. what sort of parts belong to the form and what sort not to the form, but to the concrete thing. Yet if this is not plain it is not possible to define any thing; for definition is of the universal and of the form. If then it is not evident what sort of parts are of the nature of matter and what sort are not, neither will the formula of the thing be evident.

ὅσα μὲν οὖν φαίνεται ἐπιγιγνόμενα ἐφ᾽ ἑτέρων τῷ εἴδει, οἷον κύκλος ἐν χαλκῷ καὶ λίθῳ καὶ ξύλῳ, ταῦτα μὲν δῆλα εἶναι δοκεῖ ὅτι οὐδὲν τῆς τοῦ κύκλου οὐσίας ὁ χαλκὸς οὐδ᾽ ὁ λίθος διὰ τὸ χωρίζεσθαι αὐτῶν: ὅσα δὲ [35] μὴ ὁρᾶται χωριζόμενα, οὐδὲν μὲν κωλύει ὁμοίως ἔχειν τούτοις, ὥσπερ κἂν εἰ οἱ κύκλοι πάντες ἑωρῶντο χαλκοῖ: [1036β] [1] οὐδὲν γὰρ ἂν ἧττον ἦν ὁ χαλκὸς οὐδὲν τοῦ εἴδους: χαλεπὸν δὲ ἀφελεῖν τοῦτον τῇ διανοίᾳ. οἷον τὸ τοῦ ἀνθρώπου εἶδος ἀεὶ ἐν σαρκὶ φαίνεται καὶ ὀστοῖς καὶ τοῖς τοιούτοις μέρεσιν: [5] ἆρ᾽ οὖν καὶ ἐστὶ ταῦτα μέρη τοῦ εἴδους καὶ τοῦ λόγου; οὔ, ἀλλ᾽ ὕλη, ἀλλὰ διὰ τὸ μὴ καὶ ἐπ᾽ ἄλλων ἐπιγίγνεσθαι ἀδυνατοῦμεν χωρίσαι;

Quecumque quidem igitur videntur facta in vidersis specie, ut circulus in aere et lapide et ligno, haec quidem manifesta esse videntur quia nihil circuli substantiae es neque lapis propter separari ab ipsis.Quae vero non videntur separata, nihil prohibet similiter hiis habere, ut si circuli omnes videantur aenei; nihil enim utique minus erat aes speciei. Hoc autem auferre mente est difficile. Ut hominis species semper in carnibus apparet et ossibus et talibus partibus. Utrum igitur et sunt partes haec speciei et rationis aut non, sed materia? Sed quia non et in aliis fiunt, non possumus separare.

In the case of things which are found to occur in specifically different materials, as a circle may exist in bronze or stone or wood, it seems plain that these, the bronze or the stone, are no part of the essence of the circle, since it is found apart from them. Of things which are not seen to exist apart, there [36b] is no reason why the same may not be true, just as if all circles that had ever been seen were of bronze; for none the less the bronze would be no part of the form; but it is hard to eliminate it in thought. E.g. the form of man is always found in flesh and bones and parts of this kind; are these then also parts of the form and the formula? No, they are matter; but because man is not found also in other matters we are unable to perform the abstraction.

ἐπεὶ δὲ τοῦτο δοκεῖ μὲν ἐνδέχεσθαι ἄδηλον δὲ πότε, ἀποροῦσί τινες ἤδη καὶ ἐπὶ τοῦ κύκλου καὶ τοῦ τριγώνου ὡς οὐ προσῆκον γραμμαῖς ὁρίζεσθαι καὶ τῷ [10] συνεχεῖ, ἀλλὰ πάντα καὶ ταῦτα ὁμοίως λέγεσθαι ὡσανεὶ σάρκες καὶ ὀστᾶ τοῦ ἀνθρώπου καὶ χαλκὸς καὶ λίθος τοῦ ἀνδριάντος: καὶ ἀνάγουσι πάντα εἰς τοὺς ἀριθμούς, καὶ γραμμῆς τὸν λόγον τὸν τῶν δύο εἶναί φασιν. καὶ τῶν τὰς ἰδέας λεγόντων οἱ μὲν αὐτογραμμὴν τὴν δυάδα, οἱ δὲ τὸ [15] εἶδος τῆς γραμμῆς, ἔνια μὲν γὰρ εἶναι τὸ αὐτὸ τὸ εἶδος καὶ οὗ τὸ εἶδος (οἷον δυάδα καὶ τὸ εἶδος δυάδος), ἐπὶ γραμμῆς δὲ οὐκέτι.

Quoniam autem hoc videtur contingere, immanifestum autem quando dubitant quidam iam et in circulo et in trigono, quasi non sit competens lineis diffiniri et continuo, sed omnia haec similiter dici ac si  ut carnes et ossa hominis et aes et lapis circuli; et referunt omnes ad numeros, et lineae rationem eam quae duorum esse dicunt. Et ydeas dicentium hii quidem ipsammet lineam dualitatem, hii autem speciem lineae. Quaedam enim esse eadem,  speciem et cuius species, ut dualitatem et speciem dualitatis; in linea vero non adhuc.

Since this is thought to be possible, but it is not clear when it is the case, some people already raise the question even in the case of the circle and the triangle, thinking that it is not right to define these by reference to lines and to the continuous, but that all these are to the circle or the triangle as flesh and bones are to man, and bronze or stone to the statue; and they reduce all things to numbers, and they say the formula of 'line' is that of 'two'. And of those who assert the Ideas some make 'two' the line-itself, and others make it the Form of the line; for in some cases they say the Form and that of which it is the Form are the same, e.g. 'two' and the Form of two; but in the case of 'line' they say this is no longer so.

συμβαίνει δὴ ἔν τε πολλῶν εἶδος εἶναι ὧν τὸ εἶδος φαίνεται ἕτερον (ὅπερ καὶ τοῖς Πυθαγορείοις συνέβαινεν), καὶ ἐνδέχεται ἓν πάντων ποιεῖν αὐτὸ [20] εἶδος, τὰ δ᾿ ἄλλα μὴ εἴδη: καίτοι οὕτως ἓν πάντα ἔσται. ὅτι μὲν οὖν ἔχει τινὰ ἀπορίαν τὰ περὶ τοὺς ὁρισμούς, καὶ διὰ τίν᾿ αἰτίαν, εἴρηται: διὸ καὶ τὸ πάντα ἀνάγειν οὕτω καὶ ἀφαιρεῖν τὴν ὕλην περίεργον:

Accidit itaque unum multorum esse speciem quorum species videtur esse altera (quod et Pytagoricis accidit), et contingit unam omnium facere per se speciem,  alia vero non species; quamvis sic unum omnia erunt. Quod quidem igitur habent dubitationem quandam quae sunt circa diffinitiones, et propter quam causam, dictum est.

It follows then that there is one Form for many things whose form is evidently different (a conclusion which confronted the Pythagoreans also); and it is possible to make one thing the Form-itself of all, and to hold that the others are not Forms; but thus all things will be one. We have pointed out, then, that the question of definitions contains some difficulty, and why this is so.

ἔνια γὰρ ἴσως τόδ᾽ ἐν τῷδ᾽ ἐστὶν ἢ ὡδὶ ταδὶ ἔχοντα. καὶ ἡ παραβολὴ ἡ ἐπὶ τοῦ ζῴου, [25] ἢν εἰώθει λέγειν Σωκράτης ὁ νεώτερος, οὐ καλῶς ἔχει· ἀπάγει γὰρ ἀπὸ τοῦ ἀληθοῦς, καὶ ποιεῖ ὑπολαμβάνειν ὡς ἐνδεχόμενον εἶναι τὸν ἄνθρωπον ἄνευ τῶν μερῶν, ὥσπερ ἄνευ τοῦ χαλκοῦ τὸν κύκλον. τὸ δ᾽ οὐχ ὅμοιον· αἰσθητὸν γάρ τι τὸ ζῷον, καὶ ἄνευ κινήσεως οὐκ ἔστιν ὁρίσασθαι, διὸ [30] οὐδ᾽ ἄνευ τῶν μερῶν ἐχόντων πώς. οὐ γὰρ πάντως τοῦ ἀνθρώπου μέρος ἡ χείρ, ἀλλ᾽ ἢ δυναμένη τὸ ἔργον ἀποτελεῖν, ὥστε ἔμψυχος οὖσα· μὴ ἔμψυχος δὲ οὐ μέρος.

Quare omnia reducere ita et auferre materiam superfluum est; quaedam enim forsam hoc in hoc sunt aut sic haec habentia. Et parabola de animali, quam consuevit Socrates iunior   dicere, non bene se habet; abducit enim a veritate et facit suspicari quasi contingens sit hominem esse sine partibus, sicut sine aere circulum. Sed hoc non simile; sensibile namque aliquid  forsan animal, et sine motu non est diffinire, quare nec sine partibus se habentibus qualitercumque. Non enim omni modo hominis est pars manus, sed potens opus perficere, quare animata existens; non animata vero non pars.

And so to reduce all things thus to Forms and to eliminate the matter is useless labour; for some things surely are a particular form in a particular matter, or particular things in a particular state. And the comparison which Socrates the younger used to make in the case of 'animal' is not sound; for it leads away from the truth, and makes one suppose that man can possibly exist without his parts, as the circle can without the bronze. But the case is not similar; for an animal is something perceptible, and it is not possible to define it without reference to movement – nor, therefore, without reference to the parts' being in a certain state. For it is not a hand in any and every state that is a part of man, but only when it can fulfil its work, and therefore only when it is alive; if it is not alive it is not a part.

περὶ δὲ τὰ μαθηματικὰ διὰ τί οὐκ εἰσὶ μέρη οἱ λόγοι τῶν λόγων, οἷον τοῦ κύκλου τὰ ἡμικύκλια; οὐ γάρ ἐστιν αἰσθητὰ ταῦτα. [35] ἢ οὐθὲν διαφέρει; ἔσται γὰρ ὕλη ἐνίων καὶ μὴ αἰσθητῶν· [1037α] [1] καὶ παντὸς γὰρ ὕλη τις ἔστιν ὃ μὴ ἔστι τί ἦν εἶναι καὶ εἶδος αὐτὸ καθ᾽ αὑτὸ ἀλλὰ τόδε τι. κύκλου μὲν οὖν οὐκ ἔσται τοῦ καθόλου, τῶν δὲ καθ᾽ ἕκαστα ἔσται μέρη ταῦτα, ὥσπερ εἴρηται πρότερον: ἔστι γὰρ ὕλη ἡ μὲν αἰσθητὴ ἡ [5] δὲ νοητή.

Circa mathematica autem, quare non sunt partes rationes rationum, ut circuli emikiclia? Non enim sunt sensibilia haec. Aut nil differt; erit enim materia quorundam et non sensibilium, et omnis quod non est quid erat esse et species eadem secundum se sed hoc aliquid. Circuli quidem igitur non erit eius qui universalis, singularium vero erunt partes hee, sicut dictum est prius. Est enim materia haec quidem sensibilis, haec autem intellectualis.

Regarding the objects of mathematics, why are the formulae of the parts not parts of the formulae of the wholes; e.g. why are not the semicircles included in the formula of the circle? It cannot be said, 'because these parts are perceptible things'; for they are not. But perhaps this makes no difference; for even some things [37a] which are not perceptible must have matter; indeed there is some matter in everything which is not an essence and a bare form but a 'this'. The semicircles, then, will not be parts of the universal circle, but will be parts of the individual circles, as has been said before; for while one kind of matter is perceptible, there is another which is intelligible.

δῆλον δὲ καὶ ὅτι ἡ μὲν ψυχὴ οὐσία ἡ πρώτη, τὸ δὲ σῶμα ὕλη, ὁ δ᾽ ἄνθρωπος ἢ τὸ ζῷον τὸ ἐξ ἀμφοῖν ὡς καθόλου: Σωκράτης δὲ καὶ Κορίσκος, εἰ μὲν καὶ ἡ ψυχὴ Σωκράτης, διττόν (οἱ μὲν γὰρ ὡς ψυχὴν οἱ δ᾽ ὡς τὸ σύνολον), εἰ δ᾽ ἁπλῶς ἡ ψυχὴ ἥδε καὶ <τὸ σῶμα τόδε, ὥσπερ τὸ [10] καθόλου [τε] καὶ τὸ καθ᾽ ἕκαστον.

Palam autem et quod anima quidem substantia prima, corpus autem materia; homo vero aut animal quod est ex utrisque ut universaliter. Socrates autem et Coriscus, si quidem anima, dupliciter: alii namque ut animam alii vero ut totum; si vero simpliciter anima haec et corpus hoc, ut quod quidem universale et singulare.

It is clear also that the soul is the primary substance and the body is matter, and man or animal is the compound of both taken universally; and 'Socrates' or 'Coriscus', if even the soul of Socrates may be called Socrates, has two meanings (for some mean by such a term the soul, and others mean the concrete thing), but if 'Socrates' or 'Coriscus' means simply this particular soul and this particular body, the individual is analogous to the universal in its composition.

πότερον δὲ ἔστι παρὰ τὴν ὕλην τῶν τοιούτων οὐσιῶν τις ἄλλη, καὶ δεῖ ζητεῖν οὐσίαν ἑτέραν τινὰ οἷον ἀριθμοὺς ἢ τι τοιοῦτον, σκεπτέον ὕστερον. τούτου γὰρ χάριν καὶ περὶ τῶν αἰσθητῶν οὐσιῶν πειρώμεθα διορίζειν, ἐπεὶ τρόπον τινὰ τῆς φυσικῆς καὶ [15] δευτέρας φιλοσοφίας ἔργον ἡ περὶ τὰς αἰσθητὰς οὐσίας θεωρία: οὐ γὰρ μόνον περὶ τῆς ὕλης δεῖ γνωρίζειν τὸν φυσικὸν ἀλλὰ καὶ τῆς κατὰ τὸν λόγον, καὶ μᾶλλον. ἐπὶ δὲ τῶν ὁρισμῶν πῶς μέρη τὰ ἐν τῷ λόγῳ, καὶ διὰ τί εἰς λόγος ὁ ὁρισμός (δῆλον γὰρ ὅτι τὸ πρᾶγμα ἕν, τὸ δὲ [20] πρᾶγμα τίνι ἕν, μέρη γε ἔχον;), σκεπτέον ὕστερον.

Utrum autem est praeter materiam talium aliqua substantiarum alia, et oportet quaerere substantium ipsorum alteram quandam ut numeros aut aliquid tale, perscrutandum est posterius. Huius enim gratia et de sensibilibus substantiis temptamus diffinire, quoniam modo quodam phisice et secundae philosophiae opus circa sensibiles substantias speculatio. Non enim solum de materia oportet scire phisicum sed et de ea quae secundum rationem, et magis. In diffinitionibus vero quomodo partes quae in ratione, et quare una ratio diffinitio? Palam enim quia res una. Res vero quo una partes habens, speculandum est posterius.

Whether there is, apart from the matter of such substances, another kind of matter, and one should look for some substance other than these, e.g. numbers or something of the sort, must be considered later. For it is for the sake of this that we are trying to determine the nature of perceptible substances as well, since in a sense the inquiry about perceptible substances is the work of physics, i.e. of second philosophy; for the physicist must come to know not only about the matter, but also about the substance expressed in the formula, and even more than about the other. And in the case of definitions, how the elements in the formula are parts of the definition, and why the definition is one formula (for clearly the thing is one, but in virtue of what is the thing one, although it has parts?), – this must be considered later.

τί μὲν οὖν ἐστὶ τὸ τί ἦν εἶναι καὶ πῶς αὐτὸ καθ᾽ αὑτό, καθόλου περὶ παντὸς εἴρηται, καὶ διὰ τί τῶν μὲν ὁ λόγος ὁ τοῦ τί ἦν εἶναι ἔχει τὰ μόρια τοῦ ὁριζομένου τῶν δ᾽ οὔ, καὶ ὅτι ἐν μὲν τῷ τῆς οὐσίας λόγῳ τὰ οὕτω μόρια [25] ὡς ὕλη οὐκ ἐνέσται—οὐδὲ γὰρ ἔστιν ἐκείνης μόρια τῆς οὐσίας ἀλλὰ τῆς συνόλου, ταύτης δέ γ᾽ ἔστι πως λόγος καὶ οὐκ ἔστιν: μετὰ μὲν γὰρ τῆς ὕλης οὐκ ἔστιν (ἀόριστον γάρ), κατὰ τὴν πρώτην δ᾽ οὐσίαν ἔστιν, οἷον ἀνθρώπου ὁ τῆς ψυχῆς λόγος: ἡ γὰρ οὐσία ἐστὶ τὸ εἶδος τὸ ἐνόν, ἐξ οὗ καὶ τῆς [30] ὕλης ἡ σύνολος λέγεται οὐσία, οἷον ἡ κοιλότης (ἐκ γὰρ ταύτης καὶ τῆς ῥινὸς σιμὴ ῥὶς καὶ ἡ σιμότης ἐστί [δὶς γὰρ ἐν τούτοις ὑπάρξει ἡ ῥίς])—ἐν δὲ τῇ συνόλῳ οὐσίᾳ, οἷον ῥινὶ σιμῇ ἢ Καλλίᾳ, ἐνέσται καὶ ἡ ὕλη: καὶ ὅτι τὸ τί ἦν εἶναι καὶ ἕκαστον ἐπὶ τινῶν μὲν ταὐτό, [1037β] [1] ὥσπερ ἐπὶ τῶν πρώτων οὐσιῶν, οἷον καμπυλότης καὶ καμπυλότητι εἶναι, εἰ πρώτη ἐστίν (λέγω δὲ πρώτην ἢ μὴ λέγεται τῷ ἄλλο ἐν ἄλλῳ εἶναι καὶ ὑποκειμένῳ ὡς ὕλῃ), ὅσα δὲ ὡς ὕλη ἢ [5] ὡς συνειλημμένα τῇ ὕλῃ, οὐ ταὐτό, οὐδ᾽ <εἰ κατὰ συμβεβηκὸς ἕν, οἷον Σωκράτης καὶ τὸ μουσικόν: ταῦτα γὰρ ταὐτὰ κατὰ συμβεβηκός.

Quid quidem igitur est quod quid erat esse et quomodo ipsum secundum se, universaliter de omni dictum est. Et quare horum quidem ratio quae eius quod quid erat esse habet partes diffiniti, horum autem non. Et quod in substantiae quidem ratione quae sic partes ut materia non inerunt. Neque enim sunt illius partes substantiae sed totius; huius autem est aliqualiter ratio et non est. Nam cum materia non est, indeterminatum enim; secundum primam autem substantiam est, ut hominis quae animae ratio. Substantia namque est species quae inest, ex qua et materia tota dicitur, ut concavitas; nam ex hac et naso simus nasus et simitas est; bis enim in hiis inerit nasus. In tota vero substantia, ut naso simo aut Callia, inest et materia. Et quod quod quid erat esse et unumquodque in quibusdam idem, ut in primis substantiis, ut curvitas et curvitati esse, si prima est; dico autem prima quae non dicitur per aliud in alio esse et subiecto ut materia. Quaecumque vero ut materia aut concepta cum materia, non idem, neque secundum accidens unum, ut Socrates et musicum; haec enim eadem secundum accidens.

What the essence is and in what sense it is independent, has been stated universally in a way which is true of every case, and also why the formula of the essence of some things contains the parts of the thing defined, while that of others does not. And we have stated that in the formula of the substance the material parts will not be present (for they are not even parts of the substance in that sense, but of the concrete substance; but of this there is in a sense a formula, and in a sense there is not; for there is no formula of it with its matter, for this is indefinite, but there is a formula of it with reference to its primary substance – e.g. in the case of man the formula of the soul – , for the substance is the indwelling form, from which and the matter the so-called concrete substance is derived; e.g. concavity is a form of this sort, for from this and the nose arise 'snub nose' and 'snubness'); but in the concrete substance, e.g. a snub nose or Callias, the matter also will be present. And we have stated that the essence and the [37b] thing itself are in some cases the same; ie. in the case of primary substances, e.g. curvature and the essence of curvature if this is primary. (By a 'primary' substance I mean one which does not imply the presence of something in something else, i.e. in something that underlies it which acts as matter.) But things which are of the nature of matter, or of wholes that include matter, are not the same as their essences, nor are accidental unities like that of 'Socrates' and 'musical'; for these are the same only by accident.

*Chapter* 12

νῦν δὲ λέγωμεν πρῶτον ἐφ᾽ ὅσον ἐν τοῖς ἀναλυτικοῖς περὶ ὁρισμοῦ μὴ εἴρηται: ἡ γὰρ ἐν ἐκείνοις ἀπορία [10] λεχθεῖσα πρὸ ἔργου τοῖς περὶ τῆς οὐσίας ἐστὶ λόγοις. λέγω δὲ ταύτην τὴν ἀπορίαν, διὰ τί ποτε ἕν ἐστιν οὗ τὸν λόγον ὁρισμὸν εἶναί φαμεν, οἷον τοῦ ἀνθρώπου τὸ ζῷον δίπουν: ἔστω γὰρ οὗτος αὐτοῦ λόγος. διὰ τί δὴ τοῦτο ἕν ἐστιν ἀλλ᾽ οὐ πολλά, ζῷον καὶ δίπουν;

Nunc autem dicamus primum, in quantum in Analeticis de diffinitione non dictum est; in illis enim dubitatio dicta prae opere rationibus de substantia est. Dico autem hanc dubitationem: propter quid quidem unum est cuius rationem diffinitionem esse dicimus, ut hominis animal bipes? Sit enim haec ipsius ratio. Propter quid itaque hoc unum est sed non multa, animal et bipes?

Now let us treat first of definition, in so far as we have not treated of it in the Analytics; for the problem stated in them is useful for our inquiries concerning substance. I mean this problem: – wherein can consist the unity of that, the formula of which we call a definition, as for instance, in the case of man, 'two-footed animal'; for let this be the formula of man. Why, then, is this one, and not many, viz. 'animal' and 'two-footed'?

ἐπὶ μὲν γὰρ τοῦ ἄνθρωπος [15] καὶ λευκὸν πολλὰ μέν ἐστιν ὅταν μὴ ὑπάρχῃ θατέρῳ θάτερον, ἓν δὲ ὅταν ὑπάρχῃ καὶ πάθῃ τι τὸ ὑποκείμενον, ὁ ἄνθρωπος (τότε γὰρ ἓν γίγνεται καὶ ἔστιν ὁ λευκὸς ἄνθρωπος)· ἐνταῦθα δ᾽ οὐ μετέχει θατέρου θάτερον· τὸ γὰρ γένος οὐ δοκεῖ μετέχειν τῶν διαφορῶν (ἅμα γὰρ ἂν τῶν [20] ἐναντίων τὸ αὐτὸ μετεῖχεν· αἱ γὰρ διαφοραὶ ἐναντίαι αἷς διαφέρει τὸ γένος).

In hoc namque homo et album: multa quidem sunt cum alterum non insit alteri, unum vero quando inest et patitur aliquid subiectum, homo; tunc enim fit et est albus homo. Hic autem non participat alterum altero. Genus enim non videtur participare differentiis; simul enim contrariis idem participaret; nam differentiae contrariae sunt quibus differt genus.

For in the case of 'man' and 'pale' there is a plurality when one term does not belong to the other, but a unity when it does belong and the subject, man, has a certain attribute; for then a unity is produced and we have 'the pale man'. In the present case, on the other hand, one does not share in the other; the genus is not thought to share in its differentiae (for then the same thing would share in contraries; for the differentiae by which the genus is divided are contrary).

εἰ δὲ καὶ μετέχει, ὁ αὐτὸς λόγος, εἴπερ εἰσὶν αἱ διαφοραὶ πλείους, οἷον πεζὸν δίπουν ἄπτερον. διὰ τί γὰρ ταῦθ᾽ ἓν ἀλλ᾽ οὐ πολλά; οὐ γὰρ ὅτι ἐνυπάρχει· οὕτω μὲν γὰρ ἐξ ἁπάντων ἔσται ἕν.

Si vero et participat, eadem ratio, si sunt differentiae plures, ut gressivum, bipes, non alatum. Quare namque haec unum, sed non multa? Non enim quia insunt; nam sic ex omnibus erit unum.

And even if the genus does share in them, the same argument applies, since the differentiae present in man are many, e.g. endowed with feet, two-footed, featherless. Why are these one and not many? Not because they are present in one thing; for on this principle a unity can be made out of all the attributes of a thing.

δεῖ δέ γε ἓν [25] εἶναι ὅσα ἐν τῷ ὁρισμῷ· ὁ γὰρ ὁρισμὸς λόγος τίς ἐστιν εἷς καὶ οὐσίας, ὥστε ἑνός τινος δεῖ αὐτὸν εἶναι λόγον· καὶ γὰρ ἡ οὐσία ἕν τι καὶ τόδε τι σημαίνει, ὡς φαμέν.

Oportet autem unum esse quaecumque in diffinitione; diffinitio enim ratio quaedam est una et substantia, quare unius alicuius oportet ipsam esse rationem. Et enim substantia unum quid et hoc aliquid significat, ut dicimus.

But surely all the attributes in the definition must be one; for the definition is a single formula and a formula of substance, so that it must be a formula of some one thing; for substance means a 'one' and a 'this', as we maintain.

δεῖ δὲ ἐπισκοπεῖν πρῶτον περὶ τῶν κατὰ τὰς διαιρέσεις ὁρισμῶν. οὐδὲν γὰρ ἕτερόν ἐστιν ἐν τῷ ὁρισμῷ πλὴν τὸ [30] πρῶτον λεγόμενον γένος καὶ αἱ διαφοραί· τὰ δ᾽ ἄλλα γένη ἐστὶ τό τε πρῶτον καὶ μετὰ τούτου αἱ συλλαμβανόμεναι διαφοραί, οἷον τὸ πρῶτον ζῷον, τὸ δὲ ἐχόμενον ζῷον δίπουν, καὶ πάλιν ζῷον δίπουν ἄπτερον· ὁμοίως δὲ κἂν διὰ πλειόνων λέγηται. [1038α] [1] ὅλως δ᾽ οὐδὲν διαφέρει διὰ πολλῶν ἢ δι᾽ ὀλίγων λέγεσθαι, ὥστ᾽ οὐδὲ δι᾽ ὀλίγων ἢ διὰ δυοῖν· τοῖν δυοῖν δὲ τὸ μὲν διαφορὰ τὸ δὲ γένος, οἷον τοῦ ζῷον δίπουν τὸ μὲν ζῷον γένος διαφορὰ δὲ θάτερον. [5] εἰ οὖν τὸ γένος ἁπλῶς μὴ ἔστι παρὰ τὰ ὡς γένους εἴδη, ἢ εἰ ἔστι μὲν ὡς ὕλη δ᾽ ἐστίν (ἡ μὲν γὰρ φωνὴ γένος καὶ ὕλη, αἱ δὲ διαφοραὶ τὰ εἴδη καὶ τὰ στοιχεῖα ἐκ ταύτης ποιοῦσιν), φανερὸν ὅτι ὁ ὁρισμός ἐστιν ὁ ἐκ τῶν διαφορῶν λόγος.

Oportet autem intendere primum de hiis quae secundum divisiones diffinitionibus. Nihil enim aliud est in diffinitione quam primum dictum genus et differentiae. Alia vero genera sunt primum et cum hoc comprehensae differentiae, ut primum animal, habitum vero animal bipes, et iterum animal bipes non alatum; similiter autem et si per plura dicitur. Omnino vero nihil differt per plura aut per pauca dici; quare nec per pauca aut per duo; duorum vero hoc quidem differentia illud vero genus, ut eius quod animal bipes: animal quidem genus differentia autem alterum. Si ergo genus simpliciter non est praeter eas quae ut generis species aut, si est quidem, ut materia autem est (vox enim genus est et materia, differentiae autem apecies et elementa ex hac faciunt), palam quia diffinitio est ex differentiis ratio.

We must first inquire about definitions reached by the method of divisions. There is nothing in the definition except the first-named and the differentiae. The other genera are the first genus and along with this the differentiae that are taken with it, e.g. the first may be 'animal', the next 'animal which is two-footed', and again 'animal which is two-footed and featherless', and similarly if [38a] the definition includes more terms. And in general it makes no difference whether it includes many or few terms, – nor, therefore, whether it includes few or simply two; and of the two the one is differentia and the other genus; e.g. in 'two-footed animal' 'animal' is genus, and the other is differentia.If then the genus absolutely does not exist apart from the species-of-a-genus, or if it exists but exists as matter (for the voice is genus and matter, but its differentiae make the species, i.e. the letters, out of it), clearly the definition is the formula which comprises the differentiae.

ἀλλὰ μὴν καὶ δεῖ γε διαιρεῖσθαι τῇ τῆς διαφορᾶς [10] διαφορᾷ, οἷον ζῴου διαφορὰ τὸ ὑπόπουν· πάλιν τοῦ ζῴου τοῦ ὑπόποδος τὴν διαφορὰν δεῖ εἶναι ᾗ ὑπόπουν, ὥστ᾽ οὐ λεκτέον τοῦ ὑπόποδος τὸ μὲν πτερωτὸν τὸ δὲ ἄπτερον, ἐάνπερ λέγῃ καλῶς (ἀλλὰ διὰ τὸ ἀδυνατεῖν ποιήσει τοῦτο), ἀλλ᾽ ἢ τὸ μὲν σχιζόπουν τὸ δ᾽ ἄσχιστον· αὗται [15] γὰρ διαφοραὶ ποδός· ἡ γὰρ σχιζοποδία ποδότης τις. καὶ οὕτως ἀεὶ βούλεται βαδίζειν ἕως ἂν ἔλθῃ εἰς τὰ ἀδιάφορα· τότε δ᾽ ἔσονται τοσαῦτα εἴδη ποδὸς ὅσαιπερ αἱ διαφοραί, καὶ τὰ ὑπόποδα ζῷα ἴσα ταῖς διαφοραῖς.

At vero et oportet dividi differentiae  differentiam, ut animalis differentia est pedalitas; item animalis habentis pedes differentiam oportet scire in quantum habens pedes. Quare non est dicendum habentis pedes aliud alatum aliud non alatum, siquidem bene dicit (sed propter non posse faciet hoc), sed si aliud habens fissos aliud non fissos pedes. Hae namque  sunt differentiae pedis; nam fissio pedis pedalitas quaedam est. Et sic semper vult procedere, donec utique veniat ad non differentia. Tunc autem erunt tot species pedis quot differentiae, et pedes habentia animalia aequalia differentiis.

But it is also necessary that the division be by the differentia of the differentia; e.g. 'endowed with feet' is a differentia of 'animal'; again the differentia of 'animal endowed with feet' must be of it qua endowed with feet. Therefore we must not say, if we are to speak rightly, that of that which is endowed with feet one part has feathers and one is featherless (if we do this we do it through incapacity); we must divide it only into cloven-footed and not cloven; for these are differentiae in the foot; cloven-footedness is a form of footedness. And the process wants always to go on so till it reaches the species that contain no differences. And then there will be as many kinds of foot as there are differentiae, and the kinds of animals endowed with feet will be equal in number to the differentiae.

εἰ δὴ ταῦτα οὕτως ἔχει, φανερὸν ὅτι ἡ τελευταία διαφορὰ ἡ οὐσία τοῦ [20] πράγματος ἔσται καὶ ὁ ὁρισμός, εἴπερ μὴ δεῖ πολλάκις ταὐτὰ λέγειν ἐν τοῖς ὅροις· περίεργον γάρ. συμβαίνει δέ γε τοῦτο· ὅταν γὰρ εἴπῃ ζῷον ὑπόπουν δίπουν, οὐδὲν ἄλλο εἴρηκεν ἢ ζῷον πόδας ἔχον, δύο πόδας ἔχον· κἂν τοῦτο διαιρῇ τῇ οἰκείᾳ διαιρέσει, πλεονάκις ἐρεῖ καὶ ἰσάκις ταῖς [25] διαφοραῖς. ἐὰν μὲν δὴ διαφορᾶς διαφορὰ γίγνηται, μία ἔσται ἡ τελευταία τὸ εἶδος καὶ ἡ οὐσία·

Si itaque haec sic se habent, palam quia finalis differentia substantia rei erit et diffinitio, si non oportet multotiens eadem  dicere in terminis; superfluum enim. Accidit autem hoc: nam quando dicit animal habens pedes bipes, nihil aliud dixit quam animal pedes habens duos pedes habens, et si hoc dividat propria divisione, multotiens dicet et aequaliter differentiis. Si quidem igitur differentiae differentia fiat, una erit quae finalis species et substantia;

If then this is so, clearly the last differentia will be the substance of the thing and its definition, since it is not right to state the same things more than once in our definitions; for it is superfluous. And this does happen; for when we say 'animal endowed with feet and two-footed' we have said nothing other than 'animal having feet, having two feet'; and if we divide this by the proper division, we shall be saying the same thing more than once – as many times as there are differentiae. If then a differentia of a differentia be taken at each step, one differentia – the last – will be the form and the substance;

ἐὰν δὲ κατὰ συμβεβηκός, οἷον εἰ διαιροῖ τοῦ ὑπόποδος τὸ μὲν λευκὸν τὸ δὲ μέλαν, τοσαῦται ὅσαι ἂν αἱ τομαὶ ὦσιν.

si vero secundum accidens, ut si dividat habentis pedes aliud album aliud nigrum, tot quot utique sectiones fuerint.

but if we divide according to accidental qualities, e.g. if we were to divide that which is endowed with feet into the white and the black, there will be as many differentiae as there are cuts.

ὥστε φανερὸν ὅτι ὁ ὁρισμὸς λόγος ἐστὶν ὁ ἐκ τῶν διαφορῶν, καὶ τούτων τῆς τελευταίας [30] κατά γε τὸ ὀρθόν.

Quare palam quia diffinitio ratio est quae est   ex differentiis, et harum ex finali secundum rectum.

Therefore it is plain that the definition is the formula which contains the differentiae, or, according to the right method, the last of these.

δῆλον δ᾽ ἂν εἴη, εἴ τις μετατάξειε τοὺς τοιούτους ὁρισμούς, οἷον τὸν τοῦ ἀνθρώπου, λέγων ζῷον δίπουν ὑπόπουν· περίεργον γὰρ τὸ ὑπόπουν εἰρημένου τοῦ δίποδος. τάξις δ᾽ οὐκ ἔστιν ἐν τῇ οὐσίᾳ· πῶς γὰρ δεῖ νοῆσαι τὸ μὲν ὕστερον τὸ δὲ πρότερον; περὶ μὲν οὖν τῶν κατὰ τὰς διαιρέσεις [35] ὁρισμῶν τοσαῦτα εἰρήσθω τὴν πρώτην, ποῖοί τινές εἰσιν. [1038β] [1]

Palam autem erit, si quis transponat tales diffinitiones, ut eam quae est hominis, dicens animal bipes pedes habens; superfluum enim est habens pedes dicto bipede. Sed ordo non est in substantia; quomodo namque oportet intelligere hoc quidem posterius illud vero prius? De diffinitionibus quidem igitur secundum divisiones tot dicantur primum, quales quaedam sunt.

This would be evident, if we were to change the order of such definitions, e.g. of that of man, saying 'animal which is two-footed and endowed with feet'; for 'endowed with feet' is superfluous when 'two-footed' has been said. But there is no order in the substance; for how are we to think the one element posterior and the other prior? Regarding the definitions, then, which are reached by the method of divisions, let this suffice as our first attempt at stating their nature.

*Chapter* 13

ἐπεὶ δὲ περὶ τῆς οὐσίας ἡ σκέψις ἐστί, πάλιν ἐπανέλθωμεν. λέγεται δ᾽ ὥσπερ τὸ ὑποκείμενον οὐσία εἶναι καὶ τὸ τί ἦν εἶναι καὶ τὸ ἐκ τούτων, καὶ τὸ καθόλου. περὶ μὲν οὖν τοῖν δυοῖν εἴρηται (καὶ γὰρ περὶ τοῦ τί ἦν εἶναι καὶ τοῦ [5] ὑποκειμένου, ὅτι διχῶς ὑπόκειται, ἢ τόδε τι ὄν, ὥσπερ τὸ ζῷον τοῖς πάθεσιν, ἢ ὡς ἡ ὕλη τῇ ἐντελεχείᾳ), δοκεῖ δὲ καὶ τὸ καθόλου αἴτιόν τισιν εἶναι μάλιστα, καὶ εἶναι ἀρχὴ τὸ καθόλου· διὸ ἐπέλθωμεν καὶ περὶ τούτου.

Quoniam vero de substantia perscrutatio est, iterum redeamus. Dicitur autem sicut subiectum substantia esse et quod quid erat esse et quod ex hiis, et universale. De duobus quidem igitur dictum est; et enim de quid erat esse et de subiecto, quia dupliciter subicitur: aut hoc aliquid ens, ut animal passionibus, aut ut materia actui. Videtur autem et universale causa quibusdam esse maxime, et esse principium universale; unde et de hoc tractemus.

Let us return to the subject of our inquiry, which is substance. As the substratum and the essence and the compound of these are called substance, so also is the universal. About two of these we have spoken; both about the essence and about the substratum, of which we have said that it underlies in two senses, either being a 'this' – which is the way in which an animal underlies its attributes – or as the matter underlies the complete reality. The universal also is thought by some to be in the fullest sense a cause, and a principle; therefore let us attack the discussion of this point also.

ἔοικε γὰρ ἀδύνατον εἶναι οὐσίαν εἶναι ὁτιοῦν τῶν καθόλου λεγομένων. πρῶτον [10] μὲν γὰρ οὐσία ἑκάστου ἡ ἴδιος ἑκάστῳ, ἣ οὐχ ὑπάρχει ἄλλῳ, τὸ δὲ καθόλου κοινόν· τοῦτο γὰρ λέγεται καθόλου ὃ πλείοσιν ὑπάρχειν πέφυκεν. τίνος οὖν οὐσία τοῦτ᾽ ἔσται; ἢ γὰρ πάντων ἢ οὐδενός, πάντων δ᾽ οὐχ οἷόν τε· ἑνὸς δ᾽ εἰ ἔσται, καὶ τἆλλα τοῦτ᾽ ἔσται· ὧν γὰρ μία ἡ οὐσία καὶ τὸ τί ἦν εἶναι [15] ἕν, καὶ αὐτὰ ἕν.

Videtur enim impossibile esse substantiam esse quodcumque universaliter dictorum. Primum enim substantia quae uniuscuiusque propria uniuscuiusque, quae noninest alii, universale vero commune; hoc enim dicitur universale quod pluribus inesse natum est. Cuius ergo substantia erit? Aut enim omnium aut nullius. Omnium autem non est possibile; unius autem si erit, et alia hoc erunt. Quorum enim una substantia est et quod quid erat esse unum, et ipsa unum.

For it seems impossible that any universal term should be the name of a substance. For firstly the substance of each thing is that which is peculiar to it, which does not belong to anything else; but the universal is common, since that is called universal which is such as to belong to more than one thing. Of which individual then will this be the substance? Either of all or of none; but it cannot be the substance of all. And if it is to be the substance of one, this one will be the others also; for things whose substance is one and whose essence is one are themselves also one.

ἔτι οὐσία λέγεται τὸ μὴ καθ᾽ ὑποκειμένου, τὸ δὲ καθόλου καθ᾽ ὑποκειμένου τινὸς λέγεται ἀεί.

Amplius substantia dicitur quae non de subiecto, et universale de subiecto aliquo dicitur semper.

Further, substance means that which is not predicable of a subject, but the universal is predicable of some subject always.

ἀλλ᾽ ἆρα οὕτω μὲν οὐκ ἐνδέχεται ὡς τὸ τί ἦν εἶναι, ἐν τούτῳ δὲ ἐνυπάρχειν, οἷον τὸ ζῷον ἐν τῷ ἀνθρώπῳ καὶ ἵππῳ; οὐκοῦν δῆλον ὅτι ἔστι τις αὐτοῦ λόγος. διαφέρει δ᾽ οὐθὲν οὐδ᾽ εἰ μὴ [20] πάντων λόγος ἔστι τῶν ἐν τῇ οὐσίᾳ· οὐδὲν γὰρ ἧττον οὐσία τοῦτ᾽ ἔσται τινός, ὡς ὁ ἄνθρωπος τοῦ ἀνθρώπου ἐν ᾧ ὑπάρχει, ὥστε τὸ αὐτὸ συμβήσεται πάλιν· ἔσται γὰρ ἐκείνου οὐσία, οἷον τὸ ζῷον, ἐν ᾧ ὡς ἴδιον ὑπάρχει.

Sed an sic quidem non contingit ut quod quid erat esse, in ipso autem inexistit, ut animal in homine et equo? Ergo palam quia est quaedam ipsius ratio. Differt autem nihil nec si non omnium ratio est eorum quae sunt in substantia; nihil enim minus substantia erit hoc alicuius, ut homo hominis in quo existit. Quare idem accidet iterum; erit enim substantia illius substantia, ut animal, in quo ut proprium existit.

But perhaps the universal, while it cannot be substance in the way in which the essence is so, can be present in this; e.g. 'animal' can be present in 'man' and 'horse'. Then clearly it is a formula of the essence. And it makes no difference even if it is not a formula of everything that is in the substance; for none the less the universal will be the substance of something, as 'man' is the substance of the individual man in whom it is present, so that the same result will follow once more; for the universal, e.g. 'animal', will be the substance of that in which it is present as something peculiar to it.

ἔτι δὲ καὶ ἀδύνατον καὶ ἄτοπον τὸ τόδε καὶ οὐσίαν, εἰ ἔστιν ἔκ τινων, [25] μὴ ἐξ οὐσιῶν εἶναι μηδ᾽ ἐκ τοῦ τόδε τι ἀλλ᾽ ἐκ ποιοῦ· πρότερον γὰρ ἔσται μὴ οὐσία τε καὶ τὸ ποιὸν οὐσίας τε καὶ τοῦ τόδε. ὅπερ ἀδύνατον· οὔτε λόγῳ γὰρ οὔτε χρόνῳ οὔτε γενέσει οἷόν τε τὰ πάθη τῆς οὐσίας εἶναι πρότερα· ἔσται γὰρ καὶ χωριστά.

Amplius autem et impossibile et inconveniens hoc et substantiam, si est ex aliquibus, non ex substantiis esse nec ex eo quod hoc aliquid sed ex quali; prius enim erit non substantia et quale substantia et ipso hoc, quod est impossibile. Nec enim ratione nec tempore nec generatione passiones possibilie est priores esse substantia; erunt enim separabiles.

And further it is impossible and absurd that the 'this', i.e. the substance, if it consists of parts, should not consist of substances nor of what is a 'this', but of quality; for that which is not substance, i.e. the quality, will then be prior to substance and to the 'this'. Which is impossible; for neither in formula nor in time nor in coming to be can the modifications be prior to the substance; for then they will also be separable from it.

ἔτι τῷ Σωκράτει ἐνυπάρξει οὐσία οὐσία, [30] ὥστε δυοῖν ἔσται οὐσία. ὅλως δὲ συμβαίνει, εἰ ἔστιν οὐσία ὁ ἄνθρωπος καὶ ὅσα οὕτω λέγεται, μηθὲν τῶν ἐν τῷ λόγῳ εἶναι μηδενὸς οὐσίαν μηδὲ χωρὶς ὑπάρχειν αὐτῶν μηδ᾽ ἐν ἄλλῳ, λέγω δ᾽ οἷον οὐκ εἶναί τι ζῷον παρὰ τὰ τινά, οὐδ᾽ ἄλλο τῶν ἐν τοῖς λόγοις οὐδέν. ἔκ τε δὴ τούτων θεωροῦσι [35] φανερὸν ὅτι οὐδὲν τῶν καθόλου ὑπαρχόντων οὐσία ἐστί, καὶ ὅτι οὐδὲν σημαίνει τῶν κοινῇ κατηγορουμένων τόδε τι, [1039α] [1] ἀλλὰ τοιόνδε.

Amplius Socrati inerit substantiae substantia; quare duorum erit substantia. Totaliter vero accidit, si est substantia homo et quaecumque ita dicuntur, nihil eorum quae in ratione esse nullius substantiam, neque sine ipsis existere nec in alio; dico autem ut non esse quoddam animal praeter aliqua, nec aliud eorum quae in rationibus nullum. Ex hiis itaque speculantibus palam quia nihil universaliter existentium est substantia, et quia nullum communiter praedicatorum significat hoc aliquid, sed tale.

Further, Socrates will contain a substance present in a substance, so that this will be the substance of two things. And in general it follows, if man and such things are substance, that none of the elements in their formulae is the substance of anything, nor does it exist apart from the species or in anything else; I mean, for instance, that no 'animal' exists apart from the particular kinds of animal, nor does any other of the elements present in formulae exist apart.If, then, we view the matter from these standpoints, it is plain that no universal attribute is a substance, and this is plain also from the fact that no common predicate indicates [39a] a 'this', but rather a 'such'.

εἰ δὲ μή, ἄλλα τε πολλὰ συμβαίνει καὶ ὁ τρίτος ἄνθρωπος. ἔτι δὲ καὶ ὧδε δῆλον.

Sin autem, alia quoque multa accidunt et tertius homo.

If not, many difficulties follow and especially the 'third man'.

ἀδύνατον γὰρ οὐσίαν ἐξ οὐσιῶν εἶναι ἐνυπαρχουσῶν ὡς ἐντελεχείᾳ: τὰ γὰρ δύο [5] οὕτως ἐντελεχείᾳ οὐδέποτε ἕν ἐντελεχείᾳ, ἀλλ᾿ ἐὰν δυνάμει δύο ᾖ, ἔσται ἕν (οἷον ἡ διπλασία ἐκ δύο ἡμίσεων δυνάμει γε: ἡ γὰρ ἐντελέχεια χωρίζει), ὥστ᾿ εἰ ἡ οὐσία ἕν, οὐκ ἔσται ἐξ οὐσιῶν ἐνυπαρχουσῶν καὶ κατὰ τοῦτον τὸν τρόπον, ὃν λέγει Δημόκριτος ὀρθῶς: ἀδύνατον γὰρ εἶναί φησιν ἐκ [10] δύο ἕν ἢ ἐξ ἑνὸς δύο γενέσθαι: τὰ γὰρ μεγέθη τὰ ἄτομα τὰς οὐσίας ποιεῖ. ὁμοίως τοίνυν δῆλον ὅτι καὶ ἐπ᾿ ἀριθμοῦ ἕξει, εἴπερ ἐστὶν ὁ ἀριθμὸς σύνθεσις μονάδων, ὥσπερ λέγεται ὑπό τινων: ἢ γὰρ οὐχ ἕν ἡ δυὰς ἢ οὐκ ἔστι μονὰς ἐν αὐτῇ ἐντελεχείᾳ.

Amplius autem est et ita manifestum. Impossibile enim substantiam ex substantiis esse inexistentibus sic ut actu. Duo namque sic actu numquam sunt unum actu, sed si potestate duo fuerint, erunt unum, ut quae dupla ex duobus dimidiis potestate; actus enim separat. Quare si substantia unum, non erit ex substantiis inexistentibus, et secundum hunc modum quem dicit Democritus recte. Impossibile enim esse ait ex duobus unum aut ex unno duo fieri; magnitudines enim indivisibiles substantias faciunt. Similiter igitur manifestum quia et in numero habebit, si est numerus compositio unitatum, sicut dicitur a quibusdam; aut enim non unum dualitas aut non inest unitas in ipsa actu.

The conclusion is evident also from the following consideration. A substance cannot consist of substances present in it in complete reality; for things that are thus in complete reality two are never in complete reality one, though if they are potentially two, they can be one (e.g. the double line consists of two halves – potentially; for the complete realization of the halves divides them from one another); therefore if the substance is one, it will not consist of substances present in it and present in this way, which Democritus describes rightly; he says one thing cannot be made out of two nor two out of one; for he identifies substances with his indivisible magnitudes. It is clear therefore that the same will hold good of number, if number is a synthesis of units, as is said by some; for two is either not one, or there is no unit present in it in complete reality.

ἔχει δὲ τὸ συμβαῖνον ἀπορίαν. εἰ γὰρ [15] μήτε ἐκ τῶν καθόλου οἷόν τ᾿ εἶναι μηδεμίαν οὐσίαν διὰ τὸ τοιόνδε ἀλλὰ μὴ τόδε τι σημαίνειν, μήτ᾿ ἐξ οὐσιῶν ἐνδέχεται ἐντελεχείᾳ εἶναι μηδεμίαν οὐσίαν σύνθετον, ἀσύνθετον ἂν εἴη οὐσία πᾶσα, ὥστ᾿ οὐδὲ λόγος ἂν εἴη οὐδεμιᾶς οὐσίας. ἀλλὰ μὴν δοκεῖ γε πᾶσι καὶ ἐλέχθη πάλαι ἢ [20] μόνον οὐσίας εἶναι ὅρον ἢ μάλιστα: νῦν δ᾿ οὐδὲ ταύτης. οὐδενὸς ἄρ᾿ ἔσται ὁρισμός: ἢ τρόπον μέν τινα ἔσται τρόπον δέ τινα οὔ. δῆλον δ᾿ ἔσται τὸ λεγόμενον ἐκ τῶν ὕστερον μᾶλλον.

Habet autem quod accidit dubitationem. Si enim neque ex universalibus possibile est esse nec unam substantiam propter tale sed non hoc aliquid significare, nec ex substantiis contingit actu esse neque unam substantiam, incomposita utique erit substantia omnis. Quare nec ratio utique erit neque unius substantiae. At vero videtur omnibus et dictum est dudum: aut solum substantiae esse terminum aut maxime. Nunc autem neque huius. Nullius igitur erit diffinitio; aut modo quodam erit, modo autem quodam non. Manifestum autem erit quod dicitur ex posterioribus magis.

But our result involves a difficulty. If no substance can consist of universals because a universal indicates a 'such', not a 'this', and if no substance can be composed of substances existing in complete reality, every substance would be incomposite, so that there would not even be a formula of any substance. But it is thought by all and was stated long ago that it is either only, or primarily, substance that can defined; yet now it seems that not even substance can. There cannot, then, be a definition of anything; or in a sense there can be, and in a sense there cannot. And what we are saying will be plainer from what follows.

*Chapter* 14

φανερὸν δ᾽ ἐξ αὐτῶν τούτων τὸ συμβαῖνον καὶ τοῖς [25] τὰς ἰδέας λέγουσιν οὐσίας τε χωριστὰς εἶναι καὶ ἅμα τὸ εἶδος ἐκ τοῦ γένους ποιοῦσι καὶ τῶν διαφορῶν. εἰ γὰρ ἔστι τὰ εἴδη, καὶ τὸ ζῷον ἐν τῷ ἀνθρώπῳ καὶ ἵππῳ, ἤτοι ἓν καὶ ταὐτὸν τῷ ἀριθμῷ ἐστιν ἢ ἕτερον:

Manifestum autem ex ipsis hiis accidens et ydeas dicentibus substantias et separabiles esse et simul speciem ex genere facientibus et differentiis. Si enim sunt species, et animal in homine et equo, aut unum et idem numero est aut alterum.

It is clear also from these very facts what consequence confronts those who say the Ideas are substances capable of separate existence, and at the same time make the Form consist of the genus and the differentiae. For if the Forms exist and 'animal' is present in 'man' and 'horse', it is either one and the same in number, or different.

τῷ μὲν γὰρ λόγῳ δῆλον ὅτι ἕν: τὸν γὰρ αὐτὸν διέξεισι λόγον ὁ λέγων [30] ἐν ἑκατέρῳ. εἰ οὖν ἐστί τις ἄνθρωπος αὐτὸς καθ᾽ αὑτὸν τόδε τι καὶ κεχωρισμένον, ἀνάγκη καὶ ἐξ ὧν, οἷον τὸ ζῷον καὶ τὸ δίπουν, τόδε τι σημαίνειν καὶ εἶναι χωριστὰ καὶ οὐσίας: ὥστε καὶ τὸ ζῷον.

Ratione namque palam quia unum; eandem enim exhibebit rationem dicens in utrolibet. Ergo si est aliquis homo ipsum secundum se hoc aliquid et separatum, necesse et ex quibus, ut animal et bipes, hoc aliquid significare et esse separabilia et substantias; quare et animal.

(In formula it is clearly one; for he who states the formula will go through the formula in either case.) If then there is a 'man-in-himself' who is a 'this' and exists apart, the parts also of which he consists, e.g. 'animal' and 'two-footed', must indicate 'thises', and be capable of separate existence, and substances; therefore 'animal', as well as 'man', must be of this sort.

εἰ μὲν οὖν τὸ αὐτὸ καὶ ἓν τὸ ἐν τῷ ἵππῳ καὶ τῷ ἀνθρώπῳ, ὥσπερ σὺ σαυτῷ, πῶς τὸ ἓν ἐν τοῖς οὖσι χωρὶς ἓν ἔσται,

Si quidem igitur idem et in equo sicut tu in te ipso quomodo in separatim existentibus unum erit?

Now (1) if the 'animal' in 'the horse' and in 'man' is one and the same, as you are with yourself, (a) how will the [39b]one in things that exist apart be one,

[1039β] [1] καὶ διὰ τί οὐ καὶ χωρὶς αὐτοῦ ἔσται τὸ ζῷον τοῦτο;

Et quare non et sine ipso erit animal hoc?

and how will this 'animal' escape being divided even from itself?

ἔπειτα εἰ μὲν μεθέξει τοῦ δίποδος καὶ τοῦ πολύποδος, ἀδύνατόν τι συμβαίνει, τἀναντία γὰρ ἅμα ὑπάρξει αὐτῷ ἑνὶ καὶ τῷδέ τινι ὄντι· εἰ δὲ μή, τίς ὁ τρόπος [5] ὅταν εἴπῃ τις τὸ ζῷον εἶναι δίπουν ἢ πεζόν; ἀλλ᾿ ἴσως σύγκειται καὶ ἅπτεται ἢ μέμικται· ἀλλὰ πάντα ἄτοπα.

Deinde si quidem participatione bipedis et multipedis, impossibile aliquid accidit: contraria namque simul inerunt ipsi uni et huic enti. Si autem non, quis modus, cum dixerit utique aliquis animal esse bipes aut gressibile? Sed forsam componitur et copulatur aut miscetur? Verum omnia inconvenientia.

Further, (b) if it is to share in 'two-footed' and 'many-footed', an impossible conclusion follows; for contrary attributes will belong at the same time to it although it is one and a 'this'. If it is not to share in them, what is the relation implied when one says the animal is two-footed or possessed of feet? But perhaps the two things are 'put together' and are 'in contact', or are 'mixed'. Yet all these expressions are absurd.

ἀλλ᾿ ἕτερον ἐν ἑκάστῳ· οὐκοῦν ἄπειρα ὡς ἔπος εἰπεῖν ἔσται ὧν ἡ οὐσία ζῷον· οὐ γὰρ κατὰ συμβεβηκὸς ἐκ ζῴου ἄνθρωπος.

Sed alterum in unoquoque. Infinita ergo erunt, ut consequens dicere, quorum substantia animal; non enim secundum accidens ex animali homo.

But (2) suppose the Form to be different in each species. Then there will be practically an infinite number of things whose substance is animal'; for it is not by accident that 'man' has 'animal' for one of its elements.

ἔτι πολλὰ ἔσται αὐτὸ τὸ ζῷον: οὐσία τε γὰρ τὸ [10] ἐν ἑκάστῳ ζῷον (οὐ γὰρ κατ᾽ ἄλλο λέγεται: εἰ δὲ μή, ἐξ ἐκείνου ἔσται ὁ ἄνθρωπος καὶ γένος αὐτοῦ ἐκεῖνο),

Amplius multa erit ipsum animal. Substantiaque enim quod in unoquoque animal; non enim de alio dicitur; si autem non, ex illo erit homo et genus ipsius illud.

Further, many things will be 'animal-itself'. For (i) the 'animal' in each species will be the substance of the species; for it is after nothing else that the species is called; if it were, that other would be an element in 'man', i.e. would be the genus of man.

καὶ ἔτι ἰδέαι ἅπαντα ἐξ ὧν ὁ ἄνθρωπος: οὐκοῦν οὐκ ἄλλου μὲν ἰδέα ἔσται ἄλλου δ᾽ οὐσία (ἀδύνατον γάρ): αὐτὸ ἄρα ζῷον ἓν ἕκαστον ἔσται τῶν ἐν τοῖς ζῴοις.

Et amplius ydee omnia ex quibus homo. Igitur non alterius quidem erit ydea alterius vero substantia; impossibile namque. Ipsum igitur animal erit unumquodque eorum quae in animalibus.

And further, (ii) all the elements of which 'man' is composed will be Ideas. None of them, then, will be the Idea of one thing and the substance of another; this is impossible. The 'animal', then, present in each species of animals will be animal-itself.

ἔτι ἐκ τίνος τοῦτο, καὶ [15] πῶς ἐξ αὐτοῦ ζῴου; ἢ πῶς οἷόν τε εἶναι τὸ ζῷον, ᾧ οὐσία τοῦτο αὐτό, παρ᾽ αὐτὸ τὸ ζῷον;

Amplius ex quo hoc, et quomodo ex ipso animali? Aut quomodo possibile est esse animal, quod substantia hoc ipsum, praeter ipsum animal?

Further, from what is this 'animal' in each species derived, and how will it be derived from animal-itself? Or how can this 'animal', whose essence is simply animality, exist apart from animal-itself?

ἔτι δ᾽ ἐπὶ τῶν αἰσθητῶν ταὐτά τε συμβαίνει καὶ τούτων ἀτοπώτερα. εἰ δὴ ἀδύνατον οὕτως ἔχειν, δῆλον ὅτι οὐκ ἔστιν εἴδη αὐτῶν οὕτως ὥς τινές φασιν. [20]

Amplius autem in sensibilibus haec accidunt et hiis absurdiora. Si itaque impossibile sic se habere, palam quia non est ydea ipsorum sic ut quidam dicunt.

Further, (3)in the case of sensible things both these consequences and others still more absurd follow. If, then, these consequences are impossible, clearly there are not Forms of sensible things in the sense in which some maintain their existence.

*Chapter* 15

ἐπεὶ δ᾽ ἡ οὐσία ἑτέρα, τό τε σύνολον καὶ ὁ λόγος (λέγω δ᾽ ὅτι ἡ μὲν οὕτως ἐστὶν οὐσία, σὺν τῇ ὕλῃ συνειλημμένος ὁ λόγος, ἡ δ᾽ ὁ λόγος ὅλως), ὅσαι μὲν οὖν οὕτω λέγονται, τούτων μὲν ἔστι φθορά (καὶ γὰρ γένεσις), τοῦ δὲ λόγου οὐκ ἔστιν οὕτως ὥστε φθείρεσθαι (οὐδὲ γὰρ γένεσις, οὐ [25] γὰρ γίγνεται τὸ οἰκίᾳ εἶναι ἀλλὰ τὸ τῇδε τῇ οἰκίᾳ), ἀλλ᾽ ἄνευ γενέσεως καὶ φθορᾶς εἰσὶ καὶ οὐκ εἰσίν· δέδεικται γὰρ ὅτι οὐδεὶς ταῦτα γεννᾷ οὐδὲ ποιεῖ. διὰ τοῦτο δὲ καὶ τῶν οὐσιῶν τῶν αἰσθητῶν τῶν καθ᾽ ἕκαστα οὔτε ὁρισμὸς οὔτε ἀπόδειξις ἔστιν, ὅτι ἔχουσιν ὕλην ἧς ἡ φύσις τοιαύτη ὥστ᾽ ἐνδέχεσθαι [30] καὶ εἶναι καὶ μή· διὸ φθαρτὰ πάντα τὰ καθ᾽ ἕκαστα αὐτῶν. εἰ οὖν ἥ τ᾽ ἀπόδειξις τῶν ἀναγκαίων καὶ ὁ ὁρισμὸς ἐπιστημονικόν, καὶ οὐκ ἐνδέχεται, ὥσπερ οὐδ᾽ ἐπιστήμην ὁτὲ μὲν ἐπιστήμην ὁτὲ δ᾽ ἄγνοιαν εἶναι, ἀλλὰ δόξα τὸ τοιοῦτόν ἐστιν, οὕτως οὐδ᾽ ἀπόδειξιν οὐδ᾽ ὁρισμόν, ἀλλὰ δόξα ἐστὶ τοῦ ἐνδεχομένου ἄλλως ἔχειν, [1040a] [1] δῆλον ὅτι οὐκ ἂν εἴη αὐτῶν οὔτε ὁρισμὸς οὔτε ἀπόδειξις. ἄδηλά τε γὰρ τὰ φθειρόμενα τοῖς ἔχουσι τὴν ἐπιστήμην, ὅταν ἐκ τῆς αἰσθήσεως ἀπέλθῃ, καὶ σωζομένων τῶν λόγων ἐν τῇ ψυχῇ τῶν [5] αὐτῶν οὐκ ἔσται οὔτε ὁρισμὸς ἔτι οὔτε ἀπόδειξις. διὸ δεῖ, τῶν πρὸς ὅρον ὅταν τις ὁρίζηταί τι τῶν καθ᾽ ἕκαστον, μὴ ἀγνοεῖν ὅτι ἀεὶ ἀναιρεῖν ἔστιν· οὐ γὰρ ἐνδέχεται ὁρίσασθαι.

Quoniam vero substantia altera, et quod simul totum et ratio (dico autem quia haec quidem sic est substantia, cum materia concepta ratio, illa vero ratio totaliter), quaecumque quidem igitur ita dicuntur, harum quidem est corruptio; et enim generatio. Rationis autem non est ita ut corrumpatur; neque enim generatio; non enim fit domui esse sed quod huic domui. Verum sine generatione et corruptione sunt et non sunt; ostensum est enim quia nullus haec generat nec facit.Propter hoc autem et substantiarum sensibilium singularium nec diffinitio nec demonstratio est quia habent materiam cuius natura talis est ut contingat et esse et non; quopropter corruptibilia omnia singularia ipsorum. Ergo si demonstratio necessariorum et diffinitio scientifica, et non contingit sicut nec scientiam quandoque scientiam quandoque ignorantiam esse, sed opinio quod tale est, ita nec demonstrationem nec diffinitionem, sed opinio est contingentis aliter se habere, palam quia non utique erit ipsorum nec diffinitio nec demonstratio. Non enim some manifesta corrupta scientiam habentibus, cum a sensu abscesserint; et salvatis rationibus in anima eisdem, non erit nec diffinitio amplius nec demonstratio. Propter quod oportet eorum qui ad terminum cum aliquis diffiniat aliquid singularium, non ignorare quia semper auferre est; non enim contingit diffinere.

Since substance is of two kinds, the concrete thing and the formula (I mean that one kind of substance is the formula taken with the matter, while another kind is the formula in its generality), substances in the former sense are capable of destruction (for they are capable also of generation), but there is no destruction of the formula in the sense that it is ever in course of being destroyed (for there is no generation of it either; the being of house is not generated, but only the being of this house), but without generation and destruction formulae are and are not; for it has been shown that no one begets nor makes these. For this reason, also, there is neither definition of nor demonstration about sensible individual substances, because they have matter whose nature is such that they are capable both of being and of not being; for which reason all the individual instances of them are destructible. If then demonstration is of necessary truths and definition is a scientific process, and if, just as knowledge cannot be sometimes knowledge and sometimes ignorance, but the state which varies thus is opinion, so too demonstration and definition cannot vary thus, but it is opinion that deals with [40a] that which can be otherwise than as it is, clearly there can neither be definition of nor demonstration about sensible individuals. For perishing things are obscure to those who have the relevant knowledge, when they have passed from our perception; and though the formulae remain in the soul unchanged, there will no longer be either definition or demonstration. And so when one of the definition-mongers defines any individual, he must recognize that his definition may always be overthrown; for it is not possible to define such things.

οὐδὲ δὴ ἰδέαν οὐδεμίαν ἔστιν ὁρίσασθαι. τῶν γὰρ καθ᾽ ἕκαστον ἡ ἰδέα, ὡς φασί, καὶ χωριστή:

Nec itaque ydeam nullum est diffinire. Singularium enim ydea, ut dicunt, et separabilis est.

Nor is it possible to define any Idea. For the Idea is, as its supporters say, an individual, and can exist apart;

ἀναγκαῖον δὲ ἐξ ὀνομάτων [10] εἶναι τὸν λόγον, ὄνομα δ᾽ οὐ ποιήσει ὁ ὁριζόμενος (ἄγνωστον γὰρ ἔσται), τὰ δὲ κείμενα κοινὰ πᾶσιν: ἀνάγκη ἄρα ὑπάρχειν καὶ ἄλλῳ ταῦτα: οἷον εἴ τις σὲ ὁρίσαιτο, ζῷον ἐρεῖ ἰσχνὸν ἢ λευκὸν ἢ ἕτερόν τι ὃ καὶ ἄλλῳ ὑπάρξει.

Necessarium vero ex  nominibus esse rationem, nomen autem non faciet diffiniens; ignotum enim erit. Posita autem communia omnibus. Ergo necesse inesse et alii haec; et si quis te diffiniat, animal dicet gracile aut album aut aliquid aliud quod in alio sit.

and the formula must consist of words; and he who defines must not invent a word (for it would be unknown), but the established words are common to all the members of a class; these then must apply to something besides the thing defined; e.g. if one were defining you, he would say 'an animal which is lean' or 'pale', or something else which will apply also to some one other than you.

εἰ δέ τις φαίη μηδὲν κωλύειν χωρὶς μὲν πάντα πολλοῖς [15] ἅμα δὲ μόνῳ τούτῳ ὑπάρχειν, λεκτέον πρῶτον μὲν ὅτι καὶ ἀμφοῖν, οἷον τὸ ζῷον δίπουν τῷ ζῴῳ καὶ τῷ δίποδι (καὶ τοῦτο ἐπὶ μὲν τῶν ἀϊδίων καὶ ἀνάγκη εἶναι, πρότερά γ᾽ ὄντα καὶ μέρη τοῦ συνθέτου· ἀλλὰ μὴν καὶ χωριστά, εἴπερ τὸ ἄνθρωπος χωριστόν· ἢ γὰρ οὐθὲν ἢ ἄμφω· [20] εἰ μὲν οὖν μηθέν, οὐκ ἔσται τὸ γένος παρὰ τὰ εἴδη, εἰ δ᾽ ἔσται, καὶ ἡ διαφορά)·

Si quis autem dicat nihil prohibere separatim quidem omnia multi, simul vero huic soli inesse: primum quidem quia et ambobus, ut animal bipes animali et bipedi, et hoc in sempiternis quidem, et necesse esse priora existentia et partes compositi. Quin immo et separabilia, si homo separabile; aut enim nihil aut ambo. Si quidem igitur nihil, non erit genus praeter species; si vero erit, et differentia.

If any one were to say that perhaps all the attributes taken apart may belong to many subjects, but together they belong only to this one, we must reply first that they belong also to both the elements; e.g. 'two-footed animal' belongs to animal and to the two-footed. (And in the case of eternal entities this is even necessary, since the elements are prior to and parts of the compound; nay more, they can also exist apart, if 'man' can exist apart. For either neither or both can. If, then, neither can, the genus will not exist apart from the various species; but if it does, the differentia will also.)

εἶθ᾽ ὅτι πρότερα τῷ εἶναι· ταῦτα δὲ οὐκ ἀντavaιρεῖται. ἔπειτα εἰ ἐξ ἰδεῶν αἱ ἰδέαι [23] (ἀσυνθετώτερα γὰρ τὰ ἐξ ὧν), ἔτι ἐπὶ πολλῶν δεήσει κἀκεῖνα κατηγορεῖσθαι ἐξ ὧν ἡ ἰδέα, οἷον τὸ ζῷον καὶ τὸ [25] δίπουν. εἰ δὲ μή, πῶς γνωρισθήσεται; ἔσται γὰρ ἰδέα τις ἣν ἀδύνατον ἐπὶ πλειόνων κατηγορῆσαι ἢ ἑνός. οὐ δοκεῖ δέ, ἀλλὰ πᾶσα ἰδέα εἶναι μεθεκτή.

Deinde quia priora ipso esse; haec vero non contra auferuntur. Deinde autem si ex ydeis ydee; minus enim composita ex quibus. Amplius de multis oportebit et illa praedicari ex quibus ydea, ut animal et bipes. Sin autem, quomodo cognoscetur? Erit enim ydea quaedam quam impossibile de pluribus praedicari quam uno. Non videtur autem, sed omnis ydea esse participabilis.

Secondly, we must reply that 'animal' and 'two-footed' are prior in being to 'two-footed animal'; and things which are prior to others are not destroyed when the others are.Again, if the Ideas consist of Ideas (as they must, since elements are simpler than the compound), it will be further necessary that the elements also of which the Idea consists, e.g. 'animal' and 'two-footed', should be predicated of many subjects. If not, how will they come to be known? For there will then be an Idea which cannot be predicated of more subjects than one. But this is not thought possible – every Idea is thought to be capable of being shared.

ὥσπερ οὖν εἴρηται, λανθάνει ὅτι ἀδύνατον ὁρίσασθαι ἐν τοῖς ἀϊδίοις, μάλιστα δὲ ὅσα μοναχά, οἷον ἥλιος ἢ σελήνη. οὐ μόνον γὰρ διαμαρτάνουσι [30] τῷ προστιθέναι τοιαῦτα ὧν ἀφαιρουμένων ἔτι ἔσται ἥλιος, ὥσπερ τὸ περὶ γῆν ἰὸν ἢ νυκτικρυφές (ἂν γὰρ στῇ ἢ φανῇ, οὐκέτι ἔσται ἥλιος· ἀλλ᾽ ἄτοπον εἰ μή· ὁ γὰρ ἥλιος οὐσίαν τινὰ σημαίνει)· ἔτι ὅσα ἐπ᾽ ἄλλου ἐνδέχεται, οἷον ἐὰν ἕτερος γένηται τοιοῦτος, δῆλον ὅτι ἥλιος ἔσται· κοινὸς ἄρα ὁ λόγος· [1040β] [1] ἀλλ᾽ ἦν τῶν καθ᾽ ἕκαστα ὁ ἥλιος, ὥσπερ Κλέων ἢ Σωκράτης· ἐπεὶ διὰ τί οὐδεὶς ὅρον ἐκφέρει αὐτῶν ἰδέας; γένοιτο γὰρ ἂν δῆλον πειρωμένων ὅτι ἀληθὲς τὸ νῦν εἰρημένον. [5]

Quemadmodum ergo dictum est, latet quod impossibile diffinire in sempiternis, maxime vero quaecumque unica, ut sol et luna. Non solum enim peccant additione talium quibus  ablatis adhuc erit sol, puta terram girans aut nocte absconditum; si enim steterit aut apparuerit, non adhuc erit sol. Sed absurdum si non; sol enim substantiam quandam significat. Amplius quaecumque in alio contingunt, ut si alter fiat talis, palam sol erit; communis ergo ratio. Sed erat  singularium sol, it Cleon aut Socrates.Quoniam propter quid nullus ipsorum terminum profert ydee? Fiet enim utique manifestum temptantibus quia verum quod modo dictum est.

As has been said, then, the impossibility of defining individuals escapes notice in the case of eternal things, especially those which are unique, like the sun or the moon. For people err not only by adding attributes whose removal the sun would survive, e.g. 'going round the earth' or 'night-hidden' (for from their view it follows that if it stands still or is visible, it will no longer be the sun; but it is strange if this is so; for 'the sun' means a certain substance); but also by the mention of attributes which can belong to another subject; e.g. if another thing with the stated attributes comes into existence, clearly it will be [40b] a sun; the formula therefore is general. But the sun was supposed to be an individual, like Cleon or Socrates. After all, why does not one of the supporters of the Ideas produce a definition of an Idea? It would become clear, if they tried, that what has now been said is true.

*Chapter*  16

φανερὸν δὲ ὅτι καὶ τῶν δοκουσῶν εἶναι οὐσιῶν αἱ πλεῖσται δυνάμεις εἰσί, τά τε μόρια τῶν ζῴων (οὐθὲν γὰρ κεχωρισμένον αὐτῶν ἐστίν· ὅταν δὲ χωρισθῇ, καὶ τότε ὄντα ὡς ὕλη πάντα) καὶ γῆ καὶ πῦρ καὶ ἀήρ· οὐδὲν γὰρ αὐτῶν ἕν ἐστιν, ἀλλ᾽ οἷον σωρός, πρὶν ἢ πεφθῇ καὶ γένηταί τι [10] ἐξ αὐτῶν ἕν. μάλιστα δ᾽ ἄν τις τὰ τῶν ἐμψύχων ὑπολάβοι μόρια καὶ τὰ τῆς ψυχῆς πάρεγγυς ἄμφω γίγνεσθαι, ὄντα καὶ ἐντελεχείᾳ καὶ δυνάμει, τῷ ἀρχὰς ἔχειν κινήσεως ἀπό τινος ἐν ταῖς καμπαῖς· διὸ ἔνια ζῷα διαιρούμενα ζῇ. ἀλλ᾽ ὅμως δυνάμει πάντ᾽ ἔσται, ὅταν ᾖ ἓν καὶ [15] συνεχὲς φύσει, ἀλλὰ μὴ βίᾳ ἢ συμφύσει· τὸ γὰρ τοιοῦτον πήρωσις.

Manifestum est autem quod substantiarum esse existimatarum plurime potestate sunt, et ipse partes animalium; nihil enim separatum ipsorum est. Quando autem separata fuerint, tunc entia ut materia omnia, terra, ignis et aer. Nihil enim ipsorum unum est, nisi ut cumulus, antequam digeratur et fiat aliquid ex ipsis unum. Maxime autem utique aliquis animatorum suspicabitur partes et eas quae animae propinque ambas fieri, entes et actu et potentia, eo quod principia habeant motus ab aliquo in iuncturis; propter quod quaedam animalia divisa vivunt. Sed tamen potentia omnia erunt, quando fuerit unum et continuum natura, sed non vi aut complantatione; tale namque est orbatio.

Evidently even of the things that are thought to be substances, most are only potencies, – both the parts of animals (for none of them exists separately; and when they are separated, then too they exist, all of them, merely as matter) and earth and fire and air; for none of them is a unity, but as it were a mere heap, till they are worked up and some unity is made out of them. One might most readily suppose the parts of living things and the parts of the soul nearly related to them to turn out to be both, i.e. existent in complete reality as well as in potency, because they have sources of movement in something in their joints; for which reason some animals live when divided. Yet all the parts must exist only potentially, when they are one and continuous by nature, – not by force or by growing into one, for such a phenomenon is an abnormality.

ἐπεὶ δὲ τὸ ἓν λέγεται ὥσπερ καὶ τὸ ὄν, καὶ ἡ οὐσία ἡ τοῦ ἑνὸς μία, καὶ ὧν μία ἀριθμῷ ἓν ἀριθμῷ, φανερὸν ὅτι οὔτε τὸ ἓν οὔτε τὸ ὂν ἐνδέχεται οὐσίαν εἶναι τῶν πραγμάτων, ὥσπερ οὐδὲ τὸ στοιχείῳ εἶναι ἢ ἀρχῇ· ἀλλὰ [20] ζητοῦμεν τίς οὖν ἡ ἀρχή, ἵνα εἰς γνωριμώτερον ἀναγάγωμεν. μᾶλλον μὲν οὖν τούτων οὐσία τὸ ὂν καὶ ἓν ἢ ἥ τε ἀρχὴ καὶ τὸ στοιχεῖον καὶ τὸ αἴτιον,

Quoniam vero unum dicitur sicut et ens, et substantia unius una, et quorum una numero unum numero, palam quia nec unum nec ens contingit substantium esse rerum, sicut neque elemento esse aut principio; sed quaerimus quid igitur principium, ut ad notius reducamus. Magis igitur horum substantia est ens et unum quam principium et elementum et causa;

Since the term 'unity' is used like the term 'being', and the substance of that which is one is one, and things whose substance is numerically one are numerically one, evidently neither unity nor being can be the substance of things, just as being an element or a principle cannot be the substance, but we ask what, then, the principle is, that we may reduce the thing to something more knowable. Now of these concepts 'being' and 'unity' are more substantial than 'principle' or 'element' or 'cause',

οὔπω δὲ οὐδὲ ταῦτα, εἴπερ μηδ᾽ ἄλλο κοινὸν μηδὲν οὐσία: οὐδενὶ γὰρ ὑπάρχει ἡ οὐσία ἀλλ᾽ ἢ αὑτῇ τε καὶ τῷ ἔχοντι αὐτήν, οὗ ἐστὶν οὐσία.

sed nec ista, si nec aliud commune nihil substantia. Nulli namque inest substantia sed huic et habenti ipsam, cuius est substantia.

but not even the former are substance, since in general nothing that is common is substance; for substance does not belong to anything but to itself and to that which has it, of which it is the substance.

[25] ἔτι τὸ ἓν πολλαχῇ οὐκ ἂν εἴη ἅμα, τὸ δὲ κοινὸν ἅμα πολλαχῇ ὑπάρχει: ὥστε δῆλον ὅτι οὐδὲν τῶν καθόλου ὑπάρχει παρὰ τὰ καθ᾽ ἕκαστα χωρίς.

Amplius quod unum apud multa non utique erit simul, quod autem commune simul apud multa existit; quare palam quia nullum universalium existit praeter singularia separatim.

Further, that which is one cannot be in many places at the same time, but that which is common is present in many places at the same time; so that clearly no universal exists apart from its individuals.

ἀλλ᾽ οἱ τὰ εἴδη λέγοντες τῇ μὲν ὀρθῶς λέγουσι χωρίζοντες αὐτά, εἴπερ οὐσίαι εἰσί, τῇ δ᾽ οὐκ ὀρθῶς, ὅτι τὸ ἓν ἐπὶ πολλῶν εἶδος [30] λέγουσιν. αἴτιον δ᾽ ὅτι οὐκ ἔχουσιν ἀποδοῦναι τίνες αἱ τοιαῦται οὐσίαι αἱ ἄφθαρτοι παρὰ τὰς καθ᾽ ἕκαστα καὶ αἰσθητάς: ποιοῦσιν οὖν τὰς αὐτὰς τῷ εἴδει τοῖς φθαρτοῖς (ταύτας γὰρ ἴσμεν), αὐτοάνθρωπον καὶ αὐτόϊππον, προστιθέντες τοῖς αἰσθητοῖς τὸ ῥῆμα τὸ "αὐτό". καίτοι κἂν εἰ μὴ ἑωράκειμεν τὰ ἄστρα, [1041α] [1] οὐδὲν ἂν ἧττον, οἶμαι, ἦσαν οὐσίαι ἀΐδιοι παρ᾽ ἃς ἡμεῖς ᾔδειμεν: ὥστε καὶ νῦν εἰ μὴ ἔχομεν τίνες εἰσίν, ἀλλ᾽ εἶναί γέ τινας ἴσως ἀναγκαῖον. ὅτι μὲν οὖν οὔτε τῶν καθόλου λεγομένων οὐδὲν οὐσία οὔτ᾽ ἔστιν οὐσία [5] οὐδεμία ἐξ οὐσιῶν, δῆλον.

Sed species dicentes hic quidem dicunt recte separantes eas, si substantiae sunt, illic autem non recte, quia unam in multis speciem dicunt. Causa vero quia non habent reddere quae tales substantiae incorruptibiles praeter singulares et sensibiles. Ergo faciunt easdem specie corruptibilibus (has enim scimus) auto-hominem et autoequum, addentes sensibilibus verbum auto. Quamvis utique si non videremus astra, non minus, existimo, forent substantiae sempiternae praeter eas quas nos videremus; quare et nunc si non habemus quae sunt, tamen esse quasdam forsan est necessarium. Quod quidem igitur neque universaliter dictorum nihil substantia nec est substantia neque una ex substantiis manifestum.

But those who say the Forms exist, in one respect are right, in giving the Forms separate existence, if they are substances; but in another respect they are not right, because they say the one over many is a Form. The reason for their doing this is that they cannot declare what are the substances of this sort, the imperishable substances which exist apart from the individual and sensible substances. They make them, then, the same in kind as the perishable things (for this kind of substance we know)—'man-himself' and 'horse-itself', adding to the sensible things the word [41a] 'itself'. Yet even if we had not seen the stars, none the less, I suppose, would they have been eternal substances apart from those which we knew; so that now also if we do not know what non-sensible substances there are, yet it is doubtless necessary that there should he some. – Clearly, then, no universal term is the name of a substance, and no substance is composed of substances.

*Chapter* 17

τί δὲ χρὴ λέγειν καὶ ὁποῖόν τι τὴν οὐσίαν, πάλιν ἄλλην οἷον ἀρχὴν ποιησάμενοι λέγωμεν· ἴσως γὰρ ἐκ τούτων ἔσται δῆλον καὶ περὶ ἐκείνης τῆς οὐσίας ἥτις ἐστὶ κεχωρισμένη τῶν αἰσθητῶν οὐσιῶν. ἐπεὶ οὖν ἡ οὐσία ἀρχὴ καὶ [10] αἰτία τις ἐστίν, ἐντεῦθεν μετιτέον.

Quid autem oportet dicere et quale quid substantiam, iterum aliud velut principium facientes dicamus; forsan enim ex hiis erit palam et de illa substantia quae est separata a sensibilibus substantiis. Quoniam ergo substantia principium et causa quaedam est, hinc est procedendum.

Let us state what, i.e. what kind of thing, substance should be said to be, taking once more another starting-point; for perhaps from this we shall get a clear view also of that substance which exists apart from sensible substances. Since, then, substance is a principle and a cause, let us pursue it from this starting-point.

ζητεῖται δὲ τὸ διὰ τί ἀεὶ οὕτως, διὰ τί ἄλλο ἄλλῳ τινὶ ὑπάρχει. τὸ γὰρ ζητεῖν διὰ τί ὁ μουσικὸς ἄνθρωπος μουσικὸς ἄνθρωπός ἐστιν, ἤτοι ἐστὶ τὸ εἰρημένον ζητεῖν, διὰ τί ὁ ἄνθρωπος μουσικός ἐστιν, ἢ ἄλλο. τὸ μὲν οὖν διὰ τί αὐτό ἐστιν αὐτό, οὐδέν ἐστι [15] ζητεῖν (δεῖ γὰρ τὸ ὅτι καὶ τὸ εἶναι ὑπάρχειν δῆλα ὄντα—λέγω δ᾽ οἷον ὅτι ἡ σελήνη ἐκλείπει—, αὐτὸ δὲ ὅτι αὐτό, εἷς λόγος καὶ μία αἰτία ἐπὶ πάντων, διὰ τί ὁ ἄνθρωπος ἄνθρωπος ἢ ὁ μουσικὸς μουσικός, πλὴν εἴ τις λέγοι ὅτι ἀδιαίρετον πρὸς αὐτὸ ἕκαστον, τοῦτο δ᾽ ἦν τὸ ἑνὶ εἶναι· ἀλλὰ τοῦτο [20] κοινόν γε κατὰ πάντων καὶ σύντομον)· ζητήσειε δ᾽ ἄν τις διὰ τί ἄνθρωπός ἐστι ζῷον τοιονδί. τοῦτο μὲν τοίνυν δῆλον, ὅτι οὐ ζητεῖ διὰ τί ὅς ἐστιν ἄνθρωπος ἄνθρωπός ἐστιν· τὶ ἄρα κατά τινος ζητεῖ διὰ τί ὑπάρχει (ὅτι δ᾽ ὑπάρχει, δεῖ δῆλον εἶναι· εἰ γὰρ μὴ οὕτως, οὐδὲν ζητεῖ), οἷον διὰ τί [25] βροντᾷ; διὰ τί ψόφος γίγνεται ἐν τοῖς νέφεσιν; ἄλλο γὰρ οὕτω κατ᾽ ἄλλου ἐστὶ τὸ ζητούμενον. καὶ διὰ τί ταδί, οἷον πλίνθοι καὶ λίθοι, οἰκία ἐστίν; φανερὸν τοίνυν ὅτι ζητεῖ τὸ αἴτιον· τοῦτο δ᾽ ἐστὶ τὸ τί ἦν εἶναι, ὡς εἰπεῖν λογικῶς, ὃ ἐπ᾽ ἐνίων μέν ἐστι τίνος ἕνεκα, οἷον ἴσως ἐπ᾽ οἰκίας ἢ κλίνης, [30] ἐπ᾽ ἐνίων δὲ τί ἐκίνησε πρῶτον· αἴτιον γὰρ καὶ τοῦτο. ἀλλὰ τὸ μὲν τοιοῦτον αἴτιον ἐπὶ τοῦ γίγνεσθαι ζητεῖται καὶ φθείρεσθαι, θάτερον δὲ καὶ ἐπὶ τοῦ εἶναι.

Quaeritur autem ipsum propter quid semper sic: propter quid aliud aliquid alii alicui inest? Nam quaerere propter quid musicus homo musicus homo est, aut est quod dictum est quaerere, propter quid homo musicus est, aut aliud. Hoc quidem igitur propter quid ipsum est ipsum, nihil est quaerere. Oportet enim ipsum quia et ipsum esse existere manifesta entia; dico autem ut quia luna patitur eclipsim. Ipsius autem quia ipsum una ratio et una causa in omnibus (propter quid homo homo aut musicus musicus, nisi si quis dicat quia indivisibile ad ipsum unumquodque, hoc autem erat unum esse. Sed hoc communeque de omnibus et quod breve. Quaeret autem aliquis propter quid homo est animal tale. Hoc quidem igitur palam, quia non quaerit quare qui est homo homo est; aliquid ergo de aliquo quaerit propter quid existit. Quia vero existit, oportet manifestum esse; nam si non ita, nihil quaerit. Ut propter quid tonat? Quia sonitus fit in nubibus. Aliud enim ita de alio est quod quaeritur. Et propter quid haec, puta lateres et lapides, domus sunt? Palam igitur quod quaerit causam. Hoc autem est quod quid erat esse, ut est dicere logice, quod quod in quibusdam quidem est cuius causa, ut forsan in domo aut in lecto, in quibusdam vero quid movit primum; nam causa et hoc. Sed talis quidem causa in fieri quaeritur et corrumpi, altera vero et in esse.

The 'why' is always sought in this form—'why does one thing attach to some other?' For to inquire why the musical man is a musical man, is either to inquire—as we have said why the man is musical, or it is something else. Now 'why a thing is itself' is a meaningless inquiry (for (to give meaning to the question 'why') the fact or the existence of the thing must already be evident – e.g. that the moon is eclipsed – but the fact that a thing is itself is the single reason and the single cause to be given in answer to all such questions as why the man is man, or the musician musical', unless one were to answer 'because each thing is inseparable from itself, and its being one just meant this'; this, however, is common to all things and is a short and easy way with the question). But we can inquire why man is an animal of such and such a nature. This, then, is plain, that we are not inquiring why he who is a man is a man. We are inquiring, then, why something is predicable of something (that it is predicable must be clear; for if not, the inquiry is an inquiry into nothing). E.g. why does it thunder? This is the same as 'why is sound produced in the clouds?' Thus the inquiry is about the predication of one thing of another. And why are these things, i.e. bricks and stones, a house? Plainly we are seeking the cause. And this is the essence (to speak abstractly), which in some cases is the end, e.g. perhaps in the case of a house or a bed, and in some cases is the first mover; for this also is a cause. But while the efficient cause is sought in the case of genesis and destruction, the final cause is sought in the case of being also.

λανθάνει δὲ μάλιστα τὸ ζητούμενον ἐν τοῖς μὴ κατ᾽ ἀλλήλων λεγομένοις, [1041β] [1] οἷον ἄνθρωπος τί ἐστι ζητεῖται διὰ τὸ ἁπλῶς λέγεσθαι ἀλλὰ μὴ διορίζειν ὅτι τάδε τόδε.

Latet autem maxime quod quaeritur in hiis quae non de aliis dicuntur, ut homo quid est quaeritur, propter simpliciter dici sed non diffinire quia haec aut hoc.

The object of the inquiry is most easily overlooked where one term is not expressly predicated of another (e.g. when [41b] we inquire 'what man is'), because we do not distinguish and do not say definitely that certain elements make up a certain whole.

ἀλλὰ δεῖ διαρθρώσαντας ζητεῖν: εἰ δὲ μή, κοινὸν τοῦ μηθὲν ζητεῖν καὶ τοῦ ζητεῖν τι γίγνεται. ἐπεὶ δὲ δεῖ ἔχειν τε καὶ ὑπάρχειν τὸ [5] εἶναι, δῆλον δὴ ὅτι τὴν ὕλην ζητεῖ διὰ τί <τί ἐστιν: οἷον οἰκία ταδὶ διὰ τί; ὅτι ὑπάρχει ὃ ἦν οἰκίᾳ εἶναι. καὶ ἄνθρωπος τοδί, ἢ τὸ σῶμα τοῦτο τοδὶ ἔχον. ὥστε τὸ αἴτιον ζητεῖται τῆς ὕλης (τοῦτο δ᾽ ἐστὶ τὸ εἶδος) ᾧ τί ἐστιν: τοῦτο δ᾽ ἡ οὐσία.

Sed oportet corrigentes quaerere; si autem non, commune eius quod nihil quaerere et eius quod quaerere aliquid fit. Quoniam vero oportet habere quae et existere ipsum esse, palam itaque quia materiam quaerit propter quid est; ut domus haec propter quid? Quia haec existunt, quod erat domui esse. Et homo hic aut corpus hoc hoc habens? Quare causa quaeritur materiae, hoc autem est species, qua aliquid est; hoc autem substantia.

But we must articulate our meaning before we begin to inquire; if not, the inquiry is on the border-line between being a search for something and a search for nothing. Since we must have the existence of the thing as something given, clearly the question is why the matter is some definite thing; e.g. why are these materials a house? Because that which was the essence of a house is present. And why is this individual thing, or this body having this form, a man? Therefore what we seek is the cause, i.e. the form, by reason of which the matter is some definite thing; and this is the substance of the thing.

φανερὸν τοίνυν ὅτι ἐπὶ τῶν ἁπλῶν οὐκ ἔστι ζήτησις [10] οὐδὲ δίδαξις, ἀλλ᾽ ἕτερος τρόπος τῆς ζητήσεως τῶν τοιούτων.

Palam igitur quod in simplicibus non est quaestio nec doctrina, sed alter modus quaestionis talium.

Evidently, then, in the case of simple terms no inquiry nor teaching is possible; our attitude towards such things is other than that of inquiry.

ἐπεὶ δὲ τὸ ἔκ τινος σύνθετον οὕτως ὥστε ἓν εἶναι τὸ πᾶν, [ἂν] μὴ ὡς σωρὸς ἀλλ᾽ ὡς ἡ συλλαβή—ἡ δὲ συλλαβὴ οὐκ ἔστι τὰ στοιχεῖα, οὐδὲ τῷ <βα ταὐτὸ τὸ <β καὶ <α, οὐδ᾽ ἡ σὰρξ πῦρ καὶ γῆ (διαλυθέντων γὰρ τὰ μὲν οὐκέτι ἔστιν, [15] οἷον ἡ σὰρξ καὶ ἡ συλλαβή, τὰ δὲ στοιχεῖα ἔστι, καὶ τὸ πῦρ καὶ ἡ γῆ): ἔστιν ἄρα τι ἡ συλλαβή, οὐ μόνον τὰ στοιχεῖα τὸ φωνῆεν καὶ ἄφωνον ἀλλὰ καὶ ἕτερόν τι, καὶ ἡ σὰρξ οὐ μόνον πῦρ καὶ γῆ ἢ τὸ θερμὸν καὶ ψυχρὸν ἀλλὰ καὶ ἕτερόν τι

Quoniam vero ex aliquo compositum sic ut unum sit omne, sed non ut cumulus sed ut syllaba – syllaba autem non est elementa, nec idem b et a, nec caro ignis et terra; dissolutis enim haec quidem non adhuc sunt, ut caro et syllaba, elementa vero sunt, et ignis et terra. Est igitur aliquid syllaba, non solum elementa (vocalis et consonans) sed et alterum aliquid, et caro non solum ignis et terra aut calidum et frigidum sed et alterum aliquid.

Since that which is compounded out of something so that the whole is one, not like a heap but like a syllable – now the syllable is not its elements, ba is not the same as b and a, nor is flesh fire and earth (for when these are separated the wholes, i.e. the flesh and the syllable, no longer exist, but the elements of the syllable exist, and so do fire and earth); the syllable, then, is something – not only its elements (the vowel and the consonant) but also something else, and the flesh is not only fire and earth or the hot and the cold, but also something else:

—εἰ τοίνυν ἀνάγκη κἀκεῖνο ἢ στοιχεῖον [20] ἢ ἐκ στοιχείων εἶναι, εἰ μὲν στοιχεῖον, πάλιν ὁ αὐτὸς ἔσται λόγος (ἐκ τούτου γὰρ καὶ πυρὸς καὶ γῆς ἔσται ἡ σὰρξ καὶ ἔτι ἄλλου, ὥστ᾽ εἰς ἄπειρον βαδιεῖται): εἰ δὲ ἐκ στοιχείου, δῆλον ὅτι οὐχ ἑνὸς ἀλλὰ πλειόνων, ἢ ἐκεῖνο αὐτὸ ἔσται, ὥστε πάλιν ἐπὶ τούτου τὸν αὐτὸν ἐροῦμεν λόγον καὶ ἐπὶ τῆς [25] σαρκὸς ἢ συλλαβῆς.

Si igitur necesse et illud aut elementum aut ex elementis esse, si quidem elementum, iterum eadem ratio erit; ex hoc enim et igne et terra erit caro et adhuc alio. Quare in infinitum ibit.Si vero ex elemento, palam quia non uno sed pluribus; aut illud ipsum erit. Quare rursum in hoc eandem dicemus rationem et in carne vel syllaba.

– if, then, that something must itself be either an element or composed of elements, (1) if it is an element the same argument will again apply; for flesh will

304

consist of this and fire and earth and something still further, so that the process will go on to infinity. But (2) if it is a compound, clearly it will be a compound not of one but of more than one (or else that one will be the thing itself), so that again in this case we can use the same argument as in the case of flesh or of the syllable.

δόξειε δ᾽ ἂν εἶναι τὶ τοῦτο καὶ οὐ στοιχεῖον, καὶ αἴτιόν γε τοῦ εἶναι τοδὶ μὲν σάρκα τοδὶ δὲ συλλαβήν: ὁμοίως δὲ καὶ ἐπὶ τῶν ἄλλων. οὐσία δὲ ἑκάστου μὲν τοῦτο (τοῦτο γὰρ αἴτιον πρῶτον τοῦ εἶναι)—

Videbitur autem utique esse aliquid hoc et elementum et causa essendi hoc quidem carnem hoc vero syllabam. Similiter autem et in aliis.Substantia autem uniuscuiusque quidem hoc; hoc enim causa prima essendi.

But it would seem that this 'other' is something, and not an element, and that it is the cause which makes this thing flesh and that a syllable. And similarly in all other cases. And this is the substance of each thing (for this is the primary cause of its being);

ἐπεὶ δ᾽ ἔνια οὐκ οὐσίαι τῶν πραγμάτων, ἀλλ᾽ ὅσαι οὐσίαι, κατὰ φύσιν [30] καὶ φύσει συνεστήκασι, φανείη ἂν [καὶ] αὕτη ἡ φύσις οὐσία, ἥ ἐστιν οὐ στοιχεῖον ἀλλ᾽ ἀρχή—: στοιχεῖον δ᾽ ἐστὶν εἰς ὃ διαιρεῖται ἐνυπάρχον ὡς ὕλην, οἷον τῆς συλλαβῆς τὸ <α καὶ τὸ <β.

Quoniam vero quaedam non substantiae rerum, sed quaecumque substantiae secundum naturam et natura constitutae sunt, manifestabitur utique quibusdam haec natura substantia, quae est non elementum sed principium.Elementum vero est in quod dividitur inexistens ut materiam, puta syllabe quod a et b.

and since, while some things are not substances, as many as are substances are formed in accordance with a nature of their own and by a process of nature, their substance would seem to be this kind of 'nature', which is not an element but a principle. An element, on the other hand, is that into which a thing is divided and which is present in it as matter; e.g. a and b are the elements of the syllable.

# METHAPHISICE ARISTOTILIS LIBER OCTAVUS

8 (H)

[1042α] [3] ἐκ δὴ τῶν εἰρημένων συλλογίσασθαι δεῖ καὶ συναγαγόντας τὸ κεφάλαιον τέλος ἐπιθεῖναι.

Ex dictis itaque sillogizare oportet et colligentes capitulum finem imponere.

WE must reckon up the results arising from what has been said, and compute the sum of them, and put the finishing touch to our inquiry.

εἴρηται δὴ ὅτι [5] τῶν οὐσιῶν ζητεῖται τὰ αἴτια καὶ αἱ ἀρχαὶ καὶ τὰ στοιχεῖα.

Dictum est itaque quia substantiarum quaeruntur cause et principia et elementa.

We have said that the causes, principles, and elements of substances are the object of our search.

οὐσίαι δὲ αἱ μὲν ὁμολογούμεναί εἰσιν ὑπὸ πάντων, [7] περὶ δὲ ἐνίων ἰδίᾳ τινὲς ἀπεφήναντο· ὁμολογούμεναι μὲν αἱ φυσικαί, οἷον πῦρ γῆ ὕδωρ ἀὴρ καὶ τἆλλα τὰ ἁπλᾶ σώματα, ἔπειτα τὰ φυτὰ καὶ τὰ μόρια αὐτῶν, καὶ τὰ [10] ζῷα καὶ τὰ μόρια τῶν ζῴων, καὶ τέλος ὁ οὐρανὸς καὶ τὰ μόρια τοῦ οὐρανοῦ· ἰδίᾳ δέ τινες οὐσίας λέγουσιν εἶναι τά τ᾽ εἴδη καὶ τὰ μαθηματικά.

Substantiae vero hae quidem confesse sunt ab omnibus, sed de quibusdam singulariter quidam enuntiaverunt. Confesse quidem phisice, ut ignis, terra et aqua et alia simplicia corpora, deinde plante et partes earum, et animalia et partes animalium, et tandem celum et partes celi. Singulariter vero quidam substantias dicunt esse species et mathematica.

And some substances are recognized by every one, but some have been advocated by particular schools. Those generally recognized are the natural substances, i.e. fire, earth, water, air, &c., the simple bodies; second plants and their parts, and animals and the parts of animals; and finally the physical universe and its parts; while some particular schools say that Forms and the objects of mathematics are substances.

ἄλλας δὲ δὴ συμβαίνει ἐκ τῶν λόγων οὐσίας εἶναι, τὸ τί ἦν εἶναι καὶ τὸ ὑποκείμενον· ἔτι ἄλλως τὸ γένος μᾶλλον τῶν εἰδῶν καὶ τὸ καθόλου τῶν [15] καθ᾽ ἕκαστα· τῷ δὲ καθόλου καὶ τῷ γένει καὶ αἱ ἰδέαι συνάπτουσιν (κατὰ τὸν αὐτὸν γὰρ λόγον οὐσίαι δοκοῦσιν εἶναι).

Alias vero accidit ex rationibus substantias esse: quod quid erat esse et quod subicitur. Adhuc aliter genus magis speciebus et universale singularibus. Universali vero et generi et ydee copulantur; nam secundum eandem rationem substantiae videntur esse.

But there are arguments which lead to the conclusion that there are other substances, the essence and the substratum. Again, in another way the genus seems more substantial than the various species, and the universal than the particulars. And with the universal and the genus the Ideas are connected; it is in virtue of the same argument that they are thought to be substances.

ἐπεὶ δὲ τὸ τί ἦν εἶναι οὐσία, τούτου δὲ λόγος ὁ ὁρισμός, διὰ τοῦτο περὶ ὁρισμοῦ καὶ περὶ τοῦ καθ᾽ αὑτὸ διώρισται· ἐπεὶ δὲ ὁ ὁρισμὸς λόγος, ὁ δὲ λόγος μέρη ἔχει, ἀναγκαῖον καὶ [20] περὶ μέρους ἦν ἰδεῖν, ποῖα τῆς οὐσίας μέρη καὶ ποῖα οὔ, καὶ εἰ ταῦτα καὶ τοῦ ὁρισμοῦ. ἔτι τοίνυν οὔτε τὸ καθόλου οὐσία οὔτε τὸ γένος· περὶ δὲ τῶν ἰδεῶν καὶ τῶν μαθηματικῶν ὕστερον σκεπτέον· παρὰ γὰρ τὰς αἰσθητὰς οὐσίας ταύτας λέγουσί τινες εἶναι. νῦν δὲ περὶ τῶν ὁμολογουμένων οὐσιῶν [25] ἐπέλθωμεν. αὗται δ᾽ εἰσὶν αἱ αἰσθηταί·

Quoniam autem quod quid erat esse substantia , huius autem ratio diffinitio, propter hoc de diffinitione et de secundum se  diffmitum est. Quoniam autem diffinitio ratio est, ratio autem partes  habet, necesse et de parte erat considerare quae substantiae  partes et quae non, et si hae diffinitioni opus sunt. Amplius etiam nec universale substantia nec genus. De ydeis vero et  mathematicis posterius perscrutandum est. Nam praeter sensibiles substantias quidam dicunt eas esse.  Nunc autem de confessis substantiis tractabimus. Hae vero  sensibiles;

And since the essence is substance, and the definition is a formula of the essence, for this reason we have discussed definition and essential predication. Since the definition is a formula, and a formula has parts, we had to consider also with respect to the notion of part , what are parts of the substance and what are not, and whether the parts of the substance are also parts of the definition. Further, too, neither the universal nor the genus is a substance; we must inquire later into the Ideas and the objects of mathematics; for some say these are substances as well as the sensible substances. But now let us resume the discussion of the generally recognized substances. These are the sensible substances,

αἱ δ᾽ αἰσθηταὶ οὐσίαι πᾶσαι ὕλην ἔχουσιν. ἔστι δ᾽ οὐσία τὸ ὑποκείμενον, ἄλλως μὲν ἡ ὕλη (ὕλην δὲ λέγω ἣ μὴ τόδε τι οὖσα ἐνεργείᾳ δυνάμει ἐστὶ τόδε τι), ἄλλως δ᾽ ὁ λόγος καὶ ἡ μορφή, ὃ τόδε τι ὂν τῷ λόγῳ χωριστόν ἐστιν· τρίτον δὲ τὸ [30] ἐκ τούτων, οὗ γένεσις μόνου καὶ φθορά ἐστι, καὶ χωριστὸν ἁπλῶς· τῶν γὰρ κατὰ τὸν λόγον οὐσιῶν αἱ μὲν αἱ δ᾽ οὔ.

sensibiles autem substantiae omnes materiam habent. Est autem substantia quod subicitur, aliter quidem materia ; materiam vero dico quae non hoc aliquid ens actu potestate est hoc aliquid. Aliter vero ratio et forma, quod hoc aliquid ens ratione separabile est. Tertium vero  quod est ex hiis,  cuius solius generatio et corruptio, et separabile simpliciter; nam secundum rationem substantiarum hae quidem  ille vero non.

and sensible substances all have matter. The substratum is substance, and this is in one sense the matter (and by matter I mean that which, not being a this actually, is potentially a this ), and in another sense the formula or shape (that which being a this can be separately formulated), and thirdly the complex of these two, which alone is generated and destroyed, and is, without qualification, capable of separate existence; for of substances completely expressible in a formula some are separable and some are separable and some are not.

ὅτι δ᾽ ἐστὶν οὐσία καὶ ἡ ὕλη, δῆλον: ἐν πάσαις γὰρ ταῖς ἀντικειμέναις μεταβολαῖς ἐστί τι τὸ ὑποκείμενον ταῖς μεταβολαῖς, οἷον κατὰ τόπον τὸ νῦν μὲν ἐνταῦθα πάλιν δ᾽ [35] ἄλλοθι, καὶ κατ᾽ αὔξησιν ὃ νῦν μὲν τηλικόνδε πάλιν δ᾽ ἔλαττον ἢ μεῖζον, καὶ κατ᾽ ἀλλοίωσιν ὃ νῦν μὲν ὑγιὲς πάλιν δὲ κάμνον: [1042β] [1] ὁμοίως δὲ καὶ κατ᾽ οὐσίαν ὃ νῦν μὲν ἐν γενέσει πάλιν δ᾽ ἐν φθορᾷ, καὶ νῦν μὲν ὑποκείμενον ὡς τόδε τι πάλιν δ᾽ ὑποκείμενον ὡς κατὰ στέρησιν.

Quia vero substantia est materia, palam. Nam in omnibus oppositis mutationibus est aliquid quod subicitur mutationibus, ut puta secundum locum quod nunc hic iterum alibi, et secundum augmentum quod nunc quidem est tantum iterum minus aut maius, et secundum alterationem quod nunc quidem est sanum iterum laborat. Similiter autem secundum substantiam quod nunc quidem est in generatione iterum in corruptione, et nunc quidem quod subicitur ut hoc aliquid iterum autem quod subicitur ut secundum privationem.

But clearly matter also is substance; for in all the opposite changes that occur there is something which underlies the changes, e.g. in respect of place that which is now here and again elsewhere, and in respect of increase that which is now of one size and again less or greater, and in respect of alteration that which is now healthy and again diseased; [42b] and similarly in respect of substance there is something that is now being generated and again being destroyed, and now underlies the process as a this and again underlies it in respect of a privation of positive character.

καὶ ἀκολουθοῦσι δὴ ταύτῃ αἱ ἄλλαι μεταβολαί, τῶν δ᾽ ἄλλων ἢ [5] μιᾷ ἢ δυοῖν αὕτη οὐκ ἀκολουθεῖ: οὐ γὰρ ἀνάγκη, εἴ τι ὕλην ἔχει τοπικήν, τοῦτο καὶ γεννητὴν καὶ φθαρτὴν ἔχειν. τίς μὲν οὖν διαφορὰ τοῦ ἁπλῶς γίγνεσθαι καὶ μὴ ἁπλῶς, ἐν τοῖς φυσικοῖς εἴρηται.

Et hanc sequuntur aliae mutationes. Aliarum vero aut unam aut duas haec non sequitur; non enim necesse, si quid materiam habet localem, hoc et generabilem et corruptibilem habere. Quae enim differentia simpliciter fieri et non simpliciter, in phisicis dictum est.

And in this change the others are involved. But in either one or two of the others this is not involved; for it is not necessary if a thing has matter for change of place that it should also have matter for generation and destruction. The difference between becoming in the full sense and becoming in a qualified sense has been stated in our physical works.

*Chapter* 2

ἐπεὶ δ᾽ ἡ μὲν ὡς ὑποκειμένη καὶ ὡς ὕλη οὐσία ὁμολογεῖται, [10] αὕτη δ᾽ ἐστὶν ἡ δυνάμει, λοιπὸν τὴν ὡς ἐνέργειαν οὐσίαν τῶν αἰσθητῶν εἰπεῖν τίς ἐστιν.

Quoniam autem quae quidem ut subiecta et ut materia substantia confessa est, haec autem est quae potestate, reliquum eam quae ut actum substantiam sensibilium dicere quae est.

Since the substance which exists as underlying and as matter is generally recognized, and this that which exists potentially, it remains for us to say what is the substance, in the sense of actuality, of sensible things.

Δημόκριτος μὲν οὖν τρεῖς διαφορὰς ἔοικεν οἰομένῳ εἶναι (τὸ μὲν γὰρ ὑποκείμενον σῶμα, τὴν ὕλην, ἓν καὶ ταὐτόν, διαφέρειν δὲ ἢ ῥυσμῷ, ὅ ἐστι σχῆμα, ἢ τροπῇ, ὅ ἐστι θέσις, ἢ διαθιγῇ, ὅ [15] ἐστι τάξις):

Democritus quidem igitur tres differentias similis est existimanti esse; nam subiectum corpus, materiam, unum et idem, differre autem aut rismo, quod est figura, aut tropi, quod est positio, aut dyatigi, quod est ordo.

Democritus seems to think there are three kinds of difference between things; the underlying body, the matter, is one and the same, but they differ either in rhythm, i.e. shape, or in turning, i.e. position, or in inter-contact, i.e. order.

φαίνονται δὲ πολλαὶ διαφοραὶ οὖσαι, οἷον τὰ μὲν συνθέσει λέγεται τῆς ὕλης, ὥσπερ ὅσα κράσει καθάπερ μελίκρατον, τὰ δὲ δεσμῷ οἷον φάκελος, τὰ δὲ κόλλῃ οἷον βιβλίον, τὰ δὲ γόμφῳ οἷον κιβώτιον, τὰ δὲ πλείοσι τούτων, τὰ δὲ θέσει οἷον οὐδὸς καὶ ὑπέρθυρον (ταῦτα γὰρ [20] τῷ κεῖσθαί πως διαφέρει), τὰ δὲ χρόνῳ οἷον δεῖπνον καὶ ἄριστον, τὰ δὲ τόπῳ οἷον τὰ πνεύματα: τὰ δὲ τοῖς τῶν αἰσθητῶν πάθεσιν οἷον σκληρότητι καὶ μαλακότητι, καὶ πυκνότητι καὶ ἀραιότητι, καὶ ξηρότητι καὶ ὑγρότητι, καὶ τὰ μὲν ἐνίοις τούτων τὰ δὲ πᾶσι τούτοις, καὶ ὅλως τὰ [25] μὲν ὑπεροχῇ τὰ δὲ ἐλλείψει.

Videntur autem multe differentie esse: ut alia quidem compositione dicuntur materiaei, sicut quaecumque  mixtura quemadmodum mellicratum, alia autem ligatione ut capitis ligatura, alia visco utliber, alia clavo ut archa, alia in pluribus horum, alia positione  ut liminare inferius et superius  (haec enim in poni aliqualiter differunt), alia tempore ut cena et prandium, alia loco ut spiritus, alia sensibilium passionibus ut duritie et mollitie, et spissitudine et raritate, et siccitate et humiditate. Et haec quidem  horum quibusdam alia omnibus hiis, et omnino alia superhabundantia alia defectu.

But evidently there are many differences; for instance, some things are characterized by the mode of composition of their matter, e.g. the things formed by blending, such as honey-water; and others by being bound together, e.g. bundle; and others by being glued together, e.g. a book; and others by being nailed together, e.g. a casket; and others in more than one of these ways; and others by position, e.g. threshold and lintel (for these differ by being placed in a certain way); and others by time, e.g. dinner and breakfast; and others by place, e.g. the winds; and others by the affections proper to sensible things, e.g. hardness and softness, density and rarity, dryness and wetness; and some things by some of these qualities, others by them all, and in general some by excess and some by defect.

ὥστε δῆλον ὅτι καὶ τὸ ἔστι τοσαυταχῶς λέγεται· οὐδὸς γὰρ ἔστιν ὅτι οὕτως κεῖται, καὶ τὸ εἶναι τὸ οὕτως αὐτὸ κεῖσθαι σημαίνει, καὶ τὸ κρύσταλλον εἶναι τὸ οὕτω πεπυκνῶσθαι. ἐνίων δὲ τὸ εἶναι καὶ πᾶσι τούτοις ὁρισθήσεται, τῷ τὰ μὲν μεμῖχθαι, τὰ δὲ κεκρᾶσθαι, [30] τὰ δὲ δεδέσθαι, τὰ δὲ πεπυκνῶσθαι, τὰ δὲ ταῖς ἄλλαις διαφοραῖς κεχρῆσθαι, ὥσπερ χεὶρ ἢ πούς.

Quare palam quia et le est totiens dicitur; limes enim inferior est quia ita ponitur, et esse sic ipsum poni significat, et cristallum esse sic inspissari. Quorundam vero esse et omnibus hiis diffinietur, per haec quidem misceri, haec  autem contemperari, illa vero ligari, alia inspissari, alia autem aliis differentiis uti,  sicut manus aut pes.

Clearly, then, the word is has just as many meanings; a thing is a threshold because it lies in such and such a position, and its being means its lying in that position, while being ice means having been solidified in such and such a way. And the being of some things will be defined by all these qualities, because some parts of them are mixed, others are blended, others are bound together, others are solidified, and others use the other differentiae; e.g. the hand or the foot requires such complex definition.

ληπτέα οὖν τὰ γένη τῶν διαφορῶν (αὗται γὰρ ἀρχαὶ ἔσονται τοῦ εἶναι), οἷον τὰ τῷ μᾶλλον καὶ ἧττον ἢ πυκνῷ καὶ μανῷ καὶ τοῖς ἄλλοις τοῖς τοιούτοις· πάντα γὰρ ταῦτα [35] ὑπεροχὴ καὶ ἔλλειψίς ἐστιν. εἰ δέ τι σχήματι ἢ λειότητι καὶ τραχύτητι, πάντα εὐθεῖ καὶ καμπύλῳ. τοῖς δὲ τὸ εἶναι τὸ μεμῖχθαι ἔσται, ἀντικειμένως δὲ τὸ μὴ εἶναι.

Sumenda igitur sunt genera differentiarum (hae namque erunt principia essendi), ut quae in magis et minus aut spisso et raro et aliis talibus; omnia namque haec superhabundantia et defectus sunt. Si quid autem figura aut levitate aut asperitate, omnia recto et curvo. Hiis autem esse erit misceri, opposite vero non esse.

We must grasp, then, the kinds of differentiae (for these will be the principles of the being of things), e.g. the things characterized by the more and the less, or by the dense and the rare, and by other such qualities; for all these are forms of excess and defect. And anything that is characterized by shape or by smoothness and roughness is characterized by the straight and the curved. And for [43a] other things their being will mean their being mixed, and their not being will mean the opposite.

[1043α] [1] φανερὸν δὴ ἐκ τούτων ὅτι εἴπερ ἡ οὐσία αἰτία τοῦ εἶναι ἕκαστον, ὅτι ἐν τούτοις ζητητέον τί τὸ αἴτιον τοῦ εἶναι τούτων ἕκαστον. οὐσία μὲν οὖν οὐδὲν τούτων οὐδὲ συνδυαζόμενον, ὅμως [5] δὲ τὸ ἀνάλογον ἐν ἑκάστῳ· καὶ ὡς ἐν ταῖς οὐσίαις τὸ τῆς ὕλης κατηγορούμενον αὐτὴ ἡ ἐνέργεια, καὶ ἐν τοῖς ἄλλοις ὁρισμοῖς μάλιστα. οἷον εἰ οὐδὸν δέοι ὁρίσασθαι, ξύλον ἢ λίθον ὡδὶ κείμενον ἐροῦμεν, καὶ οἰκίαν πλίνθους καὶ ξύλα ὡδὶ κείμενα (ἢ ἔτι καὶ τὸ οὗ ἕνεκα ἐπ᾽ ἐνίων ἔστιν), εἰ δὲ κρύσταλλον, [10] ὕδωρ πεπηγὸς ἢ πεπυκνωμένον ὡδί· συμφωνία δὲ ὀξέος καὶ βαρέος μῖξις τοιαδί· τὸν αὐτὸν δὲ τρόπον καὶ ἐπὶ τῶν ἄλλων.

Palam itaque ex hiis quia si substantia causa essendi unumquodque, quod in hiis quaerendum quae est causa essendi horum unumquodque. Substantia quidem igitur nihil horum nec combinatum, at tamen proportionale in quolibet. Et ut in substantiis quod de materia predicatur ipse actus, et in aliis diffinitionibus maxime. Ut si limen inferius oporteat diffiniri, lignum aut lapidem ita positum dicemus, et domum lateres et ligna sic posita (aut adhuc et quod cuius causa in quibusdam est). Si vero cristallum, aquam congelatam aut inspissatam ita; simphonia autem acuti et gravis commixtio talis; eodem quoque modo et in aliis.

It is clear, then, from these facts that, since its substance is the cause of each thing's being, we must seek in these differentiae what is the cause of the being of each of these things. Now none of these differentiae is substance, even when coupled with matter, yet it is what is analogous to substance in each case; and as in substances that which is predicated of the matter is the actuality itself, in all other definitions also it is what most resembles full actuality. E.g. if we had to define a threshold, we should say wood or stone in such and such a position , and a house we should define as bricks and timbers in such and such a position ,(or a purpose may exist as well in some cases), and if we had to define ice we should say water frozen or solidified in such and such a way , and harmony is such and such a blending of high and low ; and similarly in all other cases.

φανερὸν δὴ ἐκ τούτων ὅτι ἡ ἐνέργεια ἄλλη ἄλλης ὕλης καὶ ὁ λόγος: τῶν μὲν γὰρ ἡ σύνθεσις τῶν δ᾽ ἡ μῖξις τῶν δὲ ἄλλο τι τῶν εἰρημένων.

Palam itaque ex hiis quia actus alius alterius materiae et ratio; aliorum enim compositio, aliorum mixtio, aliorum aliud quid dictorum.

Obviously, then, the actuality or the formula is different when the matter is different; for in some cases it is the composition, in others the mixing, and in others some other of the attributes we have named.

διὸ τῶν ὁριζομένων οἱ μὲν [15] λέγοντες τί ἐστιν οἰκία, ὅτι λίθοι πλίνθοι ξύλα, τὴν δυνάμει οἰκίαν λέγουσιν, ὕλη γὰρ ταῦτα: οἱ δὲ ἀγγεῖον σκεπαστικὸν χρημάτων καὶ σωμάτων ἢ τι ἄλλο τοιοῦτον προτιθέντες, τὴν ἐνέργειαν λέγουσιν: οἱ δ᾽ ἄμφω ταῦτα συντιθέντες τὴν τρίτην καὶ τὴν ἐκ τούτων οὐσίαν (ἔοικε γὰρ ὁ μὲν διὰ τῶν διαφορῶν [20] λόγος τοῦ εἴδους καὶ τῆς ἐνεργείας εἶναι, ὁ δ᾽ ἐκ τῶν ἐνυπαρχόντων τῆς ὕλης μᾶλλον): ὁμοίως δὲ καὶ οἵους Ἀρχύτας ἀπεδέχετο ὅρους: τοῦ συνάμφω γάρ εἰσιν. οἷον τί ἐστι νηνεμία; ἠρεμία ἐν πλήθει ἀέρος: ὕλη μὲν γὰρ ὁ ἀήρ, ἐνέργεια δὲ καὶ οὐσία ἡ ἠρεμία. τί ἐστι γαλήνη; ὁμαλότης θαλάττης: [25] τὸ μὲν ὑποκείμενον ὡς ὕλη ἡ θάλαττα, ἡ δὲ ἐνέργεια καὶ ἡ μορφὴ ἡ ὁμαλότης.

Propter quod diffinientium hii quidem dicentes quid est domus, quia lapides, lateres, ligna, potestate domum dicunt; materia namque haec. Illi vero vas protectivum pecuniarum et corporum aut aliquid aliud tale addentes, actum dicunt. Alii ambo ea componentes tertiam et eam quae ex hiis substantiam. Videtur enim quae quidem per differentias ratio speciei et actus esse, quae vero est ex inexistentibus materiae magis. Similiter autem et quos architas approbavit terminos; simul utriusque enim sunt. Ut quid est serenitas? Quies in aeris pluralitate; aer quidem materia, actus et substantia quies. Quid est tranquillitas? Maris equitas; subiectum quidem ut materia mare, actus autem et forma equitas.

And so, of the people who go in for defining, those who define a house as stones, bricks, and timbers are speaking of the potential house, for these are the matter; but those who propose a receptacle to shelter chattels and living beings , or something of the sort, speak of the actuality. Those who combine both of these speak of the third kind of substance, which is composed of matter and form (for the formula that gives the differentiae seems to be an account of the form or actuality, while that which gives the components is rather an account of the matter); and the same is true of the kind of definitions which Archytas used to accept; they are accounts of the combined form and matter. E.g. what is still weather? Absence of motion in a large expanse of air; air is the matter, and absence of motion is the actuality and substance. What is a calm?

Smoothness of sea; the material substratum is the sea, and the actuality or shape is smoothness.

φανερὸν δὴ ἐκ τῶν εἰρημένων τίς ἡ αἰσθητὴ οὐσία ἐστὶ καὶ πῶς: ἡ μὲν γὰρ ὡς ὕλη, ἡ δ᾽ ὡς μορφὴ καὶ ἐνέργεια, ἡ δὲ τρίτη ἡ ἐκ τούτων.

Palam itaque ex dictis quae sit sensibilis substantia et quomodo; haec quidem enim ut materia, illa vero ut forma quia actus, tertia autem quae ex hiis.

It is obvious then, from what has been said, what sensible substance is and how it exists-one kind of it as matter, another as form or actuality, while the third kind is that which is composed of these two.

### Chapter  3

δεῖ δὲ μὴ ἀγνοεῖν ὅτι ἐνίοτε λανθάνει πότερον σημαίνει [30] τὸ ὄνομα τὴν σύνθετον οὐσίαν ἢ τὴν ἐνέργειαν καὶ τὴν μορφήν, οἷον ἡ οἰκία πότερον σημεῖον τοῦ κοινοῦ ὅτι σκέπασμα ἐκ πλίνθων καὶ λίθων ὡδὶ κειμένων, ἢ τῆς ἐνεργείας καὶ τοῦ εἴδους ὅτι σκέπασμα, καὶ γραμμὴ πότερον δυὰς ἐν μήκει ἢ [ὅτι] δυάς, καὶ ζῷον πότερον ψυχὴ ἐν [35] σώματι ἢ ψυχή: αὕτη γὰρ οὐσία καὶ ἐνέργεια σώματός τινος.

Oportet autem non ignorare quia aliquando latet utrum  significet nomen compositam substantiam aut actum et formam. Ut domus utrum signum communis quia tegumentum ex lateribus et iapidibus sic positis, aut actus et speciei quia tegumentum; et linea utrum dualitas in longitudine aut quia  dualitas, et animal utrum anima in corpore aut anima; haec namque substantia et actus corporis alicuius.

We must not fail to notice that sometimes it is not clear whether a name means the composite substance, or the actuality or form, e.g. whether house is a sign for the composite thing, a covering consisting of bricks and stones laid thus and thus , or for the actuality or form, a covering , and whether a line is twoness in length or twoness , and whether an animal is soul in a body or a soul _ ; for soul is the substance or actuality of some body.

εἴη δ᾽ ἂν καὶ ἐπ᾽ ἀμφοτέροις τὸ ζῷον, οὐχ ὡς ἑνὶ λόγῳ λεγόμενον ἀλλ᾽ ὡς πρὸς ἕν.

Erit autem utique et in utrisque animal, non ut una ratione dictum sed quasi ad unum.

Animal might even be applied to both, not as something definable by one formula, but as related to a single thing.

ἀλλὰ ταῦτα πρὸς μέν τι ἄλλο διαφέρει, πρὸς δὲ τὴν ζήτησιν τῆς οὐσίας τῆς αἰσθητῆς οὐδέν: [1043β] [1] τὸ γὰρ τί ἦν εἶναι τῷ εἴδει καὶ τῇ ἐνεργείᾳ ὑπάρχει. ψυχὴ μὲν γὰρ καὶ ψυχῇ εἶναι ταὐτόν, ἀνθρώπῳ δὲ καὶ ἄνθρωπος οὐ ταὐτόν, εἰ μὴ καὶ ἡ ψυχὴ ἄνθρωπος λεχθήσεται: οὕτω δὲ τινὶ μὲν τινὶ δ᾽ οὔ.

Sed haec ad aliquid aliud quidem differunt, ad questionem vero substantiae sensibilis nihil; nam quod quid erat esse speciei et actui existit. Nam anima et anime esse idem, homini vero esse et homo non idem, nisi et anima homo dicatur; sic autem alicui quidem, alicui vero non.

But this question, while important for another purpose, is of no importance for the inquiry into sensible substance; [43b] for the essence certainly attaches to the form and the actuality. For soul and to be soul are the same, but to be man and man are not the same, unless even the bare soul is to be called man; and thus on one interpretation the thing is the same as its essence, and on another it is not.

οὐ φαίνεται [5] δὴ ζητοῦσιν ἡ συλλαβὴ ἐκ τῶν στοιχείων οὖσα καὶ συνθέσεως, οὐδ᾽ ἡ οἰκία πλίνθοι τε καὶ σύνθεσις. καὶ τοῦτο ὀρθῶς: οὐ γάρ ἐστιν ἡ σύνθεσις οὐδ᾽ ἡ μῖξις ἐκ τούτων ὧν ἐστι σύνθεσις ἢ μῖξις. ὁμοίως δὲ οὐδὲ τῶν ἄλλων οὐθέν, οἷον εἰ ὁ οὐδὸς θέσει, οὐκ ἐκ τοῦ οὐδοῦ ἡ θέσις ἀλλὰ μᾶλλον [10] οὗτος ἐξ ἐκείνης. οὐδὲ δὴ ὁ ἄνθρωπός ἐστι τὸ ζῷον καὶ δίπουν, ἀλλά τι δεῖ εἶναι ὃ παρὰ ταῦτά ἐστιν, εἰ ταῦθ᾽ ὕλη, οὔτε δὲ στοιχεῖον οὔτ᾽ ἐκ στοιχείου, ἀλλ᾽ ἡ οὐσία: ὃ ἐξαιροῦντες [13] τὴν ὕλην λέγουσιν. εἰ οὖν τοῦτ᾽ αἴτιον τοῦ εἶναι, καὶ οὐσία τοῦτο, αὐτὴν ἂν τὴν οὐσίαν οὐ λέγοιεν.

Non videtur itaque quaerentibus sillaba ex elementis ens et compositione, nec domus lateres et compositio. Et hoc recte; non enim compositio et mixtio ex hiis quorum est compositio aut mixtio. Similiter autem nec aliorum nil; ut limes positione, non ex limine positio sed magis hoc ex illa. Nec itaque homo est animal et bipes, sed aliquid oportet esse quod praeter haec est, si haec materiae: neque autem elementum nec ex elementis, sed substantia; quod auferentes materiam dicunt. Si ergo hoc causa ipsius esse, et substantia hoc, ipsam utique substantiam non dicent.

If we examine we find that the syllable does not consist of the letters + juxtaposition, nor is the house bricks + juxtaposition. And this is right; for the juxtaposition or mixing does not consist of those things of which it is the juxtaposition or mixing. And the same is true in all other cases; e.g. if the threshold is characterized by its position, the position is not constituted by the threshold, but rather the latter is constituted by the former. Nor is man animal + biped, but there must be something besides these, if these are matter,-something which is neither an element in the whole nor a compound, but is the substance; but this people eliminate, and state only the matter. If, then, this is the cause of the thing _ s being, and if the cause of its being is its substance, they will not be stating the substance itself.

(ἀνάγκη δὴ ταύτην ἢ [15] ἀΐδιον εἶναι ἢ φθαρτὴν ἄνευ τοῦ φθείρεσθαι καὶ γεγονέναι ἄνευ τοῦ γίγνεσθαι. δέδεικται δὲ καὶ δεδήλωται ἐν ἄλλοις ὅτι τὸ εἶδος οὐθεὶς ποιεῖ οὐδὲ γεννᾷ, ἀλλὰ ποιεῖται τόδε, γίγνεται δὲ τὸ ἐκ τούτων.

Necessarium itaque hanc aut sempiternam esse aut corruptibilem sine corrumpi et factam esse sine fieri. Monstratum autem est et declaratum in aliis quia speciem nullus facit nec generatur, sed efficitur hoc, fit autem quod ex hiis.

(This, then, must either be eternal or it must be destructible without being ever in course of being destroyed, and must have come to be without ever being in course of coming to be. But it has been proved and explained elsewhere that no one makes or begets the form, but it is the individual that is made, i.e. the complex of form and matter that is generated.

εἰ δ᾿ εἰσὶ τῶν φθαρτῶν αἱ οὐσίαι χωρισταί, οὐδέν πω δῆλον:

Si autem sunt corruptibilium substantiae separabiles, nondum palam.

Whether the substances of destructible things can exist apart, is not yet at all clear;

πλὴν ὅτι γ᾿ ἐνίων οὐκ ἐνδέχεται [20] δῆλον, ὅσα μὴ οἷόν τε παρὰ τὰ τινὰ εἶναι, οἷον οἰκίαν ἢ σκεῦος.

At tamen quia quorundam non contingit, palam: quaecumque non possibile est praeter ipsa aliqua esse, ut domum aut uas.

except that obviously this is impossible in some cases-in the case of things which cannot exist apart from the individual instances, e.g. house or utensil.

ἴσως μὲν οὖν οὐδ᾿ οὐσίαι εἰσὶν οὔτ᾿ αὐτὰ ταῦτα οὔτε τι τῶν ἄλλων ὅσα μὴ φύσει συνέστηκεν: τὴν γὰρ φύσιν μόνην ἄν τις θείη τὴν ἐν τοῖς φθαρτοῖς οὐσίαν.)

Forsan quidem igitur nec substantiae sunt neque aliquid ipsa haec nec aliquid aliorum quaecumque non natura constituta sunt; naturam enim solam utique quis ponet eorum quae in corruptibilibus substantiam.

Perhaps, indeed, neither these things themselves, nor any of the other things which are not formed by nature, are substances at all; for one might say that the nature in natural objects is the only substance to be found in destructible things.)

ὥστε ἡ ἀπορία ἣν οἱ Ἀντισθένειοι καὶ οἱ οὕτως ἀπαίδευτοι ἠπόρουν [25] ἔχει τινὰ καιρόν, ὅτι οὐκ ἔστι τὸ τί ἐστιν ὁρίσασθαι (τὸν γὰρ ὅρον λόγον εἶναι μακρόν), ἀλλὰ ποῖον μέν τί ἐστιν ἐνδέχεται καὶ διδάξαι, ὥσπερ ἄργυρον, τί μέν ἐστιν οὔ, ὅτι δ᾿ οἷον καττίτερος· ὥστ᾿ οὐσίας ἔστι μὲν ἧς ἐνδέχεται εἶναι ὅρον καὶ λόγον, οἷον τῆς συνθέτου, ἐάν τε αἰσθητὴ [30] ἐάν τε νοητὴ ᾖ· ἐξ ὧν δ᾿ αὕτη πρώτων, οὐκέτι, εἴπερ τι κατὰ τινὸς σημαίνει ὁ λόγος ὁ ὁριστικὸς καὶ δεῖ τὸ μὲν ὥσπερ ὕλην εἶναι τὸ δὲ ὡς μορφήν.

Quare dubitatio quam antistenici et sic indocti dubitaverunt habet tempus quoddam: quia non est ipsum quid est diffinire (terminum enim rationem esse longam), sed quale quidem aliquid est contingit et docere; sicut argentum quid quidem est non, quia autem quale stagnum. Quare substantiae est quidem cuius contingit esse terminum et rationem, puta composite, sive sensibilis fuerit sive intellectualis; ^primorum autem ex quibus haec non est, siquidem aliquid de aliquo significat ratio diffinitiva et oportet hoc quidem ut materiam esse illud vero ut formam.

Therefore the difficulty which used to be raised by the school of Antisthenes and other such uneducated people has a certain timeliness. They said that the what cannot be defined (for the definition so called is a long rigmarole ) but of what sort a thing, e.g. silver, is, they thought it possible actually to explain, not saying what it is, but that it is like tin. Therefore one kind of substance can be defined and formulated, i.e. the composite kind, whether it be perceptible or intelligible; but the primary parts of which this consists cannot be defined, since a definitory formula predicates something of something, and one part of the definition must play the part of matter and the other that of form.

φανερὸν δὲ καὶ διότι, εἴπερ εἰσί πως ἀριθμοὶ αἱ οὐσίαι, οὕτως εἰσὶ καὶ οὐχ ὥς τινες λέγουσι μονάδων· ὅ τε γὰρ ὁρισμὸς ἀριθμός τις· [35] διαιρετός τε γὰρ καὶ εἰς ἀδιαίρετα (οὐ γὰρ ἄπειροι οἱ λόγοι), καὶ ὁ ἀριθμὸς δὲ τοιοῦτον.

Palam autem et quia, si sint aliqualiter numeri substantiae, sic sunt et non ut quidam dicunt unitatum. Nam diffinitio numerus quidam; divisibilisque enim et in indivisibilia (non enim infinite rationes), et numerus autem tale.

It is also obvious that, if substances are in a sense numbers, they are so in this sense and not, as some say, as numbers of units. For a definition is a sort of number; for (1) it is divisible, and into indivisible parts (for definitory formulae are not infinite), and number also is of this nature.

καὶ ὥσπερ οὐδ᾿ ἀπ᾿ ἀριθμοῦ ἀφαιρεθέντος τινὸς ἢ προστεθέντος ἐξ ὧν ὁ ἀριθμός ἐστιν, οὐκέτι ὁ αὐτὸς ἀριθμός ἐστιν ἀλλ᾿ ἕτερος, κἂν τοὐλάχιστον ἀφαιρεθῇ ἢ προστεθῇ, [1044a] [1] οὕτως οὐδὲ ὁ ὁρισμὸς οὐδὲ τὸ τί ἦν εἶναι οὐκέτι ἔσται ἀφαιρεθέντος τινὸς ἢ προστεθέντος.

Et quemadmodum nec a numero ablato aliquo aut addito ex quibus numerus est, non adhuc idem numerus est sed alter, quamvis minimum auferatur aut addatur, sic nec diffinitio nec quod quid erat esse non adhuc erit ablato aliquo aut addito.

And (2) as, when one of the parts of which a number consists has been taken from or added to the number, it is no longer the same number, but a different one, even if it is the very smallest part that has been taken [44a] away or added, so the definition and the essence will no longer remain when anything has been taken away or added.

καὶ τὸν ἀριθμὸν δεῖ εἶναί τι ᾧ εἷς, ὃ νῦν οὐκ ἔχουσι λέγειν τίνι εἷς, εἴπερ ἐστὶν εἷς (ἢ γὰρ οὐκ ἔστιν ἀλλ᾽ οἷον σωρός, ἢ [5] εἴπερ ἐστί, λεκτέον τί τὸ ποιοῦν ἓν ἐκ πολλῶν): καὶ ὁ ὁρισμὸς εἷς ἐστιν, ὁμοίως δὲ οὐδὲ τοῦτον ἔχουσι λέγειν. καὶ τοῦτο εἰκότως συμβαίνει: τοῦ αὐτοῦ γὰρ λόγου, καὶ ἡ οὐσία ἓν οὕτως, ἀλλ᾽ οὐχ ὡς λέγουσί τινες οἷον μονάς τις οὖσα ἢ στιγμή, ἀλλ᾽ ἐντελέχεια καὶ φύσις τις ἑκάστη.

Et numerum oportet esse aliquid quo unus, quod nunc non habent dicere quo unus, siquidem est unus; aut enim non est sed ut aceruus, aut siquidem est, dicendum quid quod est faciens unum ex multis. Et diffinitio una est, similiter autem neque hanc habent dicere. Et hoc merito accidit; eiusdem enim rationis, et substantia unum ita, sed non, ut dicunt quidam, ut unitas quaedam existens aut punctum, sed endelichia et natura quaedam unaquequae.

And (3) the number must be something in virtue of which it is one, and this these thinkers cannot state, what makes it one, if it is one (for either it is not one but a sort of heap, or if it is, we ought to say what it is that makes one out of many); and the definition is one, but similarly they cannot say what makes it one. And this is a natural result; for the same reason is applicable, and substance is one in the sense which we have explained, and not, as some say, by being a sort of unit or point; each is a complete reality and a definite nature.

καὶ ὥσπερ οὐδὲ ὁ [10] ἀριθμὸς ἔχει τὸ μᾶλλον καὶ ἧττον, οὐδ᾽ ἡ κατὰ τὸ εἶδος οὐσία, ἀλλ᾽ εἴπερ, ἡ μετὰ τῆς ὕλης.

Et quemadmodum nec numerus habet magis aut minus, nec quae secundum speciem substantia, sed siquidem, quae cum materia.

And (4) as number does not admit of the more and the less, neither does substance, in the sense of form, but if any substance does, it is only the substance which involves matter.

περὶ μὲν οὖν γενέσεως καὶ φθορᾶς τῶν λεγομένων οὐσιῶν, πῶς τ᾽ ἐνδέχεται καὶ πῶς ἀδύνατον, καὶ περὶ τῆς εἰς τὸν ἀριθμὸν ἀναγωγῆς, ἔστω μέχρι τούτων διωρισμένον. [15]

De generatione quidem igitur et corruptione dictarum substantiarum, quomodo contingit et quomodo impossibile, et de reductione ad numerum, sit usque ad haec determinatum.

Let this, then, suffice for an account of the generation and destruction of so-called substances in what sense it is possible and in what sense impossible _ and of the reduction of things to number.

*Chapter* 4

περὶ δὲ τῆς ὑλικῆς οὐσίας δεῖ μὴ λανθάνειν ὅτι εἰ καὶ ἐκ τοῦ αὐτοῦ πάντα πρώτου ἢ τῶν αὐτῶν ὡς πρώτων καὶ ἡ αὐτὴ ὕλη ὡς ἀρχὴ τοῖς γιγνομένοις, ὅμως ἔστι τις οἰκεία ἑκάστου, οἷον φλέγματος [ἐστι πρώτη ὕλη] τὰ γλυκέα ἢ λιπαρά, χολῆς δὲ τὰ πικρὰ ἢ ἄλλ᾽ ἄττα· ἴσως δὲ [20] ταῦτα ἐκ τοῦ αὐτοῦ.

De materiali autem substantia oportet non latere quia et si ex eodem omnia primo aut eisdem ut primis et eadem materia ut principium hiis quae fiunt, est tamen aliqua propria cuiuslibet, ut flegmatis est prima materia dulcia aut crassa, colere vero amara aut alia quaedam; forsan autem haec ex eodem.

Regarding material substance we must not forget that even if all things come from the same first cause or have the same things for their first causes, and if the same matter serves as starting-point for their generation, yet there is a matter proper to each, e.g. for phlegm the sweet or the fat, and for bile the bitter, or something else; though perhaps these come from the same original matter.

γίγνονται δὲ πλείους ὗλαι τοῦ αὐτοῦ ὅταν θατέρου ἡ ἑτέρα ᾖ, οἷον φλέγμα ἐκ λιπαροῦ καὶ γλυκέος εἰ τὸ λιπαρὸν ἐκ τοῦ γλυκέος, ἐκ δὲ χολῆς τῷ ἀναλύεσθαι εἰς τὴν πρώτην ὕλην τὴν χολήν. διχῶς γὰρ τόδ᾽ ἐκ τοῦδε, ἢ ὅτι πρὸ ὁδοῦ ἔσται ἢ ὅτι ἀναλυθέντος εἰς τὴν [25] ἀρχήν.

Fiunt autem plures materiae eiusdem, quando alterius altera fuerit, ut flegma ex crasso et dulci, si crassum ex dulci; ex colera vero per resolvi coleram in primam materiam. Dupliciter enim hoc ex hoc, aut quia previum erit aut quia ex resoluto in principium.

And there come to be several matters for the same thing, when the one matter is matter for the other; e.g. phlegm comes from the fat and from the sweet, if the fat comes from the sweet; and it comes from bile by analysis of the bile into its ultimate matter. For one thing comes from another in two senses, either because it will be found at a later stage, or because it is produced if the other is analysed into its original constituents.

ἐνδέχεται δὲ μιᾶς τῆς ὕλης οὔσης ἕτερα γίγνεσθαι διὰ τὴν κινοῦσαν αἰτίαν, οἷον ἐκ ξύλου καὶ κιβωτὸς καὶ κλίνη. ἐνίων δ᾽ ἑτέρα ἡ ὕλη ἐξ ἀνάγκης ἑτέρων ὄντων, οἷον πρίων οὐκ ἂν γένοιτο ἐκ ξύλου, οὐδ᾽ ἐπὶ τῇ κινούσῃ αἰτίᾳ τοῦτο: οὐ γὰρ ποιήσει πρίονα ἐξ ἐρίου ἢ ξύλου. εἰ δ᾽ ἄρα [30] τὸ αὐτὸ ἐνδέχεται ἐξ ἄλλης ὕλης ποιῆσαι, δῆλον ὅτι ἡ τέχνη καὶ ἡ ἀρχὴ ἡ ὡς κινοῦσα ἡ αὐτή: εἰ γὰρ καὶ ἡ ὕλη ἑτέρα καὶ τὸ κινοῦν, καὶ τὸ γεγονός.

Contingit autem una materia existente fieri diversa propter moventem causam, ut puta ex ligno et archa et lectus. Quorundam vero altera materia ex necessitate alteris existentibus, ut serra non utique fiet ex ligno, nec in movente causa  hoc; non enim faciet serram  ex lana aut ligno. Si ergo idem contingit ex alia materia  facere, palam quia ars et principium quod est ut movens idem; nam si et materia altera et movens, et quod factum est.

When the matter is one, different things may be produced owing to difference in the moving cause; e.g. from wood may be made both a chest and a bed. But some different things must have their matter different; e.g. a saw could not be made of wood, nor is this in the power of the moving cause; for it could not make a saw of wool or of wood. But if, as a matter of fact, the same thing can be made of different material, clearly the art, i.e. the moving principle, is the same; for if both the matter and the moving cause were different, the product would be so too.

ὅταν δή τις ζητῇ τὸ αἴτιον, ἐπεὶ πλεοναχῶς τὰ αἴτια λέγεται, πάσας δεῖ λέγειν τὰς ἐνδεχομένας αἰτίας. οἷον ἀνθρώπου τίς αἰτία ὡς [35] ὕλη; ἆρα τὰ καταμήνια; τί δ᾽ ὡς κινοῦν; ἆρα τὸ σπέρμα; τί δ᾽ ὡς τὸ εἶδος; τὸ τί ἦν εἶναι. τί δ᾽ ὡς οὗ ἕνεκα; τὸ τέλος.

Quando itaque aliquis quesierit quid  causa, quoniam pluribus modis dicuntur cause, omnes oportet dicere causas contingentes. Ut hominis quae causa ut materia? Equidem menstrua. Quid autem ut movens? Equidem sperma. Quid ut species? Quod quid erat esse. Quid ut cuius causa? Finis. Forsan  autem haec ambo idem.

When one inquires into the cause of something, one should, since causes are spoken of in several senses, state all the possible causes. what is the material cause of man? Shall we say the menstrual fluid ? What is moving cause? Shall we say the seed ?

The formal cause? His essence. The final cause? His end. But perhaps the [44b] latter two are the same.

[1044β] [1] ἴσως δὲ ταῦτα ἄμφω τὸ αὐτό. δεῖ δὲ τὰ ἐγγύτατα αἴτια λέγειν. τίς ἡ ὕλη; μὴ πῦρ ἢ γῆν ἀλλὰ τὴν ἴδιον.

Oportet autem proximas causas dicere. Quae materia? Non ignem aut terram sed propriam.

-It is the proximate causes we must state. What is the material cause? We must name not fire or earth, but the matter peculiar to the thing.

περὶ μὲν οὖν τὰς φυσικὰς οὐσίας καὶ γενητὰς ἀνάγκη οὕτω μετιέναι εἴ τις μέτεισιν ὀρθῶς, εἴπερ ἄρα [5] αἴτιά τε ταῦτα καὶ τοσαῦτα καὶ δεῖ τὰ αἴτια γνωρίζειν:

Circa naturales quidem igitur substantias et generabiles necesse sic versari si quis recte versatur, si profecto hae cause et tot et oportet causas cognoscere.

Regarding the substances that are natural and generable, if the causes are really these and of this number and we have to learn the causes, we must inquire thus, if we are to inquire rightly.

ἐπὶ δὲ τῶν φυσικῶν μὲν ἀϊδίων δὲ οὐσιῶν ἄλλος λόγος. ἴσως γὰρ ἔνια οὐκ ἔχει ὕλην, ἢ οὐ τοιαύτην ἀλλὰ μόνον κατὰ τόπον κινητήν.

In naturalibus quu dem sempiternis autem substantiis alia ratio. Forsan enim quaedam non habent materiam, aut non talem sed solum secundum locum mobilem.

But in the case of natural but eternal substances another account must be given. For perhaps some have no matter, or not matter of this sort but only such as can be moved in respect of place.

οὐδ᾽ ὅσα δὴ φύσει μέν, μὴ οὐσίαι δέ, οὐκ ἔστι τούτοις ὕλη, ἀλλὰ τὸ ὑποκείμενον ἡ οὐσία. οἷον τί [10] αἴτιον ἐκλείψεως, τίς ὕλη; οὐ γὰρ ἔστιν, ἀλλ᾽ ἡ σελήνη τὸ πάσχον. τί δ᾽ αἴτιον ὡς κινῆσαν καὶ φθεῖραν τὸ φῶς; ἡ γῆ. τὸ δ᾽ οὗ ἕνεκα ἴσως οὐκ ἔστιν. τὸ δ᾽ ὡς εἶδος ὁ λόγος, ἀλλὰ ἄδηλος ἐὰν μὴ μετὰ τῆς αἰτίας ᾖ ὁ λόγος. οἷον τί ἔκλειψις; στέρησις φωτός. ἐὰν δὲ προστεθῇ τὸ ὑπὸ γῆς ἐν [15] μέσῳ γιγνομένης, ὁ σὺν τῷ αἰτίῳ λόγος οὗτος. ὕπνου δ᾽ ἄδηλον τί τὸ πρῶτον πάσχον. ἀλλ᾽ ὅτι τὸ ζῷον; ναί, ἀλλὰ τοῦτο κατὰ τί, καὶ τί πρῶτον; καρδία ἢ ἄλλο τι. εἶτα ὑπὸ τίνος; εἶτα τί τὸ πάθος, τὸ ἐκείνου καὶ μὴ τοῦ ὅλου; ὅτι ἀκινησία τοιαδί; ναί, ἀλλ᾽ αὕτη τῷ τί πάσχειν [20] τὸ πρῶτον;

Nec quaecumque itaque natura quidem, non substantia vero, non est hiis materia, sed quod subicitur substantia. Puta quae causa eclipsis? quae materia? Non enim est, sed luna quod patitur. Quae causa ut movens et corrumpens lumen? Terra. Quod autem cuius gratia forsan non est. Quod vero ut species ratio, sed non manifesta, si non cum causa fuerit ratio. Ut quid eclipsis? Privatio luminis. Si vero addatur 4a terra in medio obiecta\ quae cum causa ratio haec. sompni vero non manifestum quid primum patiens. Sed quod animal? Etiam. Verum hoc secundum quid, et quid primum? Cor aut aliud aliquid. Deinde a quo? Deinde quid passio quae illius et non totius? Quia immobilitas talis? Vtique, sed haec per aliquid pati quod primum.

Nor does matter belong to those things which exist by nature but are not substances; their substratum is the substance. E.g what is the cause of eclipse? What is its matter? There is none; the moon is that which suffers eclipse. What is the moving cause which extinguished the light? The earth. The final cause perhaps does not exist. The formal principle is the definitory formula, but this is obscure if it does not include the cause. E.g. what is eclipse? Deprivation of light. But if we add by the earth s coming in between _ , this is the formula which includes the cause. In the case of sleep it is not clear what it is that proximately has this affection. Shall we say that it is the animal? Yes, but the animal in virtue of what, i.e. what is the proximate subject? The heart or some other part. Next, by what is it produced? Next, what is the affection-that of the proximate subject, not of the whole animal? Shall we say that it is immobility of such and such a kind? Yes, but to what process in the proximate subject is this due?

*Chapter* 5

ἐπεὶ δ᾽ ἔνια ἄνευ γενέσεως καὶ φθορᾶς ἔστι καὶ οὐκ ἔστιν, οἷον αἱ στιγμαί, εἴπερ εἰσί, καὶ ὅλως τὰ εἴδη (οὐ γὰρ τὸ λευκὸν γίγνεται ἀλλὰ τὸ ξύλον λευκόν, εἰ ἔκ τινος καὶ τὶ πᾶν τὸ γιγνόμενον γίγνεται), οὐ πάντα [25] ἂν τἀναντία γίγνοιτο ἐξ ἀλλήλων, ἀλλ᾽ ἑτέρως λευκὸς ἄνθρωπος ἐκ μέλανος ἀνθρώπου καὶ λευκὸν ἐκ μέλανος: οὐδὲ παντὸς ὕλη ἔστιν ἀλλ᾽ ὅσων γένεσις ἔστι καὶ μεταβολὴ εἰς ἄλληλα: ὅσα δ᾽ ἄνευ τοῦ μεταβάλλειν ἔστιν ἢ μή, οὐκ ἔστι τούτων ὕλη.

Quoniam vero quaedam sine generatione et corruptione sunt et non sunt, ut puncta, siquidem sunt, et totaliter species (non enim album fit sed lignum album, aut ex aliquo et aliquid omne quod fit fit), non omnia utique contraria fient ex invicem, sed aliter albus homo ex nigro homine et album ex nigro. Nec omnis materia est sed quorum generatio est et transmutatio in invicem. Quaecumque autem sine transmutari sunt aut non, non est horum materia.

Since some things are and are not, without coming to be and ceasing to be, e.g. points, if they can be said to be, and in general forms (for it is not white comes to be, but the wood comes to be white, if everything that comes to be comes from something and comes to be something), not all contraries can come from one another, but it is in different senses that a pale man comes from a dark man, and pale comes from dark. Nor has everything matter, but only those things which come to be and change into one another. Those things which, without ever being in course of changing, are or are not, have no matter.

ἔχει δ᾽ ἀπορίαν πῶς πρὸς τἀναντία ἡ [30] ὕλη ἡ ἑκάστου ἔχει. οἷον εἰ τὸ σῶμα δυνάμει ὑγιεινόν, ἐναντίον δὲ νόσος ὑγιείᾳ, ἆρα ἄμφω δυνάμει; καὶ τὸ ὕδωρ δυνάμει οἶνος καὶ ὄξος; ἢ τοῦ μὲν καθ᾽ ἕξιν καὶ κατὰ τὸ εἶδος ὕλη, τοῦ δὲ κατὰ στέρησιν καὶ φθορὰν τὴν παρὰ φύσιν;

Habet autem dubitationem quomodo ad contraria materia uniuscuiusque habet. Ut si corpus potentia sanum, contrarium vero infirmitas sanitatis, tunc ambo potentia?

There is difficulty in the question how the matter of each thing is related to its contrary states. E.g. if the body is potentially healthy, and disease is contrary to health, is it potentially both healthy and diseased?

ἀπορία δέ τις ἔστι καὶ διὰ τί ὁ οἶνος οὐχ [35] ὕλη τοῦ ὄξους οὐδὲ δυνάμει ὄξος (καίτοι γίγνεται ἐξ αὐτοῦ ὄξος) καὶ ὁ ζῶν δυνάμει νεκρός. ἢ οὔ, ἀλλὰ κατὰ συμβεβηκὸς αἱ φθοραί, [1045a] [1] ἡ δὲ τοῦ ζῴου ὕλη αὐτὴ κατὰ φθορὰν νεκροῦ δύναμις καὶ ὕλη, καὶ τὸ ὕδωρ ὄξους· γίγνεται γὰρ ἐκ τούτων ὥσπερ ἐξ ἡμέρας νύξ. καὶ ὅσα δὴ οὕτω μεταβάλλει εἰς ἄλληλα, εἰς τὴν ὕλην δεῖ ἐπανελθεῖν, οἷον εἰ [5] ἐκ νεκροῦ ζῷον, εἰς τὴν ὕλην πρῶτον, εἶθ᾽ οὕτω ζῷον· καὶ τὸ ὄξος εἰς ὕδωρ, εἶθ᾽ οὕτως οἶνος.

Et aqua potentia vinum et acetum? Aut huius quidem secundum habitum et secundum speciem materia, illius vero secundum privationem et corruptionem praeter naturam. Dubitatio autem quaedam est et quare vinum non materia aceti nec potentia acetum (quamuis fiat ex ipso acetum) et vivens potentia mortuus. Aut non, sed secundum accidens corruptiones. Animalis vero materia haec secundum corruptionem mortui potentia et materia, et aqua aceti; fit enim ex hiis ut ex die nox. Et quaecumque itaque sic transmutantur ad invicem, ad materiam oportet redire; ut si ex mortuo animal, in materiam primo, deinde sic animal; et acetum in aquam, deinde sic vinum.

And is water potentially wine and vinegar? We answer that it is the matter of one in virtue of its positive state and its form, and of the other in virtue of the privation of its positive state and the corruption of it contrary to its nature. It is also hard to say why wine is not said to be the matter of vinegar nor potentially vinegar (though

vinegar is produced from it), and why a living man is not said to be potentially dead. In fact they are not, but the corruptions in question are [45a] accidental, and it is the matter of the animal that is itself in virtue of its corruption the potency and matter of a corpse, and it is water that is the matter of vinegar. For the corpse comes from the animal, and vinegar from wine, as night from day. And all the things which change thus into one another must go back to their matter; e.g. if from a corpse is produced an animal, the corpse first goes back to its matter, and only then becomes an animal; and vinegar first goes back to water, and only then becomes wine.

*Chapter* 6

περὶ δὲ τῆς ἀπορίας τῆς εἰρημένης περί τε τοὺς ὁρισμοὺς καὶ περὶ τοὺς ἀριθμούς, τί αἴτιον τοῦ ἓν εἶναι; πάντων γὰρ ὅσα πλείω μέρη ἔχει καὶ μὴ ἔστιν οἷον σωρὸς τὸ πᾶν [10] ἀλλ᾽ ἔστι τι τὸ ὅλον παρὰ τὰ μόρια, ἔστι τι αἴτιον, ἐπεὶ καὶ ἐν τοῖς σώμασι τοῖς μὲν ἁφὴ αἰτία τοῦ ἓν εἶναι τοῖς δὲ γλισχρότης ἤ τι πάθος ἕτερον τοιοῦτον. ὁ δ᾽ ὁρισμὸς λόγος ἐστὶν εἷς οὐ συνδέσμῳ καθάπερ ἡ Ἰλιὰς ἀλλὰ τῷ ἑνὸς εἶναι. τί οὖν ἐστιν ὃ ποιεῖ ἓν τὸν ἄνθρωπον, καὶ διὰ τί [15] ἓν ἀλλ᾽ οὐ πολλά, οἷον τό τε ζῷον καὶ τὸ δίπουν,

De dubitatione vero dicta  circa diffinitiones et numeros: quae causa essendi unum? Omnium enim quaecumque  plures partes habent et non est ut aceruus quod totum sed est aliquid totum praeter partes, est aliqua causa. Quoniam et in corporibus hiis quidem tactus causa est unum essendi, aliis vero viscositas aut aliqua passio altera talis. Diffinitio vero ratio  est una non coniunctione quemadmodum Ylias sed per unius esse. Quid igitur est quod facit unum hominem, et propter quid unum sed non multa, puta animalque et bipes?

To return to the difficulty which has been stated with respect both to definitions and to numbers, what is the cause of their unity? In the case of all things which have several parts and in which the totality is not, as it were, a mere heap, but the whole is something beside the parts, there is a cause; for even in bodies contact is the cause of unity in some cases, and in others viscosity or some other such quality. And a definition is a set of words which is one not by being connected together, like the Iliad, but by dealing with one object.-What then, is it that makes man one; why is he one and not many, e.g. animal + biped,

ἄλλως τε δὴ καὶ εἰ ἔστιν, ὥσπερ φασί τινες, αὐτό τι ζῷον καὶ αὐτὸ δίπουν; διὰ τί γὰρ οὐκ ἐκεῖνα αὐτὰ ὁ ἄνθρωπός ἐστι, καὶ ἔσονται κατὰ μέθεξιν οἱ

ἄνθρωποι οὐκ ἀνθρώπου οὐδ᾽ [19] ἑνὸς ἀλλὰ δυοῖν, ζώου καὶ δίποδος, καὶ ὅλως δὴ οὐκ ἂν [20] εἴη ὁ ἄνθρωπος ἓν ἀλλὰ πλείω, ζῷον καὶ δίπουν;

Aliterque et si est, ut aiunt quidam, ipsum aliquid animal et ipsum bipes. Quare namque non illa ipsa homo est, et erunt secundum participationem homines non hominis neque unius sed duorum, scilicet animalis et bipedis, et totaliter utique non erit homo unum sed plura, animal et bipes?

especially if there are, as some say, an animal-itself and a biped-itself? Why are not those Forms themselves the man, so that men would exist by participation not in man, nor in-one Form, but in two, animal and biped, and in general man would be not one but more than one thing, animal and biped?

φανερὸν δὴ ὅτι οὕτω μὲν μετιοῦσιν ὡς εἰώθασιν ὁρίζεσθαι καὶ λέγειν, οὐκ ἐνδέχεται ἀποδοῦναι καὶ λῦσαι τὴν ἀπορίαν: εἰ δ᾽ ἐστίν, ὥσπερ λέγομεν, τὸ μὲν ὕλη τὸ δὲ μορφή, καὶ τὸ μὲν δυνάμει τὸ δὲ ἐνεργείᾳ, οὐκέτι ἀπορία δόξειεν ἂν [25] εἶναι τὸ ζητούμενον.

Palam itaque quia sic quidem acceptantibus ut consueverunt diffinire et dicere, non contingit reddere et soluere dubitationem. Si autem est, ut dicimus, hoc quidem materia illud vero forma, et hoc quidem potentia illud vero actu, non adhuc dubitatio utique videbitur esse quod quaeritur.

Clearly, then, if people proceed thus in their usual manner of definition and speech, they cannot explain and solve the difficulty. But if, as we say, one element is matter and another is form, and one is potentially and the other actually, the question will no longer be thought a difficulty.

ἔστι γὰρ αὕτη ἡ ἀπορία ἡ αὐτὴ κἂν εἰ ὁ ὅρος εἴη ἱματίου στρογγύλος χαλκός: εἴη γὰρ ἂν σημεῖον τοὔνομα τοῦτο τοῦ λόγου, ὥστε τὸ ζητούμενόν ἐστι τί αἴτιον τοῦ ἓν εἶναι τὸ στρογγύλον καὶ τὸν χαλκόν. οὐκέτι δὴ ἀπορία φαίνεται, ὅτι τὸ μὲν ὕλη τὸ δὲ μορφή. [30] τί οὖν τούτου αἴτιον, τοῦ τὸ δυνάμει ὂν ἐνεργείᾳ εἶναι, παρὰ τὸ ποιῆσαν, ἐν ὅσοις ἔστι γένεσις; οὐθὲν γάρ ἐστιν αἴτιον ἕτερον τοῦ τὴν δυνάμει σφαῖραν ἐνεργείᾳ εἶναι σφαῖραν, ἀλλὰ τοῦτ᾽ ἦν τὸ τί ἦν εἶναι ἑκατέρῳ.

Est enim haec dubitatio eadem et si terminus vestimenti sit rotundum es; sit enim utique signum nomen hoc rationis, quare quod quaeritur est: quid causa est unum essendi rotundum et es? Non adhuc itaque dubitatio videtur, quia hoc quidem materia illud vero forma. Quid igitur huius causa, eius scilicet quod potentia ens actu sit, praeter faciens, in quibuscumque generatio? Nulla namque est causa altera eius quod potestate speram actu esse speram, sed hoc erat quod quid erat esse utrique.

For this difficulty is the same as would arise if round bronze were the definition of cloak ; for this word would be a sign of the definitory formula, so that the question is, what is the cause of the unity of round and bronze? The difficulty disappears, because the one is matter, the other form. What, then, causes this-that which was potentially to be actually-except, in the case of things which are generated, the agent? For there is no other cause of the potential sphere _ s becoming actually a sphere, but this was the essence of either.

ἔστι δὲ τῆς ὕλης ἡ μὲν νοητὴ ἡ δ᾽ αἰσθητή, καὶ ἀεὶ τοῦ λόγου τὸ μὲν [35] ὕλη τὸ δὲ ἐνέργειά ἐστιν, οἷον ὁ κύκλος σχῆμα ἐπίπεδον.

Est autem materiae alia intellectualis alia sensibilis, et semper rationis hoc quidem materia illud vero actus est, ut circulus figura superficialis.

Of matter some is intelligible, some perceptible, and in a formula there is always an element of matter as well as one of actuality; e.g. the circle is a plane figure .

ὅσα δὲ μὴ ἔχει ὕλην μήτε νοητὴν μήτε αἰσθητήν, εὐθὺς ὅπερ ἕν τί [εἶναί] ἐστιν ἕκαστον, [1045β] [1] ὥσπερ καὶ ὅπερ ὄν τι, τὸ τόδε, τὸ ποιόν, τὸ ποσόν—διὸ καὶ οὐκ ἔνεστιν ἐν τοῖς ὁρισμοῖς οὔτε τὸ ὂν οὔτε τὸ ἕν—, καὶ τὸ τί ἦν εἶναι εὐθὺς ἕν τί ἐστιν ὥσπερ καὶ ὄν τι—διὸ καὶ οὐκ ἔστιν ἕτερόν τι αἴτιον τοῦ [5] ἓν εἶναι οὐθενὶ τούτων οὐδὲ τοῦ ὄν τι εἶναι: εὐθὺς γὰρ ἕκαστόν ἐστιν ὄν τι καὶ ἕν τι, οὐχ ὡς ἐν γένει τῷ ὄντι καὶ τῷ ἑνί, οὐδ᾽ ὡς χωριστῶν ὄντων παρὰ τὰ καθ᾽ ἕκαστα.

Quaecumque vero non habent materiam, nec intellectualem nec sensibilem, statim quod quidem unum ali quid esse est unumquodque quemadmodum et quod ens aliquid: quod hoc, quod quale , quod quantum. Quapropter et non inest in diffinitionibus nec ens nec unum. Et quod quid erat esse statim unum aliquid est sicut et ens aliquid. Quapropter non est aliqua alia causa unum essendi nulli horum neque essendi ens aliquid; statim enim unumquodque est ens aliquid et unum aliquid, non ut in genere ente et uno, nec ut separabilibus existentibus praeter singularia.

But of the things which have no matter, either intelligible or perceptible, each is by its [45b] nature essentially a kind of unity, as it is essentially a kind of being-individual substance, quality, or quantity (and so neither existent nor one is present in their definitions), and the essence of each of them is by its very nature a kind of unity as it is a kind of being-and so none of these has any reason outside itself, for being one, nor for being a kind of being; for each is by its nature a kind of being and a kind of unity, not as being in the genus being or one nor in the sense that being and unity can exist apart from particulars.

διὰ ταύτην δὲ τὴν ἀπορίαν οἱ μὲν μέθεξιν λέγουσι, καὶ αἴτιον τί τῆς μεθέξεως καὶ τί τὸ μετέχειν ἀποροῦσιν: οἱ δὲ συνουσίαν [10] [ψυχῆς], ὥσπερ Λυκόφρων φησὶν εἶναι τὴν ἐπιστήμην τοῦ ἐπίστασθαι καὶ ψυχῆς: οἱ δὲ σύνθεσιν ἢ σύνδεσμον ψυχῆς σώματι τὸ ζῆν.

Propter hanc vero dubitationem hii quidem participationem dicunt, et causam aliquam participationis et quid est participare dubitant; hii autem coexistentiam anime, sicut Licofron ait esse scientiam eius quod est scire et anime; alii vero compositionem aut coniunctionem anime cum corpore vivere.

Owing to the difficulty about unity some speak of participation , and raise the question, what is the cause of participation and what is it to participate; and others speak of communion , as Lycophron says knowledge is a communion of knowing with the soul; and others say life is a composition or connexion of soul with body.

καίτοι ὁ αὐτὸς λόγος ἐπὶ πάντων· καὶ γὰρ τὸ ὑγιαίνειν ἔσται ἢ συνουσία ἢ σύνδεσμος ἢ σύνθεσις ψυχῆς καὶ ὑγιείας, καὶ τὸ τὸν χαλκὸν εἶναι τρίγωνον [15] σύνθεσις χαλκοῦ καὶ τριγώνου, καὶ τὸ λευκὸν εἶναι σύνθεσις ἐπιφανείας καὶ λευκότητος.

Et quidem eadem ratio in omnibus. Et enim sanum esse erit aut coexistentia aut colligatio aut coniunctio anime et sanitatis, et es esse trigonum compositio eris et trigoni, et album esse compositio superficiei et albedinis.

Yet the same account applies to all cases; for being healthy, too, will on this showing be either a communion or a connexion or a composition of soul and health, and the fact that the bronze is a triangle will be a composition of bronze and triangle, and the fact that a thing is white will be a composition of surface and whiteness.

αἴτιον δ᾽ ὅτι δυνάμεως καὶ ἐντελεχείας ζητοῦσι λόγον ἑνοποιὸν καὶ διαφοράν. ἔστι δ᾽, ὥσπερ εἴρηται, ἡ ἐσχάτη ὕλη καὶ ἡ μορφὴ ταὐτὸ καὶ ἕν, δυνάμει, τὸ δὲ ἐνεργείᾳ, ὥστε ὅμοιον τὸ ζητεῖν τοῦ [20] ἑνὸς τί αἴτιον καὶ τοῦ ἓν εἶναι· ἓν γάρ τι ἕκαστον, καὶ τὸ δυνάμει καὶ τὸ ἐνεργείᾳ ἕν πώς ἐστιν, ὥστε αἴτιον οὐθὲν ἄλλο πλὴν εἴ τι ὡς κινῆσαν ἐκ δυνάμεως εἰς ἐνέργειαν. ὅσα δὲ μὴ ἔχει ὕλην, πάντα ἁπλῶς ὅπερ ἕν τι.

Causa vero quia potentie et actus quaerunt unum faciens et differentiam. Est autem, ut dictum est, et ultima materia et forma idem et potentia, hoc autem actu. Quare simile est quaerere unius quae causa et unum essendi; unum enim aliquid unumquodque, et quod potentia et quod actu unum aliqualiter est. Quare causa nulla alia nisi id quod ut movens ex potentia ad actum. Quaecumque vero non habent materiam, omnia simpliciter quod vere entia aliquid.

The reason is that people look for a unifying formula, and a difference, between potency and complete reality. But, as has been said, the proximate matter and the form are one and the same thing, the one potentially, and the other actually. Therefore it is like asking what in general is the cause of unity and of a thing _ s being one; for each thing is a unity, and the potential and the actual are somehow one. Therefore there is no other cause here unless there is something which caused the movement from potency into actuality. And all things which have no matter are without qualification essentially unities.

# METHAPHISICE ARISTOTILIS LIBER NONUS

## 9 (Θ)

[1045β] [27] περὶ μὲν οὖν τοῦ πρώτως ὄντος καὶ πρὸς ὃ πᾶσαι αἱ ἄλλαι κατηγορίαι τοῦ ὄντος ἀναφέρονται εἴρηται, περὶ τῆς οὐσίας (κατὰ γὰρ τὸν τῆς οὐσίας λόγον λέγεται τἆλλα [30] ὄντα, τό τε ποσὸν καὶ τὸ ποιὸν καὶ τἆλλα τὰ οὕτω λεγόμενα: πάντα γὰρ ἕξει τὸν τῆς οὐσίας λόγον, ὥσπερ εἴπομεν ἐν τοῖς πρώτοις λόγοις): ἐπεὶ δὲ λέγεται τὸ ὂν τὸ μὲν τὸ τὶ ἢ ποιὸν ἢ ποσόν, τὸ δὲ κατὰ δύναμιν καὶ ἐντελέχειαν καὶ κατὰ τὸ ἔργον, διορίσωμεν καὶ περὶ δυνάμεως [35] καὶ ἐντελεχείας, καὶ πρῶτον περὶ δυνάμεως ἣ λέγεται μὲν μάλιστα κυρίως, οὐ μὴν χρησιμωτάτη γέ ἐστι πρὸς ὃ βουλόμεθα νῦν: [1046α] [1] ἐπὶ πλέον γάρ ἐστιν ἡ δύναμις καὶ ἡ ἐνέργεια τῶν μόνον λεγομένων κατὰ κίνησιν.

De primo quidem igitur ente et ad quod omnes aliae cathegorie entis referuntur dictum est, de substantia. Nam secundum substantiae rationem dicuntur alia entia: quantitas, qualitas et alia sic dicta; omnia namque rationem habebunt substantiae, ut diximus in primis sermonibus. Quoniam vero dicitur ens hoc quidem eo quod quid aut qualitas aut quantitas, aliud secundum potentiam et actum et secundum opus, determinabimus et de potentia et actu. Et primum de potentia quae dicitur quidem maxime proprie, non tamen utilis est ad quod volumus nunc. In plus enim est potentia et actus eorum quae dicuntur secundum motum solum. Sed cum dixerimus de hac, in determinationibus de actu ostendemus et de aliis.

WE have treated of that which is primarily and to which all the other categories of being are referred-i.e. of substance. For it is in virtue of the concept of substance that the others also are said to be-quantity and quality and the like; for all will be found to involve the concept of substance, as we said in the first part of our work. And since being is in one way divided into individual thing, quality, and quantity, and is in another way distinguished in respect of potency and complete reality, and of function, let us now add a discussion of potency and complete reality. And first let us explain potency in the strictest sense, which is, how[46a]ever, not the most useful for our present purpose. For potency and actuality extend beyond the cases that involve a reference to motion. But when we have spoken of this first kind, we shall in our discussions of actuality _ explain the other kinds of potency as well.

ἀλλ᾽ εἰπόντες περὶ ταύτης, ἐν τοῖς περὶ τῆς ἐνεργείας διορισμοῖς δηλώσομεν καὶ περὶ τῶν ἄλλων. ὅτι μὲν οὖν λέγεται [5] πολλαχῶς ἡ δύναμις καὶ τὸ δύνασθαι, διώρισται ἡμῖν ἐν ἄλλοις: τούτων δ᾽ ὅσαι μὲν ὁμωνύμως λέγονται δυνάμεις ἀφείσθωσαν (ἔνιαι γὰρ ὁμοιότητί τινι λέγονται, καθάπερ ἐν γεωμετρίᾳ καὶ δυνατὰ καὶ ἀδύνατα λέγομεν τῷ εἶναί πως ἢ μὴ εἶναι), ὅσαι δὲ πρὸς τὸ αὐτὸ εἶδος, πᾶσαι ἀρχαί [10] τινές εἰσι, καὶ πρὸς πρώτην μίαν λέγονται, ἥ ἐστιν ἀρχὴ μεταβολῆς ἐν ἄλλῳ ἢ ᾗ ἄλλο. ἡ μὲν γὰρ τοῦ παθεῖν ἐστὶ δύναμις, ἡ ἐν αὐτῷ τῷ πάσχοντι ἀρχὴ μεταβολῆς παθητικῆς ὑπ᾽ ἄλλου ἢ ᾗ ἄλλο· ἡ δ᾽ ἕξις ἀπαθείας τῆς ἐπὶ τὸ χεῖρον καὶ φθορᾶς τῆς ὑπ᾽ ἄλλου ἢ ᾗ ἄλλο ὑπ᾽ ἀρχῆς [15] μεταβλητικῆς. ἐν γὰρ τούτοις ἔνεστι πᾶσι τοῖς ὅροις ὁ τῆς πρώτης δυνάμεως λόγος. πάλιν δ᾽ αὗται δυνάμεις λέγονται ἢ τοῦ μόνον ποιῆσαι ἢ [τοῦ] παθεῖν ἢ τοῦ καλῶς, ὥστε καὶ ἐν τοῖς τούτων λόγοις ἐνυπάρχουσί πως οἱ τῶν προτέρων δυνάμεων λόγοι.

Quod quidem igitur dicitur multipliciter potentia et posse, determinatum est nobis in aliis. Harum autem quaecumque quidem equivoce dicuntur potentie praetermittantur. Quaedam enim similitudine quadam dicuntur, quemadmodum in geometria et possibilia et impossibilia dicimus eo quod aliquo modo sunt aut non sunt. Quaecumque autem ad eandem speciem, omnes principia quaedam sunt, et ad primum unum dicuntur, quod est principium transmutationis in alio in quantum aliud est. Nam haec quidem patiendi potentia est, quae in ipso patiente principium mutationis passive ab alio in quantum aliud est. Haec autem habitus impassibilitatis eius quae in deterius et corruptionis ab alio in quantum aliud a principio transmutativo. In hiis enim inest omnibus terminis prime potentie ratio. Iterum autem hae potentie dicuntur aut solum faciendi aut patiendi aut ipsius bene; quare in harum rationibus insunt aliqualiter priorum rationes potentiarum.

We have pointed out elsewhere that potency and the word can have several senses. Of these we may neglect all the potencies that are so called by an equivocation. For some are called so by analogy, as in geometry we say one thing is or is not a power of another by virtue of the presence or absence of some relation between them. But all potencies that conform to the same type are originative sources of some kind, and are called potencies in reference to one primary kind of potency, which is an originative source of change in another thing or in the thing itself qua other. For one kind is a potency of being acted on, i.e. the originative source, in the very thing acted on, of its being passively changed by another thing or by itself qua other; and another kind is a state of insusceptibility to change for the worse and to destruction by another thing or by the thing itself qua other by virtue of an originative source of change. In all these definitions is implied the formula if potency in the primary sense.-And again these so-called potencies are potencies either of merely acting or being acted on, or of acting or being acted on well, so that even in the formulae of the latter the formulae of the prior kinds of potency are somehow implied.

φανερὸν οὖν ὅτι ἔστι μὲν ὡς μία δύναμις [20] τοῦ ποιεῖν καὶ πάσχειν (δυνατὸν γάρ ἐστι καὶ τῷ ἔχειν αὐτὸ δύναμιν τοῦ παθεῖν καὶ τῷ ἄλλο ὑπ᾽ αὐτοῦ), ἔστι δὲ ὡς ἄλλη. ἡ μὲν γὰρ ἐν τῷ πάσχοντι (διὰ γὰρ τὸ ἔχειν τινὰ ἀρχήν, καὶ εἶναι καὶ τὴν ὕλην ἀρχήν τινα, πάσχει τὸ πάσχον, καὶ ἄλλο ὑπ᾽ ἄλλου· τὸ λιπαρὸν μὲν

[25] γὰρ καυστὸν τὸ δ᾽ ὑπεῖκον ὡδὶ θλαστόν, ὁμοίως δὲ καὶ ἐπὶ τῶν ἄλλων), ἡ δ᾽ ἐν τῷ ποιοῦντι, οἷον τὸ θερμὸν καὶ ἡ οἰκοδομική, ἡ μὲν ἐν τῷ θερμαντικῷ ἡ δ᾽ ἐν τῷ οἰκοδομικῷ· διὸ ᾗ συμπέφυκεν, οὐθὲν πάσχει αὐτὸ ὑφ᾽ ἑαυτοῦ· ἓν γὰρ καὶ οὐκ ἄλλο.

Palam igitur quia est quidem ut una potentia faciendi et patiendi; nam possibile est et habere ipsum potentiam patiendi et eo quod aliud ab ipso. Est autem ut alia. Haec quidem enim in patiente; propter habere enim quoddam principium, et esse materiam principium quoddam, patitur patiens, et aliud ab alio. Crassum enim combustibile est, cedens autem sic impressibile, similiter autem et in aliis. Haec autem in faciente; ut calor et edificativa, haec quidem in calefactivo, haec autem in edificativo. Quapropter in quantum simul natum est, nihil patitur ipsum a se ipso; unum enim et non aliud.

Obviously, then, in a sense the potency of acting and of being acted on is one (for a thing may be capable either because it can itself be acted on or because something else can be acted on by it), but in a sense the potencies are different. For the one is in the thing acted on; it is because it contains a certain originative source, and because even the matter is an originative source, that the thing acted on is acted on, and one thing by one, another by another; for that which is oily can be burnt, and that which yields in a particular way can be crushed; and similarly in all other cases. But the other potency is in the agent, e.g. heat and the art of building are present, one in that which can produce heat and the other in the man who can build. And so, in so far as a thing is an organic unity, it cannot be acted on by itself; for it is one and not two different things.

καὶ ἡ ἀδυναμία καὶ τὸ ἀδύνατον [30] ἡ τῇ τοιαύτῃ δυνάμει ἐναντία στέρησίς ἐστιν, ὥστε τοῦ αὐτοῦ καὶ κατὰ τὸ αὐτὸ πᾶσα δύναμις ἀδυναμίᾳ. ἡ δὲ στέρησις λέγεται πολλαχῶς· καὶ γὰρ τὸ μὴ ἔχον καὶ τὸ πεφυκὸς ἂν μὴ ἔχῃ, ἢ ὅλως ἢ ὅτε πέφυκεν, καὶ ᾗ ὡδί, οἷον παντελῶς, ἢ κἂν ὁπωσοῦν. ἐπ᾽ ἐνίων δέ, ἂν πεφυκότα [35] ἔχειν μὴ ἔχῃ βίᾳ, ἐστερῆσθαι ταῦτα λέγομεν.

Et impotentia et impossibile et quae tali potentie contraria est privatio; quare eiusdem et secundum idem omnis potentia impotentia. Privatio autem dicitur multipliciter. Et enim non habens et aptum natum si non habet, aut omnino aut quando aptum natum est, et aut sic, puta perfecte, vel saltem quomodocumque. In quibusdam vero, si apta nata habere non habeant vi, privata esse haec dicimus.

And impotence and impotent stand for the privation which is contrary to potency of this sort, so that every potency belongs to the same subject and refers to the same process as a corresponding impotence. Privation has several senses; for it means (1) that which has not a certain quality and (2) that which might naturally have it but has not it, either (a) in general or (b) when it might naturally have it, and either (a) in some particular way, e.g. when it has not it completely, or (b) when it has not it at all. And in certain cases if things which naturally have a quality lose it by violence, we say they have suffered privation.

### Chapter 2

ἐπεὶ δ᾽ αἱ μὲν ἐν τοῖς ἀψύχοις ἐνυπάρχουσιν ἀρχαὶ τοιαῦται, αἱ δ᾽ ἐν τοῖς ἐμψύχοις καὶ ἐν ψυχῇ καὶ τῆς ψυχῆς ἐν τῷ λόγον ἔχοντι, [1046β] [1] δῆλον ὅτι καὶ τῶν δυνάμεων αἱ μὲν ἔσονται ἄλογοι αἱ δὲ μετὰ λόγου: διὸ πᾶσαι αἱ τέχναι καὶ αἱ ποιητικαὶ ἐπιστῆμαι δυνάμεις εἰσίν: ἀρχαὶ γὰρ μεταβλητικαί εἰσιν ἐν ἄλλῳ ἢ ᾗ ἄλλο.

Quoniam autem haec quidem in inanimatis insunt principia talia, illa vero in animatis et in anima et anime in rationem habente, palam quia et potentiarum aliae erunt irrationabiles aliae cum ratione. Quapropter omnes artes et factive scientie potentie sunt; principia namque permutativa in alio aut in quantum aliud.

Since some such originative sources are present in soulless things, and others in things possessed of soul, and in [46b] soul, and in the rational part of the soul, clearly some potencies will, be non-rational and some will be non-rational and some will be accompanied by a rational formula. This is why all arts, i.e. all productive forms of knowledge, are potencies; they are originative sources of change in another thing or in the artist himself considered as other.

καὶ αἱ μὲν [5] μετὰ λόγου πᾶσαι τῶν ἐναντίων αἱ αὐταί, αἱ δὲ ἄλογοι μία ἑνός, οἷον τὸ θερμὸν τοῦ θερμαίνειν μόνον· ἡ δὲ ἰατρικὴ νόσου καὶ ὑγιείας.

Et quae quidem cum ratione  omnes contrariorum sunt eaedem, et quae irrationabiles una unius; ut calidum calefaciendi solum, medicativa autem infirmitatis et sanitatis.

And each of those which are accompanied by a rational formula is alike capable of contrary effects, but one non-rational power produces one effect; e.g. the hot is capable only of heating, but the medical art can produce both disease and health.

αἴτιον δὲ ὅτι λόγος ἐστὶν ἡ ἐπιστήμη, ὁ δὲ λόγος ὁ αὐτὸς δηλοῖ τὸ πρᾶγμα καὶ τὴν στέρησιν, πλὴν οὐχ ὡσαύτως, καὶ ἔστιν ὡς ἀμφοῖν ἔστι δ᾽ ὡς [10] τοῦ ὑπάρχοντος μᾶλλον, ὥστ᾽ ἀνάγκη καὶ τὰς τοιαύτας ἐπιστήμας εἶναι μὲν τῶν ἐναντίων, εἶναι δὲ τοῦ μὲν καθ᾽ αὑτάς τοῦ δὲ μὴ καθ᾽ αὑτάς: καὶ γὰρ ὁ λόγος τοῦ μὲν καθ᾽ αὑτὸ τοῦ δὲ τρόπον τινὰ κατὰ συμβεβηκός: ἀποφάσει γὰρ καὶ ἀποφορᾷ δηλοῖ τὸ ἐναντίον: ἡ γὰρ στέρησις [15] ἡ πρώτη τὸ ἐναντίον, αὕτη δὲ ἀποφορὰ θατέρου.

Causa autem quia ratio est scientia; ratio autem eadem ostendit rem et privationem, tamen non similiter, et est ut amborum, est autem ut existentis magis. Quare necesse et tales scientias esse quidem contrariorum, esse vero huius quidem secundum se illius vero non secundum se; et enim ratio huius quidem secundum se illius vero modo quodam secundum accidens. Nam negatione et ablatione ostendit contrarium; etenim privatio prima contrarium, haec autem ablatio alterius.

The reason is that science is a rational formula, and the same rational formula explains a thing and its privation, only not in the same way; and in a sense it applies to both, but in a sense it applies rather to the positive fact. Therefore such sciences must deal with contraries, but with one in virtue of their own nature and with the other not in virtue of their nature; for the rational formula applies to one object in virtue of that object _ s nature, and to the other, in a sense, accidentally. For it is by denial and removal that it exhibits the contrary; for the contrary is the primary privation, and this is the removal of the positive term.

ἐπεὶ δὲ τὰ ἐναντία οὐκ ἐγγίγνεται ἐν τῷ αὐτῷ, ἡ δ᾽ ἐπιστήμη δύναμις τῷ λόγον ἔχειν, καὶ ἡ ψυχὴ κινήσεως ἔχει ἀρχήν, τὸ μὲν ὑγιεινὸν ὑγίειαν μόνον ποιεῖ καὶ τὸ θερμαντικὸν θερμότητα καὶ τὸ ψυκτικὸν ψυχρότητα, ὁ δ᾽ ἐπιστήμων [20] ἄμφω. λόγος γάρ ἐστιν ἀμφοῖν μέν, οὐχ ὁμοίως δέ, καὶ ἐν ψυχῇ ᾗ ἔχει κινήσεως ἀρχήν: ὥστε ἄμφω ἀπὸ τῆς αὐτῆς ἀρχῆς κινήσει πρὸς ταὐτὸ συνάψασα: διὸ τὰ κατὰ λόγον δυνατὰ τοῖς ἄνευ λόγου δυνατοῖς ποιεῖ τἀναντία: μιᾷ γὰρ ἀρχῇ περιέχεται, τῷ λόγῳ.

Quoniam autem contraria non fiunt in eodem, scientia autem potentia in habendo rationem, et anima motus habet principium: salubre quidem sanitatem solum facit et calefactivum caliditatem et infrigidativum frigiditatem, sciens vero ambo. Est enim amborum quidem ratio, non similiter autem, et in anima quae habet motus principium; quare ambo ab eodem principio movebit ad ipsum copulans. Propter quod secundum rationem potentia sine ratione potentibus faciunt contraria; unum enim principium continetur ratione.

Now since contraries do not occur in the same thing, but science is a potency which depends on the possession of a rational formula, and the soul possesses an originative source of movement; therefore, while the wholesome produces only health and the calorific only heat and the frigorific only cold, the scientific man produces both the contrary effects. For the rational formula is one which applies to both, though not in the same way, and it is in a soul which possesses an originative source of movement; so that the soul will start both processes from the same originative source, having linked them up with the same thing. And so the things whose potency is according to a rational formula act contrariwise to the things whose potency is non-rational; for the products of the former are included under one originative source, the rational formula.

φανερὸν δὲ καὶ ὅτι [25] τῇ μὲν τοῦ εὖ δυνάμει ἀκολουθεῖ ἡ τοῦ μόνον ποιῆσαι ἢ παθεῖν δύναμις, ταύτῃ δ᾽ ἐκείνη οὐκ ἀεί· ἀνάγκη γὰρ τὸν εὖ ποιοῦντα καὶ ποιεῖν, τὸν δὲ μόνον ποιοῦντα οὐκ ἀνάγκη καὶ εὖ ποιεῖν.

Palam autem quia ipsius bene potentiam sequitur solum faciendi aut patiendi potentia, hanc vero illa non semper. Necesse enim bene facientem facere, sed solum facientem non necesse et bene facere.

It is obvious also that the potency of merely doing a thing or having it done to one is implied in that of doing it or having it done well, but the latter is not always implied in the former: for he who does a thing well must also do it, but he who does it merely need not also do it well.

*Chapter* 3

εἰσὶ δέ τινες οἵ φασιν, οἷον οἱ Μεγαρικοί, ὅταν ἐνεργῇ [30] μόνον δύνασθαι, ὅταν δὲ μὴ ἐνεργῇ οὐ δύνασθαι, οἷον τὸν [31] μὴ οἰκοδομοῦντα οὐ δύνασθαι οἰκοδομεῖν, ἀλλὰ τὸν οἰκοδομοῦντα ὅταν οἰκοδομῇ· ὁμοίως δὲ καὶ ἐπὶ τῶν ἄλλων.

Sunt autem quidam qui dicunt, ut Megarici, quando operatur solum posse, et quando non operatur non posse, ut non edificantem non posse edificare, sed edificantem quando edificat; similiter autem et in aliis.

There are some who say, as the Megaric school does, that a thing can act only when it is acting, and when it is not acting it cannot act, e.g. that he who is not building cannot build, but only he who is building, when he is building; and so in all other cases.

οἷς τὰ συμβαίνοντα ἄτοπα οὐ χαλεπὸν ἰδεῖν. δῆλον γὰρ ὅτι οὔτ᾽ οἰκοδόμος ἔσται ἐὰν μὴ οἰκοδομῇ (τὸ γὰρ οἰκοδόμῳ [35] εἶναι τὸ δυνατῷ εἶναί ἐστιν οἰκοδομεῖν), ὁμοίως δὲ καὶ ἐπὶ τῶν ἄλλων τεχνῶν. εἰ οὖν ἀδύνατον τὰς τοιαύτας ἔχειν τέχνας μὴ μαθόντα ποτὲ καὶ λαβόντα, [1047α] [1] καὶ μὴ ἔχειν μὴ ἀποβαλόντα ποτέ (ἢ γὰρ λήθῃ ἢ πάθει τινὶ ἢ χρόνῳ· οὐ γὰρ δὴ τοῦ γε πράγματος φθαρέντος, ἀεὶ γὰρ ἔστιν), ὅταν παύσηται, οὐχ ἕξει τὴν τέχνην, πάλιν δ᾽ εὐθὺς οἰκοδομήσει πῶς λαβών;

Quibus accidentia inconvenientia non est difficile videre. Palam enim quia non est edificator si non edificet; nam edificatori esse est esse potentem edificare. Similiter autem et in aliis artibus. Si igitur impossibile est tales habere artes non discentem aliquando et accipientem, et non habere non abicientem aliquando (aut enim oblivione aut passione aliqua aut tempore; non enim utique re corrupta, semper enim est): quando cessaverit, non habebit artem, iterum qui statim edificabit aliqualiter accipiens.

It is not hard to see the absurdities that attend this view. For it is clear that on this view a man will not be a builder unless he is building (for to be a builder is to be able to build), and so with the other arts. If, then, it is impossible to have such arts if one has not at some time learnt and acquired them, and it is then impossible not to [47a] have them if one has not sometime lost them (either by forgetfulness or by some accident or by time; for it cannot be by the destruction of the object, for that lasts for ever), a man will not have the art when he has ceased to use it, and yet he may immediately build again; how then will he have got the art?

καὶ τὰ ἄψυχα δὴ ὁμοίως: οὔτε γὰρ [5] ψυχρὸν οὔτε θερμὸν οὔτε γλυκὺ οὔτε ὅλως αἰσθητὸν οὐθὲν ἔσται μὴ αἰσθανομένων: ὥστε τὸν Πρωταγόρου λόγον συμβήσεται λέγειν αὐτοῖς.

Et inanimata utique similiter. Neque enim frigidum neque calidum neque dulce neque omnino sensibile nihil erit non sentientibus; quare Protagore rationem eis dicere continget.

And similarly with regard to lifeless things; nothing will be either cold or hot or sweet or perceptible at all if people are not perceiving it; so that the upholders of this view will have to maintain the doctrine of Protagoras.

ἀλλὰ μὴν οὐδ᾽ αἴσθησιν ἕξει οὐδὲν ἂν μὴ αἰσθάνηται μηδ᾽ ἐνεργῇ. εἰ οὖν τυφλὸν τὸ μὴ ἔχον ὄψιν, πεφυκὸς δὲ καὶ ὅτε πέφυκε καὶ ἔτι ὄν, οἱ αὐτοὶ [10] τυφλοὶ ἔσονται πολλάκις τῆς ἡμέρας, καὶ κωφοί.

At vero nec sensum habebit nihil, si non sentiat nec operetur. Si ergo cecum non habens visum, aptum vero natum et quando aptum natum est et adhuc ens, iidem ceci erunt saepe die et surdi.

But, indeed, nothing will even have perception if it is not perceiving, i.e. exercising its perception. If, then, that is blind which has not sight though it would naturally have it, when it would naturally have it and when it still exists, the same people will be blind many times in the day-and deaf too.

ἔτι εἰ ἀδύνατον τὸ ἐστερημένον δυνάμεως, τὸ μὴ γιγνόμενον ἀδύνατον ἔσται γενέσθαι· τὸ δ᾽ ἀδύνατον γενέσθαι ὁ λέγων ἢ εἶναι ἢ ἔσεσθαι ψεύσεται (τὸ γὰρ ἀδύνατον τοῦτο ἐσήμαινεν), ὥστε οὗτοι οἱ λόγοι ἐξαιροῦσι καὶ κίνησιν καὶ γένεσιν. [15] ἀεὶ γὰρ τό τε ἑστηκὸς ἑστήξεται καὶ τὸ καθήμενον καθεδεῖται· οὐ γὰρ ἀναστήσεται ἂν καθέζηται· ἀδύνατον γὰρ ἔσται ἀναστῆναι ὅ γε μὴ δύναται ἀναστῆναι.

Amplius si impossibile quod privatum est potentia, quod non fit impossibile erit factum esse. Sed quod impossibile est factum esse dicens aut esse aut futurum esse, mentietur; nam impossibile hoc significavit. Quare hae rationes auferunt motum et generationem. Semper enim stans stabit et sedens sedebit, non enim surget si sedet; impossibile namque erit surgere quod non potest surgere.

Again, if that which is deprived of potency is incapable, that which is not happening will be incapable of happening; but he who says of that which is incapable of happening either that it is or that it will be will say what is untrue; for this is what incapacity meant. Therefore these views do away with both movement and becoming. For that which stands will always stand, and that which sits will always sit, since if it is sitting it will not get up; for that which, as we are told, cannot get up will be incapable of getting up.

εἰ οὖν μὴ ἐνδέχεται ταῦτα λέγειν, φανερὸν ὅτι δύναμις καὶ ἐνέργεια ἕτερόν ἐστιν (ἐκεῖνοι δ᾽ οἱ λόγοι δύναμιν καὶ ἐνέργειαν ταὐτὸ [20] ποιοῦσιν, διὸ καὶ οὐ μικρόν τι ζητοῦσιν ἀναιρεῖν), ὥστε ἐνδέχεται δυνατὸν μέν τι εἶναι μὴ εἶναι δέ, καὶ δυνατὸν μὴ εἶναι εἶναι δέ, ὁμοίως δὲ καὶ ἐπὶ τῶν ἄλλων κατηγοριῶν δυνατὸν βαδίζειν ὂν μὴ βαδίζειν, καὶ μὴ βαδίζειν δυνατὸν ὂν βαδίζειν.

Si ergo non contingit haec dicere, palam quia potentia et actus alterum sunt (ille vero rationes potentiam et actum idem faciunt, propter quod et non parvum aliquid quaerunt destruere). Quare contingit possibile quidem aliquid esse, non esse autem, et possibile non esse, esse autem. Similiter autem et in aliis cathegoriis: possibile vadere ens non vadere, et non vadens possibile esse vadere.

But we cannot say this, so that evidently potency and actuality are different (but these views make potency and actuality the same, and so it is no small thing they are seeking to annihilate), so that it is possible that a thing may be capable of being and not he, and capable of not being and yet he, and similarly with the other kinds of predicate; it may be capable of walking and yet not walk, or capable of not walking and yet walk.

ἔστι δὲ δυνατὸν τοῦτο ᾧ ἐὰν ὑπάρξῃ [25] ἡ ἐνέργεια οὗ λέγεται ἔχειν τὴν δύναμιν, οὐθὲν ἔσται ἀδύνατον. λέγω δὲ οἷον, εἰ δυνατὸν καθῆσθαι καὶ ἐνδέχεται καθῆσθαι, τούτῳ ἐὰν ὑπάρξῃ τὸ καθῆσθαι, οὐδὲν ἔσται ἀδύνατον· καὶ εἰ

κινηθῆναι ἢ κινῆσαι ἢ στῆναι ἢ στῆσαι ἢ εἶναι ἢ γίγνεσθαι ἢ μὴ εἶναι ἢ μὴ γίγνεσθαι, ὁμοίως.

Est autem possibile hoc cui si extiterit actus cuius dicitur habere potentiam, nihil erit impossibile. Dico autem puta si possibile sedere et contingit sedere, huic si inest sedere, nihil erit impossibile; et aut moveri aut movere aut statui aut statuere aut esse aut fieri aut non esse aut non fieri, similiter.

And a thing is capable of doing something if there will be nothing impossible in its having the actuality of that of which it is said to have the capacity. I mean, for instance, if a thing is capable of sitting and it is open to it to sit, there will be nothing impossible in its actually sitting; and similarly if it is capable of being moved or moving, or of standing or making to stand, or of being or coming to be, or of not being or not coming to be.

[30] ἐλήλυθε δ' ἡ ἐνέργεια τοὔνομα, ἡ πρὸς τὴν ἐντελέχειαν συντιθεμένη, καὶ ἐπὶ τὰ ἄλλα ἐκ τῶν κινήσεων μάλιστα: δοκεῖ γὰρ ἡ ἐνέργεια μάλιστα ἡ κίνησις εἶναι, διὸ καὶ τοῖς μὴ οὖσιν οὐκ ἀποδιδόασι τὸ κινεῖσθαι, ἄλλας δέ τινας κατηγορίας, οἷον διανοητὰ καὶ ἐπιθυμητὰ εἶναι τὰ μὴ ὄντα, [35] κινούμενα δὲ οὔ, τοῦτο δὲ ὅτι οὐκ ὄντα ἐνεργείᾳ ἔσονται ἐνεργείᾳ. [1047β] [1] τῶν γὰρ μὴ ὄντων ἔνια δυνάμει ἐστίν: οὐκ ἔστι δέ, ὅτι οὐκ ἐντελεχείᾳ ἐστίν.

Venit autem actus  nomen, qui ad endelichiam compositus,  et ad alia ex motibus maxime; videtur enim actus maxime motus esse. Quapropter et non existentibus non assignant moveri, alias autem quasdam cathegorias: puta intellectualia et concupiscibilia esse non entia, mota vero non. Hoc  autem, quia non entia actu erunt actu. Non entium enim quaedam potentia sunt; non sunt autem, quia non endelichia sunt.

The word actuality , which we connect with complete reality , has, in the main, been extended from movements to other things; for actuality in the strict sense is thought to be identical with movement. And so people do not assign movement to non-existent things, though they do assign some other predicates. E.g. they say that non-existent things are objects of thought and desire, but not that they are moved; and this because, while ex hypothesi they do not actually exist, they would have to exist actually if they [47b] were moved. For of non-existent things some exist potentially; but they do not exist, because they do not exist in complete reality.

*Chapter*  4

εἰ δέ ἐστι τὸ εἰρημένον τὸ δυνατὸν ἢ ἀκολουθεῖ, φανερὸν ὅτι οὐκ ἐνδέχεται ἀληθὲς εἶναι τὸ εἰπεῖν ὅτι δυνατὸν μὲν [5] τοδί, οὐκ ἔσται δέ, ὥστε τὰ ἀδύνατα εἶναι ταύτῃ διαφεύγειν· λέγω δὲ οἷον εἴ τις φαίη δυνατὸν τὴν διάμετρον μετρηθῆναι οὐ μέντοι μετρηθήσεσθαι—ὁ μὴ λογιζόμενος τὸ ἀδύνατον εἶναι—ὅτι οὐθὲν κωλύει δυνατόν τι ὂν εἶναι ἢ γενέσθαι μὴ εἶναι μηδ᾽ ἔσεσθαι. ἀλλ᾽ ἐκεῖνο ἀνάγκη ἐκ [10] τῶν κειμένων, εἰ καὶ ὑποθοίμεθα εἶναι ἢ γεγονέναι ὃ οὐκ ἔστι μὲν δυνατὸν δέ, ὅτι οὐθὲν ἔσται ἀδύνατον· συμβήσεται δέ γε, τὸ γὰρ μετρεῖσθαι ἀδύνατον. οὐ γὰρ δή ἐστι ταὐτὸ τὸ ψεῦδος καὶ τὸ ἀδύνατον· τὸ γάρ σε ἑστάναι νῦν ψεῦδος μέν, οὐκ ἀδύνατον δέ.

Si autem est quod dictum est possibile in quantum sequitur, palam quia non contingit verum esse aliquid dicere quia possibile hoc, non erit autem, ut et impossibilia esse sic diffugiant. Dico autem puta si quis dicat possibile dyametrum commensurari non tamen commensurabitur, non cogitans impossibile esse, quia nihil prohibet possibile aliquod ens esse aut fieri, non esse vero aut non futurum esse. Sed illud necesse ex positis sit, et supponamus esse aut fieri quod non est quidem possibile autem , quia nihil erit impossibile. Non enim est idem  falsum et impossibile; nam te stare nunc falsum quidem est et non impossibile.

If what we have described is identical with the capable or convertible with it, evidently it cannot be true to say this is capable of being but will not be , which would imply that the things incapable of being would on this showing vanish. Suppose, for instance, that a man-one who did not take account of that which is incapable of being-were to say that the diagonal of the square is capable of being measured but will not be measured, because a thing may well be capable of being or coming to be, and yet not be or be about to be. But from the premises this necessarily follows, that if we actually supposed that which is not, but is capable of being, to be or to have come to be, there will be nothing impossible in this; but the result will be impossible, for the measuring of the diagonal is impossible. For the false and the impossible are not the same; that you are standing now is false, but that you should be standing is not impossible.

ἅμα δὲ δῆλον καὶ ὅτι, εἰ [15] τοῦ Α ὄντος ἀνάγκη τὸ Β εἶναι, καὶ δυνατοῦ ὄντος εἶναι τοῦ Α καὶ τὸ Β ἀνάγκη εἶναι δυνατόν· εἰ γὰρ μὴ ἀνάγκη δυνατὸν εἶναι, οὐθὲν κωλύει μὴ εἶναι δυνατὸν εἶναι. ἔστω δὴ τὸ Α δυνατόν. οὐκοῦν ὅτε τὸ Α δυνατὸν εἴη εἶναι, εἰ τεθείη τὸ Α, οὐθὲν ἀδύνατον εἶναι συνέβαινεν· τὸ δέ γε Β [20] ἀνάγκη εἶναι. ἀλλ᾽ ἦν ἀδύνατον. ἔστω δὴ ἀδύνατον. εἰ δὴ ἀδύνατον [ἀνάγκη] εἶναι τὸ Β, ἀνάγκη καὶ τὸ Α εἶναι. ἀλλ᾽ ἦν ἄρα τὸ πρῶτον ἀδύνατον· καὶ τὸ δεύτερον ἄρα. ἂν ἄρα ᾖ τὸ Α δυνατόν, καὶ τὸ Β ἔσται δυνατόν, εἴπερ οὕτως εἶχον ὥστε τοῦ Α ὄντος ἀνάγκη εἶναι τὸ Β. ἐὰν δὴ οὕτως ἐχόντων [25] τῶν Α Β μὴ ᾖ δυνατὸν τὸ Β οὕτως, οὐδὲ τὰ Α Β ἕξει ὡς ἐτέθη· καὶ εἰ τοῦ Α δυνατοῦ ὄντος ἀνάγκη τὸ Β δυνατὸν εἶναι, εἰ ἔστι τὸ Α ἀνάγκη εἶναι καὶ τὸ Β. τὸ γὰρ δυνατὸν εἶναι ἐξ ἀνάγκης τὸ Β

336

εἶναι, εἰ τὸ Α δυνατόν, τοῦτο σημαίνει, ἐὰν ᾖ τὸ Α καὶ ὅτε καὶ ὡς ἦν δυνατὸν [30] εἶναι, κἀκεῖνο τότε καὶ οὕτως εἶναι ἀναγκαῖον.

Simul autem palam quia, si a ente necesse b esse, et possibili ente esse a, et b necesse esse possibile. Si enim non necesse possibile esse, nihil prohibet non esse possibile esse. Sit autem a possibile. Ergo quando a possibile erit esse, si ponatur a, nihil impossibile esse accidit; b autem necesse esse. sed erat impossibile. Sit itaque impossibile. Et si impossibile necesse esse a, necesse et b esse. Sed erat ergo primum impossibile et secundum. Si igitur sit a possibile, et b erit possibile, siquidem sic se habebant, ergo a ente necesse b esse. Si itaque sic se habentibus a b non est possibile b ita, nec a b habebunt ut positum est. Et si a possibili ente necesse b possibile esse, si est a, necesse esse b. Nam possibile esse ex necessitate b esse, si a possibile, hoc significat: si sit a et quando et ut erat possibile esse, et illud tunc et ita esse necesse.

At the same time it is clear that if, when A is real, B must be real, then, when A is possible, B also must be possible. For if B need not be possible, there is nothing to prevent its not being possible. Now let A be supposed possible. Then, when A was possible, we agreed that nothing impossible followed if A were supposed to be real; and then B must of course be real. But we supposed B to be impossible. Let it be impossible then. If, then, B is impossible, A also must be so. But the first was supposed impossible; therefore the second also is impossible. If, then, A is possible, B also will be possible, if they were so related that if A,is real, B must be real. If, then, A and B being thus related, B is not possible on this condition, and B will not be related as was supposed. And if when A is possible, B must be possible, then if A is real, B also must be real. For to say that B must be possible, if A is possible, means this, that if A is real both at the time when and in the way in which it was supposed capable of being real, B also must then and in that way be real.

*Chapter* 5

ἁπασῶν δὲ τῶν δυνάμεων οὐσῶν τῶν μὲν συγγενῶν οἷον τῶν αἰσθήσεων, τῶν δὲ ἔθει οἷον τῆς τοῦ αὐλεῖν, τῶν δὲ μαθήσει οἷον τῆς τῶν τεχνῶν, τὰς μὲν ἀνάγκη προενεργήσαντας ἔχειν, ὅσαι ἔθει καὶ λόγῳ, τὰς δὲ μὴ τοιαύτας [35] καὶ τὰς ἐπὶ τοῦ πάσχειν οὐκ ἀνάγκη.

Omnibus autem potentiis existentibus hiis quidem cognatis, ut sensibus, hiis autem consuetudine, ut quae est fistulandi, aliis autem disciplinatu, ut quae est artium:

has quidem necesse eos qui preexercitati fuerint habere, quaecumque consuetudine et ratione, non tales autem et eas quae sunt in pati non necesse.

As all potencies are either innate, like the senses, or come by practice, like the power of playing the flute, or by learning, like artistic power, those which come by practice or by rational formula we must acquire by previous exercise but this is not necessary with those which are not of this nature and which imply passivity.

[1048α] [1] ἐπεὶ δὲ τὸ δυνατὸν τὶ δυνατὸν καὶ ποτὲ καὶ πῶς καὶ ὅσα ἄλλα ἀνάγκη προσεῖναι ἐν τῷ διορισμῷ, καὶ τὰ μὲν κατὰ λόγον δύναται κινεῖν καὶ αἱ δυνάμεις αὐτῶν μετὰ λόγου, τὰ δὲ ἄλογα καὶ αἱ δυνάμεις ἄλογοι, κἀκείνας μὲν ἀνάγκη ἐν ἐμψύχῳ [5] εἶναι ταύτας δὲ ἐν ἀμφοῖν,

Quoniam autem possibile aliquid possibile et quando et quomodo et quaecumque alia necesse adesse in diffinitione, et haec quidem secundum rationem possunt movere et potentie ipsorum cum ratione, haec autem irrationabilia et potentie irrationabiles, et illas quidem necesse in animato esse has vero in ambobus:

Since that which is capable is capable of something and [48a] at some time and in some way (with all the other qualifications which must be present in the definition), and since some things can produce change according to a rational formula and their potencies involve such a formula, while other things are nonrational and their potencies are non-rational, and the former potencies must be in a living thing, while the latter can be both in the living and in the lifeless;

τὰς μὲν τοιαύτας δυνάμεις ἀνάγκη, ὅταν ὡς δύνανται τὸ ποιητικὸν καὶ τὸ παθητικὸν πλησιάζωσι, τὸ μὲν ποιεῖν τὸ δὲ πάσχειν, ἐκείνας δ᾽ οὐκ ἀνάγκη:

tales quidem potentias necesse, quando ut possint passivum et activum appropinquant, hoc quidem facere illud vero pati, illas vero non necesse.

as regards potencies of the latter kind, when the agent and the patient meet in the way appropriate to the potency in question, the one must act and the other be acted on, but with the former kind of potency this is not necessary.

αὗται μὲν γὰρ πᾶσαι μία ἑνὸς ποιητική, ἐκεῖναι δὲ τῶν ἐναντίων, ὥστε ἅμα ποιήσει τὰ ἐναντία: τοῦτο δὲ [10] ἀδύνατον.

Hae quidem enim omnes una unius factiva, ille autem contrariorum, quare simul facient contraria; hoc autem impossibile.

For the nonrational potencies are all productive of one effect each, but the rational produce contrary effects, so that if they produced their effects necessarily they would produce contrary effects at the same time; but this is impossible.

ἀνάγκη ἄρα ἕτερόν τι εἶναι τὸ κύριον: λέγω δὲ τοῦτο ὄρεξιν ἢ προαίρεσιν. ὁποτέρου γὰρ ἂν ὀρέγηται κυρίως, τοῦτο ποιήσει ὅταν ὡς δύναται ὑπάρχῃ καὶ πλησιάζῃ τῷ παθητικῷ: ὥστε τὸ δυνατὸν κατὰ λόγον ἅπαν ἀνάγκη, ὅταν ὀρέγηται οὗ ἔχει τὴν δύναμιν καὶ ὡς ἔχει, [15] τοῦτο ποιεῖν: ἔχει δὲ παρόντος τοῦ παθητικοῦ καὶ ὡδὶ ἔχοντος [ποιεῖν]: εἰ δὲ μή, ποιεῖν οὐ δυνήσεται

Necesse ergo alterum aliquid esse quod dominans . Dico autem hoc appetitum aut proheresim. Quod enim desiderabit principaliter, hoc faciet quando ut possit extiterit et appropinquaverit passivo. Quare potens secundum rationem omne necesse, quando desiderat cuius habet potentiam et ut habet, hoc facere. habet autem presente passivo et ita se habente facere. Si autem non, facere non poterit.

There must, then, be something else that decides; I mean by this, desire or will. For whichever of two things the animal desires decisively, it will do, when it is present, and meets the passive object, in the way appropriate to the potency in question. Therefore everything which has a rational potency, when it desires that for which it has a potency and in the circumstances in which it has the potency, must do this. And it has the potency in question when the passive object is present and is in a certain state; if not it will not be able to act.

(τὸ γὰρ μηθενὸς τῶν ἔξω κωλύοντος προσδιορίζεσθαι οὐθὲν ἔτι δεῖ: τὴν γὰρ δύναμιν ἔχει ὡς ἔστι δύναμις τοῦ ποιεῖν, ἔστι δ᾽ οὐ πάντως ἀλλ᾽ ἐχόντων πῶς, ἐν οἷς ἀφορισθήσεται καὶ τὰ ἔξω κωλύοντα: [20] ἀφαιρεῖται γὰρ ταῦτα τῶν ἐν τῷ διορισμῷ προσόντων ἔνια):

'Nullo namque exteriorum prohibente' adiungere nihil adhuc oportet. Potentiam enim habet [70 ut est potentia faciendi. Est autem non omnino sed habentium aliquo modo, in quibus excludentur quae exterius prohibent; removent enim haec eorum quae in determinatione apponuntur quaedam.)

(To add the qualification if nothing external prevents it is not further necessary; for it has the potency on the terms on which this is a potency of acting, and it is this not in all circumstances but on certain conditions, among which will be the exclusion of external hindrances; for these are barred by some of the positive qualifications.)

διὸ οὐδ᾽ ἐὰν ἅμα βούληται ἢ ἐπιθυμῇ ποιεῖν δύο ἢ τὰ ἐναντία, οὐ ποιήσει: οὐ γὰρ οὕτως ἔχει αὐτῶν τὴν δύναμιν οὐδ᾽ ἔστι τοῦ ἅμα ποιεῖν ἡ δύναμις, ἐπεὶ ὧν ἐστὶν οὕτως ποιήσει. [25]

Propter quod nec si simul volunt aut cupiunt facere duo aut contraria, non facient; non enim ita simul habent ipsorum potentiam nec est simul faciendi potentia, quoniam quorum est sic faciet.

And so even if one has a rational wish, or an appetite, to do two things or contrary things at the same time, one will not do them; for it is not on these terms that one has the potency for them, nor is it a potency of doing both at the same time, since one will do the things which it is a potency of doing, on the terms on which one has the potency.

*Chapter* 6

ἐπεὶ δὲ περὶ τῆς κατὰ κίνησιν λεγομένης δυνάμεως εἴρηται, περὶ ἐνεργείας διορίσωμεν τί τέ ἐστιν ἡ ἐνέργεια καὶ ποῖόν τι. καὶ γὰρ τὸ δυνατὸν ἅμα δῆλον ἔσται διαιροῦσιν, ὅτι οὐ μόνον τοῦτο λέγομεν δυνατὸν ὃ πέφυκε κινεῖν ἄλλο ἢ κινεῖσθαι ὑπ᾽ ἄλλου ἢ ἁπλῶς ἢ τρόπον τινά, ἀλλὰ [30] καὶ ἑτέρως, διὸ ζητοῦντες καὶ περὶ τούτων διήλθομεν.

Quoniam autem de potentia quae secundum motum dicitur dictum est, de actu determinemus quid est actus et quale quid. Et enim possibile simul manifestum erit dividentibus, quia non solum hoc dicimus possibile quod aptum natum est movere aliud aut moveri ab alio aut simpliciter aut modo quodam, sed et aliter.

Since we have treated of the kind of potency which is related to movement, let us discuss actuality-what, and what kind of thing, actuality is. For in the course of our analysis it will also become clear, with regard to the potential, that we not only ascribe potency to that whose nature it is to move something else, or to be moved by something else, either without qualification or in some particular way, but also use the word in another sense, which is the reason of the inquiry in the course of which we have discussed these previous senses also.

ἔστι δὴ ἐνέργεια τὸ ὑπάρχειν τὸ πρᾶγμα μὴ οὕτως ὥσπερ λέγομεν δυνάμει: λέγομεν δὲ δυνάμει οἷον ἐν τῷ ξύλῳ Ἑρμῆν καὶ ἐν τῇ ὅλῃ τὴν ἡμίσειαν, ὅτι ἀφαιρεθείη ἄν, καὶ ἐπιστήμονα καὶ τὸν μὴ θεωροῦντα, ἂν δυνατὸς ᾖ θεωρῆσαι: [35] τὸ δὲ ἐνεργείᾳ.

Quapropter quaerentes et de hiis supervenimus. Est autem actus existere rem non ita sicut dicimus potentia. Dicimus autem potentia ut in ligno Mercurium et in tota medietatem, quia auferetur utique, et scientem et non speculantem, si potens est speculari hoc actu.

Actuality, then, is the existence of a thing not in the way which we express by potentially ; we say that potentially, for instance, a statue of Hermes is in the block of wood and the half-line is in the whole, because it might be separated out, and we call even the man who is not studying a man of science, if he is capable of studying; the thing that stands in contrast to each of these exists actually.

δῆλον δ᾽ ἐπὶ τῶν καθ᾽ ἕκαστα τῇ ἐπαγωγῇ ὃ βουλόμεθα λέγειν, καὶ οὐ δεῖ παντὸς ὅρον ζητεῖν ἀλλὰ καὶ τὸ ἀνάλογον συνορᾶν, ὅτι ὡς τὸ οἰκοδομοῦν πρὸς τὸ οἰκοδομικόν, [1048β] [1] καὶ τὸ ἐγρηγορὸς πρὸς τὸ καθεῦδον, καὶ τὸ ὁρῶν πρὸς τὸ μῦον μὲν ὄψιν δὲ ἔχον, καὶ τὸ ἀποκεκριμένον ἐκ τῆς ὕλης πρὸς τὴν ὕλην, καὶ τὸ ἀπειργασμένον πρὸς τὸ ἀνέργαστον. ταύτης δὲ τῆς διαφορᾶς [5] θατέρῳ μορίῳ ἔστω ἡ ἐνέργεια ἀφωρισμένη θατέρῳ δὲ τὸ δυνατόν.

Palam autem in  singularibus inductione quod dicere volumus, et non oportet omnis terminum quaerere sed per proportionale  conspicere,  quia ut edificans ad edificabile, et vigilans ad dormiens, et videns ad claudens quidem oculum visum autem habens, et segregatum ex materia ad materiam, et elaboratum ad illaboratum est aliquid. Et huius differentiae alteri parti sit actus determinatus, alteri autem possibile.

Our meaning can be seen in the particular cases by induction, and we must not seek a definition of everything but be content to grasp the analogy, that it is as that which is building is to that [48b] which is capable of building, and the waking to the sleeping, and that which is seeing to that which has its eyes shut but has sight, and that which has been shaped out of the matter to the matter, and that which has been wrought up to the unwrought. Let actuality be defined by one member of this antithesis, and the potential by the other.

λέγεται δὲ ἐνεργείᾳ οὐ πάντα ὁμοίως ἀλλ᾽ ἢ τῷ ἀνάλογον, ὡς τοῦτο ἐν τούτῳ ἢ πρὸς τοῦτο, τόδ᾽ ἐν τῷδε ἢ πρὸς τόδε: τὰ μὲν γὰρ ὡς κίνησις πρὸς δύναμιν τὰ δ᾽ ὡς οὐσία πρός τινα ὕλην.

Dicuntur autem actu non omnia similiter sed aut proportionaliter: ut hoc in hoc aut ad hoc, hoc in hoc aut ad hoc; haec quidem enim ut motus ad potentiam, illa vero ut substantia ad aliquam materiam.

But all things are not said in the same sense to exist actually, but only by analogy-as A is in B or to B, C is in D or to D; for some are as movement to potency, and the others as substance to some sort of matter.

ἄλλως δὲ καὶ τὸ ἄπειρον [10] καὶ τὸ κενόν, καὶ ὅσα τοιαῦτα, λέγεται δυνάμει καὶ ἐνεργείᾳ <ἢ πολλοῖς τῶν ὄντων, οἷον τῷ ὁρῶντι καὶ βαδίζοντι καὶ ὁρωμένῳ. ταῦτα μὲν γὰρ ἐνδέχεται καὶ ἁπλῶς ἀληθεύεσθαί ποτε (τὸ μὲν γὰρ ὁρώμενον ὅτι ὁρᾶται, τὸ δὲ ὅτι ὁρᾶσθαι δυνατόν): τὸ δ᾽ ἄπειρον οὐχ οὕτω δυνάμει ἔστιν ὡς [15] ἐνεργείᾳ ἐσόμενον χωριστόν, ἀλλὰ γνώσει. τὸ γὰρ μὴ ὑπολείπειν τὴν διαίρεσιν ἀποδίδωσι τὸ εἶναι δυνάμει ταύτην τὴν ἐνέργειαν, τὸ δὲ χωρίζεσθαι οὔ.

Aliter autem et infinitum et uacuum, et quaecumque talia, dicuntur potentia et actu multis entium, ut videnti et vadenti et visibili. Haec quidem enim contingit et simpliciter verificari aliquando; hoc quidem enim visibile quia videtur, illud vero quia videri possibile. Sed infinitum non ita potentia est tamquam actu futurum separabile, sed notitia. Eo enim quod non deficiat divisio assignant esse potentia hunc actum, in separari vero non.

But also the infinite and the void and all similar things are said to exist potentially and actually in a different sense from that which applies to many other things, e.g. to that which sees or walks or is seen. For of the latter class these predicates can at some time be also truly asserted without qualification; for the seen is so called sometimes because it is being seen, sometimes because it is capable of being seen. But the infinite does not exist potentially in the sense that it will ever actually have separate existence; it exists potentially only for knowledge. For the fact that the process of dividing never comes to an end ensures that this activity exists potentially, but not that the infinite exists separately.

ἐπεὶ δὲ τῶν πράξεων ὧν ἔστι πέρας οὐδεμία τέλος ἀλλὰ τῶν περὶ τὸ τέλος, οἷον τὸ ἰσχναίνειν ἢ ἰσχνασία [20] [αὐτό], αὐτὰ δὲ ὅταν ἰσχναίνῃ οὕτως ἐστὶν ἐν κινήσει, μὴ ὑπάρχοντα ὧν ἕνεκα ἡ κίνησις, οὐκ ἔστι ταῦτα πρᾶξις ἢ οὐ τελεία γε (οὐ γὰρ τέλος): ἀλλ᾽ ἐκείνη <ᾗ ἐνυπάρχει τὸ τέλος καὶ [ἡ] πρᾶξις. οἷον ὁρᾷ ἅμα <καὶ ἑώρακε, καὶ φρονεῖ <καὶ πεφρόνηκε, καὶ νοεῖ καὶ νενόηκεν, ἀλλ᾽ οὐ μανθάνει καὶ μεμάθηκεν [25] οὐδ᾽ ὑγιάζεται καὶ ὑγίασται: εὖ ζῇ καὶ εὖ ἔζηκεν ἅμα, καὶ εὐδαιμονεῖ καὶ εὐδαιμόνηκεν. εἰ δὲ μή, ἔδει ἄν ποτε παύεσθαι ὥσπερ ὅταν ἰσχναίνῃ, νῦν δ᾽ οὔ, ἀλλὰ ζῇ καὶ ἔζηκεν. τούτων δὴ <δεῖ τὰς μὲν κινήσεις λέγειν, τὰς δ᾽ ἐνεργείας. πᾶσα γὰρ κίνησις ἀτελής, ἰσχνασία μάθησις βάδισις οἰκοδόμησις: [30] αὗται δὴ κινήσεις, καὶ ἀτελεῖς γε. οὐ γὰρ ἅμα βαδίζει καὶ βεβάδικεν, οὐδ᾽ οἰκοδομεῖ καὶ ᾠκοδόμηκεν, οὐδὲ γίγνεται καὶ γέγονεν ἢ κινεῖται καὶ κεκίνηται, ἀλλ᾽ ἕτερον, καὶ κινεῖ καὶ κεκίνηκεν: ἑώρακε δὲ καὶ ὁρᾷ ἅμα τὸ αὐτό, καὶ νοεῖ καὶ νενόηκεν. τὴν μὲν οὖν τοιαύτην ἐνέργειαν [35] λέγω, ἐκείνην δὲ κίνησιν. τὸ μὲν οὖν ἐνεργείᾳ τί τέ ἐστι καὶ ποῖον, ἐκ τούτων καὶ τῶν τοιούτων δῆλον ἡμῖν ἔστω.

Since of the actions which have a limit none is an end but all are relative to the end, e.g. the removing of fat, or fat-removal, and the bodily parts themselves when one is making them thin are in movement in this way (i.e. without being already that at which the movement aims), this is not an action or at least not a complete one (for it is not an end); but that movement in which the end is present is an action. E.g. at the same time we are seeing and have seen, are understanding and have understood, are thinking and have thought (while it is not true that at the same time we are learning and have learnt, or are being cured and have been cured). At the same time we are living well and have lived well, and are happy and have been happy. If not, the process would have had sometime to cease, as the process of making thin ceases: but, as things are, it does not cease; we are living and have lived. Of these processes, then, we must call the one set movements, and the other actualities. For every movement is incomplete-making thin, learning, walking, building; these are movements, and incomplete at that. For it is not true that at the same time a thing is walking and has walked, or is building and has built, or is coming to be and has come to be, or is being moved and has been moved, but what is being moved is different from what has been moved, and what is moving from what has moved. But it is the same thing that at the same time has seen and is seeing, seeing, or is thinking and has thought. The latter sort of process, then, I call an actuality, and the former a movement.

## Chapter 7

πότε δὲ δυνάμει ἔστιν ἕκαστον καὶ πότε οὔ, διοριστέον: οὐ γὰρ ὁποτεοῦν. [1049a] [1] οἷον ἡ γῆ ἆρ᾽ ἐστὶ δυνάμει ἄνθρωπος; ἢ οὔ, ἀλλὰ μᾶλλον ὅταν ἤδη γένηται σπέρμα, καὶ οὐδὲ τότε ἴσως;

Quod quidem igitur  actu et quid est et quale, ex hiis et similibus manifestum erit nobis. Quando autem potentia est unumquodque et quando  non, determinandum . Non enim quandocumque: ut terra, ergone est potentia homo? Aut non, sed magis cum iam fiat sperma. Sed neque hoc simpliciter forsan.

What, and what kind of thing, the actual is, may be taken as explained by these and similar considerations. But we must distinguish when a thing exists potentially and when it does not; for it is not at any and every time. [49a] E.g. is earth potentially a man? No-but rather when it has already become seed, and perhaps not even then.

ὥσπερ οὖν οὐδ᾽ ὑπὸ ἰατρικῆς ἅπαν ἂν ὑγιασθείη οὐδ᾽ ἀπὸ τύχης, ἀλλ᾽ ἔστι τι ὃ δυνατόν ἐστι, καὶ τοῦτ᾽ ἔστιν [5] ὑγιαῖνον δυνάμει. ὅρος δὲ τοῦ μὲν ἀπὸ διανοίας ἐντελεχείᾳ γιγνομένου ἐκ τοῦ δυνάμει ὄντος, ὅταν βουληθέντος γίγνηται μηθενὸς κωλύοντος τῶν ἐκτός, ἐκεῖ δ᾽ ἐν τῷ ὑγιαζομένῳ, ὅταν μηθὲν κωλύῃ τῶν ἐν αὐτῷ: ὁμοίως δὲ δυνάμει καὶ οἰκία: εἰ μηθὲν κωλύει τῶν ἐν τούτῳ καὶ τῇ [10] ὕλῃ τοῦ γίγνεσθαι οἰκίαν, οὐδ᾽ ἔστιν ὃ δεῖ προσγενέσθαι ἢ ἀπογενέσθαι ἢ μεταβαλεῖν, τοῦτο δυνάμει οἰκία: καὶ ἐπὶ τῶν ἄλλων ὡσαύτως ὅσων ἔξωθεν ἡ ἀρχὴ τῆς γενέσεως. καὶ ὅσων δὴ ἐν αὐτῷ τῷ ἔχοντι, ὅσα μηθενὸς τῶν ἔξωθεν ἐμποδίζοντος ἔσται δι᾽ αὐτοῦ· οἷον τὸ σπέρμα οὔπω (δεῖ γὰρ [15] ἐν ἄλλῳ <πεσεῖν καὶ μεταβάλλειν), ὅταν δ᾽ ἤδη διὰ τῆς αὐτοῦ ἀρχῆς ᾖ τοιοῦτον, ἤδη τοῦτο δυνάμει· ἐκεῖνο δὲ ἑτέρας ἀρχῆς δεῖται, ὥσπερ ἡ γῆ οὔπω ἀνδριὰς δυνάμει (μεταβαλοῦσα γὰρ ἔσται χαλκός).

Quemadmodum igitur nec a medicativa omne utique sanabitur nec a fortuna, sed est aliquid quod possibile est, et hoc est sanum potentia. Terminus autem eius quod ab intellectu actu fit ex potentia ente: quando volitum fit nullo exteriorum prohibente; ibi autem in eo quod sanatur: quando nihil prohibet eorum quae in ipso. Similiter autem potentia et domus; si nihil prohibeat eorum quae in hiis et materia fieri domum, nec est quod oporteat adici aut removeri aut permutari: hoc domus potentia. Et in aliis similiter quorumcumque extrinsecus principium est generationis. Et quorumcumque etiam in ipso habente: quaecumque nullo exteriorum impediente erunt per ipsum. Quale sperma nondum; oportet enim in alio et permutari. Quando vero iam per suum principium est tale, iam hoc est potentia. Illa vero altero egent principio, ut terra nondum est statua potentia; permutata enim erit es.

It is just as it is with being healed; not everything can be healed by the medical art or by luck, but there is a certain kind of thing which is capable of it, and only this is potentially healthy. And (1) the delimiting mark of that which as a result of thought comes to exist in complete reality from having existed potentially is that if the agent has willed it it comes to pass if nothing external hinders, while the condition on the other side-viz. in that which is healed-is that nothing in it hinders the result. It is on similar terms that we have what is potentially a house; if nothing in the thing acted on-i.e. in the matter-prevents it from becoming a house, and if there is nothing which must be added or taken away or changed, this is potentially a house; and the same is true of all other things the source of whose becoming is external. And (2) in the cases in which the source of the becoming is in the very thing which comes to be, a thing is potentially all those things which it will be of itself if nothing external hinders it. E.g. the seed is not yet potentially a man; for it must be deposited in something other than itself and undergo a change. But when through its own motive principle it has already got such and such attributes, in this state it is already potentially a man; while in the former state it needs another motive principle, just as earth is not yet potentially a statue (for it must first change in order to become brass.)

ἔοικε δὲ ὃ λέγομεν εἶναι οὐ τόδε ἀλλ᾽ ἐκείνινον—οἷον τὸ κιβώτιον οὐ ξύλον ἀλλὰ ξύλινον, [20] οὐδὲ τὸ ξύλον γῆ ἀλλὰ γήϊνον, πάλιν ἡ γῆ εἰ οὕτως μὴ ἄλλο ἀλλὰ ἐκείνινον—ἀεὶ ἐκεῖνο δυνάμει ἁπλῶς τὸ ὕστερόν ἐστιν. οἷον τὸ κιβώτιον οὐ γήϊνον οὐδὲ γῆ ἀλλὰ ξύλινον· τοῦτο γὰρ δυνάμει κιβώτιον καὶ ὕλη κιβωτίου αὕτη, ἁπλῶς μὲν τοῦ ἁπλῶς τουδὶ δὲ τοδὶ τὸ ξύλον. εἰ δέ τί ἐστι πρῶτον [25] ὃ μηκέτι κατ᾽ ἄλλο λέγεται ἐκείνινον, τοῦτο πρώτη ὕλη· οἷον εἰ ἡ γῆ ἀερίνη, ὁ δ᾽ ἀὴρ μὴ πῦρ ἀλλὰ πύρινος, τὸ πῦρ ὕλη πρώτη οὐ τόδε τι οὖσα. τούτῳ γὰρ διαφέρει τὸ καθ᾽ οὗ καὶ τὸ ὑποκείμενον, τῷ εἶναι τόδε τι ἢ μὴ εἶναι: οἷον τοῖς πάθεσι τὸ ὑποκείμενον ἄνθρωπος καὶ [30] σῶμα καὶ ψυχή, πάθος δὲ τὸ μουσικὸν καὶ λευκόν

Videtur autem quod dicimus esse non hoc sed illinum, ut archa non lignum sed lignea, nec lignum terra sed terreum, iterum terra si sic non aliud sed illinum. Semper illud potentia simpliciter quod posterius est, ut archa non terrea nec terra sed lignea. Hoc enim potentia archa et materia arche haec, simpliciter quidem ipsius simpliciter, huius vero hoc lignum. Si vero aliquid est primum quod non adhuc de alio dicitur illinum, hoc prima materia est; ut si terra aerea est et aer non ignis sed igneus, ignis est prima materia, hoc aliquid existens. In hoc enim differt universale et subiectum: per esse hoc aliquid aut non; ut puta passionibus quod subicitur homo et corpus et anima, passio autem musicum et album.

It seems that when we call a thing not something else but thaten -e.g. a casket is not wood but wooden , and wood is not earth but earthen , and again earth will illustrate our point if it is similarly not something else but thaten -that other thing is always potentially (in the full sense of that word) the thing which comes after it in this series. E.g. a casket is not earthen nor earth , but wooden ; for this is potentially a casket and this is the matter of a casket, wood in general of a casket in general, and this particular wood of this particular casket. And if there is a first thing, which is no longer, in reference to something else, called thaten , this is prime matter; e.g. if earth is airy and air is not fire but fiery , fire is prime matter, which is not a this . For the subject or substratum is differentiated by being a this or not being one; i.e. the substratum of modifications is, e.g. a man, i.e. a body and a soul, while the modification is musical or pale .

(λέγεται δὲ τῆς μουσικῆς ἐγγενομένης ἐκεῖνο οὐ μουσικὴ ἀλλὰ μουσικόν, καὶ οὐ λευκότης ὁ ἄνθρωπος ἀλλὰ λευκόν, οὐδὲ βάδισις ἢ κίνησις ἀλλὰ βαδίζον ἢ κινούμενον, ὡς τὸ ἐκείνινον):

dicitur autem musica adveniente illud non musica sed musicum, et non albedo homo sed album, nec ambulatio aut motus sed ambulans aut motum, ut illinum.

(The subject is called, when music comes to be present in it, not music but musical , and the man is not paleness but pale , and not ambulation or movement but walking or moving ,-which is akin to the thaten .)

ὅσα μὲν οὖν οὕτω, τὸ ἔσχατον οὐσία: ὅσα δὲ μὴ [35] οὕτως ἀλλ᾽ εἶδός τι καὶ τόδε τι τὸ κατηγορούμενον, τὸ ἔσχατον ὕλη καὶ οὐσία ὑλική. καὶ ὀρθῶς δὴ συμβαίνει τὸ ἐκείνινον λέγεσθαι κατὰ τὴν ὕλην καὶ τὰ πάθη: [1049β] [1] ἄμφω γὰρ ἀόριστα. πότε μὲν οὖν λεκτέον δυνάμει καὶ πότε οὔ, εἴρηται.

Quaecumque quidem igitur sic, ultimum substantia; quaecumque vero non sic sed species quaedam et hoc aliquid quod predicatur, ultimum materia et substantia materialis. Et recte itaque accidit illinum dici secundum materiam et passiones; ambo namque indeterminata. Quando quidem igitur dicendum est potentia et quando non, dictum est.

Wherever this is so, then, the ultimate subject is a substance; but when this is not so but the predicate is a form and a this , the ultimate subject is matter and material substance. And it is only right that thaten should be used with reference both to the matter [49b] and to the accidents; for both are indeterminates. We have stated, then, when a thing is to be said to exist potentially and when it is not.

*Chapter* 8

ἐπεὶ δὲ τὸ πρότερον διώρισται ποσαχῶς λέγεται, [5] φανερὸν ὅτι πρότερον ἐνέργεια δυνάμεώς ἐστιν. λέγω δὲ δυνάμεως οὐ μόνον τῆς ὡρισμένης ἣ λέγεται ἀρχὴ μεταβλητικὴ ἐν ἄλλῳ ἢ ᾗ ἄλλο, ἀλλ᾿ ὅλως πάσης ἀρχῆς κινητικῆς ἢ στατικῆς. καὶ γὰρ ἡ φύσις ἐν ταὐτῷ [γίγνεται· ἐν ταὐτῷ γὰρ] γένει τῇ δυνάμει· ἀρχὴ γὰρ κινητική, ἀλλ᾿ [10] οὐκ ἐν ἄλλῳ ἀλλ᾿ ἐν αὐτῷ ᾗ αὐτό. πάσης δὴ τῆς τοιαύτης προτέρα ἐστὶν ἡ ἐνέργεια καὶ λόγῳ καὶ τῇ οὐσίᾳ· χρόνῳ δ᾿ ἔστι μὲν ὥς, ἔστι δὲ ὡς οὔ.

Quoniam autem ipsum prius determinatum est quot modis dicitur, palam quia prior est actus potentia. Dico autem potentia non solum determinata quae dicitur principium permutativum in alio in quantum aliud , sed totaliter omni principio motivo aut immobilitativo. Et enim natura in eodem fit, in eodem enim genere ipsi potentie; principium enim motivum, sed non in alio sed in eodem in quantum idem. Omni itaque tali prior est actus ratione et substantia; tempore vero est quidem ut , est autem ut non.

From our discussion of the various senses of prior , it is clear that actuality is prior to potency. And I mean by potency not only that definite kind which is said to be a principle of change in another thing or in the thing itself regarded as other, but in general every principle of movement or of rest. For nature also is in the same genus as potency; for it is a principle of movement-not, however, in something else but in the thing itself qua itself. To all such potency, then, actuality is prior both in formula and in substantiality; and in time it is prior in one sense, and in another not.

τῷ λόγῳ μὲν οὖν ὅτι προτέρα, δῆλον (τῷ γὰρ ἐνδέχεσθαι ἐνεργῆσαι δυνατόν ἐστι τὸ πρώτως δυνατόν, οἷον λέγω οἰκοδομικὸν τὸ δυνάμενον οἰκοδομεῖν, [15] καὶ ὁρατικὸν τὸ ὁρᾶν, καὶ ὁρατὸν τὸ δυνατὸν ὁρᾶσθαι: ὁ δ᾽ αὐτὸς λόγος καὶ ἐπὶ τῶν ἄλλων, ὥστ᾽ ἀνάγκη τὸν λόγον προϋπάρχειν καὶ τὴν γνῶσιν τῆς γνώσεως):

Ratione quidem igitur quia prior , palam. Nam per contingere actu esse possibile est quod primo possibile, puta dico edificatorem potentem edificare, et speculatorem speculari, et visibile potens videri. Eadem autem ratio et in aliis. Quare necesse rationem preexistere et notitiam notitia.

(1) Clearly it is prior in formula; for that which is in the primary sense potential is potential because it is possible for it to become active; e.g. I mean by capable of building that which can build, and by capable of seeing that which can see, and by visible that which can be seen. And the same account applies to all other cases, so that the formula and the knowledge of the one must precede the knowledge of the other.

δὲ χρόνῳ πρότερον ὧδε: τὸ τῷ εἴδει τὸ αὐτὸ ἐνεργοῦν πρότερον, ἀριθμῷ δ᾽ οὔ. λέγω δὲ τοῦτο ὅτι τοῦδε μὲν τοῦ ἀνθρώπου τοῦ [20] ἤδη ὄντος κατ᾽ ἐνέργειαν καὶ τοῦ σίτου καὶ τοῦ ὁρῶντος πρότερον τῷ χρόνῳ ἡ ὕλη καὶ τὸ σπέρμα καὶ τὸ ὁρατικόν, ἃ δυνάμει μέν ἐστιν ἄνθρωπος καὶ σῖτος καὶ ὁρῶν, ἐνεργείᾳ δ᾽ οὔπω: ἀλλὰ τούτων πρότερα τῷ χρόνῳ ἕτερα ὄντα ἐνεργείᾳ ἐξ ὧν ταῦτα ἐγένετο: ἀεὶ γὰρ ἐκ τοῦ δυνάμει ὄντος [25] γίγνεται τὸ ἐνεργείᾳ ὂν ὑπὸ ἐνεργείᾳ ὄντος, οἷον ἄνθρωπος ἐξ ἀνθρώπου, μουσικὸς ὑπὸ μουσικοῦ, ἀεὶ κινοῦντός τινος πρώτου: τὸ δὲ κινοῦν ἐνεργείᾳ ἤδη ἐστίν. εἴρηται δὲ ἐν τοῖς περὶ τῆς οὐσίας λόγοις ὅτι πᾶν τὸ γιγνόμενον γίγνεται ἔκ τινος τι καὶ ὑπό τινος, καὶ τοῦτο τῷ εἴδει τὸ αὐτό.

Tempore vero prius: specie idem agens prius, sed numero non. Dico autem hoc, quia hoc quidem homine iam ente secundum actum et frumento et vidente prius est tempore materia et semen et visivum, quae potentia sunt homo et frumentum et videns, nondum autem actu. Sed hiis tempore priora altera entia actu ex quibus haec facta sunt; semper enim ex potestate ente fit actu ens ab actu ente, ut homo ex homine, musicus a musico, semper movente aliquo primo; movens autem actu iam est. Dictum est autem in sermonibus de substantia quia omne quod fit fit ex aliquo et ab aliquo, et hoc specie idem.

(2) In time it is prior in this sense: the actual which is identical in species though not in number with a potentially existing thing is to it. I mean that to this particular man who now exists actually and to the corn and to the seeing subject the matter and the seed and that which is capable of seeing, which are potentially a man and corn and seeing, but not yet actually so, are prior in time; but prior in time to these are other actually existing things, from which they were produced. For from the potentially existing the actually existing is always produced by an actually existing thing, e.g. man from man, musician by musician; there is always a first mover, and the mover already exists actually. We have said in our account of substance that everything that is

produced is something produced from something and by something, and that the same in species as it.

διὸ καὶ δοκεῖ [30] ἀδύνατον εἶναι οἰκοδόμον εἶναι μὴ οἰκοδομήσαντα μηθὲν ἢ κιθαριστὴν μηθὲν κιθαρίσαντα· ὁ γὰρ μανθάνων κιθαρίζειν κιθαρίζων μανθάνει κιθαρίζειν, ὁμοίως δὲ καὶ οἱ ἄλλοι.

Quapropter et videtur impossibile esse edificatorem esse qui non edificavit nihil aut citharedum qui non citharizavit; nam addiscens citharizare citharizans addiscit citharizare, similiter autem et alii.

This is why it is thought impossible to be a builder if one has built nothing or a harper if one has never played the harp; for he who learns to play the harp learns to play it by playing it, and all other learners do similarly.

ὅθεν ὁ σοφιστικὸς ἔλεγχος ἐγίγνετο ὅτι οὐκ ἔχων τις τὴν ἐπιστήμην ποιήσει οὗ ἡ ἐπιστήμη· ὁ γὰρ μανθάνων οὐκ ἔχει.

Unde sophisticus elenchus factus est quia non habens quis scientiam faciet cuius scientia; addiscens enim non habet.

And thence arose the sophistical quibble, that one who does not possess a science will be doing that which is the object of the science; for he who is learning it does not possess it.

[35] ἀλλὰ διὰ τὸ τοῦ γιγνομένου γεγενῆσθαί τι καὶ τοῦ ὅλως κινουμένου κεκινῆσθαί τι (δῆλον δ᾽ ἐν τοῖς περὶ κινήσεως τοῦτο) [1050α] [1] καὶ τὸν μανθάνοντα ἀνάγκη ἔχειν τι τῆς ἐπιστήμης ἴσως. ἀλλ᾽ οὖν καὶ ταύτῃ γε δῆλον ὅτι ἡ ἐνέργεια καὶ οὕτω προτέρα τῆς δυνάμεως κατὰ γένεσιν καὶ χρόνον.

Sed quia eius quod fit factum est aliquid et totaliter eius quod movetur motum est aliquid (palam autem in hiis quae de motu hoc), et discentem necesse habere aliquid scientie forsan. Sed igitur et hac palam quia actus et sic prior potentia secundum generationem et tempus.

But since, of that which is coming to be, some part must have come to be, and, of that which, in general, is changing, some part must have changed (this is shown in the [50a] treatise on movement), he who is learning must, it would seem, possess some part of the science. But here too, then, it is clear that actuality is in this sense also, viz. in order of generation and of time, prior to potency.

ἀλλὰ μὴν καὶ οὐσίᾳ γε, πρῶτον μὲν ὅτι τὰ τῇ γενέσει [5] ὕστερα τῷ εἴδει καὶ τῇ οὐσίᾳ πρότερα (οἷον ἀνὴρ παιδὸς καὶ ἄνθρωπος σπέρματος· τὸ μὲν γὰρ ἤδη ἔχει τὸ εἶδος τὸ δ᾽ οὔ),

At vero et substantia. Primum quidem quia quae generatione posteriora specie et substantia sunt priora, ut vir puero et homo spermate; hoc quidem enim iam habet speciem illud vero non.

But (3) it is also prior in substantiality; firstly, (a) because the things that are posterior in becoming are prior in form and in substantiality (e.g. man is prior to boy and human being to seed; for the one already has its form, and the other has not),

καὶ ὅτι ἅπαν ἐπ᾽ ἀρχὴν βαδίζει τὸ γιγνόμενον καὶ τέλος (ἀρχὴ γὰρ τὸ οὗ ἕνεκα, τοῦ τέλους δὲ ἕνεκα ἡ γένεσις), τέλος δ᾽ ἡ ἐνέργεια, καὶ τούτου χάριν ἡ δύναμις [10] λαμβάνεται.

Et quia omne ad principium uadit quod fit et finem. Principium enim cuius causa, finis vero causa generatio; finis autem actus, et huius gratia potentia sumitur.

and because everything that comes to be moves towards a principle, i.e. an end (for that for the sake of which a thing is, is its principle, and the becoming is for the sake of the end), and the actuality is the end, and it is for the sake of this that the potency is acquired.

οὐ γὰρ ἵνα ὄψιν ἔχωσιν ὁρῶσι τὰ ζῷα ἀλλ᾽ ὅπως ὁρῶσιν ὄψιν ἔχουσιν,

Non enim ut visum habeant vident animalia sed ut videant visum habent.

For animals do not see in order that they may have sight, but they have sight that they may see.

ὁμοίως δὲ καὶ οἰκοδομικὴν ἵνα [12] οἰκοδομῶσι καὶ τὴν θεωρητικὴν ἵνα θεωρῶσιν· ἀλλ᾽ οὐ θεωροῦσιν ἵνα θεωρητικὴν ἔχωσιν, εἰ μὴ οἱ μελετῶντες· οὗτοι δὲ οὐχὶ θεωροῦσιν ἀλλ᾽ ἢ ὡδί, ἢ ὅτι οὐδὲν δέονται θεωρεῖν.

Similiter autem et edificandi scientiam ut edificent et theoricam ut speculentur, sed non speculantur ut theoricam habeant, nisi meditantes; hii autem non speculantur sed in quantum sic, aut quia non egent speculari.

And similarly men have the art of building that they may build, and theoretical science that they may theorize; but they do not theorize that they may have theoretical science, except those who are learning by practice; and these do not theorize except in a limited sense, or because they have no need to theorize.

[15] ἔτι ἡ ὕλη ἔστι δυνάμει ὅτι ἔλθοι ἂν εἰς τὸ εἶδος· ὅταν δέ γε ἐνεργείᾳ ᾖ, τότε ἐν τῷ εἴδει ἐστίν. ὁμοίως δὲ καὶ ἐπὶ τῶν ἄλλων, καὶ ὧν κίνησις τὸ τέλος,

Amplius materia est potentia, donec veniat ad speciem; quando vero actu est, tunc est in specie. Similiter autem et in aliis, et quorum motus est finis.

Further, matter exists in a potential state, just because it may come to its form; and when it exists actually, then it is in its form. And the same holds good in all cases, even those in which the end is a movement. And so, as teachers think they have achieved their end when they have exhibited the pupil at work, nature does likewise.

διὸ ὥσπερ οἱ διδάσκοντες ἐνεργοῦντα ἐπιδείξαντες οἴονται τὸ τέλος ἀποδεδωκέναι, καὶ ἡ φύσις ὁμοίως. εἰ γὰρ μὴ οὕτω γίγνεται, ὁ [20] Παύσωνος ἔσται Ἑρμῆς: ἄδηλος γὰρ καὶ ἡ ἐπιστήμη εἰ ἔσω ἢ ἔξω, ὥσπερ κἀκεῖνος. τὸ γὰρ ἔργον τέλος, ἡ δὲ ἐνέργεια τὸ ἔργον, διὸ καὶ τοὔνομα ἐνέργεια λέγεται κατὰ τὸ ἔργον καὶ συντείνει πρὸς τὴν ἐντελέχειαν.

Propter quod sicut docentes operantem ostendentes putant finem reddidisse, et natura similiter. Nam si non fit ita, Passonos Mercurius erit; non manifestus enim, et scientia si interius aut exterius, quemadmodum ille. Opus enim finis, actus autem opus. Propter quod et nomen dicitur actus secundum opus et tendit versus endelichiam.

For if this is not the case, we shall have Pauson's Hermes over again, since it will be hard to say about the knowledge, as about the figure in the picture, whether it is within or without. For the action is the end, and the actuality is the action. And so even the word actuality is derived from action , and points to the complete reality.

ἐπεὶ δ᾽ ἐστὶ τῶν μὲν ἔσχατον ἡ χρῆσις (οἷον ὄψεως ἡ ὅρασις, καὶ οὐθὲν [25] γίγνεται παρὰ ταύτην ἕτερον ἀπὸ τῆς ὄψεως), ἀπ᾽ ἐνίων δὲ γίγνεταί τι (οἷον ἀπὸ τῆς οἰκοδομικῆς οἰκία παρὰ τὴν οἰκοδόμησιν), ὅμως οὐθὲν ἧττον ἔνθα μὲν τέλος, ἔνθα δὲ μᾶλλον τέλος τῆς δυνάμεώς ἐστιν: ἡ γὰρ οἰκοδόμησις ἐν τῷ οἰκοδομουμένῳ, καὶ ἅμα γίγνεται καὶ ἔστι τῇ οἰκίᾳ. [30] ὅσων μὲν οὖν ἕτερόν τί ἐστι παρὰ τὴν χρῆσιν τὸ γιγνόμενον, τούτων μὲν ἡ ἐνέργεια ἐν τῷ ποιουμένῳ ἐστίν (οἷον ἥ τε οἰκοδόμησις ἐν τῷ οἰκοδομουμένῳ καὶ ἡ ὕφανσις ἐν τῷ ὑφαινομένῳ, ὁμοίως δὲ καὶ ἐπὶ τῶν ἄλλων, καὶ ὅλως ἡ κίνησις ἐν τῷ κινουμένῳ): ὅσων δὲ μὴ ἔστιν ἄλλο τι ἔργον [35] παρὰ τὴν ἐνέργειαν, ἐν αὐτοῖς ὑπάρχει ἡ ἐνέργεια (οἷον ἡ ὅρασις ἐν τῷ ὁρῶντι καὶ ἡ θεωρία ἐν τῷ θεωροῦντι καὶ ἡ ζωὴ ἐν τῇ ψυχῇ, διὸ καὶ ἡ εὐδαιμονία: [1050β] [1] ζωὴ γὰρ ποιά τίς ἐστιν).

Quoniam vero est horum quidem ultimum usus, ut visus visio, et praeter hanc nullum fit alterum a visu opus, a quibusdam vero fit aliquid, ut ab edificatoria domus praeter edificationem; tamen non minus hic quidem finis, hic autem magis finis potentie est. Nam edificatio in edificato, et simul fit et est cum domo. Quorumcumque ergo aliquid alterum est quod fit praeter usum, horum actus in facto est, ut edificatio in edificato et contextio in contexto; similiter autem et in aliis, et totaliter motus in eo quod movetur. Quorum vero non est aliud aliquod opus praeter actionem, in ipsis existit actio, ut visio in vidente et speculatio in speculante et vita in anima (quare et felicitas; vita namque qualis quaedam est).

And while in some cases the exercise is the ultimate thing (e.g. in sight the ultimate thing is seeing, and no other product besides this results from sight), but from some things a product follows (e.g. from the art of building there results a house as well as the act of building), yet none the less the act is in the former case the end and in the latter more of an end than the potency is. For the act of building is realized in the thing that is being built, and comes to be, and is, at the same time as the house. Where, then, the result is something apart from the exercise, the actuality is in the thing that is being made, e.g. the act of building is in the thing that is being built and that of weaving in the thing that is being woven, and similarly in all other cases, and in general the movement is in the thing that is being moved; but where there is no product apart from the actuality, the actuality is present in the agents, e.g. the act of seeing is in the seeing subject and that of theorizing in the theorizing subject and the life is in the soul (and [50b] therefore well-being also; for it is a certain kind of life).

ὥστε φανερὸν ὅτι ἡ οὐσία καὶ τὸ εἶδος ἐνέργειά ἐστιν. κατά τε δὴ τοῦτον τὸν λόγον φανερὸν ὅτι πρότερον τῇ οὐσίᾳ ἐνέργεια δυνάμεως, καὶ ὥσπερ εἴπομεν, τοῦ χρόνου [5] ἀεὶ προλαμβάνει ἐνέργεια ἑτέρα πρὸ ἑτέρας ἕως τῆς τοῦ ἀεὶ κινοῦντος πρώτως.

Quare manifestum quod substantia et species actus quidam est. Secundum hanc itaque rationem palam quia prior substantia est actus potentia. Et ut diximus, tempore semper preaccipitur actus alius ante alium usque ad eum qui est semper moventis primum.

Obviously, therefore, the substance or form is actuality. According to this argument, then, it is obvious that actuality is prior in substantial being to potency; and as we have said, one actuality always precedes another in time right back to the actuality of the eternal prime mover.

ἀλλὰ μὴν καὶ κυριωτέρως· τὰ μὲν γὰρ ἀΐδια πρότερα τῇ οὐσίᾳ τῶν φθαρτῶν, ἔστι δ᾽ οὐθὲν δυνάμει ἀΐδιον.

At vero et magis proprie; nam sempiterna priora substantia sunt corruptibilibus, est autem nihil potentia sempiternum.

But (b) actuality is prior in a stricter sense also; for eternal things are prior in substance to perishable things, and no eternal thing exists potentially.

λόγος δὲ ὅδε· πᾶσα δύναμις ἅμα τῆς ἀντιφάσεώς ἐστιν· τὸ μὲν γὰρ μὴ δυνατὸν ὑπάρχειν οὐκ [10] ἂν ὑπάρξειεν οὐθενί, τὸ δυνατὸν δὲ πᾶν ἐνδέχεται μὴ ἐνεργεῖν. τὸ ἄρα δυνατὸν εἶναι ἐνδέχεται καὶ εἶναι καὶ μὴ εἶναι· τὸ αὐτὸ ἄρα δυνατὸν καὶ εἶναι καὶ μὴ εἶναι. τὸ δὲ δυνατὸν μὴ εἶναι ἐνδέχεται μὴ εἶναι· τὸ δὲ ἐνδεχόμενον μὴ εἶναι φθαρτόν, ἢ ἁπλῶς ἢ τοῦτο αὐτὸ ὃ λέγεται [15] ἐνδέχεσθαι μὴ εἶναι, ἢ κατὰ τόπον ἢ κατὰ τὸ ποσὸν ἢ ποιόν· ἁπλῶς δὲ τὸ κατ᾽ οὐσίαν.

Ratio vero haec. Omnis potentia simul contradictionis est;  quod quidem enim non possibile existere non utique existet in aliquo, possibile autem omne contingit non actu esse. Quod ergo possibile esse contingit esse et non esse: idem igitur possibile esse et non esse. Possibile vero non esse contingit non esse. Contingens autem non esse corruptibile, aut simpliciter aut hoc  ipsum quod dicitur contingere non esse, aut secundum locum aut secundum quantum aut secundum quale; simpliciter autem quod  secundum substantiam.

The reason is this. Every potency is at one and the same time a potency of the opposite; for, while that which is not capable of being present in a subject cannot be present, everything that is capable of being may possibly not be actual. That, then, which is capable of being may either be or not be; the same thing, then, is capable both of being and of not being. And that which is capable of not being may possibly not be; and that which may possibly not be is perishable, either in the full sense, or in the precise sense in which it is said that it possibly may not be, i.e. in respect either of place or of quantity or quality; in the full sense means in respect of substance .

οὐθὲν ἄρα τῶν ἀφθάρτων ἁπλῶς δυνάμει ἔστιν ἁπλῶς (κατά τι δὲ οὐδὲν κωλύει, οἷον ποιὸν ἢ πού)· ἐνεργείᾳ ἄρα πάντα:

Nihil ergo incorruptibilium simpliciter potentia est ens simpliciter (aliquid autem nihil prohibet, ut quale aut ubi); actu ergo  omnia.

Nothing, then, which is in the full sense imperishable is in the full sense potentially existent (though there is nothing to prevent its being so in some respect, e.g. potentially of a certain quality or in a certain place); all imperishable things, then, exist actually.

οὐδὲ τῶν ἐξ ἀνάγκης ὄντων (καίτοι ταῦτα πρῶτα· εἰ γὰρ ταῦτα μὴ ἦν, οὐθὲν ἂν ἦν):

Nec eorum quae ex necessitate sunt; et quidem ipsa prima; nam si haec  non essent, nihil utique esset.

Nor can anything which is of necessity exist potentially; yet these things are primary; for if these did not exist, nothing would exist.

[20] οὐδὲ δὴ κίνησις, εἴ τίς ἐστιν ἀΐδιος· οὐδ᾽ εἴ τι κινούμενον ἀΐδιον, οὐκ ἔστι κατὰ δύναμιν κινούμενον ἀλλ᾽ ἢ ποθὲν ποί (τούτου δ᾽ ὕλην οὐδὲν κωλύει ὑπάρχειν),

Neque utique motus, si quis est sempiternus; nec si quid motum sempiternum, non est secundum potentiam motum nisi unde quo; huius autem materiam nihil prohibet existere.

Nor does eternal movement, if there be such, exist potentially; and, if there is an eternal mobile, it is not in motion in virtue of a potentiality, except in respect of whence and whither (there is nothing to prevent its having matter which makes it capable of movement in various directions).

διὸ ἀεὶ ἐνεργεῖ ἥλιος καὶ ἄστρα καὶ ὅλος ὁ οὐρανός, καὶ οὐ φοβερὸν μή ποτε στῇ, ὃ φοβοῦνται οἱ περὶ φύσεως. οὐδὲ κάμνει τοῦτο δρῶντα· οὐ [25] γὰρ περὶ τὴν δύναμιν τῆς ἀντιφάσεως αὐτοῖς, οἷον τοῖς φθαρτοῖς, ἡ κίνησις, ὥστε ἐπίπονον εἶναι τὴν συνέχειαν τῆς κινήσεως· ἡ γὰρ οὐσία ὕλη καὶ δύναμις οὖσα, οὐκ ἐνέργεια, αἰτία τούτου.

Propter quod semper agit sol et astra et totum caelum; non est autem timendum ne quando stet, quod timent qui de natura. Neque laborant hoc agentia. Non enim super potentiam contradictionis ipsis, ut corruptibilibus, motus, ut laboriosa sit continuatio motus; nam substantia materia et potentia, non actu, causa huius.

And so the sun and the stars and the whole heaven are ever active, and there is no fear that they may sometime stand still, as the natural philosophers fear they may. Nor do they tire in this activity; for movement is not for them, as it is for perishable things, connected with the potentiality for opposites, so that the continuity of the movement should be laborious; for it is that kind of substance which is matter and potency, not actuality, that causes this.

μιμεῖται δὲ τὰ ἄφθαρτα καὶ τὰ ἐν μεταβολῇ ὄντα, οἷον γῆ καὶ πῦρ. καὶ γὰρ ταῦτα ἀεὶ ἐνεργεῖ· [30] καθ᾽ αὑτὰ γὰρ καὶ ἐν αὑτοῖς ἔχει τὴν κίνησιν.

Imitantur autem incorruptibilia et quae in transmutatione sunt entia, ut terra, ignis. Et enim haec semper agunt; nam secundum se et in ipsis habent motum.

Imperishable things are imitated by those that are involved in change, e.g. earth and fire. For these also are ever active; for they have their movement of themselves and in themselves.

αἱ δὲ ἄλλαι δυνάμεις, ἐξ ὧν διώρισται, πᾶσαι τῆς ἀντιφάσεώς εἰσιν· τὸ γὰρ δυνάμενον ὡδὶ κινεῖν δύναται καὶ μὴ ὡδί, ὅσα γε κατὰ λόγον· αἱ δ᾽ ἄλογοι τῷ παρεῖναι καὶ μὴ τῆς ἀντιφάσεως ἔσονται αἱ αὐταί.

Potentiae vero aliae, ex quibus diffinitum est, omnes contradictionis sunt. Nam possibile sic movere potest et non sic, quaecumque secundum rationem; irrationabiles vero per adesse et non contradictionis erunt eaedem.

But the other potencies, according to our previous discussion, are all potencies for opposites; for that which can move another in this way can also move it not in this way, i.e. if it acts according to a rational formula; and the same non-rational potencies will produce opposite results by their presence or absence.

εἰ ἄρα τινὲς εἰσὶ φύσεις [35] τοιαῦται ἢ οὐσίαι οἵας λέγουσιν οἱ ἐν τοῖς λόγοις τὰς ἰδέας, πολὺ μᾶλλον ἐπιστῆμον ἄν τι εἴη ἢ αὐτὸ ἐπιστήμη καὶ κινούμενον ἢ κίνησις: [1051α] [1] ταῦτα γὰρ ἐνέργειαι μᾶλλον, ἐκεῖναι δὲ δυνάμεις τούτων. ὅτι μὲν οὖν πρότερον ἡ ἐνέργεια καὶ δυνάμεως καὶ πάσης ἀρχῆς μεταβλητικῆς, φανερόν.

Si ergo alique sunt nature tales aut substantiae quales dicunt qui in rationibus ydeas, multo magis sciens utique erit aliquid quam per se scientia et motum quam motus; haec enim 105u1 actus magis, illa autem rpotentie horum1. Quod quidem igitur est prius actus potentia et omni principio mutabili, palam.

If, then, there are any entities or substances such as the dialecticians say the Ideas are, there must be something much more scientific than science-itself and something more [51a] mobile than movement-itself; for these will be more of the nature of actualities, while science-itself and movement-itself are potencies for these. Obviously, then, actuality is prior both to potency and to every principle of change.


*Chapter* 9

ὅτι δὲ καὶ βελτίων καὶ τιμιωτέρα τῆς σπουδαίας [5] δυνάμεως ἡ ἐνέργεια, ἐκ τῶνδε δῆλον. ὅσα γὰρ κατὰ τὸ δύνασθαι λέγεται, ταὐτόν ἐστι δυνατὸν τἀναντία, οἷον τὸ δύνασθαι λεγόμενον ὑγιαίνειν ταὐτόν ἐστι καὶ τὸ νοσεῖν, καὶ ἅμα: ἡ αὐτὴ γὰρ δύναμις τοῦ ὑγιαίνειν καὶ κάμνειν, καὶ ἠρεμεῖν καὶ κινεῖσθαι, καὶ οἰκοδομεῖν καὶ καταβάλλειν, [10] καὶ οἰκοδομεῖσθαι καὶ καταπίπτειν. τὸ μὲν οὖν δύνασθαι τἀναντία ἅμα ὑπάρχει: τὰ δ᾽ ἐναντία ἅμα ἀδύνατον, καὶ τὰς ἐνεργείας δὲ ἅμα ἀδύνατον ὑπάρχειν (οἷον ὑγιαίνειν καὶ κάμνειν), ὥστ᾽ ἀνάγκη τούτων θάτερον εἶναι τἀγαθόν, τὸ δὲ δύνασθαι ὁμοίως ἀμφότερον ἢ οὐδέτερον: [15] ἡ ἄρα ἐνέργεια βελτίων.

Quod autem et melior et honorabilior studiosa potentia actus, ex hiis est palam. Quaecumque enim secundum posse dicuntur, idem est potens contraria, ut rquod dicitur posse1 conualescere idem est et languens, et simul; eadem enim potentia convalescendi et laborandi, et quiescendi et movendi, et edificandi et destruendi, et

354

edificari et corruendi. Posse quidem igitur contraria simul existit; contraria vero impossibile est existere, ut sanum esse et laborare. Quare necesse horum alterum esse bonum, posse vero similiter utrumque aut neutrum. Actus ergo melior est.

That the actuality is also better and more valuable than the good potency is evident from the following argument. Everything of which we say that it can do something, is alike capable of contraries, e.g. that of which we say that it can be well is the same as that which can be ill, and has both potencies at once; for the same potency is a potency of health and illness, of rest and motion, of building and throwing down, of being built and being thrown down. The capacity for contraries, then, is present at the same time; but contraries cannot be present at the same time, and the actualities also cannot be present at the same time, e.g. health and illness. Therefore, while the good must be one of them, the capacity is both alike, or neither; the actuality, then, is better.

ἀνάγκη δὲ καὶ ἐπὶ τῶν κακῶν τὸ τέλος καὶ τὴν ἐνέργειαν εἶναι χεῖρον τῆς δυνάμεως: τὸ γὰρ δυνάμενον ταὐτὸ ἄμφω τἀναντία.

Necesse autem et in malis finem et actum esse deteriorem potentia; quod enim potens: idem ambo contraria.

Also in the case of bad things the end or actuality must be worse than the potency; for that which can is both contraries alike.

δῆλον ἄρα ὅτι οὐκ ἔστι τὸ κακὸν παρὰ τὰ πράγματα: ὕστερον γὰρ τῇ φύσει τὸ κακὸν τῆς δυνάμεως.

Palam ergo quia non est aliquid quod malum praeter res ; posterius enim ipsi nature malum quam potentia.

Clearly, then, the bad does not exist apart from bad things; for the bad is in its nature posterior to the potency.

οὐκ ἄρα οὐδ᾽ ἐν τοῖς ἐξ ἀρχῆς [20] καὶ τοῖς ἀϊδίοις οὐθὲν ἔστιν οὔτε κακὸν οὔτε ἁμάρτημα οὔτε διεφθαρμένον (καὶ γὰρ ἡ διαφθορὰ τῶν κακῶν ἐστίν).

Non ergo nec in eis quae a principio et sempiternis nihil est neque malum neque peccatum neque corruptum; et enim corruptio malorum.

And therefore we may also say that in the things which are from the beginning, i.e. in eternal things, there is nothing bad, nothing defective, nothing perverted (for perversion is something bad).

εὑρίσκεται δὲ καὶ τὰ διαγράμματα ἐνεργείᾳ: διαιροῦντες γὰρ εὑρίσκουσιν. εἰ δ᾽ ἦν διῃρημένα, φανερὰ ἂν ἦν: νῦν δ᾽ ἐνυπάρχει δυνάμει. διὰ τί δύο ὀρθαὶ τὸ τρίγωνον; ὅτι αἱ [25] περὶ μίαν στιγμὴν γωνίαι ἴσαι δύο ὀρθαῖς. εἰ οὖν ἀνῆκτο ἡ παρὰ τὴν πλευράν, ἰδόντι ἂν ἦν εὐθὺς δῆλον διὰ τί. ἐν ἡμικυκλίῳ ὀρθὴ καθόλου διὰ τί; ἐὰν ἴσαι τρεῖς, ἥ τε βάσις δύο καὶ ἡ ἐκ μέσου ἐπισταθεῖσα ὀρθή, ἰδόντι δῆλον τῷ ἐκεῖνο εἰδότι. ὥστε φανερὸν ὅτι τὰ δυνάμει ὄντα εἰς [30] ἐνέργειαν ἀγόμενα εὑρίσκεται· αἴτιον δὲ ὅτι ἡ νόησις ἐνέργεια· ὥστ᾽ ἐξ ἐνεργείας ἡ δύναμις, καὶ διὰ τοῦτο ποιοῦντες γιγνώσκουσιν (ὕστερον γὰρ γενέσει ἡ ἐνέργεια ἡ κατ᾽ ἀριθμόν).

Inveniuntur autem et dyagramata actu; nam dividentes inveniunt. Si vero essent divisa, manifesta utique essent; nunc autem insunt potentia. Propter quid duo recti trigonum? quia qui circa unum punctum anguli equales duobus rectis. Si ergo educeretur quae iuxta costam, videnti utique statim esset palam. Propter quid in semicirculo rectus universaliter? Quia si equales tres, quae bases due et quae ex medio superstans recta, videnti palam ei qui illud scivit. Quare palam quia potentia entia ad actum reducta inveniuntur. Causa vero quia intelligentia est actus. Quare ex actu potentia, et propter hoc facientes cognoscunt; posterius enim generatione qui secundum numerum actus.

It is an activity also that geometrical constructions are discovered; for we find them by dividing. If the figures had been already divided, the constructions would have been obvious; but as it is they are present only potentially. Why are the angles of the triangle equal to two right angles? Because the angles about one point are equal to two right angles. If, then, the line parallel to the side had been already drawn upwards, the reason would have been evident to any one as soon as he saw the figure. Why is the angle in a semicircle in all cases a right angle? If three lines are equal the two which form the base, and the perpendicular from the centre-the conclusion is evident at a glance to one who knows the former proposition. Obviously, therefore, the potentially existing constructions are discovered by being brought to actuality; the reason is that the geometer's thinking is an actuality; so that the potency proceeds from an actuality; and therefore it is by making constructions that people come to know them (though the single actuality is later in generation than the corresponding potency).

*Chapter* 10

ἐπεὶ δὲ τὸ ὂν λέγεται καὶ τὸ μὴ ὂν τὸ μὲν κατὰ [35] τὰ σχήματα τῶν κατηγοριῶν, τὸ δὲ κατὰ δύναμιν ἢ ἐνέργειαν τούτων ἢ τἀναντία, [1051β] [1] τὸ δὲ [κυριώτατα ὂν] ἀληθὲς ἢ ψεῦδος,

Quoniam autem ens dicitur et non ens hoc quidem secundum figuras cathegoriarum, illud vero secundum potentiam aut actum horum aut contraria, hoc autem maxime proprie aut verum aut falsum.

The terms being and non-being are employed firstly with reference to the categories, and secondly with reference to the potency or actuality of these or their non-[51b]potency or nonactuality, and thirdly in the sense of true and false.

τοῦτο δ᾽ ἐπὶ τῶν πραγμάτων ἐστὶ τῷ συγκεῖσθαι ἢ διῃρῆσθαι, ὥστε ἀληθεύει μὲν ὁ τὸ διῃρημένον οἰόμενος διῃρῆσθαι καὶ τὸ συγκείμενον συγκεῖσθαι, ἔψευσται δὲ ὁ ἐναντίως [5] ἔχων ἢ τὰ πράγματα, πότ᾽ ἔστιν ἢ οὐκ ἔστι τὸ ἀληθὲς λεγόμενον ἢ ψεῦδος; τοῦτο γὰρ σκεπτέον τί λέγομεν. οὐ γὰρ διὰ τὸ ἡμᾶς οἴεσθαι ἀληθῶς σε λευκὸν εἶναι εἶ σὺ λευκός, ἀλλὰ διὰ τὸ σὲ εἶναι λευκὸν ἡμεῖς οἱ φάντες τοῦτο ἀληθεύομεν.

Hoc autem in rebus est componi aut dividi, unde verus est divisum putans dividi et compositum componi, mentitur autem econtrario habens res quandocumque est aut non est. Quare quod verum dicitur aut falsum, hoc perscrutandum quid dicimus. Non enim propter nos existimare te vere album esse es tu albus, sed propter te esse album nos hoc dicentes verum dicimus.

This depends, on the side of the objects, on their being combined or separated, so that he who thinks the separated to be separated and the combined to be combined has the truth, while he whose thought is in a state contrary to that of the objects is in error. This being so, when is what is called truth or falsity present, and when is it not? We must consider what we mean by these terms. It is not because we think truly that you are pale, that you are pale, but because you are pale we who say this have the truth.

εἰ δὴ τὰ μὲν ἀεὶ σύγκειται καὶ ἀδύνατα διαιρεθῆναι, [10] τὰ δ᾽ ἀεὶ διῄρηται καὶ ἀδύνατα συντεθῆναι, τὰ δ᾽ ἐνδέχεται τἀναντία, τὸ μὲν εἶναί ἐστι τὸ συγκεῖσθαι καὶ ἓν εἶναι, τὸ δὲ μὴ εἶναι τὸ μὴ συγκεῖσθαι ἀλλὰ πλείω εἶναι: περὶ μὲν οὖν τὰ ἐνδεχόμενα ἡ αὐτὴ γίγνεται ψευδὴς καὶ ἀληθὴς δόξα καὶ ὁ λόγος ὁ αὐτός, καὶ ἐνδέχεται ὁτὲ [15] μὲν ἀληθεύειν ὁτὲ δὲ ψεύδεσθαι: περὶ δὲ τὰ ἀδύνατα ἄλλως ἔχειν οὐ γίγνεται ὁτὲ μὲν ἀληθὲς ὁτὲ δὲ ψεῦδος, ἀλλ᾽ ἀεὶ ταὐτὰ ἀληθῆ καὶ ψευδῆ.

Si igitur haec quidem semper componuntur et impossibilia dividi, haec vero semper divisa sunt et impossibilia componi, haec autem contingunt contraria, esse quidem est componi et unum esse, et non esse non componi sed plura esse: circa contingentia quidem igitur eadem fit falsa et vera opinio et oratio eadem et contingit quandoque veram esse et contingit quandoque esse falsam; circa impossibilia vero aliter se habere non fit aliquando verum et aliquando falsum, sed semper haec vera et falsa.

If, then, some things are always combined and cannot be separated, and others are always separated and cannot be combined, while others are capable either of combination or of separation, being is being combined and one, and not being is being not combined but more than one. Regarding contingent facts, then, the same opinion or the same statement comes to be false and true, and it is possible for it to be at one time correct and at another erroneous; but regarding things that cannot be otherwise opinions are not at one time true and at another false, but the same opinions are always true or always false.

περὶ δὲ δὴ τὰ ἀσύνθετα τί τὸ εἶναι ἢ μὴ εἶναι καὶ τὸ ἀληθὲς καὶ τὸ ψεῦδος; οὐ γάρ ἐστι σύνθετον, ὥστε εἶναι μὲν ὅταν συγκέηται, μὴ εἶναι δὲ [20] ἐὰν διῃρημένον ᾖ, ὥσπερ τὸ λευκὸν <τὸ ξύλον ἢ τὸ ἀσύμμετρον [21] τὴν διάμετρον· οὐδὲ τὸ ἀληθὲς καὶ τὸ ψεῦδος ὁμοίως ἔτι ὑπάρξει καὶ ἐπ᾽ ἐκείνων. ἢ ὥσπερ οὐδὲ τὸ ἀληθὲς ἐπὶ τούτων τὸ αὐτό, οὕτως οὐδὲ τὸ εἶναι,

Circa incomposita vero quid esse aut non esse, et verum et falsum? Non enim est compositum, ut sit quidem quando componitur et non sit quando divisum fuerit, sicut album    lignum aut incommensurabilem dyametrum; nec verum et falsum similiter adhuc existet et in illis. Aut sicut nec verum in  hiis idem, sic nec esse.

But with regard to incomposites, what is being or not being, and truth or falsity? A thing of this sort is not composite, so as to be when it is compounded, and not to be if it is separated, like that the wood is white or that the diagonal is incommensurable ; nor will truth and falsity be still present in the same way as in the previous cases. In fact, as truth is not the same in these cases, so also being is not the same;

ἀλλ᾽ ἔστι τὸ μὲν ἀληθὲς ἢ ψεῦδος, τὸ μὲν θιγεῖν καὶ φάναι ἀληθές (οὐ γὰρ ταὐτὸ κατάφασις [25] καὶ φάσις), τὸ δ᾽ ἀγνοεῖν μὴ θιγγάνειν (ἀπατηθῆναι γὰρ περὶ τὸ τί ἐστιν οὐκ ἔστιν ἀλλ᾽ ἢ κατὰ συμβεβηκός· ὁμοίως δὲ καὶ περὶ τὰς μὴ συνθετὰς οὐσίας, οὐ γὰρ ἔστιν ἀπατηθῆναι·

Sed est  verum quidem  aut falsum:  attingere quidem et representare verum (non enim idem   affirmatio et representatio), ignorare autem non attingere. Decipi enim circa quod quid est non est sed aut secundum accidens; similiter autem et circa compositas substantias, non enim est decipi.

but (a) truth or falsity is as follows – contact and assertion are truth (assertion not being the same as affirmation), and ignorance is non-contact. For it is not possible to be in error regarding the question what a thing is, save in an accidental sense; and the same holds good regarding non-composite substances (for it is not possible to be in error about them).

καὶ πᾶσαι εἰσὶν ἐνεργείᾳ, οὐ δυνάμει, ἐγίγνοντο γὰρ ἂν καὶ ἐφθείροντο, νῦν δὲ τὸ ὂν αὐτὸ οὐ γίγνεται οὐδὲ φθείρεται, [30] ἔκ τινος γὰρ ἂν ἐγίγνετο· ὅσα δὴ ἔστιν ὅπερ εἶναί τι καὶ ἐνέργειαι, περὶ ταῦτα οὐκ ἔστιν ἀπατηθῆναι ἀλλ᾽ ἢ νοεῖν ἢ μή· ἀλλὰ τὸ τί ἐστι ζητεῖται περὶ αὐτῶν, εἰ τοιαῦτά ἐστιν ἢ μή):

Et omnes sunt actu, non potentia; generarentur enim utique et corrumperentur. Nunc autem ens ipsum non generatur nec corrumpitur; ex aliquo enim utique generaretur. Quaecumque igitur sunt quod vere esse aliquid et actu, circa haec non est decipi sed aut intelligere aut non.

And they all exist actually, not potentially; for otherwise they would have come to be and ceased to be; but, as it is, being itself does not come to be (nor cease to be); for if it had done so it would have had to come out of something. About the things, then, which are essences and actualities, it is not possible to be in error, but only to know them or not to know them. But we do inquire what they are, viz. whether they are of such and such a nature or not.

τὸ δὲ εἶναι ὡς τὸ ἀληθές, καὶ τὸ μὴ εἶναι τὸ ὡς τὸ ψεῦδος, ἓν μέν ἐστιν, εἰ σύγκειται, ἀληθές, τὸ [35] δ᾿ εἰ μὴ σύγκειται, ψεῦδος: τὸ δὲ ἕν, εἴπερ ὄν, οὕτως ἐστίν, εἰ δὲ μὴ οὕτως, οὐκ ἔστιν: [1052α] [1] τὸ δὲ ἀληθὲς τὸ νοεῖν ταῦτα: τὸ δὲ ψεῦδος οὐκ ἔστιν, οὐδὲ ἀπάτη, ἀλλὰ ἄγνοια, οὐχ οἵα ἡ τυφλότης: ἡ μὲν γὰρ τυφλότης ἐστὶν ὡς ἂν εἰ τὸ νοητικὸν ὅλως μὴ ἔχοι τις.

Sed quod quid est quaeritur de ipsis, si talia sunt aut non. Esse vero ut verum et non esse ut falsum: unum quidem est si componitur, verum, hoc autem si non componitur, falsum. Unum autem, si vere ens, sic est, si vero non ita, non est. Verum autem intelligere ipsa; falsum vero non est, nec deceptio, sed ignorantia. Non qualis caecitas; caecitas enim est ut utique si intellectivum omnino non habeat aliquis.

(b) As regards the being that answers to truth and the non-being that answers to falsity, in one case there is truth if the subject and the attribute are really combined, and falsity if they are not combined; in the other case, if the object is existent it exists in a particular way, and if it does [52a] not exist in this way does not exist at all. And truth means knowing these objects, and falsity does not exist, nor error, but only ignorance-and not an ignorance which is like blindness; for blindness is akin to a total absence of the faculty of thinking.

φανερὸν δὲ καὶ ὅτι περὶ τῶν ἀκινήτων [5] οὐκ ἔστιν ἀπάτη κατὰ τὸ ποτέ, εἴ τις ὑπολαμβάνει ἀκίνητα. οἷον τὸ τρίγωνον εἰ μὴ μεταβάλλειν οἴεται, οὐκ οἰήσεται ποτὲ μὲν δύο ὀρθὰς ἔχειν ποτὲ δὲ οὔ (μεταβάλλοι γὰρ ἄν), ἀλλὰ τὶ μὲν τὶ δ᾿ οὔ, οἷον ἄρτιον ἀριθμὸν πρῶτον εἶναι μηθένα, ἢ τινὰς μὲν τινὰς δ᾿ οὔ: ἀριθμῷ δὲ περὶ ἕνα οὐδὲ [10] τοῦτο: οὐ γὰρ ἔτι τινὰ μὲν τινὰ δὲ οὔ οἰήσεται, ἀλλ᾿ ἀληθεύσει ἢ ψεύσεται ὡς ἀεὶ οὕτως ἔχοντος.

Palam etiam et quia de immobilibus non est deceptio secundum quando, si quis putet immobilia. Ut trigonum si non permutari putat, non opinabitur quandoque duos rectos habere quandoque non; permutaretur enim utique. Sed aliquid quidem aliquid vero non; ut parem numerum primum esse nullum, aut aliquos quidem aliquos autem non. Numero vero circa unum nec hoc; non enim est: aliquem quidem aliquem vero non putabit, sed verum dicet aut mentietur ut semper sic se habente.

It is evident also that about unchangeable things there can be no error in respect of time, if we assume them to be unchangeable. E.g. if we suppose that the triangle does not change, we shall not suppose that at one time its angles are equal to two right angles while at another time they are not (for that would imply change). It is possible, however, to suppose that one member of such a class has a certain attribute and another has not; e.g. while we may suppose that no even number is prime, we may suppose that some are and some are not. But regarding a numerically single number not even this form of error is possible; for we cannot in this case suppose that one instance has an attribute and another has not, but whether our judgement be true or false, it is implied that the fact is eternal.

# METHAPHISICE ARISTOTILIS LIBER DECIMUS

## 10 (I)

[1052α] [15] τὸ ἓν ὅτι μὲν λέγεται πολλαχῶς, ἐν τοῖς περὶ τοῦ ποσαχῶς διηρημένοις εἴρηται πρότερον: πλεοναχῶς δὲ λεγομένου οἱ συγκεφαλαιούμενοι τρόποι εἰσὶ τέτταρες τῶν πρώτων καὶ καθ᾽ αὑτὰ λεγομένων ἓν ἀλλὰ μὴ κατὰ συμβεβηκός. τό τε γὰρ συνεχὲς ἢ ἁπλῶς ἢ μάλιστά γε [20] τὸ φύσει καὶ μὴ ἁφῇ μηδὲ δεσμῷ (καὶ τούτων μᾶλλον ἓν καὶ πρότερον οὗ ἀδιαιρετωτέρα ἡ κίνησις καὶ μᾶλλον ἁπλῆ):

Unum quia multis modis dicitur, in divisis de quotiens dictum est prius. Multipliciter vero dicto capitales modi sunt quatuor primorum et secundum se dictorum unum sed non secundum accidens. Continuum enim, aut simpliciter aut maxime quod natura et non tactu nec ligatione; et horum magis unum et prius cuius indivisibilior motus est et magis simplex.

WE have said previously, in our distinction of the various meanings of words, that one has several meanings; the things that are directly and of their own nature and not accidentally called one may be summarized under four heads, though the word is used in more senses. (1) There is the continuous, either in general, or especially that which is continuous by nature and not by contact nor by being together; and of these, that has more unity and is prior, whose movement is more indivisible and simpler. (2)

ἔτι τοιοῦτον καὶ μᾶλλον τὸ ὅλον καὶ ἔχον τινὰ μορφὴν καὶ εἶδος, μάλιστα δ᾽ εἴ τι φύσει τοιοῦτον καὶ μὴ βίᾳ, ὥσπερ ὅσα κόλλῃ ἢ γόμφῳ ἢ συνδέσμῳ, ἀλλὰ ἔχει ἐν αὑτῷ τὸ [25] αἴτιον αὑτῷ τοῦ συνεχὲς εἶναι.

Amplius tale et magis totum et habens aliquam formam et speciem, maxime autem si quid natura est tale et non vi, ut quaecumque visco aut clauo aut coniunctione, sed habet in se quod est causa sibi ut sit continuum.

That which is a whole and has a certain shape and form is one in a still higher degree; and especially if a thing is of this sort by nature, and not by force like the things which are unified by glue or nails or by being tied together, i.e. if it has in itself the cause of its continuity.

τοιοῦτον δὲ τῷ μίαν τὴν κίνησιν εἶναι καὶ ἀδιαίρετον τόπῳ καὶ χρόνῳ, ὥστε φανερόν, εἴ τι φύσει κινήσεως ἀρχὴν ἔχει τῆς πρώτης τὴν πρώτην, οἷον λέγω φορᾶς κυκλοφορίαν, ὅτι τοῦτο πρῶτον μέγεθος ἕν. τὰ μὲν δὴ οὕτως ἕν ἢ συνεχὲς ἢ ὅλον,

Tale vero in Motum unum esse et indivisibile loco et tempore. Quare palam , si quid per naturam motus habet principium primi primum, ut puta dico lationis circulationem, quia haec prima magnitudo una. Haec quidem itaque sic unum continuum aut totum.

A thing is of this sort because its movement is one and indivisible in place and time; so that evidently if a thing has by nature a principle of movement that is of the first kind (i.e. local movement) and the first in that kind (i.e. circular movement), this is in the primary sense one extended thing. Some things, then, are one in this way, qua continuous or whole, and

τὰ δὲ ὧν ἂν ὁ λόγος [30] εἷς ᾖ, τοιαῦτα δὲ ὧν ἡ νόησις μία, τοιαῦτα δὲ ὧν ἀδιαίρετος, ἀδιαίρετος δὲ τοῦ ἀδιαιρέτου εἴδει ἢ ἀριθμῷ· ἀριθμῷ μὲν οὖν τὸ καθ᾿ ἕκαστον ἀδιαίρετον, εἴδει δὲ τὸ τῷ γνωστῷ καὶ τῇ ἐπιστήμῃ, ὥσθ᾿ ἕν ἂν εἴη πρῶτον τὸ ταῖς οὐσίαις αἴτιον τοῦ ἑνός.

Haec autem, si ratio una fuerit. Talia vero sunt  quorum intelligentia una, talia autem quorum indivisibilis; indivisibilis vero eius quod indivisibile specie aut numero. Numero vero singulare indivisibile, specie vero quod noscibili et scientie; quare unum utique erit primum quod substantiis causa unius.

the other things that are one are those whose definition is one. Of this sort are the things the thought of which is one, i.e. those the thought of which is indivisible; and it is indivisible if the thing is indivisible in kind or in number. (3) In number, then, the individual is indivisible, and (4) in kind, that which in intelligibility and in knowledge is indivisible, so that that which causes substances to be one must be one in the primary sense.

λέγεται μὲν οὖν τὸ ἓν τοσαυταχῶς, τό τε [35] συνεχὲς φύσει καὶ τὸ ὅλον, καὶ τὸ καθ᾽ ἕκαστον καὶ τὸ καθόλου, πάντα δὲ ταῦτα ἓν τῷ ἀδιαίρετον εἶναι τῶν μὲν τὴν κίνησιν τῶν δὲ τὴν νόησιν ἢ τὸν λόγον.

Dicitur quidem igitur unum tot modis: continuum natura et totum et singulare et universale. Omnia vero haec unum per indivisibile esse, horum quidem motum, illorum autem intelligentiam aut rationem.

One , then, has all these meanings – the naturally continuous and the whole, and the individual and the universal. And all these are one because in some cases the movement, in others the thought or the definition is indivisible. [52b]

[1052β] [1] —δεῖ δὲ κατανοεῖν ὅτι οὐχ ὡσαύτως ληπτέον λέγεσθαι ποῖά τε ἓν λέγεται, καὶ τί ἐστι τὸ ἑνὶ εἶναι καὶ τίς αὐτοῦ λόγος. λέγεται μὲν γὰρ τὸ ἓν τοσαυταχῶς, καὶ ἕκαστον ἔσται ἓν τούτων, ᾧ [5] ἂν ὑπάρχῃ τις τούτων τῶν τρόπων· τὸ δὲ ἑνὶ εἶναι ὁτὲ μὲν τούτων τινὶ ἔσται, ὁτὲ δὲ ἄλλῳ ὃ καὶ μᾶλλον ἐγγὺς τῷ ὀνόματί ἐστι, τῇ δυνάμει δ᾽ ἐκεῖνα, ὥσπερ καὶ περὶ στοιχείου καὶ αἰτίου εἰ δέοι λέγειν ἐπί τε τοῖς πράγμασι διορίζοντα καὶ τοῦ ὀνόματος ὅρον ἀποδιδόντα. ἔστι μὲν γὰρ ὡς [10] στοιχεῖον τὸ πῦρ (ἔστι δ᾽ ἴσως καθ᾽ αὑτὸ καὶ τὸ ἄπειρον ἢ τι ἄλλο τοιοῦτον), ἔστι δ᾽ ὡς οὔ· οὐ γὰρ τὸ αὐτὸ πυρὶ καὶ στοιχείῳ εἶναι, ἀλλ᾽ ὡς μὲν πρᾶγμά τι καὶ φύσις τὸ πῦρ στοιχεῖον, τὸ δὲ ὄνομα σημαίνει τὸ τοδὶ συμβεβηκέναι αὐτῷ, ὅτι ἐστί τι ἐκ τούτου ὡς πρώτου ἐνυπάρχοντος. οὕτω [15] καὶ ἐπὶ αἰτίου καὶ ἑνὸς καὶ τῶν τοιούτων ἁπάντων, διὸ καὶ τὸ ἑνὶ εἶναι τὸ ἀδιαιρέτῳ ἐστὶν εἶναι, ὅπερ τόδε ὄντι καὶ ἰδίᾳ χωριστῷ ἢ τόπῳ ἢ εἴδει ἢ διανοίᾳ, ἢ καὶ τὸ ὅλῳ καὶ ἀδιαιρέτῳ,

Oportet autem intelligere quia non similiter sumendum est dici qualia unum dicuntur, et quid est uni esse et quae ipsius ratio. Dicitur enim unum tot modis, et unumquodque erit unum horum cuicumque extiterit horum aliquis modorum. Uni autem esse quandoque quidem horum alicui inerit, quandoque autem alii quod et magis propinquum nomini est, potentia vero illa. Sicut de elemento et causa, si oportet dicere in rebus determinantem et nominis terminum reddentem. Est quidem enim ut elementum ignis (est autem forsan secundum se et infinitum aut aliquid aliud tale), est autem ut non. Non enim idem igni et elemento esse, sed ut quidem re et natura ignis elementum; nomen vero significat: eo quod hoc acciderit ipsi, quia est aliquid ex hoc ut primo inexistente. Sic et in causa et in uno et talibus omnibus. Propter quod et uni esse indivisibili est esse, quod quidem hoc enti et inseparabili aut loco aut specie aut mente, aut et toto et determinato.

But it must be observed that the questions, what sort of things are said to be one, and what it is to be one and what is the definition of it, should not be assumed to be the same. One has all these meanings, and each of the things to which one of these kinds of unity belongs will be one; but to be one will sometimes mean being one of these things, and sometimes being something else which is even nearer to the meaning of the word one while these other things approximate to its application. This is also true of element or cause , if one had both to specify the things of which it is predicable and to render the definition of the word. For in a sense fire is an element (and doubtless also the indefinite or something else of the sort is by its own nature the element), but in a sense it is not; for it is not the same thing to be fire and to be an element, but while as a particular thing with a nature of its own fire is an element, the name element means that it has this attribute, that there is something which is made of it as a primary constituent. And so with cause and one and all such terms. For this reason, too, to be one means to be indivisible, being essentially one means a this and capable of being isolated either in place, or in form or thought; or perhaps to be whole and indivisible ;

μάλιστα δὲ τὸ μέτρῳ εἶναι πρώτῳ ἑκάστου γένους καὶ κυριώτατα τοῦ ποσοῦ: ἐντεῦθεν γὰρ ἐπὶ τὰ ἄλλα ἐλήλυθεν. [20] μέτρον γάρ ἐστιν ᾧ τὸ ποσὸν γιγνώσκεται: γιγνώσκεται δὲ ἢ ἑνὶ ἢ ἀριθμῷ τὸ ποσὸν ᾗ ποσόν, ὁ δὲ ἀριθμὸς ἅπας ἑνί, ὥστε πᾶν τὸ ποσὸν γιγνώσκεται ᾗ ποσὸν τῷ ἑνί,

Maxime vero in eo quod est metrum esse primum uniuscuiusque generis et maxime proprie quantitatis; hinc enim ad alia venit. Metrum etenim est quo quantitas cognoscitur; cognoscitur vero aut uno aut numero quantitas in quantum quantitas, numerus autem omnis uno. Quare omnis quantitas cognoscitur in quantum quantitas uno,

but it means especially to be the first measure of a kind , and most strictly of quantity; for it is from this that it has been extended to the other categories. For measure is that by which quantity is known; and quantity qua quantity is known either by a one or by a number, and all number is known by a one . Therefore all quantity qua quantity is known by the one,

καὶ ᾧ πρώτῳ ποσὰ γιγνώσκεται, τοῦτο αὐτὸ ἕν: διὸ τὸ ἓν ἀριθμοῦ ἀρχὴ ᾗ ἀριθμός.

et quo primo cognoscitur, hoc ipsum unum; quapropter unum numeri principium secundum quod numerus.

and that by which quantities are primarily known is the one itself; and so the one is the starting-point of number qua number.

ἐντεῦθεν δὲ καὶ ἐν τοῖς ἄλλοις [25] λέγεται μέτρον τε ᾧ ἕκαστον πρώτῳ γιγνώσκεται, καὶ τὸ μέτρον ἑκάστου ἕν, ἐν μήκει, ἐν πλάτει, ἐν βάθει, ἐν βάρει, ἐν τάχει (τὸ γὰρ βάρος καὶ τάχος κοινὸν ἐν τοῖς ἐναντίοις: διττὸν γὰρ ἑκάτερον αὐτῶν, οἷον βάρος τό τε ὁποσηνοῦν ἔχον ῥοπὴν καὶ τὸ ἔχον ὑπεροχὴν ῥοπῆς, καὶ τάχος τό τε ὁποσηνοῦν [30] κίνησιν ἔχον καὶ τὸ ὑπεροχὴν κινήσεως: ἔστι γάρ τι τάχος καὶ τοῦ βραδέος καὶ βάρος τοῦ κουφοτέρου).

Hinc autem et in aliis dicitur metrum quo primo unumquodque cognoscitur. Et metrum uniuscuiusque unum, in longitudine, in latitudine, in profunditate, in gravitate, in velocitate. Gravitas enim et velocitas commune in contrariis; duplex enim eorum utrumque, ut grave et quod est quantamcumque habens inclinationem et quod est habens excessum inclinationis, et velocitas et quantumcumque motum habens et excessum motus; est enim velocitas quaedam et tardi et gravitas levioris.

And hence in the other classes too measure means that by which each is first known, and the measure of each is a unit – in length, in breadth, in depth, in weight, in speed. (The words weight and speed are common to both contraries; for each of them has two meanings – weight means both that which has any amount of gravity and that which has an excess of gravity, and speed both that which has any amount of movement and that which has an excess of movement; for even the slow has a certain speed and the comparatively light a certain weight.)

ἐν πᾶσι δὴ τούτοις μέτρον καὶ ἀρχὴ ἕν τι καὶ ἀδιαίρετον, ἐπεὶ καὶ ἐν ταῖς γραμμαῖς χρῶνται ὡς ἀτόμῳ τῇ ποδιαίᾳ. πανταχοῦ γὰρ τὸ μέτρον ἕν τι ζητοῦσι καὶ ἀδιαίρετον· τοῦτο δὲ [35] τὸ ἁπλοῦν ἢ τῷ ποιῷ ἢ τῷ ποσῷ. ὅπου μὲν οὖν δοκεῖ μὴ εἶναι ἀφελεῖν ἢ προσθεῖναι, τοῦτο ἀκριβὲς τὸ μέτρον (διὸ τὸ τοῦ ἀριθμοῦ ἀκριβέστατον· [1053α] [1] τὴν γὰρ μονάδα τιθέασι πάντη ἀδιαίρετον)· ἐν δὲ τοῖς ἄλλοις μιμοῦνται τὸ τοιοῦτον· ἀπὸ γὰρ σταδίου καὶ ταλάντου καὶ ἀεὶ τοῦ μείζονος λάθοι ἂν καὶ προστεθέν τι καὶ ἀφαιρεθὲν μᾶλλον ἢ ἀπὸ ἐλάττονος· [5] ὥστε ἀφ᾽ οὗ πρώτου κατὰ τὴν αἴσθησιν μὴ ἐνδέχεται, τοῦτο πάντες ποιοῦνται μέτρον καὶ ὑγρῶν καὶ ξηρῶν καὶ βάρους καὶ μεγέθους· καὶ τότ᾽ οἴονται εἰδέναι τὸ ποσόν, ὅταν εἰδῶσι διὰ τούτου τοῦ μέτρου.

In omnibus autem hiis metrum et principium unum aliquid et indivisibile, quoniam et in lineis utuntur quasi indivisibili pedali. Vbique namque metrum unum aliquid quaerunt et indivisibile; hoc autem quod simplex aut quali aut quanto. vbicumque quidem igitur videtur non esse aveerre aut addere, hoc est certum metrum. Quapropter numeros certissimum; unitatem enim ponunt omnino indivisibilem. In aliis vero imitantur tale. A stadio enim et talento et semper maiore latebit utique et additum aliquid et ablatum magis quam a minore; quare a quo primo secundum sensum non contingit, hoc omnes faciunt metrum et humidorum et siccorum et gravitatis et magnitudinis; et tunc putant cognoscere quantum, quando cognoscunt per hoc metrum.

In all these, then, the measure and starting-point is something one and indivisible, since even in lines we treat as indivisible the line a foot long. For everywhere we seek as the measure something one and indivisible; and this is that which is simple either in quality or in quantity. Now where it is thought impossible to take away or to add, there the measure is exact (hence that of number is [53a] most exact; for we posit the unit as indivisible in every respect); but in all other cases we

364

imitate this sort of measure. For in the case of a furlong or a talent or of anything comparatively large any addition or subtraction might more easily escape our notice than in the case of something smaller; so that the first thing from which, as far as our perception goes, nothing can be subtracted, all men make the measure, whether of liquids or of solids, whether of weight or of size; and they think they know the quantity when they know it by means of this measure.

καὶ δὴ καὶ κίνησιν τῇ ἁπλῇ κινήσει καὶ τῇ ταχίστῃ (ὀλίγιστον γὰρ αὕτη ἔχει χρόνον): [10] διὸ ἐν τῇ ἀστρολογίᾳ τὸ τοιοῦτον ἐν ἀρχῇ καὶ μέτρον (τὴν κίνησιν γὰρ ὁμαλὴν ὑποτίθενται καὶ ταχίστην τὴν τοῦ οὐρανοῦ, πρὸς ἣν κρίνουσι τὰς ἄλλας), καὶ ἐν μουσικῇ δίεσις, ὅτι ἐλάχιστον, καὶ ἐν φωνῇ στοιχεῖον. καὶ ταῦτα πάντα ἕν τι οὕτως, οὐχ ὡς κοινόν τι τὸ ἓν ἀλλ᾽ ὥσπερ εἴρηται.

Et motum autem simplici motu et velocissimo; paruissimum enim hic habet tempus. Quapropter in astrologia tale unum principium et metrum; motum enim regularem supponunt et velocissimum eum qui celi, ad quem alios iudicant. Et in musica diesis, quia minimum. Et in voce elementum. Et haec omnia unum aliquid ita, non ut commune aliquid quod unum sed sicut dictum est.

And indeed they know movement too by the simple movement and the quickest; for this occupies least time. And so in astronomy a one of this sort is the starting-point and measure (for they assume the movement of the heavens to be uniform and the quickest, and judge the others by reference to it), and in music the quarter-tone (because it is the least interval), and in speech the letter. And all these are ones in this sense – not that one is something predicable in the same sense of all of these, but in the sense we have mentioned.

οὐκ ἀεὶ [15] δὲ τῷ ἀριθμῷ ἓν τὸ μέτρον ἀλλ᾽ ἐνίοτε πλείω, οἷον αἱ διέσεις δύο, αἱ μὴ κατὰ τὴν ἀκοὴν ἀλλ᾽ ἐν τοῖς λόγοις, καὶ αἱ φωναὶ πλείους αἷς μετροῦμεν, καὶ ἡ διάμετρος δυσὶ μετρεῖται καὶ ἡ πλευρά, καὶ τὰ μεγέθη πάντα. οὕτω δὴ πάντων μέτρον τὸ ἕν, ὅτι γνωρίζομεν ἐξ ὧν ἐστὶν ἡ οὐσία διαιροῦντες [20] ἢ κατὰ τὸ ποσὸν ἢ κατὰ τὸ εἶδος. καὶ διὰ τοῦτο τὸ ἓν ἀδιαίρετον, ὅτι τὸ πρῶτον ἑκάστων ἀδιαίρετον. οὐχ ὁμοίως δὲ πᾶν ἀδιαίρετον, οἷον ποὺς καὶ μονάς, ἀλλὰ τὸ μὲν πάντῃ, τὸ δ᾽ εἰς ἀδιαίρετα πρὸς τὴν αἴσθησιν θετέον, ὥσπερ εἴρηται ἤδη: ἴσως γὰρ πᾶν συνεχὲς διαιρετόν.

Non semper autem numero unum metrum, verum aliquando plura, ut dieses due, quae non secundum auditum sed in rationibus, et voces plures quibus mensuramus, et diameter duobus mensuratur et latus, et magnitudines omnes. Sic itaque metrum omnium quod unum, quia cognoscimus ex quibus est substantia, dividentes aut secundum quantitatem aut secundum speciem. Et ideo quod unum indivisibile, quia quod primum singulorum indivisibile. Non similiter autem omne indivisibile, ut pes et unitas, sed hoc quidem omnino, illud vero in indivisibilia ad sensum voluit, sicut dictum est iam; nam forsan omne continuum est divisibile.

But the measure is not always one in number – sometimes there are several; e.g. the quarter-tones (not to the ear, but as determined by the ratios) are two, and the articulate sounds by which we measure are more than one, and the diagonal of the square and its side are measured by two quantities, and all spatial magnitudes reveal similar varieties of unit. Thus, then, the one is the measure of all things, because we come to know the elements in the substance by dividing the things either in respect of quantity or in respect of kind. And the one is indivisible just because the first of each class of things is indivisible. But it is not in the same way that every one is indivisible e.g. a foot and a unit; the latter is indivisible in every respect, while the former must be placed among things which are undivided to perception, as has been said already – only to perception, for doubtless every continuous thing is divisible.

ἀεὶ δὲ συγγενὲς [25] τὸ μέτρον: μεγεθῶν μὲν γὰρ μέγεθος, καὶ καθ᾽ ἕκαστον μήκους μῆκος, πλάτους πλάτος, φωνῆς φωνή, βάρους βάρος, μονάδων μονάς. οὕτω γὰρ δεῖ λαμβάνειν, ἀλλ᾽ οὐχ ὅτι ἀριθμῶν ἀριθμός: καίτοι ἔδει, εἰ ὁμοίως: ἀλλ᾽ οὐχ ὁμοίως ἀξιοῖ ἀλλ᾽ ὥσπερ εἰ μονάδων μονάδας ἀξιώσειε [30] μέτρον ἀλλὰ μὴ μονάδα: ὁ δ᾽ ἀριθμὸς πλῆθος μονάδων.

Semper autem cognatum est metrum. Magnitudinum quidem enim magnitudo, et secundum unumquodque longitudinis longitudo, latitudinis latitudo, vocis vox, gravitatis gravitas, unitatum unitas. Sic enim oportet accipere, sed non quod numerorum numerus, et quidem oportebat, si similiter; sed non similiter dignificat, sed ac si unitatum unitates dignificarent metrum sed non unitatem; numerus autem pluralitas unitatum est.

The measure is always homogeneous with the thing measured; the measure of spatial magnitudes is a spatial magnitude, and in particular that of length is a length, that of breadth a breadth, that of articulate sound an articulate sound, that of weight a weight, that of units a unit. (For we must state the matter so, and not say that the measure of numbers is a number; we ought indeed to say this if we were to use the corresponding form of words, but the claim does not really correspond – it is as if one claimed that the measure of units is units and not a unit; number is a plurality of units.)

καὶ τὴν ἐπιστήμην δὲ μέτρον τῶν πραγμάτων λέγομεν καὶ τὴν αἴσθησιν διὰ τὸ αὐτό, ὅτι γνωρίζομέν τι αὐταῖς, ἐπεὶ μετροῦνται μᾶλλον ἢ μετροῦσιν. ἀλλὰ συμβαίνει ἡμῖν ὥσπερ ἂν εἰ ἄλλου ἡμᾶς μετροῦντος ἐγνωρίσαμεν πηλίκοι ἐσμὲν [35] τῷ τὸν πῆχυν ἐπὶ τοσοῦτον ἡμῶν ἐπιβάλλειν. Πρωταγόρας δ᾽ ἄνθρωπόν φησι πάντων εἶναι μέτρον, ὥσπερ ἂν εἰ τὸν ἐπιστήμονα εἰπὼν ἢ τὸν αἰσθανόμενον:

[1053β] [1] τούτους δ᾿ ὅτι ἔχουσιν ὁ μὲν αἴσθησιν ὁ δὲ ἐπιστήμην, ἅ φαμεν εἶναι μέτρα τῶν ὑποκειμένων. οὐθὲν δὴ λέγοντες περιττὸν φαίνονταί τι λέγειν.

Et scientiam autem metrum rerum dicimus et sensum propter idem, quia cognoscimus aliquid ipsis, quoniam mensurantur magis quam mensurant. Sed accidit nobis veluti si alio nos mensurante cognoscamus quanti sumus per cubitum ad tantum nostri adicere. Protagoras vero hominem omnium ait esse metrum, ac utique si scientem dicens aut sentientem; hos autem quia habent hic quidem sensum ille vero scientiam, quae dicimus esse metra eorum quae subiciuntur. Nihil itaque dicentes superhabundans videntur aliquid dicere.

Knowledge, also, and perception, we call the measure of things for the same reason, because we come to know something by them – while as a matter of fact they are measured rather than measure other things. But it is with us as if some one else measured us and we came to know how big we are by seeing that he applied the cubit-measure to such and such a fraction of us. But Protagoras says "man is the measure of all things", as if he had said the man who knows or [53b] the man who perceives ; and these because they have respectively knowledge and perception, which we say are the measures of objects. Such thinkers are saying nothing, then, while they appear to be saying something remarkable.

ὅτι μὲν οὖν τὸ ἑνὶ εἶναι μάλιστά ἐστι κατὰ τὸ ὄνομα ἀφορίζοντι [5] μέτρον τι, καὶ κυριώτατα τοῦ ποσοῦ, εἶτα τοῦ ποιοῦ, φανερόν· ἔσται δὲ τοιοῦτον τὸ μὲν ἂν ᾖ ἀδιαίρετον κατὰ τὸ ποσόν, τὸ δὲ ἂν κατὰ τὸ ποιόν· διόπερ ἀδιαίρετον τὸ ἓν ἢ ἁπλῶς ἢ ᾗ ἕν.

Quod quidem igitur uni esse maxime est secundum nomen quod determinant metrum quoddam, et maxime proprie quantitatis, deinde qualitatis, palam. Erit autem tale hoc quidem si est indivisibile secundum quantitatem, illud autem si secundum qualitatem; propter quod indivisibile est quod unum aut simpliciter aut in quantum unum.

Evidently, then, unity in the strictest sense, if we define it according to the meaning of the word, is a measure, and most properly of quantity, and secondly of quality. And some things will be one if they are indivisible in quantity, and others if they are indivisible in quality; and so that which is one is indivisible, either absolutely or qua one.


## Chapter 2

κατὰ δὲ τὴν οὐσίαν καὶ τὴν φύσιν ζητητέον ποτέρως [10] ἔχει, καθάπερ ἐν τοῖς διαπορήμασιν ἐπήλθομεν τί τὸ ἕν ἐστι καὶ πῶς δεῖ περὶ αὐτοῦ λαβεῖν, πότερον ὡς οὐσίας τινὸς οὔσης αὐτοῦ τοῦ ἑνός, καθάπερ οἵ τε Πυθαγόρειοί φασι πρότερον καὶ Πλάτων ὕστερον, ἢ μᾶλλον ὑπόκειταί τις φύσις καὶ [πῶς] δεῖ γνωριμωτέρως λεχθῆναι καὶ μᾶλλον ὥσπερ οἱ [15] περὶ φύσεως· ἐκείνων γὰρ ὁ μέν τις φιλίαν εἶναί φησι τὸ ἓν ὁ δ᾽ ἀέρα ὁ δὲ τὸ ἄπειρον.

Secundum substantiam vero et naturam quaerendum est utro modo se habeat, quemadmodum in dubitationibus tractavimus quid quod unum est et quomodo oportet de eo suscipere: utrum velut substantia aliqua existente ipso uno, sicut pytagorici dicunt prius et Plato posterius, aut magis supponitur aliqua natura, et quomodo oportet notius dici et magis sicut qui de natura; illorum enim alius amicitiam esse dixit quod unum, alius aerem, alius infinitum.

With regard to the substance and nature of the one we must ask in which of two ways it exists. This is the very question that we reviewed in our discussion of problems, viz. what the one is and how we must conceive of it, whether we must take the one itself as being a substance (as both the Pythagoreans say in earlier and Plato in later times), or there is, rather, an underlying nature and the one should be described more intelligibly and more in the manner of the physical philosophers, of whom one says the one is love, another says it is air, and another the indefinite.

εἰ δὴ μηδὲν τῶν καθόλου δυνατὸν οὐσίαν εἶναι, καθάπερ ἐν τοῖς περὶ οὐσίας καὶ περὶ τοῦ ὄντος εἴρηται λόγοις, οὐδ᾽ αὐτὸ τοῦτο οὐσίαν ὡς ἕν τι παρὰ τὰ πολλὰ δυνατὸν εἶναι (κοινὸν γάρ) ἀλλ᾽ ἢ κατηγόρημα [20] μόνον, δῆλον ὡς οὐδὲ τὸ ἕν· τὸ γὰρ ὂν καὶ τὸ ἓν καθόλου κατηγορεῖται μάλιστα πάντων. ὥστε οὔτε τὰ γένη φύσεις τινὲς καὶ οὐσίαι χωρισταὶ τῶν ἄλλων εἰσίν, οὔτε τὸ ἓν γένος ἐνδέχεται εἶναι διὰ τὰς αὐτὰς αἰτίας δι᾽ ἅσπερ οὐδὲ τὸ ὂν οὐδὲ τὴν οὐσίαν.

Si itaque nullum universalium esse substantiam est possibile, sicut in sermonibus de substantia et de ente dictum est, nec ipsum hoc substantiam ut unum aliquid praeter multa possibile est esse (commune namque) sed aut predicamentum solum, palam quod neque ipsum unum. Nam ens et unum universaliter predicantur maxime de omnibus. Quare nec genera nature quaedam et substantiae separabiles ab aliis sunt, nec unum genus contingit esse propter easdem causas propter quas quidem nec ens nec substantiam.

If, then, no universal can be a substance, as has been said our discussion of substance and being, and if being itself cannot be a substance in the sense of a one apart from the many (for it is common to the many), but is only a predicate, clearly unity also cannot be a substance; for being and unity are the most universal of all predicates. Therefore, on the one hand, genera are not certain entities and substances separable from other things; and on the other hand the one cannot be a genus, for the same reasons for which being and substance cannot be genera.

ἔτι δ᾽ ὁμοίως ἐπὶ πάντων ἀναγκαῖον ἔχειν: [25] λέγεται δ᾽ ἰσαχῶς τὸ ὂν καὶ τὸ ἕν: ὥστ᾽ ἐπείπερ ἐν τοῖς ποιοῖς ἐστί τι τὸ ἓν καί τις φύσις, ὁμοίως δὲ καὶ ἐν τοῖς ποσοῖς, δῆλον ὅτι καὶ ὅλως ζητητέον τί τὸ ἕν, ὥσπερ καὶ τί τὸ ὄν, ὡς οὐχ ἱκανὸν ὅτι τοῦτο αὐτὸ ἡ φύσις αὐτοῦ. ἀλλὰ μὴν ἔν γε χρώμασίν ἐστι τὸ ἓν χρῶμα, οἷον τὸ λευκόν, εἶτα [30] τὰ ἄλλα ἐκ τούτου καὶ τοῦ μέλανος φαίνεται γιγνόμενα, τὸ δὲ μέλαν στέρησις λευκοῦ ὥσπερ καὶ φωτὸς σκότος [τοῦτο δ᾽ ἐστὶ στέρησις φωτός]: ὥστε εἰ τὰ ὄντα ἦν χρώματα, ἦν ἂν ἀριθμός τις τὰ ὄντα, ἀλλὰ τίνων; δῆλον δὴ ὅτι χρωμάτων, καὶ τὸ ἓν ἦν ἄν τι ἕν, οἷον τὸ λευκόν. ὁμοίως δὲ καὶ [35] εἰ μέλη τὰ ὄντα ἦν, ἀριθμὸς ἂν ἦν, διέσεων μέντοι, ἀλλ᾽ οὐκ ἀριθμὸς ἡ οὐσία αὐτῶν: καὶ τὸ ἓν ἦν ἄν τι οὗ ἡ οὐσία οὐ τὸ ἓν ἀλλὰ δίεσις. [1054a] [1] ὁμοίως δὲ καὶ ἐπὶ τῶν φθόγγων στοιχείων ἂν ἦν τὰ ὄντα ἀριθμός, καὶ τὸ ἓν στοιχεῖον φωνῆεν. καὶ εἰ σχήματα εὐθύγραμμα, σχημάτων ἂν ἦν ἀριθμός, καὶ τὸ ἓν τὸ τρίγωνον. ὁ δ᾽ αὐτὸς λόγος καὶ ἐπὶ τῶν ἄλλων [5] γενῶν, ὥστ᾽ εἴπερ καὶ ἐν τοῖς πάθεσι καὶ ἐν τοῖς ποιοῖς καὶ ἐν τοῖς ποσοῖς καὶ ἐν κινήσει ἀριθμῶν ὄντων καὶ ἑνός τινος ἐν ἅπασιν ὅ τε ἀριθμὸς τινῶν καὶ τὸ ἓν τὶ ἕν, ἀλλ᾽ οὐχὶ τοῦτο αὐτὸ ἡ οὐσία, καὶ ἐπὶ τῶν οὐσιῶν ἀνάγκη ὡσαύτως ἔχειν: ὁμοίως γὰρ ἔχει ἐπὶ πάντων. ὅτι μὲν οὖν τὸ ἓν ἐν [10] ἅπαντι γένει ἐστί τις φύσις, καὶ οὐδενὸς τοῦτό γ᾽ αὐτὸ ἡ φύσις τὸ ἕν, φανερόν, ἀλλ᾽ ὥσπερ ἐν χρώμασι χρῶμα ἓν ζητητέον αὐτὸ τὸ ἕν, οὕτω καὶ ἐν οὐσίᾳ οὐσίαν μίαν αὐτὸ τὸ ἕν:

Adhuc autem similiter in omnibus necesse est habere. Dicitur autem equaliter ens et unum. Ergo quoniam in qualitatibus est aliquid quod unum et aliqua natura, et similiter in quantis, palam quod et totaliter quaerendum quid quod unum, quemadmodum et quid ens, tamquam non sufficiens quod hoc ipsum natura ipsius. At vero et in coloribus est aliquid quod color unus, puta albus, deinde alii ex hoc et nigro videntur geniti, nigrum vero privatio albi est, ut et lucis tenebra (haec enim est privatio lucis). Quare si entia essent colores, essent utique numerus quidam entia. Sed quorum? Palam utique quia colorum; et ipsum unum esset utique aliquid unum, puta album. Similiter autem et si melodie entia essent, numerus utique essent, diesum equidem, sed non numerus substantia ipsorum; et ipsum unum esset utique aliquid cuius substantia non ipsum unum sed diesis. Similiter autem et in sonis elementorum utique essent entia numerus, et ipsum unum elementum vocale. Et si figure rectilinee, figurarum utique esset numerus, et ipsum unum trigonum. Eadem autem ratio et in aliis generibus. Quare siquidem in passionibus et in qualitatibus et in quantitatibus et in motu numeris existentibus et uno aliquo in omnibus, numerusque quorundam et ipsum unum aliquid unum, sed non hoc ipsius substantia: et in substantiis necesse est similiter se habere; similiter enim se habet in omnibus. Quod quidem igitur unum in omni genere est quaedam natura, et nullius natura hoc ipsum quod unum, palam. Sed sicut in coloribus colorem unum quaerendum ipsum quod unum, sic et in substantia substantiam unam ipsum unum.

Further, the position must be similar in all the kinds of unity. Now unity has just as many meanings as being; so that since in the sphere of qualities the one is something definite – some particular kind of thing – and similarly in the sphere of quantities, clearly we must in every category ask what the one is, as we must ask what the existent is, since it is not enough to say that its nature is just to be one or existent. But in colours the one is a colour, e.g. white, and then the other colours are observed to be produced out of this and black, and black is the privation of white, as darkness of light. Therefore if all existent things were colours, existent things would have been a number, indeed, but of what? Clearly of colours; and the one would have been a particular one , i.e. white. And similarly if all existing things were tunes, they would have been a number, but a number of quarter-tones, and their essence would not have been number; and the one would have been something whose substance was not to be one but to [54a] be the quarter-tone. And similarly if all existent things had been articulate sounds, they would have been a number of letters, and the one would have been a vowel. And if all existent things were rectilinear figures, they would have been a number of figures, and the one would have been the triangle. And the same argument applies to all other classes. Since, therefore, while there are numbers and a one both in affections and in qualities and in quantities and in movement, in all cases the number is a number of particular things and the one is one something, and its substance is not just to be one, the same must be true of substances also; for it is true of all cases alike. That the one, then, in every class is a definite thing, and in no case is its nature just this, unity, is evident; but as in colours the one-itself which we must seek is one colour, so too in substance the one-itself is one substance.

ὅτι δὲ ταὐτὸ σημαίνει πως τὸ ἓν καὶ τὸ ὄν, δῆλον τῷ τε παρακολουθεῖν ἰσαχῶς ταῖς κατηγορίαις καὶ μὴ εἶναι ἐν [15] μηδεμιᾷ (οἷον οὔτ᾽ ἐν τῇ τί ἐστιν οὔτ᾽ ἐν τῇ ποῖον, ἀλλ᾽ ὁμοίως ἔχει ὥσπερ τὸ ὄν) καὶ τῷ μὴ προσκατηγορεῖσθαι ἕτερόν τι τὸ εἷς ἄνθρωπος τοῦ ἄνθρωπος (ὥσπερ οὐδὲ τὸ εἶναι παρὰ τὸ τί ἢ ποῖον ἢ πόσον) καὶ <τῷ εἶναι τὸ ἑνὶ εἶναι τὸ ἑκάστῳ εἶναι. [20]

Quia vero idem significant aliqualiter unum et ens, palam per assequi equaliter cathegorias  et quia non sunt in nulla  una (ut neque in quid est neque in quale, sed similiter se habet sicut ens) et per hoc quod 'unus homo' non predicat alterum aliquid ab homine (quemadmodum nec esse praeter quid aut quale aut quantum) et uni esse id quod unicuique esse.

That in a sense unity means the same as being is clear from the facts that its meanings correspond to the categories one to one, and it is not comprised within any category (e.g. it is comprised neither in what a thing is nor in quality, but is related to them just as being is); that in one man nothing more is predicated than in man (just as being is nothing apart from substance or quality or quantity); and that to be one is just to be a particular thing.

ἀντίκειται δὲ τὸ ἓν καὶ τὰ πολλὰ κατὰ πλείους τρόπους, ὧν ἕνα τὸ ἓν καὶ τὸ πλῆθος ὡς ἀδιαίρετον καὶ διαιρετόν· τὸ μὲν γὰρ ἢ διῃρημένον ἢ διαιρετὸν πλῆθός τι λέγεται, τὸ δὲ ἀδιαίρετον ἢ μὴ διῃρημένον ἕν.

Opponuntur autem unum et multa secundum plures modos, quorum uno unum et multitudo ut indivisibile et divisibile. Quod quidem enim aut divisum aut divisibile multitudo quaedam dicitur, indivisibile vero aut non divisum unum.

The one and the many are opposed in several ways, of which one is the opposition of the one and plurality as indivisible and divisible; for that which is either divided or divisible is called a plurality, and that which is indivisible or not divided is called one.

ἐπεὶ οὖν αἱ ἀντιθέσεις τετραχῶς, καὶ τούτων κατὰ στέρησιν λέγεται θάτερον, [25] ἐναντία ἂν εἴη καὶ οὔτε ὡς ἀντίφασις οὔτε ὡς τὰ πρός τι λεγόμενα.

Quoniam ergo quatuor modis oppositiones , et horum secundum privationem dicitur alterum, contraria utique erunt et neque ut contradictio neque ut ad aliquid dicta.

Now since opposition is of four kinds, and one of these two terms is privative in meaning, they must be contraries, and neither contradictory nor correlative in meaning.

λέγεται δὲ ἐκ τοῦ ἐναντίου καὶ δηλοῦται τὸ ἕν, ἐκ τοῦ διαιρετοῦ τὸ ἀδιαίρετον, διὰ τὸ μᾶλλον αἰσθητὸν τὸ πλῆθος εἶναι καὶ τὸ διαιρετὸν ἢ τὸ ἀδιαίρετον, ὥστε τῷ λόγῳ πρότερον τὸ πλῆθος τοῦ ἀδιαιρέτου διὰ τὴν αἴσθησιν.

Dicitur autem ex contrario et ostenditur ipsum unum, ex divisibili indivisibile, propter magis sensibilem multitudinem esse et divisibile quam indivisibile. Quare ratione prior multitudo indivisibili propter sensum.

And the one derives its name and its explanation from its contrary, the indivisible from the divisible, because plurality and the divisible is more perceptible than the indivisible, so that in definition plurality is prior to the indivisible, because of the conditions of perception.

ἔστι δὲ τοῦ [30] μὲν ἑνός, ὥσπερ καὶ ἐν τῇ διαιρέσει τῶν ἐναντίων διεγράψαμεν, τὸ ταὐτὸ καὶ ὅμοιον καὶ ἴσον, τοῦ δὲ πλήθους τὸ ἕτερον καὶ ἀνόμοιον καὶ ἄνισον.

Est autem unius quidem, sicut et in divisione contrariorum descripsimus, idem et simile et equale; pluralitatis vero diversum et dissimile et inequale.

To the one belong, as we indicated graphically in our distinction of the contraries, the same and the like and the equal, and to plurality belong the other and the unlike and the unequal.

λεγομένου δὲ τοῦ ταὐτοῦ πολλαχῶς, ἕνα μὲν τρόπον κατ᾽ ἀριθμὸν λέγομεν ἐνίοτε αὐτό, τὸ δ᾽ ἐὰν καὶ λόγῳ καὶ ἀριθμῷ ἓν ᾖ, οἷον [35] σὺ σαυτῷ καὶ τῷ εἴδει καὶ τῇ ὕλῃ ἕν: ἔτι δ᾽ ἐὰν ὁ λόγος ὁ τῆς πρώτης οὐσίας εἷς ᾖ, [1054β] [1] οἷον αἱ ἴσαι γραμμαὶ εὐθεῖαι αἱ αὐταί, καὶ τὰ ἴσα καὶ ἰσογώνια τετράγωνα, καίτοι πλείω: ἀλλ᾽ ἐν τούτοις ἡ ἰσότης ἑνότης.

Dicto vero eodem multipliciter. Uno quidem modo secundum numerum, quod dicimus aliquando ipsum. Hoc autem si ratione et numero unum fuerit, ut tu tibi ipsi et specie et materia unum. Amplius autem si ratio prime substantiae una fuerit, ut equales lineae recte eaedem, et equalia et isogonia tetragona, et etiam plura; sed in hiis equalitas unitas.

The same has several meanings; (1) we sometimes mean the same numerically ; again, (2) we call a thing the same if it is one both in definition and in number, e.g. you are one with yourself both in form and in matter; and again, (3) if the definition of its primary [54b] essence is one; e.g. equal straight lines are the same, and so are equal and equal-angled quadrilaterals; there are many such, but in these equality constitutes unity.

ὅμοια δὲ ἐὰν μὴ ταὐτὰ ἁπλῶς ὄντα, μηδὲ κατὰ τὴν οὐσίαν ἀδιάφορα τὴν [5] συγκειμένην, κατὰ τὸ εἶδος ταὐτὰ ᾖ, ὥσπερ τὸ μεῖζον τετράγωνον τῷ μικρῷ ὅμοιον, καὶ αἱ ἄνισοι εὐθεῖαι: αὗται γὰρ ὅμοιαι μέν, αἱ αὐταὶ δὲ ἁπλῶς οὔ. τὰ δὲ ἐὰν τὸ αὐτὸ εἶδος ἔχοντα, ἐν οἷς τὸ μᾶλλον καὶ ἧττον ἐγγίγνεται, μήτε μᾶλλον ᾖ μήτε ἧττον. τὰ δὲ ἐὰν ᾖ τὸ αὐτὸ πάθος καὶ ἓν [10] τῷ εἴδει, οἷον τὸ λευκόν, σφόδρα καὶ ἧττον, ὅμοιά φασιν εἶναι ὅτι ἓν τὸ εἶδος αὐτῶν. τὰ δὲ ἐὰν πλείω ἔχῃ ταὐτὰ ἢ ἕτερα, ἢ ἁπλῶς ἢ τὰ πρόχειρα, οἷον καττίτερος ἀργύρῳ ἢ λευκόν, χρυσὸς δὲ πυρὶ ἢ ξανθὸν καὶ πυρρόν.

Similia vero si non sint eadem simpliciter entia nec secundum substantiam indifferentia subiectam, secundum speciem eadem sint, ut maius tetragonum minori simile, et inequales recte; hae namque similes quidem, eaedem vero simpliciter non. Alia si eandem speciem habentia, in quibus magis et minus fit, nec magis sint nec minus. Alia si sit eadem passio et una specie, ut album, valde et minus, similia dicunt esse quia una species ipsorum. Alia si plura habent eadem quam altera, aut simpliciter aut quae in promptu, ut stagnum argento vel auro ignis aut rubicundum et rufum .

Things are like if, not being absolutely the same, nor without difference in respect of their concrete substance, they are the same in form; e.g. the larger square is like the smaller, and unequal straight lines are like; they are like, but not absolutely the same. Other things are like, if, having the same form, and being things in which difference of degree is possible, they have no difference of degree. Other things, if they have a quality that is in form one and same – e.g. whiteness – in a greater or less degree, are called like because their form is one. Other things are called like if the qualities they have in common are more numerous than those in which they differ – either the qualities in general or the prominent qualities; e.g. tin is like silver, qua white, and gold is like fire, qua yellow and red.

ὥστε δῆλον ὅτι καὶ τὸ ἕτερον καὶ τὸ ἀνόμοιον πολλαχῶς λέγεται. καὶ [15] τὸ μὲν ἄλλο ἀντικειμένως καὶ τὸ ταὐτό, διὸ ἅπαν πρὸς ἅπαν ἢ ταὐτὸ ἢ ἄλλο: τὸ δ᾽ ἐὰν μὴ καὶ ἡ ὕλη καὶ ὁ λόγος εἷς, διὸ σὺ καὶ ὁ πλησίον ἕτερος: τὸ δὲ τρίτον ὡς τὰ ἐν τοῖς μαθηματικοῖς. τὸ μὲν οὖν ἕτερον ἢ ταὐτὸ διὰ τοῦτο πᾶν πρὸς πᾶν λέγεται, ὅσα λέγεται ἓν καὶ ὄν: οὐ γὰρ [20] ἀντίφασίς ἐστι τοῦ ταὐτοῦ, διὸ οὐ λέγεται ἐπὶ τῶν μὴ ὄντων (τὸ δὲ μὴ ταὐτὸ λέγεται), ἐπὶ δὲ τῶν ὄντων πάντων: ἢ γὰρ ἓν ἢ οὐχ ἓν πέφυχ᾽ ὅσα ὂν καὶ ἕν. τὸ μὲν οὖν ἕτερον καὶ ταὐτὸν οὕτως ἀντίκειται,

Quare palam quod diversum et dissimile multipliciter dicitur. Et hoc quidem aliud opposite et idem, propter quod omne ad omne aut idem aut aliud. Hoc autem si non et materia et ratio una, quapropter et tu et propinquus diversus. Tertium autem ut quae in mathematicis. Diversum quidem igitur aut idem propter hoc omne ad omne dicitur, quaecumque dicuntur unum et ens; non enim contradictio est ipsius eiusdem, quapropter non dicitur in non entibus (non idem autem dicitur). In entibus vero omnibus; aut enim unum aut non unum aptum natum et ens et unum. Diversum quidem igitur et idem ita opponuntur.

Evidently, then, other and unlike also have several meanings. And the other in one sense is the opposite of the same (so that everything is either the same as or other than everything else). In another sense things are other unless both their matter and their definition are one (so that you are other than your neighbour). The other in the third sense is exemplified in the objects of mathematics. Other or the same can therefore be predicated of everything with regard to everything else – but only if the things are one and existent, for other is not the contradictory of the same ; which is why it is not predicated of non-existent things (while not the same is so predicated). It is predicated of all existing things; for everything that is existent and one is by its very nature either one or not one with anything else.

διαφορὰ δὲ καὶ ἑτερότης ἄλλο. τὸ μὲν γὰρ ἕτερον καὶ οὗ ἕτερον οὐκ ἀνάγκη εἶναι τινὶ ἕτερον: [25] πᾶν γὰρ ἢ ἕτερον ἢ ταὐτὸ ὅ τι ἂν ᾖ ὄν: τὸ δὲ διάφορον τινὸς τινὶ διάφορον, ὥστε ἀνάγκη ταὐτό τι εἶναι ᾧ διαφέρουσιν. τοῦτο δὲ τὸ ταὐτὸ γένος ἢ εἶδος: πᾶν γὰρ τὸ διαφέρον διαφέρει ἢ γένει ἢ εἴδει, γένει μὲν ὧν μὴ ἔστι κοινὴ ἡ ὕλη μηδὲ γένεσις εἰς ἄλληλα, οἷον ὅσων ἄλλο σχῆμα τῆς κατηγορίας, [30] εἴδει δὲ ὧν τὸ αὐτὸ γένος (λέγεται δὲ γένος ὃ ἄμφω τὸ αὐτὸ λέγονται κατὰ τὴν οὐσίαν τὰ διάφορα). τὰ δ᾽ ἐναντία διάφορα, καὶ ἡ ἐναντίωσις διαφορά τις.

Differentia vero et diversitas aliud. Diversum enim et a quo est diversum non necesse aliquo esse diversum; omne namque aut diversum aut idem quodcumque est ens. Differens vero ab aliquo aliquo differens, quare necesse ipsum idem aliquid esse quo differunt. Hoc autem ipsum idem: genus aut species. Omne namque differens differt aut genere aut specie. Genere quidem quorum non est communis materia nec generatio ad invicem, ut quorumcumque alia figura cathegorie. Specie vero quorum idem est genus. Dicitur autem genus quod ambo idem dicuntur secundum substantiam differentia. Contraria vero differentia , et contrarietas differentia quaedam.

The other, then, and the same are thus opposed. But difference is not the same as otherness. For the other and that which it is other than need not be other in some definite respect (for everything that is existent is either other or the same), but that which is different is different from some particular thing in some particular respect, so that there must be something identical whereby they differ. And this identical thing is genus or species; for everything that differs differs either in genus or in species, in genus if the things have not their matter in common and are not generated out of each other (i.e. if they belong to different figures of predication), and in species if they have the same genus ( genus meaning that identical thing which is essentially predicated of both the different things). Contraries are different, and contrariety is a kind of difference.

ὅτι δὲ καλῶς τοῦτο ὑποτιθέμεθα, δῆλον ἐκ τῆς ἐπαγωγῆς: πάντα γὰρ διαφέροντα φαίνεται καὶ ταῦτα, οὐ μόνον ἕτερα [35] ὄντα ἀλλὰ τὰ μὲν τὸ γένος ἕτερα τὰ δ᾽ ἐν τῇ αὐτῇ συστοιχίᾳ τῆς κατηγορίας, [1055α] [1] ὥστ᾽ ἐν ταὐτῷ γένει καὶ ταὐτὰ τῷ γένει. διώρισται δ᾽ ἐν ἄλλοις ποῖα τῷ γένει ταὐτὰ ἢ ἕτερα.

Quod autem hoc bene supponimus, palam ex inductione. Omnia enim differentia videntur et haec, non solum diversa entia sed haec quidem genere diversa, haec autem in eadem coelementatione cathegorie, quare in eodem genere et eadem specie. Determinatum autem est in aliis quae sunt genere eadem aut diversa.

That we are right in this supposition is shown by induction. For all of these too are seen to be different; they are not merely other, but some are other in genus, [55a] and others are in the same line of predication, and therefore in the same genus, and the same in genus. We have distinguished elsewhere what sort of things are the same or other in genus.

*Chapter* 4

ἐπεὶ δὲ διαφέρειν ἐνδέχεται ἀλλήλων τὰ διαφέροντα πλεῖον καὶ ἔλαττον, ἔστι τις καὶ μεγίστη διαφορά,

Quoniam autem differre contingit ab invicem differentia plus et minus, est aliqua et maxima differentia,

Since things which differ may differ from one another more or less, there is also a greatest difference,

καὶ ταύτην [5] λέγω ἐναντίωσιν. ὅτι δ᾽ ἡ μεγίστη ἐστὶ διαφορά, δῆλον ἐκ τῆς ἐπαγωγῆς. τὰ μὲν γὰρ γένει διαφέροντα οὐκ ἔχει ὁδὸν εἰς ἄλληλα, ἀλλ᾽ ἀπέχει πλέον καὶ ἀσύμβλητα· τοῖς δ᾽ εἴδει διαφέρουσιν αἱ γενέσεις ἐκ τῶν ἐναντίων εἰσὶν ὡς ἐσχάτων, τὸ δὲ τῶν ἐσχάτων διάστημα μέγιστον, ὥστε [10] καὶ τὸ τῶν ἐναντίων.

et hanc dico contrarietatem. Quia vero maxima est differentia, palam ex inductione. Genere namque differentia non habent viam in invicem, sed distant magis et inconferibiliter. Differentibus vero specie generationes ex contrariis sunt ut ultimis, ultimorum vero distantia maxima est; quare et quae contrariorum.

and this I call contrariety. That contrariety is the greatest difference is made clear by induction. For things which differ in genus have no way to one another, but are too far distant and are not comparable; and for things that differ in species the extremes from which generation takes place are the contraries, and the distance between extremes – and therefore that between the contraries – is the greatest.

ἀλλὰ μὴν τό γε μέγιστον ἐν ἑκάστῳ γένει τέλειον. μέγιστόν τε γὰρ οὗ μὴ ἔστιν ὑπερβολή, καὶ τέλειον οὗ μὴ ἔστιν ἔξω λαβεῖν τι δυνατόν· τέλος γὰρ ἔχει ἡ τελεία διαφορά (ὥσπερ καὶ τἆλλα τῷ τέλος ἔχειν λέγεται τέλεια), τοῦ δὲ τέλους οὐθὲν ἔξω· ἔσχατον γὰρ ἐν παντὶ [15] καὶ περιέχει, διὸ οὐδὲν ἔξω τοῦ τέλους, οὐδὲ προσδεῖται οὐδενὸς τὸ τέλειον. ὅτι μὲν οὖν ἡ ἐναντιότης ἐστὶ διαφορὰ τέλειος, ἐκ τούτων δῆλον· πολλαχῶς δὲ λεγομένων τῶν ἐναντίων, ἀκολουθήσει τὸ τελείως οὕτως ὡς ἂν καὶ τὸ ἐναντίοις εἶναι ὑπάρχῃ αὐτοῖς.

At vero maximum in unoquoque genere perfectum. Maximum enim cuius non est excessus, et perfectum cuius non est adhuc extra sumere aliquid possibile; finem enim habet perfecta differentia, sicut et alia eo quod finem habeant dicuntur perfecta. Nihil autem extra finem; ultimum enim in omni et continet. Propter quod nihil extra finem, nec eget aliquo quod perfectum . Quod quidem igitur contrarietas est differentia perfecta, ex hiis palam. Multipliciter autem dictis contrariis, sequetur quod perfecte sic ut utique et quod est contrariis esse extiterit ipsis.

But surely that which is greatest in each class is complete. For that is greatest which cannot be exceeded, and that is complete beyond which nothing can be found. For the complete difference marks the end of a series (just as the other things which are called complete are so called because they have attained an end), and beyond the end there is nothing; for in everything it is the extreme and includes all else, and therefore there is nothing beyond the end, and the complete needs nothing further. From this, then, it is clear that contrariety is complete difference; and as contraries are so called in several senses, their modes of completeness will answer to the various modes of contrariety which attach to the contraries.

τούτων δὲ ὄντων φανερὸν ὅτι οὐκ ἐνδέχεται [20] ἑνὶ πλείω ἐναντία εἶναι (οὔτε γὰρ τοῦ ἐσχάτου ἐσχατώτερον εἴη ἄν τι, οὔτε τοῦ ἑνὸς διαστήματος πλείω δυοῖν ἔσχατα),

Hiis autem entibus palam quod non contingit plura uni contraria esse; nec enim ultimo ulterius erit utique aliquid, nec distantie unius plura sunt quam duo ultima.

This being so, it is clear that one thing have more than one contrary (for neither can there be anything more extreme than the extreme, nor can there be more than two extremes for the one interval),

ὅλως τε εἰ ἔστιν ἡ ἐναντιότης διαφορά, ἡ δὲ διαφορὰ δυοῖν, ὥστε καὶ ἡ τέλειος.

Totaliter autem si est contrarietas differentia, differentia vero duorum, quare et perfecta.

and, to put the matter generally, this is clear if contrariety is a difference, and if difference, and therefore also the complete difference, must be between two things.

ἀνάγκη δὲ καὶ τοὺς ἄλλους ὅρους ἀληθεῖς εἶναι τῶν ἐναντίων. καὶ γὰρ πλεῖστον διαφέρει ἡ τέλειος [25] διαφορά (τῶν τε γὰρ γένει διαφερόντων οὐκ ἔστιν ἐξωτέρω λαβεῖν καὶ τῶν εἴδει· δέδεικται γὰρ ὅτι πρὸς τὰ ἔξω τοῦ γένους οὐκ ἔστι διαφορά, τούτων δ᾽ αὕτη μεγίστη), καὶ τὰ ἐν ταὐτῷ γένει πλεῖστον διαφέροντα ἐναντία (μεγίστη γὰρ διαφορὰ τούτων ἡ τέλειος), καὶ τὰ ἐν τῷ αὐτῷ δεκτικῷ πλεῖστον [30] διαφέροντα ἐναντία (ἡ γὰρ ὕλη ἡ αὐτὴ τοῖς ἐναντίοις) καὶ τὰ ὑπὸ τὴν αὐτὴν δύναμιν πλεῖστον διαφέροντα (καὶ γὰρ ἡ ἐπιστήμη περὶ ἓν γένος ἡ μία): ἐν οἷς ἡ τελεία διαφορὰ μεγίστη.

Necesse autem et alios terminos esse veros contrariorum. Et enim plurimum differt perfecta differentia; genere namque differentibus non est magis extra accipere et hiis quae specie; ostensum est enim quia ad ea quae sunt extra genus non est differentia, horum autem haec maxima. Et in eodem genere plurimum differentia contraria ; maxima namque differentia horum quae perfecta. Et quae in eodem susceptivo plurimum differentia; eadem enim est materia contrariis. Et quae sub eadem potentia plurimum differentia; et enim scientia circa unum genus quae una, in quibus perfecta differentia maxima.

And the other commonly accepted definitions of contraries are also necessarily true. For not only is (1) the complete difference the greatest difference (for we can get no difference beyond it of things differing either in genus or in species; for it has been shown that there is no difference between anything and the things outside its genus, and among the things which differ in species the complete difference is the greatest); but also (2) the things in the same genus which differ most are contrary (for the complete difference is the greatest difference between species of the same genus); and (3) the things in the same receptive material which differ most are contrary (for the matter is the same for contraries); and (4) of the things which fall under the same faculty the most different are contrary (for one science deals with one class of things, and in these the complete difference is the greatest).

πρώτη δὲ ἐναντίωσις ἕξις καὶ στέρησίς ἐστιν: οὐ πᾶσα δὲ στέρησις (πολλαχῶς γὰρ λέγεται ἡ στέρησις) [35] ἀλλ᾽ ἥτις ἂν τελεία ᾖ.

Prima vero contrarietas habitus et privatio est; sed non omnis privatio (multipliciter enim dicitur privatio) sed quaecumquae perfecta fuerit.

The primary contrariety is that between positive state and privation – not every privation, however (for privation has several meanings), but that which is complete.

τὰ δ᾽ ἄλλα ἐναντία κατὰ ταῦτα λεχθήσεται, τὰ μὲν τῷ ἔχειν τὰ δὲ τῷ ποιεῖν ἢ ποιητικὰ εἶναι τὰ δὲ τῷ λήψεις εἶναι καὶ ἀποβολαὶ τούτων ἢ ἄλλων ἐναντίων.

Alia autem contraria secundum haec dicentur, haec quidem per habere illa vero per facere aut factiva esse, alia autem per acceptiones esse et abiectiones horum aut aliorum contrariorum.

And the other contraries must be called so with reference to these, some because they possess these, others because they produce or tend to produce them, others because they are acquisitions or losses of these or of other contraries.

εἰ δὴ ἀντίκειται μὲν ἀντίφασις καὶ στέρησις καὶ ἐναντιότης καὶ τὰ πρός τι, [1055β] [1] τούτων δὲ πρῶτον ἀντίφασις, ἀντιφάσεως δὲ μηδέν ἐστι μεταξύ, τῶν δὲ ἐναντίων ἐνδέχεται, ὅτι μὲν οὐ ταὐτὸν ἀντίφασις καὶ τἀναντία δῆλον:

Si igitur opponuntur contradictio et privatio et contrarietas et ad aliquid, horum autem primum contradictio, contradictionis autem nihil est medium, contrariorum autem contingit: quod quidem non idem contradictio et contraria, palam.

Now if the kinds of opposition are contradiction and priva[55b]tion and contrariety and relation, and of these the first is contradiction, and contradiction admits of no intermediate, while contraries admit of one, clearly contradiction and contrariety are not the same.

ἡ δὲ στέρησις ἀντίφασίς τίς ἐστιν· ἢ γὰρ τὸ ἀδύνατον ὅλως ἔχειν, [5] ἢ ὃ ἂν πεφυκὸς ἔχειν μὴ ἔχῃ, ἐστέρηται ἢ ὅλως ἢ πὼς ἀφορισθέν (πολλαχῶς γὰρ ἤδη τοῦτο λέγομεν, ὥσπερ διῄρηται ἡμῖν ἐν ἄλλοις), ὥστ᾽ ἐστὶν ἡ στέρησις ἀντίφασίς τις ἢ ἀδυναμία διορισθεῖσα ἢ συνειλημμένη τῷ δεκτικῷ· διὸ ἀντιφάσεως μὲν οὐκ ἔστι μεταξύ, στερήσεως δέ τινος ἔστιν· ἴσον [10] μὲν γὰρ ἢ οὐκ ἴσον πᾶν, ἴσον δ᾽ ἢ ἄνισον οὐ πᾶν, ἀλλ᾽ εἴπερ, μόνον ἐν τῷ δεκτικῷ τοῦ ἴσου.

Privatio vero contradictio quaedam est. Aut enim quod impossibile est totaliter habere, aut si quod aptum natum habere non habeat, privatum est aut totaliter aut aliqualiter determinatum ; multipliciter enim iam hoc dicimus, sicut divisum est a nobis in aliis. Ergo privatio quaedam est contradictio aut impotentia determinata aut concepta cum susceptivo. Quapropter contradictionis quidem non est medium, sed privationis alicuius est; equale namque aut non equale omne, equale vero aut inequale non omne, nisi solum in susceptivo equalitatis.

But privation is a kind of contradiction; for what suffers privation, either in general or in some determinate way, either that which is quite incapable of having some attribute or that which, being of such a nature as to have it, has it not; here we have already a variety of meanings, which have been distinguished elsewhere. Privation, therefore, is a contradiction or incapacity which is determinate or taken along with the receptive material. This is the reason why, while contradiction does not admit of an intermediate, privation sometimes does; for everything is equal or not equal, but not everything is equal or unequal, or if it is, it is only within the sphere of that which is receptive of equality.

εἰ δὴ αἱ γενέσεις τῇ ὕλῃ ἐκ τῶν ἐναντίων, γίγνονται δὲ ἢ ἐκ τοῦ εἴδους καὶ τῆς τοῦ εἴδους ἕξεως ἢ ἐκ στερήσεώς τινος τοῦ εἴδους καὶ τῆς μορφῆς, δῆλον ὅτι ἡ μὲν ἐναντίωσις στέρησις ἂν εἴη πᾶσα,

Si itaque generationes ipsi materie ex contrariis, fiuntque aut ex specie et ex speciei habitu aut privatione aliqua speciei et forme, palam quia contrarietas privatio quaedam utique erit omnis.

If, then, the comings-to-be which happen to the matter start from the contraries, and proceed either from the form and the possession of the form or from a privation of the form or shape, clearly all contrariety must be privation,

ἡ δὲ στέρησις [15] ἴσως οὐ πᾶσα ἐναντιότης (αἴτιον δ᾽ ὅτι πολλαχῶς ἐνδέχεται ἐστερῆσθαι τὸ ἐστερημένον)· ἐξ ὧν γὰρ αἱ μεταβολαὶ ἐσχάτων, ἐναντία ταῦτα.

Privatio vero non omnis forsan contrarietas. Causa vero quia multipliciter contingit privari privatum; ex quibus enim permutationes extremis, contraria haec .

but presumably not all privation is contrariety (the reason being that that has suffered privation may have suffered it in several ways); for it is only the extremes from which changes proceed that are contraries.

φανεϱὸν δὲ καὶ διὰ τῆς ἐπαγωγῆς. πᾶσα γὰϱ ἐναντίωσις ἔχει στέϱησιν θάτεϱον τῶν ἐναντίων, ἀλλ᾽ οὐχ ὁμοίως πάντα: ἀνισότης μὲν γὰϱ ἰσότητος ἀνομοιότης [20] δὲ ὁμοιότητος κακία δὲ ἀϱετῆς,

Palam autem et per inductionem. Omnis enim contrarietas habet privationem alterius contrariorum, sed non similiter omnia; nam inequalitas equalitatis et dissimilitudo similitudinis et malitia virtutis.

And this is obvious also by induction. For every contrariety involves, as one of its terms, a privation, but not all cases are alike; inequality is the privation of equality and unlikeness of likeness, and on the other hand vice is the privation of virtue.

διαφέϱει δὲ ὥσπεϱ εἴϱηται: τὸ μὲν γὰϱ ἐὰν μόνον ᾖ ἐστεϱημένον, τὸ δ᾽ ἐὰν ᾖ ποτὲ ᾖ ἔν τινι, οἷον ἂν ἐν ἡλικίᾳ τινὶ ᾖ τῷ κυϱίῳ, ᾖ πάντῃ: διὸ τῶν μὲν ἔστι μεταξύ, καὶ ἔστιν οὔτε ἀγαθὸς ἄνθϱωπος οὔτε κακός, τῶν δὲ οὐκ ἔστιν, ἀλλ᾽ ἀνάγκη εἶναι ᾖ πεϱιττὸν ᾖ [25] ἄϱτιον. ἔτι τὰ μὲν ἔχει τὸ ὑποκείμενον ὡϱισμένον, τὰ δ᾽ οὔ. ὥστε φανεϱὸν ὅτι ἀεὶ θάτεϱον τῶν ἐναντίων λέγεται κατὰ στέϱησιν:

Differt autem ut dictum est: hoc quidem enim si solum sit privatum, hoc autem si est aut quando aut in quo, ut si in etate aliqua aut principali aut omni. Quapropter horum quidem est medium, et est neque bonus homo neque malus, aliorum vero non est, sed necesse esse aut parem aut imparem. amplius alia quidem habent subiectum determinatum, alia autem non. Quare palam quia semper alterum contrariorum dicitur secundum privationem.

But the cases differ in a way already described; in one case we mean simply that the thing has suffered privation, in another case that it has done so either at a certain time or in a certain part (e.g. at a certain age or in the dominant part), or throughout. This is why in some cases there is a mean (there are men who are neither good nor bad), and in others there is not (a number must be either odd or even). Further, some contraries have their subject defined, others have not. Therefore it is evident that one of the contraries is always privative;

ἀπόχϱη δὲ κἂν τὰ πϱῶτα καὶ τὰ γένη τῶν ἐναντίων, οἷον τὸ ἓν καὶ τὰ πολλά: τὰ γὰϱ ἄλλα εἰς ταῦτα ἀνάγεται. [30]

Sufficit autem et si prima et genera contrariorum, puta unum et multa; alia namque ad haec reducuntur.

but it is enough if this is true of the first – i.e. the generic – contraries, e.g. the one and the many; for the others can be reduced to these.


## Chapter 5

ἐπεὶ δὲ ἓν ἑνὶ ἐναντίον, ἀπορήσειεν ἄν τις πῶς ἀντίκειται τὸ ἓν καὶ τὰ πολλά, καὶ τὸ ἴσον τῷ μεγάλῳ καὶ τῷ μικρῷ.

Quoniam autem unum uni contrarium est, dubitabit aliquis quomodo opponuntur unum et multa, et equale magno et parvo.

Since one thing has one contrary, we might raise the question how the one is opposed to the many, and the equal to the great and the small.

εἰ γὰρ τὸ πότερον ἀεὶ ἐν ἀντιθέσει λέγομεν, οἷον πότερον λευκὸν ἢ μέλαν, καὶ πότερον λευκὸν ἢ οὐ λευκόν (πότερον δὲ ἄνθρωπος ἢ λευκὸν οὐ λέγομεν, ἐὰν μὴ ἐξ [35] ὑποθέσεως καὶ ζητοῦντες οἷον πότερον ἦλθε Κλέων ἢ Σωκράτης—ἀλλ᾽ οὐκ ἀνάγκη ἐν οὐδενὶ γένει τοῦτο: ἀλλὰ καὶ τοῦτο ἐκεῖθεν ἐλήλυθεν: τὰ γὰρ ἀντικείμενα μόνα οὐκ ἐνδέχεται ἅμα ὑπάρχειν, ᾧ καὶ ἐνταῦθα χρῆται ἐν τῷ πότερος ἦλθεν: [1056α] [1] εἰ γὰρ ἅμα ἐνεδέχετο, γελοῖον τὸ ἐρώτημα: εἰ δέ, καὶ οὕτως ὁμοίως ἐμπίπτει εἰς ἀντίθεσιν, εἰς τὸ ἓν ἢ πολλά, οἷον πότερον ἀμφότεροι ἦλθον ἢ ἅτερος):

'Utrum' enim semper in oppositione dicimus, ut utrum album aut nigrum, et utrum album aut non album. utrum vero homo aut album non dicimus, nisi ex suppositione, et quaerentes puta utrum venit cleon aut Socrates — Sed non necesse in neque uno genere hoc. Sed et hoc inde venit; nam opposita sola non contingit simul existere, quo et hic utitur in eo quod uter venit; si enim simul contingeret, ridiculosa foret interrogatio. Si vero, et ita similiter incidet in oppositionem, in id quod unum aut multa, ut utrum ambo venerunt aut alter.

For if we used the word whether only in an antithesis such as whether it is white or black , or whether it is white or not white (we do not ask whether it is a man or white ), unless we are proceeding on a prior assumption and asking something such as whether it was Cleon or Socrates that came as this is not a necessary disjunction in any class of things; yet even this is an extension from the case of opposites; for opposites alone cannot be present together; and we assume this incompatibility here too in asking which of the two [56a] came; for if they might both have come, the question would have been absurd; but if they might, even so this falls just as much into an antithesis, that of the one or many , i.e. whether both came or one of the two.

εἰ δὴ ἐν τοῖς ἀντικειμένοις ἀεὶ τοῦ ποτέρου ἡ ζήτησις, λέγεται δὲ πότερον μεῖζον [5] ἢ ἔλαττον ἢ ἴσον, τίς ἐστιν ἡ ἀντίθεσις πρὸς ταῦτα τοῦ ἴσου; οὔτε γὰρ θατέρῳ μόνῳ ἐναντίον οὔτ᾽ ἀμφοῖν· τί γὰρ μᾶλλον τῷ μείζονι ἢ τῷ ἐλάττονι;

Si itaque in oppositis semper est ipsius 'utrum' interrogatio, dicitur autem utrum maius aut minus aut equale, aliqua est oppositio ad haec equalis. Non enim alteri soli contrarium nec ambobus; quid enim magis aut maiori aut minori?

If, then, the question whether is always concerned with opposites, and we can ask whether it is greater or less or equal , what is the opposition of the equal to the other two? It is not contrary either to one alone or to both; for why should it be contrary to the greater rather than to the less?

ἔτι τῷ ἀνίσῳ ἐναντίον τὸ ἴσον, ὥστε πλείοσιν ἔσται ἢ ἑνί. εἰ δὲ τὸ ἄνισον σημαίνει τὸ αὐτὸ ἅμα ἀμφοῖν, εἴη μὲν ἂν ἀντικείμενον ἀμφοῖν

Amplius inequali contrarium est equale. Quare in pluribus erit aut uno. Si vero inequale significat idem simul amborum, erit quidem utique oppositum ambobus.

Further, the equal is contrary to the unequal. Therefore if it is contrary to the greater and the less, it will be contrary to more things than one. But if the unequal means the same as both the greater and the less together, the equal will be opposite to both

[10] (καὶ ἡ ἀπορία βοηθεῖ τοῖς φάσκουσι τὸ ἄνισον δυάδα εἶναι),

Et dubitatio iuvat dicentes inequale dualitatem esse.

(and the difficulty supports those who say the unequal is a two ),

ἀλλὰ συμβαίνει ἓν δυοῖν ἐναντίον· ὅπερ ἀδύνατον.

Sed accidit unum duobus contrarium, quod est impossibile.

but it follows that one thing is contrary to two others, which is impossible.

ἔτι τὸ μὲν ἴσον μεταξὺ φαίνεται μεγάλου καὶ μικροῦ, ἐναντίωσις δὲ μεταξὺ οὐδεμία οὔτε φαίνεται οὔτε ἐκ τοῦ ὁρισμοῦ δυνατόν· οὐ γὰρ ἂν εἴη τελεία μεταξύ τινος οὖσα, ἀλλὰ μᾶλλον [15] ἔχει ἀεὶ ἑαυτῆς τι μεταξύ. λείπεται δὴ ἢ ὡς ἀπόφασιν ἀντικεῖσθαι ἢ ὡς στέρησιν.

Amplius equale quidem medium videtur esse magni et parui. Contrariatio autem intermedia neque videtur nec ex diffinitione possibile ; non enim utique erit perfecta mediatio alicuius existens, sed magis habet semper suimet aliquod medium.

Again, the equal is evidently intermediate between the great and the small, but no contrariety is either observed to be intermediate, or, from its definition, can be so; for it would not be complete if it were intermediate between any two things, but rather it always has something intermediate between its own terms.

θατέρου μὲν δὴ οὐκ ἐνδέχεται (τί γὰρ μᾶλλον τοῦ μεγάλου ἢ μικροῦ;): ἀμφοῖν ἄρα ἀπόφασις στερητική, διὸ καὶ πρὸς ἀμφότερα τὸ πότερον λέγεται, πρὸς δὲ θάτερον οὔ (οἷον πότερον μεῖζον ἢ ἴσον, ἢ πότερον ἴσον ἢ [20] ἔλαττον), ἀλλ᾽ ἀεὶ τρία.

Restat igitur aut ut negationem opponi aut ut privationem. Alterius quidem itaque non contingit; quid enim magis magni aut parvi? Amborum igitur negatio privativa . Quapropter ad ambo \jtrum' dicitur, ad alterum vero non (ut utrum maius aut equale, aut utrum equale aut minus), sed semper tria.

It remains, then, that it is opposed either as negation or as privation. It cannot be the negation or privation of one of the two; for why of the great rather than of the small? It is, then, the privative negation of both. This is why whether is said with reference to both, not to one of the two (e.g. whether it is greater or equal or whether it is equal or less ); there are always three cases.

οὐ στέρησις δὲ ἐξ ἀνάγκης· οὐ γὰρ πᾶν ἴσον ὃ μὴ μεῖζον ἢ ἔλαττον, ἀλλ᾽ ἐν οἷς πέφυκεν ἐκεῖνα. ἔστι δὴ τὸ ἴσον τὸ μήτε μέγα μήτε μικρόν, πεφυκὸς δὲ ἢ μέγα ἢ μικρὸν εἶναι· καὶ ἀντίκειται ἀμφοῖν ὡς ἀπόφασις στερητική,

Non privatio autem ex necessitate; non enim omne equale quod non maius aut minus, sed in quibus aptum natum est esse. Est itaque equale quod neque magnum neque parvum, aptum natum magnum aut parvum esse. Et opponitur ambobus ut negatio privativa.

But it is not a necessary privation; for not everything which is not greater or less is equal, but only the things which are of such a nature as to have these attributes. The equal, then, is that which is neither great nor small but is naturally fitted to be either great or small; and it is opposed to both as a privative negation

διὸ καὶ μεταξύ ἐστιν. καὶ τὸ μήτε [25] ἀγαθὸν μήτε κακὸν ἀντίκειται ἀμφοῖν, ἀλλ᾽ ἀνώνυμον· πολλαχῶς γὰρ λέγεται ἑκάτερον καὶ οὐκ ἔστιν ἓν τὸ δεκτικόν, ἀλλὰ μᾶλλον τὸ μήτε λευκὸν μήτε μέλαν. ἐν δὲ οὐδὲ τοῦτο λέγεται, ἀλλ᾽ ὡρισμένα πως ἐφ᾽ ὧν λέγεται στερητικῶς ἡ ἀπόφασις αὕτη· ἀνάγκη γὰρ ἢ φαιὸν ἢ [30] ὠχρὸν εἶναι ἢ τοιοῦτόν τι ἄλλο.

Quapropter et medium est. Et quod neque malum neque bonum opponitur ambobus, sed innominatum; multipliciter enim dicitur utrumque et non est unum susceptivum. Sed magis quod neque album neque nigrum. Unum vero non hoc

dicitur, sed determinati aliqualiter colores in quibus dicitur privative negatio haec; nam necesse aut pallidum aut rubeum esse aut tale aliquid aliud.

(and therefore is also intermediate). And that which is neither good nor bad is opposed to both, but has no name; for each of these has several meanings and the recipient subject is not one; but that which is neither white nor black has more claim to unity. Yet even this has not one name, though the colours of which this negation is privatively predicated are in a way limited; for they must be either grey or yellow or something else of the kind.

ὥστε οὐκ ὀρθῶς ἐπιτιμῶσιν οἱ νομίζοντες ὁμοίως λέγεσθαι πάντα, ὥστε ἔσεσθαι ὑποδήματος καὶ χειρὸς μεταξὺ τὸ μήτε ὑπόδημα μήτε χεῖρα, ἐπείπερ καὶ τὸ μήτε ἀγαθὸν μήτε κακὸν τοῦ ἀγαθοῦ καὶ τοῦ κακοῦ, ὡς πάντων ἐσομένου τινὸς μεταξύ. οὐκ ἀνάγκη [35] δὲ τοῦτο συμβαίνειν. ἡ μὲν γὰρ ἀντικειμένων συναπόφασίς ἐστιν ὧν ἔστι μεταξύ τι καὶ διάστημά τι πέφυκεν εἶναι· [1056β] [1] τῶν δ᾽ οὐκ ἔστι διαφορά· ἐν ἄλλῳ γὰρ γένει ὧν αἱ συναποφάσεις, ὥστ᾽ οὐχ ἓν τὸ ὑποκείμενον.

Quare non recte increpant opinantes similiter dici omnia, ut sit calcei et manus medium quod neque calceus neque manus, quoniam quidem et quod neque bonum neque malum boni et mali, tamquam omnium futuro aliquo medio. Non necesse autem hoc accidere. Haec quidem enim oppositorum connegatio est quo rum est medium ahquod et distantia aliqua nata est esse, horum autem non est differentia; nam in alio genere quorum connegationes, quare non unum quod subicitur.

Therefore it is an incorrect criticism that is passed by those who think that all such phrases are used in the same way, so that that which is neither a shoe nor a hand would be intermediate between a shoe and a hand, since that which is neither good nor bad is intermediate between the good and the bad – as if there must be an intermediate in all cases. But this does not necessarily follow. For the one phrase is a joint denial of opposites between which there is an intermediate and a certain natural [56b] interval; but between the other two there is no difference ; for the things, the denials of which are combined, belong to different classes, so that the substratum is not one.

## Chapter 6

ὁμοίως δὲ καὶ περὶ τοῦ ἑνὸς καὶ τῶν πολλῶν ἀπορήσειεν ἄν τις. εἰ γὰρ τὰ πολλὰ τῷ ἑνὶ ἁπλῶς ἀντίκειται, [5] συμβαίνει ἔνια ἀδύνατα.

Similiter autem et de uno et multis dubitabit utique aliquis. Nam si multa simpliciter uni opponuntur, accidunt quaedam impossibilia .

We might raise similar questions about the one and the many. For if the many are absolutely opposed to the one, certain impossible results follow.

τὸ γὰρ ἓν ὀλίγον ἢ ὀλίγα ἔσται· τὰ γὰρ πολλὰ καὶ τοῖς ὀλίγοις ἀντίκειται. ἔτι τὰ δύο πολλά, εἴπερ τὸ διπλάσιον πολλαπλάσιον λέγεται δὲ κατὰ τὰ δύο· ὥστε τὸ ἓν ὀλίγον· πρὸς τί γὰρ πολλὰ τὰ δύο εἰ μὴ πρὸς ἕν τε καὶ τὸ ὀλίγον; οὐθὲν γάρ ἐστιν ἔλαττον.

Nam unum paucum aut pauca erit; nam multa et paucis opponuntur. Amplius ipsa duo sunt multa, si duplex multiplex, dicitur autem secundum duo. Quare unum paucum; ad quid enim sunt multa ipsa duo nisi ad unum et paucum? Nihil enim est minus.

One will then be few, whether few be treated here as singular or plural; for the many are opposed also to the few. Further, two will be many, since the double is multiple and double derives its meaning from two ; therefore one will be few; for what is that in comparison with which two are many, except one, which must therefore be few? For there is nothing fewer.

[10] ἔτι εἰ ὡς ἐν μήκει τὸ μακρὸν καὶ βραχύ, οὕτως ἐν πλήθει τὸ πολὺ καὶ ὀλίγον, καὶ ὃ ἂν ᾖ πολὺ καὶ πολλά, καὶ τὰ πολλὰ πολύ (εἰ μή τι ἄρα διαφέρει ἐν συνεχεῖ εὐορίστῳ), τὸ ὀλίγον πλῆθός τι ἔσται. ὥστε τὸ ἓν πλῆθός τι, εἴπερ καὶ ὀλίγον· τοῦτο δ᾽ ἀνάγκη, εἰ τὰ δύο πολλά.

Amplius si ut in longitudine productum et breue, sic in multitudine multum et paucum, et quodcumque fuerit multum et multa, et multa multum (si non aliquid forte differat in continuo bene terminabili): paucum multitudo quaedam erit. Quare unum multitudo quaedam est, siquidem et paucum. Hoc autem necesse, si duo sunt multa.

Further, if the much and the little are in plurality what the long and the short are in length, and whatever is much is also many, and the many are much (unless, indeed, there is a difference in the case of an easily-bounded continuum), the little (or few) will be a plurality. Therefore one is a plurality if it is few; and this it must be, if two are many.

[15] ἴσως τὰ πολλὰ λέγεται μέν πως καὶ [τὸ] πολύ, ἀλλ᾽ ὡς διαφέρον, οἷον ὕδωρ πολύ, πολλὰ δ᾽ οὔ. ἀλλ᾽ ὅσα διαιρετά, ἐν τούτοις λέγεται,

Sed forsan multa dicuntur quidem ut et multum, sed ut differens; velut ydor id est aqua multum, multa autem non. Sed quaecumque divisa, in hiis dicitur.

But perhaps, while the many are in a sense said to be also much , it is with a difference; e.g. water is much but not many. But many is applied to the things that are divisible;

ἕνα μὲν τρόπον ἐὰν ᾖ πλῆθος ἔχον ὑπεροχὴν ἢ ἁπλῶς ἢ πρός τι (καὶ τὸ ὀλίγον ὡσαύτως πλῆθος ἔχον ἔλλειψιν), τὸ δὲ ὡς ἀριθμός, ὃ καὶ ἀντίκειται τῷ ἑνὶ [20] μόνον. οὕτως γὰρ λέγομεν ἓν ἢ πολλά, ὥσπερ εἴ τις εἴποι ἓν καὶ ἕνα ἢ λευκὸν καὶ λευκά, καὶ τὰ μεμετρημένα πρὸς τὸ μέτρον [καὶ τὸ μετρητόν]· οὕτως καὶ τὰ πολλαπλάσια λέγεται· πολλὰ γὰρ ἕκαστος ὁ ἀριθμὸς ὅτι ἕνα καὶ ὅτι μετρητὸς ἑνὶ ἕκαστος, καὶ ὡς τὸ ἀντικείμενον τῷ ἑνί, οὐ τῷ [25] ὀλίγῳ. οὕτω μὲν οὖν ἐστὶ πολλὰ καὶ τὰ δύο, ὡς δὲ πλῆθος ἔχον ὑπεροχὴν ἢ πρός τι ἢ ἁπλῶς οὐκ ἔστιν, ἀλλὰ πρῶτον. ὀλίγα δ᾽ ἁπλῶς τὰ δύο· πλῆθος γάρ ἐστιν ἔλλειψιν ἔχον πρῶτον

Uno quidem modo si fuerit multitudo habens excedentiam aut simpliciter aut ad aliquid; et paucum similiter multitudo defectum habens. Hoc autem ut numerus, quod et opponitur uni solum. Ita enim dicimus unum aut multa, ut si quis dicat unum et una aut album et alba, et mensurata ad metrum et mensurabile. Sic et multiplicia dicuntur. Multa enim unusquisque numerus quia unum et quia mensurabilis uno unusquisque, et ut quod opponitur uni, non pauco. Sic igitur sunt multa et ipsa duo, ut autem multitudo habens excedentiam aut ad aliquid aut simpliciter non sunt. Sed primum pauca simpliciter ipsa duo; multitudo enim est defectum habens prima.

in the one sense it means a plurality which is excessive either absolutely or relatively (while few is similarly a plurality which is deficient), and in another sense it means number, in which sense alone it is opposed to the one. For we say one or many , just as if one were to say one and ones or white thing and white things , or to compare the things that have been measured with the measure. It is in this sense also that multiples are so called. For each number is said to be many because it consists of ones and because each number is measurable by one; and it is many as that which is opposed to one, not to the few. In this sense, then, even two is many-not, however, in the sense of a plurality which is excessive either relatively or absolutely; it is the first plurality. But without qualification two is few; for it is first plurality which is deficient

(διὸ καὶ οὐκ ὀρθῶς ἀπέστη Ἀναξαγόρας εἰπὼν ὅτι ὁμοῦ πάντα χρήματα ἦν ἄπειρα καὶ πλήθει καὶ μικρότητι, [30] ἔδει δ᾽ εἰπεῖν ἀντὶ τοῦ "καὶ μικρότητι""καὶ ὀλιγότητι"· οὐ γὰρ ἄπειρα), ἐπεὶ τὸ ὀλίγον οὐ διὰ τὸ ἕν, ὥσπερ τινές φασιν, ἀλλὰ διὰ τὰ δύο.

Quapropter non recte destitit Anaxagoras cum dixisset quia simul omnes res erant, infinite et multitudine et parvuitate, oportebat autem dicere pro 'et paruitate' 'et paucitate'. Non enim infinite, quoniam paucum non propter unum, ut quidam dicunt, sed propter duo.

(for this reason Anaxagoras was not right in leaving the subject with the statement that "all things were together, boundless both in plurality and in smallness" – where for "and in smallness" he should have said "and in fewness"; for they could not have been boundless in fewness), since it is not one, as some say, but two, that make a few.

ἀντίκειται δὴ τὸ ἓν καὶ τὰ πολλὰ τὰ ἐν ἀριθμοῖς ὡς μέτρον μετρητῷ· ταῦτα δὲ ὡς τὰ πρός τι, ὅσα μὴ καθ᾽ αὑτὰ τῶν πρός τι. διῄρηται δ᾽ [35] ἡμῖν ἐν ἄλλοις ὅτι διχῶς λέγεται τὰ πρός τι, τὰ μὲν ὡς ἐναντία, τὰ δ᾽ ὡς ἐπιστήμη πρὸς ἐπιστητόν, τῷ λέγεσθαί τι ἄλλο πρὸς αὐτό.

Opponitur itaque unum multis ut metrum mensurabili; haec autem ut quae ad aliquid, quaecumque non secundum se eorum quae ad aliquid. Divisum autem est a nobis in aliis quia dupliciter dicuntur quae ad aliquid, alia namque ut contraria, alia ut scientia ad scibile, quia dicitur aliquid aliud ad ipsum.

The one is opposed then to the many in numbers as measure to thing measurable; and these are opposed as are the relatives which are not from their very nature relatives. We have distinguished elsewhere the two senses in which relatives are so called: – (1) as contraries; (2) as knowledge to thing known, a term being called relative [57a] because another is relative to it.

[1057α] [1] τὸ δὲ ἓν ἔλαττον εἶναι τινός, οἷον τοῖν δυοῖν, οὐδὲν κωλύει· οὐ γάρ, εἰ ἔλαττον, καὶ ὀλίγον. τὸ δὲ πλῆθος οἷον γένος ἐστὶ τοῦ ἀριθμοῦ· ἔστι γὰρ ἀριθμὸς πλῆθος ἑνὶ μετρητόν, καὶ ἀντίκειταί πως τὸ ἓν καὶ ἀριθμός, οὐχ ὡς [5] ἐναντίον ἀλλ᾽ ὥσπερ εἴρηται τῶν πρός τι ἔνια· ᾗ γὰρ μέτρον τὸ δὲ μετρητόν, ταύτῃ ἀντίκειται, διὸ οὐ πᾶν ὃ ἂν ᾖ ἓν ἀριθμός ἐστιν, οἷον εἴ τι ἀδιαίρετόν ἐστιν.

Unum autem esse minus aliquo, puta duobus, nihil prohibet; non enim si minus, et paucum. Multitudo autem quasi genus est numeri; est enim numerus multitudo uno mensurabilis. Et opponuntur aliqualiter unum et numerus, non ut contrarium sed sicut dictum est eorum quae ad aliquid quaedam; in quantum enim metrum, hoc autem mensurabile: sic opponuntur. Quapropter non omne quodcumque fuerit unum numerus est, puta si quid indivisum est.

There is nothing to prevent one from being fewer than something, e.g. than two; for if one is fewer, it is not therefore few. Plurality is as it were the class to which number belongs; for number is plurality measurable by one, and one and number are in a sense opposed, not as contrary, but as we have said some relative terms are opposed; for inasmuch as one is measure and the other measurable, they are opposed. This is why not everything that is one is a number; i.e. if the thing is indivisible it is not a number.

ὁμοίως δὲ λεγομένη ἡ ἐπιστήμη πρὸς τὸ ἐπιστητὸν οὐχ ὁμοίως ἀποδίδωσιν. δόξειε μὲν γὰρ ἂν μέτρον ἡ ἐπιστήμη εἶναι τὸ δὲ ἐπιστητὸν [10] τὸ μετρούμενον, συμβαίνει δὲ ἐπιστήμην μὲν πᾶσαν ἐπιστητὸν εἶναι τὸ δὲ ἐπιστητὸν μὴ πᾶν ἐπιστήμην, ὅτι τρόπον τινὰ ἡ ἐπιστήμη μετρεῖται τῷ ἐπιστητῷ.

Similiter autem dicta scientia ad scibile, non similiter assignatur. Videbitur enim utique scientia metrum esse, scibile vero quod mensuratur; accidit autem scientiam quidem omnem scibile esse, scibile vero non omne scientiam, quia modo quodam scientia mensuratur scibili.

But though knowledge is similarly spoken of as relative to the knowable, the relation does not work out similarly; for while knowledge might be thought to be the measure, and the knowable the thing measured, the fact that all knowledge is knowable, but not all that is knowable is knowledge, because in a sense knowledge is measured by the knowable.

τὸ δὲ πλῆθος οὔτε τῷ ὀλίγῳ ἐναντίον—ἀλλὰ τούτῳ μὲν τὸ πολὺ ὡς ὑπερέχον πλῆθος ὑπερεχομένῳ πλήθει—οὔτε τῷ ἑνὶ πάντως· ἀλλὰ τὸ μὲν [15] ὥσπερ εἴρηται, ὅτι διαιρετὸν τὸ δ' ἀδιαίρετον, τὸ δ' ὡς πρός τι ὥσπερ ἡ ἐπιστήμη ἐπιστητῷ, ἐὰν ᾖ ἀριθμὸς τὸ δ' ἓν μέτρον.

Multitudo autem nec pauco est contraria — Sed huic quidem multum sicut excedens multitudo excesse multitudini — neque ipsi uni omni modo; sed hoc quidem ut dictum est, quia divisibile illud vero indivisibile, hoc ut ad aliquid ut scientia scibili, si fuerit numerus unum vero metrum.

Plurality is contrary neither to the few (the many being contrary to this as excessive plurality to plurality exceeded), nor to the one in every sense; but in the one sense these are contrary, as has been said, because the former is divisible and the latter indivisible, while in another sense they are relative as knowledge is to knowable, if plurality is number and the one is a measure.


*Chapter* 7

ἐπεὶ δὲ τῶν ἐναντίων ἐνδέχεται εἶναί τι μεταξὺ καὶ ἐνίων ἔστιν, ἀνάγκη ἐκ τῶν ἐναντίων εἶναι τὰ μεταξύ.

Quoniam autem contrariorum contingit aliquid medium esse et quorundam est, necesse ex contrariis esse media.

Since contraries admit of an intermediate and in some cases have it, intermediates must be composed of the contraries.

πάντα [20] γὰρ τὰ μεταξὺ ἐν τῷ αὐτῷ γένει ἐστὶ καὶ ὧν ἐστι μεταξύ. μεταξὺ μὲν γὰρ ταῦτα λέγομεν εἰς ὅσα μεταβάλλειν ἀνάγκη πρότερον τὸ μεταβάλλον (οἷον ἀπὸ τῆς ὑπάτης ἐπὶ τὴν νήτην εἰ μεταβαίνοι τῷ ὀλιγίστῳ, ἥξει πρότερον εἰς τοὺς μεταξὺ φθόγγους, καὶ ἐν χρώμασιν εἰ [ἥξει] ἐκ τοῦ λευκοῦ [25] εἰς τὸ μέλαν, πρότερον ἥξει εἰς τὸ φοινικοῦν καὶ φαιὸν ἢ εἰς τὸ μέλαν· ὁμοίως δὲ καὶ ἐπὶ τῶν ἄλλων): μεταβάλλειν δ᾽ ἐξ ἄλλου γένους εἰς ἄλλο γένος οὐκ ἔστιν ἀλλ᾽ ἢ κατὰ συμβεβηκός, οἷον ἐκ χρώματος εἰς σχῆμα. ἀνάγκη ἄρα τὰ μεταξὺ καὶ αὑτοῖς καὶ ὧν μεταξύ εἰσιν ἐν τῷ αὐτῷ γένει [30] εἶναι.

Omnia namque media in eodem sunt genere et quorum sunt media. Media enim haec dicimus in quaecumque permutari prius est necesse quod permutatur, ut ab ypate in netem si transit per minimam rationem, veniet prius ad medios sonos. Et in coloribus si veniet ex albo in nigrum, prius veniet ad puniceum et plumbeum quam ad nigrum. Similiter autem et in aliis. permutari vero ex alio genere in aliud genus non est nisi secundum accidens, ut ex colore in figuram. Necesse est ergo media et quorum sunt media in eodem genere esse.

For (1) all intermediates are in the same genus as the things between which they stand. For we call those things intermediates, into which that which changes must change first; e.g. if we were to pass from the highest string to the lowest by the smallest intervals, we should come sooner to the intermediate notes, and in colours if we were to pass from white to black, we should come sooner to crimson and grey than to black; and similarly in all other cases. But to change from one genus to another genus is not possible except in an incidental way, as from colour to figure. Intermediates, then, must be in the same genus both as one another and as the things they stand between.

ἀλλὰ μὴν πάντα γε τὰ μεταξύ ἐστιν ἀντικειμένων τινῶν: ἐκ τούτων γὰρ μόνων καθ᾽ αὑτὰ ἔστι μεταβάλλειν (διὸ ἀδύνατον εἶναι μεταξὺ μὴ ἀντικειμένων: εἴη γὰρ ἂν μεταβολὴ καὶ μὴ ἐξ ἀντικειμένων).

At vero omnia media sunt oppositorum quorundam; ex hiis enim solis secundum se est permutari. Quapropter impossibile est esse media non oppositorum; esset enim permutatio et non ex oppositis.

But (2) all intermediates stand between opposites of some kind; for only between these can change take place in virtue of their own nature (so that an intermediate is impossible between things which are not opposite; for then there would be change which was not from one opposite towards the other).

τῶν δ᾽ ἀντικειμένων ἀντιφάσεως μὲν οὐκ ἔστι μεταξύ (τοῦτο γὰρ ἐστιν ἀντίφασις, [35] ἀντίθεσις ἧς ὁτῳοῦν θάτερον μόριον πάρεστιν, οὐκ ἐχούσης οὐθὲν μεταξύ), τῶν δὲ λοιπῶν τὰ μὲν πρός τι τὰ δὲ στέρησις τὰ δὲ ἐναντία ἐστίν. τῶν δὲ πρός τι ὅσα μὴ ἐναντία, οὐκ ἔχει μεταξύ: αἴτιον δ᾽ ὅτι οὐκ ἐν τῷ αὐτῷ γένει ἐστίν. [1057β] [1] τί γὰρ ἐπιστήμης καὶ ἐπιστητοῦ μεταξύ; ἀλλὰ μεγάλου καὶ μικροῦ.

Oppositorum vero contradictionis quidem medium non est; hoc enim est contradictio: oppositio cuius cuicumque altera pars adest, non habentis nullum medium. Ceterorum vero alia ad aliquid alia privatio alia contraria. Eorum autem

388

quae ad aliquid quaecumque non contraria, non habent media; causa vero quia non in eodem genere sunt. Quid enim scientie et scibilis medium? Sed magni et parvi.

Of opposites, contradictories admit of no middle term; for this is what contradiction is – an opposition, one or other side of which must attach to anything whatever, i.e. which has no intermediate. Of other opposites, some are relative, others privative, others contrary. Of relative terms, those which are not contrary have no intermediate; the reason is that they are not in the same genus. For what intermediate could there be between [57b] knowledge and knowable? But between great and small there is one. (3)

εἰ δ᾽ ἐστὶν ἐν ταὐτῷ γένει τὰ μεταξύ, ὥσπερ δέδεικται, καὶ μεταξὺ ἐναντίων, ἀνάγκη αὐτὰ συγκεῖσθαι ἐκ τούτων τῶν ἐναντίων.

Si vero sunt in eodem genere media, ut ostensum est, et media contrariorum, necesse ipsa componi ex hiis contrariis.

If intermediates are in the same genus, as has been shown, and stand between contraries, they must be composed of these contraries.

ἢ γὰρ ἔσται τι γένος αὐτῶν ἢ οὐθέν. καὶ εἰ μὲν [5] γένος ἔσται οὕτως ὥστ᾽ εἶναι πρότερόν τι τῶν ἐναντίων, αἱ διαφοραὶ πρότεραι ἐναντίαι ἔσονται αἱ ποιήσουσαι τὰ ἐναντία εἴδη ὡς γένους· ἐκ γὰρ τοῦ γένους καὶ τῶν διαφορῶν τὰ εἴδη (οἷον εἰ τὸ λευκὸν καὶ μέλαν ἐναντία, ἔστι δὲ τὸ μὲν διακριτικὸν χρῶμα τὸ δὲ συγκριτικὸν χρῶμα, αὗται αἱ διαφοραί, [10] τὸ διακριτικὸν καὶ συγκριτικόν, πρότεραι· ὥστε ταῦτα ἐναντία ἀλλήλοις πρότερα).

Nam aut erit aliquod genus ipsorum aut nullum. Et si quidem genus erit ita ut sit prius aliquid contrariis , differentie priores contrarie erunt facientes contrarias species ut generis; ex genere enim et differentiis species. Ut si album et nigrum contraria , est autem hoc quidem disgregativus color illud vero congregativus color: hae differentiae, congregativum et disgregativum, priores; quare haec contraria invicem priora. At vero contrarie differentia magis sunt contraria.

For either there will be a genus including the contraries or there will be none. And if (a) there is to be a genus in such a way that it is something prior to the contraries, the differentiae which constituted the contrary species-of-a-genus will be contraries prior to the species; for species are composed of the genus and the differentiae. (E.g. if white and black are contraries, and one is a piercing colour and the other a compressing colour, these differentiae – piercing and compressing – are prior; so that these are prior contraries of one another.) But, again, the species which differ contrariwise are the more truly contrary species.

ἀλλὰ μὴν τά γε ἐναντίως διαφέροντα μᾶλλον ἐναντία): καὶ τὰ λοιπὰ καὶ τὰ μεταξὺ ἐκ τοῦ γένους ἔσται καὶ τῶν διαφορῶν (οἷον ὅσα χρώματα τοῦ λευκοῦ καὶ μέλανός ἐστι μεταξύ, ταῦτα δεῖ ἔκ τε τοῦ γένους λέγεσθαι [15] —ἔστι δὲ γένος τὸ χρῶμα—καὶ ἐκ διαφορῶν τινων: αὗται δὲ οὐκ ἔσονται τὰ πρῶτα ἐναντία: εἰ δὲ μή, ἔσται ἕκαστον ἢ λευκὸν ἢ μέλαν: ἕτεραι ἄρα: μεταξὺ ἄρα τῶν πρώτων ἐναντίων αὗται ἔσονται,

Et reliqua et media ex genere erunt et differentiis, ut quicumque colores albi et nigri sunt medii, oportet hos ex genere dici (est autem genus color) et ex differentiis quibusdam. Hae vero non erunt prima contraria; si autem non, erit unusquisque aut albus aut niger. Altere igitur; media ergo primorum contrariorum hae erunt.

And the other species, i.e. the intermediates, must be composed of their genus and their differentiae. (E.g. all colours which are between white and black must be said to be composed of the genus, i.e. colour, and certain differentiae. But these differentiae will not be the primary contraries; otherwise every colour would be either white or black. They are different, then, from the primary contraries; and therefore they will be between the primary contraries;

αἱ πρῶται δὲ διαφοραὶ τὸ διακριτικὸν καὶ συγκριτικόν): ὥστε ταῦτα πρῶτα ζητητέον [20] ὅσα ἐναντία μὴ ἐν γένει, ἐκ τίνος τὰ μεταξὺ αὐτῶν (ἀνάγκη γὰρ τὰ ἐν τῷ αὐτῷ γένει ἐκ τῶν ἀσυνθέτων τῷ γένει συγκεῖσθαι ἢ ἀσύνθετα εἶναι). τὰ μὲν οὖν ἐναντία ἀσύνθετα ἐξ ἀλλήλων, ὥστε ἀρχαί: τὰ δὲ μεταξὺ ἢ πάντα ἢ οὐθέν. ἐκ δὲ τῶν ἐναντίων γίγνεταί τι, ὥστ᾽ ἔσται μεταβολὴ εἰς τοῦτο [25] πρὶν ἢ εἰς αὐτά: ἑκατέρου γὰρ καὶ ἧττον ἔσται καὶ μᾶλλον. μεταξὺ ἄρα ἔσται καὶ τοῦτο τῶν ἐναντίων. καὶ τἆλλα ἄρα πάντα σύνθετα τὰ μεταξύ: τὸ γὰρ τοῦ μὲν μᾶλλον τοῦ δ᾽ ἧττον σύνθετόν πως ἐξ ἐκείνων ὧν λέγεται εἶναι τοῦ μὲν μᾶλλον τοῦ δ᾽ ἧττον. ἐπεὶ δ᾽ οὐκ ἔστιν ἕτερα πρότερα ὁμογενῆ [30] τῶν ἐναντίων, ἅπαντ᾽ ἂν ἐκ τῶν ἐναντίων εἴη τὰ μεταξύ, ὥστε καὶ τὰ κάτω πάντα, καὶ τἀναντία καὶ τὰ μεταξύ, ἐκ τῶν πρώτων ἐναντίων ἔσονται.

Primae autem differentiae disgregativum et congregativum. Quare hoc primum quaerendum: quaecumque contraria non in genere, ex quo media ipsorum? Necesse enim quae sunt in eodem genere ex incompositis genere componi aut incomposita esse. Contraria namque incomposita sunt ex invicem; quare principia. Quae autem intermedia: aut omnia aut nullum. Ex contrariis vero fit aliquid, quare erit transmutatio in hoc prius quam in ipsa; utriusque enim et minus erit et magis. Medium igitur erit et hoc contrariorum. Et alia igitur omnia composita quae media; nam quod huius quidem magis illius vero minus compositum est aliqualiter ex illis quorum dicitur esse huius quidem magis illius vero minus. Quoniam autem non sunt altera priora eiusdem generis contrariis, omnia utique ex contrarus media erunt. quare et inferiora omnia, et contraria et media, ex primis contrariis erunt.

the primary differentiae are piercing and compressing .) Therefore it is (b) with regard to these contraries which do not fall within a genus that we must first ask of what their intermediates are composed. (For things which are in the same genus must be composed of terms in which the genus is not an element, or else be themselves incomposite.) Now contraries do not involve one another in their composition, and are therefore first principles; but the intermediates are either all incomposite, or none of them. But there is something compounded out of the contraries, so that there can be a change from a contrary to it sooner than to the other contrary; for it will have less of the quality in question than the one contrary and more than the other. This also, then, will come between the contraries. All the other intermediates also, therefore, are composite; for that which has more of a quality than one thing and less than another is compounded somehow out of the things than which it is said to have more and less respectively of the quality. And since there are no other things prior to the contraries and homogeneous with the intermediates, all intermediates must be compounded out of the contraries. Therefore also all the inferior classes, both the contraries and their intermediates, will be compounded out of the primary contraries.

ὅτι μὲν οὖν τὰ μεταξὺ ἔν τε ταὐτῷ γένει πάντα καὶ μεταξὺ ἐναντίων καὶ σύγκειται ἐκ τῶν ἐναντίων πάντα, δῆλον. [35]

Quod quidem igitur media et in eodem genere omnia et intermedia contrariorum et componuntur ex contrariis omnia, palam.

Clearly, then, intermediates are (1) all in the same genus and (2) intermediate between contraries, and (3) all compounded out of the contraries.

## Chapter 8

τὸ δ᾽ ἕτερον τῷ εἴδει τινὸς τὶ ἕτερόν ἐστι, καὶ δεῖ τοῦτο ἀμφοῖν ὑπάρχειν: οἷον εἰ ζῷον ἕτερον τῷ εἴδει, ἄμφω ζῷα. ἀνάγκη ἄρα ἐν γένει τῷ αὐτῷ εἶναι τὰ ἕτερα τῷ εἴδει· τὸ γὰρ τοιοῦτο γένος καλῶ ὃ ἄμφω ἓν ταὐτὸ λέγεται, μὴ κατὰ συμβεβηκὸς ἔχον διαφοράν, [1058α] [1] εἴτε ὡς ὕλη ὂν εἴτε ἄλλως. οὐ μόνον γὰρ δεῖ τὸ κοινὸν ὑπάρχειν, οἷον ἄμφω ζῷα, ἀλλὰ καὶ ἕτερον ἑκατέρῳ τοῦτο αὐτὸ τὸ ζῷον, οἷον τὸ μὲν ἵππον τὸ δὲ ἄνθρωπον, διὸ τοῦτο τὸ κοινὸν ἕτερον ἀλλήλων [5] ἐστὶ τῷ εἴδει. ἔσται δὴ καθ᾽ αὑτὰ τὸ μὲν τοιονδὶ ζῷον τὸ δὲ τοιονδί, οἷον τὸ μὲν ἵππος τὸ δ᾽ ἄνθρωπος. ἀνάγκη ἄρα τὴν διαφορὰν ταύτην ἑτερότητα τοῦ γένους εἶναι. λέγω γὰρ γένους [8] διαφορὰν ἑτερότητα ἣ ἕτερον ποιεῖ τοῦτο αὐτό.

Diversum autem specie alicuius aliquid diversum est, et oportet hoc ambobus inesse; ut si animal diversum est specie, ambo animalia. Necesse ergo in eodem genere esse diversa specie. Tale enim genus voco quod ambo unum et idem dicuntur, non secundum accidens habens differentiam, sive ut materia ens sive aliter. Non solum enim oportet commune existere, puta ambo animalia, sed et alterum utrilibet hoc ipsum animal, ut hoc quidem equum illud vero hominem. Propter quod hoc quod commune diversum ab invicem est specie. Erit itaque secundum se hoc quidem tale animal illud vero tale , ut hoc quidem equus illud vero homo. Necesse ergo differentiam hanc diversitatem esse generis. Dico enim generis differentiam diversitatem quae diversum facit hoc ipsum.

That which is other in species is other than something in something, and this must belong to both; e.g. if it is an animal other in species, both are animals. The things, then, which are other in species must be in the same genus. For by genus I mean that one identical thing which is predicated of both and is differentiated in no merely acci[58a]dental way, whether conceived as matter or otherwise. For not only must the common nature attach to the different things, e.g. not only must both be animals, but this very animality must also be different for each (e.g. in the one case equinity, in the other humanity), and so this common nature is specifically different for each from what it is for the other. One, then, will be in virtue of its own nature one sort of animal, and the other another, e.g. one a horse and the other a man. This difference, then, must be an otherness of the genus. For I give the name of difference in the genus an otherness which makes the genus itself other.

ἐναντίωσις τοίνυν ἔσται αὕτη (δῆλον δὲ καὶ ἐκ τῆς ἐπαγωγῆς): πάντα [10] γὰρ διαιρεῖται τοῖς ἀντικειμένοις,

Contrarietas igitur erit haec; palam autem et ex inductione. omnia enim dividuntur oppositis,

This, then, will be a contrariety (as can be shown also by induction). For all things are divided by opposites,

καὶ ὅτι τὰ ἐναντία ἐν ταὐτῷ γένει, δέδεικται: ἡ γὰρ ἐναντιότης ἦν διαφορὰ τελεία, ἡ δὲ διαφορὰ ἡ εἴδει πᾶσα τινὸς τί, ὥστε τοῦτο τὸ αὐτό τε καὶ γένος ἐπ᾽ ἀμφοῖν (διὸ καὶ ἐν τῇ αὐτῇ συστοιχίᾳ πάντα τὰ ἐναντία τῆς κατηγορίας ὅσα εἴδει διάφορα καὶ μὴ γένει, [15] ἕτερά τε ἀλλήλων μάλιστα—τελεία γὰρ ἡ διαφορά—καὶ ἅμα ἀλλήλοις οὐ γίγνεται). ἡ ἄρα διαφορὰ ἐναντίωσίς ἐστιν. τοῦτο ἄρα ἐστὶ τὸ ἑτέροις εἶναι τῷ εἴδει, τὸ ἐν ταὐτῷ γένει ὄντα ἐναντίωσιν ἔχειν ἄτομα ὄντα (ταὐτὰ δὲ τῷ εἴδει ὅσα μὴ ἔχει ἐναντίωσιν ἄτομα ὄντα): ἐν γὰρ τῇ διαιρέσει καὶ [20] ἐν τοῖς μεταξὺ γίγνονται ἐναντιώσεις πρὶν εἰς τὰ ἄτομα ἐλθεῖν:

et quod contraria in eodem genere sunt, ostensum est. Nam contrarietas erat differentia perfecta. Differentia vero quae specie omnis alicuius aliquid , quare hoc idemque et genus in ambobus. Quare et in eadem coelementatione omnia contraria cathegorie quaecumque specie differentia et non genere, diversaque ab invicem maxime; perfecta enim differentia, et simul invicem non fit. Ergo differentia contrarietas est. Hoc enim est diversis esse specie: in eodem genere entia contrarietatem habere, entia individua. Eadem vero specie quaecumque non habent contrarietatem, individua entia. In divisione enim et in mediis fiunt contrarietates priusquam ad individua perveniatur.

and it has been proved that contraries are in the same genus. For contrariety was seen to be complete difference; and all difference in species is a difference from something in something; so that this is the same for both and is their genus. (Hence also all contraries which are different in species and not in genus are in the same line of predication, and other than one another in the highest degree – for the difference is complete – , and cannot be present along with one another.) The difference, then, is a contrariety. This, then, is what it is to be other in species – to have a contrariety, being in the same genus and being indivisible (and those things are the same in species which have no contrariety, being indivisible); we say being indivisible , for in the process of division contrarieties arise in the intermediate stages before we come to the indivisibles.

ὥστε φανερὸν ὅτι πρὸς τὸ καλούμενον γένος οὔτε ταὐτὸν οὔτε ἕτερον τῷ εἴδει οὐθέν ἐστι τῶν ὡς γένους εἰδῶν (προσηκόντως· ἡ γὰρ ὕλη ἀποφάσει δηλοῦται, τὸ δὲ γένος ὕλη οὗ λέγεται γένος — μὴ ὡς τὸ τῶν Ἡρακλειδῶν ἀλλ᾽ ὡς τὸ [25] ἐν τῇ φύσει), οὐδὲ πρὸς τὰ μὴ ἐν ταὐτῷ γένει, ἀλλὰ διοίσει τῷ γένει ἐκείνων, εἴδει δὲ τῶν ἐν ταὐτῷ γένει. ἐναντίωσιν γὰρ ἀνάγκη εἶναι τὴν διαφορὰν οὗ διαφέρει εἴδει· αὕτη δὲ ὑπάρχει τοῖς ἐν ταὐτῷ γένει οὖσι μόνοις.

Quare palam quia ad id quod vocatur genus nec idem nec diversum specie nihil est eorum quae conveniunt ut generis specierum. Nam materia negatione ostenditur, genus autem materia quod dicitur genus, non ut quod Eraclitorum sed ut in natura. Neque ad ea quae non in eodem genere, sed different genere ab illis, specie vero ab eis quae in eodem genere. Contrarietatem enim necesse est esse differentiam, non differre specie; haec autem inest in eodem genere existentibus solis.

Evidently, therefore, with reference to that which is called the genus, none of the species-of-a-genus is either the same as it or other than it in species (and this is fitting; for the matter is indicated by negation, and the genus is the matter of that of which it is called the genus, not in the sense in which we speak of the genus or family of the Heraclidae, but in that in which the genus is an element in a thing's nature), nor is it so with reference to things which are not in the same genus, but it will differ in genus from them, and in species from things in the same genus. For a thing's difference from that from which it differs in species must be a contrariety; and this belongs only to things in the same genus.

## Chapter 9

ἀπορήσειε δ᾿ ἄν τις διὰ τί γυνὴ ἀνδρὸς οὐκ εἴδει διαφέρει, [30] ἐναντίου τοῦ θήλεος καὶ τοῦ ἄρρενος ὄντος τῆς δὲ διαφορᾶς ἐναντιώσεως, οὐδὲ ζῷον θῆλυ καὶ ἄρρεν ἕτερον τῷ εἴδει· καίτοι καθ᾿ αὑτὸ τοῦ ζῴου αὕτη ἡ διαφορὰ καὶ οὐχ ὡς λευκότης ἢ μελανία ἀλλ᾿ ᾗ ζῷον καὶ τὸ θῆλυ καὶ τὸ ἄρρεν ὑπάρχει. ἔστι δ᾿ ἡ ἀπορία αὕτη σχεδὸν ἡ αὐτὴ καὶ διὰ [35] τί ἡ μὲν ποιεῖ τῷ εἴδει ἕτερα ἐναντίωσις ἡ δ᾿ οὔ, οἷον τὸ πεζὸν καὶ τὸ πτερωτόν, λευκότης δὲ καὶ μελανία οὔ.

Dubitabit autem utique aliquis quare femina a viro non specie differt, contrario feminino et masculino existente, diffe rentia autem contrarietate. Neque animal masculinum et femininum diversum est specie, quamvis secundum se animalis haec sit differentia et non ut albedo aut nigredo sed in quantum animal femininum et masculinum inest. Est autem dubitatio haec fere eadem et quare haec quidem contrarietas facit specie diversa haec autem non, ut ambulativum et volativum, sed albedo et nigredo non.

One might raise the question, why woman does not differ from man in species, when female and male are contrary and their difference is a contrariety; and why a female and a male animal are not different in species, though this difference belongs to animal in virtue of its own nature, and not as paleness or darkness does; both female and male belong to it qua animal. This question is almost the same as the other, why one contrariety makes things different in species and another does not, e.g. with feet and with wings do, but paleness and darkness do not.

ἢ ὅτι τὰ μὲν οἰκεῖα πάθη τοῦ γένους τὰ δ᾿ ἧττον; καὶ ἐπειδή ἐστι τὸ μὲν λόγος τὸ δ᾿ ὕλη, [1058β] [1] ὅσαι μὲν ἐν τῷ λόγῳ εἰσὶν ἐναντιότητες εἴδει ποιοῦσι διαφοράν, ὅσαι δ᾿ ἐν τῷ συνειλημμένῳ τῇ ὕλῃ οὐ ποιοῦσιν. διὸ ἀνθρώπου λευκότης οὐ ποιεῖ οὐδὲ μελανία, οὐδὲ τοῦ λευκοῦ ἀνθρώπου ἔστι διαφορὰ κατ᾿ εἶδος πρὸς [5] μέλανα ἄνθρωπον, οὐδ᾿ ἂν ὄνομα ἓν τεθῇ. ὡς ὕλη γὰρ ὁ ἄνθρωπος, οὐ ποιεῖ δὲ διαφορὰν ἡ ὕλη· οὐδ᾿ ἀνθρώπου γὰρ εἴδη εἰσὶν οἱ ἄνθρωποι διὰ τοῦτο, καίτοι ἕτεραι αἱ σάρκες καὶ τὰ ὀστᾶ ἐξ ὧν ὅδε καὶ ὅδε· ἀλλὰ τὸ σύνολον ἕτερον μέν, εἴδει δ᾿ οὐχ ἕτερον, ὅτι ἐν τῷ λόγῳ οὐκ ἔστιν ἐναντίωσις. τοῦτο δ᾿ [10] ἐστὶ τὸ ἔσχατον ἄτομον· ὁ δὲ Καλλίας ἐστὶν ὁ λόγος μετὰ τῆς ὕλης· καὶ ὁ λευκὸς δὴ ἄνθρωπος, ὅτι Καλλίας λευκός· κατὰ συμβεβηκὸς οὖν ὁ ἄνθρωπος. οὐδὲ χαλκοῦς δὴ κύκλος καὶ ξύλινος· οὐδὲ τρίγωνον χαλκοῦν καὶ κύκλος ξύλινος, οὐ διὰ τὴν ὕλην εἴδει διαφέρουσιν ἀλλ᾿ ὅτι ἐν τῷ λόγῳ [15] ἔνεστιν ἐναντίωσις. πότερον δ᾿ ἡ ὕλη οὐ ποιεῖ ἕτερα τῷ εἴδει, οὖσά πως ἕτερα, ἢ ἔστιν ὡς ποιεῖ; διὰ τί γὰρ ὁδὶ ὁ ἵππος τουδὶ <τοῦ ἀνθρώπου ἕτερος τῷ εἴδει; καίτοι σὺν τῇ ὕλῃ οἱ λόγοι αὐτῶν. ἢ ὅτι ἔνεστιν ἐν τῷ λόγῳ ἐναντίωσις; καὶ γὰρ τοῦ λευκοῦ ἀνθρώπου καὶ μέλανος ἵππου, καὶ ἔστι γε [20] εἴδει, ἀλλ᾽ οὐχ ᾗ ὁ μὲν λευκὸς ὁ δὲ μέλας, ἐπεὶ καὶ εἰ ἄμφω λευκὰ ἦν, ὅμως ἂν ἦν εἴδει ἕτερα.

Aut quia haec quidem sunt propriae passiones generis illa vero minus. Quoniam est hoc quidem ratio hoc autem materia, quaecumque quidem in ratione sunt contrarietates specie faciunt differentiam, quae vero in concepto cum materia non faciunt. Quapropter hominis albedo non facit nec nigredo, nec albi hominis est differentia secundum speciem ad nigrum hominem, nec si nomen imponatur. Ut materia enim homo, non facit autem differentiam materia; non enim hominis species sunt homines propter hoc, quamvis diverse carnes et ossa ex quibus hic et hic. Sed simul totum diversum quidem, specie vero non diversum, quia in ratione non est contrarietas. Hoc autem est ultimum individuum. Callias vero est ratio cum materia; et albus itaque homo, quia Callias albus; secundum accidens ergo homo albus. Nec ereus itaque circulus et ligneus; nec triangulus ereus et circulus ligneus non propter materiam specie differunt, sed quia in ratione inest contrarietas. Vtrum autem materia non facit diversa specie, ens aliqualiter, aut est ut facit? Propter quid enim hic equus ab hoc homine diversus est specie? Equidem rationes ipsorum cum materia. Aut quia est in ratione contrarietas. Et enim albi hominis et nigri equi diversitas est specie, sed non in quantum hic albus et ille niger; quoniam et si ambo albi essent, tamen essent specie diversa.

Perhaps it is because the former are modifications peculiar to the genus, and the latter are less so. And since one [58b] element is definition and one is matter, contrarieties which are in the definition make a difference in species, but those which are in the thing taken as including its matter do not make one. And so paleness in a man, or darkness, does not make one, nor is there a difference in species between the pale man and the dark man, not even if each of them be denoted by one word. For man is here being considered on his material side, and matter does not create a difference; for it does not make individual men species of man, though the flesh and the bones of which this man and that man consist are other. The concrete thing is other, but not other in species, because in the definition there is no contrariety. This is the ultimate indivisible kind. Callias is definition + matter, the pale man, then, is so also, because it is the individual Callias that is pale; man, then, is pale only incidentally. Neither do a brazen and a wooden circle, then, differ in species; and if a brazen triangle and a wooden circle differ in species, it is not because of the matter, but because there is a contrariety in the definition. But does the matter not make things other in species, when it is other in a certain way, or is there a sense in which it does? For why is this horse other than this man in species, although their matter is included with their definitions? Doubtless because there is a contrariety in the definition. For while there is a contrariety also between pale man and dark horse, and it is a contrariety in species, it does not depend on the paleness of the one and the darkness of the other, since even if both had been pale, yet they would have been other in species.

τὸ δὲ ἄρρεν καὶ θῆλυ τοῦ ζῴου οἰκεῖα μὲν πάθη, ἀλλ᾽ οὐ κατὰ τὴν οὐσίαν ἀλλ᾽ ἐν τῇ ὕλῃ καὶ τῷ σώματι, διὸ τὸ αὐτὸ σπέρμα θῆλυ ἢ ἄρρεν γίγνεται παθόν τι πάθος.

Masculinum vero et femina animalis proprie sunt passiones, sed non secundum substantiam, verum in materia et corpore. Propter quod idem sperma femina aut masculum fit patiens passionem aliquam.

But male and female, while they are modifications peculiar to animal , are so not in virtue of its essence but in the matter, ie. the body. This is why the same seed becomes female or male by being acted on in a certain way.

τί μὲν οὖν ἐστὶ τὸ τῷ εἴδει ἕτερον [25] εἶναι, καὶ διὰ τί τὰ μὲν διαφέρει εἴδει τὰ δ᾽ οὔ, εἴρηται.

Quid quidem igitur est esse diversum specie, et quare alia differunt specie alia non, dictum est.

We have stated, then, what it is to be other in species, and why some things differ in species and others do not.

*Chapter* 10

ἐπειδὴ δὲ τὰ ἐναντία ἕτερα τῷ εἴδει, τὸ δὲ φθαρτὸν καὶ τὸ ἄφθαρτον ἐναντία (στέρησις γὰρ ἀδυναμία διωρισμένη), ἀνάγκη ἕτερον εἶναι τῷ γένει τὸ φθαρτὸν καὶ τὸ ἄφθαρτον.

Quoniam vero contraria diversa specie, corruptibile autem et incorruptibile contraria (privatio enim est impotentia determinata), necesse diversum esse genere corruptibile et incorruptibile.

Since contraries are other in form, and the perishable and the imperishable are contraries (for privation is a determinate incapacity), the perishable and the imperishable must be different in kind.

νῦν μὲν οὖν ἐπ᾽ αὐτῶν εἰρήκαμεν τῶν καθόλου [30] ὀνομάτων, ὥστε δόξειεν ἂν οὐκ ἀναγκαῖον εἶναι ὁτιοῦν ἄφθαρτον καὶ φθαρτὸν ἕτερα εἶναι τῷ εἴδει, ὥσπερ οὐδὲ λευκὸν καὶ μέλαν (τὸ γὰρ αὐτὸ ἐνδέχεται εἶναι, καὶ ἅμα, ἐὰν ᾖ τῶν καθόλου, ὥσπερ ὁ ἄνθρωπος εἴη ἂν καὶ λευκὸς καὶ μέλας, καὶ τῶν καθ᾽ ἕκαστον: εἴη γὰρ ἂν, μὴ ἅμα, ὁ αὐτὸς [35] λευκὸς καὶ μέλας: καίτοι ἐναντίον τὸ λευκὸν τῷ μέλανι):

Nunc ergo diximus de hiis universalibus nominibus, ut autem videbitur non necesse esse quodcumque incorruptibile et corruptibile diversa specie esse, quemadmodum neque album et nigrum, idem enim contingit esse, et simul, si fuerit universalium, quemadmodum homo erit utique et albus et niger, et singularium; erit enim, non simul, idem albus et niger. equidem album contrarium nigro.

Now so far we have spoken of the general terms themselves, so that it might be thought not to be necessary that every imperishable thing should be different from every perishable thing in form, just as not every pale thing is different in form from every dark thing. For the same thing can be both, and even at the same time if it is a universal (e.g. man can be both pale and dark), and if it is an individual it can still be both; for the same man can be, though not at the same time, pale and dark. Yet pale is contrary to dark.

ἀλλὰ τῶν ἐναντίων τὰ μὲν κατὰ συμβεβηκὸς ὑπάρχει ἐνίοις, οἷον καὶ τὰ νῦν εἰρημένα καὶ ἄλλα πολλά, τὰ δὲ ἀδύνατον, ὧν ἐστι καὶ τὸ φθαρτὸν καὶ τὸ ἄφθαρτον· [1059α] [1] οὐδὲν γάρ ἐστι φθαρτὸν κατὰ συμβεβηκός· τὸ μὲν γὰρ συμβεβηκὸς ἐνδέχεται μὴ ὑπάρχειν, τὸ δὲ φθαρτὸν τῶν ἐξ ἀνάγκης ὑπαρχόντων ἐστὶν οἷς ὑπάρχει· ἢ ἔσται τὸ αὐτὸ καὶ ἓν φθαρτὸν [5] καὶ ἄφθαρτον, εἰ ἐνδέχεται μὴ ὑπάρχειν αὐτῷ τὸ φθαρτόν. ἢ τὴν οὐσίαν ἄρα ἢ ἐν τῇ οὐσίᾳ ἀνάγκη ὑπάρχειν τὸ φθαρτὸν ἑκάστῳ τῶν φθαρτῶν. ὁ δ᾽ αὐτὸς λόγος καὶ περὶ τοῦ ἀφθάρτου· τῶν γὰρ ἐξ ἀνάγκης ὑπαρχόντων ἄμφω. ἢ ἄρα καὶ καθ᾽ ὃ πρῶτον τὸ μὲν φθαρτὸν τὸ δ᾽ ἄφθαρτον, [10] ἔχει ἀντίθεσιν, ὥστε ἀνάγκη γένει ἕτερα εἶναι.

Sed contrariorum haec quidem secundum accidens insunt quibusdam, ut quae nunc dicta sunt et alia multa, haec autem impossibile, quorum est et corruptibile et incorruptibile. nihil enim est corruptibile secundum accidens. Nam accidens contingit non existere, et corruptibile ex necessitate existentium est quibus inest; aut erit idem et unum corruptibile et incorruptibile, si contingit non existere ipsi corruptibile. Aut substantiam igitur aut in substantia necesse est inesse corruptibile unicuique corruptibilium. Eadem vero ratio et de incorruptibili ; ex necessitate enim existentium ambo sunt. In quantum igitur et secundum quod primum hoc quidem corruptibile hoc autem incorruptibile, habet oppositionem, unde necesse genere esse diversa.

But while some contraries belong to certain things by accident (e.g. both those now mentioned and many others), others cannot, and among these are perishable and [59a] imperishable . For nothing is by accident perishable. For what is accidental is capable of not being present, but perishableness is one of the attributes that belong of necessity to the things to which they belong; or else one and the same thing may be perishable and imperishable, if perishableness is capable of not belonging to it. Perishableness then must either be the essence or be present in the essence of each perishable thing. The same account holds good for imperishableness also; for both are attributes which are present of necessity. The characteristics, then, in respect of which and in direct consequence of which one thing is perishable and another imperishable, are opposite, so that the things must be different in kind.

φανερὸν τοίνυν ὅτι οὐκ ἐνδέχεται εἶναι εἴδη τοιαῦτα οἷα λέγουσί τινες: ἔσται γὰρ καὶ ἄνθρωπος ὁ μὲν φθαρτὸς ὁ δ᾽ ἄφθαρτος. καίτοι τῷ εἴδει ταὐτὰ λέγεται εἶναι τὰ εἴδη τοῖς τισὶ καὶ οὐχ ὁμώνυμα: τὰ δὲ γένει ἕτερα πλεῖον διέστηκεν ἢ τὰ εἴδει.

Palam igitur quod non contingit esse species tales quales dicunt quidam; erit enim homo hic quidem corruptibilis hic autem incorruptibilis. Equidem specie eadem dicuntur esse species ipsis quibusdam et non equivoca. Diversa vero genere plus distant quam quae specie.

Evidently, then, there cannot be Forms such as some maintain, for then one man would be perishable and another imperishable. Yet the Forms are said to be the same in form with the individuals and not merely to have the same name; but things which differ in kind are farther apart than those which differ in form.

# METHAPHISICE ARISTOTILIS LIBER UNDECIMUS

## 11 (K) 1

[1059α] [18] ὅτι μὲν ἡ σοφία περὶ ἀρχὰς ἐπιστήμη τίς ἐστι, δῆλον ἐκ τῶν πρώτων ἐν οἷς διηπόρηται πρὸς τὰ ὑπὸ τῶν ἄλλων [20] εἰρημένα περὶ τῶν ἀρχῶν:

Quod quidem sapientia circa principia scientia est, palam ex primis in quibus dubitatum est ad dicta ab aliis de principiis.

THAT Wisdom is a science of first principles is evident from the introductory chapters, in which we have raised objections to the statements of others about the first principles;

ἀπορήσειε δ᾽ ἄν τις πότερον μίαν ὑπολαβεῖν εἶναι δεῖ τὴν σοφίαν ἐπιστήμην ἢ πολλάς: εἰ μὲν γὰρ μίαν, μία γ᾽ ἐστὶν ἀεὶ τῶν ἐναντίων, αἱ δ᾽ ἀρχαὶ οὐκ ἐναντίαι: εἰ δὲ μὴ μία, ποίας δεῖ θεῖναι ταύτας;

Dubitabit autem utique quis utrum unam existimare esse oportet sapientiam scientiam aut multas. Si quidem enim unam, una autem est semper contrariorum, principia autem non contraria. Si autem non una, quales oportet ponere has?

but one might ask the question whether Wisdom is to be conceived as one science or as several. If as one, it may be objected that one science always deals with contraries, but the first principles are not contrary. If it is not one, what sort of sciences are those with which it is to be identified?

ἔτι τὰς ἀποδεικτικὰς ἀρχὰς θεωρῆσαι μιᾶς ἢ πλειόνων; εἰ μὲν γὰρ [25] μιᾶς, τί μᾶλλον ταύτης ἢ ὁποιασοῦν; εἰ δὲ πλειόνων, ποίας δεῖ ταύτας τιθέναι;

Adhuc demonstrativa principia speculari unius aut plurium? si quidem enim unius, quid magis huius quam cuiuscumque? si autem plurium, quales oportet has ponere?

Further, is it the business of one science, or of more than one, to examine the first principles of demonstration? If of one, why of this rather than of any other? If of more, what sort of sciences must these be said to be?

ἔτι πότερον πασῶν τῶν οὐσιῶν ἢ οὔ; εἰ μὲν γὰρ μὴ πασῶν, ποίων χαλεπὸν ἀποδοῦναι: εἰ δὲ πασῶν μία, ἄδηλον πῶς ἐνδέχεται πλειόνων τὴν αὐτὴν ἐπιστήμην εἶναι.

Adhuc utrum omnium substantiarum aut non? Si quidem enim non omnium, qualium difficile assignare. Si autem omnium una, non manifestum quomodo contingit plurium eandem scientiam esse.

Further, does Wisdom investigate all substances or not? If not all, it is hard to say which; but if, being one, it investigates them all, it is doubtful how the same science can embrace several subject-matters.

ἔτι πότερον περὶ τὰς οὐσίας μόνον ἢ καὶ τὰ [30] συμβεβηκότα [ἀπόδειξίς ἐστιν]; εἰ γὰρ περί γε τὰ συμβεβηκότα ἀπόδειξίς ἐστιν, περὶ τὰς οὐσίας οὐκ ἔστιν: εἰ δ᾽ ἑτέρα, τίς ἑκατέρα καὶ ποτέρα σοφία; ἧ μὲν γὰρ ἀποδεικτική, σοφία ἡ περὶ τὰ συμβεβηκότα: ἧ δὲ περὶ τὰ πρῶτα, ἡ τῶν οὐσιῶν.

Adhuc utrum circa substantias solum aut et circa accidentia demonstratio est? Si enim circa accidentia demonstratio est, circa substantias non est. Si autem altera, quae utraque et utra sapientia? Demonstrativa quidem enim sapientia quae circa accidentia, haec autem circa prima quae substantiarum.

Further, does it deal with substances only or also with their attributes? If in the case of attributes demonstration is possible, in that of substances it is not. But if the two sciences are different, what is each of them and which is Wisdom? If we think of it as demonstrative, the science of the attributes is Wisdom, but if as dealing with what is primary, the science of substances claims the tide.

ἀλλ’ οὐδὲ περὶ τὰς ἐν τοῖς φυσικοῖς εἰρημένας αἰτίας [35] τὴν ἐπιζητουμένην ἐπιστήμην θετέον: οὔτε γὰρ περὶ τὸ οὗ ἕνεκεν (τοιοῦτον γὰρ τὸ ἀγαθόν, τοῦτο δ’ ἐν τοῖς πρακτοῖς ὑπάρχει καὶ ταῖς οὖσιν ἐν κινήσει: καὶ τοῦτο πρῶτον κινεῖ—τοιοῦτον γὰρ τὸ τέλος—τὸ δὲ πρῶτον κινῆσαν οὐκ ἔστιν ἐν τοῖς ἀκινήτοις):

Sed neque circa dictas in phisicis causas quesitam scientiam ponendum. neque enim circa quod cuius gratia, tale enim bonum; hoc autem in operabilibus existit et existentibus in motu, et hoc primum movet (tale enim finis), primum autem movens non est in immobilibus.

But again the science we are looking for must not be supposed to deal with the causes which have been mentioned in the Physics. For (A) it does not deal with the final cause (for that is the nature of the good, and this is found in the field of action and movement; and it is the first mover-for that is the nature of the end-but in the case of things unmovable there is nothing that moved them first), and (B)

ὅλως δ’ ἀπορίαν ἔχει πότερόν ποτε περὶ τὰς αἰσθητὰς οὐσίας ἐστὶν ἡ ζητουμένη νῦν ἐπιστήμη ἢ οὔ, περὶ δέ τινας ἑτέρας. [1059β] [1] εἰ γὰρ περὶ ἄλλας, ἢ περὶ τὰ εἴδη εἴη ἂν ἢ περὶ τὰ μαθηματικά. τὰ μὲν οὖν εἴδη ὅτι οὐκ ἔστι, δῆλον

Totaliter autem dubitationem habet utrum quidem circa sensibiles substantias est quesita nunc scientia aut non, circa quas autem alteras. Si enim circa alias, aut circa species aut, si sint, circa mathematica. Species quidem enim quod non sunt, palam.

in general it is hard to say whether perchance the science we are now looking for deals with perceptible substances or not with them, but with cer[59b]tain others. If with others, it must deal either with the Forms or with the objects of mathematics. Now (a) evidently the Forms do not exist.

(ὅμως δὲ ἀπορίαν ἔχει, κἂν εἶναί τις αὐτὰ θῇ, διὰ τί ποτ’ οὐχ ὥσπερ ἐπὶ τῶν μαθηματικῶν, [5] οὕτως ἔχει καὶ ἐπὶ τῶν ἄλλων ὧν ἔστιν εἴδη: λέγω δ’ ὅτι τὰ μαθηματικὰ μὲν μεταξύ τε τῶν εἰδῶν τιθέασι καὶ τῶν αἰσθητῶν οἷον τρίτα τινὰ παρὰ τὰ εἴδη τε καὶ τὰ δεῦρο, τρίτος δ’ ἄνθρωπος οὐκ ἔστιν οὐδ’ ἵππος παρ’ αὐτόν τε καὶ τοὺς καθ’ ἕκαστον:

At tamen dubitationem habet, et si esse quis ipsas ponat, propter quid quidem non quemadmodum in mathematicis sic habet et in aliis quorum sunt species. Dico autem quia mathematica quidem intermedia specierum ponunt et sensibilium velut tertia quaedam praeter species et quae hic, tertius autem homo non est neque equus praeter auton et singulares.

(But it is hard to say, even if one suppose them to exist, why in the world the same is not true of the other things of which there are Forms, as of the objects of mathematics. I mean that these thinkers place the objects of mathematics between the

400

Forms and perceptible things, as a kind of third set of things apart both from the Forms and from the things in this world; but there is not a third man or horse besides the ideal and the individuals.

εἰ δ᾽ αὖ μὴ ἔστιν ὡς λέγουσι, [10] περὶ ποῖα θετέον πραγματεύεσθαι τὸν μαθηματικόν; οὐ γὰρ δὴ περὶ τὰ δεῦρο: τούτων γὰρ οὐθέν ἐστιν οἷον αἱ μαθηματικαὶ ζητοῦσι τῶν ἐπιστημῶν): οὐδὲ μὴν περὶ τὰ μαθηματικὰ ἡ ζητουμένη νῦν ἐστιν ἐπιστήμη (χωριστὸν γὰρ αὐτῶν οὐθέν): ἀλλ᾽ οὐδὲ τῶν αἰσθητῶν οὐσιῶν: φθαρταὶ γάρ.

Si autem iterum non est ut dicunt, circa qualia ponendum negotiari mathematicum? Non enim utique circa ea quae hic; horum enim nullum est quale mathematice quaerunt scientiarum. Neque etiam circa mathematica quesita nunc est scientia; separabile enim ipsorum nullum. Sed neque sensibilium substantiarum; corruptibiles enim.

If on the other hand it is not as they say, with what sort of things must the mathematician be supposed to deal? Certainly not with the things in this world; for none of these is the sort of thing which the mathematical sciences demand.) Nor (b) does the science which we are now seeking treat of the objects of mathematics; for none of them can exist separately. But again it does not deal with perceptible substances; for they are perishable.

ὅλως δ᾽ ἀπορήσειέ [15] τις ἂν ποίας ἐστὶν ἐπιστήμης τὸ διαπορῆσαι περὶ τῆς τῶν μαθηματικῶν ὕλης. οὔτε γὰρ τῆς φυσικῆς, διὰ τὸ περὶ τὰ ἔχοντα ἐν αὐτοῖς ἀρχὴν κινήσεως καὶ στάσεως τὴν τοῦ φυσικοῦ πᾶσαν εἶναι πραγματείαν, οὐδὲ μὴν τῆς σκοπούσης περὶ ἀποδείξεώς τε καὶ ἐπιστήμης: περὶ γὰρ αὐτὸ τοῦτο τὸ [20] γένος τὴν ζήτησιν ποιεῖται. λείπεται τοίνυν τὴν προκειμένην φιλοσοφίαν περὶ αὐτῶν τὴν σκέψιν ποιεῖσθαι.

Totaliter autem dubitabit utique quis cuius est scientie dubitare de mathematicarum materia. Neque enim phisice, propter circa habentia in ipsis principium motus et quietis naturalis omne esse negotium. Neque etiam intendentis de demonstratione et scientia; circa hoc ipsum genus enim inquisitionem facit. Relinquitur igitur propositam philosophiam de ipsis considerationem facere.

In general one might raise the question, to what kind of science it belongs to discuss the difficulties about the matter of the objects of mathematics. Neither to physics (because the whole inquiry of the physicist is about the things that have in themselves a principle. of movement and rest), nor yet to the science which inquires into demonstration and science; for this is just the subject which it investigates. It remains then that it is the philosophy which we have set before ourselves that treats of those subjects.

διαπορήσειε δ᾽ ἄν τις εἰ δεῖ θεῖναι τὴν ζητουμένην ἐπιστήμην περὶ τὰς ἀρχάς, τὰ καλούμενα ὑπό τινων στοιχεῖα· ταῦτα δὲ πάντες ἐνυπάρχοντα τοῖς συνθέτοις τιθέασιν. μᾶλλον δ᾽ ἂν δόξειε [25] τῶν καθόλου δεῖν εἶναι τὴν ζητουμένην ἐπιστήμην· πᾶς γὰρ λόγος καὶ πᾶσα ἐπιστήμη τῶν καθόλου καὶ οὐ τῶν ἐσχάτων, ὥστ᾽ εἴη ἂν οὕτω τῶν πρώτων γενῶν.

Dubitabit autem utique quis si oportet quaerere quesitam scientiam circa principia vocata ab aliquibus elementa; haec autem omnes inexistentia compositis ponunt. Magis autem utiquae videbitur universalium oportere esse quesitam scientiam. Omnis enim ratio et omnis scientia universalium et non extremorum. Quare erit utique sic primorum generum,

One might discuss the question whether the science we are seeking should be said to deal with the principles which are by some called elements; all men suppose these to be present in composite things. But it might be thought that the science we seek should treat rather of universals; for every definition and every science is of universals and not of infimae species, so that as far as this goes it would deal with the highest genera.

ταῦτα δὲ γίγνοιτ᾽ ἂν τό τε ὂν καὶ τὸ ἕν· ταῦτα γὰρ μάλιστ᾽ ἂν ὑποληφθείη περιέχειν τὰ ὄντα πάντα καὶ μάλιστα ἀρχαῖς ἐοικέναι διὰ [30] τὸ εἶναι πρῶτα τῇ φύσει· φθαρέντων γὰρ αὐτῶν συναναιρεῖται καὶ τὰ λοιπά· πᾶν γὰρ ὂν καὶ ἕν. ἧ δὲ τὰς διαφορὰς αὐτῶν ἀνάγκη μετέχειν εἰ θήσει τις αὐτὰ γένη, διαφορὰ δ᾽ οὐδεμία τοῦ γένους μετέχει, ταύτῃ δ᾽ οὐκ ἂν δόξειε δεῖν αὐτὰ τιθέναι γένη οὐδ᾽ ἀρχάς.

haec autem fient utique ens et unum; haec enim maxime utique existimabuntur continere entia omnia et maxime principia videri quia sunt prima natura. Corruptis enim ipsis cointerimuntur reliqua; omnia enim ens et unum. Secundum quod autem differentias ipsis necesse participare, si ponat quis ipsa genera, differentia autem nulla genere participat, sic non utique videbitur oportere ipsa poni genera neque principia.

These would turn out to be being and unity; for these might most of all be supposed to contain all things that are, and to be most like principles because they are by nature; for if they perish all other things are destroyed with them; for everything is and is one. But inasmuch as, if one is to suppose them to be genera, they must be predicable of their differentiae, and no genus is predicable of any of its differentiae, in this way it would seem that we should not make them genera nor principles.

ἔτι δ᾽ εἰ μᾶλλον [35] ἀρχὴ τὸ ἁπλούστερον τοῦ ἧττον τοιούτου, τὰ δ᾽ ἔσχατα τῶν ἐκ τοῦ γένους ἁπλούστερα τῶν γενῶν (ἄτομα γάρ, τὰ γένη δ᾽ εἰς εἴδη πλείω καὶ διαφέροντα διαιρεῖται), μᾶλλον ἂν ἀρχὴ δόξειεν εἶναι τὰ εἴδη τῶν γενῶν. ᾗ δὲ συναναιρεῖται τοῖς γένεσι τὰ εἴδη, τὰ γένη ταῖς ἀρχαῖς ἔοικε μᾶλλον· ἀρχὴ γὰρ τὸ συναναιροῦν. [1060α] [1] τὰ μὲν οὖν τὴν ἀπορίαν ἔχοντα ταῦτα καὶ τοιαῦτ᾽ ἐστὶν ἕτερα.

Adhuc autem si magis principium quod simplicius eo quod minus tale, ultima autem eorum quae ex genere simpliciora generibus (indivisibilia enim, genera autem in plura et differentia dividuntur), magis utique principium videbuntur esse species generibus. Qua autem cointerimuntur generibus species, genera principiis assimilantur magis; principium enim quod cointerimit. Quae quidem igitur dubitationem habent, haec et talia sunt altera.

Further, if the simpler is more of a principle than the less simple, and the ultimate members of the genus are simpler than the genera (for they are indivisible, but the genera are divided into many and differing species), the species might seem to be the principles, rather than the genera. But inasmuch as the species are involved in the destruction of the genera, the genera are more like principles; for that which involves another in its destruction is a principle of [60a] it. These and others of the kind are the subjects that involve difficulties.

## Chapter 2

ἔτι πότερον δεῖ τιθέναι τι παρὰ τὰ καθ᾽ ἕκαστα ἢ οὔ, ἀλλὰ τούτων ἡ ζητουμένη ἐπιστήμη; ἀλλὰ ταῦτα ἄπειρα: [5] τά γε μὴν παρὰ τὰ καθ᾽ ἕκαστα γένη ἢ εἴδη ἐστίν, ἀλλ᾽ οὐδετέρου τούτων ἡ ζητουμένη νῦν ἐπιστήμη. διότι γὰρ ἀδύνατον τοῦτο, εἴρηται.

Adhuc utrum oportet poni aliquid praeter singularia aut non, sed horum quesita scientia? Sed haec infinita. Quae vero praeter singularia genera aut species sunt, sed neutrius horum quesita nunc scientia; propter quod enim impossibile hoc, dictum est.

Further, must we suppose something apart from individual things, or is it these that the science we are seeking treats of? But these are infinite in number. Yet the things that are apart from the individuals are genera or species; but the science we now seek treats of neither of these. The reason why this is impossible has been stated.

καὶ γὰρ ὅλως ἀπορίαν ἔχει πότερον δεῖ τινὰ ὑπολαβεῖν οὐσίαν εἶναι χωριστὴν παρὰ τὰς αἰσθητὰς οὐσίας καὶ τὰς δεῦρο, ἢ οὔ, ἀλλὰ ταῦτ᾽ εἶναι τὰ ὄντα καὶ [10] περὶ ταῦτα τὴν σοφίαν ὑπάρχειν. ζητεῖν μὲν γὰρ ἐοίκαμεν ἄλλην τινά, καὶ τὸ προκείμενον τοῦτ᾽ ἐστιν ἡμῖν, λέγω δὲ τὸ ἰδεῖν εἴ τι χωριστὸν καθ᾽ αὑτὸ καὶ μηδενὶ τῶν αἰσθητῶν ὑπάρχον.

Et enim totaliter dubitationem habet utrum oportet aliquam existimare substantiam separabilem praeter sensibiles substantias et eas quae hic aut non, sed haec esse entia et circa haec sapientiam existere. Quaerere quidem enim videmur aliam quandam, et propositum hoc est nobis, dico autem scire si quid separabile secundum se et nulli sensibilium existens.

Indeed, it is in general hard to say whether one must assume that there is a separable substance besides the sensible substances (i.e. the substances in this world), or that these are the real things and Wisdom is concerned with them. For we seem to seek another kind of substance, and this is our problem, i.e. to see if there is something which can exist apart by itself and belongs to no sensible thing.

ἔτι δ᾽ εἰ παρὰ τὰς αἰσθητὰς οὐσίας ἔστι τις ἑτέρα οὐσία, παρὰ ποίας τῶν αἰσθητῶν δεῖ τιθέναι ταύτην εἶναι; [15] τί γὰρ μᾶλλον παρὰ τοὺς ἀνθρώπους ἢ τοὺς ἵππους ἢ τῶν ἄλλων ζῴων θήσει τις αὐτὴν ἢ καὶ τῶν ἀψύχων ὅλως; τό γε μὴν ἴσας ταῖς αἰσθηταῖς καὶ φθαρταῖς οὐσίαις ἀϊδίους ἑτέρας κατασκευάζειν ἐκτὸς τῶν εὐλόγων δόξειεν ἂν πίπτειν.

Adhuc autem si praeter sensibiles substantias est aliqua alia substantia, praeter quales sensibilium oportet ponere hanc esse? Quid enim magis praeter homines aut equos quam aliorum animalium ponet quis ipsam aut et inanimatorum totaliter? Equalesque sensibilibus et corruptibilibus substantiis perpetuas alteras construere extra rationabilia videbitur utique cadere.

-Further, if there is another substance apart from and corresponding to sensible substances, which kinds of sensible substance must be supposed to have this corresponding to them? Why should one suppose men or horses to have it, more than either the other animals or even all lifeless things? On the other hand to set up other and eternal substances equal in number to the sensible and perishable substances would seem to fall beyond the bounds of probability.

εἰ δὲ μὴ χωριστὴ τῶν σωμάτων ἡ ζητουμένη νῦν ἀρχή, [20] τίνα ἄν τις ἄλλην θείη μᾶλλον τῆς ὕλης; αὕτη γε μὴν ἐνεργείᾳ μὲν οὐκ ἔστι, δυνάμει δ᾽ ἔστιν. μᾶλλόν τ᾽ ἂν ἀρχὴ κυριωτέρα ταύτης δόξειεν εἶναι τὸ εἶδος καὶ ἡ μορφή· τοῦτο δὲ φθαρτόν, ὥσθ᾽ ὅλως οὐκ ἔστιν ἀΐδιος οὐσία χωριστὴ καὶ καθ᾽ αὑτήν. ἀλλ᾽ ἄτοπον· ἔοικε γὰρ καὶ ζητεῖται σχεδὸν [25] ὑπὸ τῶν χαριεστάτων ὡς οὖσά τις ἀρχὴ καὶ οὐσία τοιαύτη· πῶς γὰρ ἔσται τάξις μή τινος ὄντος ἀϊδίου καὶ χωριστοῦ καὶ μένοντος;

Si autem non separabile a corporibus quesitum nunc principium est, quid utique aliud quis ponet magis materia? Haec tamen actu quidem non est, potentia autem est. Magisque utique principium principalius hac videbitur esse species et forma; hoc autem corruptibile. Quare totaliter non est perpetua substantia separabilis et secundum se. Sed inconveniens. Videtur enim et quaeritur fere a gratiosissimis tamquam existens quoddam principium et substantia talis; quomodo enim erit ordo non existente aliquo perpetuo et separabili et manente?

But if the principle we now seek is not separable from corporeal things, what has a better claim to the name matter? This, however, does not exist in actuality, but exists in potency. And it would seem rather that the form or shape is a more important principle than this; but the form is perishable, so that there is no eternal substance at all which can exist apart and independent. But this is paradoxical; for such a principle and substance seems to exist and is sought by nearly all the most refined thinkers as something that exists; for how is there to be order unless there is something eternal and independent and permanent?

ἔτι δ' εἴπερ ἔστι τις οὐσία καὶ ἀρχὴ τοιαύτη τὴν φύσιν οἵαν νῦν ζητοῦμεν, καὶ αὕτη μία πάντων καὶ ἡ αὐτὴ τῶν ἀϊδίων τε καὶ φθαρτῶν, ἀπορίαν ἔχει διὰ τί ποτε τῆς [30] αὐτῆς ἀρχῆς οὔσης τὰ μέν ἐστιν ἀΐδια τῶν ὑπὸ τὴν ἀρχὴν τὰ δ' οὐκ ἀΐδια (τοῦτο γὰρ ἄτοπον): εἰ δ' ἄλλη μέν ἐστιν ἀρχὴ τῶν φθαρτῶν ἄλλη δὲ τῶν ἀϊδίων, εἰ μὲν ἀΐδιος καὶ ἡ τῶν φθαρτῶν, ὁμοίως ἀπορήσομεν (διὰ τί γὰρ οὐκ ἀϊδίου τῆς ἀρχῆς οὔσης καὶ τὰ ὑπὸ τὴν ἀρχὴν ἀΐδια;): φθαρτῆς δ' [35] οὔσης ἄλλη τις ἀρχὴ γίγνεται ταύτης κἀκείνης ἑτέρα, καὶ τοῦτ' εἰς ἄπειρον πρόεισιν.

Adhuc autem siquidem est aliqua substantia et principium tale secundum naturam quale nunc quaerimus, et hoc unum omnium et idem perpetuorum et corruptibilium, dubitationem habet propter quid quidem eodem principio existente haec quidem sunt perpetua eorum quae sub principio, haec autem non perpetua; hoc enim inconveniens. Si autem aliud quidem principium est corruptibilium aliud autem perpetuorum, si quidem perpetuum et quod corruptibilium, similiter dubitabimus; propter quid enim non, perpetuo principio existente, et quae sub principio perpetua? Corruptibili autem existente aliud aliquod principium fit huius, et illius alterum, et hoc in infinitum procedit.

Further, if there is a substance or principle of such a nature as that which we are now seeking, and if this is one for all things, and the same for eternal and for perishable things, it is hard to say why in the world, if there is the same principle, some of the things that fall under the principle are eternal, and others are not eternal; this is paradoxical. But if there is one principle of perishable and another of eternal things, we shall be in a like difficulty if the principle of perishable things, as well as that of eternal, is eternal; for why, if the principle is eternal, are not the things that fall under the principle also eternal? But if it is perishable another principle is involved to account for it, and another to account for that, and this will go on to infinity.

εἰ δ' αὖ τις τὰς δοκούσας μάλιστ' ἀρχὰς ἀκινήτους εἶναι, τό τε ὂν καὶ τὸ ἕν, θήσει, πρῶτον μὲν εἰ μὴ τόδε τι καὶ οὐσίαν ἑκάτερον αὐτῶν σημαίνει, [1060β] [1] πῶς ἔσονται χωρισταὶ καὶ καθ᾽ αὑτάς; τοιαύτας δὲ ζητοῦμεν τὰς ἀϊδίους τε καὶ πρώτας ἀρχάς. εἰ γε μὴν τόδε τι καὶ οὐσίαν ἑκάτερον αὐτῶν δηλοῖ, πάντ᾽ ἐστὶν οὐσίαι τὰ ὄντα: κατὰ [5] πάντων γὰρ τὸ ὂν κατηγορεῖται (κατ᾽ ἐνίων δὲ καὶ τὸ ἕν): οὐσίαν δ᾽ εἶναι πάντα τὰ ὄντα ψεῦδος.

Si autem rursum aliquis putata maxime principia immobilia esse, ens et unum, ponat, primo quidem si non hoc aliquid et substantiam utrumque ipsorum significat, quomodo erunt separabilia et per se? Talia autem quaerimus perpetuaque et prima principia. Si vero hoc aliquid et substantiam utrumque ipsorum significat, omnia erunt substantia entia; de omnibus enim ens predicatur, de quibusdam autem et unum. Substantiam autem esse omnia entia falsum.

If on the other hand we are to set up what are thought to be the most unchangeable principles, being and unity, firstly, if each of these does not indicate a this or sub[60b]stance, how will they be separable and independent? Yet we expect the eternal and primary principles to be so. But if each of them does signify a this or substance, all things that are are substances; for being is predicated of all things (and unity also of some); but that all things that are are substance is false.

ἔτι δὲ τοῖς τὴν πρώτην ἀρχὴν τὸ ἓν λέγουσι καὶ τοῦτ᾽ οὐσίαν, ἐκ δὲ τοῦ ἑνὸς καὶ τῆς ὕλης τὸν ἀριθμὸν γεννῶσι πρῶτον καὶ τοῦτον οὐσίαν φάσκουσιν εἶναι, πῶς ἐνδέχεται τὸ λεγόμενον ἀληθὲς εἶναι; [10] τὴν γὰρ δυάδα καὶ τῶν λοιπῶν ἕκαστον ἀριθμῶν τῶν συνθέτων πῶς ἓν δεῖ νοῆσαι; περὶ τούτου γὰρ οὔτε λέγουσιν οὐδὲν οὔτε ῥᾴδιον εἰπεῖν.

Adhuc autem primum principium quod unum dicentibus et hoc substantiam, ex uno autem et materia numerum generant primo et hunc substantiam dicunt esse, quomodo contingit quod dicitur verum esse? Dualitatem enim et reliquorum unumquemque numerum compositorum, quomodo unum oportet intelligere? De hoc enim neque dicunt nihil neque facile dicere.

Further, how can they be right who say that the first principle is unity and this is substance, and generate number as the first product from unity and from matter, assert that number is substance? How are we to think of two, and each of the other numbers composed of units, as one? On this point neither do they say anything nor is it easy to say anything.

εἴ γε μὴν γραμμὰς ἢ τὰ τούτων ἐχόμενα (λέγω δὲ ἐπιφανείας τὰς πρώτας) θήσει τις ἀρχάς, ταῦτά γ᾽ οὐκ εἰσὶν οὐσίαι χωρισταί, τομαὶ δὲ καὶ διαιρέσεις αἱ μὲν [15] ἐπιφανειῶν αἱ δὲ σωμάτων (αἱ δὲ στιγμαὶ γραμμῶν), ἔτι δὲ πέρατα τῶν αὐτῶν τούτων: πάντα δὲ ταῦτα ἐν ἄλλοις ὑπάρχει καὶ χωριστὸν οὐδέν ἐστιν.

Si vero lineas aut hiis habita (dico autem superficies) prima ponat quis principia, haec autem non sunt substantiae separabiles, decisiones autem et divisiones hae quidem superficierum hae autem corporum, puncta autem linearum, adhuc autem termini eorundem horum; omnia autem haec in aliis existunt et separabile nullum est.

But if we are to suppose lines or what comes after these (I mean the primary surfaces) to be principles, these at least are not separable substances, but sections and divisions-the former of surfaces, the latter of bodies (while points are sections and divisions of lines); and further they are limits of these same things; and all these are in other things and none is separable.

ἔτι πῶς οὐσίαν ὑπολαβεῖν εἶναι δεῖ τοῦ ἑνὸς καὶ στιγμῆς; οὐσίας μὲν γὰρ πάσης γένεσις ἔστι, στιγμῆς δ᾽ οὐκ ἔστιν: διαίρεσις γὰρ ἡ στιγμή.

Adhuc quomodo substantiam existimare esse oportet unius et puncti? Substantiae quidem enim omnis generatio est, puncti autem non est; divisio enim punctum.

Further, how are we to suppose that there is a substance of unity and the point? Every substance comes into being by a gradual process, but a point does not; for the point is a division.

παρέχει [20] δ᾽ ἀπορίαν καὶ τὸ πᾶσαν μὲν ἐπιστήμην εἶναι τῶν καθόλου καὶ τοῦ τοιουδί, τὴν δ᾽ οὐσίαν μὴ τῶν καθόλου εἶναι, μᾶλλον δὲ τόδε τι καὶ χωριστόν, ὥστ᾽ εἰ περὶ τὰς ἀρχάς ἐστιν ἐπιστήμη, πῶς δεῖ τὴν ἀρχὴν ὑπολαβεῖν οὐσίαν εἶναι;

Exhibet autem dubitationem et omnem quidem scientiam esse universalium et talis, substantiam autem non universalium esse, magis autem hoc aliquid et separabile. Quare si circa principia est scientia, quomodo oportet principium existimare substantiam esse?

A further difficulty is raised by the fact that all knowledge is of universals and of the such , but substance is not a universal, but is rather a this -a separable thing, so that if there is knowledge about the first principles, the question arises, how are we to suppose the first principle to be substance?

ἔτι πότερον ἔστι τι παρὰ τὸ σύνολον ἢ οὔ (λέγω δὲ τὴν ὕλην καὶ [25] τὸ μετὰ ταύτης); εἰ μὲν γὰρ μή, τά γε ἐν ὕλη φθαρτὰ πάντα: εἰ δ᾽ ἔστι τι, τὸ εἶδος ἂν εἴη καὶ ἡ μορφή: τοῦτ᾽ οὖν ἐπὶ τίνων ἔστι καὶ ἐπὶ τίνων οὔ, χαλεπὸν ἀφορίσαι: ἐπ᾽ ἐνίων γὰρ δῆλον οὐκ ὂν χωριστὸν τὸ εἶδος, οἷον οἰκίας.

Adhuc utrum est aliquid praeter synolon aut non? Dico autem materiam et quod cum hac. Si quidem enim non, quae quidem in materia corruptibilia omnia. Si autem est aliquid, species utique erit et forma. Hoc igitur in quibus est et in quibus non, difficile determinare; in quibusdam enim palam non existens separabilis species, puta domus.

Further, is there anything apart from the concrete thing (by which I mean the matter and that which is joined with it), or not? If not, we are met by the objection that all things that are in matter are perishable. But if there is something, it must be the form or shape. Now it is hard to determine in which cases this exists apart and in which it does not; for in some cases the form is evidently not separable, e.g. in the case of a house.

ἔτι πότερον αἱ ἀρχαὶ εἴδει ἢ ἀριθμῷ αἱ αὐταί; εἰ γὰρ ἀριθμῷ [30] ἕν, πάντ᾽ ἔσται ταὐτά.

Adhuc utrum principia specie aut numero eadem? Si enim numero, omnia erunt eadem.

Further, are the principles the same in kind or in number? If they are one in number, all things will be the same.

## Chapter 3

ἐπεὶ δ᾽ ἐστὶν ἡ τοῦ φιλοσόφου ἐπιστήμη τοῦ ὄντος ᾗ ὂν καθόλου καὶ οὐ κατὰ μέρος, τὸ δ᾽ ὂν πολλαχῶς καὶ οὐ καθ᾽ ἕνα λέγεται τρόπον· εἰ μὲν οὖν ὁμωνύμως κατὰ δὲ κοινὸν μηδέν, οὐκ ἔστιν ὑπὸ μίαν ἐπιστήμην (οὐ γὰρ ἓν γένος [35] τῶν τοιούτων), εἰ δὲ κατά τι κοινόν, εἴη ἂν ὑπὸ μίαν ἐπιστήμην.

Quoniam autem philosophi scientia entis in quantum ens universaliter et non secundum partem, ens autem multipliciter et non secundum unum dicitur modum: si quidem igitur equivoce secundum commune autem nihil, non est sub una scientia; non enim unum genus talium. Si autem secundum aliquid commune, erit utique sub una scientia.

Since the science of the philosopher treats of being qua being universally and not in respect of a part of it, and being has many senses and is not used in one only, it follows that if the word is used equivocally and in virtue of nothing common to its various uses, being does not fall under one science (for the meanings of an equivocal term do not form one genus); but if the word is used in virtue of something common, being will fall under one science.

ἔοικε δὴ τὸν εἰρημένον λέγεσθαι τρόπον καθάπερ τό τε ἰατρικὸν καὶ ὑγιεινόν· καὶ γὰρ τούτων ἑκάτερον πολλαχῶς λέγομεν. [1061α] [1] λέγεται δὲ τοῦτον τὸν τρόπον ἕκαστον τῷ τὸ μὲν πρὸς τὴν ἰατρικὴν ἐπιστήμην ἀνάγεσθαί πως τὸ δὲ πρὸς ὑγίειαν τὸ δ᾽ ἄλλως, πρὸς ταὐτὸ δ᾽ ἕκαστον. ἰατρικὸς γὰρ λόγος καὶ μαχαίριον λέγεται τῷ τὸ μὲν ἀπὸ τῆς ἰατρικῆς [5] ἐπιστήμης εἶναι τὸ δὲ ταύτῃ χρήσιμον. ὁμοίως δὲ καὶ ὑγιεινόν· τὸ μὲν γὰρ ὅτι σημαντικὸν ὑγιείας τὸ δ᾽ ὅτι ποιητικόν. ὁ δ᾽ αὐτὸς τρόπος καὶ ἐπὶ τῶν λοιπῶν. τὸν αὐτὸν δὴ τρόπον καὶ τὸ ὂν ἅπαν λέγεται· τῷ γὰρ τοῦ ὄντος ἦ ὂν πάθος ἢ ἕξις ἢ διάθεσις ἢ κίνησις ἢ τῶν ἄλλων τι τῶν τοιούτων [10] εἶναι λέγεται ἕκαστον αὐτῶν ὄν.

Videtur itaque dicto modo dici quemadmodum medicativum et salubre; et enim horum unumquodque multipliciter. Dicitur autem secundum unumquemque modorum eo quod hoc quidem ad medicativam scientiam reducatur aliqualiter hoc autem ad sanitatem hoc autem aliter, ad idem autem unumquodque. Medicativus enim sermo et cultellus dicitur eo quod hic quidem a medicativa scientia sit hic autem huic utilis. Similiter autem et salubre; hoc quidem enim quia significativum sanitatis hoc autem quia factivum. Idem autem modus et in reliquis. Eodem itaque modo et ens omne dicitur; eo enim quod entis in quantum ens passio aut habitus aut dispositio aut motus aut aliorum aliquid talium sit, dicitur unumquodque ipsorum ens.

The term seems to be used in the way we have mentioned, like medical and healthy . For each of these also we use in [61a] many senses. Terms are used in this way by virtue of some kind of reference, in the one case to medical science, in the other to health, in others to something else, but in each case to one identical concept. For a discussion and a knife are called medical because the former proceeds from medical science, and the latter is useful to it. And a thing is called healthy in a similar way; one thing because it is indicative of health, another because it is productive of it. And the same is true in the other cases. Everything that is, then, is said to be in this same way; each thing that is is said to be because it is a modification of being qua being or a permanent or a transient state or a movement of it, or something else of the sort.

ἐπεὶ δὲ παντὸς τοῦ ὄντος πρὸς ἕν τι καὶ κοινὸν ἡ ἀναγωγὴ γίγνεται, καὶ τῶν ἐναντιώσεων ἑκάστη πρὸς τὰς πρώτας διαφορὰς καὶ ἐναντιώσεις ἀναχθήσεται τοῦ ὄντος, εἴτε πλῆθος καὶ ἓν εἴθ᾽ ὁμοιότης καὶ ἀνομοιότης αἱ πρῶται τοῦ ὄντος εἰσὶ διαφοραί, εἴτ᾽ [15] ἄλλαι τινές· ἔστωσαν γὰρ αὗται τεθεωρημέναι.

Quoniam autem omnis entis ad unum aliquid et commune reductio fit, et contrarietatum unaqueque ad primas differentias et contrarietates reducetur entis, sive pluralitas et unum sive similitudo et dissimilitudo prime entis sint differentiae, sive aliae alique; sint enim hae speculatae.

And since everything that is may be referred to something single and common, each of the contrarieties also may be referred to the first differences and contrarieties of being, whether the first differences of being are plurality and unity, or likeness and unlikeness, or some other differences; let these be taken as already discussed.

διαφέρει δ᾽ οὐδὲν τὴν τοῦ ὄντος ἀναγωγὴν πρὸς τὸ ὂν ἢ πρὸς τὸ ἓν γίγνεσθαι. καὶ γὰρ εἰ μὴ ταὐτὸν ἄλλο δ᾽ ἐστίν, ἀντιστρέφει γε· τό τε γὰρ ἓν καὶ ὂν πως, τό τε ὂν ἕν.

Differt autem nihil entis reductionem ad ens aut ad unum fieri. Et enim si non idem sed est aliud, convertitur quidem; unum enim ens aliqualiter et ens unum.

It makes no difference whether that which is be referred to being or to unity. For even if they are not the same but different, at least they are convertible; for that which is one is also somehow being, and that which is being is one.

ἐπεὶ δ᾽ ἐστὶ τὰ ἐναντία πάντα τῆς αὐτῆς καὶ μιᾶς ἐπιστήμης θεωρῆσαι, λέγεται [20] δ᾽ ἕκαστον αὐτῶν κατὰ στέρησιν—καίτοι γ᾽ ἔνια ἀπορήσειέ τις ἂν πῶς λέγεται κατὰ στέρησιν, ὧν ἔστιν ἀνὰ μέσον τι, καθάπερ ἀδίκου καὶ δικαίου—περὶ πάντα δὴ τὰ τοιαῦτα τὴν στέρησιν δεῖ τιθέναι μὴ τοῦ ὅλου λόγου, τοῦ τελευταίου δὲ εἴδους: οἷον εἰ ἔστιν ὁ δίκαιος καθ᾽ ἕξιν τινὰ [25] πειθαρχικὸς τοῖς νόμοις, οὐ πάντως ὁ ἄδικος ἔσται τοῦ ὅλου στερούμενος λόγου, περὶ δὲ τὸ πείθεσθαι τοῖς νόμοις ἐκλείπων πη, καὶ ταύτη ἡ στέρησις ὑπάρξει αὐτῷ: τὸν αὐτὸν δὲ τρόπον καὶ ἐπὶ τῶν ἄλλων.

Quoniam autem sunt contraria omnia eiusdem et unius scientiae speculari, dicitur autem unumquodque ipsorum secundum privationem, et utique quaedam dubitabit aliquis quomodo dicuntur secundum privationem quorum est intermedium aliquid, quemadmodum iniusti et iusti. Circa omnia itaque talia privationem oportet poni non totius rationis, sed ultime speciei; puta si est iustus secundum habitum quendam obediens legibus, non semper iniustus erit tota privatus ratione, circa persuaderi autem legibus deficiens in aliquo, et secundum hoc privatio inest ipsi. Eodem autem modo et in aliis.

But since every pair of contraries falls to be examined by one and the same science, and in each pair one term is the privative of the other though one might regarding some contraries raise the question, how they can be privately related, viz. those which have an intermediate, e.g. unjust and just-in all such cases one must maintain that the privation is not of the whole definition, but of the infima species. if the just man is by virtue of some permanent disposition obedient to the laws , the unjust man will not in every case have the whole definition denied of him, but may be merely in some respect deficient in obedience to the laws , and in this respect the privation will attach to him; and similarly in all other cases.

καθάπερ δ᾽ ὁ μαθηματικὸς περὶ τὰ ἐξ ἀφαιρέσεως τὴν θεωρίαν ποιεῖται (περιελὼν γὰρ πάντα [30] τὰ αἰσθητὰ θεωρεῖ, οἷον βάρος καὶ κουφότητα καὶ σκληρότητα καὶ τοὐναντίον, ἔτι δὲ καὶ θερμότητα καὶ ψυχρότητα καὶ τὰς ἄλλας αἰσθητὰς ἐναντιώσεις, μόνον δὲ καταλείπει τὸ ποσὸν καὶ συνεχές, τῶν μὲν ἐφ᾽ ἓν τῶν δ᾽ ἐπὶ δύο τῶν δ᾽ ἐπὶ τρία, καὶ τὰ πάθη τὰ τούτων ᾗ ποσά ἐστι [35] καὶ συνεχῆ, καὶ οὐ καθ᾽ ἕτερόν τι θεωρεῖ, καὶ τῶν μὲν τὰς πρὸς ἄλληλα θέσεις σκοπεῖ καὶ τὰ ταύταις ὑπάρχοντα, [1061β] [1] τῶν δὲ τὰς συμμετρίας καὶ ἀσυμμετρίας, τῶν δὲ τοὺς λόγους, ἀλλ᾽ ὅμως μίαν πάντων καὶ τὴν αὐτὴν τίθεμεν ἐπιστήμην τὴν γεωμετρικήν), τὸν αὐτὸν δὴ τρόπον ἔχει καὶ περὶ τὸ ὄν.

Quemadmodum autem mathematicus circa ea quae ex ablatione theoriam facit, circumtollens enim omnia sensibilia speculatur, puta gravitatem et levitatem et duritiem et contrarium, adhuc autem caliditatem et frigiditatem et alias sensibiles contrarietates, solum autem derelinquit quantum et continuum, horum quidem ad unum horum autem ad duo horum vero ad tria, et passiones horum in quantum quanta sunt et continua et non secundum aliud aliquid speculatur, et horum quidem eas quae ad invicem positiones considerat et hiis existentia, horum autem commensurationes et incommensurationes, horum vero rationes, sed tamen omnium unam et eandem ponimus scientiam geometricam: eodem modo habet et circa ens.

As the mathematician investigates abstractions (for before beginning his investigation he strips off all the sensible qualities, e.g. weight and lightness, hardness and its contrary, and also heat and cold and the other sensible contrarieties, and leaves only the quantitative and continuous, sometimes in one, sometimes in two, sometimes in three dimensions, and the attributes of these qua quantitative and continuous, and does not consider them in any other respect, and examines the relative positions of some and the attributes of these, [61b] and the commensurabilities and incommensurabilities of others, and the ratios of others; but yet we posit one and the same science of all these things geometry) the same is true with regard to being.

τὰ γὰρ τούτῳ συμβεβηκότα καθ᾽ ὅσον ἐστὶν ὄν, καὶ [5] τὰς ἐναντιώσεις αὐτοῦ ᾗ ὄν, οὐκ ἄλλης ἐπιστήμης ἢ φιλοσοφίας θεωρῆσαι. τῇ φυσικῇ μὲν γὰρ οὐχ ᾗ ὄντα, μᾶλλον δ᾽ ᾗ κινήσεως μετέχει, τὴν θεωρίαν τις ἀπονείμειεν ἄν· ἥ γε μὴν διαλεκτικὴ καὶ ἡ σοφιστικὴ τῶν συμβεβηκότων μέν εἰσι τοῖς οὖσιν, οὐχ ᾗ δ᾽ ὄντα οὐδὲ περὶ τὸ ὂν αὐτὸ καθ᾽ ὅσον [10] ὄν ἐστιν· ὥστε λείπεται τὸν φιλόσοφον, καθ᾽ ὅσον ὄντ᾽ ἐστίν, εἶναι περὶ τὰ λεχθέντα θεωρητικόν.

Huic enim accidentia in quantum est ens et contrarietates ipsius in quantum ens non alterius scientie quam philosophiae speculari, naturali quidem enim non in quantum entia, magis autem in quantum motu participant, theoriam utique quis distribuet. Dialetica etiam et sophistica sunt accidentium quidem entibus, non autem in quantum entia neque circa ens ipsum in quantum ens est. Quare relinquitur philosophum, in quantum entis sunt, esse circa dicta speculativum.

For the attributes of this in so far as it is being, and the contrarieties in it qua being, it is the business of no other science than philosophy to investigate; for to physics one would assign the study of things not qua being, but rather qua sharing in movement; while dialectic and sophistic deal with the attributes of things that are, but not of things qua being, and not with being itself in so far as it is being; therefore it remains that it is the philosopher who studies the things we have named, in so far as they are being.

ἐπεὶ δὲ τό τε ὂν ἅπαν καθ᾽ ἕν τι καὶ κοινὸν λέγεται πολλαχῶς λεγόμενον, καὶ τἀναντία τὸν αὐτὸν τρόπον (εἰς τὰς πρώτας γὰρ ἐναντιώσεις καὶ διαφορὰς τοῦ ὄντος ἀνάγεται), τὰ δὲ τοιαῦτα δυνατὸν [15] ὑπὸ μίαν ἐπιστήμην εἶναι, διαλύοιτ᾽ ἂν ἡ κατ᾽ ἀρχὰς ἀπορία λεχθεῖσα, λέγω δ᾽ ἐν ᾗ διηπορεῖτο πῶς ἔσται πολλῶν καὶ διαφόρων ὄντων τῷ γένει μία τις ἐπιστήμη.

Quoniam autem ens omne secundum unum aliquid et commune dicitur multipliciter dictum, et contraria eodem modo (ad primas enim contrarietates et differentias entis <reducuntur), talia autem possunt sub una scientia esse, dissoluetur utique quae secundum principia dubitatio dicta. Dico autem in qua dubitatum est quomodo erit multorum et differentium genere una aliqua scientia.

Since all that is is to be in virtue of something single and common, though the term has many meanings, and contraries are in the same case (for they are referred to the first contrarieties and differences of being), and things of this sort can fall under one science, the difficulty we stated at the beginning appears to be solved,-I mean the question how there can be a single science of things which are many and different in genus.

## Chapter 4

ἐπεὶ δὲ καὶ ὁ μαθηματικὸς χρῆται τοῖς κοινοῖς ἰδίως, καὶ τὰς τούτων ἀρχὰς ἂν εἴη θεωρῆσαι τῆς πρώτης φιλοσοφίας. ὅτι γὰρ [20] ἀπὸ τῶν ἴσων ἴσων ἀφαιρεθέντων ἴσα τὰ λειπόμενα, κοινὸν μέν ἐστιν ἐπὶ πάντων τῶν ποσῶν, ἡ μαθηματικὴ δ᾽ ἀπολαβοῦσα περί τι μέρος τῆς οἰκείας ὕλης ποιεῖται τὴν θεωρίαν, οἷον περὶ γραμμὰς ἢ γωνίας ἢ ἀριθμοὺς ἢ τῶν λοιπῶν τι ποσῶν, οὐχ ᾗ δ᾽ ὄντα ἀλλ᾽ ᾗ συνεχὲς αὐτῶν ἕκαστον ἐφ᾽ [25] ἓν ἢ δύο ἢ τρία· ἡ δὲ φιλοσοφία περὶ τῶν ἐν μέρει μέν, ᾗ τούτων ἑκάστῳ τι συμβέβηκεν, οὐ σκοπεῖ, περὶ τὸ ὂν δέ, ᾗ ὂν τῶν τοιούτων ἕκαστον, θεωρεῖ.

Quoniam autem et mathematicus utitur communibus proprie, et horum principia erit utique speculari primae philosophiae. Quod enim ab equalibus equalibus ablatis quae relinquuntur equalia, commune quidem est in omnibus quantis. Mathematica autem absumens circa aliquam partem convenientis materiae facit theoriam, puta circa lineas aut angulos aut numeros aut reliquorum aliquid quantorum, non in quantum autem entia sed in quantum continuum ipsorum unumquodque ad unum aut duo aut tria. Philosophia autem de hiis quae in parte quidem in quantum horum unicuique aliquid accidit non intendit, circa ens autem in quantum ens talium unumquodque speculatur.

Since even the mathematician uses the common axioms only in a special application, it must be the business of first philosophy to examine the principles of mathematics also. That when equals are taken from equals the remainders are equal, is common to all quantities, but mathematics studies a part of its proper matter which it has detached, e.g. lines or angles or numbers or some other kind of quantity-not, however, qua being but in so far as each of them is continuous in one or two or three dimensions; but philosophy does not inquire about particular subjects in so far as each of them has some attribute or other, but speculates about being, in so far as each particular thing is.

τὸν αὐτὸν δ᾽ ἔχει τρόπον καὶ περὶ τὴν φυσικὴν ἐπιστήμην τῇ μαθηματικῇ: τὰ συμβεβηκότα γὰρ ἡ φυσικὴ καὶ τὰς ἀρχὰς θεωρεῖ τὰς τῶν ὄντων [30] ᾗ κινούμενα καὶ οὐχ ᾗ ὄντα (τὴν δὲ πρώτην εἰρήκαμεν ἐπιστήμην τούτων εἶναι καθ᾽ ὅσον ὄντα τὰ ὑποκείμενά ἐστιν, ἀλλ᾽ οὐχ ᾗ ἕτερόν τι): διὸ καὶ ταύτην καὶ τὴν μαθηματικὴν ἐπιστήμην μέρη τῆς σοφίας εἶναι θετέον.

Eodem autem habet modo et circa naturalem scientiam mathematice. Naturalis enim accidentia et principia speculatur entium in quantum mota et non in quantum entia. Primam autem scientiam diximus horum esse secundum quod entia subiecta sunt, sed non alterum aliquid. Propter quod et hanc et mathematicam scientiam partes sapientie esse ponendum.

-Physics is in the same position as mathematics; for physics studies the attributes and the principles of the things that are, qua moving and not qua being (whereas the primary science, we have said, deals with these, only in so far as the underlying subjects are existent, and not in virtue of any other character); and so both physics and mathematics must be classed as parts of Wisdom.

## Chapter 5

ἔστι δέ τις ἐν τοῖς οὖσιν ἀρχὴ περὶ ἣν οὐκ ἔστι διεψεῦσθαι, [35] τοὐναντίον δὲ ἀναγκαῖον ἀεὶ ποιεῖν, λέγω δὲ ἀληθεύειν, οἷον ὅτι οὐκ ἐνδέχεται τὸ αὐτὸ καθ᾽ ἕνα καὶ τὸν αὐτὸν χρόνον εἶναι καὶ μὴ εἶναι, [1062α] [1] καὶ τἆλλα τὰ τοῦτον αὐτοῖς ἀντικείμενα τὸν τρόπον.

Est autem quoddam in entibus principium circa quod non est mentiri, contrarium autem necessarium semper facere, dico autem verum dicere: puta quod non contingit idem secundum unum et idem tempus esse et non esse, et alia ipsis opposita hoc modo.

There is a principle in things, about which we cannot be deceived, but must always, on the contrary recognize the truth,-viz. that the same thing cannot at one and the same [62a] time be and not be, or admit any other similar pair of opposites.

καὶ περὶ τῶν τοιούτων ἁπλῶς μὲν οὐκ ἔστιν ἀπόδειξις, πρὸς τόνδε δὲ ἔστιν· οὐ γὰρ ἔστιν ἐκ πιστοτέρας ἀρχῆς αὐτοῦ τούτου ποιήσασθαι συλλογισμόν, δεῖ δέ γ᾽ [5] εἴπερ ἔσται τὸ ἁπλῶς ἀποδεδεῖχθαι.

Et de talibus simpliciter quidem non est demonstratio, ad hunc autem est. Non enim est ex credibiliori principio hoc ipso facere sillogismum; oportet autem, siquidem erit simpliciter demonstrare.

About such matters there is no proof in the full sense, though there is proof ad hominem. For it is not possible to infer this truth itself from a more certain principle, yet this is necessary if there is to be completed proof of it in the full sense.

πρὸς δὲ τὸν λέγοντα τὰς ἀντικειμένας φάσεις τῷ δεικνύντι διότι ψεῦδος ληπτέον τι τοιοῦτον ὃ ταὐτὸ μὲν ἔσται τῷ μὴ ἐνδέχεσθαι ταὐτὸ εἶναι καὶ μὴ εἶναι καθ᾽ ἕνα καὶ τὸν αὐτὸν χρόνον, μὴ δόξει δ᾽ εἶναι ταὐτόν· οὕτω γὰρ μόνως ἂν ἀποδειχθείη πρὸς τὸν [10] φάσκοντα ἐνδέχεσθαι τὰς ἀντικειμένας φάσεις ἀληθεύεσθαι κατὰ τοῦ αὐτοῦ.

Ad dicentem autem oppositas dictiones ostendenti quia falsum, sumendum aliquid tale quod idem quidem erit ei quod est non contingere idem esse et non esse secundum unum et idem tempus, non videbitur autem esse idem; sic enim solum utique demonstrabitur ad dicentem contingere oppositas dictiones verificari de eodem.

But he who wants to prove to the asserter of opposites that he is wrong must get from him an admission which shall be identical with the principle that the same thing cannot be and not be at one and the same time, but shall not seem to be identical; for thus alone can his thesis be demonstrated to the man who asserts that opposite statements can be truly made about the same subject.

τοὺς δὴ μέλλοντας ἀλλήλοις λόγου κοινωνήσειν δεῖ τι συνιέναι αὐτῶν· μὴ γιγνομένου γὰρ τούτου πῶς ἔσται κοινωνία τούτοις πρὸς ἀλλήλους λόγου; δεῖ τοίνυν τῶν ὀνομάτων ἕκαστον εἶναι γνώριμον καὶ δηλοῦν τι, καὶ μὴ [15] πολλά, μόνον δὲ ἕν· ἂν δὲ πλείονα σημαίνῃ, φανερὸν ποιεῖν ἐφ᾽ ὃ φέρει τοὔνομα τούτων. ὁ δὴ λέγων εἶναι τοῦτο καὶ μὴ εἶναι, τοῦτο ὃ φησὶν οὔ φησιν, ὥσθ᾽ ὃ σημαίνει τοὔνομα τοῦτ᾽ οὔ φησι σημαίνειν· τοῦτο δ᾽ ἀδύνατον. ὥστ᾽ εἴπερ σημαίνει τι τὸ εἶναι τόδε, τὴν ἀντίφασιν ἀδύνατον ἀληθεύειν.

Futuros itaque invicem ratione communicare oportet aliquid ipsorum intelligere; non facto autem hoc, quomodo est communicatio hiis ad invicem sermonis? Oportet igitur nominum unumquodque esse notum et significare aliquid et non multa, solum autem unum; si autem plura significet, manifestum facere ad quod fert nomen horum. Dicens itaque esse hoc et non esse, hoc quod totaliter esse dicit non dicit, quare quod significat nomen, hoc non inquit significare; hoc autem impossibile. Quare siquidem significat aliquid esse hoc, contradictionem verificari impossibile de eodem.

Those, then, who are to join in argument with one another must to some extent understand one another; for if this does not happen how are they to join in argument with one another? Therefore every word must be intelligible and indicate something, and not many things but only one; and if it signifies more than one thing, it must be made plain to which of these the word is being applied. He, then, who says this is and is not denies what he affirms, so that what the word signifies, he says it does not signify; and this is impossible. Therefore if this is signifies something, one cannot truly assert its contradictory.

ἔτι δ᾽ εἰ [20] τι σημαίνει τοὔνομα καὶ τοῦτ᾽ ἀληθεύεται, δεῖ τοῦτ᾽ ἐξ ἀνάγκης εἶναι· τὸ δ᾽ ἐξ ἀνάγκης ὂν οὐκ ἐνδέχεταί ποτε μὴ εἶναι· τὰς ἀντικειμένας ἄρα οὐκ ἐνδέχεται φάσεις καὶ ἀποφάσεις ἀληθεύειν κατὰ τοῦ αὐτοῦ.

Adhuc autem si quid significat nomen et hoc verificatur, oportet et hoc ex necessitate esse. Quod autem ex necessitate est non contingit tunc non esse; oppositas igitur non contingit dictiones et negationes verificari de eodem.

Further, if the word signifies something and this is asserted truly, this connexion must be necessary; and it is not possible that that which necessarily is should ever not be; it is not possible therefore to make the opposed affirmations and negations truly of the same subject.

ἔτι δ᾽ εἰ μηθὲν μᾶλλον ἡ φάσις ἢ ἡ ἀπόφασις ἀληθεύεται, ὁ λέγων ἄνθρωπον ἢ [25] οὐκ ἄνθρωπον οὐθὲν μᾶλλον ἀληθεύσει· δόξειε δὲ κἂν οὐχ ἵππον εἶναι φάσκων τὸν ἄνθρωπον ἢ μᾶλλον ἢ οὐχ ἧττον ἀληθεύειν ἢ οὐκ ἄνθρωπον, ὥστε καὶ ἵππον φάσκων εἶναι τὸν αὐτὸν ἀληθεύσει (τὰς γὰρ ἀντικειμένας ὁμοίως ἦν ἀληθεύειν)· συμβαίνει τοίνυν τὸν αὐτὸν ἄνθρωπον εἶναι καὶ ἵππον [30] ἢ τῶν ἄλλων τι ζῴων. ἀπόδειξις μὲν οὖν οὐδεμία τούτων ἐστὶν ἁπλῶς, πρὸς μέντοι τὸν ταῦτα τιθέμενον ἀπόδειξις.

Adhuc autem si nihil magis dictio quam negatio verificatur, dicens hominem aut non hominem nihil magis verum dicet. Videbitur autem utique non equum esse dicens hominem et magis aut non minus verum dicere quam non hominem. Quare et equum dicens esse eundem verum dicet; oppositas enim similiter erat verum dicere. Accidit igitur eundem hominem esse et equum aut aliorum aliquod animalium. Demonstratio quidem igitur nulla horum est simpliciter, ad ponentem tamen haec demonstratio.

Further, if the affirmation is no more true than the negation, he who says man will be no more right than he who says not-man . It would seem also that in saying the man is not a horse one would be either more or not less right than in saying he is not a man, so that one will also be right in saying that the same person is a horse; for it was assumed to be possible to make opposite statements equally truly. It follows then that the same person is a man and a horse, or any other animal. While, then, there is no proof of these things in the full sense, there is a proof which may suffice against one who will make these suppositions.

ταχέως δ᾽ ἄν τις καὶ αὐτὸν τὸν Ἡράκλειτον τοῦτον ἐρωτῶν τὸν τρόπον ἠνάγκασεν ὁμολογεῖν μηδέποτε τὰς ἀντικειμένας φάσεις δυνατὸν εἶναι κατὰ τῶν αὐτῶν ἀληθεύεσθαι· νῦν δ᾽ [35] οὐ συνιεὶς ἑαυτοῦ τί ποτε λέγει, ταύτην ἔλαβε τὴν δόξαν. ὅλως δ᾽ εἰ τὸ λεγόμενον ὑπ᾽ αὐτοῦ ἐστιν ἀληθές, οὐδ᾽ ἂν αὐτὸ τοῦτο εἴη ἀληθές, [1062β] [1] λέγω δὲ τὸ ἐνδέχεσθαι τὸ αὐτὸ καθ᾽ ἕνα καὶ τὸν αὐτὸν χρόνον εἶναί τε καὶ μὴ εἶναι· καθάπερ γὰρ καὶ διῃρημένων αὐτῶν οὐδὲν μᾶλλον ἡ κατάφασις ἢ ἡ ἀπόφασις ἀληθεύεται, τὸν αὐτὸν τρόπον καὶ τοῦ συναμφοτέρου [5] καὶ τοῦ συμπεπλεγμένου καθάπερ μιᾶς τινὸς καταφάσεως οὔσης οὐθὲν μᾶλλον <ἢ ἡ ἀπόφασις [ἢ] τὸ ὅλον ὡς ἐν καταφάσει τιθέμενον ἀληθεύσεται.

Cito autem utique quis et ipsum Eraclitum hoc interrogans modo cogeret confiteri numquam oppositas dictiones possibile esse de eisdem verificari. Nunc autem non intelligens se ipsum  quid quidem dicit, hanc accepit opinionem. Totaliter autem si quod dicitur ab ipso est verum, neque utique ipsum hoc verum  erit: dico autem contingere idem secundum unum et idem tempus esse et non esse. Quemadmodum enim et divisis ipsis nihil magis affirmatio quam negatio verificatur, eodem modo, et simul utriusque et simul complexi velut una quadam affirmatione existente, nihil magis negatio quam totum ut in affirmatione positum verum erit.

And perhaps if one had questioned Heraclitus himself in this way one might have forced him to confess that opposite statements can never be true of the same subjects. But, as it is, he adopted this opinion without understanding what his statement involves. But in any case if what is said by him is true, not even this [62b] itself will be true-viz. that the same thing can at one and the same time both be and not be. For as, when the statements are separated, the affirmation is no more true than the negation, in the same way-the combined and complex statement being like a single affirmation-the whole taken as an affirmation will be no more true than the negation.

ἔτι δ᾽ εἰ μηθὲν ἔστιν ἀληθῶς καταφῆσαι, κἂν αὐτὸ τοῦτο ψεῦδος εἴη τὸ φάναι μηδεμίαν ἀληθῆ κατάφασιν ὑπάρχειν. εἰ δ᾽ ἔστι τι, λύοιτ᾽ ἂν τὸ [10] λεγόμενον ὑπὸ τῶν τὰ τοιαῦτα ἐνισταμένων καὶ παντελῶς ἀναιρούντων τὸ διαλέγεσθαι.

Adhuc autem si nihil est vere affirmare, et utique hoc ipsum falsum erit: dicere nullam veram affirmationem existere. Si autem est aliquid, soluetur utique quod dicitur ab hiis qui talia instant et penitus auferentibus disputare.

Further, if it is not possible to affirm anything truly, this itself will be false-the assertion that there is no true affirmation. But if a true affirmation exists, this appears to refute what is said by those who raise such objections and utterly destroy rational discourse.

## Chapter 6

παραπλήσιον δὲ τοῖς εἰρημένοις ἐστὶ καὶ τὸ λεχθὲν ὑπὸ τοῦ Πρωταγόρου· καὶ γὰρ ἐκεῖνος ἔφη πάντων εἶναι χρημάτων μέτρον ἄνθρωπον, οὐδὲν ἕτερον λέγων ἢ τὸ δοκοῦν ἑκάστῳ [15] τοῦτο καὶ εἶναι παγίως· τούτου δὲ γιγνομένου τὸ αὐτὸ συμβαίνει καὶ εἶναι καὶ μὴ εἶναι, καὶ κακὸν καὶ ἀγαθὸν εἶναι, καὶ τἆλλα τὰ κατὰ τὰς ἀντικειμένας λεγόμενα φάσεις, διὰ τὸ πολλάκις τοισδὶ μὲν φαίνεσθαι τόδε εἶναι καλὸν τοισδὶ δὲ τοὐναντίον, μέτρον δ᾽ εἶναι τὸ φαινόμενον ἑκάστῳ.

Simile autem dictis est et quod dictum est a Protagora. et enim ille dixit omnium esse rerum mensuram hominem, nihil aliud dicens quam quod videtur unicuique hoc et esse firmiter. Hoc autem facto idem accidit et esse et non esse, et malum et bonum esse, et alia secundum oppositas dictiones dicta, propter multotiens hiis quidem videri hoc esse bonum hiis autem contrarium, mensuram autem esse quod videtur unicuique.

The saying of Protagoras is like the views we have mentioned; he said that man is the measure of all things, meaning simply that that which seems to each man also assuredly is. If this is so, it follows that the same thing both is and is not, and is bad and good, and that the contents of all other opposite statements are true, because often a particular thing appears beautiful to some and the contrary of beautiful to others, and that which appears to each man is the measure.

[20] λύοιτο δ᾽ ἂν αὕτη ἡ ἀπορία θεωρήσασι πόθεν ἐλήλυθεν ἡ ἀρχὴ [21] τῆς ὑπολήψεως ταύτης·

Solvetur autem utique haec dubitatio considerantibus unde venit principium existimationis huius.

This difficulty may be solved by considering the source of this opinion.

ἔοικε γὰρ ἐνίοις μὲν ἐκ τῆς τῶν φυσιολόγων δόξης γεγενῆσθαι, τοῖς δ᾽ ἐκ τοῦ μὴ ταὐτὰ περὶ τῶν αὐτῶν ἅπαντας γιγνώσκειν ἀλλὰ τοῖσδε μὲν ἡδὺ τόδε φαίνεσθαι τοῖσδε δὲ τοὐναντίον.

Videtur enim quibusdam quidem ex phisiologorum opinione, aliis autem ex non eadem de eisdem omnes cognoscere, sed hiis quidem delectabile  hoc videri hiis autem contrarium.

It seems to have arisen in some cases from the doctrine of the natural philosophers, and in others from the fact that all men have not the same views about the same things, but a particular thing appears pleasant to some and the contrary of pleasant to others.

τὸ γὰρ μηδὲν ἐκ μὴ ὄντος [25] γίγνεσθαι, πᾶν δ᾽ ἐξ ὄντος, σχεδὸν ἁπάντων ἐστὶ κοινὸν δόγμα τῶν περὶ φύσεως· ἐπεὶ οὖν οὐ λευκὸν γίγνεται λευκοῦ τελέως ὄντος καὶ οὐδαμῇ μὴ λευκοῦ [νῦν δὲ γεγενημένον μὴ λευκόν], γίγνοιτ᾽ ἂν ἐκ μὴ ὄντος λευκοῦ τὸ γιγνόμενον [μὴ] λευκόν· ὥστε ἐκ μὴ ὄντος γίγνοιτ᾽ ἂν κατ᾽ ἐκείνους, εἰ μὴ [30] ὑπῆρχε λευκὸν τὸ αὐτὸ καὶ μὴ λευκόν. οὐ χαλεπὸν δὲ διαλύειν τὴν ἀπορίαν ταύτην· εἴρηται γὰρ ἐν τοῖς φυσικοῖς πῶς ἐκ τοῦ μὴ ὄντος γίγνεται τὰ γιγνόμενα καὶ πῶς ἐξ ὄντος.

Nihil enim ex non ente fieri, omne autem ex ente, fere omnium est commune dogma eorum qui de natura. Quoniam igitur non album fit ex albo perfecte existente et nequaquam ex non albo, nunc autem factum non album, fiet utique ex non ente non albo quod fit non album;  quare ex non ente fiet utique secundum illos, si non extitit non album idem et album. Non difficile autem dissoluere dubitationem hanc. Dictum est enim in phisicis quomodo ex non ente fiunt quae fiunt et quomodo ex ente.

That nothing comes to be out of that which is not, but everything out of that which is, is a dogma common to nearly all the natural philosophers. Since, then, white cannot come to be if the perfectly white and in no respect not-white existed before, that which becomes white must come from that which is not white; so that it must come to be out of that which is not (so they argue), unless the same thing was at the beginning white and not-white. But it is not hard to solve this difficulty; for we have said in our works on physics in what sense things that come to be come to be from that which is not, and in what sense from that which is.

#964;ὁ γε μὴν ὁμοίως προσέχειν ταῖς δόξαις καὶ ταῖς φαντασίαις τῶν πρὸς αὐτοὺς διαμφισβητούντων εὔηθες· δῆλον [35] γὰρ ὅτι τοὺς ἑτέρους αὐτῶν ἀνάγκη διεψεῦσθαι. φανερὸν δὲ τοῦτ᾽ ἐκ τῶν γιγνομένων κατὰ τὴν αἴσθησιν· οὐδέποτε γὰρ τὸ αὐτὸ φαίνεται τοῖς μὲν γλυκὺ τοῖς δὲ τοὐναντίον, [1063α] [1] μὴ διεφθαρμένων καὶ λελωβημένων τῶν ἑτέρων τὸ αἰσθητήριον καὶ κριτήριον τῶν λεχθέντων χυμῶν. τούτου δ᾽ ὄντος τοιούτου τοὺς ἑτέρους μὲν ὑποληπτέον μέτρον εἶναι τοὺς δ' ἄλλους οὐχ [5] ὑποληπτέον. ὁμοίως δὲ τοῦτο λέγω καὶ ἐπὶ ἀγαθοῦ καὶ κακοῦ, καὶ καλοῦ καὶ αἰσχροῦ, καὶ τῶν ἄλλων τῶν τοιούτων. οὐδὲν γὰρ διαφέρει τοῦτ' ἀξιοῦν ἢ τὰ φαινόμενα τοῖς ὑπὸ τὴν ὄψιν ὑποβάλλουσι τὸν δάκτυλον καὶ ποιοῦσιν ἐκ τοῦ ἑνὸς φαίνεσθαι δύο, δύο δεῖν εἶναι διὰ τὸ φαίνεσθαι τοσαῦτα, καὶ πάλιν ἕν: [10] τοῖς γὰρ μὴ κινοῦσι τὴν ὄψιν ἓν φαίνεται τὸ ἕν.

Sed et similiter attendere utrisque opinionibus et fantasiis ad ipsos dubitantium stultum; palam enim quod alteros ipsorum necesse mentiri. Palam autem hoc ex hiis quae fiunt secundum sensum. Numquam enim idem videtur hiis quidem dulce hiis autem contrarium, non corruptis et privatis alteris secundum organum sensus et iudicatorium dictorum saporum. Hoc autem existente tali, alteros quidem existimandum mensuram esse alteros autem non putandum, similiter autem hoc dico et in bono et malo et pulcro et turpi et aliis talibus. Nihil enim differt hoc dignificare quam quae apparent submittentibus sub visu digitum et facientibus ex uno videri duo oportere esse propter apparere tanta, et iterum unum; non moventibus enim visum unum apparet quod unum.

But to attend equally to the opinions and the fancies of disputing parties is childish; for clearly one of them must be mistaken. And this is evident from what happens in respect of sensation; for the same thing never appears sweet to some [63a] and the contrary of sweet to others, unless in the one case the sense-organ which discriminates the aforesaid flavours has been perverted and injured. And if this is so the one party must be taken to be the measure, and the other must not. And say the same of good and bad, and beautiful and ugly, and all other such qualities. For to maintain the view we are opposing is just like maintaining that the things that appear to people who put their finger under their eye and make the object appear two instead of one must be two (because they appear to be of that number) and again one (for to those who do not interfere with their eye the one object appears one).

ὅλως δὲ ἄτοπον ἐκ τοῦ φαίνεσθαι τὰ δεῦρο μεταβάλλοντα καὶ μηδέποτε διαμένοντα ἐν τοῖς αὐτοῖς, ἐκ τούτου περὶ τῆς ἀληθείας τὴν κρίσιν ποιεῖσθαι: δεῖ γὰρ ἐκ τῶν ἀεὶ κατὰ ταὐτὰ ἐχόντων καὶ μηδεμίαν μεταβολὴν ποιουμένων τἀληθὲς θηρεύειν, [15] τοιαῦτα δ' ἐστὶ τὰ κατὰ τὸν κόσμον: ταῦτα γὰρ οὐχ ὁτὲ μὲν τοιαδὶ πάλιν δ' ἀλλοῖα φαίνεται, ταὐτὰ δ' ἀεὶ καὶ μεταβολῆς οὐδεμιᾶς κοινωνοῦντα.

Totaliter autem inconveniens ex videri presentia permutantia et numquam permanentia in eisdem, ex hoc de veritate iudicium facere. Oportet enim ex semper secundum eadem habentibus et neque unam permutationem facientibus verum venari. Talia autem sunt quae secundum mundum; haec enim non quandoque quidem talia iterum autem alia videntur, eadem autem semper et permutatione nulla participant.

In general, it is absurd to make the fact that the things of this earth are observed to change and never to remain in the same state, the basis of our judgement about the truth. For in pursuing the truth one must start from the things that are always in the same state and suffer no change. Such are the heavenly bodies; for these do not appear to be now of one nature and again of another, but are manifestly always the same and share in no change.

ἔτι δ᾽ εἰ κίνησίς ἐστι, καὶ κινούμενόν τι, κινεῖται δὲ πᾶν ἔκ τινος καὶ εἴς τι: δεῖ ἄρα τὸ κινούμενον εἶναι ἐν ἐκείνῳ ἐξ οὗ κινήσεται καὶ οὐκ [20] εἶναι ἐν αὐτῷ, καὶ εἰς τοδὶ κινεῖσθαι καὶ γίγνεσθαι ἐν τούτῳ, τὸ δὲ κατὰ τὴν ἀντίφασιν μὴ συναληθεύεσθαι κατ᾽ αὐτούς.

Adhuc autem si motus est, et motum aliquid, movetur autem omne ex aliquo et ad aliquid; oportet igitur quod movetur esse adhuc in illo ex quo movebit, et non esse in ipso, et ad hoc moveri et fieri in hoc, secundum contradictionem autem non verificari secundum ipsos.

Further, if there is movement, there is also something moved, and everything is moved out of something and into something; it follows that that that which is moved must first be in that out of which it is to be moved, and then not be in it, and move into the other and come to be in it, and that the contradictory statements are not true at the same time, as these thinkers assert they are.

καὶ εἰ κατὰ τὸ ποσὸν συνεχῶς τὰ δεῦρο ῥεῖ καὶ κινεῖται, καί τις τοῦτο θείη καίπερ οὐκ ἀληθὲς ὄν, διὰ τί κατὰ τὸ ποιὸν οὐ μενεῖ; φαίνονται γὰρ οὐχ ἥκιστα τὰ κατὰ τὰς ἀντιφάσεις [25] ταὐτοῦ κατηγορεῖν ἐκ τοῦ τὸ ποσὸν ὑπειληφέναι μὴ μένειν ἐπὶ τῶν σωμάτων, διὸ καὶ εἶναι τετράπηχυ τὸ αὐτὸ καὶ οὐκ εἶναι. ἡ δ᾽ οὐσία κατὰ τὸ ποιόν, τοῦτο δὲ τῆς ὡρισμένης φύσεως, τὸ δὲ ποσὸν τῆς ἀορίστου.

Et si secundum quantum continue presentia fluunt et moventur, et quis hoc ponat equidem non verum existens, propter quid secundum quale non manet? Videtur enim non minime quae secundum contradictiones eiusdem predicare ex existimare quantum non manere in corporibus, propter et esse quadricubitum idem et non esse. Substantia autem secundum quale; hoc quidem determinate nature, quantum autem indeterminate.

And if the things of this earth continuously flow and move in respect of quantity-if one were to suppose this, although it is not true-why should they not endure in respect of quality? For the assertion of contradictory statements about the same thing seems to have arisen largely from the belief that the quantity of bodies does not endure, which, our opponents hold, justifies them in saying that the same thing both is and is not four cubits long. But essence depends on quality, and this is of determinate nature, though quantity is of indeterminate.

ἔτι διὰ τί προστάττοντος τοῦ ἰατροῦ τοδὶ τὸ σιτίον προσενέγκασθαι προσφέρονται; [30] τί γὰρ μᾶλλον τοῦτο ἄρτος ἐστὶν ἢ οὐκ ἔστιν; ὥστ᾽ οὐθὲν ἂν διέχοι φαγεῖν ἢ μὴ φαγεῖν· νῦν δ᾽ ὡς ἀληθεύοντες περὶ αὐτὸ καὶ ὄντος τοῦ προσταχθέντος σιτίου τούτου προσφέρονται τοῦτο· καίτοι γ᾽ οὐκ ἔδει μὴ διαμενούσης παγίως μηδεμιᾶς φύσεως ἐν τοῖς αἰσθητοῖς ἀλλ᾽ ἀεὶ πασῶν κινουμένων [35] καὶ ῥεουσῶν.

Adhuc propter quid iubente medico hunc cibum offerre, offerunt? Quid enim magis panis est aut non est? Quare nihil utique aliquid habebit comedere aut non comedere. Nunc autem ut verum dicentes circa ipsum et existente iusso cibo hoc, offerunt hunc; quamvis non oportebat, non permanente firmiter nulla natura in sensibilibus sed semper omnibus motis et fluentibus.

Further, when the doctor orders people to take some particular food, why do they take it? In what respect is this is bread truer than this is not bread ? And so it would make no difference whether one ate or not. But as a matter of fact they take the food which is ordered, assuming that they know the truth about it and that it is bread. Yet they should not, if there were no fixed constant nature in sensible things, but all natures moved and flowed for ever.

ἔτι δ᾽ εἰ μὲν ἀλλοιούμεθα ἀεὶ καὶ μηδέποτε διαμένομεν οἱ αὐτοί, τί καὶ θαυμαστὸν εἰ μηδέποθ᾽ ἡμῖν ταὐτὰ φαίνεται καθάπερ τοῖς κάμνουσιν [1063β] [1] (καὶ γὰρ τούτοις διὰ τὸ μὴ ὁμοίως διακεῖσθαι τὴν ἕξιν καὶ ὅθ᾽ ὑγίαινον, οὐχ ὅμοια φαίνεται τὰ κατὰ τὰς αἰσθήσεις, αὐτὰ μὲν οὐδεμιᾶς διά γε τοῦτο μεταβολῆς κοινωνοῦντα τὰ αἰσθητά, αἰσθήματα δ᾽ ἕτερα ποιοῦντα τοῖς κάμνουσι καὶ μὴ τὰ αὐτά· [5] τὸν αὐτὸν δὴ τρόπον ἔχειν καὶ τῆς εἰρημένης μεταβολῆς γιγνομένης ἴσως ἀναγκαῖόν ἐστιν)· εἰ δὲ μὴ μεταβάλλομεν ἀλλ᾽ οἱ αὐτοὶ διατελοῦμεν ὄντες, εἴη ἂν τι μένον.

Adhuc si quidem alteramur semper et numquam permanemus iidem, quid mirabile si numquam nobis eadem videntur quemadmodum laborantibus? Et enim hiis propter non similiter disponi secundum habitum et quando sani erant, non similia videntur quae secundum sensus; ipsa tamen nulla propter hoc participantia permutatione sensibilia, impressiones autem alias facientia laborantibus et non eadem. Eodem itaque modo habere et dicta permutatione facta forte necessarium est. Si autem non permutamur sed iidem permanemus entes, erit utique aliquid manens.

Again, if we are always changing and never remain the same, what wonder is it if to us, as to the sick, things never [63b] appear the same? (For to them also, because they are not in the same condition as when they were well, sensible qualities do not appear alike; yet, for all that, the sensible things themselves need not share in any change, though they produce different, and not identical, sensations in the sick. And the same must surely happen to the healthy if the afore-said change takes place.) But if we do not change but remain the same, there will be something that endures.

πρὸς μὲν οὖν τοὺς ἐκ λόγου τὰς εἰρημένας ἀπορίας ἔχοντας οὐ ῥᾴδιον διαλῦσαι μὴ τιθέντων τι καὶ τούτου μηκέτι λόγον ἀπαιτούντων: [10] οὕτω γὰρ πᾶς λόγος καὶ πᾶσα ἀπόδειξις γίγνεται: μηθὲν γὰρ τιθέντες ἀναιροῦσι τὸ διαλέγεσθαι καὶ ὅλως λόγον, ὥστε πρὸς μὲν τοὺς τοιούτους οὐκ ἔστι λόγος, πρὸς δὲ τοὺς διαπωροῦντας ἐκ τῶν παραδεδομένων ἀποριῶν ῥᾴδιον ἀπαντᾶν καὶ διαλύειν τὰ ποιοῦντα τὴν ἀπορίαν ἐν αὐτοῖς: δῆλον δ᾽ ἐκ τῶν [15] εἰρημένων. ὥστε φανερὸν ἐκ τούτων.

Ad habentes quidem igitur dictas dubitationes ex ratione, non facile dissoluere non ponentibus aliquid et horum non adhuc rationem exquirentibus; sic enim omnis ratio et omnis demonstratio fit; nihil enim ponentes interimunt disputare et totaliter rationem. Quare ad tales quidem non est sermo. Ad dubitantes autem ex datis defectibus, facile obuiare et dissoluere facientia dubitationem in ipsis. Palam autem ex dictis.

As for those to whom the difficulties mentioned are suggested by reasoning, it is not easy to solve the difficulties to their satisfaction, unless they will posit something and no longer demand a reason for it; for it is only thus that all reasoning and all proof is accomplished; if they posit nothing, they destroy discussion and all reasoning. Therefore with such men there is no reasoning. But as for those who are perplexed by the traditional difficulties, it is easy to meet them and to dissipate the causes of their perplexity. This is evident from what has been said.

ὅτι οὐκ ἐνδέχεται τὰς ἀντικειμένας φάσεις περὶ τοῦ αὐτοῦ καθ᾽ ἕνα χρόνον ἀληθεύειν, οὐδὲ τὰ ἐναντία, διὰ τὸ λέγεσθαι κατὰ στέρησιν πᾶσαν ἐναντιότητα: δῆλον δὲ τοῦτ᾽ ἐπ᾽ ἀρχὴν τοὺς λόγους ἀναλύουσι τοὺς τῶν ἐναντίων. ὁμοίως δ᾽ οὐδὲ τῶν ἀνὰ μέσον οὐδὲν οἷόν τε [20] κατηγορεῖσθαι καθ᾽ ἑνὸς καὶ τοῦ αὐτοῦ: λευκοῦ γὰρ ὄντος τοῦ ὑποκειμένου λέγοντες αὐτὸ εἶναι οὔτε μέλαν οὔτε λευκὸν ψευσόμεθα: συμβαίνει γὰρ εἶναι λευκὸν αὐτὸ καὶ μὴ εἶναι: θάτερον γὰρ τῶν συμπεπλεγμένων ἀληθεύσεται κατ᾽ αὐτοῦ, τοῦτο δ᾽ ἐστὶν ἀντίφασις τοῦ λευκοῦ.

Quare manifestum ex hiis quod non contingit oppositas dictiones de eodem secundum unum tempus verificari, neque contraria, propter dici secundum privationem omnem contrarietatem. Palam autem hoc ad principium resoluentibus rationes contrariorum. Similiter autem neque intermediorum nullum possibile est predicari de uno et eodem. Albo enim existente subiecto dicentes ipsum esse neque album neque nigrum mentiemur; accidit enim esse album ipsum et non esse; alterum enim complexorum verificabitur de ipso, hoc autem est contradictio albi.

It is manifest, therefore, from these arguments that contradictory statements cannot be truly made about the same subject at one time, nor can contrary statements, because every contrariety depends on privation. This is evident if we reduce the definitions of contraries to their principle. Similarly, no intermediate between contraries can be predicated of one and the same subject, of which one of the contraries is predicated. If the subject is white we shall be wrong in saying it is neither black nor white, for then it follows that it is and is not white; for the second of the two terms we have put together is true of it, and this is the contradictory of white.

οὔτε δὴ καθ᾿ Ἡράκλειτον [25] ἐνδέχεται λέγοντας ἀληθεύειν, οὔτε κατ᾿ Ἀναξαγόραν· εἰ δὲ μή, συμβήσεται τἀναντία τοῦ αὐτοῦ κατηγορεῖν· ὅταν γὰρ ἐν παντὶ φῇ παντὸς εἶναι μοῖραν, οὐδὲν μᾶλλον εἶναί φησι γλυκὺ ἢ πικρὸν ἢ τῶν λοιπῶν ὁποιανοῦν ἐναντιώσεων, εἴπερ ἐν ἅπαντι πᾶν ὑπάρχει μὴ δυνάμει μόνον ἀλλ᾿ ἐνεργείᾳ [30] ι καὶ ἀποκεκριμένον.

Neque itaque secundum Eraclitum contingit dicentes verum dicere neque secundum Anaxagoram. Si autem non, accidet contraria de eodem predicari. Cum enim in omni dicat omnis esse partem, nihil magis esse dicit dulce quam amarum aut reliquarum quamcumque contrarietatum, siquidem in omni existit non potentia solum sed actu et segregatum.

We could not be right, then, in accepting the views either of Heraclitus or of Anaxagoras. If we were, it would follow that contraries would be predicated of the same subject; for when Anaxagoras says that in everything there is a part of everything, he says nothing is sweet any more than it is bitter, and so with any other pair of contraries, since in everything everything is present not potentially only, but actually and separately.

ὁμοίως δὲ οὐδὲ πάσας ψευδεῖς οὐδ᾿ ἀληθεῖς τὰς φάσεις δυνατὸν εἶναι, δι᾿ ἄλλα τε πολλὰ τῶν συναχθέντων ἂν δυσχερῶν διὰ ταύτην τὴν θέσιν, καὶ διότι ψευδῶν μὲν οὐσῶν πασῶν οὐδ᾿ αὐτὸ τοῦτό τις φάσκων ἀληθεύσει, ἀληθῶν δὲ ψευδεῖς εἶναι πάσας λέγων οὐ ψεύσεται. [35]

Similiter autem neque omnes falsas neque veras dictiones possibile esse, et propter alia multa collectarum utique difficultatum propter hanc positionem, et quia falsis quidem existentibus omnibus neque hoc ipsum quis dicens verum dicet, veris autem falsas esse omnes dicens non mentietur.

And similarly all statements cannot be false nor all true, both because of many other difficulties which might be adduced as arising from this position, and because if all are false it will not be true to say even this, and if all are true it will not be false to say all are false.

## Chapter 7

πᾶσα δ᾽ ἐπιστήμη ζητεῖ τινὰς ἀρχὰς καὶ αἰτίας περὶ ἕκαστον τῶν ὑφ᾽ αὑτὴν ἐπιστητῶν, [1064α] [1] οἷον ἰατρικὴ καὶ γυμναστικὴ καὶ τῶν λοιπῶν ἑκάστη τῶν ποιητικῶν καὶ μαθηματικῶν. ἑκάστη γὰρ τούτων περιγραψαμένη τι γένος αὑτῇ περὶ τοῦτο πραγματεύεται ὡς ὑπάρχον καὶ ὄν, οὐχ ᾗ δὲ ὄν, ἀλλ᾽ ἑτέρα τις αὕτη παρὰ ταύτας τὰς ἐπιστήμας ἐστὶν ἐπιστήμη.

Omnis autem scientia quaerit aliqua principia et causas circa unumquodque eorum quae sub ipsa scibilium, puta medicativa et exercitativa et reliquarum unaqueque factivarum et doctrinalium. Unaqueque enim harum circumscribens aliquod genus ipsi circa hoc negotiatur tamquam existens et ens, non in quantum autem ens; sed altera quaedam haec praeter has scientias est scientia.

Every science seeks certain principles and causes for each [64a] of its objects-e.g. medicine and gymnastics and each of the other sciences, whether productive or mathematical. For each of these marks off a certain class of things for itself and busies itself about this as about something existing and real,-not however qua real; the science that does this is another distinct from these.

τῶν δὲ [5] λεχθεισῶν ἐπιστημῶν ἑκάστη λαβοῦσά πως τὸ τί ἐστιν ἐν ἑκάστῳ γένει πειρᾶται δεικνύναι τὰ λοιπὰ μαλακώτερον ἢ ἀκριβέστερον. λαμβάνουσι δὲ τὸ τί ἐστιν αἱ μὲν δι᾽ αἰσθήσεως αἱ δ᾽ ὑποτιθέμεναι: διὸ καὶ δῆλον ἐκ τῆς τοιαύτης ἐπαγωγῆς ὅτι τῆς οὐσίας καὶ τοῦ τί ἐστιν οὐκ ἔστιν ἀπόδειξις.

Dictarum autem scientiarum unaqueque sumens aliqualiter quod quid est in unoquoque genere temptat ostendere reliqua debilius aut certius. Sumunt autem quod quid est hae quidem per sensum hae autem supponentes; propter quod et palam ex tali inductione quod substantiae et eius quod quid est non est demonstratio.

Of the sciences mentioned each gets somehow the what in some class of things and tries to prove the other truths, with more or less precision. Some get the what through perception, others by hypothesis; so that it is clear from an induction of this sort that there is no demonstration. of the substance or what .

[10] ἐπεὶ δ᾽ ἔστι τις ἡ περὶ φύσεως ἐπιστήμη, δῆλον ὅτι καὶ πρακτικῆς ἑτέρα καὶ ποιητικῆς ἔσται. ποιητικῆς μὲν γὰρ ἐν τῷ ποιοῦντι καὶ οὐ τῷ ποιουμένῳ τῆς κινήσεως ἡ ἀρχή, καὶ τοῦτ᾽ ἐστὶν εἴτε τέχνη τις εἴτ᾽ ἄλλη τις δύναμις: ὁμοίως δὲ καὶ τῆς πρακτικῆς οὐκ ἐν τῷ πρακτῷ μᾶλλον δ᾽ ἐν τοῖς [15] πράττουσιν ἡ κίνησις. ἡ δὲ τοῦ φυσικοῦ περὶ τὰ ἔχοντ᾽ ἐν ἑαυτοῖς κινήσεως ἀρχήν ἐστιν. ὅτι μὲν τοίνυν οὔτε πρακτικὴν οὔτε ποιητικὴν ἀλλὰ θεωρητικὴν ἀναγκαῖον εἶναι τὴν φυσικὴν ἐπιστήμην, δῆλον ἐκ τούτων (εἰς ἓν γάρ τι τούτων τῶν γενῶν ἀνάγκη πίπτειν):

Quoniam autem est quaedam de natura scientia, palam quia et a practica altera et a factiva erit. Factive quidem enim in faciente et non in facto motus principium, et hoc est sive ars aliqua sive aliqua alia potentia. Similiter autem et practice non in agibili, magis autem in agentibus motus. Quae autem phisici circa habentia in ipsis motus principium est. Quod quidem igitur neque activam neque factivam sed speculativam necessarium esse naturalem scientiam, palam ex hiis. In unum enim aliquod horum generum necesse cadere ipsam.

There is a science of nature, and evidently it must be different both from practical and from productive science. For in the case of productive science the principle of movement is in the producer and not in the product, and is either an art or some other faculty. And similarly in practical science the movement is not in the thing done, but rather in the doers. But the science of the natural philosopher deals with the things that have in themselves a principle of movement. It is clear from these facts, then, that natural science must be neither practical nor productive, but theoretical (for it must fall into some one of these classes).

ἐπεὶ δὲ τὸ τί ἐστιν ἀναγκαῖον [20] ἑκάστῃ πως τῶν ἐπιστημῶν εἰδέναι καὶ τούτῳ χρῆσθαι ἀρχῇ, δεῖ μὴ λανθάνειν πῶς ὁριστέον τῷ φυσικῷ καὶ πῶς ὁ τῆς οὐσίας λόγος ληπτέος, πότερον ὡς τὸ σιμὸν ἢ μᾶλλον ὡς τὸ κοῖλον. τούτων γὰρ ὁ μὲν τοῦ σιμοῦ λόγος μετὰ τῆς ὕλης λέγεται τῆς τοῦ πράγματος, ὁ δὲ τοῦ κοίλου χωρὶς τῆς ὕλης: [25] ἡ γὰρ σιμότης ἐν ῥινὶ γίγνεται, διὸ καὶ ὁ λόγος αὐτῆς μετὰ ταύτης θεωρεῖται: τὸ σιμὸν γάρ ἐστι ῥὶς κοίλη. φανερὸν οὖν ὅτι καὶ σαρκὸς καὶ ὀφθαλμοῦ καὶ τῶν λοιπῶν μορίων μετὰ τῆς ὕλης ἀεὶ τὸν λόγον ἀποδοτέον.

Quoniam autem quod quid est necessarium unicuique aliqualiter scientiarum scire et hoc uti principio, oportet non latere qualiter diffiniendum naturali et qualiter substantiae ratio sumenda, utrum ut simum aut magis ut concauum. Horum enim simi quidem ratio cum materia dicitur ea quae rei, quae autem concavi sine materia. simitas enim in naso fit, propter quod et ratio ipsius cum hoc dicta est; simum enim est nasus concavus. Manifestum igitur quod et carnis et oculi et reliquarum partium cum materia semper rationem reddendum.

And since each of the sciences must somehow know the what and use this as a principle, we must not fall to observe how the natural philosopher should define things and how he should state the definition of the essence-whether as akin to snub or rather to concave . For of these the definition of snub includes the matter of the thing, but that of concave is independent of the matter; for snubness is found in a nose, so that we look for its definition without eliminating the nose, for what is snub is a concave nose. Evidently then the definition of flesh also and of the eye and of the other parts must always be stated without eliminating the matter.

ἐπεὶ δ᾽ ἔστι τις ἐπιστήμη τοῦ ὄντος ᾗ ὂν καὶ χωριστόν, σκεπτέον πότερόν ποτε τῇ φυσικῇ [30] ι τὴν αὐτὴν θετέον εἶναι ταύτην ἢ μᾶλλον ἑτέραν. ἡ μὲν οὖν φυσικὴ περὶ τὰ κινήσεως ἔχοντ᾽ ἀρχὴν ἐν αὑτοῖς ἐστίν, ἡ δὲ μαθηματικὴ θεωρητικὴ μὲν καὶ περὶ μένοντά τις αὕτη, ἀλλ᾽ οὐ χωριστά. περὶ τὸ χωριστὸν ἄρα ὂν καὶ ἀκίνητον ἑτέρα τούτων ἀμφοτέρων τῶν ἐπιστημῶν ἔστι τις, εἴπερ [35] ὑπάρχει τις οὐσία τοιαύτη, λέγω δὲ χωριστὴ καὶ ἀκίνητος, ὅπερ πειρασόμεθα δεικνύναι. καὶ εἴπερ ἔστι τις τοιαύτη φύσις ἐν τοῖς οὖσιν, ἐνταῦθ᾽ ἂν εἴη που καὶ τὸ θεῖον, καὶ αὕτη ἂν εἴη πρώτη καὶ κυριωτάτη ἀρχή. [1064β] [1] δῆλον τοίνυν ὅτι τρία γένη τῶν θεωρητικῶν ἐπιστημῶν ἔστι, φυσική, μαθηματική, θεολογική.

Quoniam autem est quaedam scientia entis in quantum ens  et separabile, considerandum utrum quidem naturali eandem ponendum esse hanc aut magis alteram. Naturalis quidem igitur circa habentia motus principium in ipsis est; mathematica autem speculativa quidem et circa manentia quaedam haec, sed non separabilia. Circa separabile igitur ens et immobile altera  ab hiis ambabus scientiis est aliqua, siquidem existit aliqua substantia talis, dico autem separabilis et immobilis, quod quidem temptabimus ostendere. Et siquidem est aliqua talis natura in  entibus, hic utique erit alicubi et quod divinum, et haec utique erit primum et principalissimum  principium. Palam igitur quod tria genera speculativarum scientiarum sunt: naturalis, mathematica, theologica.

Since there is a science of being qua being and capable of existing apart, we must consider whether this is to be regarded as the same as physics or rather as different. Physics deals with the things that have a principle of movement in themselves; mathematics is theoretical, and is a science that deals with things that are at rest, but its subjects cannot exist apart. Therefore about that which can exist apart and is unmovable there is a science different from both of these, if there is a substance of this nature (I mean separable and unmovable), as we shall try to prove there is. And if there is such a kind of thing in the world, here must surely be the divine, and this must be the first [64b] and most dominant principle. Evidently, then, there are three kinds of theoretical sciences-physics, mathematics, theology.

βέλτιστον μὲν οὖν τὸ τῶν θεωρητικῶν γένος, τούτων δ᾽ αὐτῶν ἡ τελευταία λεχθεῖσα· περὶ τὸ τιμιώτατον [5] γάρ ἐστι τῶν ὄντων, βελτίων δὲ καὶ χείρων ἑκάστη λέγεται κατὰ τὸ οἰκεῖον ἐπιστητόν.

Optimum quidem igitur speculativarum genus, harum autem ipsarum ultima dicta;  circa honorabilissimum enim est entium. Melior autem et deterior unaqueque dicitur secundum proprium scibile.

The class of theoretical sciences is the best, and of these themselves the last named is best; for it deals with the highest of existing things, and each science is called better or worse in virtue of its proper object.

ἀπορήσειε δ' ἄν τις πότερόν ποτε τὴν τοῦ ὄντος ἢ ὂν ἐπιστήμην καθόλου δεῖ θεῖναι ἢ οὔ. τῶν μὲν γὰρ μαθηματικῶν ἑκάστη περὶ ἕν τι γένος ἀφωρισμένον ἐστίν, ἡ δὲ καθόλου κοινὴ περὶ πάντων. εἰ μὲν οὖν [10] αἱ φυσικαὶ οὐσίαι πρῶται τῶν ὄντων εἰσί, κἂν ἡ φυσικὴ πρώτη τῶν ἐπιστημῶν εἴη· εἰ δ' ἔστιν ἑτέρα φύσις καὶ οὐσία χωριστὴ καὶ ἀκίνητος, ἑτέραν ἀνάγκη καὶ τὴν ἐπιστήμην αὐτῆς εἶναι καὶ προτέραν τῆς φυσικῆς καὶ καθόλου τῷ προτέραν. [15]

Dubitabit autem utique quis utrum entis in quantum ens scientiam universalem oportet poni aut non. Mathematicarum quidem enim unaqueque circa unum aliquod genus determinatum est, quae autem universalis communiter de omnibus. Si quidem igitur naturales substantiae prime entium sunt, et naturalis utique prima scientiarum erit. Si autem est altera natura et substantia separabilis et immobilis, alteram necesse et scientiam ipsius esse et priorem naturali et universalem eo quod priorem.

One might raise the question whether the science of being qua being is to be regarded as universal or not. Each of the mathematical sciences deals with some one determinate class of things, but universal mathematics applies alike to all. Now if natural substances are the first of existing things, physics must be the first of sciences; but if there is another entity and substance, separable and unmovable, the knowledge of it must be different and prior to physics and universal because it is prior.

### Chapter 8

ἐπεὶ δὲ τὸ ἁπλῶς ὂν κατὰ πλείους λέγεται τρόπους, ὧν εἷς ἐστιν ὁ κατὰ συμβεβηκὸς εἶναι λεγόμενος, σκεπτέον πρῶτον περὶ τοῦ οὕτως ὄντος.

Quoniam autem simpliciter ens secundum plures dicitur modos, quorum unus est qui secundum accidens dicitur, considerandum primo de sic ente.

Since being in general has several senses, of which one is being by accident , we must consider first that which is in this sense.

ὅτι μὲν οὖν οὐδεμία τῶν παραδεδομένων ἐπιστημῶν πραγματεύεται περὶ τὸ συμβεβηκός, δῆλον (οὔτε γὰρ οἰκοδομικὴ σκοπεῖ τὸ συμβησόμενον τοῖς τῇ [20] οἰκίᾳ χρησομένοις, οἷον εἰ λυπηρῶς ἢ τοὐναντίον οἰκήσουσιν, οὔθ' ὑφαντικὴ οὔτε σκυτοτομικὴ οὔτε ὀψοποιική, τὸ δὲ καθ' αὑτὴν ἴδιον ἑκάστη τούτων σκοπεῖ τῶν ἐπιστημῶν μόνον, τοῦτο δ' ἐστὶ τὸ οἰκεῖον τέλος·

Quod quidem igitur nulla traditarum scientiarum negotiatur circa accidens, palam; neque enim edificativa considerat quod accidet utentibus domo, puta si triste aut contrarie habitabunt, neque textiva neque coriativa neque coquinaria. Quod autem

secundum ipsam proprium unaqueque harum considerat scientiarum solum, hoc autem est proprius finis.

Evidently none of the traditional sciences busies itself about the accidental. For neither does architecture consider what will happen to those who are to use the house (e.g. whether they have a painful life in it or not), nor does weaving, or shoemaking, or the confectioner's art, do the like; but each of these sciences considers only what is peculiar to it, i.e. its proper end.

[οὐδὲ μουσικὸν καὶ γραμματικόν,] οὐδὲ τὸν ὄντα μουσικὸν ὅτι γενόμενος γραμματικὸς ἅμα ἔσται τὰ [25] ἀμφότερα, πρότερον οὐκ ὤν, ὃ δὲ μὴ ἀεὶ ὂν ἔστιν, ἐγένετο τοῦτο, ὥσθ᾽ ἅμα μουσικὸς ἐγένετο καὶ γραμματικός, τοῦτο δὲ οὐδεμία ζητεῖ τῶν ὁμολογουμένως οὐσῶν ἐπιστημῶν πλὴν ἡ σοφιστική· περὶ τὸ συμβεβηκὸς γὰρ αὕτη μόνη πραγματεύεται, διὸ Πλάτων οὐ κακῶς εἴρηκε φήσας τὸν σοφιστὴν [30] περὶ τὸ μὴ ὂν διατρίβειν):

Neque in quantum musicum et gramaticum, neque existentem musicum quia factus gramaticus simul erit ambo prius non ens, quod autem non semper ens est factum est hoc, quare simul musicus factus est et gramaticus: hoc autem nulla quaerit confesse existentium scientiarum nisi sophistica; circa accidens enim haec sola negotiatur, propter quod Plato non male dixit dicens sophistam circa non ens versari.

And as for the argument that when he who is musical becomes lettered he will be both at once, not having been both before; and that which is, not always having been, must have come to be; therefore he must have at once become musical and lettered _ ,-this none of the recognized sciences considers, but only sophistic; for this alone busies itself about the accidental, so that Plato is not far wrong when he says that the sophist spends his time on non-being.

ὅτι δ᾽ οὐδ᾽ ἐνδεχόμενόν ἐστιν εἶναι τοῦ συμβεβηκότος ἐπιστήμην, φανερὸν ἔσται πειραθεῖσιν ἰδεῖν τί ποτ᾽ ἐστὶ τὸ συμβεβηκός. πᾶν δή φαμεν εἶναι τὸ μὲν ἀεὶ καὶ ἐξ ἀνάγκης (ἀνάγκης δ᾽ οὐ τῆς κατὰ τὸ βίαιον λεγομένης ἀλλ᾽ ᾗ χρώμεθα ἐν τοῖς κατὰ τὰς ἀποδείξεις), [35] τὸ δ᾽ ὡς ἐπὶ τὸ πολύ, τὸ δ᾽ οὔθ᾽ ὡς ἐπὶ τὸ πολὺ οὔτ᾽ ἀεὶ καὶ ἐξ ἀνάγκης ἀλλ᾽ ὅπως ἔτυχεν: οἷον ἐπὶ κυνὶ γένοιτ᾽ ἂν ψῦχος, ἀλλὰ τοῦτ᾽ οὔτ᾽ [ὡς] ἀεὶ καὶ ἐξ ἀνάγκης οὔθ᾽ ὡς ἐπὶ τὸ πολὺ γίγνεται, συμβαίη δέ ποτ᾽ ἄν. [1065α] [1] ἔστι δὴ τὸ συμβεβηκὸς ὃ γίγνεται μέν, οὐκ ἀεὶ δ᾽ οὐδ᾽ ἐξ ἀνάγκης οὐδ᾽ ὡς ἐπὶ τὸ πολύ. τί μὲν οὖν ἐστι τὸ συμβεβηκός, εἴρηται, διότι δ᾽ οὐκ ἔστιν ἐπιστήμη τοῦ τοιούτου, δῆλον: ἐπιστήμη μὲν γὰρ πᾶσα τοῦ [5] ἀεὶ ὄντος ἢ ὡς ἐπὶ τὸ πολύ, τὸ δὲ συμβεβηκὸς ἐν οὐδετέρῳ τούτων ἐστίν.

Quod autem neque contingens est esse accidentis scientiam, manifestum erit temptantibus scire quid est accidens. Omne itaque dicimus esse hoc quidem semper et ex necessitate (necessitate autem non secundum violentiam dicta sed secundum quod utimur in hiis quae secundum demonstrationes), hoc autem ut in plus, hoc vero neque ut in plus neque semper et ex necessitate sed ut contingit, puta sub cane fiet utique frigus, sed hoc neque ut semper et ex necessitate neque in plus fit, accidet tamen aliquando utique. Est itaque accidens quod fit quidem, non semper autem neque ex necessitate neque ut in plus. Quid quidem igitur est accidens, dictum est. Quia autem non est scientia talis, palam. Scientia quidem enim omnis semper entis aut ut in plus, accidens autem in neutro horum est.

That a science of the accidental is not even possible will be evident if we try to see what the accidental really is. We say that everything either is always and of necessity (necessity not in the sense of violence, but that which we appeal to in demonstrations), or is for the most part, or is neither for the most part, nor always and of necessity, but merely as it chances; e.g. there might be cold in the dogdays, but this occurs neither always and of necessity, nor for the most part [65a], though it might happen sometimes. The accidental, then, is what occurs, but not always nor of necessity, nor for the most part. Now we have said what the accidental is, and it is obvious why there is no science of such a thing; for all science is of that which is always or for the most part, but the accidental is in neither of these classes.

ὅτι δὲ τοῦ κατὰ συμβεβηκὸς ὄντος οὐκ εἰσὶν αἰτίαι καὶ ἀρχαὶ τοιαῦται οἷαίπερ τοῦ καθ᾽ αὑτὸ ὄντος, δῆλον· ἔσται γὰρ ἅπαντ᾽ ἐξ ἀνάγκης. εἰ γὰρ τόδε μὲν ἔστι τοῦδε ὄντος τόδε δὲ τοῦδε, τοῦτο δὲ μὴ ὅπως ἔτυχεν ἀλλ᾽ ἐξ [10] ἀνάγκης, ἐξ ἀνάγκης ἔσται καὶ οὗ τοῦτ᾽ ἦν αἴτιον ἕως τοῦ τελευταίου λεγομένου αἰτιατοῦ (τοῦτο δ᾽ ἦν κατὰ συμβεβηκός), ὥστ᾽ ἐξ ἀνάγκης ἅπαντ᾽ ἔσται, καὶ τὸ ὁποτέρως ἔτυχε καὶ τὸ ἐνδέχεσθαι καὶ γενέσθαι καὶ μὴ παντελῶς ἐκ τῶν γιγνομένων ἀναιρεῖται. κἂν μὴ ὂν δὲ ἀλλὰ γιγνόμενον τὸ [15] αἴτιον ὑποτεθῇ, ταὐτὰ συμβήσεται· πᾶν γὰρ ἐξ ἀνάγκης γενήσεται. ἡ γὰρ αὔριον ἔκλειψις γενήσεται ἂν τόδε γένηται, τοῦτο δ᾽ ἐὰν ἕτερόν τι, καὶ τοῦτ᾽ ἂν ἄλλο· καὶ τοῦτον δὴ τὸν τρόπον ἀπὸ πεπερασμένου χρόνου τοῦ ἀπὸ τοῦ νῦν μέχρι αὔριον ἀφαιρουμένου χρόνου ἥξει ποτὲ εἰς τὸ ὑπάρχον, ὥστ᾽ [20] ἐπεὶ τοῦτ᾽ ἔστιν, ἅπαντ᾽ ἐξ ἀνάγκης τὰ μετὰ τοῦτο γενήσεται, ὥστε πάντα ἐξ ἀνάγκης γίγνεσθαι.

Quod autem secundum accidens entis non sunt causae et principia talia qualia quidem secundum se entis, palam; erunt enim omnia ex necessitate. Si enim hoc quidem est huius entis hoc autem huius, hoc autem non ut contingit sed ex necessitate, ex necessitate erit et cuius hoc erat causa usque ad ultimum dictum causatum; hoc autem erat secundum accidens. Quare ex necessitate omnia erunt; et quod utcumque contingit et accidere et fieri et non: omnino ex generatis aufertur. Et si non existens sed quae fit causa supponatur, eadem accident; omne enim ex necessitate fiet. Si enim cras eclipsis fiet si hoc fuerit, hoc autem si alterum aliquid, et hoc si aliud; et hoc itaque modo a finito tempore eo quod a nunc usque cras ablato tempore veniet quandoque ad existens. Quare siquidem hoc est, omnia ex necessitate quae post hoc fient, ut omnia ex necessitate fiant.

Evidently there are not causes and principles of the accidental, of the same kind as there are of the essential; for if there were, everything would be of necessity. If A is when B is, and B is when C is, and if C exists not by chance but of necessity, that also of which C was cause will exist of necessity, down to the last causatum as it is called (but this was supposed to be accidental). Therefore all things will be of necessity, and chance and the possibility of a thing's either occurring or not occurring are removed entirely from the range of events. And if the cause be supposed not to exist but to be coming to be, the same results will follow; everything will occur of necessity. For to-morrow's eclipse will occur if A occurs, and A if B occurs, and B if C occurs; and in this way if we subtract time from the limited time between now and to-morrow we shall come sometime to the already existing condition. Therefore since this exists, everything after this will occur of necessity, so that all things occur of necessity.

τὸ δ᾽ ὡς ἀληθὲς ὂν καὶ κατὰ συμβεβηκὸς τὸ μέν ἐστιν ἐν συμπλοκῇ διανοίας καὶ πάθος ἐν ταύτῃ (διὸ περὶ μὲν τὸ οὕτως ὂν οὐ ζητοῦνται αἱ ἀρχαί, περὶ δὲ τὸ ἔξω ὂν καὶ χωριστόν): τὸ δ᾽ οὐκ [25] ἀναγκαῖον ἀλλ᾽ ἀόριστον, λέγω δὲ τὸ κατὰ συμβεβηκός: τοῦ τοιούτου δ᾽ ἄτακτα καὶ ἄπειρα τὰ αἴτια.

Quod autem ut vere ens et secundum accidens: hoc quidem est in complexione mentis et passio in hac, propter quod circa sic quidem ens non quaeruntur principia, circa autem quod extra ens et separabile; hoc autem non necessarium sed infinitum, dico autem quod secundum accidens, talis autem inordinatae et infinitae causae.

As to that which is in the sense of being true or of being by accident, the former depends on a combination in thought and is an affection of thought (which is the reason why it is the principles, not of that which is in this sense, but of that which is outside and can exist apart, that are sought); and the latter is not necessary but indeterminate (I mean the accidental); and of such a thing the causes are unordered and indefinite.

τὸ δὲ ἕνεκά του ἐν τοῖς φύσει γιγνομένοις ἢ ἀπὸ διανοίας ἐστίν, τύχη δέ ἐστιν ὅταν τι τούτων γένηται κατὰ συμβεβηκός: ὥσπερ γὰρ καὶ ὂν ἐστι τὸ μὲν καθ᾽ αὑτὸ τὸ δὲ κατὰ συμβεβηκός, οὕτω [30] καὶ αἴτιον. ἡ τύχη δ᾽ αἰτία κατὰ συμβεβηκὸς ἐν τοῖς κατὰ προαίρεσιν τῶν ἕνεκά του γιγνομένοις,

Quod autem gratia huius in hiis quae a natura fiunt et a mente est. Fortuna autem est quando aliquid horum fuerit secundum accidens. Sicut enim et ens est hoc quidem secundum se hoc autem secundum accidens, sic et causa. Fortuna autem causa secundum accidens in factis secundum electionem eorum quae gratia huius.

Adaptation to an end is found in events that happen by nature or as the result of thought. It is luck when one of these events happens by accident. For as a thing may exist, so it may be a cause, either by its own nature or by accident. Luck is an

430

accidental cause at work in such events adapted to an end as are usually effected in accordance with purpose.

διὸ περὶ ταὐτὰ τύχη καὶ διάνοια: προαίρεσις γὰρ οὐ χωρὶς διανοίας.

Propter quod circa eadem fortuna et mens; electio enim non sine mente.

And so luck and thought are concerned with the same sphere; for purpose cannot exist without thought.

τὰ δ᾽ αἴτια ἀόριστα ἀφ᾽ ὧν ἂν γένοιτο τὰ ἀπὸ τύχης, διὸ ἄδηλος ἀνθρωπίνῳ λογισμῷ καὶ αἴτιον κατὰ συμβεβηκός, ἁπλῶς δ᾽ [35] οὐδενός.

Causae autem infinitae a quibus utique fiet quod a fortuna; propter quod incerta humane cogitationi et causa secundum accidens, simpliciter autem nullius.

The causes from which lucky results might happen are indeterminate; and so luck is obscure to human calculation and is a cause by accident, but in the unqualified sense a cause of nothing.

ἀγαθὴ δὲ τύχη καὶ κακὴ ὅταν ἀγαθὸν ἢ φαῦλον ἀποβῇ: εὐτυχία δὲ καὶ δυστυχία περὶ μέγεθος τούτων.

bona autem fortuna et mala cum bonum aut maium euenerit; eutichia autem et infortunium circa magnitudinem horum.

It is good or bad luck when [65b] the result is good or evil; and prosperity or misfortune when the scale of the results is large.

[1065β] [1] ἐπεὶ δ᾽ οὐθὲν κατὰ συμβεβηκὸς πρότερον τῶν καθ᾽ αὑτό, οὐδ᾽ ἄρ᾽ αἴτια: εἰ ἄρα τύχη ἢ τὸ αὐτόματον αἴτιον τοῦ οὐρανοῦ, πρότερον νοῦς αἴτιος καὶ φύσις. [5]

Quoniam autem nullum secundum accidens prius hiis quae secundum se, neque igitur causa. Si igitur fortuna aut casus causa celi, prius intellectus causa et natura.

Since nothing accidental is prior to the essential, neither are accidental causes prior. If, then, luck or spontaneity is a cause of the material universe, reason and nature are causes before it.

ἔστι δὲ τὸ μὲν ἐνεργείᾳ μόνον τὸ δὲ δυνάμει τὸ δὲ δυνάμει καὶ ἐνεργείᾳ, τὸ μὲν ὂν
τὸ δὲ ποσὸν τὸ δὲ τῶν λοιπῶν. οὐκ ἔστι δέ τις κίνησις παρὰ τὰ πράγματα·
μεταβάλλει γὰρ ἀεὶ κατὰ τὰς τοῦ ὄντος κατηγορίας, κοινὸν δ᾽ ἐπὶ τούτων οὐδέν
ἐστιν ὃ οὐδ᾽ ἐν μιᾷ κατηγορίᾳ. ἕκαστον δὲ διχῶς [10] ὑπάρχει πᾶσιν (οἷον τὸ τόδε—
τὸ μὲν γὰρ μορφὴ αὐτοῦ τὸ δὲ στέρησις—καὶ κατὰ τὸ ποιὸν τὸ μὲν λευκὸν τὸ δὲ
μέλαν, καὶ κατὰ τὸ ποσὸν τὸ μὲν τέλειον τὸ δὲ ἀτελές, καὶ κατὰ φορὰν τὸ μὲν ἄνω
τὸ δὲ κάτω, ἢ κοῦφον καὶ βαρύ)· ὥστε κινήσεως καὶ μεταβολῆς τοσαῦτ᾽ εἴδη ὅσα
τοῦ ὄντος.

Est autem hoc quidem actu solum hoc autem potentia  hoc autem potentia et
actu, hoc quidem ens hoc autem quantum hoc autem reliquorum. Non est autem
aliquid motus praeter res; permutatur enim semper secundum entis cathegorias,
commune autem in hiis nullum est quod neque in una cathegoria. Unumquodque
autem dupliciter existit omnibus, ut puta quod  hoc: istud quidem forma ipsius hoc
autem privatio; et secundum quale hoc quidem album hoc autem nigrum, et
secundum quantum hoc quidem perfectum hoc autem imperfectum, et secundum
lationem hoc quidem sursum hoc autem deorsum, aut leue hoc autem grave. Quare
motus et permutationis tot species quot entis.

Some things are only actually, some potentially, some potentially and actually,
what they are, viz. in one case a particular reality, in another, characterized by a
particular quantity, or the like. There is no movement apart from things; for change is
always according to the categories of being, and there is nothing common to these and
in no one category. But each of the categories belongs to all its subjects in either of two
ways (e.g. this-ness -for one kind of it is positive form , and the other is privation ; and
as regards quality one kind is white and the other black , and as regards quantity one
kind is complete and the other incomplete , and as regards spatial movement one is
upwards and the other downwards , or one thing is light and another heavy ); so that
there are as many kinds of movement and change as of being.

διῃρημένου [15] δὲ καθ᾽ ἕκαστον γένος τοῦ μὲν δυνάμει τοῦ δ᾽ ἐντελεχείᾳ,
τὴν τοῦ δυνάμει ᾗ τοιοῦτόν ἐστιν ἐνέργειαν λέγω κίνησιν.

Diviso autem secundum unumquodque genus hoc quidem  potentia hoc autem
actu, eius quod potentia in quantum tale  est actum dico motum.

There being a distinction in each class of things between the potential and the
completely real, I call the actuality of the potential as such, movement.

ὅτι δ᾽ ἀληθῆ λέγομεν, ἐνθένδε δῆλον· ὅταν γὰρ τὸ οἰκοδομητόν, ᾗ τοιοῦτον αὐτὸ λέγομεν εἶναι, ἐνεργείᾳ ᾖ, οἰκοδομεῖται, καὶ ἔστι τοῦτο οἰκοδόμησις· ὁμοίως μάθησις, ἰάτρευσις, βάδισις, [20] ἅλσις, γήρανσις, ἅδρυνσις. συμβαίνει δὲ κινεῖσθαι ὅταν ἡ ἐντελέχεια ᾖ αὐτή, καὶ οὔτε πρότερον οὔθ᾽ ὕστερον. ἡ δὴ τοῦ δυνάμει ὄντος, ὅταν ἐντελεχείᾳ ὂν ἐνεργῇ, οὐχ ᾗ αὐτὸ ἀλλ᾽ ᾗ κινητόν, κίνησίς ἐστιν.

Quod autem vera dicimus, hinc palam. cum enim edificabile in quantum tale ipsum dicimus esse actu in quantum edificatur, et est hoc edificatio. Similiter doctrinatio, curatio, ambulatio, saltatio, orbatio, ingrossatio. Accidit autem moveri cum fuerit actu eadem, et neque prius neque posterius; iam potentia entis, cum actu ens operetur, non in quantum ipsum sed in quantum mobile, motus est. Dico autem 'in quantum' sic: est enim es potentia statua; sed tamen non eris actus in quantum es motus est.

That what we say is true, is plain from the following facts. When the buildable , in so far as it is what we mean by buildable , exists actually, it is being built, and this is the process of building. Similarly with learning, healing, walking, leaping, ageing, ripening. Movement takes when the complete reality itself exists, and neither earlier nor later. The complete reality, then, of that which exists potentially, when it is completely real and actual, not qua itself, but qua movable, is movement.

λέγω δὲ τὸ ᾗ ὧδε. ἔστι γὰρ ὁ χαλκὸς δυνάμει ἀνδριάς· ἀλλ᾽ ὅμως οὐχ ἡ τοῦ [25] χαλκοῦ ἐντελέχεια, ᾗ χαλκός, κίνησίς ἐστιν. οὐ γὰρ ταὐτὸν χαλκῷ εἶναι καὶ δυνάμει τινί, ἐπεὶ εἰ ταὐτὸν ἦν ἁπλῶς κατὰ τὸν λόγον, ἦν ἂν ἡ τοῦ χαλκοῦ ἐντελέχεια κίνησίς τις. οὐκ ἔστι δὲ ταὐτό (δῆλον δ᾽ ἐπὶ τῶν ἐναντίων· τὸ μὲν γὰρ δύνασθαι ὑγιαίνειν καὶ δύνασθαι κάμνειν οὐ ταὐτόν—καὶ γὰρ [30] ἂν τὸ ὑγιαίνειν καὶ τὸ κάμνειν ταὐτὸν ἦν—τὸ δ᾽ ὑποκείμενον καὶ ὑγιαῖνον καὶ νοσοῦν, εἴθ᾽ ὑγρότης εἴθ᾽ αἷμα, ταὐτὸ καὶ ἕν). ἐπεὶ δὲ οὐ τὸ αὐτό, ὥσπερ οὐδὲ χρῶμα ταὐτὸν καὶ ὁρατόν, ἡ τοῦ δυνατοῦ καὶ ᾗ δυνατὸν ἐντελέχεια κίνησίς ἐστιν.

Non enim idem eri esse et potentie alicui. Quoniam si idem erat simpliciter secundum rationem, erat utique eris actus motus quidam. Non est autem idem. Palam autem in contrariis; posse quidem enim sanari et posse laborare non idem (et enim si, sanari et laborare idem esset), subiectum autem et sanum et languens, sive humiditas sive sanguis, idem et unum. Quoniam autem non idem, quemadmodum neque color idem et visibile, possibilis in quantum possibile actus motus est.

By qua I mean this: bronze is potentially a statue; but yet it is not the complete reality of bronze qua bronze that is movement. For it is not the same thing to be bronze and to be a certain potency. If it were absolutely the same in its definition, the complete reality of bronze would have been a movement. But it is not the same. (This is evident in the case of contraries; for to be capable of being well and to be capable of being ill are not the same-for if they were, being well and being ill would have been the same-it is that which underlies and is healthy or diseased, whether it is moisture or blood, that is one and the same.) And since it is not. the same, as colour and the visible are not the same, it is the complete reality of the potential, and as potential, that is movement.

[34] ὅτι μὲν οὖν ἐστιν αὕτη, καὶ ὅτι συμβαίνει τότε κινεῖσθαι ὅταν [35] ἡ ἐντελέχεια ᾖ αὐτή, καὶ οὔτε πρότερον οὔθ᾽ ὕστερον, δῆλον (ἐνδέχεται γὰρ ἕκαστον ὁτὲ μὲν ἐνεργεῖν ὁτὲ δὲ μή, [1066α] [1] οἷον τὸ οἰκοδομητὸν ᾗ οἰκοδομητόν, καὶ ἡ τοῦ οἰκοδομητοῦ ἐνέργεια ᾗ οἰκοδομητὸν οἰκοδόμησίς ἐστιν: ἢ γὰρ τοῦτό ἐστιν, ἡ οἰκοδόμησις, ἡ ἐνέργεια, ἢ οἰκία: ἀλλ᾽ ὅταν οἰκία ᾖ, οὐκέτι οἰκοδομητόν, [5] οἰκοδομεῖται δὲ τὸ οἰκοδομητόν: ἀνάγκη ἄρα οἰκοδόμησιν τὴν ἐνέργειαν εἶναι, ἡ δ᾽ οἰκοδόμησις κίνησίς τις, ὁ δ᾽ αὐτὸς λόγος καὶ ἐπὶ τῶν ἄλλων κινήσεων):

Quod quidem enim est hic, et quod accidit tunc moveri quando fuerit actu hic, et neque prius neque posterius, palam. Contingit enim unumquodque aliquando quidem actu esse aliquando autem non, puta edificabile in quantum edificabile; et edificabilis actus in quantum edificabile edificatio est. Aut enim hoc domus est, aut edificatio actus. Sed cum domus fuerit, non adhuc edificabile erit, edificatur autem edificabile. Necesse igitur edificationem actum esse, edificatio autem motus quidam. Eadem autem ratio et in aliis motibus.

That it is this, and that movement takes place when the complete reality itself exists, and [66a] neither earlier nor later, is evident. For each thing is capable of being sometimes actual, sometimes not, e.g. the buildable qua buildable; and the actuality of the buildable qua buildable is building. For the actuality is either this-the act of building-or the house. But when the house exists, it is no longer buildable; the buildable is what is being built. The actuality, then, must be the act of building, and this is a movement. And the same account applies to all other movements.

ὅτι δὲ καλῶς εἴρηται, δῆλον ἐξ ὧν οἱ ἄλλοι λέγουσι περὶ αὐτῆς, καὶ ἐκ τοῦ μὴ ῥᾴδιον εἶναι διορίσαι ἄλλως αὐτήν. οὔτε γὰρ ἐν ἄλλῳ [10] τις γένει δύναιτ᾽ ἂν θεῖναι αὐτήν:

Quod autem bene dictum est, palam ex quibus alii dicunt de ipso, et ex eo quod non facile est diffinire aliter ipsum. Neque enim in alio aliquis genere poterit utique ponere ipsum.

That what we have said is right is evident from what all others say about movement, and from the fact that it is not easy to define it otherwise. For firstly one cannot put it in any class.

δῆλον δ᾽ ἐξ ὧν λέγουσιν: οἱ μὲν γὰρ ἑτερότητα καὶ ἀνισότητα καὶ τὸ μὴ ὄν,

Palam autem ex quibus dicunt. Hii quidem alteritatem et inequalitatem et non ens,

This is evident from what people say. Some call it otherness and inequality and the unreal;

ὧν οὐδὲν ἀνάγκη κινεῖσθαι, ἀλλ᾽ οὐδ᾽ ἡ μεταβολὴ οὔτ᾽ εἰς ταῦτα οὔτ᾽ ἐκ τούτων μᾶλλον ἢ τῶν ἀντικειμένων.

quorum nullum necesse moveri; sed neque permutatio neque in haec neque ex hiis magis quam ex oppositis.

none of these, however, is necessarily moved, and further, change is not either to these or from these any more than from their opposites.

αἴτιον δὲ τοῦ εἰς ταῦτα τιθέναι ὅτι ἀόριστόν τι δοκεῖ εἶναι ἡ κίνησις, τῆς [15] δ᾽ ἑτέρας συστοιχίας αἱ ἀρχαὶ διὰ τὸ στερητικαὶ εἶναι ἀόριστοι: οὔτε γὰρ τόδε οὔτε τοιόνδε οὐδεμία αὐτῶν οὔτε τῶν λοιπῶν κατηγοριῶν.

Causa autem in haec ponendi quia infinitum aliquid videtur esse motus, alterius autem coelementationis principia quia privativa sunt indeterminata; neque enim hoc neque tale nullum ipsorum neque reliquorum predicamentorum.

The reason why people put movement in these classes is that it is thought to be something indefinite, and the principles in one of the two columns of contraries are indefinite because they are privative, for none of them is either a this or a such or in any of the other categories.

τοῦ δὲ δοκεῖν ἀόριστον εἶναι τὴν κίνησιν αἴτιον ὅτι οὔτ᾽ εἰς δύναμιν τῶν ὄντων οὔτ᾽ εἰς ἐνέργειαν ἔστι θεῖναι αὐτήν: οὔτε γὰρ τὸ δυνατὸν ποσὸν εἶναι κινεῖται ἐξ [20] ἀνάγκης, οὔτε τὸ ἐνεργείᾳ ποσόν, ἥ τε κίνησις ἐνέργεια μὲν εἶναι δοκεῖ τις, ἀτελὴς δέ: αἴτιον δ᾽ ὅτι ἀτελὲς τὸ δυνατὸν οὗ ἐστιν ἐνέργεια. καὶ διὰ τοῦτο χαλεπὸν αὐτὴν λαβεῖν τί ἐστιν: ἢ γὰρ εἰς στέρησιν ἀνάγκη θεῖναι ἢ εἰς δύναμιν ἢ εἰς ἐνέργειαν ἁπλῆν, τούτων δ᾽ οὐδὲν φαίνεται ἐνδεχόμενον, ὥστε [25] λείπεται τὸ λεχθὲν εἶναι, καὶ ἐνέργειαν καὶ [μὴ] ἐνέργειαν τὴν εἰρημένην, ἰδεῖν μὲν χαλεπὴν ἐνδεχομένην δ᾽ εἶναι.

Cur autem videatur indeterminatus esse motus, causa quia neque in potentiam entium neque in actum est ponere ipsum. Neque enim possibile quantum esse movetur ex necessitate, neque quod actu quantum; motusque actus quidem esse videtur aliquis, imperfectus autem. Causa autem quia imperfectum quod possibile cuius est actus. Et propter hoc difficile ipsum sumere quid est; aut enim in privationem necesse poni aut in potentiam aut in actum simplicem, horum autem nullum videtur

contingens. Quare relinquitur quod dictum est esse, et actum et non actum dictum, videre quidem difficilem contingentem autem esse.

And the reason why movement is thought to be indefinite is that it cannot be classed either with the potency of things or with their actuality; for neither that which is capable of being of a certain quantity, nor that which is actually of a certain quantity, is of necessity moved, and movement is thought to be an actuality, but incomplete; the reason is that the potential, whose actuality it is, is incomplete. And therefore it is hard to grasp what movement is; for it must be classed either under privation or under potency or under absolute actuality, but evidently none of these is possible. Therefore what remains is that it must be what we said-both actuality and the actuality we have described-which is hard to detect but capable of existing.

καὶ ὅτι ἐστὶν ἡ κίνησις ἐν τῷ κινητῷ, δῆλον: ἐντελέχεια γάρ ἐστι τούτου ὑπὸ τοῦ κινητικοῦ.

Et quod est motus in mobili, palam; actus enim est huius a motivo, et motivi actus non alius est.

And evidently movement is in the movable; for it is the complete realization of this by that which is capable of causing movement.

καὶ ἡ τοῦ κινητικοῦ ἐνέργεια οὐκ ἄλλη ἐστίν. δεῖ μὲν γὰρ εἶναι ἐντελέχειαν ἀμφοῖν:

Oportet quidem enim esse actum amborum.

And the actuality of that which is capable of causing movement is no other than that of the movable. For it must be the complete reality of both.

κινητικὸν [30] μὲν γάρ ἐστι τῷ δύνασθαι, κινοῦν δὲ τῷ ἐνεργεῖν,

Motivum quidem enim est in posse,

For while a thing is capable of causing movement because it can do this, it is a mover because it is active;

ἀλλ᾽ ἔστιν ἐνεργητικὸν τοῦ κινητοῦ, ὥσθ᾽ ὁμοίως μία ἡ ἀμφοῖν ἐνέργεια

sed est activum mobilis. Quare similiter unus amborum actus, movens autem in operari;

but it is on the movable that it is capable of acting, so that the actuality of both is one,

ὥσπερ τὸ αὐτὸ διάστημα ἓν πρὸς δύο καὶ δύο πρὸς ἕν, καὶ τὸ ἄναντες καὶ τὸ κάταντες, ἀλλὰ τὸ εἶναι οὐχ ἕν· ὁμοίως δὲ καὶ ἐπὶ τοῦ κινοῦντος καὶ κινουμένου. [35]

quemadmodum eadem distantia unum ad duo et duo ad unum, et ascendentes et descendentes; sed esse non unum. Similiter autem et in movente et moto.

just as there is the same interval from one to two as from two to one, and as the steep ascent and the steep descent are one, but the being of them is not one; the case of the mover and the moved is similar.

## Chapter 10

τὸ δ᾽ ἄπειρον ἢ τὸ ἀδύνατον διελθεῖν τῷ μὴ πεφυκέναι διιέναι, καθάπερ ἡ φωνὴ ἀόρατος, ἢ τὸ διέξοδον ἔχον ἀτελεύτητον, ἢ ὃ μόλις, ἢ ὃ πεφυκὸς ἔχειν μὴ ἔχει διέξοδον ἢ πέρας·

Infinitum autem aut quod impossibije pertransire eo quod non sit natum pertransiri, quemadmodum vox invisibilis, aut pertransitionem habens imperfectam aut quod vix, aut quod natum est habere non habet pertransitionem aut terminum;

The infinite is either that which is incapable of being traversed because it is not its nature to be traversed (this corresponds to the sense in which the voice is invisible ), or that which admits only of incomplete traverse or scarcely admits of traverse, or that which, though it naturally admits of traverse, is not traversed or limited;

ἔτι προσθέσει ἢ ἀφαιρέσει ἢ ἄμφω.

adhuc appositione aut ablatione aut ambo.

further, a thing may be infinite in respect of addition or of subtrac[66b]tion, or both.

[1066β] [1] χωριστὸν μὲν δὴ αὐτό τι ὂν οὐχ οἷόν τ᾽ εἶναι· εἰ γὰρ μήτε μέγεθος μήτε πλῆθος, οὐσία δ᾽ αὐτὸ τὸ ἄπειρον καὶ μὴ συμβεβηκός, ἀδιαίρετον ἔσται (τὸ γὰρ διαιρετὸν ἢ μέγεθος ἢ πλῆθος), εἰ [5] δὲ ἀδιαίρετον, οὐκ ἄπειρον, εἰ μὴ καθάπερ ἡ φωνὴ ἀόρατος· ἀλλ᾽ οὐχ οὕτω λέγουσιν οὐδ᾽ ἡμεῖς ζητοῦμεν, ἀλλ᾽ ὡς ἀδιέξοδον.

Separabile quidem itaque ipsum aliquid ens non possibile esse. Si enim neque magnitudo est neque multitudo, substantia autem ipsum infinitum et non accidens, indivisibile erit; quod enim divisibile aut magnitudo aut multitudo. Si autem

indivisibile, non infinitum, nisi sicut vox inuisibilis; sed non sic dicunt neque nos quaerimus, sed tamquam impertransibile.

The infinite cannot be a separate, independent thing. For if it is neither a spatial magnitude nor a plurality, but infinity itself is its substance and not an accident of it, it will be indivisible; for the divisible is either magnitude or plurality. But if indivisible, it is not infinite, except as the voice is invisible; but people do not mean this, nor are we examining this sort of infinite, but the infinite as untraversable.

ἔτι πῶς ἐνδέχεται καθ᾽ αὑτὸ εἶναι ἄπειρον, εἰ μὴ καὶ ἀριθμὸς καὶ μέγεθος, ὧν πάθος τὸ ἄπειρον;

Adhuc quomodo contingit per se esse infinitum, si non et numerus et magnitudo, quorum passio infinitum?

Further, how can an infinite exist by itself, unless number and magnitude also exist by themselvess-since infinity is an attribute of these?

ἔτι εἰ κατὰ συμβεβηκός, οὐκ ἂν εἴη στοιχεῖον τῶν ὄντων [10] ᾗ ἄπειρον, ὥσπερ οὐδὲ τὸ ἀόρατον τῆς διαλέκτου, καίτοι ἡ φωνὴ ἀόρατος. καὶ ὅτι οὐκ ἔστιν ἐνεργείᾳ εἶναι τὸ ἄπειρον, δῆλον. ἔσται γὰρ ὁτιοῦν αὐτοῦ ἄπειρον μέρος τὸ λαμβανόμενον (τὸ γὰρ ἀπείρῳ εἶναι καὶ ἄπειρον τὸ αὐτό, εἴπερ οὐσία τὸ ἄπειρον καὶ μὴ καθ᾽ ὑποκειμένου), ὥστε ἢ ἀδιαίρετον, ἢ εἰς [15] ἄπειρα διαιρετόν, εἰ μεριστόν: πολλὰ δ᾽ εἶναι τὸ αὐτὸ ἀδύνατον ἄπειρα (ὥσπερ γὰρ ἀέρος ἀὴρ μέρος, οὕτως ἄπειρον ἀπείρου, εἰ ἔστιν οὐσία καὶ ἀρχή): ἀμέριστον ἄρα καὶ ἀδιαίρετον. ἀλλὰ ἀδύνατον τὸ ἐντελεχείᾳ ὂν ἄπειρον (ποσὸν γὰρ εἶναι ἀνάγκη): κατὰ συμβεβηκὸς ἄρα ὑπάρχει. ἀλλ᾽ εἰ [20] οὕτως, εἴρηται ὅτι οὐκ ἐνδέχεται εἶναι ἀρχήν, ἀλλ᾽ ἐκεῖνο ᾧ συμβέβηκε, τὸν ἀέρα ἢ τὸ ἄρτιον. αὕτη μὲν οὖν ἡ ζήτησις καθόλου,

Adhuc si secundum accidens, non utique erit elementum entium in quantum infinitum, quemadmodum neque inuisibile loquele, quamvis vox inuisibilis. Et quod non est actu esse infinitum, palam; erit enim quaecumque ipsius infinita pars accepta. Infinito enim esse et infinitum idem, siquidem substantia infinitum et non de subiecto. quare aut indivisibile, aut in infinita divisibile, si partibile. Multa autem esse idem impossibile infinita; quemadmodum enim pars aer aeris, sic infinitum infiniti, si est substantia et principium. Impartibile igitur et indivisibile. Sed impossibile actu ens infinitum; quantum enim esse necesse. Secundum accidens igitur existit. Sed si sic, dictum est quod non contingit esse principium, sed illud cui accidit, aerem aut parem. Haec quidem igitur inquisitio universalis.

Further, if the infinite is an accident of something else, it cannot be qua infinite an element in things, as the invisible is not an element in speech, though the voice is invisible. And evidently the infinite cannot exist actually. For then any part of it that

might be taken would be infinite (for to be infinite and the infinite are the same, if the infinite is substance and not predicated of a subject). Therefore it is either indivisible, or if it is partible, it is divisible into infinites; but the same thing cannot be many infinites (as a part of air is air, so a part of the infinite would be infinite, if the infinite is substance and a principle). Therefore it must be impartible and indivisible. But the actually infinite cannot be indivisible; for it must be of a certain quantity. Therefore infinity belongs to its subject incidentally. But if so, then (as we have said) it cannot be it that is a principle, but that of which it is an accident-the air or the even number. This inquiry is universal;

ὅτι δ᾿ ἐν τοῖς αἰσθητοῖς οὐκ ἔστιν, ἐνθένδε δῆλον: εἰ γὰρ σώματος λόγος τὸ ἐπιπέδοις ὡρισμένον, οὐκ εἴη ἂν ἄπειρον σῶμα οὔτ᾿ αἰσθητὸν οὔτε νοητόν,

Quod autem in sensibilibus non est, hinc palam. Si enim corporis ratio 'superficiebus determinatum\ non erit utique infinitum corpus neque sensibile neque intellectuale,

but that the infinite is not among sensible things, is evident from the following argument. If the definition of a body is that which is bounded by planes , there cannot be an infinite body either sensible or intelligible;

οὐδ᾿ ἀριθμὸς ὡς [25] κεχωρισμένος καὶ ἄπειρος: ἀριθμητὸν γὰρ ὁ ἀριθμὸς ἢ τὸ ἔχον ἀριθμόν.

neque numerus ut separatus et infinitus, numerabile enim numerus aut habens numerum.

nor a separate and infinite number, for number or that which has a number is numerable.

φυσικῶς δὲ ἐκ τῶνδε δῆλον: οὔτε γὰρ σύνθετον οἷόν τ᾿ εἶναι οὔθ᾿ ἁπλοῦν. σύνθετον μὲν γὰρ οὐκ ἔσται σῶμα, εἰ πεπέρανται τῷ πλήθει τὰ στοιχεῖα (δεῖ γὰρ ἰσάζειν τὰ ἐναντία καὶ μὴ εἶναι ἓν αὐτῶν ἄπειρον: εἰ γὰρ ὁτῳοῦν [30] λείπεται ἡ θατέρου σώματος δύναμις, φθαρήσεται ὑπὸ τοῦ ἀπείρου τὸ πεπερασμένον: ἕκαστον δ᾿ ἄπειρον εἶναι ἀδύνατον, σῶμα γάρ ἐστι τὸ πάντῃ ἔχον διάστασιν, ἄπειρον δὲ τὸ ἀπεράντως διεστηκός, ὥστ᾿ εἰ τὸ ἄπειρον σῶμα, πάντῃ ἔσται ἄπειρον):

Naturaliter autem ex hiis palam. Neque enim compositum possibile esse neque simplex. Compositum quidem enim non erit corpus, si finita sunt multitudine elementa. Oportet enim equari contraria et non esse unum ipsorum infinitum; si enim cuicumque deficit alterius corporis virtus, corrumpetur ab infinito finitum. Unumquodque autem infinitum esse impossibile. Corpus enim quod omnino habet

distentionem, infinitum autem quod infinite distat; quare infinitum corpus omnino erit infinitum.

Concretely, the truth is evident from the following argument. The infinite can neither be composite nor simple. For (a) it cannot be a composite body, since the elements are limited in multitude. For the contraries must be equal and no one of them must be infinite; for if one of the two bodies falls at all short of the other in potency, the finite will be destroyed by the infinite. And that each should be infinite is impossible. For body is that which has extension in all directions, and the infinite is the boundlessly extended, so that if the infinite is a body it will be infinite in every direction.

οὐδὲ ἓν δὲ καὶ ἁπλοῦν ἐνδέχεται τὸ ἄπειρον εἶναι [35] σῶμα, οὔθ᾽ ὡς λέγουσί τινες, παρὰ τὰ στοιχεῖα ἐξ οὗ γεννῶσι ταῦτα (οὐκ ἔστι γὰρ τοιοῦτο σῶμα παρὰ τὰ στοιχεῖα: ἅπαν γάρ, ἐξ οὗ ἐστί, καὶ διαλύεται εἰς τοῦτο, οὐ φαίνεται δὲ τοῦτο παρὰ τὰ ἁπλᾶ σώματα), [1067α] [1] οὐδὲ πῦρ οὐδ᾽ ἄλλο τῶν στοιχείων οὐθέν: χωρὶς γὰρ τοῦ ἄπειρον εἶναί τι αὐτῶν, ἀδύνατον τὸ ἅπαν, κἂν ᾖ πεπερασμένον, ἢ εἶναι ἢ γίγνεσθαι ἕν τι αὐτῶν, ὥσπερ Ἡράκλειτός φησιν ἅπαντα γίγνεσθαί ποτε [5] πῦρ. ὁ δ᾽ αὐτὸς λόγος καὶ ἐπὶ τοῦ ἑνὸς ὃ ποιοῦσι παρὰ τὰ στοιχεῖα οἱ φυσικοί: πᾶν γὰρ μεταβάλλει ἐξ ἐναντίου, οἷον ἐκ θερμοῦ εἰς ψυχρόν.

Neque unum autem simplex contingit infinitum esse corpus, neque ut dicunt quidam praeter elementa ex quo generant haec (non enim est tale corpus praeter elementa; omne enim ex quo est et dissolvitur in hoc, non videtur autem hoc circa simplicia corpora), neque ignis neque aliud aliquod elementorum nullum. Sine enim eo quod est infinitum esse aliquid ipsorum, impossibile omne, et si sit finitum, aut esse aut fieri unum aliquod ipsorum, quemadmodum Eraclitus ait omnia fieri aliquando ignem. Eadem autem ratio et in uno quod faciunt praeter elementa phisici; omne enim permutat ex contrario, puta ex calido in frigidum.

Nor (b) can the infinite body be one and simple-neither, as some say, something apart from the elements, from which they generate these (for there is no such body apart from the elements; for everything can be resolved into that of which it consists, but no such product of [67a] analysis is observed except the simple bodies), nor fire nor any other of the elements. For apart from the question how any of them could be infinite, the All, even if it is finite, cannot either be or become any one of them, as Heraclitus says all things sometime become fire. The same argument applies to this as to the One which the natural philosophers posit besides the elements. For everything changes from contrary to contrary, e.g. from hot to cold.

ἔτι τὸ αἰσθητὸν σῶμα πού, καὶ ὁ αὐτὸς τόπος ὅλου καὶ μορίου, οἷον τῆς γῆς,

Adhuc sensibile corpus alicubi, et idem locus totius et partis, puta terre.

Further, a sensible body is somewhere, and whole and part have the same proper place, e.g. the whole earth and part of the earth.

ὥστ᾽ εἰ μὲν ὁμοειδές, ἀκίνητον ἔσται ἢ ἀεὶ οἰσθήσεται, τοῦτο δὲ [10] ἀδύνατον (τί γὰρ μᾶλλον κάτω ἢ ἄνω ἢ ὁπουοῦν; οἷον εἰ βῶλος εἴη, ποῦ αὕτη κινήσεται ἢ μενεῖ; ὁ γὰρ τόπος τοῦ συγγενοῦς αὐτῇ σώματος ἄπειρος: καθέξει οὖν τὸν ὅλον τόπον; καὶ πῶς; τίς οὖν ἡ μονὴ καὶ ἡ κίνησις; ἢ πανταχοῦ μενεῖ—οὐ κινηθήσεται ἄρα, ἢ πανταχοῦ κινηθήσεται [15] —οὐκ ἄρα στήσεται):

Quare si quidem eiusdem speciei, immobile erit aut semper feretur; hoc autem impossibile. Quid enim magis deorsum quam sursum aut ubicumque? Puta si bolus fuerit, ubi hic movebitur aut manebit? Locus enim ipsius connaturalis corporis infinitus. Optinebit igitur totum locum. Et quomodo? Quae igitur mansio et motus? Aut ubique manet, non movebitur igitur, aut ubique, non igitur stabit.

Therefore if (a) the infinite body is homogeneous, it will be unmovable or it will be always moving. But this is impossible; for why should it rather rest, or move, down, up, or anywhere, rather than anywhere else? E.g. if there were a clod which were part of an infinite body, where will this move or rest? The proper place of the body which is homogeneous with it is infinite. Will the clod occupy the whole place, then? And how? (This is impossible.) What then is its rest or its movement? It will either rest everywhere, and then it cannot move; or it will move everywhere, and then it cannot be still.

εἰ δ᾽ ἀνόμοιον τὸ πᾶν, ἀνόμοιοι καὶ οἱ τόποι, καὶ πρῶτον μὲν οὐχ ἓν τὸ σῶμα τοῦ παντὸς ἀλλ᾽ ἢ τῷ ἅπτεσθαι, εἶτα ἢ πεπερασμένα ταῦτ᾽ ἔσται ἢ ἄπειρα εἴδει. πεπερασμένα μὲν οὖν οὐχ οἷόν τε (ἔσται γὰρ τὰ μὲν ἄπειρα τὰ δ᾽ οὔ, εἰ τὸ πᾶν ἄπειρον, οἷον πῦρ ἢ ὕδωρ: [20] φθορὰ δὲ τὸ τοιοῦτον τοῖς ἐναντίοις): εἰ δ᾽ ἄπειρα καὶ ἁπλᾶ, καὶ οἱ τόποι ἄπειροι καὶ ἔσται ἄπειρα στοιχεῖα: εἰ δὲ τοῦτ᾽ ἀδύνατον καὶ οἱ τόποι πεπερασμένοι, καὶ τὸ πᾶν ἀνάγκη πεπεράνθαι.

Si autem dissimile totum, dissimilia et loca, et primo quidem non unum corpus omnis nisi tactu. Deinde aut finita haec erunt aut infinita specie. Finita quidem igitur non possibile; erunt enim haec quidem infinita haec autem non, si omne infinitum, puta ignis aut aqua; corruptio autem quod tale contrariis. Si autem infinita et simplicia, et loca infinita et erunt infinita elementa. Si autem hoc impossibile et loca finita, et omne necesse finitum esse.

But (b) if the All has unlike parts, the proper places of the parts are unlike also, and, firstly, the body of the All is not one except by contact, and, secondly, the parts will be either finite or infinite in variety of kind. Finite they cannot be; for then those of one kind will be infinite in quantity and those of another will not (if the All is infinite), e.g. fire or water would be infinite, but such an infinite element would be destruction to the contrary elements. But if the parts are infinite and simple, their places also are infinite and there will be an infinite number of elements; and if this is impossible, and the places are finite, the All also must be limited.

ὅλως δ᾽ ἀδύνατον ἄπειρον εἶναι σῶμα καὶ τόπον τοῖς σώμασιν, εἰ πᾶν σῶμα αἰσθητὸν ἢ βάρος ἔχει [25] ἢ κουφότητα· ἢ γὰρ ἐπὶ τὸ μέσον ἢ ἄνω οἰσθήσεται, ἀδύνατον δὲ τὸ ἄπειρον ἢ πᾶν ἢ τὸ ἥμισυ ὁποτερονοῦν πεπονθέναι· πῶς γὰρ διελεῖς; ἢ πῶς τοῦ ἀπείρου ἔσται τὸ μὲν κάτω τὸ δ᾽ ἄνω, ἢ ἔσχατον καὶ μέσον;

Totaliter autem impossibile infinitum esse corpus et locum  corporibus, si omne corpus sensibile aut gravitatem aut levitatem habet; aut enim ad medium aut sursum feretur. Impossibile autem infinitum, aut omne aut dimidium, quodcumque passum esse. Quomodo enim divides, aut qualiter infiniti erit hoc quidem deorsum hoc autem sursum, aut extremum et medium?

In general, there cannot be an infinite body and also a proper place for bodies, if every sensible body has either weight or lightness. For it must move either towards the middle or upwards, and the infinite either the whole or the half of it-cannot do either; for how will you divide it? Or how will part of the infinite be down and part up, or part extreme and part middle?

ἔτι πᾶν σῶμα αἰσθητὸν ἐν τόπῳ, τόπου δὲ εἴδη ἕξ, ἀδύνατον δ᾽ ἐν τῷ [30] ἀπείρῳ σώματι ταῦτ᾽ εἶναι.

Adhuc omne sensibile corpus in loco, loci autem species sex,  impossibile autem in infinito corpore haec esse.

Further, every sensible body is in a place, and there are six kinds of place, but these cannot exist in an infinite body.

ὅλως δ᾽ εἰ ἀδύνατον τόπον ἄπειρον εἶναι, καὶ σῶμα ἀδύνατον· τὸ γὰρ ἐν τόπῳ πού, τοῦτο δὲ σημαίνει ἢ ἄνω ἢ κάτω ἢ τῶν λοιπῶν τι, τούτων δ᾽ ἕκαστον πέρας τι.

Totaliter autem si impossibile locum infinitum esse, et corpus impossibile. Quod  enim in loco alicubi, hoc autem significat aut sursum aut deorsum aut reliquorum aliquod, horum autem unumquodque terminus aliquis.

In general, if there cannot be an infinite place, there cannot be an infinite body; (and there cannot be an infinite place,) for that which is in a place is somewhere, and this means either up or down or in one of the other directions, and each of these is a limit.

τὸ δ᾽ ἄπειρον οὐ ταὐτὸν ἐν μεγέθει καὶ κινήσει καὶ χρόνῳ ὡς μία τις φύσις, ἀλλὰ τὸ ὕστερον [35] λέγεται κατὰ τὸ πρότερον, οἷον κίνησις κατὰ τὸ μέγεθος ἐφ᾽ οὗ κινεῖται ἢ ἀλλοιοῦται ἢ αὔξεται, χρόνος δὲ διὰ τὴν κίνησιν. [1067β] [1]

Infinitum autem non idem in magnitudine et motu et tempore, ut una quaedam natura, sed quod posterius dicitur secundum prius, puta motus secundum magnitudinem in qua movetur aut alteratur aut augetur, tempus autem propter motum.

The infinite is not the same in the sense that it is a single thing whether exhibited in distance or in movement or in time, but the posterior among these is called infinite in virtue of its relation to the prior; i.e. a movement is called infinite in virtue of the distance covered by the spatial movement or alteration or growth, and a time is called infinite because of the movement which occupies it.

## Chapter 11

μεταβάλλει δὲ τὸ μεταβάλλον τὸ μὲν κατὰ συμβεβηκός, [2] ὡς τὸ μουσικὸν βαδίζει, τὸ δὲ τῷ τούτου τι μεταβάλλειν ἁπλῶς λέγεται μεταβάλλειν, οἷον ὅσα κατὰ μέρη (ὑγιάζεται γὰρ τὸ σῶμα, ὅτι ὁ ὀφθαλμός), ἔστι δέ [5] τι ὃ καθ᾽ αὑτὸ πρῶτον κινεῖται, καὶ τοῦτ᾽ ἔστι τὸ καθ᾽ αὑτὸ κινητόν.

Permutatur autem quod permutatur hoc quidem secundum accidens, ut musicum ambulare, hoc autem eo quod huius aliquid permutatur simpliciter dicitur permutari, puta quaecumque secundum partes; sanatur enim corpus, quia oculus. Est autem aliquid et quod ipsum primum movetur, et hoc est per se mobile.

Of things which change, some change in an accidental sense, like that in which the musical may be said to walk, and others are said, without qualification, to change, because something in them changes, i.e. the things that change in parts; the body becomes healthy, because the eye does. But there is something which is by its own nature moved directly, and this is the essentially movable.

ἔστι δέ [τι] καὶ ἐπὶ τοῦ κινοῦντος ὡσαύτως· κινεῖ γὰρ κατὰ συμβεβηκὸς τὸ δὲ κατὰ μέρος τὸ δὲ καθ᾽ αὑτό·

Est autem aliquid et in movente eodem modo; movet enim secundum accidens, hoc quidem secundum partem, hoc autem per se.

The same distinction is found in the case of the mover; for it causes movement either in an accidental sense or in respect of a part of itself or essentially.

ἔστι δέ τι τὸ κινοῦν πρῶτον· ἔστι δέ τι τὸ κινούμενον, ἔτι ἐν ᾧ χρόνῳ καὶ ἐξ οὗ καὶ εἰς ὅ. τὰ δ᾽ εἴδη καὶ τὰ πάθη καὶ [10] ὁ τόπος, εἰς ἃ κινοῦνται τὰ κινούμενα, ἀκίνητά ἐστιν, οἷον ἐπιστήμη καὶ θερμότης· ἔστι δ᾽ οὐχ ἡ θερμότης κίνησις ἀλλ᾽ ἡ θέρμανσις.

Est autem aliquid movens primum; est autem aliquid quod movetur. Adhuc in quo tempore et ex quo et in quod. Species autem et passiones et locus, in quae moventur mota quae mobilia sunt, puta scientia et caliditas; est autem non caliditas motus sed calefactio.

There is something that directly causes movement; and there is something that is moved, also the time in which it is moved, and that from which and that into which it is moved. But the forms and the affections and the place, which are the terminals of the movement of moving things, are unmovable, e.g. knowledge or heat; it is not heat that is a movement, but heating.

ἡ δὲ μὴ κατὰ συμβεβηκὸς μεταβολὴ οὐκ ἐν ἅπασιν ὑπάρχει ἀλλ᾽ ἐν τοῖς ἐναντίοις καὶ μεταξὺ καὶ ἐν ἀντιφάσει· τούτου δὲ πίστις ἐκ τῆς ἐπαγωγῆς. μεταβάλλει [15] δὲ τὸ μεταβάλλον ἢ ἐξ ὑποκειμένου εἰς ὑποκείμενον, ἢ οὐκ ἐξ ὑποκειμένου εἰς οὐχ ὑποκείμενον, ἢ ἐξ ὑποκειμένου εἰς οὐχ ὑποκείμενον, ἢ οὐκ ἐξ ὑποκειμένου εἰς ὑποκείμενον (λέγω δὲ ὑποκείμενον τὸ καταφάσει δηλούμενον), ὥστ᾽ ἀνάγκη τρεῖς εἶναι μεταβολάς· ἡ γὰρ ἐξ οὐχ ὑποκειμένου [20] εἰς μὴ ὑποκείμενον οὐκ ἔστι μεταβολή· οὔτε γὰρ ἐναντία οὔτε ἀντίφασίς ἐστιν, ὅτι οὐκ ἀντίθεσις.

Quae autem non secundum accidens permutatio non in omnibus existit, sed in contrariis et intermediis et in contradictione; huius autem fides ex inductione. Permutatur autem quod permutatur aut ex subiecto in subiectum, aut ex non subiecto in non subiectum, aut ex subiecto in non subiectum, aut ex non subiecto in subiectum. Dico autem subiectum quod affirmatione monstramus. Quare necesse tres esse permutationes; quae enim ex non subiecto in non subiectum non est permutatio; neque enim contraria neque contradictio est, quia non oppositio.

Change which is not accidental is found not in all things, but between contraries, and their intermediates, and between contradictories. We may convince ourselves of this by induction. That which changes changes either from positive into positive, or from negative into negative, or from positive into negative, or from negative into positive. (By positive I mean that which is expressed by an affirmative term.) Therefore there must be three changes; that from negative into negative is not change, because (since the terms are neither contraries nor contradictories) there is no opposition.

ἡ μὲν οὖν οὐκ ἐξ ὑποκειμένου εἰς ὑποκείμενον κατ᾽ ἀντίφασιν γένεσίς ἐστιν, ἡ μὲν ἁπλῶς ἁπλῆ, ἡ δὲ τινὸς τίς· ἡ δ᾽ ἐξ ὑποκειμένου εἰς μὴ ὑποκείμενον φθορά, ἡ μὲν ἁπλῶς ἁπλῆ, ἡ δὲ τινὸς [25] τίς.

Quae quidem igitur ex non subiecto in subiectum secundum contradictionem generatio est, quae quidem simpliciter simplex, quae autem quaedam alicuius. Quae autem ex subiecto in non subiectum corruptio, quae quidem simpliciter simplex, quae autem alicuius quaedam.

The change from the negative into the positive which is its contradictory is generation-absolute change absolute generation, and partial change partial generation; and the change from positive to negative is destruction-absolute change absolute destruction, and partial change partial destruction.

εἰ δὴ τὸ μὴ ὂν λέγεται πλεοναχῶς, καὶ μήτε τὸ κατὰ σύνθεσιν ἢ διαίρεσιν ἐνδέχεται κινεῖσθαι μήτε τὸ κατὰ δύναμιν τὸ τῷ ἁπλῶς ὄντι ἀντικείμενον (τὸ γὰρ μὴ λευκὸν ἢ μὴ ἀγαθὸν ὅμως ἐνδέχεται κινεῖσθαι κατὰ συμβεβηκός, εἴη γὰρ ἂν ἄνθρωπος τὸ μὴ λευκόν· τὸ δ᾽ ἁπλῶς [30] μὴ τόδε οὐδαμῶς), ἀδύνατον τὸ μὴ ὂν κινεῖσθαι (εἰ δὲ τοῦτο, καὶ τὴν γένεσιν κίνησιν εἶναι· γίγνεται γὰρ τὸ μὴ ὄν· εἰ γὰρ καὶ ὅτι μάλιστα κατὰ συμβεβηκὸς γίγνεται, ἀλλ᾽ ὅμως ἀληθὲς εἰπεῖν ὅτι ὑπάρχει τὸ μὴ ὂν κατὰ τοῦ γιγνομένου ἁπλῶς)· ὁμοίως δὲ καὶ τὸ ἠρεμεῖν. ταῦτά [35] τε δὴ συμβαίνει δυσχερῆ, καὶ εἰ πᾶν τὸ κινούμενον ἐν τόπῳ, τὸ δὲ μὴ ὂν οὐκ ἔστιν ἐν τόπῳ· εἴη γὰρ ἂν πού. οὐδὲ δὴ ἡ φθορὰ κίνησις· ἐναντίον γὰρ κινήσει κίνησις ἢ ἠρεμία, φθορὰ δὲ γενέσει.

Si itaque non ens dicitur multipliciter, et neque quod secundum compositionem aut divisionem contingit moveri neque quod secundum potentiam, quod simpliciter enti oppositum (quod enim non album aut non bonum tamen contingit moveri secundum accidens; erit enim utique homo quod non album; quod autem simpliciter non hoc nequaquam): impossibile non ens moveri. Si autem hoc, et generationem motum esse; generatur enim non ens. Si enim et quam maxime secundum accidens generatur, sed tamen verum dicere quod existit non ens de generato simpliciter. Similiter autem et quiescere. Haec itaque accidunt difficilia. Et si omne quod movetur in loco, non ens autem non est in loco; erit enim utique alicubi. Neque itaque corruptio motus; contrarium enim motui motus aut quies, corruptio autem generationi.

If, then, that which is not has several senses, and movement can attach neither to that which implies putting together or separating, nor to that which implies potency and is opposed to that which is in the full sense (true, the not-white or not-good can be moved incidentally, for the not-white might be a man; but that which is not a particular thing at all can in no wise be moved), that which is not cannot be moved (and if this is so, generation cannot be movement; for that which is not is generated; for even if we admit to the full that its generation is accidental, yet it is true to say that not-being is predicable of that which is generated absolutely). Similarly rest cannot belong to that which is not. These consequences, then, turn out to be awkward, and also this, that everything that is moved is in a place, but that which is not is not in a place; for then it would be somewhere. Nor is destruction movement; for the contrary of movement is rest, but the contrary of destruction [68a] is generation.

[1068α] [1] ἐπεὶ δὲ πᾶσα κίνησις μεταβολή τις, μεταβολαὶ δὲ τρεῖς αἱ εἰρημέναι, τούτων δ' αἱ κατὰ γένεσιν καὶ φθορὰν οὐ κινήσεις, αὗται δ' εἰσὶν αἱ κατ' ἀντίφασιν, ἀνάγκη τὴν ἐξ ὑποκειμένου εἰς ὑποκείμενον κίνησιν εἶναι [5] μόνην. τὰ δ' ὑποκείμενα ἢ ἐναντία ἢ μεταξύ (καὶ γὰρ ἡ στέρησις κείσθω ἐναντίον), καὶ δηλοῦται καταφάσει, οἷον τὸ γυμνὸν καὶ νωδὸν καὶ μέλαν.

Quoniam autem omnis motus permutatio quaedam, permutationes autem tres dicte, harum autem quae secundum generationem et corruptionem non motus, hae autem sunt quae secundum contradictionem, necesse eam quae ex subiecto in subiectum motum esse solam. Subiecta autem aut contraria aut intermedia; et enim privatio ponatur contrarium, et monstratur affirmatione, puta nudum et edentulum et nigrum.

Since every movement is a change, and the kinds of change are the three named above, and of these those in the way of generation and destruction are not movements, and these are the changes from a thing to its contradictory, it follows that only the change from positive into positive is movement. And the positives are either contrary or intermediate (for even privation must be regarded as contrary), and are expressed by an affirmative term, e.g. naked or toothless or black .

## Chapter 12

εἰ οὖν αἱ κατηγορίαι διῄρηνται οὐσίᾳ, ποιότητι, τόπῳ, τῷ ποιεῖν ἢ πάσχειν, τῷ πρός τι, τῷ ποσῷ, ἀνάγκη τρεῖς [10] εἶναι κινήσεις, ποιοῦ ποσοῦ τόπου:

Si igitur predicamenta divisa sunt substantia, qualitate, ioco, facere aut pati, ad aliquid, quanto, necesse tres esse motus: qualis, quanti, loci.

If the categories are classified as substance, quality, place, acting or being acted on, relation, quantity, there must be three kinds of movement-of quality, of quantity, of place.

κατ' οὐσίαν δ' οὔ, διὰ τὸ μηθὲν εἶναι οὐσίᾳ ἐναντίον,

Secundum substantiam autem non, propter nullum esse substantiae contrarium.

There is no movement in respect of substance (because there is nothing contrary to substance),

οὐδὲ τοῦ πρός τι (ἔστι γὰρ θατέρου μεταβάλλοντος μὴ ἀληθεύεσθαι θάτερον μηδὲν μεταβάλλον, ὥστε κατὰ συμβεβηκὸς ἡ κίνησις αὐτῶν),

Neque ad aliquid; est enim altero nihil permutato verificari alterum nihil permutatum. Quare secundum accidens motus ipsorum.

nor of relation (for it is possible that if one of two things in relation changes, the relative term which was true of the other thing ceases to be true, though this other does not change at all,-so that their movement is accidental),

οὐδὲ ποιοῦντος καὶ πάσχοντος, ἢ κινοῦντος καὶ κινουμένου, ὅτι οὐκ ἔστι [15] κινήσεως κίνησις οὐδὲ γενέσεως γένεσις, οὐδ᾽ ὅλως μεταβολῆς μεταβολή. διχῶς γὰρ ἐνδέχεται κινήσεως εἶναι κίνησιν, ἢ ὡς ὑποκειμένου (οἷον ὁ ἄνθρωπος κινεῖται ὅτι ἐκ λευκοῦ εἰς μέλαν μεταβάλλει, ὥστε οὕτω καὶ ἡ κίνησις ἢ θερμαίνεται ἢ ψύχεται ἢ τόπον ἀλλάττει ἢ αὔξεται: τοῦτο [20] δὲ ἀδύνατον: οὐ γὰρ τῶν ὑποκειμένων τι ἡ μεταβολή), ἢ τῷ ἕτερόν τι ὑποκείμενον ἐκ μεταβολῆς μεταβάλλειν εἰς ἄλλο εἶδος, οἷον ἄνθρωπον ἐκ νόσου εἰς ὑγίειαν. ἀλλ᾽ οὐδὲ τοῦτο δυνατὸν πλὴν κατὰ συμβεβηκός. πᾶσα γὰρ κίνησις ἐξ ἄλλου εἰς ἄλλο ἐστὶ μεταβολή, καὶ γένεσις καὶ φθορὰ [25] ὡσαύτως: πλὴν αἱ μὲν εἰς ἀντικείμενα ὡδί, ἡ δ᾽ ὡδί, ἡ κίνησις. ἅμα οὖν μεταβάλλει ἐξ ὑγιείας εἰς νόσον, καὶ ἐξ αὐτῆς ταύτης τῆς μεταβολῆς εἰς ἄλλην. δῆλον δὴ ὅτι ἂν νοσήσῃ, μεταβεβληκὸς ἔσται εἰς ὁποιανοῦν (ἐνδέχεται γὰρ ἠρεμεῖν) καὶ ἔτι εἰς μὴ τὴν τυχοῦσαν ἀεί: κἀκείνη ἐκ τινος εἰς [30] τι ἄλλο ἔσται: ὥσθ᾽ ἡ ἀντικειμένη ἔσται, ὑγίανσις, ἀλλὰ τῷ συμβεβηκέναι, οἷον ἐξ ἀναμνήσεως εἰς λήθην μεταβάλλει ὅτι ᾧ ὑπάρχει ἐκεῖνο μεταβάλλει, ὁτὲ μὲν εἰς ἐπιστήμην ὁτὲ δὲ εἰς ἄγνοιαν.

Neque facientis et patientis aut moventis et moti, quia non est motus motus neque generationis generatio, neque totaliter permutatio permutationis. Dupliciter enim contingit motus esse motum. Aut ut subiecti, velut homo movetur quia ex albo in nigrum permutatur, quare sic et motus aut calefit aut infrigidatur aut locum permutat aut augetur. Hoc autem impossibile; non enim subiectorum aliquid permutatio. Aut eo quod alterum aliquod subiectum ex permutatione permutetur in aliam speciem, velut homo ex langore in sanitatem. Sed neque hoc possibile nisi secundum accidens. Omnis enim motus ex alio in aliud est permutatio; et generatio et corruptio eodem modo, verumptamen quae quidem ex oppositis sic aut sic non motus. Simul igitur permutat ex sanitate in egritudinem, et ex hac ipsa permutatione in aliam. Palam autem quia si languerit permutatus erit in qualiacumque; contingit enim quiescere. Et adhuc in non contingentem semper, et illa ex aliquo in aliquid aliud erit. quare opposita, sanatio. Sed per accidere, velut ex reminiscentia in oblivionem permutatur quia cui existit illud permutatur, quandoque quidem in scientiam, quandoque autem in sanitatem.

nor of agent and patient, or mover and moved, because there is no movement of movement nor generation of generation, nor, in general, change of change. For there might be movement of movement in two senses; (1) movement might be the subject moved, as a man is moved because he changes from pale to dark,-so that on this showing movement, too, may be either heated or cooled or change its place or increase. But this is impossible; for change is not a subject. Or (2) some other subject might change from change into some other form of existence (e.g. a man from disease into health). But this also is not possible except incidentally. For every movement is change from something into something. (And so are generation and destruction; only, these are changes into things opposed in certain ways while the other, movement, is into things opposed in another way.) A thing changes, then, at the same time from health into illness, and from this change itself into another. Clearly, then, if it has become ill, it will have changed into whatever may be the other change concerned (though it may be at rest), and, further, into a determinate change each time; and that new change will be from something definite into some other definite thing; therefore it will be the opposite change, that of growing well. We answer that this happens only incidentally; e.g. there is a change from the process of recollection to that of forgetting, only because that to which the process attaches is changing, now into a state of knowledge, now into one of ignorance.

ἔτι εἰς ἄπειρον βαδιεῖται, εἰ ἔσται μεταβολῆς μεταβολὴ καὶ γενέσεως γένεσις. ἀνάγκη [35] δὴ καὶ τὴν προτέραν, εἰ ἡ ὑστέρα· οἷον εἰ ἡ ἀπλῆ γένεσις ἐγίγνετό ποτε, καὶ τὸ γιγνόμενον ἐγίγνετο· [1068β] [1] ὥστε οὔπω ἦν τὸ γιγνόμενον ἀπλῶς, ἀλλά τι γιγνόμενον [ἢ] γιγνόμενον ἤδη. καὶ τοῦτ᾽ ἐγίγνετό ποτε, ὥστ᾽ οὐκ ἦν πω τότε γιγνόμενον. ἐπεὶ δὲ τῶν ἀπείρων οὐκ ἔστι τι πρῶτον, οὐκ [5] ἔσται τὸ πρῶτον, ὥστ᾽ οὐδὲ τὸ ἐχόμενον. οὔτε γίγνεσθαι οὖν οὔτε κινεῖσθαι οἷόν τε οὔτε μεταβάλλειν οὐδέν.

Adhuc in infinitum ibit, si erit permutationis permutatio et generationis generatio. Necesse igitur et priorem, si posterior; puta si simplex generatio fiebat aliquando, et quod fit fiebat; quare nondum erat quod fiebat simpliciter, sed aliquid fiens simpliciter aut factum. Si itaque et hoc fiebat aliquando, quare nondum erat tunc genitum. Quoniam autem infinitorum non est primum, non erit primum, quare neque habitum. Neque fieri igitur neque moveri possibile est neque permutari nullum.

Further, the process will go on to infinity, if there is to be change of change and coming to be of coming to be. What is true of the later, then, must be true of the earlier; e.g. if the simple coming to be was once coming to be, that which [68b] comes to be something was also once coming to be; therefore that which simply comes to be something was not yet in existence, but something which was coming to be coming to be something was already in existence. And this was once coming to be, so that at that time it was not yet coming to be something else. Now since of an infinite number of terms there is not a first, the first in this series will not exist, and therefore no following term exist. Nothing, then, can either come term wi to be or move or change.

ἔτι τοῦ αὐτοῦ κίνησις ἡ ἐναντία καὶ ἠρέμησις, καὶ γένεσις καὶ φθορά, ὥστε τὸ γιγνόμενον, ὅταν γένηται γιγνόμενον, τότε φθείρεται· οὔτε γὰρ εὐθὺς γιγνόμενον οὔθ᾽ ὕστερον· εἶναι γὰρ δεῖ [10] τὸ φθειρόμενον.

Adhuc eiusdem motus contrarius et quies et generatio et corruptio. Quare quod fit, cum fiat fiens, tunc corrumpitur; neque enim confestim factum neque posterius; esse enim oportet quod corrumpitur.

Further, that which is capable of a movement is also capable of the contrary movement and rest, and that which comes to be also ceases to be. Therefore that which is coming to be is ceasing to be when it has come to be coming to be; for it cannot cease to be as soon as it is coming to be coming to be, nor after it has come to be; for that which is ceasing to be must be.

ἔτι δεῖ ὕλην ὑπεῖναι τῷ γιγνομένῳ καὶ μεταβάλλοντι. τίς οὖν ἔσται ὥσπερ τὸ ἀλλοιωτὸν σῶμα ἢ ψυχή—οὕτω τί τὸ γιγνόμενον κίνησις ἢ γένεσις; καὶ ἔτι τί εἰς ὃ κινοῦνται; δεῖ γὰρ εἶναι τὴν τοῦδε ἐκ τοῦδε εἰς τόδε κίνησιν ἢ γένεσιν. πῶς οὖν; οὐ γὰρ ἔσται μάθησις τῆς [15] μαθήσεως, ὥστ᾽ οὐδὲ γένεσις γενέσεως.

Adhuc oportet materiam subesse ei quod fit et permutato. Quae igitur erit? Quemadmodum alterabile corpus aut anima aliquid, sic aliquid quod fit motus et generatio, et aliquid in quod moventur. Oportet enim esse aliquid eum qui huius ex hoc in hoc motum, non motum. Qualiter igitur?  neque enim erit disciplina disciplinationis, quare neque generatio generationis.

Further, there must be a matter underlying that which comes to be and changes. What will this be, then,-what is it that becomes movement or becoming, as body or soul is that which suffers alteration? And; again, what is it that they move into? For it must be the movement or becoming of something from something into something. How, then, can this condition be fulfilled? There can be no learning of learning, and therefore no becoming of becoming.

ἐπεὶ δ᾽ οὔτ᾽ οὐσίας οὔτε τοῦ πρός τι οὔτε τοῦ ποιεῖν καὶ πάσχειν, λείπεται κατὰ τὸ ποιὸν καὶ ποσὸν καὶ τόπον κίνησιν εἶναι (τούτων γὰρ ἑκάστῳ ἐναντίωσίς ἔστιν), λέγω δὲ τὸ ποιὸν οὐ τὸ ἐν τῇ οὐσίᾳ (καὶ γὰρ ἡ διαφορὰ ποιόν) ἀλλὰ τὸ παθητικόν, καθ᾽ ὃ [20] λέγεται πάσχειν ἢ ἀπαθὲς εἶναι.

Quoniam autem neque substantiae neque eius quod ad aliquid neque eius quod facere et pati, relinquitur secundum quale et quantum et ubi motum esse; horum enim unicuique contrarietas est. Dico autem quale non quod in substantia (et enim differentia quale), sed quod passivum, secundum quod dicitur pati aut impassibile esse.

Since there is not movement either of substance or of relation or of activity and passivity, it remains that movement is in respect of quality and quantity and place; for each of these admits of contrariety. By quality I mean not that which is in the substance (for even the differentia is a quality), but the passive quality, in virtue of which a thing is said to be acted on or to be incapable of being acted on.

τὸ δὲ ἀκίνητον τό τε ὅλως ἀδύνατον κινηθῆναι καὶ τὸ μόλις ἐν χρόνῳ πολλῷ ἢ βραδέως ἀρχόμενον, καὶ τὸ πεφυκὸς μὲν κινεῖσθαι καὶ δυνάμενον <μὴ κινούμενον δὲ ὅτε πέφυκε καὶ οὗ καὶ ὥς: ὃ καλῶ ἠρεμεῖν τῶν ἀκινήτων μόνον: ἐναντίον γὰρ ἠρεμία [25] κινήσει, ὥστε στέρησις ἂν εἴη τοῦ δεκτικοῦ.

Immobile autem et quod totaliter impossibile moveri, et quod vix in tempore multo tarde incipiens, et quod natum quidem moveri non potens autem quando natum est et ubi et ut; quod voco quiescere immobilium solum. Contrarium enim quies motui; quare privatio utique erit susceptivi.

The immobile is either that which is wholly incapable of being moved, or that which is moved with difficulty in a long time or begins slowly, or that which is of a nature to be moved and can be moved but is not moved when and where and as it would naturally be moved. This alone among immobiles I describe as being at rest; for rest is contrary to movement, so that it must be a privation in that which is receptive of movement.

ἅμα κατὰ τόπον ὅσα ἐν ἑνὶ τόπῳ πρώτῳ, καὶ χωρὶς ὅσα ἐν ἄλλῳ: ἅπτεσθαι δὲ ὧν τὰ ἄκρα ἅμα: μεταξὺ δ᾽ εἰς ὃ πέφυκε πρότερον ἀφικνεῖσθαι τὸ μεταβάλλον ἢ εἰς ὃ ἔσχατον μεταβάλλει κατὰ φύσιν τὸ συνεχῶς μεταβάλλον. [30] ἐναντίον κατὰ τόπον τὸ κατ᾽ εὐθεῖαν ἀπέχον πλεῖστον: ἑξῆς δὲ οὗ μετὰ τὴν ἀρχὴν ὄντος, θέσει ἢ εἴδει ἢ ἄλλως πως ἀφορισθέντος, μηθὲν μεταξύ ἐστι τῶν ἐν ταὐτῷ γένει καὶ οὗ ἐφεξῆς ἐστίν, οἷον γραμμαὶ γραμμῆς ἢ μονάδες μονάδος ἢ οἰκίας οἰκία (ἄλλο δ᾽ οὐθὲν κωλύει μεταξὺ [35] εἶναι). τὸ γὰρ ἑξῆς τινος ἐφεξῆς καὶ ὕστερόν τι: οὐ γὰρ τὸ ἓν ἑξῆς τῶν δύο οὐδ᾽ ἡ νουμηνία τῆς δευτέρας. [1069a] [1] ἐχόμενον δὲ ὃ ἂν ἑξῆς ὂν ἅπτηται. ἐπεὶ δὲ πᾶσα μεταβολὴ ἐν τοῖς ἀντικειμένοις, ταῦτα δὲ τὰ ἐναντία καὶ ἀντίφασις, ἀντιφάσεως δ᾽ οὐδὲν ἀνὰ μέσον, δῆλον ὡς ἐν τοῖς ἐναντίοις τὸ [5] μεταξύ. τὸ δὲ συνεχὲς ὅπερ ἐχόμενόν τι. λέγω δὲ συνεχὲς ὅταν ταὐτὸ γένηται καὶ ἓν τὸ ἑκατέρου πέρας οἷς ἅπτονται καὶ συνέχονται,

Simul secundum locum quaecumque in uno loco primo, et seorsum quaecumque in alio. Tangi autem quorum ultima simul. Intermedium autem in quod natum est prius pervenire quod permutatur quam in quod ultimum permutatur secundum naturam continve permutans. Contrarium secundum locum quod secundum rectam plurimum distans. Consequenter autem quo post principium ente, positione aut specie aut aliter qualiter determinato, nihil intermedium est eorum quae in eodem genere et cuius consequenter est, ut lineae lineae aut unitates unitatis aut domus domus; aliud autem nihil prohibet intermedium esse. Quod enim consequenter alicuius consequenter et posterius aliquid; non enim unum consequenter duorum neque noua luna secunde. Habitum autem quodcumque consequenter ens tangit. Quoniam autem omnis permutatio in oppositis, haec autem contraria et contradictio, contradictionis autem nullum intermedium, palam quod in contrariis intermedium. Continuum autem quod quidem habitum aliquid. Dico autem continuum cum idem fuerit et unum utriusque terminus quibus tangunt et continentur.

Things which are in one proximate place are together in place, and things which are in different places are apart: things whose extremes are together touch: that at which a changing thing, if it changes continuously according to its nature, naturally arrives before it arrives at the extreme into which it is changing, is between. That which is most distant in a straight line is contrary in place. That is successive which is after the beginning (the order being determined by position or form or in some other way) and has nothing of the same class between it and that which it succeeds, e.g. lines in the case of a line, units in that of a unit, or a house in that of a house. (There is nothing to prevent a thing of some other class from being between.) For the successive succeeds something and is something later; one does not succeed two , nor the first day of [69a] the month the second. That which, being successive, touches, is contiguous. (Since all change is between opposites, and these are either contraries or contradictories, and there is no middle term for contradictories, clearly that which is between is between contraries.) The continuous is a species of the contiguous. I call two things continuous when the limits of each, with which they touch and by which they are kept together, become one and the same,

ὥστε δῆλον ὅτι τὸ συνεχὲς ἐν τούτοις ἐξ ὧν ἕν τι πέφυκε γίγνεσθαι κατὰ τὴν σύναψιν. καὶ ὅτι πρῶτον τὸ ἐφεξῆς, δῆλον (τὸ γὰρ ἐφεξῆς οὐχ ἅπτεται, [10] τοῦτο δ᾽ ἐφεξῆς· καὶ εἰ συνεχές, ἅπτεται, εἰ δ᾽ ἅπτεται, οὔπω συνεχές· ἐν οἷς δὲ μὴ ἔστιν ἁφή, οὐκ ἔστι σύμφυσις ἐν τούτοις)· ὥστ᾽ οὐκ ἔστι στιγμὴ μονάδι ταὐτόν· ταῖς μὲν γὰρ ὑπάρχει τὸ ἅπτεσθαι, ταῖς δ᾽ οὔ, ἀλλὰ τὸ ἐφεξῆς· καὶ τῶν μὲν μεταξύ τι τῶν δ᾽ οὔ.

Quare palam quod continuum in hiis ex quibus unum aliquid natum est fieri secundum contactum. Et quia primum quod consequenter, palam. Quod enim consequenter non tangit, hoc autem consequenter; et si continuum, tangit, si autem tangit, nondum continuum; in quibus autem non est tactus, non est connascentia in hiis. Quare non est punctum unitati idem; hiis quidem enim inest tangi, hiis autem non, sed ad consequenter; et horum quidem intermedium aliquid, horum autem non.

so that plainly the continuous is found in the things out of which a unity naturally arises in virtue of their contact. And plainly the successive is the first of these concepts (for the successive does not necessarily touch, but that which touches is successive; and if a thing is continuous, it touches, but if it touches, it is not necessarily continuous; and in things in which there is no touching, there is no organic unity); therefore a point is not the same as a unit; for contact belongs to points, but not to units, which have only succession; and there is something between two of the former, but not between two of the latter.

# METHAPHISICE ARISTOTILIS LIBER DUODECIMUS

## 12 (L)1

[1069a] [18] περὶ τῆς οὐσίας ἡ θεωρία: τῶν γὰρ οὐσιῶν αἱ ἀρχαὶ καὶ τὰ αἴτια ζητοῦνται.

De substantia quidem theoria est; nam substantiarum principia et cause quaeruntur.

The subject of our inquiry is substance; for the principles and the causes we are seeking are those of substances.

καὶ γὰρ εἰ ὡς ὅλον τι τὸ πᾶν, [20] ἡ οὐσία πρῶτον μέρος: καὶ εἰ τῷ ἐφεξῆς, κἂν οὕτως πρῶτον ἡ οὐσία, εἶτα τὸ ποιόν, εἶτα τὸ ποσόν.

Et enim si ut totum quoddam  omne, substantia est prima pars; et si eo quod consequenter, et ita primum substantia, deinde qualitas aut quantitas.

For if the universe is of the nature of a whole, substance is its first part; and if it coheres merely by virtue of serial succession, on this view also substance is first, and is succeeded by quality, and then by quantity.

ἅμα δὲ οὐδ᾽ ὄντα ὡς εἰπεῖν ἁπλῶς ταῦτα, ἀλλὰ ποιότητες καὶ κινήσεις, ἢ καὶ τὸ οὐ λευκὸν καὶ τὸ οὐκ εὐθύ: λέγομεν γοῦν εἶναι καὶ ταῦτα, οἷον ἔστιν οὐ λευκόν.

Simul [/Similiter] autem nec entia ut est simpliciter dicere haec, sed qualitates et motus, qua et non album et non rectum; dicimus enim esse et haec, ut puta est non album.

At the same time these latter are not even being in the full sense, but are qualities and movements of it,-or else even the not-white and the not-straight would be being; at least we say even these are, e.g. there is a not-white .

ἔτι οὐδὲν τῶν ἄλλων χωριστόν.

Amplius nihil aliorum separabile.

Further, none of the categories other than substance can exist apart.

[25] μαρτυροῦσι δὲ καὶ οἱ ἀρχαῖοι ἔργῳ: τῆς γὰρ οὐσίας ἐζήτουν ἀρχὰς καὶ στοιχεῖα καὶ αἴτια. οἱ μὲν οὖν νῦν τὰ καθόλου οὐσίας μᾶλλον τιθέασιν (τὰ γὰρ γένη καθόλου, ἅ φασιν ἀρχὰς καὶ οὐσίας εἶναι μᾶλλον διὰ τὸ λογικῶς ζητεῖν): οἱ δὲ πάλαι τὰ καθ᾽ ἕκαστα, οἷον πῦρ καὶ γῆν, ἀλλ᾽ οὐ τὸ [30] κοινόν, σῶμα.

Testantur autem et antiqui opere; nam substantiae quaerebant principia et elementa et causas.  qui quidem nunc universalia substantias magis ponunt; nam genera universalia, quae dicunt principia et substantias esse magis propter logice inquirere. Qui vero antiquitus particularia, ut ignem et  terram, sed non commune, corpus.

And the early philosophers also in practice testify to the primacy of substance; for it was of substance that they sought the principles and elements and causes. The thinkers of the present day tend to rank universals as substances (for genera are universals, and these they tend to describe as principles and substances, owing to the abstract nature of their inquiry); but the thinkers of old ranked particular things as substances, e.g. fire and earth, not what is common to both, body.

οὐσίαι δὲ τρεῖς, μία μὲν αἰσθητή—ἧς ἡ μὲν ἀΐδιος ἡ δὲ φθαρτή, ἣν πάντες ὁμολογοῦσιν, οἷον τὰ φυτὰ καὶ τὰ ζῷα [ἡ δ᾽ ἀΐδιος]—ἧς ἀνάγκη τὰ στοιχεῖα λαβεῖν, εἴτε ἓν εἴτε πολλά: ἄλλη δὲ ἀκίνητος, καὶ ταύτην φασί τινες εἶναι χωριστήν, οἱ μὲν εἰς δύο διαιροῦντες, [35] οἱ δὲ εἰς μίαν φύσιν τιθέντες τὰ εἴδη καὶ τὰ μαθηματικά, οἱ δὲ τὰ μαθηματικὰ μόνον τούτων. ἐκεῖναι μὲν δὴ φυσικῆς (μετὰ κινήσεως γάρ), [1069β] [1] αὕτη δὲ ἑτέρας, εἰ μηδεμία αὐτοῖς ἀρχὴ κοινή.

Substantiae vero tres sunt, una quidem sensibilis, cuius alia quidem sempiterna alia corruptibilis, quam omnes  confitentur, ut plante et animalia.  Sempiterna autem, cuius elementa necesse est accipere, sive unum sive multa. Alia vero immobilis. Hanc dicunt quidam separabilem esse, hii quidem in duo dividentes, alii in unam naturam species ponentes et mathematica, alii horum mathematica solum. Ille quidem naturalis ( cum motu enim), et haec alterius, si nullum ipsis principium commune est.

There are three kinds of substance-one that is sensible (of which one subdivision is eternal and another is perishable; the latter is recognized by all men, and includes e.g. plants and animals), of which we must grasp the elements, whether one or many; and another that is immovable, and this certain thinkers assert to be capable of existing apart, some dividing it into two, others identifying the Forms and the objects of mathematics, and others positing, of these two, only the objects of mathematics. The former two kinds of substance are the subject of physics (for they [69b] imply movement); but the third kind belongs to another science, if there is no principle common to it and to the other kinds.

ἡ δ᾽ αἰσθητὴ οὐσία μεταβλητή. εἰ δ᾽ ἡ μεταβολὴ ἐκ τῶν ἀντικειμένων ἢ τῶν μεταξύ, ἀντικειμένων δὲ μὴ [5] πάντων (οὐ λευκὸν γὰρ ἡ φωνή) ἀλλ᾽ ἐκ τοῦ ἐναντίου, ἀνάγκη ὑπεῖναί τι τὸ μεταβάλλον εἰς τὴν ἐναντίωσιν: οὐ γὰρ τὰ ἐναντία μεταβάλλει.

Sensibilis vero substantia mutabilis. Si autem mutatio est ex oppositis aut mediis, oppositis autem non omnibus (non album enim vox), sed ex contrario, necesse subesse quid mutabile in contrarietatem; non enim contraria transmutantur.

Sensible substance is changeable. Now if change proceeds from opposites or from intermediates, and not from all opposites (for the voice is not-white, (but it does not therefore change to white)), but from the contrary, there must be something underlying which changes into the contrary state; for the contraries do not change.

## Chapter 2

ἔτι τὸ μὲν ὑπομένει, τὸ δ᾽ ἐναντίον οὐχ ὑπομένει: ἔστιν ἄρα τι τρίτον παρὰ τὰ ἐναντία, ἡ ὕλη.

Amplius hoc quidem manet, aliud vero contrarium non manet; est igitur aliquid tertium praeter contraria: materia.

Further, something persists, but the contrary does not persist; there is, then, some third thing besides the contraries, viz. the matter.

εἰ δὴ αἱ μεταβολαὶ τέτταρες, ἢ κατὰ τὸ τί [10] ἢ κατὰ τὸ ποῖον ἢ πόσον ἢ ποῦ, καὶ γένεσις μὲν ἡ ἁπλῆ καὶ φθορὰ ἡ κατὰ <τὸ τόδε, αὔξησις δὲ καὶ φθίσις ἡ κατὰ τὸ ποσόν, ἀλλοίωσις δὲ ἡ κατὰ τὸ πάθος, φορὰ δὲ ἡ κατὰ τόπον, εἰς ἐναντιώσεις ἂν εἶεν τὰς καθ᾽ ἕκαστον αἱ μεταβολαί. ἀνάγκη δὴ μεταβάλλειν τὴν ὕλην δυναμένην [15] ἄμφω:

Si itaque transmutationes sunt quatuor, aut secundum quid aut secundum qualitatem aut secundum quantitatem aut ubi, et generatio quidem simplex et corruptio secundum hoc, et augmentum et detrimentum quae secundum quantitatem , alteratio autem quae secundum passionem, latio autem quae secundum locum, in contrarietates utique erunt eas quae secundum unumquodque transmutationes. Necesse itaque transmutari materiam potentem ambo.

Now since changes are of four kinds-either in respect of the what or of the quality or of the quantity or of the place, and change in respect of thisness is simple generation and destruction, and change in quantity is increase and diminution, and change in respect of an affection is alteration, and change of place is motion, changes will be from given states into those contrary to them in these several respects. The matter, then, which changes must be capable of both states.

ἐπεὶ δὲ διττὸν τὸ ὄν, μεταβάλλει πᾶν ἐκ τοῦ δυνάμει ὄντος εἰς τὸ ἐνεργείᾳ ὄν (οἷον ἐκ λευκοῦ δυνάμει εἰς τὸ ἐνεργείᾳ λευκόν, ὁμοίως δὲ καὶ ἐπ᾽ αὐξήσεως καὶ φθίσεως), ὥστε οὐ μόνον κατὰ συμβεβηκὸς ἐνδέχεται γίγνεσθαι ἐκ μὴ ὄντος, ἀλλὰ καὶ ἐξ ὄντος γίγνεται πάντα, δυνάμει [20] μέντοι ὄντος, ἐκ μὴ ὄντος δὲ ἐνεργείᾳ.

Quoniam autem duplex est ens, transmutatur omne ex potentia ente in actu ens, ut puta ex albo potentia in actu album; similiter autem in augmento et detrimento. Quare non solum secundum accidens contingit fieri ex non ente, sed et ex ente fiunt omnia, potentia quidem ente, ex non ente vero actu.

And since that which is has two senses, we must say that everything changes from that which is potentially to that which is actually, e.g. from potentially white to actually white, and similarly in the case of increase and diminution. Therefore not only can a thing come to be, incidentally, out of that which is not, but also all things come to be out of that which is, but is potentially, and is not actually.

καὶ τοῦτ᾽ ἔστι τὸ Ἀναξαγόρου ἕν· βέλτιον γὰρ ἢ "ὁμοῦ πάντα"—καὶ Ἐμπεδοκλέους τὸ μῖγμα καὶ Ἀναξιμάνδρου, καὶ ὡς Δημόκριτός φησιν—"ἦν ὁμοῦ πάντα δυνάμει, ἐνεργείᾳ δ᾽ οὔ": ὥστε τῆς ὕλης ἂν εἶεν ἡμμένοι:

Et hoc est Anaxagorae unum; dignius est enim quam " simul omnia" — Et empedoclis mixtura et anaximandri et ut Democritus ait — " nobis erant omnia potentia, actu vero minime". Quare materiam utique erant tangentes.

And this is the One of Anaxagoras; for instead of all things were together -and the Mixture of Empedocles and Anaximander and the account given by Democritus-it is better to say all things were together potentially but not actually . Therefore these thinkers seem to have had some notion of matter.

πάντα δ᾽ ὕλην ἔχει ὅσα μεταβάλλει, [25] ἀλλ᾽ ἑτέραν· καὶ τῶν ἀϊδίων ὅσα μὴ γενητὰ κινητὰ δὲ φορᾷ, ἀλλ᾽ οὐ γενητὴν ἀλλὰ ποθὲν ποί.

Omnia vero materiam habent quaecumque transmutantur, sed aliam; et sempiternorum quaecumque non generabilia mobilia autem latione, verum non generabilem habent, sed unde quo.

Now all things that change have matter, but different matter; and of eternal things those which are not generable but are movable in space have matter-not matter for generation, however, but for motion [69b 26] from one place to another.

ἀπορήσειε δ᾽ ἄν τις ἐκ ποίου μὴ ὄντος ἡ γένεσις: τριχῶς γὰρ τὸ μὴ ὄν. εἰ δή τι ἔστι δυνάμει, ἀλλ᾽ ὅμως οὐ τοῦ τυχόντος ἀλλ᾽ ἕτερον ἐξ ἑτέρου: οὐδ᾽ ἱκανὸν ὅτι ὁμοῦ πάντα [30] χρήματα: διαφέρει γὰρ τῇ ὕλῃ, ἐπεὶ διὰ τί ἄπειρα ἐγένετο ἀλλ᾽ οὐχ ἕν; ὁ γὰρ νοῦς εἷς, ὥστ᾽ εἰ καὶ ἡ ὕλη μία, ἐκεῖνο ἐγένετο ἐνεργείᾳ οὗ ἡ ὕλη ἦν δυνάμει.

Dubitabit autem utique aliquis ex quali [/quo] non ente est generatio; tripliciter enim non ens. Si itaque aliquid est potentia, at tamen non ex quocumque sed alterum ex altero. Neque sufficiens quia simul res omnes; differunt enim materia, quoniam quare infinita facta sunt sed non unum? Intellectus enim unus; quare si et materia una, illud factum est actu cuius materia erat potentia.

One might raise the question from what sort of non-being generation proceeds; for non-being has three senses. If, then, one form of non-being exists potentially, still it is not by virtue of a potentiality for any and every thing, but different things come from different things; nor is it satisfactory to say that all things were together ; for they differ in their matter, since otherwise why did an infinity of things come to be, and not one thing? For reason is one, so that if matter also were one, that must have come to be in actuality which the matter was in potency.

τρία δὴ τὰ αἴτια καὶ τρεῖς αἱ ἀρχαί, δύο μὲν ἡ ἐναντίωσις, ἧς τὸ μὲν λόγος καὶ εἶδος τὸ δὲ στέρησις, τὸ δὲ τρίτον ἡ ὕλη. [35]

Tres vero sunt causae et tria principia: duo quidem contrarietas, cuius hoc quidem ratio et species illud vero privatio, tertium autem materia. 60

The causes and the principles, then, are three, two being the pair of contraries of which one is definition and form and the other is privation, and the third being the matter.

*Chapter* 3

μετὰ ταῦτα ὅτι οὐ γίγνεται οὔτε ἡ ὕλη οὔτε τὸ εἶδος, λέγω δὲ τὰ ἔσχατα. πᾶν γὰρ μεταβάλλει τὶ καὶ ὑπό τινος καὶ εἴς τι: [1070α] [1] ὑφ᾽ οὗ μέν, τοῦ πρώτου κινοῦντος: ὃ δέ, ἡ ὕλη: εἰς ὃ δέ, τὸ εἶδος. εἰς ἄπειρον οὖν εἴσιν, εἰ μὴ μόνον ὁ χαλκὸς γίγνεται στρογγύλος ἀλλὰ καὶ τὸ στρογγύλον ἢ ὁ χαλκός: ἀνάγκη δὴ στῆναι.

Postea quia nec fit materia nec species, dico autem ultima. Omne namque transmutat aliquid et ab aliquo et in quid. A quo quidem, primo movente; cuius vero, materia; in quod vero, species. In infinitum ergo sunt, si non solum es fit rotundum sed et ipsum rotundum aut es; necesse est itaque stare.

Note, next, that neither the matter nor the form comes to be-and I mean the last matter and form. For everything that changes is something and is changed by some[70a] thing and into something. That by which it is changed is the immediate mover; that which is changed, the matter; that into which it is changed, the form. The process, then, will go on to infinity, if not only the bronze comes to be round but also the round or the bronze comes to be; therefore there must be a stop.

μετὰ ταῦτα ὅτι ἑκάστη [5] ἐκ συνωνύμου γίγνεται οὐσία (τὰ γὰρ φύσει οὐσίαι καὶ τὰ ἄλλα). ἢ γὰρ τέχνῃ ἢ φύσει γίγνεται ἢ τύχῃ ἢ τῷ αὐτομάτῳ. ἡ μὲν οὖν τέχνη ἀρχὴ ἐν ἄλλῳ, ἡ δὲ φύσις ἀρχὴ ἐν αὐτῷ (ἄνθρωπος γὰρ ἄνθρωπον γεννᾷ), αἱ δὲ λοιπαὶ αἰτίαι στερήσεις τούτων.

Postea quia queque ex univoco fit substantia; nam et quae sunt natura substantia et alia. Aut enim arte aut natura foint aut fortuna aut casu. Ars igitur principium est in alio, natura autem principium in ipso (homo namque hominem generat), relique vero cause horum privationes.

Note, next, that each substance comes into being out of something that shares its name. (Natural objects and other things both rank as substances.) For things come into being either by art or by nature or by luck or by spontaneity. Now art is a principle of movement in something other than the thing moved, nature is a principle in the thing itself (for man begets man), and the other causes are privations of these two.

οὐσίαι δὲ τρεῖς, ἡ μὲν ὕλη [10] τόδε τι οὖσα τῷ φαίνεσθαι (ὅσα γὰρ ἀφῇ καὶ μὴ συμφύσει, ὕλη καὶ ὑποκείμενον), ἡ δὲ φύσις τόδε τι καὶ ἕξις τις εἰς ἥν: ἔτι τρίτη ἡ ἐκ τούτων ἡ καθ᾽ ἕκαστα, οἷον Σωκράτης ἢ Καλλίας.

Substantiae autem tres sunt, materia quidem hoc aliquid substantia in apparere; nam quaecumque tactu et non connascentia, materia et subiectum. Natura vero hoc aliquid in quam et habitus quidam . Amplius tertia quae est ex hiis singularis, ut Socrates et Callias.

There are three kinds of substance-the matter, which is a this in appearance (for all things that are characterized by contact and not, by organic unity are matter and substratum, e.g. fire, flesh, head; for these are all matter, and the last matter is the matter of that which is in the full sense substance); the nature, which is a this or positive state towards which movement takes place; and again, thirdly, the particular substance which is composed of these two, e.g. Socrates or Callias.

ἐπὶ μὲν οὖν τινῶν τὸ τόδε τι οὐκ ἔστι παρὰ τὴν συνθετὴν οὐσίαν, οἷον οἰκίας τὸ εἶδος, εἰ [15] μὴ ἡ τέχνη (οὐδ᾽ ἔστι γένεσις καὶ φθορὰ τούτων, ἀλλ᾽ ἄλλον τρόπον εἰσὶ καὶ οὐκ εἰσὶν οἰκία τε ἡ ἄνευ ὕλης καὶ ὑγίεια καὶ πᾶν τὸ κατὰ τέχνην), ἀλλ᾽ εἴπερ, ἐπὶ τῶν φύσει: διὸ δὴ οὐ κακῶς Πλάτων ἔφη ὅτι εἴδη ἔστιν ὁπόσα φύσει, εἴπερ ἔστιν εἴδη ἄλλα τούτων <οἷον πῦρ σὰρξ κεφαλή: [20] ἅπαντα γὰρ ὕλη ἐστί, καὶ τῆς μάλιστ᾽ οὐσίας ἡ τελευταία.

Igitur in quibusdam hoc non est praeter compositam substantiam, ut domus species, si non ars; nec est generatio et corruptio horum, sed alio modo sunt et non sunt domus quae sine materia et sanitas et omne quod secundum artem. Sed siquidem, in eis quae sunt natura. Quapropter non male Plato ait quia species sunt quaecumque natura, siquidem sunt species aliae horum, ut ignis, caro, caput; omnia enim materia sunt, et eius quae maxime substantiae ultima.

Now in some cases the this does not exist apart from the composite substance, e.g. the form of house does not so exist, unless the art of building exists apart (nor is there generation and destruction of these forms, but it is in another way that the house apart from its matter, and health, and all ideals of art, exist and do not exist); but if the this exists apart from the concrete thing, it is only in the case of natural objects. And so Plato was not far wrong when he said that there are as many Forms as there are kinds of natural object (if there are Forms distinct from the things of this earth).

τὰ μὲν οὖν κινοῦντα αἴτια ὡς προγεγενημένα ὄντα, τὰ δ᾽ ὡς ὁ λόγος ἅμα. ὅτε γὰρ ὑγιαίνει ὁ ἄνθρωπος, τότε καὶ ἡ ὑγίεια ἔστιν, καὶ τὸ σχῆμα τῆς χαλκῆς σφαίρας ἅμα καὶ ἡ χαλκῆ σφαῖρα (εἰ δὲ καὶ ὕστερόν τι ὑπομένει, σκεπτέον: [25] ἐπ᾽ ἐνίων γὰρ οὐδὲν κωλύει, οἷον εἰ ἡ ψυχὴ τοιοῦτον, μὴ πᾶσα ἀλλ᾽ ὁ νοῦς: πᾶσαν γὰρ ἀδύνατον ἴσως).

Moventes quidem igitur cause velut prius facte existentes, quae autem ut ratio simul. Quando enim sanatur homo, tunc et sanitas est, et figura eree spere simul et erea spera. Si autem et posterius aliquid manet, perscrutandum est. In quibusdam enim nihil prohibet, ut si anima tale, non omnis sed intellectus; omnem namque impossibile forsan.

The moving causes exist as things preceding the effects, but causes in the sense of definitions are simultaneous with their effects. For when a man is healthy, then health also exists; and the shape of a bronze sphere exists at the same time as the bronze sphere. (But we must examine whether any form also survives afterwards. For in some cases there is nothing to prevent this; e.g. the soul may be of this sort-not all soul but the reason; for presumably it is impossible that all soul should survive.)

φανερὸν δὴ ὅτι οὐδὲν δεῖ διά γε ταῦτ᾽ εἶναι τὰς ἰδέας: ἄνθρωπος γὰρ ἄνθρωπον γεννᾷ, ὁ καθ᾽ ἕκαστον τὸν τινά: ὁμοίως δὲ καὶ ἐπὶ τῶν τεχνῶν: ἡ γὰρ ἰατρικὴ τέχνη ὁ λόγος τῆς ὑγιείας [30] ἐστίν.

Palam itaque quia non oportet propter haec esse ydeas; 90 homo enim hominem generat, qui singularis aliquem. Similiter autem et in artibus; medicinalis enim ars ratio sanitatis est.

Evidently then there is no necessity, on this ground at least, for the existence of the Ideas. For man is begotten by man, a given man by an individual father; and similarly in the arts; for the medical art is the formal cause of health. [70a 31]

## Chapter 4

τὰ δ᾽ αἴτια καὶ αἱ ἀρχαὶ ἄλλα ἄλλων ἔστιν ὥς, ἔστι δ᾽ ὥς, ἂν καθόλου λέγῃ τις καὶ κατ᾽ ἀναλογίαν, ταὐτὰ πάντων.

Causae autem et principia alia aliorum est ut, est autem ut, si quis dicat universaliter et secundum proportionem, eadem omnium.

The causes and the principles of different things are in a sense different, but in a sense, if one speaks universally and analogically, they are the same for all.

ἀπορήσειε γὰρ ἄν τις πότερον ἕτεραι ἢ αἱ αὐταὶ ἀρχαὶ καὶ στοιχεῖα τῶν οὐσιῶν καὶ τῶν πρός τι, καὶ καθ᾽ [35] ἑκάστην δὴ τῶν κατηγοριῶν ὁμοίως. ἀλλ᾽ ἄτοπον εἰ ταὐτὰ πάντων: ἐκ τῶν αὐτῶν γὰρ ἔσται τὰ πρός τι καὶ αἱ οὐσίαι.

Dubitabit autem utique aliquis utrum altera aut eadem sint principia et elementa substantiarum et eorum quae sunt ad aliquid, et cuiuslibet cathegoriarum similiter.

For one might raise the question whether the principles and elements are different or the same for substances and for relative terms, and similarly in the case of each of the categories.

[1070β] [1] τί οὖν τοῦτ᾽ ἔσται; παρὰ γὰρ τὴν οὐσίαν καὶ τἆλλα τὰ κατηγορούμενα οὐδέν ἐστι κοινόν, πρότερον δὲ τὸ στοιχεῖον ἢ ὧν στοιχεῖον: ἀλλὰ μὴν οὐδ᾽ ἡ οὐσία στοιχεῖον τῶν πρός τι, οὐδὲ τούτων οὐδὲν τῆς οὐσίας.

Sed inconveniens si eadem omnium; ex eisdem enim erunt quae ad aliquid et substantia. Quid igitur hoc erit? Nam extra substantiam et alia predicamenta nihil est commune; prius autem est elementum quam quorum est elementum. At vero neque substantia elementum est eorum quae ad aliquid, nec horum aliquid substantiae.

But it would be paradoxical if they were the same for all. For then from the same elements will proceed relative terms [70b] and substances. What then will this common element be? For (1) (a) there is nothing common to and distinct from substance and the other categories, viz. those which are predicated; but an element is prior to the things of which it is an element. But again (b) substance is not an element in relative terms, nor is any of these an element in substance.

ἔτι πῶς ἐνδέχεται πάντων [5] εἶναι ταὐτὰ στοιχεῖα; οὐδὲν γὰρ οἷόν τ' εἶναι τῶν στοιχείων τῷ ἐκ στοιχείων συγκειμένῳ τὸ αὐτό, οἷον τῷ ΒΑ τὸ Β ἢ Α (οὐδὲ δὴ τῶν νοητῶν στοιχεῖόν ἐστιν, οἷον τὸ ὂν ἢ τὸ ἕν: ὑπάρχει γὰρ ταῦτα ἑκάστῳ καὶ τῶν συνθέτων). οὐδὲν ἄρ' ἔσται αὐτῶν οὔτ' οὐσία οὔτε πρός τι: ἀλλ' ἀναγκαῖον. οὐκ ἔστιν ἄρα [10] πάντων ταὐτὰ στοιχεῖα.

Amplius quomodo contingit esse omnium elementa eadem? Nullum enim possibile esse elementorum cum ex elementis composito idem, ut ei quod est BA B aut A ; nec etiam intellectualium elementorum, ut unum aut ens, insunt enim ea singulis compositorum. Nihil igitur erit eorum nec substantia nec ad aliquid; sed necessarium. Non sunt igitur omnium eadem elementa.

Further, (2) how can all things have the same elements? For none of the elements can be the same as that which is composed of elements, e.g. b or a cannot be the same as ba. (None, therefore, of the intelligibles, e.g. being or unity, is an element; for these are predicable of each of the compounds as well.) None of the elements, then, will be either a substance or a relative term; but it must be one or other. All things, then, have not the same elements.

ἢ ὥσπερ λέγομεν, ἔστι μὲν ὥς, ἔστι δ' ὡς οὔ, οἷον ἴσως τῶν αἰσθητῶν σωμάτων ὡς μὲν εἶδος τὸ θερμὸν καὶ ἄλλον τρόπον τὸ ψυχρὸν ἡ στέρησις, ὕλη δὲ τὸ δυνάμει ταῦτα πρῶτον καθ' αὑτό, οὐσίαι δὲ ταῦτά τε καὶ τὰ ἐκ τούτων, ὧν ἀρχαὶ ταῦτα, ἢ εἴ τι ἐκ θερμοῦ καὶ ψυχροῦ [15] γίγνεται ἕν, οἷον σὰρξ ἢ ὀστοῦν: ἕτερον γὰρ ἀνάγκη ἐκείνων εἶναι τὸ γενόμενον. τούτων μὲν οὖν ταὐτὰ στοιχεῖα καὶ ἀρχαί (ἄλλων δ' ἄλλα), πάντων δὲ οὕτω μὲν εἰπεῖν οὐκ ἔστιν, τῷ ἀνάλογον δέ, ὥσπερ εἴ τις εἴποι ὅτι ἀρχαί εἰσι τρεῖς, τὸ εἶδος καὶ ἡ στέρησις καὶ ἡ ὕλη. ἀλλ' ἕκαστον τούτων ἕτερον περὶ [20] ἕκαστον γένος ἐστίν, οἷον ἐν χρώματι λευκὸν μέλαν ἐπιφάνεια: φῶς σκότος ἀήρ, ἐκ δὲ τούτων ἡμέρα καὶ νύξ.

Aut ut dicimus, est quidem ut est, est vero ut non; puta forsan sensibilium corporum ut quidem species calidum et alio modo frigidum privatio, materia vero quod potentia haec primum secundum se. Substantia vero et haec et quae ex hiis, quorum sunt principia haec, aut si quid ex calido et frigido fit unum, ut caro aut os; alterum enim necesse ab illis esse quod factum est. Horum igitur eadem elementa et principia; aliorum vero alia. Omnium autem ita quidem dicere non est, sed proportionabiliter, quemadmodum si quis dicat quia principia sunt tria: species et privatio et materia. Sed horum unumquodque alterum circa genus unumquodque est, ut in colore album, nigrum, superficies; lumen, tenebre, aer, ex hiis autem dies et nox.

Or, as we are wont to put it, in a sense they have and in a sense they have not; e.g. perhaps the elements of perceptible bodies are, as form, the hot, and in another sense the cold, which is the privation; and, as matter, that which directly and of itself potentially has these attributes; and substances comprise both these and the things composed of these, of which these are the principles, or any unity which is produced out of the hot and the cold, e.g. flesh or bone; for the product must be different from the elements. These things then have the same elements and principles (though specifically different things have specifically different elements); but all things have not the same elements in this sense, but only analogically; i.e. one might say that there are three principles-the form, the privation, and the matter. But each of these is different for each class; e.g. in colour they are white, black, and surface, and in day and night they are light, darkness, and air.

ἐπεὶ δὲ οὐ μόνον τὰ ἐνυπάρχοντα αἴτια, ἀλλὰ καὶ τῶν ἐκτὸς οἷον τὸ κινοῦν, δῆλον ὅτι ἕτερον ἀρχὴ καὶ στοιχεῖον, [24] αἴτια δ' ἄμφω, καὶ εἰς ταῦτα διαιρεῖται ἡ ἀρχή, τὸ δ' [25] ὡς κινοῦν ἢ ἱστὰν ἀρχή τις καὶ οὐσία, ὥστε στοιχεῖα μὲν κατ' ἀναλογίαν τρία, αἰτίαι δὲ καὶ ἀρχαὶ τέτταρες· ἄλλο δ' ἐν ἄλλῳ, καὶ τὸ πρῶτον αἴτιον ὡς κινοῦν ἄλλο ἄλλῳ. ὑγίεια, νόσος, σῶμα· τὸ κινοῦν ἰατρική. εἶδος, ἀταξία τοιαδί, πλίνθοι· τὸ κινοῦν οἰκοδομική [καὶ εἰς ταῦτα διαιρεῖται [30] ἡ ἀρχή].

Quoniam autem non solum quae insunt cause, sed et eorum quae extra, ut puta movens, palam quia alterum principium et elementum, cause vero ambo, et in haec dividitur principium; quod autem ut movens aut sistens principium est quoddam. quare elementa secundum analogiam tria, cause autem et principia quatuor; aliud vero in alio, et prima causa quasi movens aliud alii. Sanitas, infirmitas, corpus; movens medicativa. Species, inordinatio talis, lateres; movens edificatoria. Et in ea dividitur principium.

Since not only the elements present in a thing are causes, but also something external, i.e. the moving cause, clearly while principle and element are different both are causes, and principle is divided into these two kinds; and that which acts as producing movement or rest is a principle and a substance. Therefore analogically there are three elements, and four causes and principles; but the elements are different in different things, and the proximate moving cause is different for different things.

Health, disease, body; the moving cause is the medical art. Form, disorder of a particular kind, bricks; the moving cause is the building art.

ἐπεὶ δὲ τὸ κινοῦν ἐν μὲν τοῖς φυσικοῖς ἀνθρώπῳ ἄνθρωπος, ἐν δὲ τοῖς ἀπὸ διανοίας τὸ εἶδος ἢ τὸ ἐναντίον, τρόπον τινὰ τρία αἴτια ἂν εἴη, ὡδὶ δὲ τέτταρα. ὑγίεια γάρ πως ἡ ἰατρική, καὶ οἰκίας εἶδος ἡ οἰκοδομική, καὶ ἄνθρωπος ἄνθρωπον γεννᾷ:

Quoniam autem movens in phisicis quidem homo, in hiis autem quae a mente species aut contrarium, modo quodam tres utique erunt cause, sic autem quatuor. Nam sanitas aliqualiter medicinalis, et domus species edificatoria, et homo hominem generat.

And since the moving cause in the case of natural things is-for man, for instance, man, and in the products of thought the form or its contrary, there will be in a sense three causes, while in a sense there are four. For the medical art is in some sense health, and the building art is the form of the house, and man begets man;

ἔτι παρὰ ταῦτα τὸ ὡς [35] πρῶτον πάντων κινοῦν πάντα.

Adhuc praeter haec ut primum omnium movens omnia.

further, besides these there is that which as first of all things moves all things.

## Chapter 5

ἐπεὶ δ᾽ ἐστὶ τὰ μὲν χωριστὰ τὰ δ᾽ οὐ χωριστά, οὐσίαι ἐκεῖνα. [1071α] [1] καὶ διὰ τοῦτο πάντων αἴτια ταῦτά, ὅτι τῶν οὐσιῶν ἄνευ οὐκ ἔστι τὰ πάθη καὶ αἱ κινήσεις.

Quoniam autem sunt haec quidem separabilia haec autem inseparabilia, substantiae ille . Et propter hoc omnium cause haec, quia sine substantiis non sunt passiones et motus.

Some things can exist apart and some cannot, and it is [71a] the former that are substances. And therefore all things have the same causes, because, without substances, modifications and movements do not exist.

ἔπειτα ἔσται ταῦτα ψυχὴ ἴσως καὶ σῶμα, ἢ νοῦς καὶ ὄρεξις καὶ σῶμα.

Deinde erunt haec anima forsan et corpus, aut intellectus et appetitus et corpus.

Further, these causes will probably be soul and body, or reason and desire and body.

ἔτι δ᾽ ἄλλον τρόπον τῷ ἀνάλογον ἀρχαὶ αἱ αὐταί, οἷον ἐνέργεια [5] καὶ δύναμις· ἀλλὰ καὶ ταῦτα ἄλλα τε ἄλλοις καὶ ἄλλως. ἐν ἐνίοις μὲν γὰρ τὸ αὐτὸ ὁτὲ μὲν ἐνεργείᾳ ἔστιν ὁτὲ δὲ δυνάμει, οἷον οἶνος ἢ σὰρξ ἢ ἄνθρωπος (πίπτει δὲ καὶ ταῦτα εἰς τὰ εἰρημένα αἴτια· ἐνεργείᾳ μὲν γὰρ τὸ εἶδος, ἐὰν ᾖ χωριστόν, καὶ τὸ ἐξ ἀμφοῖν στέρησις δέ, οἷον [10] σκότος ἢ κάμνον, δυνάμει δὲ ἡ ὕλη· τοῦτο γάρ ἐστι τὸ δυνάμενον γίγνεσθαι ἄμφω)· ἄλλως δ᾽ ἐνεργείᾳ καὶ δυνάμει διαφέρει ὧν μὴ ἔστιν ἡ αὐτὴ ὕλη, ὧν <ἐνίων> οὐκ ἔστι τὸ αὐτὸ εἶδος ἀλλ᾽ ἕτερον, ὥσπερ ἀνθρώπου αἴτιον τά τε στοιχεῖα, πῦρ καὶ γῆ ὡς ὕλη καὶ τὸ ἴδιον εἶδος, καὶ ἔτι τι [15] ἄλλο ἔξω οἷον ὁ πατήρ, καὶ παρὰ ταῦτα ὁ ἥλιος καὶ ὁ λοξὸς κύκλος, οὔτε ὕλη ὄντα οὔτ᾽ εἶδος οὔτε στέρησις οὔτε ὁμοειδὲς ἀλλὰ κινοῦντα.

Amplius autem alio modo proportionaliter principia eadem, ut actus et potentia; sed et haec aliaque aliis et aliter. In quibusdam quidem enim idem quandoque actu est quandoque potentia, ut vinum aut caro aut homo. Cadunt autem et haec in dictas causas. Actus quidem enim species, si sit separabilis, et quod ex ambobus, privatio vero, ut puta tenebre aut laborans; potentia autem materia; hoc enim est quod potest fieri ambo. Aliter autem actu et potestate differunt quorum non est eadem materia, quorum non est eadem species sed altera. Quemadmodum hominis causa elementa, ignis et terra ut materia et species propria; et si quid aliud extra ut pater; et praeter haec sol et obliquus circulus, neque materia entia neque species neque privatio neque conforme sed moventia.

And in yet another way, analogically identical things are principles, i.e. actuality and potency; but these also are not only different for different things but also apply in different ways to them. For in some cases the same thing exists at one time actually and at another potentially, e.g. wine or flesh or man does so. (And these too fall under the above-named causes. For the form exists actually, if it can exist apart, and so does the complex of form and matter, and the privation, e.g. darkness or disease; but the matter exists potentially; for this is that which can become qualified either by the form or by the privation.) But the distinction of actuality and potentiality applies in another way to cases where the matter of cause and of effect is not the same, in some of which cases the form is not the same but different; e.g. the cause of man is (1) the elements in man (viz. fire and earth as matter, and the peculiar form), and further (2) something else outside, i.e. the father, and (3) besides these the sun and its oblique course, which are neither matter nor form nor privation of man nor of the same species with him, but moving causes.

ἔτι δὲ ὁρᾶν δεῖ ὅτι τὰ μὲν καθόλου ἔστιν εἰπεῖν, τὰ δ᾽ οὔ. πάντων δὴ πρῶται ἀρχαὶ τὸ ἐνεργείᾳ πρῶτον τοδὶ καὶ ἄλλο ὃ δυνάμει. ἐκεῖνα μὲν [20] οὖν τὰ καθόλου οὐκ ἔστιν: ἀρχὴ γὰρ τὸ καθ᾽ ἕκαστον τῶν καθ᾽ ἕκαστον: ἄνθρωπος μὲν γὰρ ἀνθρώπου καθόλου, ἀλλ᾽ οὐκ ἔστιν οὐδείς, ἀλλὰ Πηλεὺς Ἀχιλλέως σοῦ δὲ ὁ πατήρ, καὶ τοδὶ τὸ Β τουδὶ τοῦ ΒΑ, ὅλως δὲ τὸ Β τοῦ ἁπλῶς ΒΑ. ἔπειτα, εἰ δὴ τὰ τῶν οὐσιῶν, ἄλλα δὲ ἄλλων [25] αἴτια καὶ στοιχεῖα, ὥσπερ ἐλέχθη, τῶν μὴ ἐν ταὐτῷ γένει, χρωμάτων ψόφων οὐσιῶν ποσότητος, πλὴν τῷ ἀνάλογον: καὶ τῶν ἐν ταὐτῷ εἴδει ἕτερα, οὐκ εἴδει ἀλλ᾽ ὅτι τῶν καθ᾽ ἕκαστον ἄλλο, ἥ τε σὴ ὕλη καὶ τὸ εἶδος καὶ τὸ κινῆσαν καὶ ἡ ἐμή, τῷ καθόλου δὲ λόγῳ ταὐτά.

Adhuc autem videre oportet quia haec quidem universaliter est dicere, haec autem non. Omnium etiam prima principia quod actu primum hoc et aliud quod potentia. Illa quidem igitur quae universalia non sunt; principium enim singularium singulare. Homo quidem enim hominis universaliter, sed non est nullus, verum Pileus Achillis, tui vero pater, et hoc b huius ba, totaliter vero b simpliciter ba. Deinde iam quae substantiarum; aliae autem aliorum cause et elementa, sicut dictum est, eorum quae non in eodem genere, colorum et sonorum, substantiarum, quantitatis, praeterquam proportionaliter; et eorum quae sunt in eadem specie diversa, non specie sed quia singularium aliud, tua materia et species et movens et mea, universali autem ratione eadem .

Further, one must observe that some causes can be expressed in universal terms, and some cannot. The proximate principles of all things are the this which is proximate in actuality, and another which is proximate in potentiality. The universal causes, then, of which we spoke do not exist. For it is the individual that is the originative principle of the individuals. For while man is the originative principle of man universally, there is no universal man, but Peleus is the originative principle of Achilles, and your father of you, and this particular b of this particular ba, though b in general is the originative principle of ba taken without qualification. Further, if the causes of substances are the causes of all things, yet different things have different causes and elements, as was said; the causes of things that are not in the same class, e.g. of colours and sounds, of substances and quantities, are different except in an analogical sense; and those of things in the same species are different, not in species, but in the sense that the causes of different individuals are different, your matter and form and moving cause being different from mine, while in their universal definition they are the same.

τὸ δὲ ζητεῖν [30] τίνες ἀρχαὶ ἢ στοιχεῖα τῶν οὐσιῶν καὶ πρός τι καὶ ποιῶν, πότερον αἱ αὐταὶ ἢ ἕτεραι, δῆλον ὅτι πολλαχῶς γε λεγομένων ἔστιν ἑκάστου, διαιρεθέντων δὲ οὐ ταὐτὰ ἀλλ᾽ ἕτερα, πλὴν ὡδὶ καὶ πάντων, ὡδὶ μὲν ταὐτὰ ἢ τὸ ἀνάλογον, ὅτι ὕλη, εἶδος, στέρησις, τὸ κινοῦν, καὶ ὡδὶ τὰ τῶν οὐσιῶν [35] αἴτια ὡς αἴτια πάντων, ὅτι ἀναιρεῖται ἀναιρουμένων: ἔτι τὸ πρῶτον ἐντελεχείᾳ: ὡδὶ δὲ ἕτερα πρῶτα ὅσα τὰ ἐναντία ἃ μήτε ὡς γένη λέγεται μήτε πολλαχῶς λέγεται: καὶ ἔτι αἱ ὗλαι. [1071β] [1] τίνες μὲν οὖν αἱ ἀρχαὶ τῶν αἰσθητῶν καὶ πόσαι, καὶ πῶς αἱ αὐταὶ καὶ πῶς ἕτεραι, εἴρηται.

Quaerere vero quae principia aut elementa substantiarum et ad aliquid et qualitatum, utrum eadem aut diversa, palam quia multipliciter dictorum sunt uniuscuiusque. Divisorum vero non eadem sed altera, praeterquam sic et omnium. Sic quidem eadem aut eo quod proportionaliter, quia materia, species, privatio, movens; et sic substantiarum cause ut cause omnium, quia destruuntur destructis. Amplius quod primum entelechia. Sic autem altera prima : quaecumque contraria quae nec ut genera dicuntur nec multipliciter dicuntur; et adhuc materie. Quae quidem igitur principia sensibilium et quot, et quomodo eadem et quomodo altera, dictum est.

And if we inquire what are the principles or elements of substances and relations and qualities-whether they are the same or different-clearly when the names of the causes are used in several senses the causes of each are the same, but when the senses are distinguished the causes are not the same but different, except that in the following senses the causes of all are the same. They are (1) the same or analogous in this sense, that matter, form, privation, and the moving cause are common to all things; and (2) the causes of substances may be treated as causes of all things in this sense, that when substances are removed all things are removed; further, (3) that which is first in respect of complete reality is the cause of all things. But in another sense there are different first causes, viz. all the contraries which are neither generic nor ambiguous terms; and, further, the matters of different things [71b] are different. We have stated, then, what are the principles of sensible things and how many they are, and in what sense they are the same and in what sense different.

## Chapter 6

ἐπεὶ δ᾽ ἦσαν τρεῖς οὐσίαι, δύο μὲν αἱ φυσικαὶ μία δ᾽ ἡ ἀκίνητος, περὶ ταύτης λεκτέον ὅτι ἀνάγκη εἶναι ἀΐδιόν [5] τινα οὐσίαν ἀκίνητον. αἵ τε γὰρ οὐσίαι πρῶται τῶν ὄντων, καὶ εἰ πᾶσαι φθαρταί, πάντα φθαρτά· ἀλλ᾽ ἀδύνατον κίνησιν ἢ γενέσθαι ἢ φθαρῆναι (ἀεὶ γὰρ ἦν), οὐδὲ χρόνον. οὐ γὰρ οἷόν τε τὸ πρότερον καὶ ὕστερον εἶναι μὴ ὄντος χρόνου· καὶ ἡ κίνησις ἄρα οὕτω συνεχὴς ὥσπερ καὶ ὁ χρόνος· [10] ἢ γὰρ τὸ αὐτὸ ἢ κινήσεώς τι πάθος. κίνησις δ᾽ οὐκ ἔστι συνεχὴς ἀλλ᾽ ἢ ἡ κατὰ τόπον, καὶ ταύτης ἡ κύκλῳ.

Quoniam autem tres erant substantiae, due quidem quae phisice et una quae immobilis, de hac dicendum quia necesse esse sempiternam aliquam substantiam immobilem. Nam substantiae prime entium, et si omnes corruptibiles, omnia corruptibilia. Sed impossibile motum aut fieri aut corrumpi (semper enim erat), nec tempus. Nec enim possibile prius et posterius esse, cum non sit tempus. Et motus ergo sic est continuus ut tempus; aut enim idem aut motus est aliqua passio. Motus autem non est continuus nisi qui secundum locum, et huius qui circulo.

Since there were three kinds of substance, two of them physical and one unmovable, regarding the latter we must assert that it is necessary that there should be an eternal unmovable substance. For substances are the first of existing things, and if they are all destructible, all things are destructible. But it is impossible that movement should either have come into being or cease to be (for it must always have existed), or that time should. For there could not be a before and an after if time did not exist. Movement also is continuous, then, in the sense in which time is; for time is either the same thing as movement or an attribute of movement. And there is no continuous movement except movement in place, and of this only that which is circular is continuous.

ἀλλὰ μὴν εἰ ἔστι κινητικὸν ἢ ποιητικόν, μὴ ἐνεργοῦν δέ τι, οὐκ ἔσται κίνησις· ἐνδέχεται γὰρ τὸ δύναμιν ἔχον μὴ ἐνεργεῖν. οὐθὲν ἄρα ὄφελος οὐδ᾽ ἐὰν οὐσίας ποιήσωμεν ἀϊδίους, [15] ὥσπερ οἱ τὰ εἴδη, εἰ μή τις δυναμένη ἐνέσται ἀρχὴ μεταβάλλειν· οὐ τοίνυν οὐδ᾽ αὕτη ἱκανή, οὐδ᾽ ἄλλη οὐσία παρὰ τὰ εἴδη· εἰ γὰρ μὴ ἐνεργήσει, οὐκ ἔσται κίνησις.

At vero si erit motivum aut effectivum, non operans autem aliquid, non erit motus; contingit enim potentiam habens non agere. Nihil ergo prodest, nec si substantias faciamus sempiternas, quemadmodum qui species, si non aliqua potens inerit principium transmutari. Non igitur neque ipsa sufficiens , nec alia substantia praeter species; nam si non egerit, non erit motus.

But if there is something which is capable of moving things or acting on them, but is not actually doing so, there will not necessarily be movement; for that which has a potency need not exercise it. Nothing, then, is gained even if we suppose eternal substances, as the believers in the Forms do, unless there is to be in them some principle which can cause change; nay, even this is not enough, nor is another substance besides the Forms enough; for if it is not to act, there will be no movement.

ἔτι οὐδ᾽ εἰ ἐνεργήσει, ἡ δ᾽ οὐσία αὐτῆς δύναμις· οὐ γὰρ ἔσται κίνησις ἀΐδιος· ἐνδέχεται γὰρ τὸ δυνάμει ὂν μὴ εἶναι. δεῖ [20] ἄρα εἶναι ἀρχὴν τοιαύτην ἧς ἡ οὐσία ἐνέργεια.

Adhuc neque si aget, substantia autem ipsius potentia; non enim erit motus eternus; contingit enim quod potentia est non esse. Oportet igitur esse principium tale cuius substantia actus.

Further even if it acts, this will not be enough, if its essence is potency; for there will not be eternal movement, since that which is potentially may possibly not be. There must, then, be such a principle, whose very essence is actuality.

ἔτι τοίνυν ταύτας δεῖ τὰς οὐσίας εἶναι ἄνευ ὕλης: ἀϊδίους γὰρ δεῖ, εἴπερ γε καὶ ἄλλο τι ἀΐδιον.

Amplius igitur tales oportet esse substantias sine materia; sempiternas enim esse oportet, si et aliud aliquid sempiternum; actu igitur.

Further, then, these substances must be without matter; for they must be eternal, if anything is eternal. Therefore they must be actuality.

ἐνέργεια ἄρα. καίτοι ἀπορία: δοκεῖ γὰρ τὸ μὲν ἐνεργοῦν πᾶν δύνασθαι τὸ δὲ δυνάμενον οὐ πᾶν ἐνεργεῖν, ὥστε πρότερον εἶναι τὴν δύναμιν.

Quamvis dubitatio; videtur enim agens quidem omne posse, potens vero non omne agere, quare prius esse potentiam.

Yet there is a difficulty; for it is thought that everything that acts is able to act, but that not everything that is able to act acts, so that the potency is prior.

[25] ἀλλὰ μὴν εἰ τοῦτο, οὐθὲν ἔσται τῶν ὄντων: ἐνδέχεται γὰρ δύνασθαι μὲν εἶναι μήπω δ᾽ εἶναι. καίτοι εἰ ὡς λέγουσιν οἱ θεολόγοι οἱ ἐκ νυκτὸς γεννῶντες, ἢ ὡς οἱ φυσικοὶ ὁμοῦ πάντα χρήματά φασι, τὸ αὐτὸ ἀδύνατον. πῶς γὰρ κινηθήσεται, εἰ μὴ ἔσται ἐνεργείᾳ τι αἴτιον; οὐ γὰρ ἥ γε [30] ὕλη κινήσει αὐτὴ ἑαυτήν, ἀλλὰ τεκτονική, οὐδὲ τὰ ἐπιμήνια οὐδ᾽ ἡ γῆ, ἀλλὰ τὰ σπέρματα καὶ ἡ γονή.

At vero si hoc, nihil erit entium; contingit enim posse quidem esse nondum vero esse. Et etiam si ut dicunt theologi qui ex nocte generant, aut ut phisici " erant simul res omnes" dicunt, idem impossibile. Quomodo enim movebuntur, si non fuerit actu aliqua causa? Non enim materia ipsa se ipsam movebit, sed tectonica, nec menstrua nec terra, sed semina et genitura .

But if this is so, nothing that is need be; for it is possible for all things to be capable of existing but not yet to exist. Yet if we follow the theologians who generate the world from night, or the natural philosophers who say that all things were together , the same impossible result ensues. For how will there be movement, if there is no actually existing cause? Wood will surely not move itself-the carpenter's art must act on it; nor will the menstrual blood nor the earth set themselves in motion, but the seeds must act on the earth and the semen on the menstrual blood.

διὸ ἔνιοι ποιοῦσιν ἀεὶ ἐνέργειαν, οἷον Λεύκιππος καὶ Πλάτων: ἀεὶ γὰρ εἶναί φασι κίνησιν. ἀλλὰ διὰ τί καὶ τίνα οὐ λέγουσιν, οὐδ᾽, <εἰ ὡδὶ <ἢ ὡδί, τὴν αἰτίαν. οὐδὲν γὰρ ὡς [35] ἔτυχε κινεῖται, ἀλλὰ δεῖ τι ἀεὶ ὑπάρχειν, ὥσπερ νῦν φύσει μὲν ὡδί, βίᾳ δὲ ἢ ὑπὸ νοῦ ἢ ἄλλου ὡδί. (εἶτα ποία πρώτη; διαφέρει γὰρ ἀμήχανον ὅσον). ἀλλὰ μὴν οὐδὲ Πλάτωνί γε οἷόν τε λέγειν ἣν οἴεται ἐνίοτε ἀρχὴν εἶναι, τὸ αὐτὸ ἑαυτὸ κινοῦν· ὕστερον γὰρ καὶ ἅμα τῷ οὐρανῷ ἡ ψυχή, ὡς φησίν.

Propter quod faciunt quidam semper actum, ut Leucippus et Plato; semper enim dicunt esse motum. Sed quare et quem non dicunt, nec sic nec causam. Nihil enim ut contingit movetur, sed oportet aliquid semper existere, quemadmodum nunc natura quidem sic, vi vero aut ab intellectu aut alio sic. Deinde qualis prior? Differt enim inaptabile quantum . At vero neque Platoni possibile dicere quod exjstimat aliquando principium esse, quod ipsum se ipsum movens; posterius enim et simul cum celo anima, ut ait.

This is why some suppose eternal actuality-e.g. Leucippus and Plato; for they say there is always movement. But why and what this movement is they do say, nor, if the world moves in this way or that, do they tell us the cause of its doing so. Now nothing is moved at random, but there must always be something present to move it; e.g. as a matter of fact a thing moves in one way by nature, and in another by force or through the influence of reason or something else. (Further, what sort of movement is primary? This makes a vast difference.) But again for Plato, at least, it is not permissible to name here that which [72a] he sometimes supposes to be the source of movement-that which moves itself; for the soul is later, and coeval with the heavens, according to his account.

τὸ μὲν δὴ δύναμιν οἴεσθαι ἐνεργείας πρότερον ἔστι μὲν ὡς καλῶς ἔστι δ᾽ ὡς οὔ (εἴρηται δὲ πῶς)·

Potentiam quidem igitur existimare priorem actu est quidem ut bene, est autem ut non; dictum est autem quomodo.

To suppose potency prior to actuality, then, is in a sense right, and in a sense not; and we have specified these senses.

ὅτι δ᾽ [5] ἐνέργεια πρότερον, μαρτυρεῖ Ἀναξαγόρας (ὁ γὰρ νοῦς ἐνέργεια) καὶ Ἐμπεδοκλῆς φιλίαν καὶ τὸ νεῖκος, καὶ οἱ ἀεὶ λέγοντες κίνησιν εἶναι, ὥσπερ Λεύκιππος·

Quod autem actus  prius, testatur Anaxagoras (intellectus  enim actus ), et Empedocles amicitiam et litem, et semper  dicentes motum esse, ut Leucippus.

That actuality is prior is testified by Anaxagoras (for his reason is actuality) and by Empedocles in his doctrine of love and strife, and by those who say that there is always movement, e.g. Leucippus.

ὥστ᾽ οὐκ ἦν ἄπειρον χρόνον χάος ἢ νύξ, ἀλλὰ ταὐτὰ ἀεὶ ἢ περιόδῳ ἢ ἄλλως, εἴπερ πρότερον ἐνέργεια δυνάμεως.

Quare non fuit infinito tempore chaos aut nox, sed eadem semper aut periodo aut aliter, si prius est actus potentia.

Therefore chaos or night did not exist for an infinite time, but the same things have always existed (either passing through a cycle of changes or obeying some other law), since actuality is prior to potency.

εἰ δὴ τὸ αὐτὸ [10] ἀεὶ περιόδῳ, δεῖ τι ἀεὶ μένειν ὡσαύτως ἐνεργοῦν. εἰ δὲ μέλλει γένεσις καὶ φθορὰ εἶναι, ἄλλο δεῖ εἶναι ἀεὶ ἐνεργοῦν ἄλλως καὶ ἄλλως. ἀνάγκη ἄρα ὡδὶ μὲν καθ᾽ αὑτὸ ἐνεργεῖν ὡδὶ δὲ κατ᾽ ἄλλο: ἤτοι ἄρα καθ᾽ ἕτερον ἢ κατὰ τὸ πρῶτον. ἀνάγκη δὴ κατὰ τοῦτο: πάλιν γὰρ ἐκεῖνο [15] αὑτῷ τε αἴτιον κἀκείνῳ. οὐκοῦν βέλτιον τὸ πρῶτον: καὶ γὰρ αἴτιον ἦν ἐκεῖνο τοῦ ἀεὶ ὡσαύτως: τοῦ δ᾽ ἄλλως ἕτερον, τοῦ δ᾽ ἀεὶ ἄλλως ἄμφω δηλονότι. οὐκοῦν οὕτως καὶ ἔχουσιν αἱ κινήσεις. τί οὖν ἄλλας δεῖ ζητεῖν ἀρχάς;

Si itaque idem semper periodo, oportet aliquid semper manere similiter agens. Si autem debeat fore generatio et corruptio, aliud oportet agens esse aliter et aliter. Necesse igitur sic quidem secundum se agere, sic vero secundum aliud; aut ergo secundum alterum aut secundum primum. Necesse itaque secundum hoc; iterum enim illud ipsique causa et illi. Rdignius ergo1 primum; et enim causa erat illud ipsius semper similiter; et ipsius aliter alterum, eius autem quod est semper aliter rpalam quod ambo1. Ergo si sic se habent motus, quid ergo alia oportet quaerere principia?

If, then, there is a constant cycle, something must always remain, acting in the same way. And if there is to be generation and destruction, there must be something else which is always acting in different ways. This must, then, act in one way in virtue of itself, and in another in virtue of something else-either of a third agent, therefore, or of the first. Now it must be in virtue of the first. For otherwise this again causes the motion both of the second agent and of the third. Therefore it is better to say the first . For it was the cause of eternal uniformity; and something else is the cause of variety, and evidently both together are the cause of eternal variety. This, accordingly, is the character which the motions actually exhibit. What need then is there to seek for other principles?

## Chapter 7

ἐπεὶ δ᾽ οὕτω τ᾽ ἐνδέχεται, καὶ εἰ μὴ οὕτως, ἐκ νυκτὸς [20] ἔσται καὶ ὁμοῦ πάντων καὶ ἐκ μὴ ὄντος, λύοιτ᾽ ἂν ταῦτα, καὶ ἔστι τι ἀεὶ κινούμενον κίνησιν ἄπαυστον, αὕτη δ᾽ ἡ κύκλῳ (καὶ τοῦτο οὐ λόγῳ μόνον ἀλλ᾽ ἔργῳ δῆλον), ὥστ᾽ ἀΐδιος ἂν εἴη ὁ πρῶτος οὐρανός.

Quoniam autem ita contingit, et si non sic, ex nocte erit et " simul omnium" et ex non ente, soluentur utique haec. Et est aliquid semper motum motu incessabili, hic autem qui circulo; et hoc non ratione solum sed opere palam. Quare sempiternum utique erit primum coelum.

Since (1) this is a possible account of the matter, and (2) if it were not true, the world would have proceeded out of night and all things together and out of non-being, these difficulties may be taken as solved. There is, then, something which is always moved with an unceasing motion, which is motion in a circle; and this is plain not in theory only but in fact. Therefore the first heaven must be eternal.

ἔστι τοίνυν τι καὶ ὃ κινεῖ. ἐπεὶ δὲ τὸ κινούμενον καὶ κινοῦν [καὶ] μέσον, τοίνυν [25] ἔστι τι ὃ οὐ κινούμενον κινεῖ, ἀΐδιον καὶ οὐσία καὶ ἐνέργεια οὖσα.

Est igitur aliquid et quod movet . Quoniam autem quod movetur et movens et medium, igitur est aliquid quod non motum movet, sempiternum et substantia et actus ens.

There is therefore also something which moves it. And since that which moves and is moved is intermediate, there is something which moves without being moved, being eternal, substance, and actuality.

κινεῖ δὲ ὧδε τὸ ὀρεκτὸν καὶ τὸ νοητόν: κινεῖ οὐ κινούμενα. τούτων τὰ πρῶτα τὰ αὐτά. ἐπιθυμητὸν μὲν γὰρ τὸ φαινόμενον καλόν, βουλητὸν δὲ πρῶτον τὸ ὂν καλόν: ὀρεγόμεθα δὲ διότι δοκεῖ μᾶλλον ἢ δοκεῖ διότι ὀρεγόμεθα: [30] ἀρχὴ γὰρ ἡ νόησις. νοῦς δὲ ὑπὸ τοῦ νοητοῦ κινεῖται,

Movet autem sic  appetibile et intelligibile; movent non mota. Horum autem prima  eadem. Concupiscibile quidem enim  ipsum  apparens bonum, voluntabile autem primum ipsum existens bonum. Appetimus autem quia videtur magis quam videtur quia appetimus; principium  enim  est  intelligentia. Intellectus autem ab intelligibili movetur,

And the object of desire and the object of thought move in this way; they move without being moved. The primary objects of desire and of thought are the same. For the apparent good is the object of appetite, and the real good is the primary object of rational wish. But desire is consequent on opinion rather than opinion on desire; for the thinking is the starting-point. And thought is moved by the object of thought,

νοητὴ δὲ ἡ ἑτέρα συστοιχία καθ᾽ αὑτήν: καὶ ταύτης ἡ οὐσία πρώτη, καὶ ταύτης ἡ ἁπλῆ καὶ κατ᾽ ἐνέργειαν (ἔστι δὲ τὸ ἓν καὶ τὸ ἁπλοῦν οὐ τὸ αὐτό: τὸ μὲν γὰρ ἓν μέτρον σημαίνει, τὸ δὲ ἁπλοῦν πῶς ἔχον αὐτό).

intelligibilis autem altera coelementatio secundum se; et huius substantia prima, et huius quae simplex et secundum actum. Est autem unum et simplex non idem; unum enim metrum significat, simplex autem qualiter habens ipsum.

and one of the two columns of opposites is in itself the object of thought; and in this, substance is first, and in substance, that which is simple and exists actually. (The one and the simple are not the same; for one means a measure, but simple means that the thing itself has a certain nature.)

ἀλλὰ μὴν καὶ τὸ καλὸν καὶ [35] τὸ δι᾽ αὑτὸ αἱρετὸν ἐν τῇ αὐτῇ συστοιχίᾳ· καὶ ἔστιν ἄριστον ἀεὶ ἢ ἀνάλογον τὸ πρῶτον. [1072β] [1] ὅτι δ᾽ ἔστι τὸ οὗ ἕνεκα ἐν τοῖς ἀκινήτοις, ἡ διαίρεσις δηλοῖ· ἔστι γὰρ τινὶ τὸ οὗ ἕνεκα <καὶ τινός, ὧν τὸ μὲν ἔστι τὸ δ᾽ οὐκ ἔστι. κινεῖ δὴ ὡς ἐρώμενον, κινούμενα δὲ τἆλλα κινεῖ.

At vero et quod bonum et quod propter ipsum eligibile in eadem coelementatione; et est optimum semper aut proportionale quod primum. Quia autem est quod cuius gratia in immobilibus, divisio ostendit. Est enim alicui quod cuius gratia, quorum hoc quidem est, illud vero non est.

But the beautiful, also, and that which is in itself desirable are in the same column; and the first in any class is always best, or analogous to the best. [72b] That a final cause may exist among unchangeable entities is shown by the distinction of its meanings. For the final cause is (a) some being for whose good an action is done, and (b) something at which the action aims; and of these the latter exists among unchangeable entities though the former does not.

εἰ μὲν οὖν τι κινεῖται, ἐνδέχεται καὶ [5] ἄλλως ἔχειν, ὥστ᾽ εἰ [ἡ] φορὰ πρώτη ἡ ἐνέργειά ἐστιν, ᾗ κινεῖται ταύτῃ γε ἐνδέχεται ἄλλως ἔχειν, κατὰ τόπον, καὶ εἰ μὴ κατ᾽ οὐσίαν· ἐπεὶ δὲ ἔστι τι κινοῦν αὐτὸ ἀκίνητον ὄν, ἐνεργείᾳ ὄν, τοῦτο οὐκ ἐνδέχεται ἄλλως ἔχειν οὐδαμῶς. φορὰ γὰρ ἡ πρώτη τῶν μεταβολῶν, ταύτης δὲ ἡ κύκλῳ· ταύτην [10] δὲ τοῦτο κινεῖ. ἐξ ἀνάγκης ἄρα ἐστὶν ὄν· καὶ ᾗ ἀνάγκη, καλῶς, καὶ οὕτως ἀρχή. τὸ γὰρ ἀναγκαῖον τοσαυταχῶς, τὸ μὲν βίᾳ ὅτι παρὰ τὴν ὁρμήν, τὸ δὲ οὗ οὐκ ἄνευ τὸ εὖ, τὸ δὲ μὴ ἐνδεχόμενον ἄλλως ἀλλ᾽ ἁπλῶς. ἐκ τοιαύτης ἄρα ἀρχῆς ἤρτηται ὁ οὐρανὸς καὶ ἡ φύσις.

Movet autem ut amatum, moto vero alia movet. Si quidem igitur aliquid movetur, contingit aliter habere. Quare latio quae prima et actus est; secundum quod movetur hac autem contingit aliter habere, secundum locum, et si non secundum substantiam. Quoniam autem est aliquid movens ipsum immobile ens, actu ens, hoc non contingit aliter se habere nullatenus. Latio enim prima mutationum, huius autem quae circulo; hac autem hoc movet. Ex necessitate igitur est ens; et necessitas bene et sic principium. Nam necessarium totiens : hoc quidem vi quia praeter impetum, illud vero rsine quo non bene, hoc autem non contingens aliter sed simpliciter. Ex tali igitur principio dependet coelum et natura.

The final cause, then, produces motion as being loved, but all other things move by being moved. Now if something is moved it is capable of being otherwise than as it is. Therefore if its actuality is the primary form of spatial motion, then in so far as it is subject to change, in this respect it is capable of being otherwise,-in place, even if not in substance. But since there is something which moves while itself unmoved, existing actually, this can in no way be otherwise than as it is. For motion in space is the first of the kinds of change, and motion in a circle the first kind of spatial motion; and this the first mover produces. The first mover, then, exists of necessity; and in so far as it exists by necessity, its mode of being is good, and it is in this sense a first principle. For the necessary has all these senses-that which is necessary perforce because it is contrary to the natural impulse, that without which the good is impossible, and that which cannot be otherwise but can exist only in a single way. On such a principle, then, depend the heavens and the world of nature.

διαγωγὴ δ᾽ [15] ἐστὶν οἵα ἡ ἀρίστη μικρὸν χρόνον ἡμῖν (οὕτω γὰρ ἀεὶ ἐκεῖνο: ἡμῖν μὲν γὰρ ἀδύνατον),

Deductio autem est qualis optima, paruo tempore nobis; sic enim semper illud est, nobis quidem enim impossibile.

And it is a life such as the best which we enjoy, and enjoy for but a short time (for it is ever in this state, which we cannot be),

ἐπεὶ καὶ ἡδονὴ ἡ ἐνέργεια τούτου (καὶ διὰ τοῦτο ἐγρήγορσις αἴσθησις νόησις ἥδιστον, ἐλπίδες δὲ καὶ μνῆμαι διὰ ταῦτα). ἡ δὲ νόησις ἡ καθ᾽ αὑτὴν τοῦ καθ᾽ αὑτὸ ἀρίστου, καὶ ἡ μάλιστα τοῦ μάλιστα.

Quoniam et delectatio actus huius. Et propter hoc vigilatio, sensus, intelligentia delectabilissimum. Spes vero et memorie propter haec. intelligentia autem quae secundum se eius quod secundum se optimum, et quae maxime eius quod maxime.

since its actuality is also pleasure. (And for this reason are waking, perception, and thinking most pleasant, and hopes and memories are so on account of these.) And thinking in itself deals with that which is best in itself, and that which is thinking in the fullest sense with that which is best in the fullest sense.

αὑτὸν [20] δὲ νοεῖ ὁ νοῦς κατὰ μετάληψιν τοῦ νοητοῦ: νοητὸς γὰρ γίγνεται θιγγάνων καὶ νοῶν, ὥστε ταὐτὸν νοῦς καὶ νοητόν. τὸ γὰρ δεκτικὸν τοῦ νοητοῦ καὶ τῆς οὐσίας νοῦς, ἐνεργεῖ δὲ ἔχων, ὥστ᾽ ἐκείνου μᾶλλον τοῦτο ὃ δοκεῖ ὁ νοῦς θεῖον ἔχειν, καὶ ἡ θεωρία τὸ ἥδιστον καὶ ἄριστον. εἰ οὖν οὕτως εὖ ἔχει, [25] ὡς ἡμεῖς ποτέ, ὁ θεὸς ἀεί, θαυμαστόν· εἰ δὲ μᾶλλον, ἔτι θαυμασιώτερον. ἔχει δὲ ὧδε.

Ipsum autem intelligit intellectus secundum transumptionem intelligibilis; intelligibilis enim fit attingens et intelligens, quare idem intellectus et intelligibile. Susceptivum enim intelligibilis et substantiae intellectus; actuatur autem habens. Quare illud magis isto quod videtur intellectus divinum habere, et speculatio delectabilissimum et optimum. Si igitur sic bene habet ut nos quandoque, deus semper, mirabile; si autem magis, adhuc mirabilius. Habet autem sic.

And thought thinks on itself because it shares the nature of the object of thought; for it becomes an object of thought in coming into contact with and thinking its objects, so that thought and object of thought are the same. For that which is capable of receiving the object of thought, i.e. the essence, is thought. But it is active when it possesses this object. Therefore the possession rather than the receptivity is the divine element which thought seems to contain, and the act of contemplation is what is most pleasant and best. If, then, God is always in that good state in which we sometimes are, this compels our wonder; and if in a better this compels it yet more. And God is in a better state.

καὶ ζωὴ δέ γε ὑπάρχει· ἡ γὰρ νοῦ ἐνέργεια ζωή, ἐκεῖνος δὲ ἡ ἐνέργεια· ἐνέργεια δὲ ἡ καθ᾽ αὑτὴν ἐκείνου ζωὴ ἀρίστη καὶ ἀΐδιος. φαμὲν δὴ τὸν θεὸν εἶναι ζῷον ἀΐδιον ἄριστον, ὥστε ζωὴ καὶ αἰὼν συνεχὴς [30] καὶ ἀΐδιος ὑπάρχει τῷ θεῷ· τοῦτο γὰρ ὁ θεός.

Et vita autem utique existit; etenim intellectus actus vita, illud autem ipse actus; actus autem quae secundum se illius vita optima et sempiterna. Dicimus autem deum esse animal sempiternum optimum. Quare vita et duratio continua eterna existit deo; hoc enim deus.

And life also belongs to God; for the actuality of thought is life, and God is that actuality; and God's self-dependent actuality is life most good and eternal. We say therefore that God is a living being, eternal, most good, so that life and duration continuous and eternal belong to God; for this is God.

ὅσοι δὲ ὑπολαμβάνουσιν, ὥσπερ οἱ Πυθαγόρειοι καὶ Σπεύσιππος τὸ κάλλιστον καὶ ἄριστον μὴ ἐν ἀρχῇ εἶναι, διὰ τὸ καὶ τῶν φυτῶν καὶ τῶν ζῴων τὰς ἀρχὰς αἴτια μὲν εἶναι τὸ δὲ καλὸν καὶ τέλειον ἐν τοῖς ἐκ τούτων, οὐκ ὀρθῶς οἴονται. [35] τὸ γὰρ σπέρμα ἐξ ἑτέρων ἐστὶ προτέρων τελείων, καὶ τὸ πρῶτον οὐ σπέρμα ἐστὶν ἀλλὰ τὸ τέλειον· [1073α] [1] οἷον πρότερον ἄνθρωπον ἂν φαίη τις εἶναι τοῦ σπέρματος, οὐ τὸν ἐκ τούτου γενόμενον ἀλλ᾽ ἕτερον ἐξ οὗ τὸ σπέρμα. ὅτι μὲν οὖν ἔστιν οὐσία τις ἀΐδιος καὶ ἀκίνητος καὶ κεχωρισμένη τῶν αἰσθητῶν, [5] φανερὸν ἐκ τῶν εἰρημένων·

Quicumque autem putant, ut Pytagorici et Speusippus, optimum et nobilissimum non in principio esse, quia et plantarum et animalium principia cause sunt, bonum vero et perfectum in hiis quae ex hiis, non recte existimant. Nam sperma ex alteris est prioribus perfectis, et primum non est sperma sed perfectum; ut priorem hominem dicat aliquis esse spermate, non eum qui ex hoc fit sed alterum ex quo sperma. Quod quidem igitur est substantia aliqua sempiterna et immobilis, separata a sensibilibus, manifestum ex dictis.

Those who suppose, as the Pythagoreans and Speusippus do, that supreme beauty and goodness are not present in the beginning, because the beginnings both of plants and of animals are causes, but beauty and completeness are in the effects of these, are wrong in their opinion. For the seed comes from other individuals which are prior and complete, and the first thing is not seed but the complete [73a] being; e.g. we must say that before the seed there is a man,-not the man produced from the seed, but another from whom the seed comes. It is clear then from what has been said that there is a substance which is eternal and unmovable and separate from sensible things.

δέδεικται δὲ καὶ ὅτι μέγεθος οὐδὲν ἔχειν ἐνδέχεται ταύτην τὴν οὐσίαν ἀλλ᾽ ἀμερὴς καὶ ἀδιαίρετός ἐστιν (κινεῖ γὰρ τὸν ἄπειρον χρόνον, οὐδὲν δ᾽ ἔχει δύναμιν ἄπειρον πεπερασμένον· ἐπεὶ δὲ πᾶν μέγεθος ἢ ἄπειρον ἢ πεπερασμένον, πεπερασμένον μὲν διὰ τοῦτο οὐκ [10] ἂν ἔχοι μέγεθος, ἄπειρον δ᾽ ὅτι ὅλως οὐκ ἔστιν οὐδὲν ἄπειρον μέγεθος)· ἀλλὰ μὴν καὶ ὅτι ἀπαθὲς καὶ ἀναλλοίωτον· πᾶσαι γὰρ αἱ ἄλλαι κινήσεις ὕστεραι τῆς κατὰ τόπον. ταῦτα μὲν οὖν δῆλα διότι τοῦτον ἔχει τὸν τρόπον.

Ostensum est autem et quia magnitudinem nullam contingit habere hanc substantiam, verum sine parte et indivisibilis est. Movet enim per infinitum tempus, et non habet potentiam infinitam finitum. Quoniam autem omnis magnitudo aut infinita est aut finita, finitam quidem propter hoc utique non habebit magnitudinem, infinitam vero quia totaliter non est nulla infinita magnitudo. At vero et quia impassibilis et inalterabilis; omnes enim alii motus posteriores sunt eo qui est secundum locum. Haec quidem igitur manifesta quia hunc habent modum.

It has been shown also that this substance cannot have any magnitude, but is without parts and indivisible (for it produces movement through infinite time, but nothing finite has infinite power; and, while every magnitude is either infinite or finite, it cannot, for the above reason, have finite magnitude, and it cannot have infinite magnitude because there is no infinite magnitude at all). But it has also been shown that it is impassive and unalterable; for all the other changes are posterior to change of place. It is clear, then, why these things are as they are.

*Chapter* 8

πότερον δὲ μίαν θετέον τὴν τοιαύτην οὐσίαν ἢ πλείους, [15] καὶ πόσας, δεῖ μὴ λανθάνειν, ἀλλὰ μεμνῆσθαι καὶ τὰς τῶν ἄλλων ἀποφάσεις, ὅτι περὶ πλήθους οὐθὲν εἰρήκασιν ὅ τι καὶ σαφὲς εἰπεῖν. ἡ μὲν γὰρ περὶ τὰς ἰδέας ὑπόληψις οὐδεμίαν ἔχει σκέψιν ἰδίαν (ἀριθμοὺς γὰρ λέγουσι τὰς ἰδέας οἱ λέγοντες ἰδέας, περὶ δὲ τῶν ἀριθμῶν ὁτὲ μὲν ὡς [20] περὶ ἀπείρων λέγουσιν ὁτὲ δὲ ὡς μέχρι τῆς δεκάδος ὡρισμένων· δι᾽ ἣν δ᾽ αἰτίαν τοσοῦτον τὸ πλῆθος τῶν ἀριθμῶν, οὐδὲν λέγεται μετὰ σπουδῆς ἀποδεικτικῆς):

Utrum autem unam ponendum est talem substantiam aut plures, et quot, oportet non latere, sed reminisci et aliorum negationes, quia de pluralitate nihil dixerunt quod et planum dicere. Quae enim circa ydeas existimatio nullam habet perscrutationem propriam. Numeros enim dicunt ydeas dicentes ydeas, sed de numeris quandoque quidem ut de infinitis dicunt quandoque autem ut usque ad decadem determinatis; propter quam vero causam tanta pluralitas numerorum, nihil dicitur cum studio demonstrativo.

But we must not ignore the question whether we have to suppose one such substance or more than one, and if the latter, how many; we must also mention, regarding the opinions expressed by others, that they have said nothing about the number of the substances that can even be clearly stated. For the theory of Ideas has no special discussion of the subject; for those who speak of Ideas say the Ideas are numbers, and they speak of numbers now as unlimited, now as limited by the number 10; but as for the reason why there should be just so many numbers, nothing is said with any demonstrative exactness.

ἡμῖν δ᾽ ἐκ τῶν ὑποκειμένων καὶ διωρισμένων λεκτέον. ἡ μὲν γὰρ ἀρχὴ καὶ τὸ πρῶτον τῶν ὄντων ἀκίνητον καὶ καθ᾽ αὑτὸ καὶ κατὰ [25] συμβεβηκός, κινοῦν δὲ τὴν πρώτην ἀΐδιον καὶ μίαν κίνησιν· ἐπεὶ δὲ τὸ κινούμενον ἀνάγκη ὑπό τινος κινεῖσθαι, καὶ τὸ πρῶτον κινοῦν ἀκίνητον εἶναι καθ᾽ αὑτό, καὶ τὴν ἀΐδιον κίνησιν ὑπὸ ἀϊδίου κινεῖσθαι καὶ τὴν μίαν ὑφ᾽ ἑνός,

Nobis autem est ex suppositis et determinatis dicendum. Principium quidem enim et primum entium est immobile et secundum se et secundum accidens, movens vero primum sempiternum et unum motum. Quoniam autem quod movetur necesse ab aliquo moveri, et primum movens immobile esse secundum se, et sempiternum motum a sempiterno moveri et unum ab uno.

We however must discuss the subject, starting from the presuppositions and distinctions we have mentioned. The first principle or primary being is not movable either in itself or accidentally, but produces the primary eternal and single movement. But since that which is moved must be moved by something, and the first mover must be in itself unmovable, and eternal movement must be produced by something eternal and a single movement by a single thing,

ὁρῶμεν δὲ παρὰ τὴν τοῦ παντὸς τὴν ἁπλῆν φοράν, ἣν κινεῖν φαμὲν [30] τὴν πρώτην οὐσίαν καὶ ἀκίνητον, ἄλλας φορὰς οὔσας τὰς τῶν πλανήτων ἀϊδίους (ἀΐδιον γὰρ καὶ ἄστατον τὸ κύκλῳ σῶμα: δέδεικται δ᾽ ἐν τοῖς φυσικοῖς περὶ τούτων), ἀνάγκη καὶ τούτων ἑκάστην τῶν φορῶν ὑπ᾽ ἀκινήτου τε κινεῖσθαι καθ᾽ αὐτὴν καὶ ἀϊδίου οὐσίας. ἥ τε γὰρ τῶν ἄστρων φύσις ἀΐδιος [35] οὐσία τις οὖσα, καὶ τὸ κινοῦν ἀΐδιον καὶ πρότερον τοῦ κινουμένου, καὶ τὸ πρότερον οὐσίας οὐσίαν ἀναγκαῖον εἶναι. φανερὸν τοίνυν ὅτι τοσαύτας τε οὐσίας ἀναγκαῖον εἶναι τήν τε φύσιν ἀϊδίους καὶ ἀκινήτους καθ᾽ αὐτάς, καὶ ἄνευ μεγέθους διὰ τὴν εἰρημένην αἰτίαν πρότερον. [1073β] [1] —ὅτι μὲν οὖν εἰσὶν οὐσίαι, καὶ τούτων τις πρώτη καὶ δευτέρα κατὰ τὴν αὐτὴν τάξιν ταῖς φοραῖς τῶν ἄστρων, φανερόν:

Videmus autem praeter universi simplicem lationem, quam movere dicimus primam substantiam et immobilem, alias lationes existentes planetarum sempiternas. Sempiternum enim et instabile circulare corpus; ostensum est autem in phisicis de hiis. Necesse et harum lationum unamquamque ab immobili moveri secundum se et sempiterna substantia. Astrorum enim natura sempiterna substantia quaedam ens, et movens sempiternum et prius eo quod movetur, et quod prius substantia substantiam esse necesse est. Palam itaque quia tot substantias est esse necesse, natura sempiternas et immobiles secundum se et sine magnitudine, propter predictam causam. Quod quidem igitur sint substantiae, et harum quae prima et secunda secundum ordinem eundem lationibus astrorum, palam .

and since we see that besides the simple spatial movement of the universe, which we say the first and unmovable substance produces, there are other spatial movements-those of the planets-which are eternal (for a body which moves in a circle is eternal and unresting; we have proved these points in the physical treatises), each of these movements also must be caused by a substance both unmovable in itself and eternal. For the nature of the stars is eternal just because it is a certain kind of substance, and the mover is eternal and prior to the moved, and that which is prior to a substance must be a substance. Evidently, then, there must be substances which are of the same number as the movements of the stars, and in their nature eternal, and in themselves unmovable, and without magnitude, for the reason before mentioned. [73b] That the movers are substances, then, and that one of these is first and another second according to the same order as the movements of the stars, is evident.

τὸ δὲ πλῆθος ἤδη τῶν φορῶν ἐκ τῆς οἰκειοτάτης φιλοσοφίᾳ τῶν μαθηματικῶν [5] ἐπιστημῶν δεῖ σκοπεῖν, ἐκ τῆς ἀστρολογίας: αὕτη γὰρ περὶ οὐσίας αἰσθητῆς μὲν ἀϊδίου δὲ ποιεῖται τὴν θεωρίαν, αἱ δ᾽ ἄλλαι περὶ οὐδεμιᾶς οὐσίας, οἷον ἥ τε περὶ τοὺς ἀριθμοὺς καὶ τὴν γεωμετρίαν. ὅτι μὲν οὖν πλείους τῶν φερομένων αἱ φοραί, φανερὸν τοῖς καὶ μετρίως ἡμμένοις (πλείους γὰρ ἕκαστον

[10] φέρεται μιᾶς τῶν πλανωμένων ἄστρων): πόσαι δ᾽ αὗται τυγχάνουσιν οὖσαι, νῦν μὲν ἡμεῖς ἃ λέγουσι τῶν μαθηματικῶν τινὲς ἐννοίας χάριν λέγομεν, ὅπως ᾖ τι τῇ διανοίᾳ πλῆθος ὡρισμένον ὑπολαβεῖν· τὸ δὲ λοιπὸν τὰ μὲν ζητοῦντας αὐτοὺς δεῖ τὰ δὲ πυνθανομένους παρὰ τῶν ζητούντων, [15] ἄν τι φαίνηται παρὰ τὰ νῦν εἰρημένα τοῖς ταῦτα πραγματευομένοις, φιλεῖν μὲν ἀμφοτέρους, πείθεσθαι δὲ τοῖς ἀκριβεστέροις.

Pluralitatem vero iam lationum ex maxime propria philosophia mathematicarum scientiarum intendere oportet, ex astrologia; haec enim de substantia sensibili quidem sempiterna autem facit theoriam, aliae vero de nulla substantia, puta quae circa numeros et geometriam, quod quidem igitur plures sint eorum quae feruntur lationes, manifestum est et parum attingentibus; pluribus enim quam una astrorum errantium unumquodque fertur. Sed quot sint hae, nunc quidem et nos quae dicunt mathematicorum quidam attentionis gratia dicimus, ut mente aliqua pluralitas determinata suscipiatur. Reliquum vero haec quidem quaerentes ipsos oportet, illa vero interrogantes a quaerentibus, si quid videatur praeter modo dicta ab ea tractantibus, amare quidem utrosque, persuaderi vero a certioribus.

But in the number of the movements we reach a problem which must be treated from the standpoint of that one of the mathematical sciences which is most akin to philosophy-viz. of astronomy; for this science speculates about substance which is perceptible but eternal, but the other mathematical sciences, i.e. arithmetic and geometry, treat of no substance. That the movements are more numerous than the bodies that are moved is evident to those who have given even moderate attention to the matter; for each of the planets has more than one movement. But as to the actual number of these movements, we now-to give some notion of the subject-quote what some of the mathematicians say, that our thought may have some definite number to grasp; but, for the rest, we must partly investigate for ourselves, Partly learn from other investigators, and if those who study this subject form an opinion contrary to what we have now stated, we must esteem both parties indeed, but follow the more accurate.

Εὔδοξος μὲν οὖν ἡλίου καὶ σελήνης ἑκατέρου τὴν φορὰν ἐν τρισὶν ἐτίθετ᾽ εἶναι σφαίραις, ὧν τὴν μὲν πρώτην τὴν τῶν ἀπλανῶν ἄστρων εἶναι, τὴν δὲ δευτέραν κατὰ τὸν [20] διὰ μέσων τῶν ζῳδίων, τὴν δὲ τρίτην κατὰ τὸν λελοξωμένον ἐν τῷ πλάτει τῶν ζῳδίων (ἐν μείζονι δὲ πλάτει λελοξῶσθαι καθ᾽ ὃν ἡ σελήνη φέρεται ἢ καθ᾽ ὃν ὁ ἥλιος), τῶν δὲ πλανωμένων ἄστρων ἐν τέτταρσιν ἑκάστου σφαίραις, καὶ τούτων δὲ τὴν μὲν πρώτην καὶ δευτέραν τὴν αὐτὴν εἶναι [25] ἐκείναις (τήν τε γὰρ τῶν ἀπλανῶν τὴν ἁπάσας φέρουσαν εἶναι, καὶ τὴν ὑπὸ ταύτῃ τεταγμένην καὶ κατὰ τὸν διὰ μέσων τῶν ζῳδίων τὴν φορὰν ἔχουσαν κοινὴν ἁπασῶν εἶναι), τῆς δὲ τρίτης ἁπάντων τοὺς πόλους ἐν τῷ διὰ μέσων τῶν ζῳδίων εἶναι, τῆς δὲ τετάρτης τὴν φορὰν κατὰ τὸν λελοξωμένον [30] πρὸς τὸν μέσον ταύτης· εἶναι δὲ τῆς τρίτης σφαίρας τοὺς πόλους τῶν μὲν ἄλλων ἰδίους, τοὺς δὲ τῆς Ἀφροδίτης καὶ τοῦ Ἑρμοῦ τοὺς αὐτούς·

Eudoxus quidem igitur solem et lunam utriusque lationem in tribus posuit esse speris, quarum primam aplanorum astrorum esse, secundam autem secundum eum qui per medium zodiaci, tertiam autem secundum obliquatum in latitudine animalium; in maiori autem latitudine obliquari secundum quem luna fertur quam secundum quem sol. Errantium vero astrorum in quatuor cuiusque speris. Quarum primam quidem et secundam illis eandem esse; et enim eam quae est aplanorum quae omnes est ferens, et eam quae sub ea ordinata et secundum eum qui per medium zodiaci lationem habentem communem omnium esse. Tertie vero omnium polos in eo qui per medium animalium esse. Quarte autem lationem secundum obliquatum ad medium huius. Esse vero tertie spere polos aliorum quidem proprios, veneris vero et mercurii eosdem.

Eudoxus supposed that the motion of the sun or of the moon involves, in either case, three spheres, of which the first is the sphere of the fixed stars, and the second moves in the circle which runs along the middle of the zodiac, and the third in the circle which is inclined across the breadth of the zodiac; but the circle in which the moon moves is inclined at a greater angle than that in which the sun moves. And the motion of the planets involves, in each case, four spheres, and of these also the first and second are the same as the first two mentioned above (for the sphere of the fixed stars is that which moves all the other spheres, and that which is placed beneath this and has its movement in the circle which bisects the zodiac is common to all), but the poles of the third sphere of each planet are in the circle which bisects the zodiac, and the motion of the fourth sphere is in the circle which is inclined at an angle to the equator of the third sphere; and the poles of the third sphere are different for each of the other planets, but those of Venus and Mercury are the same.

Κάλλιππος δὲ τὴν μὲν θέσιν τῶν σφαιρῶν τὴν αὐτὴν ἐτίθετο Εὐδόξῳ [τοῦτ' ἔστι τῶν ἀποστημάτων τὴν τάξιν], τὸ δὲ πλῆθος τῷ μὲν τοῦ Διὸς καὶ [35] τῷ τοῦ Κρόνου τὸ αὐτὸ ἐκείνῳ ἀπεδίδου, τῷ δ' ἡλίῳ καὶ τῇ σελήνῃ δύο ᾤετο ἔτι προσθετέας εἶναι σφαίρας, τὰ φαινόμενα [37] εἰ μέλλει τις ἀποδώσειν, τοῖς δὲ λοιποῖς τῶν πλανήτων ἑκάστῳ μίαν. ἀναγκαῖον δέ, εἰ μέλλουσι συντεθεῖσαι πᾶσαι τὰ φαινόμενα ἀποδώσειν, [1074α] [1] καθ' ἕκαστον τῶν πλανωμένων ἑτέρας σφαίρας μιᾷ ἐλάττονας εἶναι τὰς ἀνελιττούσας καὶ εἰς τὸ αὐτὸ ἀποκαθιστάσας τῇ θέσει τὴν πρώτην σφαῖραν ἀεὶ τοῦ ὑποκάτω τεταγμένου ἄστρου· οὕτω γὰρ μόνως [5] ἐνδέχεται τὴν τῶν πλανήτων φορὰν ἅπαντα ποιεῖσθαι. ἐπεὶ οὖν ἐν αἷς μὲν αὐτὰ φέρεται σφαίραις αἱ μὲν ὀκτὼ αἱ δὲ πέντε καὶ εἴκοσίν εἰσιν, τούτων δὲ μόνας οὐ δεῖ ἀνελιχθῆναι ἐν αἷς τὸ κατωτάτω τεταγμένον φέρεται, αἱ μὲν τὰς τῶν πρώτων δύο ἀνελίττουσαι ἒξ ἔσονται, αἱ δὲ τὰς [10] τῶν ὕστερον τεττάρων ἑκκαίδεκα· ὁ δὴ ἁπασῶν ἀριθμὸς τῶν τε φερουσῶν καὶ τῶν ἀνελιττουσῶν ταύτας πεντήκοντά τε καὶ πέντε. εἰ δὲ τῇ σελήνῃ τε καὶ τῷ ἡλίῳ μὴ προστιθείη τις ἃς εἴπομεν κινήσεις, αἱ πᾶσαι σφαῖραι ἔσονται ἑπτά τε καὶ τεσσαράκοντα. τὸ μὲν οὖν πλῆθος τῶν σφαιρῶν ἔστω [15] τοσοῦτον,

Callippus autem positionem quidem sperarum eandem posuit cum eudoxo, hoc est distantiarum ordinem, pluralitatem vero ei quidem quae Iovis et ei quae saturni eandem cum illo dedit, soli vero et lune duas existimabat adhuc apponendas esse speras, apparentia si quis est redditurus. Reliquis vero planetis singulis unam. Necesse autem, si simul posite omnes apparentia sunt redditure, secundum quodlibet errantium alteras speras una minores esse reuoluentes et ad idem restituentes positioni primam speram semper inferius ordinati astri; sic enim solum contingit planetarum lationem omnia facere. Quoniam ergo in quibus quidem ipsa feruntur speris hae quidem octo hae autem V et XX sunt, harum autem solas non oportet reuolui in quibus infime ordinatum fertur, quae quidem reuoluunt eas quae sunt primorum duorum sex erunt, quae autem eas quae sunt posteriorum quatuor, xvi; omnium itaque numerus et ferentium et reuoluentium eas lv. Si autem lune et soli non addiderit quis quos diximus motus, omnes spere erunt VII et XL. Pluralitas quidem igitur sperarum tanta sit.

Callippus made the position of the spheres the same as Eudoxus did, but while he assigned the same number as Eudoxus did to Jupiter and to Saturn, he thought two more spheres should be added to the sun and two to the moon, if one is to [74a] explain the observed facts; and one more to each of the other planets. But it is necessary, if all the spheres combined are to explain the observed facts, that for each of the planets there should be other spheres (one fewer than those hitherto assigned) which counteract those already mentioned and bring back to the same position the outermost sphere of the star which in each case is situated below the star in question; for only thus can all the forces at work produce the observed motion of the planets. Since, then, the spheres involved in the movement of the planets themselves are eight for Saturn and Jupiter and twenty-five for the others, and of these only those involved in the movement of the lowest-situated planet need not be counteracted the spheres which counteract those of the outermost two planets will be six in number, and the spheres which counteract those of the next four planets will be sixteen; therefore the number of all the spheres – both those which move the planets and those which counteract these – will be fifty-five. And if one were not to add to the moon and to the sun the movements we mentioned, the whole set of spheres will be forty-seven in number.

ὥστε καὶ τὰς οὐσίας καὶ τὰς ἀρχὰς τὰς ἀκινήτους [καὶ τὰς αἰσθητὰς] τοσαύτας εὔλογον ὑπολαβεῖν (τὸ γὰρ ἀναγκαῖον ἀφείσθω τοῖς ἰσχυροτέροις λέγειν):

Quare et substantias et principia immobilia et sensibilia tot rationabile existimare; necessarium enim dimittatur fortioribus dicere.

Let this, then, be taken as the number of the spheres, so that the unmovable substances and principles also may probably be taken as just so many; the assertion of necessity must be left to more powerful thinkers.

εἰ δὲ μηδεμίαν οἷόν τ᾽ εἶναι φορὰν μὴ συντείνουσαν πρὸς ἄστρου φοράν, ἔτι δὲ πᾶσαν φύσιν καὶ πᾶσαν οὐσίαν ἀπαθῆ καὶ καθ᾽ [20] αὐτὴν τοῦ ἀρίστου τετυχηκυῖαν τέλος εἶναι δεῖ νομίζειν, οὐδεμία ἂν εἴη παρὰ ταύτας ἑτέρα φύσις, ἀλλὰ τοῦτον ἀνάγκη τὸν ἀριθμὸν εἶναι τῶν οὐσιῶν. εἴτε γὰρ εἰσὶν ἕτεραι, κινοῖεν ἂν ὡς τέλος οὖσαι φορᾶς·

Si autem nullam possibile esse lationem non ordinatam ad astri lationem, amplius autem omnem naturam et omnem substantiam impassibilem et secundum se optimum sortitam finem esse oportet existimare, nulla erit praeter has altera natura, sed hunc substantiarum numerum est esse necesse. Si enim essent aliae, moverent utique ut finis existentes lationis,

But if there can be no spatial movement which does not conduce to the moving of a star, and if further every being and every substance which is immune from change and in virtue of itself has attained to the best must be considered an end, there can be no other being apart from these we have named, but this must be the number of the substances. For if there are others, they will cause change as being a final cause of movement;

ἀλλὰ εἶναί γε ἄλλας φορὰς ἀδύνατον παρὰ τὰς εἰρημένας. τοῦτο δὲ εὔλογον ἐκ τῶν [25] φερομένων ὑπολαβεῖν. εἰ γὰρ πᾶν τὸ φέρον τοῦ φερομένου χάριν πέφυκε καὶ φορὰ πᾶσα φερομένου τινός ἐστιν, οὐδεμία φορὰ αὐτῆς ἂν ἕνεκα εἴη οὐδ᾽ ἄλλης φορᾶς, ἀλλὰ τῶν ἄστρων ἕνεκα. εἰ γὰρ ἔσται φορὰ φορᾶς ἕνεκα, καὶ ἐκείνην ἑτέρου δεήσει χάριν εἶναι· ὥστ᾽ ἐπειδὴ οὐχ οἷόν τε εἰς ἄπειρον, [30] τέλος ἔσται πάσης φορᾶς τῶν φερομένων τι θείων σωμάτων κατὰ τὸν οὐρανόν. ὅτι δὲ εἷς οὐρανός, φανερόν.

sed alias quidem esse lationes impossibile est praeter dictas. Hoc autem rationabile ex latis existimare. Nam si omne ferens lati gratia natum est, et latio omnis lati est alicuius, nulla latio sui gratia erit nec alius lationis, sed astrorum gratia. Nam si fuerit latio lationis gratia, et illam alterius gratia oportebit esse. quare quoniam non possibile est in infinitum , finis erit omnis lationis latorum aliquid divinorum corporum secundum coelum.

but there cannot he other movements besides those mentioned. And it is reasonable to infer this from a consideration of the bodies that are moved; for if everything that moves is for the sake of that which is moved, and every movement belongs to something that is moved, no movement can be for the sake of itself or of another movement, but all the movements must be for the sake of the stars. For if there

480

is to be a movement for the sake of a movement, this latter also will have to be for the sake of something else; so that since there cannot be an infinite regress, the end of every movement will be one of the divine bodies which move through the heaven.

εἰ γὰρ πλείους οὐρανοὶ ὥσπερ ἄνθρωποι, ἔσται εἴδει μία ἡ περὶ ἕκαστον ἀρχή, ἀριθμῷ δέ γε πολλαί. ἀλλ᾽ ὅσα ἀριθμῷ πολλά, ὕλην ἔχει (εἷς γὰρ λόγος καὶ ὁ αὐτὸς πολλῶν, [35] οἷον ἀνθρώπου, Σωκράτης δὲ εἷς): τὸ δὲ τί ἦν εἶναι οὐκ ἔχει ὕλην τὸ πρῶτον: ἐντελέχεια γάρ. ἓν ἄρα καὶ λόγῳ καὶ ἀριθμῷ τὸ πρῶτον κινοῦν ἀκίνητον ὄν: καὶ τὸ κινούμενον ἄρα ἀεὶ καὶ συνεχῶς: εἷς ἄρα οὐρανὸς μόνος.

Quod autem unum coelum, manifestum . Si enim plures essent coeli ut homines, foret principium quod circa unumquodque specie unum, numero vero multa. Sed quaecumque sunt numero multa, materiam habent; una enim et eadem ratio multorum, ut hominis, Socrates vero unus. Quod quid autem erat esse non habet materiam, primum; entelechia enim . Unum igitur et ratione et numero primum movens mmobile ens; et motum ergo semper et continve unum solum; unum ergo solum coelum.

Evidently there is but one heaven. For if there are many heavens as there are many men, the moving principles, of which each heaven will have one, will be one in form but in number many. But all things that are many in number have matter; for one and the same definition, e.g. that of man, applies to many things, while Socrates is one. But the primary essence has not matter; for it is complete reality. So the unmovable first mover is one both in definition and in number; so too, therefore, is that which is moved always and continuously; therefore there is one heaven alone.) [74b]

[1074β] [1] παραδέδοται δὲ παρὰ τῶν ἀρχαίων καὶ παμπαλαίων ἐν μύθου σχήματι καταλελειμμένα τοῖς ὕστερον ὅτι θεοί τέ εἰσιν οὗτοι καὶ περιέχει τὸ θεῖον τὴν ὅλην φύσιν. τὰ δὲ λοιπὰ μυθικῶς ἤδη προσῆκται πρὸς τὴν πειθὼ τῶν πολλῶν καὶ [5] πρὸς τὴν εἰς τοὺς νόμους καὶ τὸ συμφέρον χρῆσιν: ἀνθρωποειδεῖς τε γὰρ τούτους καὶ τῶν ἄλλων ζῴων ὁμοίους τισὶ λέγουσι, καὶ τούτοις ἕτερα ἀκόλουθα καὶ παραπλήσια τοῖς εἰρημένοις, ὧν εἴ τις χωρίσας αὐτὸ λάβοι μόνον τὸ πρῶτον, ὅτι θεοὺς ᾤοντο τὰς πρώτας οὐσίας εἶναι, θείως ἂν εἰρῆσθαι [10] νομίσειεν, καὶ κατὰ τὸ εἰκὸς πολλάκις εὑρημένης εἰς τὸ δυνατὸν ἑκάστης καὶ τέχνης καὶ φιλοσοφίας καὶ πάλιν φθειρομένων καὶ ταύτας τὰς δόξας ἐκείνων οἷον λείψανα περισεσῶσθαι μέχρι τοῦ νῦν. ἡ μὲν οὖν πάτριος δόξα καὶ ἡ παρὰ τῶν πρώτων ἐπὶ τοσοῦτον ἡμῖν φανερὰ μόνον. [15]

Tradita sunt autem a senioribus et antiquis in fabule figura dimissa posterioribus, quia dii sunt hii et continet divinum naturam universam. Reliqua vero fabulose iam adducta sunt ad persuasionem multorum et ad oportunitatem ad leges et conferens. Conformes enim hominibus hos et aliorum animalium quibusdam similes dicunt, et hiis altera consequentia et dictis similia. A quibus si quis separans id accipiat solum quod primum, quod deos existimaverunt primas substantias esse, divine utique dictum esse putabit, et secundum verisimilitudinem saepe inventa ad possibile unaquaque et arte et philosophia et iterum corruptis, et has opiniones illorum quasi reliquias usque nunc saluatas esse. Patria quidem igitur opinio et quae a primis in tantum nobis manifesta solum.

Our forefathers in the most remote ages have handed down to their posterity a tradition, in the form of a myth, that these bodies are gods, and that the divine encloses the whole of nature. The rest of the tradition has been added later in mythical form with a view to the persuasion of the multitude and to its legal and utilitarian expediency; they say these gods are in the form of men or like some of the other animals, and they say other things consequent on and similar to these which we have mentioned. But if one were to separate the first point from these additions and take it alone-that they thought the first substances to be gods, one must regard this as an inspired utterance, and reflect that, while probably each art and each science has often been developed as far as possible and has again perished, these opinions, with others, have been preserved until the present like relics of the ancient treasure. Only thus far, then, is the opinion of our ancestors and of our earliest predecessors clear to us.

*Chapter* 9

τὰ δὲ περὶ τὸν νοῦν ἔχει τινὰς ἀπορίας: δοκεῖ μὲν γὰρ εἶναι τῶν φαινομένων θειότατον, πῶς δ᾽ ἔχων τοιοῦτος ἂν εἴη, ἔχει τινὰς δυσκολίας.

Quae autem circa intellectum habent quasdam dubitationes. Videtur quidem enim apparentium divinissimum; quomodo vero habens tajis erit utique, habet quasdam difficultates.

The nature of the divine thought involves certain problems; for while thought is held to be the most divine of things observed by us, the question how it must be situated in order to have that character involves difficulties.

εἴτε γὰρ μηδὲν νοεῖ, τί ἂν εἴη τὸ σεμνόν, ἀλλ᾽ ἔχει ὥσπερ ἂν εἰ ὁ καθεύδων: εἴτε νοεῖ, τούτου δ᾽ ἄλλο κύριον, οὐ γάρ ἐστι τοῦτο ὅ ἐστιν αὐτοῦ ἡ [20] οὐσία νόησις, ἀλλὰ δύναμις, οὐκ ἂν ἡ ἀρίστη οὐσία εἴη: διὰ γὰρ τοῦ νοεῖν τὸ τίμιον αὐτῷ ὑπάρχει.

Nam sive non intelligat, quid utique erit venerabile? Sed habet quemadmodum [ut] si dormiens . Sive intelligat, huius vero aliud principale, non enim est hoc quod est sua substantia intelligentia, sed potentia: non utique erit optima substantia; per intelligere enim honorabile ei inest.

For if it thinks of nothing, what is there here of dignity? It is just like one who sleeps. And if it thinks, but this depends on something else, then (since that which is

its substance is not the act of thinking, but a potency) it cannot be the best substance; for it is through thinking that its value belongs to it.

ἔτι δὲ εἴτε νοῦς ἡ οὐσία αὐτοῦ εἴτε νόησίς ἐστι, τί νοεῖ; ἢ γὰρ αὐτὸς αὑτὸν ἢ ἕτερόν τι: καὶ εἰ ἕτερόν τι, ἢ τὸ αὐτὸ ἀεὶ ἢ ἄλλο.

Amplius autem sive intellectus sit sua substantia sive intelligentia, quid intelligit? Aut enim se ipsum aut alterum aliquid; et si alterum aliquid, aut idem semper aut aliud.

Further, whether its substance is the faculty of thought or the act of thinking, what does it think of? Either of itself or of something else; and if of something else, either of the same thing always or of something different.

πότερον οὖν διαφέρει τι ἢ οὐδὲν τὸ νοεῖν τὸ καλὸν ἢ τὸ τυχόν; [25] ἢ καὶ ἄτοπον τὸ διανοεῖσθαι περὶ ἐνίων;

Utrum ergo differt aliquid aut nihil , intelligere bonum aut contingens? Aut et inconveniens meditari de quibusdam?

Does it matter, then, or not, whether it thinks of the good or of any chance thing? Are there not some things about which it is incredible that it should think?

δῆλον τοίνυν ὅτι τὸ θειότατον καὶ τιμιώτατον νοεῖ, καὶ οὐ μεταβάλλει: εἰς χεῖρον γὰρ ἡ μεταβολή, καὶ κίνησίς τις ἤδη τὸ τοιοῦτον.

Palam ergo quod divinissimum et honoratissimum intelligit, et non transmutatur; in indignius enim transmutatio, et motus quidam iam tale.

Evidently, then, it thinks of that which is most divine and precious, and it does not change; for change would be change for the worse, and this would be already a movement.

πρῶτον μὲν οὖν εἰ μὴ νόησίς ἐστιν ἀλλὰ δύναμις, εὔλογον ἐπίπονον εἶναι τὸ συνεχὲς αὐτῷ τῆς νοήσεως:

Primum quidem igitur si non est intelligentia sed potentia, rationabile est laboriosam esse ei continuationem intelligentie.

First, then, if thought is not the act of thinking but a potency, it would be reasonable to suppose that the continuity of its thinking is wearisome to it.

ἔπειτα δῆλον [30] ὅτι ἄλλο τι ἂν εἴη τὸ τιμιώτερον ἢ ὁ νοῦς, τὸ νοούμενον. καὶ γὰρ τὸ νοεῖν καὶ ἡ νόησις ὑπάρξει καὶ τὸ χείριστον νοοῦντι, ὥστ᾽ εἰ φευκτὸν

τοῦτο (καὶ γὰρ μὴ ὁρᾶν ἔνια κρεῖττον ἢ ὁρᾶν), οὐκ ἂν εἴη τὸ ἄριστον ἡ νόησις. αὐτὸν ἄρα νοεῖ, εἴπερ ἐστὶ τὸ κράτιστον,

Deinde palam quia aliud aliquid erit    dignius    quam intellectus, scilicet intellectum. Et enim intelligere et intelligentia inerit et indignissimum intelligenti. Quare  fugiendum hoc, et enim non videre quaedam dignius quam videre; non si sit optimum  intelligentia. Se ipsum ergo intelligit, siquidem est  potentissimum , e

Secondly, there would evidently be something else more precious than thought, viz. that which is thought of. For both thinking and the act of thought will belong even to one who thinks of the worst thing in the world, so that if this ought to be avoided (and it ought, for there are even some things which it is better not to see than to see), the act of thinking cannot be the best of things. Therefore it must be of itself that the divine thought thinks (since it is the most excellent of things),

καὶ ἔστιν ἡ νόησις νοήσεως νόησις. [35] φαίνεται δ᾽ ἀεὶ ἄλλου ἡ ἐπιστήμη καὶ ἡ αἴσθησις καὶ ἡ δόξα καὶ ἡ διάνοια, αὑτῆς δ᾽ ἐν παρέργῳ.

t est intelligentia intelligentia intelligentia. Videtur autem semper alius scientia et sensus et opinio et meditatio, ipsius autem in accessorio.

and  its thinking is a thinking on thinking. But evidently knowledge and perception and opinion and understanding have always something else as their object, and themselves only by the way.

ἔτι εἰ ἄλλο τὸ νοεῖν καὶ τὸ νοεῖσθαι, κατὰ πότερον αὐτῷ τὸ εὖ ὑπάρχει; οὐδὲ γὰρ ταὐτὸ τὸ εἶναι νοήσει καὶ νοουμένῳ.

Amplius si aliud est intelligere et intelligi, secundum quid ei ipsum bene inest? Non enim idem esse intelligentie et  intellecto.

Further, if thinking and being thought of are different, in respect of which does goodness belong to thought? For to be an act of thinking and to be an object of thought are not the same thing. [75a]

ἢ ἐπ᾽ ἐνίων ἡ ἐπιστήμη τὸ πρᾶγμα, [1075α] [1] ἐπὶ μὲν τῶν ποιητικῶν ἄνευ ὕλης ἡ οὐσία καὶ τὸ τί ἦν εἶναι, ἐπὶ δὲ τῶν θεωρητικῶν ὁ λόγος τὸ πρᾶγμα καὶ ἡ νόησις; οὐχ ἑτέρου οὖν ὄντος τοῦ νοουμένου καὶ τοῦ νοῦ, ὅσα μὴ ὕλην ἔχει, τὸ αὐτὸ ἔσται, καὶ ἡ [5] νόησις τῷ νοουμένῳ μία.

Aut in quibusdam  scientia res. In factivis quidem sine materia, substantia enim et quod quid erat esse; in theoricis vero ratio res et intelligentia. Non altero igitur existente eo quod intelligitur et intellectu, quaecumque non  materiam habent, idem erunt, et intelligentia eius quod intelligitur una.

We answer that in some cases the knowledge is the object. In the productive sciences it is the substance or essence of the object, matter omitted, and in the theoretical sciences the definition or the act of thinking is the object. Since, then, thought and the object of thought are not different in the case of things that have not matter, the divine thought and its object will be the same, i.e. the thinking will be one with the object of its thought.

ἔτι δὴ λείπεται ἀπορία, εἰ σύνθετον τὸ νοούμενον· μεταβάλλοι γὰρ ἂν ἐν τοῖς μέρεσι τοῦ ὅλου.

Adhuc autem restat dubitatio, si compositum est quod intelligitur; transmutabitur enim in partibus totius.

A further question is left-whether the object of the divine thought is composite; for if it were, thought would change in passing from part to part of the whole.

ἢ ἀδιαίρετον πᾶν τὸ μὴ ἔχον ὕλην—ὥσπερ ὁ ἀνθρώπινος νοῦς

Aut indivisibile omne quod non habet materiam, ut humanus intellectus.

We answer that everything which has not matter is indivisible - as human thought,

ἢ ὅ γε τῶν συνθέτων ἔχει ἔν τινι χρόνῳ (οὐ γὰρ ἔχει τὸ εὖ ἐν τῳδὶ ἢ ἐν τῳδί, ἀλλ᾽ ἐν ὅλῳ τινὶ τὸ ἄριστον, ὂν ἄλλο τι)— [10] οὕτως δ᾽ ἔχει αὐτὴ αὑτῆς ἡ νόησις τὸν ἅπαντα αἰῶνα;

Aut quod quidem compositorum, habet in aliquo tempore; non enim habet ipsum bene in hoc aut in hoc, sed in toto quodam quod optimum, ens aliud aliquid. Sic autem habet ipsa sui ipsius intelligentia toto eterno.

or rather the thought of composite beings, is in a certain period of time (for it does not possess the good at this moment or at that, but its best, being something different from it, is attained only in a whole period of time), so throughout eternity is the thought which has itself for its object.

*Chapter* 10

ἐπισκεπτέον δὲ καὶ ποτέρως ἔχει ἡ τοῦ ὅλου φύσις τὸ ἀγαθὸν καὶ τὸ ἄριστον, πότερον κεχωρισμένον τι καὶ αὐτὸ καθ᾽ αὑτό, ἢ τὴν τάξιν.

Perscrutandum autem est qualiter habet totius natura bonum et optimum, utrum separatum quid et ipsum secundum se, aut ordinem.

We must consider also in which of two ways the nature of the universe contains the good, and the highest good, whether as something separate and by itself, or as the order of the parts.

ἢ ἀμφοτέρως ὥσπερ στράτευμα; καὶ γὰρ ἐν τῇ τάξει τὸ εὖ καὶ ὁ στρατηγός, καὶ μᾶλλον [15] οὗτος· οὐ γὰρ οὗτος διὰ τὴν τάξιν ἀλλ᾽ ἐκείνη διὰ τοῦτόν ἐστιν.

Aut utroque modo sicut exercitus? Et enim in ordine ipsum bene et dux exercitus, et magis iste; non enim iste propter ordinem sed ille propter hunc est.

Probably in both ways, as an army does; for its good is found both in its order and in its leader, and more in the latter; for he does not depend on the order but it depends on him.

πάντα δὲ συντέτακταί πως, ἀλλ᾽ οὐχ ὁμοίως, καὶ πλωτὰ καὶ πτηνὰ καὶ φυτά· καὶ οὐχ οὕτως ἔχει ὥστε μὴ εἶναι θατέρῳ πρὸς θάτερον μηδέν, ἀλλ᾽ ἔστι τι. πρὸς μὲν γὰρ ἓν ἅπαντα συντέτακται, ἀλλ᾽ ὥσπερ ἐν οἰκίᾳ τοῖς ἐλευθέροις [20] ἥκιστα ἔξεστιν ὅ τι ἔτυχε ποιεῖν, ἀλλὰ πάντα ἢ τὰ πλεῖστα τέτακται, τοῖς δὲ ἀνδραπόδοις καὶ τοῖς θηρίοις μικρὸν τὸ εἰς τὸ κοινόν, τὸ δὲ πολὺ ὅ τι ἔτυχεν· τοιαύτη γὰρ ἑκάστου ἀρχὴ αὐτῶν ἡ φύσις ἐστίν. λέγω δ᾽ οἷον εἴς γε τὸ διακριθῆναι ἀνάγκη ἅπασιν ἐλθεῖν, καὶ ἄλλα οὕτως ἔστιν ὧν κοινωνεῖ [25] ἅπαντα εἰς τὸ ὅλον.

Omnia vero coordinata sunt aliqualiter, sed non similiter, et natatilia et volatilia et plante; et non sic se habent ut non sit alteri ad alterum nihil, sed est aliquid. Ad unum quidem enim omnia coordinata sunt. Sed quemadmodum in domo liber is non licet quod contingit facere, sed omnia aut plurima ordinata sunt, seruis vero et bestiis parvum quod ad commune, multum vero quod contingit; tale namque cuiusque principium ipsorum natura est. Dico autem puta ad discerni quidem necesse omnibus venire, et alia sic sunt quibus communicant omnia ad totum.

And all things are ordered together somehow, but not all alike,-both fishes and fowls and plants; and the world is not such that one thing has nothing to do with another, but they are connected. For all are ordered together to one end, but it is as in a house, where the freemen are least at liberty to act at random, but all things or most things are already ordained for them, while the slaves and the animals do little for the common good, and for the most part live at random; for this is the sort of principle that constitutes the nature of each. I mean, for instance, that all must at least come to be dissolved into their elements, and there are other functions similarly in which all share for the good of the whole.

ὅσα δὲ ἀδύνατα συμβαίνει ἢ ἄτοπα τοῖς ἄλλως λέγουσι, καὶ ποῖα οἱ χαριεστέρως λέγοντες, καὶ ἐπὶ ποίων ἐλάχισται ἀπορίαι, δεῖ μὴ λανθάνειν.

Quaecumque vero impossibilia accidunt aut absurda aliter dicentibus, et qualia gratiosius dicentes, et in quibus minime dubitationes, oportet non latere.

We must not fail to observe how many impossible or paradoxical results confront those who hold different views from our own, and what are the views of the subtler thinkers, and which views are attended by fewest difficulties.

πάντες γὰρ ἐξ ἐναντίων ποιοῦσι πάντα. οὔτε δὲ τὸ πάντα οὔτε τὸ ἐξ ἐναντίων ὀρθῶς, οὔτ᾽ ἐν ὅσοις τὰ ἐναντία ὑπάρχει, πῶς [30] ἐκ τῶν ἐναντίων ἔσται, οὐ λέγουσιν·

Omnes enim ex contrariis faciunt omnia. Neque autem quod omnia nec quod ex contrariis recte, nec in quibuscumque contraria existunt, quomodo ex contrariis erunt, non dicunt;

All make all things out of contraries. But neither all things nor out of contraries is right; nor do these thinkers tell us how all the things in which the contraries are present can be made out of the contraries;

ἀπαθῆ γὰρ τὰ ἐναντία ὑπ᾽ ἀλλήλων. ἡμῖν δὲ λύεται τοῦτο εὐλόγως τῷ τρίτον τι εἶναι. οἱ δὲ τὸ ἕτερον τῶν ἐναντίων ὕλην ποιοῦσιν, ὥσπερ οἱ τὸ ἄνισον τῷ ἴσῳ ἢ τῷ ἑνὶ τὰ πολλά. λύεται δὲ καὶ τοῦτο τὸν αὐτὸν τρόπον· ἡ γὰρ ὕλη ἡ μία οὐδενὶ ἐναντίον.

impassibilia namque sunt contraria ad invicem. Nobis autem solvitur hoc rationabiliter eo quod tertium aliquid sit. Alii vero alterum contrariorum materiam faciunt, quemadmodum qui inequale equali aut uni multa. Solvitur autem et hoc eodem modo; materia enim quae una nulli est contrarium.

for contraries are not affected by one another. Now for us this difficulty is solved naturally by the fact that there is a third element. These thinkers however make one of the two contraries matter; this is done for instance by those who make the unequal matter for the equal, or the many matter for the one. But this also is refuted in the same way; for the one matter which underlies any pair of contraries is contrary to nothing.

ἔτι [35] ἅπαντα τοῦ φαύλου μεθέξει ἔξω τοῦ ἑνός· τὸ γὰρ κακὸν αὐτὸ θάτερον τῶν στοιχείων.

Amplius omnia pravi participatione extra unum; nam prauum ipsum alterum elementorum.

Further, all things, except the one, will, on the view we are criticizing, partake of evil; for the bad itself is one of the two elements.

οἱ δ᾽ ἄλλοι οὐδ᾽ ἀρχὰς τὸ ἀγαθὸν καὶ τὸ κακόν· καίτοι ἐν ἅπασι μάλιστα τὸ ἀγαθὸν ἀρχή.

Alii autem nec principia bonum et malum; quamvis in omnibus maxime quod bonum principium.

But the other school does not treat the good and the bad even as principles; yet in all things the good is in the highest degree a principle.

[38] οἱ δὲ τοῦτο μὲν ὀρθῶς ὅτι ἀρχήν, ἀλλὰ πῶς τὸ ἀγαθὸν ἀρχὴ οὐ λέγουσιν, πότερον ὡς τέλος ἢ ὡς κινῆσαν ἢ ὡς εἶδος.

Alii vero hoc quidem recte quia principium, sed quomodo quod bonum principium non dicunt, utrum ut finis aut ut movens aut ut species.

The school we first mentioned is right in saying that it is a principle, but how the good is a principle they do not say-whether as end or as mover or as form. [75b]

[1075β] [1] ἀτόπως δὲ καὶ Ἐμπεδοκλῆς· τὴν γὰρ φιλίαν ποιεῖ τὸ ἀγαθόν, αὕτη δ᾽ ἀρχὴ καὶ ὡς κινοῦσα (συνάγει γάρ) καὶ ὡς ὕλη· μόριον γὰρ τοῦ μίγματος. εἰ δὴ καὶ τῷ αὐτῷ συμβέβηκεν [5] καὶ ὡς ὕλη ἀρχὴ εἶναι καὶ ὡς κινοῦντι, ἀλλὰ τό γ᾽ εἶναι οὐ ταὐτό. κατὰ πότερον οὖν φιλία; ἄτοπον δὲ καὶ τὸ ἄφθαρτον εἶναι τὸ νεῖκος· τοῦτο δ᾽ ἐστὶν αὐτῷ ἡ τοῦ κακοῦ φύσις.

inconvenienter autem et Empedocles. Amicitiam enim facit bonum, haec autem principium et ut movens (congregat enim) et ut materia (pars enim mixture). Si itaque et eidem accidit ut materiam et principium esse et ut movens , sed esse   non idem. Secundum utrum igitur amicitia? Inconveniens autem et incorruptibilem esse litem; hoc ipsum autem est mali natura.

Empedocles also has a paradoxical view; for he identifies the good with love, but this is a principle both as mover (for it brings things together) and as matter (for it is part of the mixture). Now even if it happens that the same thing is a principle both as matter and as mover, still the being, at least, of the two is not the same. In which respect then is love a principle? It is paradoxical also that strife should be imperishable; the nature of his evil is just strife.

Ἀναξαγόρας δὲ ὡς κινοῦν τὸ ἀγαθὸν ἀρχήν· ὁ γὰρ νοῦς κινεῖ. ἀλλὰ κινεῖ ἕνεκά τινος, ὥστε ἕτερον, πλὴν ὡς ἡμεῖς λέγομεν· [10] ἡ γὰρ ἰατρική ἐστί πως ἡ ὑγίεια. ἄτοπον δὲ καὶ τὸ ἐναντίον μὴ ποιῆσαι τῷ ἀγαθῷ καὶ τῷ νῷ. πάντες δ᾽ οἱ τἀναντία λέγοντες οὐ χρῶνται τοῖς ἐναντίοις, ἐὰν μὴ ῥυθμίσῃ τις.

Anaxagoras autem ut movens quod bonum principium ; intellectus enim movet. Sed gratia alicuius movet,  quare alterum , excepto ut nos dicimus; nam medicativa est quodammodo sanitas. Inconveniens autem et contrarium non facere bono et intellectui.

Anaxagoras makes the good a motive principle; for his reason moves things. But it moves them for an end, which must be something other than it, except according to our way of stating the case; for, on our view, the medical art is in a sense health. It is paradoxical also not to suppose a contrary to the good, i.e. to reason.

καὶ διὰ τί τὰ μὲν φθαρτὰ τὰ δ᾽ ἄφθαρτα, οὐδεὶς λέγει· πάντα γὰρ τὰ ὄντα ποιοῦσιν ἐκ τῶν αὐτῶν ἀρχῶν. ἔτι οἱ [15] μὲν ἐκ τοῦ μὴ ὄντος ποιοῦσι τὰ ὄντα· οἱ δ᾽ ἵνα μὴ τοῦτο ἀναγκασθῶσιν, ἓν πάντα ποιοῦσιν.

Omnes autem contraria dicentes non utuntur contrariis, nisi figuret aliquis. Et quare haec quidem corruptibilia haec vero incorruptibilia, nullus dicit; omnia namque entia faciunt ex eisdem principiis. Amplius alii quidem ex non ente faciunt entia; alii autem, ut non hoc cogantur, unum omnia faciunt.

But all who speak of the contraries make no use of the contraries, unless we bring their views into shape. And why some things are perishable and others imperishable, no one tells us; for they make all existing things out of the same principles. Further, some make existing things out of the nonexistent; and others to avoid the necessity of this make all things one.

ἔτι διὰ τί ἀεὶ ἔσται γένεσις καὶ τί αἴτιον γενέσεως, οὐδεὶς λέγει.

Amplius propter quid semper erit generatio et quae est causa generationis, nullus dicit.

Further, why should there always be becoming, and what is the cause of becoming?-this no one tells us.

καὶ τοῖς δύο ἀρχὰς ποιοῦσιν ἄλλην ἀνάγκη ἀρχὴν κυριωτέραν εἶναι, καὶ τοῖς τὰ εἴδη ἔτι ἄλλη ἀρχὴ κυριωτέρα· διὰ τί γὰρ μετέσχεν ἢ [20] μετέχει;

Et duo principia facientibus aliud necesse principium principalius esse, et hiis qui species quia aliud principium principalius; propter quid enim participavit aut participat?

And those who suppose two principles must suppose another, a superior principle, and so must those who believe in the Forms; for why did things come to participate, or why do they participate, in the Forms?

καὶ τοῖς μὲν ἄλλοις ἀνάγκη τῇ σοφίᾳ καὶ τῇ τιμιωτάτῃ ἐπιστήμῃ εἶναί τι ἐναντίον, ἡμῖν δ᾽ οὔ. οὐ γάρ ἐστιν ἐναντίον τῷ πρώτῳ οὐδέν· πάντα γὰρ τὰ ἐναντία ὕλην ἔχει, καὶ δυνάμει ταῦτα ἔστιν· ἡ δὲ ἐναντία ἄγνοια εἰς τὸ ἐναντίον, τῷ δὲ πρώτῳ ἐναντίον οὐδέν.

Et aliis quidem necesse sapientie et honoratissime scienlie aliquid esse contrarium, nobis autem non. Non enim est contrarium primo nihil. Nam omnia contraria materiam habent, et haec potentia est; contraria autem ignorantia ad contrarium; primo vero contrarium nihil.

And all other thinkers are confronted by the necessary consequence that there is something contrary to Wisdom, i.e. to the highest knowledge; but we are not. For there is nothing contrary to that which is primary; for all contraries have matter, and things that have matter exist only potentially; and the ignorance which is contrary to any knowledge leads to an object contrary to the object of the knowledge; but what is primary has no contrary.

εἴ τε μὴ ἔσται παρὰ τὰ [25] αἰσθητὰ ἄλλα, οὐκ ἔσται ἀρχὴ καὶ τάξις καὶ γένεσις καὶ τὰ οὐράνια, ἀλλ' ἀεὶ τῆς ἀρχῆς ἀρχή, ὥσπερ τοῖς θεολόγοις καὶ τοῖς φυσικοῖς πᾶσιν.

Amplius si non  erunt praeter sensibilia alia, non erit principium et ordo et generatio et celestia, sed semper principii principium, ut theologis et phisicis omnibus.

Again, if besides sensible things no others exist, there will be no first principle, no order, no becoming, no heavenly bodies, but each principle will have a principle before it, as in the accounts of the theologians and all the natural philosophers.

εἰ δ' ἔσται τὰ εἴδη· ἢ <οἱ ἀριθμοί, οὐδενὸς αἴτια· εἰ δὲ μή, οὔτι κινήσεώς γε.

Si autem erunt species aut numeri, nullius cause; sin autem, non quid motus.

But if the Forms or the numbers are to exist, they will be causes of nothing; or if not that, at least not of movement.

ἔτι πῶς ἔσται ἐξ ἀμεγεθῶν μέγεθος καὶ συνεχές; ὁ γὰρ ἀριθμὸς οὐ ποιήσει [30] συνεχές, οὔτε ὡς κινοῦν οὔτε ὡς εἶδος.

Adhuc quomodo erit ex non magnitudinibus magnitudo et continuum? Non enim numerus facit continuum, nec ut movens nec ut species.

Further, how is extension, i.e. a continuum, to be produced out of unextended parts? For number will not, either as mover or as form, produce a continuum.

ἀλλὰ μὴν οὐδέν γ' ἔσται τῶν ἐναντίων ὅπερ καὶ ποιητικὸν καὶ κινητικόν; ἐνδέχοιτο γὰρ ἂν μὴ εἶναι. ἀλλὰ μὴν ὕστερόν γε τὸ ποιεῖν δυνάμεως. οὐκ ἄρα ἀΐδια τὰ ὄντα. ἀλλ' ἔστιν· ἀναιρετέον ἄρα τούτων τι. τοῦτο δ' εἴρηται πῶς.

At vero nullum erit contrariorum quod et factivum et motivum, continget enim utique non esse. At vero posterius quidem ipsum facere potentia. Non ergo sempiterna sunt entia. Sed sunt. Interimendum igitur est horum aliquid. Et hoc dictum est ut.

But again there cannot be any contrary that is also essentially a productive or moving principle; for it would be possible for it not to be. Or at least its action would be posterior to its potency. The world, then, would not be eternal. But it is; one of these premisses, then, must be denied. And we have said how this must be done.

ἔτι τίνι οἱ ἀριθμοὶ ἓν ἢ ἡ [35] ψυχὴ καὶ τὸ σῶμα καὶ ὅλως τὸ εἶδος καὶ τὸ πρᾶγμα, οὐδὲν λέγει οὐδείς· οὐδ᾽ ἐνδέχεται εἰπεῖν, ἐὰν μὴ ὡς ἡμεῖς εἴπῃ, ὡς τὸ κινοῦν ποιεῖ.

Adhuc quo numeri unum aut anima et corpus et totaliter species et res, nihil dicit nullus; nec contingit dicere, si non ut nos dicat quod movens facit.

Further, in virtue of what the numbers, or the soul and the body, or in general the form and the thing, are one-of this no one tells us anything; nor can any one tell, unless he says, as we do, that the mover makes them one.

οἱ δὲ λέγοντες τὸν ἀριθμὸν πρῶτον τὸν μαθηματικὸν καὶ οὕτως ἀεὶ ἄλλην ἐχομένην οὐσίαν καὶ ἀρχὰς ἑκάστης ἄλλας, [1076a] [1] ἐπεισοδιώδη τὴν τοῦ παντὸς οὐσίαν ποιοῦσιν (οὐδὲν γὰρ ἡ ἑτέρα τῇ ἑτέρᾳ συμβάλλεται οὖσα ἢ μὴ οὖσα) καὶ ἀρχὰς πολλάς· τὰ δὲ ὄντα οὐ βούλεται πολιτεύεσθαι κακῶς. "οὐκ ἀγαθὸν πολυκοιρανίη· εἷς κοίρανος ἔστω."

Dicentes autem numerum primum mathematicum et sic semper aliam habitam substantiam et principia cuiuslibet alia, inconnexam universi substantiam faciunt (nihil enim alia alii confert ens aut non ens) et principia multa. Entia vero non volunt disponi male, nec bonum pluralitas principatuum. Unus ergo princeps.

And those who say mathematical number is first and go on to generate one kind of substance after another and give [76a] different principles for each, make the substance of the universe a mere series of episodes (for one substance has no influence on another by its existence or nonexistence), and they give us many governing principles; but the world refuses to be governed badly. The rule of many is not good; one ruler let there be.

# Outline of Ancient Greek Grammar

| | 1a  -η | 1b  base in-ε,ι,ρ → ᾱ/ᾰ | 1c  base in -ττ →ᾰ |
|---|---|---|---|
| ἡ | βοή | ἀπορίᾱ | θάλαττᾰ |
| τὴν / τῆς / τῇ | βοήν / βοῆς / βοῇ | ἀπορίᾱν / ἀπορίᾱς / ἀπορίᾳ | θάλαττᾰν / θαλάττης / θαλάττῃ |
| αἱ | βοαί | ἀπορίαι | θάλατται |
| τὰς / τῶν / ταῖς | βοάς(ᾱ) / βοῶν* / βοαῖς | ἀπορίᾱς / ἀποριῶν* / ἀπορίαις | θαλάττᾱς(ᾱ) / θαλαττῶν* / θαλάτταις |

**Nouns**

differences between I declension types → only in the singular!!

*all first declensions nouns (but *not* adjectives) have G.pl ῶν, no matter where their accent usually falls.

| | 1d  -ης | 1d  base in-ε,ι,ρ→ᾱ | 2a (masculine, feminine) | | 2b (neutre) |
|---|---|---|---|---|---|
| ὁ | ναύτης  ὦναῦτα! (ᾰ) | νεανίᾱς  ὦνεανίᾱ! | ἄνθρωπος  ὦ ἄνθρωπε! | τὸ | ἔργον |
| τὸν / τοῦ / τῷ | ναύτην / ναύτου / ναύτῃ | νεανίᾱν / νεανίου / νεανίᾳ | ἄνθρωπον / ἀνθρώπου / ἀνθρώπῳ | τοῦ / τῷ | ἔργου / ἔργῳ |
| οἱ | ναῦται | νεανίαι | ἄνθρωποι | τὰ | ἔργα |
| τοὺς / τῶν / τοῖς | ναύτας(ᾱ) / ναυτῶν* / ναύταις | νεανίας / νεανιῶν* / νεανίαις | ἀνθρώπους / ἀνθρώπων / ἀνθρώποις | τῶν / τοῖς | ἔργων / ἔργοις |

Accents can fall on the last three syllables (*ultima* = last, *penultima* = second from last, *antepenultima* = 3rd).
▸ the **acute**: on any of the last three:ἄνθρωπος, φόβος, βοή. On the *antepenultima* → only if the *ultima* is short: ἄνθρωπος.

▸ the **circumflex**: only on a long vowel/diphthongue; may fall on the last two syllables (βοῆς, οἱ ναῦται), on the *penultima* only if the *ultima* is short:ὦναῦτα! (ᾰ), οἱ ναῦται.

▸ the **grave**: an acute falling on the *ultima* is written as grave whenever another word (except enclitics) follows: βοή→αἱ βοαὶτῶνναυτῶν.

> **accent on the *antepenultima*** (only acute, only if the *ultima* is short) → moves forward to the *penultima* when the ending is long: N ἄνθρωπ-ος, Ac. ἄνθρωπ-ον, but G. ἀνθρώπ-ου, D.ἀνθρώπ-ῳ(see also θάλαττ-ᾰ,G. θαλάττ-ης).

> **accent on short *penultima***: acute, does not change/move: φόβος, φόβον, φόβου.
> **accent on long *penultima***: circumflex when the *ultima* is short, acute when the *ultima* is long: ὁ ναύτης, dar οἱ ναῦται, ὦναῦτα(ᾰ)

> **accent on the *ultima***: acute/grave in N.Ac.βοή, βοήν, βοαί, βοάς; always circumflex in G, D sg. and pl: βοῆς, βοῇ, βοῶν, βοαῖς;

| | 3am+f | | 3bneutr. |
|---|---|---|---|
| | N = ς (ξ, ψ) | N = Ø (vowel lengthening) -ν, ρ, ς // -οντ- | N = base |
| **N** 📖 **V= N/base** | νύξ | λιμήν (ὦ) λιμέν | πρᾶγμα |
| Ac -α/ν 📖 | νύκτα | λιμένα | |
| G -ος | νυκτός | λιμένος | πράγματος |
| D -ι | νυκτί | λιμένι | πράγματι |
| **NV -ες** | νύκτες | λιμένες | πράγματα |
| Ac -ας | νύκτας | λιμένας | |
| G -ων | νυκτῶν | λιμένων | πραγμάτων |
| D -σι | νυξί <κ+σι | λιμέσι <ν+σι | πράγμασι <τ+σι |

## 📖 NOMINATIVE

all neuters of the third declension: unmarked N → base some exceptions:**3cγένος** (γενες-
*only -ν, ρ, ς can be final consonants in Greek; all others fall:  πραγματ-→**πρᾶγμα;** the same happens when V= base: **παίς**, *child, slave* (base παιδ-) →**ὦπαῖ**

masculines, feminines: marked N:
**I.**with –ς:all consonant bases *except* -ν, ρ, ς // -οντ-; all vowel bases (**πόλι-ς, βασιλεῦ-ς**); regular phonetic changes take place when ςmeets a consonant (in Nsg and Dpl):
  ➤ **π, β, φ** + ς→ψ (ex. **κλωπ-** = thief  N.sg **κλώψ**, D.pl κλωψί;)
  ➤ **κ, γ, χ** + ς→  ξ (ex. **νύξ, κῆρυξ** – base κηρυκ-) ;
  ➤ the dentals (**τ, δ, θ**) drop out (ex. **ἐλπιδ-** = hope N. sg **ἔλπις**, D. pl **ἔλπισι;**)(**ν** is a dental too, so it drops out in Dpl **λιμέσι**)

**II.**without –ς: nouns in **-ν, ρ, ς // -οντ** → **the final vowel of the base is lengthened**
  ➤ in -ν, ρ = **λίμην** (base λιμεν-); see also **δαίμων** (δαιμον-), ὁ = god, **ῥήτωρ** (ῥητορ-) = retor; declined like this are also *adjectives*, the **εὔφρων, εὔφρον**type.
  ➤ in –οντ: **γέρων** (γέρον̶τ̶- → final -τ falls in N.sg), ὁ = old man; declines like **λίμην** except for *Dpl οντ̶+σι = **ουσι**; declined like this is also *the present active participle*, **λέγων, λεγούσα, λέγον**(-οντ-);
  ➤ bases in –σ-: type 3d (**Σωκράτης** → base Σωκρατεσ-; **τριήρης** → base τριήρες-)

VOCATIVE sg→ for allIII declension nouns: **V=N or V= base:Ζεῦς, ὦΖεῦΣωκράτης, ὦΣώκρατες**

ACCUSATIVE sg→ α/ν; ▶ α for al consonant bases, except for dental bases in which the dental is preceded by an unaccented ι or υ; **ὄρνιθ-: ὄρνιν; χάριτ-· χάριν;** some vowel bases; ▶ ν for most vowel bases (**πόλις→πόλιν**, but **βασιλεῦς→βασιλέα**)

-εσ- bases:-σ- between two vowels drops out, the vowels (usually)contract:

**γένεσος>γένους**

| 3dΠερικλεεσ-(ὁ) | 3dΣωρατεσ-(ὁ) | 3dτριηρεσ-(ἡ)*trireme* | 3cγενεσ-(τό) *family, race* |
|---|---|---|---|
| Περικλῆς<br>ὦ Περίκλεις | Σωκράτης<br>ὦ Σώκρατες | τριήρης | γένος |
| Περικλέα<br>Περικλέους<br>Περικλεῖ | Σωκράτη <sup>&lt;εα</sup><br>Σωκράτους <sup>&lt;εος</sup><br>Σωκράτει | τριήρη <sup>&lt;εα</sup><br>τριήρους <sup>&lt;εος</sup><br>τριήρει | γένους <sup>&lt;εος</sup><br>γένει |
|  |  | τριήρεις <sup>&lt;εες</sup><br>τριήρεις* | **γένη <sup>&lt;εα</sup> |
|  |  | τριήρων<br>τριήρεσι | γενῶν<br>γένεσι |

\* Ac. pl is often borrowed from the N.pl in both –εσ- and –υ/ι- bases.

\*\* See τὰχρέα, *debts*, uncontracted N/Ac.pl neuter

**vowel bases:** G. sg in either -ως or -ος; <u>in other cases than N, V, Ac. sg (± Dpl.)</u>υ and ι drop out and are replaced by -ε-, which may contract with the ending. **3h** keeps υ throughout→ no contractions.

| 3eπολι-(ἡ) *city-state* | 3eπρεσβυ- (ὁ) *old man, pl. ambass.* | 3fαστυ-(τό) *city* | 3gβασιλευ- (ὁ) *king* | 3hὀφρυ- (ἡ) *eye-brow* |
|---|---|---|---|---|
| πόλις<br>ὦ πόλι | πρέσβυς<br>ὦ πρέσβυ | ἄστυ | βασιλεύς<br>ὦ βασιλεῦ | ὀφρύς<br>ὦ ὀφρύ |
| πόλιν<br>πόλεως<br>πόλει | πρέσβυν<br>πρέσβεως<br>πρέσβει | ἄστεως<br>ἄστει | βασιλέα<br>βασιλέως<br>βασιλεῖ | ὀφρύν<br>ὀφρύος<br>ὀφρύι |
| πόλεις <sup>&lt;εες</sup> | πρέσβεις <sup>&lt;εες</sup> | ἄστη <sup>&lt;εα</sup> | βασιλεῖς/ῆς <sup>&lt;εες</sup> | ὀφρύες |
| πόλεις*<br>πόλεων<br>πόλε<u>σι</u> | πρέσβεις*<br>πρέσβεων<br>πρέσβ<u>εσι</u> | ἄστεων<br>ἄστ<u>εσι</u> | βασιλέας<br>βασιλέων<br>βασιλε<u>ῦσι</u>(ν) | ὀφρῦς<br>ὀφρύων<br>ὀφρύσι |

**irregular**

| (ὁ) *son* | (ἡ) *ship* |  |
|---|---|---|
| υἱός (2a) | ναῦς<br>ὦ ναῦ | ἡἡμετέραναῦς |
| υἱόν (2a)<br>υἱέος<br>υἱεῖ | ναῦν<br>νεώς<br>νηί | ἐγγὺςτῆςνεώς<br>ἐννηί |
| υἱεῖς <sup>&lt;εες</sup> | νῆες | αἰτῶνΠερσῶννῆες |
| υἱεῖς*<br>υἱέων<br>υἱέσι | ναῦς<br>νεῶν<br>ναυ<u>σί</u> | εἰστὰςναῦς<br>εἰσβαίνουσιν |

| (ὁ) *father* | declined like **πατήρ**: |
|---|---|
| πατήρ<br>ὦπάτερ |  |
| πατέρα<br>πατρί<br>πατρός | ἡμήτηρ (*mother*),<br>ἡθυγάτηρ (*daughter*);<br>ἀνήρ, ἀνδρός also has<br>D.pl in –ασι. |
| πατέρες |  |
| πατέρας<br>πατέρων<br>πατράσι(ν) | other strange nouns:<br>Ζεύς(Δι-), ὦΖεῦ<br>ἡγυνή(γυναικ-),<br>ὦγύναι *woman* |

**Accents:** <u>monosilabic bases</u> accent the <u>ultima</u> in the <u>G. and D,sg and pl.</u> (see *νύξ*: G νυκτ-*ός* etc)

# III *declension adjectives*

| m+f | n |
|---|---|
| εὔφρων | εὔφρον |

*<u>base -ον-</u> → like δαίμων, λίμην; for full declension see ἀμείνων bellow (except contract forms) comparative, superlative in -<u>έστερος</u>, <u>έστατος</u>(like εὐγενής)

| εὐγενής<br>ὦ εὐγενές | εὐγενές |
|---|---|
| εὐγενῆ <sup>< εα</sup><br>εὐγενοῦς <sup><εους</sup><br>εὐγενεῖ <sup><ει</sup> | εὐγενοῦς <sup>< εους</sup><br>εὐγενεῖ <sup>< ει</sup> |
| εὐγενεῖς <sup>< εες</sup><br>εὐγενεῖς* | εὐγενῆ |
| εὐγενῶν <sup>< εων</sup><br>εὐγενέσι(ν) | εὐγενῶν <sup>< εων</sup><br>εὐγενέσι(ν) |

<u>base -εσ-</u> → **masc + fem like τριηρής, neuter like γένος (types 3c-d)**

comparative, superlative:
εὐγεν<u>έστερος</u>, ᾱ, ον
εὐγεν<u>έστατος</u>, η, ον

<u>base in -υ-</u> **see types 3e-3h**→ masculine declined like πρέσβυς, neuter like ἄστυ, except for G.sg —ος and uncontracted NAc.pl. neuter -έα

*γλυκ<u>ίων</u>, ίον
    γλυκ<u>ίστος</u>, η, ον

* same as in irregular comparatives and superlatives; for declension of γλυκίων see ἀμείνων (=*better*, from ἀγαθός; superlative ἄριστος) bellow.

| γλυκύς<br>(ὦ) γλυκύ | γλυκεῖα | γλυκύ |
|---|---|---|
| γλυκύν<br>γλυκέος<br>γλυκεῖ | γλυκεῖαν<br>γλυκείας<br>γλυκείᾳ | γλυκέος<br>γλυκεῖ |
| γλυκεῖς | γλυκεῖαι | γλυκέα |
| βαθεῖς<br>γλυκέων<br>γλυκέσι(ν) | γλυκείας<br>γλυκειῶν<br>γλυκείαις | γλυκέων<br>γλυκέσι(ν) |

| ἀμείνων<br>ὦ εὐγενές | ἄμεινον |
|---|---|
| ἀμείνονα<br>/ἀμείνω*<br>ἀμείνονος<br>ἀμείνονι | ἀμείνονος<br>ἀμείνονι |
| ἀμείνονες<br>/ἀμείνους | ἀμείνονα<br>/ἀμείνω |
| ἀμείνονας<br>/ἀμείνους<br>ἀμείνονος<br>ἀμείνοσι(ν) | ἀμείνονος<br>ἀμείνοσι(ν) |

*contracted forms ἀμεινο(ν)α etc; contracted Ac. pl → borrowed from N. pl

| | Positive | *Comparative* | Superlative |
|---|---|---|---|
| **-ος type, long penult** | δεινός, -ή, -όν<br>ἐσθλός, -ή, -όν | **-ότερος, -ᾱ, -ον**<br>δεινότερος, -ᾱ, -ον<br>ἐσθλότερος, -ᾱ, -ον | **-ότατος, -η, -ον**<br>δεινότατος, -η, -ον<br>ἐσθλότατος, -η, -ον |
| **-ος type, short penult** | σοφός, -ή, -όν<br>ἄξιος, -ᾱ, -ον | **- ώτερος, -ᾱ, -ον**<br>σοφώτερος, -ᾱ, -ον<br>ἀξιώτερος, -ᾱ, -ον | **-ώτατος, -η, -ον**<br>σοφώτατος, -η,-ον<br>ἀξιώτατος, -η, -ον |
| **-ής, -ές**<br>(base in -εσ-)<br>**-ων, -ον**<br>(base in -ον-) | ἀληθής, ἀληθές<br>εὐδαίμων, -ον | **-έστερος,-ᾱ,-ον**<br>ἀληθέστερος, -ᾱ, -ον<br>εὐδαιμονέστερος, -ᾱ, -ον | **-έστατος, -η, -ον**<br>ἀληθέστατος, -η, -ον<br>εὐδαιμονέστατος, -η, -ον |
| **-υς , - εῖα, ύ**<br>and a few in -ρος<br>term. a,e = forme contr! | ἡδύς, ἡδεῖα, ἡδύ<br>αἰσχρός, -ά, -όν | **-ίων, ιον**<br>ἡδίων, ἥδιον<br>αἰσχίων, -ιον | **-ιστος, η, ον**<br>ἥδιστος, ἡδίστη, ἥδιστον<br>αἴσχιστος, -ίστη, -ιστον |
| ἀγαθός | 1. ἀγαθός, -ή, -όν*good* | **ἀμείνων, ον**<br><br>**βελτίων, ον**<br><br>**κρείττων, ον** | **ἄριστος**, η, ον<br>*(able, brave)*<br>**βέλτιστος**, η,ον<br>*(virtuous)*<br>**κράτιστος**, η, ον<br>*(strong)* |
| κακός | 2. κακός, -ή, -όν*bad*<br><br>*worse worst*<br><br><br>*inferior, less, least* | **κακίων, ον**<br>**χείρων, ον**<br>**ἥττων, ον** | **κάκιστος**, η, ον*cowardly)*<br>**χείριστος**, η, ον*(lacking, less good)*<br>**ἥκιστος**, η, ον*(weak)* |
| καλός | 3. καλός, -ή, -όν *fine finer finest* | **καλλίων, ον** | **κάλλιστος**, η, ον |
| μέγας | 4. μέγας, μεγάλη, μέγα*great greater greatest* | **μείζων, ον** | **μέγιστος**, η, ον |
| μικρός | 5. μικρός, μικρά, μικρόν *small smaller smallest* | **ἐλάττων, ον,<br>μείων, ῖον** | **ἐλάχιστος**, η, ον |
| ὀλίγος | 6. ὀλίγος, -η, -ον*little;* pl.*few fewer fewest* | **ἐλάττων/μείων** | **ὀλίγιστος**, η, ον |
| πολύς | 7. πολύς, πολλή, πολύ*much;* pl.*many more most* | **πλείων, ῖον** | **πλεῖστος**, η, ον |
| ῥᾴδιος | 8. ῥᾴδιος, ῥᾳδία, ῥᾴδιο*easy easier easiest* | **ῥᾴων, ῥᾷον** | **ῥᾷστος**, η, ον |
| ταχύς | 9. ταχύς, ταχεῖα, ταχύ*swift swifter swiftest* | **θάττων, θᾶττον** | **τάχιστος**, η, ον |

# *Regular verbs*

| present | | future* | | | |
|---|---|---|---|---|---|
| active | middle-pass. | active | middle | active | middle |
| λύω<br>λύεις<br>λύει<br><br>λύομεν<br>λύετε<br>λύουσι(ν) | λύομαι<br>λύει/ λύῃ<br>λύεται<br><br>λυόμεθα<br>λύεσθε<br>λύονται | λύσω<br>λύσεις<br>λύσει<br><br>λύσομεν<br>λύσετε<br>λύσουσι(ν) | λύσομαι<br>λύσει/ ῃ<br>λύσεται<br><br>λυσόμεθα<br>λύσεσθε<br>λύσονται | 1 aorist<br>λύω | |
| ἔλυον<br>ἔλυες<br>ἔλυε<br><br>ἐλύομεν<br>ἐλύετε<br>ἔλυον | ἐλυόμην<br>ἐλύου<br>ἐλύετο<br><br>ἐλυόμεθα<br>ἐλύεσθε<br>ἐλύοντο | Ø | | ἔλυσα<br>ἔλυσας<br>ἔλυσε(ν)<br><br>ἐλύσαμεν<br>ἐλύσατε<br>ἔλυσαν | ἐλυσάμην<br>ἐλύσω<br>ἐλύσατο<br><br>ἐλυσάμεθα<br>ἐλύσασθε<br>ἐλύσαντο |
| λύω<br>λύῃς<br>λύῃ<br><br>λύωμεν<br>λύητε<br>λύωσι(ν) | λύωμαι<br>λύῃ<br>λύηται<br><br>λυώμεθα<br>λύησθε<br>λύωνται | Ø | | λύσω<br>λύσῃς<br>λύσῃ<br><br>λύσωμεν<br>λύσητε<br>λύσωσι(ν) | λύσωμαι<br>λύσῃ<br>λύσηται<br><br>λυσώμεθα<br>λύσησθε<br>λύσωνται |
| λύοιμι<br>λύοις<br>λύοι<br><br>λύοιμεν<br>λύοιτε<br>λύοιεν | λυοίμην<br>λύοιο<br>λύοιτο<br><br>λυοίμεθα<br>λύοισθε<br>λύοιντο | λύσοιμι<br>λύσοις<br>λύσοι<br><br>λύσοιμεν<br>λύσοιτε<br>λύσοιεν | λυσοίμην<br>λύσοιο<br>λύσοιτο<br><br>λυσοίμεθα<br>λύσοισθε<br>λύσοιντο | λύσαιμι<br>λύσειας /αις<br>λύσειε(ν) /αι<br><br>λύσαιμεν<br>λύσαιτε<br>λύσειαν/αιεν | λυσαίμην<br>λύσαιο<br>λύσαιτο<br><br>λυσαίμεθα<br>λύσαισθε<br>λύσαιντο |
| λῦε<br>λύετε<br><br>λυέτω<br>λυόντων | λύου<br>λύεσθε<br><br>λυέσθω<br>λυέσθων | ←imperative→<br>II sg, pl<br><br>III sg, pl | | λῦσον<br>λύσατε<br><br>λυσάτω<br>λυσάντων | λῦσαι<br>λύσασθε<br><br>λυσάσθω<br>λυσάσθων |
| λύειν | λύεσθαι | λύσειν | λύσεσθαι | λῦσαι | λύσασθαι |
| λύων, -ουσα, -ον ⁻ουτ⁻<br>λυόμενος | | λύσων,-ουσα, -ον ⁻ουτ⁻<br>λυσόμενος | | λύσᾱς, -ᾱσα, -αν ⁻αντ⁻<br>λυσάμενος | |

*Note that verbs -ίζω and some in -νω have a different type of future, called contract future, which conjugates just like ποιέω: νομίζω→νομιῶ; μένω→μενῶ

|  | perfect |  |  |
| active | middle | active | middle-pass. | passive |

|  |  | perfect |  |  |
|---|---|---|---|---|
|  | active | middle-pass. |  | passive |
|  | λέλυκα<br>λέλυκας<br>λέλυκε(ν)<br>λελύκαμεν<br>λελύκατε<br>λελύκασι(ν) | λέλυμαι<br>λέλυσαι<br>λέλυται<br>λελύμεθα<br>λέλυσθε<br>λέλυνται |  | λυθήσομαι<br>λυθήσῃ<br>λυθήσεται<br>λυθησόμεθα<br>λυθήσεσθε<br>λυθήσονται |

**2 aorist μανθάνω**

| active | middle | active | middle-pass. | passive | future → |
|---|---|---|---|---|---|
| ἔμαθον<br>ἔμαθες<br>ἔμαθε(ν)<br>ἐμάθομεν<br>ἐμάθετε<br>ἔμαθον | ἐμαθόμην<br>ἐμάθου<br>ἐμάθετο<br>ἐμαθόμεθα<br>ἐμάθεσθε<br>ἐμάθοντο | ἐλελύκη<br>ἐλελύκης<br>ἐλελύκει(ν)<br>ἐλελύκεμεν<br>ἐλελύκετε<br>ἐλελύκεσαν | ἐλελύμην<br>ἐλέλυσο<br>ἐλέλυτο<br>ἐλελύμεθα<br>ἐλέλυσθε<br>ἐλέλυντο | ἐλύθην<br>ἐλύθης<br>ἐλύθη<br>ἐλύθημεν<br>ἐλύθητε<br>ἐλύθησαν | ←passive |
| μάθω<br>μάθῃς<br>μάθῃ<br>μάθωμεν<br>μάθητε<br>μάθωσι(ν) | μάθωμαι<br>μάθῃ<br>μάθηται<br>μαθώμεθα<br>μάθησθε<br>μάθωνται | λελύκω<br>λελύκῃς<br>λελύκη<br>λελύκωμεν<br>λελύκητε<br>λελύκωσι(ν) | λελυμένος ὦ<br>~ ᾖς<br>~ ᾖ<br>-μένοι ὦμεν<br>~ ἦτε<br>~ ὦσι | λυθῶ<br>λυθῇς<br>λυθῇ<br>λυθῶμεν<br>λυθῆτε<br>λυθῶσι(ν) |  |
| μάθοιμι<br>μάθοις<br>μάθοι<br>μάθοιμεν<br>μάθοιτε<br>μάθοιεν | μαθοίμην<br>μάθοιο<br>μάθοιτο<br>μαθοίμεθα<br>μάθοισθε<br>μάθοιντο | λελύκοιμι<br>λελύκοις<br>λελύκοι<br>λελύκοιμεν<br>λελύκοιτε<br>λελύκοιεν | -μένος εἴην<br>~ εἴης<br>~ εἴη<br>-μένοι εἶμεν<br>~ εἶτε<br>~εἶεν | λυθείην<br>λυθείης<br>λυθείη<br>λυθεῖμεν<br>λυθεῖτε<br>λυθεῖεν | λυθησοίμην<br>λυθήσοιο<br>λυθήσοιτο<br>λυθησοίμεθα<br>λυθήσοισθε<br>λυθήσοιντο |
| μάθε<br>μάθετε<br>μαθέτω<br>μαθόντων | μάθου<br>μάθεσθε<br>μαθέσθω<br>μαθέσθων | λέλυκε<br>λελύκετε<br>λελυκέτω<br>λελυκέτωσαν | λέλυσο<br>λέλυσθε<br>λελύσθω<br>λελύσθων | λύθητι<br>λύθητε<br>λυθήτω<br>λυθέντων | Ø |
| μαθεῖν | μαθέσθαι | λελυκέναι | λελῦσθαι | λυθῆναι | λυθήσεσθαι |
| μαθών, -οῦσα,-όν ⁻ᵒⁿᵗ⁻<br>μαθόμενος | | λελυκώς, -υῖα,-ός ⁻ᵒᵗ⁻<br>λελυμένος | | λυθείς, -εῖσα, -έν ⁻ᵉⁿᵗ⁻<br>λυθησόμενος | |

**future perfect**

| λελυκώς ἔσομαι | λελύσομαι |
|---|---|

## Participles

| | | present | future | 1 aorist | 2 aorist |
|---|---|---|---|---|---|
| **participle** | act. | **λύων, ουσα, ον**<br>λυοντ-<br>(λυουσῶν) | **λύσων, ουσα, ον**<br>λυσοντ-<br>(λυσουσῶν) | **λύσᾱς, ᾱσα, αν**<br>λυσαντ-<br>(λυσασῶν) | **λαβών, οῦσα, όν**<br>λαβοντ-<br>(λαβουσῶν) |
| | mid. | **λυόμενος, η, ον**<br>(λυομένων) | **λυσόμενος, η, ον**<br>(λυσομένων); | **λυσάμενος, η, ον**<br>(λυσαμένων); | **λαβόμενος, η, ον**<br>(λαβομένων) |
| **inf.** | act. | λύειν | λύσειν | λῦσαι, βουλεῦσαι | λαβεῖν |
| | mid. | λύεσθαι | λύσεσθαι | λύσασθαι | λαβέσθαι |

| λύων | λύουσα ᾰ→<br>θάλαττα | λῦον |
|---|---|---|
| λύοντα | λύουσαν | |
| λύοντος<br>λύοντι | λυούσης<br>λυούσῃ | λύοντος<br>λύοντι |
| λύοντες | λύουσαι | λύοντα |
| λύοντας | λυούσας | |
| λυόντων<br>λύουσι | λυουσῶν<br>λυούσαῖς | λυόντων<br>λύουσι |

| ὤν | οὖσᾰ | ὄν |
|---|---|---|
| ὄντα | οὖσᾰν | |
| ὄντος<br>ὄντι | οὔσης<br>οὔσῃ | ὄντος<br>ὄντι |
| ὄντες | οὖσαι | ὄντα |
| ὄντας | οὖσας | |
| ὄντων<br>οὖσι | οὐσῶν<br>οὔσαῖς | ὄντων<br>οὖσι |

second aorist
active participle

* accented like ὤν, οὖσα, ὄν

| λαβών | λαβοῦσ-ᾰ | λαβόν |
|---|---|---|
| λαβόντα | λαβοῦσᾰν | |
| λαβόντος<br>λαβόντι | λαβούσης<br>λαβούσῃ | λαβόντος<br>λαβόντι |
| λαβόντες | λαβοῦσαι | λαβόντα |
| λαβόντας | λαβούσας | |
| λαβόντων<br>λαβοῦσι | λαβουσῶν<br>λαβούσαῖς | λαβόντων<br>λαβοῦσι |

| λύσας | λύσᾱσᾰ | λῦσαν |
|---|---|---|
| λύσαντα | λύσᾱσᾰν | |
| λύσαντος<br>λύσαντι | λυσάσης<br>λυσάσῃ | λύσαντος<br>λύσαντι |
| λύσαντες | λύσᾱσαι | λύσαντα |
| λύσαντας | λυούσας | |
| λύσαντων<br>λύσᾱσι | λυσασῶν<br>λυσάσαῖς | λύσαντων<br>λύσᾱσι |

first aorist
active participle

| I am | I shall go | I know | I say | |
|---|---|---|---|---|
| εἰμί* | εἶμι | οἶδα | φημί* | *present indicative = enclitic, except for II sg. εἶ, φής |
| εἶ | εἶ | οἶσθα | φής | |
| ἐστί(ν) | εἶσι(ν) | οἶδε | φησί(ν) | |
| ἐσμέν | ἴμεν | ἴσμεν | φαμέν | |
| ἐστέ | ἴτε | ἴστε | φατέ | |
| εἰσί(ν) | ἴασι(ν) | ἴσασιν | φασί | |

| I was | I went | I knew | I said |
|---|---|---|---|
| ἦ(ν) | ἦα /ἤειν | ἤδη /ἤδειν | ἔφην |
| ἦσθα | ἤεισθα/ἤεις | ἤδησθα /ἤδεις | ἔφησθα /ἔφης |
| ἦν | ἤει(ν) | ἤδει | ἔφη |
| ἦμεν | ἦμεν | ἦσμεν /ἤδεμεν | ἔφαμεν |
| ἦτε | ἦτε | ἦστε /ἤδετε | ἔφατε |
| ἦσαν | ἦσαν/ἤεσαν | ἦσαν /ἤδεσαν | ἔφασαν |

| ἴσθι ἔστε | ἴθι ἴτε | ἴσθι ἴστε | φαθί φάτε | imp. II sg, pl |
|---|---|---|---|---|
| ἔστω, ὄντων | ἴτω, ἰόντων | ἴστω, ἴστων | φάτω, φάντων | III sg, pl |

| participle | | | φάσκων ουσα ον (-οντ-) /φάς φᾶσα φάν (-αντ-) /φάμενος,η, ον (same meaning) |
|---|---|---|---|
| ὤν, οὖσα, ὄν (ὀντ-) | ἰών, ἰοῦσα,ἰόν (ιοντ-) | εἰδώς, εἰδυῖα, ός(εἰδοτ-) | |
| Infinitive εἶναι | ἰέναι | εἰδέναι | φάναι |

| | | am | go | know | say |
|---|---|---|---|---|---|
| optative | | εἴην | ἴομι | εἰδείην | φαίην |
| | | εἴης | ἴοις | εἰδείης | φαίης |
| | | εἴη | ἴοι | εἰδείη | φαίη |
| | | εἶμεν | ἴοιμεν | εἰδεῖμεν | φαῖμεν |
| | | εἶτε | ἴοιτε | εἰδεῖτε | φαίητε |
| | | εἶεν | ἴοιεν | εἰδεῖεν | φαῖεν |
| subjonctive | | am | go | know | say |
| | | ὦ | ἴω | εἰδῶ | φῶ |
| | | ᾖς | ἴης | εἰδῆς | φῇς |
| | | ᾖ | ἴῃ | εἰδῇ | φῇ |
| | | ὦμεν | ἴωμεν | εἰδῶμεν | φῶμεν |
| | | ἦτε | ἴητε | εἰδῆτε | φῆτε |
| | | ὦσι(ν) | ἴωσι | εἰδῶ(σι)ν | φῶσι |

**future & other forms**

| I shall be (regular) | I shall go | I shall know | I shall say |
|---|---|---|---|
| ἔσομαι | = present | εἴσομαι/εἰδήσω εἴσει/εἰδήσεις … | φήσω |
| ἔσει | (the present form has future meaning in the indicative) | (regular) | (regular; |
| ἔσεται | | | same for |
| ἐσόμεθα | | | aorist ἔφησα) |
| ἔσεσθε | | | |
| ἔσονται | | | |

| ἐμός,ή,όν | | ἐγώ | σύ |
|---|---|---|---|
| | σός,σή,σόν | με /ἐμέ | σέ |
| | | μου /ἐμοῦ | σοῦ |
| | | μοι / ἐμοί | σοί |
| | | ἡμεῖς | ὑμεῖς |
| | | ἡμᾶς | ὑμᾶς |
| ἡμέτερος,ᾱ,όν | | ἡμῶν | ὑμῶν |
| ὑμέτερος,ᾱ,όν | | ἡμῖν | ὑμῖν |

| οὐδείς | οὐδεμία | οὐδέν |
|---|---|---|
| οὐδένα | οὐδεμίαν | |
| οὐδενός | οὐδεμιᾶς | οὐδενός |
| οὐδενί | οὐδεμιᾷ | οὐδενί |

The negative *pronoun*
= no one, nothing
οὐ (no) + εἷς, μία, ἕν (one)

If the context requires the negation **μή** instead of **οὐ**, <u>**μηδείς, μηδεμία, μηδέν**</u> is used (it declines in the same way and means the same thing).

| τίς γεωργός; *what farmer?* | | | γεωργός τις *a (certain) farmer* | |
|---|---|---|---|---|
| τί πλοῖον; *what ship?* | | | πλοῖόν τινα *a (certain) ship* | |
| τίς ἀφικνεῖται; *who is coming?* | | | ἀφικνεῖται τις *someone is arriving* | |
| τί ὁρᾷς; *what can you see?* | | | ἔχει τι ἐν τῇ δεξιᾷ *he has something in his right hand* | |

**which/who? what? (interrogative)**

| | τίς | | τί | someone, something / a certain (indefinite) | τις | | τι |
|---|---|---|---|---|---|---|---|
| | | τίνα | | | | τινά | |
| | τίνος | | τίνος | | τινός | | τινός |
| | τίνι | | τίνι | | τινί | | τινί |
| | τίνες | | τίνα | | τινές | | τινά |
| | | τίνας | | | | τινάς | |
| | τίνων | | τίνων | | τινῶν | | τινῶν |
| | τίσι | | τίσι | | τισί | | τισί |

*Note that the indefinite (except for Gpl) is an enclitic → it relies for its accent on the previous word.

demonstrative pronouns:
- alone: **he, she, it**
ἐκεῖνοι μὲν γὰρ κρατοῦσι κατὰ γῆν, <u>ἡμεῖς</u> δὲ κατὰ θάλατταν. 3C
but: **οὗτος**, τί ποιεῖς; *you there...*
- with nouns: **this, that**
**οὗτος** ὁ ἀνήρ / ὁ ἀνὴρ **οὗτος**
**ἐκείνη** ἡ βοή / ἡ βοὴ **ἐκείνη**
**οὗτος** begins with ου- or τ-
wherever the definite article does;
the feminine has -αυ- instead of –ου- wherever the endings contain α, η.

| ἐκεῖνος | ἐκείνη | | οὗτος | αὕτη | |
|---|---|---|---|---|---|
| | | ἐκεῖνο | | | τοῦτο |
| ἐκεῖνον | ἐκείνην | | τοῦτον | ταύτην | |
| ἐκείνου | ἐκείνης | | τούτου | ταύτης | |
| | | ἐκείνου | | | τούτου |
| ἐκείνῳ | ἐκείνῃ | | τούτῳ | ταύτῃ | |
| | | ἐκείνῳ | | | τούτῳ |
| ἐκεῖνοι | ἐκεῖναι | | οὗτοι | αὗται | |
| | | ἐκεῖνα | | | ταῦτα |
| ἐκείνους | ἐκείνας | | τούτους | ταύτας | |
| ἐκείνων | ἐκείνων | | τούτων | τούτων | |
| | | ἐκείνων | | | τούτων |
| ἐκείνοις | ἐκείναις | | τούτοις | ταύταις | |
| | | ἐκείνοις | | | τούτοις |

| | | REFLEXIVE I | REFLEXIVE II | REFLEXIVE III |
|---|---|---|---|---|
| Ac. | | ἐμαυτόν, ἐμαυτήν | σ(ε)αυτόν, σ(ε)αυτήν | ἑαυτόν, ήν/αὐτόν.. |
| G. | | ἐμαυτοῦ, ἐμαυτῆς | σ(ε)αυτοῦ, σ(ε)αυτῆς | ἑαυτοῦ,ῆς /αὐτοῦ.. |
| D. | | ἐμαυτῷ, ἐμαυτῇ | σ(ε)αυτῷ, σ(ε)αυτῇ | ἑαυτῷ,τῇ/αὐτῷ.. |
| | | Ø | Ø | Ø |
| Ac. | | ἡμᾶςαὐτούς /-άς | ὑμᾶςαὐτούς /-άς | ἑαυτούς,άς /αὐτούς |
| G. | | ἡμῶναὐτῶν | ὑμῶναὐτῶν | ἑαυτῶν /αὐτῶν |
| D. | | ἡμῖναὐτοῖς / -αῖς | ὑμῖναὐτοῖς / αὐταῖς | ἑαυτοῖς,αῖς /αὐτοῖς |

| αὐτός | αὐτή | |
|---|---|---|
| αὐτόν | αὐτήν | αὐτό |
| αὐτοῦ | αὐτῆς | αὐτοῦ |
| αὐτῷ | αὐτῇ | αὐτῷ |

| αὐτοί | αὐταί | |
|---|---|---|
| αὐτούς | αὐτάς | αὐτά |
| αὐτῶν | αὐτῶν | αὐτῶν |
| αὐτοῖς | αὐταῖς | αὐτοῖς |

- with article = *the same* (**idem**):
ὁαὐτὸς ἀνήρ/ ὁ ἀνὴρ ὁαὐτός= the *same* man

- without article = 'him/herself' (**ipse**):
αὐτός ὁἀνήρ/ὁἀνὴραὐτός = the man *himself*

- oblique cases, +pers. pronoun = reflexive pronoun (see table above): ῥίπτω ἐμαυτόν ἐκ τοῦ πλοίου= I throw myself out of the boat

- only oblique cases, alone: translated as a personal. pronoun:
ὁρῶ αὐτόν (I see *him*); δώσω αὐτοῖς (I will give *them*)

| definite article (for comparison) | | | relative who, which, that | | | relative+indefinite τις anyone who… /whoever = indefinite relative used instead of interr. τίς in indirect questions: he asked who… | | | |
|---|---|---|---|---|---|---|---|---|---|
| ὁ | ἡ | τό | ὅς | ἥ | ὅ | ὅστις | ἥτις | | ὅ, τι |
| τόν | τήν | | ὅν | ἥν | | ὅντινα | ἥντινα | | |
| τοῦ | τῆς | τοῦ | οὗ | ἧς | οὗ | οὗτινος/ὅτου | ἧστινος | | οὗτινος/ὅτου |
| τῷ | τῇ | τῷ | ᾧ | ᾗ | ᾧ | ᾧτινι/ὅτῳ | ἧτινι | | ᾧτινι/ὅτῳ |
| οἱ | αἱ | τά | οἵ | αἵ | ἅ | οἵτινες | αἵτινες | | ἄτινα/ἄττα |
| τούς | τάς | | οὕς | ἅς | | οὕστινας | ἅτινας/ἄττα | | |
| τῶν | τῶν | τῶν | ὧν | ὧν | ὧν | ὧντινων/ὅτων | ὧντινων/ὅτων | | ὧντινων/ὅτων |
| τοῖς | ταῖς | τοῖς | οἷς | αἷς | οἷς | οἷστισι/ὅτοις | αἷστισι | | οἷστισι/ὅτοις |

| ὅδε | ἥδε | |
|---|---|---|
| τόνδε | τήνδε | τόδε |
| τοῦδε | τῆσδε | τοῦδε |
| τῷδε | τῇδε | τῷδε |

| οἵδε | αἵδε | |
|---|---|---|
| τούσδε | τάσδε | τάδε |
| τῶνδε | τῶνδε | τῶνδε |
| τοῖσδε | ταῖσδε | τοῖσδε |

the last demonstrative: ὅδε, ἥδε, τόδε (definite article + δε)

Like οὗτος, it basically means 'this', but it is used more to point to something that hasn't been mentioned yet.

# Correlative pronouns

| Direct Interr. / indirect inter. | indefinite pronouns | relative / indefinite relative | demonstrative pronouns |
|---|---|---|---|
| **τίς;** *who?* qui? / **ὅστις** *(he asked) who...* | **τις** *someone, anyone* — *aliquis, quidam* | **ὅς ὅσπερ** *(the man) who/that ...* qui / **ὅστις** *whoever, anyone who...* *quisquis, quicunque* | **ὅδε**<sup>hic</sup> **οὗτος**<sup>is, ille</sup> **ἐκεῖνος**<sup>ille</sup> |
| **πόσος;** *how large? ≈much? ≈ many?* quantus? quot? / **ὁπόσος** *(he asked) how...* | **ποσός** *of some/any quantity* | **ὅσος** *as large/much/ many... as* quantus, quot / **ὁπόσος** **however large/much/many** *quantuscunque, quotquot* | **τοσόσδε** **τοσοῦτος** *this large/much/many tantus, tot* |
| **ποῖος;** *of what kind?* qualis? / **ὁποῖος** *(he asked) of what kind...* | **ποιός** *of some/any quality* | **οἷος** *of the kind that/ such as* qualis / **ὁποῖος** *of whatever kind qualiscunque* | **τοιόσδε** **τοιοῦτος** *of this kind talis* |
| **πότερος;** *which one of two?* uter? / **ὁπότερος** *(he asked) which...* | **πότερος /ποτερός** | **ὁπότερος** *utercumque* | **ἕτερος** *the other alter* |

505

## Correlative adverbs

| indir. int. / inter. | indefinite | indef.rel. / relative | demonstrative | -ι, -θι, -σι, -ου |
|---|---|---|---|---|
| **ποῦ;** where? ubi? — **ὅπου** (he asked) where... | **πού** some/anywhere alicubi | **οὗ**(ἔνθα) **οὗπερ** (the place) where.. ubi — **ὅπου** wherever, anywhere that ubiubi | **ἐνθάδε ἐνταῦθα ἐκεῖ** there ibi | **-ι, -θι, -σι, -ου** / **οὐδαμοῦ** / ἄλλοθι/ἀλλαχοῦ / πανταχοῖ / πολλαχοῦ / αὐτοῦ=in the very place / ὁμοῦ = in the same place / **ἔνδον/ἔξω** / **ἄνω/κάτω** / **οἴκοι** / Ἀθήνησι, χάμαι |
| **ποῖ;** whither? where to? quō? — **ὅποι** (he asked) whiter/where to | **ποί** to some place aliquō | **οἷ**(ἔνθα) **οἷπερ** (the place)/to which quō — **ὅποι** (to) wherever, anywhere that quōquō | **ἐνθάδε ἐνταῦθα ἐκεῖσε** thiter/(to) there eo | **-δε/-ζε, -σε** / ἄλλοσε/-αχόσε / πανταχόσε/ πάντοσε / πολλαχόσε / αὐτόσε=to the very place / ὁμόσε =to the same place / **δεῦρο** / εἴσω/ἔξω / ἄνω/κάτω / **οἰκάδε** / Ἀθήναζε |
| **πόθεν;** whence?/from where? — **ὁπόθεν** (he asked) whence... | **ποθέν** from some/anywhere alicunde | **ὅθεν**(ἔνθεν) (the place) whence unde — **ὁπόθεν** from wherever/anywhere that undecumque | **ἐνθένδε ἐντεῦθεν ἐκεῖθεν** from there inde | **-θεν** / ἄλλοθεν/-αχόθεν / πάντοθεν / πολλαχόθεν / αὐτόθεν fr. the very place / ὁμόθεν fr. the same place / /κατώθεν / **οἴκοθεν** / Ἀθήνηθεν |
| **πῇ;** which way? how? quā? — **ὅπῃ** (he asked) which way/how | **πῄ** some/anyway some/anyhow aliquā | **ᾗ** the way that quā — **ὅπῃ** whichever way quāquā | **τῇδε ταύτῃ** that way eā | οὐδαμῇ / ἄλλῃ / πάντῃ |
| **πῶς;** how? — **ὅπως** (he asked) how.. | **πώς** somehow | **ὡς** as, how — **ὅπως** however (you like) | **ὧδε οὕτω ἐκείνως** in this way | **οὐδαμῶς** / ἄλλως / πάντως / ὡσαύτως in the same way |
| **πότε;** when? quandō? — **ὁπότε** (he asked) when | **ποτέ** some/anytime aliquandō | **ὅτε** (the time) when cum — **ὁπότε** whenever, anytime when quandōcumque | **τότε** then tum | οὔποτε / ἄλλοτε / πάντοτε/ ἀεί / **νῦν/πρίν/ἔπειτα** / **ἅμα** at the same time / **ἔτι/οὐκέτι** / **ἤδη/οὐδέπω,οὔπω** |

# Patterns of formation of the perfect tense

**First perfect = verbs in vowel, liquid, or dental stop:**

λύω, λύσω, ἔλυσα, **λέλυκα**, λέλυγμαι, λελύχθην

τιμάω, τιμήσω, ἐτίμησα, **τετίμηκα**, τετίμημαι, τετιμήθην

ἀγγέλλω, ἀγγελῶ, ἤγγειλα, **ἤγγελκα,** ἤγγελμαι, ἠγγελήθην

κομίζω, κομιῶ, ἐκόμισα, **κεκόμικα, κεκόμισμαι,**

νομίζω, νομιῶ, ἐνόμισα, **νενόμικα**, νενόμισμαι, ἐνομίσθην

πείθω, πείσω, ἔπεισα, πέποιθα (*I trust*, i.e., have put confidence in); also **πέπεικα** (*I have persuaded*), πεπείσμαι, ἐπείσθην

στέλλω, στελῶ, ἔστειλα, ***ἔσταλκα,*** ἔσταλμαι (*send* ), ***ἐστάλην***

διαφθείρω, διαφθερῶ, διέφθειρα, ***διέφθαρκα***, διέφθαρμαι, διεφθάρην

> perfect in -**ηκ**-α:
> ἐθέλω, ἐθελ-**ήσ**-ω, ἠθήλ-**ησ**-αἠθέλ-**ηκ**-αØ ⮂*wish, bewilling*(+ inf.) (notfoundinm.-p.)
>
> μανθάνω, μαθ-**ήσ**-ομαι, ἔμαθον, **μεμάθ-η-κα**, Ø
>
> χαίρω, χαιρήσω, ἐχαίρησα, **κεχάρηκα**, κεχάρημαι, ***ἐχάρην***
>
> εὑρίσκω, εὑρ-**ήσ**-ω, εὗρον/ηὗρον, **ηὕρ-ηκ-α**orε**ὕρ-ηκ-α**, ηὕρ-ημαι, ***ηὑρέθην***
>
> ἔχω, ἕξω/σχ**ήσ**ω, ἔσχον, **ἔσχηκα** (regularreduplicationforstemin σχ-), ἔσχημαι
>
> + τυγχάνω, τεύξομαι, ἔτυχον, **τετύχηκα**, Ø

but:

λανθάνω, **λήσω**, ἔλαθον, **λέληθα**, Ø

λαμβάνω , λήψομαι, ἔλαβον, **εἴληφα**, εἴλημμαι, ἐλήφθην

❖ nazal verbs→perfect in -**ηκ**-α sau drop –n-

μένω, μενῶ, ἔμεινα, **μεμένηκα** Ø

κρίνω, κρινῶ, ἔκρινα, **κέκρικα**, κέκριμαι, ἐκρίθην

but: φαίνω, φανῶ, ἔφηνα, **πέφαγκα** (*I have shown*) and πέφηνα (*I have appeared*), πέφασμαι, ἐφάνθην/ἐφάνην

τείνω, τενῶ, -έτεινα, **τέτακα**< *τετνκα (*stretch*), **τέτμημαι**, **ἐτμήθην**

❖ liquid and nazal – metathesis:

ἀποθνήσκω, ἀποθανοῦμαι, ἀπέθανον, **τέθνηκα**, Ø

βάλλω, βαλῶ, ἔβαλον, **βέβληκα**, βέβλημαι

καλέωκαλε-, κλη- **κέκληκα**

κάμνωκαμ- **κέκμηκα**

τέμνω τεμ- , τεμῶ, ἔτεμον, **τέτμηκα**

τείνω, τενῶ, -έτεινα, **τέτακα**< *τετνκα (*stretch*), **τέτμημαι**, **ἐτμήθην**

πίπτω, πετ-πτο-, πεσοῦμαι, ἔπεσον, **πέπτωκα**

**Second perfect**
= formed almost always from verbs in a liquid or a stop consonant, not from a vowel

ἀκούω, ἀκούσομαι, ἤκουσα, **ἀκήκοα** (avea diggama), **ἠκούσθην**

➤ apart from vowel lengthening and v. gradation, the stem is unchanged:
φεύγω, φεύξω/φεύξομαι, ἔφυγον, **πέφευγα**

πράττω, πράξω, ἔπραξα, πέπραχα (*I have done)*; also **πέπραγα** (*I have fared*), πέπραγμαι

ἄρχω , ἄρξω, ἦρξα, **ἦρχα**, ἦργμαι

γράφω, γράψω, ἔγραψα, **γέγραφα**, γεγράμμαι

> some verbs however aspirate a final  -γ or -π:
ἄγω, ἄξω, ἤγαγον, **ἦχα**, ἦγμαι

πράττω, **πέπραχα** (*I have done*); also πέπραγα (*I have fared*), πέπραγμαι

> verbs showing variation between short and long vowel regularly lengthen the vowel.
φαίνω, φανῶ, **ἔφηνα**, πέφαγκα (*I have shown*) and **πέφηνα** (*I have appeared*), πέφασμαι

λανθάνω, **λήσω**, ἔλαθον, **λέληθα**, Ø

λαμβάνω, **λήψομαι**, ἔλαβον, **εἴληφα**, εἴλημμαι

> verbs showing vowel gradation Ø, ε, ο and –ι-, -ει-, -οι- have –οι- in the perfect:
ἀποκτείνω, ἀποκτενῶ, ἀπέκτεινα, **ἀπέκτονα**,

γίγνομαι , γενήσομαι, ἐγενόμην, **γέγονα**; note perfect active of deponent; pf. pt. *γεγώς*;
**γεγένημαι**

λείπω, λείψω, ἔλιπον, **λέλοιπα**, **λέλειμμαι**

πείθω, πείσω, ἔπεισα, **πέποιθα** (*I trust*, i.e., have put confidence in); also πέπεικα (*I have persuaded*), **πέπεισμαι**

πέμπω, πέπψω, ἔπεμψα, **πέπομφα**, **πέπεμμαι**

πάσχω, πείσομαι, ἔπαθον, **πέπονθα**

> verbs  with perfect 2 aspirated

    **ἄγω**, ἄξω, ἤγαγον, **ἦχα**, ἦγμαι, ἤχθην
    **ἀλλάττω**, ἀλλάξω, ἤλλαξα, **ἤλλαχα**, ἠλλάχθην
    **ἀνοίγω**,  **ἀνέῳχα**, **ἀνέῳγα**
    **βλάπτω**, βλάψω, ἔβλαψα/ἔβλαβον, **βέβλαφα**, βέβλαμμαι
    **θλίβω**, θλίψω, ἔθλιψα, **τέθλιφα**
    **κηρύττω**, κηρύξω, ἐκήρυξα, **κεκήρυχα**, ?κεκήρυγμαι
    **κλέπτω**, κλέψω, ἔκλεψα, **κέκλεφα**, κέκλεμμαι
    **κόπτω** , κόψω, ἔκοψα, **κέκοφα**, ?κέκομμαι
    **λαγχάνω**, λήξομαι, ἔλαχον, **εἴληχα**
    **λαμβάνω**, λήψομαι, ἔλαβον, **εἴληφα**, εἴλημμαι
    **πέμπω**, πέμψω, ἔπεμψα, **πέπομφα**, πέπεμμαι
    **πράττω**, πράξω, ἔπραξα, **πέπραχα**(I have done); also πέπραγα (I have fared),
        πέπραγμαι
    **τρέπω**, θρέψω, ἔθρεψα/ἔτραφον, **τέτροφα**, ?τέθραμμαι
    **τρίβω**, τρίψω, ἔτριψα, **τέτριφα**

**φέρω**, οἴσω, ἤνεγκον, **ἐνήνοχα**, ἐνηνεγμαι
**φυλάττω**, φυλλάξω, ἐφύλλαξα, **πεφύλαχα**, πεφύλαγμαι, ἐφυλάχθην
**δείκνυμι**, διώκω, λάπτω, λέγω , μάττω, μείγνυμι, πλέκω, πτήσσω, τάττω, …

**φέρω, οἴσω, ἤνεγκον, ἐνήνοχα, ἐνήνεγμαι**

**ἔρχομαι, ἐλεύσομαι, ἦλθον, ἐλήλυθα Ø**

**λέγω**, λέξω, ἔλεξα/**εἶπον**,  **εἴρηκα** (cf. εἶπον, used as aorist of λέγω), **εἴρημαι**

**λαγχάνω, λήξομαι, ἔλαχον, εἴληχα**
**λαμβάνω, λήψομαι, ἔλαβον, εἴληφα, εἴλημμαι**
πάσχω, πείσομαι, ἔπαθον, πέπονθα

Printed in Great Britain
by Amazon